CITE THIS VOLUME 193 L. Ed. 2d

UNITED STATES SUPREME COURT REPORTS

OCTOBER TERM, 2015

CASES CONTAINED IN U. S. REPORTS

Vol. 577 U.S. (part)

LAWYERS' EDITION

SECOND SERIES

INTERIM VOLUME 193

COMPLETE WITH HEADNOTES, ANNOTATIONS, TABLES, AND INDEX

2022

LexisNexis®

Prepared By
The Editorial Staff
United States Supreme Court Reports,
Lawyers' Edition

Barbara Kerr

Gary Knapp

Mark A. Oyer

Leah Speckhals

David B. Sweet

TABLE OF CONTENTS

JUSTICES

OF THE

SUPREME COURT OF THE UNITED STATES

DURING THE TIME OF THESE REPORTS

CHIEF JUSTICE
HON. JOHN G. ROBERTS, JR.

ASSOCIATE JUSTICES

HON. ANTONIN SCALIA   HON. STEPHEN BREYER

HON. ANTHONY M. KENNEDY   HON. SAMUEL A. ALITO, JR.

HON. CLARENCE THOMAS   HON. SONIA SOTOMAYOR

HON. RUTH BADER GINSBURG   HON. ELENA KAGAN

ATTORNEY GENERAL
LORETTA E. LYNCH

SOLICITOR GENERAL
DONALD B. VERRILLI, JR.

CLERK
SCOTT S. HARRIS

REPORTER
CHRISTINE LUCHOK FALLON

MARSHAL
PAMELA TALKIN

LIBRARIAN
LINDA S. MASLOW

ALLOTMENT, ETC., OF THE

JUSTICES OF THE SUPREME COURT OF THE UNITED STATES

TOGETHER WITH THE DATES OF THEIR COMMISSIONS AND COMMENCEMENT
OF SERVICE RESPECTIVELY

For the September 28, 2010, Order of Court Making Allotment, see 177 L. Ed. 2d, page xlii.

NAMES OF JUSTICES, AND WHENCE APPOINTED	BY WHOM APPOINTED	CIRCUITS (28 U.S.C.S. § 41)	COMMIS- SIONED	SWORN IN
CHIEF JUSTICE JOHN G. ROBERTS, JR., Maryland	President BUSH	DISTRICT OF COLUMBIA; FEDERAL	2005 (Sept. 29)	2005 (Sept. 29)
ASSOCIATE JUSTICE STEPHEN BREYER, Massachusetts	President CLINTON	FIRST ME., MASS., N. H., PUERTO RICO, R. I.	1994 (Aug. 2)	1994 (Aug. 3)
ASSOCIATE JUSTICE RUTH BADER GINSBURG, New York	President CLINTON	SECOND CONN., N. Y., VT.	1993 (Aug. 5)	1993 (Aug. 10)
ASSOCIATE JUSTICE SAMUEL A. ALITO, JR., New Jersey	President BUSH	THIRD DEL., N. J., PA., VIRGIN ISLANDS	2006 (JAN. 31)	2006 (JAN. 31)
CHIEF JUSTICE JOHN G. ROBERTS, JR., Maryland	President BUSH	FOURTH MD., N. C., S. C., VA., W. VA.	2005 (Sept. 29)	2005 (Sept. 29)
ASSOCIATE JUSTICE ANTONIN SCALIA, Virginia	President REAGAN	FIFTH CANAL ZONE, LA., MISS., TEX.	1986 (Sept. 25)	1986 (Sept. 26)
ASSOCIATE JUSTICE ELENA KAGAN, Massachusetts	President OBAMA	SIXTH KY., MICH., OHIO, TENN.	2010 (Aug. 6)	2010 (Aug. 7)
ASSOCIATE JUSTICE ELENA KAGAN, Massachusetts	President OBAMA	SEVENTH ILL., IND., WIS.	2010 (Aug. 6)	2010 (Aug. 7)
ASSOCIATE JUSTICE SAMUEL A. ALITO, JR., New Jersey	President BUSH	EIGHTH ARK., IOWA, MINN., MO., NEB., N. D., S. D.	2006 (Jan. 31)	2006 (Jan. 31)
ASSOCIATE JUSTICE ANTHONY M. KENNEDY, California	President REAGAN	NINTH ALASKA, ARIZ., CAL., IDAHO, MONT., NEV., OR., WASH., GUAM, HAWAII	1988 (Feb. 11)	1988 (Feb. 18)
ASSOCIATE JUSTICE SONIA SOTOMAYOR, New York	President OBAMA	TENTH COLO., KAN., N. M., OKLA., UTAH, WYO.	2009 (Aug. 6)	2009 (Aug. 8)
ASSOCIATE JUSTICE CLARENCE THOMAS, Georgia	President BUSH	ELEVENTH ALA., FLA., GA.	1991 (Oct. 16)	1991 (Nov. 1)

SUBJECTS ANNOTATED IN THIS VOLUME

These annotations, as well as all decisions reported in this volume, are indexed in the "Index to Decisions and Annotations" appearing at the end of this volume. For additional case and annotation references, consult appropriate topics and sections in the United States Supreme Court Digest, Lawyers' Edition, or consult the L Ed Index.

TABLE OF PARALLEL REFERENCES

FOR CASES REPORTED HEREIN AND IN OFFICIAL REPORTER'S EDITION

VOLUME 577 U.S. (part)

Also Memorandum Cases

(See 193 L. Ed. 2d pp 5-222, 223-254, 287-364, 392-420, 421-495, 517-534, 701-784, 785-813)

TABLE OF CASES REPORTED IN 193 L. Ed. 2d

Cases with opinions are **boldface**. Other cases are lightface.

Cases with opinions are **boldface.** Other cases are lightface.

Cases with opinions are **boldface.** Other cases are lightface.

Cases with opinions are **boldface.** Other cases are lightface.

Cases with opinions are **boldface**. Other cases are lightface.

U.S. SUPREME COURT REPORTS

Bluemel, In re, 306
Boca Raton Firefighters & Police Pension Fund v. Bahash, 315
Boda v. South Dakota, 73
Boddie v. Dep't of the Treasury, 21
Bodum, Inc. v. Meyer Intellectual Props. Ltd., 289
Boehner, Rangel v. 131
Boehringer Ingelheim Pharms., Inc. v. FTC, 311
Boehringer Ingelheim Pharms., Inc. v. FTC, 790
Boeing Co., Davis v. 766
Boeing Co., McDonald v. 210
Bogany v. Stephens, 58
Bogany v. Stephens, 455
Bogle, Emery v. 707
Boise, City of, James v. 694
Bolden v. Doe, 24
Bolds v. California, 403
Bolds v. California, 726
Bolds v. Cavazos, 295
Bolds v. Cavazos, 533
Bolen, Hayes v. 159
Bolin v. Florida, 534
Bolin v. Jones, 533
Bollinger v. Kansas, 721
Bolt v. Nooth, 162
Bolton v. United States, 296
Bolton v. United States, 777
Bomar v. Pennsylvania, 54
Bond v. Dep't of Educ., 239
Bond v. Holder, 468
Bondi, Marquez v. 77
Bonds v. United States, 334
Bonilla v. United States, 395
Bonner v. City of Brighton, 521
Bontrager v. United States, 730
Booker v. California, 440
Booker v. Clarke, 168
Booker, King v. 325
Booker v. United States, 210
Booker-El v. Neal, 295
Boone, In re, 770
Boone v. Griffin, 93
Boone v. Howerton, 437
Boone v. Jones, 162
Boone v. Jones, 461
Booth, In re, 214
Booth, In re, 773
Borden, Chavis v. 718
Boschini, Boswell v. 442
Bo's Food Store, Hammonds v. 488
Bosier v. Dep't of the Treasury, 197
Bost v. United States, 292
Boston Inspectional Servs. Dep't, City of, Dickey v. 469
Boswell v. Boschini, 442
Boswell v. Ector Cnty. Indep. Sch. Dist. Bd. of Trs., 298
Bouaphakeo, Tyson Foods, Inc. v. 288
Boughton, Boyd v. 795

Bouldin, Dietz v. 788
Boulware, Wannamaker v. 750
Bowden v. North Carolina, 467
Bowden v. United States, 155
Bowers v. Massachusetts, 800
Bowers v. Pollard, 746
Bowers v. United States, 172
Bowers v. United States, 245
Bowersox, Manning v. 735
Bowersox, Young v. 357
Bowling v. United States, 720
Bowring v. Raemisch, 86
Box v. Capozza, 195
Boyd v. Boughton, 795
Boyd v. Mississippi, 239
Boyd v. Mississippi, 777
Boyer, Health Grades, Inc. v. 291
Boyer v. Massachusetts, 441
Boykin v. United States, 198
Boykin v. United States, 755
BP Exploration & Prod., Sealed Appellant 2 v. 398
BP p.l.c., Veracruz v. 427
Bracken v. Missouri, 16
Bradden v. Texas, 739
Bradley v. Sabree, 132
Bradley v. Sabree, 416
Bradshaw, Savoie v. 295
Bradshaw, Savoie v. 777
Brady v. Williams, 724
Brainerd v. Schlumberger Tech. Corp., 415
Bramage v. Discover Bank, 235
Bramage v. Discover Bank, 491
Brammer v. California, 160
Bran v. United States, 722
Branch v. Dunbar, 81
Branch v. Illinois, 314
Branch, LeBlanc v. 702
Brandon v. United States, 135
Brannon v. Stevenson, 140
Brannon v. Stevenson, 460
Braun, Addai v. 69
Brawley, In re Discipline of, 494
Braxton v. Apperson, Crump & Maxwell, PLC, 716
Bray v. Premo, 245
Brayboy v. Napel, 159
Brayboy v. Napel, 531
Brayboy v. United States, 7
Brazelton, Johnson v. 795
Brazelton, McGinnis v. 167
Brazelton, Nelson v. 21
Brazelton, Nelson v. 395
Breaux v. Clarke, 403
Brelo, Pate v. 100
Brennan, Green v. 308
Brewer v. Stephens, 392
Brewer v. Stephens, 705
Bridges v. United States, 807
Briese Lichttechnik Vertriebs GmbH, Langton v. 34
Brighton, City of, Bonner v. 521

Cases with opinions are **boldface.** Other cases are lightface.

Cases with opinions are **boldface**. Other cases are lightface.

Cases with opinions are **boldface.** Other cases are lightface.

Cases with opinions are **boldface.** Other cases are lightface.

Cases with opinions are **boldface**. Other cases are lightface.

Cases with opinions are **boldface**. Other cases are lightface.

U.S. SUPREME COURT REPORTS

Cases with opinions are **boldface**. Other cases are lightface.

TABLE OF CASES REPORTED IN 193 L. Ed. 2d

Cases with opinions are **boldface.** Other cases are lightface.

Cases with opinions are **boldface.** Other cases are lightface.

Cases with opinions are **boldface.** Other cases are lightface.

Cases with opinions are **boldface.** Other cases are lightface.

Cases with opinions are **boldface**. Other cases are lightface.

Cases with opinions are **boldface**. Other cases are lightface.

Cases with opinions are **boldface.** Other cases are lightface.

Cases with opinions are **boldface.** Other cases are lightface.

TABLE OF CASES REPORTED IN 193 L. Ed. 2d

Cases with opinions are **boldface.** Other cases are lightface.

xxxiii

Cases with opinions are **boldface.** Other cases are lightface.

Cases with opinions are **boldface**. Other cases are lightface.

Cases with opinions are **boldface.** Other cases are lightface.

Cases with opinions are **boldface.** Other cases are lightface.

U.S. SUPREME COURT REPORTS

Cases with opinions are **boldface.** Other cases are lightface.

TABLE OF CASES REPORTED IN 193 L. Ed. 2d

Cases with opinions are **boldface**. Other cases are lightface.

Cases with opinions are **boldface.** Other cases are lightface.

Cases with opinions are **boldface.** Other cases are lightface.

Cases with opinions are **boldface**. Other cases are lightface.

Cases with opinions are **boldface**. Other cases are lightface.

Cases with opinions are **boldface.** Other cases are lightface.

Cases with opinions are **boldface.** Other cases are lightface.

Cases with opinions are **boldface.** Other cases are lightface.

Cases with opinions are **boldface.** Other cases are lightface.

Cases with opinions are **boldface.** Other cases are lightface.

TABLE OF CASES REPORTED IN 193 L. Ed. 2d

Cases with opinions are **boldface**. Other cases are lightface.

Cases with opinions are **boldface.** Other cases are lightface.

TABLE OF CASES REPORTED IN 193 L. Ed. 2d

Cases with opinions are **boldface.** Other cases are lightface.

Cases with opinions are **boldface.** Other cases are lightface.

Cases with opinions are **boldface**. Other cases are lightface.

Cases with opinions are **boldface.** Other cases are lightface.

Cases with opinions are **boldface**. Other cases are lightface.

Cases with opinions are **boldface.** Other cases are lightface.

Cases with opinions are **boldface.** Other cases are lightface.

Cases with opinions are **boldface.** Other cases are lightface.

Cases with opinions are **boldface.** Other cases are lightface.

Cases with opinions are **boldface.** Other cases are lightface.

TABLE OF CASES REPORTED IN 193 L. Ed. 2d

Cases with opinions are **boldface.** Other cases are lightface.

Cases with opinions are **boldface.** Other cases are lightface.

Cases with opinions are **boldface.** Other cases are lightface.

Cases with opinions are **boldface.** Other cases are lightface.

TABLE OF CASES REPORTED IN 193 L. Ed. 2d

Cases with opinions are **boldface.** Other cases are lightface.

Cases with opinions are **boldface.** Other cases are lightface.

TABLE OF CASES REPORTED IN 193 L. Ed. 2d

Cases with opinions are **boldface.** Other cases are lightface.

Cases with opinions are **boldface.** Other cases are lightface.

Cases with opinions are **boldface.** Other cases are lightface.

Cases with opinions are **boldface.** Other cases are lightface.

Cases with opinions are **boldface.** Other cases are lightface.

Cases with opinions are **boldface.** Other cases are lightface.

TABLE OF CASES REPORTED IN 193 L. Ed. 2d

Cases with opinions are **boldface.** Other cases are lightface.

Cases with opinions are **boldface.** Other cases are lightface.

Cases with opinions are **boldface.** Other cases are lightface.

Cases with opinions are **boldface.** Other cases are lightface.

Cases with opinions are **boldface.** Other cases are lightface.

Cases with opinions are **boldface.** Other cases are lightface.

TABLE OF CASES REPORTED IN 193 L. Ed. 2d

Cases with opinions are **boldface.** Other cases are lightface.

Cases with opinions are **boldface.** Other cases are lightface.

TABLE OF CASES REPORTED IN 193 L. Ed. 2d

Cases with opinions are **boldface.** Other cases are lightface.

TABLE OF FEDERAL CONSTITUTIONAL PROVISIONS, STATUTES, COURT RULES, AND REGULATIONS CITED AND CONSTRUED IN 193 L. Ed. 2d

CONSTITUTION

UNITED STATES CODE SERVICE

FEDERAL RULES OF CIVIL PROCEDURE

FEDERAL RULES OF CRIMINAL PROCEDURE

ADMINISTRATIVE RULES AND REGULATIONS

TABLE OF CLASSIFICATIONS TO THE UNITED STATES SUPREME COURT DIGEST, LAWYERS' EDITION, FROM CASES REPORTED IN 193 L. Ed. 2d

MISCELLANEOUS PROCEEDINGS

October 13, 2015

NOTING OF AMICUS CURIAE

[At oral argument in No. 14-280, Montgomery v. Louisiana] The Chief Justice said:

"Mr. Bernstein, the Court appointed you as an *amicus curiae* to brief and argue this case against this Court's jurisdiction. You have ably discharged that responsibility, for which the Court is grateful."

November 3, 2015

NOTING OF VISITORS FROM SERBIA

The Chief Justice said:

"We are pleased to have visiting with us this morning President Dragomir Milojevic, of the Supreme Court of Cassation and the High Court Council of Serbia, and his colleagues from the Serbian Judiciary. On behalf of the Court, welcome."

November 30, 2015

NOTING OF AMICUS CURIAE

[At oral argument in No. 14-613, Green v. Brennan] The Chief Justice said:

"Ms. Carroll, this Court appointed you to brief and argue this case as *amicus curiae*, in support of the judgment below. You have ably discharged that responsibility, for which the Court is grateful."

December 9, 2015

EXTENSION OF ARGUMENT TIME

[At oral argument in No. 14-981, Fisher v. Univ. of Tex.] The Chief Justice said:

"Before we get started, I advise the lawyers that this is our only case this morning, so we intend to grant the parties 10 minutes or so of extra time and the *amicus* 5 minutes."

MISCELLANEOUS PROCEEDINGS

December 31, 2015

2015 YEAR-END REPORT ON THE FEDERAL JUDICIARY

[by the Chief Justice]

In 1838, John Lyde Wilson, a former governor of South Carolina, made a grim contribution to the literature of dispute resolution by publishing *"The Code of Honor; or Rules for the Government of Principals and Seconds in Duelling."* That 22-page booklet, sized to fit comfortably alongside a gentleman's matched pair of dueling pistols, specified the procedure for issuing a challenge, the duties of seconds, and the proper conduct of the duel itself. More detailed than its predecessors, the Irish and French dueling codes, Wilson's rulebook set out time limits, the form and methods of written communications, the obligation to attempt reconciliation without bloodshed, and—if attempts at mediation failed—how to pace off the field of battle. Wilson professed that he was not advocating that adversaries settle their disputes through duels, but he claimed that dueling was inevitable "where there is no tribunal to do justice to an oppressed and deeply wronged individual." He suggested that laying out practices and procedures to ensure that duels would be conducted fairly—including provisions for resolving disputes through apology and compromise—would in fact save lives.

It may be that Wilson's code had exactly the opposite effect, glorifying and institutionalizing a barbarous practice that led to wanton death. Our Nation had lost Alexander Hamilton to a senseless duel in 1804. Abraham Lincoln and Mark Twain could have perished in duels if their seconds, in each instance, had not negotiated an amicable solution. But others were not so fortunate; one historian has calculated that, between 1798 and the Civil War, the United States Navy lost two-thirds as many officers to dueling as it did to more than 60 years of combat at sea.

Public opinion ultimately turned against dueling as a means of settling quarrels. By 1859, eighteen of the 33 States of the Union had outlawed duels. Following the Civil War, a public weary of bloodshed turned increasingly to other forums, including the courts, to settle disputes. But reminders of the practice persist. When Kentucky lawyers are admitted to the bar, they are required, by law, to swear that they have not participated in a duel.

Today, Wilson's pamphlet stands on the bookshelf as a largely forgotten relic of a happily bygone past. But it is also a stark reminder of government's responsibility to provide tribunals for the peaceful resolution of all manner of disputes. Our Nation's courts are today's guarantors of justice. Those civil tribunals, far more than the inherently uncivilized dueling fields they supplanted, must be governed by sound rules of practice and procedure.

The Rules Enabling Act, 28 U.S.C. §§ 2071 et seq., empowers the federal courts to prescribe rules for the conduct of their business. The Judicial Conference—the policy making body of the federal judiciary—has overall responsibility for formulating those rules. Consistent with that charge, Congress has directed the Conference to "carry on a continuous study of the operation and effect of the general rules of practice and procedure." 28 U.S.C. § 331. The primary work is done through the Conference's Committee on Rules of Practice and Procedure (known as the Standing Committee), which in turn enlists guidance from advisory committees that focus on the specialties of appellate, bankruptcy, civil, and criminal procedure, and the rules of evidence. Those committees solicit recommendations, conduct public hearings, draft proposed rules, and propose amendments for the Judicial Conference's consideration. If the Judicial Conference concurs, the proposed rules and amendments, together with a report on their promulgation, are submitted to the Supreme Court for its approval. If the Court approves, the rules are then laid before Congress, by the annual deadline of May 1, for its examination. Unless Congress intervenes by December 1, the new rules take effect.

This process of judicial rule formulation, now more than 80 years old, is elaborate and time-consuming, but it ensures that federal court rules of practice and procedure are developed through meticulous consideration, with input from all facets of the legal community, including judges, lawyers, law professors, and the public at large. Many rules amendments are modest and technical, even persnickety, but the 2015 amendments to the Federal Rules of Civil Procedure are different. Those amendments are the product of five years of intense study, debate, and drafting to address the most serious impediments to just, speedy, and efficient resolution of civil disputes.

The project goes back to 2010, when the Advisory Committee on Civil Rules sponsored a symposium on civil litigation, which brought together federal and state judges, law professors, and plaintiff and defense lawyers, drawn from business, government, and public interest organizations. The symposium, which generated 40 papers and 25 data compilations, confirmed that, while the federal courts are fundamentally sound, in many cases civil litigation has become too expensive, time-consuming, and contentious, inhibiting effective access to the courts. The symposium specifically identified the need for procedural reforms that would: (1) encourage greater cooperation among counsel; (2) focus discovery—the process of obtaining information within the control of the opposing party—on what is truly necessary to resolve the case; (3) engage judges in early and active case management; and (4) address serious new problems associated with vast amounts of electronically stored information.

The Advisory Committee on Civil Rules set to work on those problems. Over the next three years, the Committee drafted proposed amendments and published them for public comment. It received more than 2,300 written comments and held public hearings in Dallas, Phoenix, and Washington, D.C., eliciting input from more than 120 witnesses. The Committee then revised the amendments in response to the public recommendations. The proposed amendments received further scrutiny from the Standing Committee, the Judicial Conference, and the Supreme Court, before submission to Congress. The amended rules, which can be viewed at http://www.uscourts.gov/federal-rules-civil-procedure, went into effect one month ago, on December 1, 2015. They mark significant change, for both lawyers and judges, in the future conduct of civil trials.

The amendments may not look like a big deal at first glance, but they are. That is one reason I have chosen to highlight them in this report. For example, Rule 1 of the Federal Rules of Civil Procedure has been expanded by a mere eight words, but those are words that judges and practitioners must take to heart. Rule 1 directs that the Federal Rules "should be construed, administered, and employed by the court and the parties to secure the just, speedy, and inexpensive determination of every action and proceeding." The underscored words make express the obligation of judges and lawyers to work cooperatively in controlling the expense and time demands of litigation—an obligation given effect in the amendments that follow. The new passage highlights the point that lawyers—though representing adverse parties—have an affirmative duty to work together, and with the court, to achieve prompt and effiient resolutions of disputes.

Rule 26(b)(1) crystalizes the concept of reasonable limits on discovery through increased reliance on the common-sense concept of proportionality:

"Parties may obtain discovery regarding any nonprivileged matter that is relevant to any party's claim or defense and proportional to the needs of the case, considering the importance of the issues at stake in the action, the amount in controversy, the parties' relative access to relevant information, the parties' resources, the importance of the discovery in resolving the issues, and whether the burden or expense of the proposed discovery outweighs its likely benefit."

The amended rule states, as a fundamental principle, that lawyers must size and shape their discovery requests to the requisites of a case. Specifically, the pretrial process must provide parties with efficient access to what is needed to prove a claim or defense, but eliminate unnecessary or wasteful discovery. The key here is careful and realistic assessment of actual need. That assessment may, as a practical matter, require the active involvement of a neutral arbiter—the federal judge—to guide decisions respecting the scope of discovery.

The amended rules accordingly emphasize the crucial role of federal judges in engaging in early and effective case management. The prior rules—specifically Rule 16—already required that the judge meet with the lawyers after the complaint is filed, confer about the needs of the case, and develop a case management plan. The amended rules have shortened the deadline for that meeting and express a preference for a face-to-face encounter to enhance communication between the judge and lawyers. The amendments also identify techniques to expedite resolution of pretrial discovery disputes, including conferences with the judge before filing formal motions in aid of discovery. Such conferences can often obviate the need for a formal motion—a well-timed scowl from a trial judge can go a long way in moving things along crisply.

Recognizing the evolving role of information technology in virtually every detail of life, the amended rules specifically address the issue of "electronically stored information," which has given birth to a new acronym—"ESI." Rules 16 and 26(f) now require the parties to reach agreement on the preservation and discovery of ESI in their case management plan and discovery conferences. Amendments to Rule 37(e) effect a further refinement by specifying the consequences if a party fails to observe the generally recognized obligation to preserve ESI in the face of foreseeable litigation. If the failure to take reasonable precautions results in a loss of discoverable ESI, the courts must first focus on whether the information can be restored or replaced through alternative discovery efforts. If not, the courts may order additional measures "no greater than necessary" to cure the resulting prejudice. And if the loss of ESI is the result of one party's intent to deprive the other of the information's use in litigation, the court may impose prescribed sanctions, ranging from an adverse jury instruction to dismissal of the action or entry of a default judgment.

The rules amendments eliminate Rule 84, which referenced an appendix containing a number of civil litigation forms that were originally designed to provide lawyers and unrepresented litigants with examples of proper pleading. Over the years since their publication, many of those forms have become antiquated or obsolete. The Administrative Office of the United States Courts assembled a group of experienced judges to replace those outdated forms with modern versions that reflect current practice and procedure. They have largely completed their work. The Administrative Office has already posted 12 revised forms on the federal judiciary's website, with three more to follow in the next month. See http://www.uscourts.gov/forms/pro-se-forms.

The 2015 civil rules amendments are a major stride toward a better federal court system. But they will achieve the goal of Rule 1—"the just, speedy, and inexpensive determination of every action and proceeding"—only if the entire legal community, including the bench, bar, and legal academy, step up to the challenge of making real change.

I think we are off to a good start. The Federal Judicial Center, which is the educational and research arm of the federal judiciary, has created a training program for federal judges to ensure they are prepared to introduce the procedural reforms in their courtrooms. Training is necessary for lawyers too, and the American Bar Association and many local bar organizations have initiated educational programs and workshops across the country. The practical implementation of the rules may require some adaptation and innovation. I encourage all to support the judiciary's plans to test the workability of new case management and discovery practices through carefully conceived pilot programs. In addition, a wide variety of judicial, legal, and academic organizations have supplied key insights in the improvement of both federal and state rules of practice, and they are continuing to provide their perspectives and expertise on the rollout of the new rules. I am confident that the Advisory Committee on Civil Rules will continue to engage the full spectrum of those organizations in its ongoing work.

The success of the 2015 civil rules amendments will require more than organized educational efforts. It will also require a genuine commitment, by judges and lawyers alike, to ensure that our legal culture reflects the values we all ultimately share.

Judges must be willing to take on a stewardship role, managing their cases from the outset rather than allowing parties alone to dictate the scope of discovery and the pace of litigation. Faced with crushing dockets, judges can be tempted to postpone engagement in pretrial activities. Experience has shown, however, that judges who are knowledgeable, actively engaged, and accessible early in the process are far more effective in resolving cases fairly and efficiently, because they can identify the critical issues, determine the appropriate breadth of discovery, and curtail dilatory tactics, gamesmanship, and procedural posturing.

As for the lawyers, most will readily agree—in the abstract—that they have an obligation to their clients, and to the justice system, to avoid antagonistic tactics, wasteful procedural maneuvers, and teetering brinksmanship. I cannot believe that many members of the bar went to law school because of a burning desire to spend their professional life wearing down opponents with creatively burdensome discovery requests or evading legitimate requests through dilatory tactics. The test for plaintiffs' and defendants' counsel alike is whether they will affirmatively search out cooperative solutions, chart a cost-effective course of litigation, and assume shared responsibility with opposing counsel to achieve just results.

I am hardly the first to urge that we must engineer a change in our legal culture that places a premium on the public's interest in speedy, fair, and efficient justice. But I am motivated to address the subject now because the 2015 civil rules amendments provide a concrete opportunity for actually getting something done.

In the nineteenth century, a change in culture left dueling by the wayside and left us with lessons learned. Joseph Conrad's novella *"The Duel"* tells the tale, taken from fact, of two gallant French cavalry officers, D'Hubert and Feraud. Estranged by a trifling slight, they repeatedly duel over a 15-year period. According to newspapers of the era, the real-life antagonists, Dupont and Fournier, would cross swords and draw blood whenever their military service brought them near to one another. Conrad's characters, like the real ones, relentlessly persist in their personal feud through the rise, fall, reemergence, and ultimate exile of Napoleon, as the world transforms around them. In the end, these soldiers, who should have been comrades in a patriotic cause, spent much of their adult lives focused on a petty squabble that left them with nothing but scars. We should not miss the opportunity to help ensure that federal court litigation does not degenerate into wasteful clashes over matters that have little to do with achieving a just result.

Another year has quickly passed, and once again, I am privileged and honored to be in a position to thank all of the judges, court staff, and judicial personnel throughout the Nation for their continued excellence and dedication.

Best wishes to all in the New Year.

Appendix

Workload of the Courts

In the 12-month period ending September 30, 2015, caseloads decreased in the Supreme Court, the regional appellate courts, the district courts, the bankruptcy courts, and the pretrial services system. Growth occurred, however, in the number of persons under post-conviction supervision.

The Supreme Court of the United States

The total number of cases filed in the Supreme Court decreased by 4.65 percent from 7,376 filings in the 2013 Term to 7,033 filings in the 2014 Term. The number of cases filed in the Court's *in forma pauperis* docket decreased by 5.50 percent from 5,808 filings in the 2013 Term to 5,488 filings in the 2014 Term. The number of cases filed in the Court's paid docket decreased by 1.47 percent from 1,568 filings in the 2013 Term to 1,545 filings in the 2014 Term. During the 2014 Term, 75 cases were argued and 75 were disposed of in 66 signed opinions, compared with 79 cases argued and 77 disposed of in 67 signed opinions during the 2013 Term. The Court also issued eight per curiam decisions during the 2014 Term in cases that were not argued.

The Federal Courts of Appeals

In the regional courts of appeals, filings dropped four percent to 52,698. Appeals involving pro se litigants, which amounted to 51 percent of filings, fell four percent. Total civil appeals decreased seven percent. Criminal appeals rose three percent, as did appeals of administrative agency decisions, and bankruptcy appeals grew seven percent.

The Federal District Courts

Civil case filings in the U.S. district courts declined six percent to 279,036. Cases involving diversity of citizenship (i.e., disputes between citizens of different states) fell 14 percent, largely because of a reduction in personal injury/product liability filings. Cases with the United States as defendant dropped seven percent in response to fewer filings of prisoner petitions and Social Security cases. Cases with the United States as plaintiff went down 10 percent as filings of forfeiture and penalty cases and contract cases decreased.

Filings for criminal defendants (including those transferred from other istricts) held relatively steady, declining one percent to 80,069. Defendants accused of immigration violations dropped five percent, with the southwestern border districts receiving 79 percent of national immigration defendant filings. Defendants charged with property offenses (including fraud) fell six percent. Other reductions were reported for filings involving traffic offenses, general offenses, regulatory offenses, and justice system offenses. Drug crime defendants, who accounted for 32 percent of total filings, rose two percent. Increases also occurred in filings related to firearms and explosives, sex offenses, and violent crimes.

The Bankruptcy Courts

Bankruptcy petition filings decreased 11 percent to 860,182. Fewer petitions were filed in all bankruptcy courts but one—the Middle District of Alabama had three percent more filings this year. Consumer (i.e., nonbusiness) petitions dropped 11 percent, and business petitions fell 12 percent. Filings of petitions declined 14 percent under Chapter 7, eight percent under Chapter 11, and three percent under Chapter 13.

This year's total for bankruptcy petitions is the lowest since 2007, the first full year after the Bankruptcy Abuse Prevention and Consumer Protection Act of 2005 took effect. From 2007 to 2010, bankruptcy filings rose steadily, but they have fallen in each of the last five years.

The Federal Probation and Pretrial Services System

A total of 135,468 persons were under post-conviction supervision on September 30, 2015, an increase of two percent over the total one year earlier. Of that number, 114,961 persons were serving terms of supervised release after leaving correctional institutions, a three percent increase from the prior year.

Cases activated in the pretrial services system, including pretrial diversion cases, fell five percent to 95,013.

CASES ADJUDGED

IN THE

SUPREME COURT

OF THE

UNITED STATES

———

October Term, 2015

VOLUME 577 U.S. (part)

†

MARYLAND, Petitioner

v

JAMES KULBICKI

577 U.S. 1, 136 S. Ct. 2, 193 L. Ed. 2d 1, 2015 U.S. LEXIS 4693

[No. 14-848]

Decided October 5, 2015.

Decision: Accused's counsel not ineffective in violation of Federal Constitution's Sixth Amendment in failing to question legitimacy of Comparative Bullet Lead Analysis.

Prior history: ON PETITION FOR WRIT OF CERTIORARI TO THE COURT OF APPEALS OF MARYLAND, 440 Md. 33, 99 A.3d 730, 2014 Md. LEXIS 535

SUMMARY

Overview: HOLDINGS: [1]-Counsel was not ineffective for failing to attempt to discredit Comparative Bullet Lead Analysis (CBLA) evidence since the mode of ballistics analysis was uncontroversial and widely accepted at the time of the defendant's trial for murder, and counsel was not required to search for an obscure report questioning the methodology or to predict the subsequent demise of CBLA.

Outcome: Petition granted and judgment reversed. Unanimous Decision.

HEADNOTES

Classified to United States Supreme Court Digest, Lawyers' Edition

Right to counsel — ineffective assistance

L Ed Digest: Criminal Law §§ 46.1, 46.6, 46.10

1. A criminal defendant shall enjoy the right to have the assistance of counsel for his defense. U.S. Const. Amend. 6. This right requires effective counsel in both state and federal prosecutions, even if the defendant is unable to afford counsel. Counsel is unconstitutionally ineffective if his performance is both deficient, meaning his errors are so serious that he no longer functions as counsel, and prejudicial, meaning his errors deprive the defendant of a fair trial.

RESEARCH REFERENCES

U.S.C.S., Constitution, Amendment 6
27 Moore's Federal Practice § 644.61 (Matthew Bender 3d ed.)
L Ed Digest, Criminal Law § 46.10
L Ed Index, Attorneys at Law

Annotations:

When is attorney's representation of criminal defendant so deficient as to constitute denial of federal constitutional right to effective assistance of counsel—Supreme Court cases. 83 L. Ed. 2d 1112.

Comment Note.—What provisions of the Federal Constitution's Bill of Rights are applicable to the states. 18 L. Ed. 2d 1388, 23 L. Ed. 2d 985.

Accused's right to counsel under the Federal Constitution—Supreme Court cases. 93 L. Ed. 137, 2 L. Ed. 2d 1644, 9 L. Ed. 2d 1260, 18 L. Ed. 2d 1420.

SHEPARD'S® Citations Service. For further research of authorities referenced here, use SHEPARD'S to be sure your case or statute is still good law and to find additional authorities that support your position. SHEPARD'S is available exclusively from LexisNexis®.

SYLLABUS BY REPORTER OF DECISIONS

For text of added syllabus for this case see p 814A, infra.

OPINION OF THE COURT

[577 U.S. 2]

Per Curiam.

[1] A criminal defendant "shall enjoy the right . . . to have the Assistance of Counsel for his defence." U. S. Const., Amdt. 6. We have held that this right requires effective counsel in both state and federal prosecutions, even if the defendant is unable to afford counsel. *Gideon* v. *Wainwright*, 372 U.S. 335, 344, 83 S. Ct. 792, 9 L. Ed. 2d 799 (1963). Counsel is unconstitutionally ineffective if his performance is both deficient, meaning his errors are "so serious" that he no longer functions as "counsel," and prejudicial, meaning his errors deprive the defendant of a fair trial. *Strickland* v. *Washington*, 466 U.S. 668, 687, 104 S. Ct. 2052, 80 L. Ed. 2d 674 (1984). Applying this standard in name only, the Court of Appeals of Maryland held that James Kulbicki's defense attorneys were unconstitutionally ineffective. We summarily reverse.

In 1993, Kulbicki shot his 22-year-old mistress in the head at pointblank range. The two had been ensnarled in a paternity suit, and the killing oc-curred the weekend before a scheduled hearing about unpaid child support. At Kulbicki's trial, commencing in 1995, Agent Ernest Peele of the FBI testified as the State's expert on Comparative Bullet Lead Analysis, or CBLA. In testimony of the sort CBLA experts had provided for decades, Peele testified that the composition of elements in the molten lead of a bullet fragment found in Kulbicki's truck matched the composition of lead in a bullet fragment removed from the victim's brain; a similarity of the sort one would " 'expect' " if " 'examining two pieces of the same bullet.' " 440 Md. 33, 41, 99 A.3d

[577 U.S. 3]

730, 735 (2014). He further testified that a bullet taken from Kulbicki's gun was not an "exac[t]" match to the bullet fragments, but was similar enough that the two bullets likely came from the same package. *Id.*, at 42-44, 99 A.3d, at 735-736. After considering this ballistics evidence, additional physical evidence from Kulbicki's truck, and witness testimony, the jury convicted Kulbicki of first-degree murder.

Kulbicki then filed a petition for postconviction relief, which lingered in state court until 2006 when Kulbicki added a claim that his defense attorneys were ineffective for failing to question the legitimacy of CBLA. By then, 11 years after his conviction, CBLA had fallen out of favor. Indeed, Kulbicki supplemented his petition once more in 2006 after the Court of Appeals of Maryland held for the first time that CBLA evidence was not generally accepted by the scientific community and was therefore inadmissible. See *Clemons* v. *State*, 392 Md. 339, 371, 896 A.2d 1059, 1078 (2006).

Kulbicki lost in the lower state courts and appealed to the Court of Appeals of Maryland. At that point, Kulbicki abandoned his claim of ineffective assistance with respect to the CBLA evidence, but the high court vacated Kulbicki's conviction on that ground alone. Kulbicki's counsel, according to the court, should have found a report coauthored by Agent Peele in 1991 that "presaged the flaws in CBLA evidence." 440 Md., at 40, 99 A.3d, at 734. One of the many findings of the report was that the composition of lead in some bullets was the same as that of lead in other bullets packaged many months later in a separate box. Rather than conduct "further research to explain the existence of overlapping compositions," the authors "speculated" that coincidence (or, in one case, the likelihood that separately packaged bullets originated from the same source of lead) caused the overlap. *Id.*, at 49, 99 A.3d, at 739. The Court of Appeals opined that this lone finding should have caused the report's authors to doubt "that bullets produced from different sources of lead would have a unique chemical composition," the faulty assumption

[577 U.S. 4]

that ultimately led the court to reject CBLA evidence 15 years later. *Ibid.*; see *Clemons, supra*, at 369-370, 896 A.2d, at 1077. The authors' "failure to fully explore the variance," the Court of Appeals concluded, was "at odds with the scientific method." 440 Md., at 50, 99 A.3d, at 740.

In the Court of Appeals' view, any good attorney should have spotted this methodological flaw. The court held that counsel's failure to unearth the report, to identify one of its findings as "at odds with the scientific method," and to use this methodological flaw to cast doubt on CBLA during counsel's cross-examination of Peele, "fell short of prevailing professional norms." *Id.*, at 50-53, 99 A.3d, at 740-742. Concluding that counsel's supposed deficiency was prejudicial, the court set aside the conviction and ordered a new trial. *Id.*, at 56, 99 A.3d, at 743-744.

We reverse. The Court of Appeals offered no support for its conclusion that Kulbicki's defense attorneys were constitutionally required to predict the demise of CBLA. Instead, the court indulged in the "natural tendency to speculate as to whether a different trial strategy might have been more successful." *Lockhart* v. *Fretwell*, 506 U.S. 364, 372, 113 S. Ct. 838, 122 L. Ed. 2d 180 (1993). To combat this tendency, we have "adopted the rule of contemporary assessment of counsel's conduct." *Ibid*. Had the Court of Appeals heeded this rule, it would have "judge[d] the reasonableness of counsel's challenged conduct . . . viewed as of the time of counsel's conduct." *Strickland, supra,* at 690, 104 S. Ct. 2052, 80 L. Ed. 2d 674.

At the time of Kulbicki's trial in 1995, the validity of CBLA was widely accepted, and courts regularly admitted CBLA evidence until 2003. See *United States* v. *Higgs,* 663 F.3d 726, 738 (CA4 2011). As the Court of Appeals acknowledged, even the 1991 report itself did not question the validity of CBLA, concluding that it was a valid and useful forensic tool to match suspect to victim. 440 Md., at 51, n. 11, 99 A.3d, at 740, n. 11. Counsel did not perform deficiently by dedicating their time and focus to elements of the

[577 U.S. 5]

defense that did not involve poking methodological holes in a then-uncontroversial mode of ballistics analysis.

That is especially the case here, since there is no reason to believe that a diligent search would even have discovered the supposedly crucial report. The Court of Appeals offered a single citation in support of its sweeping statement that the report "was available" to Kulbicki's counsel in 1995—a Government Printing Office Web page accessed by the Court of Appeals, apparently conducting its own Internet research nearly two decades after the trial. *Id.,* at 51, and n. 12, 99 A.3d, at 740–741, and n. 12; see also Brief in Opposition 14. The Web page indicates that a compilation of forensic studies that included the report was "distributed to various public libraries in 1994." 440 Md., at 51, n. 12, 99 A.3d, at 741, n. 12. But which ones? And in an era of card catalogues, not a worldwide web, what

efforts would counsel have had to expend to find the compilation? And had they found it, would counsel really have combed through the entire compilation, and have identified the one (of many) findings in one of the reports, the disregard of which counsel would have recognized to be "at odds with the scientific method"? And then, would effective counsel really have brought to the attention of the jury a report whose *conclusion* was that CBLA was a valid investigative technique in cases just like Kulbicki's? Neither the Court of Appeals nor Kulbicki has answers. Given the uncontroversial nature of CBLA at the time of Kulbicki's trial, the effect of the judgment below is to demand that lawyers go "looking for a needle in a haystack," even when they have "reason to doubt there is any needle there." *Rompilla* v. *Beard,* 545 U.S. 374, 389, 125 S. Ct. 2456, 162 L. Ed. 2d 360 (2005). The Court of Appeals demanded something close to "perfect advocacy"—far more than the "reasonable competence" the right to counsel guarantees. *Yarborough* v. *Gentry,* 540 U.S. 1, 8, 124 S. Ct. 1, 157 L. Ed. 2d 1 (2003) (*per curiam*).

Kulbicki's trial counsel did not provide deficient performance when they failed to uncover the 1991 report and to use

[577 U.S. 6]

the report's so-called methodological flaw against Peele on cross-examination. (We need not, and so do not, decide whether the supposed error prejudiced Kulbicki.) The petition for writ of certiorari is granted, and the judgment of the Court of Appeals for Maryland is reversed.

It is so ordered.

MEMORANDUM CASES

No. 14-1115. Bank of America, N.A., Petitioner v. Judith L. Hackbart.

577 U.S. 801, 136 S. Ct. 31, 193 L. Ed. 2d 5, 2015 U.S. LEXIS 5196.

October 5, 2015. On petition for writ of certiorari to the United States Court of Appeals for the Eleventh Circuit. Petition for writ of certiorari granted. Judgment vacated, and case remanded to the United States Court of Appeals for the Eleventh Circuit for further consideration in light of Bank of America, N. A. v. Caulkett, 575 U.S. 790, 135 S. Ct. 1995, 192 L. Ed. 2d 52 (2015).

Same case below, 589 Fed. Appx. 477.

No. 14-1322. Jeffrey Herson, et al., Petitioners v. City of Richmond, California.

577 U.S. 801, 136 S. Ct. 46, 193 L. Ed. 2d 5, 2015 U.S. LEXIS 5279.

October 5, 2015. On petition for writ of certiorari to the United States Court of Appeals for the Ninth Circuit. Petition for writ of certiorari granted. Judgment vacated, and case remanded to the United States Court of Appeals for the Ninth Circuit for further consideration in light of Reed v. Town of Gilbert, 576 U.S. 155, 135 S. Ct. 2218, 192 L. Ed. 2d 236 (2015).

Same case below, 585 Fed. Appx. 522.

No. 14-9707. Roylin Junius Beale, Petitioner v. J. P. Madigan, et al.

577 U.S. 801, 136 S. Ct. 53, 193 L. Ed. 2d 5, 2015 U.S. LEXIS 5504.

October 5, 2015. On petition for writ of certiorari to the United States Court of Appeals for the Fourth Circuit. Motion of petitioner for leave to proceed in forma pauperis and petition for writ of certiorari granted. Judgment vacated, and case remanded to the United States Court of Appeals for the Fourth Circuit for further consideration in light of Kingsley v. Hendrickson, 576 U.S. 389, 135 S. Ct. 2466, 192 L. Ed. 2d 416 (2015).

Same case below, 589 Fed. Appx. 107.

No. 14-9971. Raymond M. Welch, II, Petitioner v. United States.

577 U.S. 801, 136 S. Ct. 78, 193 L. Ed. 2d 5, 2015 U.S. LEXIS 5161.

October 5, 2015. On petition for writ of certiorari to the United States Court of Appeals for the Sixth Circuit. Motion of petitioner for leave to proceed in forma pauperis and petition for writ of certiorari granted. Judgment vacated, and case remanded to the United States Court of Appeals for the Sixth Circuit for further consideration in light of Johnson v. United States, 576 U.S. 591, 135 S. Ct. 2551, 192 L. Ed. 2d 569 (2015).

Same case below, 774 F.3d 891.

No. 14-9996. Francisco Bernabe Gonzales, Petitioner v. United States.

577 U.S. 801, 136 S. Ct. 84, 193 L. Ed. 2d 5, 2015 U.S. LEXIS 5587.

October 5, 2015. On petition for writ of certiorari to the United States Court of

Appeals for the Fifth Circuit. Motion of petitioner for leave to proceed in forma pauperis and petition for writ of certiorari granted. Judgment vacated, and case remanded to the United States Court of Appeals for the Fifth Circuit for further consideration in light of Johnson v. United States, 576 U.S. 591, 135 S. Ct. 2551, 192 L. Ed. 2d 569 (2015).

Same case below, 598 Fed. Appx. 311.

————

No. 14-10143. Aloniza J. Williams, Petitioner v. United States.

577 U.S. 801, 136 S. Ct. 105, 193 L. Ed. 2d 6, 2015 U.S. LEXIS 5358.

October 5, 2015. On petition for writ of certiorari to the United States Court of Appeals for the Eleventh Circuit. Motion of petitioner for leave to proceed in forma pauperis and petition for writ of certiorari granted. Judgment vacated, and case remanded to the United States Court of Appeals for the Eleventh Circuit for further consideration in light of Johnson v. United States, 576 U.S. 591, 135 S. Ct. 2551, 192 L. Ed. 2d 569 (2015).

Same case below, 603 Fed. Appx. 919.

————

No. 14-10157. Tracey Lamont Coad, Petitioner v. United States.

577 U.S. 801, 136 S. Ct. 107, 193 L. Ed. 2d 6, 2015 U.S. LEXIS 5316.

October 5, 2015. On petition for writ of certiorari to the United States Court of Appeals for the Fourth Circuit. Motion of petitioner for leave to proceed in forma pauperis and petition for writ of certiorari granted. Judgment vacated, and case re-

manded to the United States Court of Appeals for the Fourth Circuit for further consideration in light of Johnson v. United States, 576 U.S. 591, 135 S. Ct. 2551, 192 L. Ed. 2d 569 (2015).

Same case below, 590 Fed. Appx. 238.

————

No. 14-10323. Tyrone Hart, Petitioner v. United States.

577 U.S. 801, 136 S. Ct. 140, 193 L. Ed. 2d 6, 2015 U.S. LEXIS 5525.

October 5, 2015. On petition for writ of certiorari to the United States Court of Appeals for the Eleventh Circuit. Motion of petitioner for leave to proceed in forma pauperis and petition for writ of certiorari granted. Judgment vacated, and case remanded to the United States Court of Appeals for the Eleventh Circuit for further consideration in light of Johnson v. United States, 576 U.S. 591, 135 S. Ct. 2551, 192 L. Ed. 2d 569 (2015).

Same case below, 597 Fed. Appx. 620.

————

No. 15-5113. John Forrest Coon, Petitioner v. United States.

577 U.S. 801, 136 S. Ct. 187, 193 L. Ed. 2d 6, 2015 U.S. LEXIS 5065.

October 5, 2015. On petition for writ of certiorari to the United States Court of Appeals for the Eleventh Circuit. Motion of petitioner for leave to proceed in forma pauperis and petition for writ of certiorari granted. Judgment is vacated, and case remanded to the United States Court of Appeals for the Eleventh Circuit for further consideration in light of Johnson v. United States, 576 U.S. 591, 135 S. Ct. 2551, 192 L. Ed. 2d 569 (2015).

Same case below, 607 Fed. Appx. 849.

No. 15-5217. Cornelius Brayboy, Petitioner v. United States.

577 U.S. 801, 136 S. Ct. 206, 193 L. Ed. 2d 7, 2015 U.S. LEXIS 5524.

October 5, 2015. On petition for writ of certiorari to the United States Court of Appeals for the Eleventh Circuit. Motion of petitioner for leave to proceed in forma pauperis and petition for writ of certiorari granted. Judgment vacated, and case remanded to the United States Court of Appeals for the Eleventh Circuit for further consideration in light of Johnson v. United States, 576 U.S. 591, 135 S. Ct. 2551, 192 L. Ed. 2d 569 (2015).

No. 15-5604. Damien Antwon Evans, Petitioner v. United States.

577 U.S. 802, 136 S. Ct. 264, 193 L. Ed. 2d 7, 2015 U.S. LEXIS 5113.

October 5, 2015. On petition for writ of certiorari to the United States Court of Appeals for the Fourth Circuit. Motion of petitioner for leave to proceed in forma pauperis and petition forwrit of certiorari granted. Judgment vacated, and case remanded to the United States Court of Appeals for the Fourth Circuit for further consideration in light of Johnson v. United States, 576 U.S. 591, 135 S. Ct. 2551, 192 L. Ed. 2d 569 (2015).

Same case below, 609 Fed. Appx. 760.

No. 14-10061. Andre J. Twitty, Petitioner v. United States.

577 U.S. 802, 136 S. Ct. 90, 193 L. Ed. 2d 7, 2015 U.S. LEXIS 5505.

October 5, 2015. On petition for writ of certiorari to the United States Court of Appeals for the Tenth Circuit. Motion of petitioner for leave to proceed in forma pauperis and petition for writ of certiorari granted. Judgment vacated, and case remanded to the United States Court of Appeals for the Tenth Circuit for further consideration in light of Elonis v. United States, 575 U.S. 723, 135 S. Ct. 2001, 192 L. Ed. 2d 1 (2015).

Same case below, 591 Fed. Appx. 676.

No. 14-10065. Anthony Lane, Petitioner v. Alabama.

577 U.S. 802, 136 S. Ct. 91, 193 L. Ed. 2d 7, 2015 U.S. LEXIS 5267.

October 5, 2015. On petition for writ of certiorari to the Court of Criminal Appeals of Alabama. Motion of petitioner for leave to proceed in forma pauperis and petition for writ of certiorari granted. Judgment vacated, and case remanded to the Court of Criminal Appeals of Alabama for further consideration in light of Hall v. Florida, 572 U.S. 701, 134 S. Ct. 1986, 188 L. Ed. 2d 1007 (2014).

Same case below, 169 So. 3d 1076.

No. 14-9532. Adil Hiramanek, Petitioner v. California.

577 U.S. 802, 136 S. Ct. 41, 193 L. Ed. 2d 7, 2015 U.S. LEXIS 6221.

October 5, 2015. Motion of petitioner for leave to proceed in forma pauperis denied, and petition for writ of certiorari to the Supreme Court of California dismissed. See Rule 39.8.

No. 14-9533. Adil Hiramanek, Petitioner v. California.

577 U.S. 802, 136 S. Ct. 41, 193 L. Ed. 2d 7, 2015 U.S. LEXIS 5956.

October 5, 2015. Motion of petitioner for leave to proceed in forma pauperis

denied, and petition for writ of certiorari to the United States Court of Appeals for the Ninth Circuit dismissed. See Rule 39.8.

No. 14-9543. Doug West, Petitioner v. Oklahoma.

577 U.S. 802, 136 S. Ct. 41, 193 L. Ed. 2d 8, 2015 U.S. LEXIS 6199.

October 5, 2015. Motion of petitioner for leave to proceed in forma pauperis denied, and petition for writ of certiorari to the Court of Criminal Appeals of Oklahoma dismissed. See Rule 39.8. As petitioner has repeatedly abused this Court's process, the Clerk is directed not to accept any further petitions in noncriminal matters from petitioner unless the docketing fee required by Rule 38(a) is paid and the petition is submitted in compliance with Rule 33.1. See Martin v. District of Columbia Court of Appeals, 506 U.S. 1, 113 S. Ct. 397, 121 L. Ed. 2d 305 (1992) (per curiam).

No. 14-9550. Antone Lamandingo Knox, Petitioner v. Oklahoma Department of Corrections.

577 U.S. 802, 136 S. Ct. 301, 193 L. Ed. 2d 8, 2015 U.S. LEXIS 6133.

October 5, 2015. Motion of petitioner for leave to proceed in forma pauperis denied, and petition for writ of certiorari to the Supreme Court of Oklahoma dismissed. See Rule 39.8.

No. 14-9617. Brandon Scott Lavergne, Petitioner v. Sheriff's Office Acadia Parish, et al.

577 U.S. 803, 136 S. Ct. 48, 193 L. Ed. 2d 8, 2015 U.S. LEXIS 6220.

October 5, 2015. Motion of petitioner for leave to proceed in forma pauperis denied, and petition for writ of certiorari to the United States Court of Appeals for the Fifth Circuit dismissed. See Rule 39.8.

Same case below, 591 Fed. Appx. 277.

No. 14-9753. Brandon Scott Lavergne, Petitioner v. Sheriff's Office of Lafayette Parish.

577 U.S. 803, 136 S. Ct. 57, 193 L. Ed. 2d 8, 2015 U.S. LEXIS 6142.

October 5, 2015. Motion of petitioner for leave to proceed in forma pauperis denied, and petition for writ of certiorari to the United States Court of Appeals for the Fifth Circuit dismissed. See Rule 39.8.

Same case below, 591 Fed. Appx. 265.

No. 14-9767. Ronald Jennings Fogle, Petitioner v. Rachel Infante.

577 U.S. 803, 136 S. Ct. 58, 193 L. Ed. 2d 8, 2015 U.S. LEXIS 5782.

October 5, 2015. Motion of petitioner for leave to proceed in forma pauperis denied, and petition for writ of certiorari to the United States Court of Appeals for the Tenth Circuit dismissed. See Rule 39.8.

Same case below, 595 Fed. Appx. 807.

No. 14-9850. William H. Evans, Jr., Petitioner v. United States District Court for the Southern District of Ohio.

577 U.S. 803, 136 S. Ct. 301, 193 L. Ed. 2d 8, 2015 U.S. LEXIS 5960.

October 5, 2015. Motion of petitioner for leave to proceed in forma pauperis

denied, and petition for writ of certiorari to the United States Court of Appeals for the Sixth Circuit dismissed. See Rule 39.8.

No. 14-9867. Louis Robenson, Petitioner v. Florida.

577 U.S. 803, 136 S. Ct. 69, 193 L. Ed. 2d 9, 2015 U.S. LEXIS 5882.

October 5, 2015. Motion of petitioner for leave to proceed in forma pauperis denied, and petition for writ of certiorari to the Supreme Court of Florida dismissed. See Rule 39.8. As petitioner has repeatedly abused this Court's process, the Clerk is directed not to accept any further petitions in noncriminal matters from petitioner unless the docketing fee required by Rule 38(a) is paid and the petition is submitted in compliance with Rule 33.1. See Martin v. District of Columbia Court of Appeals, 506 U.S. 1, 113 S. Ct. 397, 121 L. Ed. 2d 305 (1992) (per curiam).

Same case below, 163 So. 3d 512.

No. 14-9886. Derrick Allen, Petitioner v. Florida Department of Corrections.

577 U.S. 803, 136 S. Ct. 302, 193 L. Ed. 2d 9, 2015 U.S. LEXIS 6249.

October 5, 2015. Motion of petitioner for leave to proceed in forma pauperis denied, and petition for writ of certiorari to the District Court of Appeal of Florida, First District, dismissed. See Rule 39.8.

Same case below, 158 So. 3d 564.

No. 14-10064. Frederick Karl Jost, Petitioner v. California.

577 U.S. 803, 136 S. Ct. 90, 193 L. Ed. 2d 9, 2015 U.S. LEXIS 6246.

October 5, 2015. Motion of petitioner for leave to proceed in forma pauperis denied, and petition for writ of certiorari to the United States Court of Appeals for the Ninth Circuit dismissed. See Rule 39.8.

No. 14-10084. Willie Asbury, Petitioner v. South Carolina, et al.

577 U.S. 803, 136 S. Ct. 94, 193 L. Ed. 2d 9, 2015 U.S. LEXIS 6210.

October 5, 2015. Motion of petitioner for leave to proceed in forma pauperis denied, and petition for writ of certiorari to the Supreme Court of South Carolina dismissed. See Rule 39.8.

No. 14-10087. David W. Creveling, Petitioner v. Donna M. Alma, et vir, et al.

577 U.S. 803, 136 S. Ct. 95, 193 L. Ed. 2d 9, 2015 U.S. LEXIS 6281.

October 5, 2015. Motion of petitioner for leave to proceed in forma pauperis denied, and petition for writ of certiorari to the Court of Appeals of Washington, Division 3, dismissed. See Rule 39.8. As petitioner has repeatedly abused this Court's process, the Clerk is directed not to accept any further petitions in noncriminal matters from petitioner unless the docketing fee required by Rule 38(a) is paid and the petition is submitted in compliance with Rule 33.1. See Martin v. District of Columbia Court of Appeals, 506 U.S. 1, 113 S. Ct. 397, 121 L. Ed. 2d 305 (1992) (per curiam).

Same case below, 181 Wash. 2d 1020, 337 P.3d 325.

No. 14-10125. Joseph Macastle Jackson, Petitioner v. Tracy McCollum, Warden.

577 U.S. 804, 136 S. Ct. 101, 193 L. Ed. 2d 10, 2015 U.S. LEXIS 5968.

October 5, 2015. Motion of petitioner for leave to proceed in forma pauperis denied, and petition for writ of certiorari to the United States Court of Appeals for the Tenth Circuit dismissed. See Rule 39.8. As petitioner has repeatedly abused this Court's process, the Clerk is directed not to accept any further petitions in noncriminal matters from petitioner unless the docketing fee required by Rule 38(a) is paid and the petition is submitted in compliance with Rule 33.1. See Martin v. District of Columbia Court of Appeals, 506 U.S. 1, 113 S. Ct. 397, 121 L. Ed. 2d 305 (1992) (per curiam).

Same case below, 587 Fed. Appx. 502.

No. 14-10185. Armando Abreu Aceves, Petitioner v. California.

577 U.S. 804, 136 S. Ct. 113, 193 L. Ed. 2d 10, 2015 U.S. LEXIS 5923.

October 5, 2015. Motion of petitioner for leave to proceed in forma pauperis denied, and petition for writ of certiorari to the United States Court of Appeals for the Ninth Circuit dismissed. See Rule 39.8.

No. 14-10209. Arthur D'Amario, III, Petitioner v. Manhattan Housing Specialists, Inc., et al.

577 U.S. 804, 136 S. Ct. 117, 193 L. Ed. 2d 10, 2015 U.S. LEXIS 5808.

October 5, 2015. Motion of petitioner for leave to proceed in forma pauperis denied, and petition for writ of certiorari to the United States Court of Appeals for the First Circuit dismissed. See Rule 39.8. As petitioner has repeatedly abused this Court's process, the Clerk is directed not to accept any further petitions in noncriminal matters from petitioner unless the docketing fee required by Rule 38(a) is paid and the petition is submitted in compliance with Rule 33.1. See Martin v. District of Columbia Court of Appeals, 506 U.S. 1, 113 S. Ct. 397, 121 L. Ed. 2d 305 (1992) (per curiam).

No. 14-10309. Francisco Saldana, Petitioner v. United States.

577 U.S. 804, 136 S. Ct. 137, 193 L. Ed. 2d 10, 2015 U.S. LEXIS 5869.

October 5, 2015. Motion of petitioner for leave to proceed in forma pauperis denied, and petition for writ of certiorari to the United States Court of Appeals for the Eleventh Circuit dismissed. See Rule 39.8. As petitioner has repeatedly abused this Court's process, the Clerk is directed not to accept any further petitions in noncriminal matters from petitioner unless the docketing fee required by Rule 38(a) is paid and the petition is submitted in compliance with Rule 33.1. See Martin v. District of Columbia Court of Appeals, 506 U.S. 1, 113 S. Ct. 397, 121 L. Ed. 2d 305 (1992) (per curiam). Justice Kagan took no part in the consideration or decision of this motion and this petition.

No. 14-10324. Johnny Brett Gregory, Petitioner v. Deborah Denham, Warden.

577 U.S. 805, 136 S. Ct. 140, 193 L. Ed. 2d 11, 2015 U.S. LEXIS 5908.

October 5, 2015. Motion of petitioner for leave to proceed in forma pauperis denied, and petition for writ of certiorari to the United States Court of Appeals for the Eleventh Circuit dismissed. See Rule 39.8. Justice Kagan took no part in the consideration or decision of this motion and this petition.

Same case below, 581 Fed. Appx. 728.

No. 14-10335. Patrick Alexandre Missud, Petitioner v. Wayne LaPierre, et al.

577 U.S. 805, 136 S. Ct. 142, 193 L. Ed. 2d 11, 2015 U.S. LEXIS 5890.

October 5, 2015. Motion of petitioner for leave to proceed in forma pauperis denied, and petition for writ of certiorari to the United States Court of Appeals for the Ninth Circuit dismissed. See Rule 39.8.

No. 14-10451. Ronald Jennings Fogle, Petitioner v. Angelina Gonzales.

577 U.S. 805, 136 S. Ct. 161, 193 L. Ed. 2d 11, 2015 U.S. LEXIS 6102.

October 5, 2015. Motion of petitioner for leave to proceed in forma pauperis denied, and petition for writ of certiorari to the United States Court of Appeals for the Tenth Circuit dismissed. See Rule 39.8.

Same case below, 597 Fed. Appx. 485.

No. 14-10484. Adil Hiramanek, Petitioner v. Kamal A. Hiramanek, et al.

577 U.S. 805, 136 S. Ct. 167, 193 L. Ed. 2d 11, 2015 U.S. LEXIS 6168.

October 5, 2015. Motion of petitioner for leave to proceed in forma pauperis denied, and petition for writ of certiorari to the United States Court of Appeals for the Ninth Circuit dismissed. See Rule 39.8.

Same case below, 588 Fed. Appx. 681.

No. 15-5009. Rexford Tweed, Petitioner v. Rick Scott, Governor of Florida, et al.

577 U.S. 805, 136 S. Ct. 170, 193 L. Ed. 2d 11, 2015 U.S. LEXIS 5802.

October 5, 2015. Motion of petitioner for leave to proceed in forma pauperis denied, and petition for writ of certiorari to the United States Court of Appeals for the Eleventh Circuit dismissed. See Rule 39.8.

No. 15-5026. Mitchell Williams, Petitioner v. Planned Parenthood of Wisconsin, Inc.

577 U.S. 805, 136 S. Ct. 173, 193 L. Ed. 2d 11, 2015 U.S. LEXIS 5841.

October 5, 2015. Motion of petitioner for leave to proceed in forma pauperis denied, and petition for writ of certiorari to the Court of Appeals of Wisconsin, District IV, dismissed. See Rule 39.8.

Same case below, 363 Wis. 2d 479, 865 N.W.2d 502.

No. 15-5060. James Manley, Petitioner v. Indiana.

577 U.S. 805, 136 S. Ct. 178, 193 L. Ed. 2d 12, 2015 U.S. LEXIS 6105.

October 5, 2015. Motion of petitioner for leave to proceed in forma pauperis denied, and petition for writ of certiorari to the Court of Appeals of Indiana, First District, dismissed. See Rule 39.8. As petitioner has repeatedly abused this Court's process, the Clerk is directed not to accept any further petitions in noncriminal matters from petitioner unless the docketing fee required by Rule 38(a) is paid and the petition is submitted in compliance with Rule 33.1. See Martin v. District of Columbia Court of Appeals, 506 U.S. 1, 113 S. Ct. 397, 121 L. Ed. 2d 305 (1992) (per curiam).

Same case below, 31 N.E.3d 1046.

No. 15-5179. Thomas F. Williams, Petitioner v. Julie L. Jones, Secretary, Florida Department of Corrections, et al.

577 U.S. 805, 136 S. Ct. 201, 193 L. Ed. 2d 12, 2015 U.S. LEXIS 5823.

October 5, 2015. Motion of petitioner for leave to proceed in forma pauperis denied, and petition for writ of certiorari to the United States Court of Appeals for the Eleventh Circuit dismissed. See Rule 39.8. As petitioner has repeatedly abused this Court's process, the Clerk is directed not to accept any further petitions in noncriminal matters from petitioner unless the docketing fee required by Rule 38(a) is paid and the petition is submitted in compliance with Rule 33.1. See Martin v. District of Columbia Court of Appeals, 506 U.S. 1, 113 S. Ct. 397, 121 L. Ed. 2d 305 (1992) (per curiam).

No. 15-5226. David Williams, Petitioner v. Corizon, LLC, et al.

577 U.S. 806, 136 S. Ct. 208, 193 L. Ed. 2d 12, 2015 U.S. LEXIS 6114.

October 5, 2015. Motion of petitioner for leave to proceed in forma pauperis denied, and petition for writ of certiorari to the United States Court of Appeals for the Eighth Circuit dismissed. See Rule 39.8.

No. 15-5266. Mark C. Jackson, Petitioner v. Robert A. McDonald, Secretary of Veterans Affairs.

577 U.S. 806, 136 S. Ct. 214, 193 L. Ed. 2d 12, 2015 U.S. LEXIS 6208.

October 5, 2015. Motion of petitioner for leave to proceed in forma pauperis denied, and petition for writ of certiorari to the United States Court of Appeals for the Federal Circuit dismissed. See Rule 39.8. As petitioner has repeatedly abused this Court's process, the Clerk is directed not to accept any further petitions in noncriminal matters from petitioner unless the docketing fee required by Rule 38(a) is paid and the petition is submitted in compliance with Rule 33.1. See Martin v. District of Columbia Court of Appeals, 506 U.S. 1, 113 S. Ct. 397, 121 L. Ed. 2d 305 (1992) (per curiam). Justice Kagan took no part in the consideration or decision of this motion and this petition.

Same case below, 606 Fed. Appx. 999.

No. 15-5284. Edward J. Mierzwa, Petitioner v. Wal-Mart, Inc., et al.

577 U.S. 806, 136 S. Ct. 219, 193 L. Ed. 2d 12, 2015 U.S. LEXIS 6259.

October 5, 2015. Motion of petitioner for leave to proceed in forma pauperis

denied, and petition for writ of certiorari to the Supreme Court of New Jersey dismissed. See Rule 39.8. As petitioner has repeatedly abused this Court's process, the Clerk is directed not to accept any further petitions in noncriminal matters from petitioner unless the docketing fee required by Rule 38(a) is paid and the petition is submitted in compliance with Rule 33.1. See Martin v. District of Columbia Court of Appeals, 506 U.S. 1, 113 S. Ct. 397, 121 L. Ed. 2d 305 (1992) (per curiam).

Same case below, 220 N.J. 575, 108 A.3d 635.

———

No. 15-5372. Howard Herships, Petitioner v. California.

577 U.S. 806, 136 S. Ct. 233, 193 L. Ed. 2d 13, 2015 U.S. LEXIS 6262.

October 5, 2015. Motion of petitioner for leave to proceed in forma pauperis denied, and petition for writ of certiorari to the Supreme Court of California dismissed. See Rule 39.8. As petitioner has repeatedly abused this Court's process, the Clerk is directed not to accept any further petitions in noncriminal matters from petitioner unless the docketing fee required by Rule 38(a) is paid and the petition is submitted in compliance with Rule 33.1. See Martin v. District of Columbia Court of Appeals, 506 U.S. 1, 113 S. Ct. 397, 121 L. Ed. 2d 305 (1992) (per curiam).

———

No. 15-5735. John Randall Futch, Petitioner v. United States.

577 U.S. 807, 136 S. Ct. 277, 193 L. Ed. 2d 13, 2015 U.S. LEXIS 6271.

October 5, 2015. Motion of petitioner for leave to proceed in forma pauperis denied, and petition for writ of certiorari to the United States Court of Appeals for the Eleventh Circuit dismissed. See Rule 39.8. As petitioner has repeatedly abused this Court's process, the Clerk is directed

not to accept any further petitions in noncriminal matters from petitioner unless the docketing fee required by Rule 38(a) is paid and the petition is submitted in compliance with Rule 33.1. See Martin v. District of Columbia Court of Appeals, 506 U.S. 1, 113 S. Ct. 397, 121 L. Ed. 2d 305 (1992) (per curiam). Justice Kagan took no part in the consideration or decision of this motion and this petition.

Same case below, 600 Fed. Appx. 722.

———

No. 15A97. Andre J. Twitty, Applicant v. United States.

577 U.S. 807, 136 S. Ct. 284, 193 L. Ed. 2d 13, 2015 U.S. LEXIS 5219.

October 5, 2015. Application for bail, addressed to The Chief Justice and referred to the Court, denied.

Same case below, 591 Fed. Appx. 676.

———

No. 15M1. Eastman Kodak Company, Petitioner v. Collins Inkjet Corporation.

577 U.S. 807, 136 S. Ct. 284, 193 L. Ed. 2d 13, 2015 U.S. LEXIS 5330.

October 5, 2015. Motion for leave to file a petition for writ of certiorari with the supplemental appendices under seal granted.

Same case below, 781 F.3d 264.

———

No. 15M2. Rayvell Vann, Petitioner v. United States.

577 U.S. 807, 136 S. Ct. 284, 193 L. Ed. 2d 13, 2015 U.S. LEXIS 5343.

October 5, 2015. Motion for leave to file a petition for writ of certiorari with the supplemental appendices under seal granted.

Same case below, 776 F.3d 746.

Same case below, 585 Fed. Appx. 92.

No. 15M3. Louis P. Cannon, et al., Petitioners v. District of Columbia.

577 U.S. 807, 136 S. Ct. 285, 193 L. Ed. 2d 14, 2015 U.S. LEXIS 5394.

October 5, 2015. Motion for leave to file a petition for relief granted.

Same case below, 783 F.3d 327.

No. 15M4. Carol Lee Gordon, Petitioner v. Somerset Medical Center, et al.

577 U.S. 807, 136 S. Ct. 285, 193 L. Ed. 2d 14, 2015 U.S. LEXIS 5319.

October 5, 2015. Motion for leave to proceed as a veteran denied.

No. 15M5. Andrew Searcy, Jr., Petitioner v. Merit Systems Protection Board.

577 U.S. 807, 136 S. Ct. 285, 193 L. Ed. 2d 14, 2015 U.S. LEXIS 5238.

October 5, 2015. Motion for leave to proceed as a veteran granted.

No. 15M6. Shawn Sadler, Petitioner v. United States.

577 U.S. 807, 136 S. Ct. 285, 193 L. Ed. 2d 14, 2015 U.S. LEXIS 5355.

October 5, 2015. Motion to direct the Clerk to file a petition for writ of certiorari out of time denied.

No. 15M7. Arrello Barnes, Petitioner v. Carla Ross, et al.

577 U.S. 807, 136 S. Ct. 285, 193 L. Ed. 2d 14, 2015 U.S. LEXIS 5564.

October 5, 2015. Motion to direct the Clerk to file a petition for writ of certiorari out of time denied.

No. 15M8. Peter Reginald Wright, Petitioner v. United States.

577 U.S. 807, 136 S. Ct. 285, 193 L. Ed. 2d 14, 2015 U.S. LEXIS 5511.

October 5, 2015. Motion to direct the Clerk to file a petition for writ of certiorari out of time denied.

No. 15M9. Renea Justine Chafe, Petitioner v. Florida Department of Children and Families.

577 U.S. 807, 136 S. Ct. 285, 193 L. Ed. 2d 14, 2015 U.S. LEXIS 5536.

October 5, 2015. Motion for leave to proceed as a veteran denied.

No. 15M10. Darin A. Jones, Petitioner v. Merit Systems Protection Board.

577 U.S. 807, 136 S. Ct. 285, 193 L. Ed. 2d 14, 2015 U.S. LEXIS 5443.

October 5, 2015. Motion for leave to proceed as a veteran denied.

MEMORANDUM CASES

Same case below, 597 Fed. Appx. 1083.

No. 15M11. Joseph Earl Smith, Jr., Petitioner v. Daniel Paramo, Warden.

577 U.S. 807, 136 S. Ct. 286, 193 L. Ed. 2d 15, 2015 U.S. LEXIS 5521.

October 5, 2015. Motion to direct the Clerk to file a petition for writ of certiorari out of time denied.

No. 15M12. Annette C. Watkins, Petitioner v. Duke Medical Center, et al.

577 U.S. 808, 136 S. Ct. 286, 193 L. Ed. 2d 15, 2015 U.S. LEXIS 5228.

October 5, 2015. Motion to direct the Clerk to file a petition for writ of certiorari out of time denied.

Same case below, 592 Fed. Appx. 226.

No. 15M13. Wbengda Eshtu Legesse, Petitioner v. Harold W. Clarke, Director, Virginia Department of Corrections.

577 U.S. 808, 136 S. Ct. 286, 193 L. Ed. 2d 15, 2015 U.S. LEXIS 5537.

October 5, 2015. Motion to direct the Clerk to file a petition for writ of certiorari out of time denied.

No. 15M14. Tanya R. Langama, Petitioner v. Henry Buchwald, et al.

577 U.S. 808, 136 S. Ct. 286, 193 L. Ed. 2d 15, 2015 U.S. LEXIS 5200.

October 5, 2015. Motion to direct the Clerk to file a petition for writ of certiorari out of time denied.

No. 15M15. Willie Culberson, Petitioner v. Michigan Department of Corrections.

577 U.S. 808, 136 S. Ct. 286, 193 L. Ed. 2d 15, 2015 U.S. LEXIS 5428.

October 5, 2015. Motion to direct the Clerk to file a petition for writ of certiorari out of time denied.

No. 15M16. In re Douglas J. MacNeill, Petitioner.

577 U.S. 807, 136 S. Ct. 286, 193 L. Ed. 2d 15, 2015 U.S. LEXIS 5317.

October 5, 2015. Motion for leave to proceed as a veteran denied.

No. 15M17. Hratch Z. Ilanjian, Petitioner v. Kenset Corporation.

577 U.S. 808, 136 S. Ct. 286, 193 L. Ed. 2d 15, 2015 U.S. LEXIS 5251.

October 5, 2015. Motion to direct the Clerk to file a petition for writ of certiorari out of time under Rule 14.5 denied.

Same case below, 600 Fed. Appx. 827.

No. 15M18. Eric Smith, Petitioner v. California, et al.

577 U.S. 808, 136 S. Ct. 287, 193 L. Ed. 2d 15, 2015 U.S. LEXIS 5460.

October 5, 2015. Motion to direct the Clerk to file a petition for writ of certiorari out of time under Rule 14.5 denied.

Same case below, 125 App. Div. 3d 497, 4 N.Y.S.3d 20.

———

No. 15M19. Streambend Properties III, LLC, et al., Petitioners v. Sexton Lofts, LLC, et al.

577 U.S. 808, 136 S. Ct. 287, 193 L. Ed. 2d 16, 2015 U.S. LEXIS 5356.

October 5, 2015. Motion to direct the Clerk to file a petition for writ of certiorari by Jerald Hammann, pro se, as assignee to rights of petitioners denied.

Same case below, 587 Fed. Appx. 350.

———

No. 15M20. Streambend Properties II, LLC, et al., Petitioners v. Ivy Tower Minneapolis, LLC, et al.

577 U.S. 808, 136 S. Ct. 287, 193 L. Ed. 2d 16, 2015 U.S. LEXIS 5282.

October 5, 2015. Motion to direct the Clerk to file a petition for writ of certiorari by Jerald Hammann, pro se, as assignee to rights of petitioners denied.

Same case below, 781 F.3d 1003.

———

No. 15M21. Garvester Bracken, Petitioner v. Missouri, et al.

577 U.S. 808, 136 S. Ct. 287, 193 L. Ed. 2d 16, 2015 U.S. LEXIS 5571.

October 5, 2015. Motion to direct the Clerk to file a petition for writ of certiorari out of time denied.

———

No. 15M22. Deidre Holmes Clark, Petitioner v. Allen & Overy, LLP.

577 U.S. 807, 136 S. Ct. 287, 193 L. Ed. 2d 16, 2015 U.S. LEXIS 5177.

October 5, 2015. Motion for leave to file a petition for writ of certiorari with the supplemental appendix under seal granted.

———

No. 15M23. Alvia L. Lacy, Petitioner v. National Railroad Passenger Corporation, et al.

577 U.S. 808, 136 S. Ct. 287, 193 L. Ed. 2d 16, 2015 U.S. LEXIS 5054.

October 5, 2015. Motion to direct the Clerk to file a petition for writ of certiorari out of time denied.

Same case below, 600 Fed. Appx. 127.

———

No. 15M24. Learon Duvall Truss, Petitioner v. Brian Foster, Warden.

577 U.S. 808, 136 S. Ct. 288, 193 L. Ed. 2d 16, 2015 U.S. LEXIS 5158.

October 5, 2015. Motion to direct the Clerk to file a petition for writ of certiorari out of time under Rule 14.5 denied.

———

No. 15M25. Lucien Salnave, Petitioner v. Thomas Griffin, Superintendent, Green Haven Correctional Facility, et al.

577 U.S. 808, 136 S. Ct. 288, 193 L. Ed. 2d 16, 2015 U.S. LEXIS 5367.

October 5, 2015. Motion to direct the Clerk to file a petition for writ of certiorari out of time denied.

———

No. 15M26. Detelin Draganov, Petitioner v. United States.

577 U.S. 808, 136 S. Ct. 288, 193 L. Ed. 2d 16, 2015 U.S. LEXIS 5516.

October 5, 2015. Motion to direct the Clerk to file a petition for writ of certiorari out of time denied.

No. 15M27. Pablo K. Johnson, Petitioner v. Philadelphia School District.

577 U.S. 808, 136 S. Ct. 288, 193 L. Ed. 2d 17, 2015 U.S. LEXIS 5542.

October 5, 2015. Motion to direct the Clerk to file a petition for writ of certiorari out of time denied.

No. 15M28. William Carl Welsh, Petitioner v. United States.

577 U.S. 808, 136 S. Ct. 288, 193 L. Ed. 2d 17, 2015 U.S. LEXIS 5278.

October 5, 2015. Motion to direct the Clerk to file a petition for writ of certiorari out of time denied.

No. 15M29. An Thai Tu, Petitioner v. Nicole Lewis, et al.

577 U.S. 808, 136 S. Ct. 288, 193 L. Ed. 2d 17, 2015 U.S. LEXIS 5409.

October 5, 2015. Motion to direct the Clerk to file a petition for writ of certiorari out of time denied.

No. 65, Original. State of Texas, Plaintiff v. State of New Mexico.

577 U.S. 808, 136 S. Ct. 289, 193 L. Ed. 2d 17, 2015 U.S. LEXIS 5421.

October 5, 2015. Motion of the River Master for fees and expenses granted, and the River Master is awarded a total of $10,327.05 for the period July 1, 2014, through June 30, 2015, to be paid equally by the parties.

No. 137, Original. State of Montana, Plaintiff v. State of Wyoming and State of North Dakota.

577 U.S. 808, 136 S. Ct. 289, 193 L. Ed. 2d 17, 2015 U.S. LEXIS 5500.

October 5, 2015. Motion of Montana to defer consideration of this case and the Exceptions to the Special Master's Second Interim Report filed December 29, 2014, for a period of three months granted. Parties are ordered to submit a joint status report to the Court no later than December 31, 2015.

No. 141, Original. State of Texas, Plaintiff v. State of New Mexico and State of Colorado.

577 U.S. 809, 136 S. Ct. 289, 193 L. Ed. 2d 17, 2015 U.S. LEXIS 5481.

October 5, 2015. Motion of El Paso County Water Improvement District No. 1 for leave to intervene referred to the Special Master. First Interim Motion of the Special Master for allowance of fees and disbursements granted, and the Special Master is awarded a total of $195,461.53 for the period November 3, 2014, through April 30, 2015, to be paid as follows: 37.5% by Texas, 37.5% by New Mexico, 20% by the United States, and 5% by Colorado.

No. 13-1339. Spokeo, Inc., Petitioner v. Thomas Robins.

577 U.S. 809, 136 S. Ct. 289, 193 L. Ed. 2d 17, 2015 U.S. LEXIS 5499.

October 5, 2015. Motion of the Solicitor General for leave to participate in oral argument as amicus curiae and for divided argument granted.

Same case below, 742 F.3d 409.

No. 14-1055. Crystal Monique Lightfoot, et al., Petitioners v. Cendant Mortgage Corporation, dba PHH Mortgage, et al.

577 U.S. 809, 136 S. Ct. 289, 193 L. Ed. 2d 18, 2015 U.S. LEXIS 5245.

October 5, 2015. The Solicitor General is invited to file a brief in this case expressing the views of the United States.

Same case below, 769 F.3d 681.

No. 14-1132. Merrill Lynch, Pierce, Fenner & Smith, Inc., et al., Petitioners v. Greg Manning, et al.

577 U.S. 809, 136 S. Ct. 289, 193 L. Ed. 2d 18, 2015 U.S. LEXIS 5337.

October 5, 2015. Motion of petitioners to dispense with printing the joint appendix granted.

No. 14-1140. Phillip Tibbs, et al., Petitioners v. Kimberly Bunnell, Judge, Circuit Court of Kentucky, Fayette County, et al.

577 U.S. 809, 136 S. Ct. 290, 193 L. Ed. 2d 18, 2015 U.S. LEXIS 5509.

October 5, 2015. The Solicitor General is invited to file a brief in this case expressing the views of the United States.

Same case below, 448 S.W.3d 796.

No. 14-1206. Peter George Odhiambo, Petitioner v. Republic of Kenya, et al.

577 U.S. 809, 136 S. Ct. 290, 193 L. Ed. 2d 18, 2015 U.S. LEXIS 5173.

October 5, 2015. The Solicitor General is invited to file a brief in this case expressing the views of the United States.

Same case below, 412 U.S. App. D.C. 201, 764 F.3d 31.

No. 14-1538. Life Technologies Corporation, et al., Petitioners v. Promega Corporation.

577 U.S. 809, 136 S. Ct. 290, 193 L. Ed. 2d 18, 2015 U.S. LEXIS 5289.

October 5, 2015. The Solicitor General is invited to file a brief in this case expressing the views of the United States.

Same case below, 773 F.3d 1338.

No. 14-8349. Timothy Tyrone Foster, Petitioner v. Bruce Chatman, Warden.

577 U.S. 809, 136 S. Ct. 290, 193 L. Ed. 2d 18, 2015 U.S. LEXIS 5515.

October 5, 2015. Motion of petitioner for appointment of counsel granted, and Stephen B. Bright, Esquire, of Atlanta, Georgia, is appointed to serve as counsel for the petitioner in this case.

No. 14-8351. In re Thomas Edward Nesbitt, Petitioner.

577 U.S. 809, 136 S. Ct. 290, 193 L. Ed. 2d 18, 2015 U.S. LEXIS 5270.

October 5, 2015. Motion of petitioner for reconsideration of order denying leave to proceed in forma pauperis denied.

No. 14-8644. David Brian Derringer, Petitioner v. Barrie Lee Derringer.

577 U.S. 809, 136 S. Ct. 290, 193 L. Ed. 2d 19, 2015 U.S. LEXIS 5346.

October 5, 2015. Motion of petitioner for reconsideration of order denying leave to proceed in forma pauperis denied.

No. 14-8757. Thomas H. Clay, Petitioner v. Zae Young Zeon, et al.

577 U.S. 810, 136 S. Ct. 291, 193 L. Ed. 2d 19, 2015 U.S. LEXIS 5418.

October 5, 2015. Motion of petitioner for reconsideration of order denying leave to proceed in forma pauperis denied.

No. 14-9030. Brandon Scott Lavergne, Petitioner v. Mike Harson, et al.

577 U.S. 810, 136 S. Ct. 291, 193 L. Ed. 2d 19, 2015 U.S. LEXIS 5471.

October 5, 2015. Motion of petitioner for reconsideration of order denying leave to proceed in forma pauperis denied.

Same case below, 583 Fed. Appx. 361.

No. 14-9043. Brandon Scott Lavergne, Petitioner v. Public Defender 15th Judicial District Court, et al.

577 U.S. 810, 136 S. Ct. 291, 193 L. Ed. 2d 19, 2015 U.S. LEXIS 5529.

October 5, 2015. Motion of petitioner for reconsideration of order denying leave to proceed in forma pauperis denied.

Same case below, 583 Fed. Appx. 362.

No. 14-9044. Brandon Scott Lavergne, Petitioner v. Louisiana State Police.

577 U.S. 810, 136 S. Ct. 291, 193 L. Ed. 2d 19, 2015 U.S. LEXIS 5547.

October 5, 2015. Motion of petitioner for reconsideration of order denying leave to proceed in forma pauperis denied.

No. 14-9200. Brandon Scott Lavergne, Petitioner v. Steven Bajat, et al.

577 U.S. 810, 136 S. Ct. 291, 193 L. Ed. 2d 19, 2015 U.S. LEXIS 5557.

October 5, 2015. Motion of petitioner for reconsideration of order denying leave to proceed in forma pauperis denied.

No. 14-9267. William H. Evans, Jr., Petitioner v. Ohio.

577 U.S. 810, 136 S. Ct. 291, 193 L. Ed. 2d 19, 2015 U.S. LEXIS 5327.

October 5, 2015. Motion of petitioner for reconsideration of order denying leave to proceed in forma pauperis denied.

No. 14-9323. Ulysses T. Ware, Petitioner v. Securities and Exchange Commission.

577 U.S. 810, 136 S. Ct. 292, 193 L. Ed. 2d 19, 2015 U.S. LEXIS 5534.

October 5, 2015. Motion of petitioner for reconsideration of order denying leave to proceed in forma pauperis denied.

No. 14-9396. Cody Robert Judy, Petitioner v. Barack H. Obama, President of the United States, et al.

577 U.S. 810, 136 S. Ct. 292, 193 L. Ed. 2d 20, 2015 U.S. LEXIS 5115.

October 5, 2015. Motion of petitioner for reconsideration of order denying leave to proceed in forma pauperis denied.

No. 14-9530. Leon Snipes, Petitioner v. Illinois.

577 U.S. 810, 136 S. Ct. 292, 193 L. Ed. 2d 20, 2015 U.S. LEXIS 5544.

October 5, 2015. Motion of petitioner for reconsideration of order denying leave to proceed in forma pauperis denied.

No. 14-9708. Bahri Begolli, Petitioner v. Home Depot U.S.A., Inc.

577 U.S. 810, 136 S. Ct. 292, 193 L. Ed. 2d 20, 2015 U.S. LEXIS 5293, reh den 577 U.S. 1124, 136 S. Ct. 996, 194 L. Ed. 2d 14, 2016 U.S. LEXIS 961.

October 5, 2015. Motion of petitioner for leave to proceed in forma pauperis denied. Petitioner is allowed until October 26, 2015, within which to pay the docketing fee required by Rule 38(a) and to submit a petition in compliance with Rule 33.1 of the Rules of this Court.

No. 14-9816. Joseph P. McInerney, Petitioner v. Rensselaer Polytechnic Institute, et al.

577 U.S. 812, 136 S. Ct. 292, 193 L. Ed. 2d 20, 2015 U.S. LEXIS 5603.

October 5, 2015. Motion of petitioner for leave to proceed in forma pauperis denied.

Petitioner is allowed until October 26, 2015, within which to pay the docketing fee required by Rule 38(a) and to submit a petition in compliance with Rule 33.1 of the Rules of this Court. Justice Sotomayor took no part in the consideration or decision of this motion.

Same case below, 583 Fed. Appx. 17.

No. 14-9973. Justin Bergo, Petitioner v. Court of Appeal of California, Third Appellate District, et al.

577 U.S. 810, 136 S. Ct. 292, 193 L. Ed. 2d 20, 2015 U.S. LEXIS 5201.

October 5, 2015. Motion of petitioner for leave to proceed in forma pauperis denied. Petitioner is allowed until October 26, 2015, within which to pay the docketing fee required by Rule 38(a) and to submit a petition in compliance with Rule 33.1 of the Rules of this Court.

No. 14-10029. Diane King, Petitioner v. Department of Veterans Affairs.

577 U.S. 811, 136 S. Ct. 293, 193 L. Ed. 2d 20, 2015 U.S. LEXIS 5137.

October 5, 2015. Motion of petitioner for leave to proceed in forma pauperis denied. Petitioner is allowed until October 26, 2015, within which to pay the docketing fee required by Rule 38(a) and to submit a petition in compliance with Rule 33.1 of the Rules of this Court.

Same case below, 601 Fed. Appx. 956.

No. 14-10041. Edgar Leal, Petitioner v. Loretta E. Lynch, Attorney General.

577 U.S. 811, 136 S. Ct. 293, 193 L. Ed. 2d 20, 2015 U.S. LEXIS 5075.

October 5, 2015. Motion of petitioner for leave to proceed in forma pauperis

denied. Petitioner is allowed until October 26, 2015, within which to pay the docketing fee required by Rule 38(a) and to submit a petition in compliance with Rule 33.1 of the Rules of this Court.

Same case below, 771 F.3d 1140.

No. 14-10083. Erma L. Glasgow, Petitioner v. Oregon Department of Revenue.

577 U.S. 811, 136 S. Ct. 293, 193 L. Ed. 2d 21, 2015 U.S. LEXIS 5141.

October 5, 2015. Motion of petitioner for leave to proceed in forma pauperis denied. Petitioner is allowed until October 26, 2015, within which to pay the docketing fee required by Rule 38(a) and to submit a petition in compliance with Rule 33.1 of the Rules of this Court.

Same case below, 356 Or. 511, 340 P.3d 653.

No. 14-10150. Gordon Lamar Nelson, Petitioner v. P. D. Brazelton, Warden.

577 U.S. 811, 136 S. Ct. 293, 193 L. Ed. 2d 21, 2015 U.S. LEXIS 5496.

October 5, 2015. Motion of petitioner for leave to proceed in forma pauperis denied. Petitioner is allowed until October 26, 2015, within which to pay the docketing fee required by Rule 38(a) and to submit a petition in compliance with Rule 33.1 of the Rules of this Court.

No. 14-10178. Shelia Y. Cruthirds, Petitioner v. Karen Miller, et al.

577 U.S. 811, 136 S. Ct. 293, 193 L. Ed. 2d 21, 2015 U.S. LEXIS 5513.

October 5, 2015. Motion of petitioner for leave to proceed in forma pauperis denied.

Petitioner is allowed until October 26, 2015, within which to pay the docketing fee required by Rule 38(a) and to submit a petition in compliance with Rule 33.1 of the Rules of this Court.

Same case below, 600 Fed. Appx. 146.

No. 14-10183. Drew Rizzo, Petitioner v. Pennsylvania.

577 U.S. 811, 136 S. Ct. 294, 193 L. Ed. 2d 21, 2015 U.S. LEXIS 5163.

October 5, 2015. Motion of petitioner for leave to proceed in forma pauperis denied. Petitioner is allowed until October 26, 2015, within which to pay the docketing fee required by Rule 38(a) and to submit a petition in compliance with Rule 33.1 of the Rules of this Court.

Same case below, 107 A.3d 228.

No. 14-10234. Stephen Eschenbach, Petitioner v. Mortgage Electronic Registration Systems, Inc., et al.

577 U.S. 811, 136 S. Ct. 294, 193 L. Ed. 2d 21, 2015 U.S. LEXIS 5527.

October 5, 2015. Motion of petitioner for leave to proceed in forma pauperis denied. Petitioner is allowed until October 26, 2015, within which to pay the docketing fee required by Rule 38(a) and to submit a petition in compliance with Rule 33.1 of the Rules of this Court.

No. 14-10247. Anthony J. Boddie, Petitioner v. Department of the Treasury.

577 U.S. 811, 136 S. Ct. 294, 193 L. Ed. 2d 21, 2015 U.S. LEXIS 5342.

October 5, 2015. Motion of petitioner for leave to proceed in forma pauperis

denied. Petitioner is allowed until October 26, 2015, within which to pay the docketing fee required by Rule 38(a) and to submit a petition in compliance with Rule 33.1 of the Rules of this Court.

Same case below, 590 Fed. Appx. 978.

———

No. 15-5115. Jared R. Clark, Petitioner v. Federal Labor Relations Authority.

577 U.S. 811, 136 S. Ct. 294, 193 L. Ed. 2d 22, 2015 U.S. LEXIS 5621.

October 5, 2015. Motion of petitioner for leave to proceed in forma pauperis denied. Petitioner is allowed until October 26, 2015, within which to pay the docketing fee required by Rule 38(a) and to submit a petition in compliance with Rule 33.1 of the Rules of this Court.

Same case below, 782 F.3d 701.

———

No. 15-5142. Lawrence W. Passiatore, Petitioner v. Merit Systems Protection Board.

577 U.S. 811, 136 S. Ct. 294, 193 L. Ed. 2d 22, 2015 U.S. LEXIS 5111.

October 5, 2015. Motion of petitioner for leave to proceed in forma pauperis denied. Petitioner is allowed until October 26, 2015, within which to pay the docketing fee required by Rule 38(a) and to submit a petition in compliance with Rule 33.1 of the Rules of this Court.

Same case below, 607 Fed. Appx. 975.

———

No. 15-5149. Allen Maki, Petitioner v. Beverly Anderson, et al.

577 U.S. 811, 136 S. Ct. 295, 193 L. Ed. 2d 22, 2015 U.S. LEXIS 5214.

October 5, 2015. Motion of petitioner for leave to proceed in forma pauperis denied.

Petitioner is allowed until October 26, 2015, within which to pay the docketing fee required by Rule 38(a) and to submit a petition in compliance with Rule 33.1 of the Rules of this Court.

———

No. 15-5156. Rance M. Strunk, et ux., Petitioners v. Wells Fargo Bank, N.A., et al.

577 U.S. 811, 136 S. Ct. 295, 193 L. Ed. 2d 22, 2015 U.S. LEXIS 5058.

October 5, 2015. Motion of petitioner for leave to proceed in forma pauperis denied. Petitioners are allowed until October 26, 2015, within which to pay the docketing fee required by Rule 38(a) and to submit a petition in compliance with Rule 33.1 of the Rules of this Court.

Same case below, 614 Fed. Appx. 586.

———

No. 15-5197. Claude E. Pickett, Petitioner v. Michael T. Gallagher, et al.

577 U.S. 811, 136 S. Ct. 295, 193 L. Ed. 2d 22, 2015 U.S. LEXIS 5216.

October 5, 2015. Motion of petitioner for leave to proceed in forma pauperis denied. Petitioner is allowed until October 26, 2015, within which to pay the docketing fee required by Rule 38(a) and to submit a petition in compliance with Rule 33.1 of the Rules of this Court.

Same case below, 159 So. 3d 587.

———

No. 15-5222. James Edward Norris, Petitioner v. Anthony Foxx, Secretary of Transportation, et al.

577 U.S. 811, 136 S. Ct. 295, 193 L. Ed. 2d 22, 2015 U.S. LEXIS 5530, reh den 577 U.S. 1184, 136 S. Ct. 1250, 194 L. Ed. 2d 248, 2016 U.S. LEXIS 1242.

October 5, 2015. Motion of petitioner for leave to proceed in forma pauperis

denied. Petitioner is allowed until October 26, 2015, within which to pay the docketing fee required by Rule 38(a) and to submit a petition in compliance with Rule 33.1 of the Rules of this Court.

No. 15-5443. Paul Deppenbrook, Petitioner v. Pension Benefit Guaranty Corporation.

577 U.S. 811, 136 S. Ct. 295, 193 L. Ed. 2d 23, 2015 U.S. LEXIS 5436.

October 5, 2015. Motion of petitioner for leave to proceed in forma pauperis denied. Petitioner is allowed until October 26, 2015, within which to pay the docketing fee required by Rule 38(a) and to submit a petition in compliance with Rule 33.1 of the Rules of this Court.

Same case below, 414 U.S. App. D.C. 212, 778 F.3d 166.

No. 15-5610. Amy Liu, Petitioner v. Department of Industrial Relations.

577 U.S. 811, 136 S. Ct. 296, 193 L. Ed. 2d 23, 2015 U.S. LEXIS 5416.

October 5, 2015. Motion of petitioner for leave to proceed in forma pauperis denied. Petitioner is allowed until October 26, 2015, within which to pay the docketing fee required by Rule 38(a) and to submit a petition in compliance with Rule 33.1 of the Rules of this Court.

No. 15-5633. Roger Joe Ladner, Petitioner v. United States.

577 U.S. 811, 136 S. Ct. 296, 193 L. Ed. 2d 23, 2015 U.S. LEXIS 5067.

October 5, 2015. Motion of petitioner for leave to proceed in forma pauperis denied.

Petitioner is allowed until October 26, 2015, within which to pay the docketing fee required by Rule 38(a) and to submit a petition in compliance with Rule 33.1 of the Rules of this Court.

No. 15-5645. Diane King, Petitioner v. Department of the Army.

577 U.S. 811, 136 S. Ct. 296, 193 L. Ed. 2d 23, 2015 U.S. LEXIS 5528.

October 5, 2015. Motion of petitioner for leave to proceed in forma pauperis denied. Petitioner is allowed until October 26, 2015, within which to pay the docketing fee required by Rule 38(a) and to submit a petition in compliance with Rule 33.1 of the Rules of this Court.

Same case below, 602 Fed. Appx. 812.

No. 15-5670. Edo Aslanyan, Petitioner v. Mike Obenland, Superintendent, Monroe Correctional Complex.

577 U.S. 811, 136 S. Ct. 296, 193 L. Ed. 2d 23, 2015 U.S. LEXIS 5519.

October 5, 2015. Motion of petitioner for leave to proceed in forma pauperis denied. Petitioner is allowed until October 26, 2015, within which to pay the docketing fee required by Rule 38(a) and to submit a petition in compliance with Rule 33.1 of the Rules of this Court.

No. 13-1559. John B. Corr, et al., Petitioners v. Metropolitan Washington Airports Authority.

577 U.S. 815, 136 S. Ct. 29, 193 L. Ed. 2d 23, 2015 U.S. LEXIS 5503.

October 5, 2015. Petition for writ of certiorari to the United States Court of Appeals for the Fourth Circuit denied.

Same case below, 740 F.3d 295.

No. 14-1071. Richard R. Baumgartner, Petitioner v. United States.

577 U.S. 815, 136 S. Ct. 30, 193 L. Ed. 2d 24, 2015 U.S. LEXIS 5189.

October 5, 2015. Petition for writ of certiorari to the United States Court of Appeals for the Sixth Circuit denied.

Same case below, 581 Fed. Appx. 522.

No. 14-1106. William E. Bolden, Petitioner v. John Doe, et al.

577 U.S. 815, 136 S. Ct. 31, 193 L. Ed. 2d 24, 2015 U.S. LEXIS 5403.

October 5, 2015. Petition for writ of certiorari to the Supreme Court of Utah denied.

Same case below, 358 P.3d 1009.

No. 14-1133. King Ayettey Zubaidah, Petitioner v. Lorain County Bar Association.

577 U.S. 815, 136 S. Ct. 32, 193 L. Ed. 2d 24, 2015 U.S. LEXIS 5119.

October 5, 2015. Petition for writ of certiorari to the Supreme Court of Ohio denied.

Same case below, 140 Ohio St. 3d 495, 20 N.E.3d 687.

No. 14-1136. Nestle Purina PetCare Company, et al., Petitioners v. Connie Curts, et al.

577 U.S. 815, 136 S. Ct. 32, 193 L. Ed. 2d 24, 2015 U.S. LEXIS 5191.

October 5, 2015. Petition for writ of certiorari to the United States Court of Appeals for the Seventh Circuit denied.

Same case below, 779 F.3d 481.

No. 14-1177. Oklahoma, Petitioner v. Jeremiah Hobia, et al.

577 U.S. 815, 136 S. Ct. 33, 193 L. Ed. 2d 24, 2015 U.S. LEXIS 5135.

October 5, 2015. Petition for writ of certiorari to the United States Court of Appeals for the Tenth Circuit denied.

Same case below, 775 F.3d 1204.

No. 14-1184. Don Firenze, Petitioner v. National Labor Relations Board, et al.

577 U.S. 815, 136 S. Ct. 34, 193 L. Ed. 2d 24, 2015 U.S. LEXIS 5079.

October 5, 2015. Petition for writ of certiorari to the United States Court of Appeals for the First Circuit denied.

No. 14-1191. Quicken Loans Inc., Petitioner v. Lourie Brown, et al.

577 U.S. 815, 136 S. Ct. 34, 193 L. Ed. 2d 24, 2015 U.S. LEXIS 5543.

October 5, 2015. Petition for writ of certiorari to the Supreme Court of Appeals of West Virginia denied.

Same case below, 777 S.E.2d 581.

No. 14-1208. Jose Ricuarte Diaz Herrera, Petitioner v. Keith Stansell, et al.

No. 14-1336. Villarosa Investments Florida, Inc., et al., Petitioners v. Keith Stansell, et al.

No. 14-1342. Carmen Siman, et al., Petitioners v. Keith Stansell, et al.

577 U.S. 815, 136 S. Ct. 35, 193 L. Ed. 2d 24, 2015 U.S. LEXIS 5125.

October 5, 2015. Petitions for writs of certiorari to the United States Court of Appeals for the Eleventh Circuit denied.

Same cases below, 771 F.3d 713.

———

No. 14-1233. United Food and Commercial Workers Union Local 880 Pension Fund, Individually and on Behalf of All Others Similarly Situated, Petitioner v. Chesapeake Energy Corporation, et al.

577 U.S. 816, 136 S. Ct. 35, 193 L. Ed. 2d 25, 2015 U.S. LEXIS 5490.

October 5, 2015. Petition for writ of certiorari to the United States Court of Appeals for the Tenth Circuit denied.

Same case below, 774 F.3d 1229.

———

No. 14-1252. City of San Jose, California, et al., Petitioners v. Office of the Commissioner of Baseball, et al.

577 U.S. 816, 136 S. Ct. 36, 193 L. Ed. 2d 25, 2015 U.S. LEXIS 5153.

October 5, 2015. Petition for writ of certiorari to the United States Court of Appeals for the Ninth Circuit denied.

Same case below, 776 F.3d 686.

———

No. 14-1255. Richard Higbie, Petitioner v. United States.

577 U.S. 816, 136 S. Ct. 37, 193 L. Ed. 2d 25, 2015 U.S. LEXIS 5579.

October 5, 2015. Petition for writ of certiorari to the United States Court of Appeals for the Federal Circuit denied.

Same case below, 778 F.3d 990.

———

No. 14-1260. Sami Abdulaziz Allaithi, et al., Petitioners v. Donald H. Rumsfeld, former Secretary of Defense, et al.

577 U.S. 816, 136 S. Ct. 37, 193 L. Ed. 2d 25, 2015 U.S. LEXIS 5495.

October 5, 2015. Petition for writ of certiorari to the United States Court of Appeals for the District of Columbia Circuit denied.

Same case below, 410 U.S. App. D.C. 160, 753 F.3d 1327.

———

No. 14-1272. Valentino Anderson, Petitioner v. United States.

577 U.S. 816, 136 S. Ct. 38, 193 L. Ed. 2d 25, 2015 U.S. LEXIS 5517.

October 5, 2015. Petition for writ of certiorari to the United States Court of Appeals for the Second Circuit denied.

Same case below, 772 F.3d 969.

———

No. 14-1276. John Loscombe, Petitioner v. City of Scranton, Pennsylvania, et al.

577 U.S. 816, 136 S. Ct. 38, 193 L. Ed. 2d 25, 2015 U.S. LEXIS 5520.

October 5, 2015. Petition for writ of certiorari to the United States Court of Appeals for the Third Circuit denied.

Same case below, 600 Fed. Appx. 847.

Same case below, 775 F.3d 419.

No. 14-1278. Peabody Coal Company, Petitioner v. Director, Office of Workers' Compensation Programs, Department of Labor, et al.

577 U.S. 816, 136 S. Ct. 38, 193 L. Ed. 2d 26, 2015 U.S. LEXIS 5255.

October 5, 2015. Petition for writ of certiorari to the United States Court of Appeals for the Sixth Circuit denied.

Same case below, 577 Fed. Appx. 469.

No. 14-1288. Burl Cain, Warden, et al., Petitioners v. Albert Woodfox.

577 U.S. 816, 136 S. Ct. 38, 193 L. Ed. 2d 26, 2015 U.S. LEXIS 5533.

October 5, 2015. Petition for writ of certiorari to the United States Court of Appeals for the Fifth Circuit denied.

Same case below, 772 F.3d 358.

No. 14-1291. Tammy Rosebrough, Petitioner v. Buckeye Valley High School.

577 U.S. 816, 136 S. Ct. 38, 193 L. Ed. 2d 26, 2015 U.S. LEXIS 5127.

October 5, 2015. Petition for writ of certiorari to the United States Court of Appeals for the Sixth Circuit denied.

Same case below, 582 Fed. Appx. 647.

No. 14-1295. Nilo Jerez, Petitioner v. Republic of Cuba, et al.

577 U.S. 816, 136 S. Ct. 38, 193 L. Ed. 2d 26, 2015 U.S. LEXIS 5518.

October 5, 2015. Petition for writ of certiorari to the United States Court of Appeals for the District of Columbia Circuit denied.

No. 14-1299. Felder's Collision Parts, Inc., Petitioner v. All Star Advertising Agency, Inc., et al.

577 U.S. 816, 136 S. Ct. 39, 193 L. Ed. 2d 26, 2015 U.S. LEXIS 5580.

October 5, 2015. Petition for writ of certiorari to the United States Court of Appeals for the Fifth Circuit denied.

Same case below, 777 F.3d 756.

No. 14-1301. Lorraine Martin, Petitioner v. Hearst Corporation, et al.

577 U.S. 816, 136 S. Ct. 40, 193 L. Ed. 2d 26, 2015 U.S. LEXIS 5372.

October 5, 2015. Petition for writ of certiorari to the United States Court of Appeals for the Second Circuit denied.

Same case below, 777 F.3d 546.

No. 14-1302. Donald J. Yeager, Petitioner v. FirstEnergy Generation Corporation.

577 U.S. 817, 136 S. Ct. 40, 193 L. Ed. 2d 26, 2015 U.S. LEXIS 5561.

October 5, 2015. Petition for writ of certiorari to the United States Court of Appeals for the Sixth Circuit denied.

Same case below, 777 F.3d 362.

No. 14-1308. Harry L. Bierley, Petitioner v. Robert Sambroak.

577 U.S. 817, 136 S. Ct. 42, 193 L. Ed. 2d 26, 2015 U.S. LEXIS 5552.

October 5, 2015. Petition for writ of certiorari to the United States Court of Appeals for the Third Circuit denied.

No. 14-1312. Brandon Astor Jones, Petitioner v. Bruce Chatman, Warden.

577 U.S. 817, 136 S. Ct. 43, 193 L. Ed. 2d 27, 2015 U.S. LEXIS 5386, reh den 577 U.S. 1021, 136 S. Ct. 570, 193 L. Ed. 2d 452, 2015 U.S. LEXIS 7430.

October 5, 2015. Petition for writ of certiorari to the United States Court of Appeals for the Eleventh Circuit denied.

Same case below, 753 F.3d 1171.

No. 14-1313. Henry Stephens, Petitioner v. United States.

577 U.S. 817, 136 S. Ct. 43, 193 L. Ed. 2d 27, 2015 U.S. LEXIS 5588.

October 5, 2015. Petition for writ of certiorari to the United States Court of Appeals for the Fourth Circuit denied.

Same case below, 764 F.3d 327.

No. 14-1314. Telesaurus VPC, LLC, nka Verde Systems, LLC, Petitioner v. Randy Power, et al.

577 U.S. 817, 136 S. Ct. 43, 193 L. Ed. 2d 27, 2015 U.S. LEXIS 5479.

October 5, 2015. Petition for writ of certiorari to the United States Court of Appeals for the Ninth Circuit denied.

Same case below, 584 Fed. Appx. 905.

No. 14-1315. Alan Santos-Buch, Petitioner v. Financial Industry Regulatory Authority, Inc.

577 U.S. 817, 136 S. Ct. 43, 193 L. Ed. 2d 27, 2015 U.S. LEXIS 5498.

October 5, 2015. Petition for writ of certiorari to the United States Court of Appeals for the Second Circuit denied.

Same case below, 591 Fed. Appx. 32.

No. 14-1316. Jean Coulter, Petitioner v. Allegheny County Bar Association, et al.; Jean Coulter, Petitioner v. Susan Lope, et al.; Jean Coulter, Petitioner v. Mary Suzanne Ramsden, et al.; Jean Coulter, Petitioner v. Thomas Doerr, et al.; Jean Coulter, Petitioner v. Christine Gale, et al.; Jean Coulter, Petitioner v. James E. Mahood, et al.; and Jean Coulter, Petitioner v. Mary Suzanne Ramsden, et al.

577 U.S. 817, 136 S. Ct. 44, 193 L. Ed. 2d 27, 2015 U.S. LEXIS 5559, reh den 577 U.S. 1021, 136 S. Ct. 571, 193 L. Ed. 2d 452, 2015 U.S. LEXIS 7369.

October 5, 2015. Petition for writ of certiorari to the Superior Court of Pennsylvania, Pittsburgh Office, denied.

Same case below, 105 A.3d 39 (first judgment); 105 A.3d 39 (second judgment); 105 A.3d 39 (third judgment); 105 A.3d 40 (fourth judgment); 105 A.3d 39 (fifth judgment); 105 A.3d 39 (sixth judgment); and 94 A.3d 1080 (seventh judgment).

No. 14-1317. PHI Inc., Petitioner v. Rolls Royce Corporation, et al.

577 U.S. 817, 136 S. Ct. 45, 193 L. Ed. 2d 27, 2015 U.S. LEXIS 5375.

October 5, 2015. Petition for writ of certiorari to the United States Court of Appeals for the Fifth Circuit denied.

Same case below, 775 F.3d 671.

No. 14-1318. Gerald Dix, Petitioner v. Joseph P. Clancy, Director, United States Secret Service, et al.

577 U.S. 817, 136 S. Ct. 45, 193 L. Ed. 2d 27, 2015 U.S. LEXIS 5368, reh den 577 U.S. 1021, 136 S. Ct. 571, 193 L. Ed. 2d 452, 2015 U.S. LEXIS 7438.

October 5, 2015. Petition for writ of certiorari to the United States Court of Appeals for the Seventh Circuit denied.

No. 14-1319. William N. Devlin, et ux., Petitioners v. Wells Fargo Bank, N.A.

577 U.S. 817, 136 S. Ct. 46, 193 L. Ed. 2d 28, 2015 U.S. LEXIS 5569.

October 5, 2015. Petition for writ of certiorari to the United States Court of Appeals for the Fourth Circuit denied.

Same case below, 585 Fed. Appx. 171.

———

No. 14-1320. DM Records, Incorporated, Petitioner v. Alvertis Isbell, dba Alvert Music.

577 U.S. 817, 136 S. Ct. 46, 193 L. Ed. 2d 28, 2015 U.S. LEXIS 5523.

October 5, 2015. Petition for writ of certiorari to the United States Court of Appeals for the Fifth Circuit denied.

Same case below, 774 F.3d 859.

———

No. 14-1321. Gwen Stribling Henderson, et al., Petitioners v. John Richard Shanks, et al.

577 U.S. 817, 136 S. Ct. 46, 193 L. Ed. 2d 28, 2015 U.S. LEXIS 5502.

October 5, 2015. Petition for writ of certiorari to the Court of Appeals of Texas, Fourteenth District, denied.

Same case below, 449 S.W.3d 834.

———

No. 14-1323. Harvey Hoffman, Petitioner v. Baylor Health Care System, dba Baylor Medical Center at Waxahachie.

577 U.S. 818, 136 S. Ct. 45, 193 L. Ed. 2d 28, 2015 U.S. LEXIS 5258.

October 5, 2015. Petition for writ of certiorari to the United States Court of Appeals for the Fifth Circuit denied.

Same case below, 597 Fed. Appx. 231.

———

No. 14-1324. Ella Ward, Petitioner v. Robert A. McDonald, Secretary of Veterans Affairs.

577 U.S. 818, 136 S. Ct. 48, 193 L. Ed. 2d 28, 2015 U.S. LEXIS 5225.

October 5, 2015. Petition for writ of certiorari to the United States Court of Appeals for the District of Columbia Circuit denied.

Same case below, 412 U.S. App. D.C. 24, 762 F.3d 24.

———

No. 14-1326. United States ex rel. Yury Grenadyor, Petitioner v. Ukrainian Village Pharmacy, Inc., et al.

577 U.S. 818, 136 S. Ct. 49, 193 L. Ed. 2d 28, 2015 U.S. LEXIS 5538.

October 5, 2015. Petition for writ of certiorari to the United States Court of Appeals for the Seventh Circuit denied.

Same case below, 772 F.3d 1102.

———

No. 14-1327. Concepcion Amaya, Petitioner v. IndyMac Federal Bank, FSB.

577 U.S. 818, 136 S. Ct. 49, 193 L. Ed. 2d 28, 2015 U.S. LEXIS 5532.

October 5, 2015. Petition for writ of certiorari to the Supreme Court of Florida denied.

Same case below, 157 So. 3d 1040.

No. 14-1328. John J. Otrompke, Petitioner v. Lawrence Hill, President of the Illinois Board of Admissions to the Bar, et al.

577 U.S. 818, 136 S. Ct. 49, 193 L. Ed. 2d 29, 2015 U.S. LEXIS 5550.

October 5, 2015. Petition for writ of certiorari to the United States Court of Appeals for the Seventh Circuit denied.

Same case below, 592 Fed. Appx. 495.

No. 14-1335. Robert C. Tiller, Petitioner v. Indiana.

577 U.S. 818, 136 S. Ct. 50, 193 L. Ed. 2d 29, 2015 U.S. LEXIS 5531.

October 5, 2015. Petition for writ of certiorari to the Court of Appeals of Indiana, Third District, denied.

Same case below, 24 N.E.3d 1018.

No. 14-1341. Mpatanishi Tayari Garrett, et al., Petitioners v. Coventry II Developers Diversified Realty/ Trademark Montgomery Farm, L.P.

577 U.S. 818, 136 S. Ct. 52, 193 L. Ed. 2d 29, 2015 U.S. LEXIS 5526.

October 5, 2015. Petition for writ of certiorari to the United States Court of Appeals for the Fifth Circuit denied.

Same case below, 777 F.3d 792.

No. 14-1343. Gustavo Reveles, Petitioner v. Jeh Johnson, Secretary of Homeland Security.

577 U.S. 818, 136 S. Ct. 53, 193 L. Ed. 2d 29, 2015 U.S. LEXIS 5272.

October 5, 2015. Petition for writ of certiorari to the United States Court of Appeals for the Fifth Circuit denied.

Same case below, 595 Fed. Appx. 321.

No. 14-1344. Bobby Johnson, et al., Petitioners v. Draeger Safety Diagnostics, Inc.

577 U.S. 818, 136 S. Ct. 53, 193 L. Ed. 2d 29, 2015 U.S. LEXIS 5506.

October 5, 2015. Petition for writ of certiorari to the United States Court of Appeals for the Third Circuit denied.

Same case below, 594 Fed. Appx. 760.

No. 14-1346. Arlen Brown, Petitioner v. Louisiana.

577 U.S. 818, 136 S. Ct. 53, 193 L. Ed. 2d 29, 2015 U.S. LEXIS 5157.

October 5, 2015. Petition for writ of certiorari to the Court of Appeal of Louisiana, First Circuit, denied.

No. 14-1350. Schwab Money Market Fund, et al., Petitioners v. Bank of America Corporation, et al.

577 U.S. 818, 136 S. Ct. 53, 193 L. Ed. 2d 29, 2015 U.S. LEXIS 5333.

October 5, 2015. Petition for writ of certiorari to the United States Court of Appeals for the Second Circuit denied.

No. 14-1351. Knoedler Manufacturers, Inc., et al., Petitioners v. Delaware & Hudson Railway Company, Inc., dba Canadian Pacific Railway, et al.

577 U.S. 818, 136 S. Ct. 54, 193 L. Ed. 2d 30, 2015 U.S. LEXIS 5507.

October 5, 2015. Petition for writ of certiorari to the United States Court of Appeals for the Third Circuit denied.

Same case below, 781 F.3d 656.

No. 14-1352. Kenneth Earman, Petitioner v. United States.

577 U.S. 818, 136 S. Ct. 54, 193 L. Ed. 2d 30, 2015 U.S. LEXIS 5514.

October 5, 2015. Petition for writ of certiorari to the United States Court of Appeals for the Federal Circuit denied.

Same case below, 589 Fed. Appx. 991.

No. 14-1353. NetAirus Technologies, LLC, Petitioner v. Apple Inc.

577 U.S. 819, 136 S. Ct. 54, 193 L. Ed. 2d 30, 2015 U.S. LEXIS 5539, reh den 577 U.S. 1021, 136 S. Ct. 571, 193 L. Ed. 2d 452, 2015 U.S. LEXIS 7417.

October 5, 2015. Petition for writ of certiorari to the United States Court of Appeals for the Federal Circuit denied.

Same case below, 587 Fed. Appx. 658.

No. 14-1359. Terrance Owens, et al., Petitioners v. U.S. Bank N.A.

577 U.S. 819, 136 S. Ct. 55, 193 L. Ed. 2d 30, 2015 U.S. LEXIS 5250.

October 5, 2015. Petition for writ of certiorari to the Court of Appeals of Georgia denied.

No. 14-1361. Kenneth Jason Ragsdell, Petitioner v. Regional Housing Alliance of La Plata County, et al.

577 U.S. 819, 136 S. Ct. 59, 193 L. Ed. 2d 30, 2015 U.S. LEXIS 5126.

October 5, 2015. Petition for writ of certiorari to the United States Court of Appeals for the Tenth Circuit denied.

Same case below, 603 Fed. Appx. 653.

No. 14-1363. Y. W., Petitioner v. New Milford Public School, et al.

577 U.S. 819, 136 S. Ct. 63, 193 L. Ed. 2d 30, 2015 U.S. LEXIS 5264.

October 5, 2015. Petition for writ of certiorari to the Superior Court of New Jersey, Appellate Division, denied.

No. 14-1364. William Mosher, et ux., Petitioners v. Long Beach Mortgage Company, et al.

577 U.S. 819, 136 S. Ct. 64, 193 L. Ed. 2d 30, 2015 U.S. LEXIS 5156.

October 5, 2015. Petition for writ of certiorari to the United States Court of Appeals for the Tenth Circuit denied.

Same case below, 593 Fed. Appx. 766.

No. 14-1365. Mark J. Podlin, et al., Petitioners v. Nader Ghermezian, et al.

577 U.S. 819, 136 S. Ct. 64, 193 L. Ed. 2d 30, 2015 U.S. LEXIS 5462.

October 5, 2015. Petition for writ of certiorari to the United States Court of Appeals for the Second Circuit denied.

MEMORANDUM CASES

Same case below, 601 Fed. Appx. 31.

Same case below, 589 Fed. Appx. 841.

No. 14-1366. Pearl Seas Cruises, LLC, Petitioner v. Lloyd's Register North America, Inc.

577 U.S. 819, 136 S. Ct. 64, 193 L. Ed. 2d 31, 2015 U.S. LEXIS 5086.

October 5, 2015. Petition for writ of certiorari to the United States Court of Appeals for the Fifth Circuit denied.

Same case below, 780 F.3d 283.

No. 14-1367. Kawa Orthodontics, LLP, Petitioner v. Jacob J. Lew, Secretary of the Treasury, et al.

577 U.S. 819, 136 S. Ct. 64, 193 L. Ed. 2d 31, 2015 U.S. LEXIS 5273.

October 5, 2015. Petition for writ of certiorari to the United States Court of Appeals for the Eleventh Circuit denied.

Same case below, 773 F.3d 243.

No. 14-1374. James H. Goldthwaite, Petitioner v. Norfolk Southern Railway Company.

577 U.S. 819, 136 S. Ct. 67, 193 L. Ed. 2d 31, 2015 U.S. LEXIS 5280.

October 5, 2015. Petition for writ of certiorari to the Supreme Court of Alabama denied.

Same case below, 176 So. 3d 1209.

No. 14-1376. Guillermo Perez-Aguilar, Petitioner v. Loretta E. Lynch, Attorney General.

577 U.S. 819, 136 S. Ct. 67, 193 L. Ed. 2d 31, 2015 U.S. LEXIS 5535.

October 5, 2015. Petition for writ of certiorari to the United States Court of Appeals for the Ninth Circuit denied.

No. 14-1377. Baudel Velazquez-Soberanes, Petitioner v. Loretta E. Lynch, Attorney General.

577 U.S. 819, 136 S. Ct. 67, 193 L. Ed. 2d 31, 2015 U.S. LEXIS 5169.

October 5, 2015. Petition for writ of certiorari to the United States Court of Appeals for the Ninth Circuit denied.

Same case below, 589 Fed. Appx. 839.

No. 14-1378. Gene Rechtzigel, Petitioner v. Fischer Market Place, LLP, et al.

577 U.S. 819, 136 S. Ct. 71, 193 L. Ed. 2d 31, 2015 U.S. LEXIS 5522.

October 5, 2015. Petition for writ of certiorari to the Court of Appeals of Minnesota denied.

No. 14-1379. Daniel Mock, Petitioner v. Federal Home Loan Mortgage Corporation, dba Freddie Mac.

577 U.S. 819, 136 S. Ct. 71, 193 L. Ed. 2d 31, 2015 U.S. LEXIS 5287.

October 5, 2015. Petition for writ of certiorari to the United States Court of Appeals for the Fourth Circuit denied.

Same case below, 589 Fed. Appx. 127.

No. 14-1381. Rosemary Garity, Petitioner v. American Postal Workers Union, AFL-CIO, et al.

577 U.S. 820, 136 S. Ct. 71, 193 L. Ed. 2d 31, 2015 U.S. LEXIS 5194.

October 5, 2015. Petition for writ of certiorari to the United States Court of Appeals for the Ninth Circuit denied.

Same case below, 585 Fed. Appx. 383.

———

No. 14-1383. Daniel D. Williams, et ux., Petitioners v. North Carolina, et al.

577 U.S. 820, 136 S. Ct. 73, 193 L. Ed. 2d 32, 2015 U.S. LEXIS 5562.

October 5, 2015. Petition for writ of certiorari to the United States Court of Appeals for the Fourth Circuit denied.

Same case below, 585 Fed. Appx. 251.

———

No. 14-1385. Bianka Cruz, Petitioner v. Citibank, N.A.

577 U.S. 820, 136 S. Ct. 73, 193 L. Ed. 2d 32, 2015 U.S. LEXIS 5070, reh den 577 U.S. 1097, 136 S. Ct. 889, 193 L. Ed. 2d 781, 2016 U.S. LEXIS 14.

October 5, 2015. Petition for writ of certiorari to the District Court of Appeal of Florida, Fourth District, denied.

Same case below, 160 So. 3d 446.

———

No. 14-1389. Michael D. Nelson, Petitioner v. Matrixx Initiatives, Inc., et al.

577 U.S. 820, 136 S. Ct. 76, 193 L. Ed. 2d 32, 2015 U.S. LEXIS 5433.

October 5, 2015. Petition for writ of certiorari to the United States Court of Appeals for the Ninth Circuit denied.

Same case below, 592 Fed. Appx. 591.

———

No. 14-1393. Sergio Shawntez Prince, Petitioner v. Michigan.

577 U.S. 820, 136 S. Ct. 77, 193 L. Ed. 2d 32, 2015 U.S. LEXIS 5393.

October 5, 2015. Petition for writ of certiorari to the Supreme Court of Michigan denied.

Same case below, 497 Mich. 946, 857 N.W.2d 15.

———

No. 14-1394. Anthony Davila, Petitioner v. Anthony Haynes, Warden, et al.

577 U.S. 820, 136 S. Ct. 78, 193 L. Ed. 2d 32, 2015 U.S. LEXIS 5410.

October 5, 2015. Petition for writ of certiorari to the United States Court of Appeals for the Eleventh denied.

Same case below, 777 F.3d 1198.

———

No. 14-1395. Jeffrey M. Davies, Petitioner v. Waterstone Capital Management, L.P.

577 U.S. 820, 136 S. Ct. 78, 193 L. Ed. 2d 32, 2015 U.S. LEXIS 5465.

October 5, 2015. Petition for writ of certiorari to the Court of Appeals of Minnesota denied.

Same case below, 856 N.W.2d 711.

———

No. 14-1396. David Crockett, Petitioner v. Southeastern Pennsylvania Transportation Authority, dba SEPTA, et al.

577 U.S. 820, 136 S. Ct. 78, 193 L. Ed. 2d 32, 2015 U.S. LEXIS 5211.

October 5, 2015. Petition for writ of certiorari to the United States Court of Appeals for the Third Circuit denied.

Same case below, 591 Fed. Appx. 65.

Same case below, 598 Fed. Appx. 257.

No. 14-1397. Building Industry Association of Washington, Petitioner v. Robert F. Utter, et al.

577 U.S. 820, 136 S. Ct. 79, 193 L. Ed. 2d 33, 2015 U.S. LEXIS 5190.

October 5, 2015. Petition for writ of certiorari to the Supreme Court of Washington denied.

Same case below, 182 Wash. 2d 398, 341 P.3d 953.

No. 14-1399. Clayton Schulze, Petitioner v. County of Erie, Bureau of Revenue and Tax Claim.

577 U.S. 820, 136 S. Ct. 297, 193 L. Ed. 2d 33, 2015 U.S. LEXIS 5478.

October 5, 2015. Petition for writ of certiorari to the Commonwealth Court of Pennsylvania denied.

Same case below, 103 A.3d 455.

No. 14-1401. Yan Sui, Petitioner v. Stephen D. Price, et al.

577 U.S. 820, 136 S. Ct. 80, 193 L. Ed. 2d 33, 2015 U.S. LEXIS 5456.

October 5, 2015. Petition for writ of certiorari to the Appellate Division, Superior Court of California, Orange County, denied.

No. 14-1402. Kevin D. Schmidt, et ux., Petitioners v. J-Lu Company Limited, L.L.C.

577 U.S. 820, 136 S. Ct. 80, 193 L. Ed. 2d 33, 2015 U.S. LEXIS 5106.

October 5, 2015. Petition for writ of certiorari to the United States Court of Appeals for the Fifth Circuit denied.

No. 14-1403. Thomas Suchocki, Petitioner v. Chris Gilcrest, et al.

577 U.S. 820, 136 S. Ct. 81, 193 L. Ed. 2d 33, 2015 U.S. LEXIS 5226.

October 5, 2015. Petition for writ of certiorari to the United States Court of Appeals for the Third Circuit denied.

Same case below, 598 Fed. Appx. 91.

No. 14-1404. Joseph E. De Ritis, Petitioner v. Unemployment Compensation Board of Review.

577 U.S. 821, 136 S. Ct. 81, 193 L. Ed. 2d 33, 2015 U.S. LEXIS 5076.

October 5, 2015. Petition for writ of certiorari to the Commonwealth Court of Pennsylvania denied.

No. 14-1405. Eldrid Sequeira, Petitioner v. Rachel Sequeira.

577 U.S. 821, 136 S. Ct. 81, 193 L. Ed. 2d 33, 2015 U.S. LEXIS 5207.

October 5, 2015. Petition for writ of certiorari to the Appellate Division, Supreme Court of New York, First Judicial Department, denied.

Same case below, 121 App. Div. 3d 406, 993 N.Y.S.2d 309.

No. 14-1407. Douglas Eugene Camp, Petitioner v. Mary Berghuis, Warden.

577 U.S. 821, 136 S. Ct. 81, 193 L. Ed. 2d 33, 2015 U.S. LEXIS 5085.

October 5, 2015. Petition for writ of certiorari to the United States Court of Appeals for the Sixth Circuit denied.

Same case below, 601 Fed. Appx. 380.

Same case below, 775 F.3d 685.

No. 14-1410. Wendy Kelley, Director, Arkansas Department of Correction, Petitioner v. Manuel Enrique Camacho.

577 U.S. 821, 136 S. Ct. 81, 193 L. Ed. 2d 34, 2015 U.S. LEXIS 5390.

October 5, 2015. Petition for writ of certiorari to the United States Court of Appeals for the Eighth Circuit denied.

Same case below, 774 F.3d 931.

No. 14-1412. Marilyn Johnson, et al., Petitioners v. City of Memphis, Tennessee.

577 U.S. 821, 136 S. Ct. 81, 193 L. Ed. 2d 34, 2015 U.S. LEXIS 5374.

October 5, 2015. Petition for writ of certiorari to the United States Court of Appeals for the Sixth Circuit denied.

Same case below, 770 F.3d 464.

No. 14-1414. Arthur Lopez, Petitioner v. Newport Elementary School, et al.

577 U.S. 821, 136 S. Ct. 82, 193 L. Ed. 2d 34, 2015 U.S. LEXIS 5565, reh den 577 U.S. 1021, 136 S. Ct. 571, 193 L. Ed. 2d 453, 2015 U.S. LEXIS 7415.

October 5, 2015. Petition for writ of certiorari to the United States Court of Appeals for the Ninth Circuit denied.

No. 14-1415. Rodolfo Martinez, Petitioner v. Texas Workforce Commission.

577 U.S. 821, 136 S. Ct. 82, 193 L. Ed. 2d 34, 2015 U.S. LEXIS 5304.

October 5, 2015. Petition for writ of certiorari to the United States Court of Appeals for the Fifth Circuit denied.

No. 14-1416. Brent Langton, et al., Petitioners v. Briese Lichttechnik Vertriebs GmbH, et al.

577 U.S. 821, 136 S. Ct. 82, 193 L. Ed. 2d 34, 2015 U.S. LEXIS 5232.

October 5, 2015. Petition for writ of certiorari to the United States Court of Appeals for the Federal Circuit denied.

Same case below, 589 Fed. Appx. 536.

No. 14-1417. Nancy S. Stillwagon, Petitioner v. New Hampshire, et al.

577 U.S. 821, 136 S. Ct. 82, 193 L. Ed. 2d 34, 2015 U.S. LEXIS 5300.

October 5, 2015. Petition for writ of certiorari to the Supreme Court of New Hampshire denied.

No. 14-1420. John R. Mullen, II, et ux., Petitioners v. Ceres Marine Terminals, Inc., et al.

577 U.S. 821, 136 S. Ct. 84, 193 L. Ed. 2d 34, 2015 U.S. LEXIS 5422.

October 5, 2015. Petition for writ of certiorari to the Supreme Court of Virginia denied.

No. 14-1424. Nijjar Realty, Inc., dba PAMA Management Company, et al., Petitioners v. Germaine Judge.

577 U.S. 821, 136 S. Ct. 87, 193 L. Ed. 2d 34, 2015 U.S. LEXIS 5246.

October 5, 2015. Petition for writ of certiorari to the Court of Appeal of California, Second Appellate District, Division Seven, denied.

Same case below, 232 Cal. App. 4th 619, 181 Cal. Rptr. 3d 622.

No. 14-1425. Thomas P. Shoback, Petitioner v. Pennsylvania.

577 U.S. 821, 136 S. Ct. 87, 193 L. Ed. 2d 35, 2015 U.S. LEXIS 5483.

October 5, 2015. Petition for writ of certiorari to the Superior Court of Pennsylvania, Harrisburg Office, denied.

Same case below, 106 A.3d 165.

No. 14-1426. Courtney Satterwhite, Petitioner v. City of Houston, Texas.

577 U.S. 821, 136 S. Ct. 87, 193 L. Ed. 2d 35, 2015 U.S. LEXIS 5193.

October 5, 2015. Petition for writ of certiorari to the United States Court of Appeals for the Fifth Circuit denied.

Same case below, 602 Fed. Appx. 585.

No. 14-1428. David Couture, Petitioner v. Playdom, Inc.

577 U.S. 822, 136 S. Ct. 88, 193 L. Ed. 2d 35, 2015 U.S. LEXIS 5080.

October 5, 2015. Petition for writ of certiorari to the United States Court of Appeals for the Federal Circuit denied.

Same case below, 778 F.3d 1379.

No. 14-1429. Douglas E. Leightey, Petitioner v. United States.

577 U.S. 822, 136 S. Ct. 89, 193 L. Ed. 2d 35, 2015 U.S. LEXIS 5288.

October 5, 2015. Petition for writ of certiorari to the United States Court of Appeals for the Eleventh Circuit denied.

No. 14-1430. F. Harvey Whittemore, Petitioner v. United States.

577 U.S. 822, 136 S. Ct. 89, 193 L. Ed. 2d 35, 2015 U.S. LEXIS 5318.

October 5, 2015. Petition for writ of certiorari to the United States Court of Appeals for the Ninth Circuit denied.

Same case below, 776 F.3d 1074.

No. 14-1431. Farida B. Rahman, Petitioner v. Hickory Hills Property Owners Association.

577 U.S. 822, 136 S. Ct. 93, 193 L. Ed. 2d 35, 2015 U.S. LEXIS 5568.

October 5, 2015. Petition for writ of certiorari to the Superior Court of Pennsylvania, Harrisburg Office, denied.

Same case below, 104 A.3d 58.

No. 14-1432. Darrel Burditt, Petitioner v. Daniel Leedy, et al.

577 U.S. 822, 136 S. Ct. 94, 193 L. Ed. 2d 35, 2015 U.S. LEXIS 5233.

October 5, 2015. Petition for writ of certiorari to the United States Court of Appeals for the Fifth Circuit denied.

Same case below, 583 Fed. Appx. 398.

No. 14-1433. Frank M. Lombard, Petitioner v. United States.

577 U.S. 822, 136 S. Ct. 94, 193 L. Ed. 2d 35, 2015 U.S. LEXIS 5243.

October 5, 2015. Petition for writ of certiorari to the United States Court of Appeals for the District of Columbia Circuit denied.

No. 14-1434. Elizabeth Bazinski, Petitioner v. JPMorgan Chase Bank, N.A.

577 U.S. 822, 136 S. Ct. 94, 193 L. Ed. 2d 36, 2015 U.S. LEXIS 5160.

October 5, 2015. Petition for writ of certiorari to the United States Court of Appeals for the Sixth Circuit denied.

Same case below, 597 Fed. Appx. 379.

No. 14-1435. Black Farmers and Agriculturalists Association, Inc., Petitioner v. Thomas J. Vilsack, Secretary of Agriculture, et al.

577 U.S. 822, 136 S. Ct. 94, 193 L. Ed. 2d 36, 2015 U.S. LEXIS 5432.

October 5, 2015. Petition for writ of certiorari to the United States Court of Appeals for the District of Columbia Circuit denied.

No. 14-1437. Patrick Cox, Petitioner v. Select Portfolio Servicing, Inc., et al.

577 U.S. 822, 136 S. Ct. 94, 193 L. Ed. 2d 36, 2015 U.S. LEXIS 5283.

October 5, 2015. Petition for writ of certiorari to the United States Court of Appeals for the Fifth Circuit denied.

Same case below, 585 Fed. Appx. 862.

No. 14-1441. Ming Tien, Petitioner v. Paul Tien, et al.

577 U.S. 822, 136 S. Ct. 103, 193 L. Ed. 2d 36, 2015 U.S. LEXIS 5150.

October 5, 2015. Petition for writ of certiorari to the District Court of Appeal of Florida, Third District, denied.

Same case below, 155 So. 3d 359.

No. 14-1442. Corpcar Services Houston, Limited, dba Carey of Houston, et al., Petitioners v. James L. Henry, et al.

577 U.S. 822, 136 S. Ct. 104, 193 L. Ed. 2d 36, 2015 U.S. LEXIS 5476.

October 5, 2015. Petition for writ of certiorari to the United States Court of Appeals for the Fifth Circuit denied.

Same case below, 625 Fed. Appx. 607.

No. 14-1443. Benjamin Atkinson, Petitioner v. Ernie Haire Ford, Inc.

577 U.S. 822, 136 S. Ct. 104, 193 L. Ed. 2d 36, 2015 U.S. LEXIS 5197.

October 5, 2015. Petition for writ of certiorari to the United States Court of Appeals for the Eleventh Circuit denied.

Same case below, 764 F. 3d 1321.

No. 14-1444. Mary E. Stansel, Petitioner v. City of Atlanta, Georgia, et al.

577 U.S. 822, 136 S. Ct. 104, 193 L. Ed. 2d 36, 2015 U.S. LEXIS 5100.

October 5, 2015. Petition for writ of certiorari to the United States Court of Appeals for the Eleventh Circuit denied.

Same case below, 593 Fed. Appx. 866.

No. 14-1445. Nicole Phillips, Individually and on Behalf of B. P. and S. P., Minors, et al., Petitioners v. City of New York, New York, et al.

577 U.S. 822, 136 S. Ct. 104, 193 L. Ed. 2d 37, 2015 U.S. LEXIS 5363.

October 5, 2015. Petition for writ of certiorari to the United States Court of Appeals for the Second Circuit denied.

Same case below, 775 F.3d 538.

No. 14-1446. Albert J. Ragge, Jr., Petitioner v. Webster Bank, N.A.

577 U.S. 823, 136 S. Ct. 104, 193 L. Ed. 2d 37, 2015 U.S. LEXIS 5399, reh den 577 U.S. 1094, 136 S. Ct. 879, 193 L. Ed. 2d 770, 2016 U.S. LEXIS 523.

October 5, 2015. Petition for writ of certiorari to the Appeals Court of Massachusetts denied.

Same case below, 85 Mass. App. Ct. 1113, 6 N.E.3d 569.

No. 14-1447. Alina Feas, Petitioner v. United States.

577 U.S. 823, 136 S. Ct. 104, 193 L. Ed. 2d 37, 2015 U.S. LEXIS 5110.

October 5, 2015. Petition for writ of certiorari to the United States Court of Appeals for the Eleventh Circuit denied.

No. 14-1448. Nancy Kovacic, Petitioner v. Cuyahoga County Department of Children and Family Services, et al.

577 U.S. 823, 136 S. Ct. 105, 193 L. Ed. 2d 37, 2015 U.S. LEXIS 5335.

October 5, 2015. Petition for writ of certiorari to the United States Court of Appeals for the Sixth Circuit denied.

No. 14-1449. Rachael Cook, Petitioner v. Aetna Life Insurance Company, et al.

577 U.S. 823, 136 S. Ct. 109, 193 L. Ed. 2d 37, 2015 U.S. LEXIS 5475.

October 5, 2015. Petition for writ of certiorari to the United States Court of Appeals for the Eleventh Circuit denied.

Same case below, 589 Fed. Appx. 519.

No. 14-1450. Vision-Park Properties, LLC, et al., Petitioners v. Seaside Engineering & Surveying, LLC.

577 U.S. 823, 136 S. Ct. 109, 193 L. Ed. 2d 37, 2015 U.S. LEXIS 5302.

October 5, 2015. Petition for writ of certiorari to the United States Court of Appeals for the Eleventh Circuit denied.

Same case below, 780 F.3d 1070.

No. 14-1451. Mohamed Khalil and Sandra Damrah, Petitioners v. New Jersey Division of Child Protection and Permanency, et al.

577 U.S. 823, 136 S. Ct. 110, 193 L. Ed. 2d 37, 2015 U.S. LEXIS 5301.

October 5, 2015. Petition for writ of certiorari to the United States Court of Appeals for the Third Circuit denied.

Same case below, 594 Fed. Appx. 88.

No. 14-1452. John J. Dougherty, Petitioner v. Philadelphia Newspapers LLC, et al.

577 U.S. 823, 136 S. Ct. 110, 193 L. Ed. 2d 37, 2015 U.S. LEXIS 5570.

October 5, 2015. Petition for writ of certiorari to the United States Court of Appeals for the Third Circuit denied.

Same case below, 627 Fed. Appx. 97.

No. 14-1454. Preston State Bank, fka Dallas City Bank, Petitioner v. Texas, et al.

577 U.S. 823, 136 S. Ct. 111, 193 L. Ed. 2d 38, 2015 U.S. LEXIS 5136.

October 5, 2015. Petition for writ of certiorari to the Court of Appeals of Texas, Fifth District, denied.

Same case below, 443 S.W.3d 428.

No. 14-1455. Fred Martin Motor Company, Petitioner v. Spitzer Autoworld Akron, LLC, et al.

577 U.S. 823, 136 S. Ct. 111, 193 L. Ed. 2d 38, 2015 U.S. LEXIS 5412.

October 5, 2015. Petition for writ of certiorari to the United States Court of Appeals for the Sixth Circuit denied.

Same case below, 776 F.3d 411.

No. 14-1456. Billy Williams, Petitioner v. Loretta E. Lynch, Attorney General, et al.

577 U.S. 823, 136 S. Ct. 111, 193 L. Ed. 2d 38, 2015 U.S. LEXIS 5235.

October 5, 2015. Petition for writ of certiorari to the United States Court of Appeals for the Fifth Circuit denied.

Same case below, 621 Fed. Appx. 768.

No. 14-1459. Willie Meche, Petitioner v. Alex Doucet, et al.

577 U.S. 823, 136 S. Ct. 111, 193 L. Ed. 2d 38, 2015 U.S. LEXIS 5577.

October 5, 2015. Petition for writ of certiorari to the United States Court of Appeals for the Fifth Circuit denied.

Same case below, 777 F.3d 237.

No. 14-1460. Lavern R. Crump, Petitioner v. Montgomery County Education Association, et al.

577 U.S. 823, 136 S. Ct. 111, 193 L. Ed. 2d 38, 2015 U.S. LEXIS 5091.

October 5, 2015. Petition for writ of certiorari to the United States Court of Appeals for the Fourth Circuit denied.

Same case below, 590 Fed. Appx. 274.

No. 14-1461. Harris Himes, Petitioner v. Montana.

577 U.S. 824, 136 S. Ct. 111, 193 L. Ed. 2d 38, 2015 U.S. LEXIS 5583.

October 5, 2015. Petition for writ of certiorari to the Supreme Court of Montana denied.

Same case below, 378 Mont. 419, 345 P.3d 297.

No. 14-1462. John Loudermilk, et ux., Petitioners v. Joseph M. Arpaio, et al.

577 U.S. 824, 136 S. Ct. 116, 193 L. Ed. 2d 38, 2015 U.S. LEXIS 5645.

October 5, 2015. Petition for writ of certiorari to the United States Court of Appeals for the Ninth Circuit denied.

Same case below, 592 Fed. Appx. 596.

No. 14-1463. Scott Reeder, et al., Petitioners v. Michael J. Madigan, Speaker of the Illinois House of Representatives, et al.

577 U.S. 824, 136 S. Ct. 116, 193 L. Ed. 2d 39, 2015 U.S. LEXIS 5644.

October 5, 2015. Petition for writ of certiorari to the United States Court of Appeals for the Seventh Circuit denied.

Same case below, 780 F.3d 799.

—————

No. 14-1465. Andrew Fialdini, et ux., Petitioners v. Eric Cote, et al.

577 U.S. 824, 136 S. Ct. 116, 193 L. Ed. 2d 39, 2015 U.S. LEXIS 5653.

October 5, 2015. Petition for writ of certiorari to the United States Court of Appeals for the Fourth Circuit denied.

Same case below, 594 Fed. Appx. 113.

—————

No. 14-1466. William Sumner Scott, Petitioner v. Steven A. Frankel.

577 U.S. 824, 136 S. Ct. 116, 193 L. Ed. 2d 39, 2015 U.S. LEXIS 5885.

October 5, 2015. Petition for writ of certiorari to the United States Court of Appeals for the Eleventh Circuit denied.

Same case below, 606 Fed. Appx. 529.

—————

No. 14-1471. Robert J. Tretola, Petitioner v. Rebecca L. Tretola.

577 U.S. 824, 136 S. Ct. 117, 193 L. Ed. 2d 39, 2015 U.S. LEXIS 5602.

October 5, 2015. Petition for writ of certiorari to the Court of Appeals of Ohio, Logan County, denied.

No. 14-1474. George Wesley Huguely, Petitioner v. Virginia.

577 U.S. 824, 136 S. Ct. 119, 193 L. Ed. 2d 39, 2015 U.S. LEXIS 5566.

October 5, 2015. Petition for writ of certiorari to the Supreme Court of Virginia denied.

—————

No. 14-1475. U.S. Tour and Remittance, Inc., et al., Petitioners v. United States.

577 U.S. 824, 136 S. Ct. 119, 193 L. Ed. 2d 39, 2015 U.S. LEXIS 5982.

October 5, 2015. Petition for writ of certiorari to the United States Court of Appeals for the Fifth Circuit denied.

Same case below, 595 Fed. Appx. 336.

—————

No. 14-1476. JT USA, LP, et al., Petitioners v. Commissioner of Internal Revenue.

577 U.S. 824, 136 S. Ct. 120, 193 L. Ed. 2d 39, 2015 U.S. LEXIS 5553.

October 5, 2015. Petition for writ of certiorari to the United States Court of Appeals for the Ninth Circuit denied.

Same case below, 771 F.3d 654.

—————

No. 14-1477. Peter A. Prostyakov, Petitioner v. Masco Corporation.

577 U.S. 824, 136 S. Ct. 120, 193 L. Ed. 2d 39, 2015 U.S. LEXIS 5702.

October 5, 2015. Petition for writ of certiorari to the United States Court of Appeals for the Seventh Circuit denied.

Same case below, 593 Fed. Appx. 570.

Same case below, 778 F.3d 337.

No. 14-1479. Robert H. Hollander, Petitioner v. Christine R. Pembroke.

577 U.S. 824, 136 S. Ct. 128, 193 L. Ed. 2d 40, 2015 U.S. LEXIS 5572, reh den 577 U.S. 1022, 136 S. Ct. 571, 193 L. Ed. 2d 453, 2015 U.S. LEXIS 7394.

October 5, 2015. Petition for writ of certiorari to the District of Columbia Court of Appeals denied.

Same case below, 111 A.3d 647.

No. 14-1481. Kelly M. Rindfleisch, Petitioner v. Wisconsin.

577 U.S. 824, 136 S. Ct. 128, 193 L. Ed. 2d 40, 2015 U.S. LEXIS 5738.

October 5, 2015. Petition for writ of certiorari to the Court of Appeals of Wisconsin, District I, denied.

Same case below, 359 Wis. 2d 147, 857 N.W.2d 456.

No. 14-1482. Reeves A. Reeves, Petitioner v. OneBeacon America Insurance Company, et al.

577 U.S. 824, 136 S. Ct. 129, 193 L. Ed. 2d 40, 2015 U.S. LEXIS 5555.

October 5, 2015. Petition for writ of certiorari to the United States Court of Appeals for the Eleventh Circuit denied.

No. 14-1483. Federico Mendez, Petitioner v. Maya K. May.

577 U.S. 824, 136 S. Ct. 129, 193 L. Ed. 2d 40, 2015 U.S. LEXIS 5751.

October 5, 2015. Petition for writ of certiorari to the United States Court of Appeals for the First Circuit denied.

No. 14-1484. Joe O. Rodriguez, Jr., Petitioner v. Bank of America, N.A., et al.

577 U.S. 825, 136 S. Ct. 129, 193 L. Ed. 2d 40, 2015 U.S. LEXIS 5622.

October 5, 2015. Petition for writ of certiorari to the United States Court of Appeals for the Fifth Circuit denied.

Same case below, 588 Fed. Appx. 356.

No. 14-1485. Rafia Nafees Khan, Petitioner v. Regions Bank.

577 U.S. 825, 136 S. Ct. 129, 193 L. Ed. 2d 40, 2015 U.S. LEXIS 5655.

October 5, 2015. Petition for writ of certiorari to the Court of Appeals of Tennessee, Eastern Division, denied.

Same case below, 461 S.W.3d 505.

No. 14-1486. Lance T. Posner, et al., Petitioners v. Ronald Tassely, et al.

577 U.S. 825, 136 S. Ct. 129, 193 L. Ed. 2d 40, 2015 U.S. LEXIS 5628.

October 5, 2015. Petition for writ of certiorari to the Supreme Court of Nevada denied.

Same case below, 131 Nev. 1335.

No. 14-1487. Marianne Kornegay, et vir, Petitioners v. Old Republic National Title Insurance Company, et al.

577 U.S. 825, 136 S. Ct. 129, 193 L. Ed. 2d 40, 2015 U.S. LEXIS 5796.

October 5, 2015. Petition for writ of certiorari to the Court of Appeals of Nebraska denied.

No. 14-1488. Pascual Q. Olibas, et al., Petitioners v. Ronny Dodson, Sheriff, Brewster County, Texas, et al.

577 U.S. 825, 136 S. Ct. 130, 193 L. Ed. 2d 41, 2015 U.S. LEXIS 5670.

October 5, 2015. Petition for writ of certiorari to the United States Court of Appeals for the Fifth Circuit denied.

Same case below, 593 Fed. Appx. 412.

No. 14-1489. Dana Lee Orcutt, Petitioner v. Superior Court of California, Riverside County.

577 U.S. 825, 136 S. Ct. 130, 193 L. Ed. 2d 41, 2015 U.S. LEXIS 5591.

October 5, 2015. Petition for writ of certiorari to the Court of Appeal of California, Fourth Appellate District, Division Two, denied.

No. 14-1490. Mohammed Izhar, Petitioner v. Kaiser Foundation Health Plan, et al.

577 U.S. 825, 136 S. Ct. 130, 193 L. Ed. 2d 41, 2015 U.S. LEXIS 5575.

October 5, 2015. Petition for writ of certiorari to the Court of Appeal of California, Fourth Appellate District, Division Two, denied.

No. 14-1491. Hussein Nazzal, Petitioner v. United States.

577 U.S. 825, 136 S. Ct. 130, 193 L. Ed. 2d 41, 2015 U.S. LEXIS 5666.

October 5, 2015. Petition for writ of certiorari to the United States Court of Appeals for the Sixth Circuit denied.

Same case below, 607 Fed. Appx. 451.

No. 14-1493. Paulette Gardner, Petitioner v. The Bank of New York Mellon.

577 U.S. 825, 136 S. Ct. 130, 193 L. Ed. 2d 41, 2015 U.S. LEXIS 5548.

October 5, 2015. Petition for writ of certiorari to the Supreme Court of Florida denied.

Same case below, 160 So. 3d 894.

No. 14-1494. Douglas C. Charnock, Jr., Petitioner v. Virginia, et al.

577 U.S. 825, 136 S. Ct. 131, 193 L. Ed. 2d 41, 2015 U.S. LEXIS 5819.

October 5, 2015. Petition for writ of certiorari to the United States Court of Appeals for the Fourth Circuit denied.

Same case below, 587 Fed. Appx. 764.

No. 14-1495. Alvaro Adame, Petitioner v. Loretta E. Lynch, Attorney General.

577 U.S. 825, 136 S. Ct. 131, 193 L. Ed. 2d 41, 2015 U.S. LEXIS 5883.

October 5, 2015. Petition for writ of certiorari to the United States Court of Appeals for the Seventh Circuit denied.

Same case below, 762 F.3d 667.

No. 14-1496. Robert Yousefian, Petitioner v. City of Glendale, California, et al.

577 U.S. 825, 136 S. Ct. 135, 193 L. Ed. 2d 41, 2015 U.S. LEXIS 5976.

October 5, 2015. Petition for writ of certiorari to the United States Court of Appeals for the Ninth Circuit denied.

Same case below, 779 F.3d 1010.

Same case below, 588 Fed. Appx. 72.

No. 14-1500. Terry Marshall Campie, Petitioner v. United States.

577 U.S. 825, 136 S. Ct. 138, 193 L. Ed. 2d 42, 2015 U.S. LEXIS 5634.

October 5, 2015. Petition for writ of certiorari to the United States Court of Appeals for the Eighth Circuit denied.

No. 14-1501. Natasha Wrae, Petitioner v. Jan L. Eikleberry, Judge, Superior Court of California, Pima County, et al.

577 U.S. 825, 136 S. Ct. 138, 193 L. Ed. 2d 42, 2015 U.S. LEXIS 5616.

October 5, 2015. Petition for writ of certiorari to the Supreme Court of Arizona denied.

No. 14-1502. John Paul Nelson, Petitioner v. L.S. McEwen, Warden.

577 U.S. 826, 136 S. Ct. 138, 193 L. Ed. 2d 42, 2015 U.S. LEXIS 5707.

October 5, 2015. Petition for writ of certiorari to the United States Court of Appeals for the Ninth Circuit denied.

Same case below, 593 Fed. Appx. 688.

No. 14-1503. Vladimira Koch, et al., Petitioners v. Vratislva Pechota, et al.

577 U.S. 826, 136 S. Ct. 138, 193 L. Ed. 2d 42, 2015 U.S. LEXIS 5641.

October 5, 2015. Petition for writ of certiorari to the United States Court of Appeals for the Second Circuit denied.

No. 14-1509. John LaCertosa, Petitioner v. Blackman Plumbing Supply Co., Inc., et al.

577 U.S. 826, 136 S. Ct. 138, 193 L. Ed. 2d 42, 2015 U.S. LEXIS 5624, reh den 577 U.S. 1022, 136 S. Ct. 572, 193 L. Ed. 2d 453, 2015 U.S. LEXIS 7419.

October 5, 2015. Petition for writ of certiorari to the United States Court of Appeals for the Second Circuit denied.

Same case below, 582 Fed. Appx. 43.

No. 14-1510. Wu Tien Li-Shou, Petitioner v. United States.

577 U.S. 826, 136 S. Ct. 139, 193 L. Ed. 2d 42, 2015 U.S. LEXIS 5737.

October 5, 2015. Petition for writ of certiorari to the United States Court of Appeals for the Fourth Circuit denied.

Same case below, 777 F.3d 175.

No. 14-1514. William F. Holdner, Petitioner v. Ellen Rosenblum, Attorney General of Oregon, et al.

577 U.S. 826, 136 S. Ct. 148, 193 L. Ed. 2d 42, 2015 U.S. LEXIS 5828.

October 5, 2015. Petition for writ of certiorari to the United States Court of Appeals for the Ninth Circuit denied.

Same case below, 599 Fed. Appx. 327.

No. 14-1515. Evelyn Konrad, Petitioner v. Mark Epley, et al.

577 U.S. 826, 136 S. Ct. 148, 193 L. Ed. 2d 42, 2015 U.S. LEXIS 5695.

October 5, 2015. Petition for writ of certiorari to the United States Court of Appeals for the Second Circuit denied.

Same case below, 586 Fed. Appx. 72.

No. 14-1517. Walter J. Beriont, Petitioner v. GTE Laboratories, Inc., et al.

577 U.S. 826, 136 S. Ct. 148, 193 L. Ed. 2d 43, 2015 U.S. LEXIS 5665.

October 5, 2015. Petition for writ of certiorari to the United States Court of Appeals for the Federal Circuit denied.

Same case below, 601 Fed. Appx. 937.

No. 14-1518. Gloria Abram, Petitioner v. Fulton County, Georgia.

577 U.S. 826, 136 S. Ct. 149, 193 L. Ed. 2d 43, 2015 U.S. LEXIS 6028, reh den 577 U.S. 1022, 136 S. Ct. 572, 193 L. Ed. 2d 453, 2015 U.S. LEXIS 7445.

October 5, 2015. Petition for writ of certiorari to the United States Court of Appeals for the Eleventh Circuit denied.

Same case below, 598 Fed. Appx. 672.

No. 14-1519. Aaron M. Buford, Petitioner v. United States.

577 U.S. 826, 136 S. Ct. 149, 193 L. Ed. 2d 43, 2015 U.S. LEXIS 5558.

October 5, 2015. Petition for writ of certiorari to the United States Court of Appeals for the Armed Forces denied.

Same case below, 74 M.J. 98.

No. 14-1521. Vincent Torres, Petitioner v. The Santa Ynez Band of Chumash Indians.

577 U.S. 826, 136 S. Ct. 152, 193 L. Ed. 2d 43, 2015 U.S. LEXIS 5589, reh den 577 U.S. 1022, 136 S. Ct. 572, 193 L. Ed. 2d 453, 2015 U.S. LEXIS 7404.

October 5, 2015. Petition for writ of certiorari to the United States Court of Appeals for the Ninth Circuit denied.

Same case below, 599 Fed. Appx. 650.

No. 14-1522. U. L., Individually and as Father and Natural Guardian of E. L., Petitioner v. New York State Assembly, et al.

577 U.S. 826, 136 S. Ct. 153, 193 L. Ed. 2d 43, 2015 U.S. LEXIS 5581.

October 5, 2015. Petition for writ of certiorari to the United States Court of Appeals for the Second Circuit denied.

Same case below, 592 Fed. Appx. 40.

No. 14-1523. John Fazio, Jr., Petitioner v. United States.

577 U.S. 826, 136 S. Ct. 153, 193 L. Ed. 2d 43, 2015 U.S. LEXIS 5636.

October 5, 2015. Petition for writ of certiorari to the United States Court of Appeals for the Second Circuit denied.

Same case below, 770 F.3d 160.

No. 14-1525. David A. Belniak, Petitioner v. Florida Highway Patrol, et al.

577 U.S. 826, 136 S. Ct. 153, 193 L. Ed. 2d 43, 2015 U.S. LEXIS 5979.

October 5, 2015. Petition for writ of certiorari to the United States Court of Appeals for the Eleventh Circuit denied.

Same case below, 599 Fed. Appx. 357.

No. 14-1526. Arnaud Girard, Petitioner v. M/Y Quality Time.

577 U.S. 827, 136 S. Ct. 153, 193 L. Ed. 2d 43, 2015 U.S. LEXIS 5594.

October 5, 2015. Petition for writ of certiorari to the United States Court of Appeals for the Eleventh Circuit denied.

Same case below, 596 Fed. Appx. 846.

———

No. 14-1527. Eric Beeman, et al., Petitioners v. BGI Creditors' Liquidating Trust, et al. (two judgments).

577 U.S. 827, 136 S. Ct. 155, 193 L. Ed. 2d 44, 2015 U.S. LEXIS 5758.

October 5, 2015. Petition for writ of certiorari to the United States Court of Appeals for the Second Circuit denied.

Same case below, 772 F.3d 102 (first judgment); 595 Fed. Appx. 86 (second judgment).

———

No. 14-1528. Delma Jackson, Petitioner v. Carl Humphrey, et al.

577 U.S. 827, 136 S. Ct. 155, 193 L. Ed. 2d 44, 2015 U.S. LEXIS 5831.

October 5, 2015. Petition for writ of certiorari to the United States Court of Appeals for the Eleventh Circuit denied.

Same case below, 776 F.3d 1232.

———

No. 14-1529. Edward Lilly, Petitioner v. Lewiston-Porter Central School District, et al.

577 U.S. 827, 136 S. Ct. 156, 193 L. Ed. 2d 44, 2015 U.S. LEXIS 5556, reh den 577 U.S. 1094, 136 S. Ct. 879, 193 L. Ed. 2d 770, 2016 U.S. LEXIS 240.

October 5, 2015. Petition for writ of certiorari to the United States Court of Appeals for the Second Circuit denied.

Same case below, 593 Fed. Appx. 87.

———

No. 14-1530. Turnberry/MGM Grand Towers, LLC, et al., Petitioners v. Mary Ann Sussex, et al.

577 U.S. 827, 136 S. Ct. 156, 193 L. Ed. 2d 44, 2015 U.S. LEXIS 5854.

October 5, 2015. Petition for writ of certiorari to the United States Court of Appeals for the Ninth Circuit denied.

Same case below, 781 F.3d 1065.

———

No. 14-1533. Xu-Shen Zhou, Petitioner v. State University of New York Institute of Technology, et al.

577 U.S. 827, 136 S. Ct. 157, 193 L. Ed. 2d 44, 2015 U.S. LEXIS 5647.

October 5, 2015. Petition for writ of certiorari to the United States Court of Appeals for the Second Circuit denied.

Same case below, 592 Fed. Appx. 41.

———

No. 14-1534. Betshua Hernandez, Petitioner v. JPMorgan Chase Bank, N.A.

577 U.S. 827, 136 S. Ct. 157, 193 L. Ed. 2d 44, 2015 U.S. LEXIS 5753.

October 5, 2015. Petition for writ of certiorari to the Supreme Court of Florida denied.

Same case below, 157 So. 3d 1044.

———

No. 14-1537. Michael Houston and Steve Houston, Petitioners v. 42nd Judicial District Court of Louisiana.

577 U.S. 827, 136 S. Ct. 157, 193 L. Ed. 2d 44, 2015 U.S. LEXIS 5677, reh den 577 U.S. 1022, 136 S. Ct. 572, 193 L. Ed. 2d 454, 2015 U.S. LEXIS 7434.

October 5, 2015. Petition for writ of certiorari to the Supreme Court of Louisiana denied.

Same case below, 152 So. 3d 895.

No. 14-1539. Lance Koster, Petitioner v. Carol Sullivan.

577 U.S. 827, 136 S. Ct. 164, 193 L. Ed. 2d 45, 2015 U.S. LEXIS 5807.

October 5, 2015. Petition for writ of certiorari to the Supreme Court of Florida denied.

Same case below, 160 So. 3d 385.

No. 14-1540. James R. LaFrieda, et ux., Petitioners v. Black Eagle Consulting, Inc.

577 U.S. 827, 136 S. Ct. 164, 193 L. Ed. 2d 45, 2015 U.S. LEXIS 5638.

October 5, 2015. Petition for writ of certiorari to the Supreme Court of Nevada denied.

Same case below, 130 Nev. 1207.

No. 14-1541. Loren J. Zutz, et al., Petitioners v. John Nelson, et al.

577 U.S. 827, 136 S. Ct. 164, 193 L. Ed. 2d 45, 2015 U.S. LEXIS 5560.

October 5, 2015. Petition for writ of certiorari to the Court of Appeals of Minnesota denied.

No. 14-1542. Corzo Trucking Corporation, et al., Petitioners v. Bob West, aka Robert West.

577 U.S. 827, 136 S. Ct. 164, 193 L. Ed. 2d 45, 2015 U.S. LEXIS 5586.

October 5, 2015. Petition for writ of certiorari to the Court of Appeals of Georgia denied.

No. 14-1544. Tawoos Bazargani, Petitioner v. Tammy Radel, et al.

577 U.S. 827, 136 S. Ct. 167, 193 L. Ed. 2d 45, 2015 U.S. LEXIS 5708.

October 5, 2015. Petition for writ of certiorari to the United States Court of Appeals for the Third Circuit denied.

Same case below, 598 Fed. Appx. 829.

No. 14-7776. Carole M. Dean, Petitioner v. Porsche Automobil Holdings SE, et al.

577 U.S. 828, 136 S. Ct. 30, 193 L. Ed. 2d 45, 2015 U.S. LEXIS 5676, reh den 577 U.S. 1022, 136 S. Ct. 572, 193 L. Ed. 2d 454, 2015 U.S. LEXIS 7411.

October 5, 2015. Petition for writ of certiorari to the Supreme Court of Georgia denied.

No. 14-8486. Erik Diaz-Colon, Petitioner v. United States.

577 U.S. 828, 136 S. Ct. 30, 193 L. Ed. 2d 45, 2015 U.S. LEXIS 5592.

October 5, 2015. Petition for writ of certiorari to the United States Court of Appeals for the First Circuit denied.

Same case below, 763 F.3d 89.

No. 14-8575. Rodney Lamont Hunt, Petitioner v. Texas.

577 U.S. 828, 136 S. Ct. 30, 193 L. Ed. 2d 45, 2015 U.S. LEXIS 5973.

October 5, 2015. Petition for writ of certiorari to the Court of Appeals of Texas, Fifth District, denied.

Same case below, 587 Fed. Appx. 205.

No. 14-8686. Dwond Donahue, Petitioner v. Illinois.

577 U.S. 828, 136 S. Ct. 31, 193 L. Ed. 2d 46, 2015 U.S. LEXIS 5625.

October 5, 2015. Petition for writ of certiorari to the Appellate Court of Illinois, First District, denied.

Same case below, 384 Ill. Dec. 220, 16 N.E.3d 316.

No. 14-8782. Ray Dansby, Petitioner v. Wendy Kelley, Director, Arkansas Department of Correction.

577 U.S. 828, 136 S. Ct. 297, 193 L. Ed. 2d 46, 2015 U.S. LEXIS 5817.

October 5, 2015. Petition for writ of certiorari to the United States Court of Appeals for the Eighth Circuit denied.

Same case below, 766 F.3d 809.

No. 14-8791. Mohammed El Amin, Petitioner v. United States.

577 U.S. 828, 136 S. Ct. 31, 193 L. Ed. 2d 46, 2015 U.S. LEXIS 6081.

October 5, 2015. Petition for writ of certiorari to the United States Court of Appeals for the Third Circuit denied.

No. 14-8805. Contina Graham, Petitioner v. Bluebonnet Trails Community Services.

577 U.S. 828, 136 S. Ct. 31, 193 L. Ed. 2d 46, 2015 U.S. LEXIS 5816.

October 5, 2015. Petition for writ of certiorari to the United States Court of Appeals for the Fifth Circuit denied.

No. 14-8856. Alexander Alexandervi Bistrika, et al., Petitioners v. Oregon; and Svetlana Alexandrovna Bistrika, Petitioner v. Oregon.

577 U.S. 828, 136 S. Ct. 32, 193 L. Ed. 2d 46, 2015 U.S. LEXIS 6042, reh den 577 U.S. 1022, 136 S. Ct. 572, 193 L. Ed. 2d 454, 2015 U.S. LEXIS 7374.

October 5, 2015. Petition for writ of certiorari to the Court of Appeals of Oregon denied.

Same case below, 261 Or. App. 710, 322 P.3d 583 (first judgment); and 262 Or. App. 385, 324 P.3d 584 (second judgment).

No. 14-8893. Dwight Giles, Petitioner v. New York.

577 U.S. 828, 136 S. Ct. 32, 193 L. Ed. 2d 46, 2015 U.S. LEXIS 5541.

October 5, 2015. Petition for writ of certiorari to the Court of Appeals of New York denied.

Same case below, 24 N.Y.3d 1066, 2 N.Y.S.3d 30, 25 N.E.3d 943.

No. 14-8911. Paul William Pilger, Petitioner v. Department of Education, et al.

577 U.S. 828, 136 S. Ct. 32, 193 L. Ed. 2d 46, 2015 U.S. LEXIS 5836.

October 5, 2015. Petition for writ of certiorari to the United States Court of Appeals for the Ninth Circuit denied.

Same case below, 584 Fed. Appx. 452.

No. 14-8921. Arnoldo Hernandez-Gutierrez, Petitioner v. United States; Juan Miguel Alvarez-Alvarez, Petitioner v. United States; and Armando Alonzo-Solis, Petitioner v. United States.

577 U.S. 828, 136 S. Ct. 32, 193 L. Ed. 2d 47, 2015 U.S. LEXIS 5598.

October 5, 2015. Petition for writ of certiorari to the United States Court of Appeals for the Fifth Circuit denied.

Same case below, 606 Fed. Appx. 151 (first judgment); 606 Fed. Appx. 164 (second judgment); and 606 Fed. Appx. 160 (third judgment).

No. 14-8967. Mickey Fugate, Petitioner v. United States.

577 U.S. 828, 136 S. Ct. 33, 193 L. Ed. 2d 47, 2015 U.S. LEXIS 5643.

October 5, 2015. Petition for writ of certiorari to the United States Court of Appeals for the Sixth Circuit denied.

Same case below, 599 Fed. Appx. 564.

No. 14-8993. Lance McNeal, Petitioner v. Gary Kott, et al.

577 U.S. 828, 136 S. Ct. 33, 193 L. Ed. 2d 47, 2015 U.S. LEXIS 5563.

October 5, 2015. Petition for writ of certiorari to the United States Court of Appeals for the Sixth Circuit denied.

Same case below, 590 Fed. Appx. 566.

No. 14-8995. Adrian Dewayne Patterson, Petitioner v. United States.

577 U.S. 829, 136 S. Ct. 33, 193 L. Ed. 2d 47, 2015 U.S. LEXIS 5640.

October 5, 2015. Petition for writ of certiorari to the United States Court of Appeals for the Sixth Circuit denied.

Same case below, 587 Fed. Appx. 878.

No. 14-9012. Gloria Deanna Dickerson, Petitioner v. United Way of New York City, et al.

577 U.S. 829, 136 S. Ct. 33, 193 L. Ed. 2d 47, 2015 U.S. LEXIS 5658, reh den 577 U.S. 1053, 136 S. Ct. 703, 193 L. Ed. 2d 529, 2015 U.S. LEXIS 7977.

October 5, 2015. Petition for writ of certiorari to the Appellate Division, Supreme Court of New York, First Judicial Department, denied.

Same case below, 113 App. Div. 3d 452, 979 N.Y.S.2d 25.

No. 14-9036. Ludema Cruz Dorward, Petitioner v. Macy's, Inc.

577 U.S. 829, 136 S. Ct. 33, 193 L. Ed. 2d 47, 2015 U.S. LEXIS 5712.

October 5, 2015. Petition for writ of certiorari to the United States Court of Appeals for the Eleventh Circuit denied.

Same case below, 588 Fed. Appx. 951.

No. 14-9048. Jose Sierra-Villegas, Petitioner v. United States.

577 U.S. 829, 136 S. Ct. 34, 193 L. Ed. 2d 47, 2015 U.S. LEXIS 5546.

October 5, 2015. Petition for writ of certiorari to the United States Court of Appeals for the Sixth Circuit denied.

Same case below, 774 F.3d 1093.

No. 14-9078. Mamadou Barry, Petitioner v. Aissato Diallo.

577 U.S. 829, 136 S. Ct. 34, 193 L. Ed. 2d 48, 2015 U.S. LEXIS 5551, reh den 577 U.S. 1022, 136 S. Ct. 572, 193 L. Ed. 2d 454, 2015 U.S. LEXIS 7382.

October 5, 2015. Petition for writ of certiorari to the Superior Court of Pennsylvania, Philadelphia Office, denied.

Same case below, 100 A.3d 322.

No. 14-9114. Angela Darlene McAnulty, Petitioner v. Oregon.

577 U.S. 829, 136 S. Ct. 34, 193 L. Ed. 2d 48, 2015 U.S. LEXIS 5961.

October 5, 2015. Petition for writ of certiorari to the Supreme Court of Oregon denied.

Same case below, 356 Or. 432, 338 P.3d 653.

No. 14-9139. Yelkal Gelahun Ido, Petitioner v. Loretta E. Lynch, Attorney General.

577 U.S. 829, 136 S. Ct. 297, 193 L. Ed. 2d 48, 2015 U.S. LEXIS 5611.

October 5, 2015. Petition for writ of certiorari to the United States Court of Appeals for the Eleventh Circuit denied.

Same case below, 590 Fed. Appx. 897.

No. 14-9150. Norris G. Holder, Petitioner v. United States.

577 U.S. 829, 136 S. Ct. 34, 193 L. Ed. 2d 48, 2015 U.S. LEXIS 5723.

October 5, 2015. Petition for writ of certiorari to the United States Court of Appeals for the Eighth Circuit denied.

Same case below, 721 F.3d 979.

No. 14-9175. Ruben Gutierrez, Petitioner v. William Stephens, Director, Texas Department of Criminal Justice, Correctional Institutions Division.

577 U.S. 829, 136 S. Ct. 35, 193 L. Ed. 2d 48, 2015 U.S. LEXIS 5540, reh den 577 U.S. 1022, 136 S. Ct. 573, 193 L. Ed. 2d 454, 2015 U.S. LEXIS 7440.

October 5, 2015. Petition for writ of certiorari to the United States Court of Appeals for the Fifth Circuit denied.

Same case below, 590 Fed. Appx. 371.

No. 14-9239. Anthony Coles, Petitioner v. National Labor Relations Board, et al.

577 U.S. 829, 136 S. Ct. 35, 193 L. Ed. 2d 48, 2015 U.S. LEXIS 5685, reh den 577 U.S. 1022, 136 S. Ct. 573, 193 L. Ed. 2d 454, 2015 U.S. LEXIS 7387.

October 5, 2015. Petition for writ of certiorari to the United States Court of Appeals for the Sixth Circuit denied.

No. 14-9275. Robert Frazier, Petitioner v. West Virginia.

577 U.S. 829, 136 S. Ct. 35, 193 L. Ed. 2d 48, 2015 U.S. LEXIS 5728, reh den 577 U.S. 1054, 136 S. Ct. 703, 193 L. Ed. 2d 529, 2015 U.S. LEXIS 7969.

October 5, 2015. Petition for writ of certiorari to the Supreme Court of Appeals of West Virginia denied.

No. 14-9289. Earl Forrest, Petitioner v. Troy Steele, Warden.

577 U.S. 829, 136 S. Ct. 35, 193 L. Ed. 2d 48, 2015 U.S. LEXIS 5942.

October 5, 2015. Petition for writ of certiorari to the United States Court of Appeals for the Eighth Circuit denied.

Same case below, 764 F.3d 848.

No. 14-9292. Pedro Dominguez-Garcia, Petitioner v. United States.

577 U.S. 829, 136 S. Ct. 36, 193 L. Ed. 2d 49, 2015 U.S. LEXIS 5593.

October 5, 2015. Petition for writ of certiorari to the United States Court of Appeals for the Ninth Circuit denied.

Same case below, 586 Fed. Appx. 313.

No. 14-9301. Sharon L. Blount, Petitioner v. Merit Systems Protection Board.

577 U.S. 829, 136 S. Ct. 297, 193 L. Ed. 2d 49, 2015 U.S. LEXIS 5778.

October 5, 2015. Petition for writ of certiorari to the United States Court of Appeals for the Federal Circuit denied.

Same case below, 594 Fed. Appx. 987.

No. 14-9305. Patrick Miller, Petitioner v. United States.

577 U.S. 830, 136 S. Ct. 36, 193 L. Ed. 2d 49, 2015 U.S. LEXIS 5733.

October 5, 2015. Petition for writ of certiorari to the United States Court of Appeals for the Sixth Circuit denied.

Same case below, 597 Fed. Appx. 384.

No. 14-9317. Kwame A. Rockwell, Petitioner v. Texas.

577 U.S. 830, 136 S. Ct. 36, 193 L. Ed. 2d 49, 2015 U.S. LEXIS 6122.

October 5, 2015. Petition for writ of certiorari to the Court of Criminal Appeals of Texas denied.

No. 14-9320. Patrick Alexandre Missud, Petitioner v. California, et al.

577 U.S. 830, 136 S. Ct. 36, 193 L. Ed. 2d 49, 2015 U.S. LEXIS 5635.

October 5, 2015. Petition for writ of certiorari to the United States Court of Appeals for the Ninth Circuit denied.

No. 14-9336. Pablo Lucio Vasquez, Petitioner v. William Stephens, Director, Texas Department of Criminal Justice, Correctional Institutions Division.

577 U.S. 830, 136 S. Ct. 36, 193 L. Ed. 2d 49, 2015 U.S. LEXIS 5615.

October 5, 2015. Petition for writ of certiorari to the United States Court of Appeals for the Fifth Circuit denied.

Same case below, 597 Fed. Appx. 775.

No. 14-9380. David Russell Hosier, Petitioner v. Missouri.

577 U.S. 830, 136 S. Ct. 37, 193 L. Ed. 2d 49, 2015 U.S. LEXIS 5928.

October 5, 2015. Petition for writ of certiorari to the Supreme Court of Missouri denied.

Same case below, 454 S.W.3d 883.

No. 14-9405. Jack A. Morris, Petitioner v. United States.

577 U.S. 830, 136 S. Ct. 37, 193 L. Ed. 2d 49, 2015 U.S. LEXIS 5768.

October 5, 2015. Petition for writ of certiorari to the United States Court of Appeals for the Sixth Circuit denied.

Same case below, 602 Fed. Appx. 279.

No. 14-9408. Michael Wright, Petitioner v. United States.

577 U.S. 830, 136 S. Ct. 37, 193 L. Ed. 2d 50, 2015 U.S. LEXIS 5970.

October 5, 2015. Petition for writ of certiorari to the United States Court of Appeals for the Third Circuit denied.

Same case below, 777 F.3d 635.

No. 14-9425. Daniel Rodriguez, Petitioner v. United States.

577 U.S. 830, 136 S. Ct. 37, 193 L. Ed. 2d 50, 2015 U.S. LEXIS 5618.

October 5, 2015. Petition for writ of certiorari to the United States Court of Appeals for the Eleventh Circuit denied.

Same case below, 591 Fed. Appx. 897.

No. 14-9476. Marcos Sanchez-Venegas, Petitioner v. United States.

577 U.S. 830, 136 S. Ct. 39, 193 L. Ed. 2d 50, 2015 U.S. LEXIS 6098.

October 5, 2015. Petition for writ of certiorari to the United States Court of Appeals for the Ninth Circuit denied.

Same case below, 590 Fed. Appx. 709.

No. 14-9479. Valiant White, Petitioner v. Jeffrey Woods, Warden.

577 U.S. 830, 136 S. Ct. 39, 193 L. Ed. 2d 50, 2015 U.S. LEXIS 5909.

October 5, 2015. Petition for writ of certiorari to the United States Court of Appeals for the Sixth Circuit denied.

No. 14-9489. Tyrone Chalmers, Petitioner v. Tennessee.

577 U.S. 830, 136 S. Ct. 39, 193 L. Ed. 2d 50, 2015 U.S. LEXIS 5599, reh den 577 U.S. 1022, 136 S. Ct. 573, 193 L. Ed. 2d 455, 2015 U.S. LEXIS 7427.

October 5, 2015. Petition for writ of certiorari to the Court of Criminal Appeals of Tennessee, Western Division, denied.

No. 14-9495. Rodney K. Tadlock, Petitioner v. Anthony Foxx, Secretary of Transportation.

577 U.S. 830, 136 S. Ct. 39, 193 L. Ed. 2d 50, 2015 U.S. LEXIS 5614.

October 5, 2015. Petition for writ of certiorari to the United States Court of Appeals for the Tenth Circuit denied.

Same case below, 601 Fed. Appx. 595.

No. 14-9499. Posr A. Posr, Petitioner v. Barton Nachamie, et al.

577 U.S. 830, 136 S. Ct. 39, 193 L. Ed. 2d 50, 2015 U.S. LEXIS 5609.

October 5, 2015. Petition for writ of certiorari to the United States Court of Appeals for the Second Circuit denied.

No. 14-9500. Joshua Mosley, Petitioner v. Louisiana.

577 U.S. 830, 136 S. Ct. 40, 193 L. Ed. 2d 50, 2015 U.S. LEXIS 5821.

October 5, 2015. Petition for writ of certiorari to the Court of Appeal of Louisiana, First Circuit, denied.

No. 14-9506. John Joseph Kratochvil, Petitioner v. Stevenson Nixon, Warden.

577 U.S. 831, 136 S. Ct. 40, 193 L. Ed. 2d 51, 2015 U.S. LEXIS 6020.

October 5, 2015. Petition for writ of certiorari to the United States Court of Appeals for the Sixth Circuit denied.

No. 14-9515. Deon A. Leonard, Petitioner v. Richard Haskell, et al.

577 U.S. 831, 136 S. Ct. 40, 193 L. Ed. 2d 51, 2015 U.S. LEXIS 5694.

October 5, 2015. Petition for writ of certiorari to the United States Court of Appeals for the Tenth Circuit denied.

No. 14-9524. Antonio Williams, Petitioner v. Mississippi.

577 U.S. 831, 136 S. Ct. 40, 193 L. Ed. 2d 51, 2015 U.S. LEXIS 5710.

October 5, 2015. Petition for writ of certiorari to the Supreme Court of Mississippi denied.

Same case below, 158 So. 3d 309.

No. 14-9528. Gary Harrall, Petitioner v. Louisiana.

577 U.S. 831, 136 S. Ct. 41, 193 L. Ed. 2d 51, 2015 U.S. LEXIS 5605.

October 5, 2015. Petition for writ of certiorari to the Supreme Court of Louisiana denied.

Same case below, 159 So. 3d 453.

No. 14-9536. Loren Williamson, Petitioner v. Arizona.

577 U.S. 831, 136 S. Ct. 41, 193 L. Ed. 2d 51, 2015 U.S. LEXIS 5901.

October 5, 2015. Petition for writ of certiorari to the Court of Appeals of Arizona, Division Two, denied.

No. 14-9540. Wesley Schaefer, Petitioner v. Texas.

577 U.S. 831, 136 S. Ct. 41, 193 L. Ed. 2d 51, 2015 U.S. LEXIS 5812.

October 5, 2015. Petition for writ of certiorari to the Court of Appeals of Texas, Third District, denied.

No. 14-9559. Amils Barnard Drew, Petitioner v. United States.

577 U.S. 831, 136 S. Ct. 42, 193 L. Ed. 2d 51, 2015 U.S. LEXIS 5762.

October 5, 2015. Petition for writ of certiorari to the United States Court of Appeals for the Fourth Circuit denied.

Same case below, 590 Fed. Appx. 266.

No. 14-9561. Robert William Richardson, II, Petitioner v. Dean Minor, Warden, et al.

577 U.S. 831, 136 S. Ct. 42, 193 L. Ed. 2d 51, 2015 U.S. LEXIS 5739.

October 5, 2015. Petition for writ of certiorari to the United States Court of Appeals for the Eighth Circuit denied.

No. 14-9568. Robert V. Paulson, II, Petitioner v. Terry Mapes, Warden.

577 U.S. 831, 136 S. Ct. 42, 193 L. Ed. 2d 52, 2015 U.S. LEXIS 5654.

October 5, 2015. Petition for writ of certiorari to the United States Court of Appeals for the Eighth Circuit denied.

Same case below, 773 F.3d 901.

No. 14-9569. Christopher Lynn Johnson, Petitioner v. Pennsylvania.

577 U.S. 831, 136 S. Ct. 43, 193 L. Ed. 2d 52, 2015 U.S. LEXIS 5834.

October 5, 2015. Petition for writ of certiorari to the Supreme Court of Pennsylvania, Eastern District, denied.

Same case below, 630 Pa. 493, 107 A.3d 52.

No. 14-9575. Donnell Williams, Petitioner v. Illinois.

577 U.S. 831, 136 S. Ct. 43, 193 L. Ed. 2d 52, 2015 U.S. LEXIS 5584.

October 5, 2015. Petition for writ of certiorari to the Appellate Court of Illinois, First District, denied.

No. 14-9583. Christopher Ray Ingram, Petitioner v. Frances S. Stephenson.

577 U.S. 831, 136 S. Ct. 44, 193 L. Ed. 2d 52, 2015 U.S. LEXIS 5752.

October 5, 2015. Petition for writ of certiorari to the United States Court of Appeals for the Fifth Circuit denied.

No. 14-9584. Alvis C. Higgins, Petitioner v. Oklahoma.

577 U.S. 831, 136 S. Ct. 44, 193 L. Ed. 2d 52, 2015 U.S. LEXIS 5838.

October 5, 2015. Petition for writ of certiorari to the Court of Criminal Appeals of Oklahoma denied.

No. 14-9589. James Allen Higginbotham, Petitioner v. Ron King, Superintendent, South Mississippi Correctional Institution.

577 U.S. 831, 136 S. Ct. 44, 193 L. Ed. 2d 52, 2015 U.S. LEXIS 5938.

October 5, 2015. Petition for writ of certiorari to the United States Court of Appeals for the Fifth Circuit denied.

Same case below, 592 Fed. Appx. 313.

No. 14-9593. Scott Ash James Zirus, Petitioner v. William Stephens, Director, Texas Department of Criminal Justice, Correctional Institutions Division.

577 U.S. 831, 136 S. Ct. 44, 193 L. Ed. 2d 52, 2015 U.S. LEXIS 6010.

October 5, 2015. Petition for writ of certiorari to the United States Court of Appeals for the Fifth Circuit denied.

No. 14-9594. Todd Sperry, Petitioner v. Jason Maes, et al.

577 U.S. 832, 136 S. Ct. 44, 193 L. Ed. 2d 52, 2015 U.S. LEXIS 5613.

October 5, 2015. Petition for writ of certiorari to the United States Court of Appeals for the Tenth Circuit denied.

Same case below, 592 Fed. Appx. 688.

No. 14-9601. Calvin S. Secrest, Petitioner v. Dave Davey, Acting Warden.

577 U.S. 832, 136 S. Ct. 45, 193 L. Ed. 2d 53, 2015 U.S. LEXIS 5608.

October 5, 2015. Petition for writ of certiorari to the United States Court of Appeals for the Ninth Circuit denied.

No. 14-9603. Quincy Earl Stoot, Petitioner v. Kelly Santoro, Acting Warden.

577 U.S. 832, 136 S. Ct. 45, 193 L. Ed. 2d 53, 2015 U.S. LEXIS 5784.

October 5, 2015. Petition for writ of certiorari to the United States Court of Appeals for the Ninth Circuit denied.

No. 14-9611. Jonathan Miller, Petitioner v. Kenneth R. Cameron, Superintendent, State Correctional Institution at Cresson.

577 U.S. 832, 136 S. Ct. 48, 193 L. Ed. 2d 53, 2015 U.S. LEXIS 5627.

October 5, 2015. Petition for writ of certiorari to the United States Court of Appeals for the Third Circuit denied.

No. 14-9618. Frederick Lee Jackson, Petitioner v. Neil McDowell, Warden.

577 U.S. 832, 136 S. Ct. 47, 193 L. Ed. 2d 53, 2015 U.S. LEXIS 5964.

October 5, 2015. Petition for writ of certiorari to the United States Court of Appeals for the Ninth Circuit denied.

No. 14-9620. Derry Sykes, Petitioner v. City of New York Human Resources Administration, Office of Child Support Enforcement, et al.

577 U.S. 832, 136 S. Ct. 48, 193 L. Ed. 2d 53, 2015 U.S. LEXIS 5675.

October 5, 2015. Petition for writ of certiorari to the United States Court of Appeals for the Second Circuit denied.

No. 14-9625. Donald F. Mackay, Jr., Petitioner v. Mercedes Benz.

577 U.S. 832, 136 S. Ct. 47, 193 L. Ed. 2d 53, 2015 U.S. LEXIS 5606.

October 5, 2015. Petition for writ of certiorari to the United States Court of Appeals for the Second Circuit denied.

No. 14-9627. Billy Ray Turner, Jr., Petitioner v. Jay Cassady, Warden.

577 U.S. 832, 136 S. Ct. 47, 193 L. Ed. 2d 53, 2015 U.S. LEXIS 5582.

October 5, 2015. Petition for writ of certiorari to the United States Court of Appeals for the Eighth Circuit denied.

No. 14-9629. Donald B. Williams, Petitioner v. Dave Davey, Warden.

577 U.S. 832, 136 S. Ct. 46, 193 L. Ed. 2d 53, 2015 U.S. LEXIS 5633.

October 5, 2015. Petition for writ of certiorari to the United States Court of Appeals for the Ninth Circuit denied.

No. 14-9632. Durwyn Talley, Petitioner v. Christopher L. Gore, et al.

577 U.S. 832, 136 S. Ct. 47, 193 L. Ed. 2d 54, 2015 U.S. LEXIS 5652, reh den 577 U.S. 1054, 136 S. Ct. 704, 193 L. Ed. 2d 529, 2015 U.S. LEXIS 7927.

October 5, 2015. Petition for writ of certiorari to the United States Court of Appeals for the Seventh Circuit denied.

No. 14-9635. Rudy Tucker, Petitioner v. Catherine S. Bauman, Warden.

577 U.S. 832, 136 S. Ct. 46, 193 L. Ed. 2d 54, 2015 U.S. LEXIS 5860.

October 5, 2015. Petition for writ of certiorari to the United States Court of Appeals for the Sixth Circuit denied.

No. 14-9642. Timothy Paul Olmos, Petitioner v. Charles L. Ryan, Director, Arizona Department of Corrections, et al.

577 U.S. 832, 136 S. Ct. 47, 193 L. Ed. 2d 54, 2015 U.S. LEXIS 5623.

October 5, 2015. Petition for writ of certiorari to the United States Court of Appeals for the Ninth Circuit denied.

No. 14-9643. Barbara Phillips, Petitioner v. California.

577 U.S. 832, 136 S. Ct. 48, 193 L. Ed. 2d 54, 2015 U.S. LEXIS 5929.

October 5, 2015. Petition for writ of certiorari to the Court of Appeal of California, Fourth Appellate District, Division Two, denied.

No. 14-9646. Alejandro Anguiano, Petitioner v. Illinois.

577 U.S. 832, 136 S. Ct. 48, 193 L. Ed. 2d 54, 2015 U.S. LEXIS 5714.

October 5, 2015. Petition for writ of certiorari to the Appellate Court of Illinois, First District, denied.

Same case below, 378 Ill. Dec. 600, 4 N.E.3d 483.

No. 14-9648. Walter Gerald Anderson, Petitioner v. William Stephens, Director, Texas Department of Criminal Justice, Correctional Institutions Division.

577 U.S. 833, 136 S. Ct. 47, 193 L. Ed. 2d 54, 2015 U.S. LEXIS 5880, reh den 577 U.S. 1054, 136 S. Ct. 704, 193 L. Ed. 2d 530, 2015 U.S. LEXIS 7911.

October 5, 2015. Petition for writ of certiorari to the United States Court of Appeals for the Fifth Circuit denied.

No. 14-9649. Arthur Bomar, Petitioner v. Pennsylvania.

577 U.S. 833, 136 S. Ct. 49, 193 L. Ed. 2d 54, 2015 U.S. LEXIS 5595.

October 5, 2015. Petition for writ of certiorari to the Supreme Court of Pennsylvania, Middle District, denied.

Same case below, 629 Pa. 136, 104 A.3d 1179.

No. 14-9650. Ray Lee Vaughn, Petitioner v. Stu Sherman, Warden.

577 U.S. 833, 136 S. Ct. 49, 193 L. Ed. 2d 54, 2015 U.S. LEXIS 5650.

October 5, 2015. Petition for writ of certiorari to the United States Court of Appeals for the Ninth Circuit denied.

No. 14-9655. Teddest McKinney, Petitioner v. Fred Foulk, Warden.

577 U.S. 833, 136 S. Ct. 49, 193 L. Ed. 2d 55, 2015 U.S. LEXIS 5607.

October 5, 2015. Petition for writ of certiorari to the United States Court of Appeals for the Ninth Circuit denied.

No. 14-9656. Joseph Palmer, Petitioner v. Andrea Aikens, et al.

577 U.S. 833, 136 S. Ct. 50, 193 L. Ed. 2d 55, 2015 U.S. LEXIS 5549.

October 5, 2015. Petition for writ of certiorari to the United States Court of Appeals for the Sixth Circuit denied.

No. 14-9660. Craig Anderson, Petitioner v. Steven Rivard, Warden.

577 U.S. 833, 136 S. Ct. 50, 193 L. Ed. 2d 55, 2015 U.S. LEXIS 5865.

October 5, 2015. Petition for writ of certiorari to the United States Court of Appeals for the Sixth Circuit denied.

No. 14-9661. Arika Hayes, Petitioner v. Viacom, et al.

577 U.S. 833, 136 S. Ct. 297, 193 L. Ed. 2d 55, 2015 U.S. LEXIS 5731.

October 5, 2015. Petition for writ of certiorari to the United States Court of Appeals for the Ninth Circuit denied.

No. 14-9662. Kenrick Daly, Petitioner v. Connie Gipson, Acting Warden.

577 U.S. 833, 136 S. Ct. 50, 193 L. Ed. 2d 55, 2015 U.S. LEXIS 5680.

October 5, 2015. Petition for writ of certiorari to the United States Court of Appeals for the Ninth Circuit denied.

No. 14-9665. Tony Toreal Townsend, Petitioner v. Mitch Perry, Warden.

577 U.S. 833, 136 S. Ct. 50, 193 L. Ed. 2d 55, 2015 U.S. LEXIS 5682.

October 5, 2015. Petition for writ of certiorari to the United States Court of Appeals for the Sixth Circuit denied.

No. 14-9669. Morris Ricks, Petitioner v. Brian Owens, Commissioner, Georgia Department of Corrections.

577 U.S. 833, 136 S. Ct. 297, 193 L. Ed. 2d 55, 2015 U.S. LEXIS 5576.

October 5, 2015. Petition for writ of certiorari to the United States Court of Appeals for the Eleventh Circuit denied.

No. 14-9671. Charles Johnson, Jr., Petitioner v. Steven Rivard, Warden.

577 U.S. 833, 136 S. Ct. 50, 193 L. Ed. 2d 55, 2015 U.S. LEXIS 5706.

October 5, 2015. Petition for writ of certiorari to the United States Court of Appeals for the Sixth Circuit denied.

No. 14-9672. Donald Keith Burton, Petitioner v. Mississippi.

577 U.S. 833, 136 S. Ct. 51, 193 L. Ed. 2d 56, 2015 U.S. LEXIS 5910.

October 5, 2015. Petition for writ of certiorari to the Supreme Court of Mississippi denied.

No. 14-9673. Jose Jorge Andrade, Petitioner v. Clark E. Ducart, Warden.

577 U.S. 833, 136 S. Ct. 51, 193 L. Ed. 2d 56, 2015 U.S. LEXIS 5610.

October 5, 2015. Petition for writ of certiorari to the United States Court of Appeals for the Ninth Circuit denied.

No. 14-9674. Shawn Williams, Petitioner v. Raina Martin, et al.

577 U.S. 833, 136 S. Ct. 51, 193 L. Ed. 2d 56, 2015 U.S. LEXIS 5799.

October 5, 2015. Petition for writ of certiorari to the United States Court of Appeals for the Eighth Circuit denied.

Same case below, 594 Fed. Appx. 325.

No. 14-9680. Roy Nolan McKinley, Petitioner v. Michael McDonald, Warden.

577 U.S. 833, 136 S. Ct. 51, 193 L. Ed. 2d 56, 2015 U.S. LEXIS 5674.

October 5, 2015. Petition for writ of certiorari to the United States Court of Appeals for the Ninth Circuit denied.

No. 14-9682. Daniel Vassallo, Petitioner v. Jim MacDonald, Warden.

577 U.S. 833, 136 S. Ct. 51, 193 L. Ed. 2d 56, 2015 U.S. LEXIS 5629.

October 5, 2015. Petition for writ of certiorari to the United States Court of Appeals for the Ninth Circuit denied.

No. 14-9685. James George Stamos, Jr., Petitioner v. Dave Davey, Warden.

577 U.S. 834, 136 S. Ct. 51, 193 L. Ed. 2d 56, 2015 U.S. LEXIS 5545, reh den 577 U.S. 1022, 136 S. Ct. 573, 193 L. Ed. 2d 455, 2015 U.S. LEXIS 7452.

October 5, 2015. Petition for writ of certiorari to the United States Court of Appeals for the Ninth Circuit denied.

No. 14-9686. Rendell Robinson, Petitioner v. Krishna Valdamudi, et al.

577 U.S. 834, 136 S. Ct. 51, 193 L. Ed. 2d 56, 2015 U.S. LEXIS 6188, reh den 577 U.S. 1184, 136 S. Ct. 1248, 194 L. Ed. 2d 246, 2016 U.S. LEXIS 1274.

October 5, 2015. Petition for writ of certiorari to the United States Court of Appeals for the Second Circuit denied.

No. 14-9687. Jor'dan Jacqueinn Maurice Lewis, Petitioner v. Texas.

577 U.S. 834, 136 S. Ct. 52, 193 L. Ed. 2d 56, 2015 U.S. LEXIS 5958.

October 5, 2015. Petition for writ of certiorari to the Court of Appeals of Texas, Fourteenth District, denied.

Same case below, 448 S.W.3d 138.

No. 14-9691. John E. Rodarte, Sr., Petitioner v. William Stephens, Director, Texas Department of Criminal Justice, Correctional Institutions Division.

577 U.S. 834, 136 S. Ct. 52, 193 L. Ed. 2d 57, 2015 U.S. LEXIS 5631, reh den 577 U.S. 1044, 136 S. Ct. 608, 193 L. Ed. 2d 488, 2015 U.S. LEXIS 7697.

October 5, 2015. Petition for writ of certiorari to the United States Court of Appeals for the Fifth Circuit denied.

No. 14-9692. Juwaun Long, Petitioner v. Jeffrey Woods, Warden.

577 U.S. 834, 136 S. Ct. 52, 193 L. Ed. 2d 57, 2015 U.S. LEXIS 6044.

October 5, 2015. Petition for writ of certiorari to the United States Court of Appeals for the Sixth Circuit denied.

No. 14-9693. Levar Brown, Petitioner v. California, et al.

577 U.S. 834, 136 S. Ct. 52, 193 L. Ed. 2d 57, 2015 U.S. LEXIS 5955.

October 5, 2015. Petition for writ of certiorari to the United States Court of Appeals for the Ninth Circuit denied.

No. 14-9695. Daniel W. Dwyer, Petitioner v. Jeff Norman, Warden.

577 U.S. 834, 136 S. Ct. 52, 193 L. Ed. 2d 57, 2015 U.S. LEXIS 6008.

October 5, 2015. Petition for writ of certiorari to the United States Court of Appeals for the Eighth Circuit denied.

No. 14-9703. Antyane Robinson, Petitioner v. John E. Wetzel, Secretary, Pennsylvania Department of Corrections, et al.

577 U.S. 834, 136 S. Ct. 53, 193 L. Ed. 2d 57, 2015 U.S. LEXIS 5567.

October 5, 2015. Petition for writ of certiorari to the United States Court of Appeals for the Third Circuit denied.

Same case below, 762 F.3d 316.

No. 14-9717. David Alexander Bailey, Petitioner v. William Stephens, Director, Texas Department of Criminal Justice, Correctional Institutions Division.

577 U.S. 834, 136 S. Ct. 54, 193 L. Ed. 2d 57, 2015 U.S. LEXIS 5660.

October 5, 2015. Petition for writ of certiorari to the United States Court of Appeals for the Fifth Circuit denied.

No. 14-9718. Stanley Blackwood, Petitioner v. Cherry Lindamood, Warden.

577 U.S. 834, 136 S. Ct. 54, 193 L. Ed. 2d 57, 2015 U.S. LEXIS 5852.

October 5, 2015. Petition for writ of certiorari to the United States Court of Appeals for the Sixth Circuit denied.

No. 14-9719. Robert Amos Bogany, Petitioner v. William Stephens, Director, Texas Department of Criminal Justice, Correctional Institutions Division.

577 U.S. 834, 136 S. Ct. 55, 193 L. Ed. 2d 58, 2015 U.S. LEXIS 5648, reh den 577 U.S. 1022, 136 S. Ct. 574, 193 L. Ed. 2d 455, 2015 U.S. LEXIS 7425.

October 5, 2015. Petition for writ of certiorari to the United States Court of Appeals for the Fifth Circuit denied.

No. 14-9720. Fortunato Garcia, Petitioner v. Robert Hebert, et al.

577 U.S. 834, 136 S. Ct. 55, 193 L. Ed. 2d 58, 2015 U.S. LEXIS 5898.

October 5, 2015. Petition for writ of certiorari to the United States Court of Appeals for the Second Circuit denied.

Same case below, 594 Fed. Appx. 26.

No. 14-9724. Ralph Leroy Menzies, Petitioner v. Utah.

577 U.S. 834, 136 S. Ct. 55, 193 L. Ed. 2d 58, 2015 U.S. LEXIS 5971.

October 5, 2015. Petition for writ of certiorari to the Supreme Court of Utah denied.

Same case below, 344 P.3d 581.

No. 14-9726. Emilia L. Carr, Petitioner v. Florida.

577 U.S. 834, 136 S. Ct. 55, 193 L. Ed. 2d 58, 2015 U.S. LEXIS 5646.

October 5, 2015. Petition for writ of certiorari to the Supreme Court of Florida denied.

Same case below, 156 So. 3d 1052.

No. 14-9727. Kevin Epperson, Petitioner v. Delaware.

577 U.S. 835, 136 S. Ct. 55, 193 L. Ed. 2d 58, 2015 U.S. LEXIS 5725.

October 5, 2015. Petition for writ of certiorari to the Supreme Court of Delaware denied.

Same case below, 121 A.3d 1234.

No. 14-9731. Hugo Romare Jones, Petitioner v. Harold W. Clarke, Director, Virginia Department of Corrections.

577 U.S. 835, 136 S. Ct. 56, 193 L. Ed. 2d 58, 2015 U.S. LEXIS 5822, reh den 577 U.S. 1094, 136 S. Ct. 879, 193 L. Ed. 2d 771, 2016 U.S. LEXIS 581.

October 5, 2015. Petition for writ of certiorari to the United States Court of Appeals for the Fourth Circuit denied.

Same case below, 588 Fed. Appx. 259.

No. 14-9732. Ryan Patrick Madden, Petitioner v. Jeffrey Beard, Secretary, California Department of Corrections and Rehabilitation.

577 U.S. 835, 136 S. Ct. 298, 193 L. Ed. 2d 58, 2015 U.S. LEXIS 5696.

October 5, 2015. Petition for writ of certiorari to the United States Court of Appeals for the Ninth Circuit denied.

No. 14-9736. Miguel Bautista, Petitioner v. United States.

577 U.S. 835, 136 S. Ct. 56, 193 L. Ed. 2d 58, 2015 U.S. LEXIS 5661.

October 5, 2015. Petition for writ of certiorari to the United States Court of Appeals for the Second Circuit denied.

Same case below, 765 F.3d 133.

No. 14-9740. Kenneth Earl Fults, Petitioner v. Bruce Chatman, Warden.

577 U.S. 835, 136 S. Ct. 56, 193 L. Ed. 2d 59, 2015 U.S. LEXIS 5767.

October 5, 2015. Petition for writ of certiorari to the United States Court of Appeals for the Eleventh Circuit denied.

Same case below, 764 F.3d 1311.

No. 14-9741. Marco Antonio Firman, Petitioner v. California.

577 U.S. 835, 136 S. Ct. 56, 193 L. Ed. 2d 59, 2015 U.S. LEXIS 5735.

October 5, 2015. Petition for writ of certiorari to the Court of Appeal of California, Fourth Appellate District, Division One, denied.

No. 14-9742. John K. Elam, Petitioner v. Jorge L. Pastrana, Warden.

577 U.S. 835, 136 S. Ct. 56, 193 L. Ed. 2d 59, 2015 U.S. LEXIS 5711, reh den 577 U.S. 1044, 136 S. Ct. 608, 193 L. Ed. 2d 488, 2015 U.S. LEXIS 7766.

October 5, 2015. Petition for writ of certiorari to the United States Court of Appeals for the Eleventh Circuit denied.

Same case below, 588 Fed. Appx. 927.

No. 14-9743. Jean Pierre DeVaughn, Petitioner v. Georgia.

577 U.S. 835, 136 S. Ct. 56, 193 L. Ed. 2d 59, 2015 U.S. LEXIS 5795.

October 5, 2015. Petition for writ of certiorari to the Supreme Court of Georgia denied.

Same case below, 296 Ga. 475, 769 S.E.2d 70.

No. 14-9752. Jeffrey C. Jacobson, Petitioner v. Neil Colegrove, et al.

577 U.S. 835, 136 S. Ct. 57, 193 L. Ed. 2d 59, 2015 U.S. LEXIS 5769.

October 5, 2015. Petition for writ of certiorari to the Supreme Court of Michigan denied.

No. 14-9754. Michael Tony Velez, Petitioner v. New York.

577 U.S. 835, 136 S. Ct. 57, 193 L. Ed. 2d 59, 2015 U.S. LEXIS 5871, reh den 577 U.S. 1094, 136 S. Ct. 880, 193 L. Ed. 2d 771, 2016 U.S. LEXIS 415.

October 5, 2015. Petition for writ of certiorari to the Appellate Division, Supreme Court of New York, First Judicial Department, denied.

No. 14-9756. Douglas Alan Dunn, Petitioner v. William Stephens, Director, Texas Department of Criminal Justice, Correctional Institutions Division.

577 U.S. 835, 136 S. Ct. 57, 193 L. Ed. 2d 59, 2015 U.S. LEXIS 5604.

October 5, 2015. Petition for writ of certiorari to the United States Court of Appeals for the Fifth Circuit denied.

No. 14-9757. Curtin P. Crawford, Petitioner v. Mark Nooth, Superintendent, Snake River Correctional Institution.

577 U.S. 835, 136 S. Ct. 57, 193 L. Ed. 2d 59, 2015 U.S. LEXIS 5839.

October 5, 2015. Petition for writ of certiorari to the United States Court of Appeals for the Ninth Circuit denied.

No. 14-9759. David Keith McCoy, Petitioner v. Colorado.

577 U.S. 835, 136 S. Ct. 58, 193 L. Ed. 2d 60, 2015 U.S. LEXIS 5619.

October 5, 2015. Petition for writ of certiorari to the Court of Appeals of Colorado denied.

No. 14-9762. Emmanuel Von Allen Evans, Petitioner v. Texas.

577 U.S. 835, 136 S. Ct. 58, 193 L. Ed. 2d 60, 2015 U.S. LEXIS 5632.

October 5, 2015. Petition for writ of certiorari to the Court of Appeals of Texas, Fourteenth District, denied.

No. 14-9764. Christopher Horton, Petitioner v. Julie L. Jones, Secretary, Florida Department of Corrections, et al.

577 U.S. 836, 136 S. Ct. 58, 193 L. Ed. 2d 60, 2015 U.S. LEXIS 5709.

October 5, 2015. Petition for writ of certiorari to the United States Court of Appeals for the Eleventh Circuit denied.

No. 14-9766. Phillip Wayne Griffis, Petitioner v. Texas.

577 U.S. 836, 136 S. Ct. 58, 193 L. Ed. 2d 60, 2015 U.S. LEXIS 6366.

October 5, 2015. Petition for writ of certiorari to the Court of Appeals of Texas, Fourth District, denied.

Same case below, 441 S.W.3d 599.

No. 14-9768. Leroy Handy, Petitioner v. Julie L. Jones, Secretary, Florida Department of Corrections.

577 U.S. 836, 136 S. Ct. 58, 193 L. Ed. 2d 60, 2015 U.S. LEXIS 5814.

October 5, 2015. Petition for writ of certiorari to the United States Court of Appeals for the Eleventh Circuit denied.

No. 14-9770. Timothy Harrison, Petitioner v. Robert W. Obenland, Superintendent, Clallam Bay Corrections Center.

577 U.S. 836, 136 S. Ct. 59, 193 L. Ed. 2d 60, 2015 U.S. LEXIS 5713.

October 5, 2015. Petition for writ of certiorari to the United States Court of Appeals for the Ninth Circuit denied.

No. 14-9773. Karim Abdul Akbar, Petitioner v. Prison Emergency Response Team Officers, et al.

577 U.S. 836, 136 S. Ct. 59, 193 L. Ed. 2d 60, 2015 U.S. LEXIS 5554.

October 5, 2015. Petition for writ of certiorari to the United States Court of Appeals for the Fourth Circuit denied.

Same case below, 589 Fed. Appx. 215.

No. 14-9776. Montraygo Drake, Petitioner v. Burl Cain, Warden.

577 U.S. 836, 136 S. Ct. 59, 193 L. Ed. 2d 60, 2015 U.S. LEXIS 5742.

October 5, 2015. Petition for writ of certiorari to the United States Court of Appeals for the Fifth Circuit denied.

No. 14-9778. Benjamin E. Isaac, Petitioner v. Gregory McLaughlin, Warden.

577 U.S. 836, 136 S. Ct. 59, 193 L. Ed. 2d 61, 2015 U.S. LEXIS 5630.

October 5, 2015. Petition for writ of certiorari to the Superior Court of Georgia, Macon County, denied.

No. 14-9779. Charles Edward Fields, Petitioner v. Denise Gerth, et al.

577 U.S. 836, 136 S. Ct. 60, 193 L. Ed. 2d 61, 2015 U.S. LEXIS 5813.

October 5, 2015. Petition for writ of certiorari to the United States Court of Appeals for the Sixth Circuit denied.

No. 14-9780. Earnest S. Harris, Petitioner v. R. Lewis, Warden.

577 U.S. 836, 136 S. Ct. 60, 193 L. Ed. 2d 61, 2015 U.S. LEXIS 5574.

October 5, 2015. Petition for writ of certiorari to the United States Court of Appeals for the Ninth Circuit denied.

No. 14-9781. Henry Frometa Gonzalez, Petitioner v. James Greg Cox, Warden, et al.

577 U.S. 836, 136 S. Ct. 60, 193 L. Ed. 2d 61, 2015 U.S. LEXIS 5639.

October 5, 2015. Petition for writ of certiorari to the United States Court of Appeals for the Ninth Circuit denied.

No. 14-9782. Alfredo Rodriguez, Petitioner v. Gerald J. Janda, Warden.

577 U.S. 836, 136 S. Ct. 60, 193 L. Ed. 2d 61, 2015 U.S. LEXIS 5585.

October 5, 2015. Petition for writ of certiorari to the United States Court of Appeals for the Ninth Circuit denied.

No. 14-9783. Ottis J. Cummings, Jr., aka Ottis Junior Cummings, aka Otis Cummings, Petitioner v. Mississippi.

577 U.S. 836, 136 S. Ct. 60, 193 L. Ed. 2d 61, 2015 U.S. LEXIS 5726.

October 5, 2015. Petition for writ of certiorari to the Supreme Court of Mississippi denied.

No. 14-9786. Corey Cauthen, aka James Marrow, Petitioner v. New Jersey.

577 U.S. 836, 136 S. Ct. 60, 193 L. Ed. 2d 61, 2015 U.S. LEXIS 5642.

October 5, 2015. Petition for writ of certiorari to the Supreme Court of New Jersey denied.

Same case below, 220 N.J. 100, 103 A.3d 267.

No. 14-9787. Noel Galvan Cerna, Petitioner v. Texas.

577 U.S. 836, 136 S. Ct. 60, 193 L. Ed. 2d 61, 2015 U.S. LEXIS 5759.

October 5, 2015. Petition for writ of certiorari to the Court of Appeals of Texas, Fourteenth District, denied.

Same case below, 441 S.W.3d 860.

Same case below, 585 Fed. Appx. 150.

No. 14-9789. R. Kirk McDonald, Petitioner v. Zions First National Bank.

577 U.S. 836, 136 S. Ct. 61, 193 L. Ed. 2d 62, 2015 U.S. LEXIS 5600.

October 5, 2015. Petition for writ of certiorari to the Court of Appeals of Colorado denied.

No. 14-9793. Charles Horton, Petitioner v. Nicholas Degennaro, et al.

577 U.S. 837, 136 S. Ct. 61, 193 L. Ed. 2d 62, 2015 U.S. LEXIS 5933.

October 5, 2015. Petition for writ of certiorari to the United States Court of Appeals for the Eleventh Circuit denied.

No. 14-9794. Hubert Edward Ferry, Petitioner v. Virginia.

577 U.S. 837, 136 S. Ct. 61, 193 L. Ed. 2d 62, 2015 U.S. LEXIS 5612, reh den 577 U.S. 1184, 136 S. Ct. 1249, 194 L. Ed. 2d 246, 2016 U.S. LEXIS 1118.

October 5, 2015. Petition for writ of certiorari to the Supreme Court of Virginia denied.

No. 14-9797. Michael D. Goins, Petitioner v. Elbert Pearson, et al.

577 U.S. 837, 136 S. Ct. 61, 193 L. Ed. 2d 62, 2015 U.S. LEXIS 5727.

October 5, 2015. Petition for writ of certiorari to the United States Court of Appeals for the Fourth Circuit denied.

No. 14-9798. Raveon Harrell, Petitioner v. Indiana.

577 U.S. 837, 136 S. Ct. 61, 193 L. Ed. 2d 62, 2015 U.S. LEXIS 6007.

October 5, 2015. Petition for writ of certiorari to the Court of Appeals of Indiana, Third District, denied.

Same case below, 20 N.E.3d 225.

No. 14-9799. Lawson Hardrick, Petitioner v. United States.

577 U.S. 837, 136 S. Ct. 61, 193 L. Ed. 2d 62, 2015 U.S. LEXIS 5662.

October 5, 2015. Petition for writ of certiorari to the United States Court of Appeals for the Ninth Circuit denied.

Same case below, 766 F.3d 1051.

No. 14-9804. Archie Cranford, Petitioner v. Employees of Coalinga State Hospital.

577 U.S. 837, 136 S. Ct. 62, 193 L. Ed. 2d 62, 2015 U.S. LEXIS 5809.

October 5, 2015. Petition for writ of certiorari to the United States Court of Appeals for the Ninth Circuit denied.

No. 14-9806. Robert Charles Cook, Petitioner v. Unknown Cashler, et al.

577 U.S. 837, 136 S. Ct. 62, 193 L. Ed. 2d 62, 2015 U.S. LEXIS 5578.

October 5, 2015. Petition for writ of certiorari to the United States Court of Appeals for the Sixth Circuit denied.

No. 14-9810. Kevin A. Reilly, Petitioner v. Larry Cartledge, Warden.

577 U.S. 837, 136 S. Ct. 62, 193 L. Ed. 2d 63, 2015 U.S. LEXIS 6092.

October 5, 2015. Petition for writ of certiorari to the United States Court of Appeals for the Fourth Circuit denied.

Same case below, 589 Fed. Appx. 220.

No. 14-9811. Allen Fitzgerald Calton, Petitioner v. William Stephens, Director, Texas Department of Criminal Justice, Correctional Institutions Division.

577 U.S. 837, 136 S. Ct. 62, 193 L. Ed. 2d 63, 2015 U.S. LEXIS 5617.

October 5, 2015. Petition for writ of certiorari to the United States Court of Appeals for the Fifth Circuit denied.

No. 14-9814. Anthony J. DeNoma, Petitioner v. Ohio.

577 U.S. 837, 136 S. Ct. 62, 193 L. Ed. 2d 63, 2015 U.S. LEXIS 5597.

October 5, 2015. Petition for writ of certiorari to the Court of Appeals of Ohio, Hamilton County, denied.

No. 14-9817. Lawrence Mendez, Jr., Petitioner v. United States.

577 U.S. 837, 136 S. Ct. 62, 193 L. Ed. 2d 63, 2015 U.S. LEXIS 5786.

October 5, 2015. Petition for writ of certiorari to the United States Court of Appeals for the Federal Circuit denied.

Same case below, 600 Fed. Appx. 731.

No. 14-9819. George Paulk, Jr., Petitioner v. City of Orlando, Florida, et al.

577 U.S. 837, 136 S. Ct. 63, 193 L. Ed. 2d 63, 2015 U.S. LEXIS 5688, reh den 577 U.S. 1022, 136 S. Ct. 574, 193 L. Ed. 2d 455, 2015 U.S. LEXIS 7433.

October 5, 2015. Petition for writ of certiorari to the United States Court of Appeals for the Eleventh Circuit denied.

No. 14-9820. Theodore John Solano, Petitioner v. Steven R. Glunt, Superintendent, State Correctional Institution at Rockview, et al.

577 U.S. 837, 136 S. Ct. 63, 193 L. Ed. 2d 63, 2015 U.S. LEXIS 5590.

October 5, 2015. Petition for writ of certiorari to the United States Court of Appeals for the Third Circuit denied.

No. 14-9822. Mark W. Blond, Jr., Petitioner v. Harold Graham, Superintendent, Auburn Correctional Facility.

577 U.S. 837, 136 S. Ct. 63, 193 L. Ed. 2d 63, 2015 U.S. LEXIS 5649.

October 5, 2015. Petition for writ of certiorari to the United States Court of Appeals for the Second Circuit denied.

No. 14-9823. Carl Dean Sampson, Petitioner v. Robert Patton, Director, Oklahoma Department of Corrections.

577 U.S. 837, 136 S. Ct. 63, 193 L. Ed. 2d 63, 2015 U.S. LEXIS 5601, reh den 577 U.S. 1054, 136 S. Ct. 704, 193 L. Ed. 2d 530, 2015 U.S. LEXIS 7964.

October 5, 2015. Petition for writ of certiorari to the United States Court of Appeals for the Tenth Circuit denied.

Same case below, 598 Fed. Appx. 573.

No. 14-9824. Timothy Enos Edens, Sr., Petitioner v. Willie Eagleton, Warden.

577 U.S. 838, 136 S. Ct. 63, 193 L. Ed. 2d 64, 2015 U.S. LEXIS 6056.

October 5, 2015. Petition for writ of certiorari to the United States Court of Appeals for the Fourth Circuit denied.

Same case below, 580 Fed. Appx. 222.

No. 14-9825. Randall Dale Douglas, Petitioner v. William Stephens, Director, Texas Department of Criminal Justice, Correctional Institutions Division.

577 U.S. 838, 136 S. Ct. 64, 193 L. Ed. 2d 64, 2015 U.S. LEXIS 5959.

October 5, 2015. Petition for writ of certiorari to the United States Court of Appeals for the Fifth Circuit denied.

No. 14-9826. Charles Montague, Petitioner v. Howard Carlton, Warden.

577 U.S. 838, 136 S. Ct. 64, 193 L. Ed. 2d 64, 2015 U.S. LEXIS 5573.

October 5, 2015. Petition for writ of certiorari to the United States Court of Appeals for the Sixth Circuit denied.

No. 14-9827. Michael Small, Petitioner v. Cherry Lindamood, Warden.

577 U.S. 838, 136 S. Ct. 65, 193 L. Ed. 2d 64, 2015 U.S. LEXIS 5031.

October 5, 2015. Petition for writ of certiorari to the United States Court of Appeals for the Sixth Circuit denied.

No. 14-9828. Anthony Calderon, Petitioner v. Washington.

577 U.S. 838, 136 S. Ct. 65, 193 L. Ed. 2d 64, 2015 U.S. LEXIS 5311.

October 5, 2015. Petition for writ of certiorari to the Supreme Court of Washington denied.

No. 14-9829. Mary Katherine Day-Petrano, et vir, Petitioners v. Darlene P. Baylor.

577 U.S. 838, 136 S. Ct. 65, 193 L. Ed. 2d 64, 2015 U.S. LEXIS 5353.

October 5, 2015. Petition for writ of certiorari to the United States Court of Appeals for the Eleventh Circuit denied.

Same case below, 596 Fed. Appx. 741.

No. 14-9831. Keidrick L. Ewing, Petitioner v. Florida.

577 U.S. 838, 136 S. Ct. 65, 193 L. Ed. 2d 64, 2015 U.S. LEXIS 5032.

October 5, 2015. Petition for writ of certiorari to the District Court of Appeal of Florida, First District, denied.

Same case below, 145 So. 3d 833.

No. 14-9833. Darryl A. Carlos Conway, Petitioner v. Randy Pfister, Warden.

577 U.S. 838, 136 S. Ct. 65, 193 L. Ed. 2d 64, 2015 U.S. LEXIS 5020.

October 5, 2015. Petition for writ of certiorari to the United States Court of Appeals for the Seventh Circuit denied.

No. 14-9834. Joshua Delaney, Petitioner v. William Stephens, Director, Texas Department of Criminal Justice, Correctional Institutions Division.

577 U.S. 838, 136 S. Ct. 65, 193 L. Ed. 2d 65, 2015 U.S. LEXIS 5012.

October 5, 2015. Petition for writ of certiorari to the United States Court of Appeals for the Fifth Circuit denied.

No. 14-9836. Toni Clark, Petitioner v. Wells Fargo Bank, N.A.

577 U.S. 838, 136 S. Ct. 66, 193 L. Ed. 2d 65, 2015 U.S. LEXIS 4993.

October 5, 2015. Petition for writ of certiorari to the Superior Court of New Jersey, Appellate Division, denied.

No. 14-9837. Todd L. Cook, Petitioner v. Diane Sabatka-Rine, Warden, et al.

577 U.S. 838, 136 S. Ct. 66, 193 L. Ed. 2d 65, 2015 U.S. LEXIS 4996.

October 5, 2015. Petition for writ of certiorari to the United States Court of Appeals for the Eighth Circuit denied.

No. 14-9841. Robert W. Dougherty, Petitioner v. Samuel V. Pruett, Warden; and Robert W. Dougherty, Petitioner v. Virginia, et al.

577 U.S. 838, 136 S. Ct. 66, 193 L. Ed. 2d 65, 2015 U.S. LEXIS 5274, reh den 577

U.S. 1044, 136 S. Ct. 608, 193 L. Ed. 2d 489, 2015 U.S. LEXIS 7723.

October 5, 2015. Petition for writ of certiorari to the United States Court of Appeals for the Fourth Circuit denied.

Same case below, 585 Fed. Appx. 108 (first judgment); and 585 Fed. Appx. 115 (second judgment).

No. 14-9844. Licho Escamilla, Petitioner v. William Stephens, Director, Texas Department of Criminal Justice, Correctional Institutions Division.

577 U.S. 838, 136 S. Ct. 66, 193 L. Ed. 2d 65, 2015 U.S. LEXIS 5011.

October 5, 2015. Petition for writ of certiorari to the United States Court of Appeals for the Fifth Circuit denied.

Same case below, 602 Fed. Appx. 939.

No. 14-9845. Donald R. Childs, Petitioner v. Irvington Properties, LLC, dba Aruba Hotel & Spa.

577 U.S. 838, 136 S. Ct. 66, 193 L. Ed. 2d 65, 2015 U.S. LEXIS 4991.

October 5, 2015. Petition for writ of certiorari to the Supreme Court of Nevada denied.

Same case below, 131 Nev. 1263.

No. 14-9847. Jorge Martin Trinidad, Petitioner v. California.

577 U.S. 839, 136 S. Ct. 66, 193 L. Ed. 2d 65, 2015 U.S. LEXIS 5241.

October 5, 2015. Petition for writ of certiorari to the Supreme Court of California denied.

No. 14-9853. Clifford Scott Medley, Petitioner v. William Stephens, Director, Texas Department of Criminal Justice, Correctional Institutions Division.

577 U.S. 839, 136 S. Ct. 67, 193 L. Ed. 2d 66, 2015 U.S. LEXIS 5007, reh den 577 U.S. 1044, 136 S. Ct. 608, 193 L. Ed. 2d 489, 2015 U.S. LEXIS 7740.

October 5, 2015. Petition for writ of certiorari to the United States Court of Appeals for the Fifth Circuit denied.

No. 14-9854. Kem Cote, Petitioner v. Darryl Adams, Warden.

577 U.S. 839, 136 S. Ct. 67, 193 L. Ed. 2d 66, 2015 U.S. LEXIS 5027.

October 5, 2015. Petition for writ of certiorari to the United States Court of Appeals for the Ninth Circuit denied.

Same case below, 586 Fed. Appx. 414.

No. 14-9855. Victor Jordan, Petitioner v. Metropolitan Jewish Hospice, et al.

577 U.S. 839, 136 S. Ct. 67, 193 L. Ed. 2d 66, 2015 U.S. LEXIS 4970.

October 5, 2015. Petition for writ of certiorari to the Court of Appeals of New York denied.

Same case below, 24 N.Y.3d 1199, 4 N.Y.S.3d 148, 27 N.E.3d 851.

No. 14-9856. Aaron Christopher Marcus, Petitioner v. Maryland.

577 U.S. 839, 136 S. Ct. 68, 193 L. Ed. 2d 66, 2015 U.S. LEXIS 5294.

October 5, 2015. Petition for writ of certiorari to the Court of Special Appeals of Maryland denied.

Same case below, 218 Md. App. 749.

No. 14-9858. Daniel M. Lynch, Petitioner v. Laurie W. Lynch.

577 U.S. 839, 136 S. Ct. 68, 193 L. Ed. 2d 66, 2015 U.S. LEXIS 5347.

October 5, 2015. Petition for writ of certiorari to the Appellate Court of Connecticut denied.

Same case below, 153 Conn. App. 208, 100 A.3d 968.

No. 14-9860. Tracy Nixon, Petitioner v. Greg Abbott, Governor of Texas, et al.

577 U.S. 839, 136 S. Ct. 68, 193 L. Ed. 2d 66, 2015 U.S. LEXIS 5206, reh den 577 U.S. 998, 136 S. Ct. 527, 193 L. Ed. 2d 415, 2015 U.S. LEXIS 7299.

October 5, 2015. Petition for writ of certiorari to the United States Court of Appeals for the Fifth Circuit denied.

No. 14-9863. Frank Shawnte Allen, Petitioner v. Dave Davey, Acting Warden.

577 U.S. 839, 136 S. Ct. 68, 193 L. Ed. 2d 66, 2015 U.S. LEXIS 5139, reh den 577 U.S. 1094, 136 S. Ct. 880, 193 L. Ed. 2d 771, 2016 U.S. LEXIS 531.

October 5, 2015. Petition for writ of certiorari to the United States Court of Appeals for the Ninth Circuit denied.

No. 14-9864. Kayle Barrington Bates, Petitioner v. Julie L. Jones, Secretary, Florida Department of Corrections.

577 U.S. 839, 136 S. Ct. 68, 193 L. Ed. 2d 66, 2015 U.S. LEXIS 5445.

October 5, 2015. Petition for writ of certiorari to the United States Court of Appeals for the Eleventh Circuit denied.

Same case below, 768 F.3d 1278.

No. 14-9866. Jeffrey Scott Ratchford, Petitioner v. Arkansas.

577 U.S. 839, 136 S. Ct. 68, 193 L. Ed. 2d 67, 2015 U.S. LEXIS 5336.

October 5, 2015. Petition for writ of certiorari to the Supreme Court of Arkansas denied.

Same case below, 2014 Ark. 452.

No. 14-9869. Michael Paul Ralston, Petitioner v. Texas.

577 U.S. 839, 136 S. Ct. 69, 193 L. Ed. 2d 67, 2015 U.S. LEXIS 5166, reh den 577 U.S. 1054, 136 S. Ct. 704, 193 L. Ed. 2d 530, 2015 U.S. LEXIS 7955.

October 5, 2015. Petition for writ of certiorari to the Court of Criminal Appeals of Texas denied.

No. 14-9870. Marc Thomas Sylvester, Petitioner v. Colorado.

577 U.S. 839, 136 S. Ct. 69, 193 L. Ed. 2d 67, 2015 U.S. LEXIS 5371.

October 5, 2015. Petition for writ of certiorari to the Court of Appeals of Colorado denied.

No. 14-9872. Shiloh Theriault, Petitioner v. Daniel Stratton, et al.

577 U.S. 839, 136 S. Ct. 69, 193 L. Ed. 2d 67, 2015 U.S. LEXIS 5028.

October 5, 2015. Petition for writ of certiorari to the United States Court of Appeals for the Eleventh Circuit denied.

No. 14-9873. Earl Lee Wright, Petitioner v. Illinois Department of Parole, et al.

577 U.S. 839, 136 S. Ct. 69, 193 L. Ed. 2d 67, 2015 U.S. LEXIS 5254.

October 5, 2015. Petition for writ of certiorari to the United States Court of Appeals for the Seventh Circuit denied.

No. 14-9878. David Allen Knight, Petitioner v. Scott Frauenheim, Warden.

577 U.S. 839, 136 S. Ct. 69, 193 L. Ed. 2d 67, 2015 U.S. LEXIS 5021.

October 5, 2015. Petition for writ of certiorari to the United States Court of Appeals for the Ninth Circuit denied.

No. 14-9879. Rodney T. Kralovetz, Petitioner v. Marion Spearman, Warden.

577 U.S. 840, 136 S. Ct. 70, 193 L. Ed. 2d 67, 2015 U.S. LEXIS 5056, reh den 577 U.S. 1094, 136 S. Ct. 880, 193 L. Ed. 2d 771, 2016 U.S. LEXIS 587.

October 5, 2015. Petition for writ of certiorari to the United States Court of Appeals for the Ninth Circuit denied.

No. 14-9885. Roger R. Adams, Petitioner v. Clark E. Ducart, Warden.

577 U.S. 840, 136 S. Ct. 70, 193 L. Ed. 2d 67, 2015 U.S. LEXIS 5396, reh den 577 U.S. 1054, 136 S. Ct. 704, 193 L. Ed. 2d 530, 2015 U.S. LEXIS 7902.

October 5, 2015. Petition for writ of certiorari to the United States Court of Appeals for the Ninth Circuit denied.

Same case below, 554 Fed. Appx. 610.

Same case below, 588 Fed. Appx. 352.

No. 14-9893. Thomas Prado, Petitioner v. Riverside County, California, et al.

577 U.S. 840, 136 S. Ct. 70, 193 L. Ed. 2d 68, 2015 U.S. LEXIS 4985.

October 5, 2015. Petition for writ of certiorari to the Court of Appeal of California, Fourth Appellate District, Division Two, denied.

No. 14-9894. John Albert Estrada, Petitioner v. Texas.

577 U.S. 840, 136 S. Ct. 70, 193 L. Ed. 2d 68, 2015 U.S. LEXIS 5512, reh den 577 U.S. 1094, 136 S. Ct. 880, 193 L. Ed. 2d 771, 2016 U.S. LEXIS 410.

October 5, 2015. Petition for writ of certiorari to the Court of Appeals of Texas, Fifth District, denied.

No. 14-9895. Lana K. Williams, Petitioner v. Rex Lee Huha, et al.

577 U.S. 840, 136 S. Ct. 70, 193 L. Ed. 2d 68, 2015 U.S. LEXIS 5154, reh den 577 U.S. 1054, 136 S. Ct. 704, 193 L. Ed. 2d 530, 2015 U.S. LEXIS 7989.

October 5, 2015. Petition for writ of certiorari to the United States Court of Appeals for the Ninth Circuit denied.

Same case below, 584 Fed. Appx. 731.

No. 14-9897. Alvin Sheroy Terrell, Petitioner v. Charles M. Maiorana, Warden.

577 U.S. 840, 136 S. Ct. 71, 193 L. Ed. 2d 68, 2015 U.S. LEXIS 5299.

October 5, 2015. Petition for writ of certiorari to the United States Court of Appeals for the Fifth Circuit denied.

No. 14-9902. Demetreus A. Keahey, Petitioner v. Ohio.

577 U.S. 840, 136 S. Ct. 71, 193 L. Ed. 2d 68, 2015 U.S. LEXIS 4984.

October 5, 2015. Petition for writ of certiorari to the Court of Appeals of Ohio, Erie County, denied.

No. 14-9903. Richard L. Coleman, Petitioner v. Dennis Bush, Warden.

577 U.S. 840, 136 S. Ct. 72, 193 L. Ed. 2d 68, 2015 U.S. LEXIS 5195.

October 5, 2015. Petition for writ of certiorari to the United States Court of Appeals for the Fourth Circuit denied.

Same case below, 589 Fed. Appx. 225.

No. 14-9904. Nancy L. Guardia, Petitioner v. Clinical & Support Options, Inc.

577 U.S. 840, 136 S. Ct. 72, 193 L. Ed. 2d 68, 2015 U.S. LEXIS 4992.

October 5, 2015. Petition for writ of certiorari to the United States Court of Appeals for the First Circuit denied.

No. 14-9909. Claretha Ross, Petitioner v. Pamela H. Cobb.

577 U.S. 840, 136 S. Ct. 72, 193 L. Ed. 2d 68, 2015 U.S. LEXIS 5047, reh den 577 U.S. 1114, 136 S. Ct. 925, 193 L. Ed. 2d 810, 2016 U.S. LEXIS 765.

October 5, 2015. Petition for writ of certiorari to the Superior Court of Georgia, Habersham County, denied.

MEMORANDUM CASES

No. 14-9911. Cecil R. McDonald, Petitioner v. Texas.

577 U.S. 840, 136 S. Ct. 72, 193 L. Ed. 2d 69, 2015 U.S. LEXIS 5227.

October 5, 2015. Petition for writ of certiorari to the Court of Appeals of Texas, Seventh District. denied.

No. 14-9916. Marvin Cotton, Sr., Petitioner v. Terry Russell, Warden.

577 U.S. 840, 136 S. Ct. 72, 193 L. Ed. 2d 69, 2015 U.S. LEXIS 4990.

October 5, 2015. Petition for writ of certiorari to the United States Court of Appeals for the Eighth Circuit denied.

No. 14-9920. Elijah Addai, Petitioner v. Colby Braun, Warden.

577 U.S. 840, 136 S. Ct. 73, 193 L. Ed. 2d 69, 2015 U.S. LEXIS 5046.

October 5, 2015. Petition for writ of certiorari to the United States Court of Appeals for the Eighth Circuit denied.

Same case below, 776 F.3d 528.

No. 14-9923. Alveto Rivera, Petitioner v. Imo Kalla, et al.

577 U.S. 840, 136 S. Ct. 73, 193 L. Ed. 2d 69, 2015 U.S. LEXIS 5387.

October 5, 2015. Petition for writ of certiorari to the United States Court of Appeals for the Eighth Circuit denied.

Same case below, 594 Fed. Appx. 321.

No. 14-9924. Victor Paul Forward, Petitioner v. California Workers' Compensation Appeals Board, et al.

577 U.S. 840, 136 S. Ct. 73, 193 L. Ed. 2d 69, 2015 U.S. LEXIS 5143.

October 5, 2015. Petition for writ of certiorari to the Court of Appeal of California, Fourth Appellate District, Division Three, denied.

No. 14-9925. Samuel Antonio Parra, Petitioner v. Charles L. Ryan, Director, Arizona Department of Corrections, et al.

577 U.S. 841, 136 S. Ct. 74, 193 L. Ed. 2d 69, 2015 U.S. LEXIS 5108.

October 5, 2015. Petition for writ of certiorari to the United States Court of Appeals for the Ninth Circuit denied.

No. 14-9926. Omari H. Patton, Petitioner v. Robert Werlinger, et al.

577 U.S. 841, 136 S. Ct. 74, 193 L. Ed. 2d 69, 2015 U.S. LEXIS 4986.

October 5, 2015. Petition for writ of certiorari to the United States Court of Appeals for the Third Circuit denied.

Same case below, 592 Fed. Appx. 71.

No. 14-9930. Ronald E. Dudley, Petitioner v. Deb Timmerman-Cooper, Warden.

577 U.S. 841, 136 S. Ct. 74, 193 L. Ed. 2d 69, 2015 U.S. LEXIS 5000.

October 5, 2015. Petition for writ of certiorari to the United States Court of Appeals for the Sixth Circuit denied.

No. 14-9931. Anthony Lamar Fishburne, Petitioner v. Sarah L. Hamilton.

577 U.S. 841, 136 S. Ct. 74, 193 L. Ed. 2d 70, 2015 U.S. LEXIS 4971.

October 5, 2015. Petition for writ of certiorari to the United States Court of Appeals for the Fourth Circuit denied.

Same case below, 592 Fed. Appx. 228.

No. 14-9933. Archie Cranford, Petitioner v. Briandon Price, et al.

577 U.S. 841, 136 S. Ct. 74, 193 L. Ed. 2d 70, 2015 U.S. LEXIS 5029.

October 5, 2015. Petition for writ of certiorari to the United States Court of Appeals for the Ninth Circuit denied.

No. 14-9934. George Anthony Corrales, Petitioner v. California.

577 U.S. 841, 136 S. Ct. 74, 193 L. Ed. 2d 70, 2015 U.S. LEXIS 5006, reh den 577 U.S. 1054, 136 S. Ct. 704, 193 L. Ed. 2d 530, 2015 U.S. LEXIS 7939.

October 5, 2015. Petition for writ of certiorari to the Supreme Court of California denied.

No. 14-9936. Archie Cranford, Petitioner v. Vanessa Ceballos.

577 U.S. 841, 136 S. Ct. 75, 193 L. Ed. 2d 70, 2015 U.S. LEXIS 5059.

October 5, 2015. Petition for writ of certiorari to the United States Court of Appeals for the Ninth Circuit denied.

No. 14-9937. Luvell Dortch, Petitioner v. Illinois.

577 U.S. 841, 136 S. Ct. 75, 193 L. Ed. 2d 70, 2015 U.S. LEXIS 5004.

October 5, 2015. Petition for writ of certiorari to the Appellate Court of Illinois, First District. denied.

No. 14-9938. Robert Preston Clayton, Petitioner v. Wendy Kelley, Director, Arkansas Department of Correction.

577 U.S. 841, 136 S. Ct. 75, 193 L. Ed. 2d 70, 2015 U.S. LEXIS 5309.

October 5, 2015. Petition for writ of certiorari to the United States Court of Appeals for the Eighth Circuit denied.

No. 14-9939. Kevin Oniechi Jordan, Petitioner v. Dave Davey, Acting Warden.

577 U.S. 841, 136 S. Ct. 75, 193 L. Ed. 2d 70, 2015 U.S. LEXIS 5040.

October 5, 2015. Petition for writ of certiorari to the United States Court of Appeals for the Ninth Circuit denied.

No. 14-9943. Sean Tapp, Petitioner v. James Eckard, Superintendent, State Correctional Institution at Huntingdon.

577 U.S. 841, 136 S. Ct. 75, 193 L. Ed. 2d 70, 2015 U.S. LEXIS 5044, reh den 577 U.S. 1044, 136 S. Ct. 608, 193 L. Ed. 2d 489, 2015 U.S. LEXIS 7712.

October 5, 2015. Petition for writ of certiorari to the United States Court of Appeals for the Third Circuit denied.

No. 14-9945. Barry Scott Cleaveland, Petitioner v. Texas.

577 U.S. 841, 136 S. Ct. 75, 193 L. Ed. 2d 71, 2015 U.S. LEXIS 5271.

October 5, 2015. Petition for writ of certiorari to the Court of Appeals of Texas, Ninth District. denied.

No. 14-9946. Vonnie Ross Edwards, Petitioner v. J. Soto, Warden.

577 U.S. 841, 136 S. Ct. 76, 193 L. Ed. 2d 71, 2015 U.S. LEXIS 5381.

October 5, 2015. Petition for writ of certiorari to the United States Court of Appeals for the Ninth Circuit denied.

No. 14-9949. Brandon Deshawn Campbell, Petitioner v. United States.

577 U.S. 841, 136 S. Ct. 76, 193 L. Ed. 2d 71, 2015 U.S. LEXIS 5414.

October 5, 2015. Petition for writ of certiorari to the United States Court of Appeals for the Fifth Circuit denied.

Same case below, 775 F.3d 664.

No. 14-9954. Thomas Esparza, Petitioner v. Domingo Uribe, Jr., Warden.

577 U.S. 841, 136 S. Ct. 76, 193 L. Ed. 2d 71, 2015 U.S. LEXIS 5366.

October 5, 2015. Petition for writ of certiorari to the United States Court of Appeals for the Ninth Circuit denied.

Same case below, 593 Fed. Appx. 728.

No. 14-9956. Robert C. Broadway, Petitioner v. Burl Cain, Warden.

577 U.S. 842, 136 S. Ct. 76, 193 L. Ed. 2d 71, 2015 U.S. LEXIS 5024.

October 5, 2015. Petition for writ of certiorari to the United States Court of Appeals for the Fifth Circuit denied.

No. 14-9959. Milton N. Ward, III, Petitioner v. Department of Education.

577 U.S. 842, 136 S. Ct. 76, 193 L. Ed. 2d 71, 2015 U.S. LEXIS 4999.

October 5, 2015. Petition for writ of certiorari to the United States Court of Appeals for the Fourth Circuit denied.

Same case below, 588 Fed. Appx. 282.

No. 14-9960. David F. Petrano, et ux., Petitioners v. Trevor Rhodes, et al.

577 U.S. 842, 136 S. Ct. 77, 193 L. Ed. 2d 71, 2015 U.S. LEXIS 5132.

October 5, 2015. Petition for writ of certiorari to the United States Court of Appeals for the Eleventh Circuit denied.

No. 14-9961. Lindsey J. Watson, Petitioner v. Carolyn W. Colvin, Acting Commissioner of Social Security.

577 U.S. 842, 136 S. Ct. 77, 193 L. Ed. 2d 71, 2015 U.S. LEXIS 5469, reh den 577 U.S. 1054, 136 S. Ct. 705, 193 L. Ed. 2d 530, 2015 U.S. LEXIS 7961.

October 5, 2015. Petition for writ of certiorari to the United States Court of Appeals for the Eleventh Circuit denied.

Same case below, 598 Fed. Appx. 634.

Same case below, 356 Wis. 2d 830, 855 N.W.2d 720.

No. 14-9964. James Garfield Broadnax, Petitioner v. Texas.

577 U.S. 842, 136 S. Ct. 77, 193 L. Ed. 2d 72, 2015 U.S. LEXIS 5329.

October 5, 2015. Petition for writ of certiorari to the Court of Criminal Appeals of Texas denied.

No. 14-9965. Denny Benton, Petitioner v. Town of South Fork, Colorado, et al.

577 U.S. 842, 136 S. Ct. 77, 193 L. Ed. 2d 72, 2015 U.S. LEXIS 4995.

October 5, 2015. Petition for writ of certiorari to the United States Court of Appeals for the Tenth Circuit denied.

Same case below, 587 Fed. Appx. 447.

No. 14-9967. Prentice D. Jones, Petitioner v. Gary Sandor, Warden.

577 U.S. 842, 136 S. Ct. 77, 193 L. Ed. 2d 72, 2015 U.S. LEXIS 5176.

October 5, 2015. Petition for writ of certiorari to the United States Court of Appeals for the Ninth Circuit denied.

Same case below, 588 Fed. Appx. 618.

No. 14-9977. Mical Thomas, Petitioner v. Wisconsin.

577 U.S. 842, 136 S. Ct. 78, 193 L. Ed. 2d 72, 2015 U.S. LEXIS 5397.

October 5, 2015. Petition for writ of certiorari to the Court of Appeals of Wisconsin, District I, denied.

No. 14-9978. Deanglis Turner, Petitioner v. Illinois.

577 U.S. 842, 136 S. Ct. 78, 193 L. Ed. 2d 72, 2015 U.S. LEXIS 4981.

October 5, 2015. Petition for writ of certiorari to the Appellate Court of Illinois, Third District. denied.

No. 14-9980. Anthony David Urbano, Petitioner v. Jim MacDonald, Warden.

577 U.S. 842, 136 S. Ct. 79, 193 L. Ed. 2d 72, 2015 U.S. LEXIS 5181.

October 5, 2015. Petition for writ of certiorari to the United States Court of Appeals for the Ninth Circuit denied.

No. 14-9981. Robert L. Poole, Jr., Petitioner v. United States.

577 U.S. 842, 136 S. Ct. 79, 193 L. Ed. 2d 72, 2015 U.S. LEXIS 5002.

October 5, 2015. Petition for writ of certiorari to the United States Court of Appeals for the Sixth Circuit denied.

No. 14-9983. Hiram Miles, Petitioner v. Court of Appeals of Texas, Fourth District.

577 U.S. 842, 136 S. Ct. 79, 193 L. Ed. 2d 72, 2015 U.S. LEXIS 5466.

October 5, 2015. Petition for writ of certiorari to the Court of Criminal Appeals of Texas denied.

No. 14-9985. Helen Eva Spry, Petitioner v. California.

577 U.S. 842, 136 S. Ct. 79, 193 L. Ed. 2d 73, 2015 U.S. LEXIS 5257.

October 5, 2015. Petition for writ of certiorari to the Court of Appeal of California, Second Appellate District, Division Two, denied.

No. 14-9988. Morris P. Harmon, Jr., Petitioner v. Fred Foulk, Warden, et al.

577 U.S. 842, 136 S. Ct. 79, 193 L. Ed. 2d 73, 2015 U.S. LEXIS 5062.

October 5, 2015. Petition for writ of certiorari to the United States Court of Appeals for the Ninth Circuit denied.

No. 14-9989. Jesse Smith, Petitioner v. Illinois.

577 U.S. 842, 136 S. Ct. 80, 193 L. Ed. 2d 73, 2015 U.S. LEXIS 5045.

October 5, 2015. Petition for writ of certiorari to the Appellate Court of Illinois, First District, denied.

No. 14-9992. Medardo De Jesus Marroquin-Salazar, Petitioner v. United States.

577 U.S. 843, 136 S. Ct. 80, 193 L. Ed. 2d 73, 2015 U.S. LEXIS 5149.

October 5, 2015. Petition for writ of certiorari to the United States Court of Appeals for the Fifth Circuit denied.

Same case below, 595 Fed. Appx. 430.

No. 14-9994. Bernard Marks, Petitioner v. Wendy Kelley, Director, Arkansas Department of Correction.

577 U.S. 843, 136 S. Ct. 83, 193 L. Ed. 2d 73, 2015 U.S. LEXIS 5423.

October 5, 2015. Petition for writ of certiorari to the United States Court of Appeals for the Eighth Circuit denied.

No. 14-9995. Scott Bryant, Petitioner v. Joseph P. Meko, Warden.

577 U.S. 843, 136 S. Ct. 84, 193 L. Ed. 2d 73, 2015 U.S. LEXIS 5051.

October 5, 2015. Petition for writ of certiorari to the United States Court of Appeals for the Sixth Circuit denied.

No. 14-9997. Miguel Gonzalez, Petitioner v. Connecticut.

577 U.S. 843, 136 S. Ct. 84, 193 L. Ed. 2d 73, 2015 U.S. LEXIS 5291, reh den 577 U.S. 1022, 136 S. Ct. 574, 193 L. Ed. 2d 456, 2015 U.S. LEXIS 7416.

October 5, 2015. Petition for writ of certiorari to the Supreme Court of Connecticut denied.

Same case below, 315 Conn. 564, 109 A.3d 453.

No. 14-10001. Jude Joseph Boda, Petitioner v. South Dakota.

577 U.S. 843, 136 S. Ct. 82, 193 L. Ed. 2d 73, 2015 U.S. LEXIS 5224.

October 5, 2015. Petition for writ of certiorari to the Supreme Court of South Dakota denied.

No. 14-10003. Nikos Kastrinsios, Petitioner v. Illinois.

577 U.S. 843, 136 S. Ct. 82, 193 L. Ed. 2d 74, 2015 U.S. LEXIS 5030.

October 5, 2015. Petition for writ of certiorari to the Appellate Court of Illinois, Second District, denied.

No. 14-10004. Richard Motz, Petitioner v. Elizabeth A. O'Meara, Superintendent, Gouverneur Correctional Facility.

577 U.S. 843, 136 S. Ct. 83, 193 L. Ed. 2d 74, 2015 U.S. LEXIS 4994.

October 5, 2015. Petition for writ of certiorari to the United States Court of Appeals for the Second Circuit denied.

No. 14-10005. Eric Charles Olson, Petitioner v. Edmund G. Brown, Jr.

577 U.S. 843, 136 S. Ct. 83, 193 L. Ed. 2d 74, 2015 U.S. LEXIS 5248.

October 5, 2015. Petition for writ of certiorari to the United States Court of Appeals for the Ninth Circuit denied.

No. 14-10007. Alfonso Garcia Rubio, Petitioner v. Jeffrey Beard, Secretary, California Department of Corrections and Rehabilitation.

577 U.S. 843, 136 S. Ct. 83, 193 L. Ed. 2d 74, 2015 U.S. LEXIS 5102.

October 5, 2015. Petition for writ of certiorari to the United States Court of Appeals for the Ninth Circuit denied.

No. 14-10009. Ashford L. Thompson, Petitioner v. Ohio.

577 U.S. 843, 136 S. Ct. 83, 193 L. Ed. 2d 74, 2015 U.S. LEXIS 5338, reh den 577 U.S. 1022, 136 S. Ct. 574, 193 L. Ed. 2d 456, 2015 U.S. LEXIS 7469.

October 5, 2015. Petition for writ of certiorari to the Supreme Court of Ohio denied.

Same case below, 141 Ohio St. 3d 254, 23 N.E.3d 1096.

No. 14-10011. Latonia Congress, Petitioner v. Vermont.

577 U.S. 843, 136 S. Ct. 83, 193 L. Ed. 2d 74, 2015 U.S. LEXIS 5048.

October 5, 2015. Petition for writ of certiorari to the Supreme Court of Vermont denied.

Same case below, 198 Vt. 241, 114 A.3d 1128.

No. 14-10012. Hollant M. Adrien, Petitioner v. Wittenburg University, et al.

577 U.S. 843, 136 S. Ct. 85, 193 L. Ed. 2d 74, 2015 U.S. LEXIS 5484.

October 5, 2015. Petition for writ of certiorari to the United States Court of Appeals for the Sixth Circuit denied.

No. 14-10013. Eduardo Rodriguez-Ayala, Petitioner v. United States.

577 U.S. 843, 136 S. Ct. 85, 193 L. Ed. 2d 75, 2015 U.S. LEXIS 5114.

October 5, 2015. Petition for writ of certiorari to the United States Court of Appeals for the Eighth Circuit denied.

Same case below, 773 F.3d 65.

No. 14-10014. Michelle L. Kronenberg, Petitioner v. LaShann Eppinger, Warden.

577 U.S. 843, 136 S. Ct. 85, 193 L. Ed. 2d 75, 2015 U.S. LEXIS 4969.

October 5, 2015. Petition for writ of certiorari to the United States Court of Appeals for the Sixth Circuit denied.

No. 14-10016. Jesus Marquez, Petitioner v. Clark E. Ducart, Warden.

577 U.S. 844, 136 S. Ct. 85, 193 L. Ed. 2d 75, 2015 U.S. LEXIS 4979.

October 5, 2015. Petition for writ of certiorari to the United States Court of Appeals for the Ninth Circuit denied.

No. 14-10017. Richard Coleman, Petitioner v. Town of Lee, New Hampshire, et al.

577 U.S. 844, 136 S. Ct. 85, 193 L. Ed. 2d 75, 2015 U.S. LEXIS 4968.

October 5, 2015. Petition for writ of certiorari to the United States Court of Appeals for the First Circuit denied.

No. 14-10021. Travis Lequinn Sarvis, Petitioner v. Maureen Cruz, Warden.

577 U.S. 844, 136 S. Ct. 85, 193 L. Ed. 2d 75, 2015 U.S. LEXIS 5178.

October 5, 2015. Petition for writ of certiorari to the United States Court of Appeals for the Fourth Circuit denied.

Same case below, 599 Fed. Appx. 106.

No. 14-10025. Billy R. Melot, et ux., Petitioners v. United States.

577 U.S. 844, 136 S. Ct. 86, 193 L. Ed. 2d 75, 2015 U.S. LEXIS 5152, reh den 577 U.S. 1022, 136 S. Ct. 574, 193 L. Ed. 2d 456, 2015 U.S. LEXIS 7367.

October 5, 2015. Petition for writ of certiorari to the United States Court of Appeals for the Tenth Circuit denied.

Same case below, 606 Fed. Appx. 930.

No. 14-10031. Derek Wryan Wilson, Petitioner v. Texas.

577 U.S. 844, 136 S. Ct. 86, 193 L. Ed. 2d 75, 2015 U.S. LEXIS 4977.

October 5, 2015. Petition for writ of certiorari to the Court of Appeals of Texas, Second District, denied.

Same case below, 442 S.W.3d 779.

Same case below, 589 Fed. Appx. 258.

No. 14-10033. Adam Kelly Ward, Petitioner v. William Stephens, Director, Texas Department of Criminal Justice, Correctional Institutions Division.

577 U.S. 844, 136 S. Ct. 86, 193 L. Ed. 2d 76, 2015 U.S. LEXIS 5413.

October 5, 2015. Petition for writ of certiorari to the United States Court of Appeals for the Fifth Circuit denied.

Same case below, 777 F.3d 250.

No. 14-10036. Charles Devon Wasserman, Petitioner v. Texas.

577 U.S. 844, 136 S. Ct. 86, 193 L. Ed. 2d 76, 2015 U.S. LEXIS 5013.

October 5, 2015. Petition for writ of certiorari to the Court of Appeals of Texas, Thirteenth District, denied.

No. 14-10037. Daron Thomas, Petitioner v. David E. Morgan, III, et al.

577 U.S. 844, 136 S. Ct. 86, 193 L. Ed. 2d 76, 2015 U.S. LEXIS 5104.

October 5, 2015. Petition for writ of certiorari to the United States Court of Appeals for the Eleventh Circuit denied.

No. 14-10038. Darlene C. Amrhein, Petitioner v. La Madeleine, Inc., et al.

577 U.S. 844, 136 S. Ct. 86, 193 L. Ed. 2d 76, 2015 U.S. LEXIS 4965, reh den 577 U.S. 1022, 136 S. Ct. 574, 193 L. Ed. 2d 456, 2015 U.S. LEXIS 7403.

October 5, 2015. Petition for writ of certiorari to the United States Court of Appeals for the Fifth Circuit denied.

No. 14-10042. Paul Luxama, Petitioner v. Julie L. Jones, Secretary, Florida Department of Corrections.

577 U.S. 844, 136 S. Ct. 87, 193 L. Ed. 2d 76, 2015 U.S. LEXIS 5405.

October 5, 2015. Petition for writ of certiorari to the United States Court of Appeals for the Eleventh Circuit denied.

No. 14-10044. Christopher Todd Landeck and David Gregory Landeck, Petitioner v. Ivan Gilmore, Warden, et al.

577 U.S. 844, 136 S. Ct. 87, 193 L. Ed. 2d 76, 2015 U.S. LEXIS 5406.

October 5, 2015. Petition for writ of certiorari to the Supreme Court of Virginia denied.

No. 14-10045. Simon F. Ranteesi, Petitioner v. Eric Arnold, Acting Warden.

577 U.S. 844, 136 S. Ct. 87, 193 L. Ed. 2d 76, 2015 U.S. LEXIS 5345, reh den 577 U.S. 998, 136 S. Ct. 527, 193 L. Ed. 2d 415, 2015 U.S. LEXIS 7319.

October 5, 2015. Petition for writ of certiorari to the United States Court of Appeals for the Ninth Circuit denied.

No. 14-10047. Mark White, Petitioner v. Jeffrey Woods, Warden.

577 U.S. 844, 136 S. Ct. 88, 193 L. Ed. 2d 76, 2015 U.S. LEXIS 5244.

October 5, 2015. Petition for writ of certiorari to the United States Court of Appeals for the Sixth Circuit denied.

No. 14-10048. Adelbert H. Warner, II, Petitioner v. United States.

577 U.S. 844, 136 S. Ct. 88, 193 L. Ed. 2d 77, 2015 U.S. LEXIS 5487, reh den 577 U.S. 1054, 136 S. Ct. 705, 193 L. Ed. 2d 531, 2015 U.S. LEXIS 7930.

October 5, 2015. Petition for writ of certiorari to the United States Court of Appeals for the Sixth Circuit denied.

No. 14-10049. Rose McKinley, Petitioner v. CMH Homes, Inc.

577 U.S. 844, 136 S. Ct. 88, 193 L. Ed. 2d 77, 2015 U.S. LEXIS 5213.

October 5, 2015. Petition for writ of certiorari to the United States Court of Appeals for the Fourth Circuit denied.

Same case below, 597 Fed. Appx. 204.

No. 14-10050. Jimmy R. Williams, Petitioner v. Texas.

577 U.S. 845, 136 S. Ct. 88, 193 L. Ed. 2d 77, 2015 U.S. LEXIS 5451.

October 5, 2015. Petition for writ of certiorari to the Court of Appeals of Texas, First District, denied.

No. 14-10051. Cary Pickett, Petitioner v. Anthony Scillia, et al.

577 U.S. 845, 136 S. Ct. 88, 193 L. Ed. 2d 77, 2015 U.S. LEXIS 5198.

October 5, 2015. Petition for writ of certiorari to the United States Court of Appeals for the Ninth Circuit denied.

No. 14-10055. Toni Clark, Petitioner v. Jose L. Linares, Judge, United States District Court for the District of New Jersey, et al.

577 U.S. 845, 136 S. Ct. 89, 193 L. Ed. 2d 77, 2015 U.S. LEXIS 5482.

October 5, 2015. Petition for writ of certiorari to the United States Court of Appeals for the Third Circuit denied.

Same case below, 594 Fed. Appx. 81.

No. 14-10056. Jamar S. Russell, Petitioner v. Maryland.

577 U.S. 845, 136 S. Ct. 89, 193 L. Ed. 2d 77, 2015 U.S. LEXIS 5015.

October 5, 2015. Petition for writ of certiorari to the Court of Special Appeals of Maryland denied.

Same case below, 218 Md. App. 753.

No. 14-10059. Rene Marquez, Petitioner v. Pam Bondi, Attorney General of Florida.

577 U.S. 845, 136 S. Ct. 90, 193 L. Ed. 2d 77, 2015 U.S. LEXIS 5344.

October 5, 2015. Petition for writ of certiorari to the United States Court of Appeals for the Eleventh Circuit denied.

No. 14-10060. Michael Rinaldi, Petitioner v. Donna Zickefoose, Warden.

577 U.S. 845, 136 S. Ct. 90, 193 L. Ed. 2d 77, 2015 U.S. LEXIS 5208.

October 5, 2015. Petition for writ of certiorari to the United States Court of Appeals for the Third Circuit denied.

Same case below, 598 Fed. Appx. 809.

No. 14-10062. Maria A. Wimberly, Petitioner v. Alina T. Hudak, Deputy Mayor of Miami-Dade County, Florida, et al.

577 U.S. 845, 136 S. Ct. 90, 193 L. Ed. 2d 78, 2015 U.S. LEXIS 5043.

October 5, 2015. Petition for writ of certiorari to the District Court of Appeal of Florida, Third District, denied.

Same case below, 160 So. 3d 445.

No. 14-10063. Huy Trong Tran, Petitioner v. Martin Biter, Warden.

577 U.S. 845, 136 S. Ct. 90, 193 L. Ed. 2d 78, 2015 U.S. LEXIS 5183.

October 5, 2015. Petition for writ of certiorari to the United States Court of Appeals for the Ninth Circuit denied.

Same case below, 589 Fed. Appx. 365.

No. 14-10067. Arnold Zaler, Petitioner v. United States.

577 U.S. 845, 136 S. Ct. 91, 193 L. Ed. 2d 78, 2015 U.S. LEXIS 4966.

October 5, 2015. Petition for writ of certiorari to the United States Court of Appeals for the Tenth Circuit denied.

Same case below, 601 Fed. Appx. 677.

No. 14-10068. Robert J. Printz, Petitioner v. United States.

577 U.S. 845, 136 S. Ct. 91, 193 L. Ed. 2d 78, 2015 U.S. LEXIS 5380.

October 5, 2015. Petition for writ of certiorari to the United States Court of Appeals for the Seventh Circuit denied.

Same case below, 594 Fed. Appx. 883.

No. 14-10069. Jessica Medina, Petitioner v. United States.

577 U.S. 845, 136 S. Ct. 91, 193 L. Ed. 2d 78, 2015 U.S. LEXIS 4982.

October 5, 2015. Petition for writ of certiorari to the United States Court of Appeals for the Ninth Circuit denied.

Same case below, 602 Fed. Appx. 372.

No. 14-10070. Darryl Moore, Petitioner v. United States.

577 U.S. 845, 136 S. Ct. 91, 193 L. Ed. 2d 78, 2015 U.S. LEXIS 5112.

October 5, 2015. Petition for writ of certiorari to the United States Court of Appeals for the Fifth Circuit denied.

Same case below, 559 Fed. Appx. 308.

No. 14-10071. Clarence Bruce Beaulieu, Petitioner v. Minnesota.

577 U.S. 845, 136 S. Ct. 92, 193 L. Ed. 2d 78, 2015 U.S. LEXIS 5362.

October 5, 2015. Petition for writ of certiorari to the Supreme Court of Minnesota denied.

Same case below, 859 N.W.2d 275.

No. 14-10072. Lavandus Houston, Petitioner v. United States.

577 U.S. 845, 136 S. Ct. 92, 193 L. Ed. 2d 78, 2015 U.S. LEXIS 5328.

October 5, 2015. Petition for writ of certiorari to the United States Court of Appeals for the Fourth Circuit denied.

Same case below, 766 F.3d 672.

No. 14-10073. Eddie Alejandro-Montanez, Petitioner v. United States.

577 U.S. 845, 136 S. Ct. 92, 193 L. Ed. 2d 79, 2015 U.S. LEXIS 5385.

October 5, 2015. Petition for writ of certiorari to the United States Court of Appeals for the First Circuit denied.

Same case below, 778 F.3d 352.

No. 14-10074. Steven Burda, Petitioner v. Alla Korenman, fka Alla Burda (three judgments).

577 U.S. 846, 136 S. Ct. 92, 193 L. Ed. 2d 79, 2015 U.S. LEXIS 5082.

October 5, 2015. Petition for writ of certiorari to the Superior Court of Pennsylvania, Philadelphia Office, denied.

No. 14-10075. Gregory Lynn Sandreth, Petitioner v. United States.

577 U.S. 846, 136 S. Ct. 92, 193 L. Ed. 2d 79, 2015 U.S. LEXIS 4980.

October 5, 2015. Petition for writ of certiorari to the United States Court of Appeals for the Fourth Circuit denied.

Same case below, 595 Fed. Appx. 244.

No. 14-10076. Timothy S. Durham, Petitioner v. United States.

577 U.S. 846, 136 S. Ct. 92, 193 L. Ed. 2d 79, 2015 U.S. LEXIS 5240.

October 5, 2015. Petition for writ of certiorari to the United States Court of Appeals for the Seventh Circuit denied.

No. 14-10079. Webster W. Norris, III, Petitioner v. United States.

577 U.S. 846, 136 S. Ct. 93, 193 L. Ed. 2d 79, 2015 U.S. LEXIS 5165.

October 5, 2015. Petition for writ of certiorari to the United States Court of Appeals for the Ninth Circuit denied.

No. 14-10080. Anthony Whitney Norman, Petitioner v. Court of Criminal Appeals of Texas, et al.

577 U.S. 846, 136 S. Ct. 93, 193 L. Ed. 2d 79, 2015 U.S. LEXIS 4998.

October 5, 2015. Petition for writ of certiorari to the United States Court of Appeals for the Fifth Circuit denied.

Same case below, 582 Fed. Appx. 430.

No. 14-10081. Cecilia Aranda, Petitioner v. Dal-Tile Corporation.

577 U.S. 846, 136 S. Ct. 93, 193 L. Ed. 2d 79, 2015 U.S. LEXIS 5061, reh den 577 U.S. 1094, 136 S. Ct. 880, 193 L. Ed. 2d 772, 2016 U.S. LEXIS 463.

October 5, 2015. Petition for writ of certiorari to the United States Court of Appeals for the Fifth Circuit denied.

No. 14-10082. Vandaire Knox, Petitioner v. Illinois.

577 U.S. 846, 136 S. Ct. 93, 193 L. Ed. 2d 79, 2015 U.S. LEXIS 5259.

October 5, 2015. Petition for writ of certiorari to the Appellate Court of Illinois, First District, denied.

No. 14-10085. James Anthony Primus, Petitioner v. Edsel T. Taylor, Warden.

577 U.S. 846, 136 S. Ct. 95, 193 L. Ed. 2d 80, 2015 U.S. LEXIS 5204.

October 5, 2015. Petition for writ of certiorari to the United States Court of Appeals for the Fourth Circuit denied.

Same case below, 593 Fed. Appx. 235.

No. 14-10086. Alfredo Natal, Petitioner v. Tarry Williams, Warden.

577 U.S. 846, 136 S. Ct. 95, 193 L. Ed. 2d 80, 2015 U.S. LEXIS 5217.

October 5, 2015. Petition for writ of certiorari to the United States Court of Appeals for the Seventh Circuit denied.

No. 14-10088. David Gerard Jeep, Petitioner v. United States.

577 U.S. 846, 136 S. Ct. 95, 193 L. Ed. 2d 80, 2015 U.S. LEXIS 5036, reh den 577 U.S. 1022, 136 S. Ct. 574, 193 L. Ed. 2d 456, 2015 U.S. LEXIS 7383.

October 5, 2015. Petition for writ of certiorari to the United States Court of Appeals for the Eighth Circuit denied.

No. 14-10089. Akeem Alim-Nafi Abdullah-Malik, Petitioner v. South Carolina.

577 U.S. 846, 136 S. Ct. 95, 193 L. Ed. 2d 80, 2015 U.S. LEXIS 5464.

October 5, 2015. Petition for writ of certiorari to the Court of Appeals of South Carolina denied.

No. 14-10090. Johnathan Ian Burns, Petitioner v. Arizona.

577 U.S. 846, 136 S. Ct. 95, 193 L. Ed. 2d 80, 2015 U.S. LEXIS 5203.

October 5, 2015. Petition for writ of certiorari to the Supreme Court of Arizona denied.

Same case below, 237 Ariz. 1, 344 P.3d 303.

No. 14-10091. Gary Jefferson Byrd, Petitioner v. United States.

577 U.S. 846, 136 S. Ct. 96, 193 L. Ed. 2d 80, 2015 U.S. LEXIS 5009.

October 5, 2015. Petition for writ of certiorari to the United States Court of Appeals for the Fifth Circuit denied.

Same case below, 595 Fed. Appx. 431.

No. 14-10092. Carlos Melendez-Serrano, Petitioner v. United States.

577 U.S. 846, 136 S. Ct. 96, 193 L. Ed. 2d 80, 2015 U.S. LEXIS 5218.

October 5, 2015. Petition for writ of certiorari to the United States Court of Appeals for the First Circuit denied.

Same case below, 586 Fed. Appx. 709.

No. 14-10093. Brian Kerry O'Keefe, Petitioner v. Joseph Lombardo, Sheriff, Las Vegas Metropolitan Police Department, et al.

577 U.S. 846, 136 S. Ct. 96, 193 L. Ed. 2d 81, 2015 U.S. LEXIS 5351.

October 5, 2015. Petition for writ of certiorari to the United States Court of Appeals for the Ninth Circuit denied.

Same case below, 593 Fed. Appx. 626.

No. 14-10094. George Henry Midgette, Petitioner v. United States.

577 U.S. 847, 136 S. Ct. 96, 193 L. Ed. 2d 81, 2015 U.S. LEXIS 5005.

October 5, 2015. Petition for writ of certiorari to the United States Court of Appeals for the Fourth Circuit denied.

Same case below, 596 Fed. Appx. 237.

No. 14-10095. James Milton McEarchern, Petitioner v. United States.

577 U.S. 847, 136 S. Ct. 96, 193 L. Ed. 2d 81, 2015 U.S. LEXIS 5184.

October 5, 2015. Petition for writ of certiorari to the United States Court of Appeals for the Fourth Circuit denied.

Same case below, 596 Fed. Appx. 233.

No. 14-10096. Louis A. Piccone, Petitioner v. Angelo McClain, et al.

577 U.S. 847, 136 S. Ct. 96, 193 L. Ed. 2d 81, 2015 U.S. LEXIS 5234.

October 5, 2015. Petition for writ of certiorari to the United States Court of Appeals for the First Circuit denied.

No. 14-10097. Willie Branch, Petitioner v. Angela P. Dunbar, Warden.

577 U.S. 847, 136 S. Ct. 97, 193 L. Ed. 2d 81, 2015 U.S. LEXIS 5140.

October 5, 2015. Petition for writ of certiorari to the United States Court of Appeals for the Fourth Circuit denied.

Same case below, 588 Fed. Appx. 238.

No. 14-10098. Barbara Ellen Sherrill, Petitioner v. Arizona Health Care Cost Containment System, et al.

577 U.S. 847, 136 S. Ct. 97, 193 L. Ed. 2d 81, 2015 U.S. LEXIS 4976.

October 5, 2015. Petition for writ of certiorari to the United States Court of Appeals for the Ninth Circuit denied.

No. 14-10099. Rodney Rollins, Petitioner v. Allen Murphy, et al.

577 U.S. 847, 136 S. Ct. 97, 193 L. Ed. 2d 81, 2015 U.S. LEXIS 5223.

October 5, 2015. Petition for writ of certiorari to the United States Court of Appeals for the Seventh Circuit denied.

Same case below, 598 Fed. Appx. 449.

No. 14-10100. Jerry Thomas Davis, Petitioner v. United States.

577 U.S. 847, 136 S. Ct. 97, 193 L. Ed. 2d 81, 2015 U.S. LEXIS 4975.

October 5, 2015. Petition for writ of certiorari to the United States Court of Appeals for the Eleventh Circuit denied.

Same case below, 779 F.3d 1305.

No. 14-10101. Lydia Cladek, Petitioner v. United States.

577 U.S. 847, 136 S. Ct. 97, 193 L. Ed. 2d 82, 2015 U.S. LEXIS 5033, reh den 577 U.S. 1022, 136 S. Ct. 574, 193 L. Ed. 2d 456, 2015 U.S. LEXIS 7462.

October 5, 2015. Petition for writ of certiorari to the United States Court of Appeals for the Eleventh Circuit denied.

Same case below, 579 Fed. Appx. 962.

No. 14-10102. Taeshaun Javon Brown, Petitioner v. United States.

577 U.S. 847, 136 S. Ct. 97, 193 L. Ed. 2d 82, 2015 U.S. LEXIS 5377.

October 5, 2015. Petition for writ of certiorari to the United States Court of Appeals for the Fourth Circuit denied.

No. 14-10103. Scott W. Barnes, Petitioner v. United States.

No. 15-5148. Monica I. Lewis, Petitioner v. United States.

577 U.S. 847, 136 S. Ct. 98, 193 L. Ed. 2d 82, 2015 U.S. LEXIS 5441.

October 5, 2015. Petitions for writs of certiorari to the United States Court of Appeals for the Eleventh Circuit denied.

Same cases below, 777 F.3d 1234.

No. 14-10104. Nicholas Albanese, aka Stoney Oaks, Petitioner v. United States.

577 U.S. 847, 136 S. Ct. 98, 193 L. Ed. 2d 82, 2015 U.S. LEXIS 5041.

October 5, 2015. Petition for writ of certiorari to the United States Court of Appeals for the Third Circuit denied.

No. 14-10105. Simon F. Ranteesi, Petitioner v. Mark Constance, et al.

577 U.S. 847, 136 S. Ct. 98, 193 L. Ed. 2d 82, 2015 U.S. LEXIS 5025, reh den 577 U.S. 998, 136 S. Ct. 527, 193 L. Ed. 2d 416, 2015 U.S. LEXIS 7245.

October 5, 2015. Petition for writ of certiorari to the United States Court of Appeals for the Ninth Circuit denied.

Same case below, 588 Fed. Appx. 686.

No. 14-10106. Adrian G. Rangel, Petitioner v. Crystal Sanders, et al.

577 U.S. 847, 136 S. Ct. 98, 193 L. Ed. 2d 82, 2015 U.S. LEXIS 5260.

October 5, 2015. Petition for writ of certiorari to the United States Court of Appeals for the Seventh Circuit denied.

No. 14-10107. Nannette R. Heath, Petitioner v. Adam Baton, et al.

577 U.S. 847, 136 S. Ct. 98, 193 L. Ed. 2d 82, 2015 U.S. LEXIS 5096.

October 5, 2015. Petition for writ of certiorari to the United States Court of Appeals for the Sixth Circuit denied.

No. 14-10108. Robert L. Dykes-Bey, Petitioner v. Michigan Department of Corrections.

577 U.S. 847, 136 S. Ct. 98, 193 L. Ed. 2d 83, 2015 U.S. LEXIS 5494.

October 5, 2015. Petition for writ of certiorari to the Circuit Court of Michigan, Ingham County, denied.

No. 14-10109. Brian S. Hartman, Petitioner v. Indiana.

577 U.S. 847, 136 S. Ct. 99, 193 L. Ed. 2d 83, 2015 U.S. LEXIS 5472.

October 5, 2015. Petition for writ of certiorari to the Court of Appeals of Indiana, Fifth District, denied.

Same case below, 20 N.E.3d 225.

No. 14-10110. Mark Wayne Hauseur, Petitioner v. Tim V. Virga, Warden.

577 U.S. 848, 136 S. Ct. 99, 193 L. Ed. 2d 83, 2015 U.S. LEXIS 5057.

October 5, 2015. Petition for writ of certiorari to the United States Court of Appeals for the Ninth Circuit denied.

Same case below, 590 Fed. Appx. 680.

No. 14-10112. Jacobo Flores-Vasquez, Petitioner v. United States.

577 U.S. 848, 136 S. Ct. 99, 193 L. Ed. 2d 83, 2015 U.S. LEXIS 5249.

October 5, 2015. Petition for writ of certiorari to the United States Court of Appeals for the Ninth Circuit denied.

Same case below, 594 Fed. Appx. 355.

No. 14-10113. Fremandeus C. Williams, Petitioner v. United States.

577 U.S. 848, 136 S. Ct. 99, 193 L. Ed. 2d 83, 2015 U.S. LEXIS 5010.

October 5, 2015. Petition for writ of certiorari to the United States Court of Appeals for the Fourth Circuit denied.

Same case below, 589 Fed. Appx. 154.

No. 14-10114. Starsha Sewell, Petitioner v. Strayer University.

577 U.S. 848, 136 S. Ct. 100, 193 L. Ed. 2d 83, 2015 U.S. LEXIS 5018, reh den 577 U.S. 981, 136 S. Ct. 497, 193 L. Ed. 2d 361, 2015 U.S. LEXIS 7135.

October 5, 2015. Petition for writ of certiorari to the United States Court of Appeals for the Fourth Circuit denied.

Same case below, 596 Fed. Appx. 251.

No. 14-10115. Laurence Fisher, Petitioner v. Jeffrey Miller, et al.

577 U.S. 848, 136 S. Ct. 100, 193 L. Ed. 2d 83, 2015 U.S. LEXIS 4997.

October 5, 2015. Petition for writ of certiorari to the United States Court of Appeals for the Third Circuit denied.

Same case below, 571 Fed. Appx. 119.

No. 14-10116. Brian Keith Henricks, Petitioner v. William Stephens, Director, Texas Department of Criminal Justice, Correctional Institutions Division.

577 U.S. 848, 136 S. Ct. 100, 193 L. Ed. 2d 84, 2015 U.S. LEXIS 5016.

October 5, 2015. Petition for writ of certiorari to the United States Court of Appeals for the Fifth Circuit denied.

No. 14-10117. Jimmy Dewayne Hill, Petitioner v. Texas.

577 U.S. 848, 136 S. Ct. 100, 193 L. Ed. 2d 84, 2015 U.S. LEXIS 5008.

October 5, 2015. Petition for writ of certiorari to the Court of Criminal Appeals of Texas denied.

No. 14-10118. Gary Flute, Sr., Petitioner v. United States.

577 U.S. 848, 136 S. Ct. 100, 193 L. Ed. 2d 84, 2015 U.S. LEXIS 5427.

October 5, 2015. Petition for writ of certiorari to the United States Court of Appeals for the Tenth Circuit denied.

Same case below, 594 Fed. Appx. 551.

No. 14-10120. Andy Delgado Rodriguez, Petitioner v. Carl Wofford, Warden.

577 U.S. 848, 136 S. Ct. 298, 193 L. Ed. 2d 84, 2015 U.S. LEXIS 5107.

October 5, 2015. Petition for writ of certiorari to the United States Court of Appeals for the Ninth Circuit denied.

No. 14-10121. John William Campbell, Petitioner v. Florida.

577 U.S. 848, 136 S. Ct. 100, 193 L. Ed. 2d 84, 2015 U.S. LEXIS 5172.

October 5, 2015. Petition for writ of certiorari to the Supreme Court of Florida denied.

Same case below, 159 So. 3d 814.

No. 14-10122. Otis M. Drayton, Jr., Petitioner v. United States.

577 U.S. 848, 136 S. Ct. 101, 193 L. Ed. 2d 84, 2015 U.S. LEXIS 5037.

October 5, 2015. Petition for writ of certiorari to the United States Court of Appeals for the Fourth Circuit denied.

Same case below, 589 Fed. Appx. 153.

No. 14-10123. Samuel Medrano Diaz, Petitioner v. William Stephens, Director, Texas Department of Criminal Justice, Correctional Institutions Division.

577 U.S. 848, 136 S. Ct. 101, 193 L. Ed. 2d 84, 2015 U.S. LEXIS 4983.

October 5, 2015. Petition for writ of certiorari to the United States Court of Appeals for the Fifth Circuit denied.

No. 14-10124. Rigoberto Estrada, Petitioner v. California.

577 U.S. 848, 136 S. Ct. 101, 193 L. Ed. 2d 84, 2015 U.S. LEXIS 5038.

October 5, 2015. Petition for writ of certiorari to the Court of Appeal of California, Fourth Appellate District, Division Two, denied.

No. 14-10126. Jesus Manuel Rodriguez-Flores, Petitioner v. United States.

577 U.S. 848, 136 S. Ct. 101, 193 L. Ed. 2d 85, 2015 U.S. LEXIS 5388.

October 5, 2015. Petition for writ of certiorari to the United States Court of Appeals for the Fifth Circuit denied.

Same case below, 595 Fed. Appx. 442.

No. 14-10127. Pamela Allen, Petitioner v. Robert A. McDonald, Secretary of Veterans Affairs.

577 U.S. 848, 136 S. Ct. 101, 193 L. Ed. 2d 85, 2015 U.S. LEXIS 5014.

October 5, 2015. Petition for writ of certiorari to the United States Court of Appeals for the Federal Circuit denied.

Same case below, 594 Fed. Appx. 686.

No. 14-10128. Richard M. Lopez, Petitioner v. Texas.

577 U.S. 849, 136 S. Ct. 102, 193 L. Ed. 2d 85, 2015 U.S. LEXIS 5256.

October 5, 2015. Petition for writ of certiorari to the Court of Appeals of Texas, Fourth District, denied.

No. 14-10129. Lakeisha Shanae Adams, Petitioner v. James Rogers, Warden.

577 U.S. 849, 136 S. Ct. 102, 193 L. Ed. 2d 85, 2015 U.S. LEXIS 5026.

October 5, 2015. Petition for writ of certiorari to the United States Court of Appeals for the Fifth Circuit denied.

No. 14-10130. Duwane Shackelford, Petitioner v. William Stephens, Director, Texas Department of Criminal Justice, Correctional Institutions Division.

577 U.S. 849, 136 S. Ct. 102, 193 L. Ed. 2d 85, 2015 U.S. LEXIS 5001, reh den 577 U.S. 1094, 136 S. Ct. 880, 193 L. Ed. 2d 772, 2016 U.S. LEXIS 399.

October 5, 2015. Petition for writ of certiorari to the United States Court of Appeals for the Fifth Circuit denied.

No. 14-10131. Flenoid Greer, Petitioner v. Michigan.

577 U.S. 849, 136 S. Ct. 102, 193 L. Ed. 2d 85, 2015 U.S. LEXIS 5205.

October 5, 2015. Petition for writ of certiorari to the Court of Appeals of Michigan denied.

No. 14-10132. Kenyon Williams, Petitioner v. United States.

577 U.S. 849, 136 S. Ct. 102, 193 L. Ed. 2d 85, 2015 U.S. LEXIS 5212.

October 5, 2015. Petition for writ of certiorari to the United States Court of Appeals for the Eleventh Circuit denied.

Same case below, 605 Fed. Appx. 878.

No. 14-10133. Wilfred Garcia, Petitioner v. United States.

577 U.S. 849, 136 S. Ct. 102, 193 L. Ed. 2d 85, 2015 U.S. LEXIS 5109.

October 5, 2015. Petition for writ of certiorari to the United States Court of Appeals for the Ninth Circuit denied.

Same case below, 602 Fed. Appx. 363.

No. 14-10134. Julian Nevarez-Blanco, Petitioner v. United States.

577 U.S. 849, 136 S. Ct. 103, 193 L. Ed. 2d 86, 2015 U.S. LEXIS 5401.

October 5, 2015. Petition for writ of certiorari to the United States Court of Appeals for the Fifth Circuit denied.

Same case below, 595 Fed. Appx. 447.

No. 14-10135. Samuel Yeboah Duku, Petitioner v. Loretta E. Lynch, Attorney General.

577 U.S. 849, 136 S. Ct. 103, 193 L. Ed. 2d 86, 2015 U.S. LEXIS 5023.

October 5, 2015. Petition for writ of certiorari to the United States Court of Appeals for the Fourth Circuit denied.

Same case below, 589 Fed. Appx. 158.

No. 14-10136. Darius Styles, Petitioner v. United States.

577 U.S. 849, 136 S. Ct. 103, 193 L. Ed. 2d 86, 2015 U.S. LEXIS 4987.

October 5, 2015. Petition for writ of certiorari to the District of Columbia Court of Appeals denied.

Same case below, 100 A.3d 170.

No. 14-10139. Alexander Aviles-Santiago, Petitioner v. United States.

577 U.S. 849, 136 S. Ct. 103, 193 L. Ed. 2d 86, 2015 U.S. LEXIS 5446.

October 5, 2015. Petition for writ of certiorari to the United States Court of Appeals for the First Circuit denied.

No. 14-10140. Lawrence Williams, Petitioner v. Nathan B. Cain, II, Warden.

577 U.S. 849, 136 S. Ct. 105, 193 L. Ed. 2d 86, 2015 U.S. LEXIS 4963.

October 5, 2015. Petition for writ of certiorari to the United States Court of Appeals for the Fifth Circuit denied.

No. 14-10141. Merlene Jordan, Petitioner v. Carolyn W. Colvin, Acting Commissioner of Social Security.

577 U.S. 849, 136 S. Ct. 105, 193 L. Ed. 2d 86, 2015 U.S. LEXIS 5052, reh den 577 U.S. 1094, 136 S. Ct. 880, 193 L. Ed. 2d 772, 2016 U.S. LEXIS 485.

October 5, 2015. Petition for writ of certiorari to the United States Court of Appeals for the Third Circuit denied.

Same case below, 577 Fed. Appx. 107.

No. 14-10144. Ljubica Rajkovic, Petitioner v. Federal Bureau of Investigation, et al.

577 U.S. 849, 136 S. Ct. 105, 193 L. Ed. 2d 86, 2015 U.S. LEXIS 4989, reh den 577 U.S. 1022, 136 S. Ct. 575, 193 L. Ed. 2d 456, 2015 U.S. LEXIS 7399.

October 5, 2015. Petition for writ of certiorari to the United States Court of Appeals for the District of Columbia Circuit denied.

No. 14-10146. John Boyd Bowring, Petitioner v. Rick Raemisch, Executive Director, Colorado Department of Corrections.

577 U.S. 849, 136 S. Ct. 105, 193 L. Ed. 2d 86, 2015 U.S. LEXIS 5497.

October 5, 2015. Petition for writ of certiorari to the Supreme Court of Colorado denied.

No. 14-10147. Amilcar C. Butler, Petitioner v. United States.

577 U.S. 849, 136 S. Ct. 106, 193 L. Ed. 2d 87, 2015 U.S. LEXIS 5162.

October 5, 2015. Petition for writ of certiorari to the United States Court of Appeals for the Sixth Circuit denied.

No. 14-10148. Henry Benjamin, Petitioner v. Julie L. Jones, Secretary, Florida Department of Corrections.

577 U.S. 850, 136 S. Ct. 106, 193 L. Ed. 2d 87, 2015 U.S. LEXIS 5437.

October 5, 2015. Petition for writ of certiorari to the United States Court of Appeals for the Eleventh Circuit denied.

No. 14-10149. Helen Burns, Petitioner v. James Rogers, Warden.

577 U.S. 850, 136 S. Ct. 106, 193 L. Ed. 2d 87, 2015 U.S. LEXIS 4973.

October 5, 2015. Petition for writ of certiorari to the United States Court of Appeals for the Fifth Circuit denied.

No. 14-10151. Clarence T. Paige, Petitioner v. United States.

577 U.S. 850, 136 S. Ct. 106, 193 L. Ed. 2d 87, 2015 U.S. LEXIS 5003.

October 5, 2015. Petition for writ of certiorari to the District of Columbia Court of Appeals denied.

No. 14-10152. Jose Isidro Rivera-Dominguez, Petitioner v. United States.

577 U.S. 850, 136 S. Ct. 106, 193 L. Ed. 2d 87, 2015 U.S. LEXIS 5019.

October 5, 2015. Petition for writ of certiorari to the United States Court of Appeals for the Fifth Circuit denied.

Same case below, 595 Fed. Appx. 452.

No. 14-10153. Jimmy Velez, Petitioner v. Julie L. Jones, Secretary, Florida Department of Corrections.

577 U.S. 850, 136 S. Ct. 106, 193 L. Ed. 2d 87, 2015 U.S. LEXIS 4972.

October 5, 2015. Petition for writ of certiorari to the United States Court of Appeals for the Eleventh Circuit denied.

No. 14-10156. Bobby Bruce White, Petitioner v. Ray Roberts, Secretary, Kansas Department of Corrections, et al.

577 U.S. 850, 136 S. Ct. 107, 193 L. Ed. 2d 87, 2015 U.S. LEXIS 5308.

October 5, 2015. Petition for writ of certiorari to the United States Court of Appeals for the Tenth Circuit denied.

Same case below, 605 Fed. Appx. 731.

No. 14-10158. Deon Archie Powell, Petitioner v. United States.

577 U.S. 850, 136 S. Ct. 107, 193 L. Ed. 2d 87, 2015 U.S. LEXIS 5284.

October 5, 2015. Petition for writ of certiorari to the United States Court of Appeals for the Sixth Circuit denied.

Same case below, 603 Fed. Appx. 475.

Same case below, 595 Fed. Appx. 446.

No. 14-10159. Curtis Wayne Monroe, Petitioner v. District of Columbia, et al.

577 U.S. 850, 136 S. Ct. 107, 193 L. Ed. 2d 88, 2015 U.S. LEXIS 4967.

October 5, 2015. Petition for writ of certiorari to the District of Columbia Court of Appeals denied.

No. 14-10161. Arthur N. Ramirez, Petitioner v. Greg Lewis, Warden.

577 U.S. 850, 136 S. Ct. 108, 193 L. Ed. 2d 88, 2015 U.S. LEXIS 5122.

October 5, 2015. Petition for writ of certiorari to the United States Court of Appeals for the Ninth Circuit denied.

No. 14-10163. Robert Allen Byrd, Petitioner v. William Stephens, Director, Texas Department of Criminal Justice, Correctional Institutions Division.

577 U.S. 850, 136 S. Ct. 108, 193 L. Ed. 2d 88, 2015 U.S. LEXIS 5468.

October 5, 2015. Petition for writ of certiorari to the United States Court of Appeals for the Fifth Circuit denied.

No. 14-10164. Mauricio Garfias-Chaires, Petitioner v. United States.

577 U.S. 850, 136 S. Ct. 108, 193 L. Ed. 2d 88, 2015 U.S. LEXIS 5017.

October 5, 2015. Petition for writ of certiorari to the United States Court of Appeals for the Fifth Circuit denied.

No. 14-10165. Dino Wayne Kyzar, Petitioner v. Charles L. Ryan, Director, Arizona Department of Corrections, et al.

577 U.S. 850, 136 S. Ct. 108, 193 L. Ed. 2d 88, 2015 U.S. LEXIS 5277.

October 5, 2015. Petition for writ of certiorari to the United States Court of Appeals for the Ninth Circuit denied.

Same case below, 780 F.3d 940.

No. 14-10166. Samuel Saldana, Petitioner v. Clark E. Ducart, Warden.

577 U.S. 850, 136 S. Ct. 108, 193 L. Ed. 2d 88, 2015 U.S. LEXIS 5034.

October 5, 2015. Petition for writ of certiorari to the United States Court of Appeals for the Ninth Circuit denied.

Same case below, 597 Fed. Appx. 436.

No. 14-10167. Larry Cleveland, Petitioner v. California.

577 U.S. 850, 136 S. Ct. 109, 193 L. Ed. 2d 88, 2015 U.S. LEXIS 4988.

October 5, 2015. Petition for writ of certiorari to the Supreme Court of California denied.

No. 14-10168. Troy Stewart, Petitioner v. Morgan State University, et al.

577 U.S. 850, 136 S. Ct. 109, 193 L. Ed. 2d 88, 2015 U.S. LEXIS 5099.

October 5, 2015. Petition for writ of certiorari to the United States Court of Appeals for the Fourth Circuit denied.

MEMORANDUM CASES

Same case below, 606 Fed. Appx. 48.

No. 14-10169. **Herman L. Dixon, Petitioner v. Ronald O. Carlson, et al.**

577 U.S. 851, 136 S. Ct. 109, 193 L. Ed. 2d 89, 2015 U.S. LEXIS 5453.

October 5, 2015. Petition for writ of certiorari to the Supreme Court of Florida denied.

Same case below, 163 So. 3d 508.

No. 14-10170. **Thomas Coleman, Petitioner v. United States.**

577 U.S. 851, 136 S. Ct. 109, 193 L. Ed. 2d 89, 2015 U.S. LEXIS 5039.

October 5, 2015. Petition for writ of certiorari to the United States Court of Appeals for the Eighth Circuit denied.

No. 14-10171. **Michael Lugo, Petitioner v. Thomas LaValley, Superintendent, Clinton Correctional Facility, et al.**

577 U.S. 851, 136 S. Ct. 110, 193 L. Ed. 2d 89, 2015 U.S. LEXIS 5426.

October 5, 2015. Petition for writ of certiorari to the United States Court of Appeals for the Second Circuit denied.

Same case below, 601 Fed. Appx. 46.

No. 14-10172. **Oshay Johnson, Petitioner v. Robert W. Fox, Warden.**

577 U.S. 851, 136 S. Ct. 110, 193 L. Ed. 2d 89, 2015 U.S. LEXIS 5144.

October 5, 2015. Petition for writ of certiorari to the United States Court of Appeals for the Ninth Circuit denied.

Same case below, 591 Fed. Appx. 629.

No. 14-10173. **Michael Kelley, Petitioner v. United States.**

577 U.S. 851, 136 S. Ct. 110, 193 L. Ed. 2d 89, 2015 U.S. LEXIS 4978.

October 5, 2015. Petition for writ of certiorari to the United States Court of Appeals for the Eighth Circuit denied.

Same case below, 596 Fed. Appx. 529.

No. 14-10174. **Gerald Lee Latta, Jr., Petitioner v. Michigan.**

577 U.S. 851, 136 S. Ct. 110, 193 L. Ed. 2d 89, 2015 U.S. LEXIS 4974.

October 5, 2015. Petition for writ of certiorari to the Court of Appeals of Michigan denied.

No. 14-10175. **Harel Zahavi, Petitioner v. Nevada.**

577 U.S. 851, 136 S. Ct. 110, 193 L. Ed. 2d 89, 2015 U.S. LEXIS 5430.

October 5, 2015. Petition for writ of certiorari to the Supreme Court of Nevada denied.

Same case below, 131 Nev. 51, 343 P.3d 595.

No. 14-10176. **Anthony Cannon, Petitioner v. United States.**

577 U.S. 851, 136 S. Ct. 112, 193 L. Ed. 2d 89, 2015 U.S. LEXIS 5339.

October 5, 2015. Petition for writ of certiorari to the United States Court of Appeals for the Fourth Circuit denied.

Same case below, 780 F.3d 260.

Same case below, 592 Fed. Appx. 579.

No. 14-10177. Maureen Clark, Petitioner v. United States.

577 U.S. 851, 136 S. Ct. 112, 193 L. Ed. 2d 90, 2015 U.S. LEXIS 5790.

October 5, 2015. Petition for writ of certiorari to the United States Court of Appeals for the Second Circuit denied.

Same case below, 593 Fed. Appx. 53.

No. 14-10179. Mark Tompkins, Petitioner v. Robert Chetirkin, Administrator, Northern State Prison.

577 U.S. 851, 136 S. Ct. 298, 193 L. Ed. 2d 90, 2015 U.S. LEXIS 5859.

October 5, 2015. Petition for writ of certiorari to the United States Court of Appeals for the Third Circuit denied.

No. 14-10181. Joan T. Kloth-Zanard, Petitioner v. Amridge University, fka Southern Christian University & Regions University.

577 U.S. 851, 136 S. Ct. 112, 193 L. Ed. 2d 90, 2015 U.S. LEXIS 6119.

October 5, 2015. Petition for writ of certiorari to the United States Court of Appeals for the Second Circuit denied.

No. 14-10182. Robert Morris, Petitioner v. Christopher Long.

577 U.S. 851, 136 S. Ct. 112, 193 L. Ed. 2d 90, 2015 U.S. LEXIS 6152.

October 5, 2015. Petition for writ of certiorari to the United States Court of Appeals for the Ninth Circuit denied.

No. 14-10187. Feleicia Cook, Petitioner v. Beattie B. Ashmore.

577 U.S. 851, 136 S. Ct. 113, 193 L. Ed. 2d 90, 2015 U.S. LEXIS 5764.

October 5, 2015. Petition for writ of certiorari to the United States Court of Appeals for the Fourth Circuit denied.

Same case below, 585 Fed. Appx. 189.

No. 14-10188. Randy Allen Hentges, Petitioner v. United States.

577 U.S. 851, 136 S. Ct. 113, 193 L. Ed. 2d 90, 2015 U.S. LEXIS 6017.

October 5, 2015. Petition for writ of certiorari to the United States Court of Appeals for the Eighth Circuit denied.

Same case below, 790 F.3d 848.

No. 14-10190. Stanley Ray Winston, aka Stanley Wilson, aka Rashaad Winston, Petitioner v. United States.

577 U.S. 851, 136 S. Ct. 113, 193 L. Ed. 2d 90, 2015 U.S. LEXIS 5826.

October 5, 2015. Petition for writ of certiorari to the United States Court of Appeals for the Fourth Circuit denied.

Same case below, 780 F.3d 260.

No. 14-10191. Jeffrey S. Merimee, Petitioner v. United States.

577 U.S. 852, 136 S. Ct. 113, 193 L. Ed. 2d 90, 2015 U.S. LEXIS 5746.

October 5, 2015. Petition for writ of certiorari to the United States Court of Appeals for the Sixth Circuit denied.

Same case below, 106 A.3d 152.

No. 14-10193. Christopher Amos, Petitioner v. United States.

577 U.S. 852, 136 S. Ct. 114, 193 L. Ed. 2d 91, 2015 U.S. LEXIS 5966.

October 5, 2015. Petition for writ of certiorari to the United States Court of Appeals for the Sixth Circuit denied.

Same case below, 604 Fed. Appx. 418.

No. 14-10194. Randy E. Anderson, Petitioner v. First Judicial District Court of Nevada, County of Carson City, et al.

577 U.S. 852, 136 S. Ct. 114, 193 L. Ed. 2d 91, 2015 U.S. LEXIS 5935.

October 5, 2015. Petition for writ of certiorari to the Supreme Court of Nevada denied.

Same case below, 131 Nev. 1248.

No. 14-10195. Harold Blick, Petitioner v. Deutsche Bank National Trust Company.

577 U.S. 852, 136 S. Ct. 114, 193 L. Ed. 2d 91, 2015 U.S. LEXIS 6014, reh den 577 U.S. 1022, 136 S. Ct. 575, 193 L. Ed. 2d 457, 2015 U.S. LEXIS 7413.

October 5, 2015. Petition for writ of certiorari to the United States Court of Appeals for the Fourth Circuit denied.

Same case below, 591 Fed. Appx. 231.

No. 14-10196. Martha Fenchak Bell, Petitioner v. Pennsylvania.

577 U.S. 852, 136 S. Ct. 114, 193 L. Ed. 2d 91, 2015 U.S. LEXIS 5792.

October 5, 2015. Petition for writ of certiorari to the Superior Court of Pennsylvania, Pittsburgh Office, denied.

No. 14-10197. Halston M. Smith, Petitioner v. United States.

577 U.S. 852, 136 S. Ct. 114, 193 L. Ed. 2d 91, 2015 U.S. LEXIS 5620.

October 5, 2015. Petition for writ of certiorari to the United States Court of Appeals for the Fifth Circuit denied.

Same case below, 609 Fed. Appx. 180.

No. 14-10198. Steven Garrett Stoddard, Petitioner v. Julie L. Jones, Secretary, Florida Department of Corrections, et al.

577 U.S. 852, 136 S. Ct. 114, 193 L. Ed. 2d 91, 2015 U.S. LEXIS 5886.

October 5, 2015. Petition for writ of certiorari to the United States Court of Appeals for the Eleventh Circuit denied.

Same case below, 600 Fed. Appx. 696.

No. 14-10199. Niegra Egerton, Petitioner v. Nancy A. Giroux, Superintendent, State Correctional Institution at Muncy, et al.

577 U.S. 852, 136 S. Ct. 115, 193 L. Ed. 2d 91, 2015 U.S. LEXIS 5873.

October 5, 2015. Petition for writ of certiorari to the United States Court of Appeals for the Third Circuit denied.

No. 14-10200. Tony Joyce, Petitioner v. Alabama.

577 U.S. 852, 136 S. Ct. 115, 193 L. Ed. 2d 91, 2015 U.S. LEXIS 6035.

October 5, 2015. Petition for writ of certiorari to the Court of Criminal Appeals of Alabama denied.

Same case below, 605 Fed. Appx. 147.

No. 14-10201. Sherman B. Jenkins, Petitioner v. Harold W. Clarke, Director, Virginia Department of Corrections.

577 U.S. 852, 136 S. Ct. 115, 193 L. Ed. 2d 92, 2015 U.S. LEXIS 5787.

October 5, 2015. Petition for writ of certiorari to the United States Court of Appeals for the Fourth Circuit denied.

Same case below, 589 Fed. Appx. 93.

No. 14-10202. Darnell Harris, Petitioner v. United States.

577 U.S. 852, 136 S. Ct. 115, 193 L. Ed. 2d 92, 2015 U.S. LEXIS 6195.

October 5, 2015. Petition for writ of certiorari to the United States Court of Appeals for the Sixth Circuit denied.

Same case below, 617 Fed. Appx. 388.

No. 14-10203. Garner Howard Chestang, aka Howard Chestang, Petitioner v. United States.

577 U.S. 852, 136 S. Ct. 115, 193 L. Ed. 2d 92, 2015 U.S. LEXIS 5761.

October 5, 2015. Petition for writ of certiorari to the United States Court of Appeals for the Eleventh Circuit denied.

No. 14-10204. Mario Clotinho Gomes, Petitioner v. United States.

577 U.S. 852, 136 S. Ct. 115, 193 L. Ed. 2d 92, 2015 U.S. LEXIS 5911.

October 5, 2015. Petition for writ of certiorari to the United States Court of Appeals for the Fourth Circuit denied.

No. 14-10205. Ramell Sturdivant, Petitioner v. Illinois.

577 U.S. 852, 136 S. Ct. 116, 193 L. Ed. 2d 92, 2015 U.S. LEXIS 5805.

October 5, 2015. Petition for writ of certiorari to the Appellate Court of Illinois, First District, denied.

No. 14-10206. Lawrence E. Schwiger, Petitioner v. Jack Palmer, et al.

577 U.S. 853, 136 S. Ct. 116, 193 L. Ed. 2d 92, 2015 U.S. LEXIS 6083.

October 5, 2015. Petition for writ of certiorari to the United States Court of Appeals for the Ninth Circuit denied.

Same case below, 585 Fed. Appx. 488.

No. 14-10207. Carl Earl Hopkins, Petitioner v. United States.

577 U.S. 853, 136 S. Ct. 117, 193 L. Ed. 2d 92, 2015 U.S. LEXIS 5925.

October 5, 2015. Petition for writ of certiorari to the United States Court of Appeals for the Fourth Circuit denied.

Same case below, 583 Fed. Appx. 180.

No. 14-10208. Ralph Curry, Petitioner v. United States.

577 U.S. 853, 136 S. Ct. 117, 193 L. Ed. 2d 92, 2015 U.S. LEXIS 5651.

October 5, 2015. Petition for writ of certiorari to the United States Court of Appeals for the Eleventh Circuit denied.

No. 14-10211. Darryl Paul Sylvester, Petitioner v. Louisiana.

577 U.S. 853, 136 S. Ct. 117, 193 L. Ed. 2d 93, 2015 U.S. LEXIS 5741.

October 5, 2015. Petition for writ of certiorari to the Court of Appeal of Louisiana, First Circuit, denied.

No. 14-10212. Angilito Sosa, Petitioner v. United States.

577 U.S. 853, 136 S. Ct. 118, 193 L. Ed. 2d 93, 2015 U.S. LEXIS 6140.

October 5, 2015. Petition for writ of certiorari to the United States Court of Appeals for the Sixth Circuit denied.

No. 14-10213. Jeremy Bayne Lynch, Petitioner v. United States.

577 U.S. 853, 136 S. Ct. 118, 193 L. Ed. 2d 93, 2015 U.S. LEXIS 5900.

October 5, 2015. Petition for writ of certiorari to the United States Court of Appeals for the Eleventh Circuit denied.

Same case below, 595 Fed. Appx. 943.

No. 14-10214. Timothy Perri, Petitioner v. Richard M. Gerry, Warden.

577 U.S. 853, 136 S. Ct. 118, 193 L. Ed. 2d 93, 2015 U.S. LEXIS 5798.

October 5, 2015. Petition for writ of certiorari to the United States Court of Appeals for the First Circuit denied.

No. 14-10215. Lisa Meriweather, Petitioner v. Wells Fargo Bank, N.A., et al.

577 U.S. 853, 136 S. Ct. 118, 193 L. Ed. 2d 93, 2015 U.S. LEXIS 6065, reh den 577 U.S. 1094, 136 S. Ct. 881, 193 L. Ed. 2d 772, 2016 U.S. LEXIS 564.

October 5, 2015. Petition for writ of certiorari to the Court of Appeal of California, Second Appellate District, Division Five, denied.

No. 14-10216. Francis Aponte, Petitioner v. United States.

577 U.S. 853, 136 S. Ct. 118, 193 L. Ed. 2d 93, 2015 U.S. LEXIS 5672.

October 5, 2015. Petition for writ of certiorari to the United States Court of Appeals for the Third Circuit denied.

Same case below, 622 Fed. Appx. 118.

No. 14-10217. Thomas Boone, Petitioner v. Thomas Griffin, Superintendent, Green Haven Correctional Facility.

577 U.S. 853, 136 S. Ct. 118, 193 L. Ed. 2d 93, 2015 U.S. LEXIS 6058.

October 5, 2015. Petition for writ of certiorari to the United States Court of Appeals for the Second Circuit denied.

No. 14-10218. Nancy Ann Seaman, Petitioner v. Michigan.

577 U.S. 853, 136 S. Ct. 119, 193 L. Ed. 2d 93, 2015 U.S. LEXIS 5717, reh den 577 U.S. 1023, 136 S. Ct. 575, 193 L. Ed. 2d 457, 2015 U.S. LEXIS 7409.

October 5, 2015. Petition for writ of certiorari to the Court of Appeals of Michigan denied.

No. 14-10219. Marcos Rojas, Petitioner v. United States.

577 U.S. 853, 136 S. Ct. 119, 193 L. Ed. 2d 94, 2015 U.S. LEXIS 5815.

October 5, 2015. Petition for writ of certiorari to the United States Court of Appeals for the First Circuit denied.

Same case below, 780 F.3d 68.

No. 14-10220. William Adrian Roberts, Petitioner v. Texas.

577 U.S. 853, 136 S. Ct. 119, 193 L. Ed. 2d 94, 2015 U.S. LEXIS 5755.

October 5, 2015. Petition for writ of certiorari to the Court of Appeals of Texas, Second District, denied.

Same case below, 444 S.W.3d 770.

No. 14-10221. Felipe de Jesus Chavoya, Petitioner v. United States.

577 U.S. 853, 136 S. Ct. 120, 193 L. Ed. 2d 94, 2015 U.S. LEXIS 5657.

October 5, 2015. Petition for writ of certiorari to the United States Court of Appeals for the Ninth Circuit denied.

Same case below, 598 Fed. Appx. 560.

No. 14-10222. Adam Daniel Shepherd, Petitioner v. Julie L. Jones, Secretary, Florida Department of Corrections, et al.

577 U.S. 853, 136 S. Ct. 120, 193 L. Ed. 2d 94, 2015 U.S. LEXIS 6156.

October 5, 2015. Petition for writ of certiorari to the United States Court of Appeals for the Eleventh Circuit denied.

No. 14-10223. Francisco Jimenez-Arzate, Petitioner v. United States.

577 U.S. 854, 136 S. Ct. 120, 193 L. Ed. 2d 94, 2015 U.S. LEXIS 5856.

October 5, 2015. Petition for writ of certiorari to the United States Court of Appeals for the Ninth Circuit denied.

Same case below, 781 F.3d 1062.

No. 14-10224. Richard J. Vieira, Petitioner v. Wesley A. Van Winkle.

577 U.S. 854, 136 S. Ct. 120, 193 L. Ed. 2d 94, 2015 U.S. LEXIS 5671, reh den 577 U.S. 1023, 136 S. Ct. 575, 193 L. Ed. 2d 457, 2015 U.S. LEXIS 7454.

October 5, 2015. Petition for writ of certiorari to the United States Court of Appeals for the Ninth Circuit denied.

No. 14-10225. Devonne Lamar Moore, Petitioner v. United States.

577 U.S. 854, 136 S. Ct. 121, 193 L. Ed. 2d 94, 2015 U.S. LEXIS 5736.

October 5, 2015. Petition for writ of certiorari to the United States Court of Appeals for the Fourth Circuit denied.

No. 14-10226. Michael Mejia, Petitioner v. Randy Pfister, Warden.

577 U.S. 854, 136 S. Ct. 121, 193 L. Ed. 2d 94, 2015 U.S. LEXIS 6021.

October 5, 2015. Petition for writ of certiorari to the United States Court of Appeals for the Seventh Circuit denied.

Same case below, 604 Fed. Appx. 424.

No. 14-10228. Kenneth Vu, Petitioner v. United States.

577 U.S. 854, 136 S. Ct. 121, 193 L. Ed. 2d 95, 2015 U.S. LEXIS 6213.

October 5, 2015. Petition for writ of certiorari to the United States Court of Appeals for the Sixth Circuit denied.

Same case below, 622 Fed. Appx. 481.

No. 14-10229. John C. Wells, III, Petitioner v. Tennessee Board of Probation and Parole.

577 U.S. 854, 136 S. Ct. 121, 193 L. Ed. 2d 95, 2015 U.S. LEXIS 5700.

October 5, 2015. Petition for writ of certiorari to the Court of Appeals of Tennessee, Middle Division, denied.

No. 14-10230. Ronnie Roy Vera, Petitioner v. Arizona.

577 U.S. 854, 136 S. Ct. 121, 193 L. Ed. 2d 95, 2015 U.S. LEXIS 5656.

October 5, 2015. Petition for writ of certiorari to the Court of Appeals of Arizona, Division Two, denied.

Same case below, 235 Ariz. 571, 334 P.3d 754.

No. 14-10231. Pierre O. Colquitt, Petitioner v. United States.

577 U.S. 854, 136 S. Ct. 121, 193 L. Ed. 2d 95, 2015 U.S. LEXIS 5720.

October 5, 2015. Petition for writ of certiorari to the United States Court of Appeals for the Sixth Circuit denied.

No. 14-10233. Donnell Delgado, Jr., Petitioner v. United States.

577 U.S. 854, 136 S. Ct. 122, 193 L. Ed. 2d 95, 2015 U.S. LEXIS 6131.

October 5, 2015. Petition for writ of certiorari to the United States Court of Appeals for the Ninth Circuit denied.

Same case below, 592 Fed. Appx. 602.

No. 14-10235. Cedrik Piert, Petitioner v. Texas.

577 U.S. 854, 136 S. Ct. 122, 193 L. Ed. 2d 95, 2015 U.S. LEXIS 5686.

October 5, 2015. Petition for writ of certiorari to the Court of Appeals of Texas, Second District, denied.

No. 14-10236. Frank Russell McCoy, Petitioner v. United States.

577 U.S. 854, 136 S. Ct. 122, 193 L. Ed. 2d 95, 2015 U.S. LEXIS 5939.

October 5, 2015. Petition for writ of certiorari to the United States Court of Appeals for the Eleventh Circuit denied.

Same case below, 602 Fed. Appx. 501.

No. 14-10237. Douglas McClain, Jr., Petitioner v. United States.

577 U.S. 854, 136 S. Ct. 122, 193 L. Ed. 2d 95, 2015 U.S. LEXIS 5689.

October 5, 2015. Petition for writ of certiorari to the United States Court of Appeals for the Ninth Circuit denied.

Same case below, 593 Fed. Appx. 697.

Same case below, 603 Fed. Appx. 647.

No. 14-10238. Arturo Oviedo-Perez, Petitioner v. United States.

577 U.S. 854, 136 S. Ct. 122, 193 L. Ed. 2d 96, 2015 U.S. LEXIS 6078.

October 5, 2015. Petition for writ of certiorari to the United States Court of Appeals for the Fifth Circuit denied.

Same case below, 604 Fed. Appx. 331.

No. 14-10239. James Brian Rivers, Petitioner v. United States.

577 U.S. 854, 136 S. Ct. 123, 193 L. Ed. 2d 96, 2015 U.S. LEXIS 5987.

October 5, 2015. Petition for writ of certiorari to the United States Court of Appeals for the Fifth Circuit denied.

Same case below, 598 Fed. Appx. 291.

No. 14-10240. Emily Margaret Perera, Petitioner v. Georgia.

577 U.S. 854, 136 S. Ct. 123, 193 L. Ed. 2d 96, 2015 U.S. LEXIS 5917.

October 5, 2015. Petition for writ of certiorari to the Supreme Court of Georgia denied.

Same case below, 295 Ga. 880, 763 S.E.2d 687.

No. 14-10241. Spiros Romensas, Petitioner v. United States.

577 U.S. 854, 136 S. Ct. 123, 193 L. Ed. 2d 96, 2015 U.S. LEXIS 5690.

October 5, 2015. Petition for writ of certiorari to the United States Court of Appeals for the Fifth Circuit denied.

No. 14-10242. Stephen Bennett, Petitioner v. Suzanne M. Peery, Acting Warden.

577 U.S. 855, 136 S. Ct. 123, 193 L. Ed. 2d 96, 2015 U.S. LEXIS 5789.

October 5, 2015. Petition for writ of certiorari to the United States Court of Appeals for the Ninth Circuit denied.

Same case below, 598 Fed. Appx. 526.

No. 14-10243. Brandon Orlando Brown, Petitioner v. United States.

577 U.S. 855, 136 S. Ct. 123, 193 L. Ed. 2d 96, 2015 U.S. LEXIS 5760.

October 5, 2015. Petition for writ of certiorari to the United States Court of Appeals for the Fourth Circuit denied.

Same case below, 597 Fed. Appx. 203.

No. 14-10244. Daniel Blow, Petitioner v. United States.

577 U.S. 855, 136 S. Ct. 123, 193 L. Ed. 2d 96, 2015 U.S. LEXIS 6030.

October 5, 2015. Petition for writ of certiorari to the United States Court of Appeals for the Ninth Circuit denied.

Same case below, 597 Fed. Appx. 420.

No. 14-10245. Yoni Alberto Barahona-Sales, Petitioner v. United States.

577 U.S. 855, 136 S. Ct. 124, 193 L. Ed. 2d 96, 2015 U.S. LEXIS 6013.

October 5, 2015. Petition for writ of certiorari to the United States Court of Appeals for the Sixth Circuit denied.

No. 14-10248. James Joseph Platte, Jr., Petitioner v. Michigan.

577 U.S. 855, 136 S. Ct. 124, 193 L. Ed. 2d 97, 2015 U.S. LEXIS 5847.

October 5, 2015. Petition for writ of certiorari to the Court of Appeals of Michigan denied.

No. 14-10249. Antonio Moore, Petitioner v. David Frazier.

577 U.S. 855, 136 S. Ct. 124, 193 L. Ed. 2d 97, 2015 U.S. LEXIS 6139.

October 5, 2015. Petition for writ of certiorari to the United States Court of Appeals for the Eleventh Circuit denied.

Same case below, 605 Fed. Appx. 863.

No. 14-10250. Augustin Miramontes-Muniz, Petitioner v. United States.

577 U.S. 855, 136 S. Ct. 124, 193 L. Ed. 2d 97, 2015 U.S. LEXIS 5896.

October 5, 2015. Petition for writ of certiorari to the United States Court of Appeals for the Fifth Circuit denied.

No. 14-10251. Ricardo Luera Miller, Petitioner v. United States.

577 U.S. 855, 136 S. Ct. 124, 193 L. Ed. 2d 97, 2015 U.S. LEXIS 6049.

October 5, 2015. Petition for writ of certiorari to the United States Court of Appeals for the Fifth Circuit denied.

Same case below, 604 Fed. Appx. 333.

No. 14-10252. Monique Sinkfield, Petitioner v. State Farm Insurance.

577 U.S. 855, 136 S. Ct. 124, 193 L. Ed. 2d 97, 2015 U.S. LEXIS 6036.

October 5, 2015. Petition for writ of certiorari to the United States Court of Appeals for the Sixth Circuit denied.

Same case below, 580 Fed. Appx. 323.

No. 14-10254. Randy Lavern Spencer, Petitioner v. Young Kwon, et al.

577 U.S. 855, 136 S. Ct. 125, 193 L. Ed. 2d 97, 2015 U.S. LEXIS 5907.

October 5, 2015. Petition for writ of certiorari to the United States Court of Appeals for the Eleventh Circuit denied.

No. 14-10255. Courtney Donovan Wright, Petitioner v. Julie L. Jones, Secretary, Florida Department of Corrections, et al.

577 U.S. 855, 136 S. Ct. 125, 193 L. Ed. 2d 97, 2015 U.S. LEXIS 5756.

October 5, 2015. Petition for writ of certiorari to the United States Court of Appeals for the Eleventh Circuit denied.

No. 14-10256. Jeffrey R. Weinhaus, Petitioner v. Missouri.

577 U.S. 855, 136 S. Ct. 125, 193 L. Ed. 2d 97, 2015 U.S. LEXIS 5637, reh den 577 U.S. 1094, 136 S. Ct. 881, 193 L. Ed. 2d 772, 2016 U.S. LEXIS 525.

October 5, 2015. Petition for writ of certiorari to the Court of Appeals of Missouri, Eastern District, denied.

Same case below, 459 S.W.3d 916.

Same case below, 604 Fed. Appx. 702.

No. 14-10257. Thomas Caine White, Petitioner v. Ohio.

577 U.S. 855, 136 S. Ct. 125, 193 L. Ed. 2d 98, 2015 U.S. LEXIS 5664.

October 5, 2015. Petition for writ of certiorari to the Supreme Court of Ohio denied.

Same case below, 142 Ohio St. 3d 277, 29 N.E.3d 939.

No. 14-10258. Linda Sue Cheek, Petitioner v. United States.

577 U.S. 855, 136 S. Ct. 125, 193 L. Ed. 2d 98, 2015 U.S. LEXIS 6091, reh den 577 U.S. 1044, 136 S. Ct. 609, 193 L. Ed. 2d 489, 2015 U.S. LEXIS 7692.

October 5, 2015. Petition for writ of certiorari to the United States Court of Appeals for the Fourth Circuit denied.

Same case below, 592 Fed. Appx. 179.

No. 14-10259. Carline M. Curry, Petitioner v. City of Mansfield, Ohio, et al.

577 U.S. 855, 136 S. Ct. 126, 193 L. Ed. 2d 98, 2015 U.S. LEXIS 6224, reh den 577 U.S. 1023, 136 S. Ct. 575, 193 L. Ed. 2d 457, 2015 U.S. LEXIS 7410.

October 5, 2015. Petition for writ of certiorari to the United States Court of Appeals for the Sixth Circuit denied.

No. 14-10260. Jack Dowell, Petitioner v. United States.

577 U.S. 856, 136 S. Ct. 126, 193 L. Ed. 2d 98, 2015 U.S. LEXIS 6237.

October 5, 2015. Petition for writ of certiorari to the United States Court of Appeals for the Tenth Circuit denied.

No. 14-10261. Isaac Kelvin Allen, Petitioner v. Jorge L. Pastrana, Warden.

577 U.S. 856, 136 S. Ct. 126, 193 L. Ed. 2d 98, 2015 U.S. LEXIS 5626.

October 5, 2015. Petition for writ of certiorari to the United States Court of Appeals for the Eleventh Circuit denied.

Same case below, 603 Fed. Appx. 855.

No. 14-10262. Amilcar C. Butler, Petitioner v. United States.

577 U.S. 856, 136 S. Ct. 126, 193 L. Ed. 2d 98, 2015 U.S. LEXIS 5743.

October 5, 2015. Petition for writ of certiorari to the United States Court of Appeals for the Sixth Circuit denied.

No. 14-10263. Duryea Rogers, Petitioner v. United States.

577 U.S. 856, 136 S. Ct. 126, 193 L. Ed. 2d 98, 2015 U.S. LEXIS 5829.

October 5, 2015. Petition for writ of certiorari to the United States Court of Appeals for the Seventh Circuit denied.

Same case below, 777 F.3d 934.

No. 14-10264. James Oscar Douglas, Jr., Petitioner v. David W. Dunlap, Warden.

577 U.S. 856, 136 S. Ct. 126, 193 L. Ed. 2d 98, 2015 U.S. LEXIS 5667.

October 5, 2015. Petition for writ of certiorari to the United States Court of Appeals for the Fourth Circuit denied.

Same case below, 589 Fed. Appx. 106.

No. 14-10265. Rigoberto Cardenas-Borbon, Petitioner v. Sherry Burt, Warden.

577 U.S. 856, 136 S. Ct. 127, 193 L. Ed. 2d 99, 2015 U.S. LEXIS 5893.

October 5, 2015. Petition for writ of certiorari to the United States Court of Appeals for the Sixth Circuit denied.

No. 14-10266. Robert Drew, Petitioner v. United States.

577 U.S. 856, 136 S. Ct. 127, 193 L. Ed. 2d 99, 2015 U.S. LEXIS 5914.

October 5, 2015. Petition for writ of certiorari to the United States Court of Appeals for the Sixth Circuit denied.

Same case below, 610 Fed. Appx. 559.

No. 14-10267. Jorge Peter Cornell, aka King Jay, Ernesto Wilson, aka King Yayo, and Russell Lloyd Kilfoil, aka King Peaceful, aka Jonathan Hernandez, Petitioners v. United States.

577 U.S. 856, 136 S. Ct. 127, 193 L. Ed. 2d 99, 2015 U.S. LEXIS 5872.

October 5, 2015. Petition for writ of certiorari to the United States Court of Appeals for the Fourth Circuit denied.

Same case below, 780 F.3d 616.

No. 14-10268. Thomas Meadows, Petitioner v. Pennsylvania.

577 U.S. 856, 136 S. Ct. 127, 193 L. Ed. 2d 99, 2015 U.S. LEXIS 5969.

October 5, 2015. Petition for writ of certiorari to the Supreme Court of Pennsylvania, Eastern District, denied.

Same case below, 631 Pa. 282, 110 A.3d 992.

No. 14-10269. Stephen Cook, Petitioner v. United States.

577 U.S. 856, 136 S. Ct. 127, 193 L. Ed. 2d 99, 2015 U.S. LEXIS 6097.

October 5, 2015. Petition for writ of certiorari to the United States Court of Appeals for the Sixth Circuit denied.

Same case below, 607 Fed. Appx. 497.

No. 14-10270. Myron Saunders and Lamar Nero, Petitioners v. United States.

577 U.S. 856, 136 S. Ct. 127, 193 L. Ed. 2d 99, 2015 U.S. LEXIS 6079.

October 5, 2015. Petition for writ of certiorari to the United States Court of Appeals for the Fifth Circuit denied.

Same case below, 605 Fed. Appx. 285.

No. 14-10271. Christopher Ray-Bryan Rogers, Petitioner v. United States.

577 U.S. 856, 136 S. Ct. 128, 193 L. Ed. 2d 99, 2015 U.S. LEXIS 5794.

October 5, 2015. Petition for writ of certiorari to the United States Court of Appeals for the Fourth Circuit denied.

Same case below, 598 Fed. Appx. 188.

No. 14-10272. Joseph Crews, Petitioner v. United States.

577 U.S. 856, 136 S. Ct. 128, 193 L. Ed. 2d 100, 2015 U.S. LEXIS 5818.

October 5, 2015. Petition for writ of certiorari to the United States Court of Appeals for the Eleventh Circuit denied.

No. 14-10273. Adolfo Carrillo, Petitioner v. Michael Wenerowicz, Superintendent, State Correctional Institution at Graterford, et al.

577 U.S. 856, 136 S. Ct. 128, 193 L. Ed. 2d 100, 2015 U.S. LEXIS 6088.

October 5, 2015. Petition for writ of certiorari to the United States Court of Appeals for the Third Circuit denied.

No. 14-10274. Francisco Carrascal, Petitioner v. Deanna Avakian, et al.

577 U.S. 856, 136 S. Ct. 130, 193 L. Ed. 2d 100, 2015 U.S. LEXIS 5766.

October 5, 2015. Petition for writ of certiorari to the Court of Appeal of California, First Appellate District, Division Two, denied.

No. 14-10275. Donald Pate, Jr., Petitioner v. Michael Brelo, et al.

577 U.S. 856, 136 S. Ct. 131, 193 L. Ed. 2d 100, 2015 U.S. LEXIS 5983.

October 5, 2015. Petition for writ of certiorari to the United States Court of Appeals for the Sixth Circuit denied.

No. 14-10276. Philip J. Ostrander, Petitioner v. Harold W. Clarke, Director, Virginia Department of Corrections.

577 U.S. 857, 136 S. Ct. 298, 193 L. Ed. 2d 100, 2015 U.S. LEXIS 5924.

October 5, 2015. Petition for writ of certiorari to the United States Court of Appeals for the Fourth Circuit denied.

Same case below, 590 Fed. Appx. 242.

No. 14-10277. Tyler James Suong, Petitioner v. Jeffrey Beard, Secretary, California Department of Corrections and Rehabilitation.

577 U.S. 857, 136 S. Ct. 131, 193 L. Ed. 2d 100, 2015 U.S. LEXIS 5663.

October 5, 2015. Petition for writ of certiorari to the United States Court of Appeals for the Ninth Circuit denied.

No. 14-10278. Ernest Richardson, Jr., Petitioner v. South Carolina, et al.

577 U.S. 857, 136 S. Ct. 131, 193 L. Ed. 2d 100, 2015 U.S. LEXIS 5941.

October 5, 2015. Petition for writ of certiorari to the United States Court of Appeals for the Fourth Circuit denied.

Same case below, 584 Fed. Appx. 71.

No. 14-10279. Chon S. Un, Petitioner v. Deutsche Bank National Trust Company.

577 U.S. 857, 136 S. Ct. 131, 193 L. Ed. 2d 100, 2015 U.S. LEXIS 5691.

October 5, 2015. Petition for writ of certiorari to the Court of Appeals of Kansas denied.

Same case below, 324 P.3d 1153.

No. 14-10280. Rawson E. Watson, Petitioner v. United States.

577 U.S. 857, 136 S. Ct. 132, 193 L. Ed. 2d 101, 2015 U.S. LEXIS 5952.

October 5, 2015. Petition for writ of certiorari to the United States Court of Appeals for the Second Circuit denied.

Same case below, 593 Fed. Appx. 86.

No. 14-10281. Ray Turner, Petitioner v. Henry Steward, Warden.

577 U.S. 857, 136 S. Ct. 132, 193 L. Ed. 2d 101, 2015 U.S. LEXIS 5692, reh den 577 U.S. 1044, 136 S. Ct. 609, 193 L. Ed. 2d 489, 2015 U.S. LEXIS 7728.

October 5, 2015. Petition for writ of certiorari to the United States Court of Appeals for the Sixth Circuit denied.

No. 14-10282. Sebryne Walthall, aka Se'Bryne Walthall, Petitioner v. Gregory McQuiggen, Warden, et al.

577 U.S. 857, 136 S. Ct. 132, 193 L. Ed. 2d 101, 2015 U.S. LEXIS 5668, reh den 577 U.S. 1094, 136 S. Ct. 881, 193 L. Ed. 2d 772, 2016 U.S. LEXIS 507.

October 5, 2015. Petition for writ of certiorari to the United States Court of Appeals for the Sixth Circuit denied.

No. 14-10283. Daryl McEntyre, Petitioner v. Scott Semple, Commissioner, Connecticut Department of Correction.

577 U.S. 857, 136 S. Ct. 132, 193 L. Ed. 2d 101, 2015 U.S. LEXIS 5797.

October 5, 2015. Petition for writ of certiorari to the Appellate Court of Connecticut denied.

Same case below, 155 Conn. App. 283, 109 A.3d 928.

No. 14-10284. Paul David Storey, Petitioner v. William Stephens, Director, Texas Department of Criminal Justice, Correctional Institutions Division.

577 U.S. 857, 136 S. Ct. 132, 193 L. Ed. 2d 101, 2015 U.S. LEXIS 6106.

October 5, 2015. Petition for writ of certiorari to the United States Court of Appeals for the Fifth Circuit denied.

Same case below, 606 Fed. Appx. 192.

No. 14-10285. Antonio Nathaniel Speed, Petitioner v. United States.

577 U.S. 857, 136 S. Ct. 132, 193 L. Ed. 2d 101, 2015 U.S. LEXIS 5806, reh den 577 U.S. 1023, 136 S. Ct. 575, 193 L. Ed. 2d 457, 2015 U.S. LEXIS 7444.

October 5, 2015. Petition for writ of certiorari to the United States Court of Appeals for the Eighth Circuit denied.

Same case below, 587 Fed. Appx. 996.

No. 14-10286. Leonard Baugh, Petitioner v. United States.

577 U.S. 857, 136 S. Ct. 133, 193 L. Ed. 2d 101, 2015 U.S. LEXIS 5946.

October 5, 2015. Petition for writ of certiorari to the United States Court of Appeals for the Sixth Circuit denied.

Same case below, 605 Fed. Appx. 488.

No. 14-10287. Sylvester Rollins, Petitioner v. Louisiana Department of Corrections Officials.

577 U.S. 857, 136 S. Ct. 298, 193 L. Ed. 2d 102, 2015 U.S. LEXIS 5718, reh den 577 U.S. 1095, 136 S. Ct. 881, 193 L. Ed. 2d 772, 2016 U.S. LEXIS 556.

October 5, 2015. Petition for writ of certiorari to the United States Court of Appeals for the Fifth Circuit denied.

Same case below, 596 Fed. Appx. 329.

No. 14-10288. Charles Mobley, Petitioner v. United States.

577 U.S. 857, 136 S. Ct. 133, 193 L. Ed. 2d 102, 2015 U.S. LEXIS 6052.

October 5, 2015. Petition for writ of certiorari to the District of Columbia Court of Appeals denied.

Same case below, 101 A.3d 406.

No. 14-10289. Andrzej Madura, et ux., Petitioners v. Bank of America, N.A.

577 U.S. 858, 136 S. Ct. 133, 193 L. Ed. 2d 102, 2015 U.S. LEXIS 5953, reh den 577 U.S. 1023, 136 S. Ct. 575, 193 L. Ed. 2d 457, 2015 U.S. LEXIS 7375.

October 5, 2015. Petition for writ of certiorari to the United States Court of Appeals for the Eleventh Circuit denied.

Same case below, 593 Fed. Appx. 834.

No. 14-10290. James Clifford Spence, Petitioner v. Wallace Nelson, et al.

577 U.S. 858, 136 S. Ct. 133, 193 L. Ed. 2d 102, 2015 U.S. LEXIS 5967.

October 5, 2015. Petition for writ of certiorari to the United States Court of Appeals for the Fifth Circuit denied.

Same case below, 603 Fed. Appx. 250.

No. 14-10291. Willie Antoine Redd, Petitioner v. United States.

577 U.S. 858, 136 S. Ct. 133, 193 L. Ed. 2d 102, 2015 U.S. LEXIS 6123.

October 5, 2015. Petition for writ of certiorari to the United States Court of Appeals for the Ninth Circuit denied.

Same case below, 599 Fed. Appx. 324.

No. 14-10292. Alan Todd Brooks, Petitioner v. David Pierce, Warden.

577 U.S. 858, 136 S. Ct. 133, 193 L. Ed. 2d 102, 2015 U.S. LEXIS 5930.

October 5, 2015. Petition for writ of certiorari to the United States Court of Appeals for the Third Circuit denied.

No. 14-10293. Wesley Freeman Smallwood, Petitioner v. Texas.

577 U.S. 858, 136 S. Ct. 134, 193 L. Ed. 2d 102, 2015 U.S. LEXIS 5697.

October 5, 2015. Petition for writ of certiorari to the Court of Appeals of Texas, Eighth District, denied.

No. 14-10294. Felix Gabriel Castro-Davis, Petitioner v. United States.

577 U.S. 858, 136 S. Ct. 134, 193 L. Ed. 2d 102, 2015 U.S. LEXIS 5906.

October 5, 2015. Petition for writ of certiorari to the United States Court of Appeals for the First Circuit denied.

No. 14-10295. Nicandro Castaneda-Guardiola, Petitioner v. United States.

577 U.S. 858, 136 S. Ct. 134, 193 L. Ed. 2d 103, 2015 U.S. LEXIS 6047.

October 5, 2015. Petition for writ of certiorari to the United States Court of Appeals for the Ninth Circuit denied.

Same case below, 598 Fed. Appx. 501.

No. 14-10296. Yusuf Abdur Rahman, aka John Fitzgerald Presley, Petitioner v. United States.

577 U.S. 858, 136 S. Ct. 134, 193 L. Ed. 2d 103, 2015 U.S. LEXIS 5937.

October 5, 2015. Petition for writ of certiorari to the United States Court of Appeals for the Second Circuit denied.

No. 14-10297. John Ayanbadejo, Petitioner v. Jeh Johnson, Secretary of Homeland Security, et al.

577 U.S. 858, 136 S. Ct. 134, 193 L. Ed. 2d 103, 2015 U.S. LEXIS 6046.

October 5, 2015. Petition for writ of certiorari to the United States Court of Appeals for the Fifth Circuit denied.

Same case below, 586 Fed. Appx. 189.

No. 14-10298. Jarrick Earl Denewiler, Petitioner v. Gary Swarthout, Warden.

577 U.S. 858, 136 S. Ct. 134, 193 L. Ed. 2d 103, 2015 U.S. LEXIS 5747.

October 5, 2015. Petition for writ of certiorari to the United States Court of Appeals for the Ninth Circuit denied.

No. 14-10300. John Stellios Davis, Petitioner v. United States.

577 U.S. 858, 136 S. Ct. 135, 193 L. Ed. 2d 103, 2015 U.S. LEXIS 5745.

October 5, 2015. Petition for writ of certiorari to the United States Court of Appeals for the Eleventh Circuit denied.

No. 14-10301. Charles Donelson, Petitioner v. Randy Pfister, Warden, et al.

577 U.S. 858, 136 S. Ct. 135, 193 L. Ed. 2d 103, 2015 U.S. LEXIS 5679.

October 5, 2015. Petition for writ of certiorari to the United States Court of Appeals for the Seventh Circuit denied.

No. 14-10302. Felix Antonio Jimenez-Quelix, aka Harly Canales, Petitioner v. United States.

577 U.S. 858, 136 S. Ct. 135, 193 L. Ed. 2d 103, 2015 U.S. LEXIS 5853.

October 5, 2015. Petition for writ of certiorari to the United States Court of Appeals for the Fifth Circuit denied.

Same case below, 598 Fed. Appx. 270.

No. 14-10303. Rogelio Martinez-Ordonez, aka Adrian Martinez, Petitioner v. United States.

577 U.S. 858, 136 S. Ct. 136, 193 L. Ed. 2d 103, 2015 U.S. LEXIS 5724.

October 5, 2015. Petition for writ of certiorari to the United States Court of Appeals for the Fifth Circuit denied.

Same case below, 598 Fed. Appx. 292.

No. 14-10304. Peter James Martin, Petitioner v. Texas.

577 U.S. 859, 136 S. Ct. 136, 193 L. Ed. 2d 104, 2015 U.S. LEXIS 5673.

October 5, 2015. Petition for writ of certiorari to the Court of Appeals of Texas, Ninth District, denied.

No. 14-10305. Wendel Robert Wardell, Jr., Petitioner v. Rick Raesmich, Executive Director, Colorado Department of Corrections, et al.

577 U.S. 859, 136 S. Ct. 136, 193 L. Ed. 2d 104, 2015 U.S. LEXIS 5788.

October 5, 2015. Petition for writ of certiorari to the United States Court of Appeals for the Tenth Circuit denied.

Same case below, 564 Fed. Appx. 922.

No. 14-10306. Ricardo Villegas, Petitioner v. United States.

577 U.S. 859, 136 S. Ct. 136, 193 L. Ed. 2d 104, 2015 U.S. LEXIS 6084.

October 5, 2015. Petition for writ of certiorari to the United States Court of Appeals for the Ninth Circuit denied.

Same case below, 589 Fed. Appx. 372.

No. 14-10307. Margarita Lopez, Petitioner v. Illinois.

577 U.S. 859, 136 S. Ct. 136, 193 L. Ed. 2d 104, 2015 U.S. LEXIS 5902.

October 5, 2015. Petition for writ of certiorari to the Appellate Court of Illinois, First District, denied.

No. 14-10308. Hassan Thomas, Petitioner v. United States.

577 U.S. 859, 136 S. Ct. 136, 193 L. Ed. 2d 104, 2015 U.S. LEXIS 5683.

October 5, 2015. Petition for writ of certiorari to the United States Court of Appeals for the Third Circuit denied.

Same case below, 607 Fed. Appx. 157.

No. 14-10310. Rogelio Fuentes, Petitioner v. Ralph M. Diaz, Warden.

577 U.S. 859, 136 S. Ct. 137, 193 L. Ed. 2d 104, 2015 U.S. LEXIS 5703.

October 5, 2015. Petition for writ of certiorari to the United States Court of Appeals for the Ninth Circuit denied.

Same case below, 597 Fed. Appx. 426.

No. 14-10312. Louie David Goursau, Petitioner v. California.

577 U.S. 859, 136 S. Ct. 137, 193 L. Ed. 2d 104, 2015 U.S. LEXIS 6075.

October 5, 2015. Petition for writ of certiorari to the Court of Appeal of California, First Appellate District, Division Four, denied.

No. 14-10313. Omar Garron-Morales, Petitioner v. United States.

577 U.S. 859, 136 S. Ct. 137, 193 L. Ed. 2d 104, 2015 U.S. LEXIS 6120.

October 5, 2015. Petition for writ of certiorari to the United States Court of Appeals for the Fifth Circuit denied.

Same case below, 606 Fed. Appx. 187.

Same case below, 598 Fed. Appx. 273.

No. 14-10314. Jeffrey Paul Hechler, Petitioner v. United States.

577 U.S. 859, 136 S. Ct. 137, 193 L. Ed. 2d 105, 2015 U.S. LEXIS 5999.

October 5, 2015. Petition for writ of certiorari to the United States Court of Appeals for the Ninth Circuit denied.

Same case below, 588 Fed. Appx. 603.

No. 14-10315. Pedro Gomez-Pena, Petitioner v. United States.

577 U.S. 859, 136 S. Ct. 138, 193 L. Ed. 2d 105, 2015 U.S. LEXIS 5832.

October 5, 2015. Petition for writ of certiorari to the United States Court of Appeals for the Ninth Circuit denied.

Same case below, 598 Fed. Appx. 555.

No. 14-10316. Marcus Lee Harris, Petitioner v. United States.

577 U.S. 859, 136 S. Ct. 139, 193 L. Ed. 2d 105, 2015 U.S. LEXIS 5701.

October 5, 2015. Petition for writ of certiorari to the United States Court of Appeals for the Fifth Circuit denied.

Same case below, 598 Fed. Appx. 288.

No. 14-10317. Antonio Huerta-Gutierrez, Petitioner v. United States.

577 U.S. 859, 136 S. Ct. 139, 193 L. Ed. 2d 105, 2015 U.S. LEXIS 5693.

October 5, 2015. Petition for writ of certiorari to the United States Court of Appeals for the Fifth Circuit denied.

No. 14-10318. Ricardo Fernandez, Petitioner v. United States.

577 U.S. 859, 136 S. Ct. 139, 193 L. Ed. 2d 105, 2015 U.S. LEXIS 5986.

October 5, 2015. Petition for writ of certiorari to the United States Court of Appeals for the Ninth Circuit denied.

Same case below, 599 Fed. Appx. 266.

No. 14-10319. Cesar Alexis Gonzalez, Petitioner v. United States.

577 U.S. 859, 136 S. Ct. 139, 193 L. Ed. 2d 105, 2015 U.S. LEXIS 5997.

October 5, 2015. Petition for writ of certiorari to the United States Court of Appeals for the Eighth Circuit denied.

Same case below, 781 F.3d 422.

No. 14-10321. Johndrell Elliot, Petitioner v. Ohio.

577 U.S. 859, 136 S. Ct. 298, 193 L. Ed. 2d 105, 2015 U.S. LEXIS 5775.

October 5, 2015. Petition for writ of certiorari to the Court of Appeals of Ohio, Cuyahoga County, denied.

No. 14-10322. Antoine DeGrate, Petitioner v. Broadcast Music Incorporated.

577 U.S. 860, 136 S. Ct. 140, 193 L. Ed. 2d 105, 2015 U.S. LEXIS 5943.

October 5, 2015. Petition for writ of certiorari to the United States Court of Appeals for the Second Circuit denied.

No. 14-10325. John Felder, Petitioner v. United States.

577 U.S. 860, 136 S. Ct. 140, 193 L. Ed. 2d 106, 2015 U.S. LEXIS 6029.

October 5, 2015. Petition for writ of certiorari to the United States Court of Appeals for the Third Circuit denied.

No. 14-10326. Lereginald Strong, Petitioner v. United States.

577 U.S. 860, 136 S. Ct. 140, 193 L. Ed. 2d 106, 2015 U.S. LEXIS 5963.

October 5, 2015. Petition for writ of certiorari to the United States Court of Appeals for the Sixth Circuit denied.

Same case below, 606 Fed. Appx. 804.

No. 14-10327. Richard Lehman, Petitioner v. Pennsylvania.

577 U.S. 860, 136 S. Ct. 140, 193 L. Ed. 2d 106, 2015 U.S. LEXIS 5699.

October 5, 2015. Petition for writ of certiorari to the Superior Court of Pennsylvania, Harrisburg Office, denied.

Same case below, 113 A.3d 340.

No. 14-10328. Ardelia Jones, Petitioner v. Nuttall AFC Company, et al.

577 U.S. 860, 136 S. Ct. 141, 193 L. Ed. 2d 106, 2015 U.S. LEXIS 5899, reh den 577 U.S. 1044, 136 S. Ct. 609, 193 L. Ed. 2d 489, 2015 U.S. LEXIS 7839.

October 5, 2015. Petition for writ of certiorari to the Court of Appeals of Michigan denied.

No. 14-10329. Andrew P. Kalick, Petitioner v. United States, et al.

577 U.S. 860, 136 S. Ct. 141, 193 L. Ed. 2d 106, 2015 U.S. LEXIS 5975.

October 5, 2015. Petition for writ of certiorari to the United States Court of Appeals for the Third Circuit denied.

Same case below, 604 Fed. Appx. 108.

No. 14-10330. Vincent R. Lofton, Petitioner v. United States.

577 U.S. 860, 136 S. Ct. 141, 193 L. Ed. 2d 106, 2015 U.S. LEXIS 5993.

October 5, 2015. Petition for writ of certiorari to the District of Columbia Court of Appeals denied.

Same case below, 972 A.2d 327.

No. 14-10331. Kevin Mayon, Petitioner v. Louisiana.

577 U.S. 860, 136 S. Ct. 141, 193 L. Ed. 2d 106, 2015 U.S. LEXIS 6175.

October 5, 2015. Petition for writ of certiorari to the Court of Appeal of Louisiana, Fifth Circuit, denied.

No. 14-10332. David Wayne Wilson, Petitioner v. Correctional Officer Marin, et al.

577 U.S. 860, 136 S. Ct. 299, 193 L. Ed. 2d 106, 2015 U.S. LEXIS 5659.

October 5, 2015. Petition for writ of certiorari to the United States Court of Appeals for the Ninth Circuit denied.

Same case below, 570 Fed. Appx. 927.

No. 14-10333. Jeramy J. Green, Petitioner v. Illinois.

577 U.S. 860, 136 S. Ct. 141, 193 L. Ed. 2d 107, 2015 U.S. LEXIS 5978.

October 5, 2015. Petition for writ of certiorari to the Appellate Court of Illinois, Third District, denied.

Same case below, 19 N.E.3d 13.

No. 14-10334. Raymond Anthony Hanna, Petitioner v. Florida, et al.

577 U.S. 860, 136 S. Ct. 141, 193 L. Ed. 2d 107, 2015 U.S. LEXIS 6109.

October 5, 2015. Petition for writ of certiorari to the United States Court of Appeals for the Eleventh Circuit denied.

Same case below, 599 Fed. Appx. 362.

No. 14-10336. Philip Fields, Petitioner v. Housing Authority of the City of San Buena Ventura, et al.

577 U.S. 860, 136 S. Ct. 142, 193 L. Ed. 2d 107, 2015 U.S. LEXIS 5705.

October 5, 2015. Petition for writ of certiorari to the United States Court of Appeals for the Ninth Circuit denied.

No. 14-10337. Muffin Faye Anderson, Petitioner v. Kimberly-Clark Corporation.

577 U.S. 860, 136 S. Ct. 142, 193 L. Ed. 2d 107, 2015 U.S. LEXIS 6063.

October 5, 2015. Petition for writ of certiorari to the United States Court of Appeals for the Federal Circuit denied.

No. 14-10338. Troy Kenneth Scheffler, Petitioner v. Minnesota.

577 U.S. 860, 136 S. Ct. 142, 193 L. Ed. 2d 107, 2015 U.S. LEXIS 6067.

October 5, 2015. Petition for writ of certiorari to the Court of Appeals of Minnesota denied.

No. 14-10339. Rickey Lee Hutcherson, Petitioner v. Michigan.

577 U.S. 860, 136 S. Ct. 142, 193 L. Ed. 2d 107, 2015 U.S. LEXIS 5888.

October 5, 2015. Petition for writ of certiorari to the Circuit Court of Michigan, Tuscola County, denied.

No. 14-10340. Javiele Jason Frias, Petitioner v. Texas.

577 U.S. 861, 136 S. Ct. 142, 193 L. Ed. 2d 107, 2015 U.S. LEXIS 5684.

October 5, 2015. Petition for writ of certiorari to the Court of Appeals of Texas, Third District, denied.

No. 14-10341. Jamar Brandon Golson, Petitioner v. Kathleen Allison, Warden.

577 U.S. 861, 136 S. Ct. 143, 193 L. Ed. 2d 107, 2015 U.S. LEXIS 5878.

October 5, 2015. Petition for writ of certiorari to the United States Court of Appeals for the Ninth Circuit denied.

No. 14-10342. Reginald Darnell Richardson, Petitioner v. Wendy Kelley, Director, Arkansas Department of Correction.

577 U.S. 861, 136 S. Ct. 299, 193 L. Ed. 2d 108, 2015 U.S. LEXIS 5824.

October 5, 2015. Petition for writ of certiorari to the United States Court of Appeals for the Eighth Circuit denied.

No. 14-10343. Maria Isabel Ferrer, Petitioner v. Daniel Martin Garasimowicz, et al.

577 U.S. 861, 136 S. Ct. 143, 193 L. Ed. 2d 108, 2015 U.S. LEXIS 5596.

October 5, 2015. Petition for writ of certiorari to the United States Court of Appeals for the Fourth Circuit denied.

Same case below, 569 Fed. Appx. 149.

No. 14-10344. Luis M. Harris, Petitioner v. Florida.

577 U.S. 861, 136 S. Ct. 143, 193 L. Ed. 2d 108, 2015 U.S. LEXIS 5678.

October 5, 2015. Petition for writ of certiorari to the District Court of Appeal of Florida, Second District, denied.

Same case below, 169 So. 3d 1175.

No. 14-10345. Stacey Kwaimaine Grays, Petitioner v. Dewayne Estes, Warden, et al.

577 U.S. 861, 136 S. Ct. 143, 193 L. Ed. 2d 108, 2015 U.S. LEXIS 5740.

October 5, 2015. Petition for writ of certiorari to the United States Court of Appeals for the Eleventh Circuit denied.

No. 14-10346. Roberto Pablo Gutierrez, Petitioner v. United States.

577 U.S. 861, 136 S. Ct. 143, 193 L. Ed. 2d 108, 2015 U.S. LEXIS 5962.

October 5, 2015. Petition for writ of certiorari to the United States Court of Appeals for the Fourth Circuit denied.

Same case below, 581 Fed. Appx. 164.

No. 14-10347. Roy Lee Humphrey, Petitioner v. Rick Hill, Warden.

577 U.S. 861, 136 S. Ct. 143, 193 L. Ed. 2d 108, 2015 U.S. LEXIS 5996.

October 5, 2015. Petition for writ of certiorari to the United States Court of Appeals for the Ninth Circuit denied.

No. 14-10348. Jeffrey Emil Groover, Petitioner v. United States.

577 U.S. 861, 136 S. Ct. 144, 193 L. Ed. 2d 108, 2015 U.S. LEXIS 5845.

October 5, 2015. Petition for writ of certiorari to the United States Court of Appeals for the Eleventh Circuit denied.

No. 14-10349. Clarence Christopher Gloss, III, Petitioner v. John Soto, Warden.

577 U.S. 861, 136 S. Ct. 144, 193 L. Ed. 2d 108, 2015 U.S. LEXIS 6173.

October 5, 2015. Petition for writ of certiorari to the United States Court of Appeals for the Ninth Circuit denied.

No. 14-10350. Byron Harrington, Petitioner v. Kevin Jones, Warden.

577 U.S. 861, 136 S. Ct. 144, 193 L. Ed. 2d 109, 2015 U.S. LEXIS 5894.

October 5, 2015. Petition for writ of certiorari to the United States Court of Appeals for the Sixth Circuit denied.

No. 14-10351. Juan Carlos Hernandez Gonzalez, Petitioner v. United States.

577 U.S. 861, 136 S. Ct. 144, 193 L. Ed. 2d 109, 2015 U.S. LEXIS 5921.

October 5, 2015. Petition for writ of certiorari to the United States Court of Appeals for the Eighth Circuit denied.

No. 14-10352. Michael Paul Gallimore, Petitioner v. United States.

577 U.S. 861, 136 S. Ct. 144, 193 L. Ed. 2d 109, 2015 U.S. LEXIS 6203.

October 5, 2015. Petition for writ of certiorari to the United States Court of Appeals for the Fourth Circuit denied.

Same case below, 600 Fed. Appx. 132.

No. 14-10354. Kenneth Lee Lawshea, Petitioner v. Wendy Kelley, Director, Arkansas Department of Correction.

577 U.S. 861, 136 S. Ct. 145, 193 L. Ed. 2d 109, 2015 U.S. LEXIS 5698, reh den 577 U.S. 1095, 136 S. Ct. 881, 193 L. Ed. 2d 773, 2016 U.S. LEXIS 551.

October 5, 2015. Petition for writ of certiorari to the United States Court of Appeals for the Eighth Circuit denied.

No. 14-10356. Carlos Alamilla Ramirez, Petitioner v. United States.

577 U.S. 861, 136 S. Ct. 145, 193 L. Ed. 2d 109, 2015 U.S. LEXIS 5867.

October 5, 2015. Petition for writ of certiorari to the United States Court of Appeals for the Ninth Circuit denied.

Same case below, 599 Fed. Appx. 753.

No. 14-10357. Kevin J. Reid, Petitioner v. City of Flint, Michigan.

577 U.S. 861, 136 S. Ct. 145, 193 L. Ed. 2d 109, 2015 U.S. LEXIS 6099, reh den 577 U.S. 1023, 136 S. Ct. 575, 193 L. Ed. 2d 457, 2015 U.S. LEXIS 7467.

October 5, 2015. Petition for writ of certiorari to the Circuit Court of Michigan, Genesee County, denied.

No. 14-10358. William Hall, Petitioner v. Michigan.

577 U.S. 862, 136 S. Ct. 145, 193 L. Ed. 2d 109, 2015 U.S. LEXIS 5791.

October 5, 2015. Petition for writ of certiorari to the Circuit Court of Michigan, Kalamazoo County, denied.

No. 14-10359. Eric E. Garvey, Petitioner v. United States.

577 U.S. 862, 136 S. Ct. 145, 193 L. Ed. 2d 109, 2015 U.S. LEXIS 5879.

October 5, 2015. Petition for writ of certiorari to the United States Court of Appeals for the Seventh Circuit denied.

Same case below, 597 Fed. Appx. 1042.

No. 14-10360. Lionil Fernandez, Petitioner v. Elvin Valenzuela, Warden.

577 U.S. 862, 136 S. Ct. 145, 193 L. Ed. 2d 110, 2015 U.S. LEXIS 6182.

October 5, 2015. Petition for writ of certiorari to the United States Court of Appeals for the Ninth Circuit denied.

No. 14-10361. Chi Giang Ho, Petitioner v. United States.

577 U.S. 862, 136 S. Ct. 146, 193 L. Ed. 2d 110, 2015 U.S. LEXIS 5949.

October 5, 2015. Petition for writ of certiorari to the United States Court of Appeals for the Fifth Circuit denied.

Same case below, 598 Fed. Appx. 317.

No. 14-10363. Rayando Huggins, Petitioner v. John Kerestes, Superintendent, State Correctional Institution at Mahanoy, et al.

577 U.S. 862, 136 S. Ct. 146, 193 L. Ed. 2d 110, 2015 U.S. LEXIS 5981.

October 5, 2015. Petition for writ of certiorari to the United States Court of Appeals for the Third Circuit denied.

No. 14-10364. Jeffrey Scott Hall, Petitioner v. Jody Tallie, et al.

577 U.S. 862, 136 S. Ct. 146, 193 L. Ed. 2d 110, 2015 U.S. LEXIS 5985, reh den 577 U.S. 1054, 136 S. Ct. 705, 193 L. Ed. 2d 531, 2015 U.S. LEXIS 7935.

October 5, 2015. Petition for writ of certiorari to the United States Court of Appeals for the Eleventh Circuit denied.

No. 14-10365. John D. Haywood, Petitioner v. Illinois.

577 U.S. 862, 136 S. Ct. 146, 193 L. Ed. 2d 110, 2015 U.S. LEXIS 5715.

October 5, 2015. Petition for writ of certiorari to the Appellate Court of Illinois, Fourth District, denied.

No. 14-10366. Ferenc Fodor, Petitioner v. Eastern Shipbuilding Group (two judgments).

577 U.S. 862, 136 S. Ct. 146, 193 L. Ed. 2d 110, 2015 U.S. LEXIS 6215, reh den 577 U.S. 1023, 136 S. Ct. 576, 193 L. Ed. 2d 457, 2015 U.S. LEXIS 7398.

October 5, 2015. Petition for writ of certiorari to the United States Court of Appeals for the Eleventh Circuit denied.

Same case below, 598 Fed. Appx. 693 (first judgment); 599 Fed. Appx. 375 (second judgment).

No. 14-10367. Shannon Monique Gibson, Petitioner v. Valley Avenue Drive-In Restaurant, LLC.

577 U.S. 862, 136 S. Ct. 147, 193 L. Ed. 2d 110, 2015 U.S. LEXIS 5843, reh den 577 U.S. 1023, 136 S. Ct. 576, 193 L. Ed. 2d 458, 2015 U.S. LEXIS 7388.

October 5, 2015. Petition for writ of certiorari to the United States Court of Appeals for the Eleventh Circuit denied.

Same case below, 597 Fed. Appx. 568.

No. 14-10368. Miguel Angel Rodriguez-Castro, Petitioner v. United States.

577 U.S. 862, 136 S. Ct. 147, 193 L. Ed. 2d 111, 2015 U.S. LEXIS 5716.

October 5, 2015. Petition for writ of certiorari to the United States Court of Appeals for the Ninth Circuit denied.

No. 14-10369. Tracy Lee Dotson, Petitioner v. California.

577 U.S. 862, 136 S. Ct. 147, 193 L. Ed. 2d 111, 2015 U.S. LEXIS 5944.

October 5, 2015. Petition for writ of certiorari to the Supreme Court of California denied.

No. 14-10370. Miguel Lavenant, Petitioner v. United States.

577 U.S. 862, 136 S. Ct. 147, 193 L. Ed. 2d 111, 2015 U.S. LEXIS 5846, reh den 577 U.S. 1023, 136 S. Ct. 576, 193 L. Ed. 2d 458, 2015 U.S. LEXIS 7401.

October 5, 2015. Petition for writ of certiorari to the United States Court of Appeals for the Third Circuit denied.

Same case below, 607 Fed. Appx. 217.

No. 14-10371. Herbert Jena, Petitioner v. United States.

577 U.S. 862, 136 S. Ct. 147, 193 L. Ed. 2d 111, 2015 U.S. LEXIS 5779.

October 5, 2015. Petition for writ of certiorari to the United States Court of Appeals for the Fifth Circuit denied.

Same case below, 590 Fed. Appx. 324.

No. 14-10372. Gary J. Mason, Petitioner v. Wendy Kelley, Director, Arkansas Department of Correction.

577 U.S. 862, 136 S. Ct. 147, 193 L. Ed. 2d 111, 2015 U.S. LEXIS 5687.

October 5, 2015. Petition for writ of certiorari to the Supreme Court of Arkansas denied.

Same case below, 2015 Ark. 20, 453 S.W.3d 679.

No. 14-10373. Robert Earl Martin, Petitioner v. United States.

577 U.S. 863, 136 S. Ct. 148, 193 L. Ed. 2d 111, 2015 U.S. LEXIS 6016.

October 5, 2015. Petition for writ of certiorari to the United States Court of Appeals for the Fourth Circuit denied.

Same case below, 598 Fed. Appx. 199.

No. 14-10374. Lomando Mark Scott, Petitioner v. United States.

577 U.S. 863, 136 S. Ct. 148, 193 L. Ed. 2d 111, 2015 U.S. LEXIS 5895.

October 5, 2015. Petition for writ of certiorari to the United States Court of Appeals for the Ninth Circuit denied.

Same case below, 603 Fed. Appx. 573.

No. 14-10375. Jose Manuel Zavala-Marti, Petitioner v. United States.

577 U.S. 863, 136 S. Ct. 148, 193 L. Ed. 2d 111, 2015 U.S. LEXIS 6096.

October 5, 2015. Petition for writ of certiorari to the United States Court of Appeals for the First Circuit denied.

Same case below, 601 Fed. Appx. 6.

———

No. 14-10378. Juliet Wright, Petitioner v. James City County, Virginia.

577 U.S. 863, 136 S. Ct. 149, 193 L. Ed. 2d 112, 2015 U.S. LEXIS 5681.

October 5, 2015. Petition for writ of certiorari to the United States Court of Appeals for the Fourth Circuit denied.

Same case below, 589 Fed. Appx. 186.

———

No. 14-10379. Eddie Levord Taylor, Petitioner v. Dennis Daniels, Correctional Administrator, Maury Correctional Institution.

577 U.S. 863, 136 S. Ct. 149, 193 L. Ed. 2d 112, 2015 U.S. LEXIS 5800.

October 5, 2015. Petition for writ of certiorari to the United States Court of Appeals for the Fourth Circuit denied.

Same case below, 604 Fed. Appx. 269.

———

No. 14-10380. Jeffery Hamilton, Petitioner v. Mary Berghuis, Warden.

577 U.S. 863, 136 S. Ct. 149, 193 L. Ed. 2d 112, 2015 U.S. LEXIS 5868.

October 5, 2015. Petition for writ of certiorari to the United States Court of Appeals for the Sixth Circuit denied.

———

No. 14-10381. Juwan Hall, Petitioner v. Greg McConnell, et al.

577 U.S. 863, 136 S. Ct. 149, 193 L. Ed. 2d 112, 2015 U.S. LEXIS 6005.

October 5, 2015. Petition for writ of certiorari to the United States Court of Appeals for the Eleventh Circuit denied.

———

No. 14-10383. Lewis E. Fuller, Petitioner v. Julie L. Jones, Secretary, Florida Department of Corrections.

577 U.S. 863, 136 S. Ct. 299, 193 L. Ed. 2d 112, 2015 U.S. LEXIS 5934.

October 5, 2015. Petition for writ of certiorari to the Supreme Court of Florida denied.

Same case below, 139 So. 3d 297.

———

No. 14-10384. Nakia Hubbard, Petitioner v. A. Miller, Warden.

577 U.S. 863, 136 S. Ct. 150, 193 L. Ed. 2d 112, 2015 U.S. LEXIS 6086.

October 5, 2015. Petition for writ of certiorari to the United States Court of Appeals for the Ninth Circuit denied.

———

No. 14-10385. Earl William Freeman, Petitioner v. Chris Chiprez, et al.

577 U.S. 863, 136 S. Ct. 150, 193 L. Ed. 2d 112, 2015 U.S. LEXIS 5729.

October 5, 2015. Petition for writ of certiorari to the United States Court of Appeals for the Eighth Circuit denied.

Same case below, 578 Fed. Appx. 618.

———

No. 14-10386. Zane Hubbard, Petitioner v. C. Gipson, et al.

577 U.S. 863, 136 S. Ct. 150, 193 L. Ed. 2d 112, 2015 U.S. LEXIS 5861.

October 5, 2015. Petition for writ of certiorari to the United States Court of Appeals for the Ninth Circuit denied.

Same case below, 615 Fed. Appx. 264.

No. 14-10388. Anthony Ray Banks, Petitioner v. William Stephens, Director, Texas Department of Criminal Justice, Correctional Institutions Division.

577 U.S. 863, 136 S. Ct. 150, 193 L. Ed. 2d 113, 2015 U.S. LEXIS 5932.

October 5, 2015. Petition for writ of certiorari to the United States Court of Appeals for the Fifth Circuit denied.

No. 14-10390. Darryl Boyd Adkins, Petitioner v. Correctional Officer McDonald, et al.

577 U.S. 863, 136 S. Ct. 151, 193 L. Ed. 2d 113, 2015 U.S. LEXIS 5754.

October 5, 2015. Petition for writ of certiorari to the United States Court of Appeals for the Fourth Circuit denied.

Same case below, 600 Fed. Appx. 159.

No. 14-10391. Jose Francisco Jimenez Pina, aka Jose Jimenez Mancilla, Petitioner v. United States.

577 U.S. 863, 136 S. Ct. 151, 193 L. Ed. 2d 113, 2015 U.S. LEXIS 6197.

October 5, 2015. Petition for writ of certiorari to the United States Court of Appeals for the Fourth Circuit denied.

Same case below, 605 Fed. Appx. 150.

No. 14-10392. Paul Christopher Turner, Petitioner v. United States.

577 U.S. 864, 136 S. Ct. 151, 193 L. Ed. 2d 113, 2015 U.S. LEXIS 5669.

October 5, 2015. Petition for writ of certiorari to the United States Court of Appeals for the Sixth Circuit denied.

No. 14-10393. Eddie Levord Taylor, Petitioner v. Dennis Daniels, et al.

577 U.S. 864, 136 S. Ct. 151, 193 L. Ed. 2d 113, 2015 U.S. LEXIS 5833.

October 5, 2015. Petition for writ of certiorari to the United States Court of Appeals for the Fourth Circuit denied.

Same case below, 597 Fed. Appx. 192.

No. 14-10394. Christopher Lee Foster, Petitioner v. United States.

577 U.S. 864, 136 S. Ct. 151, 193 L. Ed. 2d 113, 2015 U.S. LEXIS 5842.

October 5, 2015. Petition for writ of certiorari to the United States Court of Appeals for the Fourth Circuit denied.

Same case below, 592 Fed. Appx. 217.

No. 14-10395. Dwayne Adams, Petitioner v. Thomas Mackie, Warden.

577 U.S. 864, 136 S. Ct. 151, 193 L. Ed. 2d 113, 2015 U.S. LEXIS 5840.

October 5, 2015. Petition for writ of certiorari to the United States Court of Appeals for the Sixth Circuit denied.

No. 14-10396. Robert Patrick Butters, Petitioner v. Minnesota.

577 U.S. 864, 136 S. Ct. 152, 193 L. Ed. 2d 113, 2015 U.S. LEXIS 5897.

October 5, 2015. Petition for writ of certiorari to the Court of Appeals of Minnesota denied.

No. 14-10397. Brady Lavick Adams, Petitioner v. United States.

577 U.S. 864, 136 S. Ct. 152, 193 L. Ed. 2d 114, 2015 U.S. LEXIS 5771.

October 5, 2015. Petition for writ of certiorari to the United States Court of Appeals for the Eleventh Circuit denied.

No. 14-10398. Yung Lo, Petitioner v. Golden Gaming, Inc., et al.

577 U.S. 864, 136 S. Ct. 152, 193 L. Ed. 2d 114, 2015 U.S. LEXIS 5948.

October 5, 2015. Petition for writ of certiorari to the United States Court of Appeals for the Ninth Circuit denied.

No. 14-10399. Martin J. Jonassen, Petitioner v. United States.

577 U.S. 864, 136 S. Ct. 152, 193 L. Ed. 2d 114, 2015 U.S. LEXIS 6038.

October 5, 2015. Petition for writ of certiorari to the United States Court of Appeals for the Seventh Circuit denied.

Same case below, 759 F.3d 653.

No. 14-10400. Paul Washington, Petitioner v. John Jeanes, Warden.

577 U.S. 864, 136 S. Ct. 152, 193 L. Ed. 2d 114, 2015 U.S. LEXIS 5913.

October 5, 2015. Petition for writ of certiorari to the Superior Court of Georgia, Calhoun County, denied.

No. 14-10401. Sheryl Taylor, Petitioner v. United States.

577 U.S. 864, 136 S. Ct. 152, 193 L. Ed. 2d 114, 2015 U.S. LEXIS 5892.

October 5, 2015. Petition for writ of certiorari to the United States Court of Appeals for the Federal Circuit denied.

Same case below, 590 Fed. Appx. 983.

No. 14-10402. Edward De La Cruz, Petitioner v. Arizona.

577 U.S. 864, 136 S. Ct. 153, 193 L. Ed. 2d 114, 2015 U.S. LEXIS 5827.

October 5, 2015. Petition for writ of certiorari to the Supreme Court of Arizona denied.

No. 14-10403. Maurice Elon Edwards, Petitioner v. United States.

577 U.S. 864, 136 S. Ct. 153, 193 L. Ed. 2d 114, 2015 U.S. LEXIS 5857.

October 5, 2015. Petition for writ of certiorari to the United States Court of Appeals for the Tenth Circuit denied.

Same case below, 782 F.3d 554.

No. 14-10404. Doris Stevens, Petitioner v. City of Shreveport, Louisiana, et al.

577 U.S. 864, 136 S. Ct. 154, 193 L. Ed. 2d 114, 2015 U.S. LEXIS 6025.

October 5, 2015. Petition for writ of certiorari to the Court of Appeal of Louisiana, Second Circuit, denied.

Same case below, 152 So. 3d 1071.

Same case below, 593 Fed. Appx. 633.

No. 14-10406. Trung Quang Phan, Petitioner v. Jeffrey Beard, Secretary, California Department of Corrections and Rehabilitation.

577 U.S. 864, 136 S. Ct. 154, 193 L. Ed. 2d 115, 2015 U.S. LEXIS 5803.

October 5, 2015. Petition for writ of certiorari to the United States Court of Appeals for the Ninth Circuit denied.

Same case below, 584 Fed. Appx. 841.

No. 14-10408. Gerardo Carranza-Raudales, Petitioner v. United States.

577 U.S. 864, 136 S. Ct. 154, 193 L. Ed. 2d 115, 2015 U.S. LEXIS 6000.

October 5, 2015. Petition for writ of certiorari to the United States Court of Appeals for the Fifth Circuit denied.

Same case below, 605 Fed. Appx. 325.

No. 14-10409. Arleigh Joe Esqueda, Petitioner v. United States.

577 U.S. 865, 136 S. Ct. 154, 193 L. Ed. 2d 115, 2015 U.S. LEXIS 5991.

October 5, 2015. Petition for writ of certiorari to the United States Court of Appeals for the Eighth Circuit denied.

Same case below, 599 Fed. Appx. 608.

No. 14-10410. Saul Diaz, Petitioner v. Greg Lewis, Warden.

577 U.S. 865, 136 S. Ct. 154, 193 L. Ed. 2d 115, 2015 U.S. LEXIS 5940.

October 5, 2015. Petition for writ of certiorari to the United States Court of Appeals for the Ninth Circuit denied.

No. 14-10411. Jonathan Laureano, Petitioner v. United States.

577 U.S. 865, 136 S. Ct. 154, 193 L. Ed. 2d 115, 2015 U.S. LEXIS 6217.

October 5, 2015. Petition for writ of certiorari to the United States Court of Appeals for the Eleventh Circuit denied.

No. 14-10412. Consuelo Jordan, Petitioner v. Lee Satterfield, et al.

577 U.S. 865, 136 S. Ct. 155, 193 L. Ed. 2d 115, 2015 U.S. LEXIS 6268, reh den 577 U.S. 1023, 136 S. Ct. 576, 193 L. Ed. 2d 458, 2015 U.S. LEXIS 7421.

October 5, 2015. Petition for writ of certiorari to the District of Columbia Court of Appeals denied.

No. 14-10413. Eric Laquince Brown, Petitioner v. Tim Perez, Warden.

577 U.S. 865, 136 S. Ct. 155, 193 L. Ed. 2d 115, 2015 U.S. LEXIS 6235, reh den 577 U.S. 1095, 136 S. Ct. 881, 193 L. Ed. 2d 773, 2016 U.S. LEXIS 412.

October 5, 2015. Petition for writ of certiorari to the United States Court of Appeals for the Ninth Circuit denied.

No. 14-10414. Pedro Antonio Castro Velasquez, Petitioner v. Bank of America, N.A.

577 U.S. 865, 136 S. Ct. 155, 193 L. Ed. 2d 115, 2015 U.S. LEXIS 5954.

October 5, 2015. Petition for writ of certiorari to the Supreme Court of Florida denied.

Same case below, 168 So. 3d 231.

No. 14-10415. Brian William Walpole, Petitioner v. United States.

577 U.S. 865, 136 S. Ct. 155, 193 L. Ed. 2d 116, 2015 U.S. LEXIS 6154.

October 5, 2015. Petition for writ of certiorari to the United States Court of Appeals for the Third Circuit denied.

Same case below, 599 Fed. Appx. 56.

No. 14-10416. Michael Anthony Tanzi, Petitioner v. Julie L. Jones, Secretary, Florida Department of Corrections.

577 U.S. 865, 136 S. Ct. 155, 193 L. Ed. 2d 116, 2015 U.S. LEXIS 6326.

October 5, 2015. Petition for writ of certiorari to the United States Court of Appeals for the Eleventh Circuit denied.

Same case below, 772 F.3d 644.

No. 14-10417. Evelyn H. Haynes, Petitioner v. Robert A. McDonald, Secretary of Veterans Affairs.

577 U.S. 865, 136 S. Ct. 156, 193 L. Ed. 2d 116, 2015 U.S. LEXIS 6270.

October 5, 2015. Petition for writ of certiorari to the United States Court of Appeals for the Federal Circuit denied.

Same case below, 785 F.3d 614.

No. 14-10418. Johnny Smith, Petitioner v. United States.

577 U.S. 865, 136 S. Ct. 156, 193 L. Ed. 2d 116, 2015 U.S. LEXIS 6351.

October 5, 2015. Petition for writ of certiorari to the United States Court of Appeals for the Fifth Circuit denied.

No. 14-10419. Lamarr Rowell, Petitioner v. Jack Palmer, Warden, et al.

577 U.S. 865, 136 S. Ct. 156, 193 L. Ed. 2d 116, 2015 U.S. LEXIS 6059.

October 5, 2015. Petition for writ of certiorari to the United States Court of Appeals for the Ninth Circuit denied.

Same case below, 605 Fed. Appx. 620.

No. 14-10424. Benjamin E. Isaac, Petitioner v. Gregory McLaughlin, Warden.

577 U.S. 865, 136 S. Ct. 157, 193 L. Ed. 2d 116, 2015 U.S. LEXIS 6255.

October 5, 2015. Petition for writ of certiorari to the Superior Court of Georgia, Macon County, denied.

No. 14-10425. Eric Roundtree, Petitioner v. Ed Wright, Warden.

577 U.S. 865, 136 S. Ct. 158, 193 L. Ed. 2d 116, 2015 U.S. LEXIS 6313.

October 5, 2015. Petition for writ of certiorari to the United States Court of Appeals for the Fourth Circuit denied.

Same case below, 600 Fed. Appx. 188.

Same case below, 603 Fed. Appx. 517.

No. 14-10426. Ida Mawatu, Petitioner v. Marc Valentin, et al.

577 U.S. 865, 136 S. Ct. 158, 193 L. Ed. 2d 117, 2015 U.S. LEXIS 6113.

October 5, 2015. Petition for writ of certiorari to the United States Court of Appeals for the Fifth Circuit denied.

No. 14-10428. Sean Barill, Petitioner v. New York.

577 U.S. 865, 136 S. Ct. 158, 193 L. Ed. 2d 117, 2015 U.S. LEXIS 6284.

October 5, 2015. Petition for writ of certiorari to the Appellate Division, Supreme Court of New York, Fourth Judicial Department, denied.

Same case below, 120 App. Div. 3d 951, 991 N.Y.S.2d 214.

No. 14-10429. Jarian Ricks, Petitioner v. United States.

577 U.S. 866, 136 S. Ct. 158, 193 L. Ed. 2d 117, 2015 U.S. LEXIS 6282.

October 5, 2015. Petition for writ of certiorari to the United States Court of Appeals for the Fourth Circuit denied.

Same case below, 590 Fed. Appx. 246.

No. 14-10430. David Evan Starr, Petitioner v. United States.

577 U.S. 866, 136 S. Ct. 158, 193 L. Ed. 2d 117, 2015 U.S. LEXIS 6143.

October 5, 2015. Petition for writ of certiorari to the United States Court of Appeals for the Eighth Circuit denied.

No. 14-10431. Jose Homero Rocha-Gutierrez, Petitioner v. United States.

577 U.S. 866, 136 S. Ct. 158, 193 L. Ed. 2d 117, 2015 U.S. LEXIS 6303.

October 5, 2015. Petition for writ of certiorari to the United States Court of Appeals for the Fifth Circuit denied.

Same case below, 598 Fed. Appx. 306.

No. 14-10432. Carlos Fleitas, Petitioner v. Julie L. Jones, Secretary, Florida Department of Corrections, et al.

577 U.S. 866, 136 S. Ct. 159, 193 L. Ed. 2d 117, 2015 U.S. LEXIS 6201.

October 5, 2015. Petition for writ of certiorari to the United States Court of Appeals for the Eleventh Circuit denied.

No. 14-10433. Carl D. Gordon, Petitioner v. Rena Mullins, et al.

577 U.S. 866, 136 S. Ct. 159, 193 L. Ed. 2d 117, 2015 U.S. LEXIS 6316.

October 5, 2015. Petition for writ of certiorari to the United States Court of Appeals for the Fourth Circuit denied.

Same case below, 582 Fed. Appx. 248.

No. 14-10434. Almond J. Richardson, Petitioner v. United States.

577 U.S. 866, 136 S. Ct. 159, 193 L. Ed. 2d 117, 2015 U.S. LEXIS 6308.

October 5, 2015. Petition for writ of certiorari to the United States Court of Appeals for the Fifth Circuit denied.

Same case below, 781 F.3d 237.

No. 14-10435. Ezra Hallock, Petitioner v. United States.

577 U.S. 866, 136 S. Ct. 159, 193 L. Ed. 2d 118, 2015 U.S. LEXIS 6121.

October 5, 2015. Petition for writ of certiorari to the United States Court of Appeals for the Ninth Circuit denied.

No. 14-10436. Lionel Thomas Hurd, Petitioner v. Harold W. Clarke, Director, Virginia Department of Corrections.

577 U.S. 866, 136 S. Ct. 159, 193 L. Ed. 2d 118, 2015 U.S. LEXIS 6327.

October 5, 2015. Petition for writ of certiorari to the United States Court of Appeals for the Fourth Circuit denied.

Same case below, 593 Fed. Appx. 238.

No. 14-10438. Kendall Green, Petitioner v. Robert Stevenson, Warden.

577 U.S. 866, 136 S. Ct. 159, 193 L. Ed. 2d 118, 2015 U.S. LEXIS 6094.

October 5, 2015. Petition for writ of certiorari to the United States Court of Appeals for the Fourth Circuit denied.

Same case below, 589 Fed. Appx. 209.

No. 14-10439. Jose Enrique Hernandez, Petitioner v. Florida.

577 U.S. 866, 136 S. Ct. 160, 193 L. Ed. 2d 118, 2015 U.S. LEXIS 6178.

October 5, 2015. Petition for writ of certiorari to the District Court of Appeal of Florida, Third District, denied.

Same case below, 151 So. 3d 1256.

No. 14-10440. Thomas L. Rowland, Petitioner v. Julie L. Jones, Secretary, Florida Department of Corrections.

577 U.S. 866, 136 S. Ct. 299, 193 L. Ed. 2d 118, 2015 U.S. LEXIS 6261, reh den 577 U.S. 1023, 136 S. Ct. 576, 193 L. Ed. 2d 458, 2015 U.S. LEXIS 7389.

October 5, 2015. Petition for writ of certiorari to the United States Court of Appeals for the Eleventh Circuit denied.

No. 14-10442. Ronnie Lee Johnson, Petitioner v. Tennessee.

577 U.S. 866, 136 S. Ct. 160, 193 L. Ed. 2d 118, 2015 U.S. LEXIS 6166.

October 5, 2015. Petition for writ of certiorari to the Court of Criminal Appeals of Tennessee, Middle Division, denied.

No. 14-10444. James Talley, Petitioner v. Jerome B. Simandle, Chief Judge, United States District Court for the District of New Jersey.

577 U.S. 866, 136 S. Ct. 160, 193 L. Ed. 2d 118, 2015 U.S. LEXIS 6343, reh den 577 U.S. 1044, 136 S. Ct. 609, 193 L. Ed. 2d 490, 2015 U.S. LEXIS 7693.

October 5, 2015. Petition for writ of certiorari to the United States Court of Appeals for the Third Circuit denied.

Same case below, 599 Fed. Appx. 33.

No. 14-10445. Daniel Villa, Petitioner v. United States District Court for the Northern District of Texas.

577 U.S. 866, 136 S. Ct. 299, 193 L. Ed. 2d 118, 2015 U.S. LEXIS 6307.

October 5, 2015. Petition for writ of certiorari to the United States Court of Appeals for the Fifth Circuit denied.

No. 14-10446. Marquise Leland White, Petitioner v. Hector A. Rios, Warden.

577 U.S. 867, 136 S. Ct. 160, 193 L. Ed. 2d 119, 2015 U.S. LEXIS 6293.

October 5, 2015. Petition for writ of certiorari to the United States Court of Appeals for the Tenth Circuit denied.

Same case below, 599 Fed. Appx. 849.

No. 14-10448. Maria Aide Delgado, Petitioner v. United States.

577 U.S. 867, 136 S. Ct. 160, 193 L. Ed. 2d 119, 2015 U.S. LEXIS 6247.

October 5, 2015. Petition for writ of certiorari to the United States Court of Appeals for the Fifth Circuit denied.

No. 14-10449. Jason Bo-Alan Beckman, aka Bo Beckman, Petitioner v. United States.

577 U.S. 867, 136 S. Ct. 160, 193 L. Ed. 2d 119, 2015 U.S. LEXIS 6110.

October 5, 2015. Petition for writ of certiorari to the United States Court of Appeals for the Eighth Circuit denied.

Same case below, 787 F.3d 466.

No. 14-10450. Amilcar C. Butler, Petitioner v. United States.

577 U.S. 867, 136 S. Ct. 161, 193 L. Ed. 2d 119, 2015 U.S. LEXIS 6319.

October 5, 2015. Petition for writ of certiorari to the United States Court of Appeals for the Sixth Circuit denied.

No. 14-10452. James Thomas Hancock, Petitioner v. United States.

577 U.S. 867, 136 S. Ct. 161, 193 L. Ed. 2d 119, 2015 U.S. LEXIS 6085.

October 5, 2015. Petition for writ of certiorari to the United States Court of Appeals for the Fourth Circuit denied.

Same case below, 585 Fed. Appx. 265.

No. 14-10453. Omar Sierre Folk, Petitioner v. United States.

577 U.S. 867, 136 S. Ct. 161, 193 L. Ed. 2d 119, 2015 U.S. LEXIS 6339.

October 5, 2015. Petition for writ of certiorari to the United States Court of Appeals for the Third Circuit denied.

Same case below, 577 Fed. Appx. 106.

No. 14-10454. Calvin Lee Goddard, Petitioner v. United States.

577 U.S. 867, 136 S. Ct. 161, 193 L. Ed. 2d 119, 2015 U.S. LEXIS 6214.

October 5, 2015. Petition for writ of certiorari to the United States Court of Appeals for the Sixth Circuit denied.

No. 14-10455. James Ruhallah Harrison, Petitioner v. William Muniz, Warden, et al.

577 U.S. 867, 136 S. Ct. 161, 193 L. Ed. 2d 119, 2015 U.S. LEXIS 6137.

October 5, 2015. Petition for writ of certiorari to the United States Court of Appeals for the Ninth Circuit denied.

No. 14-10456. Robert Ellis Hastings, Petitioner v. United States.

577 U.S. 867, 136 S. Ct. 162, 193 L. Ed. 2d 120, 2015 U.S. LEXIS 6292, reh den 577 U.S. 1054, 136 S. Ct. 705, 193 L. Ed. 2d 531, 2015 U.S. LEXIS 7956.

October 5, 2015. Petition for writ of certiorari to the United States Court of Appeals for the Eighth Circuit denied.

No. 14-10457. Orlando Jose Garcia-Duran, Petitioner v. United States.

577 U.S. 867, 136 S. Ct. 162, 193 L. Ed. 2d 120, 2015 U.S. LEXIS 5889.

October 5, 2015. Petition for writ of certiorari to the United States Court of Appeals for the Eleventh Circuit denied.

No. 14-10458. Mark Anthony Fregia, Petitioner v. Mike McDonald, Warden.

577 U.S. 867, 136 S. Ct. 162, 193 L. Ed. 2d 120, 2015 U.S. LEXIS 6241.

October 5, 2015. Petition for writ of certiorari to the United States Court of Appeals for the Ninth Circuit denied.

No. 14-10459. Barrett Byron Staton, Petitioner v. United States.

577 U.S. 867, 136 S. Ct. 162, 193 L. Ed. 2d 120, 2015 U.S. LEXIS 6328.

October 5, 2015. Petition for writ of certiorari to the United States Court of Appeals for the Third Circuit denied.

Same case below, 605 Fed. Appx. 110.

No. 14-10460. William Paul, Petitioner v. United States.

577 U.S. 867, 136 S. Ct. 162, 193 L. Ed. 2d 120, 2015 U.S. LEXIS 6252.

October 5, 2015. Petition for writ of certiorari to the United States Court of Appeals for the Eleventh Circuit denied.

No. 14-10461. Anderson M. Scrubb, Petitioner v. Thomas LaValley.

577 U.S. 867, 136 S. Ct. 162, 193 L. Ed. 2d 120, 2015 U.S. LEXIS 6245.

October 5, 2015. Petition for writ of certiorari to the United States Court of Appeals for the Second Circuit denied.

No. 14-10462. Gilbert O. Cameron, Petitioner v. Sandra Dolce, Superintendent, Orleans Correctional Facility.

577 U.S. 867, 136 S. Ct. 163, 193 L. Ed. 2d 120, 2015 U.S. LEXIS 6356, reh den 577 U.S. 1023, 136 S. Ct. 576, 193 L. Ed. 2d 458, 2015 U.S. LEXIS 7366.

October 5, 2015. Petition for writ of certiorari to the United States Court of Appeals for the Second Circuit denied.

No. 14-10463. Jimmy Edward Cotinola, Petitioner v. Connie Gipson, Warden.

577 U.S. 867, 136 S. Ct. 163, 193 L. Ed. 2d 120, 2015 U.S. LEXIS 6253.

October 5, 2015. Petition for writ of certiorari to the United States Court of Appeals for the Ninth Circuit denied.

No. 14-10465. Felix Alberto Castro-Davis, Petitioner v. United States.

577 U.S. 868, 136 S. Ct. 163, 193 L. Ed. 2d 121, 2015 U.S. LEXIS 6337.

October 5, 2015. Petition for writ of certiorari to the United States Court of Appeals for the First Circuit denied.

No. 14-10466. Juan Guel-Nevares, Petitioner v. United States.

577 U.S. 868, 136 S. Ct. 163, 193 L. Ed. 2d 121, 2015 U.S. LEXIS 6151.

October 5, 2015. Petition for writ of certiorari to the United States Court of Appeals for the Fifth Circuit denied.

Same case below, 598 Fed. Appx. 315.

No. 14-10467. Arlex Adalid Guzman-Bautista, Petitioner v. United States.

577 U.S. 868, 136 S. Ct. 163, 193 L. Ed. 2d 121, 2015 U.S. LEXIS 6177.

October 5, 2015. Petition for writ of certiorari to the United States Court of Appeals for the Fifth Circuit denied.

Same case below, 598 Fed. Appx. 313.

No. 14-10468. Larry Dean Cochrun, Petitioner v. Bob Dooley, Warden, et al.

577 U.S. 868, 136 S. Ct. 164, 193 L. Ed. 2d 121, 2015 U.S. LEXIS 6138.

October 5, 2015. Petition for writ of certiorari to the United States Court of Appeals for the Eighth Circuit denied.

No. 14-10469. Luis Manuel Carmona, Petitioner v. United States.

577 U.S. 868, 136 S. Ct. 164, 193 L. Ed. 2d 121, 2015 U.S. LEXIS 6289.

October 5, 2015. Petition for writ of certiorari to the United States Court of Appeals for the Sixth Circuit denied.

No. 14-10471. Suppressed, Petitioner v. Suppressed.

577 U.S. 868, 136 S. Ct. 165, 193 L. Ed. 2d 121, 2015 U.S. LEXIS 6264.

October 5, 2015. Petition for writ of certiorari to the United States Court of Appeals for the Seventh Circuit denied.

No. 14-10472. Jeosvany Salas, Petitioner v. Florida.

577 U.S. 868, 136 S. Ct. 165, 193 L. Ed. 2d 121, 2015 U.S. LEXIS 6124.

October 5, 2015. Petition for writ of certiorari to the District Court of Appeal of Florida, Third District, denied.

Same case below, 160 So. 3d 443.

No. 14-10474. Kayode Kassim, Petitioner v. United States.

577 U.S. 868, 136 S. Ct. 165, 193 L. Ed. 2d 121, 2015 U.S. LEXIS 6179.

October 5, 2015. Petition for writ of certiorari to the United States Court of Appeals for the Third Circuit denied.

Same case below, 598 Fed. Appx. 831.

No. 14-10475. Stephen Caracappa, Petitioner v. United States.

577 U.S. 868, 136 S. Ct. 165, 193 L. Ed. 2d 122, 2015 U.S. LEXIS 6358.

October 5, 2015. Petition for writ of certiorari to the United States Court of Appeals for the Second Circuit denied.

No. 14-10476. Vance Edward Johnson, Petitioner v. William Stephens, Director, Texas Department of Criminal Justice, Correctional Institutions Division.

577 U.S. 868, 136 S. Ct. 165, 193 L. Ed. 2d 122, 2015 U.S. LEXIS 6225.

October 5, 2015. Petition for writ of certiorari to the United States Court of Appeals for the Fifth Circuit denied.

No. 14-10477. Randall Sanders, Petitioner v. Georgia.

577 U.S. 868, 136 S. Ct. 165, 193 L. Ed. 2d 122, 2015 U.S. LEXIS 6134.

October 5, 2015. Petition for writ of certiorari to the Court of Appeals of Georgia denied.

No. 14-10478. Adrian Perez, Petitioner v. United States.

577 U.S. 868, 136 S. Ct. 166, 193 L. Ed. 2d 122, 2015 U.S. LEXIS 6345.

October 5, 2015. Petition for writ of certiorari to the United States Court of Appeals for the Eleventh Circuit denied.

Same case below, 625 Fed. Appx. 919.

No. 14-10479. Kirk Pennington, Petitioner v. United States.

577 U.S. 868, 136 S. Ct. 166, 193 L. Ed. 2d 122, 2015 U.S. LEXIS 6314.

October 5, 2015. Petition for writ of certiorari to the United States Court of Appeals for the Fifth Circuit denied.

Same case below, 606 Fed. Appx. 216.

No. 14-10480. John H. White, Petitioner v. Donald Uhler, Superintendent, Upstate Correctional Facility.

577 U.S. 868, 136 S. Ct. 166, 193 L. Ed. 2d 122, 2015 U.S. LEXIS 6204.

October 5, 2015. Petition for writ of certiorari to the United States Court of Appeals for the Second Circuit denied.

No. 14-10481. Carlos Rivera, Petitioner v. United States.

577 U.S. 868, 136 S. Ct. 166, 193 L. Ed. 2d 122, 2015 U.S. LEXIS 6279.

October 5, 2015. Petition for writ of certiorari to the United States Court of Appeals for the Ninth Circuit denied.

Same case below, 602 Fed. Appx. 372.

No. 14-10482. Joanenice Shields, Petitioner v. Frontier Technology LLC, dba MicroAge, LLC, et al.

577 U.S. 869, 136 S. Ct. 166, 193 L. Ed. 2d 122, 2015 U.S. LEXIS 6043.

October 5, 2015. Petition for writ of certiorari to the United States Court of Appeals for the Ninth Circuit denied.

Same case below, 593 Fed. Appx. 671.

Same case below, 106 A.3d 167.

No. 14-10485. Keith Willie Reed, Petitioner v. United States.

577 U.S. 869, 136 S. Ct. 167, 193 L. Ed. 2d 123, 2015 U.S. LEXIS 6360.

October 5, 2015. Petition for writ of certiorari to the United States Court of Appeals for the Fourth Circuit denied.

Same case below, 780 F.3d 260.

No. 14-10487. Francisco Frank Apodaca, Jr., Petitioner v. United States.

577 U.S. 869, 136 S. Ct. 167, 193 L. Ed. 2d 123, 2015 U.S. LEXIS 6146.

October 5, 2015. Petition for writ of certiorari to the United States Court of Appeals for the Fifth Circuit denied.

Same case below, 603 Fed. Appx. 303.

No. 14-10488. Benoit Otis Brookens, II, Petitioner v. Office of Disciplinary Counsel of the Supreme Court of Pennsylvania.

577 U.S. 869, 136 S. Ct. 167, 193 L. Ed. 2d 123, 2015 U.S. LEXIS 6206.

October 5, 2015. Petition for writ of certiorari to the Supreme Court of Pennsylvania, Eastern District, denied.

No. 15-2. JFT Corporation, Petitioner v. Newtel Payphone Operations, Inc., et al.

577 U.S. 869, 136 S. Ct. 169, 193 L. Ed. 2d 123, 2015 U.S. LEXIS 6244.

October 5, 2015. Petition for writ of certiorari to the Superior Court of Pennsylvania, Philadelphia Office, denied.

No. 15-3. Martin Kimber, Petitioner v. United States.

577 U.S. 869, 136 S. Ct. 170, 193 L. Ed. 2d 123, 2015 U.S. LEXIS 6260.

October 5, 2015. Petition for writ of certiorari to the United States Court of Appeals for the Second Circuit denied.

Same case below, 777 F.3d 553.

No. 15-4. William Hayes Wyttenbach, Petitioner v. R. M. P.

577 U.S. 869, 136 S. Ct. 170, 193 L. Ed. 2d 123, 2015 U.S. LEXIS 5984, reh den 577 U.S. 1054, 136 S. Ct. 705, 193 L. Ed. 2d 531, 2015 U.S. LEXIS 7981.

October 5, 2015. Petition for writ of certiorari to the Court of Appeals of Texas, Thirteenth District, denied.

No. 15-6. Medytox Solutions, Inc., et al., Petitioners v. Investorshub.com, Inc.

577 U.S. 869, 136 S. Ct. 171, 193 L. Ed. 2d 123, 2015 U.S. LEXIS 6243.

October 5, 2015. Petition for writ of certiorari to the District Court of Appeal of Florida, Fourth District, denied.

Same case below, 152 So. 3d 727.

No. 15-12. Pamela B. Johnson Trust, by Eldon E. Johnson, Trustee, Petitioner v. James Anderson, et al.

577 U.S. 869, 136 S. Ct. 167, 193 L. Ed. 2d 123, 2015 U.S. LEXIS 6304.

October 5, 2015. Petition for writ of certiorari to the Court of Appeals of Michigan denied.

No. 15-13. Svetlana Tyshkevich, Petitioner v. Countrywide Home Loans, Inc., et al.

577 U.S. 869, 136 S. Ct. 168, 193 L. Ed. 2d 124, 2015 U.S. LEXIS 6267.

October 5, 2015. Petition for writ of certiorari to the Court of Appeal of California, Third Appellate District, denied.

No. 15-14. Carlos Zelaya, et al., Petitioners v. United States.

577 U.S. 869, 136 S. Ct. 168, 193 L. Ed. 2d 124, 2015 U.S. LEXIS 6315.

October 5, 2015. Petition for writ of certiorari to the United States Court of Appeals for the Eleventh Circuit denied.

Same case below, 781 F.3d 1315.

No. 15-15. Delia Thomas, et al., Petitioners v. Virgin Islands Board of Land Use Appeals, et al.

577 U.S. 869, 136 S. Ct. 168, 193 L. Ed. 2d 124, 2015 U.S. LEXIS 6338.

October 5, 2015. Petition for writ of certiorari to the United States Court of Appeals for the Third Circuit denied.

No. 15-19. Mercer Outdoor Advertising, LLC, Petitioner v. City of Hermitage, Pennsylvania, et al.

577 U.S. 869, 136 S. Ct. 169, 193 L. Ed. 2d 124, 2015 U.S. LEXIS 6287.

October 5, 2015. Petition for writ of certiorari to the United States Court of Appeals for the Third Circuit denied.

Same case below, 605 Fed. Appx. 130.

No. 15-20. Surrendra Mangru, Petitioner v. Loretta E. Lynch, Attorney General.

577 U.S. 869, 136 S. Ct. 170, 193 L. Ed. 2d 124, 2015 U.S. LEXIS 6357.

October 5, 2015. Petition for writ of certiorari to the United States Court of Appeals for the Fourth Circuit denied.

Same case below, 592 Fed. Appx. 209.

No. 15-21. Iury Cherkovsky, Petitioner v. Mario Delgado.

577 U.S. 870, 136 S. Ct. 177, 193 L. Ed. 2d 124, 2015 U.S. LEXIS 6072, reh den 577 U.S. 1023, 136 S. Ct. 576, 193 L. Ed. 2d 458, 2015 U.S. LEXIS 7457.

October 5, 2015. Petition for writ of certiorari to the Superior Court of New Jersey, Appellate Division, denied.

No. 15-26. Elzie Fuller, III, Petitioner v. Edwin B. Stimpson Co., Inc.

577 U.S. 870, 136 S. Ct. 177, 193 L. Ed. 2d 124, 2015 U.S. LEXIS 6347.

October 5, 2015. Petition for writ of certiorari to the United States Court of Appeals for the Eleventh Circuit denied.

Same case below, 598 Fed. Appx. 652.

No. 15-29. Yan Sui, Petitioner v. 2176 Pacific Homeowners Association, et al.

577 U.S. 870, 136 S. Ct. 181, 193 L. Ed. 2d 124, 2015 U.S. LEXIS 6335.

October 5, 2015. Petition for writ of certiorari to the Court of Appeal of California, Fourth Appellate District, Division Three, denied.

No. 15-30. Ravi Sood, Petitioner v. Michael Graham.

577 U.S. 870, 136 S. Ct. 182, 193 L. Ed. 2d 125, 2015 U.S. LEXIS 6148.

October 5, 2015. Petition for writ of certiorari to the Court of Appeals of Iowa denied.

No. 15-32. Telester Powell, Petitioner v. City of Kansas City, Missouri.

577 U.S. 870, 136 S. Ct. 182, 193 L. Ed. 2d 125, 2015 U.S. LEXIS 6362.

October 5, 2015. Petition for writ of certiorari to the Court of Appeals of Missouri, Western District, denied.

Same case below, 451 S.W.3d 724.

No. 15-33. Lloyd Richard Deere, Petitioner v. Adam Paul Laxalt, Attorney General of Nevada, et al.

577 U.S. 870, 136 S. Ct. 187, 193 L. Ed. 2d 125, 2015 U.S. LEXIS 6027, reh den 577 U.S. 1023, 136 S. Ct. 576, 193 L. Ed. 2d 458, 2015 U.S. LEXIS 7373.

October 5, 2015. Petition for writ of certiorari to the United States Court of Appeals for the Ninth Circuit denied.

No. 15-34. Theresa Duperon, Petitioner v. United States.

577 U.S. 870, 136 S. Ct. 187, 193 L. Ed. 2d 125, 2015 U.S. LEXIS 6321.

October 5, 2015. Petition for writ of certiorari to the United States Court of Appeals for the Seventh Circuit denied.

Same case below, 782 F.3d 820.

No. 15-37. Linda F. Green, Petitioner v. Carolyn W. Colvin, Acting Commissioner of Social Security.

577 U.S. 870, 136 S. Ct. 187, 193 L. Ed. 2d 125, 2015 U.S. LEXIS 5989.

October 5, 2015. Petition for writ of certiorari to the United States Court of Appeals for the Seventh Circuit denied.

Same case below, 605 Fed. Appx. 553.

No. 15-38. Martin R. Taccetta, Petitioner v. Stephen D'Ilio, Administrator, New Jersey State Prison, et al.

577 U.S. 870, 136 S. Ct. 187, 193 L. Ed. 2d 125, 2015 U.S. LEXIS 6350.

October 5, 2015. Petition for writ of certiorari to the United States Court of Appeals for the Third Circuit denied.

Same case below, 601 Fed. Appx. 165.

No. 15-39. Mark Balsam, et al., Petitioners v. Kim Guadagno, New Jersey Secretary of State.

577 U.S. 870, 136 S. Ct. 189, 193 L. Ed. 2d 125, 2015 U.S. LEXIS 5793.

October 5, 2015. Petition for writ of certiorari to the United States Court of Appeals for the Third Circuit denied.

Same case below, 607 Fed. Appx. 177.

No. 15-40. Maria-Lucia Anghel, Petitioner v. Ruskin Moscou Faltischek, P.C., et al.

577 U.S. 870, 136 S. Ct. 189, 193 L. Ed. 2d 126, 2015 U.S. LEXIS 6240.

October 5, 2015. Petition for writ of certiorari to the United States Court of Appeals for the Second Circuit denied.

Same case below, 598 Fed. Appx. 805.

No. 15-42. Michael Ramon Ochoa, Petitioner v. Erin Rubin, aka Erin Rubin Ochoa.

577 U.S. 870, 136 S. Ct. 189, 193 L. Ed. 2d 126, 2015 U.S. LEXIS 6125.

October 5, 2015. Petition for writ of certiorari to the Supreme Court of Pennsylvania, Western District, denied.

Same case below, 631 Pa. 730, 112 A.3d 654.

No. 15-43. Gracie E. McBroom, Petitioner v. HR Director, Franklin County Board of Elections.

577 U.S. 870, 136 S. Ct. 190, 193 L. Ed. 2d 126, 2015 U.S. LEXIS 6039, reh den 577 U.S. 1023, 136 S. Ct. 577, 193 L. Ed. 2d 459, 2015 U.S. LEXIS 7455.

October 5, 2015. Petition for writ of certiorari to the United States Court of Appeals for the Sixth Circuit denied.

No. 15-44. Gary Olesen, Petitioner v. Douglas Stewart Carter, et al.

577 U.S. 871, 136 S. Ct. 190, 193 L. Ed. 2d 126, 2015 U.S. LEXIS 6053.

October 5, 2015. Petition for writ of certiorari to the United States Court of Appeals for the Tenth Circuit denied.

No. 15-47. Bernard J. Bagdis, Petitioner v. United States.

577 U.S. 871, 136 S. Ct. 194, 193 L. Ed. 2d 126, 2015 U.S. LEXIS 6023, reh den 577 U.S. 1023, 136 S. Ct. 577, 193 L. Ed. 2d 459, 2015 U.S. LEXIS 7442.

October 5, 2015. Petition for writ of certiorari to the United States Court of Appeals for the Third Circuit denied.

Same case below, 591 Fed. Appx. 129.

No. 15-51. Matthew Gallant, Petitioner v. Rebecca Gallant.

577 U.S. 871, 136 S. Ct. 195, 193 L. Ed. 2d 126, 2015 U.S. LEXIS 6234.

October 5, 2015. Petition for writ of certiorari to the Court of Civil Appeals of Alabama denied.

Same case below, 184 So. 3d 387.

No. 15-52. Dantone, Inc., Petitioner v. United States.

577 U.S. 871, 136 S. Ct. 196, 193 L. Ed. 2d 126, 2015 U.S. LEXIS 6066.

October 5, 2015. Petition for writ of certiorari to the United States Court of Appeals for the Third Circuit denied.

No. 15-53. Daniel E. Carpenter, Petitioner v. United States.

577 U.S. 871, 136 S. Ct. 196, 193 L. Ed. 2d 126, 2015 U.S. LEXIS 6276, reh den 577 U.S. 1044, 136 S. Ct. 609, 193 L. Ed. 2d 490, 2015 U.S. LEXIS 7738.

October 5, 2015. Petition for writ of certiorari to the United States Court of Appeals for the First Circuit denied.

Same case below, 781 F.3d 599.

No. 15-55. Dwight D. Messinger, Petitioner v. JPMorgan Chase Bank, et al.

577 U.S. 871, 136 S. Ct. 196, 193 L. Ed. 2d 127, 2015 U.S. LEXIS 6184.

October 5, 2015. Petition for writ of certiorari to the United States Court of Appeals for the Fourth Circuit denied.

No. 15-56. J. H. F., Jr., Petitioner v. Alabama.

577 U.S. 871, 136 S. Ct. 196, 193 L. Ed. 2d 127, 2015 U.S. LEXIS 6068.

October 5, 2015. Petition for writ of certiorari to the Court of Criminal Appeals of Alabama denied.

Same case below, 190 So. 3d 579.

No. 15-60. Stephen J. Williams, Petitioner v. David M. Barry, Jr.

577 U.S. 871, 136 S. Ct. 196, 193 L. Ed. 2d 127, 2015 U.S. LEXIS 6310.

October 5, 2015. Petition for writ of certiorari to the Appellate Court of Connecticut denied.

No. 15-61. Henry J. Langer, Petitioner v. Nilles, Ilvedson, Plambeck & Selbo, Ltd., nka Nilles, Plambeck, Selbo & Harrie, Ltd.

577 U.S. 871, 136 S. Ct. 196, 193 L. Ed. 2d 127, 2015 U.S. LEXIS 6222, reh den

577 U.S. 1023, 136 S. Ct. 577, 193 L. Ed. 2d 459, 2015 U.S. LEXIS 7443.

October 5, 2015. Petition for writ of certiorari to the Supreme Court of North Dakota denied.

Same case below, 2014 ND 210, 858 N.W.2d 652.

No. 15-62. Bruce Nelson, Petitioner v. Minnesota Commissioner of Revenue.

577 U.S. 871, 136 S. Ct. 198, 193 L. Ed. 2d 127, 2015 U.S. LEXIS 6344.

October 5, 2015. Petition for writ of certiorari to the Court of Appeal of California, Second Appellate District, Division Six, denied.

No. 15-66. United Refining Company, et al., Petitioners v. John Cottillion and Beverly Eldridge, Individually and on Behalf of All Others Similarly Situated.

577 U.S. 871, 136 S. Ct. 198, 193 L. Ed. 2d 127, 2015 U.S. LEXIS 5926.

October 5, 2015. Petition for writ of certiorari to the United States Court of Appeals for the Third Circuit denied.

Same case below, 781 F.3d 47.

No. 15-67. Chad William Murray, Petitioner v. Texas.

577 U.S. 871, 136 S. Ct. 198, 193 L. Ed. 2d 127, 2015 U.S. LEXIS 6333.

October 5, 2015. Petition for writ of certiorari to the Court of Criminal Appeals of Texas denied.

Same case below, 457 S.W.3d 446.

No. 15-70. Thomas Van Zandt, Executor of the Estate of Evaline Jeanne Malis, Petitioner v. Wileharda Killian Mbunda.

577 U.S. 871, 136 S. Ct. 198, 193 L. Ed. 2d 128, 2015 U.S. LEXIS 6274.

October 5, 2015. Petition for writ of certiorari to the United States Court of Appeals for the Ninth Circuit denied.

Same case below, 604 Fed. Appx. 552.

No. 15-72. Erlin Gonzalez-Isaguirre, Petitioner v. Loretta E. Lynch, Attorney General.

577 U.S. 871, 136 S. Ct. 198, 193 L. Ed. 2d 128, 2015 U.S. LEXIS 6257.

October 5, 2015. Petition for writ of certiorari to the United States Court of Appeals for the Sixth Circuit denied.

Same case below, 607 Fed. Appx. 468.

No. 15-73. Justin Basilio, Petitioner v. Nassau County, New York, et al.

577 U.S. 872, 136 S. Ct. 199, 193 L. Ed. 2d 128, 2015 U.S. LEXIS 6164.

October 5, 2015. Petition for writ of certiorari to the United States Court of Appeals for the Second Circuit denied.

No. 15-74. Mark Sallee, Petitioner v. Georgia.

577 U.S. 872, 136 S. Ct. 199, 193 L. Ed. 2d 128, 2015 U.S. LEXIS 6074.

October 5, 2015. Petition for writ of certiorari to the Court of Appeals of Georgia denied.

Same case below, 329 Ga. App. 612, 765 S.E.2d 758.

No. 15-75. William D. Burns, Petitioner v. The Florida Bar.

577 U.S. 872, 136 S. Ct. 199, 193 L. Ed. 2d 128, 2015 U.S. LEXIS 6312.

October 5, 2015. Petition for writ of certiorari to the Supreme Court of Florida denied.

Same case below, 183 So. 3d 276.

No. 15-76. Naif Al-Yousif, Petitioner v. Travis Trani, Warden, et al.

577 U.S. 872, 136 S. Ct. 199, 193 L. Ed. 2d 128, 2015 U.S. LEXIS 5931.

October 5, 2015. Petition for writ of certiorari to the United States Court of Appeals for the Tenth Circuit denied.

Same case below, 779 F.3d 1173.

No. 15-77. Vincent Pisciotta, Petitioner v. United States.

No. 15-81. Mark A. Sorrentino, Petitioner v. United States.

577 U.S. 872, 136 S. Ct. 199, 193 L. Ed. 2d 128, 2015 U.S. LEXIS 6248.

October 5, 2015. Petitions for writs of certiorari to the United States Court of Appeals for the Eighth Circuit denied.

Same cases below, 783 F.3d 727.

No. 15-78. Alejandro Mirabal, Petitioner v. HSBC Bank USA, N.A.

577 U.S. 872, 136 S. Ct. 199, 193 L. Ed. 2d 129, 2015 U.S. LEXIS 6207, reh den 577 U.S. 1097, 136 S. Ct. 889, 193 L. Ed. 2d 781, 2016 U.S. LEXIS 13.

October 5, 2015. Petition for writ of certiorari to the District Court of Appeal of Florida, Fourth District, denied.

Same case below, 162 So. 3d 1026.

No. 15-79. Eugene Bailey, Petitioner v. City of Chicago, Illinois, et al.

577 U.S. 872, 136 S. Ct. 200, 193 L. Ed. 2d 129, 2015 U.S. LEXIS 6167.

October 5, 2015. Petition for writ of certiorari to the United States Court of Appeals for the Seventh Circuit denied.

Same case below, 779 F.3d 689.

No. 15-80. David Allen, et al., Petitioners v. Robert Goguen.

577 U.S. 872, 136 S. Ct. 200, 193 L. Ed. 2d 129, 2015 U.S. LEXIS 6324.

October 5, 2015. Petition for writ of certiorari to the United States Court of Appeals for the First Circuit denied.

Same case below, 780 F.3d 437.

No. 15-82. Michael N. Sofris, Petitioner v. Superior Court of California, Los Angeles County, et al.

577 U.S. 872, 136 S. Ct. 200, 193 L. Ed. 2d 129, 2015 U.S. LEXIS 6194.

October 5, 2015. Petition for writ of certiorari to the Court of Appeal of California, Second Appellate District, Division Three, denied.

No. 15-83. Vane Line Bunkering, Inc., Petitioner v. Ciro Charles Hicks.

577 U.S. 872, 136 S. Ct. 211, 193 L. Ed. 2d 129, 2015 U.S. LEXIS 6283.

October 5, 2015. Petition for writ of certiorari to the United States Court of Appeals for the Second Circuit denied.

Same case below, 783 F.3d 939.

No. 15-86. Rocco Oppedisano, Petitioner v. Loretta E. Lynch, Attorney General.

577 U.S. 872, 136 S. Ct. 211, 193 L. Ed. 2d 129, 2015 U.S. LEXIS 6290.

October 5, 2015. Petition for writ of certiorari to the United States Court of Appeals for the Second Circuit denied.

Same case below, 769 F.3d 147.

No. 15-87. C. G., Petitioner v. Deborah Heart and Lung Center, et al.

577 U.S. 872, 136 S. Ct. 212, 193 L. Ed. 2d 129, 2015 U.S. LEXIS 6128.

October 5, 2015. Petition for writ of certiorari to the Supreme Court of New Jersey denied.

No. 15-89. Masoud Bamdad, Petitioner v. United States.

577 U.S. 872, 136 S. Ct. 212, 193 L. Ed. 2d 129, 2015 U.S. LEXIS 6301, reh den 577 U.S. 1023, 136 S. Ct. 577, 193 L. Ed. 2d 459, 2015 U.S. LEXIS 7376.

October 5, 2015. Petition for writ of certiorari to the United States Court of Appeals for the Ninth Circuit denied.

Same case below, 87 Mass. App. Ct. 1101, 23 N.E.3d 151.

No. 15-90. Angie Ceraolo, et vir, Petitioners v. Citibank, N.A.

577 U.S. 872, 136 S. Ct. 212, 193 L. Ed. 2d 130, 2015 U.S. LEXIS 6296.

October 5, 2015. Petition for writ of certiorari to the Court of Appeal of California, Sixth Appellate District, denied.

No. 15-94. Andrew S. Mackey, Petitioner v. United States.

577 U.S. 873, 136 S. Ct. 217, 193 L. Ed. 2d 130, 2015 U.S. LEXIS 6180.

October 5, 2015. Petition for writ of certiorari to the United States Court of Appeals for the Eleventh Circuit denied.

Same case below, 573 Fed. Appx. 863.

No. 15-91. Kathryn Pollard, Individually and as the Executrix of the Estate of Abram Bynum, Petitioner v. City of Columbus, Ohio, et al.

577 U.S. 872, 136 S. Ct. 217, 193 L. Ed. 2d 130, 2015 U.S. LEXIS 6323.

October 5, 2015. Petition for writ of certiorari to the United States Court of Appeals for the Sixth Circuit denied.

Same case below, 780 F.3d 395.

No. 15-95. Marsha Peshkin, et al., Petitioners v. Irving H. Picard, Trustee for the Liquidation of Bernard L. Madoff Investment Securities LLC, et al.

577 U.S. 873, 136 S. Ct. 218, 193 L. Ed. 2d 130, 2015 U.S. LEXIS 6288.

October 5, 2015. Petition for writ of certiorari to the United States Court of Appeals for the Second Circuit denied.

Same case below, 779 F.3d 74.

No. 15-92. John S. Barth, Petitioner v. Starlet McNeely, et al.

577 U.S. 873, 136 S. Ct. 217, 193 L. Ed. 2d 130, 2015 U.S. LEXIS 6001.

October 5, 2015. Petition for writ of certiorari to the United States Court of Appeals for the Eleventh Circuit denied.

Same case below, 603 Fed. Appx. 846.

No. 15-96. Chattanooga-Hamilton County Hospital Authority, dba Erlanger Medical Center, dba Erlanger Health System, Petitioner v. United States ex rel. Robert Whipple.

577 U.S. 873, 136 S. Ct. 218, 193 L. Ed. 2d 130, 2015 U.S. LEXIS 6311.

October 5, 2015. Petition for writ of certiorari to the United States Court of Appeals for the Sixth Circuit denied.

Same case below, 782 F.3d 260.

No. 15-93. John Barth, Petitioner v. City of Peabody, Massachusetts.

577 U.S. 873, 136 S. Ct. 217, 193 L. Ed. 2d 130, 2015 U.S. LEXIS 6266.

October 5, 2015. Petition for writ of certiorari to the Appeals Court of Massachusetts denied.

No. 15-97. Yurania Dolz, Petitioner v. CitiMortgage, Inc.

577 U.S. 873, 136 S. Ct. 218, 193 L. Ed. 2d 131, 2015 U.S. LEXIS 6330, reh den 577 U.S. 1097, 136 S. Ct. 889, 193 L. Ed. 2d 781, 2016 U.S. LEXIS 10.

October 5, 2015. Petition for writ of certiorari to the Supreme Court of Florida denied.

Same case below, 160 So. 3d 893.

No. 15-98. Charles B. Rangel, Petitioner v. John A. Boehner, et al.

577 U.S. 873, 136 S. Ct. 218, 193 L. Ed. 2d 131, 2015 U.S. LEXIS 6305.

October 5, 2015. Petition for writ of certiorari to the United States Court of Appeals for the District of Columbia Circuit denied.

Same case below, 785 F.3d 19.

No. 15-99. Mohammed Shaikh, Petitioner v. Florida.

577 U.S. 873, 136 S. Ct. 218, 193 L. Ed. 2d 131, 2015 U.S. LEXIS 6285, reh den 577 U.S. 1023, 136 S. Ct. 577, 193 L. Ed. 2d 459, 2015 U.S. LEXIS 7385.

October 5, 2015. Petition for writ of certiorari to the District Court of Appeal of Florida, Fifth District, denied.

Same case below, 160 So. 3d 456.

No. 15-103. Nationwide Freight Systems, Inc., et al., Petitioners v. Illinois Commerce Commission, et al.

577 U.S. 873, 136 S. Ct. 223, 193 L. Ed. 2d 131, 2015 U.S. LEXIS 6272.

October 5, 2015. Petition for writ of certiorari to the United States Court of Appeals for the Seventh Circuit denied.

Same case below, 784 F.3d 367.

No. 15-104. Eduardo Nunez, et ux., Petitioners v. CitiMortgage, Incorporated, Successor by Merger to ABN AMRO Mortgage Group, Inc.

577 U.S. 873, 136 S. Ct. 223, 193 L. Ed. 2d 131, 2015 U.S. LEXIS 6239, reh den 577 U.S. 1095, 136 S. Ct. 882, 193 L. Ed. 2d 773, 2016 U.S. LEXIS 363.

October 5, 2015. Petition for writ of certiorari to the United States Court of Appeals for the Fifth Circuit denied.

Same case below, 606 Fed. Appx. 786.

No. 15-106. David J. Waller, Petitioner v. Arizona.

577 U.S. 873, 136 S. Ct. 223, 193 L. Ed. 2d 131, 2015 U.S. LEXIS 6238.

October 5, 2015. Petition for writ of certiorari to the Court of Appeals of Arizona, Division Two, denied.

Same case below, 235 Ariz. 479, 333 P.3d 806.

No. 15-107. Sun Life and Health Insurance Company, Petitioner v. R. Jeffrey Evans.

577 U.S. 873, 136 S. Ct. 224, 193 L. Ed. 2d 131, 2015 U.S. LEXIS 6060.

October 5, 2015. Petition for writ of certiorari to the United States Court of Appeals for the Ninth Circuit denied.

Same case below, 601 Fed. Appx. 497.

No. 15-110. Lloyd G. Perry, Petitioner v. Anonymous Physician 1, et al.

577 U.S. 873, 136 S. Ct. 227, 193 L. Ed. 2d 132, 2015 U.S. LEXIS 6317.

October 5, 2015. Petition for writ of certiorari to the Court of Appeals of Indiana, Third District, denied.

Same case below, 25 N.E.3d 103.

No. 15-112. Susan Skipp-Tittle, Petitioner v. Shawn Tittle.

577 U.S. 874, 136 S. Ct. 228, 193 L. Ed. 2d 132, 2015 U.S. LEXIS 6064, reh den 577 U.S. 1044, 136 S. Ct. 609, 193 L. Ed. 2d 490, 2015 U.S. LEXIS 7746.

October 5, 2015. Petition for writ of certiorari to the Appellate Court of Connecticut denied.

Same case below, 150 Conn. App. 64, 89 A.3d 1039.

No. 15-114. Wisconsin, Petitioner v. Ho-Chunk Nation.

577 U.S. 874, 136 S. Ct. 231, 193 L. Ed. 2d 132, 2015 U.S. LEXIS 6277.

October 5, 2015. Petition for writ of certiorari to the United States Court of Appeals for the Seventh Circuit denied.

Same case below, 784 F.3d 1076.

No. 15-116. Allan Rodgers, et al., Petitioners v. Daniel K. Knight, et al.

577 U.S. 874, 136 S. Ct. 232, 193 L. Ed. 2d 132, 2015 U.S. LEXIS 6298.

October 5, 2015. Petition for writ of certiorari to the United States Court of Appeals for the Eighth Circuit denied.

Same case below, 781 F.3d 932.

No. 15-117. Home Legend, LLC, Petitioner v. Mannington Mills, Inc.

577 U.S. 874, 136 S. Ct. 232, 193 L. Ed. 2d 132, 2015 U.S. LEXIS 6190.

October 5, 2015. Petition for writ of certiorari to the United States Court of Appeals for the Eleventh Circuit denied.

Same case below, 784 F.3d 1404.

No. 15-120. Randy Holkesvig, Petitioner v. Kelly Hutton, et al.

577 U.S. 874, 136 S. Ct. 235, 193 L. Ed. 2d 132, 2015 U.S. LEXIS 6322.

October 5, 2015. Petition for writ of certiorari to the Supreme Court of North Dakota denied.

Same case below, 2015 ND 48, 861 N.W.2d 172.

No. 15-121. Pulse Electronics, Inc., et al., Petitioners v. Halo Electronics, Inc.

577 U.S. 874, 136 S. Ct. 236, 193 L. Ed. 2d 132, 2015 U.S. LEXIS 5980.

October 5, 2015. Petition for writ of certiorari to the United States Court of Appeals for the Federal Circuit denied.

Same case below, 769 F.3d 1371.

No. 15-124. Elouise Bradley, Petitioner v. Jennifer Sabree, et al.

577 U.S. 874, 136 S. Ct. 239, 193 L. Ed. 2d 132, 2015 U.S. LEXIS 6273, reh den 577 U.S. 998, 136 S. Ct. 528, 193 L. Ed. 2d 416, 2015 U.S. LEXIS 7233.

October 5, 2015. Petition for writ of certiorari to the United States Court of Appeals for the Seventh Circuit denied.

Same case below, 594 Fed. Appx. 881.

No. 15-127. R. A., Petitioner v. Louisiana Department of Children and Family Services.

577 U.S. 874, 136 S. Ct. 299, 193 L. Ed. 2d 133, 2015 U.S. LEXIS 6348.

October 5, 2015. Petition for writ of certiorari to the Court of Appeal of Louisiana, Third Circuit, denied.

No. 15-128. Kim Dahl, Petitioner v. Charles Dahl.

577 U.S. 874, 136 S. Ct. 239, 193 L. Ed. 2d 133, 2015 U.S. LEXIS 6089.

October 5, 2015. Petition for writ of certiorari to the Supreme Court of Utah denied.

No. 15-131. Sohail Abdulla, Petitioner v. Klosinski Overstreet, LLP, et al.

577 U.S. 874, 136 S. Ct. 239, 193 L. Ed. 2d 133, 2015 U.S. LEXIS 6198.

October 5, 2015. Petition for writ of certiorari to the United States Court of Appeals for the Eleventh Circuit denied.

Same case below, 591 Fed. Appx. 865.

No. 15-134. Schwab Investments, et al., Petitioners v. Northstar Financial Advisors, Inc.

577 U.S. 874, 136 S. Ct. 240, 193 L. Ed. 2d 133, 2015 U.S. LEXIS 6269.

October 5, 2015. Petition for writ of certiorari to the United States Court of Appeals for the Ninth Circuit denied.

Same case below, 779 F.3d 1036.

No. 15-136. Harlan Dale Berndt, Petitioner v. United States.

577 U.S. 874, 136 S. Ct. 242, 193 L. Ed. 2d 133, 2015 U.S. LEXIS 6349.

October 5, 2015. Petition for writ of certiorari to the United States Court of Appeals for the Eighth Circuit denied.

No. 15-137. United States, Petitioner v. Todd Newman and Anthony Chiasson.

577 U.S. 874, 136 S. Ct. 242, 193 L. Ed. 2d 133, 2015 U.S. LEXIS 6104.

October 5, 2015. Petition for writ of certiorari to the United States Court of Appeals for the Second Circuit denied.

Same case below, 773 F.3d 438.

No. 15-142. Tammy Berera, Petitioner v. Mesa Medical Group, PLLC; and Katisha Ednacot, Petitioner v. Mesa Medical Group, PLLC.

577 U.S. 874, 136 S. Ct. 243, 193 L. Ed. 2d 133, 2015 U.S. LEXIS 5951.

October 5, 2015. Petition for writ of certiorari to the United States Court of Appeals for the Sixth Circuit denied.

Same case below, 779 F.3d 352 (first judgment); and 790 F.3d 636 (second judgment).

No. 15-144. Lee Bentley Farkas, Petitioner v. United States.

577 U.S. 875, 136 S. Ct. 243, 193 L. Ed. 2d 133, 2015 U.S. LEXIS 6363.

October 5, 2015. Petition for writ of certiorari to the United States Court of Appeals for the Fourth Circuit denied.

Same case below, 592 Fed. Appx. 211.

No. 15-149. Solomon Upshaw, Petitioner v. United States.

577 U.S. 875, 136 S. Ct. 244, 193 L. Ed. 2d 134, 2015 U.S. LEXIS 6354.

October 5, 2015. Petition for writ of certiorari to the United States Court of Appeals for the Federal Circuit denied.

Same case below, 599 Fed. Appx. 387.

No. 15-150. James Hinga, Petitioner v. MIC Group, LLC.

577 U.S. 875, 136 S. Ct. 246, 193 L. Ed. 2d 134, 2015 U.S. LEXIS 6295.

October 5, 2015. Petition for writ of certiorari to the United States Court of Appeals for the Fifth Circuit denied.

Same case below, 609 Fed. Appx. 823.

No. 15-151. Stanley William Foss, III, Petitioner v. Francisco J. Quintana, Warden.

577 U.S. 875, 136 S. Ct. 246, 193 L. Ed. 2d 134, 2015 U.S. LEXIS 6341.

October 5, 2015. Petition for writ of certiorari to the United States Court of Appeals for the Sixth Circuit denied.

No. 15-153. Sabria Lossia, Petitioner v. JPMorgan Chase Bank, N.A., Successor by Merger to Chase Home Financial, LLC.

577 U.S. 875, 136 S. Ct. 246, 193 L. Ed. 2d 134, 2015 U.S. LEXIS 6107.

October 5, 2015. Petition for writ of certiorari to the United States Court of Appeals for the Sixth Circuit denied.

No. 15-154. Albert G. Hill, et al., Petitioners v. Campbell Harrison & Dagley, L.L.P., et al.

577 U.S. 875, 136 S. Ct. 247, 193 L. Ed. 2d 134, 2015 U.S. LEXIS 6336.

October 5, 2015. Petition for writ of certiorari to the United States Court of Appeals for the Fifth Circuit denied.

Same case below, 782 F.3d 240.

No. 15-159. Matthew Staton, Petitioner v. United States.

577 U.S. 875, 136 S. Ct. 255, 193 L. Ed. 2d 134, 2015 U.S. LEXIS 6256.

October 5, 2015. Petition for writ of certiorari to the United States Court of Appeals for the Third Circuit denied.

Same case below, 605 Fed. Appx. 110.

No. 15-160. Alba Nubia Senci, Petitioner v. The Bank of New York Mellon.

577 U.S. 875, 136 S. Ct. 255, 193 L. Ed. 2d 134, 2015 U.S. LEXIS 6275, reh den 577 U.S. 1044, 136 S. Ct. 609, 193 L. Ed. 2d 490, 2015 U.S. LEXIS 7859.

October 5, 2015. Petition for writ of certiorari to the Supreme Court of Florida denied.

Same case below, 168 So. 3d 228.

No. 15-164. Abraham Baca, Petitioner v. New Mexico.

577 U.S. 875, 136 S. Ct. 255, 193 L. Ed. 2d 134, 2015 U.S. LEXIS 6090.

October 5, 2015. Petition for writ of certiorari to the Supreme Court of New Mexico denied.

Same case below, 352 P.3d 1151.

Same case below, 610 Fed. Appx. 169.

No. 15-172. Millie Howard, Petitioner v. Railroad Retirement Board.

577 U.S. 875, 136 S. Ct. 260, 193 L. Ed. 2d 135, 2015 U.S. LEXIS 6070, reh den 577 U.S. 998, 136 S. Ct. 528, 193 L. Ed. 2d 416, 2015 U.S. LEXIS 7312.

October 5, 2015. Petition for writ of certiorari to the United States Court of Appeals for the Sixth Circuit denied.

No. 15-174. Ray Leonard, et al., Petitioners v. Department of Defense, et al.

577 U.S. 875, 136 S. Ct. 261, 193 L. Ed. 2d 135, 2015 U.S. LEXIS 6320.

October 5, 2015. Petition for writ of certiorari to the United States Court of Appeals for the District of Columbia Circuit denied.

Same case below, 598 Fed. Appx. 9.

No. 15-178. Kenneth McGriff, Petitioner v. United States, et al.

577 U.S. 875, 136 S. Ct. 265, 193 L. Ed. 2d 135, 2015 U.S. LEXIS 6265.

October 5, 2015. Petition for writ of certiorari to the United States Court of Appeals for the Second Circuit denied.

No. 15-179. Microbilt Corporation, Petitioner v. Maselli Warren, P.C.

577 U.S. 875, 136 S. Ct. 265, 193 L. Ed. 2d 135, 2015 U.S. LEXIS 5974.

October 5, 2015. Petition for writ of certiorari to the United States Court of Appeals for the Third Circuit denied.

No. 15-180. Ryan David Burke, Petitioner v. Utah.

577 U.S. 875, 136 S. Ct. 266, 193 L. Ed. 2d 135, 2015 U.S. LEXIS 6352.

October 5, 2015. Petition for writ of certiorari to the Court of Appeals of Utah denied.

Same case below, 342 P.3d 299.

No. 15-183. William E. Ruhaak, Petitioner v. Commissioner of Internal Revenue.

577 U.S. 876, 136 S. Ct. 266, 193 L. Ed. 2d 135, 2015 U.S. LEXIS 6192.

October 5, 2015. Petition for writ of certiorari to the United States Court of Appeals for the Seventh Circuit denied.

No. 15-188. Heather Swain, Petitioner v. Arkansas.

577 U.S. 876, 136 S. Ct. 266, 193 L. Ed. 2d 135, 2015 U.S. LEXIS 6263.

October 5, 2015. Petition for writ of certiorari to the Supreme Court of Arkansas denied.

Same case below, 2015 Ark. 132, 459 S.W.3d 283.

No. 15-189. Tarl Brandon, Petitioner v. United States.

577 U.S. 876, 136 S. Ct. 266, 193 L. Ed. 2d 135, 2015 U.S. LEXIS 6297.

October 5, 2015. Petition for writ of certiorari to the United States Court of Appeals for the Ninth Circuit denied.

Same case below, 595 Fed. Appx. 676.

No. 15-194. Uthuppan Jacob, Petitioner v. Korean Air Lines Co. Ltd.

577 U.S. 876, 136 S. Ct. 267, 193 L. Ed. 2d 136, 2015 U.S. LEXIS 6353.

October 5, 2015. Petition for writ of certiorari to the United States Court of Appeals for the Eleventh Circuit denied.

Same case below, 606 Fed. Appx. 478.

No. 15-199. Terry Hye, Jr., Petitioner v. Mississippi.

577 U.S. 876, 136 S. Ct. 267, 193 L. Ed. 2d 136, 2015 U.S. LEXIS 6176.

October 5, 2015. Petition for writ of certiorari to the Supreme Court of Mississippi denied.

Same case below, 131 So. 3d 577.

No. 15-201. Editions Limited West, Inc., Petitioner v. Victoria Ryan.

577 U.S. 876, 136 S. Ct. 267, 193 L. Ed. 2d 136, 2015 U.S. LEXIS 6294.

October 5, 2015. Petition for writ of certiorari to the United States Court of Appeals for the Ninth Circuit denied.

Same case below, 786 F.3d 754.

No. 15-204. Calvin Carrick, Petitioner v. Asa Hutchinson, Governor of Arkansas, et al.

577 U.S. 876, 136 S. Ct. 269, 193 L. Ed. 2d 136, 2015 U.S. LEXIS 6286.

October 5, 2015. Petition for writ of certiorari to the United States Court of Appeals for the Eighth Circuit denied.

Same case below, 782 F.3d 400.

No. 15-206. MobileMedia Ideas LLC, Petitioner v. Apple Inc.

577 U.S. 876, 136 S. Ct. 270, 193 L. Ed. 2d 136, 2015 U.S. LEXIS 6280.

October 5, 2015. Petition for writ of certiorari to the United States Court of Appeals for the Federal Circuit denied.

Same case below, 780 F.3d 1159.

No. 15-208. Paul Beckmann, Petitioner v. United States.

577 U.S. 876, 136 S. Ct. 270, 193 L. Ed. 2d 136, 2015 U.S. LEXIS 6174.

October 5, 2015. Petition for writ of certiorari to the United States Court of Appeals for the Eighth Circuit denied.

Same case below, 786 F.3d 672.

No. 15-217. Carole Ann Wallace, Petitioner v. Barbara Louise Hernandez.

577 U.S. 876, 136 S. Ct. 271, 193 L. Ed. 2d 136, 2015 U.S. LEXIS 6331.

October 5, 2015. Petition for writ of certiorari to the Court of Appeals of Texas, Twelfth District, denied.

No. 15-218. Danos Kallas, Petitioner v. Barbara J. Fiala, Commissioner, New York State Department of Motor Vehicles, et al.

577 U.S. 876, 136 S. Ct. 271, 193 L. Ed. 2d 137, 2015 U.S. LEXIS 6325.

October 5, 2015. Petition for writ of certiorari to the United States Court of Appeals for the Second Circuit denied.

Same case below, 591 Fed. Appx. 30.

No. 15-219. William J. Gallion, Petitioner v. United States.

577 U.S. 876, 136 S. Ct. 271, 193 L. Ed. 2d 137, 2015 U.S. LEXIS 6051.

October 5, 2015. Petition for writ of certiorari to the United States Court of Appeals for the Sixth Circuit denied.

No. 15-221. Barbara Campbell, Petitioner v. Nationstar Mortgage, et al.

577 U.S. 876, 136 S. Ct. 272, 193 L. Ed. 2d 137, 2015 U.S. LEXIS 6165.

October 5, 2015. Petition for writ of certiorari to the United States Court of Appeals for the Sixth Circuit denied.

Same case below, 611 Fed. Appx. 288.

No. 15-225. Kelly Arzate, Petitioner v. United States.

577 U.S. 876, 136 S. Ct. 273, 193 L. Ed. 2d 137, 2015 U.S. LEXIS 6318.

October 5, 2015. Petition for writ of certiorari to the United States Court of Appeals for the First Circuit denied.

No. 15-237. Brian Scott Culver, Petitioner v. United States.

577 U.S. 876, 136 S. Ct. 277, 193 L. Ed. 2d 137, 2015 U.S. LEXIS 6103.

October 5, 2015. Petition for writ of certiorari to the United States Court of Appeals for the Eleventh Circuit denied.

No. 15-239. Steven D. Dent, aka James Walker, Petitioner v. United States.

577 U.S. 877, 136 S. Ct. 279, 193 L. Ed. 2d 137, 2015 U.S. LEXIS 6189.

October 5, 2015. Petition for writ of certiorari to the United States Court of Appeals for the Sixth Circuit denied.

Same case below, 599 Fed. Appx. 584.

No. 15-248. Christopher Curtis Kelley, Petitioner v. United States.

577 U.S. 877, 136 S. Ct. 284, 193 L. Ed. 2d 137, 2015 U.S. LEXIS 6340.

October 5, 2015. Petition for writ of certiorari to the United States Court of Appeals for the Eighth Circuit denied.

Same case below, 787 F.3d 915.

No. 15-5001. Stephen Thomas Yelverton, Petitioner v. District of Columbia Office of Bar Counsel.

577 U.S. 877, 136 S. Ct. 168, 193 L. Ed. 2d 137, 2015 U.S. LEXIS 6258.

October 5, 2015. Petition for writ of certiorari to the District of Columbia Court of Appeals denied.

Same case below, 105 A.3d 413.

Same case below, 600 Fed. Appx. 89.

No. 15-5002. Gregory Arnold Richardson, Petitioner v. Virginia.

577 U.S. 877, 136 S. Ct. 168, 193 L. Ed. 2d 138, 2015 U.S. LEXIS 5785.

October 5, 2015. Petition for writ of certiorari to the Supreme Court of Virginia denied.

No. 15-5003. Kevin J. Kaylor, Petitioner v. Brian V. Coleman, Superintendent, State Correctional Institution at Fayette et al.

577 U.S. 877, 136 S. Ct. 168, 193 L. Ed. 2d 138, 2015 U.S. LEXIS 6250.

October 5, 2015. Petition for writ of certiorari to the United States Court of Appeals for the Third Circuit denied.

No. 15-5005. Levi Scott Jones, Petitioner v. Julie L. Jones, Secretary, Florida Department of Corrections, et al.

577 U.S. 877, 136 S. Ct. 169, 193 L. Ed. 2d 138, 2015 U.S. LEXIS 6024.

October 5, 2015. Petition for writ of certiorari to the United States Court of Appeals for the Eleventh Circuit denied.

No. 15-5006. Jovan Cornelius Simon, Petitioner v. United States.

577 U.S. 877, 136 S. Ct. 169, 193 L. Ed. 2d 138, 2015 U.S. LEXIS 6291.

October 5, 2015. Petition for writ of certiorari to the United States Court of Appeals for the Fourth Circuit denied.

No. 15-5007. Clinton Dewayne Smith, Petitioner v. United States.

577 U.S. 877, 136 S. Ct. 169, 193 L. Ed. 2d 138, 2015 U.S. LEXIS 6342.

October 5, 2015. Petition for writ of certiorari to the United States Court of Appeals for the Fifth Circuit denied.

Same case below, 598 Fed. Appx. 307.

No. 15-5008. Patrick J. Winters, Petitioner v. United States.

577 U.S. 877, 136 S. Ct. 170, 193 L. Ed. 2d 138, 2015 U.S. LEXIS 6302.

October 5, 2015. Petition for writ of certiorari to the United States Court of Appeals for the Sixth Circuit denied.

Same case below, 782 F.3d 289.

No. 15-5011. Jesse Evans, Petitioner v. United States.

577 U.S. 877, 136 S. Ct. 171, 193 L. Ed. 2d 138, 2015 U.S. LEXIS 6018.

October 5, 2015. Petition for writ of certiorari to the United States Court of Appeals for the Tenth Circuit denied.

Same case below, 782 F.3d 1115.

No. 15-5013. Luis Ramon Aponte-Torres, Petitioner v. United States.

577 U.S. 877, 136 S. Ct. 171, 193 L. Ed. 2d 138, 2015 U.S. LEXIS 6183.

October 5, 2015. Petition for writ of certiorari to the United States Court of Appeals for the First Circuit denied.

No. 15-5014. Susan Augustus, Petitioner v. AHRC Nassau.

577 U.S. 877, 136 S. Ct. 171, 193 L. Ed. 2d 139, 2015 U.S. LEXIS 6329, reh den 577 U.S. 1023, 136 S. Ct. 577, 193 L. Ed. 2d 459, 2015 U.S. LEXIS 7431.

October 5, 2015. Petition for writ of certiorari to the United States Court of Appeals for the Second Circuit denied.

Same case below, 596 Fed. Appx. 41.

No. 15-5015. Isaac Alcozer, Petitioner v. Randy Pfister, Warden.

577 U.S. 877, 136 S. Ct. 171, 193 L. Ed. 2d 139, 2015 U.S. LEXIS 6011.

October 5, 2015. Petition for writ of certiorari to the United States Court of Appeals for the Seventh Circuit denied.

No. 15-5017. Felipe Sanchez Avila, Petitioner v. Scott Frauenheim, Warden.

577 U.S. 877, 136 S. Ct. 172, 193 L. Ed. 2d 139, 2015 U.S. LEXIS 6157.

October 5, 2015. Petition for writ of certiorari to the United States Court of Appeals for the Ninth Circuit denied.

No. 15-5018. Earl Pierce, Petitioner v. United States.

577 U.S. 877, 136 S. Ct. 172, 193 L. Ed. 2d 139, 2015 U.S. LEXIS 6145.

October 5, 2015. Petition for writ of certiorari to the United States Court of Appeals for the Second Circuit denied.

Same case below, 785 F.3d 832.

No. 15-5020. Duy Pham, Petitioner v. L. S. McEwen, Warden.

577 U.S. 878, 136 S. Ct. 172, 193 L. Ed. 2d 139, 2015 U.S. LEXIS 6095.

October 5, 2015. Petition for writ of certiorari to the United States Court of Appeals for the Ninth Circuit denied.

Same case below, 588 Fed. Appx. 737.

No. 15-5021. Kenneth Porter, Petitioner v. United States.

577 U.S. 878, 136 S. Ct. 172, 193 L. Ed. 2d 139, 2015 U.S. LEXIS 6355.

October 5, 2015. Petition for writ of certiorari to the United States Court of Appeals for the Eleventh Circuit denied.

Same case below, 609 Fed. Appx. 1008.

No. 15-5022. David Wayne Kiehle, Petitioner v. Charles L. Ryan, Director, Arizona Department of Corrections, et al.

577 U.S. 878, 136 S. Ct. 172, 193 L. Ed. 2d 139, 2015 U.S. LEXIS 6332.

October 5, 2015. Petition for writ of certiorari to the United States Court of Appeals for the Ninth Circuit denied.

Same case below, 599 Fed. Appx. 642.

No. 15-5023. Donnie Maxwell, Petitioner v. Illinois.

577 U.S. 878, 136 S. Ct. 172, 193 L. Ed. 2d 139, 2015 U.S. LEXIS 6346.

October 5, 2015. Petition for writ of certiorari to the Appellate Court of Illinois, Fourth District, denied.

No. 15-5024. Michael David Wilson, Petitioner v. Heidi M. Lackner, Warden, et al.

577 U.S. 878, 136 S. Ct. 173, 193 L. Ed. 2d 140, 2015 U.S. LEXIS 6191.

October 5, 2015. Petition for writ of certiorari to the United States Court of Appeals for the Ninth Circuit denied.

Same case below, 599 Fed. Appx. 634.

No. 15-5025. Selomi Monge Villalta, Petitioner v. Loretta E. Lynch, Attorney General, et al.

577 U.S. 878, 136 S. Ct. 173, 193 L. Ed. 2d 140, 2015 U.S. LEXIS 5904, reh den 577 U.S. 1023, 136 S. Ct. 577, 193 L. Ed. 2d 459, 2015 U.S. LEXIS 7407.

October 5, 2015. Petition for writ of certiorari to the United States Court of Appeals for the Ninth Circuit denied.

Same case below, 599 Fed. Appx. 628.

No. 15-5027. Richard Lyon, Petitioner v. New York.

577 U.S. 878, 136 S. Ct. 173, 193 L. Ed. 2d 140, 2015 U.S. LEXIS 6299.

October 5, 2015. Petition for writ of certiorari to the Appellate Division, Supreme Court of New York, Fourth Judicial Department, denied.

Same case below, 125 App. Div. 3d 1460, 1 N.Y.S.3d 874.

No. 15-5028. Anthony Fred Martin, Petitioner v. William Byars, et al.

577 U.S. 878, 136 S. Ct. 173, 193 L. Ed. 2d 140, 2015 U.S. LEXIS 6309.

October 5, 2015. Petition for writ of certiorari to the United States Court of Appeals for the Fourth Circuit denied.

Same case below, 602 Fed. Appx. 136.

No. 15-5029. Darius Jean, Petitioner v. Steven E. Racette, Superintendent, Great Meadow Correctional Facility.

577 U.S. 878, 136 S. Ct. 173, 193 L. Ed. 2d 140, 2015 U.S. LEXIS 6300.

October 5, 2015. Petition for writ of certiorari to the United States Court of Appeals for the Second Circuit denied.

Same case below, 523 Fed. Appx. 744.

No. 15-5030. Timmy J. Reichling, Petitioner v. United States.

577 U.S. 878, 136 S. Ct. 174, 193 L. Ed. 2d 140, 2015 U.S. LEXIS 6334.

October 5, 2015. Petition for writ of certiorari to the United States Court of Appeals for the Seventh Circuit denied.

Same case below, 781 F.3d 883.

No. 15-5031. Ricky Brannon, Petitioner v. Robert M. Stevenson, Warden.

577 U.S. 878, 136 S. Ct. 174, 193 L. Ed. 2d 140, 2015 U.S. LEXIS 6170, reh den 577 U.S. 1023, 136 S. Ct. 577, 193 L. Ed. 2d 460, 2015 U.S. LEXIS 7368.

October 5, 2015. Petition for writ of certiorari to the United States Court of Appeals for the Fourth Circuit denied.

Same case below, 593 Fed. Appx. 252.

No. 15-5033. Huguens C. Southaite, Petitioner v. Nassau County, New York, et al.

577 U.S. 878, 136 S. Ct. 174, 193 L. Ed. 2d 141, 2015 U.S. LEXIS 6361.

October 5, 2015. Petition for writ of certiorari to the United States Court of Appeals for the Second Circuit denied.

No. 15-5034. Dennis Dinwiddie, Petitioner v. United States.

577 U.S. 878, 136 S. Ct. 174, 193 L. Ed. 2d 141, 2015 U.S. LEXIS 6003.

October 5, 2015. Petition for writ of certiorari to the United States Court of Appeals for the Eighth Circuit denied.

No. 15-5035. Alfredo Cervantes-Carrillo, Petitioner v. United States.

577 U.S. 878, 136 S. Ct. 174, 193 L. Ed. 2d 141, 2015 U.S. LEXIS 5424.

October 5, 2015. Petition for writ of certiorari to the United States Court of Appeals for the Fifth Circuit denied.

Same case below, 594 Fed. Appx. 275.

No. 15-5036. Hafan Antonio Riley, Petitioner v. United States.

577 U.S. 879, 136 S. Ct. 175, 193 L. Ed. 2d 141, 2015 U.S. LEXIS 5420.

October 5, 2015. Petition for writ of certiorari to the United States Court of Appeals for the Fourth Circuit denied.

Same case below, 586 Fed. Appx. 118.

No. 15-5037. Jose Roberto Pacheco-Alvarado and Cesar de la Cruz, Petitioners v. United States.

577 U.S. 879, 136 S. Ct. 175, 193 L. Ed. 2d 141, 2015 U.S. LEXIS 5088.

October 5, 2015. Petition for writ of certiorari to the United States Court of Appeals for the Fifth Circuit denied.

Same case below, 782 F.3d 213.

No. 15-5038. John Mellquist, Petitioner v. Florida.

577 U.S. 879, 136 S. Ct. 175, 193 L. Ed. 2d 141, 2015 U.S. LEXIS 5493.

October 5, 2015. Petition for writ of certiorari to the District Court of Appeal of Florida, Second District, denied.

Same case below, 200 So. 3d 1277.

No. 15-5039. Lorenzo Osvaldo Gonzalez-Robles, Petitioner v. United States.

577 U.S. 879, 136 S. Ct. 175, 193 L. Ed. 2d 141, 2015 U.S. LEXIS 5463.

October 5, 2015. Petition for writ of certiorari to the United States Court of Appeals for the Ninth Circuit denied.

Same case below, 603 Fed. Appx. 558.

No. 15-5041. Clifford Marcus Winkles, Petitioner v. No Named Respondent.

577 U.S. 879, 136 S. Ct. 175, 193 L. Ed. 2d 141, 2015 U.S. LEXIS 5171.

October 5, 2015. Petition for writ of certiorari to the United States Court of Appeals for the Tenth Circuit denied.

Same case below, 594 Fed. Appx. 550.

No. 15-5042. David Joseph Gariano, Petitioner v. United States.

577 U.S. 879, 136 S. Ct. 175, 193 L. Ed. 2d 142, 2015 U.S. LEXIS 5170.

October 5, 2015. Petition for writ of certiorari to the United States Court of Appeals for the Fourth Circuit denied.

No. 15-5044. Robert Lee Ortega, Petitioner v. William Stephens, Director, Texas Department of Criminal Justice, Correctional Institutions Division.

577 U.S. 879, 136 S. Ct. 176, 193 L. Ed. 2d 142, 2015 U.S. LEXIS 5334, reh den 577 U.S. 1095, 136 S. Ct. 883, 193 L. Ed. 2d 775, 2016 U.S. LEXIS 579.

October 5, 2015. Petition for writ of certiorari to the United States Court of Appeals for the Fifth Circuit denied.

Same case below, 784 F.3d 250.

No. 15-5045. Gordon Lamarr Moore, Petitioner v. United States.

577 U.S. 879, 136 S. Ct. 176, 193 L. Ed. 2d 142, 2015 U.S. LEXIS 5275.

October 5, 2015. Petition for writ of certiorari to the United States Court of Appeals for the Eighth Circuit denied.

Same case below, 778 F.3d 719.

No. 15-5046. Mark Razo, Petitioner v. United States.

577 U.S. 879, 136 S. Ct. 176, 193 L. Ed. 2d 142, 2015 U.S. LEXIS 5455.

October 5, 2015. Petition for writ of certiorari to the United States Court of Appeals for the First Circuit denied.

Same case below, 782 F.3d 31.

No. 15-5048. Miguel Vargas, Petitioner v. W. L. Montgomery, Warden.

577 U.S. 879, 136 S. Ct. 176, 193 L. Ed. 2d 142, 2015 U.S. LEXIS 5352.

October 5, 2015. Petition for writ of certiorari to the United States Court of Appeals for the Ninth Circuit denied.

No. 15-5049. Lewis Wright, Petitioner v. Pennsylvania, et al.

577 U.S. 879, 136 S. Ct. 176, 193 L. Ed. 2d 142, 2015 U.S. LEXIS 5055.

October 5, 2015. Petition for writ of certiorari to the United States Court of Appeals for the Third Circuit denied.

No. 15-5050. Carlos Andres Brutus, Petitioner v. United States.

577 U.S. 879, 136 S. Ct. 176, 193 L. Ed. 2d 142, 2015 U.S. LEXIS 5411.

October 5, 2015. Petition for writ of certiorari to the United States Court of Appeals for the Eleventh Circuit denied.

No. 15-5053. Willie G. Smith, Petitioner v. Phillips Winters Apartments, et al.

577 U.S. 879, 136 S. Ct. 177, 193 L. Ed. 2d 142, 2015 U.S. LEXIS 5186.

October 5, 2015. Petition for writ of certiorari to the United States Court of Appeals for the Eleventh Circuit denied.

Same case below, 599 Fed. Appx. 365.

No. 15-5055. Vandai Lapriest Irick, Petitioner v. United States.

577 U.S. 879, 136 S. Ct. 177, 193 L. Ed. 2d 143, 2015 U.S. LEXIS 5148.

October 5, 2015. Petition for writ of certiorari to the United States Court of Appeals for the Fourth Circuit denied.

Same case below, 608 Fed. Appx. 132.

No. 15-5056. Trent Alvon Smith, Petitioner v. Wood County District Attorney's Office, et al.

577 U.S. 880, 136 S. Ct. 300, 193 L. Ed. 2d 143, 2015 U.S. LEXIS 5222, reh den 577 U.S. 1023, 136 S. Ct. 578, 193 L. Ed. 2d 460, 2015 U.S. LEXIS 7386.

October 5, 2015. Petition for writ of certiorari to the Court of Appeals of Texas, Third District, denied.

No. 15-5059. Shawnton Deon Johnson, Petitioner v. United States.

577 U.S. 880, 136 S. Ct. 178, 193 L. Ed. 2d 143, 2015 U.S. LEXIS 5155.

October 5, 2015. Petition for writ of certiorari to the United States Court of Appeals for the Eleventh Circuit denied.

Same case below, 777 F.3d 1270.

No. 15-5061. Louis Michael Mann, Petitioner v. Nancy Giroux, Superintendent, State Correctional Institution at Albion, et al.

577 U.S. 880, 136 S. Ct. 178, 193 L. Ed. 2d 143, 2015 U.S. LEXIS 5263.

October 5, 2015. Petition for writ of certiorari to the United States Court of Appeals for the Third Circuit denied.

No. 15-5062. Juan Pablo Jimenez, Petitioner v. United States.

577 U.S. 880, 136 S. Ct. 178, 193 L. Ed. 2d 143, 2015 U.S. LEXIS 5306.

October 5, 2015. Petition for writ of certiorari to the United States Court of Appeals for the Ninth Circuit denied.

Same case below, 603 Fed. Appx. 601.

No. 15-5063. Stephen Richard Brown, Petitioner v. Harold W. Clarke, Director, Virginia Department of Corrections.

577 U.S. 880, 136 S. Ct. 178, 193 L. Ed. 2d 143, 2015 U.S. LEXIS 5042.

October 5, 2015. Petition for writ of certiorari to the United States Court of Appeals for the Fourth Circuit denied.

Same case below, 594 Fed. Appx. 174.

No. 15-5064. Carlos Alfonso Almanza Sanchez, Petitioner v. United States.

577 U.S. 880, 136 S. Ct. 179, 193 L. Ed. 2d 143, 2015 U.S. LEXIS 5087.

October 5, 2015. Petition for writ of certiorari to the United States Court of Appeals for the Eleventh Circuit denied.

Same case below, 606 Fed. Appx. 971.

Same case below, 599 Fed. Appx. 162.

No. 15-5065. Jesse Lin Antolin, Petitioner v. California.

577 U.S. 880, 136 S. Ct. 179, 193 L. Ed. 2d 144, 2015 U.S. LEXIS 5253.

October 5, 2015. Petition for writ of certiorari to the Court of Appeal of California, First Appellate District, denied.

No. 15-5066. Eduardo Jose Aviles, Petitioner v. United States.

577 U.S. 880, 136 S. Ct. 179, 193 L. Ed. 2d 144, 2015 U.S. LEXIS 5268.

October 5, 2015. Petition for writ of certiorari to the United States Court of Appeals for the Fifth Circuit denied.

Same case below, 599 Fed. Appx. 165.

No. 15-5067. Francisco Javier Estrada-Garcia, Petitioner v. United States.

577 U.S. 880, 136 S. Ct. 179, 193 L. Ed. 2d 144, 2015 U.S. LEXIS 5452.

October 5, 2015. Petition for writ of certiorari to the United States Court of Appeals for the Fifth Circuit denied.

Same case below, 599 Fed. Appx. 164.

No. 15-5068. Jose Guadalupe Gurrola-Perez, Petitioner v. United States.

577 U.S. 880, 136 S. Ct. 179, 193 L. Ed. 2d 144, 2015 U.S. LEXIS 5078.

October 5, 2015. Petition for writ of certiorari to the United States Court of Appeals for the Fifth Circuit denied.

No. 15-5069. Abukar Osman Beyle, Petitioner v. United States.

577 U.S. 880, 136 S. Ct. 179, 193 L. Ed. 2d 144, 2015 U.S. LEXIS 5077.

October 5, 2015. Petition for writ of certiorari to the United States Court of Appeals for the Fourth Circuit denied.

Same case below, 782 F.3d 159.

No. 15-5070. Donald Lewayne Tucker, Petitioner v. United States.

577 U.S. 880, 136 S. Ct. 180, 193 L. Ed. 2d 144, 2015 U.S. LEXIS 5202.

October 5, 2015. Petition for writ of certiorari to the United States Court of Appeals for the Tenth Circuit denied.

Same case below, 602 Fed. Appx. 463.

No. 15-5071. M. Robert Ullman, Petitioner v. Superior Court of Pennsylvania, et al. (two judgments).

577 U.S. 880, 136 S. Ct. 180, 193 L. Ed. 2d 144, 2015 U.S. LEXIS 5090.

October 5, 2015. Petition for writ of certiorari to the United States Court of Appeals for the Third Circuit denied.

Same case below, 603 Fed. Appx. 77 (second judgment).

No. 15-5072. Natalio O. Venegas, Petitioner v. Scott Frauenheim, Warden.

577 U.S. 880, 136 S. Ct. 180, 193 L. Ed. 2d 144, 2015 U.S. LEXIS 5092.

October 5, 2015. Petition for writ of certiorari to the United States Court of Appeals for the Ninth Circuit denied.

No. 15-5073. Wilbert Patrick Stewart, Petitioner v. William Stephens, Director, Texas Department of Criminal Justice, Correctional Institutions Division.

577 U.S. 881, 136 S. Ct. 300, 193 L. Ed. 2d 145, 2015 U.S. LEXIS 5461, reh den 577 U.S. 1054, 136 S. Ct. 705, 193 L. Ed. 2d 531, 2015 U.S. LEXIS 7962.

October 5, 2015. Petition for writ of certiorari to the United States Court of Appeals for the Fifth Circuit denied.

Same case below, 599 Fed. Appx. 173.

No. 15-5074. Rene Rivas, Jr., Petitioner v. William Stephens, Director, Texas Department of Correctional Justice, Correctional Institutions Division.

577 U.S. 881, 136 S. Ct. 180, 193 L. Ed. 2d 145, 2015 U.S. LEXIS 5323, reh den 577 U.S. 1095, 136 S. Ct. 883, 193 L. Ed. 2d 775, 2016 U.S. LEXIS 207.

October 5, 2015. Petition for writ of certiorari to the United States Court of Appeals for the Fifth Circuit denied.

No. 15-5075. Essie Simpson, III, Petitioner v. Elvin Valenzuela, Warden.

577 U.S. 881, 136 S. Ct. 180, 193 L. Ed. 2d 145, 2015 U.S. LEXIS 5147.

October 5, 2015. Petition for writ of certiorari to the United States Court of Appeals for the Ninth Circuit denied.

Same case below, 600 Fed. Appx. 569.

No. 15-5076. Shannon Dawson, Petitioner v. United States.

577 U.S. 881, 136 S. Ct. 180, 193 L. Ed. 2d 145, 2015 U.S. LEXIS 5089.

October 5, 2015. Petition for writ of certiorari to the United States Court of Appeals for the Eleventh Circuit denied.

No. 15-5077. Richard Kearney, Petitioner v. Brian Fischer, Commissioner, New York Department of Correctional Services, et al.

577 U.S. 881, 136 S. Ct. 181, 193 L. Ed. 2d 145, 2015 U.S. LEXIS 5146, reh den 577 U.S. 998, 136 S. Ct. 528, 193 L. Ed. 2d 416, 2015 U.S. LEXIS 7308.

October 5, 2015. Petition for writ of certiorari to the United States Court of Appeals for the Second Circuit denied.

Same case below, 609 Fed. Appx. 673.

No. 15-5078. William L. Kelley, Petitioner v. Alan J. Lazaroff, Warden.

577 U.S. 881, 136 S. Ct. 181, 193 L. Ed. 2d 145, 2015 U.S. LEXIS 5429, reh den 577 U.S. 1023, 136 S. Ct. 578, 193 L. Ed. 2d 460, 2015 U.S. LEXIS 7372.

October 5, 2015. Petition for writ of certiorari to the United States Court of Appeals for the Sixth Circuit denied.

No. 15-5079. Reuben Rivera, Petitioner v. Louis S. Folino, Superintendent, State Correctional Institution at Greene, et al.

577 U.S. 881, 136 S. Ct. 181, 193 L. Ed. 2d 145, 2015 U.S. LEXIS 5379.

October 5, 2015. Petition for writ of certiorari to the United States Court of Appeals for the Third Circuit denied.

No. 15-5080. Rafael Ramirez-Macias, Petitioner v. United States.

577 U.S. 881, 136 S. Ct. 181, 193 L. Ed. 2d 145, 2015 U.S. LEXIS 5118.

October 5, 2015. Petition for writ of certiorari to the United States Court of Appeals for the Ninth Circuit denied.

Same case below, 584 Fed. Appx. 818.

No. 15-5081. Paul Joseph Richter, Petitioner v. United States.

577 U.S. 881, 136 S. Ct. 181, 193 L. Ed. 2d 146, 2015 U.S. LEXIS 5060.

October 5, 2015. Petition for writ of certiorari to the United States Court of Appeals for the Ninth Circuit denied.

Same case below, 782 F.3d 498.

No. 15-5082. Wanda Bursey, Petitioner v. Michael McGowan, et al.

577 U.S. 881, 136 S. Ct. 182, 193 L. Ed. 2d 146, 2015 U.S. LEXIS 5370.

October 5, 2015. Petition for writ of certiorari to the Court of Appeal of California, Fourth Appellate District, Division One, denied.

No. 15-5085. Erick Perez-Chavez, Petitioner v. United States.

577 U.S. 881, 136 S. Ct. 182, 193 L. Ed. 2d 146, 2015 U.S. LEXIS 5305.

October 5, 2015. Petition for writ of certiorari to the United States Court of Appeals for the Ninth Circuit denied.

Same case below, 600 Fed. Appx. 534.

No. 15-5086. Gregory P. Nesselrode, Petitioner v. Department of Education.

577 U.S. 881, 136 S. Ct. 183, 193 L. Ed. 2d 146, 2015 U.S. LEXIS 5164, reh den 577 U.S. 998, 136 S. Ct. 528, 193 L. Ed. 2d 416, 2015 U.S. LEXIS 7295.

October 5, 2015. Petition for writ of certiorari to the United States Court of Appeals for the Ninth Circuit denied.

No. 15-5087. Santos Victorino Membreno, Petitioner v. United States.

577 U.S. 881, 136 S. Ct. 183, 193 L. Ed. 2d 146, 2015 U.S. LEXIS 5296.

October 5, 2015. Petition for writ of certiorari to the United States Court of Appeals for the Fifth Circuit denied.

Same case below, 599 Fed. Appx. 206.

No. 15-5088. Jesus Padilla-Martinez, Petitioner v. Loretta E. Lynch, Attorney General.

577 U.S. 881, 136 S. Ct. 183, 193 L. Ed. 2d 146, 2015 U.S. LEXIS 5133.

October 5, 2015. Petition for writ of certiorari to the United States Court of Appeals for the Ninth Circuit denied.

Same case below, 770 F.3d 825.

No. 15-5089. Andrew Modjewski, Petitioner v. United States.

577 U.S. 882, 136 S. Ct. 183, 193 L. Ed. 2d 146, 2015 U.S. LEXIS 5332.

October 5, 2015. Petition for writ of certiorari to the United States Court of Appeals for the Seventh Circuit denied.

Same case below, 783 F.3d 645.

No. 15-5090. Steven McCall, Petitioner v. United States.

577 U.S. 882, 136 S. Ct. 183, 193 L. Ed. 2d 146, 2015 U.S. LEXIS 5083.

October 5, 2015. Petition for writ of certiorari to the United States Court of Appeals for the Fourth Circuit denied.

No. 15-5091. Lorena Ortega-Mora, Petitioner v. United States.

577 U.S. 882, 136 S. Ct. 183, 193 L. Ed. 2d 147, 2015 U.S. LEXIS 5138.

October 5, 2015. Petition for writ of certiorari to the United States Court of Appeals for the Ninth Circuit denied.

Same case below, 585 Fed. Appx. 716.

No. 15-5092. Courtney Montez Means, Petitioner v. Brenda Jones, Warden.

577 U.S. 882, 136 S. Ct. 184, 193 L. Ed. 2d 147, 2015 U.S. LEXIS 5237.

October 5, 2015. Petition for writ of certiorari to the United States Court of Appeals for the Sixth Circuit denied.

No. 15-5094. Climpson Martin, Petitioner v. Alabama.

577 U.S. 882, 136 S. Ct. 184, 193 L. Ed. 2d 147, 2015 U.S. LEXIS 5321.

October 5, 2015. Petition for writ of certiorari to the Court of Criminal Appeals of Alabama denied.

Same case below, 195 So. 3d 1086.

No. 15-5095. Lionel Valenzuela Pereida, Petitioner v. Charles L. Ryan, et al.

577 U.S. 882, 136 S. Ct. 184, 193 L. Ed. 2d 147, 2015 U.S. LEXIS 5035.

October 5, 2015. Petition for writ of certiorari to the United States Court of Appeals for the Ninth Circuit denied.

No. 15-5097. Senen Ballesteros-Valverde, Petitioner v. United States.

577 U.S. 882, 136 S. Ct. 184, 193 L. Ed. 2d 147, 2015 U.S. LEXIS 5093.

October 5, 2015. Petition for writ of certiorari to the United States Court of Appeals for the Fifth Circuit denied.

Same case below, 599 Fed. Appx. 157.

No. 15-5098. Ponciano Mata, Petitioner v. United States.

577 U.S. 882, 136 S. Ct. 184, 193 L. Ed. 2d 147, 2015 U.S. LEXIS 5236.

October 5, 2015. Petition for writ of certiorari to the United States Court of Appeals for the Ninth Circuit denied.

Same case below, 609 Fed. Appx. 401.

No. 15-5099. Angela Nails, Petitioner v. U.S. Bank N.A.

577 U.S. 882, 136 S. Ct. 185, 193 L. Ed. 2d 147, 2015 U.S. LEXIS 5182.

October 5, 2015. Petition for writ of certiorari to the Supreme Court of North Dakota denied.

Same case below, 861 N.W.2d 172.

No. 15-5100. Gary Richard Lackey, Petitioner v. United States.

577 U.S. 882, 136 S. Ct. 185, 193 L. Ed. 2d 147, 2015 U.S. LEXIS 5131.

October 5, 2015. Petition for writ of certiorari to the United States Court of Appeals for the Fourth Circuit denied.

Same case below, 591 Fed. Appx. 202.

Same case below, 790 F.3d 26.

No. 15-5101. Robert Arthur Reed, Petitioner v. United States.

577 U.S. 882, 136 S. Ct. 185, 193 L. Ed. 2d 148, 2015 U.S. LEXIS 5408.

October 5, 2015. Petition for writ of certiorari to the United States Court of Appeals for the Tenth Circuit denied.

Same case below, 602 Fed. Appx. 436.

No. 15-5102. Terrance Cotrell Robinson, Petitioner v. Keith Cooley, Warden.

577 U.S. 882, 136 S. Ct. 185, 193 L. Ed. 2d 148, 2015 U.S. LEXIS 5407.

October 5, 2015. Petition for writ of certiorari to the United States Court of Appeals for the Fifth Circuit denied.

No. 15-5103. Jose Velez-Figueroa, Petitioner v. United States.

577 U.S. 882, 136 S. Ct. 185, 193 L. Ed. 2d 148, 2015 U.S. LEXIS 5297.

October 5, 2015. Petition for writ of certiorari to the United States Court of Appeals for the First Circuit denied.

No. 15-5104. Kenny Torres-Colon, Petitioner v. United States.

577 U.S. 882, 136 S. Ct. 185, 193 L. Ed. 2d 148, 2015 U.S. LEXIS 5425.

October 5, 2015. Petition for writ of certiorari to the United States Court of Appeals for the First Circuit denied.

No. 15-5105. Armando Ybarra, Petitioner v. Kim Holland, Warden.

577 U.S. 882, 136 S. Ct. 186, 193 L. Ed. 2d 148, 2015 U.S. LEXIS 5486.

October 5, 2015. Petition for writ of certiorari to the United States Court of Appeals for the Ninth Circuit denied.

Same case below, 595 Fed. Appx. 713.

No. 15-5106. Omar Sumpter, Petitioner v. Marylin E. Atkins, et al.

577 U.S. 882, 136 S. Ct. 186, 193 L. Ed. 2d 148, 2015 U.S. LEXIS 5049.

October 5, 2015. Petition for writ of certiorari to the United States Court of Appeals for the Sixth Circuit denied.

No. 15-5107. Rashaad Tiwania Jones, Petitioner v. Harold W. Clarke, Director, Virginia Department of Corrections.

577 U.S. 883, 136 S. Ct. 186, 193 L. Ed. 2d 148, 2015 U.S. LEXIS 5276.

October 5, 2015. Petition for writ of certiorari to the United States Court of Appeals for the Fourth Circuit denied.

Same case below, 783 F.3d 987.

No. 15-5108. Gary Ray Spears, Petitioner v. Clay Tatum, Warden.

577 U.S. 883, 136 S. Ct. 300, 193 L. Ed. 2d 148, 2015 U.S. LEXIS 5073.

October 5, 2015. Petition for writ of certiorari to the United States Court of Appeals for the Eleventh Circuit denied.

Same case below, 605 Fed. Appx. 900.

———

No. 15-5109. Vladimir Petrovich Mazur, Petitioner v. United States.

577 U.S. 883, 136 S. Ct. 186, 193 L. Ed. 2d 149, 2015 U.S. LEXIS 5074.

October 5, 2015. Petition for writ of certiorari to the United States Court of Appeals for the Fourth Circuit denied.

Same case below, 599 Fed. Appx. 109.

———

No. 15-5111. Joseph Edward Francis Lunz, Petitioner v. Elizabeth A. O'Meara, Superintendent, Gouverneur Correctional Facility.

577 U.S. 883, 136 S. Ct. 186, 193 L. Ed. 2d 149, 2015 U.S. LEXIS 5069, reh den 577 U.S. 998, 136 S. Ct. 528, 193 L. Ed. 2d 416, 2015 U.S. LEXIS 7253.

October 5, 2015. Petition for writ of certiorari to the United States Court of Appeals for the Second Circuit denied.

———

No. 15-5112. Timothy James Donahue, Petitioner v. United States.

577 U.S. 883, 136 S. Ct. 187, 193 L. Ed. 2d 149, 2015 U.S. LEXIS 5262.

October 5, 2015. Petition for writ of certiorari to the United States Court of Appeals for the Fourth Circuit denied.

Same case below, 607 Fed. Appx. 233.

———

No. 15-5114. Joel Costilla, Petitioner v. United States.

577 U.S. 883, 136 S. Ct. 188, 193 L. Ed. 2d 149, 2015 U.S. LEXIS 5123.

October 5, 2015. Petition for writ of certiorari to the United States Court of Appeals for the Fifth Circuit denied.

Same case below, 599 Fed. Appx. 194.

———

No. 15-5116. Albert Brunson, Petitioner v. Cheryl Price, Warden, et al.

577 U.S. 883, 136 S. Ct. 188, 193 L. Ed. 2d 149, 2015 U.S. LEXIS 5350.

October 5, 2015. Petition for writ of certiorari to the United States Court of Appeals for the Eleventh Circuit denied.

———

No. 15-5117. Maurice Davis, Petitioner v. United States.

577 U.S. 883, 136 S. Ct. 188, 193 L. Ed. 2d 149, 2015 U.S. LEXIS 5121.

October 5, 2015. Petition for writ of certiorari to the United States Court of Appeals for the Seventh Circuit denied.

Same case below, 761 F.3d 713.

———

No. 15-5118. Larry Falls, Petitioner v. United States.

577 U.S. 883, 136 S. Ct. 188, 193 L. Ed. 2d 149, 2015 U.S. LEXIS 5290.

October 5, 2015. Petition for writ of certiorari to the United States Court of Appeals for the Second Circuit denied.

Same case below, 543 Fed. Appx. 54.

Same case below, 597 Fed. Appx. 749.

No. 15-5119. Roni L. Medearis, Petitioner v. William Stephens, Director, Texas Department of Criminal Justice, Correctional Institutions Division.

577 U.S. 883, 136 S. Ct. 188, 193 L. Ed. 2d 150, 2015 U.S. LEXIS 5209.

October 5, 2015. Petition for writ of certiorari to the United States Court of Appeals for the Fifth Circuit denied.

No. 15-5120. David Medrano-Rodriguez, Petitioner v. United States.

577 U.S. 883, 136 S. Ct. 188, 193 L. Ed. 2d 150, 2015 U.S. LEXIS 5440.

October 5, 2015. Petition for writ of certiorari to the United States Court of Appeals for the Fifth Circuit denied.

Same case below, 606 Fed. Appx. 759.

No. 15-5121. Philip C. Tobin, Petitioner v. Kevin N. Cuddy, Justice, Superior Court of Maine.

577 U.S. 883, 136 S. Ct. 189, 193 L. Ed. 2d 150, 2015 U.S. LEXIS 5477.

October 5, 2015. Petition for writ of certiorari to the United States Court of Appeals for the First Circuit denied.

No. 15-5122. Charles Alonzo Tunstall-Bey, Petitioner v. Bryan Wells, Correctional Administrator, Pender Correctional Institution.

577 U.S. 883, 136 S. Ct. 190, 193 L. Ed. 2d 150, 2015 U.S. LEXIS 5313.

October 5, 2015. Petition for writ of certiorari to the United States Court of Appeals for the Fourth Circuit denied.

No. 15-5123. Kevin A. Tolliver, Petitioner v. Ohio.

577 U.S. 883, 136 S. Ct. 190, 193 L. Ed. 2d 150, 2015 U.S. LEXIS 5439.

October 5, 2015. Petition for writ of certiorari to the Court of Appeals of Ohio, Franklin County, denied.

No. 15-5124. Shelby Anthony Vogt, Petitioner v. Iowa, et al.

577 U.S. 884, 136 S. Ct. 190, 193 L. Ed. 2d 150, 2015 U.S. LEXIS 5431, reh den 577 U.S. 1023, 136 S. Ct. 578, 193 L. Ed. 2d 460, 2015 U.S. LEXIS 7397.

October 5, 2015. Petition for writ of certiorari to the United States Court of Appeals for the Eighth Circuit denied.

No. 15-5126. Michael D. Wright, Petitioner v. Virginia.

577 U.S. 884, 136 S. Ct. 190, 193 L. Ed. 2d 150, 2015 U.S. LEXIS 5072.

October 5, 2015. Petition for writ of certiorari to the Supreme Court of Virginia denied.

No. 15-5127. Roberto Cordova, Petitioner v. Amy Miller, Warden.

577 U.S. 884, 136 S. Ct. 191, 193 L. Ed. 2d 150, 2015 U.S. LEXIS 5199.

October 5, 2015. Petition for writ of certiorari to the United States Court of Appeals for the Ninth Circuit denied.

Same case below, 606 Fed. Appx. 744.

No. 15-5128. Virginia Frazier, Petitioner v. Deborah K. Johnson, Warden.

577 U.S. 884, 136 S. Ct. 191, 193 L. Ed. 2d 151, 2015 U.S. LEXIS 5450.

October 5, 2015. Petition for writ of certiorari to the United States Court of Appeals for the Ninth Circuit denied.

Same case below, 599 Fed. Appx. 781.

No. 15-5129. Daniel Hufstetler, Petitioner v. United States.

577 U.S. 884, 136 S. Ct. 191, 193 L. Ed. 2d 151, 2015 U.S. LEXIS 5071.

October 5, 2015. Petition for writ of certiorari to the United States Court of Appeals for the First Circuit denied.

Same case below, 782 F.3d 19.

No. 15-5130. Jesse Quinn Harrison, Petitioner v. United States.

577 U.S. 884, 136 S. Ct. 191, 193 L. Ed. 2d 151, 2015 U.S. LEXIS 5220.

October 5, 2015. Petition for writ of certiorari to the United States Court of Appeals for the Ninth Circuit denied.

Same case below, 599 Fed. Appx. 654.

No. 15-5131. Dwight L. Looney, Petitioner v. United States.

577 U.S. 884, 136 S. Ct. 191, 193 L. Ed. 2d 151, 2015 U.S. LEXIS 5378.

October 5, 2015. Petition for writ of certiorari to the United States Court of Appeals for the Fifth Circuit denied.

No. 15-5133. Christopher Sean Daniels, Petitioner v. United States.

577 U.S. 884, 136 S. Ct. 191, 193 L. Ed. 2d 151, 2015 U.S. LEXIS 5354.

October 5, 2015. Petition for writ of certiorari to the United States Court of Appeals for the Eighth Circuit denied.

Same case below, 775 F.3d 1001.

No. 15-5134. Leandro Claros, Petitioner v. Tim Perez, Warden.

577 U.S. 884, 136 S. Ct. 192, 193 L. Ed. 2d 151, 2015 U.S. LEXIS 5357.

October 5, 2015. Petition for writ of certiorari to the United States Court of Appeals for the Ninth Circuit denied.

No. 15-5135. Richard Goodwin, Petitioner v. United States.

577 U.S. 884, 136 S. Ct. 192, 193 L. Ed. 2d 151, 2015 U.S. LEXIS 5105.

October 5, 2015. Petition for writ of certiorari to the United States Court of Appeals for the Seventh Circuit denied.

Same case below, 600 Fed. Appx. 483.

No. 15-5136. Gerald Bass, Petitioner v. United States.

577 U.S. 884, 136 S. Ct. 192, 193 L. Ed. 2d 151, 2015 U.S. LEXIS 5349.

October 5, 2015. Petition for writ of certiorari to the United States Court of Appeals for the Sixth Circuit denied.

Same case below, 785 F.3d 1043.

No. 15-5138. Emmanuel Asante, Petitioner v. United States.

577 U.S. 884, 136 S. Ct. 192, 193 L. Ed. 2d 152, 2015 U.S. LEXIS 5444.

October 5, 2015. Petition for writ of certiorari to the United States Court of Appeals for the Eleventh Circuit denied.

Same case below, 782 F.3d 639.

No. 15-5139. Tony Antwann Battle, Petitioner v. Harold W. Clarke, Director, Virginia Department of Corrections.

577 U.S. 884, 136 S. Ct. 192, 193 L. Ed. 2d 152, 2015 U.S. LEXIS 5151.

October 5, 2015. Petition for writ of certiorari to the United States Court of Appeals for the Fourth Circuit denied.

Same case below, 599 Fed. Appx. 76.

No. 15-5143. Thomas Lee O'Neil, Petitioner v. Todd Kloska, et al.

577 U.S. 884, 136 S. Ct. 192, 193 L. Ed. 2d 152, 2015 U.S. LEXIS 5364.

October 5, 2015. Petition for writ of certiorari to the United States Court of Appeals for the Sixth Circuit denied.

No. 15-5144. William Jeffrey McDonough, Petitioner v. Michelle Smith, Warden.

577 U.S. 884, 136 S. Ct. 193, 193 L. Ed. 2d 152, 2015 U.S. LEXIS 5315.

October 5, 2015. Petition for writ of certiorari to the United States Court of Appeals for the Eighth Circuit denied.

No. 15-5145. David V. Rider, Petitioner v. United States.

577 U.S. 884, 136 S. Ct. 193, 193 L. Ed. 2d 152, 2015 U.S. LEXIS 5508.

October 5, 2015. Petition for writ of certiorari to the District of Columbia Court of Appeals denied.

Same case below, 103 A.3d 545.

No. 15-5146. Cassandra Scipio, Petitioner v. Carolyn W. Colvin, Acting Commissioner of Social Security.

577 U.S. 885, 136 S. Ct. 193, 193 L. Ed. 2d 152, 2015 U.S. LEXIS 5192.

October 5, 2015. Petition for writ of certiorari to the United States Court of Appeals for the Third Circuit denied.

Same case below, 611 Fed. Appx. 99.

No. 15-5151. Alfred Evans, Petitioner v. United States.

577 U.S. 885, 136 S. Ct. 193, 193 L. Ed. 2d 152, 2015 U.S. LEXIS 5168.

October 5, 2015. Petition for writ of certiorari to the District of Columbia Court of Appeals denied.

Same case below, 110 A.3d 641.

No. 15-5152. Michael D. St. Clair, Petitioner v. Kentucky.

577 U.S. 885, 136 S. Ct. 194, 193 L. Ed. 2d 152, 2015 U.S. LEXIS 5215.

October 5, 2015. Petition for writ of certiorari to the Supreme Court of Kentucky denied.

Same case below, 451 S.W.3d 597.

Same case below, 589 Fed. Appx. 200.

No. 15-5153. Jack McGee, Petitioner v. Illinois.

577 U.S. 885, 136 S. Ct. 194, 193 L. Ed. 2d 153, 2015 U.S. LEXIS 5281.

October 5, 2015. Petition for writ of certiorari to the Appellate Court of Illinois, First District, denied.

No. 15-5154. Efrain Huitron-Rocha, Petitioner v. United States.

577 U.S. 885, 136 S. Ct. 194, 193 L. Ed. 2d 153, 2015 U.S. LEXIS 5310.

October 5, 2015. Petition for writ of certiorari to the United States Court of Appeals for the Ninth Circuit denied.

Same case below, 771 F.3d 1183.

No. 15-5155. Robert Holland, Petitioner v. Stephen Feinberg, et al.

577 U.S. 885, 136 S. Ct. 194, 193 L. Ed. 2d 153, 2015 U.S. LEXIS 5266.

October 5, 2015. Petition for writ of certiorari to the United States Court of Appeals for the Seventh Circuit denied.

No. 15-5157. Anthony Quintin Kelly, Petitioner v. Frank Bishop, Warden, et al.

577 U.S. 885, 136 S. Ct. 194, 193 L. Ed. 2d 153, 2015 U.S. LEXIS 5230, reh den 577 U.S. 1044, 136 S. Ct. 610, 193 L. Ed. 2d 491, 2015 U.S. LEXIS 7824.

October 5, 2015. Petition for writ of certiorari to the United States Court of Appeals for the Fourth Circuit denied.

No. 15-5158. John Flowers, Petitioner v. Isidro Baca, Warden, et al.

577 U.S. 885, 136 S. Ct. 212, 193 L. Ed. 2d 153, 2015 U.S. LEXIS 5117.

October 5, 2015. Petition for writ of certiorari to the United States Court of Appeals for the Ninth Circuit denied.

No. 15-5161. Gary Rhines, Petitioner v. United States.

577 U.S. 885, 136 S. Ct. 195, 193 L. Ed. 2d 153, 2015 U.S. LEXIS 5128.

October 5, 2015. Petition for writ of certiorari to the United States Court of Appeals for the Third Circuit denied.

Same case below, 594 Fed. Appx. 64.

No. 15-5162. Smittie James, Petitioner v. North Carolina.

577 U.S. 885, 136 S. Ct. 195, 193 L. Ed. 2d 153, 2015 U.S. LEXIS 5373.

October 5, 2015. Petition for writ of certiorari to the Supreme Court of North Carolina denied.

Same case below, 368 N. C. 258, 771 S.E.2d 309.

No. 15-5163. Christian Paetsch, Petitioner v. United States.

577 U.S. 885, 136 S. Ct. 195, 193 L. Ed. 2d 153, 2015 U.S. LEXIS 5063.

October 5, 2015. Petition for writ of certiorari to the United States Court of Appeals for the Tenth Circuit denied.

Same case below, 782 F.3d 1162.

Same case below, 599 Fed. Appx. 729.

No. 15-5165. James Martrice Brown, Petitioner v. DeWayne Burton, Warden.

577 U.S. 885, 136 S. Ct. 195, 193 L. Ed. 2d 154, 2015 U.S. LEXIS 5265.

October 5, 2015. Petition for writ of certiorari to the United States Court of Appeals for the Sixth Circuit denied.

No. 15-5166. David Abran Anaya, Petitioner v. Texas (two judgments).

577 U.S. 885, 136 S. Ct. 195, 193 L. Ed. 2d 154, 2015 U.S. LEXIS 5448.

October 5, 2015. Petition for writ of certiorari to the Court of Criminal Appeals of Texas denied.

No. 15-5167. Terry G. Watson, Petitioner v. Nathan Stewart, Circuit Judge, Circuit Court for Jefferson County, Missouri, et al.

577 U.S. 885, 136 S. Ct. 196, 193 L. Ed. 2d 154, 2015 U.S. LEXIS 5129.

October 5, 2015. Petition for writ of certiorari to the Supreme Court of Missouri denied.

No. 15-5168. Adrian Toledo-Martinez, Petitioner v. United States.

577 U.S. 885, 136 S. Ct. 197, 193 L. Ed. 2d 154, 2015 U.S. LEXIS 5134.

October 5, 2015. Petition for writ of certiorari to the United States Court of Appeals for the Ninth Circuit denied.

No. 15-5169. Randall Raar, Petitioner v. Steven Rivard, Warden.

577 U.S. 886, 136 S. Ct. 197, 193 L. Ed. 2d 154, 2015 U.S. LEXIS 5434.

October 5, 2015. Petition for writ of certiorari to the United States Court of Appeals for the Sixth Circuit denied.

No. 15-5170. Randall Raar, Petitioner v. Steven Rivard, Warden.

577 U.S. 886, 136 S. Ct. 197, 193 L. Ed. 2d 154, 2015 U.S. LEXIS 5229.

October 5, 2015. Petition for writ of certiorari to the United States Court of Appeals for the Sixth Circuit denied.

No. 15-5173. James McCaa, Petitioner v. Thomas Mackie, Warden.

577 U.S. 886, 136 S. Ct. 197, 193 L. Ed. 2d 154, 2015 U.S. LEXIS 5053.

October 5, 2015. Petition for writ of certiorari to the United States Court of Appeals for the Sixth Circuit denied.

No. 15-5174. Adelio Rivera-Miranda, Petitioner v. United States.

577 U.S. 886, 136 S. Ct. 197, 193 L. Ed. 2d 154, 2015 U.S. LEXIS 5369.

October 5, 2015. Petition for writ of certiorari to the United States Court of Appeals for the Fifth Circuit denied.

Same case below, 599 Fed. Appx. 211.

Same case below, 603 Fed. Appx. 461.

No. 15-5175. **Gregory Todd Bowden, Petitioner v. United States.**

577 U.S. 886, 136 S. Ct. 197, 193 L. Ed. 2d 155, 2015 U.S. LEXIS 5247.

October 5, 2015. Petition for writ of certiorari to the United States Court of Appeals for the Eleventh Circuit denied.

No. 15-5177. **Patricia Hunt, Petitioner v. Ross Store, Inc.**

577 U.S. 886, 136 S. Ct. 200, 193 L. Ed. 2d 155, 2015 U.S. LEXIS 5491.

October 5, 2015. Petition for writ of certiorari to the Supreme Court of Florida denied.

Same case below, 157 So. 3d 1044.

No. 15-5178. **Santonio Turner, Petitioner v. Wendy Kelley, Director, Arkansas Department of Correction.**

577 U.S. 886, 136 S. Ct. 200, 193 L. Ed. 2d 155, 2015 U.S. LEXIS 5324.

October 5, 2015. Petition for writ of certiorari to the United States Court of Appeals for the Eighth Circuit denied.

No. 15-5180. **Thelmon F. Stuckey, III, Petitioner v. United States.**

577 U.S. 886, 136 S. Ct. 201, 193 L. Ed. 2d 155, 2015 U.S. LEXIS 5447.

October 5, 2015. Petition for writ of certiorari to the United States Court of Appeals for the Sixth Circuit denied.

No. 15-5181. **Manuel De Jesus Chicas-Guevara, Petitioner v. United States.**

577 U.S. 886, 136 S. Ct. 201, 193 L. Ed. 2d 155, 2015 U.S. LEXIS 5392.

October 5, 2015. Petition for writ of certiorari to the United States Court of Appeals for the Fifth Circuit denied.

Same case below, 599 Fed. Appx. 212.

No. 15-5182. **Anthony R. Taylor, Petitioner v. South Carolina.**

577 U.S. 886, 136 S. Ct. 201, 193 L. Ed. 2d 155, 2015 U.S. LEXIS 5068.

October 5, 2015. Petition for writ of certiorari to the Supreme Court of South Carolina denied.

No. 15-5185. **Jeffrey Robert Martin, Petitioner v. Pennsylvania.**

577 U.S. 886, 136 S. Ct. 201, 193 L. Ed. 2d 155, 2015 U.S. LEXIS 5295.

October 5, 2015. Petition for writ of certiorari to the Supreme Court of Pennsylvania, Eastern District, denied.

Same case below, 627 Pa. 623, 101 A.3d 706.

No. 15-5186. **Hussain Kamal, Petitioner v. United States.**

577 U.S. 886, 136 S. Ct. 201, 193 L. Ed. 2d 155, 2015 U.S. LEXIS 5242.

October 5, 2015. Petition for writ of certiorari to the United States Court of Appeals for the Fifth Circuit denied.

No. 15-5187. Whitney Lanier, Petitioner v. Florida.

577 U.S. 886, 136 S. Ct. 202, 193 L. Ed. 2d 156, 2015 U.S. LEXIS 5391.

October 5, 2015. Petition for writ of certiorari to the District Court of Appeal of Florida, Second District, denied.

Same case below, 160 So. 3d 427.

No. 15-5188. Ricky David Sechrest, Petitioner v. Renee Baker, Warden.

577 U.S. 886, 136 S. Ct. 202, 193 L. Ed. 2d 156, 2015 U.S. LEXIS 5474.

October 5, 2015. Petition for writ of certiorari to the United States Court of Appeals for the Ninth Circuit denied.

Same case below, 603 Fed. Appx. 548.

No. 15-5190. Daniel K. Johnson, aka Dennis D. Kelly, Petitioner v. Rissie Owens, et al.

577 U.S. 886, 136 S. Ct. 202, 193 L. Ed. 2d 156, 2015 U.S. LEXIS 5174.

October 5, 2015. Petition for writ of certiorari to the United States Court of Appeals for the Fifth Circuit denied.

Same case below, 612 Fed. Appx. 707.

No. 15-5191. Madge Matthews, Petitioner v. Anthony Stewart, Warden.

577 U.S. 886, 136 S. Ct. 202, 193 L. Ed. 2d 156, 2015 U.S. LEXIS 5457, reh den 577 U.S. 1023, 136 S. Ct. 578, 193 L. Ed. 2d 460, 2015 U.S. LEXIS 7429.

October 5, 2015. Petition for writ of certiorari to the United States Court of Appeals for the Sixth Circuit denied.

No. 15-5192. Maurice Antonio Davis, Petitioner v. United States.

577 U.S. 887, 136 S. Ct. 202, 193 L. Ed. 2d 156, 2015 U.S. LEXIS 5442.

October 5, 2015. Petition for writ of certiorari to the United States Court of Appeals for the Fourth Circuit denied.

Same case below, 606 Fed. Appx. 710.

No. 15-5193. Andres Chavira Corona, Petitioner v. United States.

577 U.S. 887, 136 S. Ct. 203, 193 L. Ed. 2d 156, 2015 U.S. LEXIS 5326.

October 5, 2015. Petition for writ of certiorari to the United States Court of Appeals for the Fifth Circuit denied.

Same case below, 599 Fed. Appx. 204.

No. 15-5194. Leticia Marie Montoya, Petitioner v. California.

577 U.S. 887, 136 S. Ct. 203, 193 L. Ed. 2d 156, 2015 U.S. LEXIS 5097.

October 5, 2015. Petition for writ of certiorari to the Court of Appeal of California, Second Appellate District, denied.

No. 15-5195. Terrell E. Newman, Petitioner v. Nebraska.

577 U.S. 887, 136 S. Ct. 203, 193 L. Ed. 2d 156, 2015 U.S. LEXIS 5331.

October 5, 2015. Petition for writ of certiorari to the Supreme Court of Nebraska denied.

MEMORANDUM CASES

Same case below, 290 Neb. 572, 861 N.W.2d 123.

No. 15-5196. Uriel Ortega, Petitioner v. California.

577 U.S. 887, 136 S. Ct. 203, 193 L. Ed. 2d 157, 2015 U.S. LEXIS 5167.

October 5, 2015. Petition for writ of certiorari to the Court of Appeal of California, Second Appellate District, Division Two, denied.

No. 15-5198. Curtis W. King, Petitioner v. Virginia.

577 U.S. 887, 136 S. Ct. 203, 193 L. Ed. 2d 157, 2015 U.S. LEXIS 5402.

October 5, 2015. Petition for writ of certiorari to the Supreme Court of Virginia denied.

No. 15-5199. Peter Sierra, Petitioner v. California.

577 U.S. 887, 136 S. Ct. 203, 193 L. Ed. 2d 157, 2015 U.S. LEXIS 5340.

October 5, 2015. Petition for writ of certiorari to the Court of Appeal of California, Second Appellate District, Division Six, denied.

No. 15-5200. Rodney Wayne Jones, Petitioner v. Jeff Macomber, Warden, et al.

577 U.S. 887, 136 S. Ct. 204, 193 L. Ed. 2d 157, 2015 U.S. LEXIS 5383.

October 5, 2015. Petition for writ of certiorari to the United States Court of Appeals for the Ninth Circuit denied.

No. 15-5201. Michael J. G. Saunders, Petitioner v. Virginia.

577 U.S. 887, 136 S. Ct. 204, 193 L. Ed. 2d 157, 2015 U.S. LEXIS 5175, reh den 577 U.S. 998, 136 S. Ct. 528, 193 L. Ed. 2d 416, 2015 U.S. LEXIS 7276.

October 5, 2015. Petition for writ of certiorari to the Supreme Court of Virginia denied.

No. 15-5202. Gary Lentz, Petitioner v. Bettina J. Wells, et al.

577 U.S. 887, 136 S. Ct. 204, 193 L. Ed. 2d 157, 2015 U.S. LEXIS 5261.

October 5, 2015. Petition for writ of certiorari to the United States Court of Appeals for the Sixth Circuit denied.

No. 15-5203. Andre David Leffebre, Petitioner v. United States.

577 U.S. 887, 136 S. Ct. 204, 193 L. Ed. 2d 157, 2015 U.S. LEXIS 5312.

October 5, 2015. Petition for writ of certiorari to the United States Court of Appeals for the Federal Circuit denied.

No. 15-5204. Manuel D. Lopes, Petitioner v. Joe A. Lizarraga, Warden.

577 U.S. 887, 136 S. Ct. 204, 193 L. Ed. 2d 157, 2015 U.S. LEXIS 5098.

October 5, 2015. Petition for writ of certiorari to the United States Court of Appeals for the Ninth Circuit denied.

Same case below, 597 Fed. Appx. 411.

No. 15-5205. Terrance Smith, Petitioner v. United States.

577 U.S. 887, 136 S. Ct. 204, 193 L. Ed. 2d 158, 2015 U.S. LEXIS 5389.

October 5, 2015. Petition for writ of certiorari to the United States Court of Appeals for the Fourth Circuit denied.

Same case below, 594 Fed. Appx. 166.

No. 15-5206. Malek M. Al-Maliki, Petitioner v. United States.

577 U.S. 887, 136 S. Ct. 204, 193 L. Ed. 2d 158, 2015 U.S. LEXIS 5365.

October 5, 2015. Petition for writ of certiorari to the United States Court of Appeals for the Sixth Circuit denied.

Same case below, 787 F.3d 784.

No. 15-5207. Floyd Pleasant Tarvin, IV, Petitioner v. William Stephens, Director, Texas Department of Criminal Justice, Correctional Institutions Division.

577 U.S. 887, 136 S. Ct. 205, 193 L. Ed. 2d 158, 2015 U.S. LEXIS 5322.

October 5, 2015. Petition for writ of certiorari to the United States Court of Appeals for the Fifth Circuit denied.

No. 15-5208. Kerry Walker, Petitioner v. United States.

577 U.S. 887, 136 S. Ct. 205, 193 L. Ed. 2d 158, 2015 U.S. LEXIS 5022.

October 5, 2015. Petition for writ of certiorari to the United States Court of Appeals for the Sixth Circuit denied.

Same case below, 599 Fed. Appx. 582.

No. 15-5209. Thomas Williams, Petitioner v. Illinois.

577 U.S. 888, 136 S. Ct. 205, 193 L. Ed. 2d 158, 2015 U.S. LEXIS 5419, reh den 577 U.S. 1095, 136 S. Ct. 884, 193 L. Ed. 2d 775, 2016 U.S. LEXIS 469.

October 5, 2015. Petition for writ of certiorari to the Appellate Court of Illinois, First District, denied.

No. 15-5210. Nicholas McCary, Petitioner v. Alabama.

577 U.S. 888, 136 S. Ct. 205, 193 L. Ed. 2d 158, 2015 U.S. LEXIS 5239.

October 5, 2015. Petition for writ of certiorari to the Court of Criminal Appeals of Alabama denied.

Same case below, 207 So. 3d 811.

No. 15-5211. Marcus Batts, Petitioner v. Keith Cooley, Warden.

577 U.S. 888, 136 S. Ct. 205, 193 L. Ed. 2d 158, 2015 U.S. LEXIS 5084.

October 5, 2015. Petition for writ of certiorari to the United States Court of Appeals for the Fifth Circuit denied.

No. 15-5212. Monica Brown, et vir, Petitioners v. Florida Department of Children and Families.

577 U.S. 888, 136 S. Ct. 205, 193 L. Ed. 2d 158, 2015 U.S. LEXIS 5252, reh den 577 U.S. 998, 136 S. Ct. 529, 193 L. Ed. 2d 417, 2015 U.S. LEXIS 7210.

October 5, 2015. Petition for writ of certiorari to the United States Court of Appeals for the Eleventh Circuit denied.

No. 15-5213. Bruce Brown, Petitioner v. United States.

577 U.S. 888, 136 S. Ct. 206, 193 L. Ed. 2d 159, 2015 U.S. LEXIS 5438.

October 5, 2015. Petition for writ of certiorari to the United States Court of Appeals for the Eleventh Circuit denied.

Same case below, 609 Fed. Appx. 969.

No. 15-5214. Edgardo Josue Aguilar, Petitioner v. United States.

577 U.S. 888, 136 S. Ct. 206, 193 L. Ed. 2d 159, 2015 U.S. LEXIS 5180.

October 5, 2015. Petition for writ of certiorari to the United States Court of Appeals for the Tenth Circuit denied.

Same case below, 609 Fed. Appx. 960.

No. 15-5215. John Lee Basey, Petitioner v. William Stephens, Director, Texas Department of Criminal Justice, Correctional Institutions Division.

577 U.S. 888, 136 S. Ct. 206, 193 L. Ed. 2d 159, 2015 U.S. LEXIS 5050, reh den 577 U.S. 1024, 136 S. Ct. 578, 193 L. Ed. 2d 461, 2015 U.S. LEXIS 7384.

October 5, 2015. Petition for writ of certiorari to the United States Court of Appeals for the Fifth Circuit denied.

No. 15-5216. Gary M. Brayboy, Petitioner v. Robert Napel, Warden.

577 U.S. 888, 136 S. Ct. 206, 193 L. Ed. 2d 159, 2015 U.S. LEXIS 5470, reh den 577 U.S. 1054, 136 S. Ct. 705, 193 L. Ed. 2d 531, 2015 U.S. LEXIS 7952.

October 5, 2015. Petition for writ of certiorari to the United States Court of Appeals for the Sixth Circuit denied.

No. 15-5218. Jose Dominguez-Garcia, Petitioner v. United States.

577 U.S. 888, 136 S. Ct. 206, 193 L. Ed. 2d 159, 2015 U.S. LEXIS 5292.

October 5, 2015. Petition for writ of certiorari to the United States Court of Appeals for the Ninth Circuit denied.

Same case below, 588 Fed. Appx. 653.

No. 15-5219. Amanda Rodriguez, Petitioner v. United States.

577 U.S. 888, 136 S. Ct. 207, 193 L. Ed. 2d 159, 2015 U.S. LEXIS 5188.

October 5, 2015. Petition for writ of certiorari to the United States Court of Appeals for the First Circuit denied.

Same case below, 609 Fed. Appx. 8.

No. 15-5220. Henry M. Hayes, aka Henry M. Mitchell, Petitioner v. R. Bolen, et al.

577 U.S. 888, 136 S. Ct. 207, 193 L. Ed. 2d 159, 2015 U.S. LEXIS 5210.

October 5, 2015. Petition for writ of certiorari to the United States Court of Appeals for the Ninth Circuit denied.

Same case below, 594 Fed. Appx. 420.

No. 15-5221. Jonathan Reyes, Petitioner v. United States.

577 U.S. 888, 136 S. Ct. 207, 193 L. Ed. 2d 159, 2015 U.S. LEXIS 5269.

October 5, 2015. Petition for writ of certiorari to the United States Court of Appeals for the Ninth Circuit denied.

Same case below, 599 Fed. Appx. 813.

No. 15-5223. Lawrence Clay McGee, Petitioner v. North Carolina.

577 U.S. 888, 136 S. Ct. 207, 193 L. Ed. 2d 160, 2015 U.S. LEXIS 5066.

October 5, 2015. Petition for writ of certiorari to the Supreme Court of North Carolina denied.

Same case below, 368 N.C. 270, 772 S.E.2d 727 and 772 S.E.2d 728.

No. 15-5224. Samuel Ortiz-Lopez, Petitioner v. Florida.

577 U.S. 888, 136 S. Ct. 207, 193 L. Ed. 2d 160, 2015 U.S. LEXIS 5095.

October 5, 2015. Petition for writ of certiorari to the District Court of Appeal of Florida, Second District, denied.

Same case below, 153 So. 3d 313.

No. 15-5225. James E. Price, III, Petitioner v. United States.

577 U.S. 888, 136 S. Ct. 207, 193 L. Ed. 2d 160, 2015 U.S. LEXIS 5286, reh den 578 U.S. 942, 136 S. Ct. 1706, 194 L. Ed. 2d 803, 2016 U.S. LEXIS 2454.

October 5, 2015. Petition for writ of certiorari to the United States Court of Appeals for the Eleventh Circuit denied.

Same case below, 582 Fed. Appx. 846.

No. 15-5227. Stevon Warren, Petitioner v. United States.

577 U.S. 889, 136 S. Ct. 208, 193 L. Ed. 2d 160, 2015 U.S. LEXIS 5454, reh den

577 U.S. 1124, 136 S. Ct. 996, 194 L. Ed. 2d 14, 2016 U.S. LEXIS 874.

October 5, 2015. Petition for writ of certiorari to the United States Court of Appeals for the Eighth Circuit denied.

No. 15-5228. Jonathan Russell Wright, Petitioner v. United States.

577 U.S. 889, 136 S. Ct. 208, 193 L. Ed. 2d 160, 2015 U.S. LEXIS 5395.

October 5, 2015. Petition for writ of certiorari to the United States Court of Appeals for the Eighth Circuit denied.

No. 15-5229. Breon Thompson, Petitioner v. Illinois.

577 U.S. 889, 136 S. Ct. 208, 193 L. Ed. 2d 160, 2015 U.S. LEXIS 5415.

October 5, 2015. Petition for writ of certiorari to the Appellate Court of Illinois, First District, denied.

No. 15-5230. Antonio Turner, Petitioner v. United States.

577 U.S. 889, 136 S. Ct. 208, 193 L. Ed. 2d 160, 2015 U.S. LEXIS 5185.

October 5, 2015. Petition for writ of certiorari to the United States Court of Appeals for the Eighth Circuit denied.

Same case below, 781 F.3d 374.

No. 15-5231. James William Brammer, Petitioner v. California.

577 U.S. 889, 136 S. Ct. 208, 193 L. Ed. 2d 160, 2015 U.S. LEXIS 5360.

October 5, 2015. Petition for writ of certiorari to the Court of Appeal of California, Second Appellate District, Division One, denied.

No. 15-5232. Norman L. Allen, Petitioner v. Florida.

577 U.S. 889, 136 S. Ct. 209, 193 L. Ed. 2d 161, 2015 U.S. LEXIS 5458.

October 5, 2015. Petition for writ of certiorari to the District Court of Appeal of Florida, Second District, denied.

Same case below, 173 So. 3d 971.

No. 15-5233. Dennys Acevedo, Petitioner v. Michael Capra, Superintendent, Sing Sing Correctional Facility.

577 U.S. 889, 136 S. Ct. 209, 193 L. Ed. 2d 161, 2015 U.S. LEXIS 5159.

October 5, 2015. Petition for writ of certiorari to the United States Court of Appeals for the Second Circuit denied.

Same case below, 600 Fed. Appx. 801.

No. 15-5234. Steven Burton, Petitioner v. South Carolina.

577 U.S. 889, 136 S. Ct. 209, 193 L. Ed. 2d 161, 2015 U.S. LEXIS 5435.

October 5, 2015. Petition for writ of certiorari to the Court of Common Pleas of South Carolina, Aiken County, denied.

No. 15-5236. Nazario Rodriguez-Grado, Petitioner v. United States.

577 U.S. 889, 136 S. Ct. 209, 193 L. Ed. 2d 161, 2015 U.S. LEXIS 5449.

October 5, 2015. Petition for writ of certiorari to the United States Court of Appeals for the Ninth Circuit denied.

No. 15-5237. Lester R. Shinault, Petitioner v. Dick Hawks, et al.

577 U.S. 889, 136 S. Ct. 209, 193 L. Ed. 2d 161, 2015 U.S. LEXIS 5101.

October 5, 2015. Petition for writ of certiorari to the United States Court of Appeals for the Ninth Circuit denied.

Same case below, 782 F.3d 1053.

No. 15-5240. Anthony Yawn, Petitioner v. Julie L. Jones, Secretary, Florida Department of Corrections.

577 U.S. 889, 136 S. Ct. 210, 193 L. Ed. 2d 161, 2015 U.S. LEXIS 5145.

October 5, 2015. Petition for writ of certiorari to the United States Court of Appeals for the Eleventh Circuit denied.

No. 15-5241. Keith Taylor, Petitioner v. United States.

577 U.S. 889, 136 S. Ct. 210, 193 L. Ed. 2d 161, 2015 U.S. LEXIS 5398.

October 5, 2015. Petition for writ of certiorari to the United States Court of Appeals for the Sixth Circuit denied.

No. 15-5242. Daniel Taylor, Petitioner v. United States.

577 U.S. 889, 136 S. Ct. 210, 193 L. Ed. 2d 161, 2015 U.S. LEXIS 5361.

October 5, 2015. Petition for writ of certiorari to the United States Court of Appeals for the Fourth Circuit denied.

Same case below, 601 Fed. Appx. 212.

No. 15-5243. Juan Alberto Mendez-Sosa, Petitioner v. United States.

577 U.S. 889, 136 S. Ct. 210, 193 L. Ed. 2d 162, 2015 U.S. LEXIS 5348.

October 5, 2015. Petition for writ of certiorari to the United States Court of Appeals for the Ninth Circuit denied.

Same case below, 782 F.3d 1061.

No. 15-5244. M.C., the Father, Petitioner v. Florida Department of Children and Families, et al. (two judgments).

577 U.S. 889, 136 S. Ct. 210, 193 L. Ed. 2d 162, 2015 U.S. LEXIS 5341.

October 5, 2015. Petition for writ of certiorari to the Supreme Court of Florida denied.

Same case below, 171 So. 3d 118 (first judgment); and 166 So. 3d 791 (second judgment).

No. 15-5245. Andrew Lamar Coley, Petitioner v. United States.

577 U.S. 890, 136 S. Ct. 210, 193 L. Ed. 2d 162, 2015 U.S. LEXIS 5303.

October 5, 2015. Petition for writ of certiorari to the United States Court of Appeals for the Fourth Circuit denied.

Same case below, 589 Fed. Appx. 161.

No. 15-5246. Eugenia Woodard, Petitioner v. Fortress Insurance Company, et al.

577 U.S. 890, 136 S. Ct. 211, 193 L. Ed. 2d 162, 2015 U.S. LEXIS 5485, reh den 577 U.S. 1095, 136 S. Ct. 884, 193 L. Ed. 2d 775, 2016 U.S. LEXIS 312.

October 5, 2015. Petition for writ of certiorari to the Court of Appeals of Texas, First District, denied.

No. 15-5247. John Russell Allard, Petitioner v. Tonia Baldwin, et al.

577 U.S. 890, 136 S. Ct. 211, 193 L. Ed. 2d 162, 2015 U.S. LEXIS 5400.

October 5, 2015. Petition for writ of certiorari to the United States Court of Appeals for the Eighth Circuit denied.

Same case below, 779 F.3d 768.

No. 15-5248. Raymond Bolt, Petitioner v. Mark Nooth, Superintendent, Snake River Correctional Institution.

577 U.S. 890, 136 S. Ct. 211, 193 L. Ed. 2d 162, 2015 U.S. LEXIS 5320.

October 5, 2015. Petition for writ of certiorari to the United States Court of Appeals for the Ninth Circuit denied.

Same case below, 605 Fed. Appx. 680.

No. 15-5249. Willie James Boone, Petitioner v. Julie L. Jones, Secretary, Florida Department of Corrections.

577 U.S. 890, 136 S. Ct. 211, 193 L. Ed. 2d 162, 2015 U.S. LEXIS 5187, reh den 577 U.S. 1024, 136 S. Ct. 578, 193 L. Ed. 2d 461, 2015 U.S. LEXIS 7381.

October 5, 2015. Petition for writ of certiorari to the United States Court of Appeals for the Eleventh Circuit denied.

No. 15-5250. Antwion E. Thompson, Petitioner v. United States District Court for the Northern District of California.

577 U.S. 890, 136 S. Ct. 300, 193 L. Ed. 2d 162, 2015 U.S. LEXIS 5094, reh den 577 U.S. 1024, 136 S. Ct. 579, 193 L. Ed. 2d 461, 2015 U.S. LEXIS 7405.

October 5, 2015. Petition for writ of certiorari to the United States Court of Appeals for the Ninth Circuit denied.

No. 15-5251. Allen Ray Williams, Petitioner v. United States.

577 U.S. 890, 136 S. Ct. 212, 193 L. Ed. 2d 163, 2015 U.S. LEXIS 5116.

October 5, 2015. Petition for writ of certiorari to the United States Court of Appeals for the Eighth Circuit denied.

No. 15-5253. Carl Cumby, Petitioner v. Colorado.

577 U.S. 890, 136 S. Ct. 212, 193 L. Ed. 2d 163, 2015 U.S. LEXIS 5359.

October 5, 2015. Petition for writ of certiorari to the Court of Appeals of Colorado denied.

No. 15-5254. Jan Michael Edmonds, Petitioner v. United States.

577 U.S. 890, 136 S. Ct. 213, 193 L. Ed. 2d 163, 2015 U.S. LEXIS 5307.

October 5, 2015. Petition for writ of certiorari to the United States Court of Appeals for the Third Circuit denied.

Same case below, 606 Fed. Appx. 656.

No. 15-5255. Melvin Colon, aka Sealed Defendant 2, Petitioner v. United States.

577 U.S. 890, 136 S. Ct. 213, 193 L. Ed. 2d 163, 2015 U.S. LEXIS 5298.

October 5, 2015. Petition for writ of certiorari to the United States Court of Appeals for the Second Circuit denied.

Same case below, 785 F.3d 832.

No. 15-5256. David Andrew Diehl, aka David A. Diehl, Petitioner v. United States.

577 U.S. 890, 136 S. Ct. 213, 193 L. Ed. 2d 163, 2015 U.S. LEXIS 5404, reh den 577 U.S. 1024, 136 S. Ct. 579, 193 L. Ed. 2d 461, 2015 U.S. LEXIS 7426.

October 5, 2015. Petition for writ of certiorari to the United States Court of Appeals for the Fifth Circuit denied.

Same case below, 775 F.3d 714.

No. 15-5258. Jason Robert Widdison, Petitioner v. United States.

577 U.S. 890, 136 S. Ct. 213, 193 L. Ed. 2d 163, 2015 U.S. LEXIS 5314.

October 5, 2015. Petition for writ of certiorari to the United States Court of Appeals for the Eleventh Circuit denied.

Same case below, 783 F.3d 1216.

No. 15-5259. Bill Paul Marquardt, Petitioner v. Florida.

577 U.S. 890, 136 S. Ct. 213, 193 L. Ed. 2d 163, 2015 U.S. LEXIS 5459.

October 5, 2015. Petition for writ of certiorari to the Supreme Court of Florida denied.

Same case below, 156 So. 3d 464.

No. 15-5260. Charles G. Kinney, Petitioner v. Luis Lavin, Judge, Superior Court of California, Los Angeles County, et al.

577 U.S. 890, 136 S. Ct. 214, 193 L. Ed. 2d 163, 2015 U.S. LEXIS 5221.

October 5, 2015. Petition for writ of certiorari to the United States Court of Appeals for the Ninth Circuit denied.

Same case below, 781 F.3d 532.

No. 15-5261. Raymond L. Rogers, Petitioner v. United States.

577 U.S. 891, 136 S. Ct. 214, 193 L. Ed. 2d 164, 2015 U.S. LEXIS 5179, reh den 577 U.S. 1024, 136 S. Ct. 579, 193 L. Ed. 2d 461, 2015 U.S. LEXIS 7448.

October 5, 2015. Petition for writ of certiorari to the United States Court of Appeals for the Tenth Circuit denied.

Same case below, 599 Fed. Appx. 850.

No. 15-5268. Edward Clyde Silvis, Petitioner v. Steven R. Glunt, Superintendent, State Correctional Institution at Rockview.

577 U.S. 891, 136 S. Ct. 215, 193 L. Ed. 2d 164, 2015 U.S. LEXIS 5376.

October 5, 2015. Petition for writ of certiorari to the United States Court of Appeals for the Third Circuit denied.

No. 15-5262. Loranzo Square, III, Petitioner v. North Carolina.

577 U.S. 891, 136 S. Ct. 214, 193 L. Ed. 2d 164, 2015 U.S. LEXIS 5081.

October 5, 2015. Petition for writ of certiorari to the Court of Appeals of North Carolina denied.

No. 15-5269. Danny Ruben, Petitioner v. Timothy Keith, Warden.

577 U.S. 891, 136 S. Ct. 215, 193 L. Ed. 2d 164, 2015 U.S. LEXIS 5492, reh den 577 U.S. 1054, 136 S. Ct. 706, 193 L. Ed. 2d 532, 2015 U.S. LEXIS 7896.

October 5, 2015. Petition for writ of certiorari to the United States Court of Appeals for the Fifth Circuit denied.

No. 15-5263. Frank Morales, Petitioner v. United States.

577 U.S. 891, 136 S. Ct. 214, 193 L. Ed. 2d 164, 2015 U.S. LEXIS 5142.

October 5, 2015. Petition for writ of certiorari to the United States Court of Appeals for the Fifth Circuit denied.

Same case below, 600 Fed. Appx. 269.

No. 15-5270. Richard Sanders, Petitioner v. Steven Rivard, Warden.

577 U.S. 891, 136 S. Ct. 215, 193 L. Ed. 2d 164, 2015 U.S. LEXIS 5325.

October 5, 2015. Petition for writ of certiorari to the United States Court of Appeals for the Sixth Circuit denied.

No. 15-5264. Beatrice Munyenyezi, Petitioner v. United States.

577 U.S. 891, 136 S. Ct. 214, 193 L. Ed. 2d 164, 2015 U.S. LEXIS 5473.

October 5, 2015. Petition for writ of certiorari to the United States Court of Appeals for the First Circuit denied.

No. 15-5271. Jose Rodriguez Sosa, Petitioner v. United States.

577 U.S. 891, 136 S. Ct. 215, 193 L. Ed. 2d 164, 2015 U.S. LEXIS 5231.

October 5, 2015. Petition for writ of certiorari to the United States Court of Appeals for the Eleventh Circuit denied.

No. 15-5272. Charlotte G., Petitioner v. Arizona Department of Child Safety, et al.

577 U.S. 891, 136 S. Ct. 215, 193 L. Ed. 2d 165, 2015 U.S. LEXIS 5120.

October 5, 2015. Petition for writ of certiorari to the Court of Appeals of Arizona, Division One, denied.

No. 15-5273. Abel Lucio, Petitioner v. Venerio M. Santos, et al.

577 U.S. 891, 136 S. Ct. 215, 193 L. Ed. 2d 165, 2015 U.S. LEXIS 5382.

October 5, 2015. Petition for writ of certiorari to the United States Court of Appeals for the Seventh Circuit denied.

Same case below, 600 Fed. Appx. 480.

No. 15-5274. Daryl Jerome Robinson, Petitioner v. William Stephens, Director, Texas Department of Criminal Justice, Correctional Institution Division.

577 U.S. 891, 136 S. Ct. 216, 193 L. Ed. 2d 165, 2015 U.S. LEXIS 5130.

October 5, 2015. Petition for writ of certiorari to the United States Court of Appeals for the Fifth Circuit denied.

No. 15-5275. Louis Murray, Petitioner v. Alabama.

577 U.S. 891, 136 S. Ct. 216, 193 L. Ed. 2d 165, 2015 U.S. LEXIS 5510.

October 5, 2015. Petition for writ of certiorari to the Court of Criminal Appeals of Alabama denied.

Same case below, 184 So. 3d 465.

No. 15-5276. Vincent T. Neely, Petitioner v. Jeffrey Woods, Warden.

577 U.S. 891, 136 S. Ct. 216, 193 L. Ed. 2d 165, 2015 U.S. LEXIS 5064.

October 5, 2015. Petition for writ of certiorari to the United States Court of Appeals for the Sixth Circuit denied.

No. 15-5277. Alfredo Javier Luna, Petitioner v. Carmen Palmer, Warden.

577 U.S. 891, 136 S. Ct. 216, 193 L. Ed. 2d 165, 2015 U.S. LEXIS 5285.

October 5, 2015. Petition for writ of certiorari to the United States Court of Appeals for the Sixth Circuit denied.

No. 15-5280. Claretha Ross, Petitioner v. Robert Struble, Judge, Superior Court of Georgia, Habersham County.

577 U.S. 891, 136 S. Ct. 216, 193 L. Ed. 2d 165, 2015 U.S. LEXIS 5124.

October 5, 2015. Petition for writ of certiorari to the Superior Court of Georgia, Habersham County, denied.

No. 15-5281. Victor Lacayo, Petitioner v. United States.

577 U.S. 892, 136 S. Ct. 217, 193 L. Ed. 2d 165, 2015 U.S. LEXIS 5103.

October 5, 2015. Petition for writ of certiorari to the United States Court of Appeals for the Fifth Circuit denied.

Same case below, 598 Fed. Appx. 296.

Same case below, 781 F.3d 563.

No. 15-5283. Edwin Rivera-Otero, Petitioner v. United States.

577 U.S. 892, 136 S. Ct. 218, 193 L. Ed. 2d 166, 2015 U.S. LEXIS 5417.

October 5, 2015. Petition for writ of certiorari to the United States Court of Appeals for the Fifth Circuit denied.

Same case below, 603 Fed. Appx. 306.

No. 15-5285. Jesus Pacheco, Petitioner v. United States.

577 U.S. 892, 136 S. Ct. 219, 193 L. Ed. 2d 166, 2015 U.S. LEXIS 5467.

October 5, 2015. Petition for writ of certiorari to the United States Court of Appeals for the Ninth Circuit denied.

Same case below, 599 Fed. Appx. 809.

No. 15-5286. Jack D. McCullough, Petitioner v. Illinois.

577 U.S. 892, 136 S. Ct. 219, 193 L. Ed. 2d 166, 2015 U.S. LEXIS 5488.

October 5, 2015. Petition for writ of certiorari to the Appellate Court of Illinois, Second District, denied.

Same case below, 38 N. E. 3d 1.

No. 15-5287. Yamil Navedo-Ramirez, Petitioner v. United States.

577 U.S. 892, 136 S. Ct. 219, 193 L. Ed. 2d 166, 2015 U.S. LEXIS 5384.

October 5, 2015. Petition for writ of certiorari to the United States Court of Appeals for the First Circuit denied.

No. 15-5288. Leo Adams, Petitioner v. United States.

577 U.S. 892, 136 S. Ct. 219, 193 L. Ed. 2d 166, 2015 U.S. LEXIS 4883.

October 5, 2015. Petition for writ of certiorari to the United States Court of Appeals for the Eighth Circuit denied.

No. 15-5289. Mazen Arakji, Petitioner v. Cliff Hess, et al.

577 U.S. 892, 136 S. Ct. 220, 193 L. Ed. 2d 166, 2015 U.S. LEXIS 4808.

October 5, 2015. Petition for writ of certiorari to the United States Court of Appeals for the Tenth Circuit denied.

No. 15-5290. Gary Wayne Bush, Petitioner v. Tennessee.

577 U.S. 892, 136 S. Ct. 220, 193 L. Ed. 2d 166, 2015 U.S. LEXIS 4902.

October 5, 2015. Petition for writ of certiorari to the Court of Criminal Appeals of Tennessee, Middle Division, denied.

No. 15-5291. Clifford Eric Burgess, Petitioner v. James M. Holloway, Warden.

577 U.S. 892, 136 S. Ct. 220, 193 L. Ed. 2d 166, 2015 U.S. LEXIS 4853.

October 5, 2015. Petition for writ of certiorari to the United States Court of Appeals for the Sixth Circuit denied.

No. 15-5292. Donald Morris Lee, Petitioner v. Patrick Glebe, Superintendent, Stafford Creek Corrections Center.

577 U.S. 892, 136 S. Ct. 220, 193 L. Ed. 2d 167, 2015 U.S. LEXIS 4791.

October 5, 2015. Petition for writ of certiorari to the United States Court of Appeals for the Ninth Circuit denied.

No. 15-5293. Joseph Michael Ladeairous, Petitioner v. Eric T. Schneiderman, Attorney General of New York, et al.

577 U.S. 892, 136 S. Ct. 220, 193 L. Ed. 2d 167, 2015 U.S. LEXIS 4783, reh den 577 U.S. 1024, 136 S. Ct. 579, 193 L. Ed. 2d 461, 2015 U.S. LEXIS 7408.

October 5, 2015. Petition for writ of certiorari to the United States Court of Appeals for the Second Circuit denied.

Same case below, 592 Fed. Appx. 47.

No. 15-5295. Roger Stevenson, Petitioner v. Sorrell Saunders.

577 U.S. 892, 136 S. Ct. 220, 193 L. Ed. 2d 167, 2015 U.S. LEXIS 4857, reh den 577 U.S. 998, 136 S. Ct. 529, 193 L. Ed. 2d 417, 2015 U.S. LEXIS 7197.

October 5, 2015. Petition for writ of certiorari to the United States Court of Appeals for the Fourth Circuit denied.

Same case below, 594 Fed. Appx. 190.

No. 15-5296. Norman McGinnis, Jr., Petitioner v. P. D. Brazelton, Warden.

577 U.S. 892, 136 S. Ct. 221, 193 L. Ed. 2d 167, 2015 U.S. LEXIS 4774.

October 5, 2015. Petition for writ of certiorari to the United States Court of Appeals for the Ninth Circuit denied.

No. 15-5297. Kenneth McGee, Petitioner v. Michigan.

577 U.S. 892, 136 S. Ct. 221, 193 L. Ed. 2d 167, 2015 U.S. LEXIS 4820.

October 5, 2015. Petition for writ of certiorari to the Circuit Court of Michigan, Wayne County, Criminal Division, denied.

No. 15-5298. Denard Darnell Neal, Petitioner v. Richard Ives, Warden.

577 U.S. 892, 136 S. Ct. 221, 193 L. Ed. 2d 167, 2015 U.S. LEXIS 4842.

October 5, 2015. Petition for writ of certiorari to the United States Court of Appeals for the Ninth Circuit denied.

No. 15-5300. Gerald Watkins, Petitioner v. Pennsylvania.

577 U.S. 893, 136 S. Ct. 221, 193 L. Ed. 2d 167, 2015 U.S. LEXIS 4887.

October 5, 2015. Petition for writ of certiorari to the Supreme Court of Pennsylvania, Eastern District, denied.

Same case below, 630 Pa. 652, 108 A.3d 692.

No. 15-5301. Larry Demond Williams, Petitioner v. United States.

577 U.S. 893, 136 S. Ct. 221, 193 L. Ed. 2d 167, 2015 U.S. LEXIS 4899.

October 5, 2015. Petition for writ of certiorari to the United States Court of Appeals for the Eleventh Circuit denied.

Same case below, 586 Fed. Appx. 576.

No. 15-5302. Feng Xian, Petitioner v. United States.

577 U.S. 893, 136 S. Ct. 221, 193 L. Ed. 2d 168, 2015 U.S. LEXIS 4913.

October 5, 2015. Petition for writ of certiorari to the United States Court of Appeals for the Ninth Circuit denied.

Same case below, 602 Fed. Appx. 399.

No. 15-5303. Walter Delany Booker, Jr., Petitioner v. Harold W. Clarke, Director, Virginia Department of Corrections, et al.

577 U.S. 893, 136 S. Ct. 222, 193 L. Ed. 2d 168, 2015 U.S. LEXIS 4769.

October 5, 2015. Petition for writ of certiorari to the Supreme Court of Virginia denied.

No. 15-5304. Arthur Belcher, Petitioner v. Kim Thomas, et al.

577 U.S. 893, 136 S. Ct. 222, 193 L. Ed. 2d 168, 2015 U.S. LEXIS 4792.

October 5, 2015. Petition for writ of certiorari to the Supreme Court of Alabama denied.

Same case below, 215 So. 3d 1027.

No. 15-5305. Earl Charles Martin, Petitioner v. Texas.

577 U.S. 893, 136 S. Ct. 222, 193 L. Ed. 2d 168, 2015 U.S. LEXIS 4768.

October 5, 2015. Petition for writ of certiorari to the Court of Appeals of Texas, First District, denied.

No. 15-5306. Raymond Leon Johnson, Petitioner v. Shankiri Reddy.

577 U.S. 893, 136 S. Ct. 222, 193 L. Ed. 2d 168, 2015 U.S. LEXIS 4932.

October 5, 2015. Petition for writ of certiorari to the United States Court of Appeals for the Ninth Circuit denied.

Same case below, 586 Fed. Appx. 405.

No. 15-5308. Kiran Sharma, Petitioner v. United States.

577 U.S. 893, 136 S. Ct. 222, 193 L. Ed. 2d 168, 2015 U.S. LEXIS 4766.

October 5, 2015. Petition for writ of certiorari to the United States Court of Appeals for the Fifth Circuit denied.

Same case below, 609 Fed. Appx. 797.

No. 15-5309. Arun Sharma, Petitioner v. United States.

577 U.S. 893, 136 S. Ct. 222, 193 L. Ed. 2d 168, 2015 U.S. LEXIS 4805.

October 5, 2015. Petition for writ of certiorari to the United States Court of Appeals for the Fifth Circuit denied.

Same case below, 609 Fed. Appx. 797.

No. 15-5311. Ronnie Edward Cupp, Petitioner v. United States.

577 U.S. 893, 136 S. Ct. 223, 193 L. Ed. 2d 168, 2015 U.S. LEXIS 4840.

October 5, 2015. Petition for writ of certiorari to the United States Court of Appeals for the Fourth Circuit denied.

Same case below, 598 Fed. Appx. 183.

Same case below, 783 F.3d 487.

No. 15-5312. Eduardo Barnes, Petitioner v. United States.

577 U.S. 893, 136 S. Ct. 223, 193 L. Ed. 2d 169, 2015 U.S. LEXIS 4949.

October 5, 2015. Petition for writ of certiorari to the United States Court of Appeals for the Eleventh Circuit denied.

Same case below, 596 Fed. Appx. 821.

No. 15-5313. Vincent Bazemore, Petitioner v. United States.

577 U.S. 893, 136 S. Ct. 223, 193 L. Ed. 2d 169, 2015 U.S. LEXIS 4855.

October 5, 2015. Petition for writ of certiorari to the United States Court of Appeals for the Fifth Circuit denied.

Same case below, 608 Fed. Appx. 207.

No. 15-5314. Rico Green, Petitioner v. Pennsylvania.

577 U.S. 893, 136 S. Ct. 224, 193 L. Ed. 2d 169, 2015 U.S. LEXIS 4795.

October 5, 2015. Petition for writ of certiorari to the Superior Court of Pennsylvania, Pittsburgh Office, denied.

Same case below, 106 A.3d 155.

No. 15-5316. Marlon Flores-Granados, Petitioner v. United States.

577 U.S. 893, 136 S. Ct. 224, 193 L. Ed. 2d 169, 2015 U.S. LEXIS 4816.

October 5, 2015. Petition for writ of certiorari to the United States Court of Appeals for the Fourth Circuit denied.

No. 15-5318. Houston Douglas, aka Douglas Houston, Petitioner v. Bughrara, et al.

577 U.S. 893, 136 S. Ct. 224, 193 L. Ed. 2d 169, 2015 U.S. LEXIS 4958, reh den 577 U.S. 1024, 136 S. Ct. 579, 193 L. Ed. 2d 462, 2015 U.S. LEXIS 7393.

October 5, 2015. Petition for writ of certiorari to the United States Court of Appeals for the Second Circuit denied.

Same case below, 590 Fed. Appx. 99.

No. 15-5319. Michael Chew, Petitioner v. Frank Bishop, Warden, et al.

577 U.S. 894, 136 S. Ct. 224, 193 L. Ed. 2d 169, 2015 U.S. LEXIS 4927.

October 5, 2015. Petition for writ of certiorari to the United States Court of Appeals for the Fourth Circuit denied.

Same case below, 591 Fed. Appx. 203.

No. 15-5320. Julio Alejandro Diaz, Petitioner v. M.D. Biter, Warden.

577 U.S. 894, 136 S. Ct. 224, 193 L. Ed. 2d 169, 2015 U.S. LEXIS 4813.

October 5, 2015. Petition for writ of certiorari to the United States Court of Appeals for the Ninth Circuit denied.

No. 15-5321. Isaiah James Coleman, Petitioner v. Virginia.

577 U.S. 894, 136 S. Ct. 225, 193 L. Ed. 2d 169, 2015 U.S. LEXIS 4833.

October 5, 2015. Petition for writ of certiorari to the Supreme Court of Virginia denied.

No. 15-5322. Rodolfo Gavilanes-Ocaranza, Petitioner v. United States.

577 U.S. 894, 136 S. Ct. 225, 193 L. Ed. 2d 170, 2015 U.S. LEXIS 4829.

October 5, 2015. Petition for writ of certiorari to the United States Court of Appeals for the Ninth Circuit denied.

Same case below, 772 F.3d 624 and 585 Fed. Appx. 321.

No. 15-5323. Ikeisha Perry, Petitioner v. Angelia Rawski, Warden.

577 U.S. 894, 136 S. Ct. 225, 193 L. Ed. 2d 170, 2015 U.S. LEXIS 4767.

October 5, 2015. Petition for writ of certiorari to the United States Court of Appeals for the Fourth Circuit denied.

Same case below, 600 Fed. Appx. 166.

No. 15-5324. John Anthony Lee, Petitioner v. United States.

577 U.S. 894, 136 S. Ct. 225, 193 L. Ed. 2d 170, 2015 U.S. LEXIS 4807.

October 5, 2015. Petition for writ of certiorari to the United States Court of Appeals for the Fifth Circuit denied.

Same case below, 600 Fed. Appx. 254.

No. 15-5325. Keith LeFlore, Petitioner v. Illinois.

577 U.S. 894, 136 S. Ct. 225, 193 L. Ed. 2d 170, 2015 U.S. LEXIS 4845.

October 5, 2015. Petition for writ of certiorari to the Supreme Court of Illinois denied.

Same case below, 392 Ill. Dec. 467, 32 N.E.3d 1043.

No. 15-5326. David Willan, Petitioner v. Ohio.

577 U.S. 894, 136 S. Ct. 225, 193 L. Ed. 2d 170, 2015 U.S. LEXIS 4940.

October 5, 2015. Petition for writ of certiorari to the Supreme Court of Ohio denied.

Same case below, 144 Ohio St. 3d 94, 41 N.E.3d 366.

No. 15-5327. Alexander Walls, Petitioner v. United States.

577 U.S. 894, 136 S. Ct. 226, 193 L. Ed. 2d 170, 2015 U.S. LEXIS 4882.

October 5, 2015. Petition for writ of certiorari to the United States Court of Appeals for the Ninth Circuit denied.

Same case below, 784 F.3d 543.

No. 15-5328. Ricardo Antione King, Petitioner v. Susan Ann Kessler.

577 U.S. 894, 136 S. Ct. 226, 193 L. Ed. 2d 170, 2015 U.S. LEXIS 4888.

October 5, 2015. Petition for writ of certiorari to the United States Court of Appeals for the Fourth Circuit denied.

Same case below, 599 Fed. Appx. 513.

No. 15-5329. Richard M. Plato, Petitioner v. United States.

577 U.S. 894, 136 S. Ct. 226, 193 L. Ed. 2d 170, 2015 U.S. LEXIS 4942.

October 5, 2015. Petition for writ of certiorari to the United States Court of Appeals for the Fifth Circuit denied.

Same case below, 593 Fed. Appx. 364.

No. 15-5331. Mario Gibson, Petitioner v. United States.

577 U.S. 894, 136 S. Ct. 226, 193 L. Ed. 2d 171, 2015 U.S. LEXIS 4930.

October 5, 2015. Petition for writ of certiorari to the United States Court of Appeals for the Eighth Circuit denied.

Same case below, 600 Fed. Appx. 491.

No. 15-5332. Juan Brandon Gray-Sommerville, Petitioner v. United States.

577 U.S. 894, 136 S. Ct. 226, 193 L. Ed. 2d 171, 2015 U.S. LEXIS 4785.

October 5, 2015. Petition for writ of certiorari to the United States Court of Appeals for the Fourth Circuit denied.

Same case below, 618 Fed. Appx. 165.

No. 15-5333. Steven L. Hunter, Petitioner v. United States.

577 U.S. 894, 136 S. Ct. 226, 193 L. Ed. 2d 171, 2015 U.S. LEXIS 4914.

October 5, 2015. Petition for writ of certiorari to the United States Court of Appeals for the Seventh Circuit denied.

No. 15-5334. James Edward Green, Jr., Petitioner v. Wendy Kelley, Director, Arkansas Department of Correction.

577 U.S. 894, 136 S. Ct. 227, 193 L. Ed. 2d 171, 2015 U.S. LEXIS 4828.

October 5, 2015. Petition for writ of certiorari to the United States Court of Appeals for the Eighth Circuit denied.

No. 15-5335. Tommy L. Fitzgerald, Petitioner v. Ted House, Judge, 11th Judicial Circuit, St. Charles County, Missouri, et al.

577 U.S. 895, 136 S. Ct. 227, 193 L. Ed. 2d 171, 2015 U.S. LEXIS 4926.

October 5, 2015. Petition for writ of certiorari to the Supreme Court of Missouri denied.

No. 15-5338. Marcos Isidro Mercado Villalobos, Petitioner v. William Stephens, Director, Texas Department of Criminal Justice, Correctional Institutions Division.

577 U.S. 895, 136 S. Ct. 227, 193 L. Ed. 2d 171, 2015 U.S. LEXIS 4931.

October 5, 2015. Petition for writ of certiorari to the United States Court of Appeals for the Fifth Circuit denied.

No. 15-5339. Marcus Tillman, Petitioner v. Michigan.

577 U.S. 895, 136 S. Ct. 227, 193 L. Ed. 2d 171, 2015 U.S. LEXIS 4788.

October 5, 2015. Petition for writ of certiorari to the Circuit Court of Michigan, Wayne County, Criminal Division, denied.

No. 15-5340. Samuel L. Surles, Petitioner v. G. Leach, et al.

577 U.S. 895, 136 S. Ct. 228, 193 L. Ed. 2d 171, 2015 U.S. LEXIS 4773.

October 5, 2015. Petition for writ of certiorari to the United States Court of Appeals for the Sixth Circuit denied.

No. 15-5341. Mario Solorzano, Petitioner v. Jeffrey Beard, Secretary, California Department of Corrections and Rehabilitation.

577 U.S. 895, 136 S. Ct. 228, 193 L. Ed. 2d 172, 2015 U.S. LEXIS 4878.

October 5, 2015. Petition for writ of certiorari to the United States Court of Appeals for the Ninth Circuit denied.

No. 15-5342. Armando Leyva-Munoz, Petitioner v. United States.

577 U.S. 895, 136 S. Ct. 228, 193 L. Ed. 2d 172, 2015 U.S. LEXIS 4793.

October 5, 2015. Petition for writ of certiorari to the United States Court of Appeals for the Fifth Circuit denied.

Same case below, 605 Fed. Appx. 393.

No. 15-5343. Danny Ray McBride, Petitioner v. William Stephens, Director, Texas Department of Criminal Justice, Correctional Institutions Division.

577 U.S. 895, 136 S. Ct. 228, 193 L. Ed. 2d 172, 2015 U.S. LEXIS 4945.

October 5, 2015. Petition for writ of certiorari to the United States Court of Appeals for the Fifth Circuit denied.

No. 15-5344. Thaddeus M. McKinnon, Petitioner v. Julie L. Jones, Secretary, Florida Department of Corrections.

577 U.S. 895, 136 S. Ct. 228, 193 L. Ed. 2d 172, 2015 U.S. LEXIS 4771.

October 5, 2015. Petition for writ of certiorari to the United States Court of Appeals for the Eleventh Circuit denied.

No. 15-5345. Donald Ray Palmer, Petitioner v. Charles L. Ryan, Director, Arizona Department of Corrections, et al.

577 U.S. 895, 136 S. Ct. 229, 193 L. Ed. 2d 172, 2015 U.S. LEXIS 4885.

October 5, 2015. Petition for writ of certiorari to the United States Court of Appeals for the Ninth Circuit denied.

No. 15-5346. Dmitry Shteyman, Petitioner v. United States.

577 U.S. 895, 136 S. Ct. 229, 193 L. Ed. 2d 172, 2015 U.S. LEXIS 4814.

October 5, 2015. Petition for writ of certiorari to the United States Court of Appeals for the Second Circuit denied.

Same case below, 610 Fed. Appx. 60.

No. 15-5347. Kathleen Chytka, Petitioner v. Wright Tree Service, Inc.

577 U.S. 895, 136 S. Ct. 229, 193 L. Ed. 2d 172, 2015 U.S. LEXIS 4789.

October 5, 2015. Petition for writ of certiorari to the United States Court of Appeals for the Tenth Circuit denied.

Same case below, 617 Fed. Appx. 841.

No. 15-5348. Norman Seneka Bowers, Petitioner v. United States.

577 U.S. 895, 136 S. Ct. 229, 193 L. Ed. 2d 172, 2015 U.S. LEXIS 4905.

October 5, 2015. Petition for writ of certiorari to the United States Court of Appeals for the Fourth Circuit denied.

Same case below, 616 Fed. Appx. 620.

Same case below, 600 Fed. Appx. 937.

No. 15-5349. Rigaud Andre, Petitioner v. United States.

577 U.S. 895, 136 S. Ct. 229, 193 L. Ed. 2d 173, 2015 U.S. LEXIS 4937.

October 5, 2015. Petition for writ of certiorari to the United States Court of Appeals for the Eleventh Circuit denied.

Same case below, 605 Fed. Appx. 954.

No. 15-5351. Kenneth A. Roberts, Petitioner v. Deborah McCulloch, Director, Sand Ridge Secure Treatment Facility.

577 U.S. 895, 136 S. Ct. 230, 193 L. Ed. 2d 173, 2015 U.S. LEXIS 4924.

October 5, 2015. Petition for writ of certiorari to the United States Court of Appeals for the Seventh Circuit denied.

No. 15-5352. Joaquin Garduno-Castillo, Petitioner v. United States.

577 U.S. 896, 136 S. Ct. 230, 193 L. Ed. 2d 173, 2015 U.S. LEXIS 4904.

October 5, 2015. Petition for writ of certiorari to the United States Court of Appeals for the Fifth Circuit denied.

Same case below, 600 Fed. Appx. 938.

No. 15-5353. Roberto Simon Garcia-Lara, Petitioner v. United States.

577 U.S. 896, 136 S. Ct. 230, 193 L. Ed. 2d 173, 2015 U.S. LEXIS 4801.

October 5, 2015. Petition for writ of certiorari to the United States Court of Appeals for the Fifth Circuit denied.

No. 15-5354. Jerrin Lavazie Hickman, Petitioner v. Oregon.

577 U.S. 896, 136 S. Ct. 230, 193 L. Ed. 2d 173, 2015 U.S. LEXIS 4847, reh den 577 U.S. 1054, 136 S. Ct. 706, 193 L. Ed. 2d 532, 2015 U.S. LEXIS 7940.

October 5, 2015. Petition for writ of certiorari to the Supreme Court of Oregon denied.

Same case below, 355 Or. 715, 330 P.3d 551, and 356 Or. 687, 343 P.3d 634.

No. 15-5355. Daniel L. Hanson, Petitioner v. Timothy Haines, Warden.

577 U.S. 896, 136 S. Ct. 230, 193 L. Ed. 2d 173, 2015 U.S. LEXIS 4775.

October 5, 2015. Petition for writ of certiorari to the United States Court of Appeals for the Seventh Circuit denied.

No. 15-5356. Henry Lee Hutchinson, Petitioner v. Texas.

577 U.S. 896, 136 S. Ct. 230, 193 L. Ed. 2d 173, 2015 U.S. LEXIS 4894.

October 5, 2015. Petition for writ of certiorari to the Court of Appeals of Texas, Tenth District, denied.

No. 15-5357. Sherman Stillwell Griffin, Petitioner v. Texas.

577 U.S. 896, 136 S. Ct. 230, 193 L. Ed. 2d 173, 2015 U.S. LEXIS 4925.

October 5, 2015. Petition for writ of certiorari to the Court of Appeals of Texas, Fourteenth District, denied.

No. 15-5358. Anthony Golston, Petitioner v. Kenneth Sconyers, Warden, et al.

577 U.S. 896, 136 S. Ct. 231, 193 L. Ed. 2d 174, 2015 U.S. LEXIS 4962.

October 5, 2015. Petition for writ of certiorari to the United States Court of Appeals for the Eleventh Circuit denied.

No. 15-5359. Charles A. Hood, Petitioner v. United States.

577 U.S. 896, 136 S. Ct. 231, 193 L. Ed. 2d 174, 2015 U.S. LEXIS 4830, reh den 577 U.S. 1024, 136 S. Ct. 579, 193 L. Ed. 2d 462, 2015 U.S. LEXIS 7396.

October 5, 2015. Petition for writ of certiorari to the District of Columbia Court of Appeals denied.

No. 15-5360. Joseph W. Farmer, Petitioner v. Michael Potteiger, et al.

577 U.S. 896, 136 S. Ct. 231, 193 L. Ed. 2d 174, 2015 U.S. LEXIS 4802, reh den 577 U.S. 1024, 136 S. Ct. 579, 193 L. Ed. 2d 462, 2015 U.S. LEXIS 7463.

October 5, 2015. Petition for writ of certiorari to the United States Court of Appeals for the Third Circuit denied.

No. 15-5361. Glenn J. Hopkins, Petitioner v. Springfield Housing Authority.

577 U.S. 896, 136 S. Ct. 231, 193 L. Ed. 2d 174, 2015 U.S. LEXIS 4865.

October 5, 2015. Petition for writ of certiorari to the United States Court of Appeals for the Seventh Circuit denied.

Same case below, 592 Fed. Appx. 528.

No. 15-5362. Freddie Crayton, Petitioner v. Florida.

577 U.S. 896, 136 S. Ct. 231, 193 L. Ed. 2d 174, 2015 U.S. LEXIS 4872, reh den 577 U.S. 1044, 136 S. Ct. 610, 193 L. Ed. 2d 491, 2015 U.S. LEXIS 7715.

October 5, 2015. Petition for writ of certiorari to the Supreme Court of Florida denied.

Same case below, 160 So. 3d 893.

No. 15-5363. Corey Sanders, Petitioner v. Wendy Kelley, Director, Arkansas Department of Correction, et al.

577 U.S. 896, 136 S. Ct. 232, 193 L. Ed. 2d 174, 2015 U.S. LEXIS 4954.

October 5, 2015. Petition for writ of certiorari to the United States Court of Appeals for the Eighth Circuit denied.

Same case below, 773 F.3d 186.

No. 15-5364. Milton Ohlsen, III, Petitioner v. United States.

577 U.S. 896, 136 S. Ct. 232, 193 L. Ed. 2d 174, 2015 U.S. LEXIS 4851.

October 5, 2015. Petition for writ of certiorari to the United States Court of Appeals for the Eighth Circuit denied.

No. 15-5365. Charles W. Parsons, Petitioner v. Craig Adkins, Administrator, Southwestern Regional Jail.

577 U.S. 896, 136 S. Ct. 232, 193 L. Ed. 2d 174, 2015 U.S. LEXIS 4891.

October 5, 2015. Petition for writ of certiorari to the Supreme Court of Appeals of West Virginia denied.

No. 15-5366. Santosh Ram, Petitioner v. United States.

577 U.S. 897, 136 S. Ct. 232, 193 L. Ed. 2d 175, 2015 U.S. LEXIS 4811.

October 5, 2015. Petition for writ of certiorari to the United States Court of Appeals for the Eighth Circuit denied.

Same case below, 594 Fed. Appx. 317.

No. 15-5367. Patrick E. Noel, Petitioner v. Jeff Macomber, Warden.

577 U.S. 897, 136 S. Ct. 233, 193 L. Ed. 2d 175, 2015 U.S. LEXIS 4778.

October 5, 2015. Petition for writ of certiorari to the United States Court of Appeals for the Ninth Circuit denied.

Same case below, 605 Fed. Appx. 606.

No. 15-5369. Thomas Jackson, Petitioner v. United States.

577 U.S. 897, 136 S. Ct. 233, 193 L. Ed. 2d 175, 2015 U.S. LEXIS 4818.

October 5, 2015. Petition for writ of certiorari to the United States Court of Appeals for the Eleventh Circuit denied.

No. 15-5370. Larry G. Harris, Petitioner v. Jonathan R. Walls, et al.

577 U.S. 897, 136 S. Ct. 233, 193 L. Ed. 2d 175, 2015 U.S. LEXIS 4772.

October 5, 2015. Petition for writ of certiorari to the United States Court of Appeals for the Seventh Circuit denied.

Same case below, 604 Fed. Appx. 518.

No. 15-5371. Raymond Alfred Gagnon, Petitioner v. United States.

577 U.S. 897, 136 S. Ct. 233, 193 L. Ed. 2d 175, 2015 U.S. LEXIS 4907.

October 5, 2015. Petition for writ of certiorari to the United States Court of Appeals for the Fifth Circuit denied.

No. 15-5373. Robert Hazen, Petitioner v. Ellen Hazen.

577 U.S. 897, 136 S. Ct. 233, 193 L. Ed. 2d 175, 2015 U.S. LEXIS 4875.

October 5, 2015. Petition for writ of certiorari to the District Court of Appeal of Florida, Fourth District, denied.

Same case below, 158 So. 3d 597.

No. 15-5374. Roger Randolph, Petitioner v. Nevada.

577 U.S. 897, 136 S. Ct. 234, 193 L. Ed. 2d 175, 2015 U.S. LEXIS 4881.

October 5, 2015. Petition for writ of certiorari to the Supreme Court of Nevada denied.

Same case below, 131 Nev. 1336.

No. 15-5375. John Kevin Waldrip, Petitioner v. United States.

577 U.S. 897, 136 S. Ct. 234, 193 L. Ed. 2d 175, 2015 U.S. LEXIS 4911.

October 5, 2015. Petition for writ of certiorari to the United States Court of Appeals for the Fifth Circuit denied.

Same case below, 600 Fed. Appx. 949.

Same case below, 588 Fed. Appx. 256.

No. 15-5376. Charlie Sanders, Petitioner v. Georgia.

577 U.S. 897, 136 S. Ct. 234, 193 L. Ed. 2d 176, 2015 U.S. LEXIS 4880.

October 5, 2015. Petition for writ of certiorari to the Supreme Court of Georgia denied.

No. 15-5377. Kurt Huy Pham, Petitioner v. Financial Industry Regulatory Authority, Inc., et al.

577 U.S. 897, 136 S. Ct. 234, 193 L. Ed. 2d 176, 2015 U.S. LEXIS 4892.

October 5, 2015. Petition for writ of certiorari to the United States Court of Appeals for the Ninth Circuit denied.

Same case below, 589 Fed. Appx. 345.

No. 15-5378. Jonathan Butler, Petitioner v. Mary Berghuis, Warden.

577 U.S. 897, 136 S. Ct. 234, 193 L. Ed. 2d 176, 2015 U.S. LEXIS 4867.

October 5, 2015. Petition for writ of certiorari to the United States Court of Appeals for the Sixth Circuit denied.

No. 15-5379. Arlington Ashley, Petitioner v. United States.

577 U.S. 897, 136 S. Ct. 234, 193 L. Ed. 2d 176, 2015 U.S. LEXIS 4890.

October 5, 2015. Petition for writ of certiorari to the United States Court of Appeals for the Fourth Circuit denied.

No. 15-5381. Quincy Deshan Butler, Petitioner v. Texas.

577 U.S. 897, 136 S. Ct. 235, 193 L. Ed. 2d 176, 2015 U.S. LEXIS 4912.

October 5, 2015. Petition for writ of certiorari to the Court of Appeals of Texas, Tenth District, denied.

No. 15-5383. Troy Douglas Brimm, Petitioner v. United States.

577 U.S. 897, 136 S. Ct. 235, 193 L. Ed. 2d 176, 2015 U.S. LEXIS 4779.

October 5, 2015. Petition for writ of certiorari to the United States Court of Appeals for the Eleventh Circuit denied.

Same case below, 608 Fed. Appx. 795.

No. 15-5384. Ernesto Alvarado, Petitioner v. California.

577 U.S. 897, 136 S. Ct. 235, 193 L. Ed. 2d 176, 2015 U.S. LEXIS 4879.

October 5, 2015. Petition for writ of certiorari to the Court of Appeal of California, Fourth Appellate District, Division Two, denied.

No. 15-5385. Oscar Romero-Molina, Petitioner v. United States.

577 U.S. 897, 136 S. Ct. 236, 193 L. Ed. 2d 176, 2015 U.S. LEXIS 4794.

October 5, 2015. Petition for writ of certiorari to the United States Court of Appeals for the Fifth Circuit denied.

Same case below, 600 Fed. Appx. 286.

No. 15-5386. Louis Edwin Smock, Petitioner v. Julie L. Jones, Secretary, Florida Department of Corrections.

577 U.S. 898, 136 S. Ct. 236, 193 L. Ed. 2d 177, 2015 U.S. LEXIS 4781.

October 5, 2015. Petition for writ of certiorari to the United States Court of Appeals for the Eleventh Circuit denied.

No. 15-5387. Anson Chi, Petitioner v. John Doe #1.

577 U.S. 898, 136 S. Ct. 236, 193 L. Ed. 2d 177, 2015 U.S. LEXIS 4850.

October 5, 2015. Petition for writ of certiorari to the United States Court of Appeals for the Fifth Circuit denied.

Same case below, 600 Fed. Appx. 258.

No. 15-5389. Roberto Cruz, Petitioner v. Massachusetts.

577 U.S. 898, 136 S. Ct. 236, 193 L. Ed. 2d 177, 2015 U.S. LEXIS 4868.

October 5, 2015. Petition for writ of certiorari to the Appeals Court of Massachusetts denied.

Same case below, 86 Mass. App. Ct. 1123, 20 N.E.3d 981.

No. 15-5390. Fred Johnson, Petitioner v. Darin Young, Warden, et al.

577 U.S. 898, 136 S. Ct. 237, 193 L. Ed. 2d 177, 2015 U.S. LEXIS 4916.

October 5, 2015. Petition for writ of certiorari to the United States Court of Appeals for the Eighth Circuit denied.

Same case below, 779 F.3d 495.

No. 15-5391. Dion Nelson, Petitioner v. United States.

577 U.S. 898, 136 S. Ct. 237, 193 L. Ed. 2d 177, 2015 U.S. LEXIS 4901.

October 5, 2015. Petition for writ of certiorari to the United States Court of Appeals for the Second Circuit denied.

Same case below, 591 Fed. Appx. 37.

No. 15-5393. Thad C. Theall, Petitioner v. United States.

577 U.S. 898, 136 S. Ct. 237, 193 L. Ed. 2d 177, 2015 U.S. LEXIS 4786.

October 5, 2015. Petition for writ of certiorari to the United States Court of Appeals for the Fifth Circuit denied.

Same case below, 609 Fed. Appx. 807.

No. 15-5394. Jose Guillermo Verdugo-Beltran, Petitioner v. United States.

577 U.S. 898, 136 S. Ct. 237, 193 L. Ed. 2d 177, 2015 U.S. LEXIS 4934.

October 5, 2015. Petition for writ of certiorari to the United States Court of Appeals for the Ninth Circuit denied.

Same case below, 598 Fed. Appx. 556.

No. 15-5395. Timothy M. Strain, Petitioner v. United States District Court for the Middle District of Louisiana.

577 U.S. 898, 136 S. Ct. 300, 193 L. Ed. 2d 177, 2015 U.S. LEXIS 4876, reh den 577 U.S. 1054, 136 S. Ct. 706, 193 L. Ed. 2d 532, 2015 U.S. LEXIS 7897.

October 5, 2015. Petition for writ of certiorari to the United States Court of Appeals for the Fifth Circuit denied.

No. 15-5396. Robert Scheiring, Petitioner v. United States.

577 U.S. 898, 136 S. Ct. 237, 193 L. Ed. 2d 178, 2015 U.S. LEXIS 4871.

October 5, 2015. Petition for writ of certiorari to the United States Court of Appeals for the Eighth Circuit denied.

No. 15-5397. Henry L. Shell, Jr., Petitioner v. Indiana.

577 U.S. 898, 136 S. Ct. 238, 193 L. Ed. 2d 178, 2015 U.S. LEXIS 4921.

October 5, 2015. Petition for writ of certiorari to the Court of Appeals of Indiana, Second District, denied.

Same case below, 16 N.E.3d 488.

No. 15-5398. Andrew Gareth Nelson, Petitioner v. United States.

577 U.S. 898, 136 S. Ct. 238, 193 L. Ed. 2d 178, 2015 U.S. LEXIS 4961.

October 5, 2015. Petition for writ of certiorari to the United States Court of Appeals for the Eleventh Circuit denied.

Same case below, 609 Fed. Appx. 559.

No. 15-5400. Anthony Dewayne Lester, Petitioner v. William Stephens,

Director, Texas Department of Criminal Justice, Correctional Institutions Division.

577 U.S. 898, 136 S. Ct. 238, 193 L. Ed. 2d 178, 2015 U.S. LEXIS 4938, reh den 577 U.S. 1054, 136 S. Ct. 706, 193 L. Ed. 2d 532, 2015 U.S. LEXIS 7934.

October 5, 2015. Petition for writ of certiorari to the United States Court of Appeals for the Fifth Circuit denied.

No. 15-5401. Felix A. Okafor, Petitioner v. United States.

577 U.S. 898, 136 S. Ct. 238, 193 L. Ed. 2d 178, 2015 U.S. LEXIS 4922.

October 5, 2015. Petition for writ of certiorari to the United States Court of Appeals for the Fourth Circuit denied.

Same case below, 602 Fed. Appx. 108.

No. 15-5402. William Henry Krieg, Petitioner v. Stephen L. Steele, et al.

577 U.S. 898, 136 S. Ct. 238, 193 L. Ed. 2d 178, 2015 U.S. LEXIS 4928.

October 5, 2015. Petition for writ of certiorari to the United States Court of Appeals for the Fifth Circuit denied.

Same case below, 599 Fed. Appx. 231.

No. 15-5403. Jeffrey R. LeBlanc, Petitioner v. Macomb Regional Facility.

577 U.S. 898, 136 S. Ct. 238, 193 L. Ed. 2d 178, 2015 U.S. LEXIS 4957, reh den 577 U.S. 1095, 136 S. Ct. 884, 193 L. Ed. 2d 776, 2016 U.S. LEXIS 332.

October 5, 2015. Petition for writ of certiorari to the United States Court of Appeals for the Sixth Circuit denied.

No. 15-5404. **William Torres, Petitioner v. Thomas Read, et al.**

577 U.S. 899, 136 S. Ct. 239, 193 L. Ed. 2d 179, 2015 U.S. LEXIS 4835.

October 5, 2015. Petition for writ of certiorari to the United States Court of Appeals for the Ninth Circuit denied.

Same case below, 593 Fed. Appx. 742.

No. 15-5405. **Eppie McClain, Jr., Petitioner v. W. L. Montgomery, Warden.**

577 U.S. 899, 136 S. Ct. 239, 193 L. Ed. 2d 179, 2015 U.S. LEXIS 4948.

October 5, 2015. Petition for writ of certiorari to the United States Court of Appeals for the Ninth Circuit denied.

Same case below, 600 Fed. Appx. 549.

No. 15-5406. **Maurice Darnell Tyler, Petitioner v. Derrick D. Schofield, Commissioner, Tennessee Department of Correction, et al.**

577 U.S. 899, 136 S. Ct. 239, 193 L. Ed. 2d 179, 2015 U.S. LEXIS 4815.

October 5, 2015. Petition for writ of certiorari to the United States Court of Appeals for the Sixth Circuit denied.

Same case below, 610 Fed. Appx. 445.

No. 15-5407. **Oscar Rodriguez, Petitioner v. United States.**

577 U.S. 899, 136 S. Ct. 240, 193 L. Ed. 2d 179, 2015 U.S. LEXIS 4884.

October 5, 2015. Petition for writ of certiorari to the United States Court of Appeals for the Ninth Circuit denied.

Same case below, 598 Fed. Appx. 534.

No. 15-5408. **Christina Sajor-Reeder, Petitioner v. J. Cavazos, Warden.**

577 U.S. 899, 136 S. Ct. 240, 193 L. Ed. 2d 179, 2015 U.S. LEXIS 6359.

October 5, 2015. Petition for writ of certiorari to the United States Court of Appeals for the Ninth Circuit denied.

Same case below, 605 Fed. Appx. 679.

No. 15-5409. **Rodney Sparks, Petitioner v. Michael A. Trumbull, et ux.**

577 U.S. 899, 136 S. Ct. 240, 193 L. Ed. 2d 179, 2015 U.S. LEXIS 4782.

October 5, 2015. Petition for writ of certiorari to the Court of Special Appeals of Maryland denied.

Same case below, 220 Md. App. 726 and 220 Md. App. 727.

No. 15-5410. **James Willie Norman, Petitioner v. Florida.**

577 U.S. 899, 136 S. Ct. 240, 193 L. Ed. 2d 179, 2015 U.S. LEXIS 4839, reh den 577 U.S. 1024, 136 S. Ct. 580, 193 L. Ed. 2d 462, 2015 U.S. LEXIS 7447.

October 5, 2015. Petition for writ of certiorari to the District Court of Appeal of Florida, First District, denied.

Same case below, 162 So. 3d 991.

No. 15-5411. **Earl Lee Wright, Petitioner v. Ronald King.**

577 U.S. 899, 136 S. Ct. 240, 193 L. Ed. 2d 179, 2015 U.S. LEXIS 4906.

October 5, 2015. Petition for writ of certiorari to the Supreme Court of Mississippi denied.

Same case below, 166 So. 3d 38.

No. 15-5412. Jamie A. Watkins, Petitioner v. Ian Wallace, Warden.

577 U.S. 899, 136 S. Ct. 241, 193 L. Ed. 2d 180, 2015 U.S. LEXIS 4859.

October 5, 2015. Petition for writ of certiorari to the United States Court of Appeals for the Eighth Circuit denied.

No. 15-5413. Anthony Walker, Petitioner v. United States.

577 U.S. 899, 136 S. Ct. 241, 193 L. Ed. 2d 180, 2015 U.S. LEXIS 4849.

October 5, 2015. Petition for writ of certiorari to the United States Court of Appeals for the Fourth Circuit denied.

Same case below, 607 Fed. Appx. 247.

No. 15-5414. Kerry Devin O'Bryan, Petitioner v. Jason A. Terris, Warden.

577 U.S. 899, 136 S. Ct. 241, 193 L. Ed. 2d 180, 2015 U.S. LEXIS 4959.

October 5, 2015. Petition for writ of certiorari to the United States Court of Appeals for the Sixth Circuit denied.

No. 15-5415. Melvin Johnson, III, Petitioner v. Texas.

577 U.S. 899, 136 S. Ct. 241, 193 L. Ed. 2d 180, 2015 U.S. LEXIS 4809.

October 5, 2015. Petition for writ of certiorari to the Court of Criminal Appeals of Texas denied.

No. 15-5416. Douglas Paul Wright, Petitioner v. Trevor Wingard, Superintendent, State Correctional Institution at Somerset, et al.

577 U.S. 899, 136 S. Ct. 241, 193 L. Ed. 2d 180, 2015 U.S. LEXIS 4825, reh den 577 U.S. 1024, 136 S. Ct. 580, 193 L. Ed. 2d 462, 2015 U.S. LEXIS 7449.

October 5, 2015. Petition for writ of certiorari to the United States Court of Appeals for the Third Circuit denied.

Same case below, 601 Fed. Appx. 115.

No. 15-5417. Michael David Williams, Petitioner v. Texas.

577 U.S. 899, 136 S. Ct. 241, 193 L. Ed. 2d 180, 2015 U.S. LEXIS 4861.

October 5, 2015. Petition for writ of certiorari to the Court of Appeals of Texas, Seventh District, denied.

No. 15-5418. Ivan Cabrera, Petitioner v. United States.

577 U.S. 899, 136 S. Ct. 242, 193 L. Ed. 2d 180, 2015 U.S. LEXIS 4951.

October 5, 2015. Petition for writ of certiorari to the United States Court of Appeals for the Fifth Circuit denied.

Same case below, 600 Fed. Appx. 279.

No. 15-5419. Joel Mazariegos-Soto, Petitioner v. United States.

577 U.S. 900, 136 S. Ct. 242, 193 L. Ed. 2d 180, 2015 U.S. LEXIS 6364.

October 5, 2015. Petition for writ of certiorari to the United States Court of Appeals for the Ninth Circuit denied.

Same case below, 592 Fed. Appx. 641.

No. 15-5420. Eric Jerome Johnson, Petitioner v. Minnesota.

577 U.S. 900, 136 S. Ct. 242, 193 L. Ed. 2d 181, 2015 U.S. LEXIS 4923.

October 5, 2015. Petition for writ of certiorari to the Court of Appeals of Minnesota denied.

No. 15-5422. Beverly Allen Baker, Petitioner v. United States.

577 U.S. 900, 136 S. Ct. 242, 193 L. Ed. 2d 181, 2015 U.S. LEXIS 4856, reh den 577 U.S. 1024, 136 S. Ct. 580, 193 L. Ed. 2d 462, 2015 U.S. LEXIS 7422.

October 5, 2015. Petition for writ of certiorari to the United States Court of Appeals for the Fourth Circuit denied.

Same case below, 601 Fed. Appx. 231.

No. 15-5423. Carl Moore, Petitioner v. United States.

577 U.S. 900, 136 S. Ct. 243, 193 L. Ed. 2d 181, 2015 U.S. LEXIS 4800.

October 5, 2015. Petition for writ of certiorari to the United States Court of Appeals for the Sixth Circuit denied.

Same case below, 604 Fed. Appx. 458.

No. 15-5424. Stanley Yelardy, Petitioner v. David Pierce, Warden, et al.

577 U.S. 900, 136 S. Ct. 243, 193 L. Ed. 2d 181, 2015 U.S. LEXIS 4863.

October 5, 2015. Petition for writ of certiorari to the United States Court of Appeals for the Third Circuit denied.

No. 15-5425. Carlos Ivan Llera-Plaza, Petitioner v. United States.

577 U.S. 900, 136 S. Ct. 243, 193 L. Ed. 2d 181, 2015 U.S. LEXIS 4896.

October 5, 2015. Petition for writ of certiorari to the United States Court of Appeals for the Third Circuit denied.

No. 15-5426. Rogerio Chaves Scotton, Petitioner v. United States.

577 U.S. 900, 136 S. Ct. 243, 193 L. Ed. 2d 181, 2015 U.S. LEXIS 4964, reh den 577 U.S. 1024, 136 S. Ct. 580, 193 L. Ed. 2d 462, 2015 U.S. LEXIS 7377.

October 5, 2015. Petition for writ of certiorari to the United States Court of Appeals for the Eleventh Circuit denied.

No. 15-5427. David Warren, Petitioner v. Illinois.

577 U.S. 900, 136 S. Ct. 244, 193 L. Ed. 2d 181, 2015 U.S. LEXIS 4935.

October 5, 2015. Petition for writ of certiorari to the Appellate Court of Illinois, Fifth District, denied.

No. 15-5428. Michael Taffaro, Petitioner v. Daniel Ng.

577 U.S. 900, 136 S. Ct. 244, 193 L. Ed. 2d 181, 2015 U.S. LEXIS 4841.

October 5, 2015. Petition for writ of certiorari to the Superior Court of New Jersey, Appellate Division, denied.

No. 15-5429. Luis D. Cabrera Mejia, Petitioner v. Wal-Mart.

577 U.S. 900, 136 S. Ct. 244, 193 L. Ed. 2d 182, 2015 U.S. LEXIS 4832, reh den 577 U.S. 1024, 136 S. Ct. 580, 193 L. Ed. 2d 463, 2015 U.S. LEXIS 7441.

October 5, 2015. Petition for writ of certiorari to the United States Court of Appeals for the Fourth Circuit denied.

Same case below, 599 Fed. Appx. 520.

No. 15-5430. Ronald Gary Moore, Petitioner v. Florida.

577 U.S. 900, 136 S. Ct. 244, 193 L. Ed. 2d 182, 2015 U.S. LEXIS 4812.

October 5, 2015. Petition for writ of certiorari to the District Court of Appeal of Florida, Fifth District, denied.

Same case below, 162 So. 3d 1036.

No. 15-5431. Ricardo Guerrero, Petitioner v. United States.

577 U.S. 900, 136 S. Ct. 244, 193 L. Ed. 2d 182, 2015 U.S. LEXIS 4790.

October 5, 2015. Petition for writ of certiorari to the United States Court of Appeals for the Fifth Circuit denied.

Same case below, 603 Fed. Appx. 328.

No. 15-5432. Donald F. Mackay, Petitioner v. United States, et al.

577 U.S. 900, 136 S. Ct. 245, 193 L. Ed. 2d 182, 2015 U.S. LEXIS 4874.

October 5, 2015. Petition for writ of certiorari to the United States Court of Appeals for the Ninth Circuit denied.

No. 15-5433. Marvell Antonio Culp, Petitioner v. United States.

577 U.S. 900, 136 S. Ct. 245, 193 L. Ed. 2d 182, 2015 U.S. LEXIS 4898.

October 5, 2015. Petition for writ of certiorari to the United States Court of Appeals for the Sixth Circuit denied.

Same case below, 608 Fed. Appx. 390.

No. 15-5434. Jeffrey R. LeBlanc, Petitioner v. Kalamazoo County Sheriff's Department.

577 U.S. 900, 136 S. Ct. 245, 193 L. Ed. 2d 182, 2015 U.S. LEXIS 4817, reh den 577 U.S. 1096, 136 S. Ct. 884, 193 L. Ed. 2d 776, 2016 U.S. LEXIS 488.

October 5, 2015. Petition for writ of certiorari to the United States Court of Appeals for the Sixth Circuit denied.

No. 15-5436. Dominick Jean Philippe, Petitioner v. United States.

No. 15-5439. Trevor Cole, Petitioner v. United States.

577 U.S. 900, 136 S. Ct. 245, 193 L. Ed. 2d 182, 2015 U.S. LEXIS 4893.

October 5, 2015. Petitions for writs of certiorari to the United States Court of Appeals for the Second Circuit denied.

Same cases below, 594 Fed. Appx. 35.

No. 15-5437. Rhett U., Petitioner v. Arizona Department of Child Safety, et al.

577 U.S. 901, 136 S. Ct. 245, 193 L. Ed. 2d 182, 2015 U.S. LEXIS 4858.

October 5, 2015. Petition for writ of certiorari to the Court of Appeals of Arizona, Division One, denied.

No. 15-5438. Martin Ramos, Petitioner v. Anthony A. Lamarque, Warden.

577 U.S. 901, 136 S. Ct. 246, 193 L. Ed. 2d 183, 2015 U.S. LEXIS 4944.

October 5, 2015. Petition for writ of certiorari to the United States Court of Appeals for the Ninth Circuit denied.

No. 15-5440. Jeffrey R. LeBlanc, Petitioner v. Michigan Department of Corrections.

577 U.S. 901, 136 S. Ct. 300, 193 L. Ed. 2d 183, 2015 U.S. LEXIS 4886, reh den 577 U.S. 1096, 136 S. Ct. 884, 193 L. Ed. 2d 776, 2016 U.S. LEXIS 479.

October 5, 2015. Petition for writ of certiorari to the United States Court of Appeals for the Sixth Circuit denied.

No. 15-5441. Corry Mency, Petitioner v. Florida.

577 U.S. 901, 136 S. Ct. 246, 193 L. Ed. 2d 183, 2015 U.S. LEXIS 4796.

October 5, 2015. Petition for writ of certiorari to the District Court of Appeal of Florida, First District, denied.

Same case below, 158 So. 3d 569.

No. 15-5442. John Vaughn Neil, Petitioner v. Loretta E. Lynch, Attorney General.

577 U.S. 901, 136 S. Ct. 247, 193 L. Ed. 2d 183, 2015 U.S. LEXIS 4787.

October 5, 2015. Petition for writ of certiorari to the United States Court of Appeals for the Second Circuit denied.

No. 15-5444. Rafael Salas, Petitioner v. Clark E. Ducart, Warden.

577 U.S. 901, 136 S. Ct. 247, 193 L. Ed. 2d 183, 2015 U.S. LEXIS 4837.

October 5, 2015. Petition for writ of certiorari to the United States Court of Appeals for the Ninth Circuit denied.

No. 15-5445. Will L. Dawson, Petitioner v. United States.

577 U.S. 901, 136 S. Ct. 247, 193 L. Ed. 2d 183, 2015 U.S. LEXIS 4824.

October 5, 2015. Petition for writ of certiorari to the United States Court of Appeals for the Seventh Circuit denied.

No. 15-5447. Will Gross, Petitioner v. United States.

577 U.S. 901, 136 S. Ct. 247, 193 L. Ed. 2d 183, 2015 U.S. LEXIS 4870.

October 5, 2015. Petition for writ of certiorari to the United States Court of Appeals for the District of Columbia Circuit denied.

Same case below, 784 F.3d 784.

No. 15-5448. Francisco Javier Gomez, Petitioner v. United States.

577 U.S. 901, 136 S. Ct. 247, 193 L. Ed. 2d 183, 2015 U.S. LEXIS 4804.

October 5, 2015. Petition for writ of certiorari to the United States Court of Appeals for the Ninth Circuit denied.

Same case below, 595 Fed. Appx. 726.

No. 15-5449. Leon Carmichael, Jr., Petitioner v. Dewayne Estes, Warden, et al.

577 U.S. 901, 136 S. Ct. 248, 193 L. Ed. 2d 184, 2015 U.S. LEXIS 4910.

October 5, 2015. Petition for writ of certiorari to the United States Court of Appeals for the Eleventh Circuit denied.

No. 15-5450. Shawn Allen Cleaver, Petitioner v. Florida.

577 U.S. 901, 136 S. Ct. 248, 193 L. Ed. 2d 184, 2015 U.S. LEXIS 4889.

October 5, 2015. Petition for writ of certiorari to the District Court of Appeal of Florida, Second District, denied.

Same case below, 173 So. 3d 972.

No. 15-5451. Paul Alan Roberts, Petitioner v. Donald Barrow, Warden.

577 U.S. 901, 136 S. Ct. 248, 193 L. Ed. 2d 184, 2015 U.S. LEXIS 4933.

October 5, 2015. Petition for writ of certiorari to the United States Court of Appeals for the Eleventh Circuit denied.

No. 15-5452. Francisco Sanchez, Petitioners v. Jeffrey Beard, Secretary, California Department of Corrections and Rehabilitation.

577 U.S. 901, 136 S. Ct. 248, 193 L. Ed. 2d 184, 2015 U.S. LEXIS 4846.

October 5, 2015. Petition for writ of certiorari to the United States Court of Appeals for the Ninth Circuit denied.

No. 15-5453. Stephen Eikelboom, Petitioner v. United States.

577 U.S. 901, 136 S. Ct. 248, 193 L. Ed. 2d 184, 2015 U.S. LEXIS 4797.

October 5, 2015. Petition for writ of certiorari to the United States Court of Appeals for the Fifth Circuit denied.

Same case below, 609 Fed. Appx. 224.

No. 15-5454. Francisco Ramirez, Jr., Petitioner v. Greg Lewis, Warden.

577 U.S. 901, 136 S. Ct. 248, 193 L. Ed. 2d 184, 2015 U.S. LEXIS 4819.

October 5, 2015. Petition for writ of certiorari to the United States Court of Appeals for the Ninth Circuit denied.

No. 15-5455. Phillip Michael Thomas, Petitioner v. Florida.

577 U.S. 901, 136 S. Ct. 249, 193 L. Ed. 2d 184, 2015 U.S. LEXIS 4960.

October 5, 2015. Petition for writ of certiorari to the Supreme Court of Florida denied.

Same case below, 168 So. 3d 231.

No. 15-5456. Brandon Jerome James, Petitioner v. United States.

577 U.S. 902, 136 S. Ct. 249, 193 L. Ed. 2d 185, 2015 U.S. LEXIS 4943.

October 5, 2015. Petition for writ of certiorari to the United States Court of Appeals for the Eleventh Circuit denied.

Same case below, 598 Fed. Appx. 714.

No. 15-5457. Reis Lopez, Petitioner v. George Tapia, Warden.

577 U.S. 902, 136 S. Ct. 249, 193 L. Ed. 2d 185, 2015 U.S. LEXIS 4946.

October 5, 2015. Petition for writ of certiorari to the District Court of New Mexico, Valencia County, denied.

No. 15-5458. Gary D. Easterling, aka Gary Easterling, aka Gary Smith, Petitioner v. United States.

577 U.S. 902, 136 S. Ct. 249, 193 L. Ed. 2d 185, 2015 U.S. LEXIS 4952.

October 5, 2015. Petition for writ of certiorari to the United States Court of Appeals for the Fourth Circuit denied.

Same case below, 602 Fed. Appx. 919.

No. 15-5459. Rocke William Dilbert, Petitioner v. United States.

577 U.S. 902, 136 S. Ct. 249, 193 L. Ed. 2d 185, 2015 U.S. LEXIS 4920.

October 5, 2015. Petition for writ of certiorari to the United States Court of Appeals for the Eleventh Circuit denied.

No. 15-5460. Jose Maria Felix-Villalobos, Petitioner v. United States.

577 U.S. 902, 136 S. Ct. 249, 193 L. Ed. 2d 185, 2015 U.S. LEXIS 4770.

October 5, 2015. Petition for writ of certiorari to the United States Court of Appeals for the Ninth Circuit denied.

Same case below, 600 Fed. Appx. 574.

No. 15-5461. Martin Gonzalez-Gonzalez, Petitioner v. United States.

577 U.S. 902, 136 S. Ct. 250, 193 L. Ed. 2d 185, 2015 U.S. LEXIS 4953.

October 5, 2015. Petition for writ of certiorari to the United States Court of Appeals for the Fifth Circuit denied.

Same case below, 600 Fed. Appx. 297.

No. 15-5462. Cristobal Figueroa-Magana, Petitioner v. United States.

577 U.S. 902, 136 S. Ct. 250, 193 L. Ed. 2d 185, 2015 U.S. LEXIS 4822.

October 5, 2015. Petition for writ of certiorari to the United States Court of Appeals for the Ninth Circuit denied.

Same case below, 608 Fed. Appx. 500.

No. 15-5463. Mark Starkey, Petitioner v. Heath Spackler, Warden.

577 U.S. 902, 136 S. Ct. 301, 193 L. Ed. 2d 185, 2015 U.S. LEXIS 4821.

October 5, 2015. Petition for writ of certiorari to the Supreme Court of Missouri denied.

No. 15-5464. Johnny Brown, Petitioner v. United States.

577 U.S. 902, 136 S. Ct. 250, 193 L. Ed. 2d 186, 2015 U.S. LEXIS 4810.

October 5, 2015. Petition for writ of certiorari to the United States Court of Appeals for the Ninth Circuit denied.

Same case below, 784 F.3d 1301.

No. 15-5465. Miguel Arciba, Petitioner v. William Stephens, Director, Texas Department of Criminal Justice, Correctional Institutions Division.

577 U.S. 902, 136 S. Ct. 250, 193 L. Ed. 2d 186, 2015 U.S. LEXIS 4919.

October 5, 2015. Petition for writ of certiorari to the United States Court of Appeals for the Fifth Circuit denied.

No. 15-5466. William M. Watts, Petitioner v. United States.

577 U.S. 902, 136 S. Ct. 250, 193 L. Ed. 2d 186, 2015 U.S. LEXIS 4860.

October 5, 2015. Petition for writ of certiorari to the United States Court of Appeals for the Seventh Circuit denied.

Same case below, 590 Fed. Appx. 637.

No. 15-5467. Steven Floyd Voss, Petitioner v. Isidro Baca, Warden.

577 U.S. 902, 136 S. Ct. 250, 193 L. Ed. 2d 186, 2015 U.S. LEXIS 4915.

October 5, 2015. Petition for writ of certiorari to the Court of Appeals of Nevada denied.

Same case below, 131 Nev. 1360.

No. 15-5468. Bunthoen Roeung and Son Thanh Bui, Petitioners v. Domingo Uribe, Jr., Warden, et al.

577 U.S. 902, 136 S. Ct. 251, 193 L. Ed. 2d 186, 2015 U.S. LEXIS 4803.

October 5, 2015. Petition for writ of certiorari to the United States Court of Appeals for the Ninth Circuit denied.

Same case below, 596 Fed. Appx. 575.

No. 15-5469. David Saguil, Petitioner v. United States.

577 U.S. 902, 136 S. Ct. 251, 193 L. Ed. 2d 186, 2015 U.S. LEXIS 4918.

October 5, 2015. Petition for writ of certiorari to the United States Court of Appeals for the Fifth Circuit denied.

Same case below, 600 Fed. Appx. 945.

No. 15-5470. Enrique Rodriguez-Lopez, Petitioner v. United States.

577 U.S. 902, 136 S. Ct. 251, 193 L. Ed. 2d 186, 2015 U.S. LEXIS 4806.

October 5, 2015. Petition for writ of certiorari to the United States Court of Appeals for the Ninth Circuit denied.

Same case below, 601 Fed. Appx. 549.

No. 15-5471. Carlos Mercado, Petitioner v. United States.

577 U.S. 903, 136 S. Ct. 251, 193 L. Ed. 2d 186, 2015 U.S. LEXIS 4838.

October 5, 2015. Petition for writ of certiorari to the United States Court of Appeals for the Fifth Circuit denied.

Same case below, 603 Fed. Appx. 327.

No. 15-5473. Carlos Alfredo Landaverde-Escalante, Petitioner v. United States.

577 U.S. 903, 136 S. Ct. 251, 193 L. Ed. 2d 187, 2015 U.S. LEXIS 4848.

October 5, 2015. Petition for writ of certiorari to the United States Court of Appeals for the Fifth Circuit denied.

Same case below, 604 Fed. Appx. 335.

No. 15-5475. Karl Kraus, Jr., Petitioner v. Randy White, Warden.

577 U.S. 903, 136 S. Ct. 251, 193 L. Ed. 2d 187, 2015 U.S. LEXIS 4780.

October 5, 2015. Petition for writ of certiorari to the United States Court of Appeals for the Sixth Circuit denied.

No. 15-5476. Enoc Ramirez-Garcia, Petitioner v. United States.

577 U.S. 903, 136 S. Ct. 252, 193 L. Ed. 2d 187, 2015 U.S. LEXIS 4877.

October 5, 2015. Petition for writ of certiorari to the United States Court of Appeals for the Fifth Circuit denied.

Same case below, 600 Fed. Appx. 293.

No. 15-5477. Merced Eliseo Romero-Guevara, Petitioner v. United States.

577 U.S. 903, 136 S. Ct. 252, 193 L. Ed. 2d 187, 2015 U.S. LEXIS 4827.

October 5, 2015. Petition for writ of certiorari to the United States Court of Appeals for the Fifth Circuit denied.

Same case below, 600 Fed. Appx. 292.

No. 15-5478. Claude V. Jones, Jr., Petitioner v. Leroy Cartledge, Warden.

577 U.S. 903, 136 S. Ct. 252, 193 L. Ed. 2d 187, 2015 U.S. LEXIS 4903, reh den 577 U.S. 1044, 136 S. Ct. 610, 193 L. Ed. 2d 491, 2015 U.S. LEXIS 7701.

October 5, 2015. Petition for writ of certiorari to the United States Court of Appeals for the Fourth Circuit denied.

Same case below, 597 Fed. Appx. 190.

No. 15-5480. Wilfredo Sanchez, Petitioner v. United States.

577 U.S. 903, 136 S. Ct. 252, 193 L. Ed. 2d 187, 2015 U.S. LEXIS 4941.

October 5, 2015. Petition for writ of certiorari to the United States Court of Appeals for the Second Circuit denied.

Same case below, 610 Fed. Appx. 42.

No. 15-5481. Charles Stanley Kowaleski, III, Petitioner v. United States.

577 U.S. 903, 136 S. Ct. 252, 193 L. Ed. 2d 187, 2015 U.S. LEXIS 4936.

October 5, 2015. Petition for writ of certiorari to the United States Court of Appeals for the Ninth Circuit denied.

Same case below, 593 Fed. Appx. 645.

No. 15-5482. Renee Ferebee, Petitioner v. Temple Hills Post Office.

577 U.S. 903, 136 S. Ct. 252, 193 L. Ed. 2d 187, 2015 U.S. LEXIS 4866.

October 5, 2015. Petition for writ of certiorari to the United States Court of Appeals for the Fourth Circuit denied.

Same case below, 590 Fed. Appx. 276.

Same case below, 611 Fed. Appx. 261.

No. 15-5483. Carlos Lorenzo Chacon-Arviso, aka Carlos Chacon-Arviso, Petitioner v. United States.

577 U.S. 903, 136 S. Ct. 253, 193 L. Ed. 2d 188, 2015 U.S. LEXIS 4897.

October 5, 2015. Petition for writ of certiorari to the United States Court of Appeals for the Fifth Circuit denied.

Same case below, 600 Fed. Appx. 948.

No. 15-5485. Robert Williams, Petitioner v. City University of New York, Brooklyn College.

577 U.S. 903, 136 S. Ct. 253, 193 L. Ed. 2d 188, 2015 U.S. LEXIS 4908, reh den 577 U.S. 1024, 136 S. Ct. 580, 193 L. Ed. 2d 463, 2015 U.S. LEXIS 7466.

October 5, 2015. Petition for writ of certiorari to the United States Court of Appeals for the Second Circuit denied.

Same case below, 590 Fed. Appx. 84.

No. 15-5486. Israel Mata-Camacho, Petitioner v. Greg Fizer, Warden, et al.

577 U.S. 903, 136 S. Ct. 253, 193 L. Ed. 2d 188, 2015 U.S. LEXIS 4798.

October 5, 2015. Petition for writ of certiorari to the United States Court of Appeals for the Ninth Circuit denied.

No. 15-5491. Angel Hernandez, Petitioner v. United States.

577 U.S. 903, 136 S. Ct. 253, 193 L. Ed. 2d 188, 2015 U.S. LEXIS 4900.

October 5, 2015. Petition for writ of certiorari to the United States Court of Appeals for the Sixth Circuit denied.

No. 15-5492. Myles W. Robinson, Petitioner v. United States.

577 U.S. 903, 136 S. Ct. 253, 193 L. Ed. 2d 188, 2015 U.S. LEXIS 4873.

October 5, 2015. Petition for writ of certiorari to the United States Court of Appeals for the Fifth Circuit denied.

Same case below, 609 Fed. Appx. 180.

No. 15-5493. David C. Stinson, Sr., Petitioner v. Florida.

577 U.S. 903, 136 S. Ct. 253, 193 L. Ed. 2d 188, 2015 U.S. LEXIS 4950.

October 5, 2015. Petition for writ of certiorari to the District Court of Appeal of Florida, Fourth District, denied.

Same case below, 195 So. 3d 391.

No. 15-5498. William Billy Gene Carter, Petitioner v. Jason Kefer, et al.

577 U.S. 904, 136 S. Ct. 254, 193 L. Ed. 2d 188, 2015 U.S. LEXIS 4864.

October 5, 2015. Petition for writ of certiorari to the United States Court of Appeals for the Eighth Circuit denied.

No. 15-5499. Zack Zafer Dyab, Petitioner v. United States.

577 U.S. 904, 136 S. Ct. 254, 193 L. Ed. 2d 188, 2015 U.S. LEXIS 4947.

October 5, 2015. Petition for writ of certiorari to the United States Court of Appeals for the Eighth Circuit denied.

No. 15-5500. Dalton Fletcher, Petitioner v. Louisiana.

577 U.S. 904, 136 S. Ct. 254, 193 L. Ed. 2d 189, 2015 U.S. LEXIS 4831.

October 5, 2015. Petition for writ of certiorari to the Court of Appeal of Louisiana, Second Circuit, denied.

Same case below, 149 So. 3d 934.

No. 15-5504. Ronald J. Gardner, Jr., Petitioner v. United States.

577 U.S. 904, 136 S. Ct. 254, 193 L. Ed. 2d 189, 2015 U.S. LEXIS 4869.

October 5, 2015. Petition for writ of certiorari to the United States Court of Appeals for the Third Circuit denied.

No. 15-5507. Bernard Roemmele, Petitioner v. United States.

577 U.S. 904, 136 S. Ct. 255, 193 L. Ed. 2d 189, 2015 U.S. LEXIS 4955.

October 5, 2015. Petition for writ of certiorari to the United States Court of Appeals for the Eleventh Circuit denied.

Same case below, 589 Fed. Appx. 470.

No. 15-5508. Infinite Allah, Petitioner v. Virginia.

577 U.S. 904, 136 S. Ct. 255, 193 L. Ed. 2d 189, 2015 U.S. LEXIS 4895.

October 5, 2015. Petition for writ of certiorari to the United States Court of Appeals for the Fourth Circuit denied.

Same case below, 601 Fed. Appx. 201.

No. 15-5510. Rui Novo, Petitioner v. Massachusetts.

577 U.S. 904, 136 S. Ct. 255, 193 L. Ed. 2d 189, 2015 U.S. LEXIS 4799.

October 5, 2015. Petition for writ of certiorari to the Superior Court of Massachusetts, Bristol County, denied.

No. 15-5511. Abraham Carrillo-Morones, Petitioner v. United States.

577 U.S. 904, 136 S. Ct. 256, 193 L. Ed. 2d 189, 2015 U.S. LEXIS 4854.

October 5, 2015. Petition for writ of certiorari to the United States Court of Appeals for the Fifth Circuit denied.

No. 15-5516. David Louis Lee, Petitioner v. United States.

577 U.S. 904, 136 S. Ct. 256, 193 L. Ed. 2d 189, 2015 U.S. LEXIS 4909.

October 5, 2015. Petition for writ of certiorari to the United States Court of Appeals for the Sixth Circuit denied.

Same case below, 608 Fed. Appx. 375.

No. 15-5517. Robert O'Campo, Petitioner v. United States.

577 U.S. 904, 136 S. Ct. 256, 193 L. Ed. 2d 189, 2015 U.S. LEXIS 4844.

October 5, 2015. Petition for writ of certiorari to the United States Court of Appeals for the Ninth Circuit denied.

Same case below, 599 Fed. Appx. 783.

No. 15-5518. Richard A. Thurston, Petitioner v. Maryland.

577 U.S. 904, 136 S. Ct. 256, 193 L. Ed. 2d 190, 2015 U.S. LEXIS 4836, reh den 577 U.S. 1096, 136 S. Ct. 884, 193 L. Ed. 2d 776, 2016 U.S. LEXIS 195.

October 5, 2015. Petition for writ of certiorari to the United States Court of Appeals for the Fourth Circuit denied.

Same case below, 611 Fed. Appx. 112.

No. 15-5519. Charles James Robinson, Petitioner v. Jeremy Andrews, et al.

577 U.S. 904, 136 S. Ct. 257, 193 L. Ed. 2d 190, 2015 U.S. LEXIS 4929.

October 5, 2015. Petition for writ of certiorari to the United States Court of Appeals for the Eighth Circuit denied.

Same case below, 594 Fed. Appx. 325.

No. 15-5523. Shawn McWhorter, Petitioner v. United States.

577 U.S. 904, 136 S. Ct. 257, 193 L. Ed. 2d 190, 2015 U.S. LEXIS 4862.

October 5, 2015. Petition for writ of certiorari to the United States Court of Appeals for the First Circuit denied.

No. 15-5529. Quincy Maurice Nash, Petitioner v. Leroy Cartledge, Warden.

577 U.S. 904, 136 S. Ct. 257, 193 L. Ed. 2d 190, 2015 U.S. LEXIS 4823.

October 5, 2015. Petition for writ of certiorari to the United States Court of Appeals for the Fourth Circuit denied.

Same case below, 597 Fed. Appx. 200.

No. 15-5530. Granville Lloyd Tribble, Jr., Petitioner v. Harold W. Clarke, Director, Virginia Department of Corrections, et al.

577 U.S. 904, 136 S. Ct. 257, 193 L. Ed. 2d 190, 2015 U.S. LEXIS 4834.

October 5, 2015. Petition for writ of certiorari to the United States Court of Appeals for the Fourth Circuit denied.

Same case below, 599 Fed. Appx. 512.

No. 15-5533. Christopher Joseph Maes, Petitioner v. Heidi M. Lackner, Warden.

577 U.S. 905, 136 S. Ct. 258, 193 L. Ed. 2d 190, 2015 U.S. LEXIS 4917.

October 5, 2015. Petition for writ of certiorari to the United States Court of Appeals for the Ninth Circuit denied.

Same case below, 792 F.3d 1132.

No. 15-5534. Richard Layne LaBelle, Petitioner v. United States.

577 U.S. 905, 136 S. Ct. 258, 193 L. Ed. 2d 190, 2015 U.S. LEXIS 4826, reh den 577 U.S. 1096, 136 S. Ct. 885, 193 L. Ed. 2d 776, 2016 U.S. LEXIS 384.

October 5, 2015. Petition for writ of certiorari to the United States Court of Appeals for the Sixth Circuit denied.

No. 15-5535. Javier Uribe, Petitioner v. United States.

577 U.S. 905, 136 S. Ct. 258, 193 L. Ed. 2d 190, 2015 U.S. LEXIS 4852.

October 5, 2015. Petition for writ of certiorari to the United States Court of Appeals for the Ninth Circuit denied.

Same case below, 596 Fed. Appx. 563.

No. 15-5536. Luis Santillan, Petitioner v. United States.

577 U.S. 905, 136 S. Ct. 258, 193 L. Ed. 2d 191, 2015 U.S. LEXIS 4776.

October 5, 2015. Petition for writ of certiorari to the United States Court of Appeals for the Ninth Circuit denied.

Same case below, 601 Fed. Appx. 548.

No. 15-5537. Mark C. Anderson, Petitioner v. United States.

577 U.S. 905, 136 S. Ct. 258, 193 L. Ed. 2d 191, 2015 U.S. LEXIS 4784.

October 5, 2015. Petition for writ of certiorari to the United States Court of Appeals for the Ninth Circuit denied.

Same case below, 617 Fed. Appx. 742.

No. 15-5538. Andres Ruiz-Huertas, Petitioner v. United States.

577 U.S. 905, 136 S. Ct. 258, 193 L. Ed. 2d 191, 2015 U.S. LEXIS 4777.

October 5, 2015. Petition for writ of certiorari to the United States Court of Appeals for the First Circuit denied.

Same case below, 792 F.3d 223.

No. 15-5540. Antonio Bealer, Petitioner v. Tarry Williams, et al.

577 U.S. 905, 136 S. Ct. 259, 193 L. Ed. 2d 191, 2015 U.S. LEXIS 4843.

October 5, 2015. Petition for writ of certiorari to the United States Court of Appeals for the Seventh Circuit denied.

No. 15-5543. Michael Blakes, Petitioner v. Linda Foutch, et al.

577 U.S. 905, 136 S. Ct. 259, 193 L. Ed. 2d 191, 2015 U.S. LEXIS 4956.

October 5, 2015. Petition for writ of certiorari to the United States Court of Appeals for the Seventh Circuit denied.

Same case below, 600 Fed. Appx. 1004.

No. 15-5544. Keith Dewayne Smith, Petitioner v. United States.

577 U.S. 905, 136 S. Ct. 259, 193 L. Ed. 2d 191, 2015 U.S. LEXIS 5866.

October 5, 2015. Petition for writ of certiorari to the United States Court of Appeals for the Sixth Circuit denied.

No. 15-5545. Carl Smith, Petitioner v. Pennsylvania.

577 U.S. 905, 136 S. Ct. 259, 193 L. Ed. 2d 191, 2015 U.S. LEXIS 6069.

October 5, 2015. Petition for writ of certiorari to the Superior Court of Pennsylvania, Philadelphia Office, denied.

Same case below, 107 A.3d 227.

No. 15-5547. Coy Cotham, Jr., Petitioner v. Tennessee.

577 U.S. 905, 136 S. Ct. 259, 193 L. Ed. 2d 191, 2015 U.S. LEXIS 6226.

October 5, 2015. Petition for writ of certiorari to the Court of Criminal Appeals of Tennessee, Middle Division, denied.

No. 15-5548. Mark David Chanley, Petitioner v. United States.

577 U.S. 905, 136 S. Ct. 259, 193 L. Ed. 2d 192, 2015 U.S. LEXIS 5884.

October 5, 2015. Petition for writ of certiorari to the United States Court of Appeals for the Ninth Circuit denied.

No. 15-5549. Kent Douglas Easton, Petitioner v. United States.

577 U.S. 905, 136 S. Ct. 260, 193 L. Ed. 2d 192, 2015 U.S. LEXIS 5749.

October 5, 2015. Petition for writ of certiorari to the United States Court of Appeals for the Fourth Circuit denied.

Same case below, 601 Fed. Appx. 236.

No. 15-5551. Carlos Aponte-Sobrado, Petitioner v. United States.

577 U.S. 905, 136 S. Ct. 260, 193 L. Ed. 2d 192, 2015 U.S. LEXIS 5874.

October 5, 2015. Petition for writ of certiorari to the United States Court of Appeals for the First Circuit denied.

Same case below, 763 F.3d 89.

No. 15-5554. Jeffrey R. LeBlanc, Petitioner v. Kalamazoo County, Michigan.

577 U.S. 905, 136 S. Ct. 260, 193 L. Ed. 2d 192, 2015 U.S. LEXIS 5977, reh den 577 U.S. 1096, 136 S. Ct. 885, 193 L. Ed. 2d 777, 2016 U.S. LEXIS 352.

October 5, 2015. Petition for writ of certiorari to the United States Court of Appeals for the Sixth Circuit denied.

No. 15-5557. Robert Edwards, Jr., Petitioner v. United States.

577 U.S. 905, 136 S. Ct. 260, 193 L. Ed. 2d 192, 2015 U.S. LEXIS 6132.

October 5, 2015. Petition for writ of certiorari to the United States Court of Appeals for the Eleventh Circuit denied.

Same case below, 601 Fed. Appx. 928.

No. 15-5559. Frenchitt Su-Dell Collins, Petitioner v. United States.

577 U.S. 906, 136 S. Ct. 260, 193 L. Ed. 2d 192, 2015 U.S. LEXIS 6136.

October 5, 2015. Petition for writ of certiorari to the United States Court of Appeals for the Fifth Circuit denied.

Same case below, 774 F.3d 256.

No. 15-5561. Charles Adkins, Petitioner v. United States.

577 U.S. 906, 136 S. Ct. 261, 193 L. Ed. 2d 192, 2015 U.S. LEXIS 5858.

October 5, 2015. Petition for writ of certiorari to the United States Court of Appeals for the Fourth Circuit denied.

No. 15-5563. Eve Olivarez, Petitioner v. United States.

577 U.S. 906, 136 S. Ct. 261, 193 L. Ed. 2d 192, 2015 U.S. LEXIS 5719.

October 5, 2015. Petition for writ of certiorari to the United States Court of Appeals for the Sixth Circuit denied.

Same case below, 617 Fed. Appx. 391.

Same case below, 158 So. 3d 603.

No. 15-5564. Olufemi Adigun, Petitioner v. United States.

577 U.S. 906, 136 S. Ct. 261, 193 L. Ed. 2d 193, 2015 U.S. LEXIS 5994.

October 5, 2015. Petition for writ of certiorari to the United States Court of Appeals for the Third Circuit denied.

Same case below, 609 Fed. Appx. 718.

No. 15-5565. Jerome Allen Bargo, Petitioner v. Wendy Kelley, Director, Arkansas Department of Correction, et al.

577 U.S. 906, 136 S. Ct. 261, 193 L. Ed. 2d 193, 2015 U.S. LEXIS 5776.

October 5, 2015. Petition for writ of certiorari to the United States Court of Appeals for the Eighth Circuit denied.

Same case below, 592 Fed. Appx. 538.

No. 15-5566. Courtenay Robertson Price, aka Courtenay Robertson, Petitioner v. Shawn Phillips, Warden.

577 U.S. 906, 136 S. Ct. 261, 193 L. Ed. 2d 193, 2015 U.S. LEXIS 5855.

October 5, 2015. Petition for writ of certiorari to the United States Court of Appeals for the Sixth Circuit denied.

No. 15-5569. Ronald Hill, Petitioner v. Florida.

577 U.S. 906, 136 S. Ct. 262, 193 L. Ed. 2d 193, 2015 U.S. LEXIS 5877.

October 5, 2015. Petition for writ of certiorari to the District Court of Appeal of Florida, Fifth District, denied.

No. 15-5574. Bradley Cook, Petitioner v. United States.

577 U.S. 906, 136 S. Ct. 262, 193 L. Ed. 2d 193, 2015 U.S. LEXIS 6150.

October 5, 2015. Petition for writ of certiorari to the United States Court of Appeals for the Eighth Circuit denied.

Same case below, 782 F.3d 983.

No. 15-5575. Merrell Hobbs, Petitioner v. United States.

577 U.S. 906, 136 S. Ct. 262, 193 L. Ed. 2d 193, 2015 U.S. LEXIS 6031.

October 5, 2015. Petition for writ of certiorari to the United States Court of Appeals for the Third Circuit denied.

Same case below, 612 Fed. Appx. 94.

No. 15-5576. Joseph Duquette, Petitioner v. United States.

577 U.S. 906, 136 S. Ct. 262, 193 L. Ed. 2d 193, 2015 U.S. LEXIS 6229.

October 5, 2015. Petition for writ of certiorari to the United States Court of Appeals for the First Circuit denied.

Same case below, 778 F.3d 314.

No. 15-5577. David Guerra, Petitioner v. United States.

577 U.S. 906, 136 S. Ct. 262, 193 L. Ed. 2d 193, 2015 U.S. LEXIS 5947.

October 5, 2015. Petition for writ of certiorari to the United States Court of Appeals for the Fifth Circuit denied.

Same case below, 605 Fed. Appx. 295.

No. 15-5578. Christopher Hitchcock, Petitioner v. United States.

577 U.S. 906, 136 S. Ct. 262, 193 L. Ed. 2d 194, 2015 U.S. LEXIS 6147.

October 5, 2015. Petition for writ of certiorari to the United States Court of Appeals for the First Circuit denied.

No. 15-5580. Harry W. Maisonet, Petitioner v. United States.

577 U.S. 906, 136 S. Ct. 263, 193 L. Ed. 2d 194, 2015 U.S. LEXIS 5905.

October 5, 2015. Petition for writ of certiorari to the United States Court of Appeals for the First Circuit denied.

Same case below, 785 F.3d 757.

No. 15-5581. Marvin Ray Wilburn, Petitioner v. United States.

577 U.S. 906, 136 S. Ct. 263, 193 L. Ed. 2d 194, 2015 U.S. LEXIS 6212.

October 5, 2015. Petition for writ of certiorari to the United States Court of Appeals for the Fourth Circuit denied.

Same case below, 596 Fed. Appx. 241.

No. 15-5582. Sherman George Wimberly, Petitioner v. United States.

577 U.S. 906, 136 S. Ct. 263, 193 L. Ed. 2d 194, 2015 U.S. LEXIS 6230.

October 5, 2015. Petition for writ of certiorari to the United States Court of Appeals for the Sixth Circuit denied.

No. 15-5583. Desiree M. Brown, Petitioner v. Office of Personnel Management.

577 U.S. 907, 136 S. Ct. 301, 193 L. Ed. 2d 194, 2015 U.S. LEXIS 6034.

October 5, 2015. Petition for writ of certiorari to the United States Court of Appeals for the Federal Circuit denied.

Same case below, 608 Fed. Appx. 934.

No. 15-5584. Trevor Alston, Petitioner v. United States.

577 U.S. 907, 136 S. Ct. 263, 193 L. Ed. 2d 194, 2015 U.S. LEXIS 6209.

October 5, 2015. Petition for writ of certiorari to the United States Court of Appeals for the Third Circuit denied.

No. 15-5585. Cody William Marble, Petitioner v. Timothy C. Fox, Attorney General of Montana, et al.

577 U.S. 907, 136 S. Ct. 263, 193 L. Ed. 2d 194, 2015 U.S. LEXIS 5870.

October 5, 2015. Petition for writ of certiorari to the United States Court of Appeals for the Ninth Circuit denied.

Same case below, 601 Fed. Appx. 591.

No. 15-5586. Anthony Jackson, Petitioner v. South Carolina.

577 U.S. 907, 136 S. Ct. 264, 193 L. Ed. 2d 194, 2015 U.S. LEXIS 5744.

October 5, 2015. Petition for writ of certiorari to the Court of Appeals of South Carolina denied.

No. 15-5592. David Lewis Anderson, Petitioner v. United States.

577 U.S. 907, 136 S. Ct. 264, 193 L. Ed. 2d 195, 2015 U.S. LEXIS 5916.

October 5, 2015. Petition for writ of certiorari to the United States Court of Appeals for the Sixth Circuit denied.

Same case below, 608 Fed. Appx. 369.

No. 15-5593. Earl Eugene Box, Petitioner v. Mark V. Capozza, Superintendent, State Correctional Institution at Pittsburgh, et al.

577 U.S. 907, 136 S. Ct. 264, 193 L. Ed. 2d 195, 2015 U.S. LEXIS 5781.

October 5, 2015. Petition for writ of certiorari to the United States Court of Appeals for the Third Circuit denied.

No. 15-5598. Monique Smith, Petitioner v. United States.

577 U.S. 907, 136 S. Ct. 264, 193 L. Ed. 2d 195, 2015 U.S. LEXIS 5722.

October 5, 2015. Petition for writ of certiorari to the United States Court of Appeals for the Sixth Circuit denied.

No. 15-5606. Thomas C. McGee, Petitioner v. Jeff Norman, Warden.

577 U.S. 907, 136 S. Ct. 264, 193 L. Ed. 2d 195, 2015 U.S. LEXIS 5734.

October 5, 2015. Petition for writ of certiorari to the United States Court of Appeals for the Eighth Circuit denied.

No. 15-5607. Ramel Moten, Petitioner v. United States.

577 U.S. 907, 136 S. Ct. 265, 193 L. Ed. 2d 195, 2015 U.S. LEXIS 6100.

October 5, 2015. Petition for writ of certiorari to the United States Court of Appeals for the Third Circuit denied.

Same case below, 617 Fed. Appx. 186.

No. 15-5608. Rodney Lee Riggins, Petitioner v. Amy Miller, Warden, et al.

577 U.S. 907, 136 S. Ct. 265, 193 L. Ed. 2d 195, 2015 U.S. LEXIS 6019.

October 5, 2015. Petition for writ of certiorari to the United States Court of Appeals for the Ninth Circuit denied.

No. 15-5611. Jose Santos Zepeda-Gonzalez, Petitioner v. United States.

577 U.S. 907, 136 S. Ct. 265, 193 L. Ed. 2d 195, 2015 U.S. LEXIS 5876.

October 5, 2015. Petition for writ of certiorari to the United States Court of Appeals for the Ninth Circuit denied.

Same case below, 611 Fed. Appx. 394.

No. 15-5612. Thomas Chambliss, Petitioner v. United States.

577 U.S. 907, 136 S. Ct. 265, 193 L. Ed. 2d 195, 2015 U.S. LEXIS 6144, reh den 577 U.S. 1096, 136 S. Ct. 885, 193 L. Ed. 2d 777, 2016 U.S. LEXIS 309.

October 5, 2015. Petition for writ of certiorari to the United States Court of Appeals for the Second Circuit denied.

Same case below, 582 Fed. Appx. 22.

No. 15-5617. Casey Dooley, Petitioner v. Pennsylvania, et al.

577 U.S. 907, 136 S. Ct. 266, 193 L. Ed. 2d 196, 2015 U.S. LEXIS 5765.

October 5, 2015. Petition for writ of certiorari to the Supreme Court of Pennsylvania, Eastern District, denied.

Same case below, 631 Pa. 679, 115 A.3d 875.

No. 15-5618. Shawn F. Engle, aka Shawn Forrest Engle, Petitioner v. United States.

577 U.S. 907, 136 S. Ct. 266, 193 L. Ed. 2d 196, 2015 U.S. LEXIS 6169.

October 5, 2015. Petition for writ of certiorari to the United States Court of Appeals for the Fourth Circuit denied.

Same case below, 590 Fed. Appx. 234.

No. 15-5619. Joseph Dyson, Petitioner v. Pennsylvania.

577 U.S. 907, 136 S. Ct. 267, 193 L. Ed. 2d 196, 2015 U.S. LEXIS 5811.

October 5, 2015. Petition for writ of certiorari to the Superior Court of Pennsylvania, Philadelphia Office, denied.

Same case below, 113 A.3d 355.

No. 15-5620. Joseph Reyes and Richard Daniels, Petitioners v. United States.

577 U.S. 908, 136 S. Ct. 267, 193 L. Ed. 2d 196, 2015 U.S. LEXIS 6161.

October 5, 2015. Petition for writ of certiorari to the United States Court of Appeals for the Second Circuit denied.

No. 15-5625. Carlos Cancel, Petitioner v. Julie L. Jones, Secretary, Florida Department of Corrections, et al.

577 U.S. 908, 136 S. Ct. 268, 193 L. Ed. 2d 196, 2015 U.S. LEXIS 6211.

October 5, 2015. Petition for writ of certiorari to the United States Court of Appeals for the Eleventh Circuit denied.

No. 15-5626. Jeffrey P. Taylor, Petitioner v. United States.

577 U.S. 908, 136 S. Ct. 268, 193 L. Ed. 2d 196, 2015 U.S. LEXIS 6006.

October 5, 2015. Petition for writ of certiorari to the United States Court of Appeals for the Seventh Circuit denied.

Same case below, 777 F.3d 434.

No. 15-5629. Bani Moreno, Petitioner v. United States.

577 U.S. 908, 136 S. Ct. 268, 193 L. Ed. 2d 196, 2015 U.S. LEXIS 5950.

October 5, 2015. Petition for writ of certiorari to the United States Court of Appeals for the Tenth Circuit denied.

Same case below, 607 Fed. Appx. 775.

No. 15-5631. Sandra Huarte, Petitioner v. United States.

577 U.S. 908, 136 S. Ct. 268, 193 L. Ed. 2d 196, 2015 U.S. LEXIS 6057.

October 5, 2015. Petition for writ of certiorari to the United States Court of Appeals for the Eleventh Circuit denied.

Same case below, 778 F.3d 942.

No. 15-5637. Markus Dwayne Chopane, Petitioner v. United States.

577 U.S. 908, 136 S. Ct. 268, 193 L. Ed. 2d 197, 2015 U.S. LEXIS 6002.

October 5, 2015. Petition for writ of certiorari to the United States Court of Appeals for the Fifth Circuit denied.

Same case below, 603 Fed. Appx. 325.

No. 15-5638. Casey Alan Castles, Petitioner v. United States.

577 U.S. 908, 136 S. Ct. 268, 193 L. Ed. 2d 197, 2015 U.S. LEXIS 6233.

October 5, 2015. Petition for writ of certiorari to the United States Court of Appeals for the Eleventh Circuit denied.

No. 15-5642. James E. Johnston, Petitioner v. United States.

577 U.S. 908, 136 S. Ct. 269, 193 L. Ed. 2d 197, 2015 U.S. LEXIS 5844.

October 5, 2015. Petition for writ of certiorari to the United States Court of Appeals for the Ninth Circuit denied.

Same case below, 789 F.3d 934.

No. 15-5643. Willie V. Jones, Petitioner v. United States.

577 U.S. 908, 136 S. Ct. 269, 193 L. Ed. 2d 197, 2015 U.S. LEXIS 5936.

October 5, 2015. Petition for writ of certiorari to the United States Court of Appeals for the Eighth Circuit denied.

No. 15-5644. Mario Rios-Pintado, Petitioner v. United States.

577 U.S. 908, 136 S. Ct. 269, 193 L. Ed. 2d 197, 2015 U.S. LEXIS 6236.

October 5, 2015. Petition for writ of certiorari to the United States Court of Appeals for the Fifth Circuit denied.

Same case below, 612 Fed. Appx. 741.

No. 15-5646. Harold James Bosier, Petitioner v. Department of the Treasury.

577 U.S. 908, 136 S. Ct. 269, 193 L. Ed. 2d 197, 2015 U.S. LEXIS 5875.

October 5, 2015. Petition for writ of certiorari to the United States Court of Appeals for the Fifth Circuit denied.

Same case below, 597 Fed. Appx. 803.

No. 15-5647. Kathea G. Adams, Petitioner v. United States.

577 U.S. 908, 136 S. Ct. 269, 193 L. Ed. 2d 197, 2015 U.S. LEXIS 6082.

October 5, 2015. Petition for writ of certiorari to the United States Court of Appeals for the Eleventh Circuit denied.

No. 15-5651. Perla Yesenia Perez, Petitioner v. United States.

577 U.S. 908, 136 S. Ct. 270, 193 L. Ed. 2d 197, 2015 U.S. LEXIS 5863.

October 5, 2015. Petition for writ of certiorari to the United States Court of Appeals for the Ninth Circuit denied.

Same case below, 603 Fed. Appx. 620.

Same case below, 600 Fed. Appx. 141.

No. 15-5652. Harry Rhyne McCall, Petitioner v. United States.

577 U.S. 908, 136 S. Ct. 270, 193 L. Ed. 2d 198, 2015 U.S. LEXIS 5988.

October 5, 2015. Petition for writ of certiorari to the United States Court of Appeals for the Fourth Circuit denied.

Same case below, 595 Fed. Appx. 236.

No. 15-5653. Joshua Meregildo, Petitioner v. United States.

577 U.S. 908, 136 S. Ct. 270, 193 L. Ed. 2d 198, 2015 U.S. LEXIS 6048.

October 5, 2015. Petition for writ of certiorari to the United States Court of Appeals for the Second Circuit denied.

Same case below, 785 F.3d 832.

No. 15-5656. Efrain J. Rosa, Petitioner v. United States.

577 U.S. 909, 136 S. Ct. 270, 193 L. Ed. 2d 198, 2015 U.S. LEXIS 5721.

October 5, 2015. Petition for writ of certiorari to the United States Court of Appeals for the Second Circuit denied.

Same case below, 785 F.3d 856.

No. 15-5659. Norman Alan Kerr, Petitioner v. United States.

577 U.S. 909, 136 S. Ct. 271, 193 L. Ed. 2d 198, 2015 U.S. LEXIS 5965, reh den 577 U.S. 1024, 136 S. Ct. 580, 193 L. Ed. 2d 463, 2015 U.S. LEXIS 7465.

October 5, 2015. Petition for writ of certiorari to the United States Court of Appeals for the Fourth Circuit denied.

No. 15-5660. Julian Okeayainneh, Petitioner v. United States.

577 U.S. 909, 136 S. Ct. 271, 193 L. Ed. 2d 198, 2015 U.S. LEXIS 5730.

October 5, 2015. Petition for writ of certiorari to the United States Court of Appeals for the Ninth Circuit denied.

No. 15-5664. Donald Nash, Petitioner v. Ronda J. Pash, Warden, et al.

577 U.S. 909, 136 S. Ct. 271, 193 L. Ed. 2d 198, 2015 U.S. LEXIS 5891.

October 5, 2015. Petition for writ of certiorari to the United States Court of Appeals for the Eighth Circuit denied.

No. 15-5669. Anthony Boykin, Petitioner v. United States.

577 U.S. 909, 136 S. Ct. 272, 193 L. Ed. 2d 198, 2015 U.S. LEXIS 5849.

October 5, 2015. Petition for writ of certiorari to the United States Court of Appeals for the Ninth Circuit denied.

Same case below, 785 F.3d 1352.

No. 15-5671. Christopher Thomas Mejia, Petitioner v. United States.

577 U.S. 909, 136 S. Ct. 272, 193 L. Ed. 2d 198, 2015 U.S. LEXIS 6216.

October 5, 2015. Petition for writ of certiorari to the United States Court of Appeals for the Ninth Circuit denied.

Same case below, 611 Fed. Appx. 407.

No. 15-5677. Paul L. Williams, Petitioner v. United States.

577 U.S. 909, 136 S. Ct. 272, 193 L. Ed. 2d 199, 2015 U.S. LEXIS 6159.

October 5, 2015. Petition for writ of certiorari to the United States Court of Appeals for the Ninth Circuit denied.

Same case below, 597 Fed. Appx. 916.

No. 15-5678. Ronald A. Dobek, Petitioner v. United States.

577 U.S. 909, 136 S. Ct. 272, 193 L. Ed. 2d 199, 2015 U.S. LEXIS 6101.

October 5, 2015. Petition for writ of certiorari to the United States Court of Appeals for the Seventh Circuit denied.

Same case below, 789 F.3d 698.

No. 15-5679. Hainze Elias Diaz-Arroyo, Petitioner v. United States.

577 U.S. 909, 136 S. Ct. 272, 193 L. Ed. 2d 199, 2015 U.S. LEXIS 6117.

October 5, 2015. Petition for writ of certiorari to the United States Court of Appeals for the First Circuit denied.

Same case below, 797 F.3d 125.

No. 15-5683. Gerald Armstrong, Petitioner v. Julie L. Jones, Secretary, Florida Department of Corrections.

577 U.S. 909, 136 S. Ct. 273, 193 L. Ed. 2d 199, 2015 U.S. LEXIS 6231.

October 5, 2015. Petition for writ of certiorari to the United States Court of Appeals for the Eleventh Circuit denied.

No. 15-5685. Arteria Bibbs, Petitioner v. Karen Edenfield, Warden.

577 U.S. 909, 136 S. Ct. 273, 193 L. Ed. 2d 199, 2015 U.S. LEXIS 6187.

October 5, 2015. Petition for writ of certiorari to the United States Court of Appeals for the Sixth Circuit denied.

No. 15-5687. Richard Alexander Heyn, Petitioner v. United States.

577 U.S. 909, 136 S. Ct. 273, 193 L. Ed. 2d 199, 2015 U.S. LEXIS 6050.

October 5, 2015. Petition for writ of certiorari to the United States Court of Appeals for the Eleventh Circuit denied.

Same case below, 605 Fed. Appx. 801.

No. 15-5688. Vernon James Hill, Petitioner v. United States.

577 U.S. 909, 136 S. Ct. 273, 193 L. Ed. 2d 199, 2015 U.S. LEXIS 5957.

October 5, 2015. Petition for writ of certiorari to the United States Court of Appeals for the Tenth Circuit denied.

Same case below, 604 Fed. Appx. 759.

No. 15-5690. Luel Hayes, Jr., Petitioner v. United States.

577 U.S. 909, 136 S. Ct. 273, 193 L. Ed. 2d 199, 2015 U.S. LEXIS 5763.

October 5, 2015. Petition for writ of certiorari to the District of Columbia Court of Appeals denied.

Same case below, 111 A.3d 647.

No. 15-5691. Andre Saint Cyr, Petitioner v. United States.

577 U.S. 909, 136 S. Ct. 274, 193 L. Ed. 2d 200, 2015 U.S. LEXIS 6135.

October 5, 2015. Petition for writ of certiorari to the United States Court of Appeals for the Eleventh Circuit denied.

Same case below, 618 Fed. Appx. 569.

No. 15-5692. Junior H. De La Cruz-Feliciano, Petitioner v. United States.

577 U.S. 909, 136 S. Ct. 274, 193 L. Ed. 2d 200, 2015 U.S. LEXIS 6158.

October 5, 2015. Petition for writ of certiorari to the United States Court of Appeals for the First Circuit denied.

Same case below, 786 F.3d 78.

No. 15-5693. Alaa M. Al Jaber, Petitioner v. United States.

577 U.S. 910, 136 S. Ct. 274, 193 L. Ed. 2d 200, 2015 U.S. LEXIS 5887.

October 5, 2015. Petition for writ of certiorari to the United States Court of Appeals for the Second Circuit denied.

No. 15-5694. Shedrick D. Hollis, Petitioner v. United States.

577 U.S. 910, 136 S. Ct. 274, 193 L. Ed. 2d 200, 2015 U.S. LEXIS 5732.

October 5, 2015. Petition for writ of certiorari to the United States Court of Appeals for the Eleventh Circuit denied.

Same case below, 780 F.3d 1064.

No. 15-5701. Ronnie Gerald Belt, Petitioner v. United States.

577 U.S. 910, 136 S. Ct. 274, 193 L. Ed. 2d 200, 2015 U.S. LEXIS 5810.

October 5, 2015. Petition for writ of certiorari to the United States Court of Appeals for the Fourth Circuit denied.

Same case below, 609 Fed. Appx. 745.

No. 15-5702. Andrew Brown, Petitioner v. United States.

577 U.S. 910, 136 S. Ct. 275, 193 L. Ed. 2d 200, 2015 U.S. LEXIS 5945.

October 5, 2015. Petition for writ of certiorari to the United States Court of Appeals for the Fifth Circuit denied.

No. 15-5704. Hector Bruno, Jr., Petitioner v. United States.

577 U.S. 910, 136 S. Ct. 275, 193 L. Ed. 2d 200, 2015 U.S. LEXIS 6062.

October 5, 2015. Petition for writ of certiorari to the United States Court of Appeals for the Eleventh Circuit denied.

Same case below, 604 Fed. Appx. 912.

Same case below, 602 Fed. Appx. 402.

No. 15-5705. Richard Pacell, Petitioner v. Lawrence Mahally, Superintendent, State Correctional Institution at Dallas, et al.

577 U.S. 910, 136 S. Ct. 275, 193 L. Ed. 2d 201, 2015 U.S. LEXIS 6004.

October 5, 2015. Petition for writ of certiorari to the United States Court of Appeals for the Third Circuit denied.

No. 15-5716. Jason Best, Petitioner v. J. C. Holland, Warden.

577 U.S. 910, 136 S. Ct. 276, 193 L. Ed. 2d 201, 2015 U.S. LEXIS 6041.

October 5, 2015. Petition for writ of certiorari to the United States Court of Appeals for the Sixth Circuit denied.

No. 15-5710. Julio Moronta, Petitioner v. Patrick Griffin, Superintendent, Sullivan Correctional Facility.

577 U.S. 910, 136 S. Ct. 275, 193 L. Ed. 2d 201, 2015 U.S. LEXIS 5830.

October 5, 2015. Petition for writ of certiorari to the United States Court of Appeals for the Second Circuit denied.

Same case below, 610 Fed. Appx. 78.

No. 15-5717. J. Lee Barnard, Petitioner v. Tim Perez, Warden.

577 U.S. 910, 136 S. Ct. 276, 193 L. Ed. 2d 201, 2015 U.S. LEXIS 6223.

October 5, 2015. Petition for writ of certiorari to the United States Court of Appeals for the Ninth Circuit denied.

No. 15-5713. Brandon Danielle Collier, Petitioner v. United States.

577 U.S. 910, 136 S. Ct. 275, 193 L. Ed. 2d 201, 2015 U.S. LEXIS 5995.

October 5, 2015. Petition for writ of certiorari to the United States Court of Appeals for the Fifth Circuit denied.

Same case below, 603 Fed. Appx. 339.

No. 15-5723. Vladimyr Jean Baptiste, Petitioner v. United States.

577 U.S. 910, 136 S. Ct. 276, 193 L. Ed. 2d 201, 2015 U.S. LEXIS 6045.

October 5, 2015. Petition for writ of certiorari to the United States Court of Appeals for the Eleventh Circuit denied.

Same case below, 607 Fed. Appx. 950.

No. 15-5714. Adalberto Rivera, Petitioner v. United States.

577 U.S. 910, 136 S. Ct. 275, 193 L. Ed. 2d 201, 2015 U.S. LEXIS 6251.

October 5, 2015. Petition for writ of certiorari to the United States Court of Appeals for the Ninth Circuit denied.

No. 15-5724. Glen Baughman, Petitioner v. United States.

577 U.S. 910, 136 S. Ct. 276, 193 L. Ed. 2d 201, 2015 U.S. LEXIS 6126.

October 5, 2015. Petition for writ of certiorari to the United States Court of Appeals for the Eighth Circuit denied.

Same case below, 597 Fed. Appx. 899.

No. 15-5728. Jason Michael Stewart-Hanson, Petitioner v. United States.

577 U.S. 910, 136 S. Ct. 276, 193 L. Ed. 2d 202, 2015 U.S. LEXIS 5704.

October 5, 2015. Petition for writ of certiorari to the United States Court of Appeals for the Ninth Circuit denied.

Same case below, 613 Fed. Appx. 600.

No. 15-5729. Anthony Wynn, Petitioner v. United States.

577 U.S. 910, 136 S. Ct. 276, 193 L. Ed. 2d 202, 2015 U.S. LEXIS 6040.

October 5, 2015. Petition for writ of certiorari to the United States Court of Appeals for the Fourth Circuit denied.

Same case below, 786 F.3d 339.

No. 15-5734. Andres Fermin, Petitioner v. United States.

577 U.S. 911, 136 S. Ct. 277, 193 L. Ed. 2d 202, 2015 U.S. LEXIS 6129.

October 5, 2015. Petition for writ of certiorari to the United States Court of Appeals for the Third Circuit denied.

No. 15-5736. Mike Garcia, Petitioner v. United States.

577 U.S. 911, 136 S. Ct. 277, 193 L. Ed. 2d 202, 2015 U.S. LEXIS 6127.

October 5, 2015. Petition for writ of certiorari to the United States Court of Appeals for the Fifth Circuit denied.

No. 15-5737. William George Fagan, III, Petitioner v. United States.

577 U.S. 911, 136 S. Ct. 277, 193 L. Ed. 2d 202, 2015 U.S. LEXIS 5780.

October 5, 2015. Petition for writ of certiorari to the United States Court of Appeals for the Eleventh Circuit denied.

No. 15-5741. Carlos Jaimez Reyes, Petitioner v. G. Ellis, et al.

577 U.S. 911, 136 S. Ct. 278, 193 L. Ed. 2d 202, 2015 U.S. LEXIS 6055.

October 5, 2015. Petition for writ of certiorari to the United States Court of Appeals for the Ninth Circuit denied.

Same case below, 605 Fed. Appx. 682.

No. 15-5745. Ronald Demetrious Thomas, Petitioner v. United States.

577 U.S. 911, 136 S. Ct. 278, 193 L. Ed. 2d 202, 2015 U.S. LEXIS 6071.

October 5, 2015. Petition for writ of certiorari to the United States Court of Appeals for the Fourth Circuit denied.

Same case below, 598 Fed. Appx. 214.

No. 15-5746. Stylios Alton Trachanas, Petitioner v. United States.

577 U.S. 911, 136 S. Ct. 278, 193 L. Ed. 2d 202, 2015 U.S. LEXIS 6172.

October 5, 2015. Petition for writ of certiorari to the United States Court of Appeals for the Tenth Circuit denied.

Same case below, 605 Fed. Appx. 751.

No. 15-5751. Troy V. Cleveland, Petitioner v. Timothy S. Stewart, Warden.

577 U.S. 911, 136 S. Ct. 278, 193 L. Ed. 2d 203, 2015 U.S. LEXIS 6037.

October 5, 2015. Petition for writ of certiorari to the United States Court of Appeals for the Fourth Circuit denied.

Same case below, 602 Fed. Appx. 931.

No. 15-5752. Bruce Wayne Ervin, Petitioner v. United States.

577 U.S. 911, 136 S. Ct. 278, 193 L. Ed. 2d 203, 2015 U.S. LEXIS 6162.

October 5, 2015. Petition for writ of certiorari to the United States Court of Appeals for the Fifth Circuit denied.

No. 15-5755. Quinton D. Manning, Petitioner v. United States.

577 U.S. 911, 136 S. Ct. 278, 193 L. Ed. 2d 203, 2015 U.S. LEXIS 5773.

October 5, 2015. Petition for writ of certiorari to the United States Court of Appeals for the Eighth Circuit denied.

Same case below, 786 F.3d 684.

No. 15-5759. Ramon M. Molina, aka Ray Molina, Petitioner v. Charles L. Lockett, Warden.

577 U.S. 911, 136 S. Ct. 279, 193 L. Ed. 2d 203, 2015 U.S. LEXIS 6254.

October 5, 2015. Petition for writ of certiorari to the United States Court of Appeals for the Eleventh Circuit denied.

No. 15-5761. Rickey Thompson, Petitioner v. United States.

577 U.S. 911, 136 S. Ct. 279, 193 L. Ed. 2d 203, 2015 U.S. LEXIS 5750.

October 5, 2015. Petition for writ of certiorari to the United States Court of Appeals for the Eleventh Circuit denied.

Same case below, 608 Fed. Appx. 726.

No. 15-5764. Andrew Maxwell Parker, Petitioner v. United States.

577 U.S. 911, 136 S. Ct. 279, 193 L. Ed. 2d 203, 2015 U.S. LEXIS 6130.

October 5, 2015. Petition for writ of certiorari to the United States Court of Appeals for the Fifth Circuit denied.

No. 15-5765. Marlin Eugene Mette, Petitioner v. United States.

577 U.S. 911, 136 S. Ct. 279, 193 L. Ed. 2d 203, 2015 U.S. LEXIS 6155.

October 5, 2015. Petition for writ of certiorari to the United States Court of Appeals for the Eleventh Circuit denied.

Same case below, 608 Fed. Appx. 890.

No. 15-5766. Carlos Hernandez, Petitioner v. United States.

577 U.S. 911, 136 S. Ct. 279, 193 L. Ed. 2d 203, 2015 U.S. LEXIS 5774.

October 5, 2015. Petition for writ of certiorari to the United States Court of Appeals for the Fifth Circuit denied.

Same case below, 781 F.3d 374.

No. 15-5768. Samuel Dixon, Petitioner v. United States.

577 U.S. 911, 136 S. Ct. 280, 193 L. Ed. 2d 204, 2015 U.S. LEXIS 6022.

October 5, 2015. Petition for writ of certiorari to the United States Court of Appeals for the First Circuit denied.

Same case below, 787 F.3d 55.

No. 15-5769. Antonio Esquivel-Rios, Petitioner v. United States.

577 U.S. 911, 136 S. Ct. 280, 193 L. Ed. 2d 204, 2015 U.S. LEXIS 6012.

October 5, 2015. Petition for writ of certiorari to the United States Court of Appeals for the Tenth Circuit denied.

Same case below, 786 F.3d 1299.

No. 15-5771. Archie Cabello, aka Archibaldo Cabello, aka Archie Cabello, Jr., aka Archie P. Cabello, aka Arquimedes Cabello, aka Archie Palumbo, Petitioner v. United States.

577 U.S. 912, 136 S. Ct. 280, 193 L. Ed. 2d 204, 2015 U.S. LEXIS 6073.

October 5, 2015. Petition for writ of certiorari to the United States Court of Appeals for the Ninth Circuit denied.

Same case below, 599 Fed. Appx. 761.

No. 15-5773. Corey E. Turner, Sr., Petitioner v. United States.

577 U.S. 912, 136 S. Ct. 280, 193 L. Ed. 2d 204, 2015 U.S. LEXIS 6032, reh den 577 U.S. 998, 136 S. Ct. 529, 193 L. Ed. 2d 417, 2015 U.S. LEXIS 7313.

October 5, 2015. Petition for writ of certiorari to the United States Court of Appeals for the Eighth Circuit denied.

No. 15-5777. Ike David Simmons, Petitioner v. United States.

577 U.S. 912, 136 S. Ct. 280, 193 L. Ed. 2d 204, 2015 U.S. LEXIS 5835.

October 5, 2015. Petition for writ of certiorari to the United States Court of Appeals for the Fourth Circuit denied.

Same case below, 604 Fed. Appx. 280.

No. 15-5779. Ricardo Garcia-Chihuahua, Petitioner v. United States.

577 U.S. 912, 136 S. Ct. 280, 193 L. Ed. 2d 204, 2015 U.S. LEXIS 6061.

October 5, 2015. Petition for writ of certiorari to the United States Court of Appeals for the Tenth Circuit denied.

Same case below, 613 Fed. Appx. 686.

No. 15-5781. Roger Bruce, Petitioner v. South Carolina.

577 U.S. 912, 136 S. Ct. 281, 193 L. Ed. 2d 204, 2015 U.S. LEXIS 5920.

October 5, 2015. Petition for writ of certiorari to the Supreme Court of South Carolina denied.

Same case below, 412 S.C. 504, 772 S.E.2d 753.

No. 15-5782. Moises Hernandez-Osorio, Petitioner v. United States.

577 U.S. 912, 136 S. Ct. 281, 193 L. Ed. 2d 204, 2015 U.S. LEXIS 6160.

October 5, 2015. Petition for writ of certiorari to the United States Court of Appeals for the Fourth Circuit denied.

Same case below, 604 Fed. Appx. 278.

No. 15-5783. Robert Harris, Petitioner v. United States.

577 U.S. 912, 136 S. Ct. 281, 193 L. Ed. 2d 205, 2015 U.S. LEXIS 6181.

October 5, 2015. Petition for writ of certiorari to the United States Court of Appeals for the Eleventh Circuit denied.

Same case below, 603 Fed. Appx. 858.

No. 15-5785. Arthur James Chappell, Petitioner v. United States.

577 U.S. 912, 136 S. Ct. 281, 193 L. Ed. 2d 205, 2015 U.S. LEXIS 6115.

October 5, 2015. Petition for writ of certiorari to the United States Court of Appeals for the Eighth Circuit denied.

Same case below, 779 F.3d 872.

No. 15-5788. Craig Jackson, Petitioner v. United States.

577 U.S. 912, 136 S. Ct. 281, 193 L. Ed. 2d 205, 2015 U.S. LEXIS 5820.

October 5, 2015. Petition for writ of certiorari to the United States Court of Appeals for the Eleventh Circuit denied.

No. 15-5789. Matthew Kolodesh, Petitioner v. United States.

577 U.S. 912, 136 S. Ct. 281, 193 L. Ed. 2d 205, 2015 U.S. LEXIS 6033.

October 5, 2015. Petition for writ of certiorari to the United States Court of Appeals for the Third Circuit denied.

Same case below, 787 F.3d 224.

No. 15-5791. Galvin Gibson, Petitioner v. United States.

No. 15-5792. Vagan Adzhemyan, Petitioner v. United States.

577 U.S. 912, 136 S. Ct. 282, 193 L. Ed. 2d 205, 2015 U.S. LEXIS 5777.

October 5, 2015. Petitions for writs of certiorari to the United States Court of Appeals for the Ninth Circuit denied.

Same cases below, 598 Fed. Appx. 487.

No. 15-5794. Jamel Chawlone Brown, Petitioner v. United States.

577 U.S. 912, 136 S. Ct. 282, 193 L. Ed. 2d 205, 2015 U.S. LEXIS 5804.

October 5, 2015. Petition for writ of certiorari to the United States Court of Appeals for the Fourth Circuit denied.

Same case below, 614 Fed. Appx. 632.

No. 15-5800. Michael E. Pettit, Petitioner v. United States.

577 U.S. 912, 136 S. Ct. 282, 193 L. Ed. 2d 205, 2015 U.S. LEXIS 6149.

October 5, 2015. Petition for writ of certiorari to the United States Court of Appeals for the Tenth Circuit denied.

Same case below, 785 F.3d 1374.

No. 15-5802. Jose Delores Vanegas, Petitioner v. United States.

577 U.S. 912, 136 S. Ct. 282, 193 L. Ed. 2d 206, 2015 U.S. LEXIS 6076.

October 5, 2015. Petition for writ of certiorari to the United States Court of Appeals for the Fourth Circuit denied.

Same case below, 612 Fed. Appx. 664.

No. 15-5806. Clifford Darden, Petitioner v. Jorge L. Pastrana, Warden.

577 U.S. 913, 136 S. Ct. 282, 193 L. Ed. 2d 206, 2015 U.S. LEXIS 6228.

October 5, 2015. Petition for writ of certiorari to the United States Court of Appeals for the Eleventh Circuit denied.

No. 15-5809. David J. Cullen, Petitioner v. United States.

577 U.S. 913, 136 S. Ct. 283, 193 L. Ed. 2d 206, 2015 U.S. LEXIS 6242.

October 5, 2015. Petition for writ of certiorari to the United States Court of Appeals for the Fourth Circuit denied.

Same case below, 600 Fed. Appx. 172.

No. 15-5812. Miguel Osuna-Alvarez, Petitioner v. United States.

577 U.S. 913, 136 S. Ct. 283, 193 L. Ed. 2d 206, 2015 U.S. LEXIS 6087.

October 5, 2015. Petition for writ of certiorari to the United States Court of Appeals for the Ninth Circuit denied.

Same case below, 788 F.3d 1183.

No. 15-5814. Damien Gouse, Petitioner v. United States.

577 U.S. 913, 136 S. Ct. 283, 193 L. Ed. 2d 206, 2015 U.S. LEXIS 6093.

October 5, 2015. Petition for writ of certiorari to the United States Court of Appeals for the First Circuit denied.

Same case below, 798 F.3d 39.

No. 15-5815. Shabasco Dakota Shineed Gray, Petitioner v. United States.

577 U.S. 913, 136 S. Ct. 283, 193 L. Ed. 2d 206, 2015 U.S. LEXIS 6141.

October 5, 2015. Petition for writ of certiorari to the United States Court of Appeals for the Fourth Circuit denied.

Same case below, 611 Fed. Appx. 778.

No. 14-972. ABB Incorporated, et al., Petitioners v. Arizona Board of Regents, et al.

No. 14-1019. Arizona, Petitioner v. Ashton Company Incorporated Contractors and Engineers, et al.

577 U.S. 913, 136 S. Ct. 30, 193 L. Ed. 2d 206, 2015 U.S. LEXIS 5864.

October 5, 2015. Petitions for writs of certiorari to the United States Court of Appeals for the Ninth Circuit denied. Justice Alito took no part in the consideration or decision of these petitions.

Same cases below, 761 F.3d 1005.

No. 14-1358. I/P Engine, Inc., Petitioner v. AOL Inc., et al.

577 U.S. 913, 136 S. Ct. 54, 193 L. Ed. 2d 206, 2015 U.S. LEXIS 5801.

October 5, 2015. Petition for writ of certiorari to the United States Court of

Appeals for the Federal Circuit denied. The Chief Justice took no part in the consideration or decision of this petition.

Same case below, 576 Fed. Appx. 982.

———

No. 14-1362. Interval Licensing LLC, Petitioner v. AOL Inc., et al.

577 U.S. 913, 136 S. Ct. 59, 193 L. Ed. 2d 207, 2015 U.S. LEXIS 5850.

October 5, 2015. Petition for writ of certiorari to the United States Court of Appeals for the Federal Circuit denied. The Chief Justice took no part in the consideration or decision of this petition.

Same case below, 766 F.3d 1364.

———

No. 14-1380. Erica Y. Bryant, et al., Petitioners v. United States.

577 U.S. 913, 136 S. Ct. 71, 193 L. Ed. 2d 207, 2015 U.S. LEXIS 6118.

October 5, 2015. Motion of petitioners to defer consideration of the petition for writ of certiorari denied. Petition for writ of certiorari to the United States Court of Appeals for the Eleventh Circuit denied.

Same case below, 768 F.3d 1378.

———

No. 14-1384. Ohio, Petitioner v. Thomas Caine White.

577 U.S. 913, 136 S. Ct. 73, 193 L. Ed. 2d 207, 2015 U.S. LEXIS 5770.

October 5, 2015. Motion of respondent for leave to proceed in forma pauperis granted. Petition for writ of certiorari to the Supreme Court of Ohio denied.

Same case below, 142 Ohio St. 3d 277, 29 N.E.3d 939.

———

No. 14-1398. Eric Arnold, Acting Warden, Petitioner v. Tio Dinero Sessoms.

577 U.S. 913, 136 S. Ct. 80, 193 L. Ed. 2d 207, 2015 U.S. LEXIS 5825.

October 5, 2015. Motion of respondent for leave to proceed in forma pauperis granted. Petition for writ of certiorari to the United States Court of Appeals for the Ninth Circuit denied.

Same case below, 776 F.3d 615.

———

No. 14-1400. Riva Janes, et al., Petitioners v. Triborough Bridge and Tunnel Authority, et al.

577 U.S. 914, 136 S. Ct. 80, 193 L. Ed. 2d 207, 2015 U.S. LEXIS 5862.

October 5, 2015. Petition for writ of certiorari to the United States Court of Appeals for the Second Circuit denied. Justice Alito took no part in the consideration or decision of this petition.

Same case below, 774 F.3d 1052.

———

No. 14-1419. Sac and Fox Nation of Oklahoma, et al., Petitioners v. Borough of Jim Thorpe, Pennsylvania, et al.

577 U.S. 914, 136 S. Ct. 84, 193 L. Ed. 2d 207, 2015 U.S. LEXIS 6218.

October 5, 2015. Motion of Senator Ben Nighthorse Campbell, et al. for leave to file a brief as amici curiae granted.

Motion of National Congress of American Indians for leave to file a brief as amicus curiae granted. Petition for writ of certiorari to the United States Court of Appeals for the Third Circuit denied.

Same case below, 770 F.3d 255.

No. 14-1423. Chuan Wang, Petitioner v. International Business Machines Corporation, et al.

577 U.S. 914, 136 S. Ct. 301, 193 L. Ed. 2d 208, 2015 U.S. LEXIS 5881.

October 5, 2015. Petition for writ of certiorari to the Appeals Court of Massachusetts denied. Justice Breyer took no part in the consideration or decision of this petition.

Same case below, 86 Mass. App. Ct. 1113, 17 N.E.3d 1118.

No. 14-1438. William B. Jolley, Petitioner v. Department of Justice.

577 U.S. 914, 136 S. Ct. 99, 193 L. Ed. 2d 208, 2015 U.S. LEXIS 6171.

October 5, 2015. Petition for writ of certiorari to the United States Court of Appeals for the Federal Circuit denied. Justice Kagan took no part in the consideration or decision of this petition.

Same case below, 602 Fed. Appx. 805.

No. 14-1473. Content Extraction and Transmission LLC, Petitioner v. Wells Fargo Bank, National Association, et al.

577 U.S. 914, 136 S. Ct. 119, 193 L. Ed. 2d 208, 2015 U.S. LEXIS 6112.

October 5, 2015. Petition for writ of certiorari to the United States Court of

Appeals for the Federal Circuit denied. Justice Alito took no part in the consideration or decision of this petition.

Same case below, 776 F.3d 1343.

No. 14-1498. Daniel Anthony Lucas, Petitioner v. Carl Humphrey, Warden.

577 U.S. 914, 136 S. Ct. 135, 193 L. Ed. 2d 208, 2015 U.S. LEXIS 6116, reh den 577 U.S. 1022, 136 S. Ct. 571, 193 L. Ed. 2d 453, 2015 U.S. LEXIS 7391.

October 5, 2015. Motion of petitioner to defer consideration of the petition for writ of certiorari denied. Petition for writ of certiorari to the United States Court of Appeals for the Eleventh Circuit denied.

Same case below, 771 F.3d 785.

No. 14-7733. Dustin Lee Honken, Petitioner v. United States.

577 U.S. 914, 136 S. Ct. 29, 193 L. Ed. 2d 208, 2015 U.S. LEXIS 5912.

October 5, 2015. Petition for writ of certiorari to the United States Court of Appeals for the Eighth Circuit denied. Justice Kagan took no part in the consideration or decision of this petition.

No. 14-9645. Shawn William Sherman, Petitioner v. Mary Edwards-Fears, et al.

577 U.S. 914, 136 S. Ct. 301, 193 L. Ed. 2d 208, 2015 U.S. LEXIS 6205.

October 5, 2015. Petition for writ of certiorari before judgment to the United States Court of Appeals for the Eighth Circuit denied.

No. 14-9914. Ernest Paul Cassidy, III, Petitioner v. Clark E. Ducart, Warden.

577 U.S. 914, 136 S. Ct. 72, 193 L. Ed. 2d 209, 2015 U.S. LEXIS 6185.

October 5, 2015. Petition for writ of certiorari to the United States Court of Appeals for the Ninth Circuit denied. Justice Breyer took no part in the consideration or decision of this petition.

No. 14-10111. Tyrone Alan Ganoe, Petitioner v. United States.

577 U.S. 914, 136 S. Ct. 99, 193 L. Ed. 2d 209, 2015 U.S. LEXIS 6227.

October 5, 2015. Petition for writ of certiorari to the United States Court of Appeals for the Ninth Circuit denied. Justice Kagan took no part in the consideration or decision of this petition.

Same case below, 588 Fed. Appx. 650.

No. 14-10138. Glen Thomas Dotson, Petitioner v. United States.

577 U.S. 915, 136 S. Ct. 103, 193 L. Ed. 2d 209, 2015 U.S. LEXIS 5757.

October 5, 2015. Petition for writ of certiorari to the United States Court of Appeals for the Eighth Circuit denied. Justice Kagan took no part in the consideration or decision of this petition.

No. 14-10162. Samuel Saldana, Petitioner v. Clark E. Ducart, Warden.

577 U.S. 915, 136 S. Ct. 108, 193 L. Ed. 2d 209, 2015 U.S. LEXIS 6232.

October 5, 2015. Petition for writ of certiorari to the United States Court of Appeals for the Ninth Circuit denied. Justice Breyer took no part in the consideration or decision of this petition.

Same case below, 597 Fed. Appx. 423.

No. 14-10184. Allah Burman, Petitioner v. R. A. Perdue, Warden, et al.

577 U.S. 915, 136 S. Ct. 112, 193 L. Ed. 2d 209, 2015 U.S. LEXIS 5992.

October 5, 2015. Petition for writ of certiorari before judgment to the United States Court of Appeals for the Fourth Circuit denied.

No. 14-10362. Mark Raymond Ford, Petitioner v. United States.

577 U.S. 915, 136 S. Ct. 146, 193 L. Ed. 2d 209, 2015 U.S. LEXIS 6163.

October 5, 2015. Petition for writ of certiorari to the United States Court of Appeals for the Eleventh Circuit denied. Justice Kagan took no part in the consideration or decision of this petition.

No. 14-10437. Kevin Patrick Flood, Petitioner v. United States District Court for the Western District of Pennsylvania.

577 U.S. 915, 136 S. Ct. 302, 193 L. Ed. 2d 209, 2015 U.S. LEXIS 6193.

October 5, 2015. Petition for writ of certiorari to the United States Court of Appeals for the Third Circuit denied. Justice Kagan took no part in the consideration or decision of this petition.

Same case below, 600 Fed. Appx. 867.

No. 15-18. Richard Bistline, Petitioner v. United States.

577 U.S. 915, 136 S. Ct. 169, 193 L. Ed. 2d 210, 2015 U.S. LEXIS 6077.

October 5, 2015. Petition for writ of certiorari to the United States Court of Appeals for the Sixth Circuit denied. Justice Kagan took no part in the consideration or decision of this petition.

Same case below, 605 Fed. Appx. 529.

No. 15-41. W. L. Gore & Associates, Inc., Petitioner v. Bard Peripheral Vascular, Inc., et al.

577 U.S. 915, 136 S. Ct. 189, 193 L. Ed. 2d 210, 2015 U.S. LEXIS 6015.

October 5, 2015. Petition for writ of certiorari to the United States Court of Appeals for the Federal Circuit denied. Justice Alito took no part in the consideration or decision of this petition.

Same case below, 776 F.3d 837.

No. 15-63. Ernest McDonald, Petitioner v. The Boeing Company.

577 U.S. 915, 136 S. Ct. 198, 193 L. Ed. 2d 210, 2015 U.S. LEXIS 6200.

October 5, 2015. Petition for writ of certiorari to the United States Court of Appeals for the Tenth Circuit denied. Justice Alito took no part in the consideration or decision of this petition.

Same case below, 602 Fed. Appx. 452.

No. 15-5032. Philip M. Sebolt, Petitioner v. United States.

577 U.S. 915, 136 S. Ct. 174, 193 L. Ed. 2d 210, 2015 U.S. LEXIS 5919.

October 5, 2015. Petition for writ of certiorari to the United States Court of Appeals for the Seventh Circuit denied. Justice Kagan took no part in the consideration or decision of this petition.

No. 15-5052. Michael Phillip Telemaque, Petitioner v. United States.

577 U.S. 915, 136 S. Ct. 177, 193 L. Ed. 2d 210, 2015 U.S. LEXIS 5772.

October 5, 2015. Petition for writ of certiorari to the United States Court of Appeals for the Fifth Circuit denied. Justice Kagan took no part in the consideration or decision of this petition.

No. 15-5058. Jeffrey Lynn Myers, Petitioner v. United States.

577 U.S. 915, 136 S. Ct. 178, 193 L. Ed. 2d 210, 2015 U.S. LEXIS 5998.

October 5, 2015. Petition for writ of certiorari to the United States Court of Appeals for the Fourth Circuit denied. Justice Kagan took no part in the consideration or decision of this petition.

Same case below, 597 Fed. Appx. 153.

No. 15-5083. Edward Booker, Petitioner v. United States.

577 U.S. 916, 136 S. Ct. 182, 193 L. Ed. 2d 210, 2015 U.S. LEXIS 5922.

October 5, 2015. Petition for writ of certiorari to the United States Court of Appeals for the Eighth Circuit denied. Justice Kagan took no part in the consideration or decision of this petition.

No. 15-5093. Casey Dale Mayer, Petitioner v. United States.

577 U.S. 916, 136 S. Ct. 184, 193 L. Ed. 2d 211, 2015 U.S. LEXIS 5903.

October 5, 2015. Petition for writ of certiorari to the United States Court of Appeals for the Ninth Circuit denied. Justice Kagan took no part in the consideration or decision of this petition.

No. 15-5110. Victor Torres and Jorge Torres, Petitioners v. United States.

577 U.S. 916, 136 S. Ct. 186, 193 L. Ed. 2d 211, 2015 U.S. LEXIS 5915.

October 5, 2015. Petition for writ of certiorari to the United States Court of Appeals for the Second Circuit denied. Justice Sotomayor took no part in the consideration or decision of this petition.

No. 15-5189. John Johnson, aka Duke Hardcore, aka Johnnie Johnson, Petitioner v. United States.

577 U.S. 916, 136 S. Ct. 202, 193 L. Ed. 2d 211, 2015 U.S. LEXIS 6202.

October 5, 2015. Petition for writ of certiorari to the United States Court of Appeals for the Second Circuit denied. Justice Sotomayor took no part in the consideration or decision of this petition.

Same case below, 786 F.3d 241.

No. 15-5239. Leonard C. Johnson, Petitioner v. United States.

577 U.S. 916, 136 S. Ct. 209, 193 L. Ed. 2d 211, 2015 U.S. LEXIS 6054.

October 5, 2015. Petition for writ of certiorari to the United States Court of Appeals for the Second Circuit denied. Justice Sotomayor took no part in the consideration or decision of this petition.

Same case below, 779 F.3d 125.

No. 15-5279. Philip Michael Sebolt, Petitioner v. United States.

577 U.S. 916, 136 S. Ct. 216, 193 L. Ed. 2d 211, 2015 U.S. LEXIS 6009.

October 5, 2015. Petition for writ of certiorari to the United States Court of Appeals for the Fourth Circuit denied. Justice Kagan took no part in the consideration or decision of this petition.

Same case below, 598 Fed. Appx. 159.

No. 15-5350. Julio Acuna, Petitioner v. United States.

577 U.S. 916, 136 S. Ct. 229, 193 L. Ed. 2d 211, 2015 U.S. LEXIS 5748.

October 5, 2015. Petition for writ of certiorari to the United States Court of Appeals for the Eleventh Circuit denied. Justice Kagan took no part in the consideration or decision of this petition.

No. 15-5388. Stephen Caracappa, Petitioner v. United States.

577 U.S. 916, 136 S. Ct. 236, 193 L. Ed. 2d 211, 2015 U.S. LEXIS 5972.

October 5, 2015. Petition for writ of certiorari to the United States Court of Appeals for the Second Circuit denied. Justice Sotomayor took no part in the consideration or decision of this petition.

No. 15-5392. Kenneth Wilk, Petitioner v. Louis W. Winn, Jr., Complex Warden.

577 U.S. 916, 136 S. Ct. 237, 193 L. Ed. 2d 212, 2015 U.S. LEXIS 5851.

October 5, 2015. Petition for writ of certiorari to the United States Court of Appeals for the Ninth Circuit denied. Justice Kagan took no part in the consideration or decision of this petition.

———

No. 15-5514. Emerson Davis, aka John Calvin, aka Stanford Robinson, Petitioner v. United States.

577 U.S. 916, 136 S. Ct. 256, 193 L. Ed. 2d 212, 2015 U.S. LEXIS 6278.

October 5, 2015. Petition for writ of certiorari to the United States Court of Appeals for the Eleventh Circuit denied. Justice Kagan took no part in the consideration or decision of this petition.

Same case below, 604 Fed. Appx. 871.

———

No. 15-5515. Terry Lamell Ezell, Petitioner v. United States.

577 U.S. 916, 136 S. Ct. 256, 193 L. Ed. 2d 212, 2015 U.S. LEXIS 5927.

October 5, 2015. Petition for writ of certiorari to the United States Court of Appeals for the Ninth Circuit denied. Justice Kagan took no part in the consideration or decision of this petition.

Same case below, 778 F.3d 762.

———

No. 15-5532. Kelly Edward Wadford, Jr., Petitioner v. United States.

577 U.S. 917, 136 S. Ct. 257, 193 L. Ed. 2d 212, 2015 U.S. LEXIS 5848.

October 5, 2015. Petition for writ of certiorari to the United States Court of Appeals for the Fourth Circuit denied. Justice Kagan took no part in the consideration or decision of this petition.

Same case below, 594 Fed. Appx. 168.

———

No. 15-5579. Cirilo Flores-Perez, Petitioner v. United States.

577 U.S. 917, 136 S. Ct. 263, 193 L. Ed. 2d 212, 2015 U.S. LEXIS 6219, reh den 577 U.S. 1209, 136 S. Ct. 1404, 194 L. Ed. 2d 384, 2016 U.S. LEXIS 1638.

October 5, 2015. Petition for writ of certiorari to the United States Court of Appeals for the Ninth Circuit denied. Justice Kagan took no part in the consideration or decision of this petition.

Same case below, 599 Fed. Appx. 735.

———

No. 15-5624. Marcus Rivers, Petitioner v. United States.

577 U.S. 917, 136 S. Ct. 267, 193 L. Ed. 2d 212, 2015 U.S. LEXIS 5837.

October 5, 2015. Petition for writ of certiorari to the United States Court of Appeals for the Eleventh Circuit denied. Justice Kagan took no part in the consideration or decision of this petition.

Same case below, 777 F.3d 1306.

———

No. 15-5700. Mauricio Aguilera, Petitioner v. United States.

577 U.S. 917, 136 S. Ct. 274, 193 L. Ed. 2d 212, 2015 U.S. LEXIS 6186.

October 5, 2015. Petition for writ of certiorari to the United States Court of Appeals for the Ninth Circuit denied. Justice Breyer took no part in the consideration or decision of this petition.

Same case below, 591 Fed. Appx. 555.

No. 14-10155. In re Justin Wells, Petitioner.

577 U.S. 812, 136 S. Ct. 107, 193 L. Ed. 2d 213, 2015 U.S. LEXIS 6196.

October 5, 2015. Petition for writ of habeas corpus denied.

No. 14-10192. In re Michael Edward Kennedy, Petitioner.

577 U.S. 812, 136 S. Ct. 113, 193 L. Ed. 2d 213, 2015 U.S. LEXIS 5918.

October 5, 2015. Petition for writ of habeas corpus denied.

No. 14-10210. In re Kelly Patrick Riggs, Petitioner.

577 U.S. 812, 136 S. Ct. 117, 193 L. Ed. 2d 213, 2015 U.S. LEXIS 6153.

October 5, 2015. Petition for writ of habeas corpus denied.

No. 14-10232. In re Robert L. Sisk, Bradley Shane Sheppard, Gregory Lynn Sitz, and Richard C. Moon, Petitioners.

577 U.S. 812, 136 S. Ct. 122, 193 L. Ed. 2d 213, 2015 U.S. LEXIS 5783.

October 5, 2015. Petition for writ of habeas corpus denied.

No. 14-10246. In re Christopher D. Brown, Petitioner.

577 U.S. 812, 136 S. Ct. 124, 193 L. Ed. 2d 213, 2015 U.S. LEXIS 6026.

October 5, 2015. Petition for writ of habeas corpus denied.

No. 14-10253. In re Levon Spaulding, Petitioner.

577 U.S. 812, 136 S. Ct. 125, 193 L. Ed. 2d 213, 2015 U.S. LEXIS 5990.

October 5, 2015. Petition for writ of habeas corpus denied.

No. 14-10320. In re Alejandro Rodriguez, Petitioner.

577 U.S. 812, 136 S. Ct. 139, 193 L. Ed. 2d 213, 2015 U.S. LEXIS 6108.

October 5, 2015. Petition for writ of habeas corpus denied.

No. 14-10353. In re Daniel T. Loeffler, Petitioner.

577 U.S. 812, 136 S. Ct. 144, 193 L. Ed. 2d 213, 2015 U.S. LEXIS 4710.

October 5, 2015. Petition for writ of habeas corpus denied.

No. 14-10387. In re Edward Wright, Petitioner.

577 U.S. 812, 136 S. Ct. 150, 193 L. Ed. 2d 213, 2015 U.S. LEXIS 4733.

October 5, 2015. Petition for writ of habeas corpus denied.

No. 14-10389. In re Ricky Dewayne Booth, Petitioner.

577 U.S. 812, 136 S. Ct. 150, 193 L. Ed. 2d 214, 2015 U.S. LEXIS 4743, reh den 577 U.S. 1095, 136 S. Ct. 881, 193 L. Ed. 2d 773, 2016 U.S. LEXIS 330.

October 5, 2015. Petition for writ of habeas corpus denied.

No. 14-10420. In re Corey Rowe, Petitioner.

577 U.S. 812, 136 S. Ct. 157, 193 L. Ed. 2d 214, 2015 U.S. LEXIS 4728, reh den 577 U.S. 1044, 136 S. Ct. 609, 193 L. Ed. 2d 490, 2015 U.S. LEXIS 7772.

October 5, 2015. Petition for writ of habeas corpus denied.

No. 14-10464. In re Coleman Tavon Edwards, Petitioner.

577 U.S. 812, 136 S. Ct. 163, 193 L. Ed. 2d 214, 2015 U.S. LEXIS 4696.

October 5, 2015. Petition for writ of habeas corpus denied.

No. 14-10483. In re Ricky Louis Jackson, Petitioner.

577 U.S. 812, 136 S. Ct. 166, 193 L. Ed. 2d 214, 2015 U.S. LEXIS 4746.

October 5, 2015. Petition for writ of habeas corpus denied.

No. 15-49. In re Robert L. Rehberger, Petitioner.

577 U.S. 812, 136 S. Ct. 195, 193 L. Ed. 2d 214, 2015 U.S. LEXIS 4754.

October 5, 2015. Petition for writ of habeas corpus denied.

No. 15-250. In re Colton Aaron Pitonyak, Petitioner.

577 U.S. 812, 136 S. Ct. 284, 193 L. Ed. 2d 214, 2015 U.S. LEXIS 4742.

October 5, 2015. Petition for writ of habeas corpus denied.

No. 15-5010. In re Tommy Walker, Petitioner.

577 U.S. 812, 136 S. Ct. 170, 193 L. Ed. 2d 214, 2015 U.S. LEXIS 4700.

October 5, 2015. Petition for writ of habeas corpus denied.

No. 15-5016. In re Darrell Burrows, Petitioner.

577 U.S. 812, 136 S. Ct. 172, 193 L. Ed. 2d 214, 2015 U.S. LEXIS 4716, reh den 577 U.S. 1054, 136 S. Ct. 705, 193 L. Ed. 2d 531, 2015 U.S. LEXIS 7991.

October 5, 2015. Petition for writ of habeas corpus denied.

No. 15-5084. In re Muntu Akili, Petitioner.

577 U.S. 812, 136 S. Ct. 182, 193 L. Ed. 2d 214, 2015 U.S. LEXIS 4718.

October 5, 2015. Petition for writ of habeas corpus denied.

No. 15-5125. In re Ramon Williamson, Petitioner.

577 U.S. 812, 136 S. Ct. 190, 193 L. Ed. 2d 214, 2015 U.S. LEXIS 4731, reh den 577 U.S. 1095, 136 S. Ct. 884, 193 L. Ed. 2d 775, 2016 U.S. LEXIS 604.

October 5, 2015. Petition for writ of habeas corpus denied.

No. 15-5252. In re Alexander Rivera, Petitioner.

577 U.S. 812, 136 S. Ct. 212, 193 L. Ed. 2d 215, 2015 U.S. LEXIS 4727.

October 5, 2015. Petition for writ of habeas corpus denied.

No. 15-5257. In re Anthony Dwayne Washington, Petitioner.

577 U.S. 812, 136 S. Ct. 213, 193 L. Ed. 2d 215, 2015 U.S. LEXIS 4708.

October 5, 2015. Petition for writ of habeas corpus denied.

No. 15-5282. In re Derron Jackson, Petitioner.

577 U.S. 812, 136 S. Ct. 217, 193 L. Ed. 2d 215, 2015 U.S. LEXIS 4697.

October 5, 2015. Petition for writ of habeas corpus denied.

No. 15-5337. In re Lorenzo Tavarez, Petitioner.

577 U.S. 812, 136 S. Ct. 227, 193 L. Ed. 2d 215, 2015 U.S. LEXIS 4719.

October 5, 2015. Petition for writ of habeas corpus denied.

No. 15-5380. In re Gregory Richardson, Petitioner.

577 U.S. 812, 136 S. Ct. 235, 193 L. Ed. 2d 215, 2015 U.S. LEXIS 4701.

October 5, 2015. Petition for writ of habeas corpus denied.

No. 15-5435. In re Brian McInnis, Petitioner.

577 U.S. 812, 136 S. Ct. 245, 193 L. Ed. 2d 215, 2015 U.S. LEXIS 4737.

October 5, 2015. Petition for writ of habeas corpus denied.

No. 15-5446. In re Richard A. Smith, Jr., Petitioner.

577 U.S. 812, 136 S. Ct. 247, 193 L. Ed. 2d 215, 2015 U.S. LEXIS 4698.

October 5, 2015. Petition for writ of habeas corpus denied.

No. 15-5503. In re Roy Finley Faulkner, Petitioner.

577 U.S. 812, 136 S. Ct. 254, 193 L. Ed. 2d 215, 2015 U.S. LEXIS 4694.

October 5, 2015. Petition for writ of habeas corpus denied.

No. 15-5531. In re Roland Thompson, Petitioner.

577 U.S. 812, 136 S. Ct. 257, 193 L. Ed. 2d 215, 2015 U.S. LEXIS 4720.

October 5, 2015. Petition for writ of habeas corpus denied.

No. 15-5560. In re Lakeith Debrow, Petitioner.

577 U.S. 812, 136 S. Ct. 261, 193 L. Ed. 2d 215, 2015 U.S. LEXIS 4723.

October 5, 2015. Petition for writ of habeas corpus denied.

No. 15-5739. In re Kenneth R. Truitt, Jr., Petitioner.

577 U.S. 812, 136 S. Ct. 277, 193 L. Ed. 2d 216, 2015 U.S. LEXIS 4750.

October 5, 2015. Petition for writ of habeas corpus denied.

No. 15-5786. In re Bui Phu Xuan, Petitioner.

577 U.S. 812, 136 S. Ct. 281, 193 L. Ed. 2d 216, 2015 U.S. LEXIS 4715.

October 5, 2015. Petition for writ of habeas corpus denied.

No. 15-5816. In re Leroy Dean Dennis, Petitioner.

577 U.S. 812, 136 S. Ct. 283, 193 L. Ed. 2d 216, 2015 U.S. LEXIS 4758.

October 5, 2015. Petition for writ of habeas corpus denied.

No. 15-5894. In re Edward R. Vashey, Petitioner.

577 U.S. 813, 136 S. Ct. 284, 193 L. Ed. 2d 216, 2015 U.S. LEXIS 4707.

October 5, 2015. Petition for writ of habeas corpus denied.

No. 14-10057. In re William Staples, Petitioner.

577 U.S. 813, 136 S. Ct. 89, 193 L. Ed. 2d 216, 2015 U.S. LEXIS 4757.

October 5, 2015. Motion of petitioner for leave to proceed in forma pauperis denied,

and petition for writ of habeas corpus dismissed. See Rule 39.8. Justice Kagan took no part in the consideration or decision of this motion and this petition.

No. 14-10421. In re Echo Westley Dixon, Petitioner.

577 U.S. 813, 136 S. Ct. 157, 193 L. Ed. 2d 216, 2015 U.S. LEXIS 4756.

October 5, 2015. Motion of petitioner for leave to proceed in forma pauperis denied, and petition for writ of habeas corpus dismissed. See Rule 39.8.

No. 15-5012. In re James Darnell Scott, Petitioner.

577 U.S. 813, 136 S. Ct. 171, 193 L. Ed. 2d 216, 2015 U.S. LEXIS 4762.

October 5, 2015. Motion of petitioner for leave to proceed in forma pauperis denied, and petition for writ of habeas corpus dismissed. See Rule 39.8. As petitioner has repeatedly abused this Court's process, the Clerk is directed not to accept any further petitions in noncriminal matters from petitioner unless the docketing fee required by Rule 38(a) is paid and the petition is submitted in compliance with Rule 33.1. See Martin v. District of Columbia Court of Appeals, 506 U.S. 1, 113 S. Ct. 397, 121 L. Ed. 2d 305 (1992) (per curiam).

No. 15-5150. In re Ronnie M. Lyles, Petitioner.

577 U.S. 813, 136 S. Ct. 193, 193 L. Ed. 2d 216, 2015 U.S. LEXIS 4724.

October 5, 2015. Motion of petitioner for leave to proceed in forma pauperis

denied, and petition for writ of habeas corpus dismissed. See Rule 39.8. As petitioner has repeatedly abused this Court's process, the Clerk is directed not to accept any further petitions in noncriminal matters from petitioner unless the docketing fee required by Rule 38(a) is paid and the petition is submitted in compliance with Rule 33.1. See Martin v. District of Columbia Court of Appeals, 506 U.S. 1, 113 S. Ct. 397, 121 L. Ed. 2d 305 (1992) (per curiam).

No. 15-5506. In re Roberto Beras, Petitioner.

577 U.S. 813, 136 S. Ct. 254, 193 L. Ed. 2d 217, 2015 U.S. LEXIS 4740.

October 5, 2015. Motion of petitioner for leave to proceed in forma pauperis denied, and petition for writ of habeas corpus dismissed. See Rule 39.8. As petitioner has repeatedly abused this Court's process, the Clerk is directed not to accept any further petitions in noncriminal matters from petitioner unless the docketing fee required by Rule 38(a) is paid and the petition is submitted in compliance with Rule 33.1. See Martin v. District of Columbia Court of Appeals, 506 U.S. 1, 113 S. Ct. 397, 121 L. Ed. 2d 305 (1992) (per curiam). Justice Kagan took no part in the consideration or decision of this motion and this petition.

No. 15-5820. In re Lemuel L. Cole, Petitioner.

577 U.S. 814, 136 S. Ct. 283, 193 L. Ed. 2d 217, 2015 U.S. LEXIS 4765.

October 5, 2015. Motion of petitioner for leave to proceed in forma pauperis denied, and petition for writ of habeas corpus dismissed. See Rule 39.8. As petitioner has repeatedly abused this Court's process, the Clerk is directed not to accept any further petitions in noncriminal matters from petitioner unless the docketing fee required by Rule 38(a) is paid and the

petition is submitted in compliance with Rule 33.1. See Martin v. District of Columbia Court of Appeals, 506 U.S. 1, 113 S. Ct. 397, 121 L. Ed. 2d 305 (1992) (per curiam).

No. 14-1427. In re Modesta Sabeniano, Petitioner.

577 U.S. 814, 136 S. Ct. 87, 193 L. Ed. 2d 217, 2015 U.S. LEXIS 4695, reh den 577 U.S. 1022, 136 S. Ct. 571, 193 L. Ed. 2d 453, 2015 U.S. LEXIS 7371.

October 5, 2015. Petition for writ of mandamus denied.

No. 14-1480. In re Graham Schreiber, Petitioner.

577 U.S. 814, 136 S. Ct. 128, 193 L. Ed. 2d 217, 2015 U.S. LEXIS 4709.

October 5, 2015. Petition for writ of mandamus denied.

No. 14-1532. In re Derrick Tartt, Petitioner.

577 U.S. 814, 136 S. Ct. 156, 193 L. Ed. 2d 217, 2015 U.S. LEXIS 4711.

October 5, 2015. Petition for writ of mandamus denied.

No. 14-9676. In re Otis Ervin, Petitioner.

577 U.S. 814, 136 S. Ct. 51, 193 L. Ed. 2d 217, 2015 U.S. LEXIS 4704, reh den 577 U.S. 1022, 136 S. Ct. 573, 193 L. Ed. 2d 455, 2015 U.S. LEXIS 7456.

October 5, 2015. Petition for writ of mandamus denied.

No. 14-9751. In re Charles Rentschler, Petitioner.

577 U.S. 814, 136 S. Ct. 57, 193 L. Ed. 2d 218, 2015 U.S. LEXIS 4736.

October 5, 2015. Petition for writ of mandamus denied.

No. 14-9791. In re Michael Schneider, Petitioner.

577 U.S. 814, 136 S. Ct. 61, 193 L. Ed. 2d 218, 2015 U.S. LEXIS 4712, reh den 577 U.S. 1094, 136 S. Ct. 880, 193 L. Ed. 2d 771, 2016 U.S. LEXIS 462.

October 5, 2015. Petition for writ of mandamus denied.

No. 14-10058. In re Zdravko Kotzev, Petitioner.

577 U.S. 814, 136 S. Ct. 89, 193 L. Ed. 2d 218, 2015 U.S. LEXIS 4732.

October 5, 2015. Petition for writ of mandamus denied.

No. 14-10470. In re Jacob Ben-Ari, Petitioner.

577 U.S. 814, 136 S. Ct. 164, 193 L. Ed. 2d 218, 2015 U.S. LEXIS 4730, reh den 577 U.S. 1125, 136 S. Ct. 979, 194 L. Ed. 2d 16, 2016 U.S. LEXIS 869.

October 5, 2015. Petition for writ of mandamus denied.

No. 15-148. In re OMS, LLC, et al., Petitioners.

577 U.S. 814, 136 S. Ct. 244, 193 L. Ed. 2d 218, 2015 U.S. LEXIS 4751.

October 5, 2015. Petition for writ of mandamus denied.

No. 15-5051. In re Benjardi B. Viray, Petitioner.

577 U.S. 814, 136 S. Ct. 176, 193 L. Ed. 2d 218, 2015 U.S. LEXIS 4744, reh den 577 U.S. 1023, 136 S. Ct. 578, 193 L. Ed. 2d 460, 2015 U.S. LEXIS 7439.

October 5, 2015. Petition for writ of mandamus denied.

No. 15-5054. In re Gregory Scott Savoy, Petitioner.

577 U.S. 814, 136 S. Ct. 177, 193 L. Ed. 2d 218, 2015 U.S. LEXIS 4722.

October 5, 2015. Petition for writ of mandamus denied.

No. 15-5488. In re James C. Platts, Petitioner.

577 U.S. 814, 136 S. Ct. 253, 193 L. Ed. 2d 218, 2015 U.S. LEXIS 4706.

October 5, 2015. Petition for writ of mandamus denied.

No. 14-9565. In re Stephen G. Kraemer, Petitioner.

577 U.S. 814, 136 S. Ct. 42, 193 L. Ed. 2d 218, 2015 U.S. LEXIS 4729.

October 5, 2015. Petition for writ of mandamus and/or prohibition denied.

No. 14-10077. In re David Andrew Christenson, Petitioner.

577 U.S. 814, 136 S. Ct. 93, 193 L. Ed. 2d 218, 2015 U.S. LEXIS 4726, reh den 577 U.S. 969, 136 S. Ct. 439, 193 L. Ed. 2d 341, 2015 U.S. LEXIS 6773.

October 5, 2015. Petition for writ of mandamus and/or prohibition denied.

No. 14-10160. In re Roy Perkins, Petitioner.

577 U.S. 814, 136 S. Ct. 107, 193 L. Ed. 2d 219, 2015 U.S. LEXIS 4714.

October 5, 2015. Petition for writ of mandamus and/or prohibition denied.

No. 14-10180. In re Jack R. Koch, Petitioner.

577 U.S. 814, 136 S. Ct. 112, 193 L. Ed. 2d 219, 2015 U.S. LEXIS 4713.

October 5, 2015. Motion of petitioner for leave to proceed in forma pauperis denied, and petition for writ of mandamus and/or prohibition dismissed. See Rule 39.8.

No. 14-10299. In re Echo Westley Dixon, Petitioner.

577 U.S. 814, 136 S. Ct. 135, 193 L. Ed. 2d 219, 2015 U.S. LEXIS 4752.

October 5, 2015. Motion of petitioner for leave to proceed in forma pauperis denied, and petition for writ of mandamus dismissed. See Rule 39.8.

No. 14-10382. In re Norman E. Gregory, Petitioner.

577 U.S. 814, 136 S. Ct. 150, 193 L. Ed. 2d 219, 2015 U.S. LEXIS 4749.

October 5, 2015. Motion of petitioner for leave to proceed in forma pauperis denied, and petition for writ of mandamus dismissed. See Rule 39.8.

No. 14-1439. In re Donald Steven Charles, Petitioner.

577 U.S. 814, 136 S. Ct. 103, 193 L. Ed. 2d 219, 2015 U.S. LEXIS 4735.

October 5, 2015. Petition for writ of prohibition denied.

No. 14-9887. In re Robert H. Ajamian, Petitioner.

577 U.S. 814, 136 S. Ct. 70, 193 L. Ed. 2d 219, 2015 U.S. LEXIS 4739.

October 5, 2015. Petition for writ of prohibition denied.

No. 14-9888. In re Robert H. Ajamian, Petitioner.

577 U.S. 814, 136 S. Ct. 70, 193 L. Ed. 2d 219, 2015 U.S. LEXIS 4755.

October 5, 2015. Petition for writ of prohibition denied.

No. 14-9889. In re Robert H. Ajamian, Petitioner.

577 U.S. 814, 136 S. Ct. 70, 193 L. Ed. 2d 219, 2015 U.S. LEXIS 4721.

October 5, 2015. Petition for writ of prohibition denied.

No. 14-9544. In re Ronnie M. Lyles, Petitioner.

577 U.S. 815, 136 S. Ct. 42, 193 L. Ed. 2d 219, 2015 U.S. LEXIS 4763.

October 5, 2015. Motion of petitioner for leave to proceed in forma pauperis

denied, and petition for writ of prohibition dismissed. See Rule 39.8. Justice Kagan took no part in the consideration or decision of this motion and this petition.

No. 14-10422. In re Echo Westley Dixon, Petitioner.

577 U.S. 815, 136 S. Ct. 157, 193 L. Ed. 2d 220, 2015 U.S. LEXIS 4764.

October 5, 2015. Motion of petitioner for leave to proceed in forma pauperis denied, and petition for writ of prohibition dismissed. See Rule 39.8.

No. 15-5382. In re Twain Newman Ayers, Petitioner.

577 U.S. 815, 136 S. Ct. 235, 193 L. Ed. 2d 220, 2015 U.S. LEXIS 4760.

October 5, 2015. Motion of petitioner for leave to proceed in forma pauperis denied, and petition for writ of prohibition dismissed. See Rule 39.8.

No. 14-1241. Christopher Lawrence, Petitioner v. Gwinnett County, Georgia, et al.

577 U.S. 917, 136 S. Ct. 302, 193 L. Ed. 2d 220, 2015 U.S. LEXIS 4705.

October 5, 2015. Petition for rehearing denied.

Former decision, 576 U.S. 1036, 135 S. Ct. 2861, 192 L. Ed. 2d 896, 2015 U.S. LEXIS 4097, 83 U.S.L.W. 3911.

No. 14-1258. Evelyn Leyva, Petitioner v. Wells Fargo Bank, N.A.

577 U.S. 917, 136 S. Ct. 302, 193 L. Ed. 2d 220, 2015 U.S. LEXIS 4748.

October 5, 2015. Petition for rehearing denied.

Former decision, 576 U.S. 1036, 135 S. Ct. 2864, 192 L. Ed. 2d 897, 2015 U.S. LEXIS 4202.

No. 14-7190. Vicente Garcia, Petitioner v. United States.

577 U.S. 917, 136 S. Ct. 302, 193 L. Ed. 2d 220, 2015 U.S. LEXIS 4699.

October 5, 2015. Petition for rehearing denied.

Former decision, 574 U.S. 1095, 135 S. Ct. 991, 191 L. Ed. 2d 869, 2015 U.S. LEXIS 255.

No. 14-9069. John S. Codiga, Petitioner v. Jeffrey A. Uttecht, Superintendent, Coyote Ridge Corrections Center.

577 U.S. 917, 136 S. Ct. 302, 193 L. Ed. 2d 220, 2015 U.S. LEXIS 4759.

October 5, 2015. Petition for rehearing denied.

Former decision, 575 U.S. 1031, 135 S. Ct. 2362, 192 L. Ed. 2d 154, 2015 U.S. LEXIS 3558.

No. 14-9422. Abu Bakarr Kargbo, Petitioner v. New Hampshire.

577 U.S. 917, 136 S. Ct. 302, 193 L. Ed. 2d 220, 2015 U.S. LEXIS 4741.

October 5, 2015. Petition for rehearing denied.

Former decision, 576 U.S. 1039, 135 S. Ct. 2866, 192 L. Ed. 2d 903, 2015 U.S. LEXIS 4140.

No. 14-9459. Steve Lester, Petitioner v. Michael Henthorne.

577 U.S. 917, 136 S. Ct. 303, 193 L. Ed. 2d 221, 2015 U.S. LEXIS 4734.

October 5, 2015. Petition for rehearing denied.

Former decision, 576 U.S. 1059, 135 S. Ct. 2896, 192 L. Ed. 2d 932, 2015 U.S. LEXIS 4414.

No. 14-9523. Floyd E. Cross, Petitioner v. John Fayram, Warden.

577 U.S. 917, 136 S. Ct. 303, 193 L. Ed. 2d 221, 2015 U.S. LEXIS 4747.

October 5, 2015. Petition for rehearing denied.

Former decision, 576 U.S. 1059, 135 S. Ct. 2898, 192 L. Ed. 2d 933, 2015 U.S. LEXIS 4471.

No. 14-9647. Cedrick S. Barriner, Petitioner v. Julie L. Jones, Secretary, Florida Department of Corrections, et al.

577 U.S. 917, 136 S. Ct. 303, 193 L. Ed. 2d 221, 2015 U.S. LEXIS 4702.

October 5, 2015. Petition for rehearing denied.

Former decision, 576 U.S. 1060, 135 S. Ct. 2899, 192 L. Ed. 2d 934, 2015 U.S. LEXIS 4311.

No. 14-9652. Euphrem Dohou, Petitioner v. United States.

577 U.S. 917, 136 S. Ct. 303, 193 L. Ed. 2d 221, 2015 U.S. LEXIS 4761.

October 5, 2015. Petition for rehearing denied.

Former decision, 576 U.S. 1012, 135 S. Ct. 2823, 192 L. Ed. 2d 861, 2015 U.S. LEXIS 3844.

No. 14-9664. Bobby Collins, Jr., Petitioner v. Troy Steele, Warden.

577 U.S. 917, 136 S. Ct. 303, 193 L. Ed. 2d 221, 2015 U.S. LEXIS 4717.

October 5, 2015. Petition for rehearing denied.

Former decision, 576 U.S. 1041, 135 S. Ct. 2870, 192 L. Ed. 2d 905, 2015 U.S. LEXIS 4173.

No. 14-9744. Craig Thomas Dawson, Petitioner v. Jeff Premo, Superintendent, Oregon State Penitentiary.

577 U.S. 917, 136 S. Ct. 303, 193 L. Ed. 2d 221, 2015 U.S. LEXIS 4725.

October 5, 2015. Petition for rehearing denied.

Former decision, 576 U.S. 1060, 135 S. Ct. 2901, 192 L. Ed. 2d 935, 2015 U.S. LEXIS 4313.

No. 14-9839. Darrell R. Johns, Petitioner v. United States.

577 U.S. 917, 136 S. Ct. 303, 193 L. Ed. 2d 221, 2015 U.S. LEXIS 4753.

October 5, 2015. Petition for rehearing denied.

Former decision, 576 U.S. 1042, 135 S. Ct. 2874, 192 L. Ed. 2d 907, 2015 U.S. LEXIS 4177.

No. 14-9876. Kenneth Michael Wilcox, Petitioner v. United States.

577 U.S. 917, 136 S. Ct. 303, 193 L. Ed. 2d 222, 2015 U.S. LEXIS 4738.

October 5, 2015. Petition for rehearing denied.

Former decision, 576 U.S. 1061, 135 S. Ct. 2903, 192 L. Ed. 2d 936, 2015 U.S. LEXIS 4391.

No. 14-9882. Jermaine Leon Copeland, Petitioner v. Julie L. Jones, Secretary, Florida Department of Corrections, et al.

577 U.S. 917, 136 S. Ct. 304, 193 L. Ed. 2d 222, 2015 U.S. LEXIS 4745.

October 5, 2015. Petition for rehearing denied.

Former decision, 576 U.S. 1061, 135 S. Ct. 2904, 192 L. Ed. 2d 936, 2015 U.S. LEXIS 4390.

No. 14-8628. Ulysses Thomas Ware, Petitioner v. United States.

577 U.S. 918, 136 S. Ct. 304, 193 L. Ed. 2d 222, 2015 U.S. LEXIS 4703.

October 5, 2015. Petition for rehearing denied. Justice Sotomayor took no part in the consideration or decision of this petition.

Former decision, 575 U.S. 946, 135 S. Ct. 1725, 191 L. Ed. 2d 696, 2015 U.S. LEXIS 2147.

No. 15-5725 (R46-001). Michael Bischoff, Petitioner v. Tony Gallo, et al.

577 U.S. 918, 136 S. Ct. 304, 193 L. Ed. 2d 222, 2015 U.S. LEXIS 6367.

October 6, 2015. The petition for writ of certiorari to the United States Court of Appeals for the Sixth Circuit was dismissed today pursuant to Rule 46 of the Rules of this Court.

MEMORANDUM CASES

No. 14-1422. The First Marblehead Corporation, et al., Petitioners v. Massachusetts Commissioner of Revenue.

577 U.S. 918, 136 S. Ct. 317, 193 L. Ed. 2d 223, 2015 U.S. LEXIS 6423.

October 13, 2015. On petition for writ of certiorari to the Supreme Judicial Court of Massachusetts. Petition for writ of certiorari granted. Judgment vacated, and case remanded to the Supreme Judicial Court of Massachusetts for further consideration in light of Comptroller of the Treasury of Md. v. Wynne, 575 U.S. 542, 135 S. Ct. 1787, 191 L. Ed. 2d 813 (2015).

Same case below, 470 Mass. 497, 23 N.E.3d 892.

———

No. 15-5330. Richard Wally Rose, Petitioner v. United States.

577 U.S. 918, 136 S. Ct. 320, 193 L. Ed. 2d 223, 2015 U.S. LEXIS 6526.

October 13, 2015. On petition for writ of certiorari to the United States Court of Appeals for the Eleventh Circuit. Motion of petitioner for leave to proceed in forma pauperis and petition for writ of certiorari granted. Judgment vacated, and case remanded to the United States Court of Appeals for the Eleventh Circuit for further consideration in light of Johnson v. United States, 576 U.S. 591, 135 S. Ct. 2551, 192 L. Ed. 2d 569 (2015).

Same case below, 590 Fed. Appx. 937.

———

No. 15-5654. Bacari McCarthren, Petitioner v. United States.

577 U.S. 918, 136 S. Ct. 332, 193 L. Ed. 2d 223, 2015 U.S. LEXIS 6489.

October 13, 2015. On petition for writ of certiorari to the United States Court of Appeals for the Eleventh Circuit. Motion of petitioner for leave to proceed in forma pauperis and petition for writ of certiorari granted. Judgment vacated, and case remanded to the United States Court of Appeals for the Eleventh Circuit for further consideration in light of Johnson v. United States, 576 U.S. 591, 135 S. Ct. 2551, 192 L. Ed. 2d 569 (2015).

Same case below, 575 Fed. Appx. 873.

———

No. 15-5667. James Bernard Jones, Jr., Petitioner v. United States.

577 U.S. 918, 136 S. Ct. 333, 193 L. Ed. 2d 223, 2015 U.S. LEXIS 6585.

October 13, 2015. On petition for writ of certiorari to the United States Court of Appeals for the Eleventh Circuit. Motion of petitioner for leave to proceed in forma pauperis and petition for writ of certiorari granted. Judgment vacated, and case remanded to the United States Court of Appeals for the Eleventh Circuit for further consideration in light of Johnson v. United States, 576 U.S. 591, 135 S. Ct. 2551, 192 L. Ed. 2d 569 (2015).

Same case below, 597 Fed. Appx. 1064.

———

No. 15-5601. Patrick A. Missud, Petitioner v. Court of Appeal of California, First Appellate District, et al.

577 U.S. 918, 136 S. Ct. 329, 193 L. Ed. 2d 223, 2015 U.S. LEXIS 6507.

October 13, 2015. Because the Court lacks a quorum, 28 U.S.C. § 1, and since the only qualified Justices are of the opinion that the case cannot be heard and determined at the next Term of the Court, the judgment is affirmed under 28 U.S.C. § 2109, which provides that under these circumstances "the court shall enter its order affirming the judgment of the court from which the case was brought for review with the same effect as upon affirmance by an equally divided court." The Chief Justice, Justice Scalia, Justice Kennedy, Justice Thomas, and Justice Alito took no part in the consideration or decision of this petition.

No. 15-5489. Bret D. Landrith, Petitioner v. Don Jordan, et al.

577 U.S. 919, 136 S. Ct. 321, 193 L. Ed. 2d 224, 2015 U.S. LEXIS 6389.

October 13, 2015. Motion of petitioner for leave to proceed in forma pauperis denied, and petition for writ of certiorari to the Court of Appeals of Kansas dismissed. See Rule 39.8.

Same case below, 321 P.3d 36.

No. 15-5495. Juan Enriquez, Petitioner v. William Stephens, Director, Texas Department of Criminal Justice, Correctional Institutions Division.

577 U.S. 919, 136 S. Ct. 322, 193 L. Ed. 2d 224, 2015 U.S. LEXIS 6390.

October 13, 2015. Motion of petitioner for leave to proceed in forma pauperis denied, and petition for writ of certiorari to the United States Court of Appeals for the Fifth Circuit dismissed. See Rule 39.8. As petitioner has repeatedly abused this Court's process, the Clerk is directed not to accept any further petitions in noncriminal matters from petitioner unless

the docketing fee required by Rule 38(a) is paid and petition is submitted in compliance with Rule 33.1. See Martin v. District of Columbia Court of Appeals, 506 U.S. 1, 113 S. Ct. 397, 121 L. Ed. 2d 305 (1992) (per curiam).

No. 15-5527. Richard Kearney, Petitioner v. New York Department of Correctional Services, et al.

577 U.S. 919, 136 S. Ct. 355, 193 L. Ed. 2d 224, 2015 U.S. LEXIS 6377.

October 13, 2015. Motion of petitioner for leave to proceed in forma pauperis denied, and petition for writ of certiorari to the United States Court of Appeals for the Second Circuit dismissed. See Rule 39.8.

No. 15-5589. Donald Turnpaugh, Petitioner v. Michigan.

577 U.S. 919, 136 S. Ct. 328, 193 L. Ed. 2d 224, 2015 U.S. LEXIS 6380.

October 13, 2015. Motion of petitioner for leave to proceed in forma pauperis denied, and petition for writ of certiorari to the Court of Appeals of Michigan dismissed. See Rule 39.8.

Same case below, 497 Mich. 1015, 862 N.W.2d 211.

No. 15-5748. James B. Campbell, Petitioner v. Julie L. Jones, Secretary, Florida Department of Corrections.

577 U.S. 919, 136 S. Ct. 335, 193 L. Ed. 2d 224, 2015 U.S. LEXIS 6375.

October 13, 2015. Motion of petitioner for leave to proceed in forma pauperis

denied, and petition for writ of certiorari to the Supreme Court of Florida dismissed. See Rule 39.8. As petitioner has repeatedly abused this Court's process, the Clerk is directed not to accept any further petitions in noncriminal matters from petitioner unless the docketing fee required by Rule 38(a) is paid and petition submitted in compliance with Rule 33.1. See Martin v. District of Columbia Court of Appeals, 506 U.S. 1, 113 S. Ct. 397, 121 L. Ed. 2d 305 (1992) (per curiam).

Same case below, 171 So. 3d 114.

No. 15-5811. Nyka Tassiant O'Connor, Petitioner v. Julie L. Jones, Secretary, Florida Department of Corrections.

577 U.S. 919, 136 S. Ct. 336, 193 L. Ed. 2d 225, 2015 U.S. LEXIS 6376.

October 13, 2015. Motion of petitioner for leave to proceed in forma pauperis denied, and petition for writ of certiorari to the United States Court of Appeals for the Eleventh Circuit dismissed. See Rule 39.8. As petitioner has repeatedly abused this Court's process, the Clerk is directed not to accept any further petitions in noncriminal matters from petitioner unless the docketing fees required by Rule 38(a) is paid and petition is submitted in compliance with Rule 33.1. See Martin v. District of Columbia Court of Appeals, 506 U.S. 1, 113 S. Ct. 397, 121 L. Ed. 2d 305 (1992) (per curiam).

No. 15-5819. Gary DeWilliams, Petitioner v. United States.

577 U.S. 920, 136 S. Ct. 337, 193 L. Ed. 2d 225, 2015 U.S. LEXIS 6378.

October 13, 2015. Motion of petitioner for leave to proceed in forma pauperis denied, and petition for writ of certiorari to the United States Court of Appeals for

the Tenth Circuit dismissed. See Rule 39.8. As petitioner has repeatedly abused this Court's process, the Clerk is directed not to accept any further petitions in noncriminal matters from petitioner unless the docketing fee required by Rule 38(a) is paid and petition is submitted in compliance with Rule 33.1. See Martin v. District of Columbia Court of Appeals, 506 U.S. 1, 113 S. Ct. 397, 121 L. Ed. 2d 305 (1992) (per curiam). Justice Kagan took no part in the consideration or decision of this motion and this petition.

Same case below, 612 Fed. Appx. 489.

No. 15-5921. Alvin Harvey, Petitioner v. Louisiana.

577 U.S. 920, 136 S. Ct. 345, 193 L. Ed. 2d 225, 2015 U.S. LEXIS 6391.

October 13, 2015. Motion of petitioner for leave to proceed in forma pauperis denied, and petition for writ of certiorari to the Supreme Court of Louisiana dismissed. See Rule 39.8. As petitioner has repeatedly abused this Court's process, the Clerk is directed not to accept any further petitions in noncriminal matters from petitioner unless the docketing fee required by Rule 38(a) is paid and petition submitted in compliance with Rule 33.1. See Martin v. District of Columbia Court of Appeals, 506 U.S. 1, 113 S. Ct. 397, 121 L. Ed. 2d 305 (1992) (per curiam).

Same case below, 171 So. 3d 945.

No. 14A1153. Pete Nechovski, Applicant v. United States.

577 U.S. 920, 136 S. Ct. 352, 193 L. Ed. 2d 225, 2015 U.S. LEXIS 6495.

October 13, 2015. Application for a certificate of appealability, addressed to Justice Sotomayor and referred to the Court, denied.

Same case below, 598 Fed. Appx. 457.

No. 15A216. Christopher Lee Manska, Applicant v. Minnesota.

577 U.S. 920, 136 S. Ct. 352, 193 L. Ed. 2d 226, 2015 U.S. LEXIS 6422.

October 13, 2015. Application for stay, addressed to Justice Sotomayor and referred to the Court, denied.

No. 15A293. Laura M. Watson, Applicant v. Florida Judicial Qualifications Commission.

577 U.S. 920, 136 S. Ct. 352, 193 L. Ed. 2d 226, 2015 U.S. LEXIS 6578.

October 13, 2015. Application for stay, addressed to Justice Sotomayor and referred to the Court, denied.

Same case below, 174 So. 3d 364.

No. 15M30. Christian R. Colon, Petitioner v. Brian Foster, Warden.

577 U.S. 921, 136 S. Ct. 353, 193 L. Ed. 2d 226, 2015 U.S. LEXIS 6586.

October 13, 2015. Motion to direct the Clerk to file a petition for writ of certiorari out of time denied.

No. 15M31. Beverly Thompson, et al., Petitioners v. Gregory P. Ruddy, et al.

577 U.S. 921, 136 S. Ct. 353, 193 L. Ed. 2d 226, 2015 U.S. LEXIS 6401.

October 13, 2015. Motion to direct the Clerk to file a petition for writ of certiorari out of time denied.

No. 15M32. Darwin M. Nealy, Petitioner v. United States Postal Service.

577 U.S. 921, 136 S. Ct. 353, 193 L. Ed. 2d 226, 2015 U.S. LEXIS 6576.

October 13, 2015. Motion to direct the Clerk to file a petition for writ of certiorari out of time under Rule 14.5 denied.

Same case below, 593 Fed. Appx. 1000.

No. 15M33. Michael Brock, Petitioner v. Larry Small, Warden.

577 U.S. 921, 136 S. Ct. 353, 193 L. Ed. 2d 226, 2015 U.S. LEXIS 6454.

October 13, 2015. Motion to direct the Clerk to file a petition for writ of certiorari out of time denied.

No. 15M34. Willie D. Upson, Petitioner v. Julie L. Jones, Secretary, Florida Department of Corrections, et al.

577 U.S. 921, 136 S. Ct. 353, 193 L. Ed. 2d 226, 2015 U.S. LEXIS 6564.

October 13, 2015. Motion to direct the Clerk to file a petition for writ of certiorari out of time denied.

No. 142, Original. State of Florida, Plaintiff v. State of Georgia.

577 U.S. 921, 136 S. Ct. 353, 193 L. Ed. 2d 226, 2015 U.S. LEXIS 6471.

October 13, 2015. Motion of the Special Master for allowance of fees and disbursements granted, and the Special Master is awarded a total of $70,245.52, for the period April 1, 2015, through August 31, 2015, to be paid equally by the parties.

———

No. 15-5539. Tracy Brown, Petitioner v. Janet Kleerekoper.

577 U.S. 921, 136 S. Ct. 354, 193 L. Ed. 2d 227, 2015 U.S. LEXIS 6455.

October 13, 2015. Motion of petitioner for leave to proceed in forma pauperis denied. Petitioner is allowed until November 3, 2015, within which to pay the docketing fees required by Rule 38(a) and to submit a petition in compliance with Rule 33.1 of the Rules of this Court.

———

No. 15-5686. Marvin Antonio Franco-Bardales, Petitioner v. Loretta E. Lynch, Attorney General.

577 U.S. 921, 136 S. Ct. 354, 193 L. Ed. 2d 227, 2015 U.S. LEXIS 6569.

October 13, 2015. Motion of petitioner for leave to proceed in forma pauperis denied. Petitioner is allowed until November 3, 2015, within which to pay the docketing fees required by Rule 38(a) and to submit a petition in compliance with Rule 33.1 of the Rules of this Court.

Same case below, 599 Fed. Appx. 684.

———

No. 14-1153. Edmund D. LaChance, Jr., Petitioner v. Massachusetts.

577 U.S. 922, 136 S. Ct. 317, 193 L. Ed. 2d 227, 2015 U.S. LEXIS 6476.

October 13, 2015. Petition for writ of certiorari to the Supreme Judicial Court of Massachusetts denied.

Same case below, 469 Mass. 854, 17 N.E.3d 1101.

———

No. 14-1286. United Healthcare of Arizona, et al., Petitioners v. Spinedex Physical Therapy USA, Inc., et al.

577 U.S. 922, 136 S. Ct. 317, 193 L. Ed. 2d 227, 2015 U.S. LEXIS 6538.

October 13, 2015. Petition for writ of certiorari to the United States Court of Appeals for the Ninth Circuit denied.

Same case below, 770 F.3d 1282.

———

No. 14-1331. Kenneth Kirschenbaum, Chapter 7 Trustee of the Estate of the Robert Plan Corporation, Petitioner v. Department of Labor.

577 U.S. 922, 136 S. Ct. 317, 193 L. Ed. 2d 227, 2015 U.S. LEXIS 6435.

October 13, 2015. Petition for writ of certiorari to the United States Court of Appeals for the Second Circuit denied.

Same case below, 777 F.3d 594.

———

No. 14-1436. Michael Hambleton, as Successor Personal Representative of the Estate of Helen M. Hambleton, et al., Petitioners v. Washington Department of Revenue.

577 U.S. 922, 136 S. Ct. 318, 193 L. Ed. 2d 227, 2015 U.S. LEXIS 6490.

October 13, 2015. Petition for writ of certiorari to the Supreme Court of Washington denied.

Same case below, 181 Wash. 2d 802, 335 P.3d 398.

No. 14-1464. Oakland Port Services Corp., Petitioner v. Lavon Godfrey, et al.

577 U.S. 922, 136 S. Ct. 318, 193 L. Ed. 2d 228, 2015 U.S. LEXIS 6572.

October 13, 2015. Petition for writ of certiorari to the Court of Appeal of California, First Appellate District, District Two, denied.

Same case below, 230 Cal. App. 4th 1267, 179 Cal. Rptr. 3d 498.

No. 14-1497. Kane County, Utah, Petitioner v. United States.

No. 15-27. Utah, Petitioner v. United States.

577 U.S. 922, 136 S. Ct. 318, 193 L. Ed. 2d 228, 2015 U.S. LEXIS 6453.

October 13, 2015. Petitions for writs of certiorari to the United States Court of Appeals for the Tenth Circuit denied.

Same cases below, 772 F.3d 1205.

No. 14-9416. Rafael Diaz, Petitioner v. Francisco J. Quintana, Warden.

577 U.S. 922, 136 S. Ct. 317, 193 L. Ed. 2d 228, 2015 U.S. LEXIS 6399.

October 13, 2015. Petition for writ of certiorari to the United States Court of Appeals for the Sixth Circuit denied.

No. 14-9470. Ledell Lee, Petitioner v. Wendy Kelley, Director, Arkansas Department of Correction.

577 U.S. 922, 136 S. Ct. 354, 193 L. Ed. 2d 228, 2015 U.S. LEXIS 6544.

October 13, 2015. Petition for writ of certiorari to the United States Court of Appeals for the Eighth Circuit denied.

No. 14-9875. Bernard West, Petitioner v. United States.

577 U.S. 922, 136 S. Ct. 317, 193 L. Ed. 2d 228, 2015 U.S. LEXIS 6528.

October 13, 2015. Petition for writ of certiorari to the District of Columbia Court of Appeals denied.

Same case below, 100 A.3d 1076.

No. 14-10066. Charles Alston Smith, Petitioner v. Colorado.

577 U.S. 922, 136 S. Ct. 354, 193 L. Ed. 2d 228, 2015 U.S. LEXIS 6502.

October 13, 2015. Petition for writ of certiorari to the Court of Appeals of Colorado denied.

No. 14-10405. Victor Lopez, Petitioner v. United States.

577 U.S. 923, 136 S. Ct. 318, 193 L. Ed. 2d 228, 2015 U.S. LEXIS 6448.

October 13, 2015. Petition for writ of certiorari to the United States Court of Appeals for the Fifth Circuit denied.

No. 14-10443. Rocky Joe Williams, Petitioner v. United States.

577 U.S. 923, 136 S. Ct. 318, 193 L. Ed. 2d 228, 2015 U.S. LEXIS 6539.

October 13, 2015. Petition for writ of certiorari to the United States Court of Appeals for the Fifth Circuit denied.

No. 15-16. Allen Raymond Johnson, Petitioner v. United States.

577 U.S. 923, 136 S. Ct. 318, 193 L. Ed. 2d 229, 2015 U.S. LEXIS 6552.

October 13, 2015. Petition for writ of certiorari to the United States Court of Appeals for the Ninth Circuit denied.

Same case below, 588 Fed. Appx. 743.

No. 15-17. Carolyn L. Davis, Petitioner v. U.S. Bank N.A., et al.

577 U.S. 923, 136 S. Ct. 319, 193 L. Ed. 2d 229, 2015 U.S. LEXIS 6545.

October 13, 2015. Petition for writ of certiorari to the United States Court of Appeals for the Ninth Circuit denied.

Same case below, 778 F.3d 809.

No. 15-22. William N. Gerhartz, Petitioner v. David Richert, et al.

577 U.S. 923, 136 S. Ct. 319, 193 L. Ed. 2d 229, 2015 U.S. LEXIS 6541.

October 13, 2015. Petition for writ of certiorari to the United States Court of Appeals for the Seventh Circuit denied.

Same case below, 779 F.3d 682.

No. 15-23. Prairie County, Montana, et al., Petitioners v. United States.

577 U.S. 923, 136 S. Ct. 319, 193 L. Ed. 2d 229, 2015 U.S. LEXIS 6524.

October 13, 2015. Petition for writ of certiorari to the United States Court of Appeals for the Federal Circuit denied.

Same case below, 782 F.3d 685.

No. 15-130. Martha L. Anglin, Petitioner v. Ceres Gulf, Incorporated, et al.

577 U.S. 923, 136 S. Ct. 320, 193 L. Ed. 2d 229, 2015 U.S. LEXIS 6581.

October 13, 2015. Petition for writ of certiorari to the United States Court of Appeals for the Fifth Circuit denied.

Same case below, 588 Fed. Appx. 342.

No. 15-135. Michael Rubin, et al., Petitioners v. Alex Padilla, California Secretary of State, et al.

577 U.S. 923, 136 S. Ct. 320, 193 L. Ed. 2d 229, 2015 U.S. LEXIS 6571.

October 13, 2015. Petition for writ of certiorari to the Court of Appeal of California, First Appellate District, Division One, denied.

Same case below, 233 Cal. App. 4th 1128, 183 Cal. Rptr. 3d 373.

No. 15-139. Leanna Volk, Petitioner v. Nicholas Grant Williams.

577 U.S. 923, 136 S. Ct. 320, 193 L. Ed. 2d 229, 2015 U.S. LEXIS 6577.

October 13, 2015. Petition for writ of certiorari to the Court of Appeals of Ohio, Coshocton County, denied.

No. 15-143. Shace Gjokaj, et vir, Petitioners v. HSBC Mortgage Services, Inc., et al.

577 U.S. 923, 136 S. Ct. 321, 193 L. Ed. 2d 229, 2015 U.S. LEXIS 6413.

October 13, 2015. Petition for writ of certiorari to the United States Court of Appeals for the Sixth Circuit denied.

Same case below, 602 Fed. Appx. 275.

No. 15-165. Nazar R. Hindo, et ux., Petitioners v. Bank of New York Mellon.

577 U.S. 923, 136 S. Ct. 324, 193 L. Ed. 2d 230, 2015 U.S. LEXIS 6400.

October 13, 2015. Petition for writ of certiorari to the United States Court of Appeals for the Sixth Circuit denied.

Same case below, 596 Fed. Appx. 484.

No. 15-167. Pagona Christakis, Petitioner v. Jeanne D'Arc Credit Union.

577 U.S. 923, 136 S. Ct. 325, 193 L. Ed. 2d 230, 2015 U.S. LEXIS 6488.

October 13, 2015. Petition for writ of certiorari to the Supreme Judicial Court of Massachusetts denied.

Same case below, 471 Mass. 365, 29 N.E.3d 823.

No. 15-171. James P. DeFazio, et al., Petitioners v. Hollister, Inc., et al.

577 U.S. 923, 136 S. Ct. 325, 193 L. Ed. 2d 230, 2015 U.S. LEXIS 6437, reh den 577 U.S. 1044, 136 S. Ct. 610, 193 L. Ed. 2d 490, 2015 U.S. LEXIS 7689.

October 13, 2015. Petition for writ of certiorari to the United States Court of Appeals for the Ninth Circuit denied.

Same case below, 612 Fed. Appx. 439.

No. 15-177. Noatex Corporation, et al., Petitioners v. Auto Parts Manufacturing Mississippi Inc., et al.

577 U.S. 924, 136 S. Ct. 330, 193 L. Ed. 2d 230, 2015 U.S. LEXIS 6392.

October 13, 2015. Petition for writ of certiorari to the United States Court of Appeals for the Fifth Circuit denied.

Same case below, 782 F.3d 186.

No. 15-184. Alan Lee Overton, Petitioner v. Tennessee Department of Children's Services.

577 U.S. 924, 136 S. Ct. 330, 193 L. Ed. 2d 230, 2015 U.S. LEXIS 6517.

October 13, 2015. Petition for writ of certiorari to the Court of Appeals of Tennessee, Eastern Division, denied.

Same case below, 464 S.W.3d 311.

No. 15-190. Ruth Hardin, Personal Representative for Zane Hardin, Petitioner v. Wal-Mart Stores, Inc.

577 U.S. 924, 136 S. Ct. 331, 193 L. Ed. 2d 230, 2015 U.S. LEXIS 6462.

October 13, 2015. Petition for writ of certiorari to the United States Court of Appeals for the Ninth Circuit denied.

Same case below, 604 Fed. Appx. 545.

No. 15-192. Glenn Henderson, Petitioner v. Town of Hope Mills, North Carolina, et al.

577 U.S. 924, 136 S. Ct. 331, 193 L. Ed. 2d 230, 2015 U.S. LEXIS 6416, reh den 577 U.S. 1095, 136 S. Ct. 882, 193 L. Ed. 2d 773, 2016 U.S. LEXIS 582.

October 13, 2015. Petition for writ of certiorari to the United States Court of Appeals for the Fourth Circuit denied.

Same case below, 594 Fed. Appx. 195.

No. 15-207. Lynn A. Van Tassel, Petitioner v. Thomas Piccione, Judge, Court of Common Pleas of Pennsylvania, Lawrence County, et al.

577 U.S. 924, 136 S. Ct. 332, 193 L. Ed. 2d 231, 2015 U.S. LEXIS 6520.

October 13, 2015. Petition for writ of certiorari to the United States Court of Appeals for the Third Circuit denied.

Same case below, 608 Fed. Appx. 66.

No. 15-211. Aaron Hollier, et ux., Individually and as Next Friends of M. H., a minor, and L. H., a minor, Petitioners v. Randy Watson, et al.

577 U.S. 924, 136 S. Ct. 332, 193 L. Ed. 2d 231, 2015 U.S. LEXIS 6565.

October 13, 2015. Petition for writ of certiorari to the United States Court of Appeals for the Fifth Circuit denied.

Same case below, 605 Fed. Appx. 255.

No. 15-212. Jay Marc Harris, Petitioner v. Fiesta Texas, Inc., dba Six Flags-FiestaTexas, et al.

577 U.S. 924, 136 S. Ct. 332, 193 L. Ed. 2d 231, 2015 U.S. LEXIS 6553.

October 13, 2015. Petition for writ of certiorari to the Court of Appeals of Texas, Fourth District, denied.

No. 15-213. Chang Lim, Petitioner v. Terumo Corporation, et al.

577 U.S. 924, 136 S. Ct. 332, 193 L. Ed. 2d 231, 2015 U.S. LEXIS 6582.

October 13, 2015. Petition for writ of certiorari to the United States Court of Appeals for the Sixth Circuit denied.

No. 15-223. E. Frank Cornelius, Petitioner v. Dykema Gossett PLLC Retirement Plan, et al.

577 U.S. 924, 136 S. Ct. 333, 193 L. Ed. 2d 231, 2015 U.S. LEXIS 6534.

October 13, 2015. Petition for writ of certiorari to the United States Court of Appeals for the Sixth Circuit denied.

No. 15-231. David R. Smith, Petitioner v. United States.

577 U.S. 924, 136 S. Ct. 334, 193 L. Ed. 2d 231, 2015 U.S. LEXIS 6427.

October 13, 2015. Petition for writ of certiorari to the United States Court of Appeals for the Federal Circuit denied.

Same case below, 611 Fed. Appx. 1000.

No. 15-246. Maxitrate Tratamento Termico E Controles, et al., Petitioners v. Allianz Seguros S.A., fka AGF Brasil Seguros S.A.

577 U.S. 924, 136 S. Ct. 336, 193 L. Ed. 2d 231, 2015 U.S. LEXIS 6493.

October 13, 2015. Petition for writ of certiorari to the United States Court of Appeals for the Sixth Circuit denied.

Same case below, 617 Fed. Appx. 406.

No. 15-251. Margie McRae, Petitioner v. Matthew Doering, et al.

577 U.S. 924, 136 S. Ct. 338, 193 L. Ed. 2d 232, 2015 U.S. LEXIS 6561.

October 13, 2015. Petition for writ of certiorari to the Court of Appeals of Georgia denied.

No. 15-261. Rossco Holdings, Inc., et al., Petitioners v. Michael McConnell, et al.

577 U.S. 925, 136 S. Ct. 339, 193 L. Ed. 2d 232, 2015 U.S. LEXIS 6518.

October 13, 2015. Petition for writ of certiorari to the United States Court of Appeals for the Fifth Circuit denied.

Same case below, 613 Fed. Appx. 302.

No. 15-271. Samuel Reed, Petitioner v. Kansas.

577 U.S. 925, 136 S. Ct. 344, 193 L. Ed. 2d 232, 2015 U.S. LEXIS 6516.

October 13, 2015. Petition for writ of certiorari to the Supreme Court of Kansas denied.

Same case below, 302 Kan. 227, 352 P.3d 530.

No. 15-275. Jeramiah Chamberlain, Petitioner v. Virginia.

577 U.S. 925, 136 S. Ct. 345, 193 L. Ed. 2d 232, 2015 U.S. LEXIS 6486.

October 13, 2015. Petition for writ of certiorari to the Supreme Court of Virginia denied.

No. 15-279. Kensho Sone, et al., Petitioners v. Harvest Natural Resources, Inc.

577 U.S. 925, 136 S. Ct. 345, 193 L. Ed. 2d 232, 2015 U.S. LEXIS 6558, reh den 577 U.S. 1044, 136 S. Ct. 610, 193 L. Ed. 2d 490, 2015 U.S. LEXIS 7744.

October 13, 2015. Petition for writ of certiorari to the United States Court of Appeals for the Fifth Circuit denied.

Same case below, 605 Fed. Appx. 452.

No. 15-285. Rodney J. Anderson, Petitioner v. United States.

577 U.S. 925, 136 S. Ct. 347, 193 L. Ed. 2d 232, 2015 U.S. LEXIS 6501.

October 13, 2015. Petition for writ of certiorari to the United States Court of Appeals for the Eighth Circuit denied.

Same case below, 783 F.3d 727.

No. 15-309. Jerry D. Kerley, Petitioner v. United States.

577 U.S. 925, 136 S. Ct. 350, 193 L. Ed. 2d 232, 2015 U.S. LEXIS 6443.

October 13, 2015. Petition for writ of certiorari to the United States Court of Appeals for the Sixth Circuit denied.

Same case below, 784 F.3d 327.

No. 15-5137. Norman Scott Allen, Petitioner v. United States.

577 U.S. 925, 136 S. Ct. 319, 193 L. Ed. 2d 232, 2015 U.S. LEXIS 6499.

October 13, 2015. Petition for writ of certiorari to the United States Court of Appeals for the Eighth Circuit denied.

Same case below, 778 F.3d 719.

Same case below, 778 F.3d 586.

No. 15-5140. Jesse Driskill, Petitioner v. Missouri.

577 U.S. 925, 136 S. Ct. 320, 193 L. Ed. 2d 233, 2015 U.S. LEXIS 6468.

October 13, 2015. Petition for writ of certiorari to the Supreme Court of Missouri denied.

Same case below, 459 S.W.3d 412.

No. 15-5474. Kim Raymond Kopatz, Petitioner v. California.

577 U.S. 925, 136 S. Ct. 321, 193 L. Ed. 2d 233, 2015 U.S. LEXIS 6556.

October 13, 2015. Petition for writ of certiorari to the Supreme Court of California denied.

Same case below, 61 Cal. 4th 62, 186 Cal. Rptr. 3d 797, 347 P.3d 952.

No. 15-5479. Twana Fisher, Petitioner v. City of Ironton, Ohio.

577 U.S. 925, 136 S. Ct. 321, 193 L. Ed. 2d 233, 2015 U.S. LEXIS 6475, reh den 577 U.S. 1044, 136 S. Ct. 610, 193 L. Ed. 2d 491, 2015 U.S. LEXIS 7857.

October 13, 2015. Petition for writ of certiorari to the Court of Appeals of Ohio, Lawrence County, denied.

No. 15-5484. Richard Wagoner, Petitioner v. Bruce Lemmon, Commissioner, Indiana Department of Correction, et al.

577 U.S. 925, 136 S. Ct. 321, 193 L. Ed. 2d 233, 2015 U.S. LEXIS 6445.

October 13, 2015. Petition for writ of certiorari to the United States Court of Appeals for the Seventh Circuit denied.

No. 15-5487. Rodney Landers, Petitioner v. Marcia L. Norris.

577 U.S. 925, 136 S. Ct. 321, 193 L. Ed. 2d 233, 2015 U.S. LEXIS 6494.

October 13, 2015. Petition for writ of certiorari to the United States Court of Appeals for the Eleventh Circuit denied.

No. 15-5490. Eliahu Mazin, Petitioner v. Norwood Police Department, et al.

577 U.S. 925, 136 S. Ct. 322, 193 L. Ed. 2d 233, 2015 U.S. LEXIS 6508.

October 13, 2015. Petition for writ of certiorari to the Appeals Court of Massachusetts denied.

Same case below, 86 Mass. App. Ct. 1121, 19 N.E.3d 868.

No. 15-5494. Rejeanne M. Bernier, Petitioner v. Court of Appeal of California, Fourth Appellate District, Division One, et al.

577 U.S. 925, 136 S. Ct. 322, 193 L. Ed. 2d 233, 2015 U.S. LEXIS 6419.

October 13, 2015. Petition for writ of certiorari to the Supreme Court of California denied.

No. 15-5496. Gardell Cowart, Petitioner v. Stu Sherman, Warden.

577 U.S. 926, 136 S. Ct. 322, 193 L. Ed. 2d 233, 2015 U.S. LEXIS 6450, reh den 577 U.S. 1096, 136 S. Ct. 884, 193 L. Ed. 2d 776, 2016 U.S. LEXIS 307.

October 13, 2015. Petition for writ of certiorari to the United States Court of Appeals for the Ninth Circuit denied.

No. 15-5497. James A. Harnage, Petitioner v. Raquel Torres, et al.

577 U.S. 926, 136 S. Ct. 322, 193 L. Ed. 2d 234, 2015 U.S. LEXIS 6403.

October 13, 2015. Petition for writ of certiorari to the Appellate Court of Connecticut denied.

Same case below, 155 Conn. App. 792, 111 A.3d 523.

No. 15-5501. Richard Houswerth, Petitioner v. Julie L. Jones, Secretary, Florida Department of Corrections, et al.

577 U.S. 926, 136 S. Ct. 354, 193 L. Ed. 2d 234, 2015 U.S. LEXIS 6514.

October 13, 2015. Petition for writ of certiorari to the United States Court of Appeals for the Eleventh Circuit denied.

No. 15-5502. J. C. Higginbotham, Petitioner v. Mississippi.

577 U.S. 926, 136 S. Ct. 322, 193 L. Ed. 2d 234, 2015 U.S. LEXIS 6428.

October 13, 2015. Petition for writ of certiorari to the United States Court of Appeals for the Fifth Circuit denied.

No. 15-5505. James A. Harnage, Petitioner v. Jodi M. Rell, et al.

577 U.S. 926, 136 S. Ct. 323, 193 L. Ed. 2d 234, 2015 U.S. LEXIS 6447.

October 13, 2015. Petition for writ of certiorari to the Appellate Court of Connecticut denied.

Same case below, 154 Conn. App. 905, 105 A.3d 367.

No. 15-5512. Gloria Ann Clayton, Petitioner v. Bank of America, et al.

577 U.S. 926, 136 S. Ct. 323, 193 L. Ed. 2d 234, 2015 U.S. LEXIS 6464.

October 13, 2015. Petition for writ of certiorari to the United States Court of Appeals for the Sixth Circuit denied.

No. 15-5513. Kenneth F. Creamer, Petitioner v. Virginia.

577 U.S. 926, 136 S. Ct. 323, 193 L. Ed. 2d 234, 2015 U.S. LEXIS 6418.

October 13, 2015. Petition for writ of certiorari to the Supreme Court of Virginia denied.

No. 15-5520. Therl Taylor, Petitioner v. John R. Pate, Warden.

577 U.S. 926, 136 S. Ct. 323, 193 L. Ed. 2d 234, 2015 U.S. LEXIS 6549.

October 13, 2015. Petition for writ of certiorari to the United States Court of Appeals for the Fourth Circuit denied.

Same case below, 594 Fed. Appx. 186.

No. 15-5521. Anthony Lewis, Petitioner v. American Airlines, Inc.

577 U.S. 926, 136 S. Ct. 323, 193 L. Ed. 2d 234, 2015 U.S. LEXIS 6407.

October 13, 2015. Petition for writ of certiorari to the United States Court of Appeals for the Eighth Circuit denied.

Same case below, 590 Fed. Appx. 653.

No. 15-5522. Antonio Lebaron Melton, Petitioner v. Julie L. Jones, Secretary, Florida Department of Corrections, et al.

577 U.S. 926, 136 S. Ct. 324, 193 L. Ed. 2d 235, 2015 U.S. LEXIS 6444.

October 13, 2015. Petition for writ of certiorari to the United States Court of Appeals for the Eleventh Circuit denied.

No. 15-5524. Kenis Ray Johnson, Petitioner v. Frank L. Perry, Secretary, North Carolina Department of Public Safety.

577 U.S. 926, 136 S. Ct. 324, 193 L. Ed. 2d 235, 2015 U.S. LEXIS 6398.

October 13, 2015. Petition for writ of certiorari to the United States Court of Appeals for the Fourth Circuit denied.

Same case below, 602 Fed. Appx. 128.

No. 15-5525. Miguel Martinez, Petitioner v. Thomas Winn, Warden.

577 U.S. 926, 136 S. Ct. 324, 193 L. Ed. 2d 235, 2015 U.S. LEXIS 6396.

October 13, 2015. Petition for writ of certiorari to the United States Court of Appeals for the Sixth Circuit denied.

No. 15-5526. Herman P. Johnson, Petitioner v. Dushan Zatecky, Superintendent, Pendleton Correctional Facility.

577 U.S. 926, 136 S. Ct. 324, 193 L. Ed. 2d 235, 2015 U.S. LEXIS 6421.

October 13, 2015. Petition for writ of certiorari to the United States Court of Appeals for the Seventh Circuit denied.

No. 15-5528. Thaddeus Johnson, Petitioner v. Tennessee.

577 U.S. 926, 136 S. Ct. 324, 193 L. Ed. 2d 235, 2015 U.S. LEXIS 6404.

October 13, 2015. Petition for writ of certiorari to the Court of Criminal Appeals of Tennessee, Western Division, denied.

No. 15-5541. Walter J. Bramage, Petitioner v. Discover Bank.

577 U.S. 927, 136 S. Ct. 325, 193 L. Ed. 2d 235, 2015 U.S. LEXIS 6513, reh den 577 U.S. 1044, 136 S. Ct. 610, 193 L. Ed. 2d 491, 2015 U.S. LEXIS 7854.

October 13, 2015. Petition for writ of certiorari to the Court of Appeals of Indiana, Fourth District, denied.

Same case below, 16 N.E.3d 1039.

No. 15-5542. Jerry Neil Alfred, Petitioner v. Julie L. Jones, Secretary, Florida Department of Corrections, et al.

577 U.S. 927, 136 S. Ct. 325, 193 L. Ed. 2d 235, 2015 U.S. LEXIS 6440, reh den 577 U.S. 1096, 136 S. Ct. 885, 193 L. Ed. 2d 776, 2016 U.S. LEXIS 509.

October 13, 2015. Petition for writ of certiorari to the United States Court of Appeals for the Eleventh Circuit denied.

No. 15-5546. Loren Reyna, Petitioner v. Darin Young, Warden, et al.

577 U.S. 927, 136 S. Ct. 325, 193 L. Ed. 2d 236, 2015 U.S. LEXIS 6527.

October 13, 2015. Petition for writ of certiorari to the United States Court of Appeals for the Eighth Circuit denied.

Same case below, 597 Fed. Appx. 401.

No. 15-5550. Carey Abney, Petitioner v. Court of Common Pleas of Pennsylvania, First Judicial District, et al.

577 U.S. 927, 136 S. Ct. 325, 193 L. Ed. 2d 236, 2015 U.S. LEXIS 6483.

October 13, 2015. Petition for writ of certiorari to the Supreme Court of Pennsylvania, Eastern District, denied.

Same case below, 631 Pa. 602, 114 A.3d 1035.

No. 15-5552. Cash Wallace Pawley, Petitioner v. Florida.

577 U.S. 927, 136 S. Ct. 326, 193 L. Ed. 2d 236, 2015 U.S. LEXIS 6533.

October 13, 2015. Petition for writ of certiorari to the District Court of Appeal of Florida, Third District, denied.

Same case below, 166 So. 3d 792.

No. 15-5553. Steve Skinner, Petitioner v. Debra K. Johnson, Warden.

577 U.S. 927, 136 S. Ct. 326, 193 L. Ed. 2d 236, 2015 U.S. LEXIS 6433.

October 13, 2015. Petition for writ of certiorari to the United States Court of Appeals for the Sixth Circuit denied.

No. 15-5555. Bobby L. Magwood, Petitioner v. Florida.

577 U.S. 927, 136 S. Ct. 326, 193 L. Ed. 2d 236, 2015 U.S. LEXIS 6463.

October 13, 2015. Petition for writ of certiorari to the District Court of Appeal of Florida, First District, denied.

Same case below, 162 So. 3d 991.

No. 15-5556. Yvette Castaneda, Petitioner v. Margaret Burton-Cahill, et al.

577 U.S. 927, 136 S. Ct. 326, 193 L. Ed. 2d 236, 2015 U.S. LEXIS 6439.

October 13, 2015. Petition for writ of certiorari to the United States Court of Appeals for the Ninth Circuit denied.

Same case below, 586 Fed. Appx. 373.

No. 15-5558. Michael Donofrio, Petitioner v. New York.

577 U.S. 927, 136 S. Ct. 326, 193 L. Ed. 2d 236, 2015 U.S. LEXIS 6537.

October 13, 2015. Petition for writ of certiorari to the Appellate Division, Supreme Court of New York, Second Judicial Department, denied.

Same case below, 123 App. Div. 3d 941, 1 N.Y.S.3d 127.

No. 15-5562. Thomas Powers, Petitioner v. Wexford Health Services, et al.

577 U.S. 927, 136 S. Ct. 327, 193 L. Ed. 2d 236, 2015 U.S. LEXIS 6459.

October 13, 2015. Petition for writ of certiorari to the United States Court of Appeals for the Seventh Circuit denied.

Same case below, 163 So. 3d 507.

No. 15-5567. David F. Petrano, et ux., Petitioners v. Nationwide Mutual Fire Insurance Company, et al.

577 U.S. 927, 136 S. Ct. 327, 193 L. Ed. 2d 237, 2015 U.S. LEXIS 6575.

October 13, 2015. Petition for writ of certiorari to the United States Court of Appeals for the Eleventh Circuit denied.

Same case below, 590 Fed. Appx. 927.

No. 15-5568. Franklin H. Wright, Petitioner v. United States Interagency Council on Homelessness, et al.

577 U.S. 927, 136 S. Ct. 327, 193 L. Ed. 2d 237, 2015 U.S. LEXIS 6546, reh den 577 U.S. 1024, 136 S. Ct. 580, 193 L. Ed. 2d 463, 2015 U.S. LEXIS 7432.

October 13, 2015. Petition for writ of certiorari to the United States Court of Appeals for the Ninth Circuit denied.

No. 15-5570. Garceia Coleman, Petitioner v. Bryan Bartow, Director, Wisconsin Resource Center.

577 U.S. 927, 136 S. Ct. 327, 193 L. Ed. 2d 237, 2015 U.S. LEXIS 6426.

October 13, 2015. Petition for writ of certiorari to the United States Court of Appeals for the Seventh Circuit denied.

No. 15-5571. Norman E. Caison, Petitioner v. Julie L. Jones, Secretary, Florida Department of Corrections.

577 U.S. 927, 136 S. Ct. 327, 193 L. Ed. 2d 237, 2015 U.S. LEXIS 6592.

October 13, 2015. Petition for writ of certiorari to the Supreme Court of Florida denied.

No. 15-5572. Eric Raymond Crowell, aka Eric Raymond Carter, Petitioner v. Harold W. Clarke, Director, Virginia Department of Corrections.

577 U.S. 928, 136 S. Ct. 327, 193 L. Ed. 2d 237, 2015 U.S. LEXIS 6424.

October 13, 2015. Petition for writ of certiorari to the Supreme Court of Virginia denied.

No. 15-5573. Eric Raymond Crowell, aka Eric Raymond Carter, Petitioner v. Harold W. Clarke, Director, Virginia Department of Corrections.

577 U.S. 928, 136 S. Ct. 354, 193 L. Ed. 2d 237, 2015 U.S. LEXIS 6420.

October 13, 2015. Petition for writ of certiorari to the United States Court of Appeals for the Fourth Circuit denied.

Same case below, 594 Fed. Appx. 213.

No. 15-5590. Pauline Moody, Petitioner v. City of Delray Beach, Florida, et al.

577 U.S. 928, 136 S. Ct. 328, 193 L. Ed. 2d 237, 2015 U.S. LEXIS 6425, reh den 577 U.S. 1045, 136 S. Ct. 610, 193 L. Ed. 2d 491, 2015 U.S. LEXIS 7736.

October 13, 2015. Petition for writ of certiorari to the United States Court of Appeals for the Eleventh Circuit denied.

Same case below, 609 Fed. Appx. 966.

Same case below, 575 Fed. Appx. 173.

No. 15-5591. Richard W. McCarthy, Petitioner v. Florida.

577 U.S. 928, 136 S. Ct. 328, 193 L. Ed. 2d 238, 2015 U.S. LEXIS 6438.

October 13, 2015. Petition for writ of certiorari to the District Court of Appeal of Florida, Second District, denied.

Same case below, 163 So. 3d 1197.

No. 15-5594. Wade W. Bell, Petitioner v. Virginia Natural Gas, Inc.

577 U.S. 928, 136 S. Ct. 328, 193 L. Ed. 2d 238, 2015 U.S. LEXIS 6588.

October 13, 2015. Petition for writ of certiorari to the Supreme Court of Virginia denied.

No. 15-5596. Daniel J. Bakalik, Petitioner v. Pat Quinn, et al.

577 U.S. 928, 136 S. Ct. 328, 193 L. Ed. 2d 238, 2015 U.S. LEXIS 6414.

October 13, 2015. Petition for writ of certiorari to the United States Court of Appeals for the Seventh Circuit denied.

No. 15-5597. Brandon Michael Pickens, Petitioner v. Brad Perritt, Superintendent, Lumberton Correctional Institution.

577 U.S. 928, 136 S. Ct. 329, 193 L. Ed. 2d 238, 2015 U.S. LEXIS 6395, reh den 577 U.S. 1096, 136 S. Ct. 885, 193 L. Ed. 2d 777, 2016 U.S. LEXIS 468.

October 13, 2015. Petition for writ of certiorari to the United States Court of Appeals for the Fourth Circuit denied.

No. 15-5599. Carlos Jessie Ramirez, Petitioner v. California.

577 U.S. 928, 136 S. Ct. 329, 193 L. Ed. 2d 238, 2015 U.S. LEXIS 6506.

October 13, 2015. Petition for writ of certiorari to the Court of Appeal of California, Sixth Appellate District, denied.

No. 15-5600. Marlon L. Watford, Petitioner v. Pat Quinn.

577 U.S. 928, 136 S. Ct. 329, 193 L. Ed. 2d 238, 2015 U.S. LEXIS 6594.

October 13, 2015. Petition for writ of certiorari to the United States Court of Appeals for the Seventh Circuit denied.

No. 15-5602. Isaac Fermin Arriaga, Petitioner v. Jeffrey Beard, Secretary, California Department of Corrections and Rehabilitation.

577 U.S. 928, 136 S. Ct. 329, 193 L. Ed. 2d 238, 2015 U.S. LEXIS 6470.

October 13, 2015. Petition for writ of certiorari to the United States Court of Appeals for the Ninth Circuit denied.

No. 15-5603. Beulah Davis, Petitioner v. Carolyn W. Colvin, Acting Commissioner of Social Security.

577 U.S. 928, 136 S. Ct. 330, 193 L. Ed. 2d 238, 2015 U.S. LEXIS 6547.

October 13, 2015. Petition for writ of certiorari to the United States Court of Appeals for the Fifth Circuit denied.

Same case below, 600 Fed. Appx. 249.

No. 15-5609. Arrie Frank Roberts, Petitioner v. Florida.

577 U.S. 928, 136 S. Ct. 330, 193 L. Ed. 2d 239, 2015 U.S. LEXIS 6566.

October 13, 2015. Petition for writ of certiorari to the District Court of Appeal of Florida, First District, denied.

Same case below, 166 So. 3d 774.

No. 15-5614. Gregg McNamara, Petitioner v. California.

577 U.S. 928, 136 S. Ct. 355, 193 L. Ed. 2d 239, 2015 U.S. LEXIS 6412.

October 13, 2015. Petition for writ of certiorari to the Court of Appeal of California, Second Appellate District, Division Two, denied.

No. 15-5615. Malachy DeHenre, Petitioner v. Mississippi, et al.

577 U.S. 928, 136 S. Ct. 330, 193 L. Ed. 2d 239, 2015 U.S. LEXIS 6394.

October 13, 2015. Petition for writ of certiorari to the United States Court of Appeals for the Fifth Circuit denied.

No. 15-5616. Morris Dean Davis, Petitioner v. Arkansas.

577 U.S. 929, 136 S. Ct. 330, 193 L. Ed. 2d 239, 2015 U.S. LEXIS 6568.

October 13, 2015. Petition for writ of certiorari to the Supreme Court of Arkansas denied.

Same case below, 2015 Ark. 122.

No. 15-5621. Victor Barrera, Petitioner v. Industrial Claim Appeals Office of Colorado, et al.

577 U.S. 929, 136 S. Ct. 331, 193 L. Ed. 2d 239, 2015 U.S. LEXIS 6466.

October 13, 2015. Petition for writ of certiorari to the Court of Appeals of Colorado denied.

No. 15-5622. Terence O'Neal Boyd, Petitioner v. Mississippi.

577 U.S. 929, 136 S. Ct. 331, 193 L. Ed. 2d 239, 2015 U.S. LEXIS 6417, reh den 577 U.S. 1096, 136 S. Ct. 885, 193 L. Ed. 2d 777, 2016 U.S. LEXIS 585.

October 13, 2015. Petition for writ of certiorari to the Supreme Court of Mississippi denied.

No. 15-5623. Pamela Bond, Petitioner v. Department of Education.

577 U.S. 929, 136 S. Ct. 331, 193 L. Ed. 2d 239, 2015 U.S. LEXIS 6405.

October 13, 2015. Petition for writ of certiorari to the United States Court of Appeals for the Fourth Circuit denied.

Same case below, 588 Fed. Appx. 293.

No. 15-5640. Joseph Osmond Danihel, Petitioner v. Office of the President of the United States, et al.

577 U.S. 929, 136 S. Ct. 331, 193 L. Ed. 2d 239, 2015 U.S. LEXIS 6523.

October 13, 2015. Petition for writ of certiorari to the United States Court of Appeals for the Third Circuit denied.

Same case below, 616 Fed. Appx. 467.

No. 15-5641. Charles Chukwumeze Eleri, aka Charles C. Eleri, Petitioner v. James D. Hartley, Warden.

577 U.S. 929, 136 S. Ct. 332, 193 L. Ed. 2d 240, 2015 U.S. LEXIS 6436, reh den 577 U.S. 1054, 136 S. Ct. 706, 193 L. Ed. 2d 532, 2015 U.S. LEXIS 7899.

October 13, 2015. Petition for writ of certiorari to the United States Court of Appeals for the Ninth Circuit denied.

No. 15-5655. Maurice Vernon, Petitioner v. United States.

577 U.S. 929, 136 S. Ct. 333, 193 L. Ed. 2d 240, 2015 U.S. LEXIS 6409.

October 13, 2015. Petition for writ of certiorari to the United States Court of Appeals for the Eleventh Circuit denied.

Same case below, 593 Fed. Appx. 883.

No. 15-5663. Juan Antonio Partida-Rodriguez, Petitioner v. Frank Perry.

577 U.S. 929, 136 S. Ct. 333, 193 L. Ed. 2d 240, 2015 U.S. LEXIS 6485.

October 13, 2015. Petition for writ of certiorari to the United States Court of Appeals for the Fourth Circuit denied.

Same case below, 600 Fed. Appx. 103.

No. 15-5665. Lawrence Udukobraye Pela, Petitioner v. John N. Katavich, Warden.

577 U.S. 929, 136 S. Ct. 333, 193 L. Ed. 2d 240, 2015 U.S. LEXIS 6441.

October 13, 2015. Petition for writ of certiorari to the United States Court of Appeals for the Ninth Circuit denied.

No. 15-5672. James David Ofeldt, Petitioner v. James G. Cox, Director, Nevada Department of Corrections, et al.

577 U.S. 929, 136 S. Ct. 333, 193 L. Ed. 2d 240, 2015 U.S. LEXIS 6492.

October 13, 2015. Petition for writ of certiorari to the United States Court of Appeals for the Ninth Circuit denied.

Same case below, 603 Fed. Appx. 619.

No. 15-5675. Shelby Anthony Vogt, Petitioner v. Iowa State Penitentiary, et al.

577 U.S. 929, 136 S. Ct. 334, 193 L. Ed. 2d 240, 2015 U.S. LEXIS 6408, reh den 577 U.S. 998, 136 S. Ct. 529, 193 L. Ed. 2d 417, 2015 U.S. LEXIS 7294.

October 13, 2015. Petition for writ of certiorari to the United States Court of Appeals for the Eighth Circuit denied.

No. 15-5676. Shawn Michael Wagner, Petitioner v. Willie Smith, Warden.

577 U.S. 929, 136 S. Ct. 334, 193 L. Ed. 2d 240, 2015 U.S. LEXIS 6567.

October 13, 2015. Petition for writ of certiorari to the United States Court of Appeals for the Sixth Circuit denied.

No. 15-5680. Larry E. Clark, Petitioner v. United States District Court for the Western District of Louisiana.

577 U.S. 929, 136 S. Ct. 355, 193 L. Ed. 2d 240, 2015 U.S. LEXIS 6478.

October 13, 2015. Petition for writ of certiorari to the United States Court of Appeals for the Fifth Circuit denied.

No. 15-5681. Rickey Lee Sabin, Petitioners v. Ernest Trujillo, et al.

577 U.S. 929, 136 S. Ct. 334, 193 L. Ed. 2d 241, 2015 U.S. LEXIS 6584.

October 13, 2015. Petition for writ of certiorari to the United States Court of Appeals for the Ninth Circuit denied.

No. 15-5707. Deloris Phillips, Petitioner v. Texas Department of Public Safety.

577 U.S. 929, 136 S. Ct. 334, 193 L. Ed. 2d 241, 2015 U.S. LEXIS 6480, reh den 577 U.S. 1231, 136 S. Ct. 1487, 194 L. Ed. 2d 578, 2016 U.S. LEXIS 1912.

October 13, 2015. Petition for writ of certiorari to the Supreme Court of Texas denied.

No. 15-5726. Wendell Duncan, aka Wendell Avery Duncan, Petitioner v. Mississippi.

577 U.S. 930, 136 S. Ct. 334, 193 L. Ed. 2d 241, 2015 U.S. LEXIS 6532.

October 13, 2015. Petition for writ of certiorari to the Court of Appeals of Mississippi denied.

Same case below, 170 So. 3d 579.

No. 15-5727. Raid Elfadly, Petitioner v. Carolyn W. Colvin, Acting Commissioner of Social Security.

577 U.S. 930, 136 S. Ct. 335, 193 L. Ed. 2d 241, 2015 U.S. LEXIS 6505.

October 13, 2015. Petition for writ of certiorari to the United States Court of Appeals for the Third Circuit denied.

Same case below, 588 Fed. Appx. 93.

No. 15-5747. Charles Todd Clugston, Petitioner v. Mike Batista, Director, Montana Department of Corrections, et al.

577 U.S. 930, 136 S. Ct. 335, 193 L. Ed. 2d 241, 2015 U.S. LEXIS 6473, reh den 577 U.S. 1045, 136 S. Ct. 611, 193 L. Ed. 2d 491, 2015 U.S. LEXIS 7803.

October 13, 2015. Petition for writ of certiorari to the United States Court of Appeals for the Ninth Circuit denied.

No. 15-5763. Derryel Lee, Petitioner v. Jeff Premo, Superintendent, Oregon State Penitentiary.

577 U.S. 930, 136 S. Ct. 355, 193 L. Ed. 2d 241, 2015 U.S. LEXIS 6497.

October 13, 2015. Petition for writ of certiorari to the United States Court of Appeals for the Ninth Circuit denied.

Same case below, 613 Fed. Appx. 566.

No. 15-5772. Edward Thomas Kendrick, III, Petitioner v. Tennessee.

577 U.S. 930, 136 S. Ct. 335, 193 L. Ed. 2d 241, 2015 U.S. LEXIS 6487.

October 13, 2015. Petition for writ of certiorari to the Supreme Court of Tennessee, Eastern Division, denied.

Same case below, 454 S.W.3d 450.

No. 15-5784. John D. Stanton, III, Petitioner v. United States.

577 U.S. 930, 136 S. Ct. 335, 193 L. Ed. 2d 241, 2015 U.S. LEXIS 6560.

October 13, 2015. Petition for writ of certiorari to the United States Court of Appeals for the Eleventh Circuit denied.

Same case below, 579 Fed. Appx. 982.

———

No. 15-5790. Dawna Valentine, Petitioner v. JPMorgan Chase Bank, N.A.

577 U.S. 930, 136 S. Ct. 336, 193 L. Ed. 2d 242, 2015 U.S. LEXIS 6430.

October 13, 2015. Petition for writ of certiorari to the United States Court of Appeals for the Fifth Circuit denied.

———

No. 15-5803. John Nelson, Petitioner v. Kathleen Kane, Attorney General of Pennsylvania, et al.

577 U.S. 930, 136 S. Ct. 336, 193 L. Ed. 2d 242, 2015 U.S. LEXIS 6500.

October 13, 2015. Petition for writ of certiorari to the United States Court of Appeals for the Third Circuit denied.

———

No. 15-5817. D'Angelo Domingo Davis, aka D'Angelo Dominico Davis, Petitioner v. United States.

577 U.S. 930, 136 S. Ct. 336, 193 L. Ed. 2d 242, 2015 U.S. LEXIS 6460.

October 13, 2015. Petition for writ of certiorari to the United States Court of Appeals for the Ninth Circuit denied.

———

No. 15-5818. Jorge Correa-Osorio, Petitioner v. United States.

577 U.S. 930, 136 S. Ct. 336, 193 L. Ed. 2d 242, 2015 U.S. LEXIS 6531.

October 13, 2015. Petition for writ of certiorari to the United States Court of Appeals for the First Circuit denied.

Same case below, 784 F.3d 11.

———

No. 15-5821. Michael Carlton Lowe, Sr., Petitioner v. Minnesota.

577 U.S. 930, 136 S. Ct. 337, 193 L. Ed. 2d 242, 2015 U.S. LEXIS 6456.

October 13, 2015. Petition for writ of certiorari to the Court of Appeals of Minnesota denied.

———

No. 15-5822. Muhammed Nasiru Usman, Petitioner v. United States.

577 U.S. 930, 136 S. Ct. 337, 193 L. Ed. 2d 242, 2015 U.S. LEXIS 6550.

October 13, 2015. Petition for writ of certiorari to the United States Court of Appeals for the Fifth Circuit denied.

———

No. 15-5829. John E. Barrington, Petitioner v. Michael Babcock, Warden, et al.

577 U.S. 930, 136 S. Ct. 337, 193 L. Ed. 2d 242, 2015 U.S. LEXIS 6469.

October 13, 2015. Petition for writ of certiorari to the United States Court of Appeals for the Ninth Circuit denied.

Same case below, 585 Fed. Appx. 698.

No. 15-5830. Patrick Smith, Petitioner v. Brian Fischer, Commissioner, New York Department of Corrections and Community Supervision.

577 U.S. 930, 136 S. Ct. 337, 193 L. Ed. 2d 243, 2015 U.S. LEXIS 6434.

October 13, 2015. Petition for writ of certiorari to the United States Court of Appeals for the Second Circuit denied.

Same case below, 780 F.3d 556.

No. 15-5831. Daniel Nunez, Petitioner v. United States.

577 U.S. 931, 136 S. Ct. 338, 193 L. Ed. 2d 243, 2015 U.S. LEXIS 6590.

October 13, 2015. Petition for writ of certiorari to the United States Court of Appeals for the Fifth Circuit denied.

Same case below, 604 Fed. Appx. 353.

No. 15-5833. Earl William Freeman, Petitioner v. United States.

577 U.S. 931, 136 S. Ct. 338, 193 L. Ed. 2d 243, 2015 U.S. LEXIS 6496.

October 13, 2015. Petition for writ of certiorari to the United States Court of Appeals for the Eighth Circuit denied.

Same case below, 611 Fed. Appx. 886.

No. 15-5836. Donnell Young, Petitioner v. United States.

577 U.S. 931, 136 S. Ct. 338, 193 L. Ed. 2d 243, 2015 U.S. LEXIS 6522.

October 13, 2015. Petition for writ of certiorari to the United States Court of Appeals for the Sixth Circuit denied.

No. 15-5838. David Arturo Martinez-Montalvo, Petitioner v. United States.

577 U.S. 931, 136 S. Ct. 338, 193 L. Ed. 2d 243, 2015 U.S. LEXIS 6554.

October 13, 2015. Petition for writ of certiorari to the United States Court of Appeals for the Fifth Circuit denied.

Same case below, 604 Fed. Appx. 345.

No. 15-5841. Thomas W. Qualls, Petitioner v. United States.

577 U.S. 931, 136 S. Ct. 338, 193 L. Ed. 2d 243, 2015 U.S. LEXIS 6432.

October 13, 2015. Petition for writ of certiorari to the United States Court of Appeals for the Second Circuit denied.

Same case below, 613 Fed. Appx. 25.

No. 15-5843. Richard Enyart, Petitioner v. Ronald Erdos, Warden.

577 U.S. 931, 136 S. Ct. 339, 193 L. Ed. 2d 243, 2015 U.S. LEXIS 6503.

October 13, 2015. Petition for writ of certiorari to the United States Court of Appeals for the Sixth Circuit denied.

No. 15-5844. Santos Diaz-Soto, aka Jason A. Duran-Mejia, Petitioner v. United States.

577 U.S. 931, 136 S. Ct. 339, 193 L. Ed. 2d 243, 2015 U.S. LEXIS 6559.

October 13, 2015. Petition for writ of certiorari to the United States Court of Appeals for the Fifth Circuit denied.

Same case below, 599 Fed. Appx. 154.

No. 15-5848. Keith Bryant Webb, Petitioner v. United States.

577 U.S. 931, 136 S. Ct. 339, 193 L. Ed. 2d 244, 2015 U.S. LEXIS 6580, reh den 577 U.S. 998, 136 S. Ct. 529, 193 L. Ed. 2d 417, 2015 U.S. LEXIS 7179.

October 13, 2015. Petition for writ of certiorari to the United States Court of Appeals for the Fifth Circuit denied.

No. 15-5849. Anthony Watson, Petitioner v. United States.

577 U.S. 931, 136 S. Ct. 339, 193 L. Ed. 2d 244, 2015 U.S. LEXIS 6512.

October 13, 2015. Petition for writ of certiorari to the United States Court of Appeals for the Fourth Circuit denied.

Same case below, 592 Fed. Appx. 213.

No. 15-5852. Randy Lavern Spencer, Petitioner v. R.P. Tifft, Warden, et al.

577 U.S. 931, 136 S. Ct. 339, 193 L. Ed. 2d 244, 2015 U.S. LEXIS 6511.

October 13, 2015. Petition for writ of certiorari to the United States Court of Appeals for the Eleventh Circuit denied.

No. 15-5855. Edgar Keaton Martin, Petitioner v. United States.

577 U.S. 931, 136 S. Ct. 340, 193 L. Ed. 2d 244, 2015 U.S. LEXIS 6467, reh den 577 U.S. 1114, 136 S. Ct. 925, 193 L. Ed. 2d 810, 2016 U.S. LEXIS 643.

October 13, 2015. Petition for writ of certiorari to the United States Court of Appeals for the Eighth Circuit denied.

No. 15-5857. Ernest Cornelius Williams, Petitioner v. Cindy Griffith, Warden.

577 U.S. 931, 136 S. Ct. 340, 193 L. Ed. 2d 244, 2015 U.S. LEXIS 6406.

October 13, 2015. Petition for writ of certiorari to the United States Court of Appeals for the Eighth Circuit denied.

No. 15-5859. David B. Leverette, Petitioner v. Florida.

577 U.S. 931, 136 S. Ct. 340, 193 L. Ed. 2d 244, 2015 U.S. LEXIS 6593.

October 13, 2015. Petition for writ of certiorari to the District Court of Appeal of Florida, Second District, denied.

Same case below, 174 So. 3d 1004.

No. 15-5861. John Andries Bal, Jr., Petitioner v. ITEX Corporation, et al.

577 U.S. 931, 136 S. Ct. 340, 193 L. Ed. 2d 244, 2015 U.S. LEXIS 6509.

October 13, 2015. Petition for writ of certiorari to the United States Court of Appeals for the Second Circuit denied.

No. 15-5862. Kevin Bartholomew, Petitioner v. A. F. Muhammad, et al.

577 U.S. 931, 136 S. Ct. 340, 193 L. Ed. 2d 244, 2015 U.S. LEXIS 6530.

October 13, 2015. Petition for writ of certiorari to the United States Court of Appeals for the Ninth Circuit denied.

Same case below, 599 Fed. Appx. 313.

Same case below, 166 So. 3d 769.

No. 15-5863. Tony Vines, Jr., Petitioner v. United States.

577 U.S. 931, 136 S. Ct. 340, 193 L. Ed. 2d 245, 2015 U.S. LEXIS 6574.

October 13, 2015. Petition for writ of certiorari to the United States Court of Appeals for the Fourth Circuit denied.

Same case below, 594 Fed. Appx. 158.

No. 15-5871. John Michael Bray, Petitioner v. Jeff Premo, Superintendent, Oregon State Penitentiary.

577 U.S. 932, 136 S. Ct. 341, 193 L. Ed. 2d 245, 2015 U.S. LEXIS 6397.

October 13, 2015. Petition for writ of certiorari to the United States Court of Appeals for the Ninth Circuit denied.

Same case below, 605 Fed. Appx. 631.

No. 15-5872. Jared Thomas Bowers, Petitioner v. United States.

577 U.S. 932, 136 S. Ct. 341, 193 L. Ed. 2d 245, 2015 U.S. LEXIS 6410.

October 13, 2015. Petition for writ of certiorari to the United States Court of Appeals for the Ninth Circuit denied.

Same case below, 611 Fed. Appx. 407.

No. 15-5873. Dennis Creamer, Petitioner v. Florida Commission on Offender Review.

577 U.S. 932, 136 S. Ct. 341, 193 L. Ed. 2d 245, 2015 U.S. LEXIS 6498.

October 13, 2015. Petition for writ of certiorari to the District Court of Appeal of Florida, First District, denied.

No. 15-5876. Pedro Soto, Petitioner v. United States.

577 U.S. 932, 136 S. Ct. 341, 193 L. Ed. 2d 245, 2015 U.S. LEXIS 6570.

October 13, 2015. Petition for writ of certiorari to the United States Court of Appeals for the First Circuit denied.

Same case below, 799 F.3d 68.

No. 15-5877. Jerome Totten, Petitioner v. Mississippi.

577 U.S. 932, 136 S. Ct. 355, 193 L. Ed. 2d 245, 2015 U.S. LEXIS 6595.

October 13, 2015. Petition for writ of certiorari to the Supreme Court of Mississippi denied.

Same case below, 166 So. 3d 32.

No. 15-5881. Jeffery White, Petitioner v. United States.

577 U.S. 932, 136 S. Ct. 341, 193 L. Ed. 2d 245, 2015 U.S. LEXIS 6465.

October 13, 2015. Petition for writ of certiorari to the United States Court of Appeals for the Sixth Circuit denied.

Same case below, 617 Fed. Appx. 545.

No. 15-5883. Julie Choi, Petitioner v. United States.

577 U.S. 932, 136 S. Ct. 341, 193 L. Ed. 2d 245, 2015 U.S. LEXIS 6540.

October 13, 2015. Petition for writ of certiorari to the United States Court of Appeals for the Ninth Circuit denied.

Same case below, 613 Fed. Appx. 597.

No. 15-5885. Gregory Brent Christian, Petitioner v. Marvin Plumley, Warden.

577 U.S. 932, 136 S. Ct. 342, 193 L. Ed. 2d 246, 2015 U.S. LEXIS 6529.

October 13, 2015. Petition for writ of certiorari to the United States Court of Appeals for the Fourth Circuit denied.

Same case below, 792 F.3d 427.

No. 15-5887. Maria Lourdes Moe, Petitioner v. United States.

577 U.S. 932, 136 S. Ct. 342, 193 L. Ed. 2d 246, 2015 U.S. LEXIS 6458.

October 13, 2015. Petition for writ of certiorari to the United States Court of Appeals for the Ninth Circuit denied.

Same case below, 781 F.3d 1120.

No. 15-5888. Mark A. Baine, Petitioner v. Dewayne Estes, Warden.

577 U.S. 932, 136 S. Ct. 342, 193 L. Ed. 2d 246, 2015 U.S. LEXIS 6519.

October 13, 2015. Petition for writ of certiorari to the United States Court of Appeals for the Eleventh Circuit denied.

No. 15-5889. Zane Balsam, Petitioner v. United States.

577 U.S. 932, 136 S. Ct. 342, 193 L. Ed. 2d 246, 2015 U.S. LEXIS 6484, reh den 577 U.S. 1096, 136 S. Ct. 887, 193 L. Ed. 2d 779, 2016 U.S. LEXIS 562.

October 13, 2015. Petition for writ of certiorari to the United States Court of Appeals for the Eleventh Circuit denied.

No. 15-5891. Shuntrell Jones, Petitioner v. United States.

577 U.S. 932, 136 S. Ct. 342, 193 L. Ed. 2d 246, 2015 U.S. LEXIS 6461, reh den 577 U.S. 1096, 136 S. Ct. 887, 193 L. Ed. 2d 779, 2016 U.S. LEXIS 571.

October 13, 2015. Petition for writ of certiorari to the United States Court of Appeals for the Sixth Circuit denied.

No. 15-5892. Maurice Charles Maxwell, Petitioner v. United States.

577 U.S. 932, 136 S. Ct. 342, 193 L. Ed. 2d 246, 2015 U.S. LEXIS 6442.

October 13, 2015. Petition for writ of certiorari to the United States Court of Appeals for the Tenth Circuit denied.

Same case below, 613 Fed. Appx. 740.

No. 15-5893. Jose Marquez, Petitioner v. United States.

577 U.S. 932, 136 S. Ct. 343, 193 L. Ed. 2d 246, 2015 U.S. LEXIS 6446.

October 13, 2015. Petition for writ of certiorari to the United States Court of Appeals for the Fifth Circuit denied.

No. 15-5896. Shaddy Whittaker, Petitioner v. United States.

577 U.S. 932, 136 S. Ct. 343, 193 L. Ed. 2d 246, 2015 U.S. LEXIS 6525.

October 13, 2015. Petition for writ of certiorari to the United States Court of Appeals for the Eleventh Circuit denied.

No. 15-5897. Shaddy Whittaker, Petitioner v. United States.

577 U.S. 933, 136 S. Ct. 343, 193 L. Ed. 2d 247, 2015 U.S. LEXIS 6551.

October 13, 2015. Petition for writ of certiorari to the United States Court of Appeals for the Eleventh Circuit denied.

No. 15-5899. Fortino Elenes, Jr., Petitioner v. United States.

577 U.S. 933, 136 S. Ct. 343, 193 L. Ed. 2d 247, 2015 U.S. LEXIS 6429.

October 13, 2015. Petition for writ of certiorari to the United States Court of Appeals for the Ninth Circuit denied.

Same case below, 591 Fed. Appx. 562.

No. 15-5902. James P. Burg, Petitioner v. United States.

577 U.S. 933, 136 S. Ct. 343, 193 L. Ed. 2d 247, 2015 U.S. LEXIS 6472.

October 13, 2015. Petition for writ of certiorari to the United States Court of Appeals for the Tenth Circuit denied.

Same case below, 605 Fed. Appx. 724.

No. 15-5909. William C. Lanham, Petitioner v. United States.

577 U.S. 933, 136 S. Ct. 344, 193 L. Ed. 2d 247, 2015 U.S. LEXIS 6583.

October 13, 2015. Petition for writ of certiorari to the United States Court of Appeals for the Sixth Circuit denied.

No. 15-5911. Jean Mari Lindor, Petitioner v. United States.

577 U.S. 933, 136 S. Ct. 344, 193 L. Ed. 2d 247, 2015 U.S. LEXIS 6589, reh den 577 U.S. 1045, 136 S. Ct. 611, 193 L. Ed. 2d 492, 2015 U.S. LEXIS 7848.

October 13, 2015. Petition for writ of certiorari to the United States Court of Appeals for the Eleventh Circuit denied.

Same case below, 613 Fed. Appx. 777.

No. 15-5913. Marcus Hahn, Petitioner v. United States.

577 U.S. 933, 136 S. Ct. 344, 193 L. Ed. 2d 247, 2015 U.S. LEXIS 6555.

October 13, 2015. Petition for writ of certiorari to the United States Court of Appeals for the Tenth Circuit denied.

No. 15-5922. Katarie Sahndal Prince Leake, Petitioner v. United States.

577 U.S. 933, 136 S. Ct. 345, 193 L. Ed. 2d 247, 2015 U.S. LEXIS 6479.

October 13, 2015. Petition for writ of certiorari to the United States Court of Appeals for the Fourth Circuit denied.

Same case below, 604 Fed. Appx. 313.

No. 15-5931. Alexis Amador-Huggins, Petitioner v. United States.

577 U.S. 933, 136 S. Ct. 345, 193 L. Ed. 2d 247, 2015 U.S. LEXIS 6562.

October 13, 2015. Petition for writ of certiorari to the United States Court of Appeals for the First Circuit denied.

Same case below, 799 F.3d 124.

No. 15-5936. James Whitfield, Petitioner v. Julie L. Jones, Secretary, Florida Department of Corrections, et al.

577 U.S. 933, 136 S. Ct. 346, 193 L. Ed. 2d 248, 2015 U.S. LEXIS 6587.

October 13, 2015. Petition for writ of certiorari to the United States Court of Appeals for the Eleventh Circuit denied.

No. 15-5937. Kareem Milhouse, Petitioner v. United States.

577 U.S. 933, 136 S. Ct. 346, 193 L. Ed. 2d 248, 2015 U.S. LEXIS 6474.

October 13, 2015. Petition for writ of certiorari to the United States Court of Appeals for the Third Circuit denied.

Same case below, 605 Fed. Appx. 83.

No. 15-5938. David Joseph Rezendes, Petitioner v. United States.

577 U.S. 933, 136 S. Ct. 346, 193 L. Ed. 2d 248, 2015 U.S. LEXIS 6415.

October 13, 2015. Petition for writ of certiorari to the United States Court of Appeals for the Tenth Circuit denied.

Same case below, 605 Fed. Appx. 744.

No. 15-5939. Daniel Imperato, Petitioner v. Securities and Exchange Commission.

577 U.S. 933, 136 S. Ct. 346, 193 L. Ed. 2d 248, 2015 U.S. LEXIS 6563, reh den 577 U.S. 998, 136 S. Ct. 529, 193 L. Ed. 2d 417, 2015 U.S. LEXIS 7260.

October 13, 2015. Petition for writ of certiorari to the United States Court of Appeals for the Eleventh Circuit denied.

Same case below, 594 Fed. Appx. 957.

No. 15-5943. James Spencer, aka Troy Buxton, Petitioner v. United States.

577 U.S. 933, 136 S. Ct. 346, 193 L. Ed. 2d 248, 2015 U.S. LEXIS 6393, reh den 577 U.S. 1096, 136 S. Ct. 887, 193 L. Ed. 2d 779, 2016 U.S. LEXIS 570.

October 13, 2015. Petition for writ of certiorari to the United States Court of Appeals for the Third Circuit denied.

No. 15-5949. David Jose Argueta-Bonilla, Petitioner v. United States;Oscar Asael Gonzales-Matute, Petitioner v. United States;Jose Ruben Medina, aka Jose Rios Medina, aka Jose Medina, Petitioner v. United States;Jose Alfredo Snowball-Padron, Petitioner v. United States;Fernando Tovar-Espinoza, Petitioner v. United States;Oliverio Valencia-Garcia, aka Oliverio Garcia Valencia, aka Oliverio Garza Valencia, aka Oliverio Valencia Garcia, Petitioner v. United States;Napoleon De Jesus Velasquez-Lopez, Petitioner v. United States;and Heliodoro Vela-Cavazos, aka Heliodoro Vela, aka Eliodoro Vela, aka Eliodoro Cavazos Vela, aka Eliodoro Vela-Cavazos, aka Helidoro Cavazos Vela, aka Jose Vela, Petitioner v. United States.

577 U.S. 933, 136 S. Ct. 346, 193 L. Ed. 2d 248, 2015 U.S. LEXIS 6510.

October 13, 2015. Petition for writ of certiorari to the United States Court of Appeals for the Fifth Circuit denied.

Same case below, 613 Fed. Appx. 369 (first judgment); 613 Fed. Appx. 415 (second judgment); 607 Fed. Appx. 389 (third judgment); 613 Fed. Appx. 374 (fourth judgment); 607 Fed. Appx. 413 (fifth judgment); 607 Fed. Appx.402 (sixth judgment); 607 Fed. Appx. 414 (seventh judgment); and 613 Fed. Appx. 411 (eighth judgment).

No. 15-5950. Chris Darrell Joseph Sage, Petitioner v. United States.

577 U.S. 934, 136 S. Ct. 347, 193 L. Ed. 2d 249, 2015 U.S. LEXIS 6521.

October 13, 2015. Petition for writ of certiorari to the United States Court of Appeals for the Ninth Circuit denied.

Same case below, 609 Fed. Appx. 410.

No. 15-5951. Luis Alberto Diaz-Agramonte, aka Jose Luis Torres, Petitioner v. United States.

577 U.S. 934, 136 S. Ct. 347, 193 L. Ed. 2d 249, 2015 U.S. LEXIS 6515.

October 13, 2015. Petition for writ of certiorari to the United States Court of Appeals for the Second Circuit denied.

No. 15-5952. John Doe, Petitioner v. United States.

577 U.S. 934, 136 S. Ct. 347, 193 L. Ed. 2d 249, 2015 U.S. LEXIS 6481.

October 13, 2015. Petition for writ of certiorari to the United States Court of Appeals for the Ninth Circuit denied.

Same case below, 613 Fed. Appx. 625.

No. 15-5953. Johnny Colondres, Petitioner v. Massachusetts.

577 U.S. 934, 136 S. Ct. 347, 193 L. Ed. 2d 249, 2015 U.S. LEXIS 6542.

October 13, 2015. Petition for writ of certiorari to the Supreme Judicial Court of Massachusetts denied.

Same case below, 471 Mass. 192, 27 N.E.3d 1272.

No. 15-5955. Charles Sacus, Petitioner v. United States.

577 U.S. 934, 136 S. Ct. 348, 193 L. Ed. 2d 249, 2015 U.S. LEXIS 6543.

October 13, 2015. Petition for writ of certiorari to the United States Court of Appeals for the Eighth Circuit denied.

Same case below, 784 F.3d 1214.

No. 15-5956. Derrick Ivan Jim, Petitioner v. United States.

577 U.S. 934, 136 S. Ct. 348, 193 L. Ed. 2d 249, 2015 U.S. LEXIS 6452.

October 13, 2015. Petition for writ of certiorari to the United States Court of Appeals for the Tenth Circuit denied.

Same case below, 786 F.3d 802.

No. 15-5960. Donald Mitchell, Petitioner v. United States.

577 U.S. 934, 136 S. Ct. 348, 193 L. Ed. 2d 249, 2015 U.S. LEXIS 6504.

October 13, 2015. Petition for writ of certiorari to the United States Court of Appeals for the Eleventh Circuit denied.

Same case below, 617 Fed. Appx. 976.

No. 15-5962. Jorge Luis Reyes-Lopez, Petitioner v. United States.

577 U.S. 934, 136 S. Ct. 348, 193 L. Ed. 2d 250, 2015 U.S. LEXIS 6573.

October 13, 2015. Petition for writ of certiorari to the United States Court of Appeals for the Fifth Circuit denied.

Same case below, 605 Fed. Appx. 451.

No. 15-5966. Paul H. Volkman, Petitioner v. United States.

577 U.S. 934, 136 S. Ct. 348, 193 L. Ed. 2d 250, 2015 U.S. LEXIS 6591.

October 13, 2015. Petition for writ of certiorari to the United States Court of Appeals for the Sixth Circuit denied.

Same case below, 797 F.3d 377.

No. 15-5968. Sabil M. Mujahid, Petitioner v. United States.

577 U.S. 934, 136 S. Ct. 348, 193 L. Ed. 2d 250, 2015 U.S. LEXIS 6548.

October 13, 2015. Petition for writ of certiorari to the United States Court of Appeals for the Ninth Circuit denied.

Same case below, 611 Fed. Appx. 402.

No. 15-5972. Anthony Antonio Cox, Petitioner v. United States.

577 U.S. 934, 136 S. Ct. 349, 193 L. Ed. 2d 250, 2015 U.S. LEXIS 6482.

October 13, 2015. Petition for writ of certiorari to the United States Court of Appeals for the Eleventh Circuit denied.

No. 15-5975. Manoj Kumar Jha, Petitioner v. United States.

577 U.S. 934, 136 S. Ct. 349, 193 L. Ed. 2d 250, 2015 U.S. LEXIS 6457, reh den 577 U.S. 1045, 136 S. Ct. 611, 193 L. Ed. 2d 492, 2015 U.S. LEXIS 7727.

October 13, 2015. Petition for writ of certiorari to the United States Court of Appeals for the Fourth Circuit denied.

Same case below, 613 Fed. Appx. 212.

No. 15-5978. Jacorey Taylor, Petitioner v. United States.

577 U.S. 934, 136 S. Ct. 349, 193 L. Ed. 2d 250, 2015 U.S. LEXIS 6402.

October 13, 2015. Petition for writ of certiorari to the United States Court of Appeals for the Ninth Circuit denied.

Same case below, 617 Fed. Appx. 671.

No. 15-5981. Edward J. Woodward, Petitioner v. United States.

577 U.S. 935, 136 S. Ct. 349, 193 L. Ed. 2d 250, 2015 U.S. LEXIS 6477.

October 13, 2015. Petition for writ of certiorari to the United States Court of Appeals for the Fourth Circuit denied.

Same case below, 614 Fed. Appx. 101.

No. 15-5982. Daryl Warren, Petitioner v. United States.

577 U.S. 935, 136 S. Ct. 349, 193 L. Ed. 2d 250, 2015 U.S. LEXIS 6449.

October 13, 2015. Petition for writ of certiorari to the United States Court of Appeals for the Eighth Circuit denied.

Same case below, 788 F.3d 805.

No. 15-5992. Adrian Lamonte Shankle, Petitioner v. United States.

577 U.S. 935, 136 S. Ct. 350, 193 L. Ed. 2d 251, 2015 U.S. LEXIS 6557.

October 13, 2015. Petition for writ of certiorari to the United States Court of Appeals for the Fourth Circuit denied.

Same case below, 614 Fed. Appx. 105.

No. 15-5993. Alexander Robbins, Petitioner v. United States.

577 U.S. 935, 136 S. Ct. 350, 193 L. Ed. 2d 251, 2015 U.S. LEXIS 6411.

October 13, 2015. Petition for writ of certiorari to the United States Court of Appeals for the Fourth Circuit denied.

Same case below, 622 Fed. Appx. 209.

No. 15-5994. Marco Cesar Retta-Reyes, Petitioner v. United States;Dayna Alexa Velasquez, Petitioner v. United States; Hugo Aguirre, Petitioner v. United States; Jose Miguel Andrade-Rocha, Petitioner v. United States; Oscar Delgadillo, Petitioner v. United States; Luis Andrade-Rodriguez, Petitioner v. United States; Roslyn Kay Collins, Petitioner v. United States; Orlando Giovanni Hernandez, Petitioner v. United States; and Silverio Loera-Velasco, Petitioner v. United States.

577 U.S. 935, 136 S. Ct. 350, 193 L. Ed. 2d 251, 2015 U.S. LEXIS 6579.

October 13, 2015. Petition for writ of certiorari to the United States Court of Appeals for the Fifth Circuit denied.

Same case below, 607 Fed. Appx. 416 (first judgment); 607 Fed. Appx. 384 (second judgment); 607 Fed. Appx. 397 (third judgment); 609 Fed. Appx. 830 (fourth judgment); 607 Fed. Appx. 410 (fifth judg-

ment); 604 Fed. Appx. 376 (sixth judgment); 604 Fed. Appx. 384 (seventh judgment); 613 Fed. Appx. 406 (eighth judgment); and 613 Fed. Appx. 391 (ninth judgment).

No. 15-5997. Timothy Massey, Petitioner v. United States.

577 U.S. 935, 136 S. Ct. 350, 193 L. Ed. 2d 251, 2015 U.S. LEXIS 6385.

October 13, 2015. Petition for writ of certiorari to the United States Court of Appeals for the Fourth Circuit denied.

No. 15-5999. Jose David Cortez-Guzman, Petitioner v. United States.

577 U.S. 935, 136 S. Ct. 351, 193 L. Ed. 2d 251, 2015 U.S. LEXIS 6383.

October 13, 2015. Petition for writ of certiorari to the United States Court of Appeals for the Fifth Circuit denied.

Same case below, 606 Fed. Appx. 241.

No. 15-6000. Tedric Jameil Chin, Petitioner v. United States.

577 U.S. 935, 136 S. Ct. 351, 193 L. Ed. 2d 251, 2015 U.S. LEXIS 6368.

October 13, 2015. Petition for writ of certiorari to the United States Court of Appeals for the Eleventh Circuit denied.

Same case below, 606 Fed. Appx. 538.

No. 15-6010. Jorge Villarreal-Flores, Petitioner v. United States.

577 U.S. 935, 136 S. Ct. 351, 193 L. Ed. 2d 251, 2015 U.S. LEXIS 6372.

October 13, 2015. Petition for writ of certiorari to the United States Court of Appeals for the Fifth Circuit denied.

No. 15-6011. Lovonne Williams, Petitioner v. United States.

577 U.S. 935, 136 S. Ct. 351, 193 L. Ed. 2d 252, 2015 U.S. LEXIS 6371.

October 13, 2015. Petition for writ of certiorari to the United States Court of Appeals for the Eleventh Circuit denied.

No. 15-6024. Russell Merriweather, Petitioner v. Julie L. Jones, Secretary, Florida Department of Corrections, et al.

577 U.S. 935, 136 S. Ct. 351, 193 L. Ed. 2d 252, 2015 U.S. LEXIS 6373.

October 13, 2015. Petition for writ of certiorari to the United States Court of Appeals for the Eleventh Circuit denied.

No. 15-6034. Keith D. Courville, Petitioner v. Colorado.

577 U.S. 935, 136 S. Ct. 352, 193 L. Ed. 2d 252, 2015 U.S. LEXIS 6596.

October 13, 2015. Petition for writ of certiorari to the Court of Appeals of Colorado denied.

No. 15-31. Alfredo Prieto, Petitioner v. Harold W. Clarke, Director, Virginia Department of Corrections, et al.

577 U.S. 919, 136 S. Ct. 319, 193 L. Ed. 2d 252, 2015 U.S. LEXIS 6388.

October 13, 2015. Motion of Mark Eric Lawlor for leave to intervene denied. Petition for writ of certiorari to the United States Court of Appeals for the Fourth Circuit dismissed as moot.

Same case below, 780 F.3d 245.

No. 15-173. Sidney B. Harr, Petitioner v. Richard H. Brodhead, et al.

577 U.S. 935, 136 S. Ct. 326, 193 L. Ed. 2d 252, 2015 U.S. LEXIS 6491.

October 13, 2015. Petition for writ of certiorari to the United States Court of Appeals for the Fourth Circuit denied. Justice Breyer took no part in the consideration or decision of this petition.

Same case below, 588 Fed. Appx. 285.

No. 15-5895. William A. White, Petitioner v. United States.

577 U.S. 936, 136 S. Ct. 343, 193 L. Ed. 2d 252, 2015 U.S. LEXIS 6384.

October 13, 2015. Petition for writ of certiorari to the United States Court of Appeals for the Fourth Circuit denied. Justice Kagan took no part in the consideration or decision of this petition.

Same case below, 608 Fed. Appx. 160.

No. 15-5907. Adrian Payne, Petitioner v. United States.

577 U.S. 936, 136 S. Ct. 344, 193 L. Ed. 2d 253, 2015 U.S. LEXIS 6381.

October 13, 2015. Petition for writ of certiorari to the United States Court of Appeals for the Second Circuit denied. Justice Kagan took no part in the consideration or decision of this petition.

No. 15-5973. Leon King, Petitioner v. United States.

577 U.S. 936, 136 S. Ct. 349, 193 L. Ed. 2d 253, 2015 U.S. LEXIS 6369.

October 13, 2015. Petition for writ of certiorari to the United States Court of Appeals for the Eleventh Circuit denied. Justice Kagan took no part in the consideration or decision of this petition.

Same case below, 610 Fed. Appx. 825.

No. 15-6007. Thomas Johnson, Petitioner v. United States.

577 U.S. 936, 136 S. Ct. 351, 193 L. Ed. 2d 253, 2015 U.S. LEXIS 6535.

October 13, 2015. Petition for writ of certiorari to the United States Court of Appeals for the Eleventh Circuit denied. Justice Kagan took no part in the consideration or decision of this petition.

No. 15-6143. In re Robert Eugene Eason, Petitioner.

577 U.S. 921, 136 S. Ct. 352, 193 L. Ed. 2d 253, 2015 U.S. LEXIS 6386.

October 13, 2015. Petition for writ of habeas corpus denied.

No. 15-6113. In re Terry Middleton, Petitioner.

577 U.S. 921, 136 S. Ct. 352, 193 L. Ed. 2d 253, 2015 U.S. LEXIS 6379.

October 13, 2015. Motion of petitioner for leave to proceed in forma pauperis denied, and petition for writ of habeas corpus dismissed. See Rule 39.8. Justice Kagan took no part in the consideration or decision of this motion and this petition.

No. 15-5708. In re James C. Platts, Petitioner.

577 U.S. 921, 136 S. Ct. 334, 193 L. Ed. 2d 253, 2015 U.S. LEXIS 6370.

October 13, 2015. Petition for writ of mandamus denied.

No. 15-5868. In re Consuelo Jordan, Petitioner.

577 U.S. 921, 136 S. Ct. 341, 193 L. Ed. 2d 253, 2015 U.S. LEXIS 6382, reh den 577 U.S. 1024, 136 S. Ct. 581, 193 L. Ed. 2d 463, 2015 U.S. LEXIS 7459.

October 13, 2015. Petition for writ of mandamus denied.

No. 15-5903. In re Kendal Taylor, aka Shamsideen Salaam, Petitioner.

577 U.S. 921, 136 S. Ct. 344, 193 L. Ed. 2d 254, 2015 U.S. LEXIS 6374.

October 13, 2015. Petition for writ of mandamus denied.

No. 15-5509. In re Toufic Naddi, Petitioner.

577 U.S. 921, 136 S. Ct. 323, 193 L. Ed. 2d 254, 2015 U.S. LEXIS 6431.

October 13, 2015. Motion of petitioner for leave to proceed in forma pauperis denied, and petition for writ of mandamus dismissed. See Rule 39.8. As petitioner has repeatedly abused this Court's process, the Clerk is directed not to accept any further petitions in noncriminal matters from petitioner unless the docketing fee required by Rule 38(a) is paid and petition submitted in compliance with Rule 33.1. See Martin v. District of Columbia Court of Appeals, 506 U.S. 1, 113 S. Ct. 397, 121 L. Ed. 2d 305 (1992) (per curiam).

No. 15-5588. In re Kenneth W. Pratt and Cleo Dixon, Petitioners.

577 U.S. 922, 136 S. Ct. 328, 193 L. Ed. 2d 254, 2015 U.S. LEXIS 6536.

October 13, 2015. Petition for writ of mandamus and/or prohibition denied.

No. 14-8938. Tyrone Samuel Fields, Petitioner v. United States.

577 U.S. 936, 136 S. Ct. 355, 193 L. Ed. 2d 254, 2015 U.S. LEXIS 6387.

October 13, 2015. Petition for rehearing denied.

Former decision, 575 U.S. 976, 135 S. Ct. 1878, 191 L. Ed. 2d 750, 2015 U.S. LEXIS 2575.

[577 U.S. 7]

CHADRIN LEE MULLENIX, Petitioner

v

BEATRICE LUNA, Individually and as Representative of the ESTATE OF
ISRAEL LEIJA, JR., et al.

577 U.S. 7, 136 S. Ct. 305, 193 L. Ed. 2d 255, 2015 U.S. LEXIS 7160

[No. 14-1143]

Decided November 9, 2015.

Decision: Police officer entitled to qualified immunity from 42 U.S.C.S. § 1983
civil-rights action alleging violation of Fourth Amendment by using excessive force in shooting and killing reportedly intoxicated fugitive who was
fleeing in motor vehicle.

Prior history: ON PETITION FOR WRIT OF CERTIORARI TO THE UNITED
STATES COURT OF APPEALS FOR THE FIFTH CIRCUIT, 773 F.3d 712, 2014 U.S.
App. LEXIS 24067

SUMMARY

Overview: HOLDINGS: [1]-A police officer was entitled to qualified immunity for
his conduct in shooting and killing a reportedly intoxicated fugitive who was fleeing in
a vehicle at high speed, twice threatened to kill officers, and was racing toward another
officer's location before the vehicle reached a spike strip placed on the road, since it was
not beyond debate that the officer acted unreasonably in the unclear border between
excessive and acceptable force.

Outcome: Petition granted and decision summarily reversed. 8-1 Decision; 1
Concurrence; 1 Dissent.

SUBJECT OF ANNOTATION

Beginning on page 831, infra

Supreme Court's views as to application or applicability of doctrine of
qualified immunity in action under 42 U.S.C.S. § 1983, or in Bivens
action, seeking damages for alleged civil rights violations involving law
enforcement activities or treatment of prisoners

HEADNOTES

Classified to United States Supreme Court Digest, Lawyers' Edition

**Violation of right — qualified im-
munity**

L Ed Digest: Public Officers § 56

1. The doctrine of qualified immunity shields officials from civil liability
so long as their conduct does not violate clearly established statutory or
constitutional rights of which a reasonable person would have known. A
clearly established right is one that is
sufficiently clear that every reasonable
official would have understood that
what he is doing violates that right. A
court does not require a case directly

on point, but existing precedent must
have placed the statutory or constitutional question beyond debate. Put
simply, qualified immunity protects all
but the plainly incompetent or those
who knowingly violate the law. (Per
curiam opinion of Roberts, Ch. J., and
Kennedy, Thomas, Ginsburg, Breyer,
Alito, and Kagan, JJ.)

[See annotation p 831, infra]

**Fourth Amendment violation —
qualified immunity**

L Ed Digest: Public Officers § 56

2. For purposes of qualified immunity, courts are not to define clearly established law at a high level of generality. The dispositive question is whether the violative nature of particular conduct is clearly established. This inquiry must be undertaken in light of the specific context of the case, not as a broad general proposition. Such specificity is especially important in the Fourth Amendment context, where it is sometimes difficult for an officer to determine how the relevant legal doctrine will apply to the factual situation the officer confronts. (Per curiam opinion of Roberts, Ch. J., and Kennedy, Thomas, Ginsburg, Breyer, Alito, and Kagan, JJ.)

[See annotation p 831, infra]

RESEARCH REFERENCES

U.S.C.S., Constitution, Amendment 4; 42 U.S.C.S. § 1983

Antieau on Local Government Law § 77.04 (Matthew Bender 2d ed.)

L Ed Digest, Civil Rights § 32; Public Officers § 56

L Ed Index, Qualified Immunity

Annotations:

Supreme Court's views as to extent of prosecutorial immunity from liability for damages for alleged violations of civil rights. 172 L. Ed. 2d 905.

Supreme Court's views as to application or applicability of doctrine of qualified immunity in action under 42 U.S.C.S. § 1983 or in Bivens action, seeking damages for alleged civil rights violations. 116 L. Ed. 2d 965.

Supreme Court's construction of Civil Rights Act of 1871 (42 U.S.C.S. § 1983) providing private right of action for violation of federal rights. 43 L. Ed. 2d 833.

Unconstitutional conduct by state or federal officer as affecting governmental immunity from suit in federal court—Supreme Court cases. 12 L. Ed. 2d 1110.

SHEPARD'S® Citations Service. For further research of authorities referenced here, use SHEPARD'S to be sure your case or statute is still good law and to find additional authorities that support your position. SHEPARD'S is available exclusively from LexisNexis®.

SYLLABUS BY REPORTER OF DECISIONS

For text of added syllabus for this case see p 814B, infra.

OPINION OF THE COURT

[577 U.S. 8]

Per Curiam.

On the night of March 23, 2010, Sergeant Randy Baker of the Tulia, Texas, Police Department followed Israel Leija, Jr., to a drive-in restaurant, with a warrant for his arrest. 773 F.3d 712, 715-716 (CA5 2014). When Baker approached Leija's car and informed him that he was under arrest, Leija sped off, headed for Interstate 27. 2013 U.S. Dist. LEXIS 111414, 2013 WL 4017124, *1 (ND Tex., Aug. 7, 2013). Baker gave chase and was quickly joined by Trooper

Gabriel Rodriguez of the Texas Department of Public Safety (DPS). 773 F.3d, at 716.

Leija entered the interstate and led the officers on an 18-minute chase at speeds between 85 and 110 miles per hour. *Ibid.* Twice during the chase, Leija called the Tulia Police dispatcher, claiming to have a gun and threatening to shoot at police officers if they did not abandon their pursuit. The dispatcher relayed Leija's threats, together with a report that Leija might be intoxicated, to all concerned officers.

As Baker and Rodriguez maintained their pursuit, other law enforcement officers set up tire spikes at three locations. Officer Troy Ducheneaux of the Canyon Police Department manned the spike strip at the first location Leija was expected to reach, beneath the overpass at Cemetery Road. Ducheneaux and the other officers had received training on the deployment of spike strips, including on how to take a defensive position so as to minimize the risk posed by the passing driver. *Ibid.*

[577 U.S. 9]

DPS Trooper Chadrin Mullenix also responded. He drove to the Cemetery Road overpass, initially intending to set up a spike strip there. Upon learning of the other spike strip positions, however, Mullenix began to consider another tactic: shooting at Leija's car in order to disable it. 2013 U.S. Dist. LEXIS 111414, 2013 WL 4017124, *1. Mullenix had not received training in this tactic and had not attempted it before, but he radioed the idea to Rodriguez. Rodriguez responded "10-4," gave Mullenix his position, and said that Leija had slowed to 85 miles per hour. Mullenix then asked the DPS dispatcher to inform his supervisor, Sergeant Byrd, of his plan and ask if Byrd thought it was " 'worth doing.' " 773 F.3d, at 716-717. Before receiving Byrd's response, Mullenix exited his vehicle and, armed with his service rifle, took a shooting position on the overpass, 20 feet above I-27. Respondents allege that from this position, Mullenix still could hear Byrd's response to " 'stand by' " and " 'see if the spikes work first.' " *Ibid.**

As Mullenix waited for Leija to arrive, he and another officer, Randall County Sheriff's Deputy Tom Shipman, discussed whether Mullenix's plan would work and how and where to shoot the vehicle to best carry it out. 2013 U.S. Dist. LEXIS 111414, 2013 WL 4017124, *2. Shipman also informed Mullenix that another officer was located beneath the overpass. 773 F.3d, at 717.

Approximately three minutes after Mullenix took up his shooting position, he spotted Leija's vehicle, with Rodriguez in pursuit. As Leija approached the overpass, Mullenix fired six shots. Leija's car continued forward beneath the overpass, where it engaged the spike strip, hit the median, and rolled 2½ times. It was later determined that Leija had been killed by Mullenix's shots, four of which struck his upper body. There was no evidence that any of Mullenix's

[577 U.S. 10]

shots hit the car's radiator, hood, or engine block. *Id.*, at 716-717;

---

* Although Mullenix disputes hearing Byrd's response, we view the facts in the light most favorable to respondents, who oppose Mullenix's motion for summary judgment. See *Tolan* v. *Cotton*, 572 U.S. 650, 651, 134 S. Ct. 1861, 188 L. Ed. 2d 895 (2014) (*per curiam*).

2013 U.S. Dist. LEXIS 111414, 2013 WL 4017124, *2-*3.

Respondents sued Mullenix under Rev. Stat. § 1979, 42 U.S.C. § 1983, alleging that he had violated the Fourth Amendment by using excessive force against Leija. Mullenix moved for summary judgment on the ground of qualified immunity, but the District Court denied his motion, finding that "[t]here are genuine issues of fact as to whether Trooper Mullenix acted recklessly, or acted as a reasonable, trained peace officer would have acted in the same or similar circumstances." 2013 U.S. Dist. LEXIS 111414, 2013 WL 4017124, *6.

Mullenix appealed, and the Court of Appeals for the Fifth Circuit affirmed. 765 F.3d 531 (2014). The court agreed with the District Court that the "immediacy of the risk posed by Leija is a disputed fact that a reasonable jury could find either in the plaintiffs' favor or in the officer's favor, precluding us from concluding that Mullenix acted objectively reasonably as a matter of law." *Id.*, at 538.

Judge King dissented. She described the " 'fact issue' referenced by the majority" as "simply a restatement of the objective reasonableness test that applies to Fourth Amendment excessive force claims," which, she noted, the Supreme Court has held " 'is a pure question of law.' " *Id.*, at 544-545 (quoting *Scott* v. *Harris*, 550 U.S. 372, 381, n. 8, 127 S. Ct. 1769, 167 L. Ed. 2d 686 (2007)). Turning to that legal question, Judge King concluded that Mullenix's actions were objectively reasonable. When Mullenix fired, she emphasized, he knew not only that Leija had threatened to shoot the officers involved in his pursuit, but also that Leija was seconds away from encountering such an officer beneath the overpass. Judge King also dismissed the notion that Mullenix should have given the spike strips a chance to work. She explained that because spike strips are often ineffective, and because officers operating them are vulnerable to gunfire from passing cars, Mullenix reasonably feared that the officers manning them faced a significant risk of harm. 765 F.3d, at 548-549.

[577 U.S. 11]

Mullenix sought rehearing en banc before the Fifth Circuit, but the court denied his petition. Judge Jolly dissented, joined by six other members of the court. Judge King, who joined Judge Jolly's dissent, also filed a separate dissent of her own. 777 F.3d 221 (2014) (*per curiam*). On the same day, however, the two members forming the original panel's majority withdrew their previous opinion and substituted a new one. 773 F.3d 712. The revised opinion recognized that objective unreasonableness is a question of law that can be resolved on summary judgment—as Judge King had explained in her dissent—but reaffirmed the denial of qualified immunity. *Id.*, at 715, 718. The majority concluded that Mullenix's actions were objectively unreasonable because several of the factors that had justified deadly force in previous cases were absent here: There were no innocent bystanders, Leija's driving was relatively controlled, Mullenix had not first given the spike strips a chance to work, and Mullenix's decision was not a split-second judgment. *Id.*, at 720-724. The court went on to conclude that Mullenix was not entitled to qualified immunity because "the law was clearly established such that a reasonable officer would have known that the use of deadly force, absent a sufficiently substantial and immediate threat, violated the Fourth Amendment." *Id.*, at 725.

We address only the qualified immunity question, not whether there was a Fourth Amendment violation in the first place, and now reverse.

[1] The doctrine of qualified immunity shields officials from civil liability so long as their conduct " 'does not violate clearly established statutory or constitutional rights of which a reasonable person would have known.' " *Pearson* v. *Callahan*, 555 U.S. 223, 231, 129 S. Ct. 808, 172 L. Ed. 2d 565 (2009) (quoting *Harlow* v. *Fitzgerald*, 457 U.S. 800, 818, 102 S. Ct. 2727, 73 L. Ed. 2d 396 (1982)). A clearly established right is one that is "sufficiently clear that every reasonable official would have understood that what he is doing violates that right." *Reichle* v. *Howards*, 566 U.S. 658, 664, 132 S. Ct. 2088, 182 L. Ed. 2d 985 (2012) (internal quotation

[577 U.S. 12]

marks and alteration omitted). "We do not require a case directly on point, but existing precedent must have placed the statutory or constitutional question beyond debate." *Ashcroft* v. *al-Kidd*, 563 U.S. 731, 741, 131 S. Ct. 2074, 179 L. Ed. 2d 1149 (2011). Put simply, qualified immunity protects "all but the plainly incompetent or those who knowingly violate the law." *Malley* v. *Briggs*, 475 U.S. 335, 341, 106 S. Ct. 1092, 89 L. Ed. 2d 271 (1986).

[2] "We have repeatedly told courts . . . not to define clearly established law at a high level of generality." *al-Kidd, supra,* at 742, 131 S. Ct. 2074, 179 L. Ed. 2d 1149. The dispositive question is "whether the violative

nature of *particular* conduct is clearly established." *Ibid.* (emphasis added). This inquiry " 'must be undertaken in light of the specific context of the case, not as a broad general proposition.' " *Brosseau* v. *Haugen*, 543 U.S. 194, 198, 125 S. Ct. 596, 160 L. Ed. 2d 583 (2004) (*per curiam*) (quoting *Saucier* v. *Katz*, 533 U.S. 194, 201, 121 S. Ct. 2151, 150 L. Ed. 2d 272 (2001)). Such specificity is especially important in the Fourth Amendment context, where the Court has recognized that "[i]t is sometimes difficult for an officer to determine how the relevant legal doctrine, here excessive force, will apply to the factual situation the officer confronts." 533 U.S., at 205, 121 S. Ct. 2151, 150 L. Ed. 2d 272.

In this case, the Fifth Circuit held that Mullenix violated the clearly established rule that a police officer may not " 'use deadly force against a fleeing felon who does not pose a sufficient threat of harm to the officer or others.' " 773 F.3d, at 725. Yet this Court has previously considered—and rejected—almost that exact formulation of the qualified immunity question in the Fourth Amendment context. In *Brosseau*, which also involved the shooting of a suspect fleeing by car, the Ninth Circuit denied qualified immunity on the ground that the officer had violated the clearly established rule, set forth in *Tennessee* v. *Garner*, 471 U.S. 1, 105 S. Ct. 1694, 85 L. Ed. 2d 1 (1985), that "deadly force is only permissible where the officer has probable cause to believe that the suspect poses a threat of serious physical harm, either to the officer or to others." *Haugen* v. *Brosseau*, 339 F.3d 857, 873 (CA9 2003) (internal quotation

[577 U.S. 13]

marks omitted). This Court summarily reversed, holding that use of *Garner's* "general" test for excessive force was "mistaken." *Brosseau*, 543 U.S., at 199, 125 S. Ct. 596, 160 L. Ed. 2d 583. The correct inquiry, the Court explained, was whether it was clearly established that the Fourth Amendment prohibited the officer's conduct in the " 'situation [she] confronted': whether to shoot a disturbed felon, set on avoiding capture through vehicular flight, when persons in the immediate area are at risk from that flight." *Id.*, at 199-200, 125 S. Ct. 596, 160 L. Ed. 2d 583. The Court considered three Court of Appeals cases discussed by the parties, noted that "this area is one in which the result depends very much on the facts of each case," and concluded that the officer was entitled to qualified immunity because "[n]one of [the cases] *squarely governs* the case here." *Id.*, at 201, 125 S. Ct. 596, 160 L. Ed. 2d 583 (emphasis added).

Anderson v. *Creighton*, 483 U.S. 635, 107 S. Ct. 3034, 97 L. Ed. 2d 523 (1987), is also instructive on the required degree of specificity. There, the lower court had denied qualified immunity based on the clearly established "right to be free from warrantless searches of one's home unless the searching officers have probable cause and there are exigent circumstances." *Id.*, at 640, 107 S. Ct. 3034, 97 L. Ed. 2d 523. This Court faulted that formulation for failing to address the actual question at issue: whether "the circumstances with which Anderson was confronted . . . constitute[d] probable cause and exigent circumstances." *Id.*, at 640-641, 107 S. Ct. 3034, 97 L. Ed. 2d 523. Without answering that question, the Court explained, the conclusion that Anderson's search was objectively unreasonable did not "follow immedi-

ately" from—and thus was not clearly established by—the principle that warrantless searches not supported by probable cause and exigent circumstances violate the Fourth Amendment. *Id.*, at 641, 107 S. Ct. 3034, 97 L. Ed. 2d 523.

In this case, Mullenix confronted a reportedly intoxicated fugitive, set on avoiding capture through high-speed vehicular flight, who twice during his flight had threatened to shoot police officers, and who was moments away from encountering an officer at Cemetery Road. The relevant inquiry is

[577 U.S. 14]

whether existing precedent placed the conclusion that Mullenix acted unreasonably in these circumstances "beyond debate." *al-Kidd, supra,* at 741, 131 S. Ct. 2074, 179 L. Ed. 2d 1149. The general principle that deadly force requires a sufficient threat hardly settles this matter. See *Pasco* v. *Knoblauch*, 566 F.3d 572, 580 (CA5 2009) ("[I]t would be unreasonable to expect a police officer to make the numerous legal conclusions necessary to apply *Garner* to a high-speed car chase . . . ").

Far from clarifying the issue, excessive force cases involving car chases reveal the hazy legal backdrop against which Mullenix acted. In *Brosseau* itself, the Court held that an officer did not violate clearly established law when she shot a fleeing suspect out of fear that he endangered "other officers on foot who [she] *believed* were in the immediate area," "the occupied vehicles in [his] path," and "any other citizens who *might* be in the area." 543 U.S., at 197, 125 S. Ct. 596, 160 L. Ed. 2d 583 (first alteration in original; internal quotation marks omitted; emphasis added).

The threat Leija posed was at least as immediate as that presented by a suspect who had just begun to drive off and was headed only in the general direction of officers and bystanders. *Id.*, at 196-197, 125 S. Ct. 596, 160 L. Ed. 2d 583. By the time Mullenix fired, Leija had led police on a 25-mile chase at extremely high speeds, was reportedly intoxicated, had twice threatened to shoot officers, and was racing toward an officer's location.

This Court has considered excessive force claims in connection with high-speed chases on only two occasions since *Brosseau*. In *Scott* v. *Harris*, 550 U.S. 372, 127 S. Ct. 1769, 167 L. Ed. 2d 686, the Court held that an officer did not violate the Fourth Amendment by ramming the car of a fugitive whose reckless driving "posed an actual and imminent threat to the lives of any pedestrians who might have been present, to other civilian motorists, and to the officers involved in the chase." *Id.,* at 384, 127 S. Ct. 1769, 167 L. Ed. 2d 686. And in *Plumhoff* v. *Rickard*, 572 U.S. 765, 134 S. Ct. 2012, 188 L. Ed. 2d 1056 (2014), the Court reaffirmed *Scott* by holding that an officer acted reasonably when he fatally shot a fugitive who was "intent on resuming" a

[577 U.S. 15]

chase that "pose[d] a deadly threat for others on the road." 572 U.S., at 777, 134 S. Ct. 2012, 188 L. Ed. 2d 1056. The Court has thus never found the use of deadly force in connection with a dangerous car chase to violate the Fourth Amendment, let alone to be a basis for denying qualified immunity. Leija in his flight did not pass as many cars as the drivers in *Scott* or *Plumhoff*; traffic was light on I-27. At the same time, the fleeing fugitives in *Scott* and *Plumhoff* had not verbally threatened

to kill any officers in their path, nor were they about to come upon such officers. In any event, none of our precedents "squarely governs" the facts here. Given Leija's conduct, we cannot say that only someone "plainly incompetent" or who "knowingly violate[s] the law" would have perceived a sufficient threat and acted as Mullenix did. *Malley*, 475 U.S., at 341, 106 S. Ct. 1092, 89 L. Ed. 2d 271.

The dissent focuses on the availability of spike strips as an alternative means of terminating the chase. It argues that even if Leija posed a threat sufficient to justify deadly force in some circumstances, Mullenix nevertheless contravened clearly established law because he did not wait to see if the spike strips would work before taking action. Spike strips, however, present dangers of their own, not only to drivers who encounter them at speeds between 85 and 110 miles per hour, but also to officers manning them. See, *e.g., Thompson* v. *Mercer*, 762 F.3d 433, 440 (CA5 2014); Brief for National Association of Police Organizations et al. as *Amici Curiae* 15-16. Nor are spike strips always successful in ending the chase. See, *e.g., Cordova* v. *Aragon*, 569 F.3d 1183, 1186 (CA10 2009); Brief for National Association of Police Organizations et al. as *Amici Curiae* 16 (citing examples). The dissent can cite no case from this Court denying qualified immunity because officers entitled to terminate a high-speed chase selected one dangerous alternative over another.

Even so, the dissent argues, there was no governmental interest that justified acting before Leija's car hit the spikes. Mullenix explained, however, that he feared Leija might attempt to shoot at or run over the officers manning the spike

[577 U.S. 16]

strips. Mullenix also feared that even if Leija hit the spike strips, he might still be able to continue driving in the direction of other officers. The dissent ignores these interests by suggesting that there was no "possible marginal gain in shooting at the car over using the spike strips already in place." *Post*, at 23, 193 L. Ed. 2d, at 267 (opinion of Sotomayor, J.). In fact, Mullenix hoped his actions would stop the car in a manner that avoided the risks to other officers and other drivers that relying on spike strips would entail. The dissent disputes the merits of the options available to Mullenix, *post*, at 22–23, 193 L. Ed. 2d, at 266-267, but others with more experience analyze the issues differently. See, *e.g.,* Brief for National Association of Police Organizations et al. as *Amici Curiae* 15-16. Ultimately, whatever can be said of the wisdom of Mullenix's choice, this Court's precedents do not place the conclusion that he acted unreasonably in these circumstances "beyond debate." *al-Kidd*, 563 U.S., at 741, 131 S. Ct. 2074, 179 L. Ed. 2d 1149.

More fundamentally, the dissent repeats the Fifth Circuit's error. It defines the qualified immunity inquiry at a high level of generality—whether any governmental interest justified choosing one tactic over another—and then fails to consider that question in "the specific context of the case." *Brosseau, supra*, at 198, 125 S. Ct. 596, 160 L. Ed. 2d 583 (internal quotation marks omitted). As in *Anderson*, the conclusion that Mullenix's reasons were insufficient to justify his actions simply does not "follow immediately" from the general proposition that

force must be justified. 483 U.S., at 641, 107 S. Ct. 3034, 97 L. Ed. 2d 523.

Cases decided by the lower courts since *Brosseau* likewise have not clearly established that deadly force is inappropriate in response to conduct like Leija's. The Fifth Circuit here principally relied on its own decision in *Lytle* v. *Bexar County*, 560 F.3d 404 (2009), denying qualified immunity to a police officer who had fired at a fleeing car and killed one of its passengers. That holding turned on the court's assumption, for purposes of summary judgment, that the car was moving away from the officer and had already traveled

[577 U.S. 17]

some distance at the moment the officer fired. See *id.*, at 409. The court held that a reasonable jury could conclude that a receding car "did not pose a sufficient threat of harm such that the use of deadly force was reasonable." *Id.*, at 416. But, crucially, the court also recognized that if the facts were as the officer alleged, and he fired as the car was coming toward him, "he would likely be entitled to qualified immunity" based on the "threat of immediate and severe physical harm." *Id.*, at 412. Without implying that *Lytle* was either correct or incorrect, it suffices to say that *Lytle* does not clearly dictate the conclusion that Mullenix was unjustified in perceiving grave danger and responding accordingly, given that Leija was speeding toward a confrontation with officers he had threatened to kill.

Cases that the Fifth Circuit ignored also suggest that Mullenix's assessment of the threat Leija posed was reasonable. In *Long* v. *Slaton*, 508 F.3d 576 (2007), for example, the Eleventh Circuit held that a sheriff's deputy did not violate the Fourth Amendment by fatally shooting a mentally unstable individual who was attempting to flee in the deputy's car, even though at the time of the shooting the individual had not yet operated the cruiser dangerously. The court explained that "the law does not require officers in a tense and dangerous situation to wait until the moment a suspect uses a deadly weapon to act to stop the suspect" and concluded that the deputy had reason to believe Long was dangerous based on his unstable state of mind, theft of the cruiser, and failure to heed the deputy's warning to stop. *Id.*, at 581-582. The court also rejected the notion that the deputy should have first tried less lethal methods, such as spike strips. "[C]onsidering the unpredictability of Long's behavior and his fleeing in a marked police cruiser," the court held, "we think the police need not have taken that chance and hoped for the best." *Id.*, at 583 (alteration and internal quotation marks omitted). But see *Smith* v. *Cupp*, 430 F.3d 766, 774-777 (CA6 2005) (denying qualified immunity to an

[577 U.S. 18]

officer who shot an intoxicated suspect who had stolen the officer's cruiser where a reasonable jury could have concluded that the suspect's flight did not immediately threaten the officer or any other bystander).

Other cases cited by the Fifth Circuit and respondents are simply too factually distinct to speak clearly to the specific circumstances here. Several involve suspects who may have done little more than flee at relatively low speeds. See, *e.g.*, *Walker* v. *Davis*, 649 F.3d 502, 503 (CA6 2011); *Kirby* v.

Duva, 530 F.3d 475, 479-480 (CA6 2008); *Adams* v. *Speers*, 473 F.3d 989, 991 (CA9 2007); *Vaughan* v. *Cox*, 343 F.3d 1323, 1330-1331, and n. 7 (CA11 2003). These cases shed little light on whether the far greater danger of a speeding fugitive threatening to kill police officers waiting in his path could warrant deadly force. The court below noted that "no weapon was ever seen," 773 F.3d, at 723, but surely in these circumstances the police were justified in taking Leija at his word when he twice told the dispatcher he had a gun and was prepared to use it.

Finally, respondents argue that the danger Leija represented was less substantial than the threats that courts have found sufficient to justify deadly force. But the mere fact that courts have approved deadly force in more extreme circumstances says little, if anything, about whether such force was reasonable in the circumstances here. The fact is that when Mullenix fired, he reasonably understood Leija to be a fugitive fleeing arrest, at speeds over 100 miles per hour, who was armed and possibly intoxicated, who had threatened to kill any officer he saw if the police did not abandon their pursuit, and who was racing toward Officer Ducheneaux's position. Even accepting that these circumstances fall somewhere between the two sets of cases respondents discuss, qualified immunity protects actions in the " 'hazy border between excessive and acceptable force.' " *Brosseau*, 543 U.S., at 201, 125 S. Ct. 596, 160 L. Ed. 2d 583 (quoting *Saucier*, 533 U.S., at 206, 121 S. Ct. 2151, 150 L. Ed. 2d 272; some internal quotation marks omitted).

[577 U.S. 19]

Because the constitutional rule applied by the Fifth Circuit was not " 'beyond debate,' " *Stanton* v. *Sims*, 571 U.S. 3, 11, 134 S. Ct. 3, 187 L. Ed. 2d 341 (2013) (*per curiam*), we grant Mullenix's petition for certiorari and reverse the Fifth Circuit's determination that Mullenix is not entitled to qualified immunity.

It is so ordered.

SEPARATE OPINIONS

Justice **Scalia**, concurring in the judgment.

I join the judgment of the Court, but would not describe what occurred here as the application of deadly force in effecting an arrest. Our prior cases have reserved that description to the directing of force sufficient to kill *at the person* of the desired arrestee. See, *e.g.*, *Plumhoff* v. *Rickard*, 572 U.S. 765, 134 S. Ct. 2012, 188 L. Ed. 2d 1056 (2014); *Brosseau* v. *Haugen*, 543 U.S. 194, 125 S. Ct. 596, 160 L. Ed. 2d 583 (2004) (*per curiam*); *Tennessee* v. *Garner*, 471 U.S. 1, 105 S. Ct. 1694, 85 L. Ed. 2d 1 (1985). It does not assist analysis to refer to all use of force that happens to kill the arrestee as the application of deadly force. The police might, for example, attempt to stop a fleeing felon's car by felling a large tree across the road; if they drop the tree too late, so that it crushes the car and its occupant, I would not call that the application of deadly force. Though it was force sufficient to kill, it was not applied with the object of harming the body of the felon.

Thus, in *Scott* v. *Harris*, 550 U.S. 372, 127 S. Ct. 1769, 167 L. Ed. 2d 686 (2007), we declined to characterize officer Scott's use of his pursuing vehicle's bumper to push the fleeing vehicle off the road as the application of deadly force. Whether or not it was that, we said, "all that matters is whether Scott's actions were reasonable." *Id.*, at 383, 127 S. Ct. 1769, 167 L. Ed. 2d 686. So also here. But it stacks the deck against the officer, it seems to me, to describe his action as the application of deadly force.

It was at least arguable in *Scott* that pushing a speeding vehicle off the road is targeting its occupant for injury or death. Here, however, it is conceded that Trooper Mullenix did not shoot to wound or kill the fleeing Leija, nor even to drive Leija's car off the road, but only to cause the car to

[577 U.S. 20]

stop by destroying its engine. That was a risky enterprise, as the outcome demonstrated; but determining whether it violated the Fourth Amendment requires us to ask, not whether it was reasonable to kill Leija, but whether it was reasonable to shoot at the engine in light of the risk to Leija. It distorts that inquiry, I think, to make the question whether it was reasonable for Mullenix to "apply deadly force."

Justice **Sotomayor**, dissenting.

Chadrin Mullenix fired six rounds in the dark at a car traveling 85 miles per hour. He did so without any training in that tactic, against the wait order of his superior officer, and less than a second before the car hit spike strips deployed to stop it. Mullenix's rogue conduct killed the driver, Israel Leija, Jr. Because it was clearly established under the Fourth Amendment that an officer in Mullenix's position should not have fired the shots, I respectfully dissent from the grant of summary reversal.

I

Resolving all factual disputes in favor of plaintiffs, as the Court must on a motion for summary judgment, Mullenix knew the following facts before he shot at Leija's engine block: Leija had led police officers on an 18-minute car chase, at speeds ranging from 85 to 110 miles per hour. 773 F.3d 712, 716 (CA5 2014). Leija had twice called the police dispatcher threatening to shoot at officers if they did not cease the pursuit. *Ibid.* Police officers were deploying three sets of spike strips in order to stop Leija's flight. *Ibid.* The officers were trained to stop a car using spike strips. This training included how to take a defensive position to minimize the risk of danger from the target car. *Ibid.* Mullenix knew that spike strips were being set up directly beneath the overpass where he was stationed. *Id.,* at 723. There is no evidence below that any of the officers with whom Mullenix

[577 U.S. 21]

was in communication—including Officer Troy Ducheneaux, whom Mullenix believed to be below the overpass—had expressed any concern for their safety. *Id.,* at 720.

Mullenix had no training in shooting to disable a moving vehicle and had never seen the tactic done before. *Id.,* at 716. He also lacked permission to take the shots: When Mullenix relayed his plan to his superior officer, Robert Byrd, Byrd responded "stand by" and "see if the spikes work first." *Id.,* at 716-717. Three minutes after arriving at the overpass, Mullenix fired six rounds at Leija's car. None hit the car's engine block; at least four struck Leija in the upper body, killing Leija. *Id.,* at 717.

II

When confronting a claim of qualified immunity, a court asks two questions. First, the court considers whether the officer in fact violated a constitutional right. *Saucier* v. *Katz,* 533 U.S. 194, 201, 121 S. Ct. 2151, 150 L. Ed. 2d 272 (2001). Second, the court asks whether the contours of the right were "sufficiently clear that a reasonable official would [have understood] that what he is doing violates that right." *Id.,* at 202, 121 S. Ct. 2151, 150 L. Ed. 2d 272 (quoting *Anderson* v. *Creighton,* 483 U.S. 635, 640, 107 S. Ct. 3034, 97 L. Ed. 2d 523 (1987)). This Court has rejected the idea that "an official action is protected by qualified immunity unless the very action in question has previously been held unlawful." *Id.,* at 640, 107 S. Ct. 3034, 97 L. Ed. 2d 523. Instead, the crux of the qualified immunity test is whether officers have "fair notice" that they are acting unconstitutionally. *Hope* v. *Pelzer,* 536 U.S. 730, 739, 122 S. Ct. 2508, 153 L. Ed. 2d 666 (2002).

Respondents here allege that Mullenix violated the Fourth Amendment's prohibition on unreasonable seizures by using deadly force to apprehend Leija. This Court's precedents clearly establish that the Fourth Amendment is violated unless the " 'governmental interests' " in effectuating a particular kind of seizure outweigh the " 'nature and quality of the intrusion on the individual's Fourth Amendment interests.' " *Scott* v. *Harris,* 550 U.S. 372, 383, 127 S. Ct. 1769, 167 L. Ed. 2d 686 (2007) (quoting *United*

[577 U.S. 22]

States v. *Place,* 462 U.S. 696, 703, 103 S. Ct. 2637, 77 L. Ed. 2d 110 (1983)). There must be a "governmental interes[t]" not only in effectuating a seizure, but also in "how [the seizure] is carried out." *Tennessee* v. *Garner*, 471 U.S. 1, 8, 105 S. Ct. 1694, 85 L. Ed. 2d 1 (1985).

Balancing a particular governmental interest in the use of deadly force against the intrusion occasioned by the use of that force is inherently a fact-specific inquiry, not susceptible to bright lines. But it is clearly established that the government must have *some* interest in using deadly force over other kinds of force.

Here, then, the clearly established legal question—the question a reasonable officer would have asked—is whether, under all the circumstances as known to Mullenix, there was a governmental interest in shooting at the car rather than waiting for it to run over spike strips.

The Court does not point to *any* such interest here. It claims that Mullenix's goal was not merely to stop the car, but to stop the car "in a manner that avoided the risks" of relying on spike strips. *Ante*, at 16, 193 L. Ed. 2d, at 262. But there is no evidence in the record that shooting at Leija's engine block would stop the car in such a manner.

The majority first suggests that Mullenix did not wait for the results of the spikes, as his superior advised, because of his concern for the officers manning the strips. But Leija was going to come upon those officers whether or not Mullenix's shooting tactic was successful: Mullenix took his shot when Leija was between 25 and 30 yards away from the spike strip, traveling at 85 miles per hour. Even if his shots hit Leija's engine block, the car would not have stopped instantly. Mullenix would have bought the officers he was trying to

protect—officers who had been trained to take defensive positions—less than three-quarters of a second over waiting for the spike strips. And whatever threat Leija posed after his car was stopped existed whether the car was stopped by a shot to the engine block or by the spike strips.

Nor was there any evidence that shooting at the car was more reliable than the spike strips. The majority notes that

[577 U.S. 23]

spike strips are fallible. *Ante*, at 15, 193 L. Ed. 2d, at 261. But Mullenix had no information to suggest that shooting to disable a car had a higher success rate, much less that doing so with no training and at night was more likely to succeed. Moreover, not only did officers have training in setting up the spike strips, but they had also placed two backup strips farther north along the highway in case the first set failed. A reasonable officer could not have thought that shooting would stop the car with less danger or greater certainty than waiting.

The majority cites *Long* v. *Slaton*, 508 F.3d 576 (CA11 2007), for the proposition that Mullenix need not have "first tried less lethal methods, such as spike strips." *Ante*, at 17, 193 L. Ed. 2d, at 262. But in that case, there was a clear reason to prefer deadly force over the alternatives. In *Long*, an officer fired to stop a suspect from fleeing in a stolen police cruiser. 508 F.3d, at 583. When the officer fired, there were no alternative means of stopping the car in place. The Eleventh Circuit held that the governmental interest against waiting for a future deployment of spike strips that may never materialize justified the use of deadly force. *Ibid.*

In this case, by contrast, neither petitioner nor the majority can point to any possible marginal gain in shooting at the car over using the spike strips already in place. It is clearly established that there must be some governmental interest that necessitates deadly force, even if it is not always clearly established what level of governmental interest is sufficient.

Under the circumstances known to him at the time, Mullenix puts forth no plausible reason to choose shooting at Leija's engine block over waiting for the results of the spike strips. I would thus hold that Mullenix violated Leija's clearly established right to be free of intrusion absent some governmental interest.

III

The majority largely evades this key legal question by focusing primarily on the governmental interest in *whether* the car should be stopped rather than the dispositive question of *how* the car should be stopped. But even assuming

[577 U.S. 24]

that Leija posed a "sufficient," *ante,* at 15, 193 L. Ed. 2d, at 261, or "immediate," *ante,* at 14, 193 L. Ed. 2d, at 260–261, threat, Mullenix did not face a "choice between two evils" of shooting at a suspect's car or letting him go. *Scott,* 550 U.S., at 384, 127 S. Ct. 1769, 167 L. Ed. 2d 686; see, *e.g., Plumhoff* v. *Rickard,* 572 U.S. 765, 769–770, 134 S. Ct. 2012, 188 L. Ed. 2d 1056 (2014); *Brosseau* v. *Haugen,* 543 U.S. 194,

196-197, 125 S. Ct. 596, 160 L. Ed. 2d 583 (2004) *per curiam.* Instead, Mullenix chose to employ a potentially lethal tactic (shooting at Leija's engine block) in addition to a tactic specifically designed to accomplish the same result (spike strips).* By granting Mullenix qualified immunity, this Court goes a step further than our previous cases and does so without full briefing or argument.

Thus framed, it is apparent that the majority's exhortation that the right at stake not be defined at "a high level of generality," *ante,* at 16, 193 L. Ed. 2d, at 262, is a red herring. The majority adduces various facts that the Fifth Circuit supposedly ignored in its qualified immunity analysis, including that Leija was "a reportedly intoxicated fugitive, set on avoiding capture through high-speed vehicular flight, who twice during his flight had threatened to shoot police officers, and who was moments away from encountering an officer at Cemetery Road." *Ante,* at 13, 193 L. Ed. 2d, at 260. But not one of those facts goes to the governmental interest in shooting over awaiting the spike strips. The majority also claims that established law does not make clear that "Mullenix's reasons were insufficient to justify" his choice of shooting over following his superior's orders to wait for the spikes. *Ante,* at 16, 193 L. Ed. 2d, at 262. But Mullenix

[577 U.S. 25]

seemed to have *no* reasons to prefer shooting to following orders.

---

* The majority describes the choice between spike strips and shooting as the choice between "one dangerous alternative" and another, noting that spike strips can pose a danger to drivers that encounter them. *Ante,* at 15, 193 L. Ed. 2d, at 261. But Mullenix could not have thought that awaiting the spikes was anywhere near as dangerous as shooting immediately before Leija hit the spikes. For one thing, Mullenix had no training in shooting to disable the vehicle and so no idea of the relative danger that shooting posed to a driver. For another, Leija would be subjected to the danger posed by the spike strips whether Mullenix shot or not. And, in fact, that is what happened: Leija's car hit the spike strips and then rolled 2½ times.

Instead of dealing with the question whether Mullenix could constitutionally fire on Leija's car rather than waiting for the spike strips, the majority dwells on the imminence of the threat posed by Leija. The majority recharacterizes Mullenix's decision to shoot at Leija's engine block as a split-second, heat-of-the-moment choice, made when the suspect was "moments away." *Ante*, at 13, 193 L. Ed. 2d, at 260. Indeed, reading the majority opinion, one would scarcely believe that Mullenix arrived at the overpass several minutes before he took his shot, or that the rural road where the car chase occurred had few cars and no bystanders or businesses. 773 F.3d, at 717, 720. The majority also glosses over the facts that Mullenix had time to ask Byrd for permission to fire upon Leija and that Byrd—Mullenix's superior officer—told Mullenix to "stand by." *Id.*, at 717. There was no reason to believe that Byrd did not have all the same information Mullenix did, including the knowledge that an officer was stationed beneath the overpass. Even after receiving Byrd's response, Mullenix spent minutes in shooting position discussing his next step with a fellow officer, minutes during which he received no information that would have made his plan more suitable or his superior's orders less so. *Ibid.*

An appropriate reading of the record on summary judgment would thus render Mullenix's choice even more unreasonable. And asking the appropriate legal question would leave the majority with no choice but to conclude that Mullenix ignored the longstanding and well-settled Fourth Amendment rule that there must be a governmental interest not just in seizing a suspect, but in the level of force used to effectuate that seizure.

* * *

When Mullenix confronted his superior officer after the shooting, his first words were, "How's that for proactive?"

[577 U.S. 26]
Ibid. (Mullenix was apparently referencing an earlier counseling session in which Byrd suggested that he was not enterprising enough. *Ibid.*) The glib comment does not impact our legal analysis; an officer's actual intentions are irrelevant to the Fourth Amendment's "objectively reasonable" inquiry. See *Graham* v. *Connor*, 490 U.S. 386, 397, 109 S. Ct. 1865, 104 L. Ed. 2d 443 (1989). But the comment seems to me revealing of the culture this Court's decision supports when it calls it reasonable—or even reasonably reasonable—to use deadly force for no discernible gain and over a supervisor's express order to "stand by." By sanctioning a "shoot first, think later" approach to policing, the Court renders the protections of the Fourth Amendment hollow.

For the reasons discussed, I would deny Mullenix's petition for a writ of certiorari. I thus respectfully dissent.

OBB PERSONENVERKEHR AG, Petitioner

v

CAROL P. SACHS

577 U.S. 27, 136 S. Ct. 390, 193 L. Ed. 2d 269, 2015 U.S. LEXIS 7670

[No. 13-1067]

Argued October 5, 2015. Decided December 1, 2015.

Decision: American passenger's suit for injury against Austrian state-owned railway was barred by sovereign immunity, as suit fell outside 28 U.S.C.S. § 1605(a)(2)'s commercial-activity exception.

Prior history: ON WRIT OF CERTIORARI TO THE UNITED STATES COURT OF APPEALS FOR THE NINTH CIRCUIT, 737 F.3d 584, 2013 U.S. App. LEXIS 24290

SUMMARY

Overview: HOLDINGS: [1]-An injured rail passenger failed to show that her action against a foreign railway operator fell within the commercial activity exception of 28 U.S.C.S. § 1605(a)(2) where she sought to recover for injuries suffered when she fell when attempting to board a train in Austria, thus, the essentials of her suit were found in Austria, and the mere fact that she bought the Eurail pass in the United States was insufficient to show that her claims were based upon that sale for purposes of § 1605(a)(2); [2]-The passenger's argument that her claims were based upon the operator's overall commercial railway enterprise was not considered as she had not presented it to the lower court.

Outcome: Judgment reversed; Unanimous decision.

HEADNOTES

Classified to United States Supreme Court Digest, Lawyers' Edition

Sovereign immunity
L Ed Digest: International Law § 15.5
   1. The Foreign Sovereign Immunities Act shields foreign states and their agencies from suit in United States courts unless the suit falls within one of the Act's specifically enumerated exceptions.

Sovereign immunity — exception
L Ed Digest: International Law § 15.5
   2. The commercial activity exception of the Foreign Sovereign Immunities Act withdraws sovereign

immunity in any case in which the action is based upon a commercial activity carried on in the United States by a foreign state. 28 U.S.C.S. § 1605(a)(2).

Sovereign immunity
L Ed Digest: Courts § 254; International Law § 15.5
   3. The Foreign Sovereign Immunities Act provides the sole basis for obtaining jurisdiction over a foreign state in the courts of the United States. The Act defines foreign state

to include a state agency or instrumentality, 28 U.S.C.S. § 1603(a).

Sovereign immunity — exception
L Ed Digest: International Law § 15.5
4. See 28 U.S.C.S. § 1605(a)(2), which, in part, withdraws sovereign immunity in any case in which an action against a foreign state is based upon a commercial activity carried on in the United States by the foreign state.

Sovereign immunity — exception
L Ed Digest: International Law § 15.5
5. The Foreign Sovereign Immunities Act's "based upon" inquiry first requires a court to identify the particular conduct on which the plaintiff's action is based. Considering dictionary definitions and lower court decisions, judicial precedent explains that a court should identify that particular conduct by looking to the basis or foundation for a claim, those elements that, if proven, would entitle a plaintiff to relief, and the gravamen of the complaint.

Sovereign immunity — exception
L Ed Digest: International Law § 15.5
6. Under judicial precedent, the mere fact that the sale of the Eurail pass would establish a single element of a claim is insufficient to demonstrate that the claim is "based upon" that sale for purposes of 28 U.S.C.S. § 1605(a)(2).

Sovereign immunity — exception
L Ed Digest: International Law § 15.5
7. Judicial precedent teaches that, for purposes of 28 U.S.C.S. § 1605(a)(2), an action is based upon the particular conduct that constitutes the gravamen of the suit. Rather than individually analyzing each of the plaintiff's causes of action, courts are to zero in on the core of the plaintiff's suit.

Sovereign immunity — exception
L Ed Digest: International Law § 15.5
8. Commercial activity carried on in the United States by the foreign state, as used in 28 U.S.C.S. § 1605(a)(2), is defined to mean commercial activity carried on by such state and having substantial contact with the United States. 28 U.S.C.S. § 1603(e).

Argument not made below
L Ed Digest: Appeal § 1104
9. Absent unusual circumstances, appellate courts will not entertain arguments not made below.

RESEARCH REFERENCES

28 U.S.C.S. § 1605(a)(2)

2 International Business Planning: Law and Taxation § 14.14 (Matthew Bender)

L Ed Digest, International Law § 15.5

L Ed Index, Foreign Sovereign Immunities Act

Annotations:

Supreme Court's views as to constitutionality, construction, and application of Foreign Sovereign Immunities Act of 1976 (28 U.S.C.S. §§1330, 1332(a)(2)-(4), 1391(f), 1441(d), 1602-1611). 102 L. Ed. 2d 1093.

Supreme Court's views as to right of foreign nation or its representative to sue in courts of United States. 54 L. Ed. 2d 854.

OBB PERSONENVERKEHR AG v. SACHS

(2015) 577 U.S. 27, 136 S. Ct. 390, 193 L. Ed. 2d 269, 2015 U.S. LEXIS 7670

APPEARANCES OF COUNSEL ARGUING CASE

Juan C. Basombrio argued the cause for petitioner.

Edwin S. Kneedler argued the cause for the United States, as amicus curiae, by special leave of court.

Jeffrey L. Fisher argued the cause for respondent.

SYLLABUS BY REPORTER OF DECISIONS

Respondent Carol Sachs, a California resident, purchased a Eurail pass over the Internet from a Massachusetts-based travel agent. While using that pass to board a train in Austria operated by petitioner OBB Personenverkehr AG (OBB), the Austrian state-owned railway, Sachs fell to the tracks and suffered traumatic personal injuries. She sued OBB in Federal District Court. OBB moved to dismiss, claiming that her suit was barred by the Foreign Sovereign Immunities Act, which shields foreign states and their agencies and instrumentalities from suit in United States courts, unless a specified exception applies. Sachs countered that her suit fell within the Act's commercial activity exception, which abrogates sovereign immunity for suits "based upon a commercial activity carried on in the United States by [a] foreign state," 28 U.S.C. § 1605(a)(2), reasoning that her suit was "based upon" the Massachusetts-based travel agent's sale of the Eurail pass in the United States, and that the travel agent's sale of that pass could be attributed to OBB through common law principles of agency. The District Court held that Sachs's suit did not fall within § 1605(a)(2) and dismissed the suit,

but the en banc Ninth Circuit reversed. The court first concluded that the Eurail pass sale by the travel agent could be attributed to OBB through common law principles of agency, and then determined that Sachs's suit was "based upon" that Eurail pass sale because the sale established a single element necessary to recover under each cause of action brought by Sachs.

Held: Sachs's suit falls outside the commercial activity exception and is therefore barred by sovereign immunity. Pp. 32–38, 193 L. Ed. 2d, at 275-278.

(a) Sachs's suit is not "based upon" the sale of the Eurail pass for purposes of § 1605(a)(2). Therefore, the Court has no need to address whether the Act allows the travel agent's sale of the Eurail pass to be attributed to OBB through common law principles of agency. Pp. 32–36, 193 L. Ed. 2d, at 275-277.

(1) Although the Act does not elaborate on the phrase "based upon," *Saudi Arabia* v. *Nelson*, 507 U.S. 349, 113 S. Ct. 1471, 123 L. Ed. 2d 47, provides sufficient guidance to resolve this case. There, the Court held that the "based upon" inquiry requires a

court to determine the "particular conduct on which the action is 'based,'" *id.*, at 356, 113 S. Ct. 1471, 123 L. Ed. 2d 47, and identified that conduct by looking to "the 'gravamen of the complaint,'" *id.*, at 357, 113 S. Ct. 1471, 123 L. Ed. 2d 47. Pp. 33–34, 193 L. Ed. 2d, at 275.

(2) The Ninth Circuit used a flawed approach when it found that the "based upon" inquiry would be satisfied if the sale of the Eurail pass provided *"an element"* of each of Sachs's claims. This Court's approach in *Nelson* is flatly incompatible with such a one-element approach, which necessarily requires a court to identify all the elements of each claim before finding that the claim falls outside § 1605(a)(2). The *Nelson* Court did not undertake such an exhaustive claim-by-claim, element-by-element analysis or engage in the choice-of-law analysis necessary to such an undertaking. See 507 U.S., at 356–358, 113 S. Ct. 1471, 123 L. Ed. 2d 47. Pp. 34–35, 193 L. Ed. 2d, at 276.

(3) As opposed to adopting a one-element test, the *Nelson* Court zeroed in on the core of the plaintiffs' suit—

the conduct that actually injured the plaintiffs—to identify the conduct that the suit was "based upon." See 507 U.S., at 358, 113 S. Ct. 1471, 123 L. Ed. 2d 47. All of Sachs's claims turn on the same tragic episode in Austria, allegedly caused by wrongful conduct and dangerous conditions in Austria, which led to injuries suffered in Austria. However Sachs frames her suit, the incident in Innsbruck, Austria, remains at its foundation. Any other approach would allow plaintiffs to evade the Act's restrictions through artful pleading. See *id.*, at 363, 113 S. Ct. 1471, 123 L. Ed. 2d 47. Pp. 35–36, 193 L. Ed. 2d, at 276-277.

(b) Sachs now contends that her claims are "based upon" OBB's entire railway enterprise. Because that argument was never presented to any lower court, it is forfeited. See *Taylor v. Freeland & Kronz*, 503 U.S. 638, 645-646, 112 S. Ct. 1644, 118 L. Ed. 2d 280. Pp. 36–38, 193 L. Ed. 2d, at 277-278.

737 F.3d 584, reversed.

Roberts, C. J., delivered the opinion for a unanimous Court.

OPINION OF THE COURT

[577 U.S. 29]

Chief Justice **Roberts** delivered the opinion of the Court.

[1] The Foreign Sovereign Immunities Act shields foreign states and their agencies from suit in United States courts unless the suit falls within one of the Act's specifically enumerated exceptions. This case concerns the scope of [2] the commercial activity exception, which withdraws sovereign immunity in any case "in which the action is based

upon a commercial activity carried on in the United States by [a] foreign state." 28 U.S.C. § 1605(a)(2).

Respondent Carol Sachs is a resident of California who purchased in the United States a Eurail pass for rail travel in Europe. She suffered traumatic personal injuries when she fell onto the tracks at the Innsbruck, Austria, train station while attempting to board a train operated by the Austrian state-owned railway. She sued the railway in Federal District Court, arguing that her suit was not barred by sovereign immunity because it is "based upon" the railway's sale of the pass to her in the United States. We disagree and conclude that her action is instead "based upon" the railway's conduct in Innsbruck. We therefore hold that her suit falls outside the commercial activity exception and is barred by sovereign immunity.

I

A

Petitioner OBB Personenverkehr AG (OBB) operates a railway that carries nearly 235 million passengers each year on routes within Austria and to and from points beyond Austria's frontiers. OBB is wholly owned by OBB Holding Group, a joint-stock company created by the Republic of Austria. OBB Holding Group in turn is wholly owned by the Austrian Federal Ministry of Transport, Innovation, and Technology. *Sachs* v. *Republic of Austria*, 737 F.3d 584, 587 (CA9 2013).

OBB—along with 29 other railways throughout Europe—is a member of the Eurail Group, an association responsible

[577 U.S. 30]

for the marketing and management of the Eurail pass program. Brief for International Rail Transport Committee as *Amicus Curiae* 12; 737 F.3d, at 587. Eurail passes allow their holders unlimited passage for a set period of time on participating Eurail Group railways. They are available only to non-Europeans, who may purchase them both directly from the Eurail Group and indirectly through a worldwide network of travel agents. Brief for International Rail Transport Committee as *Amicus Curiae* 12-13, and n. 3; Brief for Respondent 4-5.

Carol Sachs is a resident of Berkeley, California. In March 2007, she purchased a Eurail pass over the Internet from The Rail Pass Experts, a Massachusetts-based travel agent. The following month, Sachs arrived at the Innsbruck train station, planning to use her Eurail pass to ride an OBB train to Prague. As she attempted to board the train, Sachs fell from the platform onto the tracks. OBB's moving train crushed her legs, both of which had to be amputated above the knee. 737 F.3d, at 587-588.

Sachs sued OBB in the United States District Court for the Northern District of California, asserting five causes of action: (1) negligence; (2) strict liability for design defects in the train and platform; (3) strict liability for failure to warn of those design defects; (4) breach of an implied warranty of merchantability for providing a train and platform unsafe for their intended uses; and (5) breach of an implied warranty of fitness for providing a train and platform unfit for their intended uses. App. 14-18. OBB claimed sovereign immunity and moved to dismiss the suit for lack of subject matter jurisdiction. 737 F.3d, at 588.

B

[3] The Foreign Sovereign Immunities Act "provides the sole basis for obtaining jurisdiction over a foreign state in the courts of this country." *Argentine Republic* v. *Amerada Hess Shipping Corp.*, 488 U.S. 428, 443, 109 S. Ct. 683, 102 L. Ed. 2d 818 (1989). The Act defines "foreign state" to include a state "agency or instrumentality,"

[577 U.S. 31]

28 U.S.C. § 1603(a), and both parties agree that OBB qualifies as a "foreign state" for purposes of the Act. OBB is therefore "presumptively immune from the jurisdiction of United States courts" unless one of

the Act's express exceptions to sovereign immunity applies. *Saudi Arabia v. Nelson*, 507 U.S. 349, 355, 113 S. Ct. 1471, 123 L. Ed. 2d 47 (1993). Sachs argues that her suit falls within the Act's commercial activity exception, which provides in part that a foreign state does not enjoy immunity when "the action is based upon a commercial activity carried on in the United States by the foreign state." § 1605(a)(2).[1]

The District Court concluded that Sachs's suit did not fall within § 1605(a)(2) and therefore granted OBB's motion to dismiss. 2011 U.S. Dist. LEXIS 27149, 2011 WL 816854, *1, *4 (ND Cal., Jan. 28, 2011). A divided panel of the United States Court of Appeals for the Ninth Circuit affirmed. 695 F.3d 1021 (2012). The full court ordered rehearing en banc and, with three judges dissenting, reversed the panel decision. 737 F.3d 584.

The en banc majority first observed that, "based on the agreement of the parties," "the only relevant commercial activity within the United States was [Sachs's] March 2007 purchase of a Eurail pass from the Rail Pass Experts," a Massachusetts company. *Id.*, at 591, n. 4 (internal quotation marks omitted). The court concluded that The Rail Pass Experts had acted as OBB's agent and, using common law principles of agency, attributed that Eurail pass sale to OBB. *Id.*, at 591-598.

[577 U.S. 32]

The court next asked whether Sachs's claims were "based upon" the sale of the Eurail pass within the meaning of § 1605(a)(2). The "based upon" determination, the court explained, requires that the commercial activity within the United States be "connected with the conduct that gives rise to the plaintiff's cause of action." *Id.*, at 590. But, the court continued, "it is not necessary that the entire claim be based upon the commercial activity of OBB." *Id.*, at 599. Rather, in the court's view, Sachs would satisfy the "based upon" requirement for a particular claim "if *an element* of [that] claim consists in conduct that occurred in commercial activity carried on in the United States." *Ibid.* (internal quotation marks omitted).

Applying California law, see *id.*, at 600, n. 14, the court analyzed Sachs's causes of action individually and concluded that the sale of the Eurail pass established a necessary element of each of her claims. Turning first to the negligence claim, the court found that Sachs was required to show that OBB owed her a duty of care as a passenger as one element of that claim. The court concluded that such a duty arose from the sale of the Eurail pass. *Id.*, at 600-602. Turning next to the other claims, the court determined that the existence of a "transaction between a seller and a consumer" was a necessary element of Sachs's strict liability and breach of implied war-

---

1. Section 1605(a)(2) contains three separate clauses. In full, the section provides:

[4] "A foreign state shall not be immune from the jurisdiction of courts of the United States or of the States in any case . . . in which the action is based upon a commercial activity carried on in the United States by the foreign state; or upon an act performed in the United States in connection with a commercial activity of the foreign state elsewhere; or upon an act outside the territory of the United States in connection with a commercial activity of the foreign state elsewhere and that act causes a direct effect in the United States."

As Sachs relies only on the first clause to establish jurisdiction over her suit, we limit our inquiry to that clause.

ranty claims. *Id.*, at 602. The sale of the Eurail pass, the court noted, provided proof of such a transaction. *Ibid.* Having found that "the sale of the Eurail pass in the United States forms an essential element of each of Sachs's claims," the court concluded that each claim was "based upon a commercial activity carried on in the United States" by OBB. *Ibid.*

We granted certiorari. 574 U.S. 1133, 135 S. Ct. 1172, 190 L. Ed. 2d 929 (2015).

II

OBB contends that the sale of the Eurail pass is not attributable to the railway, reasoning that the Foreign Sovereign

[577 U.S. 33]
Immunities Act does not allow attribution through principles found in the common law of agency. OBB also argues that even if such attribution were allowed under the Act, Sachs's suit is not "based upon" the sale of the Eurail pass for purposes of § 1605(a)(2). We agree with OBB on the second point and therefore do not reach the first.

A

The Act itself does not elaborate on the phrase "based upon." Our decision in *Saudi Arabia* v. *Nelson*, 507 U.S. 349, 113 S. Ct. 1471, 123 L. Ed. 2d 47, however, provides sufficient guidance to resolve this case. In *Nelson*, a husband and wife brought suit against Saudi Arabia and its state-owned hospital, seeking damages for intentional and negligent torts stemming from the husband's allegedly wrongful arrest, imprisonment, and torture by Saudi police while he was employed at a hospital in Saudi Arabia. *Id.*, at 351, 353-354, 113 S. Ct. 1471, 123 L. Ed. 2d 47. The Saudi defendants claimed sovereign immunity under the Act, arguing, *inter alia*, that § 1605(a)(2) was inapplicable because the suit was "based upon" sovereign acts—the exercise of Saudi police authority—and not upon commercial activity. See Brief for Petitioners in *Saudi Arabia* v. *Nelson*, O. T. 1992, No. 91-552, pp. 12-14. The Nelsons countered that their suit was "based upon" the defendants' commercial activities in "recruit[ing] Scott Nelson for work at the hospital, sign[ing] an employment contract with him, and subsequently employ[ing] him." 507 U.S., at 358, 113 S. Ct. 1471, 123 L. Ed. 2d 47. We rejected the Nelsons' arguments.

[5] The Act's "based upon" inquiry, we reasoned, first requires a court to "identify[] the particular conduct on which the [plaintiff's] action is 'based.'" *Id.*, at 356, 113 S. Ct. 1471, 123 L. Ed. 2d 47. Considering dictionary definitions and lower court decisions, we explained that a court should identify that "particular conduct" by looking to the "basis" or "foundation" for a claim, *id.*, at 357, 113 S. Ct. 1471, 123 L. Ed. 2d 47 (citing dictionary definitions), "those elements . . . that, if proven, would entitle a plaintiff to relief," *ibid.*, and "the

[577 U.S. 34]
'gravamen of the complaint,'" *ibid.* (quoting *Callejo* v. *Bancomer, S. A.*, 764 F.2d 1101, 1109 (CA5 1985)). Under that analysis, we found that the commercial activities, while they "led to the conduct that eventually injured the Nelsons," were not the particular conduct upon which their suit was based. The suit was instead based upon the Saudi sovereign acts that actually injured them. 507 U.S., at 358, 113 S. Ct. 1471, 123 L. Ed. 2d 47. The Nelsons' suit therefore did not fit within § 1605(a)(2). *Id.*, at 361-362, 113 S. Ct. 1471, 123 L. Ed. 2d 47.

B

The Ninth Circuit held that Sachs's claims were "based upon" the sale of the Eurail pass because the sale of the pass provided *"an element"* of each of her claims. 737 F.3d, at 599. **[6]** Under *Nelson*, however, the mere fact that the sale of the Eurail pass would establish a single element of a claim is insufficient to demonstrate that the claim is "based upon" that sale for purposes of § 1605(a)(2).

The Ninth Circuit apparently derived its one-element test from an overreading of one part of one sentence in *Nelson*, in which we observed that "the phrase ['based upon'] is read most naturally to mean those elements of a claim that, if proven, would entitle a plaintiff to relief under his theory of the case." 507 U.S., at 357, 113 S. Ct. 1471, 123 L. Ed. 2d 47. We do not see how that mention of elements—plural—could be considered an endorsement of a *one*-element test, nor how the particular element the Ninth Circuit singled out for each of Sachs's claims could be construed to entitle her to relief.

Be that as it may, our analysis in *Nelson* is flatly incompatible with a one-element approach. A one-element test necessarily requires a court to identify *all* the elements of each claim in a complaint before that court may reject those claims for falling outside § 1605(a)(2). But we did not undertake such an exhaustive claim-by-claim, element-by-element analysis of the Nelsons' 16 causes of action, nor did we engage in the choice-of-law analysis that would have been a necessary prelude to such an undertaking. Compare *id.*, at

[577 U.S. 35]

356-358, 113 S. Ct. 1471, 123 L. Ed. 2d 47, with 737 F.3d, at 600, n. 14 (noting disagreement over whether state or federal common law principles govern suits under the Foreign Sovereign Immunities Act).

[7] *Nelson* instead teaches that an action is "based upon" the "particular conduct" that constitutes the "gravamen" of the suit. Rather than individually analyzing each of the Nelsons' causes of action, we zeroed in on the core of their suit: the Saudi sovereign acts that actually injured them. As the Court explained:

"Even taking each of the Nelsons' allegations about Scott Nelson's recruitment and employment as true, those facts alone entitle the Nelsons to nothing under their theory of the case. The Nelsons have . . . alleged . . . personal injuries caused by [the defendants'] intentional wrongs and by [the defendants'] negligent failure to warn Scott Nelson that they might commit those wrongs. Those torts, and not the arguably commercial activities that preceded their commission, form the basis for the Nelsons' suit." 507 U.S., at 358, 113 S. Ct. 1471, 123 L. Ed. 2d 47.

Under this analysis, the conduct constituting the gravamen of Sachs's suit plainly occurred abroad. All of her claims turn on the same tragic episode in Austria, allegedly caused by wrongful conduct and dangerous conditions in Austria, which led to injuries suffered in Austria.

Sachs maintains that some of those claims are not limited to negligent conduct or unsafe conditions in Austria, but rather involve at least some wrongful action in the United States. Her strict liability claim for failure to warn, for example, alleges that OBB should have alerted her to the dangerous conditions at the Innsbruck train station when OBB sold the Eurail pass to her *in the United States*. Under any theory of the case that Sachs presents, however, there is nothing wrongful about the sale of the Eurail pass standing alone. Without the existence of the unsafe boarding conditions in Innsbruck, there would have been nothing to warn

[577 U.S. 36]

Sachs about when she bought the Eurail pass. However Sachs frames her suit, the incident in Innsbruck remains at its foundation.

As we explained in *Nelson*, any other approach would allow plaintiffs to evade the Act's restrictions through artful pleading. For example, any plaintiff "could recast virtually any claim of intentional tort . . . as a claim of failure to warn, simply by charging the defendant with an obligation to announce its own tortious propensity before indulging it." *Id.*, at 363, 113 S. Ct. 1471, 123 L. Ed. 2d 47. To allow such "recast[ing]" of a complaint, we reasoned, would "give jurisdictional significance to [a] feint of language," thereby "effectively thwart[ing] the Act's manifest purpose." *Ibid.*

A century ago, in a letter to then-Professor Frankfurter, Justice Holmes wrote that the "essentials" of a personal injury narrative will be found at the "point of contact"—"the place where the boy got his fingers pinched." Letter (Dec. 19, 1915), in Holmes and Frankfurter: Their Correspondence, 1912-1934, p. 40 (R. Mennel & C. Compston eds. 1996). At least in this case, that insight holds true. Regardless of whether Sachs seeks relief under claims for negligence, strict liability for failure to warn, or breach of implied warranty, the "essentials" of her suit for purposes of § 1605(a)(2) are found in Austria.[2]

III

Sachs raises a new argument in this Court in an attempt to fit her claims within § 1605(a)(2). In addition to arguing that her claims are "based upon" the sale of the Eurail pass, she now contends that her suit is "based upon" "OBB's overall

[577 U.S. 37]

commercial railway enterprise." Brief for Respondent 24; see also Tr. of Oral Arg. 38.

[8] "[C]ommercial activity carried on in the United States by the foreign state," as used in § 1605(a)(2), is defined to mean "commercial activity carried on by such state and having substantial contact with the United States." § 1603(e). Sachs's new theory is that OBB's *entire* railway enterprise constitutes the "commercial activity" that has the requisite "substantial contact with the United States," because OBB reaches out to American customers by marketing and selling Eurail passes in the United States.

That argument was never presented to any lower court and is therefore forfeited. Sachs argued in the courts below only that her claims were "based upon" the sale of the Eurail pass, and the lower courts resolved the case on that understanding. See, *e.g.*, 737 F.3d, at 591, n. 4 ("The district court concluded, based

---

2. We cautioned in *Nelson* that the reach of our decision was limited, see *Saudi Arabia* v. *Nelson*, 507 U.S. 349, 358, n. 4, 113 S. Ct. 1471, 123 L. Ed. 2d 47 (1993), and similar caution is warranted here. Domestic conduct with respect to different types of commercial activity may play a more significant role in other suits under the first clause of § 1605(a)(2). In addition, we consider here only a case in which the gravamen of each claim is found in the same place.

on the agreement of the parties, that 'the only relevant commercial activity within the United States was plaintiff's March 2007 purchase of a Eurail Pass from the Rail Pass Experts.' We consider only the relevant conduct as defined by the district court.").[3] Indeed, when we granted certiorari, the relevant question presented for our review was whether Sachs's claims were "based upon" the "sale of the ticket in the United States." Pet. for Cert.

[577 U.S. 38]

i; accord, Brief for Respondent i. We have answered that question in the negative. [9] Absent unusual circumstances—none of which is present here—we will not entertain arguments not made below. *Taylor* v. *Freeland & Kronz*, 503 U.S. 638, 645-646, 112 S. Ct. 1644, 118 L. Ed. 2d 280 (1992).

We therefore conclude that Sachs has failed to demonstrate that her suit falls within the commercial activity exception in § 1605(a)(2). OBB has sovereign immunity under the Act, and accordingly the courts of the United States lack jurisdiction over the suit.

The judgment of the United States Court of Appeals for the Ninth Circuit is reversed.

It is so ordered.

---

3. See also Points and Authorities in Opposition to OBB Personenverkehr AG's Motion To Dismiss in No. 08-01840 (ND Cal.), p. 8 ("The claims herein are based on the purchase of the Eurail pass."); Appellant's Opening Brief in No. 11-15458 (CA9), p. 10 ("[T]he claims are 'based upon' the purchase of the ticket which occurred in the United States."); Appellant's Reply Brief in No. 11-15458 (CA9), p. 8 ("[H]er claim was based on the purchase/sale of the ticket."). The District Court decided the case on that understanding of Sachs's argument. See 2011 U.S. Dist. LEXIS 27149, 2011 WL 816854, *2 (ND Cal., Jan. 28, 2011); see also 2010 U.S. Dist. LEXIS 130316, 2010 WL 4916394, *1 (ND Cal., Nov. 22, 2010). As did the Ninth Circuit panel, see 695 F.3d 1021, 1024 (2012), and, as noted, the Ninth Circuit en banc. When OBB petitioned this Court for writ of certiorari, Sachs's brief in opposition repeated her earlier arguments. See Brief in Opposition 2; see also this Court's Rule 15.2.

STEPHEN M. SHAPIRO, et al., Petitioners

v

DAVID J. McMANUS, JR., CHAIRMAN, MARYLAND STATE BOARD OF
ELECTIONS, et al.

577 U.S. 39, 136 S. Ct. 450, 193 L. Ed. 2d 279, 2015 U.S. LEXIS 7868

[No. 14-990]

Argued November 4, 2015. Decided December 8, 2015.

Decision: Parties alleging that congressional redistricting plan burdened
right of political association under Federal Constitution's First Amendment
were entitled under 28 U.S.C.S. § 2284 to make case before three-judge
Federal District Court.

Prior history: ON WRIT OF CERTIORARI TO THE UNITED STATES
COURT OF APPEALS FOR THE FOURTH CIRCUIT, 584 Fed. Appx. 140,
2014 U.S. App. LEXIS 19122

SUMMARY

Overview: HOLDINGS: [1]-All the district judge had to determine was
whether the request for three judges was made in a case covered by 28 U.S.C.S.
§ 2284(a) because § 2284(a) admitted of no exception, and the subsequent
provision of § 2284(b)(1), that the district judge shall commence the process for
appointment of a three-judge panel unless he determined that three judges
were not required, need not and therefore should not have been read as a grant
of discretion to the district judge to ignore § 2284(a); [2]-The district judge was
required to refer the case to a three-judge court because the present suit was
an action challenging the constitutionality of the apportionment of congressional districts; [3]-The district judge should not have dismissed the claim as
constitutionally insubstantial.

Outcome: Judgment reversed. Case remanded. Unanimous Decision.

HEADNOTES
Classified to United States Supreme Court Digest, Lawyers' Edition

**Three-judge court — when re-
quired**

L Ed Digest: Courts § 225.6

1. In 1976, Congress substantially
curtailed the circumstances under
which a three-judge court is required.
It was no longer required for the
grant of an injunction against state
statutes, Pub. L. No. 94-381, § 1, 90
Stat. 1119, but was mandated for an
action challenging the constitutionality of the apportionment of congressional districts or the apportionment
of any statewide legislative body. 28
U.S.C.S. § 2284(a). Simultaneously,
Congress amended the procedures governing three-judge District Courts.

Three-judge court

L Ed Digest: Courts § 225.3

2. Upon the filing of a request for three judges, the judge to whom the request is presented shall, unless he determines that three judges are not required, immediately notify the chief judge of the circuit, who shall designate two other judges to serve. 28 U.S.C.S. § 2284(b)(1).

Three-judge court — congressional apportionment

L Ed Digest: Courts § 225.6

3. See 28 U.S.C.S. § 2284(a), which provides in part that a Federal District Court of three judges shall be convened when an action is filed challenging the federal constitutionality of the apportionment of congressional districts.

Three-judge court — discretion

L Ed Digest: Courts § 225.5

4. 28 U.S.C.S. § 2284(a) admits of no exception, and the mandatory "shall" normally creates an obligation impervious to judicial discretion. The subsequent provision of § 2284(b)(1), that the District Judge shall commence the process for appointment of a three-judge panel unless he determines that three judges are not required, need not and therefore should not be read as a grant of discretion to the District Judge to ignore § 2284(a). It is not even framed as a proviso, or an exception from that provision, but rather as an administrative detail that is entirely compatible with § 2284(a). The old § 2284(1) triggered the District Judge's duty to refer the matter for the convening of a three-judge court on the filing of the application to enjoin an unconstitutional state law. The current § 2254(b)(1) triggers the judge's duty upon the filing of a request for three judges.

But of course a party may—whether in good faith or bad, through ignorance or hope or malice—file a request for a three-judge court even if the case does not merit one under § 2284(a). Section 2284(b)(1) merely clarifies that a judge need not unthinkingly initiate the procedures to convene a three-judge court without first examining the allegations in the complaint. In short, all the District Judge must determine is whether the request for three judges is made in a case covered by § 2284(a)—no more, no less.

Single judge

L Ed Digest: Courts § 225.5

5. See 28 U.S.C.S. § 2284(b)(3), which provides in part that a single Federal District Court Judge shall not enter judgment on the merits.

Three-judge court — jurisdiction — discretion — judgment on merits

L Ed Digest: Courts §§ 225.5, 256

6. Constitutional claims will not lightly be found insubstantial for purposes of the three-judge-court statute. The U.S. Supreme Court has long distinguished between failing to raise a substantial federal question for jurisdictional purposes and failing to state a claim for relief on the merits; only wholly insubstantial and frivolous claims implicate the former. Absent such frivolity, the failure to state a proper cause of action calls for a judgment on the merits and not for a dismissal for want of jurisdiction. Consistent with this principle, the U.S. Supreme Court's decision in Goosby clarified that "constitutional insubstantiality" for this purpose has been equated with such concepts as essentially fictitious, wholly insubstantial, obviously frivolous, and obvi-

ously without merit. And the adverbs are no mere throwaways; the limiting words "wholly" and "obviously" have cogent legal significance.

RESEARCH REFERENCES

28 U.S.C.S. § 2284

22 Moore's Federal Practice §§404.01, 404.02 (Matthew Bender 3d ed.)

L Ed Digest, Courts §§225.5, 225.6

L Ed Index, Three-Judge Courts

Annotations:

Construction and application of 28 U.S.C.S. § 1253 permitting direct appeal to Supreme Court from order of three-judge District Court granting or denying injunction. 26 L. Ed. 2d 947.

APPEARANCES OF COUNSEL ARGUING CASE

Michael B. Kimberly argued the cause for petitioners.

Steven M. Sullivan argued the cause for respondents.

SYLLABUS BY REPORTER OF DECISIONS

Since 1976, federal law has mandated that a "district court of three judges shall be convened . . . when an action is filed challenging the constitutionality of the apportionment of congressional districts . . . ," 28 U.S.C. § 2284(a), and has provided that "the judge [presented with a request for a three-judge court] shall, unless he determines that three judges are not required, immediately notify the chief judge of the circuit, who shall designate two other judges" to serve, § 2284(b)(1).

Petitioners requested that a three-judge court be convened to consider their claim that Maryland's 2011 congressional redistricting plan burdens their First Amendment right of politi-cal association. Concluding that no relief could be granted for this claim, the District Judge dismissed the action instead of notifying the Chief Judge of the Circuit to convene a three-judge court. The Fourth Circuit affirmed.

Held: Section 2284 entitles petitioners to make their case before a three-judge court. Pp. 42–46, 193 L. Ed. 2d, at 284-286.

(a) Section 2284(a)'s prescription could not be clearer. Because the present suit is indisputably "an action . . . challenging the constitutionality of the apportionment of congressional districts," the District Judge was *required* to refer the case to a three-judge court. Section 2284(a) admits of no exception, and "the mandatory 'shall' . . . normally creates an obligation impervious to judicial discretion." *Lexecon Inc.* v. *Milberg Weiss Bershad Hynes & Lerach*, 523 U.S. 26, 35, 118 S. Ct. 956, 140 L. Ed. 2d 62. The subsequent provision of § 2284(b)(1), that the district judge shall commence the process for appointment of a three-judge panel "unless he determines that three judges are not required," should be read not as a grant of discretion to the district judge to ignore § 2284(a), but as a compatible administrative detail requiring district judges to "determin[e]" only whether the "request for three judges" is made in a case covered by § 2284(a). This conclusion is bolstered by § 2284(b)(3)'s explicit command that "[a] single judge shall not . . . enter judgment on the merits." Pp. 42–44, 193 L. Ed. 2d, at 284-285.

(b) Respondents' alternative argument, that the District Judge should have dismissed petitioners' claim as "constitutionally insubstantial" under *Goosby* v. *Osser*, 409 U.S. 512, 93 S. Ct. 854, 35 L. Ed. 2d 36, is unpersuasive. This Court has long distinguished between failing to raise a substantial federal question for jurisdictional purposes—what *Goosby* addressed—and failing to state a claim for relief on the merits—what the District Judge found here; only "wholly insubstantial and frivolous" claims implicate the former, *Bell* v. *Hood*, 327 U.S. 678, 682-683, 66 S. Ct. 773, 90 L. Ed. 939. Absent such obvious frivolity, "the failure to state a proper cause of action calls for a judgment on the merits and not for a dismissal for want of jurisdiction." *Id.*, at 682, 66 S. Ct. 773, 90 L. Ed. 939. Petitioners' plea for relief, which was based on a legal theory put forward in Justice Kennedy's concurrence in *Vieth* v. *Jubelirer*, 541 U.S. 267, 315, 124 S. Ct. 1769, 158 L. Ed. 2d 546, and uncontradicted in subsequent majority opinions, easily clears *Goosby*'s low bar. Pp. 44–46, 193 L. Ed. 2d, at 285-286.

584 Fed. Appx. 140, reversed and remanded.

Scalia, J., delivered the opinion for a unanimous Court.

OPINION OF THE COURT

[577 U.S. 40]

Justice **Scalia** delivered the opinion of the Court.

We consider under what circumstances, if any, a district judge is free to "determin[e] that three judges are not required" for an action "challenging the constitutionality of the apportionment of congressional districts." 28 U.S.C. §§ 2284(a), (b)(1).

I

A

Rare today, three-judge district courts were more common in the decades before 1976, when they were required for various adjudications, including the grant of an "interlocutory

[577 U.S. 41]

or permanent injunction restraining the enforcement, operation or execution of any State statute . . . upon the ground of the unconstitutionality of such statute." 28 U.S.C. § 2281 (1970 ed.), repealed, Pub. L. 94-381, § 1, 90 Stat. 1119. See Currie, The Three-Judge District Court in Constitutional Litigation, 32 U. Chi. L. Rev. 1,

3-12 (1964). Decisions of three-judge courts could, then as now, be appealed as of right directly to this Court. 28 U.S.C. § 1253.

[1] In 1976, Congress substantially curtailed the circumstances under which a three-judge court is required. It was no longer required for the grant of an injunction against state statutes, see Pub. L. 94-381, § 1, 90 Stat. 1119 (repealing 28 U.S.C. § 2281), but was mandated for "an action . . . challenging the constitutionality of the apportionment of congressional districts or the apportionment of any statewide legislative body." *Id.*, § 3, now codified at 28 U.S.C. § 2284(a).

Simultaneously, Congress amended the procedures governing three-judge district courts. The prior statute had provided: "The district judge to whom the application for injunction or other relief is presented shall constitute one member of [the three-judge] court. On the filing of the application, he shall immediately notify the chief judge of the circuit, who shall designate two other judges" to serve. 28 U.S.C. § 2284(1) (1970 ed.). The amended statute provides: [2] "Upon the filing of a request for three judges, the judge to whom the request is presented shall, *unless he determines that three judges are not required*, immediately notify the chief judge of the circuit, who shall designate two other judges" to serve. 28 U.S.C. § 2284(b)(1) (2012 ed.) (emphasis added). The dispute here concerns the scope of the italicized text.

B

In response to the 2010 Census, Maryland enacted a statute in October 2011 establishing—or, more pejoratively, gerrymandering—the districts for the State's eight congressional

[577 U.S. 42]

seats. Dissatisfied with the crazy-quilt results, see App. to Pet. for Cert. 23a, petitioners, a bipartisan group of citizens, filed suit *pro se* in Federal District Court. Their amended complaint alleges, *inter alia*, that Maryland's redistricting plan burdens their First Amendment right of political association. Petitioners also requested that a three-judge court be convened to hear the case.

The District Judge, however, thought the claim "not one for which relief can be granted." *Benisek* v. *Mack*, 11 F. Supp. 3d 516, 526 (Md. 2014). "[N]othing about the congressional districts at issue in this case affects in any proscribed way [petitioners'] ability to participate in the political debate in any of the Maryland congressional districts in which they might find themselves. They are free to join preexisting political committees, form new ones, or use whatever other means are at their disposal to influence the opinions of their congressional representatives." *Ibid.* (brackets, ellipsis, and internal quotation marks omitted).

For that reason, instead of notifying the Chief Judge of the Circuit of the need for a three-judge court, the District Judge dismissed the action. The Fourth Circuit summarily affirmed in an unpublished disposition. *Benisek* v. *Mack*, 584 Fed. Appx. 140 (CA4 2014). Seeking review in this Court, petitioners pointed out that at least two other Circuits consider it reversible error for a district judge to dismiss a case under § 2284 for failure to state a claim for relief rather than refer it for transfer to a three-judge court. See *LaRouche* v. *Fowler*, 152 F.3d 974, 981-983 (CADC 1998); *LULAC* v.

Texas, 113 F.3d 53, 55-56 (CA5 1997) (*per curiam*). We granted certiorari. *Shapiro* v. *Mack*, 576 U.S. 1003, 135 S. Ct. 2805, 192 L. Ed. 2d 846 (2015).

II

Petitioners' sole contention is that the District Judge had no authority to dismiss the case rather than initiate the procedures to convene a three-judge court. Not so, argue respondents; the 1976 addition to § 2284(b)(1) of the clause "unless

[577 U.S. 43]

he determines that three judges are not required" is precisely such a grant of authority. Moreover, say respondents, Congress declined to specify a standard to constrain the exercise of this authority. Choosing, as the District Judge did, the familiar standard for dismissal under Federal Rule of Civil Procedure 12(b)(6) best serves the purposes of a three-judge court, which (in respondents' view) is to protect States from "hasty, imprudent invalidation" of their statutes by rogue district judges acting alone. Brief for Respondents 27.

Whatever the purposes of a three-judge court may be, respondents' argument needlessly produces a contradiction in the statutory text. That text's initial prescription could not be clearer: **[3]** "A district court of three judges *shall be convened* . . . when an action is filed challenging the constitutionality of the apportionment of congressional districts . . . ." 28 U.S.C. § 2284(a) (emphasis added). Nobody disputes that the present suit is "an action . . . challenging the constitutionality of the apportionment of congressional districts." It follows that the district judge was *required* to refer the case to a three-judge court, for **[4]** § 2284(a) admits of no exception, and "the mandatory 'shall' . . . nor-

mally creates an obligation impervious to judicial discretion." *Lexecon Inc.* v. *Milberg Weiss Bershad Hynes & Lerach*, 523 U.S. 26, 35, 118 S. Ct. 956, 140 L. Ed. 2d 62 (1998); see also *National Assn. of Home Builders* v. *Defenders of Wildlife*, 551 U.S. 644, 661-662, 127 S. Ct. 2518, 168 L. Ed. 2d 467 (2007) (same).

The subsequent provision of § 2284(b)(1), that the district judge shall commence the process for appointment of a three-judge panel "unless he determines that three judges are not required," need not and therefore should not be read as a grant of discretion to the district judge to ignore § 2284(a). It is not even framed as a proviso, or an exception from that provision, but rather as an administrative detail that is entirely compatible with § 2284(a). The old § 2284(1) triggered the district judge's duty to refer the matter for the convening of a three-judge court "[o]n the filing of the application" to

[577 U.S. 44]

enjoin an unconstitutional state law. By contrast, the current § 2284(b)(1) triggers the district judge's duty "[u]pon the filing of a *request* for three judges" (emphasis added). But of course a party may— whether in good faith or bad, through ignorance or hope or malice—file a *request* for a three-judge court even if the case does not merit one under § 2284(a). Section 2284(b)(1) merely clarifies that a district judge need not unthinkingly initiate the procedures to convene a three-judge court without first examining the allegations in the complaint. In short, all the district judge must "determin[e]" is whether the "request for three judges" is made in a case covered by § 2284(a)—no more, no less.

That conclusion is bolstered by § 2284(b)(3)'s explicit command that

[5] "[a] single judge shall not . . . enter judgment on the merits." It would be an odd interpretation that allowed a district judge to do under § 2284(b)(1) what he is forbidden to do under § 2284(b)(3). More likely that Congress intended a three-judge court, and not a single district judge, to enter all final judgments in cases satisfying the criteria of § 2284(a).

III

Respondents argue in the alternative that a district judge is not required to refer a case for the convening of a three-judge court if the constitutional claim is (as they assert petitioners' claim to be) "insubstantial." In *Goosby* v. *Osser*, 409 U.S. 512, 93 S. Ct. 854, 35 L. Ed. 2d 36 (1973), we stated that the filing of a "constitutionally insubstantial" claim did not trigger the three-judge-court requirement under the pre-1976 statutory regime. *Id.*, at 518, 93 S. Ct. 854, 35 L. Ed. 2d 36. *Goosby* rested not on an interpretation of statutory text, but on the familiar proposition that "[i]n the absence of diversity of citizenship, it is essential to jurisdiction that a *substantial* federal question should be presented." *Ex parte Poresky*, 290 U.S. 30, 31, 54 S. Ct. 3, 78 L. Ed. 152 (1933) (*per curiam*) (emphasis added). Absent a substantial federal question, even a single-judge district court lacks jurisdiction, and "[a] three-judge court is not required where the district court itself lacks jurisdiction of the complaint or the complaint is not

[577 U.S. 45]

justiciable in the federal courts." *Gonzalez* v. *Automatic Employees Credit Union*, 419 U.S. 90, 100, 95 S. Ct. 289, 42 L. Ed. 2d 249 (1974).

In the present case, however, the District Judge dismissed petitioners' complaint not because he thought he lacked jurisdiction, but because he concluded that the allegations failed to state a claim for relief on the merits, citing *Ashcroft* v. *Iqbal*, 556 U.S. 662, 129 S. Ct. 1937, 173 L. Ed. 2d 868 (2009), and *Bell Atlantic Corp.* v. *Twombly*, 550 U.S. 544, 127 S. Ct. 1955, 167 L. Ed. 2d 929 (2007). See 11 F. Supp. 3d, at 520. That was in accord with Fourth Circuit precedent, which holds that where the "pleadings do not state a claim, then *by definition they are insubstantial* and so properly are subject to dismissal by the district court without convening a three-judge court." *Duckworth* v. *State Admin. Bd. of Election Laws*, 332 F.3d 769, 772-773 (CA4 2003) (emphasis added).

We think this standard both too demanding and inconsistent with our precedents. **[6]** "[C]onstitutional claims will not lightly be found insubstantial for purposes of" the three-judge-court statute. *Washington* v. *Confederated Tribes of Colville Reservation*, 447 U.S. 134, 147-148, 100 S. Ct. 2069, 65 L. Ed. 2d 10 (1980). We have long distinguished between failing to raise a substantial federal question for jurisdictional purposes—which is what *Goosby* addressed—and failing to state a claim for relief on the merits; only "wholly insubstantial and frivolous" claims implicate the former. *Bell* v. *Hood*, 327 U.S. 678, 682-683, 66 S. Ct. 773, 90 L. Ed. 939 (1946); see also *Hannis Distilling Co.* v. *Mayor and City Council of Baltimore*, 216 U.S. 285, 288, 30 S. Ct. 326, 54 L. Ed. 482 (1910) ("obviously frivolous or plainly insubstantial"); *Bailey* v. *Patterson*, 369 U.S. 31, 33, 82 S. Ct. 549, 7 L. Ed. 2d 512 (1962) (*per curiam*) ("wholly insubstantial," "legally speaking nonexistent," "essentially fictitious"); *Steel Co.* v. *Citizens for Better Environment*, 523 U.S. 83, 89, 118 S. Ct. 1003, 140 L. Ed. 2d 210 (1998) ("frivolous or immaterial"). Absent such frivolity, "the failure to state a proper cause of action calls for a judgment on the merits and not for a dismissal for want of jurisdiction." *Bell, supra,* at 682, 66 S. Ct. 773, 90 L. Ed. 939. Consistent with this principle, *Goosby* clarified that " '[c]onstitutional insubstantiality' for this purpose has been equated with such concepts as 'essentially fictitious,' 'wholly insubstantial,' 'obviously frivolous,'

[577 U.S. 46]

and 'obviously without merit.' " 409 U.S., at 518, 93 S. Ct. 854, 35 L. Ed. 2d 36 (citations omitted). And the adverbs were no mere throwaways; "[t]he limiting words 'wholly' and 'obviously' have cogent legal significance." *Ibid.*

Without expressing any view on the merits of petitioners' claim, we believe it easily clears *Goosby*'s low bar; after all, the amended complaint specifically challenges Maryland's apportionment "along the lines suggested by Justice Kennedy in his concurrence in *Vieth* [v. *Jubelirer*, 541 U.S. 267, 124 S. Ct. 1769, 158 L. Ed. 2d 546 (2004)]." App. to Brief in Opposition 44. Although the *Vieth* plurality thought all political gerrymandering claims nonjusticiable, Justice Kennedy, concurring in the judgment, surmised that if "a State did impose burdens and restrictions on groups or persons by reason of their views, there would likely be a First Amendment violation, unless the State shows some compelling interest. . . . Where it is alleged that a gerrymander had the purpose and effect of imposing burdens on a disfavored party and its voters, the First Amendment may offer a sounder and more prudential basis for intervention than does the Equal Protection Clause." *Vieth* v. *Jubelirer*, 541 U.S. 267, 315, 124 S. Ct. 1769, 158 L. Ed. 2d 546 (2004). Whatever "wholly insubstantial," "obviously frivolous," etc., mean, at a minimum they cannot include a plea for relief based on a legal theory put forward by a Justice of this Court and uncontradicted by the majority in any of our cases. Accordingly, the District Judge should not have dismissed the claim as "constitutionally insubstantial" under *Goosby*. Perhaps petitioners will ultimately fail on the merits of their suit, but § 2284 entitles them to make their case before a three-judge district court.

* * *

The judgment of the Fourth Circuit is reversed, and the case is remanded for further proceedings consistent with this opinion.

It is so ordered.

MEMORANDUM CASES

No. 15-5722. Joseph Banks, Petitioner v. United States.

577 U.S. 936, 136 S. Ct. 365, 193 L. Ed. 2d 287, 2015 U.S. LEXIS 6740.

October 19, 2015. On petition for writ of certiorari to the United States Court of Appeals for the Sixth Circuit. Motion of petitioner for leave to proceed in forma pauperis and petition for writ of certiorari granted. Judgment vacated, and case remanded to the United States Court of Appeals for the Sixth Circuit for further consideration in light of Johnson v. United States, 576 U.S. 591, 135 S. Ct. 2551, 192 L. Ed. 2d 569 (2015).

Same case below, 606 Fed. Appx. 804.

No. 15-5712. Nella Manko, Petitioner v. David A. Gabay, et al.

577 U.S. 936, 136 S. Ct. 364, 193 L. Ed. 2d 287, 2015 U.S. LEXIS 6753.

October 19, 2015. Motion of petitioner for leave to proceed in forma pauperis denied, and petition for writ of certiorari to the Court of Appeals of New York dismissed. See Rule 39.8. As petitioner has repeatedly abused this Court's process, the Clerk is directed not to accept any further petitions in noncriminal matters from petitioner unless the docketing fee required by Rule 38(a) is paid and petition submitted in compliance with Rule 33.1. See Martin v. District of Columbia Court of Appeals, 506 U.S. 1, 113 S. Ct. 397, 121 L. Ed. 2d 305 (1992) (per curiam).

Same case below, 24 N.Y.3d 1206, 4 N.Y.S.3d 588, 28 N.E.3d 22.

No. 15M35. Carrie M. Williams, Petitioner v. Carolyn W. Colvin, Acting Commissioner of Social Security.

577 U.S. 937, 136 S. Ct. 380, 193 L. Ed. 2d 287, 2015 U.S. LEXIS 6690.

October 19, 2015. Motion to direct the Clerk to file a petition for writ of certiorari out of time denied.

Same case below, 604 Fed. Appx. 294.

No. 15M36. Usir Nynetjer El Bey, Petitioner v. Michigan, et al.

577 U.S. 937, 136 S. Ct. 380, 193 L. Ed. 2d 287, 2015 U.S. LEXIS 6607.

October 19, 2015. Motion to direct the Clerk to file a petition for writ of certiorari out of time denied.

No. 15M37. Michael S. Ross, Petitioner v. United States, et al.

577 U.S. 937, 136 S. Ct. 380, 193 L. Ed. 2d 287, 2015 U.S. LEXIS 6619.

October 19, 2015. Motion to direct the Clerk to file a petition for writ of certiorari out of time denied.

No. 15M38. Clifford W. Jones, Sr., Petitioner v. Department of Health and Human Services.

577 U.S. 937, 136 S. Ct. 381, 193 L. Ed. 2d 287, 2015 U.S. LEXIS 6622.

October 19, 2015. Motion to direct the Clerk to file a petition for writ of certiorari out of time denied.

Same case below, 602 Fed. Appx. 808.

No. 15M39. Manuel Rodriguez, Petitioner v. School Board of Polk County, Florida, et al.

577 U.S. 937, 136 S. Ct. 381, 193 L. Ed. 2d 288, 2015 U.S. LEXIS 6601.

October 19, 2015. Motion to direct the Clerk to file a petition for writ of certiorari out of time denied.

Same case below, 599 Fed. Appx. 371.

No. 15M40. Marion S. Blades, Petitioner v. Norman C. Blades, Jr.

577 U.S. 937, 136 S. Ct. 381, 193 L. Ed. 2d 288, 2015 U.S. LEXIS 6637.

October 19, 2015. Motion to direct the Clerk to file a petition for writ of certiorari out of time denied.

Same case below, 442 Md. 194, 112 A.3d 373.

No. 14-940. Sue Evenwel, et al., Appellants v. Greg Abbott, Governor of Texas, et al.

577 U.S. 937, 136 S. Ct. 381, 193 L. Ed. 2d 288, 2015 U.S. LEXIS 6725.

October 19, 2015. Motion of the Solicitor General for leave to participate in oral argument as amicus curiae and for divided argument granted.

No. 14-1146. Tyson Foods, Inc., Petitioner v. Peg Bouaphakeo, et al.,

Individually and on Behalf of All Others Similarly Situated.

577 U.S. 937, 136 S. Ct. 381, 193 L. Ed. 2d 288, 2015 U.S. LEXIS 6628.

October 19, 2015. Motion of the Solicitor General for leave to participate in oral argument as amicus curiae and for divided argument granted.

No. 15-5635. Renee Stephens, Petitioner v. Nike, Inc.

577 U.S. 937, 136 S. Ct. 381, 193 L. Ed. 2d 288, 2015 U.S. LEXIS 6670.

October 19, 2015. Motion of petitioner for leave to proceed in forma pauperis denied. Petitioner is allowed until November 9, 2015, within which to pay the docketing fee required by Rule 38(a) and to submit a petition in compliance with Rule 33.1 of the Rules of this Court.

Same case below, 611 Fed. Appx. 896.

No. 14-614. W. Kevin Hughes, Chairman, Maryland Public Service Commission, et al., Petitioners v. Talen Energy Marketing, LLC, fka PPL EnergyPlus, LLC, et al.

No. 14-623. CPV Maryland, LLC, Petitioner v. Talen Energy Marketing, LLC, fka PPL EnergyPlus, LLC, et al.

577 U.S. 938, 136 S. Ct. 382, 193 L. Ed. 2d 288, 2015 U.S. LEXIS 6659.

October 19, 2015. Petitions for writs of certiorari to the United States Court of Appeals for the Fourth Circuit granted. The cases are consolidated and a total of one hour is allotted for oral argument.

Same cases below, 753 F.3d 467.

No. 14-1513. Halo Electronics, Inc., Petitioner v. Pulse Electronics, Inc., et al.

No. 14-1520. Stryker Corporation, et al., Petitioners v. Zimmer, Inc., et al.

577 U.S. 938, 136 S. Ct. 356, 193 L. Ed. 2d 289, 2015 U.S. LEXIS 6634.

October 19, 2015. Motion of Independent Inventor Groups for leave to file a brief as amici curiae granted. Motion of Nokia Technologies OY, et al. for leave to file a brief as amici curiae granted. Petition for writ of certiorari to the United States Court of Appeals for the Federal Circuit granted in No. 14-1513 limited to Question 1 presented by the petition. Petition for writ of certiorari to the United States Court of Appeals for the Federal Circuit in No. 14-1520 granted. The cases are consolidated and a total of one hour is allotted for oral argument.

Same cases below, 769 F.3d 1371 (first judgment); 782 F.3d 649 (second judgment).

No. 14-1337. Jesus Manuel Diaz, Petitioner v. United States.

577 U.S. 938, 136 S. Ct. 356, 193 L. Ed. 2d 289, 2015 U.S. LEXIS 6646.

October 19, 2015. Petition for writ of certiorari to the United States Court of Appeals for the Tenth Circuit denied.

Same case below, 598 Fed. Appx. 591.

No. 14-10227. Bruce Earl Ward, Petitioner v. Arkansas.

577 U.S. 938, 136 S. Ct. 356, 193 L. Ed. 2d 289, 2015 U.S. LEXIS 6721.

October 19, 2015. Petition for writ of certiorari to the Supreme Court of Arkansas denied.

Same case below, 2015 Ark. 61, 455 S.W.3d 818.

No. 15-36. Edward Michael Glasmann, Petitioner v. Washington.

577 U.S. 938, 136 S. Ct. 357, 193 L. Ed. 2d 289, 2015 U.S. LEXIS 6684.

October 19, 2015. Petition for writ of certiorari to the Supreme Court of Washington denied.

Same case below, 183 Wash. 2d 117, 349 P.3d 829.

No. 15-48. Mujahid Carswell, as Personal Representative of the Estate of Luqman A. Abdullah, Petitioner v. Andrew G. Arena, et al.

577 U.S. 938, 136 S. Ct. 357, 193 L. Ed. 2d 289, 2015 U.S. LEXIS 6653.

October 19, 2015. Petition for writ of certiorari to the United States Court of Appeals for the Sixth Circuit denied.

Same case below, 601 Fed. Appx. 389.

No. 15-176. Irene S. Dische, Petitioner v. Kelly A. Preyer, et al.

577 U.S. 938, 136 S. Ct. 357, 193 L. Ed. 2d 289, 2015 U.S. LEXIS 6609.

October 19, 2015. Petition for writ of certiorari to the Appellate Division, Supreme Court of New York, Third Judicial Department, denied.

Same case below, 121 App. Div. 3d 1216, 994 N.Y.S.2d 449.

No. 15-185. Bodum, Inc., Petitioner v. Meyer Intellectual Properties Limited, et al.

577 U.S. 938, 136 S. Ct. 358, 193 L. Ed. 2d 289, 2015 U.S. LEXIS 6626.

October 19, 2015. Petition for writ of certiorari to the United States Court of Appeals for the Federal Circuit denied.

Same case below, 604 Fed. Appx. 931.

———————

No. 15-197. Brian M. Allen, Petitioner v. Ann Keller, et al.

577 U.S. 939, 136 S. Ct. 358, 193 L. Ed. 2d 290, 2015 U.S. LEXIS 6733.

October 19, 2015. Petition for writ of certiorari to the United States Court of Appeals for the Fifth Circuit denied.

Same case below, 602 Fed. Appx. 200.

———————

No. 15-198. John W. Oller, Petitioner v. Nancye C. Roussel, Individually and in Her Official Capacity as Head of the Department of Communicative Disorders, University of Louisiana at Lafayette, et al.

577 U.S. 939, 136 S. Ct. 358, 193 L. Ed. 2d 290, 2015 U.S. LEXIS 6702.

October 19, 2015. Petition for writ of certiorari to the United States Court of Appeals for the Fifth Circuit denied.

Same case below, 609 Fed. Appx. 770.

———————

No. 15-200. Kenneth J. Taggart, Petitioner v. GMAC Mortgage, LLC, et al.

577 U.S. 939, 136 S. Ct. 358, 193 L. Ed. 2d 290, 2015 U.S. LEXIS 6694, reh den 577 U.S. 1095, 136 S. Ct. 882, 193 L. Ed. 2d 773, 2016 U.S. LEXIS 334.

October 19, 2015. Petition for writ of certiorari to the United States Court of Appeals for the Third Circuit denied.

Same case below, 600 Fed. Appx. 859.

———————

No. 15-202. Maureen Uche, Petitioner v. Montgomery Hospice, Inc., et al.

577 U.S. 939, 136 S. Ct. 359, 193 L. Ed. 2d 290, 2015 U.S. LEXIS 6662.

October 19, 2015. Petition for writ of certiorari to the United States Court of Appeals for the Fourth Circuit denied.

Same case below, 599 Fed. Appx. 97.

———————

No. 15-205. William Phipps, Petitioner v. Cathy C. Phipps.

577 U.S. 939, 136 S. Ct. 360, 193 L. Ed. 2d 290, 2015 U.S. LEXIS 6710.

October 19, 2015. Petition for writ of certiorari to the Court of Appeals of Tennessee, Eastern Division, denied.

———————

No. 15-220. Sandra Sue Grazzini-Rucki, Individually and on Behalf of Her Children, N.J.R., S.V.R., G.J.R., N.G.R., and G.P.R., Petitioner v. David Knutson, et al.

577 U.S. 939, 136 S. Ct. 361, 193 L. Ed. 2d 290, 2015 U.S. LEXIS 6606.

October 19, 2015. Petition for writ of certiorari to the United States Court of Appeals for the Eighth Circuit denied.

Same case below, 597 Fed. Appx. 902.

———————

No. 15-224. Hector R. Garza-Mata, Petitioner v. United States, et al.

577 U.S. 939, 136 S. Ct. 361, 193 L. Ed. 2d 290, 2015 U.S. LEXIS 6695.

October 19, 2015. Petition for writ of certiorari to the United States Court of Appeals for the Fifth Circuit denied.

Same case below, 598 Fed. Appx. 295.

No. 15-228. Mark Kevin Miller, Petitioner v. Wal-Mart Stores, Inc.

577 U.S. 939, 136 S. Ct. 363, 193 L. Ed. 2d 291, 2015 U.S. LEXIS 6633.

October 19, 2015. Petition for writ of certiorari to the United States Court of Appeals for the Fourth Circuit denied.

Same case below, 606 Fed. Appx. 99.

No. 15-240. Carolyn Mizukami, Petitioner v. Don Quijote (USA) Co. Ltd., et al.

577 U.S. 939, 136 S. Ct. 366, 193 L. Ed. 2d 291, 2015 U.S. LEXIS 6599.

October 19, 2015. Petition for writ of certiorari to the Intermediate Court of Appeals of Hawaii denied.

Same case below, 134 Haw. 539, 345 P.3d 205.

No. 15-258. Health Grades, Inc., Petitioner v. Christopher Boyer, et al.

577 U.S. 939, 136 S. Ct. 367, 193 L. Ed. 2d 291, 2015 U.S. LEXIS 6654.

October 19, 2015. Petition for writ of certiorari to the Supreme Court of Colorado denied.

Same case below, 359 P.3d 25.

No. 15-268. Danny R. Love, Petitioner v. Memphis-Shelby County Airport Authority.

577 U.S. 939, 136 S. Ct. 368, 193 L. Ed. 2d 291, 2015 U.S. LEXIS 6701.

October 19, 2015. Petition for writ of certiorari to the United States Court of Appeals for the Sixth Circuit denied.

No. 15-286. William D. Rogers, et ux., Petitioners v. Commissioner of Internal Revenue.

577 U.S. 939, 136 S. Ct. 369, 193 L. Ed. 2d 291, 2015 U.S. LEXIS 6689.

October 19, 2015. Petition for writ of certiorari to the United States Court of Appeals for the District of Columbia Circuit denied.

Same case below, 783 F.3d 320.

No. 15-296. Eric C. Onyango, Petitioner v. Nick & Howard, LLC, et al.

577 U.S. 939, 136 S. Ct. 369, 193 L. Ed. 2d 291, 2015 U.S. LEXIS 6664.

October 19, 2015. Petition for writ of certiorari to the United States Court of Appeals for the Seventh Circuit denied.

Same case below, 607 Fed. Appx. 552.

No. 15-301. Ian Aulden Campbell, Petitioner v. North Carolina.

577 U.S. 939, 136 S. Ct. 369, 193 L. Ed. 2d 291, 2015 U.S. LEXIS 6703.

October 19, 2015. Petition for writ of certiorari to the Superior Court of North Carolina, Wake County, denied.

No. 15-312. Ohan Karagozian, Petitioner v. Commissioner of Internal Revenue.

577 U.S. 940, 136 S. Ct. 370, 193 L. Ed. 2d 291, 2015 U.S. LEXIS 6708.

October 19, 2015. Petition for writ of certiorari to the United States Court of Appeals for the Second Circuit denied.

Same case below, 595 Fed. Appx. 87.

Same case below, 786 F.3d 1287.

No. 15-313. Ralph Stanley Cooper, Petitioner v. Kevin Bennett.

577 U.S. 940, 136 S. Ct. 372, 193 L. Ed. 2d 292, 2015 U.S. LEXIS 6644.

October 19, 2015. Petition for writ of certiorari to the United States Court of Appeals for the Ninth Circuit denied.

Same case below, 621 Fed. Appx. 875.

No. 15-315. Daryl Overka, et al., Petitioners v. American Airlines, Inc.

577 U.S. 940, 136 S. Ct. 372, 193 L. Ed. 2d 292, 2015 U.S. LEXIS 6603.

October 19, 2015. Petition for writ of certiorari to the United States Court of Appeals for the First Circuit denied.

Same case below, 790 F.3d 36.

No. 15-317. William L. Bost, Petitioner v. United States.

577 U.S. 940, 136 S. Ct. 372, 193 L. Ed. 2d 292, 2015 U.S. LEXIS 6696.

October 19, 2015. Petition for writ of certiorari to the United States Court of Appeals for the Sixth Circuit denied.

Same case below, 606 Fed. Appx. 821.

No. 15-325. Todd Cahill, Petitioner v. Pre-Paid Legal Services, Inc.

577 U.S. 940, 136 S. Ct. 373, 193 L. Ed. 2d 292, 2015 U.S. LEXIS 6748.

October 19, 2015. Petition for writ of certiorari to the United States Court of Appeals for the Tenth Circuit denied.

No. 15-337. Charles J. Conway, Jr., et al., Petitioners v. California State Water Resources Control Board, et al.

577 U.S. 940, 136 S. Ct. 374, 193 L. Ed. 2d 292, 2015 U.S. LEXIS 6671.

October 19, 2015. Petition for writ of certiorari to the Court of Appeal of California, Second Appellate District, Division Six, denied.

Same case below, 235 Cal. App. 4th 671, 185 Cal. Rptr. 3d 490.

No. 15-347. Charles W. McCall, Petitioner v. United States.

577 U.S. 940, 136 S. Ct. 374, 193 L. Ed. 2d 292, 2015 U.S. LEXIS 6657.

October 19, 2015. Petition for writ of certiorari to the United States Court of Appeals for the Ninth Circuit denied.

No. 15-5132. John Steven Huggins, Petitioner v. Florida, et al.

577 U.S. 940, 136 S. Ct. 357, 193 L. Ed. 2d 292, 2015 U.S. LEXIS 6649.

October 19, 2015. Petition for writ of certiorari to the Supreme Court of Florida denied.

Same case below, 161 So. 3d 335.

No. 15-5265. Steven LaWayne Nelson, Petitioner v. Texas.

577 U.S. 940, 136 S. Ct. 357, 193 L. Ed. 2d 292, 2015 U.S. LEXIS 6666.

October 19, 2015. Petition for writ of certiorari to the Court of Criminal Appeals of Texas denied.

No. 15-5299. Shedran Williams, Petitioner v. Louisiana.

577 U.S. 940, 136 S. Ct. 357, 193 L. Ed. 2d 293, 2015 U.S. LEXIS 6612.

October 19, 2015. Petition for writ of certiorari to the District Court of Louisiana, East Baton Rouge Parish, denied.

No. 15-5627. Jeremy Crespin, Petitioner v. Texas (two judgments).

577 U.S. 940, 136 S. Ct. 359, 193 L. Ed. 2d 293, 2015 U.S. LEXIS 6625.

October 19, 2015. Petition for writ of certiorari to the Court of Criminal Appeals of Texas denied.

No. 15-5630. Marcus Lynn Perkins, Petitioner v. Superior Court of California, Los Angeles County, et al.

577 U.S. 940, 136 S. Ct. 359, 193 L. Ed. 2d 293, 2015 U.S. LEXIS 6681.

October 19, 2015. Petition for writ of certiorari to the Court of Appeal of California, Second Appellate District, Division One, denied.

No. 15-5632. Kristin S. Hill, Petitioner v. Indiana.

577 U.S. 940, 136 S. Ct. 359, 193 L. Ed. 2d 293, 2015 U.S. LEXIS 6639.

October 19, 2015. Petition for writ of certiorari to the Court of Appeals of Indiana, Second District, denied.

No. 15-5634. Donald L. Vos, Petitioner v. Jefferson Gough, et al.

577 U.S. 940, 136 S. Ct. 359, 193 L. Ed. 2d 293, 2015 U.S. LEXIS 6700.

October 19, 2015. Petition for writ of certiorari to the Court of Appeals of Ohio, Columbiana County, denied.

No. 15-5636. Antonio Sustaita, Petitioner v. Illinois.

577 U.S. 941, 136 S. Ct. 359, 193 L. Ed. 2d 293, 2015 U.S. LEXIS 6709.

October 19, 2015. Petition for writ of certiorari to the Appellate Court of Illinois, Fourth District, denied.

No. 15-5639. Mitchell Eads, Petitioner v. David Sexton, Warden.

577 U.S. 941, 136 S. Ct. 360, 193 L. Ed. 2d 293, 2015 U.S. LEXIS 6647.

October 19, 2015. Petition for writ of certiorari to the United States Court of Appeals for the Sixth Circuit denied.

No. 15-5649. Jack Lee King, Petitioner v. William Stephens, Director, Texas Department of Criminal Justice, Correctional Institutions Division.

577 U.S. 941, 136 S. Ct. 360, 193 L. Ed. 2d 293, 2015 U.S. LEXIS 6663.

October 19, 2015. Petition for writ of certiorari to the United States Court of Appeals for the Fifth Circuit denied.

No. 15-5650. Q. O., Petitioner v. Ohio.

577 U.S. 941, 136 S. Ct. 360, 193 L. Ed. 2d 294, 2015 U.S. LEXIS 6630.

October 19, 2015. Petition for writ of certiorari to the Court of Appeals of Ohio, Hamilton County, denied.

No. 15-5657. Michael Scott Nelson, Petitioner v. Burl Cain, Warden.

577 U.S. 941, 136 S. Ct. 360, 193 L. Ed. 2d 294, 2015 U.S. LEXIS 6597.

October 19, 2015. Petition for writ of certiorari to the United States Court of Appeals for the Fifth Circuit denied.

No. 15-5658. Lamonte Lake, Petitioner v. Brad Robert, et al.

577 U.S. 941, 136 S. Ct. 361, 193 L. Ed. 2d 294, 2015 U.S. LEXIS 6677.

October 19, 2015. Petition for writ of certiorari to the Appellate Court of Illinois, Fifth District, denied.

No. 15-5661. LaCarlton Dewayne Mitchell, Petitioner v. William Stephens, Director, Texas Department of Criminal Justice, Correctional Institutions Division.

577 U.S. 941, 136 S. Ct. 361, 193 L. Ed. 2d 294, 2015 U.S. LEXIS 6734.

October 19, 2015. Petition for writ of certiorari to the United States Court of Appeals for the Fifth Circuit denied.

No. 15-5662. Carol Johnene Morris, Petitioner v. William Stephens, Director, Texas Department of Criminal Justice, Correctional Institutions Division.

577 U.S. 941, 136 S. Ct. 361, 193 L. Ed. 2d 294, 2015 U.S. LEXIS 6755, reh den 577 U.S. 1054, 136 S. Ct. 706, 193 L. Ed. 2d 532, 2015 U.S. LEXIS 7890.

October 19, 2015. Petition for writ of certiorari to thioe United States Court of Appeals for the Fifth Circuit denied.

No. 15-5666. Kevin A. Williams, Petitioner v. Riliwan Ojelade, et al.

577 U.S. 941, 136 S. Ct. 361, 193 L. Ed. 2d 294, 2015 U.S. LEXIS 6636.

October 19, 2015. Petition for writ of certiorari to the United States Court of Appeals for the Seventh Circuit denied.

No. 15-5668. Shane Johnson, Petitioner v. Colorado.

577 U.S. 941, 136 S. Ct. 362, 193 L. Ed. 2d 294, 2015 U.S. LEXIS 6736.

October 19, 2015. Petition for writ of certiorari to the Court of Appeals of Colorado denied.

No. 15-5673. Jeffrey R. LeBlanc, Petitioner v. Kalamazoo County, Michigan.

577 U.S. 941, 136 S. Ct. 362, 193 L. Ed. 2d 294, 2015 U.S. LEXIS 6750.

October 19, 2015. Petition for writ of certiorari to the United States Court of Appeals for the Sixth Circuit denied.

Same case below, 590 Fed. Appx. 629 and 785 F.3d 1174.

No. 15-5674. Casey Rafael Tyler, Petitioner v. Oliver Washington.

577 U.S. 941, 136 S. Ct. 362, 193 L. Ed. 2d 295, 2015 U.S. LEXIS 6732.

October 19, 2015. Petition for writ of certiorari to the United States Court of Appeals for the Fourth Circuit denied.

Same case below, 599 Fed. Appx. 120.

No. 15-5689. Sylvester J. Hoffart, Petitioner v. Scott Wiggins, et al.

577 U.S. 941, 136 S. Ct. 362, 193 L. Ed. 2d 295, 2015 U.S. LEXIS 6705, reh den 577 U.S. 1054, 136 S. Ct. 707, 193 L. Ed. 2d 532, 2015 U.S. LEXIS 7908.

October 19, 2015. Petition for writ of certiorari to the United States Court of Appeals for the Fifth Circuit denied.

Same case below, 600 Fed. Appx. 261.

No. 15-5698. Frank D. Maki, Petitioner v. New York, et al.

577 U.S. 941, 136 S. Ct. 362, 193 L. Ed. 2d 295, 2015 U.S. LEXIS 6656, reh den 577 U.S. 1096, 136 S. Ct. 885, 193 L. Ed. 2d 777, 2016 U.S. LEXIS 589.

October 19, 2015. Petition for writ of certiorari to the United States Court of Appeals for the Second Circuit denied.

Same case below, 597 Fed. Appx. 36.

No. 15-5699. Lee Blankenship, Petitioner v. Kimberly Birch.

577 U.S. 942, 136 S. Ct. 363, 193 L. Ed. 2d 295, 2015 U.S. LEXIS 6623.

October 19, 2015. Petition for writ of certiorari to the United States Court of Appeals for the Seventh Circuit denied.

No. 15-5703. Willie Bolds, Petitioner v. J. Cavazos, et al.

577 U.S. 942, 136 S. Ct. 363, 193 L. Ed. 2d 295, 2015 U.S. LEXIS 6621, reh den 577 U.S. 1054, 136 S. Ct. 707, 193 L. Ed. 2d 533, 2015 U.S. LEXIS 7993.

October 19, 2015. Petition for writ of certiorari to the United States Court of Appeals for the Ninth Circuit denied.

Same case below, 599 Fed. Appx. 307.

No. 15-5706. Roswitha Ann Savoie, Petitioner v. Ric Bradshaw, Sheriff, Palm Beach County, Florida, et al.

577 U.S. 942, 136 S. Ct. 363, 193 L. Ed. 2d 295, 2015 U.S. LEXIS 6674, reh den 577 U.S. 1096, 136 S. Ct. 885, 193 L. Ed. 2d 777, 2016 U.S. LEXIS 417.

October 19, 2015. Petition for writ of certiorari to the United States Court of Appeals for the Eleventh Circuit denied.

No. 15-5709. David D. Palmer, Petitioner v. Ohio.

577 U.S. 942, 136 S. Ct. 363, 193 L. Ed. 2d 295, 2015 U.S. LEXIS 6635.

October 19, 2015. Petition for writ of certiorari to the Court of Appeals of Ohio, Montgomery County, denied.

No. 15-5711. Sammie L. Booker-El, Petitioner v. Ron Neal, Superintendent, Indiana State Prison.

577 U.S. 942, 136 S. Ct. 363, 193 L. Ed. 2d 295, 2015 U.S. LEXIS 6598.

October 19, 2015. Petition for writ of certiorari to the United States Court of Appeals for the Seventh Circuit denied.

No. 15-5715. James Earl Smith, Petitioner v. Martin Biter, Warden.

577 U.S. 942, 136 S. Ct. 364, 193 L. Ed. 2d 296, 2015 U.S. LEXIS 6667.

October 19, 2015. Petition for writ of certiorari to the United States Court of Appeals for the Ninth Circuit denied.

No. 15-5718. Julio C. Benitez, Petitioner v. Julie L. Jones, Secretary, Florida Department of Corrections, et al.

577 U.S. 942, 136 S. Ct. 364, 193 L. Ed. 2d 296, 2015 U.S. LEXIS 6692.

October 19, 2015. Petition for writ of certiorari to the United States Court of Appeals for the Eleventh Circuit denied.

No. 15-5719. Brad Bolton, Petitioner v. United States.

577 U.S. 942, 136 S. Ct. 364, 193 L. Ed. 2d 296, 2015 U.S. LEXIS 6629, reh den 577 U.S. 1096, 136 S. Ct. 886, 193 L. Ed. 2d 777, 2016 U.S. LEXIS 573.

October 19, 2015. Petition for writ of certiorari to the United States Court of Appeals for the Sixth Circuit denied.

No. 15-5720. Kai Brost, Petitioner v. Iowa.

577 U.S. 942, 136 S. Ct. 364, 193 L. Ed. 2d 296, 2015 U.S. LEXIS 6602, reh den 577 U.S. 1096, 136 S. Ct. 886, 193 L. Ed. 2d 778, 2016 U.S. LEXIS 282.

October 19, 2015. Petition for writ of certiorari to the United States Court of Appeals for the Eighth Circuit denied.

No. 15-5721. Orrin C. Hudson, Petitioner v. Clairerencia Hudson.

577 U.S. 942, 136 S. Ct. 364, 193 L. Ed. 2d 296, 2015 U.S. LEXIS 6620.

October 19, 2015. Petition for writ of certiorari to the Court of Civil Appeals of Alabama denied.

Same case below, 178 So. 3d 861.

No. 15-5730. Justin White, Petitioner v. Alabama.

577 U.S. 942, 136 S. Ct. 365, 193 L. Ed. 2d 296, 2015 U.S. LEXIS 6683.

October 19, 2015. Petition for writ of certiorari to the Court of Criminal Appeals of Alabama denied.

No. 15-5731. Marvin Green, Petitioner v. Jerry Lester, Warden.

577 U.S. 942, 136 S. Ct. 365, 193 L. Ed. 2d 296, 2015 U.S. LEXIS 6747.

October 19, 2015. Petition for writ of certiorari to the United States Court of Appeals for the Sixth Circuit denied.

No. 15-5732. Isaac K. Fullman, Petitioner v. Thomas King Kistler, et al.

577 U.S. 942, 136 S. Ct. 365, 193 L. Ed. 2d 296, 2015 U.S. LEXIS 6714, reh den 577 U.S. 1024, 136 S. Ct. 581, 193 L. Ed. 2d 463, 2015 U.S. LEXIS 7464.

October 19, 2015. Petition for writ of certiorari to the United States Court of Appeals for the Third Circuit denied.

Same case below, 608 Fed. Appx. 124.

No. 15-5733. Isaac K. Fullman, Petitioner v. Thomas King Kistler, et al.

577 U.S. 942, 136 S. Ct. 365, 193 L. Ed. 2d 297, 2015 U.S. LEXIS 6715, reh den 577 U.S. 1024, 136 S. Ct. 581, 193 L. Ed. 2d 463, 2015 U.S. LEXIS 7390.

October 19, 2015. Petition for writ of certiorari to the United States Court of Appeals for the Third Circuit denied.

Same case below, 617 Fed. Appx. 124.

No. 15-5743. Tykee Ross, Petitioner v. Tony Trierweiler, Warden.

577 U.S. 942, 136 S. Ct. 366, 193 L. Ed. 2d 297, 2015 U.S. LEXIS 6697.

October 19, 2015. Petition for writ of certiorari to the United States Court of Appeals for the Sixth Circuit denied.

No. 15-5744. Robert Ray Young, Petitioner v. Truman Medical Center, Administrative Department, et al.

577 U.S. 943, 136 S. Ct. 366, 193 L. Ed. 2d 297, 2015 U.S. LEXIS 6754.

October 19, 2015. Petition for writ of certiorari to the United States Court of Appeals for the Eighth Circuit denied.

No. 15-5750. Dianne Ewing, Petitioner v. Lucas County Department of Job and Family Services.

577 U.S. 943, 136 S. Ct. 366, 193 L. Ed. 2d 297, 2015 U.S. LEXIS 6641.

October 19, 2015. Petition for writ of certiorari to the United States Court of Appeals for the Sixth Circuit denied.

No. 15-5753. Anthony Rucano, Petitioner v. New York.

577 U.S. 943, 136 S. Ct. 366, 193 L. Ed. 2d 297, 2015 U.S. LEXIS 6650.

October 19, 2015. Petition for writ of certiorari to the Supreme Court of New York, Richmond County, denied.

No. 15-5757. Lewis Price, III, Petitioner v. Leroy Kirkegard, Warden, et al.

577 U.S. 943, 136 S. Ct. 366, 193 L. Ed. 2d 297, 2015 U.S. LEXIS 6699.

October 19, 2015. Petition for writ of certiorari to the United States Court of Appeals for the Ninth Circuit denied.

Same case below, 617 Fed. Appx. 646.

No. 15-5793. Oluwagbenga Rotimi Awoleye, Petitioner v. Loretta E. Lynch, Attorney General.

577 U.S. 943, 136 S. Ct. 367, 193 L. Ed. 2d 297, 2015 U.S. LEXIS 6722.

October 19, 2015. Petition for writ of certiorari to the United States Court of Appeals for the Eleventh Circuit denied.

Same case below, 608 Fed. Appx. 868.

No. 15-5797. Edmond McClinton, Petitioner v. Arkansas.

577 U.S. 943, 136 S. Ct. 367, 193 L. Ed. 2d 297, 2015 U.S. LEXIS 6605.

October 19, 2015. Petition for writ of certiorari to the Supreme Court of Arkansas denied.

Same case below, 2015 Ark. 245, 464 S.W.3d 913.

———

No. 15-5807. Ricky O. Ray, Petitioner v. Louisiana.

577 U.S. 943, 136 S. Ct. 367, 193 L. Ed. 2d 298, 2015 U.S. LEXIS 6719.

October 19, 2015. Petition for writ of certiorari to the Supreme Court of Louisiana denied.

Same case below, 171 So. 3d 928.

———

No. 15-5834. Vern Kills On Top, Petitioner v. Leroy Kirkegard, Warden.

577 U.S. 943, 136 S. Ct. 367, 193 L. Ed. 2d 298, 2015 U.S. LEXIS 6642.

October 19, 2015. Petition for writ of certiorari to the United States Court of Appeals for the Ninth Circuit denied.

———

No. 15-5850. Myron Roderick Nunn, Petitioner v. Ricky Matthews, et al.

577 U.S. 943, 136 S. Ct. 368, 193 L. Ed. 2d 298, 2015 U.S. LEXIS 6737.

October 19, 2015. Petition for writ of certiorari to the United States Court of Appeals for the Fourth Circuit denied.

Same case below, 604 Fed. Appx. 298.

———

No. 15-5854. Donovan Craig Matthews, Petitioner v. Kris Kline, Warden, et al.

577 U.S. 943, 136 S. Ct. 368, 193 L. Ed. 2d 298, 2015 U.S. LEXIS 6716.

October 19, 2015. Petition for writ of certiorari to the United States Court of Appeals for the Tenth Circuit denied.

Same case below, 605 Fed. Appx. 741.

———

No. 15-5870. James Boswell, Petitioner v. Ector County Independent School District Board of Trustees, et al.

577 U.S. 943, 136 S. Ct. 382, 193 L. Ed. 2d 298, 2015 U.S. LEXIS 6749.

October 19, 2015. Petition for writ of certiorari to the United States Court of Appeals for the Sixth Circuit denied.

———

No. 15-5900. Juan D. White, Petitioner v. Harold W. Clarke, Director, Virginia Department of Corrections.

577 U.S. 943, 136 S. Ct. 368, 193 L. Ed. 2d 298, 2015 U.S. LEXIS 6645.

October 19, 2015. Petition for writ of certiorari to the United States Court of Appeals for the Fourth Circuit denied.

Same case below, 604 Fed. Appx. 310.

———

No. 15-5917. Bruce Elliott, Petitioner v. Debra K. Johnson, Warden.

577 U.S. 943, 136 S. Ct. 368, 193 L. Ed. 2d 298, 2015 U.S. LEXIS 6613.

October 19, 2015. Petition for writ of certiorari to the United States Court of Appeals for the Sixth Circuit denied.

No. 15-5925. Dontaye Malik DeShields, Petitioner v. John Kerestes, Superintendent, State Correctional Institution at Mahanoy, et al.

577 U.S. 943, 136 S. Ct. 368, 193 L. Ed. 2d 299, 2015 U.S. LEXIS 6682.

October 19, 2015. Petition for writ of certiorari to the United States Court of Appeals for the Third Circuit denied.

No. 15-5930. Derek J. Brown, Petitioner v. Larry Cartledge, Warden.

577 U.S. 944, 136 S. Ct. 369, 193 L. Ed. 2d 299, 2015 U.S. LEXIS 6691.

October 19, 2015. Petition for writ of certiorari to the United States Court of Appeals for the Fourth Circuit denied.

Same case below, 599 Fed. Appx. 102.

No. 15-5942. Charles G. Kinney, Petitioner v. Michele Clark.

577 U.S. 944, 136 S. Ct. 369, 193 L. Ed. 2d 299, 2015 U.S. LEXIS 6673.

October 19, 2015. Petition for writ of certiorari to the United States Court of Appeals for the Ninth Circuit denied.

No. 15-5988. Marquis Anthony Nelson, Petitioner v. United States.

577 U.S. 944, 136 S. Ct. 369, 193 L. Ed. 2d 299, 2015 U.S. LEXIS 6706.

October 19, 2015. Petition for writ of certiorari to the United States Court of Appeals for the Fourth Circuit denied.

Same case below, 600 Fed. Appx. 130.

No. 15-5990. Alfred Maurice Blackley, Petitioner v. United States.

577 U.S. 944, 136 S. Ct. 370, 193 L. Ed. 2d 299, 2015 U.S. LEXIS 6704.

October 19, 2015. Petition for writ of certiorari to the United States Court of Appeals for the Eleventh Circuit denied.

No. 15-6013. Lamarr Scott, Petitioner v. New York.

577 U.S. 944, 136 S. Ct. 370, 193 L. Ed. 2d 299, 2015 U.S. LEXIS 6618.

October 19, 2015. Petition for writ of certiorari to the Appellate Division, Supreme Court of New York, Fourth Judicial Department, denied.

Same case below, 126 App. Div. 3d 1425, 3 N.Y.S.3d 661.

No. 15-6015. Elvin Alisuretove, Petitioner v. United States.

577 U.S. 944, 136 S. Ct. 370, 193 L. Ed. 2d 299, 2015 U.S. LEXIS 6627.

October 19, 2015. Petition for writ of certiorari to the United States Court of Appeals for the Tenth Circuit denied.

Same case below, 788 F.3d 1247.

No. 15-6018. Kenneth Robert Simpson, Petitioner v. United States, et al.

577 U.S. 944, 136 S. Ct. 370, 193 L. Ed. 2d 299, 2015 U.S. LEXIS 6729.

October 19, 2015. Petition for writ of certiorari to the United States Court of Appeals for the Sixth Circuit denied.

Same case below, 754 F.3d 569.

No. 15-6019. Kenneth Robert Simpson, Petitioner v. Joseph Coakley, Warden.

577 U.S. 944, 136 S. Ct. 370, 193 L. Ed. 2d 300, 2015 U.S. LEXIS 6693.

October 19, 2015. Petition for writ of certiorari to the United States Court of Appeals for the Sixth Circuit denied.

No. 15-6021. Eduardo Ivanez, Petitioner v. Wisconsin.

577 U.S. 944, 136 S. Ct. 371, 193 L. Ed. 2d 300, 2015 U.S. LEXIS 6720.

October 19, 2015. Petition for writ of certiorari to the Court of Appeals of Wisconsin, District I, denied.

Same case below, 361 Wis. 2d 283, 862 N.W.2d 618.

No. 15-6023. Marvin Garrett, Petitioner v. United States.

577 U.S. 944, 136 S. Ct. 371, 193 L. Ed. 2d 300, 2015 U.S. LEXIS 6723.

October 19, 2015. Petition for writ of certiorari to the United States Court of Appeals for the Fourth Circuit denied.

Same case below, 606 Fed. Appx. 71.

No. 15-6025. Lonnie Goodrich, Petitioner v. United States.

577 U.S. 944, 136 S. Ct. 371, 193 L. Ed. 2d 300, 2015 U.S. LEXIS 6717, reh den 577 U.S. 1096, 136 S. Ct. 887, 193 L. Ed. 2d 779, 2016 U.S. LEXIS 321.

October 19, 2015. Petition for writ of certiorari to the United States Court of Appeals for the Eighth Circuit denied.

No. 15-6029. A. M. G., Petitioner v. Oregon Department of Human Services.

577 U.S. 944, 136 S. Ct. 371, 193 L. Ed. 2d 300, 2015 U.S. LEXIS 6660.

October 19, 2015. Petition for writ of certiorari to the Court of Appeals of Oregon denied.

Same case below, 270 Or. App. 1, 346 P.3d 1254.

No. 15-6032. Jorge Sosa, Petitioner v. United States.

577 U.S. 944, 136 S. Ct. 371, 193 L. Ed. 2d 300, 2015 U.S. LEXIS 6698.

October 19, 2015. Petition for writ of certiorari to the United States Court of Appeals for the Ninth Circuit denied.

Same case below, 608 Fed. Appx. 464.

No. 15-6035. Viengxay Chantharath, Petitioner v. United States.

577 U.S. 944, 136 S. Ct. 371, 193 L. Ed. 2d 300, 2015 U.S. LEXIS 6707.

October 19, 2015. Petition for writ of certiorari to the United States Court of Appeals for the Eighth Circuit denied.

No. 15-6036. Marvin Cesar Carabali-Diaz, aka Alex Omar Aponte-Ortiz, Petitioner v. United States.

577 U.S. 944, 136 S. Ct. 372, 193 L. Ed. 2d 300, 2015 U.S. LEXIS 6746.

October 19, 2015. Petition for writ of certiorari to the United States Court of Appeals for the Fifth Circuit denied.

Same case below, 603 Fed. Appx. 306.

No. 15-6039. Eric Dexter Welch, Petitioner v. United States.

577 U.S. 945, 136 S. Ct. 372, 193 L. Ed. 2d 301, 2015 U.S. LEXIS 6661.

October 19, 2015. Petition for writ of certiorari to the United States Court of Appeals for the Sixth Circuit denied.

No. 15-6040. Vincent L. Ruchlewicz, Petitioner v. United States.

577 U.S. 945, 136 S. Ct. 372, 193 L. Ed. 2d 301, 2015 U.S. LEXIS 6678.

October 19, 2015. Petition for writ of certiorari to the United States Court of Appeals for the Third Circuit denied.

Same case below, 610 Fed. Appx. 204.

No. 15-6042. Reginald S. Myers, Petitioner v. United States.

577 U.S. 945, 136 S. Ct. 373, 193 L. Ed. 2d 301, 2015 U.S. LEXIS 6739.

October 19, 2015. Petition for writ of certiorari to the United States Court of Appeals for the Sixth Circuit denied.

No. 15-6044. Aubrey Davis, Petitioner v. United States.

577 U.S. 945, 136 S. Ct. 373, 193 L. Ed. 2d 301, 2015 U.S. LEXIS 6724.

October 19, 2015. Petition for writ of certiorari to the United States Court of Appeals for the Fifth Circuit denied.

Same case below, 606 Fed. Appx. 257.

No. 15-6045. Ray Allen Dicks, Jr., Petitioner v. United States.

577 U.S. 945, 136 S. Ct. 373, 193 L. Ed. 2d 301, 2015 U.S. LEXIS 6686.

October 19, 2015. Petition for writ of certiorari to the United States Court of Appeals for the Fourth Circuit denied.

Same case below, 614 Fed. Appx. 628.

No. 15-6047. Julio Cesar Cardenas, Petitioner v. United States.

577 U.S. 945, 136 S. Ct. 373, 193 L. Ed. 2d 301, 2015 U.S. LEXIS 6651, reh den 577 U.S. 1045, 136 S. Ct. 611, 193 L. Ed. 2d 492, 2015 U.S. LEXIS 7840.

October 19, 2015. Petition for writ of certiorari to the United States Court of Appeals for the Fifth Circuit denied.

Same case below, 606 Fed. Appx. 246.

No. 15-6052. Clay O'Brien Mann, Petitioner v. United States.

577 U.S. 945, 136 S. Ct. 373, 193 L. Ed. 2d 301, 2015 U.S. LEXIS 6745.

October 19, 2015. Petition for writ of certiorari to the United States Court of Appeals for the Tenth Circuit denied.

Same case below, 786 F.3d 1244.

No. 15-6054. Paul Starner, Petitioner v. United States.

577 U.S. 945, 136 S. Ct. 374, 193 L. Ed. 2d 301, 2015 U.S. LEXIS 6611.

October 19, 2015. Petition for writ of certiorari to the United States Court of Appeals for the Fourth Circuit denied.

Same case below, 620 Fed. Appx. 156.

No. 15-6057. Leopold Ronald Casias, Jr., Petitioner v. United States.

577 U.S. 945, 136 S. Ct. 374, 193 L. Ed. 2d 302, 2015 U.S. LEXIS 6658.

October 19, 2015. Petition for writ of certiorari to the United States Court of Appeals for the Ninth Circuit denied.

Same case below, 614 Fed. Appx. 885.

No. 15-6058. George Michael Turner, Petitioner v. United States.

577 U.S. 945, 136 S. Ct. 374, 193 L. Ed. 2d 302, 2015 U.S. LEXIS 6685.

October 19, 2015. Petition for writ of certiorari to the United States Court of Appeals for the Fourth Circuit denied.

Same case below, 608 Fed. Appx. 149.

No. 15-6067. Ricky Smith, Petitioner v. United States.

577 U.S. 945, 136 S. Ct. 374, 193 L. Ed. 2d 302, 2015 U.S. LEXIS 6711.

October 19, 2015. Petition for writ of certiorari to the United States Court of Appeals for the Eleventh Circuit denied.

No. 15-6069. Abraham Betranos Rasgado, Petitioner v. United States.

577 U.S. 945, 136 S. Ct. 375, 193 L. Ed. 2d 302, 2015 U.S. LEXIS 6615.

October 19, 2015. Petition for writ of certiorari to the United States Court of Appeals for the Ninth Circuit denied.

No. 15-6072. Juan Estrada-Zolorzano, Petitioner v. United States.

577 U.S. 945, 136 S. Ct. 375, 193 L. Ed. 2d 302, 2015 U.S. LEXIS 6731.

October 19, 2015. Petition for writ of certiorari to the United States Court of Appeals for the Fifth Circuit denied.

Same case below, 604 Fed. Appx. 369.

No. 15-6073. Henry Alexander Calix, Petitioner v. United States.

577 U.S. 945, 136 S. Ct. 375, 193 L. Ed. 2d 302, 2015 U.S. LEXIS 6751.

October 19, 2015. Petition for writ of certiorari to the United States Court of Appeals for the Fifth Circuit denied.

Same case below, 607 Fed. Appx. 419.

No. 15-6074. Jose Chavez-Perez, Petitioner v. United States.

577 U.S. 945, 136 S. Ct. 375, 193 L. Ed. 2d 302, 2015 U.S. LEXIS 6672.

October 19, 2015. Petition for writ of certiorari to the United States Court of Appeals for the Fifth Circuit denied.

Same case below, 607 Fed. Appx. 403.

No. 15-6079. Jose Nicanor Escobar-Lopez, Petitioner v. United States.

577 U.S. 945, 136 S. Ct. 375, 193 L. Ed. 2d 302, 2015 U.S. LEXIS 6680.

October 19, 2015. Petition for writ of certiorari to the United States Court of Appeals for the Fourth Circuit denied.

Same case below, 609 Fed. Appx. 150.

No. 15-6083. Daniel L. Ushery, Jr., Petitioner v. United States.

577 U.S. 946, 136 S. Ct. 375, 193 L. Ed. 2d 303, 2015 U.S. LEXIS 6728.

October 19, 2015. Petition for writ of certiorari to the United States Court of Appeals for the Sixth Circuit denied.

Same case below, 785 F.3d 210.

No. 15-6085. Terrence Terrell Matthews, Petitioner v. United States.

577 U.S. 946, 136 S. Ct. 376, 193 L. Ed. 2d 303, 2015 U.S. LEXIS 6624.

October 19, 2015. Petition for writ of certiorari to the United States Court of Appeals for the Eighth Circuit denied.

Same case below, 784 F.3d 1232.

No. 15-6088. Marquis Deron Heard, Petitioner v. United States.

577 U.S. 946, 136 S. Ct. 376, 193 L. Ed. 2d 303, 2015 U.S. LEXIS 6679.

October 19, 2015. Petition for writ of certiorari to the United States Court of Appeals for the Sixth Circuit denied.

Same case below, 762 F.3d 538.

No. 15-6089. Jose De La Cruz Saenz-Aranda, Petitioner v. United States.

577 U.S. 946, 136 S. Ct. 376, 193 L. Ed. 2d 303, 2015 U.S. LEXIS 6726.

October 19, 2015. Petition for writ of certiorari to the United States Court of Appeals for the Fifth Circuit denied.

Same case below, 607 Fed. Appx. 417.

No. 15-6093. Randy Sam Jackson, Petitioner v. United States.

577 U.S. 946, 136 S. Ct. 376, 193 L. Ed. 2d 303, 2015 U.S. LEXIS 6614.

October 19, 2015. Petition for writ of certiorari to the United States Court of Appeals for the Eleventh Circuit denied.

Same case below, 618 Fed. Appx. 472.

No. 15-6095. Albert Espinal, Petitioner v. United States.

577 U.S. 946, 136 S. Ct. 376, 193 L. Ed. 2d 303, 2015 U.S. LEXIS 6676.

October 19, 2015. Petition for writ of certiorari to the United States Court of Appeals for the Eleventh Circuit denied.

Same case below, 596 Fed. Appx. 800.

No. 15-6103. Jeremy Thomas Trogdon, Petitioner v. United States.

577 U.S. 946, 136 S. Ct. 376, 193 L. Ed. 2d 303, 2015 U.S. LEXIS 6713.

October 19, 2015. Petition for writ of certiorari to the United States Court of Appeals for the Eighth Circuit denied.

Same case below, 789 F.3d 907.

No. 15-6108. Julio Aleman Triana, aka Julio Aleman, aka Julio Aleman-Triana, Petitioner v. United States; Mario Ramos-Martinez, Petitioner v. United States; and Francisco Armando Chan-Vicente, Petitioner v. United States.

577 U.S. 946, 136 S. Ct. 377, 193 L. Ed. 2d 304, 2015 U.S. LEXIS 6617.

October 19, 2015. Petition for writ of certiorari to the United States Court of Appeals for the Fifth Circuit denied.

Same case below, 604 Fed. Appx. 376 (first judgment); 617 Fed. Appx. 287 (second judgment); and 612 Fed. Appx. 240 (third judgment).

No. 15-6111. Jefferson Gatewood, Petitioner v. United States.

577 U.S. 946, 136 S. Ct. 377, 193 L. Ed. 2d 304, 2015 U.S. LEXIS 6712.

October 19, 2015. Petition for writ of certiorari to the United States Court of Appeals for the Ninth Circuit denied.

Same case below, 601 Fed. Appx. 580.

No. 15-6112. William Peppers, Petitioner v. United States.

577 U.S. 946, 136 S. Ct. 377, 193 L. Ed. 2d 304, 2015 U.S. LEXIS 6652.

October 19, 2015. Petition for writ of certiorari to the United States Court of Appeals for the Sixth Circuit denied.

No. 15-6114. James E. McLean, Petitioner v. Andrew Mansukhani, Warden.

577 U.S. 946, 136 S. Ct. 377, 193 L. Ed. 2d 304, 2015 U.S. LEXIS 6610.

October 19, 2015. Petition for writ of certiorari to the United States Court of Appeals for the Fourth Circuit denied.

Same case below, 599 Fed. Appx. 78.

No. 15-6118. Dejaun Leshae Hill, Petitioner v. United States.

577 U.S. 946, 136 S. Ct. 377, 193 L. Ed. 2d 304, 2015 U.S. LEXIS 6631.

October 19, 2015. Petition for writ of certiorari to the United States Court of Appeals for the Tenth Circuit denied.

Same case below, 786 F.3d 1254.

No. 15-6129. Michael Balice, Petitioner v. United States.

577 U.S. 946, 136 S. Ct. 377, 193 L. Ed. 2d 304, 2015 U.S. LEXIS 6735.

October 19, 2015. Petition for writ of certiorari to the United States Court of Appeals for the Third Circuit denied.

No. 15-6132. Deandre Antonio Hopkins, Petitioner v. United States.

577 U.S. 946, 136 S. Ct. 378, 193 L. Ed. 2d 304, 2015 U.S. LEXIS 6655.

October 19, 2015. Petition for writ of certiorari to the United States Court of Appeals for the Tenth Circuit denied.

Same case below, 608 Fed. Appx. 637.

No. 15-6133. Markevin Faucette, Petitioner v. United States.

577 U.S. 946, 136 S. Ct. 378, 193 L. Ed. 2d 304, 2015 U.S. LEXIS 6643.

October 19, 2015. Petition for writ of certiorari to the United States Court of Appeals for the First Circuit denied.

Same case below, 607 Fed. Appx. 5.

––––––––

No. 15-6135. Jack Baker, Petitioner v. United States.

577 U.S. 947, 136 S. Ct. 378, 193 L. Ed. 2d 305, 2015 U.S. LEXIS 6742.

October 19, 2015. Petition for writ of certiorari to the United States Court of Appeals for the Fifth Circuit denied.

Same case below, 607 Fed. Appx. 431.

––––––––

No. 15-6138. Derrick Chappelle, Petitioner v. United States.

577 U.S. 947, 136 S. Ct. 378, 193 L. Ed. 2d 305, 2015 U.S. LEXIS 6632.

October 19, 2015. Petition for writ of certiorari to the United States Court of Appeals for the Third Circuit denied.

Same case below, 591 Fed. Appx. 71.

––––––––

No. 15-6140. Jerome Creighton, Petitioner v. United States.

577 U.S. 947, 136 S. Ct. 378, 193 L. Ed. 2d 305, 2015 U.S. LEXIS 6738.

October 19, 2015. Petition for writ of certiorari to the United States Court of Appeals for the Eighth Circuit denied.

––––––––

No. 15-6144. Mauriosantana Cowan, Petitioner v. United States.

577 U.S. 947, 136 S. Ct. 378, 193 L. Ed. 2d 305, 2015 U.S. LEXIS 6741.

October 19, 2015. Petition for writ of certiorari to the United States Court of Appeals for the Eighth Circuit denied.

No. 15-6157. Sheikh Bilaal Muhammad Arafat, Petitioner v. United States.

577 U.S. 947, 136 S. Ct. 379, 193 L. Ed. 2d 305, 2015 U.S. LEXIS 6608.

October 19, 2015. Petition for writ of certiorari to the United States Court of Appeals for the Eighth Circuit denied.

Same case below, 789 F.3d 839.

––––––––

No. 15-6159. Bradley Michael Abbring, Petitioner v. United States.

577 U.S. 947, 136 S. Ct. 379, 193 L. Ed. 2d 305, 2015 U.S. LEXIS 6668.

October 19, 2015. Petition for writ of certiorari to the United States Court of Appeals for the Sixth Circuit denied.

Same case below, 788 F.3d 565.

––––––––

No. 15-6160. Sylvester Andrews, Petitioner v. United States; and Sylvester Andrews, Petitioner v. United States District Court for the Eastern District of Pennsylvania.

577 U.S. 947, 136 S. Ct. 379, 193 L. Ed. 2d 305, 2015 U.S. LEXIS 6744, reh den 577 U.S. 1054, 136 S. Ct. 707, 193 L. Ed. 2d 533, 2015 U.S. LEXIS 7926.

October 19, 2015. Petition for writ of certiorari to the United States Court of Appeals for the Third Circuit denied.

Same case below, 610 Fed. Appx. 101 (second judgment).

––––––––

No. 15-6164. Donnell Durant Cogdell, Petitioner v. United States.

577 U.S. 947, 136 S. Ct. 379, 193 L. Ed. 2d 305, 2015 U.S. LEXIS 6648.

October 19, 2015. Petition for writ of certiorari to the United States Court of Appeals for the Fifth Circuit denied.

Same case below, 608 Fed. Appx. 241.

———

No. 15-6169. Cirilo Chilo Lara Madrid, Petitioner v. United States.

577 U.S. 947, 136 S. Ct. 379, 193 L. Ed. 2d 306, 2015 U.S. LEXIS 6688.

October 19, 2015. Petition for writ of certiorari to the United States Court of Appeals for the Fifth Circuit denied.

Same case below, 610 Fed. Appx. 359.

———

No. 15-6172. Vanessa Cooper, Petitioner v. United States.

577 U.S. 947, 136 S. Ct. 379, 193 L. Ed. 2d 306, 2015 U.S. LEXIS 6600.

October 19, 2015. Petition for writ of certiorari to the United States Court of Appeals for the Eleventh Circuit denied.

Same case below, 608 Fed. Appx. 764.

———

No. 15-6183. John Dwayne Garvin, Petitioner v. Chuck Wright, et al.

577 U.S. 947, 136 S. Ct. 380, 193 L. Ed. 2d 306, 2015 U.S. LEXIS 6640, reh den 577 U.S. 1184, 136 S. Ct. 1251, 194 L. Ed. 2d 248, 2016 U.S. LEXIS 1080.

October 19, 2015. Petition for writ of certiorari to the United States Court of Appeals for the Fourth Circuit denied.

Same case below, 583 Fed. Appx. 287.

———

No. 15-193. Andrew Kane, Individually and as Personal Representative of the Estate of Andrew Dwayne Cornish, Petitioner v. Brian Lewis, et al.

577 U.S. 947, 136 S. Ct. 358, 193 L. Ed. 2d 306, 2015 U.S. LEXIS 6687.

October 19, 2015. Motion of Seth Stoughton for leave to file a brief as amicus curiae granted. Motion of Cato Institute for leave to file a brief as amicus curiae granted. Petition for writ of certiorari to the United States Court of Appeals for the Fourth Circuit denied.

Same case below, 604 Fed. Appx. 229.

———

No. 15-203. David Louis Whitehead, Petitioner v. White & Case LLP, et al.

577 U.S. 947, 136 S. Ct. 360, 193 L. Ed. 2d 306, 2015 U.S. LEXIS 6604.

October 19, 2015. Petition for writ of certiorari to the United States Court of Appeals for the Fifth Circuit denied. The Chief Justice took no part in the consideration or decision of this petition.

———

No. 15-6238. In re Darren C. Bluemel, Petitioner.

577 U.S. 937, 136 S. Ct. 380, 193 L. Ed. 2d 306, 2015 U.S. LEXIS 6718, reh den 577 U.S. 1184, 136 S. Ct. 1251, 194 L. Ed. 2d 248, 2016 U.S. LEXIS 1366.

October 19, 2015. Petition for writ of habeas corpus denied.

———

No. 15-6286. In re John Lee Cockerham, Petitioner.

577 U.S. 937, 136 S. Ct. 380, 193 L. Ed. 2d 306, 2015 U.S. LEXIS 6665.

October 19, 2015. Petition for writ of habeas corpus denied.

No. 15-6328. In re Curtis Smith, Petitioner.

577 U.S. 937, 136 S. Ct. 380, 193 L. Ed. 2d 307, 2015 U.S. LEXIS 6730.

October 19, 2015. Petition for writ of habeas corpus denied.

No. 15-5890. In re Aretha D. Brown, Petitioner.

577 U.S. 937, 136 S. Ct. 368, 193 L. Ed. 2d 307, 2015 U.S. LEXIS 6752, reh den 577 U.S. 1024, 136 S. Ct. 581, 193 L. Ed. 2d 463, 2015 U.S. LEXIS 7379.

October 19, 2015. Petition for writ of mandamus denied.

No. 15-6061. In re John Joseph Tatar, Petitioner.

577 U.S. 937, 136 S. Ct. 374, 193 L. Ed. 2d 307, 2015 U.S. LEXIS 6669, reh den 577 U.S. 1054, 136 S. Ct. 707, 193 L. Ed. 2d 533, 2015 U.S. LEXIS 7983.

October 19, 2015. Petition for writ of mandamus denied.

No. 15-5684. In re Isaiah Jerome Anderson, Petitioner.

577 U.S. 937, 136 S. Ct. 362, 193 L. Ed. 2d 307, 2015 U.S. LEXIS 6675.

October 19, 2015. Petition for writ of mandamus and/or prohibition denied.

No. 15-5826. In re Sakima Iban Salih El Bey, Petitioner.

577 U.S. 937, 136 S. Ct. 367, 193 L. Ed. 2d 307, 2015 U.S. LEXIS 6743.

October 19, 2015. Motion of petitioner for leave to proceed in forma pauperis denied, and petition for writ of prohibition dismissed. See Rule 39.8.

No. 14-9173. Margaret A. Moline, Petitioner v. CBS News Inc.

577 U.S. 947, 136 S. Ct. 382, 193 L. Ed. 2d 307, 2015 U.S. LEXIS 6638.

October 19, 2015. Petition for rehearing denied.

Former decision, 576 U.S. 1007, 135 S. Ct. 2808, 192 L. Ed. 2d 852, 2015 U.S. LEXIS 3886.

No. 15-345 (R46-002). Yolanda Crawford, et vir, Petitioners v. Household Finance Corp. III.

577 U.S. 948, 136 S. Ct. 382, 193 L. Ed. 2d 307, 2015 U.S. LEXIS 6756.

October 22, 2015. The petition for writ of certiorari to the Court of Appeals of Indiana, Fifth District, was dismissed today pursuant to Rule 46.1 of the Rules of this Court.

Same case below, 29 N.E.3d 123.

No. 15-6551 (15A424). Jerry William Correll, Petitioner v. Florida.

577 U.S. 948, 193 L. Ed. 2d 307, 2015 U.S. LEXIS 6757.

October 29, 2015. Application for stay of execution of sentence of death, presented to Justice Thomas, and by him referred to the Court, denied. Petition for writ of certiorari to the Supreme Court of Florida denied.

Justice **Breyer**, dissenting from denial of certiorari and application for stay of execution.

Jerry William Correll was sentenced to death on February 7, 1986, and has now been incarcerated on death row by the State of Florida for over 29 years. Correll requests a stay of execution to allow the Court to consider his claims that Florida's sentencing procedures violate the Sixth and Eighth Amendments and that his lengthy period of incarceration under threat of execution constitutes cruel and unusual punishment.

I remain convinced that the Court should consider whether nearly 30 years of incarceration under sentence of death is cruel and unusual punishment. See *Lackey* v. *Texas*, 514 U.S. 1045, 115 S. Ct. 1421, 131 L. Ed. 2d 304 (1995) (Stevens, J., memorandum respecting denial of certiorari); *Knight* v. *Florida*, 528 U.S. 990, 993, 120 S. Ct. 459, 145 L. Ed. 2d 370 (1999) (Breyer, J., dissenting from denial of certiorari); see also *Glossip* v. *Gross*, 576 U.S. 863, 908, 135 S. Ct. 2726, 192 L. Ed. 2d 761 (2015) (Breyer, J., dissenting).

In addition, whether Florida's sentencing procedures violate the Sixth and Eighth Amendments is now pending before the Court. *Hurst* v. *Florida*, No. 14-7505. In my view, we should hold this petition for resolution of those issues in *Hurst*.

I respectfully dissent from the order of the Court to deny the application for stay of execution and the petition for a writ of certiorari

Justice **Sotomayor**, dissenting from denial of stay and petition for writ of certiorari.

I agree with Justice Breyer that we should hold this petition for resolution of the issues in *Hurst* v. *Florida*, No. 14-7505, now pending before the Court. I therefore respectfully dissent from the order of the Court to deny the petition for a writ of certiorari and the application for stay of execution.

No. 14-419. Sila Luis, Petitioner v. United States.

577 U.S. 949, 136 S. Ct. 386, 193 L. Ed. 2d 308, 2015 U.S. LEXIS 6758.

October 30, 2015. Motion out of time of Americans for Forfeiture Reform for leave to participate in oral argument as amicus curiae and for divided argument denied.

No. 14-613. Marvin Green, Petitioner v. Megan J. Brennan, Postmaster General.

577 U.S. 949, 136 S. Ct. 386, 193 L. Ed. 2d 308, 2015 U.S. LEXIS 6760.

October 30, 2015. Motion of respondent for allocation of argument time granted.

No. 14-723. Robert Montanile, Petitioner v. Board of Trustees of the National Elevator Industry Health Benefit Plan.

577 U.S. 949, 136 S. Ct. 386, 193 L. Ed. 2d 308, 2015 U.S. LEXIS 6759.

October 30, 2015. Motion of the Solicitor General for leave to participate in oral argument as amicus curiae and for divided argument granted.

No. 14-10154. Stephen L. Voisine and William E. Armstrong, III, Petitioners v. United States.

577 U.S. 949, 136 S. Ct. 386, 193 L. Ed. 2d 309, 2015 U.S. LEXIS 6761.

October 30, 2015. Motion of petitioners for leave to proceed in forma pauperis granted. Petition for writ of certiorari to the United States Court of Appeals for the First Circuit granted limited to Question 1 presented by the petition.

Same case below, 778 F.3d 176.

No. 15-5970. Larry Lavonne Berry, Petitioner v. United States.

577 U.S. 949, 136 S. Ct. 417, 193 L. Ed. 2d 309, 2015 U.S. LEXIS 6873.

November 2, 2015. Motion of petitioner for leave to proceed in forma pauperis and petition for writ of certiorari granted. Judgment vacated, and case remanded to the United States Court of Appeals for the Fourth Circuit for further consideration in light of Johnson v. United States, 576 U.S. 591, 135 S. Ct. 2551, 192 L. Ed. 2d 569 (2015).

Same case below, 598 Fed. Appx. 205.

No. 15-5984. Shawn Caldwell, Petitioner v. United States.

577 U.S. 949, 136 S. Ct. 417, 193 L. Ed. 2d 309, 2015 U.S. LEXIS 6882.

November 2, 2015. Motion of petitioner for leave to proceed in forma pauperis and petition for writ of certiorari granted. Judgment vacated, and case remanded to the United States Court of Appeals for the Sixth Circuit for further consideration in light of Johnson v. United States, 576 U.S. 591, 135 S. Ct. 2551, 192 L. Ed. 2d 569 (2015).

Same case below, 614 Fed. Appx. 325.

No. 15-5776. Barbara Ellen Sherrill, Petitioner v. Estate of Thomas Michael Pico, Jr.

577 U.S. 949, 136 S. Ct. 405, 193 L. Ed. 2d 309, 2015 U.S. LEXIS 6784.

November 2, 2015. Motion of petitioner for leave to proceed in forma pauperis denied, and petition for writ of certiorari to the Supreme Court of the United States dismissed. See Rule 39.8.

Same case below, 134 Hawaii 305, 339 P.3d 1106.

No. 15-5904. Annette Fluker, Petitioner v. United States, et al.; and Annette Fluker, Petitioner v. Reynolds American Inc., et al.

577 U.S. 950, 136 S. Ct. 413, 193 L. Ed. 2d 309, 2015 U.S. LEXIS 6819.

November 2, 2015. Motion of petitioner for leave to proceed in forma pauperis denied, and petition for writ of certiorari to the United States Court of Appeals for the Second Circuit dismissed. See Rule 39.8. As petitioner has repeatedly abused this Court's process, the Clerk is directed not to accept any further petitions in noncriminal matters from petitioner unless the docketing fee required by Rule 38(a) is paid and the petition is submitted in compliance with Rule 33.1. See Martin v. District of Columbia Court of Appeals, 506 U.S. 1, 113 S. Ct. 397, 121 L. Ed. 2d 305 (1992) (per curiam).

No. 15-5905. Annette Fluker, Petitioner v. Division of Youth and Family Services.

577 U.S. 950, 136 S. Ct. 413, 193 L. Ed. 2d 310, 2015 U.S. LEXIS 6788.

November 2, 2015. Motion of petitioner for leave to proceed in forma pauperis denied, and petition for writ of certiorari to the United States Court of Appeals for the Second Circuit dismissed. See Rule 39.8. As petitioner has repeatedly abused this Court's process, the Clerk is directed not to accept any further petitions in non-criminal matters from petitioner unless the docketing fee required by Rule 38(a) is paid and the petition is submitted in compliance with Rule 33.1. See Martin v. District of Columbia Court of Appeals, 506 U.S. 1, 113 S. Ct. 397, 121 L. Ed. 2d 305 (1992) (per curiam).

No. 15-5923. Hunter R. Levi, Petitioner v. Thomas E. Perez, Secretary of Labor, et al.

577 U.S. 950, 136 S. Ct. 415, 193 L. Ed. 2d 310, 2015 U.S. LEXIS 6786.

November 2, 2015. Motion of petitioner for leave to proceed in forma pauperis denied, and petition for writ of certiorari to the United States Court of Appeals for the Tenth Circuit dismissed. See Rule 39.8.

Same case below, 614 Fed. Appx. 926.

No. 15-6027. Burl Anderson Howell, Petitioner v. United States.

577 U.S. 950, 136 S. Ct. 418, 193 L. Ed. 2d 310, 2015 U.S. LEXIS 6789.

November 2, 2015. Motion of petitioner for leave to proceed in forma pauperis denied, and petition for writ of certiorari to the United States Court of Appeals for the Fourth Circuit dismissed. See Rule 39.8. As petitioner has repeatedly abused this Court's process, the Clerk is directed not to accept any further petitions in non-criminal matters from petitioner unless the docketing fee required by Rule 38(a) is paid and the petition is submitted in compliance with Rule 33.1. See Martin v. District of Columbia Court of Appeals, 506 U.S. 1, 113 S. Ct. 397, 121 L. Ed. 2d 305 (1992) (per curiam).

Same case below, 612 Fed. Appx. 184.

No. 15-6165. Michael Charles DeSue, Petitioner v. Julie L. Jones, Secretary, Florida Department of Corrections.

577 U.S. 950, 136 S. Ct. 422, 193 L. Ed. 2d 310, 2015 U.S. LEXIS 6793.

November 2, 2015. Motion of petitioner for leave to proceed in forma pauperis denied, and petition for writ of certiorari to the United States Court of Appeals for the Eleventh Circuit dismissed. See Rule 39.8.

No. 15A137. Moones Mellouli, Applicant v. Loretta E. Lynch, Attorney General.

577 U.S. 950, 136 S. Ct. 436, 193 L. Ed. 2d 310, 2015 U.S. LEXIS 6991.

November 2, 2015. Joint motion to vacate the Court's order of August 21, 2015, granting the application for stay granted. The stay of proceedings heretofore issued by the Court on August 21, 2015, is hereby vacated.

No. 15M41. Ronald Rafferty, Petitioner v. United States.

577 U.S. 953, 136 S. Ct. 437, 193 L. Ed. 2d 311, 2015 U.S. LEXIS 6894.

November 2, 2015. Motion for leave to proceed as a veteran denied.

No. 15M42. Boehringer Ingelheim Pharmaceuticals, Inc., Petitioner v. Federal Trade Commission.

577 U.S. 953, 136 S. Ct. 437, 193 L. Ed. 2d 311, 2015 U.S. LEXIS 6880.

November 2, 2015. Motion for leave to file petition for writ of certiorari with supplemental appendix under seal granted.

Same case below, 414 U.S. App. D.C. 188, 778 F.3d 142.

No. 15M43. Douglas L. Prestidge, Petitioner v. United States.

577 U.S. 953, 136 S. Ct. 437, 193 L. Ed. 2d 311, 2015 U.S. LEXIS 6881.

November 2, 2015. Motion for leave to proceed as a veteran denied.

Same case below, 611 Fed. Appx. 979.

No. 15M44. Durwyn Talley, Petitioner v. Christopher L. Gore, et al.

577 U.S. 953, 136 S. Ct. 437, 193 L. Ed. 2d 311, 2015 U.S. LEXIS 6864.

November 2, 2015. Motion to direct the Clerk to file a petition for writ of certiorari out of time denied.

No. 15M45. Mark K. Arness, Petitioner v. United States.

577 U.S. 953, 136 S. Ct. 437, 193 L. Ed. 2d 311, 2015 U.S. LEXIS 6970.

November 2, 2015. Motion for leave to proceed as a veteran denied.

No. 15-5767. Cynthia E. Collie, Petitioner v. South Carolina Commission on Lawyer Conduct.

577 U.S. 953, 136 S. Ct. 437, 193 L. Ed. 2d 311, 2015 U.S. LEXIS 6989.

November 2, 2015. Motion of petitioner for leave to proceed in forma pauperis denied. Petitioner is allowed until November 23, 2015, within which to pay the docketing fee required by Rule 38(a) and to submit a petition in compliance with Rule 33.1 of the Rules of this Court.

No. 15-5798. Joshua Schwager, Petitioner v. Chana Ahuva Schwager.

577 U.S. 953, 136 S. Ct. 438, 193 L. Ed. 2d 311, 2015 U.S. LEXIS 6933.

November 2, 2015. Motion of petitioner for leave to proceed in forma pauperis denied. Petitioner is allowed until November 23, 2015, within which to pay the docketing fee required by Rule 38(a) and to submit a petition in compliance with Rule 33.1 of the Rules of this Court.

No. 15-5867. Vladimir Leon, Petitioner v. Columbia University Medical Center.

577 U.S. 954, 136 S. Ct. 438, 193 L. Ed. 2d 311, 2015 U.S. LEXIS 6869.

November 2, 2015. Motion of petitioner for leave to proceed in forma pauperis denied. Petitioner is allowed until November 23, 2015, within which to pay the docketing fee required by Rule 38(a) and to submit a petition in compliance with Rule 33.1 of the Rules of this Court.

No. 15-6099. Don Martin Fleming, Petitioner v. Shore Health System, Inc.

577 U.S. 954, 136 S. Ct. 438, 193 L. Ed. 2d 312, 2015 U.S. LEXIS 6929.

November 2, 2015. Motion of petitioner for leave to proceed in forma pauperis denied. Petitioner is allowed until November 23, 2015, within which to pay the docketing fee required by Rule 38(a) and to submit a petition in compliance with Rule 33.1 of the Rules of this Court.

Same case below, 443 Md. 235, 116 A.3d 474.

No. 14-1306. Christopher Erwin, Petitioner v. United States.

577 U.S. 954, 136 S. Ct. 400, 193 L. Ed. 2d 312, 2015 U.S. LEXIS 6886.

November 2, 2015. Petition for writ of certiorari to the United States Court of Appeals for the Third Circuit denied.

Same case below, 765 F.3d 219.

No. 14-1499. DIRECTV, LLC, et al., Petitioners v. Massachusetts Department of Revenue.

577 U.S. 954, 136 S. Ct. 401, 193 L. Ed. 2d 312, 2015 U.S. LEXIS 6946.

November 2, 2015. Petition for writ of certiorari to the Supreme Judicial Court of Massachusetts denied.

Same case below, 470 Mass. 647, 25 N.E.3d 258.

No. 14-1524. DIRECTV, Inc., et al., Petitioners v. Richard H. Roberts, Tennessee Commissioner of Revenue.

577 U.S. 954, 136 S. Ct. 401, 193 L. Ed. 2d 312, 2015 U.S. LEXIS 6988.

November 2, 2015. Petition for writ of certiorari to the Court of Appeals of Tennessee, Middle Division, denied.

Same case below, 477 S.W.3d 293.

No. 14-1535. George Georgiou, Petitioner v. United States.

577 U.S. 954, 136 S. Ct. 401, 193 L. Ed. 2d 312, 2015 U.S. LEXIS 6926.

November 2, 2015. Petition for writ of certiorari to the United States Court of Appeals for the Third Circuit denied.

Same case below, 777 F.3d 125.

No. 14-1536. IDT Corporation, et al., Petitioners v. Blackstone Advisory Partners LP, et al.

577 U.S. 954, 136 S. Ct. 402, 193 L. Ed. 2d 312, 2015 U.S. LEXIS 6874.

November 2, 2015. Petition for writ of certiorari to the United States Court of Appeals for the Third Circuit denied.

Same case below, 591 Fed. Appx. 58.

No. 14-9255. Roderick D. Sinclair, Petitioner v. United States.

577 U.S. 954, 136 S. Ct. 399, 193 L. Ed. 2d 312, 2015 U.S. LEXIS 6912.

November 2, 2015. Petition for writ of certiorari to the United States Court of Appeals for the Seventh Circuit denied.

Same case below, 770 F.3d 1148.

No. 14-9438. Ronald Patterson, Petitioner v. Illinois.

577 U.S. 955, 136 S. Ct. 399, 193 L. Ed. 2d 313, 2015 U.S. LEXIS 6846.

November 2, 2015. Petition for writ of certiorari to the Supreme Court of Illinois denied.

Same case below, 388 Ill. Dec. 834, 25 N.E.3d 526.

No. 14-9448. Frederick Claiborne, Petitioner v. Illinois.

577 U.S. 955, 136 S. Ct. 401, 193 L. Ed. 2d 313, 2015 U.S. LEXIS 6834.

November 2, 2015. Petition for writ of certiorari to the Appellate Court of Illinois, First District, denied.

No. 14-9453. Nickolas Santos, Petitioner v. Illinois.

577 U.S. 955, 136 S. Ct. 399, 193 L. Ed. 2d 313, 2015 U.S. LEXIS 6903.

November 2, 2015. Petition for writ of certiorari to the Appellate Court of Illinois, First District, denied.

No. 14-9504. Kevin Watson, Petitioner v. Illinois.

577 U.S. 955, 136 S. Ct. 399, 193 L. Ed. 2d 313, 2015 U.S. LEXIS 6898.

November 2, 2015. Petition for writ of certiorari to the Appellate Court of Illinois, First District, denied.

No. 14-9505. Terrel Jenkins, Petitioner v. Illinois.

577 U.S. 955, 136 S. Ct. 399, 193 L. Ed. 2d 313, 2015 U.S. LEXIS 7009.

November 2, 2015. Petition for writ of certiorari to the Appellate Court of Illinois, First District, denied.

No. 14-9508. Jesus Rodriguez, Petitioner v. Illinois.

577 U.S. 955, 136 S. Ct. 399, 193 L. Ed. 2d 313, 2015 U.S. LEXIS 6883.

November 2, 2015. Petition for writ of certiorari to the Appellate Court of Illinois, First District, denied.

No. 14-9525. Ryan T. Harmon, Petitioner v. Illinois.

577 U.S. 955, 136 S. Ct. 400, 193 L. Ed. 2d 313, 2015 U.S. LEXIS 6981.

November 2, 2015. Petition for writ of certiorari to the Appellate Court of Illinois, Second District, denied.

Same case below, 26 N.E.3d 344.

No. 14-9548. Maria S. Pacheco, Petitioner v. Illinois.

577 U.S. 955, 136 S. Ct. 438, 193 L. Ed. 2d 313, 2015 U.S. LEXIS 6987.

November 2, 2015. Petition for writ of certiorari to the Appellate Court of Illinois, Fourth District, denied.

Same case below, 991 N.E.2d 896.

No. 14-9552. Demetrius Warren, Petitioner v. Illinois.

577 U.S. 955, 136 S. Ct. 400, 193 L. Ed. 2d 314, 2015 U.S. LEXIS 6990.

November 2, 2015. Petition for writ of certiorari to the Appellate Court of Illinois, First District, denied.

No. 14-9554. Renard Branch, Petitioner v. Illinois.

577 U.S. 955, 136 S. Ct. 400, 193 L. Ed. 2d 314, 2015 U.S. LEXIS 6902.

November 2, 2015. Petition for writ of certiorari to the Appellate Court of Illinois, First District, denied.

No. 14-9560. Eric Diaz, Petitioner v. Illinois.

577 U.S. 955, 136 S. Ct. 400, 193 L. Ed. 2d 314, 2015 U.S. LEXIS 6899.

November 2, 2015. Petition for writ of certiorari to the Appellate Court of Illinois, First District, denied.

No. 14-9701. Cleophus Mooney, Petitioner v. Illinois.

577 U.S. 955, 136 S. Ct. 401, 193 L. Ed. 2d 314, 2015 U.S. LEXIS 6907.

November 2, 2015. Petition for writ of certiorari to the Appellate Court of Illinois, First District, denied.

No. 14-9723. James Perry, Petitioner v. United States.

577 U.S. 955, 136 S. Ct. 401, 193 L. Ed. 2d 314, 2015 U.S. LEXIS 6922.

November 2, 2015. Petition for writ of certiorari to the United States Court of Appeals for the Ninth Circuit denied.

Same case below, 588 Fed. Appx. 727.

No. 14-10441. Eddie Lee Anthony, Petitioner v. Wisconsin.

577 U.S. 955, 136 S. Ct. 402, 193 L. Ed. 2d 314, 2015 U.S. LEXIS 6900.

November 2, 2015. Petition for writ of certiorari to the Supreme Court of Wisconsin denied.

Same case below, 361 Wis. 2d 116, 860 N.W.2d 10.

No. 14-10473. John P. Tomkins, Petitioner v. United States.

577 U.S. 955, 136 S. Ct. 402, 193 L. Ed. 2d 314, 2015 U.S. LEXIS 6928, reh den 577 U.S. 1095, 136 S. Ct. 881, 193 L. Ed. 2d 773, 2016 U.S. LEXIS 403.

November 2, 2015. Petition for writ of certiorari to the United States Court of Appeals for the Seventh Circuit denied.

Same case below, 782 F.3d 338.

No. 15-10. Thomas Edwin Loden, Jr., Petitioner v. Marshall L. Fisher, Commissioner, Mississippi Department of Corrections.

577 U.S. 956, 136 S. Ct. 402, 193 L. Ed. 2d 315, 2015 U.S. LEXIS 6851.

November 2, 2015. Petition for writ of certiorari to the United States Court of Appeals for the Fifth Circuit denied.

———

No. 15-88. Boca Raton Firefighters and Police Pension Fund, Petitioner v. Robert J. Bahash, et al.

577 U.S. 956, 136 S. Ct. 402, 193 L. Ed. 2d 315, 2015 U.S. LEXIS 6893.

November 2, 2015. Petition for writ of certiorari to the United States Court of Appeals for the Second Circuit denied.

Same case below, 574 Fed. Appx. 21.

———

No. 15-123. California Dump Truck Owners Association, Petitioner v. Mary D. Nichols, et al.

577 U.S. 956, 136 S. Ct. 403, 193 L. Ed. 2d 315, 2015 U.S. LEXIS 6941.

November 2, 2015. Petition for writ of certiorari to the United States Court of Appeals for the Ninth Circuit denied.

Same case below, 784 F.3d 500.

———

No. 15-226. Andrew L. Shirvell, Petitioner v. Christopher Armstrong.

577 U.S. 956, 136 S. Ct. 403, 193 L. Ed. 2d 315, 2015 U.S. LEXIS 6842.

November 2, 2015. Petition for writ of certiorari to the United States Court of Appeals for the Sixth Circuit denied.

Same case below, 596 Fed. Appx. 433.

———

No. 15-229. Derrick Price, Petitioner v. Independence Federal Savings Bank, et al.

577 U.S. 956, 136 S. Ct. 438, 193 L. Ed. 2d 315, 2015 U.S. LEXIS 6958.

November 2, 2015. Petition for writ of certiorari to the District of Columbia Court of Appeals denied.

Same case below, 110 A.3d 567.

———

No. 15-230. Harold Werkheiser, Individually and in His Official Capacity as Supervisor for Pocono Township, Pennsylvania, Petitioner v. Pocono Township, Pennsylvania, et al.

577 U.S. 956, 136 S. Ct. 404, 193 L. Ed. 2d 315, 2015 U.S. LEXIS 6953.

November 2, 2015. Petition for writ of certiorari to the United States Court of Appeals for the Third Circuit denied.

Same case below, 780 F.3d 172.

———

No. 15-234. Joseph Raimondo, Petitioner v. Village of Armada, Michigan, et al.

577 U.S. 956, 136 S. Ct. 404, 193 L. Ed. 2d 315, 2015 U.S. LEXIS 6918.

November 2, 2015. Petition for writ of certiorari to the United States Court of Appeals for the Sixth Circuit denied.

No. 15-235. Maged Labib Karas, Petitioner v. Daniel Paramo, Warden.

577 U.S. 956, 136 S. Ct. 404, 193 L. Ed. 2d 316, 2015 U.S. LEXIS 6865.

November 2, 2015. Petition for writ of certiorari to the United States Court of Appeals for the Ninth Circuit denied.

No. 15-242. Luv N' Care, Ltd., Petitioner v. Munchkin, Inc.

577 U.S. 956, 136 S. Ct. 405, 193 L. Ed. 2d 316, 2015 U.S. LEXIS 6936.

November 2, 2015. Petition for writ of certiorari to the United States Court of Appeals for the Federal Circuit denied.

Same case below, 599 Fed. Appx. 958.

No. 15-247. Gene Rechtzigel, Petitioner v. Fischer Sand and Aggregate, LLP.

577 U.S. 956, 136 S. Ct. 407, 193 L. Ed. 2d 316, 2015 U.S. LEXIS 6935.

November 2, 2015. Petition for writ of certiorari to the Court of Appeals of Minnesota denied.

No. 15-252. William Sumner Scott, Petitioner v. Commodity Futures Trading Commission, et al.

577 U.S. 956, 136 S. Ct. 409, 193 L. Ed. 2d 316, 2015 U.S. LEXIS 6943.

November 2, 2015. Petition for writ of certiorari to the United States Court of Appeals for the Eleventh Circuit denied.

No. 15-254. Brad Edwards, Petitioner v. Lockheed Martin Corporation.

577 U.S. 956, 136 S. Ct. 409, 193 L. Ed. 2d 316, 2015 U.S. LEXIS 6878.

November 2, 2015. Petition for writ of certiorari to the United States Court of Appeals for the Ninth Circuit denied.

Same case below, 617 Fed. Appx. 648.

No. 15-256. Kathryn Walker, Petitioner v. United States.

577 U.S. 956, 136 S. Ct. 409, 193 L. Ed. 2d 316, 2015 U.S. LEXIS 6852.

November 2, 2015. Petition for writ of certiorari to the United States Court of Appeals for the Federal Circuit denied.

Same case below, 587 Fed. Appx. 651.

No. 15-260. Anh Nguyet Tran, et al., Petitioners v. Bank of New York, nka Bank of New York Mellon, et al.

577 U.S. 956, 136 S. Ct. 409, 193 L. Ed. 2d 316, 2015 U.S. LEXIS 6927.

November 2, 2015. Petition for writ of certiorari to the United States Court of Appeals for the Second Circuit denied.

Same case below, 610 Fed. Appx. 82.

No. 15-262. Martha Echeverry, Petitioner v. Deutsche Bank National Trust Company.

577 U.S. 957, 136 S. Ct. 410, 193 L. Ed. 2d 316, 2015 U.S. LEXIS 6976, reh den 577 U.S. 1095, 136 S. Ct. 882, 193 L. Ed. 2d 774, 2016 U.S. LEXIS 544.

November 2, 2015. Petition for writ of certiorari to the District Court of Appeal of Florida, Fourth District, denied.

Same case below, 163 So. 3d 1216.

No. 15-263. Freddy Locarno Baloco, et al., Petitioners v. Drummond Company, Inc., et al.

577 U.S. 957, 136 S. Ct. 410, 193 L. Ed. 2d 317, 2015 U.S. LEXIS 6875.

November 2, 2015. Petition for writ of certiorari to the United States Court of Appeals for the Eleventh Circuit denied.

Same case below, 767 F.3d 1229.

No. 15-264. A.V.E.L.A., Inc., et al., Petitioners v. Fifty-Six Hope Road Music, Ltd., et al.

577 U.S. 957, 136 S. Ct. 410, 193 L. Ed. 2d 317, 2015 U.S. LEXIS 6962.

November 2, 2015. Petition for writ of certiorari to the United States Court of Appeals for the Ninth Circuit denied.

Same case below, 778 F.3d 1059.

No. 15-273. Kenneth Butler, Sr., Petitioner v. Balkamp Inc., et al.

577 U.S. 957, 136 S. Ct. 415, 193 L. Ed. 2d 317, 2015 U.S. LEXIS 6888.

November 2, 2015. Petition for writ of certiorari to the United States Court of Appeals for the Federal Circuit denied.

Same case below, 607 Fed. Appx. 982.

No. 15-284. Sheri L. Barron, Petitioner v. University of Michigan, et al.

577 U.S. 957, 136 S. Ct. 416, 193 L. Ed. 2d 317, 2015 U.S. LEXIS 6940.

November 2, 2015. Petition for writ of certiorari to the United States Court of Appeals for the Sixth Circuit denied.

Same case below, 613 Fed. Appx. 480.

No. 15-295. Raymond H. Pierson, III, Petitioner v. Bruce S. Rogow, et al.

577 U.S. 957, 136 S. Ct. 416, 193 L. Ed. 2d 317, 2015 U.S. LEXIS 6942, reh den 577 U.S. 1095, 136 S. Ct. 882, 193 L. Ed. 2d 774, 2016 U.S. LEXIS 592.

November 2, 2015. Petition for writ of certiorari to the United States Court of Appeals for the Eleventh Circuit denied.

Same case below, 589 Fed. Appx. 499.

No. 15-297. Alfredia Pruitt, Petitioner v. ResCap Liquidating Trust.

577 U.S. 957, 136 S. Ct. 416, 193 L. Ed. 2d 317, 2015 U.S. LEXIS 6895.

November 2, 2015. Petition for writ of certiorari to the United States Court of Appeals for the Second Circuit denied.

No. 15-299. Anthony J. Russo, Petitioner v. New York City Department of Education.

577 U.S. 957, 136 S. Ct. 416, 193 L. Ed. 2d 317, 2015 U.S. LEXIS 6916, reh den 577 U.S. 1095, 136 S. Ct. 882, 193 L. Ed. 2d 774, 2016 U.S. LEXIS 609.

November 2, 2015. Petition for writ of certiorari to the Court of Appeals of New York denied.

Same case below, 25 N.Y.3d 946, 6 N.Y.S.3d 549, 29 N.E.3d 896.

No. 15-306. Marco A. Cantu, et ux., Petitioners v. Michael B. Schmidt, Trustee.

577 U.S. 957, 136 S. Ct. 417, 193 L. Ed. 2d 317, 2015 U.S. LEXIS 6915.

November 2, 2015. Petition for writ of certiorari to the United States Court of Appeals for the Fifth Circuit denied.

Same case below, 784 F.3d 253.

No. 15-310. Majida Salem, Petitioner v. United States.

577 U.S. 957, 136 S. Ct. 418, 193 L. Ed. 2d 318, 2015 U.S. LEXIS 6892.

November 2, 2015. Petition for writ of certiorari to the United States Court of Appeals for the Fifth Circuit denied.

Same case below, 789 F.3d 547.

No. 15-320. David Balfour, Petitioner v. Carol Howes, Warden.

577 U.S. 957, 136 S. Ct. 419, 193 L. Ed. 2d 318, 2015 U.S. LEXIS 6965.

November 2, 2015. Petition for writ of certiorari to the United States Court of Appeals for the Sixth Circuit denied.

Same case below, 611 Fed. Appx. 862.

No. 15-326. Automated Merchandising Systems, Inc., Petitioner v. Michelle K. Lee, Director, United States Patent and Trademark Office.

577 U.S. 957, 136 S. Ct. 419, 193 L. Ed. 2d 318, 2015 U.S. LEXIS 6947.

November 2, 2015. Petition for writ of certiorari to the United States Court of Appeals for the Federal Circuit denied.

Same case below, 782 F.3d 1376.

No. 15-333. Jason Senne, Petitioner v. Village of Palatine, Illinois.

577 U.S. 957, 136 S. Ct. 419, 193 L. Ed. 2d 318, 2015 U.S. LEXIS 6828.

November 2, 2015. Petition for writ of certiorari to the United States Court of Appeals for the Seventh Circuit denied.

Same case below, 784 F.3d 444.

No. 15-336. Lura Hess Bechtel, et al., Petitioners v. Sandel Avionics, Inc.

577 U.S. 958, 136 S. Ct. 419, 193 L. Ed. 2d 318, 2015 U.S. LEXIS 6868.

November 2, 2015. Petition for writ of certiorari to the Court of Appeal of California, Fourth Appellate District, Division One, denied.

No. 15-341. Irwin R. Eisenstein, Petitioner v. Committee on Character and Fitness, Appellate Division, Supreme Court of New York, Third Judicial Department.

577 U.S. 958, 136 S. Ct. 420, 193 L. Ed. 2d 318, 2015 U.S. LEXIS 6855.

November 2, 2015. Petition for writ of certiorari to the Appellate Division, Supreme Court of New York, Third Judicial Department, denied.

Same case below, 123 App. Div. 3d 1371, 997 N.Y.S.2d 332.

No. 15-344. Daniel Thibeault, Petitioner v. Merit Systems Protection Board.

577 U.S. 958, 136 S. Ct. 438, 193 L. Ed. 2d 318, 2015 U.S. LEXIS 6980.

November 2, 2015. Petition for writ of certiorari to the United States Court of Appeals for the Federal Circuit denied.

Same case below, 611 Fed. Appx. 975.

Same case below, 599 Fed. Appx. 767.

No. 15-350. Samuel Zook, et al., Petitioners v. Environmental Protection Agency, et al.

577 U.S. 958, 136 S. Ct. 421, 193 L. Ed. 2d 319, 2015 U.S. LEXIS 6982.

November 2, 2015. Petition for writ of certiorari to the United States Court of Appeals for the District of Columbia Circuit denied.

Same case below, 611 Fed. Appx. 725.

No. 15-355. Anna E. Charlton, et vir, Petitioners v. Commissioner of Internal Revenue.

577 U.S. 958, 136 S. Ct. 421, 193 L. Ed. 2d 319, 2015 U.S. LEXIS 6896.

November 2, 2015. Petition for writ of certiorari to the United States Court of Appeals for the Third Circuit denied.

Same case below, 611 Fed. Appx. 91.

No. 15-360. Richard E. Crayton, Petitioner v. United States.

577 U.S. 958, 136 S. Ct. 424, 193 L. Ed. 2d 319, 2015 U.S. LEXIS 6932.

November 2, 2015. Petition for writ of certiorari to the United States Court of Appeals for the Seventh Circuit denied.

Same case below, 799 F.3d 623.

No. 15-364. Ruth Milano, Petitioner v. Ashton B. Carter, Secretary of Defense, et al.

577 U.S. 958, 136 S. Ct. 424, 193 L. Ed. 2d 319, 2015 U.S. LEXIS 6955.

November 2, 2015. Petition for writ of certiorari to the United States Court of Appeals for the Ninth Circuit denied.

No. 15-373. Howard Grant, Petitioner v. United States.

577 U.S. 958, 136 S. Ct. 427, 193 L. Ed. 2d 319, 2015 U.S. LEXIS 6973.

November 2, 2015. Petition for writ of certiorari to the United States Court of Appeals for the Fifth Circuit denied.

Same case below, 605 Fed. Appx. 448.

No. 15-382. Gerald Morawski, Petitioner v. Lightstorm Entertainment, Inc., et al.

577 U.S. 958, 136 S. Ct. 427, 193 L. Ed. 2d 319, 2015 U.S. LEXIS 6870.

November 2, 2015. Petition for writ of certiorari to the United States Court of Appeals for the Ninth Circuit denied.

Same case below, 599 Fed. Appx. 779.

No. 15-383. Vito Antonio Laera, Petitioner v. Blanco GmbH + Co. KG.

577 U.S. 958, 136 S. Ct. 427, 193 L. Ed. 2d 319, 2015 U.S. LEXIS 6919.

November 2, 2015. Petition for writ of certiorari to the United States Court of Appeals for the Eleventh Circuit denied.

Same case below, 620 Fed. Appx. 718.

No. 15-391. James Wilbur Fondren, Jr., Petitioner v. United States.

577 U.S. 958, 136 S. Ct. 428, 193 L. Ed. 2d 319, 2015 U.S. LEXIS 6884.

November 2, 2015. Petition for writ of certiorari to the United States Court of Appeals for the Fourth Circuit denied.

Same case below, 600 Fed. Appx. 895.

Same case below, 786 F.3d 873.

No. 15-392. James W. Hall, Petitioner v. Edward L. Gilbert, et al.

577 U.S. 958, 136 S. Ct. 428, 193 L. Ed. 2d 320, 2015 U.S. LEXIS 6863, reh den 577 U.S. 1095, 136 S. Ct. 883, 193 L. Ed. 2d 774, 2016 U.S. LEXIS 439.

November 2, 2015. Petition for writ of certiorari to the Court of Appeals of Ohio, Cuyahoga County, denied.

No. 15-409. Jack Rosga, Petitioner v. United States.

577 U.S. 959, 136 S. Ct. 431, 193 L. Ed. 2d 320, 2015 U.S. LEXIS 6996.

November 2, 2015. Petition for writ of certiorari to the United States Court of Appeals for the Fourth Circuit denied.

Same case below, 608 Fed. Appx. 166.

No. 15-399. Sean David Pickett, Petitioner v. United States.

577 U.S. 958, 136 S. Ct. 428, 193 L. Ed. 2d 320, 2015 U.S. LEXIS 6972.

November 2, 2015. Petition for writ of certiorari to the United States Court of Appeals for the Eleventh Circuit denied.

Same case below, 602 Fed. Appx. 774.

No. 15-414. Gregg Germain Williams, Petitioner v. United States.

577 U.S. 959, 136 S. Ct. 434, 193 L. Ed. 2d 320, 2015 U.S. LEXIS 6910.

November 2, 2015. Petition for writ of certiorari to the United States Court of Appeals for the Eleventh Circuit denied.

Same case below, 618 Fed. Appx. 541.

No. 15-401. Louis Ruggiero, Petitioner v. United States.

577 U.S. 959, 136 S. Ct. 429, 193 L. Ed. 2d 320, 2015 U.S. LEXIS 6974.

November 2, 2015. Petition for writ of certiorari to the United States Court of Appeals for the Eleventh Circuit denied.

Same case below, 791 F.3d 1281.

No. 15-5368. Derrick Jones, Petitioner v. Louisiana.

577 U.S. 959, 136 S. Ct. 403, 193 L. Ed. 2d 320, 2015 U.S. LEXIS 7025.

November 2, 2015. Petition for writ of certiorari to the Court of Appeal of Louisiana, Fourth Circuit, denied.

No. 15-402. Michael A. Rosin, Petitioner v. United States.

577 U.S. 959, 136 S. Ct. 429, 193 L. Ed. 2d 320, 2015 U.S. LEXIS 6985.

November 2, 2015. Petition for writ of certiorari to the United States Court of Appeals for the Eleventh Circuit denied.

No. 15-5472. Oscar Leyva-Samaripa, Petitioner v. United States.

577 U.S. 959, 136 S. Ct. 403, 193 L. Ed. 2d 320, 2015 U.S. LEXIS 6847.

November 2, 2015. Petition for writ of certiorari to the United States Court of Appeals for the Fifth Circuit denied.

No. 15-5595. Robert Louis Brown, Petitioner v. Marriott Hotel.

577 U.S. 959, 136 S. Ct. 403, 193 L. Ed. 2d 321, 2015 U.S. LEXIS 6897.

November 2, 2015. Petition for writ of certiorari to the United States Court of Appeals for the Tenth Circuit denied.

Same case below, 602 Fed. Appx. 726.

No. 15-5682. Terry Darnell Edwards, Petitioner v. William Stephens, Director, Texas Department of Criminal Justice, Correctional Institutions Division.

577 U.S. 959, 136 S. Ct. 403, 193 L. Ed. 2d 321, 2015 U.S. LEXIS 6911.

November 2, 2015. Petition for writ of certiorari to the United States Court of Appeals for the Fifth Circuit denied.

Same case below, 612 Fed. Appx. 719.

No. 15-5742. Michael Shane Shuster, Petitioner v. Ohio (two judgments).

577 U.S. 959, 136 S. Ct. 404, 193 L. Ed. 2d 321, 2015 U.S. LEXIS 6831.

November 2, 2015. Petition for writ of certiorari to the Court of Appeals of Ohio, Morgan County, denied.

No. 15-5754. Mark Irving Shapiro, Petitioner v. California.

577 U.S. 959, 136 S. Ct. 404, 193 L. Ed. 2d 321, 2015 U.S. LEXIS 6964.

November 2, 2015. Petition for writ of certiorari to the Court of Appeal of California, Fourth Appellate District, Division Three, denied.

No. 15-5758. Michael E. Olive, Petitioner v. Florida.

577 U.S. 959, 136 S. Ct. 404, 193 L. Ed. 2d 321, 2015 U.S. LEXIS 6960, reh den 578 U.S. 916, 136 S. Ct. 1537, 194 L. Ed. 2d 621, 2016 U.S. LEXIS 2316.

November 2, 2015. Petition for writ of certiorari to the District Court of Appeal of Florida, Fifth District, denied.

Same case below, 162 So. 3d 1037.

No. 15-5760. Aurel Smith, Petitioner v. Thomas LaValley, Superintendent, Clinton Correctional Facility.

577 U.S. 959, 136 S. Ct. 405, 193 L. Ed. 2d 321, 2015 U.S. LEXIS 6951.

November 2, 2015. Petition for writ of certiorari to the United States Court of Appeals for the Second Circuit denied.

Same case below, 610 Fed. Appx. 23.

No. 15-5762. Ricardo Jaimes, Petitioner v. Illinois.

577 U.S. 959, 136 S. Ct. 405, 193 L. Ed. 2d 321, 2015 U.S. LEXIS 6963.

November 2, 2015. Petition for writ of certiorari to the Appellate Court of Illinois, Second District, denied.

Same case below, 21 N.E.3d 501.

No. 15-5774. Jeremiah Jackson, Petitioner v. Ohio.

577 U.S. 959, 136 S. Ct. 405, 193 L. Ed. 2d 321, 2015 U.S. LEXIS 6845.

November 2, 2015. Petition for writ of certiorari to the Supreme Court of Ohio denied.

Same case below, 141 Ohio St. 3d 171, 23 N.E.3d 1023.

No. 15-5775. Russell David Wood, Petitioner v. Harold W. Clarke, Director, Virginia Department of Corrections.

577 U.S. 960, 136 S. Ct. 405, 193 L. Ed. 2d 322, 2015 U.S. LEXIS 6997.

November 2, 2015. Petition for writ of certiorari to the United States Court of Appeals for the Fourth Circuit denied.

Same case below, 602 Fed. Appx. 140.

No. 15-5778. James Charles Fudge, Petitioner v. Arkansas.

577 U.S. 960, 136 S. Ct. 406, 193 L. Ed. 2d 322, 2015 U.S. LEXIS 7015.

November 2, 2015. Petition for writ of certiorari to the Supreme Court of Arkansas denied.

Same case below, 2015 Ark. 230, 463 S.W.3d 292.

No. 15-5780. Joel L. Beling, Petitioner v. Ennis, Inc.

577 U.S. 960, 136 S. Ct. 406, 193 L. Ed. 2d 322, 2015 U.S. LEXIS 6861.

November 2, 2015. Petition for writ of certiorari to the United States Court of Appeals for the Federal Circuit denied.

Same case below, 613 Fed. Appx. 924.

No. 15-5787. William M. Johnson, Petitioner v. Jeffrey Woods, Warden.

577 U.S. 960, 136 S. Ct. 406, 193 L. Ed. 2d 322, 2015 U.S. LEXIS 6961.

November 2, 2015. Petition for writ of certiorari to the United States Court of Appeals for the Sixth Circuit denied.

No. 15-5795. Steven Beasley, Petitioner v. Florida.

577 U.S. 960, 136 S. Ct. 406, 193 L. Ed. 2d 322, 2015 U.S. LEXIS 6924.

November 2, 2015. Petition for writ of certiorari to the District Court of Appeal of Florida, First District, denied.

Same case below, 162 So. 3d 986.

No. 15-5796. Curtis Lee Sheppard, Petitioner v. Brad Livingston, et al.

577 U.S. 960, 136 S. Ct. 406, 193 L. Ed. 2d 322, 2015 U.S. LEXIS 6923.

November 2, 2015. Petition for writ of certiorari to the United States Court of Appeals for the Fifth Circuit denied.

No. 15-5799. Warren Parks, Petitioner v. Wendy Knight.

577 U.S. 960, 136 S. Ct. 406, 193 L. Ed. 2d 322, 2015 U.S. LEXIS 6999.

November 2, 2015. Petition for writ of certiorari to the United States Court of Appeals for the Seventh Circuit denied.

No. 15-5801. Donald E. Ware, Petitioner v. Dushan Zatecky, Superintendent, Pendleton Correctional Facility.

577 U.S. 960, 136 S. Ct. 407, 193 L. Ed. 2d 323, 2015 U.S. LEXIS 6948.

November 2, 2015. Petition for writ of certiorari to the United States Court of Appeals for the Seventh Circuit denied.

No. 15-5805. William Tavares Dunn, Petitioner v. William Stephens, Director, Texas Department of Criminal Justice, Correctional Institutions Division.

577 U.S. 960, 136 S. Ct. 407, 193 L. Ed. 2d 323, 2015 U.S. LEXIS 6838.

November 2, 2015. Petition for writ of certiorari to the United States Court of Appeals for the Fifth Circuit denied.

No. 15-5813. James D. Moore, Petitioner v. Pennsylvania.

577 U.S. 960, 136 S. Ct. 407, 193 L. Ed. 2d 323, 2015 U.S. LEXIS 6956.

November 2, 2015. Petition for writ of certiorari to the Superior Court of Pennsylvania, Philadelphia Office, denied.

Same case below, 105 A.3d 796.

No. 15-5823. Philip Maier, Petitioner v. Lawrence Mahally, Superintendent, State Correctional Institution at Dallas, et al.

577 U.S. 960, 136 S. Ct. 407, 193 L. Ed. 2d 323, 2015 U.S. LEXIS 6992.

November 2, 2015. Petition for writ of certiorari to the United States Court of Appeals for the Third Circuit denied.

No. 15-5824. Steven Allen Jones, Petitioner v. Suzanne M. Peery, Acting Warden, et al.

577 U.S. 960, 136 S. Ct. 407, 193 L. Ed. 2d 323, 2015 U.S. LEXIS 6995.

November 2, 2015. Petition for writ of certiorari to the United States Court of Appeals for the Ninth Circuit denied.

Same case below, 593 Fed. Appx. 674.

No. 15-5825. Darryl D. Streeter, Petitioner v. Florida.

577 U.S. 960, 136 S. Ct. 408, 193 L. Ed. 2d 323, 2015 U.S. LEXIS 6908.

November 2, 2015. Petition for writ of certiorari to the Supreme Court of Florida denied.

Same case below, 147 So. 3d 527.

No. 15-5827. Carl E. Brown, as Next Friend of James E. Carter, Petitioner v. Corrections Corporation of America.

577 U.S. 960, 136 S. Ct. 408, 193 L. Ed. 2d 323, 2015 U.S. LEXIS 6977.

November 2, 2015. Petition for writ of certiorari to the United States Court of Appeals for the Ninth Circuit denied.

Same case below, 586 Fed. Appx. 430.

No. 15-5828. Jose Zamarripa Alvarado, Petitioner v. Texas.

577 U.S. 961, 136 S. Ct. 408, 193 L. Ed. 2d 323, 2015 U.S. LEXIS 6994.

November 2, 2015. Petition for writ of certiorari to the Court of Criminal Appeals of Texas denied.

No. 15-5832. Frederick D. Moore, Petitioner v. Rick Raemisch, Executive Director, Colorado Department of Corrections, et al.

577 U.S. 961, 136 S. Ct. 439, 193 L. Ed. 2d 324, 2015 U.S. LEXIS 6986.

November 2, 2015. Petition for writ of certiorari to the Supreme Court of Colorado denied.

No. 15-5835. Robert L. White, Petitioner v. Burl Cain, Warden.

577 U.S. 961, 136 S. Ct. 408, 193 L. Ed. 2d 324, 2015 U.S. LEXIS 6904.

November 2, 2015. Petition for writ of certiorari to the United States Court of Appeals for the Fifth Circuit denied.

No. 15-5837. Dorian Frank O'Kelley, Petitioner v. Bruce Chatman, Warden.

577 U.S. 961, 136 S. Ct. 408, 193 L. Ed. 2d 324, 2015 U.S. LEXIS 6860.

November 2, 2015. Petition for writ of certiorari to the Superior Court of Georgia, Butts County, denied.

No. 15-5840. Ernest Littleton, Petitioner v. Illinois.

577 U.S. 961, 136 S. Ct. 409, 193 L. Ed. 2d 324, 2015 U.S. LEXIS 6891.

November 2, 2015. Petition for writ of certiorari to the Appellate Court of Illinois, First District, denied.

Same case below, 14 N.E.3d 555.

No. 15-5842. Joel Carter, Petitioner v. Michigan Department of Corrections, et al.

577 U.S. 961, 136 S. Ct. 439, 193 L. Ed. 2d 324, 2015 U.S. LEXIS 6856, reh den 577 U.S. 1096, 136 S. Ct. 886, 193 L. Ed. 2d 778, 2016 U.S. LEXIS 552.

November 2, 2015. Petition for writ of certiorari to the United States Court of Appeals for the Sixth Circuit denied.

No. 15-5845. Bennie K. Ellison, Petitioner v. Joseph G. Kazmierski, Supervising Judge, Circuit Court of Illinois, Cook County, et al.

577 U.S. 961, 136 S. Ct. 410, 193 L. Ed. 2d 324, 2015 U.S. LEXIS 7022, reh den 577 U.S. 1096, 136 S. Ct. 886, 193 L. Ed. 2d 778, 2016 U.S. LEXIS 618.

November 2, 2015. Petition for writ of certiorari to the Supreme Court of Illinois denied.

No. 15-5846. Omar R. Wilkins, Petitioner v. Nick Ludwick, Warden.

577 U.S. 961, 136 S. Ct. 410, 193 L. Ed. 2d 324, 2015 U.S. LEXIS 6889.

November 2, 2015. Petition for writ of certiorari to the United States Court of Appeals for the Eighth Circuit denied.

No. 15-5847. Chester Staples, Petitioner v. Texas.

577 U.S. 961, 136 S. Ct. 410, 193 L. Ed. 2d 324, 2015 U.S. LEXIS 6853, reh den 577 U.S. 1096, 136 S. Ct. 886, 193 L. Ed. 2d 778, 2016 U.S. LEXIS 545.

November 2, 2015. Petition for writ of certiorari to the Court of Appeals of Texas, Twelfth District, denied.

No. 15-5853. Keenan King, Petitioner v. Raymond Booker, Warden.

577 U.S. 961, 136 S. Ct. 411, 193 L. Ed. 2d 325, 2015 U.S. LEXIS 6840.

November 2, 2015. Petition for writ of certiorari to the United States Court of Appeals for the Sixth Circuit denied.

———

No. 15-5856. Boaz Pleasant-Bey, Petitioner v. Tennessee.

577 U.S. 961, 136 S. Ct. 411, 193 L. Ed. 2d 325, 2015 U.S. LEXIS 6905.

November 2, 2015. Petition for writ of certiorari to the Supreme Court of Tennessee, Western Division, denied.

———

No. 15-5858. David Kelsey Sparre, Petitioner v. Florida.

577 U.S. 961, 136 S. Ct. 411, 193 L. Ed. 2d 325, 2015 U.S. LEXIS 7005.

November 2, 2015. Petition for writ of certiorari to the Supreme Court of Florida denied.

Same case below, 164 So. 3d 1183.

———

No. 15-5860. Corielle Johnson, Petitioner v. Leslie Beak, et al.

577 U.S. 961, 136 S. Ct. 411, 193 L. Ed. 2d 325, 2015 U.S. LEXIS 6876, reh den

577 U.S. 1096, 136 S. Ct. 886, 193 L. Ed. 2d 778, 2016 U.S. LEXIS 588.

November 2, 2015. Petition for writ of certiorari to the United States Court of Appeals for the Sixth Circuit denied.

———

No. 15-5864. Jorge Vazquez, Petitioner v. Orange County Service Unit.

577 U.S. 961, 136 S. Ct. 411, 193 L. Ed. 2d 325, 2015 U.S. LEXIS 6934.

November 2, 2015. Petition for writ of certiorari to the United States Court of Appeals for the Eleventh Circuit denied.

Same case below, 598 Fed. Appx. 760.

———

No. 15-5865. Anthony Marco Ramirez, Petitioner v. James A. Yates, Warden.

577 U.S. 962, 136 S. Ct. 411, 193 L. Ed. 2d 325, 2015 U.S. LEXIS 6917.

November 2, 2015. Petition for writ of certiorari to the United States Court of Appeals for the Ninth Circuit denied.

———

No. 15-5866. John O. Study, Petitioner v. Indiana.

577 U.S. 962, 136 S. Ct. 412, 193 L. Ed. 2d 325, 2015 U.S. LEXIS 7008.

November 2, 2015. Petition for writ of certiorari to the Supreme Court of Indiana denied.

Same case below, 24 N.E.3d 947.

Same case below, 607 Fed. Appx. 688.

No. 15-5869. Damion Leafey, Petitioner v. Mark Garman, Superintendent, State Correctional Institution at Rockview, et al.

577 U.S. 962, 136 S. Ct. 412, 193 L. Ed. 2d 326, 2015 U.S. LEXIS 6921.

November 2, 2015. Petition for writ of certiorari to the United States Court of Appeals for the Third Circuit denied.

No. 15-5875. Ivan Almeida, Petitioner v. Illinois.

577 U.S. 962, 136 S. Ct. 412, 193 L. Ed. 2d 326, 2015 U.S. LEXIS 6829.

November 2, 2015. Petition for writ of certiorari to the Appellate Court of Illinois, First District, denied.

No. 15-5878. Walter Lee Wright, Petitioner v. Julie L. Jones, Secretary, Florida Department of Corrections.

577 U.S. 962, 136 S. Ct. 412, 193 L. Ed. 2d 326, 2015 U.S. LEXIS 6887.

November 2, 2015. Petition for writ of certiorari to the United States Court of Appeals for the Eleventh Circuit denied.

No. 15-5879. Anthony L. Taylor, Petitioner v. Elvin Valenzuela, Warden, et al.

577 U.S. 962, 136 S. Ct. 412, 193 L. Ed. 2d 326, 2015 U.S. LEXIS 6890.

November 2, 2015. Petition for writ of certiorari to the United States Court of Appeals for the Ninth Circuit denied.

No. 15-5880. Gary Taylor, Petitioner v. Raythel Fisher, Jr., Acting Warden.

577 U.S. 962, 136 S. Ct. 412, 193 L. Ed. 2d 326, 2015 U.S. LEXIS 6837.

November 2, 2015. Petition for writ of certiorari to the United States Court of Appeals for the Ninth Circuit denied.

No. 15-5882. Benjamin R. Ragan, Petitioner v. Susan Wilson, et al.

577 U.S. 962, 136 S. Ct. 413, 193 L. Ed. 2d 326, 2015 U.S. LEXIS 6832.

November 2, 2015. Petition for writ of certiorari to the United States Court of Appeals for the Sixth Circuit denied.

No. 15-5884. Carline M. Curry, Petitioner v. Martin Berger, et al.

577 U.S. 962, 136 S. Ct. 413, 193 L. Ed. 2d 326, 2015 U.S. LEXIS 6885, reh den 577 U.S. 1096, 136 S. Ct. 886, 193 L. Ed. 2d 778, 2016 U.S. LEXIS 476.

November 2, 2015. Petition for writ of certiorari to the United States Court of Appeals for the Sixth Circuit denied.

No. 15-5898. Lonnie Huckabone, Petitioner v. City of Jamestown, New York, et al.

577 U.S. 962, 136 S. Ct. 413, 193 L. Ed. 2d 326, 2015 U.S. LEXIS 6833.

November 2, 2015. Petition for writ of certiorari to the United States Court of Appeals for the Second Circuit denied.

No. 15-5901. Willie Baldwin, Petitioner v. Illinois.

577 U.S. 962, 136 S. Ct. 413, 193 L. Ed. 2d 327, 2015 U.S. LEXIS 6913.

November 2, 2015. Petition for writ of certiorari to the Appellate Court of Illinois, First District, denied.

Same case below, 17 N.E.3d 746.

No. 15-5906. Tina Lachief Patterson, Petitioner v. United States District Court for the Southern District of Texas.

577 U.S. 962, 136 S. Ct. 439, 193 L. Ed. 2d 327, 2015 U.S. LEXIS 6931.

November 2, 2015. Petition for writ of certiorari to the United States Court of Appeals for the Fifth Circuit denied.

No. 15-5908. Harold Moore, Petitioner v. Mary Berghuis, Warden.

577 U.S. 962, 136 S. Ct. 414, 193 L. Ed. 2d 327, 2015 U.S. LEXIS 6966.

November 2, 2015. Petition for writ of certiorari to the United States Court of Appeals for the Sixth Circuit denied.

No. 15-5910. Luis Rodolfo Lopez, Petitioner v. Texas.

577 U.S. 962, 136 S. Ct. 414, 193 L. Ed. 2d 327, 2015 U.S. LEXIS 7018.

November 2, 2015. Petition for writ of certiorari to the Court of Appeals of Texas, Fifth District, denied.

No. 15-5912. Timothy Jay Kaprelian, Petitioner v. John Barrett.

577 U.S. 962, 136 S. Ct. 414, 193 L. Ed. 2d 327, 2015 U.S. LEXIS 6867.

November 2, 2015. Petition for writ of certiorari to the United States Court of Appeals for the Seventh Circuit denied.

Same case below, 607 Fed. Appx. 583.

No. 15-5914. Jesley Audley Moran, Petitioner v. California.

577 U.S. 963, 136 S. Ct. 414, 193 L. Ed. 2d 327, 2015 U.S. LEXIS 6920.

November 2, 2015. Petition for writ of certiorari to the Court of Appeal of California, Second Appellate District, Division Eight, denied.

No. 15-5915. Victor Paleologus, aka Victor Lawrence Paleologus, Petitioner v. R. Lopez, Warden.

577 U.S. 963, 136 S. Ct. 414, 193 L. Ed. 2d 327, 2015 U.S. LEXIS 6979.

November 2, 2015. Petition for writ of certiorari to the United States Court of Appeals for the Ninth Circuit denied.

No. 15-5916. John Willie Carter, Jr., Petitioner v. Harold W. Clarke, Director, Virginia Department of Corrections.

577 U.S. 963, 136 S. Ct. 415, 193 L. Ed. 2d 327, 2015 U.S. LEXIS 6983.

November 2, 2015. Petition for writ of certiorari to the Supreme Court of Virginia denied.

No. 15-5920. Vincent Harper-Bey, Petitioner v. Jeffrey Beard, Secretary, California Department of Corrections and Rehabilitation.

577 U.S. 963, 136 S. Ct. 415, 193 L. Ed. 2d 328, 2015 U.S. LEXIS 6914.

November 2, 2015. Petition for writ of certiorari to the United States Court of Appeals for the Ninth Circuit denied.

No. 15-5926. Marvin Douglas, Petitioner v. Jerry Goodwin, Warden.

577 U.S. 963, 136 S. Ct. 415, 193 L. Ed. 2d 328, 2015 U.S. LEXIS 6939.

November 2, 2015. Petition for writ of certiorari to the United States Court of Appeals for the Fifth Circuit denied.

No. 15-5941. Demetric McGowan, Petitioner v. Sherry Burt, Warden.

577 U.S. 963, 136 S. Ct. 415, 193 L. Ed. 2d 328, 2015 U.S. LEXIS 6849.

November 2, 2015. Petition for writ of certiorari to the United States Court of Appeals for the Sixth Circuit denied.

Same case below, 788 F.3d 510.

No. 15-5969. Douglas Morin, Petitioner v. Florida.

577 U.S. 963, 136 S. Ct. 416, 193 L. Ed. 2d 328, 2015 U.S. LEXIS 7019.

November 2, 2015. Petition for writ of certiorari to the District Court of Appeal of Florida, Fifth District, denied.

Same case below, 171 So. 3d 737.

No. 15-5983. Keith Burks, Petitioner v. Florida.

577 U.S. 963, 136 S. Ct. 417, 193 L. Ed. 2d 328, 2015 U.S. LEXIS 6945.

November 2, 2015. Petition for writ of certiorari to the District Court of Appeal of Florida, First District, denied.

Same case below, 163 So. 3d 571.

No. 15-5995. Shawn Lessieur, Petitioner v. Massachusetts.

577 U.S. 963, 136 S. Ct. 418, 193 L. Ed. 2d 328, 2015 U.S. LEXIS 6971.

November 2, 2015. Petition for writ of certiorari to the Supreme Judicial Court of Massachusetts denied.

Same case below, 472 Mass. 317, 34 N.E.3d 321.

No. 15-6005. Nathan Marquis LeBaron, Petitioner v. Osvaldo Vidal, Superintendent, Souza-Baranowski Correctional Center.

577 U.S. 963, 136 S. Ct. 418, 193 L. Ed. 2d 328, 2015 U.S. LEXIS 7006.

November 2, 2015. Petition for writ of certiorari to the United States Court of Appeals for the First Circuit denied.

No. 15-6009. Harold E. Wallis, Petitioner v. Florida.

577 U.S. 963, 136 S. Ct. 418, 193 L. Ed. 2d 328, 2015 U.S. LEXIS 7021.

November 2, 2015. Petition for writ of certiorari to the Supreme Court of Florida denied.

Same case below, 157 So. 3d 1051.

———

No. 15-6028. Jamie Douglas Geer, Petitioner v. Florida.

577 U.S. 963, 136 S. Ct. 418, 193 L. Ed. 2d 329, 2015 U.S. LEXIS 6975.

November 2, 2015. Petition for writ of certiorari to the District Court of Appeal of Florida, Second District, denied.

Same case below, 200 So. 3d 1274.

———

No. 15-6033. Ingrid Cotterell Ingram, Petitioner v. Just Energy.

577 U.S. 963, 136 S. Ct. 419, 193 L. Ed. 2d 329, 2015 U.S. LEXIS 7011, reh den 578 U.S. 942, 136 S. Ct. 1706, 194 L. Ed. 2d 803, 2016 U.S. LEXIS 2542.

November 2, 2015. Petition for writ of certiorari to the United States Court of Appeals for the Second Circuit denied.

———

No. 15-6041. Jamie D. Geer, Petitioner v. Florida.

577 U.S. 963, 136 S. Ct. 419, 193 L. Ed. 2d 329, 2015 U.S. LEXIS 6841.

November 2, 2015. Petition for writ of certiorari to the District Court of Appeal of Florida, Second District, denied.

———

No. 15-6062. Ricky Lamar Turner, Petitioner v. Harold W. Clarke, Director, Virginia Department of Corrections.

577 U.S. 963, 136 S. Ct. 420, 193 L. Ed. 2d 329, 2015 U.S. LEXIS 7002.

November 2, 2015. Petition for writ of certiorari to the United States Court of Appeals for the Fourth Circuit denied.

Same case below, 591 Fed. Appx. 217.

———

No. 15-6066. Ernest D. Shields, Petitioner v. United States.

577 U.S. 964, 136 S. Ct. 420, 193 L. Ed. 2d 329, 2015 U.S. LEXIS 7020.

November 2, 2015. Petition for writ of certiorari to the United States Court of Appeals for the Seventh Circuit denied.

Same case below, 789 F.3d 733.

———

No. 15-6077. Rick Jean, Petitioner v. United States.

No. 15-6256. Neheme Ductant, Petitioner v. United States.

No. 15-6337. Jude Sereme, Petitioner v. United States.

577 U.S. 964, 136 S. Ct. 420, 193 L. Ed. 2d 329, 2015 U.S. LEXIS 7016.

November 2, 2015. Petitions for writs of certiorari to the United States Court of Appeals for the Eleventh Circuit denied.

Same cases below, 609 Fed. Appx. 597.

———

No. 15-6086. Ricardo Woods, Petitioner v. Ohio.

577 U.S. 964, 136 S. Ct. 420, 193 L. Ed. 2d 329, 2015 U.S. LEXIS 6859.

November 2, 2015. Petition for writ of certiorari to the Court of Appeals of Ohio, Hamilton County, denied.

No. 15-6109. Augustine Sanchez-Hernandez, aka Agustin Sanchez, Petitioner v. United States; Jesus Rodriguez-Pena, Petitioner v. United States; Jose Walter Navarrete-Cordova, Petitioner v. United States; Milton Enrique Ulin Subieta, aka Milton Ulin, aka Jose Milton, aka Jose Ulin-Zubieta, Petitioner v. United States; Enrique Vasquez-Martinez, Petitioner v. United States; Omar Guadalupe Perez-Barra, Petitioner v. United States; Rodrigo Jimenez-Binagra, Petitioner v. United States; and Jared Villarreal-De La Fuente, Petitioner v. United States.

577 U.S. 964, 136 S. Ct. 420, 193 L. Ed. 2d 330, 2015 U.S. LEXIS 6830.

November 2, 2015. Petition for writ of certiorari to the United States Court of Appeals for the Fifth Circuit denied.

Same case below, 607 Fed. Appx. 409 (first judgment); 604 Fed. Appx. 381 (second judgment); 607 Fed. Appx. 389 (third judgment); 613 Fed. Appx. 353 fourth judgment); 613 Fed. Appx. 356 (fifth judgment); 613 Fed. Appx. 355 (sixth judgment); 613 Fed. Appx. 394 (seventh judgment); and 613 Fed. Appx. 368 (eighth judgment).

No. 15-6123. Carmen Soto, Petitioner v. United States.

577 U.S. 964, 136 S. Ct. 421, 193 L. Ed. 2d 330, 2015 U.S. LEXIS 7010.

November 2, 2015. Petition for writ of certiorari to the United States Court of Appeals for the First Circuit denied.

Same case below, 799 F.3d 68.

No. 15-6125. Jonathan Eugene Brunson, Petitioner v. Felix Taylor, Warden.

577 U.S. 964, 136 S. Ct. 421, 193 L. Ed. 2d 330, 2015 U.S. LEXIS 7004, reh den 577 U.S. 1114, 136 S. Ct. 926, 193 L. Ed. 2d 811, 2016 U.S. LEXIS 719.

November 2, 2015. Petition for writ of certiorari to the United States Court of Appeals for the Fourth Circuit denied.

Same case below, 606 Fed. Appx. 86.

No. 15-6162. Christopher J. Martin, Petitioner v. Virginia.

577 U.S. 964, 136 S. Ct. 422, 193 L. Ed. 2d 330, 2015 U.S. LEXIS 7003.

November 2, 2015. Petition for writ of certiorari to the Supreme Court of Virginia denied.

No. 15-6170. James Strouse, Petitioner v. Bureau of Prisons, et al.

577 U.S. 964, 136 S. Ct. 422, 193 L. Ed. 2d 330, 2015 U.S. LEXIS 6944.

November 2, 2015. Petition for writ of certiorari to the United States Court of Appeals for the Fourth Circuit denied.

Same case below, 610 Fed. Appx. 329.

No. 15-6185. Bobby Henry Holt, Petitioner v. United States.

577 U.S. 964, 136 S. Ct. 422, 193 L. Ed. 2d 330, 2015 U.S. LEXIS 7026.

November 2, 2015. Petition for writ of certiorari to the United States Court of Appeals for the Eleventh Circuit denied.

No. 15-6187. Virgil Hall, Petitioner v. United States.

577 U.S. 964, 136 S. Ct. 422, 193 L. Ed. 2d 330, 2015 U.S. LEXIS 7023.

November 2, 2015. Petition for writ of certiorari to the United States Court of Appeals for the Tenth Circuit denied.

Same case below, 605 Fed. Appx. 766.

No. 15-6188. William Humberto Granados, Petitioner v. United States.

577 U.S. 964, 136 S. Ct. 422, 193 L. Ed. 2d 331, 2015 U.S. LEXIS 6952.

November 2, 2015. Petition for writ of certiorari to the United States Court of Appeals for the Fourth Circuit denied.

Same case below, 586 Fed. Appx. 115.

No. 15-6189. Juan Garcia-Hernandez, Petitioner v. United States.

577 U.S. 964, 136 S. Ct. 423, 193 L. Ed. 2d 331, 2015 U.S. LEXIS 6872.

November 2, 2015. Petition for writ of certiorari to the United States Court of Appeals for the First Circuit denied.

No. 15-6192. Kelvin J. Lewis, Petitioner v. United States.

577 U.S. 965, 136 S. Ct. 423, 193 L. Ed. 2d 331, 2015 U.S. LEXIS 6871.

November 2, 2015. Petition for writ of certiorari to the United States Court of Appeals for the Sixth Circuit denied.

Same case below, 615 Fed. Appx. 332.

No. 15-6193. Pablo Lopez-Vasquez, Petitioner v. United States.

577 U.S. 965, 136 S. Ct. 423, 193 L. Ed. 2d 331, 2015 U.S. LEXIS 6978.

November 2, 2015. Petition for writ of certiorari to the United States Court of Appeals for the Fourth Circuit denied.

No. 15-6197. Gabriel Granado, Petitioner v. United States.

577 U.S. 965, 136 S. Ct. 423, 193 L. Ed. 2d 331, 2015 U.S. LEXIS 7017.

November 2, 2015. Petition for writ of certiorari to the United States Court of Appeals for the Fifth Circuit denied.

Same case below, 608 Fed. Appx. 247.

No. 15-6199. Maria E. Villegas, Petitioner v. United States.

577 U.S. 965, 136 S. Ct. 423, 193 L. Ed. 2d 331, 2015 U.S. LEXIS 6950.

November 2, 2015. Petition for writ of certiorari to the United States Court of Appeals for the Fifth Circuit denied.

Same case below, 606 Fed. Appx. 277.

No. 15-6201. Trevis Starks, Petitioner v. United States.

577 U.S. 965, 136 S. Ct. 423, 193 L. Ed. 2d 331, 2015 U.S. LEXIS 6879.

November 2, 2015. Petition for writ of certiorari to the United States Court of Appeals for the Sixth Circuit denied.

No. 15-6210. Joseph Morgan Rogers, Jr., Petitioner v. United States.

577 U.S. 965, 136 S. Ct. 424, 193 L. Ed. 2d 331, 2015 U.S. LEXIS 6984.

November 2, 2015. Petition for writ of certiorari to the United States Court of Appeals for the Eleventh Circuit denied.

No. 15-6213. Alfredo Vergara-Escobar, Petitioner v. United States.

577 U.S. 965, 136 S. Ct. 424, 193 L. Ed. 2d 332, 2015 U.S. LEXIS 6850.

November 2, 2015. Petition for writ of certiorari to the United States Court of Appeals for the Fourth Circuit denied.

Same case below, 616 Fed. Appx. 586.

No. 15-6214. Alvaro Arreola-Escalante, Petitioner v. United States.

577 U.S. 965, 136 S. Ct. 424, 193 L. Ed. 2d 332, 2015 U.S. LEXIS 6862.

November 2, 2015. Petition for writ of certiorari to the United States Court of Appeals for the Fifth Circuit denied.

Same case below, 609 Fed. Appx. 248.

No. 15-6217. Anthony Anderson, Petitioner v. United States.

577 U.S. 965, 136 S. Ct. 424, 193 L. Ed. 2d 332, 2015 U.S. LEXIS 6954.

November 2, 2015. Petition for writ of certiorari to the United States Court of Appeals for the Sixth Circuit denied.

No. 15-6220. Giovanni Bell, Petitioner v. United States.

577 U.S. 965, 136 S. Ct. 425, 193 L. Ed. 2d 332, 2015 U.S. LEXIS 6925.

November 2, 2015. Petition for writ of certiorari to the United States Court of Appeals for the Fourth Circuit denied.

Same case below, 599 Fed. Appx. 505.

No. 15-6222. Mustafa Muhammad, Petitioner v. United States.

577 U.S. 965, 136 S. Ct. 425, 193 L. Ed. 2d 332, 2015 U.S. LEXIS 6909.

November 2, 2015. Petition for writ of certiorari to the United States Court of Appeals for the Fourth Circuit denied.

Same case below, 601 Fed. Appx. 226.

No. 15-6229. Deangelo D. Dixon, Petitioner v. United States.

577 U.S. 965, 136 S. Ct. 425, 193 L. Ed. 2d 332, 2015 U.S. LEXIS 7001.

November 2, 2015. Petition for writ of certiorari to the United States Court of Appeals for the Seventh Circuit denied.

Same case below, 790 F.3d 758.

No. 15-6230. Jimmy Alonzo Wright, Petitioner v. United States.

577 U.S. 965, 136 S. Ct. 425, 193 L. Ed. 2d 332, 2015 U.S. LEXIS 6848.

November 2, 2015. Petition for writ of certiorari to the United States Court of Appeals for the Fourth Circuit denied.

Same case below, 600 Fed. Appx. 189.

No. 15-6233. Stephen G. Kraemer, Petitioner v. United States District Court for the Northern District of Illinois.

577 U.S. 965, 136 S. Ct. 439, 193 L. Ed. 2d 332, 2015 U.S. LEXIS 6877.

November 2, 2015. Petition for writ of certiorari to the United States Court of Appeals for the Seventh Circuit denied.

No. 15-6235. Alfredo Davis, Petitioner v. United States.

577 U.S. 965, 136 S. Ct. 425, 193 L. Ed. 2d 333, 2015 U.S. LEXIS 7024.

November 2, 2015. Petition for writ of certiorari to the United States Court of Appeals for the Second Circuit denied.

Same case below, 607 Fed. Appx. 112.

No. 15-6240. Robert Marshall, Petitioner v. United States.

577 U.S. 965, 136 S. Ct. 425, 193 L. Ed. 2d 333, 2015 U.S. LEXIS 6937.

November 2, 2015. Petition for writ of certiorari to the United States Court of Appeals for the Eleventh Circuit denied.

Same case below, 611 Fed. Appx. 961.

No. 15-6243. Frank Davis Moore, Jr., Petitioner v. United States.

577 U.S. 966, 136 S. Ct. 426, 193 L. Ed. 2d 333, 2015 U.S. LEXIS 7014.

November 2, 2015. Petition for writ of certiorari to the United States Court of Appeals for the Eleventh Circuit denied.

Same case below, 611 Fed. Appx. 572.

No. 15-6247. Michael Kekoa Ciacci, Petitioner v. United States.

577 U.S. 966, 136 S. Ct. 426, 193 L. Ed. 2d 333, 2015 U.S. LEXIS 6969.

November 2, 2015. Petition for writ of certiorari to the District of Columbia Court of Appeals denied.

Same case below, 117 A.3d 1043.

No. 15-6249. Mark Brown, Petitioner v. United States.

577 U.S. 966, 136 S. Ct. 426, 193 L. Ed. 2d 333, 2015 U.S. LEXIS 6967, reh den 577 U.S. 1097, 136 S. Ct. 888, 193 L. Ed. 2d 780, 2016 U.S. LEXIS 454.

November 2, 2015. Petition for writ of certiorari to the United States Court of Appeals for the Eleventh Circuit denied.

No. 15-6254. Osman Norales, Petitioner v. United States.

577 U.S. 966, 136 S. Ct. 426, 193 L. Ed. 2d 333, 2015 U.S. LEXIS 6938.

November 2, 2015. Petition for writ of certiorari to the United States Court of Appeals for the Ninth Circuit denied.

Same case below, 597 Fed. Appx. 463.

No. 15-6260. Mark Corrigan, Petitioner v. United States.

577 U.S. 966, 136 S. Ct. 427, 193 L. Ed. 2d 333, 2015 U.S. LEXIS 6930.

November 2, 2015. Petition for writ of certiorari to the United States Court of Appeals for the Fourth Circuit denied.

Same case below, 594 Fed. Appx. 177.

Same case below, 609 Fed. Appx. 525.

No. 15-6261. Trudy Eliana Munoz Rueda, Petitioner v. Harold W. Clarke, Director, Virginia Department of Corrections.

577 U.S. 966, 136 S. Ct. 427, 193 L. Ed. 2d 334, 2015 U.S. LEXIS 7007.

November 2, 2015. Petition for writ of certiorari to the United States Court of Appeals for the Fourth Circuit denied.

Same case below, 607 Fed. Appx. 306.

No. 15-6265. Christopher Patterson, Petitioner v. United States.

577 U.S. 966, 136 S. Ct. 427, 193 L. Ed. 2d 334, 2015 U.S. LEXIS 6957.

November 2, 2015. Petition for writ of certiorari to the United States Court of Appeals for the Eleventh Circuit denied.

Same case below, 615 Fed. Appx. 594.

No. 15-6269. Joseph Guerino, Petitioner v. United States.

577 U.S. 966, 136 S. Ct. 428, 193 L. Ed. 2d 334, 2015 U.S. LEXIS 7000.

November 2, 2015. Petition for writ of certiorari to the United States Court of Appeals for the Second Circuit denied.

Same case below, 607 Fed. Appx. 117.

No. 15-6272. Roberto Bello-Urquiza, Jr., Petitioner v. United States.

577 U.S. 966, 136 S. Ct. 428, 193 L. Ed. 2d 334, 2015 U.S. LEXIS 6844.

November 2, 2015. Petition for writ of certiorari to the United States Court of Appeals for the Ninth Circuit denied.

No. 15-6273. Johnny Joseph Bonds, Petitioner v. United States.

577 U.S. 966, 136 S. Ct. 428, 193 L. Ed. 2d 334, 2015 U.S. LEXIS 6998.

November 2, 2015. Petition for writ of certiorari to the United States Court of Appeals for the Ninth Circuit denied.

Same case below, 608 Fed. Appx. 526.

No. 15-6291. Anibal Diaz-Rodriguez, Petitioner v. United States.

577 U.S. 966, 136 S. Ct. 429, 193 L. Ed. 2d 334, 2015 U.S. LEXIS 6858.

November 2, 2015. Petition for writ of certiorari to the United States Court of Appeals for the Ninth Circuit denied.

Same case below, 592 Fed. Appx. 636.

No. 15-6292. Mujo Bektas, Petitioner v. United States.

577 U.S. 966, 136 S. Ct. 429, 193 L. Ed. 2d 334, 2015 U.S. LEXIS 7012.

November 2, 2015. Petition for writ of certiorari to the United States Court of Appeals for the Sixth Circuit denied.

No. 15-6295. Jorge Armando Betancourt Mendoza, Petitioner v. United States.

577 U.S. 966, 136 S. Ct. 429, 193 L. Ed. 2d 334, 2015 U.S. LEXIS 6959.

November 2, 2015. Petition for writ of certiorari to the United States Court of Appeals for the Ninth Circuit denied.

Same case below, 608 Fed. Appx. 506.

Same case below, 790 F.3d 270.

No. 15-6298. Raymond Julius Melton, Petitioner v. Brent Reinke, Director, Idaho Department of Corrections.

577 U.S. 966, 136 S. Ct. 429, 193 L. Ed. 2d 335, 2015 U.S. LEXIS 6857.

November 2, 2015. Petition for writ of certiorari to the United States Court of Appeals for the Ninth Circuit denied.

No. 15-6302. Dacota Robert Rogers, Petitioner v. United States.

577 U.S. 966, 136 S. Ct. 430, 193 L. Ed. 2d 335, 2015 U.S. LEXIS 6854.

November 2, 2015. Petition for writ of certiorari to the United States Court of Appeals for the Ninth Circuit denied.

Same case below, 603 Fed. Appx. 602.

No. 15-6311. Christopher Seifer, Petitioner v. United States.

577 U.S. 967, 136 S. Ct. 430, 193 L. Ed. 2d 335, 2015 U.S. LEXIS 6993.

November 2, 2015. Petition for writ of certiorari to the United States Court of Appeals for the Seventh Circuit denied.

Same case below, 800 F.3d 328.

No. 15-6316. Santos J. Miranda-Martinez, Petitioner v. United States.

577 U.S. 967, 136 S. Ct. 430, 193 L. Ed. 2d 335, 2015 U.S. LEXIS 6906.

November 2, 2015. Petition for writ of certiorari to the United States Court of Appeals for the First Circuit denied.

No. 15-6320. Jacqueline Mosti, Petitioner v. United States.

577 U.S. 967, 136 S. Ct. 430, 193 L. Ed. 2d 335, 2015 U.S. LEXIS 6968.

November 2, 2015. Petition for writ of certiorari to the United States Court of Appeals for the Ninth Circuit denied.

Same case below, 597 Fed. Appx. 451.

No. 15-6334. Ramon Rosa Valle Zuniga, Petitioner v. United States.

577 U.S. 967, 136 S. Ct. 430, 193 L. Ed. 2d 335, 2015 U.S. LEXIS 6839.

November 2, 2015. Petition for writ of certiorari to the United States Court of Appeals for the Ninth Circuit denied.

Same case below, 598 Fed. Appx. 558.

No. 15-6348. Kendrick Jermaine Fulton, Petitioner v. United States.

577 U.S. 967, 136 S. Ct. 431, 193 L. Ed. 2d 335, 2015 U.S. LEXIS 6835, reh den 577 U.S. 1097, 136 S. Ct. 888, 193 L. Ed. 2d 780, 2016 U.S. LEXIS 18.

November 2, 2015. Petition for writ of certiorari to the United States Court of Appeals for the Fifth Circuit denied.

Same case below, 780 F.3d 683.

No. 15-6350. Charles Nave, III, Petitioner v. United States.

577 U.S. 967, 136 S. Ct. 431, 193 L. Ed. 2d 335, 2015 U.S. LEXIS 6836.

November 2, 2015. Petition for writ of certiorari to the United States Court of Appeals for the Eleventh Circuit denied.

Same case below, 608 Fed. Appx. 888.

Same case below, 609 Fed. Appx. 934.

No. 15-6353. Angelo Williams, Petitioner v. United States.

577 U.S. 967, 136 S. Ct. 431, 193 L. Ed. 2d 336, 2015 U.S. LEXIS 6866.

November 2, 2015. Petition for writ of certiorari to the United States Court of Appeals for the Fourth Circuit denied.

Same case below, 613 Fed. Appx. 221.

No. 15-6355. Gary Dixon, aka Lamos Hadley, Petitioner v. United States.

577 U.S. 967, 136 S. Ct. 431, 193 L. Ed. 2d 336, 2015 U.S. LEXIS 6949.

November 2, 2015. Petition for writ of certiorari to the United States Court of Appeals for the First Circuit denied.

No. 15-6357. Alberto Rivera-Nevarez, Petitioner v. United States.

577 U.S. 967, 136 S. Ct. 432, 193 L. Ed. 2d 336, 2015 U.S. LEXIS 6843.

November 2, 2015. Petition for writ of certiorari to the United States Court of Appeals for the Fifth Circuit denied.

Same case below, 609 Fed. Appx. 209.

No. 15-6359. Matthew Taylor, Petitioner v. United States.

577 U.S. 967, 136 S. Ct. 432, 193 L. Ed. 2d 336, 2015 U.S. LEXIS 7013.

November 2, 2015. Petition for writ of certiorari to the United States Court of Appeals for the Ninth Circuit denied.

No. 15-6362. Omar Jones, Petitioner v. United States.

577 U.S. 967, 136 S. Ct. 432, 193 L. Ed. 2d 336, 2015 U.S. LEXIS 6767.

November 2, 2015. Petition for writ of certiorari to the United States Court of Appeals for the Sixth Circuit denied.

No. 15-6363. Onan Herrera-Sanchez, Petitioner v. United States.

577 U.S. 967, 136 S. Ct. 432, 193 L. Ed. 2d 336, 2015 U.S. LEXIS 6798.

November 2, 2015. Petition for writ of certiorari to the United States Court of Appeals for the Fifth Circuit denied.

Same case below, 608 Fed. Appx. 278.

No. 15-6365. Manuel Gomez-Gutierrez, Petitioner v. United States.

577 U.S. 967, 136 S. Ct. 432, 193 L. Ed. 2d 336, 2015 U.S. LEXIS 6821.

November 2, 2015. Petition for writ of certiorari to the United States Court of Appeals for the Ninth Circuit denied.

Same case below, 592 Fed. Appx. 651.

No. 15-6366. Michael A. Galluzzo, Petitioner v. City of Dayton, Ohio.

577 U.S. 967, 136 S. Ct. 432, 193 L. Ed. 2d 336, 2015 U.S. LEXIS 6785.

November 2, 2015. Petition for writ of certiorari to the Court of Appeals of Ohio, Montgomery County, denied.

No. 15-6368. Haoren Ma, Petitioner v. United States.

577 U.S. 967, 136 S. Ct. 433, 193 L. Ed. 2d 337, 2015 U.S. LEXIS 6822.

November 2, 2015. Petition for writ of certiorari to the United States Court of Appeals for the Ninth Circuit denied.

Same case below, 609 Fed. Appx. 397.

No. 15-6371. Raul Flores Wong, Petitioner v. United States.

577 U.S. 967, 136 S. Ct. 433, 193 L. Ed. 2d 337, 2015 U.S. LEXIS 6771.

November 2, 2015. Petition for writ of certiorari to the United States Court of Appeals for the Ninth Circuit denied.

Same case below, 600 Fed. Appx. 584.

No. 15-6372. Dwayne A. Johnson, Petitioner v. United States.

577 U.S. 968, 136 S. Ct. 433, 193 L. Ed. 2d 337, 2015 U.S. LEXIS 6818.

November 2, 2015. Petition for writ of certiorari to the United States Court of Appeals for the Sixth Circuit denied.

Same case below, 586 Fed. Appx. 664.

No. 15-6374. Jeffrey Bernard Joyner, Petitioner v. United States.

577 U.S. 968, 136 S. Ct. 433, 193 L. Ed. 2d 337, 2015 U.S. LEXIS 6792.

November 2, 2015. Petition for writ of certiorari to the United States Court of Appeals for the Fourth Circuit denied.

Same case below, 614 Fed. Appx. 119.

No. 15-6375. James Raymonda, Petitioner v. United States.

577 U.S. 968, 136 S. Ct. 433, 193 L. Ed. 2d 337, 2015 U.S. LEXIS 6763.

November 2, 2015. Petition for writ of certiorari to the United States Court of Appeals for the Second Circuit denied.

Same case below, 780 F.3d 105.

No. 15-6376. Christopher E. Reese, Petitioner v. United States.

577 U.S. 968, 136 S. Ct. 433, 193 L. Ed. 2d 337, 2015 U.S. LEXIS 6782.

November 2, 2015. Petition for writ of certiorari to the United States Court of Appeals for the Second Circuit denied.

Same case below, 603 Fed. Appx. 63.

No. 15-6378. Brian Lamont Copeland, Petitioner v. United States.

577 U.S. 968, 136 S. Ct. 434, 193 L. Ed. 2d 337, 2015 U.S. LEXIS 6799.

November 2, 2015. Petition for writ of certiorari to the District of Columbia Court of Appeals denied.

Same case below, 111 A.3d 627.

No. 15-6379. Paul C. Schumacher, Petitioner v. United States.

577 U.S. 968, 136 S. Ct. 434, 193 L. Ed. 2d 337, 2015 U.S. LEXIS 6804.

November 2, 2015. Petition for writ of certiorari to the United States Court of Appeals for the Sixth Circuit denied.

Same case below, 611 Fed. Appx. 337.

Same case below, 608 Fed. Appx. 698.

No. 15-6382. Gregory Allen Blue, Petitioner v. United States.

577 U.S. 968, 136 S. Ct. 434, 193 L. Ed. 2d 338, 2015 U.S. LEXIS 6815.

November 2, 2015. Petition for writ of certiorari to the United States Court of Appeals for the Eleventh Circuit denied.

Same case below, 604 Fed. Appx. 922.

No. 15-6396. Rayvell Vann, Petitioner v. United States.

577 U.S. 968, 136 S. Ct. 434, 193 L. Ed. 2d 338, 2015 U.S. LEXIS 6796.

November 2, 2015. Petition for writ of certiorari to the United States Court of Appeals for the Tenth Circuit denied.

Same case below, 776 F.3d 746.

No. 15-6402. Antowan Thorne, Petitioner v. United States.

577 U.S. 968, 136 S. Ct. 434, 193 L. Ed. 2d 338, 2015 U.S. LEXIS 6801.

November 2, 2015. Petition for writ of certiorari to the United States Court of Appeals for the Fourth Circuit denied.

Same case below, 614 Fed. Appx. 646.

No. 15-6403. Aaron Ramirez-Saucedo, Petitioner v. United States.

577 U.S. 968, 136 S. Ct. 435, 193 L. Ed. 2d 338, 2015 U.S. LEXIS 6790.

November 2, 2015. Petition for writ of certiorari to the United States Court of Appeals for the Tenth Circuit denied.

No. 15-6406. Edgar Jaime Alegria-Mera, Petitioner v. United States.

577 U.S. 968, 136 S. Ct. 435, 193 L. Ed. 2d 338, 2015 U.S. LEXIS 6765.

November 2, 2015. Petition for writ of certiorari to the United States Court of Appeals for the Fifth Circuit denied.

Same case below, 609 Fed. Appx. 251.

No. 15-6409. Willie Jones, Petitioner v. United States.

577 U.S. 968, 136 S. Ct. 435, 193 L. Ed. 2d 338, 2015 U.S. LEXIS 6826.

November 2, 2015. Petition for writ of certiorari to the United States Court of Appeals for the Seventh Circuit denied.

Same case below, 792 F.3d 831.

No. 15-6413. Stuart Ray Mitchell, Petitioner v. United States.

577 U.S. 968, 136 S. Ct. 435, 193 L. Ed. 2d 338, 2015 U.S. LEXIS 6824.

November 2, 2015. Petition for writ of certiorari to the United States Court of Appeals for the Fifth Circuit denied.

Same case below, 608 Fed. Appx. 290.

No. 15-6414. Jose Santos Quinino-Salome, Petitioner v. United States.

577 U.S. 968, 136 S. Ct. 435, 193 L. Ed. 2d 338, 2015 U.S. LEXIS 6794.

November 2, 2015. Petition for writ of certiorari to the United States Court of Appeals for the Fifth Circuit denied.

Same case below, 609 Fed. Appx. 241.

No. 15-6417. Hoang Ai Le, Petitioner v. United States.

577 U.S. 968, 136 S. Ct. 436, 193 L. Ed. 2d 339, 2015 U.S. LEXIS 6780.

November 2, 2015. Petition for writ of certiorari to the United States Court of Appeals for the Ninth Circuit denied.

Same case below, 610 Fed. Appx. 598.

No. 15-6420. Antonio M. Taylor, Petitioner v. United States.

577 U.S. 968, 136 S. Ct. 436, 193 L. Ed. 2d 339, 2015 U.S. LEXIS 6802, reh den 577 U.S. 1097, 136 S. Ct. 888, 193 L. Ed. 2d 781, 2016 U.S. LEXIS 15.

November 2, 2015. Petition for writ of certiorari to the United States Court of Appeals for the Eighth Circuit denied.

Same case below, 606 Fed. Appx. 315.

No. 15-6431. Michael Orlando Champagnie, Petitioner v. United States.

577 U.S. 969, 136 S. Ct. 436, 193 L. Ed. 2d 339, 2015 U.S. LEXIS 6810.

November 2, 2015. Petition for writ of certiorari to the United States Court of Appeals for the Eleventh Circuit denied.

Same case below, 609 Fed. Appx. 625.

No. 15-6439. Antonio Butler, Petitioner v. United States.

577 U.S. 969, 136 S. Ct. 436, 193 L. Ed. 2d 339, 2015 U.S. LEXIS 6769.

November 2, 2015. Petition for writ of certiorari to the United States Court of Appeals for the Eleventh Circuit denied.

No. 15-6444. Lazaro Rivero, Petitioner v. United States.

577 U.S. 969, 136 S. Ct. 436, 193 L. Ed. 2d 339, 2015 U.S. LEXIS 6800.

November 2, 2015. Petition for writ of certiorari to the United States Court of Appeals for the Eleventh Circuit denied.

Same case below, 619 Fed. Appx. 784.

No. 14-9590. J.D.T., Juvenile Male, Petitioner v. United States.

577 U.S. 969, 136 S. Ct. 400, 193 L. Ed. 2d 339, 2015 U.S. LEXIS 6764, reh den 577 U.S. 1044, 136 S. Ct. 608, 193 L. Ed. 2d 488, 2015 U.S. LEXIS 7776.

November 2, 2015. Motion of petitioner for leave to file a reply brief under seal with redacted copies for the public record granted. Petition for writ of certiorari to the United States Court of Appeals for the Ninth Circuit denied.

Same case below, 762 F.3d 984.

No. 15-50. Darrill M. Henry, Petitioner v. Louisiana.

577 U.S. 969, 136 S. Ct. 402, 193 L. Ed. 2d 339, 2015 U.S. LEXIS 6770.

November 2, 2015. Motion of Innocence Project New Orleans, et al. for leave to file a brief as amici curiae granted. Petition for writ of certiorari to the Court of Appeal of Louisiana, Fourth Circuit, denied.

Same case below, 147 So. 3d 1143.

No. 15-249. David Louis Whitehead, Petitioner v. White & Case LLP, et al.

577 U.S. 969, 136 S. Ct. 408, 193 L. Ed. 2d 339, 2015 U.S. LEXIS 6777.

November 2, 2015. Petition for writ of certiorari to the United States Court of

Appeals for the Fifth Circuit denied. The Chief Justice took no part in the consideration or decision of this petition.

No. 15-257. Christina Wong, Petitioner v. Ellen Anderson, et al.

577 U.S. 969, 136 S. Ct. 409, 193 L. Ed. 2d 340, 2015 U.S. LEXIS 6809.

November 2, 2015. Petition for writ of certiorari before judgment to the Supreme Court of the United States denied. Justice Breyer took no part in the consideration or decision of this petition.

No. 15-292. Rory M. Walsh, Petitioner v. James L. Jones, Jr., et al.

577 U.S. 969, 136 S. Ct. 416, 193 L. Ed. 2d 340, 2015 U.S. LEXIS 6772, reh den 577 U.S. 1054, 136 S. Ct. 707, 193 L. Ed. 2d 533, 2015 U.S. LEXIS 7959.

November 2, 2015. Petition for writ of certiorari to the United States Court of Appeals for the District of Columbia Circuit denied. Justice Kagan took no part in the consideration or decision of this petition.

No. 15-304. John R. Behrmann, et ux., Petitioners v. National Heritage Foundation, Inc.

577 U.S. 969, 136 S. Ct. 417, 193 L. Ed. 2d 340, 2015 U.S. LEXIS 6775.

November 2, 2015. Motion of Jeffrey H. Hartje for leave to file a brief as amicus curiae granted. Petition for writ of certiorari to the United States Court of Appeals for the Fourth Circuit denied.

Same case below, 599 Fed. Appx. 107.

No. 15-351. Rory M. Walsh, Petitioner v. Federal Bureau of Investigation, et al.

577 U.S. 969, 136 S. Ct. 421, 193 L. Ed. 2d 340, 2015 U.S. LEXIS 6803, reh den 577 U.S. 1055, 136 S. Ct. 707, 193 L. Ed. 2d 533, 2015 U.S. LEXIS 7963.

November 2, 2015. Petition for writ of certiorari to the United States Court of Appeals for the District of Columbia Circuit denied. Justice Kagan took no part in the consideration or decision of this petition.

No. 15-6338. Steven Allen Schwartz, Petitioner v. United States.

577 U.S. 969, 136 S. Ct. 431, 193 L. Ed. 2d 340, 2015 U.S. LEXIS 6781.

November 2, 2015. Petition for writ of certiorari to the United States Court of Appeals for the Third Circuit denied. Justice Kagan took no part in the consideration or decision of this petition.

No. 15-6404. In re Paul Amaro, Petitioner.

577 U.S. 954, 136 S. Ct. 435, 193 L. Ed. 2d 340, 2015 U.S. LEXIS 6807.

November 2, 2015. Petition for writ of habeas corpus denied.

No. 15-6501. In re Azhar Lal, Petitioner.

577 U.S. 954, 136 S. Ct. 436, 193 L. Ed. 2d 340, 2015 U.S. LEXIS 6768.

November 2, 2015. Petition for writ of habeas corpus denied.

No. 15-5839. In re GwanJun Kim, Petitioner.

577 U.S. 954, 136 S. Ct. 409, 193 L. Ed. 2d 341, 2015 U.S. LEXIS 6774, reh den 577 U.S. 1096, 136 S. Ct. 886, 193 L. Ed. 2d 778, 2016 U.S. LEXIS 563.

November 2, 2015. Petition for writ of mandamus denied.

No. 15-6241. In re Bakari Mackey, Petitioner.

577 U.S. 954, 136 S. Ct. 426, 193 L. Ed. 2d 341, 2015 U.S. LEXIS 6816.

November 2, 2015. Petition for writ of mandamus denied. Justice Kagan took no part in the consideration or decision of this petition.

No. 15-6101. In re Corey Michaels, Petitioner.

577 U.S. 954, 136 S. Ct. 420, 193 L. Ed. 2d 341, 2015 U.S. LEXIS 6806, reh den 577 U.S. 1124, 136 S. Ct. 996, 194 L. Ed. 2d 14, 2016 U.S. LEXIS 917.

November 2, 2015. Petition for writ of prohibition denied.

No. 14-10077. In re David Andrew Christenson, Petitioner.

577 U.S. 969, 136 S. Ct. 439, 193 L. Ed. 2d 341, 2015 U.S. LEXIS 6773.

November 2, 2015. Petition for rehearing denied.

Former decision, 577 U.S. 814, 136 S. Ct. 93, 193 L. Ed. 2d 218, 2015 U.S. LEXIS 4726.

No. D-2837. In the Matter of Discipline of John. H. Wyman.

577 U.S. 950, 136 S. Ct. 439, 193 L. Ed. 2d 341, 2015 U.S. LEXIS 6808.

November 2, 2015. John H. Wyman, of Plymouth, Massachusetts, is suspended from the practice of law in this Court and a rule will issue, returnable within 40 days, requiring him to show cause why he should not be disbarred from the practice of law in this Court.

No. D-2838. In the Matter of Discipline of Daniel A. Beck.

577 U.S. 951, 136 S. Ct. 440, 193 L. Ed. 2d 341, 2015 U.S. LEXIS 6791.

November 2, 2015. Daniel A. Beck, of Saluda, North Carolina, is suspended from the practice of law in this Court and a rule will issue, returnable within 40 days, requiring him to show cause why he should not be disbarred from the practice of law in this Court.

No. D-2839. In the Matter of Discipline of Mark H. Allenbaugh.

577 U.S. 951, 136 S. Ct. 440, 193 L. Ed. 2d 341, 2015 U.S. LEXIS 6817.

November 2, 2015. Mark H. Allenbaugh, of Conneaut, Ohio, is suspended from the practice of law in this Court and a rule will issue, returnable within 40 days, requiring him to show cause why he should not be disbarred from the practice of law in this Court.

No. D-2840. In the Matter of Discipline of Charles Jeffrey Broida.

577 U.S. 951, 136 S. Ct. 440, 193 L. Ed. 2d 341, 2015 U.S. LEXIS 6778.

November 2, 2015. Charles Jeffrey Broida, of Ellicott City, Maryland, is suspended from the practice of law in this Court and a rule will issue, returnable within 40 days, requiring him to show cause why he should not be disbarred from the practice of law in this Court.

from the practice of law in this Court and a rule will issue, returnable within 40 days, requiring him to show cause why he should not be disbarred from the practice of law in this Court.

No. D-2841. In the Matter of Discipline of Laurence M. Starr.

577 U.S. 951, 136 S. Ct. 440, 193 L. Ed. 2d 342, 2015 U.S. LEXIS 6787.

November 2, 2015. Laurence M. Starr, of West Roxbury, Massachusetts, is suspended from the practice of law in this Court and a rule will issue, returnable within 40 days, requiring him to show cause why he should not be disbarred from the practice of law in this Court.

No. D-2842. In the Matter of Discipline of Douglas Frederick Tracia.

577 U.S. 951, 136 S. Ct. 440, 193 L. Ed. 2d 342, 2015 U.S. LEXIS 6812.

November 2, 2015. Douglas Frederick Tracia, of Wakefield, Massachusetts, is suspended from the practice of law in this Court and a rule will issue, returnable within 40 days, requiring him to show cause why he should not be disbarred from the practice of law in this Court.

No. D-2843. In the Matter of Discipline of Richard S. Hanlon.

577 U.S. 951, 136 S. Ct. 440, 193 L. Ed. 2d 342, 2015 U.S. LEXIS 6766.

November 2, 2015. Richard S. Hanlon, of Bayonne, New Jersey, is suspended

---

No. D-2844. In the Matter of Discipline of Jenny R. Armstrong.

577 U.S. 951, 136 S. Ct. 441, 193 L. Ed. 2d 342, 2015 U.S. LEXIS 6805.

November 2, 2015. Jenny R. Armstrong, of Madison, Wisconsin, is suspended from the practice of law in this Court and a rule will issue, returnable within 40 days, requiring her to show cause why she should not be disbarred from the practice of law in this Court.

No. D-2845. In the Matter of Discipline of Patricia Jamie Doran.

577 U.S. 952, 136 S. Ct. 441, 193 L. Ed. 2d 342, 2015 U.S. LEXIS 6783.

November 2, 2015. Patricia Jamie Doran, of Tiburon, California, is suspended from the practice of law in this Court and a rule will issue, returnable within 40 days, requiring her to show cause why she should not be disbarred from the practice of law in this Court.

No. D-2846. In the Matter of Discipline of Kevin Purcell.

577 U.S. 952, 136 S. Ct. 441, 193 L. Ed. 2d 342, 2015 U.S. LEXIS 6820.

November 2, 2015. Kevin Purcell, of Rocky River, Ohio, is suspended from the practice of law in this Court and a rule will issue, returnable within 40 days, requiring him to show cause why he should not be disbarred from the practice of law in this Court.

No. D-2847. In the Matter of Discipline of Paul Stephen Kormanik.

577 U.S. 952, 136 S. Ct. 441, 193 L. Ed. 2d 343, 2015 U.S. LEXIS 6797.

November 2, 2015. Paul Stephen Kormanik, of Columbus, Ohio, is suspended from the practice of law in this Court and a rule will issue, returnable within 40 days, requiring him to show cause why he should not be disbarred from the practice of law in this Court.

No. D-2848. In the Matter of Discipline of Lee Daniel Gottesman.

577 U.S. 952, 136 S. Ct. 441, 193 L. Ed. 2d 343, 2015 U.S. LEXIS 6779.

November 2, 2015. Lee Daniel Gottesman, of Toms River, New Jersey, is suspended from the practice of law in this Court and a rule will issue, returnable within 40 days, requiring him to show cause why he should not be disbarred from the practice of law in this Court.

Same case below, 185 N.J. 318, 885 A.2d 439.

No. D-2849. In the Matter of Discipline of Robert Langston Williams.

577 U.S. 952, 136 S. Ct. 442, 193 L. Ed. 2d 343, 2015 U.S. LEXIS 6823.

November 2, 2015. Robert Langston Williams, of Pittsburgh, Pennsylvania, is suspended from the practice of law in this Court and a rule will issue, returnable within 40 days, requiring him to show cause why he should not be disbarred from the practice of law in this Court.

No. D-2850. In the Matter of Discipline of Peter Floyd Anderson, Jr.

577 U.S. 952, 136 S. Ct. 442, 193 L. Ed. 2d 343, 2015 U.S. LEXIS 6825.

November 2, 2015. Peter Floyd Anderson, Jr., of Garnerville, New York, is suspended from the practice of law in this Court and a rule will issue, returnable within 40 days, requiring him to show cause why he should not be disbarred from the practice of law in this Court.

No. D-2851. In the Matter of Discipline of Gerald Isadore Katz.

577 U.S. 952, 136 S. Ct. 442, 193 L. Ed. 2d 343, 2015 U.S. LEXIS 6813.

November 2, 2015. Gerald Isadore Katz, of Bethesda, Maryland, is suspended from the practice of law in this Court and a rule will issue, returnable within 40 days, requiring him to show cause why he should not be disbarred from the practice of law in this Court.

No. D-2852. In the Matter of Discipline of James Francis Donohue.

577 U.S. 952, 136 S. Ct. 442, 193 L. Ed. 2d 343, 2015 U.S. LEXIS 6762.

November 2, 2015. James Francis Donohue, of Butler, Pennsylvania, is suspended from the practice of law in this Court and a rule will issue, returnable within 40 days, requiring him to show cause why he should not be disbarred from the practice of law in this Court.

––––––––

No. D-2853. In the Matter of Discipline of James Marshall Biddle.

577 U.S. 953, 136 S. Ct. 442, 193 L. Ed. 2d 344, 2015 U.S. LEXIS 6814.

November 2, 2015. James Marshall Biddle, of Myrtle Beach, South Carolina, is suspended from the practice of law in this Court and a rule will issue, returnable within 40 days, requiring him to show cause why he should not be disbarred from the practice of law in this Court.

––––––––

No. D-2854. In the Matter of Discipline of Lawrence S. Cumberbatch.

577 U.S. 953, 136 S. Ct. 443, 193 L. Ed. 2d 344, 2015 U.S. LEXIS 6776.

November 2, 2015. Lawrence S. Cumberbatch, of New York, New York, is suspended from the practice of law in this Court and a rule will issue, returnable within 40 days, requiring him to show cause why he should not be disbarred from the practice of law in this Court.

––––––––

No. D-2855. In the Matter of Discipline of Daniel James Halloran, III.

577 U.S. 953, 136 S. Ct. 443, 193 L. Ed. 2d 344, 2015 U.S. LEXIS 6811.

November 2, 2015. Daniel James Halloran, III, of Bayside, New York, is suspended from the practice of law in this Court and a rule will issue, returnable within 40 days, requiring him to show cause why he should not be disbarred from the practice of law in this Court.

––––––––

No. D-2856. In the Matter of Discipline of Dean Gary Weber.

577 U.S. 953, 136 S. Ct. 443, 193 L. Ed. 2d 344, 2015 U.S. LEXIS 6795.

November 2, 2015. Dean Gary Weber, of Hauppauge, New York, is suspended from the practice of law in this Court and a rule will issue, returnable within 40 days, requiring him to show cause why he should not be disbarred from the practice of law in this Court.

––––––––

No. 15A473. Ernest Lee Johnson, Applicant v. George A. Lombardi, et al.

577 U.S. 970, 136 S. Ct. 443, 193 L. Ed. 2d 344, 2015 U.S. LEXIS 7028.

November 3, 2015. The application for stay of execution of sentence of death, presented to Justice Alito, and by him referred to the Court, is treated as an application for stay pending appeal in the Eighth Circuit. The application is granted pending the disposition of petitioner's appeal. Petitioner's complaint alleges that Missouri's method of execution violates the Eighth Amendment as applied to a person with his particular medical condition. A supporting affidavit by a medical expert states that "[a]s a result of Mr. Johnson's brain tumor, brain defect, and brain scar, a substantial risk of serious harm will occur during his execution as result of a violent seizure that may be induced by [the] Pentobarbital injection." Because petitioner's complaint was dismissed for failure to state a claim, the State was not required to submit any evidence refuting this allegation. In the currently pending appeal, the Court of

Appeals will be required to decide whether petitioner's complaint was properly dismissed for failure to state a claim or whether the case should have been permitted to progress to the summary judgment stage.

No. 15A478. Ernest Lee Johnson, Applicant v. Cindy Griffith, Warden.

577 U.S. 970, 136 S. Ct. 444, 193 L. Ed. 2d 345, 2015 U.S. LEXIS 7027.

November 3, 2015. Application for stay of execution of sentence of death, presented to Justice Alito, and by him referred to the Court, denied.

No. 14-916. Kingdomware Technologies, Inc., Petitioner v. United States.

577 U.S. 970, 136 S. Ct. 444, 193 L. Ed. 2d 345, 2015 U.S. LEXIS 7029.

November 4, 2015. This case is removed from the argument calendar for Monday, November 9, 2015. The parties are directed to file supplemental briefs addressing the following question: "Whether the Department of Veterans Affairs procurements at issue in this case have been fully performed, and if so, whether the case is moot." The briefs, limited to 6,000 words each, are to be filed simultaneously with the Clerk and served upon opposing counsel on or before Friday, November 20, 2015. Reply briefs, not to exceed 3,000 words each, are to be filed simultaneously with the Clerk and served upon opposing counsel on or before Tuesday, December 1, 2015.

No. 15-232 (R46-003). Omega S.A., Petitioner v. Costco Wholesale Corporation.

577 U.S. 971, 136 S. Ct. 445, 193 L. Ed. 2d 345, 2015 U.S. LEXIS 7040.

November 6, 2015. The petition for writ of certiorari to the United States Court of Appeals for the Ninth Circuit was dismissed today pursuant to Rule 46.1 of the Rules of this Court.

Same case below, 776 F.3d 692.

No. 14-1418. David A. Zubik, et al., Petitioners v. Sylvia Burwell, Secretary of Health and Human Services, et al.

No. 14-1453. Priests for Life, et al., Petitioners v. Department of Health and Human Services, et al.

No. 14-1505. Roman Catholic Archbishop of Washington, et al., Petitioners v. Sylvia Burwell, Secretary of Health and Human Services, et al.

No. 15-35. East Texas Baptist University, et al., Petitioners v. Sylvia Burwell, Secretary of Health and Human Services, et al.

No. 15-105. Little Sisters of the Poor Home for the Aged, Denver, Colorado, et al., Petitioners v. Sylvia Burwell, Secretary of Health and Human Services, et al.

No. 15-119. Southern Nazarene University, et al., Petitioners v. Sylvia Burwell, Secretary of Health and Human Services, et al.

No. 15-191. Geneva College, Petitioner v. Sylvia Burwell, Secretary of Health and Human Services, et al.

577 U.S. 971, 136 S. Ct. 444, 193 L. Ed. 2d 345, 2015 U.S. LEXIS 7030.

November 6, 2015. Petition for writ of certiorari to the United States Court of Appeals for the Third Circuit granted in No. 14-1418 limited to Question 1 presented by the petition. Petition for writ of certiorari to the United States Court of Appeals for the District of Columbia Circuit granted in No. 14-1453. Petition for writ of certiorari to the United States Court of Appeals for the District of Columbia Circuit granted in No. 14-1505. Petition for writ of certiorari to the United States Court of Appeals for the Fifth Circuit granted in No. 15-35. Petition for writ of certiorari to the United States Court of Appeals for the Tenth Circuit granted in No. 15-105 limited to Questions 1 and 2 presented by the petition. Petition for writ of certiorari to the United States Court of Appeals for the Tenth Circuit granted in No. 15-119. Petition for writ of certiorari to the United States Court of Appeals for the Third Circuit granted in No. 15-191. The cases are consolidated.

Same case below, 778 F.3d 422 (first judgment); 772 F.3d 229 (second judgment); 772 F.3d 229 (third judgment); 793 F.3d 449 (fourth judgment); 794 F.3d 1151 (fifth judgment); 794 F.3d 1151 (sixth judgment); 778 F.3d 422; (seventh judgment).

No. 15-109. Jermaine Simmons, et al., Petitioners v. Walter J. Himmelreich.

577 U.S. 971, 136 S. Ct. 445, 193 L. Ed. 2d 346, 2015 U.S. LEXIS 7035.

November 6, 2015. Motion of respondent for leave to proceed in forma pauperis granted, Petition for writ of certiorari to the United States Court of Appeals for the Sixth Circuit granted.

Same case below, 766 F.3d 576.

No. 15-145. Husky International Electronics, Inc., Petitioner v. Daniel Lee Ritz, Jr.

577 U.S. 971, 136 S. Ct. 445, 193 L. Ed. 2d 346, 2015 U.S. LEXIS 7036.

November 6, 2015. Petition for writ of certiorari to the United States Court of Appeals for the Fifth Circuit granted.

Same case below, 787 F.3d 312.

No. 15-5238. Lester Ray Nichols, Petitioner v. United States.

577 U.S. 972, 136 S. Ct. 445, 193 L. Ed. 2d 346, 2015 U.S. LEXIS 7039.

November 6, 2015. Motion of petitioner for leave to proceed in forma pauperis granted. Petition for writ of certiorari to the United States Court of Appeals for the Tenth Circuit granted limited to Question 1 presented by the petition.

Same case below, 775 F.3d 1225.

No. 14-1492. Brandon Pickens, et al., Petitioners v. Erma Aldaba, Personal Representative and Next of Kin of Johnny Manuel Leija, Deceased.

577 U.S. 972, 136 S. Ct. 479, 193 L. Ed. 2d 347, 2015 U.S. LEXIS 7063.

November 9, 2015. On petition for writ of certiorari to the United States Court of Appeals for the Tenth Circuit. Petition for writ of certiorari granted. Judgment vacated, and case remanded to the United States Court of Appeals for the Tenth Circuit for further consideration in light of Mullenix v. Luna, 577 U.S. 7, 136 S. Ct. 305, 193 L. Ed. 2d 255 (2015) (per curiam).

Same case below, 777 F.3d 1148.

No. 15-5965. Domenic Tricome, Petitioner v. Paul LaRiviere, et al.

577 U.S. 972, 136 S. Ct. 484, 193 L. Ed. 2d 347, 2015 U.S. LEXIS 7137.

November 9, 2015. Motion of petitioner for leave to proceed in forma pauperis denied, and petition for writ of certiorari to the Superior Court of Pennsylvania, Philadelphia Office, dismissed. See Rule 39.8. As petitioner has repeatedly abused this Court's process, the Clerk is directed not to accept any further petitions in noncriminal matters from petitioner unless the docketing fee required by Rule 38(a) is paid and petition submitted in compliance with Rule 33.1. See Martin v. District of Columbia Court of Appeals, 506 U.S. 1, 113 S. Ct. 397, 121 L. Ed. 2d 305 (1992) (per curiam).

Same case below, 106 A.3d 178.

No. 15-6002. Teddy Moore, Petitioner v. T-Mobile USA, Inc.

577 U.S. 972, 136 S. Ct. 486, 193 L. Ed. 2d 347, 2015 U.S. LEXIS 7096.

November 9, 2015. Motion of petitioner for leave to proceed in forma pauperis denied, and petition for writ of certiorari to the United States Court of Appeals for the Second Circuit dismissed. See Rule 39.8.

No. 15-6177. David E. Hill, Petitioner v. Rudolph Contreras, Judge, United States District Court for the District of Columbia.

577 U.S. 972, 136 S. Ct. 488, 193 L. Ed. 2d 347, 2015 U.S. LEXIS 7130.

November 9, 2015. Motion of petitioner for leave to proceed in forma pauperis denied, and petition for writ of certiorari to the United States Court of Appeals for the District of Columbia Circuit dismissed. See Rule 39.8.

Same case below, 598 Fed. Appx. 6.

No. 15M46. Kendall Jevon Jackson, Petitioner v. United States.

577 U.S. 973, 136 S. Ct. 495, 193 L. Ed. 2d 347, 2015 U.S. LEXIS 7091.

November 9, 2015. Motion to direct the Clerk to file a petition for writ of certiorari out of time denied.

No. 15M47. Henry E. Gossage, Petitioner v. Richard Terrill, et al.

577 U.S. 973, 136 S. Ct. 495, 193 L. Ed. 2d 347, 2015 U.S. LEXIS 7058.

November 9, 2015. Motion for leave to proceed as a veteran denied.

Same case below, 586 Fed. Appx. 393.

Same case below, 598 Fed. Appx. 470.

―――――

No. 15M48. Qin Zhang, Petitioner v. Google, Inc., et al.

577 U.S. 973, 136 S. Ct. 495, 193 L. Ed. 2d 348, 2015 U.S. LEXIS 7050.

November 9, 2015. Motion to direct the Clerk to file a petition for writ of certiorari out of time denied.

Same case below, 609 Fed. Appx. 459.

―――――

No. 15M49. Salvador Reyes-Garcia, Petitioner v. Loretta E. Lynch, Attorney General.

577 U.S. 973, 136 S. Ct. 495, 193 L. Ed. 2d 348, 2015 U.S. LEXIS 7113.

November 9, 2015. Motion to direct the Clerk to file a petition for writ of certiorari out of time denied.

Same case below, 617 Fed. Appx. 884.

―――――

No. 15M50. Michael Edwards, Petitioner v. Olukunle Obadina.

577 U.S. 973, 136 S. Ct. 495, 193 L. Ed. 2d 348, 2015 U.S. LEXIS 7158.

November 9, 2015. Motion to direct the Clerk to file a petition for writ of certiorari out of time under Rule 14.5 denied.

―――――

No. 15M51. Michael A. Hoelscher, et al., Petitioners v. Millers First Insurance Co., et al.

577 U.S. 973, 136 S. Ct. 496, 193 L. Ed. 2d 348, 2015 U.S. LEXIS 7072.

November 9, 2015. Motion to direct the Clerk to file a petition for writ of certiorari out of time denied.

―――――

No. 13-1496. Dollar General Corporation, et al., Petitioners v. Mississippi Band of Choctaw Indians, et al.

577 U.S. 973, 136 S. Ct. 496, 193 L. Ed. 2d 348, 2015 U.S. LEXIS 7121.

November 9, 2015. Motion of the Solicitor General for leave to participate in oral argument as amicus curiae and for divided argument granted.

―――――

No. 14-181. Alfred Gobeille, in His Official Capacity as Chair of the Vermont Green Mountain Care Board, Petitioner v. Liberty Mutual Insurance Company.

577 U.S. 973, 136 S. Ct. 496, 193 L. Ed. 2d 348, 2015 U.S. LEXIS 7061.

November 9, 2015. Motion of the Solicitor General for leave to participate in oral argument as amicus curiae and for divided argument granted.

―――――

No. 15-5266. Mark C. Jackson, Petitioner v. Robert A. McDonald, Secretary of Veterans Affairs.

577 U.S. 974, 136 S. Ct. 496, 193 L. Ed. 2d 348, 2015 U.S. LEXIS 7079.

November 9, 2015. Motion of petitioner for reconsideration of order denying leave to proceed in forma pauperis denied. Justice Kagan took no part in the consideration or decision of this motion.

Same case below, 461 S.W.3d 469.

No. 15-6070. Gary S. Roup, Petitioner v. Commercial Research, LLC.

577 U.S. 974, 136 S. Ct. 496, 193 L. Ed. 2d 349, 2015 U.S. LEXIS 7129.

November 9, 2015. Motion of petitioner for leave to proceed in forma pauperis denied. Petitioner is allowed until November 30, 2015, within which to pay the docketing fee required by Rule 38(a) and to submit a petition in compliance with Rule 33.1 of the Rules of this Court.

Same case below, 349 P.3d 273.

No. 15-6491. Phyllis Dorothy Mabbett, Petitioner v. Commissioner of Internal Revenue.

577 U.S. 974, 136 S. Ct. 496, 193 L. Ed. 2d 349, 2015 U.S. LEXIS 7067.

November 9, 2015. Motion of petitioner for leave to proceed in forma pauperis denied. Petitioner is allowed until November 30, 2015, within which to pay the docketing fee required by Rule 38(a) and to submit a petition in compliance with Rule 33.1 of the Rules of this Court.

Same case below, 610 Fed. Appx. 760.

No. 14-1413. Ministerio Roca Solida, Inc., Petitioner v. United States.

577 U.S. 974, 136 S. Ct. 479, 193 L. Ed. 2d 349, 2015 U.S. LEXIS 7044.

November 9, 2015. Petition for writ of certiorari to the United States Court of Appeals for the Federal Circuit denied.

Same case below, 778 F.3d 1351.

No. 14-10311. William Eugene Hall, Petitioner v. Tennessee.

577 U.S. 974, 136 S. Ct. 479, 193 L. Ed. 2d 349, 2015 U.S. LEXIS 7117.

November 9, 2015. Petition for writ of certiorari to the Supreme Court of Tennessee, Middle Division, denied.

No. 15-8. Applied Underwriters, Inc., et al., Petitioners v. Arrow Recycling Solutions, Inc., et al.

577 U.S. 974, 136 S. Ct. 479, 193 L. Ed. 2d 349, 2015 U.S. LEXIS 7102.

November 9, 2015. Petition for writ of certiorari to the Court of Appeal of California, Second Appellate District, Division Three, denied.

No. 15-102. Robert A. Politte, et al., Petitioners v. United States.

577 U.S. 974, 136 S. Ct. 479, 193 L. Ed. 2d 349, 2015 U.S. LEXIS 7073.

November 9, 2015. Petition for writ of certiorari to the United States Court of Appeals for the Ninth Circuit denied.

Same case below, 587 Fed. Appx. 406.

No. 15-146. Quartavius Davis, Petitioner v. United States.

577 U.S. 975, 136 S. Ct. 479, 193 L. Ed. 2d 349, 2015 U.S. LEXIS 7148.

November 9, 2015. Petition for writ of certiorari to the United States Court of Appeals for the Eleventh Circuit denied.

Same case below, 785 F.3d 498.

No. 15-152. Center for Competitive Politics, Petitioner v. Kamala D. Harris, Attorney General of California.

577 U.S. 975, 136 S. Ct. 480, 193 L. Ed. 2d 349, 2015 U.S. LEXIS 7065.

November 9, 2015. Petition for writ of certiorari to the United States Court of Appeals for the Ninth Circuit denied.

Same case below, 784 F.3d 1307.

No. 15-156. Richard Joseph, et al., Petitioners v. City of Burlington, Vermont, et al.

577 U.S. 975, 136 S. Ct. 480, 193 L. Ed. 2d 350, 2015 U.S. LEXIS 7111.

November 9, 2015. Petition for writ of certiorari to the Supreme Court of Vermont denied.

Same case below, 117 A.3d 457.

No. 15-163. Todd R. Rochow, Personal Representative of the Estate of Daniel J. Rochow, et al., Petitioners v. Life Insurance Company of North America.

577 U.S. 975, 136 S. Ct. 480, 193 L. Ed. 2d 350, 2015 U.S. LEXIS 7070.

November 9, 2015. Petition for writ of certiorari to the United States Court of Appeals for the Sixth Circuit denied.

Same case below, 780 F.3d 364.

No. 15-265. Alabama Gas Corporation, Petitioner v. Gas Fitters Local Union No. 548 of the United Association, AFL-CIO-CLC.

577 U.S. 975, 136 S. Ct. 480, 193 L. Ed. 2d 350, 2015 U.S. LEXIS 7095.

November 9, 2015. Petition for writ of certiorari to the United States Court of Appeals for the Eleventh Circuit denied.

Same case below, 599 Fed. Appx. 382.

No. 15-269. Walter Lee Whitaker, Petitioner v. Nash-Rocky Mount Board of Education, et al.

577 U.S. 975, 136 S. Ct. 480, 193 L. Ed. 2d 350, 2015 U.S. LEXIS 7071.

November 9, 2015. Petition for writ of certiorari to the United States Court of Appeals for the Fourth Circuit denied.

Same case below, 585 Fed. Appx. 60.

No. 15-327. Westgate Resorts, Ltd., L.P., Petitioner v. Nathan B. Overton, et ux.

577 U.S. 975, 136 S. Ct. 486, 193 L. Ed. 2d 350, 2015 U.S. LEXIS 7049.

November 9, 2015. Petition for writ of certiorari to the Court of Appeals of Tennessee, Eastern Division, denied.

No. 15-334. John Baker, et ux., Petitioners v. City of Iowa City, Iowa, et al.

577 U.S. 975, 136 S. Ct. 487, 193 L. Ed. 2d 350, 2015 U.S. LEXIS 7126.

November 9, 2015. Petition for writ of certiorari to the Supreme Court of Iowa denied.

Same case below, 867 N.W.2d 44.

No. 15-346. Manuel J. Gonzalez-Acevedo and Edmarie Mendez-Salas, Petitioners v. United States, et al.

577 U.S. 975, 136 S. Ct. 487, 193 L. Ed. 2d 350, 2015 U.S. LEXIS 7100.

November 9, 2015. Petition for writ of certiorari to the United States Court of Appeals for the First Circuit denied.

No. 15-359. Frederick V. Greene, Petitioner v. Department of Education.

577 U.S. 975, 136 S. Ct. 488, 193 L. Ed. 2d 351, 2015 U.S. LEXIS 7075.

November 9, 2015. Petition for writ of certiorari to the United States Court of Appeals for the Seventh Circuit denied.

Same case below, 770 F.3d 667.

No. 15-366. Nolan Estes, Petitioner v. JPMorgan Chase Bank, N.A.

577 U.S. 975, 136 S. Ct. 489, 193 L. Ed. 2d 351, 2015 U.S. LEXIS 7141.

November 9, 2015. Petition for writ of certiorari to the United States Court of Appeals for the Fifth Circuit denied.

Same case below, 613 Fed. Appx. 277.

No. 15-377. Raymond Pardon, Petitioner v. Julie L. Jones, Secretary, Florida Department of Corrections.

577 U.S. 975, 136 S. Ct. 490, 193 L. Ed. 2d 351, 2015 U.S. LEXIS 7157.

November 9, 2015. Petition for writ of certiorari to the United States Court of Appeals for the Eleventh Circuit denied.

Same case below, 607 Fed. Appx. 908.

No. 15-388. Andrea K. Silverthorne, Petitioner v. CitiMortgage, Inc.

577 U.S. 975, 136 S. Ct. 490, 193 L. Ed. 2d 351, 2015 U.S. LEXIS 7114.

November 9, 2015. Petition for writ of certiorari to the Court of Appeal of Florida, Third District, denied.

Same case below, 169 So. 3d 1186.

No. 15-411. Daniel Makiel, Petitioner v. Kim Butler, Warden.

577 U.S. 976, 136 S. Ct. 491, 193 L. Ed. 2d 351, 2015 U.S. LEXIS 7101.

November 9, 2015. Petition for writ of certiorari to the United States Court of Appeals for the Seventh Circuit denied.

Same case below, 782 F.3d 882.

No. 15-413. Andrew Searcy, Jr., Petitioner v. Merit Systems Protection Board.

577 U.S. 976, 136 S. Ct. 497, 193 L. Ed. 2d 351, 2015 U.S. LEXIS 7088, reh den 577 U.S. 1095, 136 S. Ct. 883, 193 L. Ed. 2d 775, 2016 U.S. LEXIS 539.

November 9, 2015. Petition for writ of certiorari to the United States Court of Appeals for the Federal Circuit denied.

No. 15-425. Megan Coffman, et al., Petitioners v. United States.

577 U.S. 976, 136 S. Ct. 491, 193 L. Ed. 2d 351, 2015 U.S. LEXIS 7156.

November 9, 2015. Petition for writ of certiorari to the United States Court of Appeals for the Sixth Circuit denied.

Same case below, 612 Fed. Appx. 278.

No. 15-435. City of Cleveland Board of Review, et al., Petitioners v. Hunter T. Hillenmeyer; and City of Cleveland Board of Review, et al., Petitioners v. Jeffrey B. Saturday, et ux.

577 U.S. 976, 136 S. Ct. 491, 193 L. Ed. 2d 352, 2015 U.S. LEXIS 7109.

November 9, 2015. Petition for writ of certiorari to the Supreme Court of Ohio denied.

Same case below, 144 Ohio St. 3d 165, 41 N.E.3d 1164 (first judgment); and 142 Ohio St. 3d 528, 33 N.E.3d 46 (second judgment).

No. 15-445. William Patrick Clark, Petitioner v. United States.

577 U.S. 976, 136 S. Ct. 492, 193 L. Ed. 2d 352, 2015 U.S. LEXIS 7106.

November 9, 2015. Petition for writ of certiorari to the United States Court of Appeals for the Seventh Circuit denied.

Same case below, 787 F.3d 451.

No. 15-481. Bearing Fund LP, et al., Petitioners v. PricewaterhouseCoopers LLP.

577 U.S. 976, 136 S. Ct. 497, 193 L. Ed. 2d 352, 2015 U.S. LEXIS 7057.

November 9, 2015. Petition for writ of certiorari to the United States Court of Appeals for the Second Circuit denied.

Same case below, 611 Fed. Appx. 34.

No. 15-5918. Larry Lee Russell, Jr., Petitioner v. Contra Costa County Martinez Detention Facility.

577 U.S. 976, 136 S. Ct. 481, 193 L. Ed. 2d 352, 2015 U.S. LEXIS 7083.

November 9, 2015. Petition for writ of certiorari to the United States Court of Appeals for the Ninth Circuit denied.

No. 15-5919. Lawrence Hall, Petitioner v. Howard Prince, Warden.

577 U.S. 976, 136 S. Ct. 481, 193 L. Ed. 2d 352, 2015 U.S. LEXIS 7087.

November 9, 2015. Petition for writ of certiorari to the United States Court of Appeals for the Fifth Circuit denied.

No. 15-5924. Richard James Johnson, Petitioner v. G. S. David, Warden, et al.

577 U.S. 976, 136 S. Ct. 481, 193 L. Ed. 2d 352, 2015 U.S. LEXIS 7099.

November 9, 2015. Petition for writ of certiorari to the United States Court of Appeals for the Fifth Circuit denied.

No. 15-5927. Valerie Carey, Petitioner v. Georgia.

577 U.S. 976, 136 S. Ct. 481, 193 L. Ed. 2d 352, 2015 U.S. LEXIS 7046.

November 9, 2015. Petition for writ of certiorari to the Supreme Court of Georgia denied.

Same case below, 293 Ga. 624, 748 S.E.2d 891.

No. 15-5928. Alrelio Evans, Petitioner v. Daniel H. Heyns, Director, Michigan Department of Corrections, et al.

577 U.S. 976, 136 S. Ct. 481, 193 L. Ed. 2d 352, 2015 U.S. LEXIS 7124.

November 9, 2015. Petition for writ of certiorari to the United States Court of Appeals for the Sixth Circuit denied.

No. 15-5929. Preston Cooper, Petitioner v. Illinois.

577 U.S. 976, 136 S. Ct. 482, 193 L. Ed. 2d 353, 2015 U.S. LEXIS 7090.

November 9, 2015. Petition for writ of certiorari to the Appellate Court of Illinois, First District, denied.

No. 15-5933. Odell Lance Douglas, Petitioner v. Gerald J. Janda, Warden.

577 U.S. 976, 136 S. Ct. 482, 193 L. Ed. 2d 353, 2015 U.S. LEXIS 7143.

November 9, 2015. Petition for writ of certiorari to the United States Court of Appeals for the Ninth Circuit denied.

No. 15-5934. Rohan Campbell, Petitioner v. William Lee, Superintendent, Green Haven Correctional Facility.

577 U.S. 976, 136 S. Ct. 482, 193 L. Ed. 2d 353, 2015 U.S. LEXIS 7125.

November 9, 2015. Petition for writ of certiorari to the United States Court of Appeals for the Second Circuit denied.

No. 15-5935. Mitchell E. Edwards, Petitioner v. Ken Cameron, Superintendent, State Correctional Institution at Houtzdale, et al.

577 U.S. 977, 136 S. Ct. 482, 193 L. Ed. 2d 353, 2015 U.S. LEXIS 7153.

November 9, 2015. Petition for writ of certiorari to the United States Court of Appeals for the Third Circuit denied.

No. 15-5944. Antonio DeShawn Robinson, Petitioner v. Charles D. Griffith, Jr.

577 U.S. 977, 136 S. Ct. 482, 193 L. Ed. 2d 353, 2015 U.S. LEXIS 7066.

November 9, 2015. Petition for writ of certiorari to the United States Court of Appeals for the Fourth Circuit denied.

No. 15-5945. Albin Adalin Zelaya-Zelaya, Petitioner v. Texas.

577 U.S. 977, 136 S. Ct. 482, 193 L. Ed. 2d 353, 2015 U.S. LEXIS 7086.

November 9, 2015. Petition for writ of certiorari to the Court of Criminal Appeals of Texas denied.

No. 15-5946. Carlton Parks, Petitioner v. Burl Cain, Warden.

577 U.S. 977, 136 S. Ct. 483, 193 L. Ed. 2d 353, 2015 U.S. LEXIS 7068.

November 9, 2015. Petition for writ of certiorari to the United States Court of Appeals for the Fifth Circuit denied.

No. 15-5948. David Reeves, Petitioner v. Homer Bryson, Commissioner, Georgia Department of Corrections.

577 U.S. 977, 136 S. Ct. 483, 193 L. Ed. 2d 353, 2015 U.S. LEXIS 7112.

November 9, 2015. Petition for writ of certiorari to the United States Court of Appeals for the Eleventh Circuit denied.

No. 15-5954. Washington Davis, Petitioner v. Kenneth L. Thompson, Justice, Supreme Court of New York, Bronx County, et al.

577 U.S. 977, 136 S. Ct. 483, 193 L. Ed. 2d 354, 2015 U.S. LEXIS 7149.

November 9, 2015. Petition for writ of certiorari to the Court of Appeals of New York denied.

Same case below, 25 N.Y.3d 907, 10 N.Y.S.3d 527, 32 N.E.3d 964.

No. 15-5957. Steven M. Leonhart, Petitioner v. Ohio.

577 U.S. 977, 136 S. Ct. 483, 193 L. Ed. 2d 354, 2015 U.S. LEXIS 7054.

November 9, 2015. Petition for writ of certiorari to the Court of Appeals of Ohio, Washington County, denied.

No. 15-5959. Jovany Peredes, Petitioner v. Texas.

577 U.S. 977, 136 S. Ct. 483, 193 L. Ed. 2d 354, 2015 U.S. LEXIS 7144.

November 9, 2015. Petition for writ of certiorari to the Court of Criminal Appeals of Texas denied.

Same case below, 462 S.W.3d 510.

No. 15-5961. Kelly Nobles, Petitioner v. Jeffrey Woods, Warden.

577 U.S. 977, 136 S. Ct. 483, 193 L. Ed. 2d 354, 2015 U.S. LEXIS 7133.

November 9, 2015. Petition for writ of certiorari to the United States Court of Appeals for the Sixth Circuit denied.

Same case below, 613 Fed. Appx. 487.

No. 15-5963. Gosundi Wusiya, aka James A. Johnson, Petitioner v. City of Miami Beach, Florida, et al.

577 U.S. 977, 136 S. Ct. 484, 193 L. Ed. 2d 354, 2015 U.S. LEXIS 7051.

November 9, 2015. Petition for writ of certiorari to the United States Court of Appeals for the Eleventh Circuit denied.

Same case below, 614 Fed. Appx. 389.

No. 15-5967. Paul James Koumjian, Petitioner v. William Stephens, Director, Texas Department of Criminal Justice, Correctional Institutions Division.

577 U.S. 977, 136 S. Ct. 484, 193 L. Ed. 2d 354, 2015 U.S. LEXIS 7115.

November 9, 2015. Petition for writ of certiorari to the United States Court of Appeals for the Fifth Circuit denied.

No. 15-5971. Sean P. Stoll, Petitioner v. Washington.

577 U.S. 977, 136 S. Ct. 484, 193 L. Ed. 2d 354, 2015 U.S. LEXIS 7103.

November 9, 2015. Petition for writ of certiorari to the Supreme Court of Washington denied.

Same case below, 183 Wash. 2d 1013, 353 P.3d 639.

No. 15-5974. Marcia L. Jackson, Petitioner v. Park Place Condominiums Association, Inc.

577 U.S. 977, 136 S. Ct. 484, 193 L. Ed. 2d 355, 2015 U.S. LEXIS 7123, reh den 577 U.S. 1096, 136 S. Ct. 887, 193 L. Ed. 2d 779, 2016 U.S. LEXIS 475.

November 9, 2015. Petition for writ of certiorari to the United States Court of Appeals for the Tenth Circuit denied.

Same case below, 619 Fed. Appx. 699.

No. 15-5977. Bruce Ward, Petitioner v. Arkansas.

577 U.S. 978, 136 S. Ct. 485, 193 L. Ed. 2d 355, 2015 U.S. LEXIS 7152.

November 9, 2015. Petition for writ of certiorari to the Supreme Court of Arkansas denied.

Same case below, 2015 Ark. 62, 455 S.W.3d 830.

No. 15-5986. Sher Qureshi, Petitioner v. New York (two judgments).

577 U.S. 978, 136 S. Ct. 485, 193 L. Ed. 2d 355, 2015 U.S. LEXIS 7084, reh den 577 U.S. 1096, 136 S. Ct. 887, 193 L. Ed. 2d 779, 2016 U.S. LEXIS 318.

November 9, 2015. Petition for writ of certiorari to the Appellate Term of the Supreme Court of New York, 9th & 10th Judicial Districts, denied.

Same case below, 998 N.Y.S.2d 307 (first judgment); 996 N.Y.S.2d 462 (second judgment).

No. 15-5987. Carolyn Barnes, Petitioner v. Dennis Tumlinson, et al.

577 U.S. 978, 136 S. Ct. 485, 193 L. Ed. 2d 355, 2015 U.S. LEXIS 7069.

November 9, 2015. Petition for writ of certiorari to the United States Court of Appeals for the Fifth Circuit denied.

Same case below, 597 Fed. Appx. 798.

No. 15-5996. Billy Lee Lisenby, Jr., Petitioner v. South Carolina.

577 U.S. 978, 136 S. Ct. 485, 193 L. Ed. 2d 355, 2015 U.S. LEXIS 7042.

November 9, 2015. Petition for writ of certiorari to the Supreme Court of South Carolina denied.

No. 15-6001. Reynaldo Morales, Petitioner v. Travelers Indemnity Company of Connecticut.

577 U.S. 978, 136 S. Ct. 485, 193 L. Ed. 2d 355, 2015 U.S. LEXIS 7118.

November 9, 2015. Petition for writ of certiorari to the Court of Appeals of Texas, First District, denied.

No. 15-6008. Kumar Jones, Petitioner v. Dale Artus, Superintendent, Attica Correctional Facility.

577 U.S. 978, 136 S. Ct. 486, 193 L. Ed. 2d 355, 2015 U.S. LEXIS 7131.

November 9, 2015. Petition for writ of certiorari to the United States Court of Appeals for the Second Circuit denied.

No. 15-6046. Alex Carreon, Petitioner v. Neil McDowell, Warden.

577 U.S. 978, 136 S. Ct. 486, 193 L. Ed. 2d 355, 2015 U.S. LEXIS 7154.

November 9, 2015. Petition for writ of certiorari to the United States Court of Appeals for the Ninth Circuit denied.

Same case below, 612 Fed. Appx. 877.

Same case below, 599 Fed. Appx. 714.

No. 15-6048. Malik Al-Mustafa El-Alamin, Petitioner v. Scott Moats, et al.

577 U.S. 978, 136 S. Ct. 486, 193 L. Ed. 2d 356, 2015 U.S. LEXIS 7110.

November 9, 2015. Petition for writ of certiorari to the United States Court of Appeals for the Seventh Circuit denied.

No. 15-6056. Leon Michael T. Kornegay, Petitioner v. New York, et al.

577 U.S. 978, 136 S. Ct. 486, 193 L. Ed. 2d 356, 2015 U.S. LEXIS 7108, reh den 577 U.S. 1096, 136 S. Ct. 887, 193 L. Ed. 2d 779, 2016 U.S. LEXIS 326.

November 9, 2015. Petition for writ of certiorari to the United States Court of Appeals for the Second Circuit denied.

No. 15-6065. Richard Cunningham, Petitioner v. Mary Berghuis, Warden.

577 U.S. 978, 136 S. Ct. 487, 193 L. Ed. 2d 356, 2015 U.S. LEXIS 7092.

November 9, 2015. Petition for writ of certiorari to the United States Court of Appeals for the Sixth Circuit denied.

No. 15-6076. Karen Krushwitz, Petitioner v. University of California.

577 U.S. 978, 136 S. Ct. 487, 193 L. Ed. 2d 356, 2015 U.S. LEXIS 7119, reh den 577 U.S. 1124, 136 S. Ct. 996, 194 L. Ed. 2d 14, 2016 U.S. LEXIS 967.

November 9, 2015. Petition for writ of certiorari to the United States Court of Appeals for the Ninth Circuit denied.

No. 15-6091. Marc Sturdivant, Petitioner v. Joe A. Lizarraga, Warden.

577 U.S. 978, 136 S. Ct. 487, 193 L. Ed. 2d 356, 2015 U.S. LEXIS 7055.

November 9, 2015. Petition for writ of certiorari to the United States Court of Appeals for the Ninth Circuit denied.

No. 15-6097. Christopher A. Jones, Petitioner v. E. K. McDaniel, Warden, et al.

577 U.S. 978, 136 S. Ct. 487, 193 L. Ed. 2d 356, 2015 U.S. LEXIS 7120.

November 9, 2015. Petition for writ of certiorari to the United States Court of Appeals for the Ninth Circuit denied.

Same case below, 607 Fed. Appx. 710.

No. 15-6100. Aaron Crump, Petitioner v. New York.

577 U.S. 978, 136 S. Ct. 488, 193 L. Ed. 2d 356, 2015 U.S. LEXIS 7093.

November 9, 2015. Petition for writ of certiorari to Appellate Division, Supreme Court of New York, Second Judicial Department, denied.

Same case below, 125 App. Div. 3d 999, 1 N.Y.S.3d 866.

No. 15-6104. Mark Ronald Pray, Petitioner v. Craig Farwell, Warden, et al.

577 U.S. 979, 136 S. Ct. 488, 193 L. Ed. 2d 356, 2015 U.S. LEXIS 7045.

November 9, 2015. Petition for writ of certiorari to the United States Court of Appeals for the Ninth Circuit denied.

Same case below, 620 Fed. Appx. 561.

No. 15-6139. Eric Darnell Cook, Petitioner v. William Muniz, Acting Warden.

577 U.S. 979, 136 S. Ct. 488, 193 L. Ed. 2d 357, 2015 U.S. LEXIS 7089.

November 9, 2015. Petition for writ of certiorari to the United States Court of Appeals for the Ninth Circuit denied.

No. 15-6154. Pearlie Mae Dunigan, Petitioner v. Tennessee Department of Corrections.

577 U.S. 979, 136 S. Ct. 497, 193 L. Ed. 2d 357, 2015 U.S. LEXIS 7076.

November 9, 2015. Petition for writ of certiorari to the United States Court of Appeals for the Sixth Circuit denied.

No. 15-6156. Daniel K. Teal, Petitioner v. James Campbell, et al.

577 U.S. 979, 136 S. Ct. 488, 193 L. Ed. 2d 357, 2015 U.S. LEXIS 7142.

November 9, 2015. Petition for writ of certiorari to the United States Court of Appeals for the Eleventh Circuit denied.

Same case below, 603 Fed. Appx. 820.

No. 15-6179. Ronald J. Hamilton, Jr., Petitioner v. Angelita Smarjesse, et al.

577 U.S. 979, 136 S. Ct. 489, 193 L. Ed. 2d 357, 2015 U.S. LEXIS 7104.

November 9, 2015. Petition for writ of certiorari to the United States Court of Appeals for the Eighth Circuit denied.

No. 15-6195. Joseph Cornett, Petitioner v. Raymond Madden, Warden.

577 U.S. 979, 136 S. Ct. 489, 193 L. Ed. 2d 357, 2015 U.S. LEXIS 7085.

November 9, 2015. Petition for writ of certiorari to the United States Court of Appeals for the Ninth Circuit denied.

Same case below, 610 Fed. Appx. 626.

No. 15-6209. Keith Stanley Young, Petitioner v. Michael Bowersox, Warden.

577 U.S. 979, 136 S. Ct. 489, 193 L. Ed. 2d 357, 2015 U.S. LEXIS 7122.

November 9, 2015. Petition for writ of certiorari to the United States Court of Appeals for the Eighth Circuit denied.

No. 15-6225. Troy K. Scheffler, Petitioner v. Ramona Dohman, Commissioner, Minnesota Department of Public Safety, et al.

577 U.S. 979, 136 S. Ct. 489, 193 L. Ed. 2d 357, 2015 U.S. LEXIS 7080.

November 9, 2015. Petition for writ of certiorari to the United States Court of Appeals for the Eighth Circuit denied.

Same case below, 785 F.3d 1260.

No. 15-6252. Chong Su Yi, Petitioner v. Cable News Network.

577 U.S. 979, 136 S. Ct. 489, 193 L. Ed. 2d 357, 2015 U.S. LEXIS 7138.

November 9, 2015. Petition for writ of certiorari to the United States Court of Appeals for the Fourth Circuit denied.

Same case below, 600 Fed. Appx. 116.

No. 15-6276. James Edward Smith, Petitioner v. Wendy Kelley, Director, Arkansas Department of Correction.

577 U.S. 979, 136 S. Ct. 490, 193 L. Ed. 2d 358, 2015 U.S. LEXIS 7059.

November 9, 2015. Petition for writ of certiorari to the United States Court of Appeals for the Eighth Circuit denied.

No. 15-6312. Byrias Roberson, Petitioner v. Texas.

577 U.S. 979, 136 S. Ct. 490, 193 L. Ed. 2d 358, 2015 U.S. LEXIS 7150.

November 9, 2015. Petition for writ of certiorari to the Court of Appeals of Texas, Second District, denied.

Same case below, 455 S.W.3d 257.

No. 15-6331. Byron L. Wallace, Petitioner v. Charles Walker, et al.

577 U.S. 979, 136 S. Ct. 490, 193 L. Ed. 2d 358, 2015 U.S. LEXIS 7048.

November 9, 2015. Petition for writ of certiorari to the United States Court of Appeals for the Eighth Circuit denied.

No. 15-6342. Russell Dwayne Rodgers, Petitioner v. Greg Munks, et al.

577 U.S. 979, 136 S. Ct. 490, 193 L. Ed. 2d 358, 2015 U.S. LEXIS 7043.

November 9, 2015. Petition for writ of certiorari to the United States Court of Appeals for the Ninth Circuit denied.

Same case below, 608 Fed. Appx. 555.

No. 15-6367. Donald Sullivan, Petitioner v. United States.

577 U.S. 979, 136 S. Ct. 491, 193 L. Ed. 2d 358, 2015 U.S. LEXIS 7140, reh den 577 U.S. 1097, 136 S. Ct. 888, 193 L. Ed. 2d 780, 2016 U.S. LEXIS 12.

November 9, 2015. Petition for writ of certiorari to the United States Court of Appeals for the Fourth Circuit denied.

Same case below, 608 Fed. Appx. 136.

No. 15-6380. Jack Norman Rukes, Petitioner v. Martin Frink, Warden, et al.

577 U.S. 979, 136 S. Ct. 491, 193 L. Ed. 2d 358, 2015 U.S. LEXIS 7056.

November 9, 2015. Petition for writ of certiorari to the United States Court of Appeals for the Ninth Circuit denied.

Same case below, 611 Fed. Appx. 479.

No. 15-6451. Stephen G. Fields, Petitioner v. United States.

577 U.S. 979, 136 S. Ct. 492, 193 L. Ed. 2d 358, 2015 U.S. LEXIS 7053.

November 9, 2015. Petition for writ of certiorari to the United States Court of Appeals for the Fourth Circuit denied.

Same case below, 614 Fed. Appx. 101.

No. 15-6452. Dario Gomez-Juarez, Petitioner v. United States.

577 U.S. 980, 136 S. Ct. 492, 193 L. Ed. 2d 358, 2015 U.S. LEXIS 7127.

November 9, 2015. Petition for writ of certiorari to the United States Court of Appeals for the Fourth Circuit denied.

Same case below, 609 Fed. Appx. 155.   Same case below, 802 F.3d 690.

No. 15-6454. Gerson Fletes-Ramos, Petitioner v. United States.

577 U.S. 980, 136 S. Ct. 492, 193 L. Ed. 2d 359, 2015 U.S. LEXIS 7081.

November 9, 2015. Petition for writ of certiorari to the United States Court of Appeals for the Ninth Circuit denied.

Same case below, 612 Fed. Appx. 484.

No. 15-6455. Oswald Miles, Jr., Petitioner v. United States.

577 U.S. 980, 136 S. Ct. 492, 193 L. Ed. 2d 359, 2015 U.S. LEXIS 7077.

November 9, 2015. Petition for writ of certiorari to the United States Court of Appeals for the Fourth Circuit denied.

Same case below, 616 Fed. Appx. 610.

No. 15-6456. Luis Carlos Castro-Gomez, Petitioner v. United States.

577 U.S. 980, 136 S. Ct. 492, 193 L. Ed. 2d 359, 2015 U.S. LEXIS 7105.

November 9, 2015. Petition for writ of certiorari to the United States Court of Appeals for the Tenth Circuit denied.

Same case below, 792 F.3d 1216.

No. 15-6461. Anthony Bender, Petitioner v. United States Parole Commission.

577 U.S. 980, 136 S. Ct. 493, 193 L. Ed. 2d 359, 2015 U.S. LEXIS 7155.

November 9, 2015. Petition for writ of certiorari to the United States Court of Appeals for the Fifth Circuit denied.

No. 15-6471. Jose Jair Sainz-Camacho, Petitioner v. United States.

577 U.S. 980, 136 S. Ct. 493, 193 L. Ed. 2d 359, 2015 U.S. LEXIS 7060.

November 9, 2015. Petition for writ of certiorari to the United States Court of Appeals for the Ninth Circuit denied.

Same case below, 597 Fed. Appx. 449.

No. 15-6475. Donald R. Turner, Jr., Petitioner v. United States.

577 U.S. 980, 136 S. Ct. 493, 193 L. Ed. 2d 359, 2015 U.S. LEXIS 7094.

November 9, 2015. Petition for writ of certiorari to the United States Court of Appeals for the Eighth Circuit denied.

Same case below, 781 F.3d 374.

No. 15-6476. Sean Douglas Marchan, Petitioner v. United States.

577 U.S. 980, 136 S. Ct. 493, 193 L. Ed. 2d 359, 2015 U.S. LEXIS 7146.

November 9, 2015. Petition for writ of certiorari to the United States Court of Appeals for the Ninth Circuit denied.

Same case below, 597 Fed. Appx. 448.

No. 15-6478. John Louis Lewandowski, Petitioner v. United States.

577 U.S. 980, 136 S. Ct. 493, 193 L. Ed. 2d 359, 2015 U.S. LEXIS 7052.

November 9, 2015. Petition for writ of certiorari to the United States Court of Appeals for the Fourth Circuit denied.

Same case below, 608 Fed. Appx. 168.

No. 15-6480. Carlos Ayala Lopez, Petitioner v. United States.

577 U.S. 980, 136 S. Ct. 493, 193 L. Ed. 2d 360, 2015 U.S. LEXIS 7159.

November 9, 2015. Petition for writ of certiorari to the United States Court of Appeals for the First Circuit denied.

Same case below, 611 Fed. Appx. 3.

No. 15-6497. David McLellan, Petitioner v. United States.

577 U.S. 980, 136 S. Ct. 494, 193 L. Ed. 2d 360, 2015 U.S. LEXIS 7145.

November 9, 2015. Petition for writ of certiorari to the United States Court of Appeals for the First Circuit denied.

Same case below, 792 F.3d 200.

No. 15-6499. Robert Padgett, Petitioner v. United States.

577 U.S. 980, 136 S. Ct. 494, 193 L. Ed. 2d 360, 2015 U.S. LEXIS 7139.

November 9, 2015. Petition for writ of certiorari to the United States Court of Appeals for the Fourth Circuit denied.

Same case below, 788 F.3d 370.

No. 15-6500. Ryan Ridens, Petitioner v. United States.

577 U.S. 980, 136 S. Ct. 494, 193 L. Ed. 2d 360, 2015 U.S. LEXIS 7151.

November 9, 2015. Petition for writ of certiorari to the United States Court of Appeals for the Tenth Circuit denied.

Same case below, 792 F.3d 1270.

No. 15-6558. Nasedra Lumpkin, Petitioner v. Julie L. Jones, Secretary, Florida Department of Corrections.

577 U.S. 980, 136 S. Ct. 494, 193 L. Ed. 2d 360, 2015 U.S. LEXIS 7062.

November 9, 2015. Petition for writ of certiorari to the Supreme Court of Florida denied.

No. 15-157. Kawasaki Kisen Kaisha, Ltd., et al., Petitioners v. Plano Molding Company.

577 U.S. 980, 136 S. Ct. 480, 193 L. Ed. 2d 360, 2015 U.S. LEXIS 7116.

November 9, 2015. Petition for writ of certiorari to the United States Court of Appeals for the Seventh Circuit denied. Justice Kagan took no part in the consideration or decision of this petition.

Same case below, 782 F.3d 353.

No. 15-281. Daiichi Sankyo, Inc., et al., Petitioners v. Apotex Inc.

No. 15-307. Mylan Pharmaceuticals Inc., Petitioner v. Apotex Inc.

577 U.S. 980, 136 S. Ct. 481, 193 L. Ed. 2d 360, 2015 U.S. LEXIS 7078.

November 9, 2015. Petitions for writs of certiorari to the United States Court of Appeals for the Federal Circuit denied. Justice Alito took no part in the consideration or decision of these petitions.

Same cases below, 781 F.3d 1356.

_____

No. 15-419. Louis P. Cannon, et al., Petitioners v. District of Columbia.

577 U.S. 981, 136 S. Ct. 491, 193 L. Ed. 2d 361, 2015 U.S. LEXIS 7128.

November 9, 2015. Petition for relief to the United States Court of Appeals for the District of Columbia Circuit denied.

Same case below, 783 F.3d 327.

_____

No. 15-6529. In re Donald Lee McDonald, Petitioner.

577 U.S. 974, 136 S. Ct. 494, 193 L. Ed. 2d 361, 2015 U.S. LEXIS 7074.

November 9, 2015. Petition for writ of habeas corpus denied.

_____

No. 15-6562. In re Edward D. Curtis, Petitioner.

577 U.S. 974, 136 S. Ct. 495, 193 L. Ed. 2d 361, 2015 U.S. LEXIS 7136.

November 9, 2015. Petition for writ of habeas corpus denied.

_____

No. 15-6559. In re Terrance James-Bey, Petitioner.

577 U.S. 974, 136 S. Ct. 494, 193 L. Ed. 2d 361, 2015 U.S. LEXIS 7134.

November 9, 2015. Motion of petitioner for leave to proceed in forma pauperis denied, and petition for writ of habeas corpus dismissed. See Rule 39.8. As petitioner has repeatedly abused this Court's process, the Clerk is directed not to accept any further petitions in noncriminal matters from petitioner unless the docketing fee required by Rule 38(a) is paid and petition submitted in compliance with Rule 33.1. See Martin v. District of Columbia Court of Appeals, 506 U.S. 1, 113 S. Ct. 397, 121 L. Ed. 2d 305 (1992) (per curiam).

_____

No. 14-10114. Starsha Sewell, Petitioner v. Strayer University.

577 U.S. 981, 136 S. Ct. 497, 193 L. Ed. 2d 361, 2015 U.S. LEXIS 7135.

November 9, 2015. Petition for rehearing denied.

Former decision, 577 U.S. 848, 136 S. Ct. 100, 193 L. Ed. 2d 83, 2015 U.S. LEXIS 5018.

_____

No. D-2829. In the Matter of Disbarment of Vito Matteo Evola.

577 U.S. 972, 136 S. Ct. 497, 193 L. Ed. 2d 361, 2015 U.S. LEXIS 7132.

November 9, 2015. Disbarment entered.

Former order, 576 U.S. 1051, 135 S. Ct. 2922, 192 L. Ed. 2d 955, 2015 U.S. LEXIS 4275.

No. D-2830. In the Matter of Disbarment of Michael Lawrence Flynn.

577 U.S. 972, 136 S. Ct. 497, 193 L. Ed. 2d 362, 2015 U.S. LEXIS 7047.

November 9, 2015. Disbarment entered.

Former order, 576 U.S. 1051, 135 S. Ct. 2922, 192 L. Ed. 2d 955, 2015 U.S. LEXIS 4263.

No. D-2831. In the Matter of Disbarment of Robert S. Seguin.

577 U.S. 973, 136 S. Ct. 497, 193 L. Ed. 2d 362, 2015 U.S. LEXIS 7041.

November 9, 2015. Disbarment entered.

Former order, 576 U.S. 1051, 135 S. Ct. 2922, 192 L. Ed. 2d 956, 2015 U.S. LEXIS 4264.

No. D-2832. In the Matter of Disbarment of Richard David Feldman.

577 U.S. 973, 136 S. Ct. 498, 193 L. Ed. 2d 362, 2015 U.S. LEXIS 7098.

November 9, 2015. Disbarment entered.

Former order, 576 U.S. 1051, 135 S. Ct. 2922, 192 L. Ed. 2d 956, 2015 U.S. LEXIS 4259.

No. D-2833. In the Matter of Disbarment of Geoffrey Parker Damon.

577 U.S. 973, 136 S. Ct. 498, 193 L. Ed. 2d 362, 2015 U.S. LEXIS 7064.

November 9, 2015. Disbarment entered.

Former order, 576 U.S. 1051, 135 S. Ct. 2922, 192 L. Ed. 2d 956, 2015 U.S. LEXIS 4268.

No. D-2834. In the Matter of Disbarment of Ricky Lawton.

577 U.S. 973, 136 S. Ct. 498, 193 L. Ed. 2d 362, 2015 U.S. LEXIS 7107.

November 9, 2015. Disbarment entered.

Former order, 576 U.S. 1051, 135 S. Ct. 2923, 192 L. Ed. 2d 956, 2015 U.S. LEXIS 4261.

No. D-2835. In the Matter of Disbarment of Jon Charles Cooper.

577 U.S. 973, 136 S. Ct. 498, 193 L. Ed. 2d 362, 2015 U.S. LEXIS 7147.

November 9, 2015. Disbarment entered.

Former order, 576 U.S. 1051, 135 S. Ct. 2923, 192 L. Ed. 2d 956, 2015 U.S. LEXIS 4257.

No. D-2836. In the Matter of Disbarment of Lawrence J. Fleming.

577 U.S. 973, 136 S. Ct. 498, 193 L. Ed. 2d 362, 2015 U.S. LEXIS 7082.

November 9, 2015. Disbarment entered.

Former order, 576 U.S. 1051, 135 S. Ct. 2923, 192 L. Ed. 2d 956, 2015 U.S. LEXIS 4270 .

No. 15-412 (R46-004). Eastman Kodak Company, Petitioner v. Collins Inkjet Corporation.

577 U.S. 981, 136 S. Ct. 498, 193 L. Ed. 2d 362, 2015 U.S. LEXIS 7162.

November 10, 2015. The petition for writ of certiorari to the United States

Court of Appeals for the Sixth Circuit was dismissed today pursuant to Rule 46.1 of the Rules of this Court.

Same case below, 781 F.3d 264.

No. 15-6094 (R46-005). James L. Colvin, Petitioner v. Jeffery E. Thomas, Warden.

577 U.S. 981, 136 S. Ct. 498, 193 L. Ed. 2d 363, 2015 U.S. LEXIS 7163.

November 10, 2015. The petition for writ of certiorari to the United States Court of Appeals for the Fifth Circuit was dismissed today pursuant to Rule 46 of the Rules of this Court.

No. 143, Original. State of Mississippi, Plaintiff v. State of Tennessee, City of Memphis, Tennessee, and Memphis Light, Gas & Water Division.

577 U.S. 981, 136 S. Ct. 499, 193 L. Ed. 2d 363, 2015 U.S. LEXIS 7161.

November 10, 2015. It is ordered that the Honorable Eugene E. Siler, Jr., of London, Kentucky, is appointed Special Master in this case with authority to fix the time and conditions for the filing of additional pleadings, to direct subsequent proceedings, to summon witnesses, to issue subpoenas, and to take such evidence as may be introduced and such as he may deem it necessary to call for. The Special Master is directed to submit Reports as he may deem appropriate. The cost of printing his Reports, and all other proper expenses, including travel expenses shall be submitted to the Court.

No. 15-323 (R46-006). Trinity Wall Street, Petitioner v. Wal-Mart Stores, Inc.

577 U.S. 982, 136 S. Ct. 499, 193 L. Ed. 2d 363, 2015 U.S. LEXIS 7164.

November 12, 2015. The petition for writ of certiorari to the United States Court of Appeals for the Third Circuit was dismissed today pursuant to Rule 46 of the Rules of this Court.

Same case below, 792 F.3d 323.

No. 15-140 (R46-007). Daniel J. Taylor, Petitioner v. Patipan Nakkhumpun.

577 U.S. 981, 136 S. Ct. 499, 193 L. Ed. 2d 363, 2015 U.S. LEXIS 7165.

November 12, 2015. The petition for writ of certiorari to the United States Court of Appeals for the Tenth Circuit was dismissed today pursuant to Rule 46 of the Rules of this Court.

Same case below, 782 F.3d 1142.

No. 14-1516 (15A475). Stephen Duncan, Warden, Petitioner v. Lawrence Owens.

577 U.S. 982, 136 S. Ct. 500, 193 L. Ed. 2d 363, 2015 U.S. LEXIS 7166.

November 13, 2015. Application to recall and stay the mandate of the United States Court of Appeals for the Seventh Circuit in case No. 14-1419, presented to Justice Kagan and by her referred to the Court granted, pending the sending down of the judgment of this Court. The request seeking that the respondent be returned to applicant's custody pending final disposition of this case denied, thus leaving that determination for the state court.

Same case below, 781 F.3d 360.

————

No. 14-1504. Robert J. Wittman, et al., Appellants v. Gloria Personhuballah, et al.

577 U.S. 982, 136 S. Ct. 499, 193 L. Ed. 2d 364, 2015 U.S. LEXIS 7167.

November 13, 2015. Further consideration of the question of jurisdiction is postponed to the hearing of the case on the merits. In addition to the questions presented by the jurisdictional statement, parties are directed to brief and argue the following question: Whether appellants lack standing because none reside in or represent the only congressional district whose constitutionality is at issue in this case.

————

No. 15-274. Whole Woman's Health, et al., Petitioners v. Kirk Cole, Commissioner, Texas Department of State Health Services, et al.

577 U.S. 982, 136 S. Ct. 499, 193 L. Ed. 2d 364, 2015 U.S. LEXIS 7168.

November 13, 2015. Petition for writ of certiorari to the United States Court of Appeals for the Fifth Circuit granted.

Same case below, 790 F.3d 563.

[577 U.S. 47]

DIRECTV, INC., Petitioner

v

AMY IMBURGIA, et al.

577 U.S. 47, 136 S. Ct. 463, 193 L. Ed. 2d 365, 2015 U.S. LEXIS 7999

[No. 14-462]

Argued October 6, 2015. Decided December 14, 2015.

Decision: Interpretation, by state appellate court—which refused to enforce contract's arbitration provision—of contract phrase "law of your state" (1) did not place arbitration contracts on equal footing with all other contracts, and (2) was pre-empted by Federal Arbitration Act (9 U.S.C.S. § 1 et seq.).

Prior history: ON WRIT OF CERTIORARI TO THE COURT OF APPEAL OF CALIFORNIA, SECOND APPELLATE DISTRICT, 225 Cal. App. 4th 338, 170 Cal. Rptr. 3d 190, 2014 Cal. App. LEXIS 312

SUMMARY

Overview: ISSUE: Whether a reference in an arbitration provision to "the law of your state" rendered a waiver of class arbitration unenforceable under California's anti-waiver rule, which had been held to be pre-empted by the Federal Arbitration Act. HOLDINGS: [1]-The state court's incorporation into the arbitration provision of invalid California law was unique and restricted to the arbitration field. There was no indication that the state court would generally interpret a "law of your state" contract provision to include state laws that had been invalidated by federal law; [2]-Because the state court's interpretation of "law of your state" did not place arbitration contracts on equal footing with all other contracts, that interpretation was pre-empted, and the arbitration provision had to be enforced under 9 U.S.C.S. § 2.

Outcome: Judgment reversed; case remanded. 6-3 decision; 2 dissents.

HEADNOTES

Classified to United States Supreme Court Digest, Lawyers' Edition

Validity of contract provision
L Ed Digest: Arbitration § 5
1. The Federal Arbitration Act states that a written provision in a contract providing for settlement by arbitration of a controversy arising out of that contract shall be valid, irrevocable, and enforceable, save upon such grounds as exist at law or in equity for the revocation of any contract. 9 U.S.C.S. § 2.

Federal Arbitration Act — preemption
L Ed Digest: States, Territories, and Possessions § 46
2. In 2005, the California Supreme Court held that a waiver of class arbitration in a consumer contract of adhesion that predictably involves small amounts of damages and meets certain other criteria is unconscionable under California law and

should not be enforced. But in 2011, the United States Supreme Court held that California's Discover Bank rule stands as an obstacle to the accomplishment and execution of the full purposes and objectives of Congress embodied in the Federal Arbitration Act. The Federal Arbitration Act therefore pre-empts and invalidates that rule. (Breyer, J., joined by Roberts, Ch. J., and Scalia, Kennedy, Alito, and Kagan, JJ.)

Federal law — disagreement by state court

L Ed Digest: Courts § 781

3. Lower court judges are certainly free to note their disagreement with a decision of the U.S. Supreme Court. But the Supremacy Clause, U.S. Const. Art. VI, cl. 2, forbids state courts to dissociate themselves from federal law because of disagreement with its content or a refusal to recognize the superior authority of its source. (Breyer, J., joined by Roberts, Ch. J., and Scalia, Kennedy, Alito, and Kagan, JJ.)

Federal law — state judges — arbitration

L Ed Digest: Courts § 846

4. The Federal Arbitration Act is a law of the United States, and AT&T Mobility LLC v. Concepcion (2011) 563 U.S. 333, 131 S. Ct. 1740, 179 L. Ed. 2d 742, is an authoritative interpretation of that Act. Consequently, the judges of every state must follow it. U.S. Const. Art. VI, cl. 2 provides that the judges in every state shall be bound by the laws of the United States. (Breyer, J., joined by Roberts, Ch. J., and Scalia, Kennedy, Alito, and Kagan, JJ.)

Federal Arbitration Act — choice of law

L Ed Digest: Arbitration § 2

5. The Federal Arbitration Act allows parties to an arbitration contract considerable latitude to choose what law governs some or all of its provisions, including the law governing enforceability of a class-arbitration waiver. (Breyer, J., joined by Roberts, Ch. J., and Scalia, Kennedy, Alito, and Kagan, JJ.)

Contract interpretation — state law — deference

L Ed Digest: Appeal § 779

6. The interpretation of a contract is ordinarily a matter of state law to which a federal court defers. (Breyer, J., joined by Roberts, Ch. J., and Scalia, Kennedy, Alito, and Kagan, JJ.)

State laws — authority

L Ed Digest: Courts § 171

7. State courts are the ultimate authority on that state's law. (Breyer, J., joined by Roberts, Ch. J., and Scalia, Kennedy, Alito, and Kagan, JJ.)

Judicial construction — retroactivity

L Ed Digest: Statutes § 208

8. Under general contract principles, references to California law incorporate the California Legislature's power to change the law retroactively. And judicial construction of a statute ordinarily applies retroactively. (Breyer, J., joined by Roberts, Ch. J., and Scalia, Kennedy, Alito, and Kagan, JJ.)

Specific words

L Ed Digest: Contracts § 48

9. Specific words of a contract govern only when a general and a particular provision are inconsistent.

DIRECTV, INC. v. IMBURGIA

(2015) 577 U.S. 47, 136 S. Ct. 463, 193 L. Ed. 2d 365, 2015 U.S. LEXIS 7999

(Breyer, J., joined by Roberts, Ch. J., and Scalia, Kennedy, Alito, and Kagan, JJ.)

Construing against drafter

L Ed Digest: Contracts § 54

10. The reach of the canon construing contract language against the drafter must have limits, no matter who the drafter was. (Breyer, J., joined by Roberts, Ch. J., and Scalia, Kennedy, Alito, and Kagan, JJ.)

Federal Arbitration Act — pre-emption

L Ed Digest: States, Territories, and Possessions § 46

11. The Federal Arbitration Act pre-empts decisions that take their meaning precisely from the fact that a contract to arbitrate is at issue. (Breyer, J., joined by Roberts, Ch. J., and Scalia, Kennedy, Alito, and Kagan, JJ.)

RESEARCH REFERENCES

U.S.C.S., Constitution, Art. VI, cl. 2; 9 U.S.C.S. § 2

17A Moore's Federal Practice § 124.08 (Matthew Bender 3d ed.)

L Ed Digest, States, Territories, and Possessions § 46

L Ed Index, Arbitration and Award

Annotations:

Federal Arbitration Act (FAA) (9 U.S.C.S. § 1 et seq.) as pre-empting state law—Supreme Court cases. 169 L. Ed. 2d 995.

What kinds of contracts containing arbitration agreements are subject to stay and enforcement provisions of §§1-4 and 8 of Federal Arbitration Act (FAA) (9 U.S.C.S. §§1-4 and 8, and similar predecessor provisions)—Supreme Court cases. 130 L. Ed. 2d 1189.

Validity, under Federal Constitution, of arbitration statutes—Supreme Court cases. 87 L. Ed. 2d 787.

APPEARANCES OF COUNSEL ARGUING CASE

Christopher Landau argued the cause for petitioner.

Thomas C. Goldstein argued the cause for respondents.

SYLLABUS BY REPORTER OF DECISIONS

Petitioner DIRECTV, Inc., and its customers entered into a service agreement that included a binding arbitration provision with a class-arbitration waiver. It specified that the entire arbitration provision was unenforceable if the "law of your state" made class-arbitration waivers unenforceable. The agreement also declared that the arbitration clause was governed by the Federal Arbitration Act. At the time that respondents, California residents, entered into that agreement with DIRECTV, California law made class-arbitration waivers unenforceable, see *Discover Bank* v. *Superior Court*, 36 Cal. 4th 148, 113 P.3d 1100. This Court subsequently held in *AT&T Mobility LLC* v. *Concepcion*, 563 U.S. 333, 131 S. Ct. 1740, 179 L. Ed. 2d 742, however, that California's *Discover Bank* rule was pre-empted by the Federal Arbitration Act, 9 U.S.C. § 2.

When respondents sued petitioner, the trial court denied DIRECTV's request to order the matter to arbitration, and the California Court of Appeal affirmed. The court thought that California law would render class-arbitration waivers unenforceable, so it held the entire arbitration provision was unenforceable under the agreement. The fact that the Federal Arbitration Act pre-empted that California law did not change the result, the court said, because the parties were free to refer in the contract to California law as it would have been absent federal pre-emption. The court reasoned that the phrase "law of your state" was both a specific provision that should govern more general provisions and an ambiguous provision that should be construed against the drafter. Therefore, the court held, the parties had in fact included California law as it would have been without federal pre-emption.

Held: Because the California Court of Appeal's interpretation is pre-empted by the Federal Arbitra-

tion Act, that court must enforce the arbitration agreement. Pp. 53–59, 193 L. Ed. 2d, at 371-375.

(a) No one denies that lower courts must follow *Concepcion*, but that elementary point of law does not resolve the case because the parties are free to choose the law governing an arbitration provision, including California law as it would have been if not pre-empted. The state court interpreted the contract to mean that the parties did so, and the interpretation of a contract is ordinarily a matter of state law to which this Court defers, *Volt Information Sciences, Inc.* v. *Board of Trustees of Leland Stanford Junior Univ.*, 489 U.S. 468, 474, 109 S. Ct. 1248, 103 L. Ed. 2d 488. The issue here is not whether the court's decision is a correct statement of California law but whether it is consistent with the Federal Arbitration Act. Pp. 53–54, 193 L. Ed. 2d, at 371-372.

(b) The California court's interpretation does not place arbitration contracts "on equal footing with all other contracts," *Buckeye Check Cashing, Inc.* v. *Cardegna*, 546 U.S. 440, 443, 126 S. Ct. 1204, 163 L. Ed. 2d 1038, because California courts would not interpret contracts other than arbitration contracts the same way. Several considerations lead to this conclusion.

First, the phrase "law of your state" is not ambiguous and takes its ordinary meaning: valid state law. Second, California case law—that under "general contract principles," references to California law incorporate the California Legislature's power to change the law retroactively, *Doe* v. *Harris*, 57 Cal. 4th 64, 69-70, 302 P.3d 598, 601-602—clarifies any doubt about how to interpret it. Third, because the court nowhere suggests that California courts would reach the same interpretation in any other context, its conclusion appears to reflect the subject matter, rather than a general principle that would include state statutes invalidated by other federal law. Fourth, the language the court uses to frame the issue focuses only on arbitration. Fifth, the view that state law retains independent force after being authoritatively invalidated is one courts are unlikely to apply in other contexts. Sixth, none of the principles of contract interpretation relied on by the California court suggests that other California courts would reach the same interpretation elsewhere. The court applied the canon that contracts are construed against the drafter, but the lack of any similar case interpreting similar language to include invalid laws indicates that the antidrafter canon would not lead California courts to reach a similar conclusion in cases not involving arbitration. Pp. 54–58, 193 L. Ed. 2d, at 372-375.

225 Cal. App. 4th 338, 170 Cal. Rptr. 3d 190, reversed and remanded.

Breyer, J., delivered the opinion of the Court, in which Roberts, C. J., and Scalia, Kennedy, Alito, and Kagan, JJ., joined. Thomas, J., filed a dissenting opinion. Ginsburg, J., filed a dissenting opinion, in which Sotomayor, J., joined.

OPINION OF THE COURT

[577 U.S. 49]

Justice **Breyer** delivered the opinion of the Court.

[1] The Federal Arbitration Act states that a "written provision" in a contract providing for "settle[ment] by arbitration" of "a controversy . . . arising out of" that "contract . . . shall be valid, irrevocable, and enforceable, save upon such grounds as exist at law or in equity for the revocation of any contract." 9 U.S.C. § 2. We here consider a California court's refusal to enforce an arbitration provision in a contract. In our view, that decision does not rest "upon such grounds as exist . . . for the revocation of any contract," and we consequently set that judgment aside.

I

DIRECTV, Inc., the petitioner, entered into a service agreement with its customers, including respondents Amy

[577 U.S. 50]

Imburgia and Kathy Greiner. Section 9 of that contract provides that "any Claim either of us asserts will be resolved only by binding arbitration." App. 128. It then sets forth a waiver of class arbitration, stating that "[n]either you nor we shall be entitled to join or consolidate claims in arbitration." Id., at 128-129. It adds that if the "law of your state" makes the waiver of class arbitration unenforceable, then the entire arbitration provision "is unenforceable." Id., at 129. Section 10 of the contract states that § 9, the arbitration provision, "shall be governed by the Federal Arbitration Act." Ibid.

In 2008, the two respondents brought this lawsuit against DIRECTV in a California state court. They seek damages for early termination fees that they believe violate California law. After various proceedings not here relevant, DIRECTV, pointing to the arbitration provision, asked the court to send the matter to arbitration. The state trial court denied that request, and DIRECTV appealed.

The California Court of Appeal thought that the critical legal question concerned the meaning of the contractual phrase "law of your state," in this case the law of California. Does the law of California make the contract's class-arbitration waiver unenforceable? If so, as the contract provides, the entire arbitration provision is unenforceable. Or does California law permit the parties to agree to waive the right to proceed as a class in arbitration? If so, the arbitration provision is enforceable.

At one point, the law of California would have made the contract's class-arbitration waiver unenforceable. [2] In 2005, the California Supreme Court held in *Discover Bank* v. *Superior Court*, 36 Cal. 4th 148, 162-163, 113 P.3d 1100, 1110, that a "waiver" of class arbitration in a "consumer contract of adhesion" that "predictably involve[s] small amounts of damages" and meets certain other criteria not contested here is "unconscionable under California law and should not be enforced." See *Cohen* v. *DirecTV, Inc.*, 142 Cal. App. 4th

[577 U.S. 51]

1442, 1446-1447, 48 Cal. Rptr. 3d 813, 815-816 (2006) (holding a class-action waiver similar to the one at issue here unenforceable pursuant to *Discover Bank*); see also Consumers Legal Remedies Act, Cal. Civ. Code Ann. §§ 1751, 1781(a) (West 2009) (invalidating class-action waivers for claims brought under that statute). But in 2011, this Court held that California's *Discover Bank* rule " 'stands as an obstacle to the accomplishment and execution of the full purposes and objectives of Congress' " embodied in the Federal Arbitration Act. *AT&T Mobility LLC* v. *Concep-*

cion, 563 U.S. 333, 352, 131 S. Ct. 1740, 179 L. Ed. 2d 742 (2011) (quoting *Hines* v. *Davidowitz*, 312 U.S. 52, 67, 61 S. Ct. 399, 85 L. Ed. 581 (1941)); see *Sanchez* v. *Valencia Holding Co., LLC*, 61 Cal. 4th 899, 923-924, 353 P.3d 741, 757 (2015) (holding that *Concepcion* applies to the Consumers Legal Remedies Act to the extent that it would have the same effect as *Discover Bank*). The Federal Arbitration Act therefore pre-empts and invalidates that rule. 563 U.S., at 352, 131 S. Ct. 1740, 179 L. Ed. 2d 742; see U.S. Const., Art. VI, cl. 2.

The California Court of Appeal subsequently held in this case that, despite this Court's holding in *Concepcion*, "the law of California would find the class action waiver unenforceable." 225 Cal. App. 4th 338, 342, 170 Cal. Rptr. 3d 190, 194 (2014). The court noted that *Discover Bank* had held agreements to dispense with class-arbitration procedures unenforceable under circumstances such as these. 225 Cal. App. 4th, at 341, 170 Cal. Rptr. 3d, at 194. It conceded that this Court in *Concepcion* had held that the Federal Arbitration Act invalidated California's rule. 225 Cal. App. 4th, at 341, 170 Cal. Rptr. 3d, at 194. But it then concluded that this latter circumstance did not change the result—that the "class action waiver is unenforceable under California law." *Id.*, at 347, 170 Cal. Rptr. 3d, at 198.

In reaching that conclusion, the Court of Appeal referred to two sections of California's Consumers Legal Remedies Act, §§ 1751, 1781(a), rather than *Discover Bank* itself. See 225 Cal. App. 4th, at 344, 170 Cal. Rptr. 3d, at 195. Section

[577 U.S. 52]

1751 renders invalid any waiver of the right under § 1781(a) to bring a class action for violations of that Act. The Court of Appeal thought that applying "state law alone" (that is, those two sections) would render unenforceable the class-arbitration waiver in § 9 of the contract. *Id.*, at 344, 170 Cal. Rptr. 3d, at 195. But it nonetheless recognized that if it applied federal law "then the class action waiver is enforceable and any state law to the contrary is preempted." *Ibid.* As far as those sections apply to class-arbitration waivers, they embody the *Discover Bank* rule. The California Supreme Court has recognized as much, see *Sanchez, supra*, at 923-924, 353 P.3d, at 757, and no party argues to the contrary, see Supp. Brief for Respondents 2 ("The ruling in *Sanchez* tracks respondents' position precisely"). We shall consequently refer to the here-relevant rule as the *Discover Bank* rule.

The court reasoned that just as the parties were free in their contract to refer to the laws of different States or different nations, so too were they free to refer to California law as it would have been without this Court's holding invalidating the *Discover Bank* rule. The court thought that the parties in their contract had done just that. And it set forth two reasons for believing so.

First, § 10 of the contract, stating that the Federal Arbitration Act governs § 9 (the arbitration provision), is a *general* provision. But the provision voiding arbitration if the "law of your state" would find the class-arbitration waiver unenforceable is a *specific* provision. The court believed that the specific provision " 'is paramount to' " and must govern the general. 225 Cal. App. 4th, at 344, 170 Cal. Rptr. 3d, at 195 (quoting *Prouty* v. *Gores Technology Group*, 121 Cal. App. 4th 1225,

1235, 18 Cal. Rptr. 3d 178, 185-186 (2004); brackets omitted).

Second, the court said that " 'a court should construe ambiguous language against the interest of the party that drafted it.' " 225 Cal. App. 4th, at 345, 170 Cal. Rptr. 3d, at

[577 U.S. 53]

196

(quoting *Mastrobuono* v. *Shearson Lehman Hutton, Inc.*, 514 U.S. 52, 62, 115 S. Ct. 1212, 131 L. Ed. 2d 76 (1995)). DIRECTV had drafted the language; to void the arbitration provision was against its interest. Hence the arbitration provision was void. The Court of Appeal consequently affirmed the trial court's denial of DIRECTV's motion to enforce the arbitration provision.

The California Supreme Court denied discretionary review. App. to Pet. for Cert. 1a. DIRECTV then filed a petition for a writ of certiorari, noting that the Ninth Circuit had reached the opposite conclusion on precisely the same interpretive question decided by the California Court of Appeal. *Murphy* v. *DirecTV, Inc.*, 724 F.3d 1218, 1226-1228 (2013). We granted the petition.

II

No one denies that lower courts must follow this Court's holding in *Concepcion*. The fact that *Concepcion* was a closely divided case, resulting in a decision from which four Justices dissented, has no bearing on that undisputed obligation. [3] Lower court judges are certainly free to note their disagreement with a decision of this Court. But the "Supremacy Clause forbids state courts to dissociate themselves from federal law because of disagreement with its content or a refusal to recognize the superior authority of its source." *Howlett* v. *Rose*,

496 U.S. 356, 371, 110 S. Ct. 2430, 110 L. Ed. 2d 332 (1990); cf. *Khan v. State Oil Co.*, 93 F.3d 1358, 1363-1364 (CA7 1996), vacated, 522 U.S. 3, 118 S. Ct. 275, 139 L. Ed. 2d 199 (1997). **[4]** The Federal Arbitration Act is a law of the United States, and *Concepcion* is an authoritative interpretation of that Act. Consequently, the judges of every State must follow it. U. S. Const., Art. VI, cl. 2 ("[T]he Judges in every State shall be bound" by "the Laws of the United States").

While all accept this elementary point of law, that point does not resolve the issue in this case. As the Court of Appeal noted, **[5]** the Federal Arbitration Act allows parties to an arbitration contract considerable latitude to choose what law

[577 U.S. 54]

governs some or all of its provisions, including the law governing enforceability of a class-arbitration waiver. 225 Cal. App. 4th, at 342-343, 170 Cal. Rptr. 3d, at 194. In principle, they might choose to have portions of their contract governed by the law of Tibet, the law of pre-revolutionary Russia, or (as is relevant here) the law of California including the *Discover Bank* rule and irrespective of that rule's invalidation in *Concepcion*. The Court of Appeal decided that, as a matter of contract law, the parties did mean the phrase "law of your state" to refer to this last possibility. Since **[6]** the interpretation of a contract is ordinarily a matter of state law to which we defer, *Volt Information Sciences, Inc. v. Board of Trustees of Leland Stanford Junior Univ.*, 489 U.S. 468, 474, 109 S. Ct. 1248, 103 L. Ed. 2d 488 (1989), we must decide not whether its decision is a correct statement of California law but whether (assuming it is) that state law is consistent with the Federal Arbitration Act.

III

Although we may doubt that the Court of Appeal has correctly interpreted California law, we recognize that **[7]** California courts are the ultimate authority on that law. While recognizing this, we must decide whether the decision of the California court places arbitration contracts "on equal footing with all other contracts." *Buckeye Check Cashing, Inc. v. Cardegna*, 546 U.S. 440, 443, 126 S. Ct. 1204, 163 L. Ed. 2d 1038 (2006). And in doing so, we must examine whether the Court of Appeal's decision in fact rests upon "grounds as exist at law or in equity for the revocation of any contract." 9 U.S.C. § 2. That is to say, we look not to grounds that the California court might have offered but rather to those it did in fact offer. Neither this approach nor our result "steps beyond *Concepcion*" or any other aspect of federal arbitration law. See *post*, at 67, 193 L. Ed. 2d, at 380 (Ginsburg, J., dissenting) (hereinafter the dissent).

We recognize, as the dissent points out, *post*, at 62, 193 L. Ed. 2d, at 377, that when DIRECTV drafted the contract, the parties likely believed that the words "law of your state" included California

[577 U.S. 55]

law that then made class-arbitration waivers unenforceable. But that does not answer the legal question before us. That is because this Court subsequently held in *Concepcion* that the *Discover Bank* rule was invalid. Thus the underlying question of contract law at the time the Court of Appeal made its decision was whether the "law of your state" included *invalid* California law. We must now decide whether answering *that* question in the affirmative is consistent with the Federal Arbitration Act. After examining the grounds upon which the Court of Appeal rested its decision, we conclude that California courts would not interpret contracts other than arbitration contracts the same way. Rather, several considerations lead us to conclude that the court's interpretation of this arbitration contract is unique, restricted to that field.

First, we do not believe that the relevant contract language is ambiguous. The contract says that "[i]f . . . the law of your state would find this agreement to dispense with class arbitration procedures unenforceable, then this entire Section 9 [the arbitration section] is unenforceable." App. 129. Absent any indication in the contract that this language is meant to refer to *invalid* state law, it presumably takes its ordinary meaning: *valid* state law. Indeed, neither the parties nor the dissent refer us to any contract case from California or from any other State that interprets similar language to refer to state laws authoritatively held to be invalid. While we recognize that the dissent believes this phrase to be "ambiguous," *post,* at 65, 67, 193 L. Ed. 2d, at 379, 380, or "anomalous," *post,* at 68, 193 L. Ed. 2d, at 381, we cannot agree with that characterization.

Second, California case law itself clarifies any doubt about how to interpret the language. The California Supreme Court has held that **[8]** under "general contract principles," references to California law incorporate the California Legislature's power to change the law retroactively. *Doe* v. *Harris,* 57 Cal. 4th 64, 69-70, 302 P.3d 598, 601-602 (2013) (holding that plea agreements, which are governed by general contract

[577 U.S. 56]

principles, are " ' "deemed to incorporate and con-

template not only the existing law but the reserve power of the state to amend the law or enact additional laws" ' " (quoting *People* v. *Gipson,* 117 Cal. App. 4th 1065, 1070, 12 Cal. Rptr. 3d 478, 481 (2004))). And judicial construction of a statute ordinarily applies retroactively. *Rivers* v. *Roadway Express, Inc.,* 511 U.S. 298, 312-313, 114 S. Ct. 1510, 128 L. Ed. 2d 274 (1994). As far as we are aware, the principle of California law announced in *Harris,* not the Court of Appeal's decision here, would ordinarily govern the scope of phrases such as "law of your state."

Third, nothing in the Court of Appeal's reasoning suggests that a California court would reach the same interpretation of "law of your state" in any context other than arbitration. The Court of Appeal did not explain why parties might generally intend the words "law of your state" to encompass "*invalid* law of your state." To the contrary, the contract refers to "state law" that makes the waiver of class arbitration "unenforceable," while an invalid state law would not make a contractual provision unenforceable. Assuming—as we must—that the court's reasoning is a correct statement as to the meaning of "law of your state" in this arbitration provision, we can find nothing in that opinion (nor in any other California case) suggesting that California would generally interpret words such as "law of your state" to include state laws held invalid because they conflict with, say, federal labor statutes, federal pension statutes, federal antidiscrimination laws, the Equal Protection Clause, or the like. Even given our assumption that the Court of Appeal's conclusion is correct, its conclusion appears to reflect the subject matter at issue here (arbitration), rather than a general principle that would apply to contracts using similar language but involving state statutes invalidated by other federal law.

Fourth, the language used by the Court of Appeal focused only on arbitration. The court asked whether "law of your

[577 U.S. 57]

state" "mean[s] 'the law of your state to the extent it is not preempted by the [Federal Arbitration Act],' or 'the law of your state without considering the preemptive effect, if any, of the [Federal Arbitration Act].'" 225 Cal. App. 4th, at 344, 170 Cal. Rptr. 3d, at 195. Framing the question in such terms, rather than in generally applicable terms, suggests that the Court of Appeal could well have meant that its holding was limited to the specific subject matter of this contract—arbitration.

Fifth, the Court of Appeal reasoned that invalid state arbitration law, namely, the *Discover Bank* rule, maintained legal force despite this Court's holding in *Concepcion*. The court stated that "[i]f we apply state law alone . . . to the class action waiver, then the waiver is unenforceable." 225 Cal. App. 4th, at 344, 170 Cal. Rptr. 3d, at 195. And at the end of its opinion it reiterated that "[t]he class action waiver is unenforceable under California law, so the entire arbitration agreement is unenforceable." *Id.,* at 347, 170 Cal. Rptr. 3d, at 198. But those statements do not describe California law. See *Concepcion,* 563 U.S., at 344, 352, 131 S. Ct. 1740, 179 L. Ed. 2d 742; *Sanchez,* 61 Cal. 4th, at 923-924, 353 P.3d, at 757. The view that state law retains independent force even after it has been authoritatively invalidated by this Court is one courts are unlikely to accept as a general matter and to apply in other contexts.

Sixth, there is no other principle invoked by the Court of Appeal that suggests that California courts would reach the same interpretation of the words "law of your state" in other contexts. The court said that the phrase "law of your state" constitutes "'a specific *exception*'" to the agreement's "'*general* adoption of the [Federal Arbitration Act].'" 225 Cal. App. 4th, at 344, 170 Cal. Rptr. 3d, at 195. But that tells us nothing about how to interpret the words "law of your state" elsewhere. It does not answer the relevant question: whether those words encompass laws that have been authoritatively

[577 U.S. 58]

held invalid. Cf. *Prouty,* 121 Cal. App. 4th, at 1235, 18 Cal. Rptr. 3d, at 185-186 ([9] specific words govern only "when a general and a particular provision are inconsistent").

The court added that it would interpret "'ambiguous language against the interest of the party that drafted it,'" namely, DIRECTV. 225 Cal. App. 4th, at 345, 170 Cal. Rptr. 3d, at 196 (quoting *Mastrobuono,* 514 U.S., at 62, 115 S. Ct. 1212, 131 L. Ed. 2d 76). The dissent adopts a similar argument. See *post,* at 65–67, 193 L. Ed. 2d, at 379-380. But, as we have pointed out, *supra,* at 56, 193 L. Ed. 2d, at 373, were the phrase "law of your state" ambiguous, surely some court would have construed that term to incorporate state laws invalidated by, for example, federal labor law, federal pension law, or federal civil rights law. Yet, we have found no such case. Moreover, [10] the reach of the canon construing contract language against the drafter must have limits, no matter who the drafter was. The fact that we can find no similar case interpreting the words "law of your state" to include *invalid* state laws indicates, at the least, that the anti-drafter canon would not lead California courts to reach a similar conclusion in similar cases that do not involve arbitration.

* * *

Taking these considerations together, we reach a conclusion that, in our view, falls well within the confines of (and goes no further than) present well-established law. California's interpretation of the phrase "law of your state" does not place arbitration contracts "on equal footing with all other contracts," *Buckeye Check Cashing, Inc.*, 546 U.S., at 443, 126 S. Ct. 1204, 163 L. Ed. 2d 1038. For that reason, it does not give "due regard . . . to the federal policy favoring arbitration." *Volt Information Sciences*, 489 U.S., at 476, 109 S. Ct. 1248, 103 L. Ed. 2d

488. Thus, the Court of Appeal's interpretation is pre-empted by the Federal Arbitration Act. See *Perry* v. *Thomas*, 482 U.S. 483, 493, n. 9, 107 S. Ct. 2520, 96 L. Ed. 2d 426 (1987) (noting that [11] the Federal Arbitration Act pre-empts decisions that take their "meaning precisely from the fact that a contract to arbitrate

[577 U.S. 59]

is at issue"). Hence, the California Court of Appeal must "enforc[e]" the arbitration agreement. 9 U.S.C. § 2.

The judgment of the California Court of Appeal is reversed, and the case is remanded for further proceedings not inconsistent with this opinion.

It is so ordered.

SEPARATE OPINIONS

Justice **Thomas**, dissenting.

I remain of the view that the Federal Arbitration Act (FAA), 9 U.S.C. § 1 *et seq.*, does not apply to proceedings in state courts. See *Allied-Bruce Terminix Cos.* v. *Dobson*, 513 U.S. 265, 285-297, 115 S. Ct. 834, 130 L. Ed. 2d 753 (1995) (dissenting opinion); see also *Preston* v. *Ferrer*, 552 U.S. 346, 363, 128 S. Ct. 978, 169 L. Ed. 2d 917 (2008) (same); *Buckeye Check Cashing, Inc.* v. *Cardegna*, 546 U.S. 440, 449, 126 S. Ct. 1204, 163 L. Ed. 2d 1038 (2006) (same); *Green Tree Financial Corp.* v. *Bazzle*, 539 U.S. 444, 460, 123 S. Ct. 2402, 156 L. Ed. 2d 414 (2003) (same); *Doctor's Associates, Inc.* v. *Casarotto*, 517 U.S. 681, 689, 116 S. Ct. 1652, 134 L. Ed. 2d 902 (1996) (same). Thus, the FAA does not require state courts to order arbitration. Accordingly, I would affirm the judgment of the California Court of Appeal.

Justice **Ginsburg**, with whom Justice **Sotomayor** joins, dissenting.

It has become routine, in a large part due to this Court's decisions, for powerful economic enterprises to write into their form contracts with consumers and employees no-class-action arbitration clauses. The form contract in this case contains a Delphic provision stating that "if the law of your state" does not permit agreements barring class arbitration, then the entire agreement to arbitrate becomes unenforceable, freeing the aggrieved customer to commence class-based litigation in court. This Court reads that provision in a manner most protective of the drafting enterprise. I would read it, as the California court did, to give the customer, not the drafter, the benefit of the doubt. Acknowledging the precedent so far set by the Court, I would take

[577 U.S. 60]

no further

step to disarm consumers, leaving them without effective access to justice.

I

This case began as a putative class action in state court claiming that DIRECTV, by imposing hefty early-termination fees, violated California consumer-protective legislation, including the Consumers Legal Remedies Act (CLRA), Cal. Civ. Code Ann. § 1750 *et seq.* (West 2015). App. 58. DIRECTV did not initially seek to stop the lawsuit and compel bilateral arbitration. See *id.,* at 52-53. The reason for DIRECTV's failure to oppose the litigation is no mystery. The version of DIRECTV's service agreement applicable in this case (the 2007 version) requires consumers to arbitrate all disputes and to forgo class arbitration. *Id.,* at 128-129. If the relevant provision stopped there, the Court's recent precedent, see *American Express Co.* v. *Italian Colors Restaurant,* 570 U.S. 228, 133 S. Ct. 2304, 186 L. Ed. 2d 417 (2013); *AT&T Mobility LLC* v. *Concepcion,* 563 U.S. 333, 131 S. Ct. 1740, 179 L. Ed. 2d 742 (2011), would control, and DIRECTV could have resisted the lawsuit. But DIRECTV's form contract continued: The entire arbitration clause is unenforceable "[i]f . . . the law of your state would find" unenforceable the agreement's class-arbitration prohibition. App. 129. At the time plaintiff-respondents Imburgia and Greiner commenced their court action, class-arbitration bars like the one in DIRECTV's agreement were *per se* unenforceable as unconscionable under the law of California. See *Discover Bank* v. *Superior Court,* 36 Cal. 4th 148, 162-163, 113 P.3d 1100, 1110 (2005).

Nearly three years into the litigation, this Court held in *Concepcion,* 563 U.S., at 338-351, 131 S. Ct. 1740, 179 L. Ed. 2d 742, that the Federal Arbitration Act (FAA), 9 U.S.C. § 1 *et seq.,* preempts state rules that render class-arbitration bans unenforceable. DIRECTV then moved to halt the long-pending lawsuit and compel bilateral arbitration. App. to Pet. for Cert. 4a. The California Superior Court denied DIRECTV's motion, No. BC398295 (Super. Ct. Los Angeles Cty., Jan. 26, 2012), App. to Pet. for Cert. 17a-20a, and the California Court of Appeal

[577 U.S. 61]

affirmed. The Court of Appeal first observed that, under the California law DIRECTV confronted when it drafted the clause in question, provisions relinquishing the right to proceed under the CLRA on behalf of a class would not be enforced. 225 Cal. App. 4th 338, 342, 170 Cal. Rptr. 3d 190, 194 (2014). The question dispositive of DIRECTV's motion, the California court explained, trains on the meaning of the atypical contractual phrase "the law of your state": "[D]oes it mean 'the law of your state to the extent it is not preempted by the FAA,' or 'the law of your state without considering the preemptive effect, if any, of the FAA'?" *Id.,* at 344, 170 Cal. Rptr. 3d, at 195.

In resolving this question, the California court emphasized that DIRECTV drafted the service agreement, giving its customers no say in the matter, and reserving to itself the right to modify the agreement unilaterally at any time. *Id.,* at 345, 170 Cal. Rptr. 3d, at 196. See also Brief for Respondents 1-2. DIRECTV used the same take-it-or-leave-it contract everywhere it did business. *Ibid.* "[T]o protect the party who did not choose the language from an unintended or unfair result," the California court applied "the common-law rule of contract interpretation that a court should construe ambiguous language against the interest of the party that drafted it." 225 Cal. App. 4th, at 345, 170 Cal. Rptr. 3d, at 196 (quoting *Mastrobuono* v. *Shearson Lehman Hutton, Inc.*, 514 U.S. 52, 62-63, 115 S. Ct. 1212, 131 L. Ed. 2d 76 (1995)). That rule was particularly appropriate in this case, the court reasoned, for, "as a practical matter, it seems unlikely that plaintiffs anticipated in 2007 that the Supreme Court would hold in 2011 that the FAA preempts" state-law protection against compelled class-arbitration waivers. 225 Cal. App. 4th, at 345, 170 Cal. Rptr. 3d, at 196 (internal quotation marks omitted).

II

The Court today holds that the California Court of Appeal interpreted the language in DIRECTV's service agreement so unreasonably as to suggest discrimination against arbitration

[577 U.S. 62]

in violation of the FAA. *Ante*, at 58, 193 L. Ed. 2d, at 374. As I see it, the California court's interpretation of the "law of your state" provision is not only reasonable, it is entirely right.

Arbitration is a matter of "consent, not coercion." *Stolt-Nielsen S. A.* v. *AnimalFeeds Int'l Corp.*, 559 U.S. 662, 681, 130 S. Ct. 1758, 176 L. Ed. 2d 605 (2010) (internal quotation marks omitted). The FAA "requires courts to enforce privately negotiated agreements to arbitrate, like other contracts, in accordance with their terms." *Volt Information Sciences, Inc.* v. *Board of Trustees of Leland Stanford Junior Univ.*, 489 U.S. 468, 478, 109 S. Ct. 1248, 103 L. Ed. 2d 488 (1989). "[T]he interpretation of pri-

vate contracts is ordinarily a question of state law, which this Court does not sit to review." *Id.*, at 474, 109 S. Ct. 1248, 103 L. Ed. 2d 488. See also *First Options of Chicago, Inc.* v. *Kaplan*, 514 U.S. 938, 944, 115 S. Ct. 1920, 131 L. Ed. 2d 985 (1995) (when interpreting arbitration agreements, courts "should apply ordinary state-law principles that govern the formation of contracts"). Historically, this Court has respected state-court interpretations of arbitration agreements. See *Mastrobuono*, 514 U.S., at 60, n. 4, 115 S. Ct. 1212, 131 L. Ed. 2d 76; *Volt Information Sciences*, 489 U.S., at 484, 109 S. Ct. 1248, 103 L. Ed. 2d 488. Indeed, in the more than 25 years between *Volt Information Sciences* and this case, not once has this Court reversed a state-court decision on the ground that the state court misapplied state contract law when it determined the meaning of a term in a particular arbitration agreement. Today's decision is a dangerous first.

Beyond genuine debate, DIRECTV originally meant the "law of your state" clause to refer to its customer's home state law untouched by federal preemption. As DIRECTV explained in a state-court filing, the clause prevented enforcement of the arbitration agreement in those States, California among them, where the class-arbitration proscription was unenforceable as a matter of state law, while requiring bilateral arbitration in States that did not outlaw purported waivers of class proceedings. App. 52 ("The Customer Agreement between DIRECTV and its customers provides that the customer's home state laws will govern the relationship,

[577 U.S. 63]

and that any disputes will be resolved in individual arbitration *if* the customer's home state laws enforce the parties' arbitration agreement." (emphasis added)).

According to DIRECTV, because the class-arbitration ban, post-*Concepcion*, is enforceable in all States, this case must now be resolved, if at all, in bilateral arbitration. The Court agrees. After *Concepcion*, the Court maintains, it no longer matters whether DIRECTV meant California's "home state laws" when it drafted the 2007 version of its service agreement. But *Concepcion* held only that a State cannot *compel* a party to engage in class arbitration when the controlling agreement unconditionally prohibits class procedures. See 563 U.S., at 351, 352, 131 S. Ct. 1740, 179 L. Ed. 2d 742 ("Arbitration is a matter of contract, and the FAA requires courts to honor parties' expectations," so parties may consent to class procedures even though such procedures "may not be required by state law."). Just as a contract itself may provide for class arbitration, so the parties may *choose* to be bound by a particular state law, in this case, the CLRA, even if the FAA would otherwise displace that state law. *Hall Street Associates, L. L. C. v. Mattel, Inc.*, 552 U.S. 576, 586, 128 S. Ct. 1396, 170 L. Ed. 2d 254 (2008) ("[T]he FAA lets parties tailor some, even many, features of arbitration by contract, including . . . procedure and choice of substantive law.").[1] "In principle," the Court acknowledges, parties "might choose to have portions of their contract governed by the law of Tibet, [or] the law of prerevolutionary Russia." *Ante*, at 54, 193 L. Ed. 2d, at 372; see Brief for Petitioner 20 (observing that the FAA would allow parties "to bind themselves by reference to the rules of a

[577 U.S. 64]

board game"). Prerevolutionary Russian law, but not California's "home state laws" operative and unquestionably valid in 2007? Makes little sense to me.

Nothing in *Concepcion* or the FAA nullifies provisions of the CLRA. They hold sway when parties elect judicial resolution of their disputes, and should similarly control when parties choose that consumer-protective law to govern their arbitration agreements. See *Volt Information Sciences*, 489 U.S., at 475, 109 S. Ct. 1248, 103 L. Ed. 2d 488 (where parties had "incorporat[ed] . . . California rules of arbitration into their agreement," they had no "FAA-guaranteed right to compel arbitration" on terms inconsistent with those California rules).[2] Thus, even after *Concepcion*, one could properly refer to the CLRA's class-waiver proscription as "California law." To repeat, the dispositive

---

1. FAA preemption is distinct from federal preemption in other contexts. Unlike "state laws invalidated by, for example, federal labor law, federal pension law, or federal civil rights law," *ante*, at 58, 193 L. Ed. 2d, at 374, state laws are preempted by the FAA only to the extent that they conflict with the contracting parties' intent. See *Mastrobuono* v. *Shearson Lehman Hutton, Inc.*, 514 U.S. 52, 59, 115 S. Ct. 1212, 131 L. Ed. 2d 76 (1995) ("*[I]n the absence of contractual intent to the contrary*, the FAA would pre-empt" a particular state law. (emphasis added)); Brief for Law Professors as *Amici Curiae* 10 ("FAA preemption cannot occur without reference to a particular agreement of the parties . . . .").

2. The Court refers to the relevant California law as the "*Discover Bank* rule" and suggests that, "under 'general contract principles,' references to California law incorporate the California Legislature's power to change the law retroactively." *Ante*, at 55, 193 L. Ed. 2d, at 373. But despite this Court's rejection of the *Discover Bank* rule in *Concepcion*, the California Legislature has not capitulated; it has retained without change the CLRA's class-waiver prohibition. The

question in this case is whether the parties intended the "law of your state" provision to mean state law as preempted by federal law, as the Court today reads the provision, or home state law as framed by the California Legislature, without considering the preemptive effect of federal law, as the California court read it.

The latter reading is the better one. DIRECTV had no occasion to refer to "the law of [its customer's] state" had it meant to incorporate state law as preempted by the FAA. That is, DIRECTV, like virtually every other company with a similar service agreement, could have employed a clause directly conditioning enforceability of the arbitration agreement on the exclusion of class arbitration. Indeed, DIRECTV

[577 U.S. 65]

has done just that in service agreements both before and after 2007. App. 121 (the 2004 version provides that "[a] court may sever any portion of [the arbitration agreement] that it finds to be unenforceable, except for the prohibition on class or representative arbitration"); Brief for Respondents 35-36 (stating that the June 2015 version of DIRECTV's agreement provides that "[a] court may sever any portion of [the arbitration agreement] that it finds to be unenforceable, except for the prohibition on [class arbitration]" (internal quotation marks omitted)). Had DIRECTV followed this pattern in its 2007 form contract, the arbitration agreement, post-*Concepcion*, unquestionably would have been enforceable in all States. In the 2007 version, however, DIRECTV chose a different formulation, one referring to the "law of [its customer's] state." I would not

translate that term to be synonymous with "federal law." If DIRECTV meant to exclude the application of California legislation, it surely chose a bizarre way to accomplish that result.

As earlier noted, see *supra,* at 61, 193 L. Ed. 2d, at 376, and as the California court appreciated, courts generally construe ambiguous contractual terms against the drafter. See *Mastrobuono,* 514 U.S., at 63, 115 S. Ct. 1212, 131 L. Ed. 2d 76 ("Respondents drafted an ambiguous document, and they cannot now claim the benefit of the doubt."). This "common-law rule of contract interpretation," *id.,* at 62, 115 S. Ct. 1212, 131 L. Ed. 2d 76, reflects the principle that a party should not be permitted to write an ambiguous term, lock another party into agreeing to that term, and then reap the benefit of the ambiguity once a dispute emerges. The rule has particular force where, as here, a court is interpreting a "standardized contrac[t]" that was not the product of bilateral bargaining. Restatement (Second) of Contracts § 206, Comment *a* (1979).

Allowing DIRECTV to reap the benefit of an ambiguity it could have avoided would ignore not just the hugely unequal bargaining power of the parties, but also their reasonable expectations at the time the contract was formed. See

[577 U.S. 66]

Mastrobuono, 514 U.S., at 63, 115 S. Ct. 1212, 131 L. Ed. 2d 76 (it is particularly appropriate to construe terms against the drafter where the other party had no reason to anticipate or intend the drafter's preferred result). See also *Trans World Airlines, Inc. v. Franklin Mint*

Discover Bank rule relied on an interpretation of the FAA, see 36 Cal. 4th 148, 162-173, 113 P.3d 1100, 1100-1117 (2005); in contrast, the CLRA's class-waiver proscription reflects California's legislative policy judgment.

Corp., 466 U.S. 243, 262, 104 S. Ct. 1776, 80 L. Ed. 2d 273 (1984) ("[C]ontract[s] . . . are to be read in the light of the conditions and circumstances existing at the time they were entered into, with a view to effecting the objects and purposes of the [parties] thereby contracting." (quoting *Rocca v. Thompson*, 223 U.S. 317, 331-332, 32 S. Ct. 207, 56 L. Ed. 453 (1912); ellipsis in original)). At the time DIRECTV imposed this agreement on its customers, it assumed that the arbitration clause would be unenforceable in California. App. 52 (explaining in state-court filing that, "[b]ecause California law would not enforce the arbitration agreement . . ., DIRECTV has not sought and will not seek to arbitrate disputes with California customers"). Likewise, any California customer who read the agreement would scarcely have understood that she had submitted to bilateral arbitration of any and all disputes with DIRECTV. She certainly would have had no reason to anticipate the Court's decision in *Concepcion*, rendered four years later, or to consider whether "law of your state" is a chameleon term meaning California legislation when she received her service contract, but preemptive federal law later on.

DIRECTV primarily responds that the FAA requires construction of all terms in arbitration agreements in favor of arbitrability. True, this Court has found in the FAA a "federal policy favoring arbitration." *Ante*, at 58, 193 L. Ed. 2d, at 375 (quoting *Volt Information Sciences*, 489 U.S., at 476, 109 S. Ct. 1248, 103 L. Ed. 2d 488). But the Court has also cautioned that an arbitration-favoring presumption applies "only where it reflects, and derives its legitimacy from, a judicial conclusion that arbitration of a par-

ticular dispute is what the parties intended because their express agreement to arbitrate was validly formed[, is] legally enforceable[,] and [is] best construed to encompass the dispute." *Granite Rock Co.* v. *Teamsters*, 561 U.S. 287, 303, 130 S. Ct. 2847, 177 L. Ed. 2d 567 (2010).

[577 U.S. 67]

　　　　　DIRECTV acknowledges that "[t]his case . . . involves a threshold dispute over the enforceability of the parties' arbitration agreement" in its entirety. Reply Brief 7. Like the California court, I would resolve that dispute by employing traditional rules of contract interpretation *sans* any arbitration-favoring presumption, including the rule that ambiguous language should be construed against the drafter. See *supra*, at 61, 65, 193 L. Ed. 2d, at 376, 379.

III

Today's decision steps beyond *Concepcion* and *Italian Colors*. There, as here, the Court misread the FAA to deprive consumers of effective relief against powerful economic entities that write no-class-action arbitration clauses into their form contracts. In *Concepcion*, 563 U.S., at 336, 131 S. Ct. 1740, 179 L. Ed. 2d 742, customers brought a class action claiming that AT&T Mobility had improperly charged $30.22 in sales tax while advertising cellular telephones as free. AT&T Mobility's form consumer contract contained a mandatory arbitration clause and a class-arbitration proscription. Because consumers lacked input into the contractual terms, and because few rational consumers would go through the hassle of pursuing a $30.22 claim in bilateral arbitration, the California courts deemed the arbitration agreement unenforceable as unconscionable. See *id.*, at 365, 131 S. Ct. 1740, 179 L. Ed. 2d 742 (Breyer, J., dissenting) (" '[T]he maximum gain to a customer for the hassle of arbitrating a $30.22 dispute is still just $30.22.' " (quoting *Laster* v. *AT&T Mobility LLC*, 584 F.3d 849, 856 (CA9 2009))); *Carnegie* v. *Household Int'l, Inc.*, 376 F.3d 656, 661 (CA7 2004) ("The *realistic* alternative to a class action is not 17 million individual suits, but zero individual suits, as only a lunatic or a fanatic sues for $30."), cert. denied, 543 U.S. 1051, 125 S. Ct. 877, 160 L. Ed. 2d 772 (2005). Nonetheless, the Court held that the FAA mandated enforcement of the entire arbitration agreement, including the class-arbitration ban. *Concepcion*, 563 U.S., at 343, 131 S. Ct. 1740, 179 L. Ed. 2d 742. Two years later, in *Italian Colors*, 570 U.S., at 235, 133 S. Ct. 2304, 186 L. Ed. 2d 417, the Court reaffirmed that class-arbitration prohibitions are enforceable even where claimants

[577 U.S. 68]

"have no economic incentive to pursue their . . . claims individually in arbi-

tration." Today, the Court holds that consumers lack not only protection against unambiguous class-arbitration bans in adhesion contracts. They lack even the benefit of the doubt when anomalous terms in such contracts reasonably could be construed to protect their rights.[3]

These decisions have predictably resulted in the deprivation of consumers' rights to seek redress for losses, and, turning the coin, they have insulated powerful economic interests from liability for violations of consumer-protection laws. See N. Y. Times, Nov. 1, 2015, p. A1, col. 5 ("By inserting

[577 U.S. 69]

individual arbitration clauses into a soaring number of consumer and employment contracts, companies [have] devised a way to circumvent the courts and bar people from joining together in class-action lawsuits, realistically the only tool citizens have to fight illegal or deceitful business practices."). Studies confirm that hardly any consumers take

---

3. It has not always been this way. In *Wilko* v. *Swan*, 346 U.S. 427, 435, 438, 74 S. Ct. 182, 98 L. Ed. 168 (1953), the Court unanimously held that an arbitration clause in a brokerage agreement was unenforceable. The Court noted that the Securities Act was "drafted with an eye to the disadvantages under which buyers labor" when negotiating brokerage agreements, *id.*, at 435, 438, 74 S. Ct. 182, 98 L. Ed. 168, and described arbitration as less protective of the rights of stock buyers than litigation, *id.*, at 435-437, 438, 74 S. Ct. 182, 98 L. Ed. 168. The Court later overruled *Wilko*, rejecting what it described as *Wilko*'s "suspicion of arbitration as a method of weakening the protections afforded in the substantive law." *Rodriguez de Quijas* v. *Shearson/American Express, Inc.*, 490 U.S. 477, 481, 109 S. Ct. 1917, 104 L. Ed. 2d 526 (1989). See also *Gilmer* v. *Interstate/Johnson Lane Corp.*, 500 U.S. 20, 33, 111 S. Ct. 1647, 114 L. Ed. 2d 26 (1991) (relying on *Rodriguez de Quijas* to conclude that "[m]ere inequality in bargaining power . . . is not a sufficient reason to hold that arbitration agreements are never enforceable in the employment context"). Similarly, before *Italian Colors*, the Court had suggested that "the existence of large arbitration costs could preclude a litigant . . . from effectively vindicating her federal statutory rights in the arbitral forum," and when that is so, an arbitration agreement may be unenforceable. *Green Tree Financial Corp.-Ala.* v. *Randolph*, 531 U.S. 79, 90, 121 S. Ct. 513, 148 L. Ed. 2d 373 (2000). Although the Court in *Italian Colors* did not expressly reject this "effective vindication" principle, the Court's refusal to apply the principle in that case suggests that the principle will no longer apply in any case. See 570 U.S., at 240–241, 133 S. Ct. 2304, 186 L. Ed. 2d 417 (Kagan, J., dissenting); *CompuCredit Corp.* v. *Greenwood*, 565 U.S. 95, 110, 132 S. Ct. 665, 181 L. Ed. 2d 586 (2012) (Ginsburg, J., dissenting) (criticizing the Court for ignoring a federal statutory "right to sue" and for holding "that credit repair organizations can escape suit by providing in their take-it-or-leave-it contracts that arbitration will serve as the parties' sole dispute-resolution mechanism").

advantage of bilateral arbitration to pursue small-dollar claims. Resnik, Diffusing Disputes: The Public in the Private of Arbitration, the Private in Courts, and the Erasure of Rights, 124 Yale L. J. 2804, 2900-2910 (2015) (Resnik, Diffusing Disputes). Because consumers lack bargaining power to change the terms of consumer adhesion contracts *ex ante*, "[t]he providers [have] won the power to impose a mandatory, no-opt-out system in their own private 'courts' designed to preclude aggregate litigation." Resnik, Fairness in Numbers: A Comment on *AT&T* v. *Concepcion*, *Wal-Mart* v. *Dukes*, and *Turner* v. *Rogers*, 125 Harv. L. Rev. 78, 133 (2011). See also Miller, Simplified Pleading, Meaningful Days in Court, and Trials on the Merits: Reflections on the Deformation of Federal Procedure, 88 N. Y. U. L. Rev. 286, 323 (2013) ("[P]owerful economic entities can impose no-class-action-arbitration clauses on people with little or no bargaining position—through adhesion contracts involving securities accounts, credit cards, mobile phones, car rentals, and many other social amenities and necessities.").[4] The proliferation of take-it-or-leave-it agreements mandating arbitration and banning class procedures, and this Court's readiness to enforce such one-sided agreements, have disabled consumers from "shop[ping] to avoid arbitration mandates." Resnik, Diffusing Disputes 2839. See also *id.,* at

[577 U.S. 70]

2872 ("[T]he numbers of clauses mandating arbitration are soaring across many sectors.").

The Court has suggested that these anticonsumer outcomes flow inexorably from the text and purpose of the FAA. But Congress passed the FAA in 1925 as a response to the reluctance of some judges to enforce commercial arbitration agreements between merchants with relatively equal bargaining power. Moses, Arbitration Law: Who's in Charge? 40 Seton Hall L. Rev. 147, 170-171 (2010). See also *id.,* at 170 (contract disputes between merchants have been a proper subject of arbitration since the 1600's). The FAA's purpose was to "make the contracting party live up to his agreement." H. R. Rep. No. 68-96, p. 1 (1924). See also Moses, *supra,* at 147 (Congress sought to "provide federal courts with procedural law that would permit the enforcement of arbitration agreements between merchants in diversity cases."). Congress in 1925 could not have anticipated that the Court would apply the FAA to render consumer adhesion contracts invulnerable to attack by parties who never meaningfully agreed to arbitration in the first place. See Resnik, Diffusing Disputes 2860 ("The merchants and lawyers who forged the public law of arbitration in the United States sought federal legislation to enforce *consensual* agreements." (emphasis added)).

Nor does the text of the FAA compel this result. Section 2, on which the Court relied in *Concepcion, Italian Colors*, and this case, prescribes simply that arbitration provisions are to be treated the same as other contractual terms: "A written provision in . . . a contract evidencing a transac-

---

4. The Consumer Financial Protection Bureau recently published a study documenting the proliferation of mandatory arbitration clauses containing class-arbitration waivers in consumer financial-services contracts, as well as the vanishingly small number of claims brought by financial-services consumers in bilateral arbitration. See Consumer Financial Protection Bureau, Arbitration Study § 1, pp. 9-13 (2015).

tion involving commerce to settle by arbitration a controversy . . . shall be valid, irrevocable, and enforceable, save upon such grounds as exist at law or in equity for the revocation of any contract." 9 U.S.C. § 2. As Justice O'Connor observed when the Court was just beginning to transform the FAA into what it has become, "the Court has abandoned all pretense of ascertaining congressional intent with respect to the Federal Arbitration Act, building instead, case by case,

[577 U.S. 71]

an edifice of its own creation." *Allied-Bruce Terminix Cos.* v. *Dobson,* 513 U.S. 265, 283, 115 S. Ct. 834, 130 L. Ed. 2d 753 (1995) (concurring opinion). See also Miller, *supra,* at 324 ("[O]ver the years the Act has been transformed by the Supreme Court through constant expansion into an expression of a 'federal policy' favoring arbitration, whether it involves a bilateral business dispute or not.").

The Court's ever-larger expansion of the FAA's scope contrasts sharply with how other countries treat mandatory arbitration clauses in consumer contracts of adhesion. A 1993 European Union Directive forbids binding consumers to unfair contractual terms, defined as those "not . . . individually negotiated" that "caus[e] a significant imbalance in the parties' rights and obligations . . . to the detriment of the consumer." Coun. Directive 93/13, Art. 3, 1993 O. J. (L. 95) 31. A subsequent EU Recommendation interpreted this Directive to bar enforcement of one-party-dictated mandatory consumer arbitration agreements. Comm'n Recommenda-

tion 98/257, 1998 O. J. (L. 115) 34 ("The consumer's recourse to the out-of-court procedure may not be the result of a commitment prior to the materialisation of the dispute, where such commitment has the effect of depriving the consumer of his right to bring an action before the courts for the settlement of the dispute."). As a result of this Directive and Recommendation, disputes between providers and consumers in the EU are arbitrated only when the parties mutually agree to arbitration on a "post-dispute basis." Sternlight, Is the U. S. Out on a Limb? Comparing the U. S. Approach to Mandatory Consumer and Employment Arbitration to That of the Rest of the World, 56 U. Miami L. Rev. 831, 847-848 (2002) (emphasis deleted); see *id.,* at 852 (enforcement of mandatory arbitration clauses in consumer contracts of adhesion "is quite rare, if not nonexistent," outside the United States).

* * *

The California Court of Appeal appropriately applied traditional tools of state contract law to interpret DIRECTV's

[577 U.S. 72]

reference to the home state laws of its customers. Demeaning that court's judgment through harsh construction, this Court has again expanded the scope of the FAA, further degrading the rights of consumers and further insulating already powerful economic entities from liability for unlawful acts. I resist the Court's bent, and would affirm the judgment of the California Court of Appeal.

RANDY WHITE, WARDEN, Petitioner

v

ROGER L. WHEELER

577 U.S. 73, 136 S. Ct. 456, 193 L. Ed. 2d 384, 2015 U.S. LEXIS 7998

[No. 14-1372]

Decided December 14, 2015.

Decision: For purposes of 28 U.S.C.S. § 2254(d)(1) habeas corpus petition, state court did not unreasonably apply clearly established federal law in concluding that exclusion of juror who equivocated about ability to impose death penalty did not violate Federal Constitution's Sixth Amendment.

Prior history: ON PETITION FOR WRIT OF CERTIORARI TO THE UNITED STATES COURT OF APPEALS FOR THE SIXTH CIRCUIT, 779 F.3d 366, 2015 U.S. App. LEXIS 2601

SUMMARY

Overview: HOLDINGS: [1]-The U.S. Court of Appeals for the Sixth Circuit erred when it found that a Kentucky judge who presided over defendant's trial on two counts of murder violated defendant's rights under the Sixth Amendment to the U.S. Constitution because she dismissed a juror who provided equivocal answers when asked if he could impose the death penalty if defendant was convicted; [2]-The Sixth Circuit did not properly apply the deference it was required to accord the state court's ruling under the Antiterrorism and Effective Death Penalty Act of 1996 and failed to ask the critical question: Was the Kentucky Supreme Court's decision affirming the trial judge's decision so lacking in justification that there was an error well understood and comprehended in existing law beyond any possibility for fairminded disagreement?

Outcome: Judgment reversed; case remanded. Unanimous decision.

HEADNOTES

Classified to United States Supreme Court Digest, Lawyers' Edition

Federal law — contrary decision — unreasonable application

L Ed Digest: Habeas Corpus §§ 26, 121.5

1. Under the Antiterrorism and Effective Death Penalty Act of 1996 (AEDPA), habeas relief is authorized if a state court's decision was contrary to, or involved an unreasonable application of, clearly established federal law, as determined by the Supreme Court of the United States. 28 U.S.C.S. § 2254(d)(1). The Supreme Court, time and again, has instructed that the AEDPA, by setting forth necessary predicates before state-court judgments may be set aside, erects a formidable barrier to federal habeas relief for prisoners whose claims have been adjudicated in state court. Under § 2254(d)(1), a state prisoner must show that the state court's rul-

ing on the claim being presented in federal court was so lacking in justification that there was an error understood and comprehended in existing law beyond any possibility for fairminded disagreement.

Juror disqualification — capital cases

L Ed Digest: Criminal Law § 93.5; Jury § 38.5

2. In Witherspoon v. Illinois, 391 U.S. 510 (1968), the United States Supreme Court set forth the rule for juror disqualification in capital cases. Witherspoon recognized that the Sixth Amendment's guarantee of an impartial jury confers on capital defendants the right to a jury not uncommonly willing to condemn a man to die. But the court with equal clarity has acknowledged the state's strong interest in having jurors who are able to apply capital punishment within the framework state law prescribes. To ensure the proper balance between these two interests, only a juror who is substantially impaired in his or her ability to impose the death penalty under the state-law framework can be excused for cause. As the Supreme Court explained in Wainwright v. Witt, 469 U.S. 412 (1985), a juror may be excused for cause where the trial judge is left with the definite impression that a prospective juror would be unable to faithfully and impartially apply the law.

Striking of juror — death penalty — ineffective assistance

L Ed Digest: Habeas Corpus §§ 121, 121.5

3. Reviewing courts owe deference to a trial court's ruling on whether to strike a particular juror regardless of whether the trial court engages in explicit analysis regarding substantial impairment; even the granting of a motion to excuse for cause constitutes an implicit finding of bias. A trial court's finding may be upheld even in the absence of clear statements from the juror that he or she is impaired. And where the federal courts review a state-court ruling under the constraints imposed by the Antiterrorism and Effective Death Penalty Act of 1996, the federal court must accord an additional and independent, high standard of deference. As a result, federal habeas review of a Witherspoon-Witt claim, much like federal habeas review of an ineffective-assistance-of-counsel claim, must be doubly deferential.

Striking of juror

L Ed Digest: Habeas Corpus § 34

4. The United States Supreme Court made clear in Uttecht v. Brown, 551 U.S. 1 (2007), that when there is ambiguity in a prospective juror's statements, the trial court is entitled to resolve it in favor of the state.

Striking of juror — deference

L Ed Digest: Habeas Corpus §§ 34, 121.5

5. Nothing in the United States Supreme Court's decision in Uttecht v. Brown, 551 U.S. 1 (2007), limits a trial court to evaluating demeanor alone and not the substance of a juror's response. And the implicit suggestion that a trial judge is entitled to less deference for having deliberated after her initial ruling is wrong. In the ordinary case, the conclusion should be quite the opposite. It is true that a trial court's contemporaneous assessment of a juror's demeanor, and its bearing on how to interpret or understand the juror's responses, are entitled to substantial deference; but a trial court ruling is likewise entitled to deference when made after a careful review of a formal transcript or recording. If a trial judge chooses to reflect and deliberate further, that is not to be faulted; it is to be commended.

Death penalty

L Ed Digest: Habeas Corpus § 121.5

6. The provisions of the Antiterrorism and Effective Death Penalty Act of 1996 apply with full force even when reviewing a conviction and sentence imposing the death penalty.

RESEARCH REFERENCES

U.S.C.S., Constitution, Amendment 6; 28 U.S.C.S. § 2254(d)(1)

28 Moore's Federal Practice § 671.08 (Matthew Bender 3d ed.)

L Ed Digest, Habeas Corpus § 34

L Ed Index, Capital Offenses and Punishment

Annotations:

Propriety of excluding prospective juror in capital case on basis of juror's views concerning capital punishment—Supreme Court cases. 167 L. Ed. 2d 1223.

Supreme Court's construction and application of Antiterrorism and Effective Death Penalty Act of 1996 (AEDPA) provision (28 U.S.C.S. § 2254(d)), restricting grant of federal habeas corpus relief to state prisoner on claim already adjudicated by state court on merits. 154 L. Ed. 2d 1147.

Effect of accused's federal constitutional rights on scope of voir dire examination of prospective jurors—Supreme Court cases. 114 L. Ed. 2d 763.

Supreme Court's views on constitutionality of death penalty and procedures under which it is impose or carried out. 90 L. Ed. 2d 1001.

SYLLABUS BY REPORTER OF DECISIONS

For text of added syllabus for this case see p 814D, infra.

OPINION OF THE COURT

[577 U.S. 74]

Per Curiam.

A death sentence imposed by a Kentucky trial court and affirmed by the Kentucky Supreme Court has been overturned, on habeas corpus review, by the Court of Appeals for the Sixth Circuit. During the jury selection process, the state trial court excused a juror after concluding he could not give sufficient assurance of neutrality or impartiality in considering whether the death penalty should be imposed. The Court of Appeals, despite the substantial deference it must accord to state-court rulings in federal habeas proceedings, determined that excusing the juror in the circumstances of this case violated the Sixth and Fourteenth Amendments. That ruling contravenes controlling precedents from this Court, and it is now necessary to reverse the Court of Appeals by this summary disposition.

Warden Randy White is the petitioner here, and the convicted prisoner, Roger Wheeler, is the respondent.

In October 1997, police in Louisville, Kentucky, found the bodies of Nigel Malone and Nairobi Warfield in the apartment the couple shared. Malone had been stabbed nine times. Warfield had been strangled to death and a pair of scissors stuck out from her neck. She was pregnant. DNA taken from blood at the crime scene matched respondent's. Respondent was charged with the murders.

During *voir dire,* Juror 638 gave equivocal and inconsistent answers when questioned about whether he could consider voting to impose the death penalty. In response to the judge's questions about his personal beliefs on the death penalty, Juror 638 said, "I'm not sure that I have formed an opinion one way or the other. I believe there are arguments on both sides of the—of it." App. to Pet. for Cert. 126a. When asked by the prosecution about his ability to consider

[577 U.S. 75]

all available penalties, Juror 638 noted he had "never been confronted with that situation in a, in a real-life sense of having to make that kind of determination." *Id.*, at 131a. "So it's difficult for me," he explained, "to judge how I would I guess act, uh."

Ibid. The prosecution sought to clarify Juror 638's answer, asking if the juror meant he was "not absolutely certain whether [he] could realistically consider" the death penalty. *Id.*, at 132a. Juror 638 replied, "I think that would be the most accurate way I could answer your question." *Ibid.* During defense counsel's examination, Juror 638 described himself as "a bit more contemplative on the issue of taking a life and, uh, whether or not we have the right to take that life." *Id.*, at 133a. Later, however, he expressed his belief that he could consider all the penalty options. *Id.*, at 134a.

The prosecution moved to strike Juror 638 for cause based on his inconsistent replies, as illustrated by his statement that he was not absolutely certain he could realistically consider the death penalty. The defense opposed the motion, arguing that Juror 638's answers indicated his ability to consider all the penalty options, despite having some reservations about the death penalty. The judge said that when she was done questioning Juror 638, she wrote in her notes that the juror " 'could consider [the] entire range' " of penalties. *Id.*, at 138a. She further stated that she did not "see him as problematic" at the end of her examination. *Ibid.* But she also noted that she did not "hear him say that he couldn't realistically consider the death penalty," and reserved ruling on the motion until she could review Juror 638's testimony. *Ibid.* The next day, after reviewing the relevant testimony, the judge struck Juror 638 for cause. When she announced her decision to excuse the juror, the trial judge stated, "And when I went back and reviewed [the juror's] entire testimony, [the prosecution] concluded with saying, 'Would it be accurate to say that you couldn't, couldn't consider the entire range?' And his response is—I think was, 'I think that

[577 U.S. 76]

would be pretty accurate.' So, I'm going to sustain that one, too." *Id.*, at 139a-140a.

The case proceeded to trial. Respondent was convicted of both murders and sentenced to death. The Kentucky Supreme Court affirmed the convictions and the sentence. *Wheeler* v. *Commonwealth*, 121 S.W.3d 173, 189 (2003). In considering respondent's challenges to the trial court's excusal of certain jurors for cause, the Kentucky Supreme Court held that the trial judge "appropriately struck for cause those jurors that could not impose the death penalty. . . . There was no error and the rights of the defendant to a fair trial by a fair and impartial jury . . . under both the federal and state constitutions were not violated." *Id.*, at 179.

After exhausting available state postconviction procedures, respondent sought a writ of habeas corpus under 28 U.S.C. § 2254 from the United States District Court for the Western District of Kentucky. He asserted, *inter alia*, that the Kentucky trial court erred in striking Juror 638 during *voir dire* on the ground that the juror could not give assurances that he could consider the death penalty as a sentencing option. The District Court dismissed the petition; but a divided panel of the Court of Appeals for the Sixth Circuit reversed, granting habeas relief as to respondent's sentence. *Wheeler* v. *Simpson*, 779 F.3d 366, 379 (2015). While acknowledging the deferential standard required on federal habeas review of a state conviction, the Court of Appeals held that allowing the exclusion of Juror 638 was an unreasonable appli-

cation of *Witherspoon* v. *Illinois*, 391 U.S. 510, 88 S. Ct. 1770, 20 L. Ed. 2d 776 (1968), *Wainwright* v. *Witt*, 469 U.S. 412, 105 S. Ct. 844, 83 L. Ed. 2d 841 (1985), and their progeny. 779 F.3d, at 372-374.

[1] Under the Antiterrorism and Effective Death Penalty Act of 1996 (AEDPA), habeas relief is authorized if the state court's decision "was contrary to, or involved an unreasonable application of, clearly established Federal law, as determined by the Supreme Court of the United States." 28 U.S.C. § 2254(d)(1). This Court, time and again, has instructed

[577 U.S. 77]

that AEDPA, by setting forth necessary predicates before state-court judgments may be set aside, "erects a formidable barrier to federal habeas relief for prisoners whose claims have been adjudicated in state court." *Burt* v. *Titlow*, 571 U.S. 12, 19, 134 S. Ct. 10, 187 L. Ed. 2d 348 (2013). Under § 2254(d)(1), " 'a state prisoner must show that the state court's ruling on the claim being presented in federal court was so lacking in justification that there was an error well understood and comprehended in existing law beyond any possibility for fair-minded disagreement.' " *White* v. *Woodall*, 572 U.S. 415, 419–420, 134 S. Ct. 1697, 188 L. Ed. 2d 698 (2014) (quoting *Harrington* v. *Richter*, 562 U.S. 86, 103, 131 S. Ct. 770, 178 L. Ed. 2d 624 (2011)).

The Court of Appeals was required to apply this deferential standard to the state court's analysis of respondent's juror exclusion claim. [2] In *Witherspoon*, this Court set forth the rule for juror disqualification in capital cases. *Witherspoon* recognized that the Sixth Amendment's guarantee of an impartial jury confers on capital defendants the right to a jury not "uncommonly willing to condemn a man to die." 391 U.S., at 521, 88 S. Ct. 1770, 20 L. Ed. 2d 776. But the Court with equal clarity has acknowledged the State's "strong interest in having jurors who are able to apply capital punishment within the framework state law prescribes." *Uttecht* v. *Brown*, 551 U.S. 1, 9, 127 S. Ct. 2218, 167 L. Ed. 2d 1014 (2007). To ensure the proper balance between these two interests, only "a juror who is substantially impaired in his or her ability to impose the death penalty under the state-law framework can be excused for cause." *Ibid.* As the Court explained in *Witt*, a juror may be excused for cause "where the trial judge is left with the definite impression that a prospective juror would be unable to faithfully and impartially apply the law." 469 U.S., at 425-426, 105 S. Ct. 844, 83 L. Ed. 2d 841.

[3] Reviewing courts owe deference to a trial court's ruling on whether to strike a particular juror "regardless of whether the trial court engages in explicit analysis regarding substantial impairment; even the granting of a motion to excuse for cause constitutes an implicit finding of bias." *Uttecht*, 551 U.S., at 7, 127 S. Ct. 2218, 167 L. Ed. 2d 1014. A trial court's "finding may be upheld

[577 U.S. 78]

even in the absence of clear statements from the juror that he or she is impaired . . . ." *Ibid.* And where, as here, the federal courts review a state-court ruling under the constraints imposed by AEDPA, the federal court must accord an additional and "independent, high standard" of deference. *Id.*, at 10, 127 S. Ct. 2218, 167 L. Ed. 2d 1014. As a result, federal habeas review of a *Witherspoon-Witt* claim—much like federal habeas review of an ineffective-assistance-of-counsel claim—must be " ' "doubly deferential." ' " *Burt*, *supra*, at 15, 134 S. Ct. 10, 187 L. Ed. 2d 348 (quoting *Cullen* v. *Pinholster*, 563 U.S. 170, 190, 131 S. Ct. 1388, 179 L. Ed. 2d 557 (2011)).

The Court of Appeals held that the Kentucky Supreme Court unreasonably applied *Witherspoon*, *Witt*, and their progeny when it determined that removing Juror 638 for cause was constitutional. 779 F.3d, at 372-374. The Court of Appeals determined Juror 638 "understood the decisions he would face and engaged with them in a thoughtful, honest, and conscientious manner." *Id.*, at 373. In the Court of Appeals' estimation, the trial judge concluded the juror was not qualified only by "misapprehending a single question and answer exchange" between Juror 638 and the prosecution, *id.*, at 374, the exchange in which Juror 638 stated he was not absolutely certain he could realistically consider the death penalty, *id.*, at 372. According to the Court of Appeals, Juror 638 "agreed *he did not know* to an absolute certainty whether he could realistically consider the death penalty, but the court proceeded as if *he knew he could not*." *Ibid*. The Court of Appeals further determined that if the trial judge, when reviewing Juror 638's examination, had "properly processed that exchange" between Juror 638 and the prosecution, Juror 638 would not have been excused. *Id.*, at 374.

Both the analysis and the conclusion in the decision under review were incorrect. While the Court of Appeals acknowledged that deference was required under AEDPA, it failed to ask the critical question: Was the Kentucky Supreme Court's decision to affirm the excusal of Juror 638 for

[577 U.S. 79]

cause " 'so lacking in justification that there was an error well understood and comprehended in existing law beyond any possibility for fairminded disagreement' "? *Woodall, supra,* at 420, 134 S. Ct. 1697, 188 L. Ed. 2d 698 (quoting *Harrington, supra,* at 103, 131 S. Ct. 770, 178 L. Ed. 2d 624.

The Court of Appeals did not properly apply the deference it was required to accord the state-court ruling. A fairminded jurist could readily conclude that the trial judge's exchange with Juror 638 reflected a "diligent and thoughtful *voir dire*"; that she considered with care the juror's testimony; and that she was fair in the exercise of her "broad discretion" in determining whether the juror was qualified to serve in this capital case. *Uttecht,* 551 U.S., at 20, 127 S. Ct. 2218, 167 L. Ed. 2d 1014. Juror 638's answers during *voir dire* were at least ambiguous as to whether he would be able to give appropriate consideration to imposing the death penalty. [4] And as this Court made clear in *Uttecht,* "when there is ambiguity in the prospective juror's statements," the trial court is " 'entitled to resolve it in favor of the State.' " *Id.,* at 7, 127 S. Ct. 2218, 167 L. Ed. 2d 1014 (quoting *Witt,* 469 U.S., at 434, 105 S. Ct. 844, 83 L. Ed. 2d 841).

The Court of Appeals erred in its assessment of the trial judge's reformulation of an important part of Juror 638's questioning. 779 F.3d, at 372. When excusing the juror the day after the *voir dire*, the trial judge said that the prosecution had asked whether the juror "couldn't consider the entire range" of penalties. App. to Pet. for Cert. 139a. The prosecution in fact asked if the juror was "not abso-

lutely certain whether [he] could realistically consider" the entire range of penalties. *Id.,* at 132a. The juror's confirmation that he was "not absolutely certain whether [he] could realistically consider" the death penalty, *ibid.,* was a reasonable basis for the trial judge to conclude that the juror was unable to give that penalty fair consideration. The trial judge's decision to excuse Juror 638 did not violate clearly established federal law by concluding that Juror 638 was not qualified to serve as a member of this capital jury. See *Witt, supra,* at 424-426, 105 S. Ct. 844, 83 L. Ed. 2d 841. And similarly, the Kentucky Supreme Court's

[577 U.S. 80]

ruling that there was no error is not beyond any possibility for fairminded disagreement.

The Court of Appeals noted that the deference toward trial courts recognized in *Uttecht* "was largely premised on the trial judge's ability to 'observe the demeanor of' " the juror. 779 F.3d, at 373 (quoting 551 U.S., at 17, 127 S. Ct. 2218, 167 L. Ed. 2d 1014). It concluded that deference to the trial court here supported habeas relief, because the trial judge's "initial assessment of [the juror's] answers and demeanor" did not lead her to immediately strike Juror 638 for cause. 779 F.3d, at 373-374.

The Court of Appeals' conclusion conflicts with the meaning and holding of *Uttecht* and with a commonsense understanding of the jury selection process. [5] Nothing in *Uttecht* limits the trial court to evaluating demeanor alone and not the substance of a juror's response. And the implicit suggestion that a trial judge is entitled to less deference for having deliberated after her initial ruling is wrong. In the ordinary case the conclusion should be quite the opposite. It is true that a trial court's contemporaneous assessment of a juror's demeanor and its bearing on how to interpret or understand the juror's responses are entitled to substantial deference; but a trial court ruling is likewise entitled to deference when made after a careful review of a formal transcript or recording. If the trial judge chooses to reflect and deliberate further, as this trial judge did after the proceedings recessed for the day, that is not to be faulted; it is to be commended.

This is not a case where "the record discloses no basis for a finding of substantial impairment." *Uttecht, supra*, at 20, 127 S. Ct. 2218, 167 L. Ed. 2d 1014. The two federal judges in the majority below might have reached a different conclusion had they been presiding over this *voir dire*. But simple disagreement does not overcome the two layers of deference owed by a federal habeas court in this context.

[577 U.S. 81]

* * *

The Kentucky Supreme Court was not unreasonable in its application of clearly established federal law when it concluded that the exclusion of Ju-ror 638 did not violate the Sixth Amendment. Given this conclusion, there is no need to consider petitioner's further contention that, if there were an error by the trial court in excluding the juror, it should be subject to harmless-error analysis. And this Court does not review the other rulings of the Court of Appeals that are not addressed in this opinion.

As a final matter, this Court again advises the Court of Appeals that **[6]** the provisions of AEDPA apply with full force even when reviewing a conviction and sentence imposing the death penalty. See, *e.g., Parker* v. *Matthews*, 567 U.S. 37, 132 S. Ct. 2148, 183 L. Ed. 2d 32 (2012) (*per curiam*); *Bobby* v. *Dixon*, 565 U.S. 23, 132 S. Ct. 26, 181 L. Ed. 2d 328 (2011) (*per curiam*); *Bobby* v. *Mitts*, 563 U.S. 395, 131 S. Ct. 1762, 179 L. Ed. 2d 819 (2011) (*per curiam*); *Bobby* v. *Van Hook*, 558 U.S. 4, 130 S. Ct. 13, 175 L. Ed. 2d 255 (2009) (*per curiam*).

The petition for certiorari and respondent's motion to proceed *in forma pauperis* are granted. The judgment of the Court of Appeals for the Sixth Circuit is reversed, and the case is remanded for further proceedings consistent with this opinion.

It is so ordered.

MEMORANDUM CASES

No. 15-6134. Antonio Maldonado, Petitioner v. United States.

577 U.S. 982, 136 S. Ct. 510, 193 L. Ed. 2d 392, 2015 U.S. LEXIS 7284.

November 16, 2015. Motion of petitioner for leave to proceed in forma pauperis and petition for writ of certiorari granted. Judgment vacated, and case remanded to the United States Court of Appeals for the Fifth Circuit for further consideration in light of Johnson v. United States, 576 U.S. 591, 135 S. Ct. 2551, 192 L. Ed. 2d 569 (2015).

Same case below, 608 Fed. Appx. 244.

No. 15-6087. Steven Hairl Wilhelm, Petitioner v. Raythel Fisher, Jr., Warden.

577 U.S. 983, 136 S. Ct. 508, 193 L. Ed. 2d 392, 2015 U.S. LEXIS 7226.

November 16, 2015. Motion of petitioner for leave to proceed in forma pauperis denied, and petition for writ of certiorari to the United States Court of Appeals for the Ninth Circuit dismissed. See Rule 39.8.

No. 15-6122. Echo W. Dixon, Petitioner v. United States; and Echo Westley Dixon, Petitioner v. United States, et al.

577 U.S. 983, 136 S. Ct. 509, 193 L. Ed. 2d 392, 2015 U.S. LEXIS 7212.

November 16, 2015. Motion of petitioner for leave to proceed in forma pau-

peris denied, and petition for writ of certiorari to the United States Court of Appeals for the Second Circuit dismissed. See Rule 39.8.

No. 15-6127. Van Lee Brewer, Petitioner v. William Stephens, Director, Texas Department of Criminal Justice, Correctional Institutions Division.

577 U.S. 983, 136 S. Ct. 510, 193 L. Ed. 2d 392, 2015 U.S. LEXIS 7348.

November 16, 2015. Motion of petitioner for leave to proceed in forma pauperis denied, and petition for writ of certiorari to the United States Court of Appeals for the Fifth Circuit dismissed. See Rule 39.8. As petitioner has repeatedly abused this Court's process, the Clerk is directed not to accept any further petitions in noncriminal matters from petitioner unless the docketing fee required by Rule 38(a) is paid and petition submitted in compliance with Rule 33.1. See Martin v. District of Columbia Court of Appeals, 506 U.S. 1, 113 S. Ct. 397, 121 L. Ed. 2d 305 (1992) (per curiam).

Same case below, 605 Fed. Appx. 417.

No. 15-6205. Stephen W. Carlson, Petitioner v. Mark Dayton, Governor of Minnesota, et al.

577 U.S. 983, 136 S. Ct. 512, 193 L. Ed. 2d 392, 2015 U.S. LEXIS 7219.

November 16, 2015. Motion of petitioner for leave to proceed in forma pauperis denied, and petition for writ of certiorari to the Supreme Court of Minnesota dismissed. See Rule 39.8.

No. 15A370 (15-6130). Ash Israni, Petitioner v. Crystal Lake 960 Assoc., Inc.

577 U.S. 983, 136 S. Ct. 524, 193 L. Ed. 2d 393, 2015 U.S. LEXIS 7172.

November 16, 2015. Application for stay, addressed to Justice Alito and referred to the Court, denied.

Same case below, 171 So. 3d 117.

No. 15M52. Elena Sturdza, Petitioner v. United Arab Emirates, et al.

577 U.S. 983, 136 S. Ct. 524, 193 L. Ed. 2d 393, 2015 U.S. LEXIS 7341.

November 16, 2015. Motion to direct the Clerk to file a petition for writ of certiorari out of time denied.

Same case below, 587 Fed. Appx. 660.

No. 14-9973. Justin Bergo, Petitioner v. Court of Appeal of California, Third Appellate District, et al.

577 U.S. 983, 136 S. Ct. 525, 193 L. Ed. 2d 393, 2015 U.S. LEXIS 7321.

November 16, 2015. Motion of petitioner for reconsideration of order denying leave to proceed in forma pauperis denied.

No. 15-5149. Allen Maki, Petitioner v. Beverly Anderson, et al.

577 U.S. 983, 136 S. Ct. 525, 193 L. Ed. 2d 393, 2015 U.S. LEXIS 7322.

November 16, 2015. Motion of petitioner for reconsideration of order denying leave to proceed in forma pauperis granted. The order entered October 5, 2015, vacated.

No. 15-5284. Edward J. Mierzwa, Petitioner v. Wal-Mart, Inc., et al.

577 U.S. 984, 136 S. Ct. 525, 193 L. Ed. 2d 393, 2015 U.S. LEXIS 7224.

November 16, 2015. Motion of petitioner for reconsideration of order denying leave to proceed in forma pauperis denied.

No. 15-5648. Landry Dixon, Petitioner v. 24th District Court of Louisiana, et al.

577 U.S. 984, 136 S. Ct. 525, 193 L. Ed. 2d 393, 2015 U.S. LEXIS 7347.

November 16, 2015. Motion of petitioner for leave to proceed in forma pauperis denied. Petitioner is allowed until December 7, 2015, within which to pay the docketing fees required by Rule 38(a) and to submit petition in compliance with Rule 33.1 of the Rules of this Court.

Same case below, 591 Fed. Appx. 281.

No. 15-6060. John W. Wood, Jr., Petitioner v. Florida Atlantic University Board of Trustees.

577 U.S. 984, 136 S. Ct. 525, 193 L. Ed. 2d 393, 2015 U.S. LEXIS 7278.

November 16, 2015. Motion of petitioner for leave to proceed in forma pauperis denied. Petitioner is allowed until December 7, 2015, within which to pay the docketing fee required by Rule 38(a) and to submit a petition in compliance with Rule 33.1 of the Rules of this Court.

Same case below, 162 So. 3d 1028.

———

No. 15-6068. Amna Salahuddin, Petitioner v. Zoning Hearing Board of West Chester, et al.

577 U.S. 984, 136 S. Ct. 525, 193 L. Ed. 2d 394, 2015 U.S. LEXIS 7346, reh den 577 U.S. 1184, 136 S. Ct. 1250, 194 L. Ed. 2d 248, 2016 U.S. LEXIS 1059.

November 16, 2015. Motion of petitioner for leave to proceed in forma pauperis denied. Petitioner is allowed until December 7, 2015, within which to pay the docketing fee required by Rule 38(a) and to submit a petition in compliance with Rule 33.1 of the Rules of this Court.

Same case below, 103 A.3d 888.

———

No. 15-6082. Jose J. Hernandez, Petitioner v. Dignity Health.

577 U.S. 984, 136 S. Ct. 526, 193 L. Ed. 2d 394, 2015 U.S. LEXIS 7186.

November 16, 2015. Motion of petitioner for leave to proceed in forma pauperis denied. Petitioner is allowed until December 7, 2015, within which to pay the docketing fee required by Rule 38(a) and to submit a petition in compliance with Rule 33.1 of the Rules of this Court.

———

No. 15-6181. Louis T. Faison, Sr., Petitioner v. United States.

577 U.S. 984, 136 S. Ct. 526, 193 L. Ed. 2d 394, 2015 U.S. LEXIS 7184.

November 16, 2015. Motion of petitioner for leave to proceed in forma pauperis denied. Petitioner is allowed until December 7, 2015, within which to pay the docketing fee required by Rule 38(a) and

to submit a petition in compliance with Rule 33.1 of the Rules of this Court.

Same case below, 547 Fed. Appx. 88.

———

No. 15-6211. Joseph White, Petitioner v. Detroit East Community Mental Health, et al.

577 U.S. 984, 136 S. Ct. 526, 193 L. Ed. 2d 394, 2015 U.S. LEXIS 7345, reh den 577 U.S. 1209, 136 S. Ct. 1403, 194 L. Ed. 2d 383, 2016 U.S. LEXIS 1635.

November 16, 2015. Motion of petitioner for leave to proceed in forma pauperis denied. Petitioner is allowed until December 7, 2015, within which to pay the docketing fee required by Rule 38(a) and to submit a petition in compliance with Rule 33.1 of the Rules of this Court.

———

No. 15-6593. George Hoey Morris, Petitioner v. United States.

577 U.S. 984, 136 S. Ct. 526, 193 L. Ed. 2d 394, 2015 U.S. LEXIS 7289.

November 16, 2015. Motion of petitioner for leave to proceed in forma pauperis denied. Petitioner is allowed until December 7, 2015, within which to pay the docketing fee required by Rule 38(a) and to submit a petition in compliance with Rule 33.1 of the Rules of this Court.

———

No. 14-10029. Diane King, Petitioner v. Department of Veterans Affairs.

577 U.S. 984, 136 S. Ct. 526, 193 L. Ed. 2d 394, 2015 U.S. LEXIS 7290.

November 16, 2015. Petition for writ of certiorari to the United States Court of Appeals for the Federal Circuit denied.

Same case below, 601 Fed. Appx. 956.

Same case below, 600 Fed. Appx. 146.

No. 14-10083. Erma L. Glasgow, Petitioner v. Oregon Department of Revenue.

577 U.S. 984, 136 S. Ct. 500, 193 L. Ed. 2d 395, 2015 U.S. LEXIS 7316.

November 16, 2015. Petition for writ of certiorari to the Supreme Court of Oregon denied.

Same case below, 356 Or. 511, 340 P.3d 653.

No. 14-10145. Ricardo Bonilla, Petitioner v. United States.

577 U.S. 984, 136 S. Ct. 500, 193 L. Ed. 2d 395, 2015 U.S. LEXIS 7304.

November 16, 2015. Petition for writ of certiorari to the United States Court of Appeals for the Ninth Circuit denied.

Same case below, 602 Fed. Appx. 667.

No. 14-10150. Gordon Lamar Nelson, Petitioner v. P. D. Brazelton, Warden.

577 U.S. 984, 136 S. Ct. 500, 193 L. Ed. 2d 395, 2015 U.S. LEXIS 7336.

November 16, 2015. Petition for writ of certiorari to the United States Court of Appeals for the Ninth Circuit denied.

No. 14-10178. Shelia Y. Cruthirds, Petitioner v. Karen Miller, et al.

577 U.S. 985, 136 S. Ct. 500, 193 L. Ed. 2d 395, 2015 U.S. LEXIS 7171.

November 16, 2015. Petition for writ of certiorari to the United States Court of Appeals for the Fourth Circuit denied.

No. 14-10189. Dontez Shelton Flowers, Petitioner v. United States.

577 U.S. 985, 136 S. Ct. 500, 193 L. Ed. 2d 395, 2015 U.S. LEXIS 7180.

November 16, 2015. Petition for writ of certiorari to the United States Court of Appeals for the Sixth Circuit denied.

No. 15-11. Benny Garay, Petitioner v. New York.

577 U.S. 985, 136 S. Ct. 501, 193 L. Ed. 2d 395, 2015 U.S. LEXIS 7306.

November 16, 2015. Petition for writ of certiorari to the Court of Appeals of New York denied.

Same case below, 25 N.Y.3d 62, 7 N.Y.S.3d 254, 30 N.E.3d 145.

No. 15-59. Ronald Marquet Cheadle, Petitioner v. United States.

577 U.S. 985, 136 S. Ct. 501, 193 L. Ed. 2d 395, 2015 U.S. LEXIS 7269.

November 16, 2015. Petition for writ of certiorari to the District of Columbia Court of Appeals denied.

Same case below, 109 A.3d 594.

No. 15-175. Amerijet International, Inc., Petitioner v. International Brotherhood of Teamsters.

577 U.S. 985, 136 S. Ct. 502, 193 L. Ed. 2d 395, 2015 U.S. LEXIS 7237.

November 16, 2015. Petition for writ of certiorari to the United States Court of Appeals for the Eleventh Circuit denied.

Same case below, 604 Fed. Appx. 841.

Same case below, 779 F.3d 1360.

No. 15-187. Louis Castro Perez, Petitioner v. William Stephens, Director, Texas Department of Criminal Justice, Correctional Institutions Division.

577 U.S. 985, 136 S. Ct. 502, 193 L. Ed. 2d 396, 2015 U.S. LEXIS 7267.

November 16, 2015. Petition for writ of certiorari to the United States Court of Appeals for the Fifth Circuit denied.

Same case below, 784 F.3d 276.

No. 15-227. Yamaha Motor Corporation, U.S.A., et al., Petitioners v. Jacklyn McMahon.

577 U.S. 985, 136 S. Ct. 502, 193 L. Ed. 2d 396, 2015 U.S. LEXIS 7335.

November 16, 2015. Petition for writ of certiorari to the Supreme Court of Alabama denied.

Same case below, 183 So. 3d 145.

No. 15-282. Tony E. Mathis, Petitioner v. City of Morrow, Georgia, et al.

577 U.S. 985, 136 S. Ct. 502, 193 L. Ed. 2d 396, 2015 U.S. LEXIS 7211.

November 16, 2015. Petition for writ of certiorari to the United States Court of Appeals for the Eleventh Circuit denied.

Same case below, 601 Fed. Appx. 805.

No. 15-288. Chunghwa Picture Tubes, Ltd., et al., Petitioners v. Eidos Display, LLC, et al.

577 U.S. 985, 136 S. Ct. 502, 193 L. Ed. 2d 396, 2015 U.S. LEXIS 7251.

November 16, 2015. Petition for writ of certiorari to the United States Court of Appeals for the Federal Circuit denied.

No. 15-291. Arthrex, Inc., Petitioner v. KFx Medical Corporation.

577 U.S. 985, 136 S. Ct. 503, 193 L. Ed. 2d 396, 2015 U.S. LEXIS 7261.

November 16, 2015. Petition for writ of certiorari to the United States Court of Appeals for the Federal Circuit denied.

Same case below, 589 Fed. Appx. 538.

No. 15-294. Brandon Raub, Petitioner v. Michael Campbell.

577 U.S. 985, 136 S. Ct. 503, 193 L. Ed. 2d 396, 2015 U.S. LEXIS 7250.

November 16, 2015. Petition for writ of certiorari to the United States Court of Appeals for the Fourth Circuit denied.

Same case below, 785 F.3d 876.

No. 15-298. OMG, L.P., et al., Petitioners v. Heritage Auctions, Inc.

577 U.S. 985, 136 S. Ct. 503, 193 L. Ed. 2d 396, 2015 U.S. LEXIS 7255.

November 16, 2015. Petition for writ of certiorari to the United States Court of Appeals for the Fifth Circuit denied.

Same case below, 612 Fed. Appx. 207.

No. 15-300. David J. Ellrich, et al., Petitioners v. Molly A. Hays.

577 U.S. 985, 136 S. Ct. 503, 193 L. Ed. 2d 396, 2015 U.S. LEXIS 7235.

November 16, 2015. Petition for writ of certiorari to the Supreme Judicial Court of Massachusetts denied.

Same case below, 471 Mass. 592, 31 N.E.3d 1064.

No. 15-303. Christopher Ruben Zavala, Petitioner v. Texas, et al.

577 U.S. 986, 136 S. Ct. 503, 193 L. Ed. 2d 397, 2015 U.S. LEXIS 7279.

November 16, 2015. Petition for writ of certiorari to the United States Court of Appeals for the Fifth Circuit denied.

No. 15-311. Michael Houston and Steve Houston, Petitioners v. Vernetta Queen, et al.

577 U.S. 986, 136 S. Ct. 503, 193 L. Ed. 2d 397, 2015 U.S. LEXIS 7199, reh den 577 U.S. 1095, 136 S. Ct. 882, 193 L. Ed. 2d 774, 2016 U.S. LEXIS 508.

November 16, 2015. Petition for writ of certiorari to the United States Court of Appeals for the Fifth Circuit denied.

Same case below, 606 Fed. Appx. 725.

No. 15-318. Micheline Baptiste, Petitioner v. C & F Properties, LLC.

577 U.S. 986, 136 S. Ct. 505, 193 L. Ed. 2d 397, 2015 U.S. LEXIS 7263.

November 16, 2015. Petition for writ of certiorari to the Supreme Court of Florida Circuit denied.

Same case below, 171 So. 3d 113.

No. 15-319. UnitedHealth Group, Inc., et al., Petitioners v. Jonathan Denbo, et al.

577 U.S. 986, 136 S. Ct. 506, 193 L. Ed. 2d 397, 2015 U.S. LEXIS 7243.

November 16, 2015. Petition for writ of certiorari to the United States Court of Appeals for the Second Circuit denied.

Same case below, 798 F.3d 125.

No. 15-322. Lewis Wu, et ux., Petitioners v. Capital One, N.A., et al.

577 U.S. 986, 136 S. Ct. 506, 193 L. Ed. 2d 397, 2015 U.S. LEXIS 7204, reh den 577 U.S. 1095, 136 S. Ct. 883, 193 L. Ed. 2d 774, 2016 U.S. LEXIS 231.

November 16, 2015. Petition for writ of certiorari to the United States Court of Appeals for the Third Circuit denied.

Same case below, 617 Fed. Appx. 214.

No. 15-332. Joseph W. Lewicki, Jr., et al., Petitioners v. Washington County, Pennsylvania, et al.

577 U.S. 986, 136 S. Ct. 507, 193 L. Ed. 2d 397, 2015 U.S. LEXIS 7193, reh den 577 U.S. 1095, 136 S. Ct. 883, 193 L. Ed. 2d 774, 2016 U.S. LEXIS 541.

November 16, 2015. Petition for writ of certiorari to the Commonwealth Court of Pennsylvania denied.

Same case below, 105 A.3d 855.

No. 15-340. David Raoul, Petitioner v. City of New York Police Department, et al.

577 U.S. 986, 136 S. Ct. 507, 193 L. Ed. 2d 397, 2015 U.S. LEXIS 7221.

November 16, 2015. Petition for writ of certiorari to the United States Court of Appeals for the Second Circuit denied.

No. 15-342. Deanthony Thomas, et al., Petitioners v. U.S. Bank N.A., et al.

577 U.S. 986, 136 S. Ct. 507, 193 L. Ed. 2d 397, 2015 U.S. LEXIS 7248.

November 16, 2015. Petition for writ of certiorari to the United States Court of Appeals for the Eighth Circuit denied.

Same case below, 789 F.3d 900.

Same case below, 174 So. 3d 1001.

No. 15-343. James G. Wong, et al., Petitioners v. Wells Fargo Bank, N.A., et al.

577 U.S. 986, 136 S. Ct. 507, 193 L. Ed. 2d 398, 2015 U.S. LEXIS 7329.

November 16, 2015. Petition for writ of certiorari to the United States Court of Appeals for the Eighth Circuit denied.

Same case below, 789 F.3d 889.

No. 15-368. Dirk Beukes, et ux., Petitioners v. GMAC Mortgage, LLC, as Successor in Interest to Homecomings Financial, LLC, et al.

577 U.S. 986, 136 S. Ct. 513, 193 L. Ed. 2d 398, 2015 U.S. LEXIS 7206.

November 16, 2015. Petition for writ of certiorari to the United States Court of Appeals for the Eighth Circuit denied.

Same case below, 786 F.3d 649.

No. 15-393. Bridget M. Long, Petitioner v. Libertywood Nursing Center, et al.

577 U.S. 986, 136 S. Ct. 513, 193 L. Ed. 2d 398, 2015 U.S. LEXIS 7178, reh den 577 U.S. 1095, 136 S. Ct. 883, 193 L. Ed. 2d 775, 2016 U.S. LEXIS 317.

November 16, 2015. Petition for writ of certiorari to the United States Court of Appeals for the Fourth Circuit denied.

Same case below, 603 Fed. Appx. 224.

No. 15-417. Dennis J. Plews, et al., Petitioners v. Jeffrey Luhrsen, et al.

577 U.S. 986, 136 S. Ct. 514, 193 L. Ed. 2d 398, 2015 U.S. LEXIS 7258.

November 16, 2015. Petition for writ of certiorari to the District Court of Appeal of Florida, Second District, denied.

No. 15-427. William Wayne Lee, Jr., Petitioner v. Burl Cain, Warden.

577 U.S. 986, 136 S. Ct. 515, 193 L. Ed. 2d 398, 2015 U.S. LEXIS 7174.

November 16, 2015. Petition for writ of certiorari to the United States Court of Appeals for the Fifth Circuit denied.

No. 15-434. Kenneth B. Davenport, Petitioner v. Pennsylvania.

577 U.S. 987, 136 S. Ct. 516, 193 L. Ed. 2d 398, 2015 U.S. LEXIS 7282.

November 16, 2015. Petition for writ of certiorari to the Superior Court of Pennsylvania, Philadelphia Office, denied.

Same case below, 120 A.3d 1056.

No. 15-508. Sealed Appellant 2, et al., Petitioners v. BP Exploration & Production, Inc., et al.

577 U.S. 987, 136 S. Ct. 523, 193 L. Ed. 2d 398, 2015 U.S. LEXIS 7293.

November 16, 2015. Petition for writ of certiorari to the United States Court of Appeals for the Fifth Circuit denied.

Same case below, 584 Fed. Appx. 230.

No. 15-519. Aircraft Check Services Co., et al., Individually and on Behalf of All Others Similarly Situated, Petitioners v. Verizon Wireless, et al.

577 U.S. 987, 136 S. Ct. 524, 193 L. Ed. 2d 398, 2015 U.S. LEXIS 7218.

November 16, 2015. Petition for writ of certiorari to the United States Court of Appeals for the Seventh Circuit denied.

Same case below, 782 F.3d 867.

Same case below, 414 U.S. App. D.C. 212, 778 F.3d 166.

No. 15-5164. Antonio Almanza, Petitioner v. California.

577 U.S. 987, 136 S. Ct. 501, 193 L. Ed. 2d 399, 2015 U.S. LEXIS 7332.

November 16, 2015. Petition for writ of certiorari to the Court of Appeal of California, Sixth Appellate District, denied.

Same case below, 233 Cal. App. 4th 990, 183 Cal. Rptr. 3d 335.

No. 15-5171. Andreus O'Bryant, Petitioner v. United States.

577 U.S. 987, 136 S. Ct. 501, 193 L. Ed. 2d 399, 2015 U.S. LEXIS 7176.

November 16, 2015. Petition for writ of certiorari to the United States Court of Appeals for the Eighth Circuit denied.

Same case below, 782 F.3d 1006.

No. 15-5197. Claude E. Pickett, Petitioner v. Michael T. Gallagher, et al.

577 U.S. 987, 136 S. Ct. 501, 193 L. Ed. 2d 399, 2015 U.S. LEXIS 7249.

November 16, 2015. Petition for writ of certiorari to the Court of Appeals of Mississippi denied.

Same case below, 159 So. 3d 587.

No. 15-5443. Paul Deppenbrook, Petitioner v. Pension Benefit Guaranty Corporation.

577 U.S. 987, 136 S. Ct. 501, 193 L. Ed. 2d 399, 2015 U.S. LEXIS 7188.

November 16, 2015. Petition for writ of certiorari to the United States Court of Appeals for the District of Columbia Circuit denied.

No. 15-5610. Amy Liu, Petitioner v. Department of Industrial Relations.

577 U.S. 987, 136 S. Ct. 502, 193 L. Ed. 2d 399, 2015 U.S. LEXIS 7342.

November 16, 2015. Petition for writ of certiorari to the Court of Appeal of California, First Appellate District, Division Five, denied.

No. 15-5989. Coy Smith, Petitioner v. William Stephens, Director, Texas Department of Criminal Justice, Correctional Institutions Division.

577 U.S. 987, 136 S. Ct. 504, 193 L. Ed. 2d 399, 2015 U.S. LEXIS 7288.

November 16, 2015. Petition for writ of certiorari to the United States Court of Appeals for the Fifth Circuit denied.

No. 15-5998. Danny Kim, Petitioner v. W. L. Montgomery, Warden.

577 U.S. 987, 136 S. Ct. 504, 193 L. Ed. 2d 399, 2015 U.S. LEXIS 7236.

November 16, 2015. Petition for writ of certiorari to the United States Court of Appeals for the Ninth Circuit denied.

Same case below, 604 Fed. Appx. 619.

No. 15-6003. Eugenia Pinkard, Petitioner v. New York City Department of Education, et al.

577 U.S. 987, 136 S. Ct. 504, 193 L. Ed. 2d 399, 2015 U.S. LEXIS 7339.

November 16, 2015. Petition for writ of certiorari to the United States Court of Appeals for the Second Circuit denied.

No. 15-6004. Emerson Osborne, Petitioner v. Ron King, Superintendent, South Mississippi Correctional Institution.

577 U.S. 987, 136 S. Ct. 504, 193 L. Ed. 2d 400, 2015 U.S. LEXIS 7305.

November 16, 2015. Petition for writ of certiorari to the United States Court of Appeals for the Fifth Circuit denied.

Same case below, 617 Fed. Appx. 308.

No. 15-6012. Anthony Wimberly, Petitioner v. Jeffrey B. Julius, et al.

577 U.S. 987, 136 S. Ct. 504, 193 L. Ed. 2d 400, 2015 U.S. LEXIS 7215.

November 16, 2015. Petition for writ of certiorari to the United States Court of Appeals for the Seventh Circuit denied.

Same case below, 606 Fed. Appx. 309.

No. 15-6014. Dwight David Bell, Petitioner v. New Jersey, et al.

577 U.S. 988, 136 S. Ct. 504, 193 L. Ed. 2d 400, 2015 U.S. LEXIS 7220.

November 16, 2015. Petition for writ of certiorari to the United States Court of Appeals for the Third Circuit denied.

No. 15-6017. Juan R. Soto, Petitioner v. Stephen D'Ilio, Administrator, New Jersey State Prison, et al.

577 U.S. 988, 136 S. Ct. 527, 193 L. Ed. 2d 400, 2015 U.S. LEXIS 7201.

November 16, 2015. Petition for writ of certiorari to the United States Court of Appeals for the Third Circuit denied.

No. 15-6020. Philip Fields, Petitioner v. Bob Stone.

577 U.S. 988, 136 S. Ct. 505, 193 L. Ed. 2d 400, 2015 U.S. LEXIS 7239.

November 16, 2015. Petition for writ of certiorari to the Supreme Court of California denied.

No. 15-6026. John Ivy, Petitioner v. Richard Brown, Superintendent, Wabash Valley Correctional Facility.

577 U.S. 988, 136 S. Ct. 505, 193 L. Ed. 2d 400, 2015 U.S. LEXIS 7170, reh den 577 U.S. 1114, 136 S. Ct. 926, 193 L. Ed. 2d 811, 2016 U.S. LEXIS 764.

November 16, 2015. Petition for writ of certiorari to the United States Court of Appeals for the Seventh Circuit denied.

No. 15-6031. Charles Tyson, Petitioner v. Larry Cartledge, Warden, et al.

577 U.S. 988, 136 S. Ct. 505, 193 L. Ed. 2d 400, 2015 U.S. LEXIS 7173.

November 16, 2015. Petition for writ of certiorari to the Supreme Court of South Carolina denied.

No. 15-6038. Daniel W. Taylor, Petitioner v. Terry E. Barnard, et al.; and Daniel Webster Taylor, Petitioner v. Cathelene Robinson, Clerk, Superior Court of Georgia, Fulton County.

577 U.S. 988, 136 S. Ct. 505, 193 L. Ed. 2d 401, 2015 U.S. LEXIS 7203.

November 16, 2015. Petition for writ of certiorari to the Supreme Court of Georgia denied.

No. 15-6043. Keith Lamonte Hill, Petitioner v. Virginia.

577 U.S. 988, 136 S. Ct. 506, 193 L. Ed. 2d 401, 2015 U.S. LEXIS 7281.

November 16, 2015. Petition for writ of certiorari to the Supreme Court of Virginia denied.

No. 15-6049. Roy A. Smith, Petitioner v. Richard Brown.

577 U.S. 988, 136 S. Ct. 506, 193 L. Ed. 2d 401, 2015 U.S. LEXIS 7273.

November 16, 2015. Petition for writ of certiorari to the United States Court of Appeals for the Seventh Circuit denied.

Same case below, 764 F.3d 790.

No. 15-6051. David Leon Riley, Petitioner v. California.

577 U.S. 988, 136 S. Ct. 506, 193 L. Ed. 2d 401, 2015 U.S. LEXIS 7231.

November 16, 2015. Petition for writ of certiorari to the Court of Appeal of California, Fourth Appellate District, Division One, denied.

No. 15-6055. Houston Douglas, Petitioner v. Lester N. Wright, et al.

577 U.S. 988, 136 S. Ct. 506, 193 L. Ed. 2d 401, 2015 U.S. LEXIS 7181, reh den 577 U.S. 1185, 136 S. Ct. 1253, 194 L. Ed. 2d 251, 2016 U.S. LEXIS 1004.

November 16, 2015. Petition for writ of certiorari to the United States Court of Appeals for the Second Circuit denied.

No. 15-6059. Victor Brian Vega, Petitioner v. William Stephens, Director, Texas Department of Criminal Justice, Correctional Institutions Division.

577 U.S. 988, 136 S. Ct. 507, 193 L. Ed. 2d 401, 2015 U.S. LEXIS 7175.

November 16, 2015. Petition for writ of certiorari to the United States Court of Appeals for the Fifth Circuit denied.

No. 15-6071. Jeffrey Charles Burfeindt, Petitioner v. Nina Postupack, et al.

577 U.S. 988, 136 S. Ct. 507, 193 L. Ed. 2d 401, 2015 U.S. LEXIS 7285.

November 16, 2015. Petition for writ of certiorari to the United States Court of Appeals for the Second Circuit denied.

No. 15-6080. Johneil Watkins, Petitioner v. James Stern, et al.

577 U.S. 988, 136 S. Ct. 508, 193 L. Ed. 2d 401, 2015 U.S. LEXIS 7310.

November 16, 2015. Petition for writ of certiorari to the United States Court of Appeals for the Fifth Circuit denied.

Same case below, 615 Fed. Appx. 582.

No. 15-6084. Harry Jackson, Petitioner v. Pennsylvania.

577 U.S. 988, 136 S. Ct. 508, 193 L. Ed. 2d 402, 2015 U.S. LEXIS 7190.

November 16, 2015. Petition for writ of certiorari to the Superior Court of Pennsylvania, Philadelphia Office, denied.

Same case below, 121 A.3d 1123.

No. 15-6096. Carol Johnene Morris, Petitioner v. Court of Appeals of Texas, Eleventh District.

577 U.S. 988, 136 S. Ct. 508, 193 L. Ed. 2d 402, 2015 U.S. LEXIS 7207, reh den 578 U.S. 916, 136 S. Ct. 1537, 194 L. Ed. 2d 621, 2016 U.S. LEXIS 2343.

November 16, 2015. Petition for writ of certiorari to the Supreme Court of Texas denied.

No. 15-6102. Andre Deshawn Pickens, Petitioner v. California.

577 U.S. 989, 136 S. Ct. 508, 193 L. Ed. 2d 402, 2015 U.S. LEXIS 7271.

November 16, 2015. Petition for writ of certiorari to the Supreme Court of California denied.

No. 15-6105. Preston Lee Johnson, Jr., Petitioner v. United States.

577 U.S. 989, 136 S. Ct. 508, 193 L. Ed. 2d 402, 2015 U.S. LEXIS 7256, reh den 577 U.S. 1124, 136 S. Ct. 996, 194 L. Ed. 2d 14, 2016 U.S. LEXIS 887.

November 16, 2015. Petition for writ of certiorari to the United States Court of Appeals for the Eleventh Circuit denied.

No. 15-6106. Joshua Dewayne Moore, Petitioner v. Oklahoma.

577 U.S. 989, 136 S. Ct. 509, 193 L. Ed. 2d 402, 2015 U.S. LEXIS 7301.

November 16, 2015. Petition for writ of certiorari to the Court of Criminal Appeals of Oklahoma denied.

No. 15-6115. LaKeith L. McCoy, aka LaKeith LeRoy McCoy, Petitioner v. Toni Carel O'Neill, et al.

577 U.S. 989, 136 S. Ct. 509, 193 L. Ed. 2d 402, 2015 U.S. LEXIS 7334.

November 16, 2015. Petition for writ of certiorari to the United States Court of Appeals for the Ninth Circuit denied.

Same case below, 609 Fed. Appx. 450.

No. 15-6116. Thomas James Fox, Petitioner v. Minnesota.

577 U.S. 989, 136 S. Ct. 509, 193 L. Ed. 2d 402, 2015 U.S. LEXIS 7227.

November 16, 2015. Petition for writ of certiorari to the Supreme Court of Minnesota denied.

Same case below, 868 N.W.2d 206.

No. 15-6120. Robin Lynn Evans, Petitioner v. Elmer's Products, Inc., et al.

577 U.S. 989, 136 S. Ct. 509, 193 L. Ed. 2d 402, 2015 U.S. LEXIS 7314.

November 16, 2015. Petition for writ of certiorari to the United States Court of Appeals for the Fourth Circuit denied.

Same case below, 599 Fed. Appx. 515.

No. 15-6124. Abdul Aziz, Petitioner v. New Jersey.

577 U.S. 989, 136 S. Ct. 509, 193 L. Ed. 2d 403, 2015 U.S. LEXIS 7242.

November 16, 2015. Petition for writ of certiorari to the Superior Court of New Jersey, Appellate Division, denied.

No. 15-6126. Steven Alexander Breaux, Petitioner v. Harold W. Clarke, Director, Virginia Department of Corrections.

577 U.S. 989, 136 S. Ct. 510, 193 L. Ed. 2d 403, 2015 U.S. LEXIS 7343.

November 16, 2015. Petition for writ of certiorari to the United States Court of Appeals for the Fourth Circuit denied.

Same case below, 606 Fed. Appx. 106.

No. 15-6128. Willie Bolds, Petitioner v. California.

577 U.S. 989, 136 S. Ct. 510, 193 L. Ed. 2d 403, 2015 U.S. LEXIS 7262.

November 16, 2015. Petition for writ of certiorari to the Supreme Court of California denied.

No. 15-6130. Ash Israni, Petitioner v. Crystal Lake 960 Assoc., Inc.

577 U.S. 989, 136 S. Ct. 510, 193 L. Ed. 2d 403, 2015 U.S. LEXIS 7338, reh den 577 U.S. 1124, 136 S. Ct. 996, 194 L. Ed. 2d 14, 2016 U.S. LEXIS 909.

November 16, 2015. Petition for writ of certiorari to the District Court of Appeal of Florida, Fourth District, denied.

No. 15-6131. Troy Kenneth Scheffler, Petitioner v. Minnesota.

577 U.S. 989, 136 S. Ct. 510, 193 L. Ed. 2d 403, 2015 U.S. LEXIS 7277.

November 16, 2015. Petition for writ of certiorari to the Court of Appeals of Minnesota denied.

No. 15-6136. Curtis J. Cole, Petitioner v. United States.

577 U.S. 989, 136 S. Ct. 511, 193 L. Ed. 2d 403, 2015 U.S. LEXIS 7311.

November 16, 2015. Petition for writ of certiorari to the United States Court of Appeals for the Eighth Circuit denied.

Same case below, 592 Fed. Appx. 542.

No. 15-6153. Laquinces D. Davis, Petitioner v. Robert M. Stevenson, III, Warden.

577 U.S. 989, 136 S. Ct. 511, 193 L. Ed. 2d 403, 2015 U.S. LEXIS 7202.

November 16, 2015. Petition for writ of certiorari to the United States Court of Appeals for the Fourth Circuit denied.

Same case below, 593 Fed. Appx. 255.

No. 15-6158. David V. Alston, Petitioner v. Kean University, et al.

577 U.S. 989, 136 S. Ct. 511, 193 L. Ed. 2d 403, 2015 U.S. LEXIS 7229, reh den 577 U.S. 1114, 136 S. Ct. 926, 193 L. Ed. 2d 811, 2016 U.S. LEXIS 651.

November 16, 2015. Petition for writ of certiorari to the United States Court of Appeals for the Third Circuit denied.

Same case below, 604 Fed. Appx. 216.

No. 15-6174. Jesus Garcia, Petitioner v. Lawrence Mahally, Superintendent, State Correctional Institution at Dallas, et al.

577 U.S. 989, 136 S. Ct. 511, 193 L. Ed. 2d 404, 2015 U.S. LEXIS 7266.

November 16, 2015. Petition for writ of certiorari to the United States Court of Appeals for the Third Circuit denied.

No. 15-6203. Milovan Rajko Urosevic, Petitioner v. Department of Homeland Security, et al.

577 U.S. 990, 136 S. Ct. 511, 193 L. Ed. 2d 404, 2015 U.S. LEXIS 7270.

November 16, 2015. Petition for writ of certiorari to the United States Court of Appeals for the Ninth Circuit denied.

No. 15-6227. Terrell Taylor, Petitioner v. Karen Crowley, Superintendent, Orleans Correctional Facility.

577 U.S. 990, 136 S. Ct. 512, 193 L. Ed. 2d 404, 2015 U.S. LEXIS 7296, reh den 577 U.S. 1096, 136 S. Ct. 888, 193 L. Ed. 2d 780, 2016 U.S. LEXIS 346.

November 16, 2015. Petition for writ of certiorari to the United States Court of Appeals for the Second Circuit denied.

No. 15-6246. Maurice Bradley Christian, Petitioner v. 43rd District Court of Michigan, et al.

577 U.S. 990, 136 S. Ct. 512, 193 L. Ed. 2d 404, 2015 U.S. LEXIS 7228.

November 16, 2015. Petition for writ of certiorari to the United States Court of Appeals for the Sixth Circuit denied.

No. 15-6255. Kinoll McCormick, Petitioner v. Lawrence Mahally, Superintendent, State Correctional Institution at Dallas, et al.

577 U.S. 990, 136 S. Ct. 512, 193 L. Ed. 2d 404, 2015 U.S. LEXIS 7265, reh den 577 U.S. 1097, 136 S. Ct. 888, 193 L. Ed. 2d 780, 2016 U.S. LEXIS 16.

November 16, 2015. Petition for writ of certiorari to the United States Court of Appeals for the Third Circuit denied.

No. 15-6257. Johnny Lee Lucas, Petitioner v. Leroy Cartledge, Warden.

577 U.S. 990, 136 S. Ct. 512, 193 L. Ed. 2d 404, 2015 U.S. LEXIS 7195.

November 16, 2015. Petition for writ of certiorari to the Supreme Court of South Carolina denied.

No. 15-6259. Robert Lee Johnson, Petitioner v. Department of Labor, et al.

577 U.S. 990, 136 S. Ct. 512, 193 L. Ed. 2d 404, 2015 U.S. LEXIS 7280, reh den 577 U.S. 1097, 136 S. Ct. 888, 193 L. Ed. 2d 780, 2016 U.S. LEXIS 9.

November 16, 2015. Petition for writ of certiorari to the United States Court of Appeals for the District of Columbia Circuit denied.

Same case below, 589 Fed. Appx. 545.

No. 15-6271. Larry Flenoid, Petitioner v. Chris Koster, Attorney General of Missouri, et al.

577 U.S. 990, 136 S. Ct. 513, 193 L. Ed. 2d 404, 2015 U.S. LEXIS 7252.

November 16, 2015. Petition for writ of certiorari to the United States Court of Appeals for the Eighth Circuit denied.

No. 15-6274. Noel Adams, Petitioner v. Florida.

577 U.S. 990, 136 S. Ct. 513, 193 L. Ed. 2d 405, 2015 U.S. LEXIS 7309.

November 16, 2015. Petition for writ of certiorari to the Supreme Court of Florida denied.

Same case below, 173 So. 3d 960.

No. 15-6280. Jason O. Riley, Petitioner v. Leroy Cartledge, Warden.

577 U.S. 990, 136 S. Ct. 513, 193 L. Ed. 2d 405, 2015 U.S. LEXIS 7182.

November 16, 2015. Petition for writ of certiorari to the United States Court of Appeals for the Fourth Circuit denied.

Same case below, 607 Fed. Appx. 308.

No. 15-6332. Curtis Lee Watson, Petitioner v. United States.

577 U.S. 990, 136 S. Ct. 513, 193 L. Ed. 2d 405, 2015 U.S. LEXIS 7225.

November 16, 2015. Petition for writ of certiorari to the District of Columbia Court of Appeals denied.

No. 15-6343. Ernest Adkins, Petitioner v. John E. Wetzel, Secretary, Pennsylvania Department of Corrections, et al.

577 U.S. 990, 136 S. Ct. 514, 193 L. Ed. 2d 405, 2015 U.S. LEXIS 7230, reh den 577 U.S. 1125, 136 S. Ct. 997, 194 L. Ed. 2d 15, 2016 U.S. LEXIS 968.

November 16, 2015. Petition for writ of certiorari to the United States Court of Appeals for the Third Circuit denied.

No. 15-6377. Jeffrey Gray, Petitioner v. New Hampshire.

577 U.S. 990, 136 S. Ct. 514, 193 L. Ed. 2d 405, 2015 U.S. LEXIS 7328.

November 16, 2015. Petition for writ of certiorari to the Superior Court of New Hampshire, Rockingham County, denied.

No. 15-6387. Alan B. Fabian, Petitioner v. Jeffery E. Thomas, Warden.

577 U.S. 990, 136 S. Ct. 514, 193 L. Ed. 2d 405, 2015 U.S. LEXIS 7240.

November 16, 2015. Petition for writ of certiorari to the United States Court of Appeals for the Third Circuit denied.

Same case below, 588 Fed. Appx. 203.

No. 15-6392. Victor Eugene Mason, Petitioner v. United States.

577 U.S. 990, 136 S. Ct. 514, 193 L. Ed. 2d 405, 2015 U.S. LEXIS 7185.

November 16, 2015. Petition for writ of certiorari to the United States Court of Appeals for the Fourth Circuit denied.

Same case below, 774 F.3d 824.

No. 15-6400. Antoinette Renee Lampkin, Petitioner v. Ajilon Professional Staffing.

577 U.S. 991, 136 S. Ct. 514, 193 L. Ed. 2d 405, 2015 U.S. LEXIS 7213.

November 16, 2015. Petition for writ of certiorari to the United States Court of Appeals for the Fifth Circuit denied.

Same case below, 608 Fed. Appx. 285.

Same case below, 588 Fed. Appx. 100.

No. 15-6415. Miles J. Julison, Petitioner v. United States.

577 U.S. 991, 136 S. Ct. 515, 193 L. Ed. 2d 406, 2015 U.S. LEXIS 7246.

November 16, 2015. Petition for writ of certiorari to the United States Court of Appeals for the Ninth Circuit denied.

Same case below, 635 Fed. Appx. 342.

No. 15-6416. Eugene Talik, Petitioner v. Jeffery E. Thomas, Warden, et al.

577 U.S. 991, 136 S. Ct. 515, 193 L. Ed. 2d 406, 2015 U.S. LEXIS 7274.

November 16, 2015. Petition for writ of certiorari to the United States Court of Appeals for the Third Circuit denied.

Same case below, 621 Fed. Appx. 94.

No. 15-6422. Francesk Shkambi, Petitioner v. United States.

577 U.S. 991, 136 S. Ct. 515, 193 L. Ed. 2d 406, 2015 U.S. LEXIS 7303.

November 16, 2015. Petition for writ of certiorari to the United States Court of Appeals for the Fifth Circuit denied.

Same case below, 620 Fed. Appx. 260.

No. 15-6425. Raymond Zareck, Petitioner v. United States.

577 U.S. 991, 136 S. Ct. 515, 193 L. Ed. 2d 406, 2015 U.S. LEXIS 7247.

November 16, 2015. Petition for writ of certiorari to the United States Court of Appeals for the Third Circuit denied.

No. 15-6428. Raul Preciado-Ovalles, Petitioner v. United States.

577 U.S. 991, 136 S. Ct. 515, 193 L. Ed. 2d 406, 2015 U.S. LEXIS 7268.

November 16, 2015. Petition for writ of certiorari to the United States Court of Appeals for the Ninth Circuit denied.

Same case below, 615 Fed. Appx. 437.

No. 15-6433. Mark Green, Petitioner v. United States.

577 U.S. 991, 136 S. Ct. 516, 193 L. Ed. 2d 406, 2015 U.S. LEXIS 7320.

November 16, 2015. Petition for writ of certiorari to the United States Court of Appeals for the Third Circuit denied.

No. 15-6434. James Brown, Petitioner v. United States.

577 U.S. 991, 136 S. Ct. 516, 193 L. Ed. 2d 406, 2015 U.S. LEXIS 7200.

November 16, 2015. Petition for writ of certiorari to the United States Court of Appeals for the Second Circuit denied.

Same case below, 613 Fed. Appx. 58.

No. 15-6446. Charles Ray Deese, Petitioner v. United States.

577 U.S. 991, 136 S. Ct. 516, 193 L. Ed. 2d 406, 2015 U.S. LEXIS 7196.

November 16, 2015. Petition for writ of certiorari to the United States Court of Appeals for the Fourth Circuit denied.

Same case below, 591 Fed. Appx. 200.

No. 15-6458. James Jamal Williams, Petitioner v. Leroy Cartledge, Warden.

577 U.S. 991, 136 S. Ct. 516, 193 L. Ed. 2d 407, 2015 U.S. LEXIS 7217.

November 16, 2015. Petition for writ of certiorari to the United States Court of Appeals for the Fourth Circuit denied.

Same case below, 605 Fed. Appx. 196.

No. 15-6463. Pedro Vargas, Petitioner v. United States.

577 U.S. 991, 136 S. Ct. 516, 193 L. Ed. 2d 407, 2015 U.S. LEXIS 7287.

November 16, 2015. Petition for writ of certiorari to the United States Court of Appeals for the Ninth Circuit denied.

Same case below, 608 Fed. Appx. 462.

No. 15-6481. Darryl Lee, Petitioner v. United States.

577 U.S. 991, 136 S. Ct. 517, 193 L. Ed. 2d 407, 2015 U.S. LEXIS 7333.

November 16, 2015. Petition for writ of certiorari to the United States Court of Appeals for the Sixth Circuit denied.

Same case below, 793 F.3d 680.

No. 15-6487. Arthur Anthony Gonzales, Petitioner v. Utah.

577 U.S. 991, 136 S. Ct. 517, 193 L. Ed. 2d 407, 2015 U.S. LEXIS 7317, reh den

578 U.S. 966, 136 S. Ct. 1839, 194 L. Ed. 2d 842, 2016 U.S. LEXIS 2995.

November 16, 2015. Petition for writ of certiorari to the United States Court of Appeals for the Tenth Circuit denied.

Same case below, 592 Fed. Appx. 749.

No. 15-6489. Jack E. Howton, Petitioner v. United States.

577 U.S. 991, 136 S. Ct. 517, 193 L. Ed. 2d 407, 2015 U.S. LEXIS 7326.

November 16, 2015. Petition for writ of certiorari to the United States Court of Appeals for the Fifth Circuit denied.

No. 15-6502. Arron Adams, Petitioner v. United States.

577 U.S. 991, 136 S. Ct. 517, 193 L. Ed. 2d 407, 2015 U.S. LEXIS 7216.

November 16, 2015. Petition for writ of certiorari to the United States Court of Appeals for the Eleventh Circuit denied.

No. 15-6503. Terrance Joseph Kilburg, Petitioner v. United States.

577 U.S. 991, 136 S. Ct. 517, 193 L. Ed. 2d 407, 2015 U.S. LEXIS 7183.

November 16, 2015. Petition for writ of certiorari to the United States Court of Appeals for the Eighth Circuit denied.

Same case below, 615 Fed. Appx. 386.

No. 15-6507. Louis Askew, Petitioner v. United States.

577 U.S. 992, 136 S. Ct. 517, 193 L. Ed. 2d 407, 2015 U.S. LEXIS 7327.

November 16, 2015. Petition for writ of certiorari to the United States Court of Appeals for the Eleventh Circuit denied.

Same case below, 591 Fed. Appx. 910.

Same case below, 626 Fed. Appx. 785.

No. 15-6512. Clinton Lemont Pettway, Petitioner v. Marion Feather, Warden.

577 U.S. 992, 136 S. Ct. 518, 193 L. Ed. 2d 408, 2015 U.S. LEXIS 7286.

November 16, 2015. Petition for writ of certiorari to the United States Court of Appeals for the Ninth Circuit denied.

No. 15-6513. Joseph Pirosko, Petitioner v. United States.

577 U.S. 992, 136 S. Ct. 518, 193 L. Ed. 2d 408, 2015 U.S. LEXIS 7238.

November 16, 2015. Petition for writ of certiorari to the United States Court of Appeals for the Sixth Circuit denied.

Same case below, 787 F.3d 358.

No. 15-6519. Freddie Wilson, Petitioner v. United States.

577 U.S. 992, 136 S. Ct. 518, 193 L. Ed. 2d 408, 2015 U.S. LEXIS 7318.

November 16, 2015. Petition for writ of certiorari to the United States Court of Appeals for the Eleventh Circuit denied.

Same case below, 788 F.3d 1298.

No. 15-6522. Santana James, Petitioner v. United States.

577 U.S. 992, 136 S. Ct. 518, 193 L. Ed. 2d 408, 2015 U.S. LEXIS 7234.

November 16, 2015. Petition for writ of certiorari to the United States Court of Appeals for the Eleventh Circuit denied.

No. 15-6523. Kenneth Keatings, Petitioner v. United States.

577 U.S. 992, 136 S. Ct. 518, 193 L. Ed. 2d 408, 2015 U.S. LEXIS 7191.

November 16, 2015. Petition for writ of certiorari to the United States Court of Appeals for the Eighth Circuit denied.

Same case below, 787 F.3d 1197.

No. 15-6524. Ryan Masters, Petitioner v. United States.

577 U.S. 992, 136 S. Ct. 518, 193 L. Ed. 2d 408, 2015 U.S. LEXIS 7257.

November 16, 2015. Petition for writ of certiorari to the United States Court of Appeals for the Ninth Circuit denied.

Same case below, 613 Fed. Appx. 618.

No. 15-6525. Rudy Soto, Petitioner v. United States.

577 U.S. 992, 136 S. Ct. 519, 193 L. Ed. 2d 408, 2015 U.S. LEXIS 7209.

November 16, 2015. Petition for writ of certiorari to the United States Court of Appeals for the Ninth Circuit denied.

Same case below, 603 Fed. Appx. 634.

No. 15-6526. Raymond Camacho, aka Jesus Mendoza-Nunez, Petitioner v. United States.

577 U.S. 992, 136 S. Ct. 519, 193 L. Ed. 2d 408, 2015 U.S. LEXIS 7205.

November 16, 2015. Petition for writ of certiorari to the United States Court of Appeals for the Ninth Circuit denied.

Same case below, 612 Fed. Appx. 437.

Same case below, 618 Fed. Appx. 569.

No. 15-6527. Sabino Duque-Diaz, aka Jorge Ivan Medina, aka Saul Gomez-Duval, Petitioner v. United States.

577 U.S. 992, 136 S. Ct. 519, 193 L. Ed. 2d 409, 2015 U.S. LEXIS 7208.

November 16, 2015. Petition for writ of certiorari to the United States Court of Appeals for the Fourth Circuit denied.

Same case below, 606 Fed. Appx. 133.

No. 15-6528. Juan Pablo Pena-Aguilar, Petitioner v. United States.

577 U.S. 992, 136 S. Ct. 519, 193 L. Ed. 2d 409, 2015 U.S. LEXIS 7344.

November 16, 2015. Petition for writ of certiorari to the United States Court of Appeals for the Eighth Circuit denied.

No. 15-6531. Otto Rodriguez, Petitioner v. United States.

577 U.S. 992, 136 S. Ct. 519, 193 L. Ed. 2d 409, 2015 U.S. LEXIS 7272.

November 16, 2015. Petition for writ of certiorari to the United States Court of Appeals for the Eleventh Circuit denied.

Same case below, 609 Fed. Appx. 619.

No. 15-6537. Jean Cazy, Petitioner v. United States.

577 U.S. 992, 136 S. Ct. 519, 193 L. Ed. 2d 409, 2015 U.S. LEXIS 7337.

November 16, 2015. Petition for writ of certiorari to the United States Court of Appeals for the Eleventh Circuit denied.

No. 15-6543. Amanda May Richter, Petitioner v. United States.

577 U.S. 992, 136 S. Ct. 520, 193 L. Ed. 2d 409, 2015 U.S. LEXIS 7223.

November 16, 2015. Petition for writ of certiorari to the United States Court of Appeals for the Ninth Circuit denied.

Same case below, 609 Fed. Appx. 503.

No. 15-6545. John Simmons, Petitioner v. United States.

577 U.S. 992, 136 S. Ct. 520, 193 L. Ed. 2d 409, 2015 U.S. LEXIS 7254.

November 16, 2015. Petition for writ of certiorari to the United States Court of Appeals for the Second Circuit denied.

Same case below, 599 Fed. Appx. 404.

No. 15-6550. John Kaiser, Petitioner v. United States.

577 U.S. 993, 136 S. Ct. 520, 193 L. Ed. 2d 409, 2015 U.S. LEXIS 7291.

November 16, 2015. Petition for writ of certiorari to the United States Court of Appeals for the Second Circuit denied.

No. 15-6553. John That Luong, Thongsouk Theng Lattanaphon, and Minh Huynh, Petitioners v. United States.

577 U.S. 993, 136 S. Ct. 520, 193 L. Ed. 2d 409, 2015 U.S. LEXIS 7187.

November 16, 2015. Petition for writ of certiorari to the United States Court of Appeals for the Ninth Circuit denied.

Same case below, 610 Fed. Appx. 598.

———

No. 15-6554. Bryan Ross, Petitioner v. United States.

577 U.S. 993, 136 S. Ct. 520, 193 L. Ed. 2d 410, 2015 U.S. LEXIS 7292.

November 16, 2015. Petition for writ of certiorari to the United States Court of Appeals for the Sixth Circuit denied.

Same case below, 619 Fed. Appx. 453.

———

No. 15-6555. Delvin Deon Tinker, Petitioner v. United States.

577 U.S. 993, 136 S. Ct. 520, 193 L. Ed. 2d 410, 2015 U.S. LEXIS 7189.

November 16, 2015. Petition for writ of certiorari to the United States Court of Appeals for the Eleventh Circuit denied.

Same case below, 618 Fed. Appx. 635.

———

No. 15-6564. Kenneth J. Rowe, Petitioner v. United States.

577 U.S. 993, 136 S. Ct. 521, 193 L. Ed. 2d 410, 2015 U.S. LEXIS 7177, reh den 577 U.S. 1097, 136 S. Ct. 889, 193 L. Ed. 2d 781, 2016 U.S. LEXIS 11.

November 16, 2015. Petition for writ of certiorari to the United States Court of Appeals for the Sixth Circuit denied.

———

No. 15-6569. Joey Chibuko, aka Steven Buckley, aka Joseph Pride, aka Stephen Ray Buckley, aka Steven

Buckeley, aka Steven R. Buckley, Petitioner v. United States.

577 U.S. 993, 136 S. Ct. 521, 193 L. Ed. 2d 410, 2015 U.S. LEXIS 7297.

November 16, 2015. Petition for writ of certiorari to the United States Court of Appeals for the Second Circuit denied.

Same case below, 617 Fed. Appx. 82.

———

No. 15-6570. Royland Rice, Petitioner v. United States.

577 U.S. 993, 136 S. Ct. 521, 193 L. Ed. 2d 410, 2015 U.S. LEXIS 7298.

November 16, 2015. Petition for writ of certiorari to the United States Court of Appeals for the Ninth Circuit denied.

Same case below, 607 Fed. Appx. 748.

———

No. 15-6571. Arturo Martinez, Petitioner v. United States.

577 U.S. 993, 136 S. Ct. 521, 193 L. Ed. 2d 410, 2015 U.S. LEXIS 7283.

November 16, 2015. Petition for writ of certiorari to the United States Court of Appeals for the Tenth Circuit denied.

Same case below, 608 Fed. Appx. 692.

———

No. 15-6573. Eddie C. Outlaw, Petitioner v. United States.

577 U.S. 993, 136 S. Ct. 521, 193 L. Ed. 2d 410, 2015 U.S. LEXIS 7259.

November 16, 2015. Petition for a writ of certiorari to the United States Court of Appeals for the Fifth Circuit denied.

Same case below, 610 Fed. Appx. 420.

No. 15-6577. Gary E. Peel, Petitioner v. Michael Sepanek, Warden.

577 U.S. 993, 136 S. Ct. 521, 193 L. Ed. 2d 411, 2015 U.S. LEXIS 7315.

November 16, 2015. Petition for writ of certiorari to the United States Court of Appeals for the Sixth Circuit denied.

No. 15-6580. Myron Dewayne Tibbs, Petitioner v. United States.

577 U.S. 993, 136 S. Ct. 522, 193 L. Ed. 2d 411, 2015 U.S. LEXIS 7232.

November 16, 2015. Petition for writ of certiorari to the United States Court of Appeals for the Eleventh Circuit denied.

Same case below, 603 Fed. Appx. 744.

No. 15-6585. Cristobal Veliz, Petitioner v. United States.

577 U.S. 993, 136 S. Ct. 522, 193 L. Ed. 2d 411, 2015 U.S. LEXIS 7194.

November 16, 2015. Petition for writ of certiorari to the United States Court of Appeals for the Second Circuit denied.

Same case below, 623 Fed. Appx. 538.

No. 15-6589. Versiah M. Taylor, Petitioner v. United States District Court for the Northern District of Florida.

577 U.S. 993, 136 S. Ct. 527, 193 L. Ed. 2d 411, 2015 U.S. LEXIS 7323, reh den 577 U.S. 1185, 136 S. Ct. 1252, 194 L. Ed. 2d 250, 2016 U.S. LEXIS 1106.

November 16, 2015. Petition for writ of certiorari to the United States Court of Appeals for the Eleventh Circuit denied.

No. 15-6592. Anthony McGee, Petitioner v. United States.

577 U.S. 993, 136 S. Ct. 522, 193 L. Ed. 2d 411, 2015 U.S. LEXIS 7307.

November 16, 2015. Petition for writ of certiorari to the United States Court of Appeals for the Ninth Circuit denied.

Same case below, 606 Fed. Appx. 351.

No. 15-6598. Jose Trevino Morales, Petitioner v. United States.

577 U.S. 993, 136 S. Ct. 522, 193 L. Ed. 2d 411, 2015 U.S. LEXIS 7241.

November 16, 2015. Petition for writ of certiorari to the United States Court of Appeals for the Fifth Circuit denied.

Same case below, 785 F.3d 165.

No. 15-6599. Omar Dominguez-Valencia, Petitioner v. United States.

577 U.S. 994, 136 S. Ct. 522, 193 L. Ed. 2d 411, 2015 U.S. LEXIS 7340.

November 16, 2015. Petition for writ of certiorari to the United States Court of Appeals for the Ninth Circuit denied.

Same case below, 608 Fed. Appx. 459.

No. 15-6601. Melvin Hernandez-Maldonado, Petitioner v. United States.

577 U.S. 994, 136 S. Ct. 522, 193 L. Ed. 2d 411, 2015 U.S. LEXIS 7222.

November 16, 2015. Petition for writ of certiorari to the United States Court of Appeals for the First Circuit denied.

Same case below, 793 F.3d 223.

No. 15-6604. Rauf Abdul Salam, Petitioner v. United States.

577 U.S. 994, 136 S. Ct. 523, 193 L. Ed. 2d 412, 2015 U.S. LEXIS 7214.

November 16, 2015. Petition for writ of certiorari to the United States Court of Appeals for the Fourth Circuit denied.

Same case below, 611 Fed. Appx. 110.

No. 15-6609. Erick Herrera, Petitioner v. United States.

577 U.S. 994, 136 S. Ct. 523, 193 L. Ed. 2d 412, 2015 U.S. LEXIS 7325.

November 16, 2015. Petition for writ of certiorari to the United States Court of Appeals for the Ninth Circuit denied.

Same case below, 610 Fed. Appx. 621.

No. 15-6610. Richard Franklin, Petitioner v. United States.

577 U.S. 994, 136 S. Ct. 523, 193 L. Ed. 2d 412, 2015 U.S. LEXIS 7275.

November 16, 2015. Petition for writ of certiorari to the United States Court of Appeals for the Tenth Circuit denied.

Same case below, 785 F.3d 1365.

No. 15-6614. Kenneth Bullard, Petitioner v. United States.

577 U.S. 994, 136 S. Ct. 523, 193 L. Ed. 2d 412, 2015 U.S. LEXIS 7300.

November 16, 2015. Petition for writ of certiorari to the United States Court of Appeals for the Eleventh Circuit denied.

Same case below, 610 Fed. Appx. 898.

No. 15-6616. Jose Luis Castillo, Petitioner v. United States.

577 U.S. 994, 136 S. Ct. 523, 193 L. Ed. 2d 412, 2015 U.S. LEXIS 7244.

November 16, 2015. Petition for writ of certiorari to the United States Court of Appeals for the Ninth Circuit denied.

Same case below, 607 Fed. Appx. 754.

No. 15-6627. Edward Robinson, Petitioner v. United States.

577 U.S. 994, 136 S. Ct. 524, 193 L. Ed. 2d 412, 2015 U.S. LEXIS 7264.

November 16, 2015. Petition for writ of certiorari to the United States Court of Appeals for the Sixth Circuit denied.

No. 15-6629. John D. Hayes, Petitioner v. United States.

577 U.S. 994, 136 S. Ct. 524, 193 L. Ed. 2d 412, 2015 U.S. LEXIS 7331.

November 16, 2015. Petition for writ of certiorari to the United States Court of Appeals for the Fourth Circuit denied.

Same case below, 612 Fed. Appx. 673.

No. 14-1273. New Hampshire Right to Life, Petitioner v. Department of Health and Human Services.

577 U.S. 994, 136 S. Ct. 383, 193 L. Ed. 2d 412, 2015 U.S. LEXIS 7169.

November 16, 2015. Petition for writ of certiorari to the United States Court of Appeals for the First Circuit denied.

Same case below, 778 F.3d 43.

Justice **Thomas**, with whom Justice **Scalia** joins, dissenting from denial of the petition for writ of certiorari.

The Freedom of Information Act (FOIA), 5 U.S.C. § 552, requires federal agencies to "make [agency] records promptly available to any person" who requests them, unless the information that they contain falls under a specifically enumerated exemption. §§ 552(a)(3)(A), (b). One of those exemptions, Exemption 4, authorizes agencies to withhold documents that contain "trade secrets and commercial or financial information obtained from a person and privileged or confidential." § 552(b)(4).

We have long maintained that "FOIA reflects a general philosophy of full agency disclosure unless information is exempted under clearly delineated statutory language." *Department of Defense* v. *FLRA*, 510 U.S. 487, 494, 114 S. Ct. 1006, 127 L. Ed. 2d 325 (1994) (internal quotation marks omitted). And we have rejected interpretations of other FOIA exemptions that diverge from the text. *E.g., Milner* v. *Department of Navy*, 562 U.S. 562, 573, 131 S. Ct. 1259, 179 L. Ed. 2d 268 (2011) (rejecting interpretation due to its "patent flaw: It is disconnected from Exemption 2's text").

Though we often have considered other FOIA exemptions, we have never interpreted Exemption 4's exception for "trade secrets and commercial or financial information obtained from a person and privileged or confidential." § 552(b)(4). In the meantime, Courts of Appeals have declined to interpret the word "confidential" in Exemption 4 according to its ordinary meaning. Here, for instance, the Court of Appeals for the First Circuit upheld the Department of Health and Human Services' refusal to disclose Planned Parenthood's Manual of Medical Standards and Guidelines, a document that the Govern-

ment had required Planned Parenthood to submit in connection with a non-competitive grant application. See *New Hampshire Right to Life* v. *Department of Health and Human Services*, 778 F.3d 43, 49-52 (2015). The First Circuit based this conclusion not on the ordinary meaning of the term "confidential," but on conjectures as to whether disclosure could harm Planned Parenthood's competitive position. The court deemed the manual confidential because "[a] potential future competitor could take advantage of the institutional knowledge contained in the Manual" to compete with Planned Parenthood at some later date. *Id.,* at 51.

The decision below reflects a wider development. Courts of Appeals have embraced varying versions of a convoluted test that rests on judicial speculation about whether disclosure will cause competitive harm to the entity from which the information was obtained. In 1974, the Court of Appeals for the D. C. Circuit decided *National Parks & Conservation Assn.* v. *Morton*, 498 F.2d 765, which construed the word "confidential" in Exemption 4 by looking to legislative history and the "legislative purpose which underlies the exemption." *Id.,* at 767; see *id.,* at 766-770. That court determined that commercial information is "confidential" if, *inter alia*, disclosure would "cause substantial harm to the competitive position of the person from whom the information was obtained." *Id.,* at 770. The D. C. Circuit later elaborated that there was no need to "show actual competitive harm," and that "[a]ctual competition and the likelihood of substantial competitive injury" sufficed. *Public Citizen Health Research Group* v. *FDA*, 704 F.2d 1280, 1291 (1983) (internal quotation marks omitted). Seven other Circuits adopted the *National Parks* test. See *Critical Mass Energy Project* v. *NRC*, 975 F.2d 871, 876 (CADC 1992) (en banc) (collecting cases).

In 1992, the D. C. Circuit granted rehearing en banc to reconsider *National Parks*, after two judges of that court described its test as "fabricated, out of whole cloth." *Critical Mass*, 975 F.2d, at 875 (internal quotation marks omitted). The full court declined to overrule it entirely. *Id.*, at 876-877, 880. Instead, the court "confine[d]" the *National Parks* test "to information that persons are required to provide the Government," and adopted a different test for voluntarily provided information. 975 F.2d, at 872, 880.

Since then, every Court of Appeals to consider Exemption 4 has interpreted it by parsing *National Parks*' nebulous language about "actual competition" and a "substantial likelihood of competitive harm." The courts' reliance on *National Parks* to determine whether information is "confidential" commercial information has produced confusion. Courts cannot seem to agree on what kind of "actual competition" must be shown. Some require factual justifications and market definitions to show that there is "actual competition in the relevant market" in which the entity opposing the disclosure of its information operates. *Watkins* v. *Bureau of Customs and Border Protection*, 643 F.3d 1189, 1196 (CA9 2011). Others, including the First Circuit below, take an expansive view of what the relevant market is, and do not require any connection between that market and the context in which an entity supplied the requested information. 778 F.3d, at 51.

Courts of Appeals also disagree over what a "substantial likelihood of competitive harm" means. In some courts, there must be evidence that the entity whose information is being disclosed would likely suffer some defined competitive harm (like lost market share) if competitors used the information. *E.g., McDonnell Douglas Corp.* v. *Department of Air Force*, 375 F.3d 1182, 1187 (CADC 2004); *GC Micro Corp.* v. *Defense Logistics*

Agency, 33 F.3d 1109, 1115 (CA9 1994). But the First Circuit here accepted that competitors' possible use of the information alone constitutes harm—even if this would not likely result in any negative consequences for the entity whose information was disclosed. See 778 F.3d, at 51. Similarly, some courts hold that competitive harm exists if a competitor could use the disclosed information to publicly embarrass the originator of the information. *E.g., Nadler* v. *FDIC*, 92 F.3d 93, 96-97 (CA2 1996). Others hold that this can never be competitive harm. *E.g., United Technologies Corp.* v. *Department of Defense*, 601 F.3d 557, 563-564 (CADC 2010). We should not leave the meaning of Exemption 4 up to an atextual test that has different limits in different Circuits.*

By failing to address the Courts of Appeals' abrogation of Exemption 4's text, we have also created a disconcerting anomaly. We have interpreted FOIA Exemption 5—applicable to agency memoranda that "would not be available by law to a party . . . in litigation with the agency," § 552(b)(5)—to encompass a "privilege for confidential commercial information" created by the Government. *Federal Open Market Comm.* v. *Merrill*, 443 U.S. 340, 360, 99 S. Ct. 2800, 61 L. Ed. 2d 587 (1979). Yet, in that context, we defined confidential commercial information to mean information "generated in the process of awarding a contract," which "would in fact be privileged in civil discovery." *Id.*, at 361, 99 S. Ct. 2800, 61 L. Ed. 2d 587. It is odd for one definition of confidential commercial information to apply to Government-generated records and for a different test to apply if nongovernmental actors created them. It is especially strange given our recognition that the only difference between confidential commercial information covered by Exemption 4 and Exemption 5 is that the latter "is necessarily confined to informa-

---

* The Government apparently agrees. Rather than defending the Courts of Appeals' tests, the Government's brief opposing certiorari states that every court that has adopted the *National Parks* definition of "confidential" information has turned its back on the statutory text.

tion generated by the Federal Government itself." *Id.,* at 360, 99 S. Ct. 2800, 61 L. Ed. 2d 587.

* * *

The First Circuit's decision warrants review. It perpetuates an unsupported interpretation of an important federal statute and further muddies an already amorphous test. For these reasons, I respectfully dissent from the denial of certiorari.

_____

No. 15-510. Meso Scale Diagnostics, LLC, et al., Petitioners v. Roche Diagnostics GmbH, et al.

577 U.S. 997, 136 S. Ct. 524, 193 L. Ed. 2d 415, 2015 U.S. LEXIS 7324.

November 16, 2015. Motion of Leonard A. White, et al. for leave to file a brief as amici curiae granted. Petition for writ of certiorari to the Supreme Court of Delaware denied.

Same case below, 116 A.3d 1244.

_____

No. 15-6016. Claire Brainerd, Petitioner v. Schlumberger Technology Corporation.

577 U.S. 997, 136 S. Ct. 505, 193 L. Ed. 2d 415, 2015 U.S. LEXIS 7192.

November 16, 2015. Petition for writ of certiorari to the United States Court of Appeals for the Tenth Circuit denied. Justice Alito took no part in the consideration or decision of this petition.

Same case below, 589 Fed. Appx. 406.

_____

No. 15-6494. Deon Delguato Roundtree, Petitioner v. United States.

577 U.S. 998, 136 S. Ct. 527, 193 L. Ed. 2d 415, 2015 U.S. LEXIS 7330.

November 16, 2015. Petition for writ of certiorari to the United States Court of Appeals for the Eleventh Circuit denied. Justice Kagan took no part in the consideration or decision of this petition.

_____

No. 15-6665. In re Marcus O. Tate, Petitioner.

577 U.S. 984, 136 S. Ct. 524, 193 L. Ed. 2d 415, 2015 U.S. LEXIS 7198.

November 16, 2015. Petition for writ of habeas corpus denied.

_____

No. 15-6078. In re Gregory Johnson, Petitioner.

577 U.S. 984, 136 S. Ct. 508, 193 L. Ed. 2d 415, 2015 U.S. LEXIS 7302.

November 16, 2015. Petition for writ of prohibition denied.

_____

No. 14-9860. Tracy Nixon, Petitioner v. Greg Abbott, Governor of Texas, et al.

577 U.S. 998, 136 S. Ct. 527, 193 L. Ed. 2d 415, 2015 U.S. LEXIS 7299.

November 16, 2015. Petition for rehearing denied.

Former decision, 577 U.S. 839, 136 S. Ct. 68, 193 L. Ed. 2d 66, 2015 U.S. LEXIS 5206.

_____

No. 14-10045. Simon F. Ranteesi, Petitioner v. Eric Arnold, Acting Warden.

577 U.S. 998, 136 S. Ct. 527, 193 L. Ed. 2d 415, 2015 U.S. LEXIS 7319.

November 16, 2015. Petition for rehearing denied.

Former decision, 577 U.S. 844, 136 S. Ct. 87, 193 L. Ed. 2d 76, 2015 U.S. LEXIS 5345.

————

No. 14-10105. Simon F. Ranteesi, Petitioner v. Mark Constance, et al.

577 U.S. 998, 136 S. Ct. 527, 193 L. Ed. 2d 416, 2015 U.S. LEXIS 7245.

November 16, 2015. Petition for rehearing denied.

Former decision, 577 U.S. 847, 136 S. Ct. 98, 193 L. Ed. 2d 82, 2015 U.S. LEXIS 5025.

————

No. 15-124. Elouise Bradley, Petitioner v. Jennifer Sabree, et al.

577 U.S. 998, 136 S. Ct. 528, 193 L. Ed. 2d 416, 2015 U.S. LEXIS 7233.

November 16, 2015. Petition for rehearing denied.

Former decision, 577 U.S. 874, 136 S. Ct. 239, 193 L. Ed. 2d 132, 2015 U.S. LEXIS 6273.

————

No. 15-172. Millie Howard, Petitioner v. Railroad Retirement Board.

577 U.S. 998, 136 S. Ct. 528, 193 L. Ed. 2d 416, 2015 U.S. LEXIS 7312.

November 16, 2015. Petition for rehearing denied.

Former decision, 577 U.S. 875, 136 S. Ct. 260, 193 L. Ed. 2d 135, 2015 U.S. LEXIS 6070.

————

No. 15-5077. Richard Kearney, Petitioner v. Brian Fischer, Commissioner, New York Department of Correctional Services, et al.

577 U.S. 998, 136 S. Ct. 528, 193 L. Ed. 2d 416, 2015 U.S. LEXIS 7308.

November 16, 2015. Petition for rehearing denied.

Former decision, 577 U.S. 881, 136 S. Ct. 181, 193 L. Ed. 2d 145, 2015 U.S. LEXIS 5146.

————

No. 15-5086. Gregory P. Nesselrode, Petitioner v. Department of Education.

577 U.S. 998, 136 S. Ct. 528, 193 L. Ed. 2d 416, 2015 U.S. LEXIS 7295.

November 16, 2015. Petition for rehearing denied.

Former decision, 577 U.S. 881, 136 S. Ct. 183, 193 L. Ed. 2d 146, 2015 U.S. LEXIS 5164.

————

No. 15-5111. Joseph Edward Francis Lunz, Petitioner v. Elizabeth A. O'Meara, Superintendent, Gouverneur Correctional Facility.

577 U.S. 998, 136 S. Ct. 528, 193 L. Ed. 2d 416, 2015 U.S. LEXIS 7253.

November 16, 2015. Petition for rehearing denied.

Former decision, 577 U.S. 883, 136 S. Ct. 186, 193 L. Ed. 2d 149, 2015 U.S. LEXIS 5069.

————

No. 15-5201. Michael J. G. Saunders, Petitioner v. Virginia.

577 U.S. 998, 136 S. Ct. 528, 193 L. Ed. 2d 416, 2015 U.S. LEXIS 7276.

November 16, 2015. Petition for rehearing denied.

Former decision, 577 U.S. 887, 136 S. Ct. 204, 193 L. Ed. 2d 157, 2015 U.S. LEXIS 5175.

———

No. 15-5212. Monica Brown, et vir, Petitioners v. Florida Department of Children and Families.

577 U.S. 998, 136 S. Ct. 529, 193 L. Ed. 2d 417, 2015 U.S. LEXIS 7210.

November 16, 2015. Petition for rehearing denied.

Former decision, 577 U.S. 888, 126 S. Ct. 205, 193 L. Ed. 2d 158, 2015 U.S. LEXIS 5252.

———

No. 15-5295. Roger Stevenson, Petitioner v. Sorrell Saunders.

577 U.S. 998, 136 S. Ct. 529, 193 L. Ed. 2d 417, 2015 U.S. LEXIS 7197.

November 16, 2015. Petition for rehearing denied.

Former decision, 577 U.S. 892, 136 S. Ct. 220, 193 L. Ed. 2d 167, 2015 U.S. LEXIS 4857.

———

No. 15-5675. Shelby Anthony Vogt, Petitioner v. Iowa State Penitentiary, et al.

577 U.S. 998, 136 S. Ct. 529, 193 L. Ed. 2d 417, 2015 U.S. LEXIS 7294.

November 16, 2015. Petition for rehearing denied.

Former decision, 577 U.S. 929, 136 S. Ct. 334, 193 L. Ed. 2d 240, 2015 U.S. LEXIS 6408.

———

No. 15-5773. Corey E. Turner, Sr., Petitioner v. United States.

577 U.S. 998, 136 S. Ct. 529, 193 L. Ed. 2d 417, 2015 U.S. LEXIS 7313.

November 16, 2015. Petition for rehearing denied.

Former decision, 577 U.S. 912, 136 S. Ct. 280, 193 L. Ed. 2d 204, 2015 U.S. LEXIS 6032.

———

No. 15-5848. Keith Bryant Webb, Petitioner v. United States.

577 U.S. 998, 136 S. Ct. 529, 193 L. Ed. 2d 417, 2015 U.S. LEXIS 7179.

November 16, 2015. Petition for rehearing denied.

Former decision, 577 U.S. 931, 136 S. Ct. 339, 193 L. Ed. 2d 244, 2015 U.S. LEXIS 6580.

———

No. 15-5939. Daniel Imperato, Petitioner v. Securities and Exchange Commission.

577 U.S. 998, 136 S. Ct. 529, 193 L. Ed. 2d 417, 2015 U.S. LEXIS 7260.

November 16, 2015. Petition for rehearing denied.

Former decision, 577 U.S. 933, 136 S. Ct. 346, 193 L. Ed. 2d 248, 2015 U.S. LEXIS 6563.

No. 14-1418. David A. Zubik, et al., Petitioners v. Sylvia Burwell, Secretary of Health and Human Services, et al.

No. 14-1453. Priests for Life, et al., Petitioners v. Department of Health and Human Services, et al.

No. 14-1505. Roman Catholic Archbishop of Washington, et al., Petitioners v. Sylvia Burwell, Secretary of Health and Human Services, et al.

No. 15-35. East Texas Baptist University, et al., Petitioners v. Sylvia Burwell, Secretary of Health and Human Services, et al.

No. 15-105. Little Sisters of the Poor Home for the Aged, Denver, Colorado, et al., Petitioners v. Sylvia Burwell, Secretary of Health and Human Services, et al.

No. 15-119. Southern Nazarene University, et al., Petitioners v. Sylvia Burwell, Secretary of Health and Human Services, et al.

No. 15-191. Geneva College, Petitioner v. Sylvia Burwell, Secretary of Health and Human Services, et al.

577 U.S. 998, 136 S. Ct. 529, 193 L. Ed. 2d 418, 2015 U.S. LEXIS 7353.

November 17, 2015. Briefing proposal set forth in the parties' letter of November 16, 2015, adopted. Petitioners in Nos. 14-1418, 14-1453, and 14-1505, will file one consolidated opening brief and one reply brief. Petitioners in Nos. 15-35, 15-105, 15-119, and 15-191 will file one consolidated opening brief and one reply brief. Petitioners' opening briefs, not to exceed 20,000 words each, are to be filed on or before January 4, 2016. Respondents will file one consolidated brief, not to exceed 22,500 words, on or before February 10, 2016. Petitioners' reply briefs, not to exceed 8,000 words each, are to be filed on or before March 11, 2016.

———

No. 15-6956 (15A520). Raphael Deon Holiday, Petitioner v. William Stephens, Director, Texas Department of Criminal Justice, Correctional Institutions Division.

577 U.S. 999, 136 S. Ct. 387, 193 L. Ed. 2d 418, 2015 U.S. LEXIS 7357.

November 18, 2015. Application for stay of execution of sentence of death, presented to Justice Scalia, and by him referred to the Court, denied. Petition for writ of certiorari to the United States Court of Appeals for the Fifth Circuit denied.

Statement of Justice **Sotomayor**, respecting the application for stay of execution and denial of certiorari.

A federal statute entitles defendants sentenced to death to court-appointed counsel during "all available post-conviction process." 18 U.S.C. § 3599(e). This statute requires counsel to "represent the defendant in . . . proceedings for executive or other clemency as may be available to the defendant." *Ibid.*; see *Harbison* v. *Bell*, 556 U.S. 180, 185-186, 129 S. Ct. 1481, 173 L. Ed. 2d 347 (2009). Pursuant to § 3599, Raphael Holiday asked his court-appointed counsel—Seth Kretzer and James Volberding—to petition the State of Texas for clemency. App. to Pet. for Cert. 5a. His attorneys declined, however, because of their belief that there was "no chance at all that a clemency petition would be granted." Id., at 11a (internal quotation marks omitted).

Holiday asked a Federal District Court to appoint a new attorney who would file his petition for clemency. The court denied his request. The court recognized that § 3599 compelled it to appoint new counsel if "the interests of justice" require. Ibid. (quoting Martel v. Clair, 565 U.S. 648, 658, 132 S. Ct. 1276, 182 L. Ed. 2d 135 (2012); (internal quotation marks omitted). But given the "representations" of Holiday's attorneys, the court found new counsel unwarranted. App. to Pet. for Cert. 11a.

This denial was an abuse of discretion. When Congress authorized federally funded counsel to represent clients in clemency proceedings, it plainly "did not want condemned men and women to be abandoned by their counsel at the last moment and left to navigate the sometimes labyrinthine clemency process from their jail cells." Harbison, 556 U.S., at 194, 129 S. Ct. 1481, 173 L. Ed. 2d 347 (quoting Hain v. Mullin, 436 F.3d 1168, 1175 (CA10 2006) (en banc); internal quotation marks omitted). Yet this is exactly what happened here. Although the " 'interests of justice' standard contemplates a peculiarly context-specific inquiry," Martel, 565 U.S., at 663, 132 S. Ct. 1276, 182 L. Ed. 2d 135, it surely precludes a court from rejecting a substitution motion solely because it agrees with the appointed attorneys' premonitions about clemency.

Executive clemency is fundamentally unpredictable. Clemency officials typically have "complete discretion" to commute a defendant's sentence based on "a wide range of factors not comprehended by earlier judicial proceedings and sentencing determinations." Ohio Adult Parole Authority v. Woodard, 523 U.S. 272, 278, 281, 118 S. Ct. 1244, 140 L. Ed. 2d 387 (1998) (principal opinion); see Tex. Const., Art. IV, § 11; Tex. Code Crim. Proc. Ann., Art. 48.01 (Vernon Supp. 2014). By granting death-eligible defendants an attorney, "Congress ensured that no prisoner would be put to death without meaningful access to th[is] ' "fail safe" ' of our justice system." Harbison, 556 U.S., at 194, 129 S. Ct. 1481, 173 L. Ed. 2d 347 (quoting Herrera v. Collins, 506 U.S. 390, 415, 113 S. Ct. 853, 122 L. Ed. 2d 203 (1993)). So long as clemency proceedings were "available" to Holiday, § 3599(e), the interests of justice required the appointment of attorneys who would represent him in that process. Cf. Christeson v. Roper, 574 U.S. 373, 377, 135 S. Ct. 891, 190 L. Ed. 2d 763 (2015) (per curiam) (reversing the denial of a substitution motion under § 3599 despite the "host of procedural obstacles" confronting the petitioner's claims). The District Court's denial did not adequately account for Holiday's statutory right.

Despite the District Court's error, I reluctantly join the Court's decision to deny Holiday's petition for certiorari. After the court rejected Holiday's request for new counsel, his original attorneys eventually submitted a clemency application on his behalf. This application proved unsuccessful—and likely would have benefited from additional preparation by more zealous advocates. Yet this Court, unlike a state court, is likely to have no power to order Texas to reconsider its clemency decision with new attorneys representing Holiday.

No. 14-471 (R46-008). Joseph Contorinis, Petitioner v. Securities and Exchange Commission.

577 U.S. 1001, 136 S. Ct. 531, 193 L. Ed. 2d 419, 2015 U.S. LEXIS 7360.

November 19, 2015. The petition for writ of certiorari to the United States Court of Appeals for the Second Circuit was dismissed today pursuant to Rule 46 of the Rules of this Court.

Same case below, 743 F.3d 296.

No. 15-7015 (15A535). Marcus Ray Johnson, Petitioner v. Bruce Chatman, Warden.

577 U.S. 1001, 136 S. Ct. 532, 193 L. Ed. 2d 420, 2015 U.S. LEXIS 7358.

November 19, 2015. Application for stay of execution of sentence of death, presented to Justice Thomas, and by him referred to the Court, denied. Petition for writ of certiorari to the Supreme Court of Georgia denied.

No. 15-7022 (15A539). Marcus Ray Johnson, Petitioner v. Bruce Chatman, Warden.

577 U.S. 1001, 136 S. Ct. 532, 193 L. Ed. 2d 420, 2015 U.S. LEXIS 7359.

November 19, 2015. Application for stay of execution of sentence of death, presented to Justice Thomas, and by him referred to the Court, denied. Petition for writ of certiorari to the United States Court of Appeals for the Eleventh Circuit denied.

Same case below, 805 F.3d 1317.

No. 14-232. Wesley W. Harris, et al., Appellants v. Arizona Independent Redistricting Commission, et al.

577 U.S. 1001, 136 S. Ct. 533, 193 L. Ed. 2d 420, 2015 U.S. LEXIS 7361.

November 24, 2015. Motion of appellee, Arizona Secretary of State Michele Reagan, in support of appellants, for divided argument granted. Motion of the Solicitor General for leave to participate in oral argument as amicus curiae and for divided argument granted.

No. 14-981. Abigail Noel Fisher, Petitioner v. University of Texas at Austin, et al.

577 U.S. 1002, 136 S. Ct. 533, 193 L. Ed. 2d 420, 2015 U.S. LEXIS 7362.

November 24, 2015. Motion of the Solicitor General for leave to participate in oral argument as amicus curiae and for divided argument granted. Justice Kagan took no part in the consideration or decision of this motion.

No. 15A551. Keli'i Akina, et al., Applicants v. Hawaii, et al.

193 L. Ed. 2d 420, 2015 U.S. LEXIS 7363.

November 27, 2015. UPON CONSIDERATION of the application of counsel for the applicants, the responses filed thereto, and the reply.

IT IS ORDERED that the respondents are enjoined from counting the ballots cast in, and certifying the winners of, the election described in the application, pending further order of the undersigned or of the Court. [Per Justice Kennedy, as individual Justice.]

Same case below, 141 F. Supp. 3d 1106.

MEMORANDUM CASES

No. 15-587 (R46–009). Allergan PLC, fka Actavis PLC, et al., Petitioners v. New York, By and Through Eric T. Schneiderman, Attorney General.

577 U.S. 1002, 136 S. Ct. 581, 193 L. Ed. 2d 421, 2015 U.S. LEXIS 7671.

November 30, 2015. The petition for writ of certiorari to the United States Court of Appeals for the Second Circuit was dismissed today pursuant to Rule 46 of the Rules of this Court.

Same case below, 787 F.3d 638.

No. 15-454. Kenneth L. Smith, Petitioner v. Antonin Scalia, Associate Justice, Supreme Court of the United States, et al.

577 U.S. 1002, 136 S. Ct. 554, 193 L. Ed. 2d 421, 2015 U.S. LEXIS 7579.

November 30, 2015. Because the Court lacks a quorum, 28 U.S.C. §1, and since the only qualified Justices are of the opinion that the case cannot be heard and determined at the next Term of the Court, the judgment is affirmed under 28 U.S.C. §2109, which provides that under these circumstances "the court shall enter its order affirming the judgment of the court from which the case was brought for review with the same effect as upon affirmance by an equally divided court." The Chief Justice, Justice Scalia, Justice Thomas, and Justice Kagan took no part in the consideration or decision of this petition.

No. 15-6219. Jorge Baez-Martinez, Petitioner v. United States.

577 U.S. 1002, 136 S. Ct. 545, 193 L. Ed. 2d 421, 2015 U.S. LEXIS 7524.

November 30, 2015. On petition for writ of certiorari to the United States Court of Appeals for the First Circuit. Motion of petitioner for leave to proceed in forma pauperis and petition for writ of certiorari granted. Judgment vacated, and case remanded to the United States Court of Appeals for the First Circuit for further consideration in light of Johnson v. United States, 576 U.S. 591, 135 S. Ct. 2551, 192 L. Ed. 2d 569 (2015).

Same case below, 786 F.3d 121.

No. 15-6142. Thomas H. Clay, Petitioner v. William Stephens, Director, Texas Department of Criminal Justice, Correctional Institutions Division.

577 U.S. 1002, 136 S. Ct. 539, 193 L. Ed. 2d 421, 2015 U.S. LEXIS 7423.

November 30, 2015. Motion of petitioner for leave to proceed in forma pauperis denied, and petition for writ of certiorari to the United States Court of Appeals for the Fifth Circuit dismissed. See Rule 39.8. As petitioner has repeatedly abused this Court's process, the Clerk is directed not to accept any further petitions in noncriminal matters from petitioner unless the docketing fee required by Rule 38(a) is paid and petition submitted in compliance with Rule 33.1. See Martin v. District of Columbia Court of Appeals, 506 U.S. 1, 113 S. Ct. 397, 121 L. Ed. 2d 305 (1992) (per curiam).

Same case below, 597 Fed. Appx. 261.

No. 15-6168. Jeffrey R. LeBlanc, Petitioner v. City of Kalamazoo, Michigan.

577 U.S. 1003, 136 S. Ct. 542, 193 L. Ed. 2d 422, 2015 U.S. LEXIS 7424.

November 30, 2015. Motion of petitioner for leave to proceed in forma pauperis denied, and petition for writ of certiorari to the United States Court of Appeals for the Sixth Circuit dismissed. See Rule 39.8.

No. 15-6228. Jesse L. Youngblood, Petitioner v. Superior Court of California, Butte County, et al.

577 U.S. 1003, 136 S. Ct. 546, 193 L. Ed. 2d 422, 2015 U.S. LEXIS 7395.

November 30, 2015. Motion of petitioner for leave to proceed in forma pauperis denied, and petition for writ of certiorari to the United States Court of Appeals for the Ninth Circuit dismissed. See Rule 39.8. As petitioner has repeatedly abused this Court's process, the Clerk is directed not to accept any further petitions in noncriminal matters from petitioner unless the docketing fee required by Rule 38(a) is paid and petition submitted in compliance with Rule 33.1. See Martin v. District of Columbia Court of Appeals, 506 U.S. 1, 113 S. Ct. 397, 121 L. Ed. 2d 305 (1992) (per curiam).

Same case below, 610 Fed. Appx. 664.

No. 15-6321. Tommy Ray Mosley, Petitioner v. Michael Harmon, et al.

577 U.S. 1003, 136 S. Ct. 551, 193 L. Ed. 2d 422, 2015 U.S. LEXIS 7461.

November 30, 2015. Motion of petitioner for leave to proceed in forma pau-

peris denied, and petition for writ of certiorari to the United States Court of Appeals for the Eighth Circuit dismissed. See Rule 39.8.

No. 15-6538. Renea J. Chafe, Petitioner v. Florida Department of Children and Families.

577 U.S. 1003, 136 S. Ct. 557, 193 L. Ed. 2d 422, 2015 U.S. LEXIS 7420.

November 30, 2015. Motion of petitioner for leave to proceed in forma pauperis denied, and petition for writ of certiorari to the District Court of Appeals of Florida, Fourth District, dismissed. See Rule 39.8.

Same case below, 162 So. 3d 1025.

No. 15M53. Walter Ralph Wood, Petitioner v. United States.

577 U.S. 1003, 136 S. Ct. 565, 193 L. Ed. 2d 422, 2015 U.S. LEXIS 7563.

November 30, 2015. Motion to direct the Clerk to file a petition for writ of certiorari out of time denied.

Same case below, 594 Fed. Appx. 171.

No. 15M54. McWane, Inc., Petitioner v. Federal Trade Commission.

577 U.S. 1004, 136 S. Ct. 565, 193 L. Ed. 2d 422, 2015 U.S. LEXIS 7475.

November 30, 2015. Motion for leave to file a petition for writ of certiorari with supplemental appendix under seal is granted.

Same case below, 783 F.3d 814.

Same case below, 612 Fed. Appx. 41.

No. 15M55. Norton, Petitioner v. Maine Department of Health and Human Services, et al.

577 U.S. 1004, 136 S. Ct. 565, 193 L. Ed. 2d 423, 2015 U.S. LEXIS 7629.

November 30, 2015. Motion for leave to file a petition for writ of certiorari with supplemental appendix under seal granted.

Same case below, 121 A.3d 105.

No. 15M56. Equarn White, Petitioner v. Steven E. Racette, Superintendent, Great Meadow Correctional Facility.

577 U.S. 1003, 136 S. Ct. 565, 193 L. Ed. 2d 423, 2015 U.S. LEXIS 7571.

November 30, 2015. Motion to direct the Clerk to file a petition for writ of certiorari out of time denied.

Same case below, 601 Fed. Appx. 62.

No. 15M57. Chao Ho Lin, et ux., Petitioners v. Chi Chu Wu.

577 U.S. 1003, 136 S. Ct. 565, 193 L. Ed. 2d 423, 2015 U.S. LEXIS 7626.

November 30, 2015. Motion to direct the Clerk to file a petition for writ of certiorari out of time denied.

Same case below, 392 Ill. Dec. 364, 32 N.E.3d 672.

No. 15M58. Timothy M. Cohane, Petitioner v. National Collegiate Athletic Association, et al.

577 U.S. 1003, 136 S. Ct. 565, 193 L. Ed. 2d 423, 2015 U.S. LEXIS 7561.

November 30, 2015. Motion to direct the Clerk to file a petition for writ of certiorari out of time denied.

No. 15M59. John M. Esposito, Petitioner v. Lucy A. Esposito.

577 U.S. 1003, 136 S. Ct. 566, 193 L. Ed. 2d 423, 2015 U.S. LEXIS 7496.

November 30, 2015. Motion to direct the Clerk to file a petition for writ of certiorari out of time denied.

Same case below, 152 So. 3d 583.

No. 15M60. Gregory D. Rowe, Petitioner v. Ruben Gonzalez, et al.

577 U.S. 1004, 136 S. Ct. 566, 193 L. Ed. 2d 423, 2015 U.S. LEXIS 7485.

November 30, 2015. Motion to direct the Clerk to file a petition for writ of certiorari out of time denied.

Same case below, 605 Fed. Appx. 466.

No. 14-770. Bank Markazi, aka The Central Bank of Iran, Petitioner v. Deborah Peterson, et al.

577 U.S. 1004, 136 S. Ct. 566, 193 L. Ed. 2d 423, 2015 U.S. LEXIS 7643.

November 30, 2015. Motion of petitioner to dispense with printing the joint appendix granted.

No. 14-915. Rebecca Friedrichs, et al., Petitioners v. California Teachers Association, et al.

577 U.S. 1004, 136 S. Ct. 566, 193 L. Ed. 2d 423, 2015 U.S. LEXIS 7660.

November 30, 2015. Motion of respondent Attorney General of California for divided argument granted. Motion of the Solicitor General for leave to participate in oral argument as amicus curiae, for enlargement of time for oral argument, and for divided argument granted; and the time is divided as follows: 40 minutes for petitioners, 15 minutes for the Union Respondents, 15 minutes for respondent Attorney General of California, and 10 minutes for the Solicitor General.

No. 14-9753. Brandon Scott Lavergne, Petitioner v. Sheriff's Office of Lafayette Parish.

577 U.S. 1004, 136 S. Ct. 566, 193 L. Ed. 2d 424, 2015 U.S. LEXIS 7661.

November 30, 2015. Motion of petitioner for reconsideration of order denying leave to proceed in forma pauperis denied.

No. 14-9816. Joseph P. McInerney, Petitioner v. Rensselaer Polytechnic Institute, et al.

577 U.S. 1004, 136 S. Ct. 566, 193 L. Ed. 2d 424, 2015 U.S. LEXIS 7470.

November 30, 2015. Motion of petitioner for reconsideration of order denying leave to proceed in forma pauperis denied. Justice Sotomayor took no part in the consideration or decision of this motion.

No. 14-10084. Willie Asbury, Petitioner v. South Carolina, et al.

577 U.S. 1004, 136 S. Ct. 567, 193 L. Ed. 2d 424, 2015 U.S. LEXIS 7481.

November 30, 2015. Motion of petitioner for reconsideration of order denying leave to proceed in forma pauperis denied.

No. 15-118. Jesus C. Hernandez, et al., Petitioners v. Jesus Mesa, Jr.

577 U.S. 1004, 136 S. Ct. 567, 193 L. Ed. 2d 424, 2015 U.S. LEXIS 7622.

November 30, 2015. The Solicitor General is invited to file a brief in this case expressing the views of the United States.

Same case below, 785 F.3d 117.

No. 15-138. RJR Nabisco, Inc., et al., Petitioners v. The European Community, et al.

577 U.S. 1004, 136 S. Ct. 567, 193 L. Ed. 2d 424, 2015 U.S. LEXIS 7604.

November 30, 2015. Motion of petitioners to dispense with printing the joint appendix granted. Justice Sotomayor took no part in the consideration or decision of this motion.

No. 15-5009. Rexford Tweed, Petitioner v. Rick Scott, Governor of Florida, et al.

577 U.S. 1005, 136 S. Ct. 567, 193 L. Ed. 2d 424, 2015 U.S. LEXIS 7525.

November 30, 2015. Motion of petitioner for reconsideration of order denying leave to proceed in forma pauperis denied.

No. 15-5226. David Williams, Petitioner v. Corizon, LLC, et al.

577 U.S. 1005, 136 S. Ct. 567, 193 L. Ed. 2d 424, 2015 U.S. LEXIS 7557.

November 30, 2015. Motion of petitioner for reconsideration of order denying leave to proceed in forma pauperis denied.

No. 15-5670. Edo Aslanyan, Petitioner v. Mike Obenland, Superintendent, Monroe Correctional Complex.

577 U.S. 1005, 136 S. Ct. 567, 193 L. Ed. 2d 425, 2015 U.S. LEXIS 7637.

November 30, 2015. Motion of petitioner for reconsideration of order denying leave to proceed in forma pauperis denied.

No. 15-5826. In re Sakima Iban Salih El Bey, Petitioner.

577 U.S. 1005, 136 S. Ct. 568, 193 L. Ed. 2d 425, 2015 U.S. LEXIS 7536.

November 30, 2015. Motion of petitioner for reconsideration of order denying leave to proceed in forma pauperis denied.

No. 15-6244. Darrell J. Moore, Sr., Petitioner v. Rudolf Montiel, et al.

577 U.S. 1005, 136 S. Ct. 568, 193 L. Ed. 2d 425, 2015 U.S. LEXIS 7646.

November 30, 2015. Motion of petitioner for leave to proceed in forma pauperis denied. Petitioner is allowed until December 21, 2015, within which to pay the docketing fees required by Rule 38(a) and to submit a petition in compliance with Rule 33.1 of the Rules of this Court.

Same case below, 599 Fed. Appx. 787.

No. 15-6335. David Alan Van Houten, Petitioner v. William Stephens, Director, Texas Department of Criminal Justice, Correctional Institutions Division.

577 U.S. 1005, 136 S. Ct. 568, 193 L. Ed. 2d 425, 2015 U.S. LEXIS 7511.

November 30, 2015. Motion of petitioner for leave to proceed in forma pauperis denied. Petitioner is allowed until December 21, 2015, within which to pay the docketing fees required by Rule 38(a) and to submit a petition in compliance with Rule 33.1 of the Rules of this Court.

No. 15-6341. Laura Randolph-Kennedy, Petitioner v. Verizon Services Corp.

577 U.S. 1005, 136 S. Ct. 568, 193 L. Ed. 2d 425, 2015 U.S. LEXIS 7668.

November 30, 2015. Motion of petitioner for leave to proceed in forma pauperis denied. Petitioner is allowed until December 21, 2015, within which to pay the docketing fee required by Rule 38(a) and to submit a petition in compliance with Rule 33.1 of the Rules of this Court.

No. 15-6384. William Henry Harrison, Petitioner v. Carolyn W. Colvin, Acting Commissioner of Social Security.

577 U.S. 1005, 136 S. Ct. 568, 193 L. Ed. 2d 425, 2015 U.S. LEXIS 7583.

November 30, 2015. Motion of petitioner for leave to proceed in forma pauperis denied. Petitioner is allowed until December 21, 2015, within which to pay the docketing fee required by Rule 38(a) and to submit a petition in compliance with Rule 33.1 of the Rules of this Court.

Same case below, 587 Fed. Appx. 762.

Same case below, 167 N.H. 429, 113 A.3d 239.

No. 15-6492. Pio Peter Zammit, Petitioner v. City of New Baltimore, Michigan.

577 U.S. 1005, 136 S. Ct. 569, 193 L. Ed. 2d 426, 2015 U.S. LEXIS 7586.

November 30, 2015. Motion of petitioner for leave to proceed in forma pauperis denied. Petitioner is allowed until December 21, 2015, within which to pay the docketing fee required by Rule 38(a) and to submit a petition in compliance with Rule 33.1 of the Rules of this Court.

Same case below, 497 Mich. 949, 857 N.W.2d 28.

No. 15-6493. Tom Lan, Petitioner v. Comcast Corporation, LLC.

577 U.S. 1005, 136 S. Ct. 569, 193 L. Ed. 2d 426, 2015 U.S. LEXIS 7576, reh den 577 U.S. 1185, 136 S. Ct. 1252, 194 L. Ed. 2d 250, 2016 U.S. LEXIS 1185.

November 30, 2015. Motion of petitioner for leave to proceed in forma pauperis denied. Petitioner is allowed until December 21, 2015, within which to pay the docketing fee required by Rule 38(a) and to submit a petition in compliance with Rule 33.1 of the Rules of this Court.

No. 14-1388. Peter McDonough, et al., Petitioners v. Gregory Dupont.

577 U.S. 1006, 136 S. Ct. 533, 193 L. Ed. 2d 426, 2015 U.S. LEXIS 7596.

November 30, 2015. Petition for writ of certiorari to the Supreme Court of New Hampshire denied.

No. 14-1543. Ronald S. Hines, Petitioner v. Bud E. Alldredge, Jr., et al.

577 U.S. 1006, 136 S. Ct. 534, 193 L. Ed. 2d 426, 2015 U.S. LEXIS 7664.

November 30, 2015. Petition for writ of certiorari to the United States Court of Appeals for the Fifth Circuit denied.

Same case below, 783 F.3d 197.

No. 14-9708. Bahri Begolli, Petitioner v. Home Depot U.S.A., Inc.

577 U.S. 1006, 136 S. Ct. 533, 193 L. Ed. 2d 426, 2015 U.S. LEXIS 7555, reh den 577 U.S. 1124, 136 S. Ct. 996, 194 L. Ed. 2d 14, 2016 U.S. LEXIS 961.

November 30, 2015. Petition for writ of certiorari to the United States Court of Appeals for the Seventh Circuit denied.

No. 14-10355. Juan Francisco Martinez-Lugo, Petitioner v. United States.

577 U.S. 1006, 136 S. Ct. 533, 193 L. Ed. 2d 426, 2015 U.S. LEXIS 7503.

November 30, 2015. Petition for writ of certiorari to the United States Court of Appeals for the Fifth Circuit denied.

Same case below, 782 F.3d 198.

No. 14-10377. Desmond Wilson, Petitioner v. United States.

No. 14-10407. Yugool Persaud, Petitioner v. United States.

577 U.S. 1006, 136 S. Ct. 533, 193 L. Ed. 2d 427, 2015 U.S. LEXIS 7548.

November 30, 2015. Petitions for writs of certiorari to the United States Court of Appeals for the Eleventh Circuit denied.

Same cases below, 605 Fed. Appx. 791.

No. 15-9. Joshua Cintron, Petitioner v. Massachusetts.

577 U.S. 1006, 136 S. Ct. 534, 193 L. Ed. 2d 427, 2015 U.S. LEXIS 7500.

November 30, 2015. Petition for writ of certiorari to the Supreme Judicial Court of Massachusetts denied.

No. 15-45. William Joseph Birhanzl, Petitioner v. Oregon.

577 U.S. 1006, 136 S. Ct. 534, 193 L. Ed. 2d 427, 2015 U.S. LEXIS 7529.

November 30, 2015. Petition for writ of certiorari to the Court of Appeals of Oregon denied.

Same case below, 264 Or. App. 466, 332 P.3d 371.

No. 15-46. Wendy Davis, et al., Petitioners v. Greg Abbott, Governor of Texas, et al.

577 U.S. 1006, 136 S. Ct. 534, 193 L. Ed. 2d 427, 2015 U.S. LEXIS 7550.

November 30, 2015. Petition for writ of certiorari to the United States Court of Appeals for the Fifth Circuit denied.

Same case below, 781 F.3d 207.

No. 15-69. Biolitec AG, et al., Petitioners v. AngioDynamics, Inc. (two judgments).

577 U.S. 1007, 136 S. Ct. 535, 193 L. Ed. 2d 427, 2015 U.S. LEXIS 7572.

November 30, 2015. Petition for writ of certiorari to the United States Court of Appeals for the First Circuit denied.

Same case below, 780 F.3d 420 (first judgment); 780 F.3d 429 (second judgment).

No. 15-101. Walter Edward Hardin, Petitioner v. United States.

577 U.S. 1007, 136 S. Ct. 535, 193 L. Ed. 2d 427, 2015 U.S. LEXIS 7638.

November 30, 2015. Petition for writ of certiorari to the United States Court of Appeals for the Sixth Circuit denied.

Same case below, 595 Fed. Appx. 460.

No. 15-132. Samuel L. Uveges, Petitioner v. Betty Uveges.

577 U.S. 1007, 136 S. Ct. 536, 193 L. Ed. 2d 427, 2015 U.S. LEXIS 7666.

November 30, 2015. Petition for writ of certiorari to the Superior Court of Pennsylvania, Pittsburgh Office, denied.

Same case below, 103 A.3d 825.

No. 15-155. State of Veracruz, Republic of Mexico, et al., Petitioners v. BP p.l.c., et al.

577 U.S. 1007, 136 S. Ct. 536, 193 L. Ed. 2d 427, 2015 U.S. LEXIS 7484.

November 30, 2015. Petition for writ of certiorari to the United States Court of Appeals for the Fifth Circuit denied.

Same case below, 784 F.3d 1019.

No. 15-162. Peter J. Paske, Jr., Petitioner v. Joel Fitzgerald, Individually and in His Official Capacity as Chief of Police of the City of Missouri City, Texas, et al.

577 U.S. 1007, 136 S. Ct. 536, 193 L. Ed. 2d 428, 2015 U.S. LEXIS 7652.

November 30, 2015. Petition for writ of certiorari to the United States Court of Appeals for the Fifth Circuit denied.

Same case below, 785 F.3d 977.

No. 15-215. Jimmy Yamada, et al., Petitioners v. Gregory Shoda, in His Official Capacity as Chair and Member of the Hawaii Campaign Spending Commission, et al.

577 U.S. 1007, 136 S. Ct. 569, 193 L. Ed. 2d 428, 2015 U.S. LEXIS 7545.

November 30, 2015. Petition for writ of certiorari to the United States Court of Appeals for the Ninth Circuit denied.

Same case below, 786 F.3d 1182.

No. 15-241. William Douglas Fulghum, et al., Petitioners v. Embarq Corporation, et al.

No. 15-244. Embarq Corporation, et al., Petitioners v. William Douglas Fulghum, et al.

577 U.S. 1007, 136 S. Ct. 537, 193 L. Ed. 2d 428, 2015 U.S. LEXIS 7497.

November 30, 2015. Petitions for writs of certiorari to the United States Court of Appeals for the Tenth Circuit denied.

Same cases below, 785 F.3d 395.

No. 15-329. A. M. Kelly Grove, Petitioner v. South Carolina Department of Health and Environmental Control, et al.

577 U.S. 1007, 136 S. Ct. 569, 193 L. Ed. 2d 428, 2015 U.S. LEXIS 7527.

November 30, 2015. Petition for writ of certiorari to the Court of Appeals of South Carolina denied.

No. 15-335. Robert Blake Adams, Petitioner v. William Stephens, Director, Texas Department of Criminal Justice, Correctional Institutions Division.

577 U.S. 1007, 136 S. Ct. 538, 193 L. Ed. 2d 428, 2015 U.S. LEXIS 7665.

November 30, 2015. Petition for writ of certiorari to the United States Court of Appeals for the Fifth Circuit denied.

No. 15-352. Miguel Zaragoza Fuentes, Petitioner v. 245th Judicial District Court of Harris County, Texas, et al.

577 U.S. 1007, 136 S. Ct. 538, 193 L. Ed. 2d 428, 2015 U.S. LEXIS 7507.

November 30, 2015. Petition for writ of certiorari to the Supreme Court of Texas denied.

No. 15-354. Kirk Carmichael, Petitioner v. JPMorgan Chase Bank, N.A.

577 U.S. 1007, 136 S. Ct. 540, 193 L. Ed. 2d 428, 2015 U.S. LEXIS 7492.

November 30, 2015. Petition for writ of certiorari to the Court of Appeal of California, Fourth Appellate District, Division One, denied.

No. 15-356. **Eric S. Clark, Petitioner v. City of Olathe, Kansas.**

577 U.S. 1007, 136 S. Ct. 541, 193 L. Ed. 2d 429, 2015 U.S. LEXIS 7490.

November 30, 2015. Petition for writ of certiorari to the Court of Appeals of Kansas denied.

Same case below, 338 P.3d 24.

No. 15-357. **James M. Tennant, Petitioner v. City of Georgetown, South Carolina, et al.**

577 U.S. 1008, 136 S. Ct. 541, 193 L. Ed. 2d 429, 2015 U.S. LEXIS 7623.

November 30, 2015. Petition for writ of certiorari to the United States Court of Appeals for the Fourth Circuit denied.

Same case below, 597 Fed. Appx. 752.

No. 15-358. **Westlake Legal Group, dba Thomas K. Plofchan, Jr., PLLC, et al., Petitioners v. Yelp, Inc.**

577 U.S. 1008, 136 S. Ct. 541, 193 L. Ed. 2d 429, 2015 U.S. LEXIS 7480.

November 30, 2015. Petition for writ of certiorari to the United States Court of Appeals for the Fourth Circuit denied.

Same case below, 599 Fed. Appx. 481.

No. 15-369. **Vivek Pampattiwar, Petitioner v. Rupali Chitre.**

577 U.S. 1008, 136 S. Ct. 548, 193 L. Ed. 2d 429, 2015 U.S. LEXIS 7551.

November 30, 2015. Petition for writ of certiorari to the Court of Appeals of Georgia denied.

No. 15-395. **Jason A. Calhoun, Petitioner v. Julie L. Jones, Secretary, Florida Department of Corrections.**

577 U.S. 1008, 136 S. Ct. 549, 193 L. Ed. 2d 429, 2015 U.S. LEXIS 7520.

November 30, 2015. Petition for writ of certiorari to the United States Court of Appeals for the Eleventh Circuit denied.

Same case below, 607 Fed. Appx. 968.

No. 15-400. **Dzmitry Sergeyevich Dauksh, Petitioner v. Loretta E. Lynch, Attorney General.**

577 U.S. 1008, 136 S. Ct. 549, 193 L. Ed. 2d 429, 2015 U.S. LEXIS 7491.

November 30, 2015. Petition for writ of certiorari to the United States Court of Appeals for the Ninth Circuit denied.

Same case below, 607 Fed. Appx. 640.

No. 15-444. **Frances Endencia, Petitioner v. Rush Behavioral Health, et al.**

577 U.S. 1008, 136 S. Ct. 554, 193 L. Ed. 2d 429, 2015 U.S. LEXIS 7658.

November 30, 2015. Petition for writ of certiorari to the Appellate Court of Illinois, First District, denied.

No. 15-452. **Gary L. Leonard, et ux., Petitioners v. Ocwen Loan Servicing, LLC, et al.**

577 U.S. 1008, 136 S. Ct. 554, 193 L. Ed. 2d 429, 2015 U.S. LEXIS 7599.

November 30, 2015. Petition for writ of certiorari to the United States Court of Appeals for the Fifth Circuit denied.

Same case below, 616 Fed. Appx. 677.

No. 15-459. Jed Laften Nagel, Petitioner v. Alabama.

577 U.S. 1008, 136 S. Ct. 556, 193 L. Ed. 2d 430, 2015 U.S. LEXIS 7494.

November 30, 2015. Petition for writ of certiorari to the Court of Criminal Appeals of Alabama denied.

No. 15-476. Harvey R. Johnson, Petitioner v. Maureen Cruz, Warden.

577 U.S. 1008, 136 S. Ct. 556, 193 L. Ed. 2d 430, 2015 U.S. LEXIS 7580.

November 30, 2015. Petition for writ of certiorari to the United States Court of Appeals for the Fourth Circuit denied.

Same case below, 597 Fed. Appx. 161.

No. 15-477. James Albert Beckman, Jr., Petitioner v. United States.

577 U.S. 1008, 136 S. Ct. 556, 193 L. Ed. 2d 430, 2015 U.S. LEXIS 7537.

November 30, 2015. Petition for writ of certiorari to the United States Court of Appeals for the Sixth Circuit denied.

Same case below, 624 Fed. Appx. 909.

No. 15-482. Joseph Parr, et ux., Individually and as Parents and Natural Guardians of Samantha Parr, Petitioners v. Ford Motor Company, et al.

577 U.S. 1008, 136 S. Ct. 557, 193 L. Ed. 2d 430, 2015 U.S. LEXIS 7547.

November 30, 2015. Petition for writ of certiorari to the Superior Court of Pennsylvania, Philadelphia Office, denied.

Same case below, 109 A.3d 682.

No. 15-487. Umeme Raysor, Petitioner v. United States.

577 U.S. 1008, 136 S. Ct. 558, 193 L. Ed. 2d 430, 2015 U.S. LEXIS 7642.

November 30, 2015. Petition for writ of certiorari to the United States Court of Appeals for the Second Circuit denied.

No. 15-496. Richard H. Rosario, Petitioner v. Chief Justice Thomas G. Saylor, et al.

577 U.S. 1008, 136 S. Ct. 558, 193 L. Ed. 2d 430, 2015 U.S. LEXIS 7606.

November 30, 2015. Petition for writ of certiorari to the United States Court of Appeals for the Third Circuit denied.

Same case below, 799 F.3d 216.

No. 15-503. Eli Chabot, et ux., Petitioners v. United States.

577 U.S. 1009, 136 S. Ct. 559, 193 L. Ed. 2d 430, 2015 U.S. LEXIS 7528.

November 30, 2015. Petition for writ of certiorari to the United States Court of Appeals for the Third Circuit denied.

Same case below, 793 F.3d 338.

Same case below, 795 F.3d 343.

No. 15-523. Ronald Deandrea Solomon, Petitioner v. United States.

577 U.S. 1009, 136 S. Ct. 560, 193 L. Ed. 2d 431, 2015 U.S. LEXIS 7522.

November 30, 2015. Petition for writ of certiorari to the United States Court of Appeals for the Eleventh Circuit denied.

Same case below, 610 Fed. Appx. 956.

No. 15-540. Sundersingh Bala, Petitioner v. Virginia Department of Conservation and Recreation.

577 U.S. 1009, 136 S. Ct. 563, 193 L. Ed. 2d 431, 2015 U.S. LEXIS 7488.

November 30, 2015. Petition for writ of certiorari to the United States Court of Appeals for the Fourth Circuit denied.

Same case below, 614 Fed. Appx. 636.

No. 15-561. Nautilus, Inc., Petitioner v. Biosig Instruments, Inc.

577 U.S. 1009, 136 S. Ct. 569, 193 L. Ed. 2d 431, 2015 U.S. LEXIS 7644.

November 30, 2015. Petition for writ of certiorari to the United States Court of Appeals for the Federal Circuit denied.

Same case below, 783 F.3d 1374.

No. 15-568. City of Concord, New Hampshire, Petitioner v. Northern New England Telephone Operations LLC.

577 U.S. 1009, 136 S. Ct. 564, 193 L. Ed. 2d 431, 2015 U.S. LEXIS 7546.

November 30, 2015. Petition for writ of certiorari to the United States Court of Appeals for the Second Circuit denied.

No. 15-5047. Fermin Rodriguez-Bernal, Petitioner v. United States.

577 U.S. 1009, 136 S. Ct. 534, 193 L. Ed. 2d 431, 2015 U.S. LEXIS 7598.

November 30, 2015. Petition for writ of certiorari to the United States Court of Appeals for the Fifth Circuit denied.

Same case below, 783 F.3d 1002.

No. 15-5172. Ricci Mobley, Petitioner v. Georgia.

577 U.S. 1009, 136 S. Ct. 535, 193 L. Ed. 2d 431, 2015 U.S. LEXIS 7570.

November 30, 2015. Petition for writ of certiorari to the Supreme Court of Georgia denied.

Same case below, 296 Ga. 876, 770 S.E.2d 1.

No. 15-5222. James Edward Norris, Petitioner v. Anthony Foxx, Secretary of Transportation, et al.

577 U.S. 1009, 136 S. Ct. 535, 193 L. Ed. 2d 431, 2015 U.S. LEXIS 7474, reh den 577 U.S. 1184, 136 S. Ct. 1250, 194 L. Ed. 2d 248, 2016 U.S. LEXIS 1242.

November 30, 2015. Petition for writ of certiorari to the United States Court of Appeals for the Ninth Circuit denied.

No. 15-5235. Miguel Riscajche-Siquina, Petitioner v. United States.

577 U.S. 1009, 136 S. Ct. 535, 193 L. Ed. 2d 431, 2015 U.S. LEXIS 7667.

November 30, 2015. Petition for writ of certiorari to the United States Court of Appeals for the Fifth Circuit denied.

Same case below, 605 Fed. Appx. 412.

No. 15-5317. David W. Hollingsworth, Petitioner v. United States.

577 U.S. 1009, 136 S. Ct. 535, 193 L. Ed. 2d 432, 2015 U.S. LEXIS 7477.

November 30, 2015. Petition for writ of certiorari to the United States Court of Appeals for the Fifth Circuit denied.

Same case below, 783 F.3d 556.

No. 15-5336. James Lewis, Petitioner v. United States.

577 U.S. 1009, 136 S. Ct. 536, 193 L. Ed. 2d 432, 2015 U.S. LEXIS 7633.

November 30, 2015. Petition for writ of certiorari to the United States Court of Appeals for the Fifth Circuit denied.

Same case below, 587 Fed. Appx. 223.

No. 15-5686. Marvin Antonio Franco-Bardales, Petitioner v. Loretta E. Lynch, Attorney General.

577 U.S. 1009, 136 S. Ct. 537, 193 L. Ed. 2d 432, 2015 U.S. LEXIS 7593.

November 30, 2015. Petition for writ of certiorari to the United States Court of Appeals for the Ninth Circuit denied.

Same case below, 599 Fed. Appx. 684.

No. 15-5696. Cary Michael Lambrix, Petitioner v. Julie L. Jones, Secretary, Florida Department of Corrections.

577 U.S. 1009, 136 S. Ct. 537, 193 L. Ed. 2d 432, 2015 U.S. LEXIS 7595.

November 30, 2015. Petition for writ of certiorari to the United States Court of Appeals for the Eleventh Circuit denied.

No. 15-5738. Dana J. Huff, Petitioner v. United States.

577 U.S. 1009, 136 S. Ct. 537, 193 L. Ed. 2d 432, 2015 U.S. LEXIS 7620.

November 30, 2015. Petition for writ of certiorari to the United States Court of Appeals for the Tenth Circuit denied.

Same case below, 782 F.3d 1221.

No. 15-5756. Dana E. Tuomi, Petitioner v. United States.

577 U.S. 1010, 136 S. Ct. 537, 193 L. Ed. 2d 432, 2015 U.S. LEXIS 7605, reh den 577 U.S. 1184, 136 S. Ct. 1250, 194 L. Ed. 2d 248, 2016 U.S. LEXIS 1144.

November 30, 2015. Petition for writ of certiorari to the United States Court of Appeals for the Eleventh Circuit denied.

Same case below, 605 Fed. Appx. 956.

No. 15-5770. Michael F. Durante, Petitioner v. United States.

577 U.S. 1010, 136 S. Ct. 537, 193 L. Ed. 2d 432, 2015 U.S. LEXIS 7534.

November 30, 2015. Petition for writ of certiorari to the United States Court of Appeals for the Third Circuit denied.

Same case below, 612 Fed. Appx. 129.

No. 15-5804. John R. Tomikel, Petitioner v. Virginia.

577 U.S. 1010, 136 S. Ct. 538, 193 L. Ed. 2d 432, 2015 U.S. LEXIS 7471.

November 30, 2015. Petition for writ of certiorari to the Supreme Court of Virginia denied.

No. 15-6117. James D. Ford, Petitioner v. Florida, et al.

577 U.S. 1010, 136 S. Ct. 538, 193 L. Ed. 2d 433, 2015 U.S. LEXIS 7648.

November 30, 2015. Petition for writ of certiorari to the Supreme Court of Florida denied.

Same case below, 168 So. 3d 224.

No. 15-6121. Josue Carius, Petitioner v. Florida.

577 U.S. 1010, 136 S. Ct. 538, 193 L. Ed. 2d 433, 2015 U.S. LEXIS 7531.

November 30, 2015. Petition for writ of certiorari to the District Court of Appeal of Florida, Third District, denied.

Same case below, 163 So. 3d 1204.

No. 15-6137. Jose Lorenzo Esparza, Petitioner v. William Stephens, Director, Texas Department of Criminal Justice, Correctional Institutions Division.

577 U.S. 1010, 136 S. Ct. 539, 193 L. Ed. 2d 433, 2015 U.S. LEXIS 7560.

November 30, 2015. Petition for writ of certiorari to the United States Court of Appeals for the Fifth Circuit denied.

No. 15-6141. Kim Wade Dillon, Petitioner v. Robert Bob Dooley, Jr., Warden, et al.

577 U.S. 1010, 136 S. Ct. 539, 193 L. Ed. 2d 433, 2015 U.S. LEXIS 7608, reh den 577 U.S. 1184, 136 S. Ct. 1250, 194 L. Ed. 2d 248, 2016 U.S. LEXIS 1224.

November 30, 2015. Petition for writ of certiorari to the United States Court of Appeals for the Eighth Circuit denied.

No. 15-6145. Gatdet G. Chuol, Petitioner v. Nebraska.

577 U.S. 1010, 136 S. Ct. 539, 193 L. Ed. 2d 433, 2015 U.S. LEXIS 7617.

November 30, 2015. Petition for writ of certiorari to the Court of Appeals of Nebraska denied.

No. 15-6146. Michelle Croskey, Petitioner v. James Crawford, aka C&B Association Montgomery.

577 U.S. 1010, 136 S. Ct. 539, 193 L. Ed. 2d 433, 2015 U.S. LEXIS 7558.

November 30, 2015. Petition for writ of certiorari to the Court of Civil Appeals of Alabama denied.

Same case below, 177 So. 3d 468.

No. 15-6147. Kevin Terry Dotson, Petitioner v. Jeffery B. Kiser, Warden.

577 U.S. 1010, 136 S. Ct. 539, 193 L. Ed. 2d 433, 2015 U.S. LEXIS 7574.

November 30, 2015. Petition for writ of certiorari to the United States Court of Appeals for the Fourth Circuit denied.

Same case below, 603 Fed. Appx. 235.

No. 15-6148. Angelo Keith Clark, Petitioner v. William Stephens, Director, Texas Department of Criminal Justice, Correctional Intitutions Division.

577 U.S. 1010, 136 S. Ct. 540, 193 L. Ed. 2d 433, 2015 U.S. LEXIS 7487.

November 30, 2015. Petition for writ of certiorari to the United States Court of Appeals for the Fifth Circuit denied.

No. 15-6149. Heriberto Castro-Gutierrez, Petitioner v. Scott Frauenheim, Warden.

577 U.S. 1010, 136 S. Ct. 540, 193 L. Ed. 2d 434, 2015 U.S. LEXIS 7564.

November 30, 2015. Petition for writ of certiorari to the United States Court of Appeals for the Ninth Circuit denied.

Same case below, 590 Fed. Appx. 674.

No. 15-6150. Andy E., Petitioner v. John Doe, et al.

577 U.S. 1010, 136 S. Ct. 540, 193 L. Ed. 2d 434, 2015 U.S. LEXIS 7482.

November 30, 2015. Petition for writ of certiorari to the Supreme Court of Appeals of West Virginia denied.

No. 15-6151. Steven Joseph D'Amico, Petitioner v. Julie L. Jones, Secretary, Florida Department of Corrections, et al.

577 U.S. 1010, 136 S. Ct. 540, 193 L. Ed. 2d 434, 2015 U.S. LEXIS 7567.

November 30, 2015. Petition for writ of certiorari to the United States Court of Appeals for the Eleventh Circuit denied.

No. 15-6152. Marvin Lewis Doleman, Petitioner v. Dwight Neven, Warden, et al.

577 U.S. 1011, 136 S. Ct. 540, 193 L. Ed. 2d 434, 2015 U.S. LEXIS 7523.

November 30, 2015. Petition for writ of certiorari to the United States Court of Appeals for the Ninth Circuit denied.

No. 15-6155. Stanley Daniels, Petitioner v. Cindi Curtin, Warden.

577 U.S. 1011, 136 S. Ct. 541, 193 L. Ed. 2d 434, 2015 U.S. LEXIS 7649.

November 30, 2015. Petition for writ of certiorari to the United States Court of Appeals for the Sixth Circuit denied.

No. 15-6161. Nathaniel D. Banks, Petitioner v. Kim Butler, Warden.

577 U.S. 1011, 136 S. Ct. 541, 193 L. Ed. 2d 434, 2015 U.S. LEXIS 7624.

November 30, 2015. Petition for writ of certiorari to the United States Court of Appeals for the Seventh Circuit denied.

No. 15-6166. Robert J. Cooke, Petitioner v. New York.

577 U.S. 1011, 136 S. Ct. 542, 193 L. Ed. 2d 434, 2015 U.S. LEXIS 7632.

November 30, 2015. Petition for writ of certiorari to the Court of Appeals of New York denied.

Same case below, 24 N.Y.3d 1196, 3 N.Y.S.3d 755, 27 N.E.3d 469.

No. 15-6171. Donn Deveral Martin, Petitioner v. William Stephens, Director, Texas Department of Criminal Justice, Correctional Institutions Division.

577 U.S. 1011, 136 S. Ct. 542, 193 L. Ed. 2d 434, 2015 U.S. LEXIS 7552, reh den 577 U.S. 1125, 136 S. Ct. 997, 194 L. Ed. 2d 15, 2016 U.S. LEXIS 929.

November 30, 2015. Petition for writ of certiorari to the United States Court of Appeals for the Fifth Circuit denied.

No. 15-6173. Joseph Garivay, Petitioner v. David Long, Warden.

577 U.S. 1011, 136 S. Ct. 542, 193 L. Ed. 2d 435, 2015 U.S. LEXIS 7607.

November 30, 2015. Petition for writ of certiorari to the United States Court of Appeals for the Ninth Circuit denied.

No. 15-6175. Arthur Lewis Ghee, Petitioner v. Alabama Department of Human Resources, et al.

577 U.S. 1011, 136 S. Ct. 542, 193 L. Ed. 2d 435, 2015 U.S. LEXIS 7602.

November 30, 2015. Petition for writ of certiorari to the United States Court of Appeals for the Eleventh Circuit denied.

Same case below, 589 Fed. Appx. 486.

No. 15-6176. Conraad L. Hoever, Petitioner v. S. Porter, Warden, et al.

577 U.S. 1011, 136 S. Ct. 543, 193 L. Ed. 2d 435, 2015 U.S. LEXIS 7512, reh den 578 U.S. 956, 136 S. Ct. 1730, 194 L. Ed. 2d 826, 2016 U.S. LEXIS 2823.

November 30, 2015. Petition for writ of certiorari to the United States Court of Appeals for the Eleventh Circuit denied.

No. 15-6178. Vicki Casseday M. Howard, Petitioner v. Luther Strange, Governor of Alabama, et al.

577 U.S. 1011, 136 S. Ct. 543, 193 L. Ed. 2d 435, 2015 U.S. LEXIS 7559.

November 30, 2015. Petition for writ of certiorari to the United States Court of Appeals for the Eleventh Circuit denied.

No. 15-6180. Jimmie Harrell, Jr., Petitioner v. United States.

577 U.S. 1011, 136 S. Ct. 543, 193 L. Ed. 2d 435, 2015 U.S. LEXIS 7612.

November 30, 2015. Petition for writ of certiorari to the United States Court of Appeals for the Eleventh Circuit denied.

Same case below, 603 Fed. Appx. 877.

No. 15-6182. Ricky Leander Gamble, Petitioner v. George Kenworthy, et al.

577 U.S. 1011, 136 S. Ct. 543, 193 L. Ed. 2d 435, 2015 U.S. LEXIS 7627.

November 30, 2015. Petition for writ of certiorari to the United States Court of Appeals for the Fourth Circuit denied.

Same case below, 604 Fed. Appx. 301.

No. 15-6184. Randall Travis Green, Petitioner v. Mike Addison, Warden.

577 U.S. 1011, 136 S. Ct. 543, 193 L. Ed. 2d 435, 2015 U.S. LEXIS 7483.

November 30, 2015. Petition for writ of certiorari to the United States Court of Appeals for the Tenth Circuit denied.

Same case below, 613 Fed. Appx. 704.

No. 15-6186. Alfredo Holguin, Petitioner v. Texas.

577 U.S. 1011, 136 S. Ct. 543, 193 L. Ed. 2d 435, 2015 U.S. LEXIS 7568.

November 30, 2015. Petition for writ of certiorari to the Court of Appeals of Texas, Eighth District, denied.

No. 15-6190. Ravon Ramsey, Petitioner v. William Muniz, Acting Warden.

577 U.S. 1011, 136 S. Ct. 544, 193 L. Ed. 2d 436, 2015 U.S. LEXIS 7517.

November 30, 2015. Petition for writ of certiorari to the United States Court of Appeals for the Ninth Circuit denied.

No. 15-6194. Steven Jacob Seibert, Petitioner v. Georgia.

577 U.S. 1011, 136 S. Ct. 544, 193 L. Ed. 2d 436, 2015 U.S. LEXIS 7510, reh den 577 U.S. 1125, 136 S. Ct. 997, 194 L. Ed. 2d 15, 2016 U.S. LEXIS 902.

November 30, 2015. Petition for writ of certiorari to the Court of Appeals of Georgia denied.

No. 15-6196. William Michael Hart, Petitioner v. Sherry A. Salois, et al.

577 U.S. 1012, 136 S. Ct. 544, 193 L. Ed. 2d 436, 2015 U.S. LEXIS 7509.

November 30, 2015. Petition for writ of certiorari to the United States Court of Appeals for the Tenth Circuit denied.

Same case below, 605 Fed. Appx. 694.

No. 15-6200. Durwyn Talley, Petitioner v. Thomas Baker, et al.

577 U.S. 1012, 136 S. Ct. 544, 193 L. Ed. 2d 436, 2015 U.S. LEXIS 7556, reh den 577 U.S. 1125, 136 S. Ct. 997, 194 L. Ed. 2d 15, 2016 U.S. LEXIS 877.

November 30, 2015. Petition for writ of certiorari to the United States Court of Appeals for the Seventh Circuit denied.

No. 15-6204. Lacey Mark Sivak, Petitioner v. Idaho.

577 U.S. 1012, 136 S. Ct. 544, 193 L. Ed. 2d 436, 2015 U.S. LEXIS 7635.

November 30, 2015. Petition for writ of certiorari to the Court of Appeals of Idaho denied.

No. 15-6207. Tracy Lee Thurman, Petitioner v. William Stephens, Director, Texas Department of Criminal Justice, Correctional Institutions Division.

577 U.S. 1012, 136 S. Ct. 544, 193 L. Ed. 2d 436, 2015 U.S. LEXIS 7588.

November 30, 2015. Petition for writ of certiorari to the United States Court of Appeals for the Fifth Circuit denied.

No. 15-6208. Milton Leon Terry, Petitioner v. Virginia.

577 U.S. 1012, 136 S. Ct. 544, 193 L. Ed. 2d 436, 2015 U.S. LEXIS 7636.

November 30, 2015. Petition for writ of certiorari to the Supreme Court of Virginia denied.

No. 15-6212. Larry Thomas, Jr., Petitioner v. Jerry Goodwin, Warden.

577 U.S. 1012, 136 S. Ct. 545, 193 L. Ed. 2d 436, 2015 U.S. LEXIS 7630.

November 30, 2015. Petition for writ of certiorari to the United States Court of Appeals for the Fifth Circuit denied.

Same case below, 786 F.3d 395.

No. 15-6215. Stephen Corey Bryant, Petitioner v. South Carolina.

577 U.S. 1012, 136 S. Ct. 545, 193 L. Ed. 2d 437, 2015 U.S. LEXIS 7516.

November 30, 2015. Petition for writ of certiorari to the Court of Common Pleas of South Carolina, Sumter County, denied.

No. 15-6216. Rebecca Regina Boone, Petitioner v. Tony Howerton, Warden.

577 U.S. 1012, 136 S. Ct. 545, 193 L. Ed. 2d 437, 2015 U.S. LEXIS 7499.

November 30, 2015. Petition for writ of certiorari to the Superior Court of Georgia, Habersham County, denied.

No. 15-6218. Christopher Barksdale, Petitioner v. United States District Court for the Northern District of Ohio.

577 U.S. 1012, 136 S. Ct. 569, 193 L. Ed. 2d 437, 2015 U.S. LEXIS 7577, reh den 577 U.S. 1096, 136 S. Ct. 887, 193 L. Ed. 2d 779, 2016 U.S. LEXIS 555.

November 30, 2015. Petition for writ of certiorari to the United States Court of Appeals for the Sixth Circuit denied.

No. 15-6226. Albert Verlee, Petitioner v. Texas (two judgments).

577 U.S. 1012, 136 S. Ct. 545, 193 L. Ed. 2d 437, 2015 U.S. LEXIS 7566.

November 30, 2015. Petition for writ of certiorari to the Court of Criminal Appeals of Texas denied.

No. 15-6231. Jose F. Valencia, Petitioner v. City of Santa Fe, New Mexico, et al.

577 U.S. 1012, 136 S. Ct. 546, 193 L. Ed. 2d 437, 2015 U.S. LEXIS 7584, reh den 577 U.S. 1125, 136 S. Ct. 997, 194 L. Ed. 2d 15, 2016 U.S. LEXIS 905.

November 30, 2015. Petition for writ of certiorari to the United States Court of Appeals for the Tenth Circuit denied.

Same case below, 599 Fed. Appx. 353.

No. 15-6232. Jose Valencia, Petitioner v. Heinz De Luca, et al.

577 U.S. 1012, 136 S. Ct. 546, 193 L. Ed. 2d 437, 2015 U.S. LEXIS 7505, reh den 577 U.S. 1125, 136 S. Ct. 997, 194 L. Ed. 2d 15, 2016 U.S. LEXIS 872.

November 30, 2015. Petition for writ of certiorari to the United States Court of Appeals for the Tenth Circuit denied.

Same case below, 612 Fed. Appx. 512.

No. 15-6234. Steven Lee, Petitioner v. Paul Hymowitz, et al.

577 U.S. 1012, 136 S. Ct. 546, 193 L. Ed. 2d 437, 2015 U.S. LEXIS 7533, reh den 577 U.S. 1097, 136 S. Ct. 888, 193 L. Ed. 2d 780, 2016 U.S. LEXIS 598.

November 30, 2015. Petition for writ of certiorari to the United States Court of Appeals for the Second Circuit denied.

No. 15-6237. Corielle Johnson, Petitioner v. Jeffrey Dauphanus, et al.

577 U.S. 1012, 136 S. Ct. 546, 193 L. Ed. 2d 437, 2015 U.S. LEXIS 7641, reh den 577 U.S. 1114, 136 S. Ct. 926, 193 L. Ed. 2d 811, 2016 U.S. LEXIS 638.

November 30, 2015. Petition for writ of certiorari to the United States Court of Appeals for the Sixth Circuit denied.

No. 15-6239. Tod Jack, Petitioner v. Virginia Bureau of Insurance.

577 U.S. 1012, 136 S. Ct. 546, 193 L. Ed. 2d 438, 2015 U.S. LEXIS 7655.

November 30, 2015. Petition for writ of certiorari to the United States Court of Appeals for the Fourth Circuit denied.

Same case below, 610 Fed. Appx. 295.

No. 15-6242. Anne E. Mitchell, Petitioner v. Monica P. Navarro, et al.

577 U.S. 1013, 136 S. Ct. 547, 193 L. Ed. 2d 438, 2015 U.S. LEXIS 7600.

November 30, 2015. Petition for writ of certiorari to the United States Court of Appeals for the Sixth Circuit denied.

No. 15-6245. Fred B. Salas, Petitioner v. Independent Electrical Contractors Inc., et al.

577 U.S. 1013, 136 S. Ct. 547, 193 L. Ed. 2d 438, 2015 U.S. LEXIS 7625.

November 30, 2015. Petition for writ of certiorari to the United States Court of Appeals for the Ninth Circuit denied.

Same case below, 603 Fed. Appx. 607.

No. 15-6248. James Benjamin Barstad, Petitioner v. Washington Department of Corrections, et al.

577 U.S. 1013, 136 S. Ct. 547, 193 L. Ed. 2d 438, 2015 U.S. LEXIS 7601.

November 30, 2015. Petition for writ of certiorari to the United States Court of Appeals for the Ninth Circuit denied.

Same case below, 609 Fed. Appx. 427.

No. 15-6250. Jimmy Reid, Petitioner v. Oliver Washington.

577 U.S. 1013, 136 S. Ct. 547, 193 L. Ed. 2d 438, 2015 U.S. LEXIS 7585.

November 30, 2015. Petition for writ of certiorari to the United States Court of Appeals for the Fourth Circuit denied.

Same case below, 599 Fed. Appx. 502.

No. 15-6253. Prentice Wheatley, Petitioner v. Michelle Smith, et al.

577 U.S. 1013, 136 S. Ct. 547, 193 L. Ed. 2d 438, 2015 U.S. LEXIS 7573.

November 30, 2015. Petition for writ of certiorari to the United States Court of Appeals for the Eighth Circuit denied.

Same case below, 593 Fed. Appx. 589.

No. 15-6262. Juan Celso Zavaleta Perez, Petitioner v. Frank L. Perry, Secretary, North Carolina Department of Public Safety.

577 U.S. 1013, 136 S. Ct. 547, 193 L. Ed. 2d 438, 2015 U.S. LEXIS 7619.

November 30, 2015. Petition for writ of certiorari to the United States Court of Appeals for the Fourth Circuit denied.

Same case below, 600 Fed. Appx. 184.

No. 15-6263. Ronald A. Nurse, Petitioner v. Sheraton Atlanta Hotel, et al.

577 U.S. 1013, 136 S. Ct. 548, 193 L. Ed. 2d 438, 2015 U.S. LEXIS 7575, reh den 577 U.S. 1184, 136 S. Ct. 1251, 194 L. Ed. 2d 249, 2016 U.S. LEXIS 1256.

November 30, 2015. Petition for writ of certiorari to the United States Court of Appeals for the Eleventh Circuit denied.

Same case below, 618 Fed. Appx. 987.

Same case below, 471 Mass. 537, 31 N.E.3d 575.

No. 15-6264. Calvin Neyland, Jr., Petitioner v. Ohio.

577 U.S. 1013, 136 S. Ct. 548, 193 L. Ed. 2d 439, 2015 U.S. LEXIS 7472.

November 30, 2015. Petition for writ of certiorari to the Court of Appeals of Ohio, Wood County, denied.

No. 15-6266. Marti Lundahl, Petitioner v. American Bankers Insurance Company of Florida.

577 U.S. 1013, 136 S. Ct. 548, 193 L. Ed. 2d 439, 2015 U.S. LEXIS 7609.

November 30, 2015. Petition for writ of certiorari to the United States Court of Appeals for the Tenth Circuit denied.

Same case below, 610 Fed. Appx. 734.

No. 15-6267. Bobby Joe Peyronel, Petitioner v. Texas.

577 U.S. 1013, 136 S. Ct. 548, 193 L. Ed. 2d 439, 2015 U.S. LEXIS 7542.

November 30, 2015. Petition for writ of certiorari to the Court of Criminal Appeals of Texas denied.

Same case below, 465 S.W.3d 650.

No. 15-6268. Juan Pagan, Petitioner v. Massachusetts.

577 U.S. 1013, 136 S. Ct. 548, 193 L. Ed. 2d 439, 2015 U.S. LEXIS 7592.

November 30, 2015. Petition for writ of certiorari to the Supreme Judicial Court of Massachusetts denied.

No. 15-6270. Jeremy Garrett, Petitioner v. Tennessee.

577 U.S. 1013, 136 S. Ct. 549, 193 L. Ed. 2d 439, 2015 U.S. LEXIS 7501.

November 30, 2015. Petition for writ of certiorari to the Court of Criminal Appeals of Tennessee, Western Division, denied.

No. 15-6277. John David Wilson, Jr., Petitioner v. Florida.

577 U.S. 1013, 136 S. Ct. 549, 193 L. Ed. 2d 439, 2015 U.S. LEXIS 7657.

November 30, 2015. Petition for writ of certiorari to the Supreme Court of Florida denied.

Same case below, 173 So. 3d 968.

No. 15-6279. Chong Su Yi, Petitioner v. Capital One, N.A.

577 U.S. 1014, 136 S. Ct. 549, 193 L. Ed. 2d 439, 2015 U.S. LEXIS 7538.

November 30, 2015. Petition for writ of certiorari to the United States Court of Appeals for the Fourth Circuit denied.

Same case below, 600 Fed. Appx. 124.

No. 15-6281. David Reeves, Petitioner v. Bruce Chatman, Warden.

577 U.S. 1014, 136 S. Ct. 549, 193 L. Ed. 2d 439, 2015 U.S. LEXIS 7565.

November 30, 2015. Petition for writ of certiorari to the Superior Court of Georgia, Tattnall County, denied.

No. 15-6285. Marcus Elliot King, Petitioner v. Thomas Mackie, Warden.

577 U.S. 1014, 136 S. Ct. 550, 193 L. Ed. 2d 440, 2015 U.S. LEXIS 7530.

November 30, 2015. Petition for writ of certiorari to the United States Court of Appeals for the Sixth Circuit denied.

No. 15-6293. Dennis R. Brock, Petitioner v. Brian Cook, Warden.

577 U.S. 1014, 136 S. Ct. 550, 193 L. Ed. 2d 440, 2015 U.S. LEXIS 7493.

November 30, 2015. Petition for writ of certiorari to the Supreme Court of Ohio denied.

Same case below, 142 Ohio St. 3d 1473, 31 N.E.3d 652.

No. 15-6294. Zolo Agona Azania, Petitioner v. Ron Neal, Superintendent, Indiana State Prison.

577 U.S. 1014, 136 S. Ct. 550, 193 L. Ed. 2d 440, 2015 U.S. LEXIS 7615.

November 30, 2015. Petition for writ of certiorari to the United States Court of Appeals for the Seventh Circuit denied.

No. 15-6313. David Reeves, Petitioner v. Frederick Head, Warden, et al.

577 U.S. 1014, 136 S. Ct. 550, 193 L. Ed. 2d 440, 2015 U.S. LEXIS 7508.

November 30, 2015. Petition for writ of certiorari to the Superior Court of Georgia, Baldwin County, denied.

No. 15-6314. John Scales, Petitioner v. Laurel Harry, Superintendent, State Correctional Institution at Camp Hill, et al.

577 U.S. 1014, 136 S. Ct. 550, 193 L. Ed. 2d 440, 2015 U.S. LEXIS 7479.

November 30, 2015. Petition for writ of certiorari to the United States Court of Appeals for the Third Circuit denied.

No. 15-6315. Herbert Nicholson, Petitioner v. Louisiana.

577 U.S. 1014, 136 S. Ct. 551, 193 L. Ed. 2d 440, 2015 U.S. LEXIS 7669.

November 30, 2015. Petition for writ of certiorari to the Supreme Court of Louisiana denied.

Same case below, 169 So. 3d 344.

No. 15-6318. Stephanie Denise Olson, Petitioner v. Jeff Little, Warden.

577 U.S. 1014, 136 S. Ct. 551, 193 L. Ed. 2d 440, 2015 U.S. LEXIS 7541.

November 30, 2015. Petition for writ of certiorari to the United States Court of Appeals for the Sixth Circuit denied.

Same case below, 604 Fed. Appx. 387.

No. 15-6322. Andre Ledon Booker, Petitioner v. California.

577 U.S. 1014, 136 S. Ct. 551, 193 L. Ed. 2d 440, 2015 U.S. LEXIS 7587.

November 30, 2015. Petition for writ of certiorari to the Supreme Court of California denied.

No. 15-6323. Scott Boyer, Petitioner v. Massachusetts.

577 U.S. 1014, 136 S. Ct. 570, 193 L. Ed. 2d 441, 2015 U.S. LEXIS 7540.

November 30, 2015. Petition for writ of certiorari to the Appeals Court of Massachusetts denied.

Same case below, 87 Mass. App. Ct. 1111, 26 N.E.3d 1141.

No. 15-6324. Franklin Donell Aikins, Petitioner v. Florida.

577 U.S. 1014, 136 S. Ct. 551, 193 L. Ed. 2d 441, 2015 U.S. LEXIS 7590.

November 30, 2015. Petition for writ of certiorari to the District Court of Appeal of Florida, Fifth District, denied.

Same case below, 169 So. 3d 1191.

No. 15-6329. Marcus Isaiah Washington, Petitioner v. William Morris Endeavor Entertainment, LLC, et al.

577 U.S. 1014, 136 S. Ct. 551, 193 L. Ed. 2d 441, 2015 U.S. LEXIS 7518, reh den 577 U.S. 1184, 136 S. Ct. 1251, 194 L. Ed. 2d 249, 2016 U.S. LEXIS 1352.

November 30, 2015. Petition for writ of certiorari to the United States Court of Appeals for the Second Circuit denied.

No. 15-6333. Marcus Vargas, Petitioner v. Steven Johnson, Administrator, New Jersey State Prison.

577 U.S. 1014, 136 S. Ct. 552, 193 L. Ed. 2d 441, 2015 U.S. LEXIS 7651.

November 30, 2015. Petition for writ of certiorari to the United States Court of Appeals for the Third Circuit denied.

No. 15-6339. Michael Doyle Ruggles, Petitioner v. Dominic Yagong, et al.

577 U.S. 1015, 136 S. Ct. 552, 193 L. Ed. 2d 441, 2015 U.S. LEXIS 7502.

November 30, 2015. Petition for writ of certiorari to the Supreme Court of Hawaii denied.

Same case below, 135 Hawaii 411, 353 P.3d 953.

No. 15-6345. Reginald Lee Rogers, Sr., Petitioner v. Frank L. Perry, Secretary, North Carolina Department of Public Safety.

577 U.S. 1015, 136 S. Ct. 552, 193 L. Ed. 2d 441, 2015 U.S. LEXIS 7581.

November 30, 2015. Petition for writ of certiorari to the United States Court of Appeals for the Fourth Circuit denied.

Same case below, 608 Fed. Appx. 147.

No. 15-6347. Scott Powers, Petitioner v. Terry A. Tibbals, Warden.

577 U.S. 1015, 136 S. Ct. 552, 193 L. Ed. 2d 441, 2015 U.S. LEXIS 7495.

November 30, 2015. Petition for writ of certiorari to the United States Court of Appeals for the Sixth Circuit denied.

No. 15-6349. Carlos Esquivel, Petitioner v. Al Ramirez.

577 U.S. 1015, 136 S. Ct. 552, 193 L. Ed. 2d 441, 2015 U.S. LEXIS 7618.

November 30, 2015. Petition for writ of certiorari to the United States Court of Appeals for the Ninth Circuit denied.

Same case below, 605 Fed. Appx. 661.

No. 15-6351. Jarvis Wolfe, Petitioner v. Jacquelyn Banks, Superintendent, South Mississippi Correctional Institution.

577 U.S. 1015, 136 S. Ct. 552, 193 L. Ed. 2d 442, 2015 U.S. LEXIS 7535.

November 30, 2015. Petition for writ of certiorari to the United States Court of Appeals for the Fifth Circuit denied.

No. 15-6381. James Boswell, Petitioner v. Victor J. Boschini, Jr., et al.

577 U.S. 1015, 136 S. Ct. 553, 193 L. Ed. 2d 442, 2015 U.S. LEXIS 7631.

November 30, 2015. Petition for writ of certiorari to the United States Court of Appeals for the Fifth Circuit denied.

Same case below, 581 Fed. Appx. 372.

No. 15-6383. David J. Haddow, Petitioner v. United States.

577 U.S. 1015, 136 S. Ct. 553, 193 L. Ed. 2d 442, 2015 U.S. LEXIS 7640.

November 30, 2015. Petition for writ of certiorari to the United States Court of Appeals for the Third Circuit denied.

Same case below, 598 Fed. Appx. 117.

No. 15-6385. Cesar Guadalupe Garcia, Petitioner v. Jeffrey Beard, Secretary, California Department of Corrections and Rehabilitation.

577 U.S. 1015, 136 S. Ct. 553, 193 L. Ed. 2d 442, 2015 U.S. LEXIS 7597.

November 30, 2015. Petition for writ of certiorari to the United States Court of Appeals for the Ninth Circuit denied.

No. 15-6388. Joel Christopher Holmes, Petitioner v. Washington.

577 U.S. 1015, 136 S. Ct. 553, 193 L. Ed. 2d 442, 2015 U.S. LEXIS 7486.

November 30, 2015. Petition for writ of certiorari to the Court of Appeals of Washington, Division 1, denied.

Same case below, 183 Wash. App. 1037.

No. 15-6393. James Mario Pridgen, Petitioner v. John Kerestes, Superintendent, State Correctional Institution at Mahanoy, et al.

577 U.S. 1015, 136 S. Ct. 553, 193 L. Ed. 2d 442, 2015 U.S. LEXIS 7621, reh den 577 U.S. 1114, 136 S. Ct. 926, 193 L. Ed. 2d 811, 2016 U.S. LEXIS 641.

November 30, 2015. Petition for writ of certiorari to the United States Court of Appeals for the Third Circuit denied.

No. 15-6397. Deidre Holmes Clark, Petitioner v. Allen & Overy, LLP.

577 U.S. 1015, 136 S. Ct. 553, 193 L. Ed. 2d 442, 2015 U.S. LEXIS 7504.

November 30, 2015. Petition for writ of certiorari to the Appellate Division, Supreme Court of New York, First Judicial Department, denied.

Same case below, 125 App. Div. 3d 497, 4 N.Y.S.3d 20.

No. 15-6399. Clarence B. Jackson, Petitioner v. Wal-Mart Stores, Inc.

577 U.S. 1015, 136 S. Ct. 554, 193 L. Ed. 2d 443, 2015 U.S. LEXIS 7569.

November 30, 2015. Petition for writ of certiorari to the United States Court of Appeals for the Seventh Circuit denied.

No. 15-6419. Dennis R. Walker, Petitioner v. Jeffrey Beard, Secretary, California Department of Corrections and Rehabilitation, et al.

577 U.S. 1015, 136 S. Ct. 570, 193 L. Ed. 2d 443, 2015 U.S. LEXIS 7519.

November 30, 2015. Petition for writ of certiorari to the United States Court of Appeals for the Ninth Circuit denied.

Same case below, 789 F.3d 1125.

No. 15-6424. Troy K. Scheffler, Petitioner v. Messerli & Kramer, P.A.

577 U.S. 1015, 136 S. Ct. 554, 193 L. Ed. 2d 443, 2015 U.S. LEXIS 7506.

November 30, 2015. Petition for writ of certiorari to the United States Court of Appeals for the Eighth Circuit denied.

Same case below, 791 F.3d 847.

No. 15-6440. Johnny Ray Luna, Petitioner v. Burl Cain, Warden.

577 U.S. 1016, 136 S. Ct. 555, 193 L. Ed. 2d 443, 2015 U.S. LEXIS 7611.

November 30, 2015. Petition for writ of certiorari to the United States Court of Appeals for the Fifth Circuit denied.

No. 15-6441. Kenneth Deangelo Thomas, Petitioner v. Tennessee.

577 U.S. 1016, 136 S. Ct. 555, 193 L. Ed. 2d 443, 2015 U.S. LEXIS 7544.

November 30, 2015. Petition for writ of certiorari to the Court of Criminal Appeals of Tennessee, Middle Division, denied.

No. 15-6447. Gary Raymond Harvey, Petitioner v. United States.

577 U.S. 1016, 136 S. Ct. 555, 193 L. Ed. 2d 443, 2015 U.S. LEXIS 7662.

November 30, 2015. Petition for writ of certiorari to the United States Court of Appeals for the Ninth Circuit denied.

Same case below, 597 Fed. Appx. 455.

No. 15-6457. Jamie D. Yoak, Petitioner v. Sprint Nextel Corporation, et al.

577 U.S. 1016, 136 S. Ct. 555, 193 L. Ed. 2d 443, 2015 U.S. LEXIS 7515.

November 30, 2015. Petition for writ of certiorari to the United States Court of Appeals for the Eighth Circuit denied.

No. 15-6466. David Lopez Moreno, Petitioner v. California.

577 U.S. 1016, 136 S. Ct. 555, 193 L. Ed. 2d 443, 2015 U.S. LEXIS 7634.

November 30, 2015. Petition for writ of certiorari to the Court of Appeal of California, Second Appellate District, Division Three, denied.

No. 15-6467. Eugene Herman Paulson, Petitioner v. South Dakota.

577 U.S. 1016, 136 S. Ct. 555, 193 L. Ed. 2d 444, 2015 U.S. LEXIS 7610.

November 30, 2015. Petition for writ of certiorari to the Supreme Court of South Dakota denied.

Same case below, 861 N.W.2d 504.

No. 15-6470. Joseph Bland, Petitioner v. Daniel T. French, et al.

577 U.S. 1016, 136 S. Ct. 556, 193 L. Ed. 2d 444, 2015 U.S. LEXIS 7473.

November 30, 2015. Petition for writ of certiorari to the United States Court of Appeals for the Sixth Circuit denied.

No. 15-6483. Lindsay Harding, Petitioner v. Colorado.

577 U.S. 1016, 136 S. Ct. 556, 193 L. Ed. 2d 444, 2015 U.S. LEXIS 7498.

November 30, 2015. Petition for writ of certiorari to the Court of Appeals of Colorado denied.

No. 15-6505. Robert W. Brooks, Petitioner v. Julie L. Jones, Secretary, Florida Department of Corrections, et al.

577 U.S. 1016, 136 S. Ct. 556, 193 L. Ed. 2d 444, 2015 U.S. LEXIS 7478.

November 30, 2015. Petition for writ of certiorari to the United States Court of Appeals for the Eleventh Circuit denied.

No. 15-6509. Joseph L. Bell, Jr., Petitioner v. United States.

577 U.S. 1016, 136 S. Ct. 557, 193 L. Ed. 2d 444, 2015 U.S. LEXIS 7650.

November 30, 2015. Petition for writ of certiorari to the United States Court of Appeals for the Seventh Circuit denied.

No. 15-6511. David Clum, Jr., Petitioner v. United States.

577 U.S. 1016, 136 S. Ct. 557, 193 L. Ed. 2d 444, 2015 U.S. LEXIS 7539, reh den 577 U.S. 1185, 136 S. Ct. 1252, 194 L. Ed. 2d 250, 2016 U.S. LEXIS 1355.

November 30, 2015. Petition for writ of certiorari to the United States Court of Appeals for the Eleventh Circuit denied.

Same case below, 607 Fed. Appx. 922.

No. 15-6515. James Strouse, Petitioner v. E. D. Wilson, Warden, et al.

577 U.S. 1016, 136 S. Ct. 557, 193 L. Ed. 2d 444, 2015 U.S. LEXIS 7562.

November 30, 2015. Petition for writ of certiorari to the United States Court of Appeals for the Ninth Circuit denied.

No. 15-6532. Antoine Richardson, Petitioner v. United States.

577 U.S. 1016, 136 S. Ct. 557, 193 L. Ed. 2d 444, 2015 U.S. LEXIS 7476.

November 30, 2015. Petition for writ of certiorari to the District of Columbia Court of Appeals denied.

Same case below, 104 A.3d 115.

No. 15-6556. Joseph Lobaito, Jr., Petitioner v. Financial Industry Regulatory Authority, Inc.

577 U.S. 1016, 136 S. Ct. 570, 193 L. Ed. 2d 445, 2015 U.S. LEXIS 7553.

November 30, 2015. Petition for writ of certiorari to the United States Court of Appeals for the Second Circuit denied.

Same case below, 599 Fed. Appx. 400.

No. 15-6572. David McCann, Petitioner v. Federal Deposit Insurance Corporation, as Receiver for Lakeside Community Bank.

577 U.S. 1016, 136 S. Ct. 558, 193 L. Ed. 2d 445, 2015 U.S. LEXIS 7554, reh den 577 U.S. 1125, 136 S. Ct. 997, 194 L. Ed. 2d 16, 2016 U.S. LEXIS 950.

November 30, 2015. Petition for writ of certiorari to the United States Court of Appeals for the Sixth Circuit denied.

No. 15-6590. Seidy Maria Tiburcio, Petitioner v. United States Capitol.

577 U.S. 1017, 136 S. Ct. 558, 193 L. Ed. 2d 445, 2015 U.S. LEXIS 7616, reh den 577 U.S. 1114, 136 S. Ct. 926, 193 L. Ed. 2d 811, 2016 U.S. LEXIS 639.

November 30, 2015. Petition for writ of certiorari to the United States Court of Appeals for the District of Columbia Circuit denied.

Same case below, 602 Fed. Appx. 540.

No. 15-6595. James Arthur Woodley, Petitioner v. Esker Tatum, Warden.

577 U.S. 1017, 136 S. Ct. 558, 193 L. Ed. 2d 445, 2015 U.S. LEXIS 7614.

November 30, 2015. Petition for writ of certiorari to the United States Court of Appeals for the First Circuit denied.

No. 15-6596. Keon Thomas and Styles Taylor, Petitioners v. United States.

577 U.S. 1017, 136 S. Ct. 558, 193 L. Ed. 2d 445, 2015 U.S. LEXIS 7514.

November 30, 2015. Petition for writ of certiorari to the United States Court of Appeals for the Seventh Circuit denied.

Same case below, 794 F.3d 705.

No. 15-6600. Alejandro Figueroa-Lugo, Petitioner v. United States.

577 U.S. 1017, 136 S. Ct. 559, 193 L. Ed. 2d 445, 2015 U.S. LEXIS 7647.

November 30, 2015. Petition for writ of certiorari to the United States Court of Appeals for the First Circuit denied.

Same case below, 793 F.3d 179.

No. 15-6606. Carlos Antonio Montanez, Petitioner v. Julie L. Jones, Secretary, Florida Department of Corrections, et al.

577 U.S. 1017, 136 S. Ct. 570, 193 L. Ed. 2d 445, 2015 U.S. LEXIS 7489.

November 30, 2015. Petition for writ of certiorari to the United States Court of Appeals for the Eleventh Circuit denied.

No. 15-6613. Pierre Yates, Petitioner v. Ohio.

577 U.S. 1017, 136 S. Ct. 559, 193 L. Ed. 2d 445, 2015 U.S. LEXIS 7659.

November 30, 2015. Petition for writ of certiorari to the Court of Appeals of Ohio, Cuyahoga County, denied.

No. 15-6617. Christopher Lovin, Petitioner v. David Osborne, Warden.

577 U.S. 1017, 136 S. Ct. 559, 193 L. Ed. 2d 446, 2015 U.S. LEXIS 7543.

November 30, 2015. Petition for writ of certiorari to the United States Court of Appeals for the Sixth Circuit denied.

No. 15-6621. Joshua Wayne Bevill, Petitioner v. United States.

577 U.S. 1017, 136 S. Ct. 570, 193 L. Ed. 2d 446, 2015 U.S. LEXIS 7654.

November 30, 2015. Petition for writ of certiorari to the United States Court of Appeals for the Fifth Circuit denied.

Same case below, 611 Fed. Appx. 180.

No. 15-6622. Isiah Taylor, III, Petitioner v. United States.

577 U.S. 1017, 136 S. Ct. 559, 193 L. Ed. 2d 446, 2015 U.S. LEXIS 7513, reh den 577 U.S. 1125, 136 S. Ct. 997, 194 L. Ed. 2d 16, 2016 U.S. LEXIS 866.

November 30, 2015. Petition for writ of certiorari to the United States Court of Appeals for the Sixth Circuit denied.

No. 15-6623. James Edward Smith, Petitioner v. Wendy Kelley, Director, Arkansas Department of Correction.

577 U.S. 1017, 136 S. Ct. 560, 193 L. Ed. 2d 446, 2015 U.S. LEXIS 7663.

November 30, 2015. Petition for writ of certiorari to the United States Court of Appeals for the Eighth Circuit denied.

No. 15-6624. Patrick Dewayne Smith, Petitioner v. United States.

577 U.S. 1017, 136 S. Ct. 560, 193 L. Ed. 2d 446, 2015 U.S. LEXIS 7532.

November 30, 2015. Petition for writ of certiorari to the United States Court of Appeals for the Sixth Circuit denied.

Same case below, 609 Fed. Appx. 340.

No. 15-6625. Dwight Moss, Petitioner v. United States.

577 U.S. 1017, 136 S. Ct. 560, 193 L. Ed. 2d 446, 2015 U.S. LEXIS 7578.

November 30, 2015. Petition for writ of certiorari to the United States Court of Appeals for the Eleventh Circuit denied.

No. 15-6631. Mark Anthony Beckford, Petitioner v. United States.

577 U.S. 1017, 136 S. Ct. 560, 193 L. Ed. 2d 446, 2015 U.S. LEXIS 7591.

November 30, 2015. Petition for writ of certiorari to the United States Court of Appeals for the Eleventh Circuit denied.

No. 15-6634. Timothy Eric Alston, Petitioner v. United States.

577 U.S. 1017, 136 S. Ct. 560, 193 L. Ed. 2d 446, 2015 U.S. LEXIS 7645.

November 30, 2015. Petition for writ of certiorari to the United States Court of Appeals for the Eleventh Circuit denied.

Same case below, 598 Fed. Appx. 730.

No. 15-6635. William Bell, Petitioner v. Rob Persson, Superintendent, Oregon State Correctional Institution.

577 U.S. 1017, 136 S. Ct. 561, 193 L. Ed. 2d 447, 2015 U.S. LEXIS 7639.

November 30, 2015. Petition for writ of certiorari to the United States Court of Appeals for the Ninth Circuit denied.

Same case below, 610 Fed. Appx. 619.

No. 15-6636. Fred L. Jones, Petitioner v. Marc Clements, Warden.

577 U.S. 1018, 136 S. Ct. 561, 193 L. Ed. 2d 447, 2015 U.S. LEXIS 7653.

November 30, 2015. Petition for writ of certiorari to the United States Court of Appeals for the Seventh Circuit denied.

No. 15-6637. Howard O. Kieffer, Petitioner v. Delbert G. Sauers, Warden.

577 U.S. 1018, 136 S. Ct. 561, 193 L. Ed. 2d 447, 2015 U.S. LEXIS 7582.

November 30, 2015. Petition for writ of certiorari to the United States Court of Appeals for the Third Circuit denied.

Same case below, 616 Fed. Appx. 464.

No. 15-6644. Ava Ramey, Petitioner v. United States.

577 U.S. 1018, 136 S. Ct. 561, 193 L. Ed. 2d 447, 2015 U.S. LEXIS 7603.

November 30, 2015. Petition for writ of certiorari to the United States Court of Appeals for the Fourth Circuit denied.

Same case below, 608 Fed. Appx. 165.

No. 15-6647. Allan Marcus Harvey, Petitioner v. United States.

577 U.S. 1018, 136 S. Ct. 561, 193 L. Ed. 2d 447, 2015 U.S. LEXIS 7589.

November 30, 2015. Petition for writ of certiorari to the United States Court of Appeals for the Sixth Circuit denied.

Same case below, 794 F.3d 617.

No. 15-6649. Isabel Gonzalez, Petitioner v. United States.

577 U.S. 1018, 136 S. Ct. 561, 193 L. Ed. 2d 447, 2015 U.S. LEXIS 7613.

November 30, 2015. Petition for writ of certiorari to the United States Court of Appeals for the Fourth Circuit denied.

Same case below, 616 Fed. Appx. 631.

No. 15-6650. Derek Zar, Susanne Zar, and Michael Jacoby, Petitioners v. United States.

577 U.S. 1018, 136 S. Ct. 562, 193 L. Ed. 2d 447, 2015 U.S. LEXIS 7521.

November 30, 2015. Petition for writ of certiorari to the United States Court of Appeals for the Tenth Circuit denied.

Same case below, 790 F.3d 1036.

No. 15-6651. Karen Davis, Petitioner v. Maryland State Department of Education Office of Child Care.

577 U.S. 1018, 136 S. Ct. 562, 193 L. Ed. 2d 447, 2015 U.S. LEXIS 7594.

November 30, 2015. Petition for writ of certiorari to the Court of Special Appeals of Maryland denied.

Same case below, 222 Md. App. 709.

No. 15-6655. Douglas Whisnant, Petitioner v. United States.

577 U.S. 1018, 136 S. Ct. 562, 193 L. Ed. 2d 448, 2015 U.S. LEXIS 7656.

November 30, 2015. Petition for writ of certiorari to the United States Court of Appeals for the Sixth Circuit denied.

No. 15-6656. Domingo Ventura, Petitioner v. United States.

577 U.S. 1018, 136 S. Ct. 562, 193 L. Ed. 2d 448, 2015 U.S. LEXIS 7526.

November 30, 2015. Petition for writ of certiorari to the United States Court of Appeals for the Second Circuit denied.

No. 15-6658. David Kirkland, Petitioner v. United States.

577 U.S. 1018, 136 S. Ct. 562, 193 L. Ed. 2d 448, 2015 U.S. LEXIS 7412.

November 30, 2015. Petition for writ of certiorari to the United States Court of Appeals for the Third Circuit denied.

Same case below, 612 Fed. Appx. 133.

No. 15-6671. Michael Short, Petitioner v. United States.

577 U.S. 1018, 136 S. Ct. 562, 193 L. Ed. 2d 448, 2015 U.S. LEXIS 7437.

November 30, 2015. Petition for writ of certiorari to the United States Court of Appeals for the Fifth Circuit denied.

No. 15-6678. Juan Manuel Medrano-Hernandez, Petitioner v. United States.

577 U.S. 1018, 136 S. Ct. 563, 193 L. Ed. 2d 448, 2015 U.S. LEXIS 7392.

November 30, 2015. Petition for writ of certiorari to the United States Court of Appeals for the Ninth Circuit denied.

Same case below, 604 Fed. Appx. 586.

No. 15-6680. Mario Oliver Perez-Sanchez, Petitioner v. United States.

577 U.S. 1018, 136 S. Ct. 563, 193 L. Ed. 2d 448, 2015 U.S. LEXIS 7414.

November 30, 2015. Petition for writ of certiorari to the United States Court of Appeals for the Fourth Circuit denied.

Same case below, 626 Fed. Appx. 412.

No. 15-6690. Leighton Fay, Petitioner v. Claude Maye, Warden.

577 U.S. 1018, 136 S. Ct. 563, 193 L. Ed. 2d 448, 2015 U.S. LEXIS 7436.

November 30, 2015. Petition for writ of certiorari to the United States Court of Appeals for the Tenth Circuit denied.

Same case below, 608 Fed. Appx. 667.

No. 15-6702. Phillip E. LaPointe, Petitioner v. Illinois.

577 U.S. 1018, 136 S. Ct. 563, 193 L. Ed. 2d 448, 2015 U.S. LEXIS 7428.

November 30, 2015. Petition for writ of certiorari to the Appellate Court of Illinois, Second District, denied.

Same case below, 396 Ill. Dec. 419, 40 N.E.3d 72.

No. 15-6705. Dijon McClurkin, Petitioner v. Maryland.

577 U.S. 1019, 136 S. Ct. 564, 193 L. Ed. 2d 449, 2015 U.S. LEXIS 7380.

November 30, 2015. Petition for writ of certiorari to the Court of Special Appeals of Maryland denied.

Same case below, 222 Md. App. 461, 113 A.3d 1111.

No. 15-115. Tyco Healthcare Group LP, et al., Petitioners v. Ethicon Endo-Surgery, Inc.

577 U.S. 1019, 136 S. Ct. 536, 193 L. Ed. 2d 449, 2015 U.S. LEXIS 7378.

November 30, 2015. Petition for writ of certiorari to the United States Court of Appeals for the Federal Circuit denied. Justice Alito took no part in the consideration or decision of this petition.

Same case below, 774 F.3d 968.

No. 15-161. Lloyd Rapelje, Warden, Petitioner v. Junior Fred Blackston.

577 U.S. 1019, 136 S. Ct. 388, 193 L. Ed. 2d 449, 2015 U.S. LEXIS 7364.

November 30, 2015. Petition for writ of certiorari to the United States Court of Appeals for the Sixth Circuit denied.

Same case below, 780 F.3d 340.

Justice **Scalia**, with whom Justice **Thomas** and Justice **Alito** join, dissenting from denial of certiorari.

A criminal defendant "shall enjoy the right . . . to be confronted with the witnesses against him." U. S. Const., Amdt. 6.

We have held that this right entitles the accused to cross-examine witnesses who testify at trial, and to exclude certain out-of-court statements that the defendant did not have a prior opportunity to cross-examine. *Crawford* v. *Washington*, 541 U.S. 36, 50-51, 124 S. Ct. 1354, 158 L. Ed. 2d 177 (2004); *Davis* v. *Alaska*, 415 U.S. 308, 315-317, 94 S. Ct. 1105, 39 L. Ed. 2d 347 (1974). We have never held— nor would the verb "to confront" support the holding—that confrontation includes the right to *admit* out-of-court statements into evidence. Nevertheless, the Sixth Circuit held not only that the Confrontation Clause guarantees the right to admit such evidence but that our cases have "clearly established" as much. We should grant certiorari and summarily reverse.

Respondent Junior Fred Blackston was convicted in Michigan state court of first-degree murder on the strength of the testimony of five people, some of whom participated in the crime. For reasons not relevant here, the court ordered a new trial. Before Blackston's retrial, however, two of the five witnesses signed written statements recanting their trial testimony. The prosecution called them at the second trial, but they refused to answer any questions. The trial court therefore pronounced them "unavailable" and, pursuant to a venerable hearsay exception, see Mich. Rule Evid. 804(b)(1) (2012); cf. 5 J. Wigmore, Evidence § 1370, p. 55 (J. Chadbourn rev. 1974), allowed their earlier testimony to be read to the jury. But the court refused to admit into evidence their written recantations.

Blackston was once again convicted of first-degree murder and sentenced to life imprisonment. Affirming the conviction, the Supreme Court of Michigan held that the trial court's exclusion of the recantations was not error and, even if it was, was harmless beyond a reasonable doubt. 481 Mich. 451, 751 N.W.2d 408 (2008).

This petition for federal habeas relief followed. The District Court conditionally granted the writ, finding that the exclusion of the recantations violated Blackston's Sixth and Fourteenth Amendment rights. 907 F. Supp. 2d 878 (ED Mich. 2012). A divided Sixth Circuit panel affirmed. 780 F.3d 340 (2015). In the Court of Appeals' view, "[t]here is a clearly established right to impeach the credibility of an adverse witness using the witness's own inconsistent statements." *Id.,* at 348. The recantations, reasoned the court, were inconsistent statements that had obvious impeachment value.

The Antiterrorism and Effective Death Penalty Act of 1996 (AEDPA) prohibits federal courts from granting habeas relief unless the state court's decision "involved an unreasonable application of . . . *clearly established* Federal law, as determined by the Supreme Court of the United States." 28 U.S.C. § 2254(d)(1) (emphasis added). As the dissenting judge below pointed out, no case of ours establishes, clearly or otherwise, that the Confrontation Clause bestows a right to *admit* this kind of evidence. 780 F.3d, at 363-364 (opinion of Kethledge, J.). In fact we long ago suggested just the opposite. *Mattox* v. *United States*, 156 U.S. 237, 245-250, 15 S. Ct. 337, 39 L. Ed. 409 (1895). Each of the cases the Sixth Circuit relied on involved the defendant's attempting during cross-examination to impeach *testifying witnesses*, not unavailable declarants. See *Olden* v. *Kentucky*, 488 U.S. 227, 230, 109 S. Ct. 480, 102 L. Ed. 2d 513 (1988) (*per curiam*); *Delaware* v. *Van Arsdall*, 475 U.S. 673, 676, 106 S. Ct. 1431, 89 L. Ed. 2d 674 (1986); *Alford* v. *United States*, 282 U.S. 687, 693, 51 S. Ct. 218, 75 L. Ed. 624 (1931). And just recently we said in *Nevada* v. *Jackson*, 569 U.S. 505, 512, 133 S. Ct. 1990, 186 L. Ed. 2d 62 (2013) (*per curiam*), that "this Court has never held that the Confrontation Clause entitles a criminal defendant to introduce *extrinsic evidence* for impeachment purposes." The Sixth Circuit thought the recantations here intrinsic, not extrinsic, and so beyond *Jackson*'s ambit. That is quite irrelevant. The pertinent question under AEDPA is whether our cases have clearly established a right, not whether they have failed to clearly foreclose it.

There may well be a plausible argument why the recantations ought to have been admitted under state law. See Mich. Rule Evid. 806. But nothing in our precedents clearly establishes their admissibility as a matter of federal constitutional law. AEDPA "provides a remedy for instances in which a state court unreasonably *applies* this Court's precedent; it does not require state courts to *extend* that precedent or license federal courts to treat the failure to do so as error." *White* v. *Woodall*, 572 U.S. 415, 426, 134 S. Ct. 1697, 188 L. Ed. 2d 698 (2014). By framing the confrontation right at a high level of generality (making it the right "to impeach the credibility of an adverse witness"), the Sixth Circuit in effect "transform[ed] . . . [an] imaginative extension of existing case law into 'clearly established'" law. *Jackson, supra,* at 512, 133 S. Ct. 1990, 186 L. Ed. 2d 62. That will not do.

The Sixth Circuit seems to have acquired a taste for disregarding AEDPA. *E.g., Woods* v. *Donald*, 575 U.S. 312, 135 S. Ct. 1372, 191 L. Ed. 2d 464 (2015) (*per curiam*); *White* v. *Woodall, supra*; *Burt* v. *Titlow*, 571 U.S. 12, 134 S. Ct. 10, 187 L. Ed. 2d 348 (2013); *Metrish* v. *Lancaster*, 569 U.S. 351, 133 S. Ct. 1781, 185 L. Ed. 2d 988 (2013); *Howes* v. *Fields*, 565 U.S. 499, 132 S. Ct. 1181, 182 L. Ed. 2d 17 (2012). We should grant certiorari to discourage this appetite.

No. 15-5628. Albert Holland, Jr., Petitioner v. Florida.

577 U.S. 1021, 136 S. Ct. 536, 193 L. Ed. 2d 450, 2015 U.S. LEXIS 7460.

November 30, 2015. Petition for writ of certiorari to the United States Court of Appeals for the Eleventh Circuit denied.

Justice Kagan took no part in the consideration or decision of this petition.

Same case below, 775 F.3d 1294.

––––––

No. 15-6296. Anthony Robert Mizner, Petitioner v. Randy Grounds, Warden.

577 U.S. 1021, 136 S. Ct. 550, 193 L. Ed. 2d 451, 2015 U.S. LEXIS 7446.

November 30, 2015. Petition for writ of certiorari to the United States Court of Appeals for the Ninth Circuit denied. Justice Breyer took no part in the consideration or decision of this petition.

Same case below, 591 Fed. Appx. 577.

––––––

No. 15-6612. Steven Martinez, Petitioner v. Tamyra Jarvis, Warden.

577 U.S. 1021, 136 S. Ct. 559, 193 L. Ed. 2d 451, 2015 U.S. LEXIS 7365.

November 30, 2015. Petition for writ of certiorari to the United States Court of Appeals for the Eleventh Circuit denied. Justice Kagan took no part in the consideration or decision of this petition.

Same case below, 609 Fed. Appx. 630.

––––––

No. 15-6163. In re Cary Michael Lambrix, Petitioner.

577 U.S. 1005, 136 S. Ct. 541, 193 L. Ed. 2d 451, 2015 U.S. LEXIS 7435.

November 30, 2015. Petition for writ of habeas corpus denied.

––––––

No. 15-6167. In re Michael Alonza Rufus, Petitioner.

577 U.S. 1005, 136 S. Ct. 542, 193 L. Ed. 2d 451, 2015 U.S. LEXIS 7406.

November 30, 2015. Petition for writ of habeas corpus denied.

––––––

No. 15-6738. In re Andrew Cox, Petitioner.

577 U.S. 1005, 136 S. Ct. 564, 193 L. Ed. 2d 451, 2015 U.S. LEXIS 7402.

November 30, 2015. Petition for writ of habeas corpus denied.

––––––

No. 15-6759. In re Robert Ramsey, Petitioner.

577 U.S. 1005, 136 S. Ct. 564, 193 L. Ed. 2d 451, 2015 U.S. LEXIS 7418.

November 30, 2015. Petition for writ of habeas corpus denied.

––––––

No. 15-6870. In re Levon Mintz, Petitioner.

577 U.S. 1006, 136 S. Ct. 564, 193 L. Ed. 2d 451, 2015 U.S. LEXIS 7450.

November 30, 2015. Petition for writ of habeas corpus denied.

––––––

No. 15-6223. In re Shawn P. Shelton, Petitioner.

577 U.S. 1006, 136 S. Ct. 545, 193 L. Ed. 2d 451, 2015 U.S. LEXIS 7370.

November 30, 2015. Petition for writ of mandamus denied.

No. 15-6698. In re Arturo Solis, Petitioner.

577 U.S. 1006, 136 S. Ct. 563, 193 L. Ed. 2d 452, 2015 U.S. LEXIS 7451.

November 30, 2015. Motion of petitioner for leave to proceed in forma pauperis denied, and petition for writ of mandamus and/or prohibition dismissed. See Rule 39.8. As petitioner has repeatedly abused this Court's process, the Clerk is directed not to accept any further petition in noncriminal matters from petitioner unless the docketing fees required by Rule 38(a) is paid and petition submitted in compliance with Rule 33.1. See Martin v. District of Columbia Court of Appeals, 506 U.S. 1, 113 S. Ct. 397, 121 L. Ed. 2d 305 (1992) (per curiam).

No. 15-6704. In re Arturo Solis, Petitioner.

577 U.S. 1006, 136 S. Ct. 564, 193 L. Ed. 2d 452, 2015 U.S. LEXIS 7468.

November 30, 2015. Motion of petitioner for leave to proceed in forma pauperis denied, and petition for writ of mandamus and/or prohibition dismissed. See Rule 39.8. As petitioner has repeatedly abused this Court's process, the Clerk is directed not to accept any further petition in noncriminal matters from petitioner unless the docketing fees required by Rule 38(a) is paid and petition submitted in compliance with Rule 33.1. See Martin v. District of Columbia Court of Appeals, 506 U.S. 1, 113 S. Ct. 397, 121 L. Ed. 2d 305 (1992) (per curiam).

No. 14-1312. Brandon Astor Jones, Petitioner v. Bruce Chatman, Warden.

577 U.S. 1021, 136 S. Ct. 570, 193 L. Ed. 2d 452, 2015 U.S. LEXIS 7430.

November 30, 2015. Petition for rehearing denied.

Former decision, 577 U.S. 817, 136 S. Ct. 43, 193 L. Ed. 2d 27, 2015 U.S. LEXIS 5386.

No. 14-1316. Jean Coulter, Petitioner v. Allegheny County Bar Association, et al.; Jean Coulter, Petitioner v. Susan Lope, et al.; Jean Coulter, Petitioner v. Mary Suzanne Ramsden, et al.; Jean Coulter, Petitioner v. Thomas Doerr, et al.; Jean Coulter, Petitioner v. Christine Gale, et al.; Jean Coulter, Petitioner v. James E. Mahood, et al.; and Jean Coulter, Petitioner v. Mary Suzanne Ramsden, et al.

577 U.S. 1021, 136 S. Ct. 571, 193 L. Ed. 2d 452, 2015 U.S. LEXIS 7369.

November 30, 2015. Petition for rehearing denied.

Former decision, 577 U.S. 817, 136 S. Ct. 44, 193 L. Ed. 2d 27, 2015 U.S. LEXIS 5559.

No. 14-1318. Gerald Dix, Petitioner v. Joseph P. Clancy, Director, United States Secret Service, et al.

577 U.S. 1021, 136 S. Ct. 571, 193 L. Ed. 2d 452, 2015 U.S. LEXIS 7438.

November 30, 2015. Petition for rehearing denied.

Former decision, 577 U.S. 817, 136 S. Ct. 45, 193 L. Ed. 2d 27, 2015 U.S. LEXIS 5368.

No. 14-1353. NetAirus Technologies, LLC, Petitioner v. Apple Inc.

577 U.S. 1021, 136 S. Ct. 571, 193 L. Ed. 2d 452, 2015 U.S. LEXIS 7417.

November 30, 2015. Petition for rehearing denied.

Former decision, 577 U.S. 819, 136 S. Ct. 54, 193 L. Ed. 2d 30, 2015 U.S. LEXIS 5539.

No. 14-1414. Arthur Lopez, Petitioner v. Newport Elementary School, et al.

577 U.S. 1021, 136 S. Ct. 571, 193 L. Ed. 2d 453, 2015 U.S. LEXIS 7415.

November 30, 2015. Petition for rehearing denied.

Former decision, 577 U.S. 821, 136 S. Ct. 82, 193 L. Ed. 2d 34, 2015 U.S. LEXIS 5565.

No. 14-1427. In re Modesta Sabeniano, Petitioner.

577 U.S. 1022, 136 S. Ct. 571, 193 L. Ed. 2d 453, 2015 U.S. LEXIS 7371.

November 30, 2015. Petition for rehearing denied.

Former decision, 577 U.S. 814, 136 S. Ct. 87, 193 L. Ed. 2d 217, 2015 U.S. LEXIS 4695.

No. 14-1479. Robert H. Hollander, Petitioner v. Christine R. Pembroke.

577 U.S. 1022, 136 S. Ct. 571, 193 L. Ed. 2d 453, 2015 U.S. LEXIS 7394.

November 30, 2015. Petition for rehearing denied.

Former decision, 577 U.S. 824, 136 S. Ct. 128, 193 L. Ed. 2d 40, 2015 U.S. LEXIS 5572.

No. 14-1498. Daniel Anthony Lucas, Petitioner v. Carl Humphrey, Warden.

577 U.S. 1022, 136 S. Ct. 571, 193 L. Ed. 2d 453, 2015 U.S. LEXIS 7391.

November 30, 2015. Petition for rehearing denied.

Former decision, 577 U.S. 914, 136 S. Ct. 135, 193 L. Ed. 2d 208, 2015 U.S. LEXIS 6116.

No. 14-1509. John LaCertosa, Petitioner v. Blackman Plumbing Supply Co., Inc., et al.

577 U.S. 1022, 136 S. Ct. 572, 193 L. Ed. 2d 453, 2015 U.S. LEXIS 7419.

November 30, 2015. Petition for rehearing denied.

Former decision, 577 U.S. 826, 136 S. Ct. 138, 193 L. Ed. 2d 42, 2015 U.S. LEXIS 5624.

No. 14-1518. Gloria Abram, Petitioner v. Fulton County, Georgia.

577 U.S. 1022, 136 S. Ct. 572, 193 L. Ed. 2d 453, 2015 U.S. LEXIS 7445.

November 30, 2015. Petition for rehearing denied.

Former decision, 577 U.S. 826, 136 S. Ct. 149, 193 L. Ed. 2d 43, 2015 U.S. LEXIS 6028.

No. 14-1521. Vincent Torres, Petitioner v. The Santa Ynez Band of Chumash Indians.

577 U.S. 1022, 136 S. Ct. 572, 193 L. Ed. 2d 453, 2015 U.S. LEXIS 7404.

November 30, 2015. Petition for rehearing denied.

Former decision, 577 U.S. 826, 136 S. Ct. 152, 193 L. Ed. 2d 43, 2015 U.S. LEXIS 5589.

Former decision, 577 U.S. 828, 136 S. Ct. 32, 193 L. Ed. 2d 46, 2015 U.S. LEXIS 6042.

No. 14-1537. Michael Houston and Steve Houston, Petitioners v. 42nd Judicial District Court of Louisiana.

577 U.S. 1022, 136 S. Ct. 572, 193 L. Ed. 2d 454, 2015 U.S. LEXIS 7434.

November 30, 2015. Petition for rehearing denied.

Former decision, 577 U.S. 827, 136 S. Ct. 157, 193 L. Ed. 2d 44, 2015 U.S. LEXIS 5677.

No. 14-7776. Carole M. Dean, Petitioner v. Porsche Automobile Holdings SE, et al.

577 U.S. 1022, 136 S. Ct. 572, 193 L. Ed. 2d 454, 2015 U.S. LEXIS 7411.

November 30, 2015. Petition for rehearing denied.

Former decision, 577 U.S. 828, 136 S. Ct. 30, 193 L. Ed. 2d 45, 2015 U.S. LEXIS 5676.

No. 14-8856. Alexander Alexandervi Bistrika, et al., Petitioners v. Oregon; and Svetlana Alexandrovna Bistrika, et al., Petitioners v. Oregon.

577 U.S. 1022, 136 S. Ct. 572, 193 L. Ed. 2d 454, 2015 U.S. LEXIS 7374.

November 30, 2015. Petition for rehearing denied.

No. 14-9078. Mamadou Barry, Petitioner v. Aissato Diallo.

577 U.S. 1022, 136 S. Ct. 572, 193 L. Ed. 2d 454, 2015 U.S. LEXIS 7382.

November 30, 2015. Petition for rehearing denied.

Former decision, 577 U.S. 829, 136 S. Ct. 34, 193 L. Ed. 2d 48, 2015 U.S. LEXIS 5551.

No. 14-9175. Ruben Gutierrez, Petitioner v. William Stephens, Director, Texas Department of Criminal Justice, Correctional Institutions Division.

577 U.S. 1022, 136 S. Ct. 573, 193 L. Ed. 2d 454, 2015 U.S. LEXIS 7440.

November 30, 2015. Petition for rehearing denied.

Former decision, 577 U.S. 829, 136 S. Ct. 35, 193 L. Ed. 2d 48, 2015 U.S. LEXIS 5540.

No. 14-9239. Anthony Coles, Petitioner v. National Labor Relations Board, et al.

577 U.S. 1022, 136 S. Ct. 573, 193 L. Ed. 2d 454, 2015 U.S. LEXIS 7387.

November 30, 2015. Petition for rehearing denied.

Former decision, 577 U.S. 829, 136 S. Ct. 35, 193 L. Ed. 2d 48, 2015 U.S. LEXIS 5685.

No. 14-9369. Cecil Ray Garcia, Petitioner v. Texas.

577 U.S. 1022, 136 S. Ct. 573, 193 L. Ed. 2d 455, 2015 U.S. LEXIS 7458.

November 30, 2015. Petition for rehearing denied.

Former decision, 576 U.S. 1038, 135 S. Ct. 2862, 192 L. Ed. 2d 900, 2015 U.S. LEXIS 4092.

No. 14-9397. Andrew Hutchinson, Petitioner v. Sanjay Razdan.

577 U.S. 1022, 136 S. Ct. 573, 193 L. Ed. 2d 455, 2015 U.S. LEXIS 7400.

November 30, 2015. Petition for rehearing denied.

Former decision, 576 U.S. 1025, 135 S. Ct. 2843, 192 L. Ed. 2d 880, 2015 U.S. LEXIS 4017.

No. 14-9489. Tyrone Chalmers, Petitioner v. Tennessee.

577 U.S. 1022, 136 S. Ct. 573, 193 L. Ed. 2d 455, 2015 U.S. LEXIS 7427.

November 30, 2015. Petition for rehearing denied.

Former decision, 577 U.S. 830, 136 S. Ct. 39, 193 L. Ed. 2d 50, 2015 U.S. LEXIS 5599.

No. 14-9676. In re Otis Ervin, Petitioner.

577 U.S. 1022, 136 S. Ct. 573, 193 L. Ed. 2d 455, 2015 U.S. LEXIS 7456.

November 30, 2015. Petition for rehearing denied.

Former decision, 577 U.S. 814, 136 S. Ct. 51, 193 L. Ed. 2d 217, 2015 U.S. LEXIS 4704.

No. 14-9685. James George Stamos, Jr., Petitioner v. Dave Davey, Warden.

577 U.S. 1022, 136 S. Ct. 573, 193 L. Ed. 2d 455, 2015 U.S. LEXIS 7452.

November 30, 2015. Petition for rehearing denied.

Former decision, 577 U.S. 834, 136 S. Ct. 51, 193 L. Ed. 2d 56, 2015 U.S. LEXIS 5545.

No. 14-9719. Robert Amos Bogany, Petitioner v. William Stephens, Director, Texas Department of Criminal Justice, Correctional Institutions Division.

577 U.S. 1022, 136 S. Ct. 574, 193 L. Ed. 2d 455, 2015 U.S. LEXIS 7425.

November 30, 2015. Petition for rehearing denied.

Former decision, 577 U.S. 834, 136 S. Ct. 55, 193 L. Ed. 2d 58, 2015 U.S. LEXIS 5648.

No. 14-9819. George Paulk, Jr., Petitioner v. City of Orlando, Florida, et al.

577 U.S. 1022, 136 S. Ct. 574, 193 L. Ed. 2d 455, 2015 U.S. LEXIS 7433.

November 30, 2015. Petition for rehearing denied.

Former decision, 577 U.S. 837, 136 S. Ct. 63, 193 L. Ed. 2d 63, 2015 U.S. LEXIS 5688.

No. 14-9997. Miguel Gonzalez, Petitioner v. Connecticut.

577 U.S. 1022, 136 S. Ct. 574, 193 L. Ed. 2d 456, 2015 U.S. LEXIS 7416.

November 30, 2015. Petition for rehearing denied.

Former decision, 577 U.S. 843, 136 S. Ct. 84, 193 L. Ed. 2d 73, 2015 U.S. LEXIS 5291.

No. 14-10009. Ashford L. Thompson, Petitioner v. Ohio.

577 U.S. 1022, 136 S. Ct. 574, 193 L. Ed. 2d 456, 2015 U.S. LEXIS 7469.

November 30, 2015. Petition for rehearing denied.

Former decision, 577 U.S. 843, 136 S. Ct. 83, 193 L. Ed. 2d 74, 2015 U.S. LEXIS 5338.

No. 14-10025. Billy R. Melot, et ux., Petitioners v. United States.

577 U.S. 1022, 136 S. Ct. 574, 193 L. Ed. 2d 456, 2015 U.S. LEXIS 7367.

November 30, 2015. Petition for rehearing denied.

Former decision, 577 U.S. 844, 136 S. Ct. 86, 193 L. Ed. 2d 75, 2015 U.S. LEXIS 5152.

No. 14-10038. Darlene C. Amrhein, Petitioner v. La Madeleine, Inc., et al.

577 U.S. 1022, 136 S. Ct. 574, 193 L. Ed. 2d 456, 2015 U.S. LEXIS 7403.

November 30, 2015. Petition for rehearing denied.

Former decision, 577 U.S. 844, 136 S. Ct. 86, 193 L. Ed. 2d 76, 2015 U.S. LEXIS 4965.

No. 14-10088. David Gerard Jeep, Petitioner v. United States.

577 U.S. 1022, 136 S. Ct. 574, 193 L. Ed. 2d 456, 2015 U.S. LEXIS 7383.

November 30, 2015. Petition for rehearing denied.

Former decision, 577 U.S. 46, 136 S. Ct. 95, 193 L. Ed. 2d 80, 2015 U.S. LEXIS 5036.

No. 14-10101. Lydia Cladek, Petitioner v. United States.

577 U.S. 1022, 136 S. Ct. 574, 193 L. Ed. 2d 456, 2015 U.S. LEXIS 7462.

November 30, 2015. Petition for rehearing denied.

Former decision, 577 U.S. 847, 136 S. Ct. 97, 193 L. Ed. 2d 82, 2015 U.S. LEXIS 5033.

No. 14-10144. Ljubica Rajkovic, Petitioner v. Federal Bureau of Investigation, et al.

577 U.S. 1022, 136 S. Ct. 575, 193 L. Ed. 2d 456, 2015 U.S. LEXIS 7399.

November 30, 2015. Petition for rehearing denied.

Former decision, 577 U.S. 849, 136 S. Ct. 105, 193 L. Ed. 2d 86, 2015 U.S. LEXIS 4989.

No. 14-10195. Harold Blick, Petitioner v. Deutsche Bank National Trust Company.

577 U.S. 1022, 136 S. Ct. 575, 193 L. Ed. 2d 457, 2015 U.S. LEXIS 7413.

November 30, 2015. Petition for rehearing denied.

Former decision, 577 U.S. 852, 136 S. Ct. 114, 193 L. Ed. 2d 91, 2015 U.S. LEXIS 6014.

No. 14-10218. Nancy Ann Seaman, Petitioner v. Michigan.

577 U.S. 1023, 136 S. Ct. 575, 193 L. Ed. 2d 457, 2015 U.S. LEXIS 7409.

November 30, 2015. Petition for rehearing denied.

Former decision, 577 U.S. 853, 136 S. Ct. 119, 193 L. Ed. 2d 93, 2015 U.S. LEXIS 5717.

No. 14-10224. Richard J. Vieira, Petitioner v. Wesley A. Van Winkle.

577 U.S. 1023, 136 S. Ct. 575, 193 L. Ed. 2d 457, 2015 U.S. LEXIS 7454.

November 30, 2015. Petition for rehearing denied.

Former decision, 577 U.S. 854, 136 S. Ct. 120, 193 L. Ed. 2d 94, 2015 U.S. LEXIS 5671.

No. 14-10259. Carline M. Curry, Petitioner v. City of Mansfield, Ohio, et al.

577 U.S. 1023, 136 S. Ct. 575, 193 L. Ed. 2d 457, 2015 U.S. LEXIS 7410.

November 30, 2015. Petition for rehearing denied.

Former decision, 577 U.S. 855, 136 S. Ct. 126, 193 L. Ed. 2d 98, 2015 U.S. LEXIS 6224.

No. 14-10285. Antonio Nathaniel Speed, Petitioner v. United States.

577 U.S. 1023, 136 S. Ct. 575, 193 L. Ed. 2d 457, 2015 U.S. LEXIS 7444.

November 30, 2015. Petition for rehearing denied.

Former decision, 577 U.S. 857, 136 S. Ct. 132, 193 L. Ed. 2d 101, 2015 U.S. LEXIS 5806.

No. 14-10289. Andrzej Madura, et ux., Petitioners v. Bank of America, N.A.

577 U.S. 1023, 136 S. Ct. 575, 193 L. Ed. 2d 457, 2015 U.S. LEXIS 7375.

November 30, 2015. Petition for rehearing denied.

Former decision, 577 U.S. 858, 136 S. Ct. 133, 193 L. Ed. 2d 102, 2015 U.S. LEXIS 5953.

No. 14-10357. Kevin J. Reid, Petitioner v. City of Flint, Michigan.

577 U.S. 1023, 136 S. Ct. 575, 193 L. Ed. 2d 457, 2015 U.S. LEXIS 7467.

November 30, 2015. Petition for rehearing denied.

Former decision, 577 U.S. 861, 136 S. Ct. 145, 193 L. Ed. 2d 109, 2015 U.S. LEXIS 6099.

No. 14-10366. Ferenc Fodor, Petitioner v. Eastern Shipbuilding Group (two judgments).

577 U.S. 1023, 136 S. Ct. 576, 193 L. Ed. 2d 457, 2015 U.S. LEXIS 7398.

November 30, 2015. Petition for rehearing denied.

Former decision, 577 U.S. 862, 136 S. Ct. 146, 193 L. Ed. 2d 110, 2015 U.S. LEXIS 6215.

No. 14-10367. Shannon Monique Gibson, Petitioner v. Valley Avenue Drive-In Restaurant, LLC.

577 U.S. 1023, 136 S. Ct. 576, 193 L. Ed. 2d 458, 2015 U.S. LEXIS 7388.

November 30, 2015. Petition for rehearing denied.

Former decision, 577 U.S. 862, 136 S. Ct. 147, 193 L. Ed. 2d 110, 2015 U.S. LEXIS 5843.

No. 14-10370. Miguel Lavenant, Petitioner v. United States.

577 U.S. 1023, 136 S. Ct. 576, 193 L. Ed. 2d 458, 2015 U.S. LEXIS 7401.

November 30, 2015. Petition for rehearing denied.

Former decision, 577 U.S. 862, 136 S. Ct. 147, 193 L. Ed. 2d 111, 2015 U.S. LEXIS 5846.

No. 14-10412. Consuelo Jordan, Petitioner v. Lee Satterfield, et al.

577 U.S. 1023, 136 S. Ct. 576, 193 L. Ed. 2d 458, 2015 U.S. LEXIS 7421.

November 30, 2015. Petition for rehearing denied.

Former decision, 577 U.S. 865, 136 S. Ct. 155, 193 L. Ed. 2d 115, 2015 U.S. LEXIS 6268.

No. 14-10440. Thomas L. Rowland, Petitioner v. Julie L. Jones, Secretary, Florida Department of Corrections.

577 U.S. 1023, 136 S. Ct. 576, 193 L. Ed. 2d 458, 2015 U.S. LEXIS 7389.

November 30, 2015. Petition for rehearing denied.

Former decision, 577 U.S. 866, 136 S. Ct. 299, 193 L. Ed. 2d 118, 2015 U.S. LEXIS 6261.

No. 14-10462. Gilbert O. Cameron, Petitioner v. Sandra Dolce, Superintendent, Orleans Correctional Facility.

577 U.S. 1023, 136 S. Ct. 576, 193 L. Ed. 2d 458, 2015 U.S. LEXIS 7366.

November 30, 2015. Petition for rehearing denied.

Former decision, 577 U.S. 867, 136 S. Ct. 163, 193 L. Ed. 2d 120, 2015 U.S. LEXIS 6356.

No. 15-21. Iury Cherkovsky, Petitioner v. Mario Delgado.

577 U.S. 1023, 136 S. Ct. 576, 193 L. Ed. 2d 458, 2015 U.S. LEXIS 7457.

November 30, 2015. Petition for rehearing denied.

Former decision, 577 U.S. 870, 136 S. Ct. 177, 193 L. Ed. 2d 124, 2015 U.S. LEXIS 6072.

No. 15-33. Lloyd Richard Deere, Petitioner v. Adam Paul Laxalt, Attorney General of Nevada, et al.

577 U.S. 1023, 136 S. Ct. 576, 193 L. Ed. 2d 458, 2015 U.S. LEXIS 7373.

November 30, 2015. Petition for rehearing denied.

Former decision, 577 U.S. 870, 136 S. Ct. 187, 193 L. Ed. 2d 125, 2015 U.S. LEXIS 6027.

No. 15-43. Gracie E. McBroom, Petitioner v. HR Director, Franklin County Board of Elections.

577 U.S. 1023, 136 S. Ct. 577, 193 L. Ed. 2d 459, 2015 U.S. LEXIS 7455.

November 30, 2015. Petition for rehearing denied.

Former decision, 577 U.S. 870, 136 S. Ct. 190, 193 L. Ed. 2d 126, 2015 U.S. LEXIS 6039.

No. 15-47. Bernard J. Bagdis, Petitioner v. United States.

577 U.S. 1023, 136 S. Ct. 577, 193 L. Ed. 2d 459, 2015 U.S. LEXIS 7442.

November 30, 2015. Petition for rehearing denied.

Former decision, 577 U.S. 871, 136 S. Ct. 194, 193 L. Ed. 2d 126, 2015 U.S. LEXIS 6023.

No. 15-61. Henry J. Langer, Petitioner v. Nilles, Ilvedson, Plambeck & Selbo, Ltd., nka Nilles, Plambeck, Selbo & Harrie, Ltd.

577 U.S. 1023, 136 S. Ct. 577, 193 L. Ed. 2d 459, 2015 U.S. LEXIS 7443.

November 30, 2015. Petition for rehearing denied.

Former decision, 577 U.S. 871, 136 S. Ct. 196, 193 L. Ed. 2d 127, 2015 U.S. LEXIS 6222.

No. 15-89. Masoud Bamdad, Petitioner v. United States.

577 U.S. 1023, 136 S. Ct. 577, 193 L. Ed. 2d 459, 2015 U.S. LEXIS 7376.

November 30, 2015. Petition for rehearing denied.

Former decision, 577 U.S. 872, 136 S. Ct. 212, 193 L. Ed. 2d 129, 2015 U.S. LEXIS 6301.

No. 15-99. Mohammed Shaikh, Petitioner v. Florida.

577 U.S. 1023, 136 S. Ct. 577, 193 L. Ed. 2d 459, 2015 U.S. LEXIS 7385.

November 30, 2015. Petition for rehearing denied.

Former decision, 577 U.S. 873, 136 S. Ct. 218, 193 L. Ed. 2d 131, 2015 U.S. LEXIS 6285.

No. 15-5014. Susan Augustus, Petitioner v. AHRC Nassau.

577 U.S. 1023, 136 S. Ct. 577, 193 L. Ed. 2d 459, 2015 U.S. LEXIS 7431.

November 30, 2015. Petition for rehearing denied.

Former decision, 577 U.S. 877, 136 S. Ct. 171, 193 L. Ed. 2d 139, 2015 U.S. LEXIS 6329.

No. 15-5025. Selomi Monge Villalta, Petitioner v. Loretta E. Lynch, Attorney General, et al.

577 U.S. 1023, 136 S. Ct. 577, 193 L. Ed. 2d 459, 2015 U.S. LEXIS 7407.

November 30, 2015. Petition for rehearing denied.

Former decision, 577 U.S. 878, 136 S. Ct. 173, 193 L. Ed. 2d 140, 2015 U.S. LEXIS 5904.

No. 15-5031. Ricky Brannon, Petitioner v. Robert M. Stevenson, Warden.

577 U.S. 1023, 136 S. Ct. 577, 193 L. Ed. 2d 460, 2015 U.S. LEXIS 7368.

November 30, 2015. Petition for rehearing denied.

Former decision, 577 U.S. 878, 136 S. Ct. 174, 193 L. Ed. 2d 140, 2015 U.S. LEXIS 6170.

No. 15-5051. In re Benjardi B. Viray, Petitioner.

577 U.S. 1023, 136 S. Ct. 578, 193 L. Ed. 2d 460, 2015 U.S. LEXIS 7439.

November 30, 2015. Petition for rehearing denied.

Former decision, 577 U.S. 814, 136 S. Ct. 176, 193 L. Ed. 2d 218, 2015 U.S. LEXIS 4744.

No. 15-5056. Trent Alvon Smith, Petitioner v. Wood County District Attorney's Office, et al.

577 U.S. 1023, 136 S. Ct. 578, 193 L. Ed. 2d 460, 2015 U.S. LEXIS 7386.

November 30, 2015. Petition for rehearing denied.

Former decision, 577 U.S. 880, 136 S. Ct. 300, 193 L. Ed. 2d 143, 2015 U.S. LEXIS 5222.

No. 15-5078. William L. Kelley, Petitioner v. Alan J. Lazaroff, Warden.

577 U.S. 1023, 136 S. Ct. 578, 193 L. Ed. 2d 460, 2015 U.S. LEXIS 7372.

November 30, 2015. Petition for rehearing denied.

Former decision, 577 U.S. 881, 136 S. Ct. 181, 193 L. Ed. 2d 145, 2015 U.S. LEXIS 5429.

No. 15-5116. Albert Brunson, Petitioner v. Cheryl Price, Warden, et al.

577 U.S. 1023, 136 S. Ct. 578, 193 L. Ed. 2d 460, 2015 U.S. LEXIS 7453.

November 30, 2015. Petition for rehearing denied.

Former decision, 577 U.S. 883, 136 S. Ct. 188, 193 L. Ed. 2d 149, 2015 U.S. LEXIS 5350.

No. 15-5124. Shelby Anthony Vogt, Petitioner v. Iowa, et al.

577 U.S. 1023, 136 S. Ct. 578, 193 L. Ed. 2d 460, 2015 U.S. LEXIS 7397.

November 30, 2015. Petition for rehearing denied.

Former decision, 577 U.S. 884, 136 S. Ct. 190, 193 L. Ed. 2d 150, 2015 U.S. LEXIS 5431.

No. 15-5191. Madge Matthews, Petitioner v. Anthony Stewart, Warden.

577 U.S. 1023, 136 S. Ct. 578, 193 L. Ed. 2d 460, 2015 U.S. LEXIS 7429.

November 30, 2015. Petition for rehearing denied.

Former decision, 577 U.S. 886, 136 S. Ct. 202, 193 L. Ed. 2d 156, 2015 U.S. LEXIS 5457.

Former decision, 577 U.S. 890, 136 S. Ct. 300, 193 L. Ed. 2d 162, 2015 U.S. LEXIS 5094.

———

No. 15-5215. John Lee Basey, Petitioner v. William Stephens, Director, Texas Department of Criminal Justice, Correctional Institutions Division.

577 U.S. 1024, 136 S. Ct. 578, 193 L. Ed. 2d 461, 2015 U.S. LEXIS 7384.

November 30, 2015. Petition for rehearing denied.

Former decision, 577 U.S. 888, 136 S. Ct. 206, 193 L. Ed. 2d 159, 2015 U.S. LEXIS 5050.

———

No. 15-5249. Willie James Boone, Petitioner v. Julie L. Jones, Secretary, Florida Department of Corrections.

577 U.S. 1024, 136 S. Ct. 578, 193 L. Ed. 2d 461, 2015 U.S. LEXIS 7381.

November 30, 2015. Petition for rehearing denied.

Former decision, 577 U.S. 890, 136 S. Ct. 211, 193 L. Ed. 2d 162, 2015 U.S. LEXIS 5187.

———

No. 15-5250. Antwion E. Thompson, Petitioner v. United States District Court for the Northern District of California.

577 U.S. 1024, 136 S. Ct. 579, 193 L. Ed. 2d 461, 2015 U.S. LEXIS 7405.

November 30, 2015. Petition for rehearing denied.

No. 15-5256. David Andrew Diehl, aka David A. Diehl, Petitioner v. United States.

577 U.S. 1024, 136 S. Ct. 579, 193 L. Ed. 2d 461, 2015 U.S. LEXIS 7426.

November 30, 2015. Petition for rehearing denied.

Former decision, 577 U.S. 890, 136 S. Ct. 213, 193 L. Ed. 2d 163, 2015 U.S. LEXIS 5404.

———

No. 15-5261. Raymond L. Rogers, Petitioner v. United States.

577 U.S. 1024, 136 S. Ct. 579, 193 L. Ed. 2d 461, 2015 U.S. LEXIS 7448.

November 30, 2015. Petition for rehearing denied.

Former decision, 577 U.S. 891, 136 S. Ct. 214, 193 L. Ed. 2d 164, 2015 U.S. LEXIS 5179.

———

No. 15-5293. Joseph Michael Ladeairous, Petitioner v. Eric T. Schneiderman, Attorney General of New York, et al.

577 U.S. 1024, 136 S. Ct. 579, 193 L. Ed. 2d 461, 2015 U.S. LEXIS 7408.

November 30, 2015. Petition for rehearing denied.

Former decision, 577 U.S. 892, 136 S. Ct. 220, 193 L. Ed. 2d 167, 2015 U.S. LEXIS 4783.

No. 15-5318. Houston Douglas, aka Douglas Houston, Petitioner v. Bughrara, et al.

577 U.S. 1024, 136 S. Ct. 579, 193 L. Ed. 2d 462, 2015 U.S. LEXIS 7393.

November 30, 2015. Petition for rehearing denied.

Former decision, 577 U.S. 893, 136 S. Ct. 224, 193 L. Ed. 2d 169, 2015 U.S. LEXIS 4958.

No. 15-5359. Charles A. Hood, Petitioner v. United States.

577 U.S. 1024, 136 S. Ct. 579, 193 L. Ed. 2d 462, 2015 U.S. LEXIS 7396.

November 30, 2015. Petition for rehearing denied.

Former decision, 577 U.S. 896, 136 S. Ct. 231, 193 L. Ed. 2d 174, 2015 U.S. LEXIS 4830.

No. 15-5360. Joseph W. Farmer, Petitioner v. Michael Potteiger, et al.

577 U.S. 1024, 136 S. Ct. 579, 193 L. Ed. 2d 462, 2015 U.S. LEXIS 7463.

November 30, 2015. Petition for rehearing denied.

Former decision, 577 U.S. 896, 136 S. Ct. 231, 193 L. Ed. 2d 174, 2015 U.S. LEXIS 4802.

No. 15-5410. James Willie Norman, Petitioner v. Florida.

577 U.S. 1024, 136 S. Ct. 580, 193 L. Ed. 2d 462, 2015 U.S. LEXIS 7447.

November 30, 2015. Petition for rehearing denied.

Former decision, 577 U.S. 899, 136 S. Ct. 240, 193 L. Ed. 2d 179, 2015 U.S. LEXIS 4839.

No. 15-5416. Douglas Paul Wright, Petitioner v. Trevor Wingard, Superintendent, State Correctional Institution at Somerset, et al.

577 U.S. 1024, 136 S. Ct. 580, 193 L. Ed. 2d 462, 2015 U.S. LEXIS 7449.

November 30, 2015. Petition for rehearing denied.

Former decision, 577 U.S. 899, 136 S. Ct. 241, 193 L. Ed. 2d 180, 2015 U.S. LEXIS 4825.

No. 15-5422. Beverly Allen Baker, Petitioner v. United States.

577 U.S. 1024, 136 S. Ct. 580, 193 L. Ed. 2d 462, 2015 U.S. LEXIS 7422.

November 30, 2015. Petition for rehearing denied.

Former decision, 577 U.S. 900, 136 S. Ct. 242, 193 L. Ed. 2d 181, 2015 U.S. LEXIS 4856.

No. 15-5426. Rogerio Chaves Scotton, Petitioner v. United States.

577 U.S. 1024, 136 S. Ct. 580, 193 L. Ed. 2d 462, 2015 U.S. LEXIS 7377.

November 30, 2015. Petition for rehearing denied.

Former decision, 577 U.S. 900, 136 S. Ct. 243, 193 L. Ed. 2d 181, 2015 U.S. LEXIS 4964.

No. 15-5429. Luis D. Cabrera Mejia, Petitioner v. Wal-Mart.

577 U.S. 1024, 136 S. Ct. 580, 193 L. Ed. 2d 463, 2015 U.S. LEXIS 7441.

November 30, 2015. Petition for rehearing denied.

Former decision, 577 U.S. 900, 136 S. Ct. 244, 193 L. Ed. 2d 182, 2015 U.S. LEXIS 4832.

No. 15-5485. Robert Williams, Petitioner v. City University of New York, Brooklyn College.

577 U.S. 1024, 136 S. Ct. 580, 193 L. Ed. 2d 463, 2015 U.S. LEXIS 7466.

November 30, 2015. Petition for rehearing denied.

Former decision, 577 U.S. 903, 136 S. Ct. 253, 193 L. Ed. 2d 188, 2015 U.S. LEXIS 4908.

No. 15-5568. Franklin H. Wright, Petitioner v. United States Interagency Council on Homelessness, et al.

577 U.S. 1024, 136 S. Ct. 580, 193 L. Ed. 2d 463, 2015 U.S. LEXIS 7432.

November 30, 2015. Petition for rehearing denied.

Former decision, 577 U.S. 927, 136 S. Ct. 327, 193 L. Ed. 2d 237, 2015 U.S. LEXIS 6546.

No. 15-5659. Norman Alan Kerr, Petitioner v. United States.

577 U.S. 1024, 136 S. Ct. 580, 193 L. Ed. 2d 463, 2015 U.S. LEXIS 7465.

November 30, 2015. Petition for rehearing denied.

Former decision, 577 U.S. 909, 136 S. Ct. 271, 193 L. Ed. 2d 198, 2015 U.S. LEXIS 5965.

No. 15-5732. Isaac K. Fullman, Petitioner v. Thomas King Kistler, et al.

577 U.S. 1024, 136 S. Ct. 581, 193 L. Ed. 2d 463, 2015 U.S. LEXIS 7464.

November 30, 2015. Petition for rehearing denied.

Former decision, 577 U.S. 942, 136 S. Ct. 365, 193 L. Ed. 2d 296, 2015 U.S. LEXIS 6714.

No. 15-5733. Isaac K. Fullman, Petitioner v. Thomas King Kistler, et al.

577 U.S. 1024, 136 S. Ct. 581, 193 L. Ed. 2d 463, 2015 U.S. LEXIS 7390.

November 30, 2015. Petition for rehearing denied.

Former decision, 577 U.S. 942, 136 S. Ct. 365, 193 L. Ed. 2d 297, 2015 U.S. LEXIS 6715.

No. 15-5868. In re Consuelo Jordan, Petitioner.

577 U.S. 1024, 136 S. Ct. 581, 193 L. Ed. 2d 463, 2015 U.S. LEXIS 7459.

November 30, 2015. Petition for rehearing denied.

Former decision, 577 U.S. 921, 136 S. Ct. 341, 193 L. Ed. 2d 253, 2015 U.S. LEXIS 6382.

No. 15-5890. In re Aretha D. Brown, Petitioner.

577 U.S. 1024, 136 S. Ct. 581, 193 L. Ed. 2d 463, 2015 U.S. LEXIS 7379.

November 30, 2015. Petition for rehearing denied.

Former decision, 577 U.S. 937, 136 S. Ct. 368, 193 L. Ed. 2d 307, 2015 U.S. LEXIS 6752.

No. 15A551. Keli'i Akina, et al., Applicants v. Hawaii, et al.

577 U.S. 1024, 136 S. Ct. 581, 193 L. Ed. 2d 464, 2015 U.S. LEXIS 7672.

December 2, 2015. Application for injunction pending appellate review, presented to Justice Kennedy and by him referred to the Court, granted. Respondents are enjoined from counting the ballots cast in, and certifying winners of, the election described in the application, pending final disposition of the appeal by the United States Court of Appeals for the Ninth Circuit.

Justice Ginsburg, Justice Breyer, Justice Sotomayor, and Justice Kagan would deny the application.

No. 15-28 (R46-010). Jerome Listecki, as Trustee of the Archdiocese of Milwaukee Catholic Cemetery Perpetual Care Trust, Petitioner v. Official Committee of Unsecured Creditors.

577 U.S. 1025, 136 S. Ct. 581, 193 L. Ed. 2d 464, 2015 U.S. LEXIS 7673.

December 3, 2015. The petition for writ of certiorari to the United States Court of Appeals for the Seventh Circuit was dismissed today pursuant to Rule 46.1 of the Rules of this Court.

Same case below, 780 F.3d 731.

No. 15-436 (R46-011). In re Moones Mellouli, Petitioner.

No. 15-437 (R46-011). Moones Mellouli, Petitioner v. Loretta E. Lynch, Attorney General.

577 U.S. 1025, 136 S. Ct. 1155, 193 L. Ed. 2d 464, 2015 U.S. LEXIS 7680.

December 4, 2015. The petition for writ of mandamus and/or prohibition and the petition for writ of certiorari to the United States Court of Appeals for the Eighth Circuit were dismissed today pursuant to Rule 46.1 of the Rules of this Court.

No. 14-1382. Americold Logistics, LLC, et al., Petitioners v. ConAgra Foods, Inc., et al.

577 U.S. 1025, 136 S. Ct. 583, 193 L. Ed. 2d 464, 2015 U.S. LEXIS 7675.

December 4, 2015. Joint motion of the parties to dismiss Americold Logistics, LLC as a dispensable party granted.

No. 14-1375. CRST Van Expedited, Inc., Petitioner v. Equal Employment Opportunity Commission.

577 U.S. 1025, 136 S. Ct. 582, 193 L. Ed. 2d 464, 2015 U.S. LEXIS 7678.

December 4, 2015. Petition for writ of certiorari to the United States Court of Appeals for the Eighth Circuit granted.

Same case below, 774 F.3d 1169.

No. 14-1457. Brandon Thomas Betterman, Petitioner v. Montana.

577 U.S. 1025, 136 S. Ct. 582, 193 L. Ed. 2d 464, 2015 U.S. LEXIS 7674.

December 4, 2015. Petition for writ of certiorari to the Supreme Court of Montana granted.

Same case below, 378 Mont. 182, 342 P.3d 971.

No. 15-7. Universal Health Services, Inc., Petitioner v. United States and Massachusetts ex rel. Julio Escobar and Carmen Correa.

577 U.S. 1025, 136 S. Ct. 582, 193 L. Ed. 2d 465, 2015 U.S. LEXIS 7677.

December 4, 2015. Petition for writ of certiorari to the United States Court of Appeals for the First Circuit granted limited to Questions 2 & 3 presented by the petition.

Same case below, 780 F.3d 504.

No. 15-233. Commonwealth of Puerto Rico, et al., Petitioners v. Franklin California Tax-Free Trust, et al.

No. 15-255. Melba Acosta-Febo, et al., Petitioners v. Franklin California Tax-Free Trust, et al.

577 U.S. 1025, 136 S. Ct. 582, 193 L. Ed. 2d 465, 2015 U.S. LEXIS 7676.

December 4, 2015. Motion of Fundacion Angel Ramos, Inc., et al. for leave to file a brief as amici curiae in No. 15-233 granted. Petitions for writs of certiorari to the United States Court of Appeals for the First Circuit granted. The cases are consolidated and a total of one hour is allotted for oral argument. Justice Alito took no part in the consideration or decision of this motion and these petitions.

Same cases below, 805 F.3d 322.

No. 15-545 (R46-012). Freeman Marine Equipment, Inc., Petitioner v. CHMM, LLC.

577 U.S. 1026, 136 S. Ct. 597, 193 L. Ed. 2d 465, 2015 U.S. LEXIS 7867.

December 7, 2015. The petition for writ of certiorari to the United States Court of Appeals for the Ninth Circuit was dismissed today pursuant to Rule 46.1 of the Rules of this Court.

Same case below, 791 F.3d 1059.

No. 15-24. Gary L. France, Petitioner v. United States.

577 U.S. 1026, 136 S. Ct. 583, 193 L. Ed. 2d 465, 2015 U.S. LEXIS 7862.

December 7, 2015. On petition for writ of certiorari to the United States Court of Appeals for the Seventh Circuit. Petition for writ of certiorari granted. Judgment vacated, and case remanded to the United States Court of Appeals for the Seventh Circuit for further consideration in light of the confession of error by the Solicitor General in his brief for the United States filed on November 6, 2015.

Same case below, 782 F.3d 820.

No. 15-6373. Charles Christopher Lancaster, Petitioner v. Texas (two judgments).

577 U.S. 1026, 136 S. Ct. 590, 193 L. Ed. 2d 465, 2015 U.S. LEXIS 7725.

December 7, 2015. Motion of petitioner for leave to proceed in forma pauperis denied, and petition for writ of certiorari to the Court of Criminal Appeals of Texas dismissed. See Rule 39.8. As petitioner has repeatedly abused this Court's process, the Clerk is directed not to accept any further petitions in noncriminal matters from petitioner unless the docketing fee required by Rule 38(a) is paid and petition submitted in compliance with Rule 33.1. See Martin v. District of Columbia Court of Appeals, 506 U.S. 1, 113 S. Ct. 397, 121 L. Ed. 2d 305 (1992) (per curiam).

No. 15A458 (15-595). Jerold R. Sorensen, Petitioner v. United States.

577 U.S. 1026, 136 S. Ct. 606, 193 L. Ed. 2d 466, 2015 U.S. LEXIS 7809.

December 7, 2015. Application for stay, addressed to The Chief Justice and referred to the Court, denied.

Same case below, 801 F.3d 1217.

No. 15A479. Mary Wilkerson, Applicant v. United States.

577 U.S. 1026, 136 S. Ct. 606, 193 L. Ed. 2d 466, 2015 U.S. LEXIS 7710.

December 7, 2015. Application for release on bond pending appeal, addressed to Justice Ginsburg and referred to the Court, denied.

No. 15M61. David Hardy, Petitioner v. Thomas Birkett, Warden.

577 U.S. 1028, 136 S. Ct. 606, 193 L. Ed. 2d 466, 2015 U.S. LEXIS 7752.

December 7, 2015. Motion to direct the Clerk to file a petition for writ of certiorari out of time denied.

No. 15M62. Reginald Wilkinson, Petitioner v. The GEO Group, Inc., et al.

577 U.S. 1028, 136 S. Ct. 606, 193 L. Ed. 2d 466, 2015 U.S. LEXIS 7729.

December 7, 2015. Motion to direct the Clerk to file a petition for writ of certiorari out of time denied.

Same case below, 617 Fed. Appx. 915.

No. 15-5527. Richard Kearney, Petitioner v. New York Department of Correctional Services, et al.

577 U.S. 1028, 136 S. Ct. 606, 193 L. Ed. 2d 466, 2015 U.S. LEXIS 7719.

December 7, 2015. Motion of petitioner for reconsideration of order denying leave to proceed in forma pauperis denied.

No. 15-5748. James B. Campbell, Petitioner v. Julie L. Jones, Secretary, Florida Department of Corrections.

577 U.S. 1028, 136 S. Ct. 606, 193 L. Ed. 2d 466, 2015 U.S. LEXIS 7846.

December 7, 2015. Motion of petitioner for reconsideration of order denying leave to proceed in forma pauperis denied.

No. 15-5767. Cynthia E. Collie, Petitioner v. South Carolina Commission on Lawyer Conduct.

577 U.S. 1028, 136 S. Ct. 606, 193 L. Ed. 2d 466, 2015 U.S. LEXIS 7704.

December 7, 2015. Motion of petitioner for reconsideration of order denying leave to proceed in forma pauperis denied.

No. 15-6027. Burl Anderson Howell, Petitioner v. United States.

577 U.S. 1029, 136 S. Ct. 607, 193 L. Ed. 2d 467, 2015 U.S. LEXIS 7774.

December 7, 2015. Motion of petitioner for reconsideration of order denying leave to proceed in forma pauperis denied.

No. 15-6370. Bill D. Jackson, Petitioner v. Jesse White, Illinois Secretary of State, et al.

577 U.S. 1029, 136 S. Ct. 607, 193 L. Ed. 2d 467, 2015 U.S. LEXIS 7770, reh den 578 U.S. 956, 136 S. Ct. 1730, 194 L. Ed. 2d 826, 2016 U.S. LEXIS 2878.

December 7, 2015. Motion of petitioner for leave to proceed in forma pauperis denied. Petitioner is allowed until December 28, 2015, within which to pay the docketing fees required by Rule 38(a) and to submit a petition in compliance with Rule 33.1 of the Rules of this Court.

Same case below, 581 Fed. Appx. 556.

No. 15-6806. Addie E. Dixon, Petitioner v. Robert A. McDonald, Secretary of Veterans Affairs.

577 U.S. 1029, 136 S. Ct. 607, 193 L. Ed. 2d 467, 2015 U.S. LEXIS 7860.

December 7, 2015. Motion of petitioner for leave to proceed in forma pauperis denied. Petitioner is allowed until December 28, 2015, within which to pay the docketing fees required by Rule 38(a) and to submit a petition in compliance with Rule 33.1 of the Rules of this Court.

Same case below, 778 F.3d 1339.

No. 14-1391. Bobby E. Bowden, Petitioner v. North Carolina.

577 U.S. 1029, 136 S. Ct. 583, 193 L. Ed. 2d 467, 2015 U.S. LEXIS 7702.

December 7, 2015. Petition for writ of certiorari to the Supreme Court of North Carolina denied.

Same case below, 367 N.C. 680, 766 S.E.2d 320.

No. 14-9299. Andrew D. Marshall, Petitioner v. Federal Bureau of Prisons.

577 U.S. 1029, 136 S. Ct. 583, 193 L. Ed. 2d 467, 2015 U.S. LEXIS 7798, reh den 577 U.S. 1184, 136 S. Ct. 1248, 194 L. Ed. 2d 246, 2016 U.S. LEXIS 1119.

December 7, 2015. Petition for writ of certiorari to the United States Court of Appeals for the Eleventh Circuit denied.

Same case below, 580 Fed. Appx. 896.

No. 14-10447. Todd Russell Fries, Petitioner v. United States.

577 U.S. 1029, 136 S. Ct. 583, 193 L. Ed. 2d 467, 2015 U.S. LEXIS 7836.

December 7, 2015. Petition for writ of certiorari to the United States Court of Appeals for the Ninth Circuit denied.

Same case below, 781 F.3d 1137.

No. 15-65. Juan Lizcano, Petitioner v. Texas.

577 U.S. 1029, 136 S. Ct. 584, 193 L. Ed. 2d 467, 2015 U.S. LEXIS 7829.

December 7, 2015. Petition for writ of certiorari to the Court of Criminal Appeals of Texas denied.

No. 15-147. Brian T. Sullivan, Petitioner v. Michael R. Glenn, Jr. et ux.

577 U.S. 1029, 136 S. Ct. 584, 193 L. Ed. 2d 468, 2015 U.S. LEXIS 7855.

December 7, 2015. Petition for writ of certiorari to the United States Court of Appeals for the Seventh Circuit denied.

Same case below, 782 F.3d 378.

No. 15-210. Lorrie Geoffrey, Petitioner v. Bryan Geoffrey.

577 U.S. 1030, 136 S. Ct. 585, 193 L. Ed. 2d 468, 2015 U.S. LEXIS 7782.

December 7, 2015. Petition for writ of certiorari to the District Court of Appeal of Florida, Fourth District, denied.

Same case below, 162 So. 3d 1025.

No. 15-245. Stewart Conrad Mann, Petitioner v. United States.

577 U.S. 1030, 136 S. Ct. 585, 193 L. Ed. 2d 468, 2015 U.S. LEXIS 7783.

December 7, 2015. Petition for writ of certiorari to the United States Court of Appeals for the Ninth Circuit denied.

No. 15-270. Allena Burge Smiley, Petitioner v. Hartford Life and Accident Insurance Company, et al.

577 U.S. 1030, 136 S. Ct. 585, 193 L. Ed. 2d 468, 2015 U.S. LEXIS 7789.

December 7, 2015. Petition for writ of certiorari to the United States Court of Appeals for the Eleventh Circuit denied.

Same case below, 610 Fed. Appx. 8.

No. 15-272. Charles J. Hawkins, Petitioner v. JPMorgan Chase Bank, N.A.

577 U.S. 1030, 136 S. Ct. 585, 193 L. Ed. 2d 468, 2015 U.S. LEXIS 7810.

December 7, 2015. Petition for writ of certiorari to the United States Court of Appeals for the Fifth Circuit denied.

Same case below, 616 Fed. Appx. 662.

No. 15-381. Fivetech Technology Inc., Petitioner v. Southco, Inc.

577 U.S. 1030, 136 S. Ct. 587, 193 L. Ed. 2d 468, 2015 U.S. LEXIS 7747.

December 7, 2015. Petition for writ of certiorari to the United States Court of Appeals for the Federal Circuit denied.

Same case below, 611 Fed. Appx. 681.

No. 15-384. Sitka Enterprises, Inc., et al., Petitioners v. Wilfredo Segarra Miranda, et al.

577 U.S. 1030, 136 S. Ct. 587, 193 L. Ed. 2d 468, 2015 U.S. LEXIS 7773.

December 7, 2015. Petition for writ of certiorari to the United States Court of Appeals for the First Circuit denied.

Same case below, 795 F.3d 288.

No. 15-385. Frederick O. Bond, Petitioner v. Eric H. Holder, Jr., et al.

577 U.S. 1030, 136 S. Ct. 587, 193 L. Ed. 2d 468, 2015 U.S. LEXIS 7775.

December 7, 2015. Petition for writ of certiorari to the United States Court of Appeals for the Eighth Circuit denied.

No. 15-389. James Dickey, Petitioner v. City of Boston Inspectional Services Department, et al.

577 U.S. 1030, 136 S. Ct. 587, 193 L. Ed. 2d 469, 2015 U.S. LEXIS 7760.

December 7, 2015. Petition for writ of certiorari to the Appeals Court of Massachusetts denied.

Same case below, 87 Mass. App. Ct. 1119, 30 N.E.3d 134.

No. 15-390. Tony Ing, Petitioner v. Thomas Lee.

577 U.S. 1030, 136 S. Ct. 587, 193 L. Ed. 2d 469, 2015 U.S. LEXIS 7852.

December 7, 2015. Petition for writ of certiorari to the Court of Appeal of California, Second Appellate District, Division Four, denied.

No. 15-394. Jose S. Cunda, Petitioner v. The Bank of New York Mellon.

577 U.S. 1030, 136 S. Ct. 588, 193 L. Ed. 2d 469, 2015 U.S. LEXIS 7781.

December 7, 2015. Petition for writ of certiorari to the Supreme Court of Florida denied.

Same case below, 177 So. 3d 1264.

No. 15-396. Ambrosio Rouse, Petitioner v. II-VI Inc., et al.

577 U.S. 1030, 136 S. Ct. 588, 193 L. Ed. 2d 469, 2015 U.S. LEXIS 7755.

December 7, 2015. Petition for writ of certiorari to the United States Court of Appeals for the Third Circuit denied.

Same case below, 609 Fed. Appx. 62.

No. 15-397. John Racz, Petitioner v. William Knipp, Warden.

577 U.S. 1030, 136 S. Ct. 588, 193 L. Ed. 2d 469, 2015 U.S. LEXIS 7816.

December 7, 2015. Petition for writ of certiorari to the United States Court of Appeals for the Ninth Circuit denied.

No. 15-398. Diane Petrella, Next Friend and Guardian of Minor N. P. and Minor C. P., et al., Petitioners v. Sam Brownback, Governor of Kansas, et al.

577 U.S. 1030, 136 S. Ct. 588, 193 L. Ed. 2d 469, 2015 U.S. LEXIS 7733.

December 7, 2015. Petition for writ of certiorari to the United States Court of Appeals for the Tenth Circuit denied.

Same case below, 787 F.3d 1242.

No. 15-407. John E. Villegas, et al., Petitioners v. Michael B. Schmidt, Trustee.

577 U.S. 1031, 136 S. Ct. 588, 193 L. Ed. 2d 469, 2015 U.S. LEXIS 7787.

December 7, 2015. Petition for writ of certiorari to the United States Court of Appeals for the Fifth Circuit denied.

Same case below, 788 F.3d 156.

No. 15-408. Joan C. Lipin, Petitioner v. Danske Bank, et al.

577 U.S. 1031, 136 S. Ct. 589, 193 L. Ed. 2d 469, 2015 U.S. LEXIS 7720.

December 7, 2015. Petition for writ of certiorari to the United States Court of Appeals for the Second Circuit denied.

No. 15-418. Deborah Jane Wynn, Petitioner v. Callan Appraisal Incorporated, et al.

577 U.S. 1031, 136 S. Ct. 590, 193 L. Ed. 2d 470, 2015 U.S. LEXIS 7863.

December 7, 2015. Petition for writ of certiorari to the United States Court of Appeals for the Ninth Circuit denied.

Same case below, 592 Fed. Appx. 584.

No. 15-422. Laverne Jones, et al., Petitioners v. Bernaldo Dancel, et al.

577 U.S. 1031, 136 S. Ct. 591, 193 L. Ed. 2d 470, 2015 U.S. LEXIS 7767.

December 7, 2015. Petition for writ of certiorari to the United States Court of Appeals for the Fourth Circuit denied.

Same case below, 792 F.3d 395.

No. 15-426. Nathalee Evans, Executor of the Estate of Eugenia M. Ringgold, et al., Petitioners v. Thomas B. McCullough, Jr., Special Administrator and Administrator with Will Annexed, et al.; Dorian Carter, Petitioner v. Nathalee Evans; Myer J. Sankary, Petitioner v. Justin Ringgold-Lockhart, et al.; Myer Sankary, Petitioner v. Nina Ringgold, et al.; and Justin Ringgold-Lockhart, et al., Petitioners v. Myer J. Sankary, et al.

577 U.S. 1031, 136 S. Ct. 592, 193 L. Ed. 2d 470, 2015 U.S. LEXIS 7797.

December 7, 2015. Petition for writ of certiorari to the United States Court of Appeals for the Ninth Circuit denied.

Same case below, 600 Fed. Appx. 577 (first judgment); 601 Fed. Appx. 527 (second judgment); 611 Fed. Appx. 893 (third judgment); 601 Fed. Appx. 529 (fourth judgment); and 600 Fed. Appx. 592 (fifth judgment).

No. 15-431. Marshall Hunn, Petitioner v. Dan Wilson Homes Inc., et al.

577 U.S. 1031, 136 S. Ct. 592, 193 L. Ed. 2d 470, 2015 U.S. LEXIS 7812.

December 7, 2015. Petition for writ of certiorari to the United States Court of Appeals for the Fifth Circuit denied.

Same case below, 789 F.3d 573.

No. 15-433. Robert Jackson Crider, II, Petitioner v. Texas.

577 U.S. 1031, 136 S. Ct. 593, 193 L. Ed. 2d 470, 2015 U.S. LEXIS 7850.

December 7, 2015. Petition for writ of certiorari to the Court of Appeals of Texas, Eighth District, denied.

No. 15-441. Thomas Hill, Petitioner v. Cindi S. Curtin, Warden.

577 U.S. 1031, 136 S. Ct. 593, 193 L. Ed. 2d 470, 2015 U.S. LEXIS 7815.

December 7, 2015. Petition for writ of certiorari to the United States Court of Appeals for the Sixth Circuit denied.

Same case below, 792 F.3d 670.

No. 15-455. Dirk Askew, et ux., Petitioners v. United States.

577 U.S. 1031, 136 S. Ct. 593, 193 L. Ed. 2d 470, 2015 U.S. LEXIS 7822.

December 7, 2015. Petition for writ of certiorari to the United States Court of Appeals for the Eighth Circuit denied.

Same case below, 786 F.3d 1091.

No. 15-462. Christopher Thomas Wenthe, Petitioner v. Minnesota.

577 U.S. 1031, 136 S. Ct. 595, 193 L. Ed. 2d 471, 2015 U.S. LEXIS 7684.

December 7, 2015. Petition for writ of certiorari to the Supreme Court of Minnesota denied.

Same case below, 865 N.W.2d 293.

No. 15-542. Michael A. Katz, Petitioner v. Cellco Partnership, dba Verizon Wireless.

577 U.S. 1031, 136 S. Ct. 596, 193 L. Ed. 2d 471, 2015 U.S. LEXIS 7820.

December 7, 2015. Petition for writ of certiorari to the United States Court of Appeals for the Second Circuit denied.

Same case below, 794 F.3d 341.

No. 15-5043. Ricardo Josue Gutierrez, Petitioner v. United States.

577 U.S. 1031, 136 S. Ct. 583, 193 L. Ed. 2d 471, 2015 U.S. LEXIS 7817.

December 7, 2015. Petition for writ of certiorari to the United States Court of Appeals for the Fifth Circuit denied.

Same case below, 600 Fed. Appx. 259.

No. 15-5147. Gilberto Lara-Ruiz, Petitioner v. United States.

577 U.S. 1031, 136 S. Ct. 584, 193 L. Ed. 2d 471, 2015 U.S. LEXIS 7788.

December 7, 2015. Petition for writ of certiorari to the United States Court of Appeals for the Eighth Circuit denied.

Same case below, 781 F.3d 919.

No. 15-5149. Allen Maki, Petitioner v. Beverly Anderson, et al.

577 U.S. 1032, 136 S. Ct. 584, 193 L. Ed. 2d 471, 2015 U.S. LEXIS 7748.

December 7, 2015. Petition for writ of certiorari to the Court of Appeals of Texas, Second District, denied.

No. 15-5635. Renee Stephens, Petitioner v. Nike, Inc.

577 U.S. 1032, 136 S. Ct. 584, 193 L. Ed. 2d 471, 2015 U.S. LEXIS 7838.

December 7, 2015. Petition for writ of certiorari to the United States Court of Appeals for the Ninth Circuit denied.

Same case below, 611 Fed. Appx. 896.

No. 15-5740. William Earl Rayford, Petitioner v. William Stephens, Director, Texas Department of Criminal Justice, Correctional Institutions Division.

577 U.S. 1032, 136 S. Ct. 585, 193 L. Ed. 2d 471, 2015 U.S. LEXIS 7708.

December 7, 2015. Petition for writ of certiorari to the United States Court of Appeals for the Fifth Circuit denied.

Same case below, 622 Fed. Appx. 315.

No. 15-5886. Mark Pickens, Petitioner v. Ohio.

577 U.S. 1032, 136 S. Ct. 585, 193 L. Ed. 2d 471, 2015 U.S. LEXIS 7745.

December 7, 2015. Petition for writ of certiorari to the Supreme Court of Ohio denied.

Same case below, 141 Ohio St. 3d 462, 25 N.E.3d 1023.

No. 15-5940. Ramiro F. Gonzales, Petitioner v. William Stephens, Director, Texas Department of Criminal Justice, Correctional Institutions Division.

577 U.S. 1032, 136 S. Ct. 586, 193 L. Ed. 2d 472, 2015 U.S. LEXIS 7813.

December 7, 2015. Petition for writ of certiorari to the United States Court of Appeals for the Fifth Circuit denied.

Same case below, 606 Fed. Appx. 767.

No. 15-5958. Gabriel Plascencia-Acosta, aka Jose Maro Sanchez, Petitioner v. United States; Jorge Lopez-Merino, Petitioner v. United States; J. Consepcion Garcia-Jasso, Petitioner v. United States; Noe Zepeda-Rangel, Petitioner v. United States; Julio Sarabia-Baltazar, aka Jose Noel Mercado, Petitioner v. United States; Rosali Mauricio Ramos-Sorto, aka Sorto Ramos-Mauricio, Petitioner v. United States; Vincente Placios-Pascacio, Petitioner v. United States; Juan Alvarado-Aranda, Petitioner v. United States; Luis Alberto Sepulveda-Uribe, Petitioner v. United States; Victor Manuel Mendoza-Toledo, Petitioner v. United States; Noel David Ramirez-Bertran, Petitioner v. United States; Cristobal Sarceno-Sarceno, Petitioner v. United States; Fernando Bautista-Sanchez, Petitioner v. United States; Jorge Eduardo Espinoza-Nunez, aka Jorge Espinoza, Petitioner v. United States; Elevi Ortiz-Aguirre, Petitioner v. United States; Manuel Uresti-Garza, Petitioner v. United States; Jorge Luis Rebollar-Bautista, aka Jorge Luis Rebollar, aka Jorge L. Rebollar, Petitioner v. United States; Antonio Rosales-Vargas, aka Antonio Rosales, Petitioner v. United States; and Rocardo Posas-Torres, aka Ricardo Alonso Posas, Petitioner v. United States.

577 U.S. 1032, 136 S. Ct. 586, 193 L. Ed. 2d 472, 2015 U.S. LEXIS 7731.

December 7, 2015. Petition for writ of certiorari to the United States Court of Appeals for the Fifth Circuit denied.

Same case below, 607 Fed. Appx. 419 (first judgment); 608 Fed. Appx. 296 (second judgment); 608 Fed. Appx. 295 (third judgment); 609 Fed. Appx. 216 (fourth judgment); 609 Fed. Appx. 223 (fifth judgment); 609 Fed. Appx. 248 (sixth judgment); 609 Fed. Appx. 280 (seventh judgment); 610 Fed. Appx. 402 (eighth judgment); 610 Fed. Appx. 413 (ninth judgment); 610 Fed. Appx. 418 (tenth judgment); 611 Fed. Appx. 838 (eleventh judgment); 612 Fed. Appx. 251 (twelfth judgment); 613 Fed. Appx. 416 (thirteenth judgment); (613 Fed. Appx. 375 (fourteenth judgment); 613 Fed. Appx. 386 (fifteenth judgment); 613 Fed. Appx. 388 (sixteenth judgment); 613 Fed. Appx. 398 (seventeenth judgment); 613 Fed. Appx. 353 (eighteenth judgment); and 614 Fed. Appx. 225 (ninteenth judgment).

No. 15-5964. Benjamin Rodriguez-Rodriguez, Petitioner v. United States; Joel Torres-Salas, Petitioner v. United States; Sotero Ramirez-Ballejo, Petitioner v. United States; Juan Manuel Torres-Rodriguez, aka Juan Manuel Rodriguez, aka Juan Torres-Rodriguez, Petitioner v. United States; Jose Manuel De La Cruz-Gutierrez, aka Victor Taveras, aka Jose Manuel Taveras De La Cruz-Gutierrez, Petitioner v. United States; Pablo Cortes, Petitioner v. United States; Trinidad Jaimes-Jaimes, Petitioner v. United States; Omar Rivera-Diaz, Petitioner v. United States; Marta Gonzalez-Lopez, aka Matha Gonzalez-Lopez, aka Maricela R. Lopez, aka Maricela Recendez Lopez, Petitioner v. United States; Mario Eduardo Acosta-Juarez, aka Jose R. Chavez, aka Mario Acosta, Petitioner v. United States; and Humberto Yecid Castro Gomez, aka Humberto Yecid Castro, aka Humberto Castro Gomez, aka Humberto

Yacid Castro Gomez, aka Robert Gomez, Petitioner v. United States.

577 U.S. 1032, 136 S. Ct. 586, 193 L. Ed. 2d 472, 2015 U.S. LEXIS 7743.

December 7, 2015. Petition for writ of certiorari to the United States Court of Appeals for the Fifth Circuit denied.

Same case below, 606 Fed. Appx. 255 (first judgment); 607 Fed. Appx. 416 (second judgment); 606 Fed. Appx. 268 (third judgment); 606 Fed. Appx. 276 (fourth judgment); 609 Fed. Appx. 263 (fifth judgment); 610 Fed. Appx. 427 (sixth judgment); 611 Fed. Appx. 205 (seventh judgment); 611 Fed. Appx. 246 (eighth judgment); 612 Fed. Appx. 247 (ninth judgment); 613 Fed. Appx. 380 (tenth judgment); and 613 Fed. Appx. 410 (eleventh judgment).

No. 15-6282. Robert Leslie Roberson, III, Petitioner v. William Stephens, Director, Texas Department of Criminal Justice, Correctional Institutions Division.

577 U.S. 1033, 136 S. Ct. 607, 193 L. Ed. 2d 473, 2015 U.S. LEXIS 7847.

December 7, 2015. Petition for writ of certiorari to the United States Court of Appeals for the Fifth Circuit denied.

No. 15-6344. William Robert Parker, Petitioner v. Texas.

577 U.S. 1033, 136 S. Ct. 588, 193 L. Ed. 2d 473, 2015 U.S. LEXIS 7769.

December 7, 2015. Petition for writ of certiorari to the Court of Appeals of Texas, Sixth District, denied.

No. 15-6346. George Escamilla, Petitioner v. Kathleen T. Escamilla, et al.

577 U.S. 1033, 136 S. Ct. 589, 193 L. Ed. 2d 473, 2015 U.S. LEXIS 7724.

December 7, 2015. Petition for writ of certiorari to the United States Court of Appeals for the Second Circuit denied.

No. 15-6352. Andre Demond Traylor, Petitioner v. Gregory McLaughlin, Warden.

577 U.S. 1033, 136 S. Ct. 589, 193 L. Ed. 2d 473, 2015 U.S. LEXIS 7754.

December 7, 2015. Petition for writ of certiorari to the Superior Court of Georgia, Macon County, denied.

No. 15-6354. Nadine Leach, Petitioner v. New York.

577 U.S. 1033, 136 S. Ct. 589, 193 L. Ed. 2d 473, 2015 U.S. LEXIS 7821.

December 7, 2015. Petition for writ of certiorari to the Appellate Division, Supreme Court of New York, First Judicial Department, denied.

Same case below, 125 App. Div. 3d 568, 5 N.Y.S.3d 28.

No. 15-6358. Adrian Robles, Petitioner v. California.

577 U.S. 1033, 136 S. Ct. 589, 193 L. Ed. 2d 473, 2015 U.S. LEXIS 7843.

December 7, 2015. Petition for writ of certiorari to the Court of Appeal of California, Second Appellate District, Division Six, denied.

No. 15-6364. Biven Hudson, Petitioner v. United States.

577 U.S. 1033, 136 S. Ct. 589, 193 L. Ed. 2d 473, 2015 U.S. LEXIS 7717.

December 7, 2015. Petition for writ of certiorari to the United States Court of Appeals for the Eleventh Circuit denied.

Same case below, 608 Fed. Appx. 915.

––––––––

No. 15-6369. Sherman O. Wagner, Petitioner v. Sherry L. Burt, Warden.

577 U.S. 1033, 136 S. Ct. 590, 193 L. Ed. 2d 474, 2015 U.S. LEXIS 7688.

December 7, 2015. Petition for writ of certiorari to the United States Court of Appeals for the Sixth Circuit denied.

Same case below, 620 Fed. Appx. 375.

––––––––

No. 15-6386. Rodney A. Hubbard, Petitioner v. Jeffrey Woods, Warden.

577 U.S. 1033, 136 S. Ct. 590, 193 L. Ed. 2d 474, 2015 U.S. LEXIS 7841.

December 7, 2015. Petition for writ of certiorari to the United States Court of Appeals for the Sixth Circuit denied.

––––––––

No. 15-6389. Michael Hegewald, Petitioner v. Pat Glebe.

577 U.S. 1033, 136 S. Ct. 590, 193 L. Ed. 2d 474, 2015 U.S. LEXIS 7722.

December 7, 2015. Petition for writ of certiorari to the United States Court of Appeals for the Ninth Circuit denied.

––––––––

No. 15-6390. Keith D. Goodman, Petitioner v. Harold W. Clarke, Director, Virginia Department of Corrections, et al.

577 U.S. 1034, 136 S. Ct. 591, 193 L. Ed. 2d 474, 2015 U.S. LEXIS 7764.

December 7, 2015. Petition for writ of certiorari to the United States Court of Appeals for the Fourth Circuit denied.

Same case below, 606 Fed. Appx. 82.

––––––––

No. 15-6391. Alex Gu, Petitioner v. Presence Saint Joseph Medical Center, et al.

577 U.S. 1034, 136 S. Ct. 591, 193 L. Ed. 2d 474, 2015 U.S. LEXIS 7808.

December 7, 2015. Petition for writ of certiorari to the United States Court of Appeals for the Seventh Circuit denied.

Same case below, 557 Fed. Appx. 581.

––––––––

No. 15-6394. Dewey Lee McBride, Petitioner v. Arizona.

577 U.S. 1034, 136 S. Ct. 591, 193 L. Ed. 2d 474, 2015 U.S. LEXIS 7825.

December 7, 2015. Petition for writ of certiorari to the Court of Appeals of Arizona, Division Two, denied.

––––––––

No. 15-6395. Derrick Dewayne Davis, Petitioner v. Pat Thomas, et al.

577 U.S. 1034, 136 S. Ct. 591, 193 L. Ed. 2d 474, 2015 U.S. LEXIS 7777, reh den 577 U.S. 1184, 136 S. Ct. 1251, 194 L. Ed. 2d 249, 2016 U.S. LEXIS 1060.

December 7, 2015. Petition for writ of certiorari to the United States Court of Appeals for the Fifth Circuit denied.

Same case below, 615 Fed. Appx. 240.

No. 15-6405. Rejeanne M. Bernier, Petitioner v. Court of Appeal of California, Fourth Appellate District, Division One, et al.

577 U.S. 1034, 136 S. Ct. 592, 193 L. Ed. 2d 475, 2015 U.S. LEXIS 7834.

December 7, 2015. Petition for writ of certiorari to the Supreme Court of California denied.

No. 15-6410. Manuel Villa, Petitioner v. California.

577 U.S. 1034, 136 S. Ct. 592, 193 L. Ed. 2d 475, 2015 U.S. LEXIS 7790.

December 7, 2015. Petition for writ of certiorari to the Court of Appeal of California, Sixth Appellate District, denied.

No. 15-6411. Doshee S. Towery, Petitioner v. Williams Stephens, Diector, Texas Department of Criminal Justice, Correctional Institutions Division.

577 U.S. 1034, 136 S. Ct. 592, 193 L. Ed. 2d 475, 2015 U.S. LEXIS 7690.

December 7, 2015. Petition for writ of certiorari to the United States Court of Appeals for the Fifth Circuit denied.

No. 15-6412. Michael J. Reid, Petitioner v. Florida.

577 U.S. 1034, 136 S. Ct. 592, 193 L. Ed. 2d 475, 2015 U.S. LEXIS 7806.

December 7, 2015. Petition for writ of certiorari to the District Court of Appeal of Florida, Fifth District, denied.

Same case below, 166 So. 3d 809.

No. 15-6421. Tyrone Tittle, Petitioner v. California.

577 U.S. 1034, 136 S. Ct. 593, 193 L. Ed. 2d 475, 2015 U.S. LEXIS 7753.

December 7, 2015. Petition for writ of certiorari to the Supreme Court of California denied.

No. 15-6423. Earla G. Redman, Petitioner v. New York State Department of Correctional Service, et al.

577 U.S. 1034, 136 S. Ct. 607, 193 L. Ed. 2d 475, 2015 U.S. LEXIS 7844.

December 7, 2015. Petition for writ of certiorari to the United States Court of Appeals for the Second Circuit denied.

No. 15-6427. John B. Laschkewitsch, Petitioner v. ReliaStar Life Insurance Company.

577 U.S. 1034, 136 S. Ct. 593, 193 L. Ed. 2d 475, 2015 U.S. LEXIS 7849, reh den 577 U.S. 1184, 136 S. Ct. 1251, 194 L. Ed. 2d 249, 2016 U.S. LEXIS 1022.

December 7, 2015. Petition for writ of certiorari to the United States Court of Appeals for the Fourth Circuit denied.

Same case below, 597 Fed. Appx. 159.

No. 15-6436. Noel Wentworth Adams, Petitioner v. Loretta E. Lynch, Attorney General.

577 U.S. 1034, 136 S. Ct. 593, 193 L. Ed. 2d 475, 2015 U.S. LEXIS 7682.

December 7, 2015. Petition for writ of certiorari to the United States Court of Appeals for the Eleventh Circuit denied.

Same case below, 603 Fed. Appx. 223.

No. 15-6453. Henry Gonzales, Jr., Petitioner v. Texas.

577 U.S. 1034, 136 S. Ct. 594, 193 L. Ed. 2d 476, 2015 U.S. LEXIS 7793.

December 7, 2015. Petition for writ of certiorari to the United States Court of Appeals for the Court of Appeals of Texas, Third District, denied.

No. 15-6465. Rejeanne Bernier, Petitioner v. Court of Appeal of California, Fourth Appellate District, Division One, et al.

577 U.S. 1034, 136 S. Ct. 594, 193 L. Ed. 2d 476, 2015 U.S. LEXIS 7771.

December 7, 2015. Petition for writ of certiorari to the Supreme Court of California denied.

No. 15-6474. Deborah Elizabeth Gouch-Onassis, Petitioner v. United States.

577 U.S. 1035, 136 S. Ct. 594, 193 L. Ed. 2d 476, 2015 U.S. LEXIS 7700, reh den 577 U.S. 1231, 136 S. Ct. 1487, 194 L. Ed. 2d 578, 2016 U.S. LEXIS 1867.

December 7, 2015. Petition for writ of certiorari to the United States Court of Appeals for the Ninth Circuit denied.

No. 15-6477. Alfred Robinson, Jr., Petitioner v. Carolyn W. Colvin, Acting Commissioner of Social Security.

577 U.S. 1035, 136 S. Ct. 594, 193 L. Ed. 2d 476, 2015 U.S. LEXIS 7739.

December 7, 2015. Petition for writ of certiorari to the United States Court of Appeals for the Fourth Circuit denied.

No. 15-6486. Nexis Rene Gomez, Petitioner v. Connie Gipson, Warden.

577 U.S. 1035, 136 S. Ct. 594, 193 L. Ed. 2d 476, 2015 U.S. LEXIS 7818.

December 7, 2015. Petition for writ of certiorari to the United States Court of Appeals for the Ninth Circuit denied.

No. 15-6498. Angel Mayora Medrano, Petitioner v. Charles L. Ryan, Director, Arizona Department of Corrections, et al.

577 U.S. 1035, 136 S. Ct. 594, 193 L. Ed. 2d 476, 2015 U.S. LEXIS 7687.

December 7, 2015. Petition for writ of certiorari to the United States Court of Appeals for the Ninth Circuit denied.

Same case below, 614 Fed. Appx. 351.

No. 15-6530. Michael A. McNew, Petitioner v. Terry A. Tibbals, Warden.

577 U.S. 1035, 136 S. Ct. 595, 193 L. Ed. 2d 476, 2015 U.S. LEXIS 7830.

December 7, 2015. Petition for writ of certiorari to the United States Court of Appeals for the Sixth Circuit denied.

No. 15-6533. Arturo Franco Palomar, Jr., Petitioner v. Ron Barnes, Warden.

577 U.S. 1035, 136 S. Ct. 595, 193 L. Ed. 2d 476, 2015 U.S. LEXIS 7683.

December 7, 2015. Petition for writ of certiorari to the United States Court of Appeals for the Ninth Circuit denied.

Same case below, 599 Fed. Appx. 455.

No. 15-6534. Markos N. Pappas, Petitioner v. United States.

577 U.S. 1035, 136 S. Ct. 595, 193 L. Ed. 2d 477, 2015 U.S. LEXIS 7699.

December 7, 2015. Petition for writ of certiorari to the United States Court of Appeals for the Tenth Circuit denied.

Same case below, 617 Fed. Appx. 879.

No. 15-6542. Charles P. White, Petitioner v. Indiana.

577 U.S. 1035, 136 S. Ct. 595, 193 L. Ed. 2d 477, 2015 U.S. LEXIS 7735.

December 7, 2015. Petition for writ of certiorari to the Court of Appeals of Indiana, Fifth District, denied.

Same case below, 25 N.E.3d 107.

No. 15-6546. Elias Rosado, Petitioner v. Julie L. Jones, Secretary, Florida Department of Corrections, et al.

577 U.S. 1035, 136 S. Ct. 596, 193 L. Ed. 2d 477, 2015 U.S. LEXIS 7685.

December 7, 2015. Petition for writ of certiorari to the United States Court of Appeals for the Eleventh Circuit denied.

No. 15-6547. Carlos Javier Ponce Silva, Petitioner v. Loretta E. Lynch, Attorney General.

577 U.S. 1035, 136 S. Ct. 596, 193 L. Ed. 2d 477, 2015 U.S. LEXIS 7695.

December 7, 2015. Petition for writ of certiorari to the United States Court of Appeals for the Third Circuit denied.

No. 15-6576. Jeffery Pedersen, Petitioner v. Reed Richardson, Warden.

577 U.S. 1035, 136 S. Ct. 596, 193 L. Ed. 2d 477, 2015 U.S. LEXIS 7718.

December 7, 2015. Petition for writ of certiorari to the United States Court of Appeals for the Seventh Circuit denied.

No. 15-6639. Benjamin Puentes, Petitioner v. Santa Clara County, California, et al.

577 U.S. 1035, 136 S. Ct. 596, 193 L. Ed. 2d 477, 2015 U.S. LEXIS 7711.

December 7, 2015. Petition for writ of certiorari to the United States Court of Appeals for the Ninth Circuit denied.

Same case below, 606 Fed. Appx. 339.

No. 15-6652. Fred W. Robinson, Petitioner v. United States.

577 U.S. 1035, 136 S. Ct. 596, 193 L. Ed. 2d 477, 2015 U.S. LEXIS 7819.

December 7, 2015. Petition for writ of certiorari to the United States Court of Appeals for the Eighth Circuit denied.

Same case below, 781 F.3d 453.

No. 15-6676. Scott Brandon Hutcheson, Petitioner v. United States.

577 U.S. 1035, 136 S. Ct. 597, 193 L. Ed. 2d 477, 2015 U.S. LEXIS 7762.

December 7, 2015. Petition for writ of certiorari to the United States Court of Appeals for the Fifth Circuit denied.

Same case below, 608 Fed. Appx. 300.

No. 15-6692. Che Rose, Petitioner v. United States.

577 U.S. 1036, 136 S. Ct. 597, 193 L. Ed. 2d 478, 2015 U.S. LEXIS 7786.

December 7, 2015. Petition for writ of certiorari to the United States Court of Appeals for the Third Circuit denied.

Same case below, 613 Fed. Appx. 125.

No. 15-6707. Leonard Uchenna Nwafor, Petitioner v. United States.

577 U.S. 1036, 136 S. Ct. 597, 193 L. Ed. 2d 478, 2015 U.S. LEXIS 7763.

December 7, 2015. Petition for writ of certiorari to the United States Court of Appeals for the Ninth Circuit denied.

No. 15-6715. David Lee Hardin, Jr., Petitioner v. United States.

577 U.S. 1036, 136 S. Ct. 597, 193 L. Ed. 2d 478, 2015 U.S. LEXIS 7732.

December 7, 2015. Petition for writ of certiorari to the United States Court of Appeals for the Seventh Circuit denied.

Same case below, 571 Fed. Appx. 480.

No. 15-6720. Amir Hosseini, Petitioner v. United States.

577 U.S. 1036, 136 S. Ct. 597, 193 L. Ed. 2d 478, 2015 U.S. LEXIS 7694.

December 7, 2015. Petition for writ of certiorari to the United States Court of Appeals for the Seventh Circuit denied.

No. 15-6721. Frank Z. Guajardo, Petitioner v. Robert A. McDonald, Secretary of Veterans Affairs.

577 U.S. 1036, 136 S. Ct. 598, 193 L. Ed. 2d 478, 2015 U.S. LEXIS 7865.

December 7, 2015. Petition for writ of certiorari to the United States Court of Appeals for the Federal Circuit denied.

Same case below, 607 Fed. Appx. 985.

No. 15-6726. Kandace Rhean Griffin, Petitioner v. United States.

577 U.S. 1036, 136 S. Ct. 598, 193 L. Ed. 2d 478, 2015 U.S. LEXIS 7833.

December 7, 2015. Petition for writ of certiorari to the United States Court of Appeals for the Fourth Circuit denied.

No. 15-6727. Noe Farid Medrano, Petitioner v. United States.

577 U.S. 1036, 136 S. Ct. 598, 193 L. Ed. 2d 478, 2015 U.S. LEXIS 7780.

December 7, 2015. Petition for writ of certiorari to the United States Court of Appeals for the Fourth Circuit denied.

Same case below, 606 Fed. Appx. 51.

No. 15-6728. Markos Pappas, Petitioner v. Donna Zickefoose, Warden.

577 U.S. 1036, 136 S. Ct. 598, 193 L. Ed. 2d 478, 2015 U.S. LEXIS 7751.

December 7, 2015. Petition for writ of certiorari to the United States Court of Appeals for the Third Circuit denied.

Same case below, 608 Fed. Appx. 122.

No. 15-6729. Julio Cesar Garcia-Rosas, Petitioner v. United States.

577 U.S. 1036, 136 S. Ct. 598, 193 L. Ed. 2d 479, 2015 U.S. LEXIS 7791.

December 7, 2015. Petition for writ of certiorari to the United States Court of Appeals for the Ninth Circuit denied.

Same case below, 610 Fed. Appx. 652.

No. 15-6732. Leslie Dewayne Allen, Petitioner v. United States.

577 U.S. 1036, 136 S. Ct. 598, 193 L. Ed. 2d 479, 2015 U.S. LEXIS 7831.

December 7, 2015. Petition for writ of certiorari to the United States Court of Appeals for the Sixth Circuit denied.

No. 15-6736. Maurice Xavier Cruell, Petitioner v. United States.

577 U.S. 1036, 136 S. Ct. 599, 193 L. Ed. 2d 479, 2015 U.S. LEXIS 7827.

December 7, 2015. Petition for writ of certiorari to the United States Court of Appeals for the Fourth Circuit denied.

No. 15-6737. Jessica Lynn Tran, Petitioner v. United States.

577 U.S. 1036, 136 S. Ct. 599, 193 L. Ed. 2d 479, 2015 U.S. LEXIS 7765.

December 7, 2015. Petition for writ of certiorari to the United States Court of Appeals for the Eighth Circuit denied.

No. 15-6739. Edison Burgos-Montes, Petitioner v. United States.

577 U.S. 1036, 136 S. Ct. 599, 193 L. Ed. 2d 479, 2015 U.S. LEXIS 7721.

December 7, 2015. Petition for writ of certiorari to the United States Court of Appeals for the First Circuit denied.

Same case below, 786 F.3d 92.

No. 15-6741. Juan Diaz, Petitioner v. United States.

577 U.S. 1036, 136 S. Ct. 599, 193 L. Ed. 2d 479, 2015 U.S. LEXIS 7757.

December 7, 2015. Petition for writ of certiorari to the United States Court of Appeals for the Ninth Circuit denied.

Same case below, 607 Fed. Appx. 730.

No. 15-6742. Jean-Daniel Perkins, Petitioner v. United States.

577 U.S. 1036, 136 S. Ct. 599, 193 L. Ed. 2d 479, 2015 U.S. LEXIS 7686.

December 7, 2015. Petition for writ of certiorari to the United States Court of Appeals for the Eleventh Circuit denied.

Same case below, 787 F.3d 1329.

No. 15-6744. Pedro Rosales, Petitioner v. United States.

577 U.S. 1036, 136 S. Ct. 600, 193 L. Ed. 2d 479, 2015 U.S. LEXIS 7794.

December 7, 2015. Petition for writ of certiorari to the United States Court of Appeals for the Fifth Circuit denied.

Same case below, 612 Fed. Appx. 778.

Same case below, 163 So. 3d 1219.

No. 15-6749. Darran Lohse, Petitioner v. United States.

577 U.S. 1037, 136 S. Ct. 600, 193 L. Ed. 2d 480, 2015 U.S. LEXIS 7814.

December 7, 2015. Petition for writ of certiorari to the United States Court of Appeals for the Eighth Circuit denied.

Same case below, 797 F.3d 515.

No. 15-6772. Russell Lee Collins, Petitioner v. United States.

577 U.S. 1037, 136 S. Ct. 601, 193 L. Ed. 2d 480, 2015 U.S. LEXIS 7796.

December 7, 2015. Petition for writ of certiorari to the United States Court of Appeals for the Sixth Circuit denied.

Same case below, 799 F.3d 554.

No. 15-6752. Samuel J. T. Moore, III, Petitioner v. United States.

577 U.S. 1037, 136 S. Ct. 600, 193 L. Ed. 2d 480, 2015 U.S. LEXIS 7705.

December 7, 2015. Petition for writ of certiorari to the United States Court of Appeals for the Fourth Circuit denied.

No. 15-6773. Ernest Lee Johnson, Petitioner v. George A. Lombardi, et al.

577 U.S. 1037, 136 S. Ct. 601, 193 L. Ed. 2d 480, 2015 U.S. LEXIS 7784.

December 7, 2015. Petition for writ of certiorari to the United States Court of Appeals for the Eighth Circuit denied.

Same case below, 809 F.3d 388.

No. 15-6770. Donald Vickers, Petitioner v. Julie L. Jones, Secretary, Florida Department of Corrections, et al.

577 U.S. 1037, 136 S. Ct. 600, 193 L. Ed. 2d 480, 2015 U.S. LEXIS 7741.

December 7, 2015. Petition for writ of certiorari to the United States Court of Appeals for the Eleventh Circuit denied.

No. 15-6775. Pedro Mauricio-Trujillo, Petitioner v. United States.

577 U.S. 1037, 136 S. Ct. 601, 193 L. Ed. 2d 480, 2015 U.S. LEXIS 7845.

December 7, 2015. Petition for writ of certiorari to the United States Court of Appeals for the Ninth Circuit denied.

Same case below, 610 Fed. Appx. 716.

No. 15-6771. Thomas A. Sandelier, III, Petitioner v. Florida.

577 U.S. 1037, 136 S. Ct. 600, 193 L. Ed. 2d 480, 2015 U.S. LEXIS 7866.

December 7, 2015. Petition for writ of certiorari to the District Court of Appeal of Florida, Fourth District, denied.

No. 15-6776. Kathy Medlock, Petitioner v. United States.

577 U.S. 1037, 136 S. Ct. 601, 193 L. Ed. 2d 480, 2015 U.S. LEXIS 7779.

December 7, 2015. Petition for writ of certiorari to the United States Court of Appeals for the Sixth Circuit denied.

Same case below, 792 F.3d 700.

No. 15-6777. Kenneth Kraeger, Petitioner v. United States.

577 U.S. 1037; 136 S. Ct. 601, 193 L. Ed. 2d 481, 2015 U.S. LEXIS 7714.

December 7, 2015. Petition for writ of certiorari to the United States Court of Appeals for the Third Circuit denied.

Same case below, 615 Fed. Appx. 747.

No. 15-6780. Leslie Lyle Camick, Petitioner v. United States.

577 U.S. 1037, 136 S. Ct. 601, 193 L. Ed. 2d 481, 2015 U.S. LEXIS 7703.

December 7, 2015. Petition for writ of certiorari to the United States Court of Appeals for the Tenth Circuit denied.

Same case below, 796 F.3d 1206.

No. 15-6781. Manuel Salazar-Espinoza, Petitioner v. Suzanne R. Hastings, Warden.

577 U.S. 1037, 136 S. Ct. 602, 193 L. Ed. 2d 481, 2015 U.S. LEXIS 7792.

December 7, 2015. Petition for writ of certiorari to the United States Court of Appeals for the Eleventh Circuit denied.

No. 15-6782. Ernest Lee Johnson, Petitioner v. Cindy Griffith, Warden.

577 U.S. 1037, 136 S. Ct. 602, 193 L. Ed. 2d 481, 2015 U.S. LEXIS 7828.

December 7, 2015. Petition for writ of certiorari to the Supreme Court of Missouri denied.

No. 15-6785. Dwayne Calais, Petitioner v. United States.

577 U.S. 1037, 136 S. Ct. 602, 193 L. Ed. 2d 481, 2015 U.S. LEXIS 7756.

December 7, 2015. Petition for writ of certiorari to the United States Court of Appeals for the Eighth Circuit denied.

No. 15-6787. Amin A. Rashid, Petitioner v. David E. Ortiz, Warden.

577 U.S. 1037, 136 S. Ct. 602, 193 L. Ed. 2d 481, 2015 U.S. LEXIS 7851, reh den 577 U.S. 1209, 136 S. Ct. 1404, 194 L. Ed. 2d 383, 2016 U.S. LEXIS 1616.

December 7, 2015. Petition for writ of certiorari to the United States Court of Appeals for the Third Circuit denied.

Same case below, 617 Fed. Appx. 221.

No. 15-6791. Leonard Moore, Petitioner v. United States.

577 U.S. 1037, 136 S. Ct. 602, 193 L. Ed. 2d 481, 2015 U.S. LEXIS 7696, reh den 577 U.S. 1114, 136 S. Ct. 926, 193 L. Ed. 2d 811, 2016 U.S. LEXIS 642.

December 7, 2015. Petition for writ of certiorari to the United States Court of Appeals for the Sixth Circuit denied.

No. 15-6795. Hayzen Turner, Jr., Petitioner v. United States.

577 U.S. 1037, 136 S. Ct. 602, 193 L. Ed. 2d 481, 2015 U.S. LEXIS 7795.

December 7, 2015. Petition for writ of certiorari to the United States Court of Appeals for the Eleventh Circuit denied.

Same case below, 614 Fed. Appx. 108.

No. 15-6799. Donald P. Cipra, Petitioner v. United States.

577 U.S. 1038, 136 S. Ct. 602, 193 L. Ed. 2d 482, 2015 U.S. LEXIS 7835.

December 7, 2015. Petition for writ of certiorari to the United States Court of Appeals for the Seventh Circuit denied.

Same case below, 795 F.3d 735.

No. 15-6800. Efrain Armenta-Aguilar, aka Efrain Sanchez-Armenta, aka Jose Sanchez-Armenta, Petitioner v. United States.

577 U.S. 1038, 136 S. Ct. 603, 193 L. Ed. 2d 482, 2015 U.S. LEXIS 7864.

December 7, 2015. Petition for writ of certiorari to the United States Court of Appeals for the Ninth Circuit denied.

Same case below, 610 Fed. Appx. 638.

No. 15-6803. Donald G. Jackman Jr., Petitioner v. United States.

577 U.S. 1038, 136 S. Ct. 603, 193 L. Ed. 2d 482, 2015 U.S. LEXIS 7800, reh den 577 U.S. 1125, 136 S. Ct. 979, 194 L. Ed. 2d 16, 2016 U.S. LEXIS 923.

December 7, 2015. Petition for writ of certiorari to the United States Court of Appeals for the Third Circuit denied.

No. 15-6804. Jakota Raye Brown and Jikeem Gabriel Tyler, Petitioners v. United States.

577 U.S. 1038, 136 S. Ct. 603, 193 L. Ed. 2d 482, 2015 U.S. LEXIS 7837.

December 7, 2015. Petition for writ of certiorari to the United States Court of Appeals for the Fourth Circuit denied.

No. 15-6818. Charles M. Woolsey, Petitioner v. United States.

577 U.S. 1038, 136 S. Ct. 603, 193 L. Ed. 2d 482, 2015 U.S. LEXIS 7706.

December 7, 2015. Petition for writ of certiorari to the United States Court of Appeals for the Ninth Circuit denied.

Same case below, 608 Fed. Appx. 524.

No. 15-6819. Lodise Wadley, Petitioner v. Robert Farley, Warden.

577 U.S. 1038, 136 S. Ct. 603, 193 L. Ed. 2d 482, 2015 U.S. LEXIS 7742.

December 7, 2015. Petition for writ of certiorari to the United States Court of Appeals for the Sixth Circuit denied.

No. 15-6820. Myron Young, Petitioner v. United States.

577 U.S. 1038, 136 S. Ct. 604, 193 L. Ed. 2d 482, 2015 U.S. LEXIS 7853.

December 7, 2015. Petition for writ of certiorari to the United States Court of Appeals for the Sixth Circuit denied.

No. 15-6838. Jeffrey Dan Williams, Petitioner v. United States.

577 U.S. 1038, 136 S. Ct. 604, 193 L. Ed. 2d 482, 2015 U.S. LEXIS 7749.

December 7, 2015. Petition for writ of certiorari to the United States Court of Appeals for the Tenth Circuit denied.

Same case below, 790 F.3d 1059.

No. 15-6842. Irina Shelikhova, Petitioner v. United States.

577 U.S. 1038, 136 S. Ct. 604, 193 L. Ed. 2d 483, 2015 U.S. LEXIS 7805.

December 7, 2015. Petition for writ of certiorari to the United States Court of Appeals for the Second Circuit denied.

Same case below, 613 Fed. Appx. 4.

No. 15-6844. James Butler, Petitioner v. United States.

577 U.S. 1038, 136 S. Ct. 604, 193 L. Ed. 2d 483, 2015 U.S. LEXIS 7761.

December 7, 2015. Petition for writ of certiorari to the United States Court of Appeals for the Sixth Circuit denied.

No. 15-6848. Adelmo Isidro Rosales-Velasquez, Petitioner v. United States.

577 U.S. 1038, 136 S. Ct. 604, 193 L. Ed. 2d 483, 2015 U.S. LEXIS 7778.

December 7, 2015. Petition for writ of certiorari to the United States Court of Appeals for the Ninth Circuit denied.

Same case below, 609 Fed. Appx. 399.

No. 15-6850. Robert Lindsey, Petitioner v. United States.

577 U.S. 1038, 136 S. Ct. 605, 193 L. Ed. 2d 483, 2015 U.S. LEXIS 7811.

December 7, 2015. Petition for writ of certiorari to the United States Court of Appeals for the Eighth Circuit denied.

No. 15-6851. Porfirio Lopez-Vences, Petitioner v. United States.

577 U.S. 1038, 136 S. Ct. 605, 193 L. Ed. 2d 483, 2015 U.S. LEXIS 7698.

December 7, 2015. Petition for writ of certiorari to the United States Court of Appeals for the Fifth Circuit denied.

Same case below, 611 Fed. Appx. 226.

No. 15-6854. Ricardo Montero-Ornelas, Petitioner v. United States.

577 U.S. 1038, 136 S. Ct. 605, 193 L. Ed. 2d 483, 2015 U.S. LEXIS 7802.

December 7, 2015. Petition for writ of certiorari to the United States Court of Appeals for the Fifth Circuit denied.

Same case below, 615 Fed. Appx. 219.

No. 15-6855. Ruben Nino-Guererro, Petitioner v. United States.

577 U.S. 1038, 136 S. Ct. 605, 193 L. Ed. 2d 483, 2015 U.S. LEXIS 7858.

December 7, 2015. Petition for writ of certiorari to the United States Court of Appeals for the Fifth Circuit denied.

No. 15-133. Arie S. Friedman, et al., Petitioners v. City of Highland Park, Illinois.

577 U.S. 1039, 136 S. Ct. 447, 193 L. Ed. 2d 483, 2015 U.S. LEXIS 7681.

December 7, 2015. Petition for writ of certiorari to the United States Court of Appeals for the Seventh Circuit denied.

Same case below, 784 F.3d 406.

Justice **Thomas**, with whom Justice **Scalia** joins, dissenting from the denial of certiorari.

"[O]ur central holding in" *District of Columbia* v. *Heller*, 554 U.S. 570, 128 S. Ct. 2783, 171 L. Ed. 2d 637 (2008), was "that the Second Amendment protects a personal right to keep and bear arms for lawful purposes, most notably for self-defense within the home." *McDonald* v. *Chicago*, 561 U.S. 742, 780, 130 S. Ct. 3020, 177 L. Ed. 2d 894 (2010) (plurality opinion). And in *McDonald*, we recognized that the Second Amendment applies fully against the States as well as the Federal Government. *Id.*, at 750, 130 S. Ct. 3020, 177 L. Ed. 2d 894; *id.*, at 805, 130 S. Ct. 3020, 177 L. Ed. 2d 894 (Thomas, J., concurring in part and concurring in judgment).

Despite these holdings, several Courts of Appeals—including the Court of Appeals for the Seventh Circuit in the decision below—have upheld categorical bans on firearms that millions of Americans commonly own for lawful purposes. See 784 F.3d 406, 410-412 (2015). Because noncompliance with our Second Amendment precedents warrants this Court's attention as much as any of our precedents, I would grant certiorari in this case.

I

The City of Highland Park, Illinois, bans manufacturing, selling, giving, lending, acquiring, or possessing many of the most commonly owned semiautomatic firearms, which the City branded "Assault Weapons." See Highland Park, Ill., City Code §§ 136.001(C), 136.005 (2015), App. to Pet. for Cert. 65a, 71a. For instance, the ordinance criminalizes modern sporting rifles (*e.g.*, AR-style semiautomatic rifles), which many Americans own for lawful purposes like self-defense, hunting, and

target shooting. The City also prohibited "Large Capacity Magazines," a term the City used to refer to nearly all ammunition feeding devices that "accept more than ten rounds." § 136.001(G), *id.*, at 70a.

The City gave anyone who legally possessed "an Assault Weapon or Large Capacity Magazine" 60 days to move these items outside city limits, disable them, or surrender them for destruction. § 136.020, *id.*, at 73a. Anyone who violates the ordinance can be imprisoned for up to six months, fined up to $1,000, or both. § 136.999, *id.*, at 74a.

Petitioners—a Highland Park resident who sought to keep now-prohibited firearms and magazines to defend his home, and an advocacy organization—brought a suit to enjoin the ordinance on the ground that it violates the Second Amendment. The District Court for the Northern District of Illinois granted summary judgment to the City.

A divided panel of the Seventh Circuit affirmed. The panel majority acknowledged that the prohibited weapons "can be beneficial for self-defense because they are lighter than many rifles and less dangerous per shot than larger-caliber pistols or revolvers," and thus "[h]ouseholders too frightened or infirm to aim carefully may be able to wield them more effectively." 784 F.3d, at 411.

The majority nonetheless found no constitutional problem with the ordinance. It recognized that *Heller* "holds that a law banning the possession of handguns in the home . . . violates" the Second Amendment. 784 F.3d, at 407. But beyond *Heller*'s rejection of banning handguns in the home, the majority believed, *Heller* and *McDonald* "leave matters open" on the scope of the Second Amendment. 784 F.3d, at 412. The majority thus adopted a new test for gauging the constitutionality of bans on firearms: "[W]e [will] ask whether a regulation bans weapons that were common at the time of ratification or those that have some reasonable relationship to the preservation or efficiency of a well regulated militia, . . . and whether law-abiding citizens retain adequate means of self-defense." *Id.*, at 410 (internal quotation marks omitted).

Judge Manion dissented, reasoning that "[b]oth the ordinance and this court's opinion upholding it are directly at odds with the central holdings of *Heller* and *McDonald.*" *Id.*, at 412.

II

The Second Amendment provides: "A well regulated Militia, being necessary to the security of a free State, the right of the people to keep and bear Arms, shall not be infringed." We explained in *Heller* and *McDonald* that the Second Amendment "guarantee[s] the individual right to possess and carry weapons in case of confrontation." *Heller, supra,* at 592, 128 S. Ct. 2783, 171 L. Ed. 2d 637; see also *McDonald, supra,* at 767-769, 130 S. Ct. 3020, 177 L. Ed. 2d 894. We excluded from protection only "those weapons not typically possessed by law-abiding citizens for lawful purposes." *Heller,* 554 U.S., at 625, 128 S. Ct. 2783, 171 L. Ed. 2d 637. And we stressed that "[t]he very enumeration of the right takes out of the hands of government—even the Third Branch of Government—the power to decide on a case-by-case basis whether the right is really worth insisting upon." *Id.*, at 634, 128 S. Ct. 2783, 171 L. Ed. 2d 637 (emphasis deleted).

Instead of adhering to our reasoning in *Heller,* the Seventh Circuit limited *Heller* to its facts, and read *Heller* to forbid only total bans on handguns used for self-defense in the home. See 784 F.3d, at 407, 412. All other questions about the Second Amendment, the Seventh Circuit concluded, should be defined by "the political process and scholarly debate." *Id.*, at 412. But *Heller* repudiates that approach. We explained in *Heller* that "since th[e] case represent[ed] this Court's first in-depth

examination of the Second Amendment, one should not expect it to clarify the entire field." 554 U.S., at 635, 128 S. Ct. 2783, 171 L. Ed. 2d 637. We cautioned courts against leaving the rest of the field to the legislative process: "Constitutional rights are enshrined with the scope they were understood to have when the people adopted them, whether or not future legislatures or (yes) even future judges think that scope too broad." *Id.*, at 634-635, 128 S. Ct. 2783, 171 L. Ed. 2d 637.

Based on its crabbed reading of *Heller,* the Seventh Circuit felt free to adopt a test for assessing firearm bans that eviscerates many of the protections recognized in *Heller* and *McDonald.* The court asked in the first instance whether the banned firearms "were common at the time of ratification" in 1791. 784 F.3d, at 410. But we said in *Heller* that "the Second Amendment extends, prima facie, to all instruments that constitute bearable arms, even those that were not in existence at the time of the founding." 554 U.S., at 582, 128 S. Ct. 2783, 171 L. Ed. 2d 637.

The Seventh Circuit alternatively asked whether the banned firearms relate "to the preservation or efficiency of a well regulated militia." 784 F.3d, at 410 (internal quotation marks omitted). The court concluded that state and local ordinances never run afoul of that objective, since "states, which are in charge of militias, should be allowed to decide when civilians can possess military-grade firearms." *Ibid.* But that ignores *Heller's* fundamental premise: The right to keep and bear arms is an independent, individual right. Its scope is defined not by what the militia needs, but by what private citizens commonly possess. 554 U.S., at 592, 627-629, 128 S. Ct. 2783, 171 L. Ed. 2d 637. Moreover, the Seventh Circuit endorsed the view of the militia that *Heller* rejected. We explained that "*Congress* retains plenary authority to organize the militia," not States. *Id.*, at 600, 128 S. Ct. 2783, 171 L. Ed. 2d 637 (emphasis added). Because the

Second Amendment confers rights upon individual citizens—not state governments—it was doubly wrong for the Seventh Circuit to delegate to States and localities the power to decide which firearms people may possess.

Lastly, the Seventh Circuit considered "whether law-abiding citizens retain adequate means of self-defense," and reasoned that the City's ban was permissible because "[i]f criminals can find substitutes for banned assault weapons, then so can law-abiding homeowners." 784 F.3d, at 410, 411. Although the court recognized that *"Heller* held that the availability of long guns does not save a ban on handgun ownership," it thought that *"Heller* did not foreclose the possibility that allowing the use of most long guns plus pistols and revolvers . . . gives householders adequate means of defense." *Id.*, at 411.

That analysis misreads *Heller.* The question under *Heller* is not whether citizens have adequate alternatives available for self-defense. Rather, *Heller* asks whether the law bans types of firearms commonly used for a lawful purpose— regardless of whether alternatives exist. 554 U.S., at 627-629, 128 S. Ct. 2783, 171 L. Ed. 2d 637. And *Heller* draws a distinction between such firearms and weapons specially adapted to unlawful uses and not in common use, such as sawed-off shotguns. *Id.*, at 624-625, 128 S. Ct. 2783, 171 L. Ed. 2d 637. The City's ban is thus highly suspect because it broadly prohibits common semiautomatic firearms used for lawful purposes. Roughly five million Americans own AR-style semiautomatic rifles. See 784 F.3d, at 415, n. 3. The overwhelming majority of citizens who own and use such rifles do so for lawful purposes, including self-defense and target shooting. See *ibid.* Under our precedents, that is all that is needed for citizens to have a right under the Second Amendment to keep such weapons. See *McDonald*, 561 U.S., at 767-768, 130 S. Ct. 3020, 177 L. Ed. 2d 894; *Heller, supra,* at 628-629, 128 S. Ct. 2783, 171 L. Ed. 2d 637.

The Seventh Circuit ultimately upheld a ban on many common semiautomatic firearms based on speculation about the law's potential policy benefits. See 784 F.3d, at 411-412. The court conceded that handguns—not "assault weapons"—"are responsible for the vast majority of gun violence in the United States." *Id.*, at 409. Still, the court concluded, the ordinance "may increase the public's sense of safety," which alone is "a substantial benefit." *Id.*, at 412. *Heller*, however, forbids subjecting the Second Amendment's "core protection . . . to a freestanding 'interest-balancing' approach." *Heller, supra,* at 634, 128 S. Ct. 2783, 171 L. Ed. 2d 637. This case illustrates why. If a broad ban on firearms can be upheld based on conjecture that the public might *feel* safer (while being no safer at all), then the Second Amendment guarantees nothing.

III

The Court's refusal to review a decision that flouts two of our Second Amendment precedents stands in marked contrast to the Court's willingness to summarily reverse courts that disregard our other constitutional decisions. *E.g., Maryland* v. *Kulbicki, ante,* at 1, 136 S. Ct. 2, 193 L. Ed. 2d 1 (*per curiam*) (summarily reversing because the court below applied *Strickland* v. *Washington*, 466 U.S. 668, 104 S. Ct. 2052, 80 L. Ed. 2d 674 (1984), "in name only"); *Grady* v. *North Carolina*, 575 U.S. 306, 135 S. Ct. 1368, 191 L. Ed. 2d 459 (2015) (*per curiam*) (summarily reversing a judgment inconsistent with this Court's recent Fourth Amendment precedents); *Martinez* v. *Illinois*, 572 U.S. 833, 843, 134 S. Ct. 2070, 188 L. Ed. 2d 1112 (2014) (*per curiam*) (summarily reversing judgment that rested on an "understandable" double jeopardy holding that nonetheless "r[an] directly counter to our precedents").

There is no basis for a different result when our Second Amendment precedents are at stake. I would grant certiorari to prevent the Seventh Circuit from relegating the Second Amendment to a second-class right.

No. 15-416. Michigan, Petitioner v. Rahim Omarkhan Lockridge.

577 U.S. 1043, 136 S. Ct. 590, 193 L. Ed. 2d 487, 2015 U.S. LEXIS 7709.

December 7, 2015. Motion of respondent for leave to proceed in forma pauperis granted. Petition for writ of certiorari to the Supreme Court of Michigan denied.

Same case below, 498 Mich. 358, 870 N.W.2d 502.

No. 15-471. Energy and Environment Legal Institute, et al., Petitioners v. Joshua Epel, et al.

577 U.S. 1043, 136 S. Ct. 595, 193 L. Ed. 2d 487, 2015 U.S. LEXIS 7750.

December 7, 2015. Motion of Pacific Legal Foundation, et al. for leave to file a brief as amici curiae granted. Motion of Chamber of Commerce of the United States of America, et al. for leave to file a brief as amici curiae granted. Motion of Association des Eleveurs de Canards et d'Oies du Quebec, et al. for leave to file a brief as amici curiae granted. Petition for writ of certiorari to the United States Court of Appeals for the Tenth Circuit denied.

Same case below, 793 F.3d 1169.

No. 15-6735. Tracy Alan Barnett, Petitioner v. Claude Maye, Warden.

577 U.S. 1043, 136 S. Ct. 599, 193 L. Ed. 2d 487, 2015 U.S. LEXIS 7726.

December 7, 2015. Petition for writ of certiorari to the United States Court of Appeals for the Tenth Circuit denied. Justice Kagan took no part in the consideration or decision of this petition.

Same case below, 602 Fed. Appx. 717.

No. 15-6758. Johnny Scott Warren, Petitioner v. United States.

577 U.S. 1043, 136 S. Ct. 600, 193 L. Ed. 2d 487, 2015 U.S. LEXIS 7832.

December 7, 2015. Petition for writ of certiorari to the United States Court of Appeals for the Tenth Circuit denied. Justice Kagan took no part in the consideration or decision of this petition.

No. 15-6826. Wilfredo Gonzalez Lora, Petitioner v. United States.

577 U.S. 1044, 136 S. Ct. 604, 193 L. Ed. 2d 487, 2015 U.S. LEXIS 7707.

December 7, 2015. Petition for writ of certiorari to the United States Court of Appeals for the Fourth Circuit denied. Justice Kagan took no part in the consideration or decision of this petition.

No. 15-6931. In re George H. Gage, Petitioner.

577 U.S. 1029, 136 S. Ct. 605, 193 L. Ed. 2d 487, 2015 U.S. LEXIS 7807.

December 7, 2015. Petition for writ of habeas corpus denied.

No. 15-6955. In re John H. Jones, Petitioner.

577 U.S. 1029, 136 S. Ct. 605, 193 L. Ed. 2d 487, 2015 U.S. LEXIS 7823.

December 7, 2015. Petition for writ of habeas corpus denied.

No. 15-6972. In re Marvin Green, Petitioner.

577 U.S. 1029, 136 S. Ct. 605, 193 L. Ed. 2d 488, 2015 U.S. LEXIS 7804.

December 7, 2015. Petition for writ of habeas corpus denied.

No. 15-6807. In re Wilfredo Gonzalez Lora, Petitioner.

577 U.S. 1029, 136 S. Ct. 603, 193 L. Ed. 2d 488, 2015 U.S. LEXIS 7856.

December 7, 2015. Petition for writ of habeas corpus denied. Justice Kagan took no part in the consideration or decision of this petition.

No. 15-6398. In re Otis Fitzgerald Ervin, Petitioner.

577 U.S. 1029, 136 S. Ct. 591, 193 L. Ed. 2d 488, 2015 U.S. LEXIS 7691.

December 7, 2015. Petition for writ of mandamus denied.

No. 14-8863. Gary Ray Debolt, Petitioner v. United States.

577 U.S. 1044, 136 S. Ct. 607, 193 L. Ed. 2d 488, 2015 U.S. LEXIS 7785.

December 7, 2015. Petition for rehearing denied.

Former decision, 575 U.S. 974, 135 S. Ct. 1873, 191 L. Ed. 2d 746, 2015 U.S. LEXIS 2505.

No. 14-9429. Anthony Dwayne Hammonds, Petitioner v. Bo's Food Store.

577 U.S. 1044, 136 S. Ct. 608, 193 L. Ed. 2d 488, 2015 U.S. LEXIS 7799.

December 7, 2015. Petition for rehearing denied.

Former decision, 575 U.S. 1042, 135 S. Ct. 2389, 192 L. Ed. 2d 174, 2015 U.S. LEXIS 3585.

No. 14-9590. J. D. T., Juvenile Male, Petitioner v. United States.

577 U.S. 1044, 136 S. Ct. 608, 193 L. Ed. 2d 488, 2015 U.S. LEXIS 7776.

December 7, 2015. Petition for rehearing denied.

Former decision, 577 U.S. 969, 136 S. Ct. 400, 193 L. Ed. 2d 339, 2015 U.S. LEXIS 6764.

No. 14-9691. John E. Rodarte, Sr., Petitioner v. William Stephens, Director, Texas Department of Criminal Justice, Correctional Institutions Division.

577 U.S. 1044, 136 S. Ct. 608, 193 L. Ed. 2d 488, 2015 U.S. LEXIS 7697.

December 7, 2015. Petition for rehearing denied.

Former decision, 577 U.S. 834, 136 S. Ct. 52, 193 L. Ed. 2d 57, 2015 U.S. LEXIS 5631.

No. 14-9742. John K. Elam, Petitioner v. Jorge L. Pastrana, Warden.

577 U.S. 1044, 136 S. Ct. 608, 193 L. Ed. 2d 488, 2015 U.S. LEXIS 7766.

December 7, 2015. Petition for rehearing denied.

Former decision, 577 U.S. 835, 136 S. Ct. 56, 193 L. Ed. 2d 59, 2015 U.S. LEXIS 5711.

————

No. 14-9841. Robert W. Dougherty, Petitioner v. Samuel V. Pruett, Warden; and Robert W. Dougherty, Petitioner v. Virginia, et al.

577 U.S. 1044, 136 S. Ct. 608, 193 L. Ed. 2d 489, 2015 U.S. LEXIS 7723.

December 7, 2015. Petition for rehearing denied.

Former decision, 577 U.S. 838, 136 S. Ct. 66, 193 L. Ed. 2d 65, 2015 U.S. LEXIS 5274.

————

No. 14-9853. Clifford Scott Medley, Petitioner v. William Stephens, Director, Texas Department of Criminal Justice, Correctional Institutions Division.

577 U.S. 1044, 136 S. Ct. 608, 193 L. Ed. 2d 489, 2015 U.S. LEXIS 7740.

December 7, 2015. Petition for rehearing denied.

Former decision, 577 U.S. 839, 136 S. Ct. 67, 193 L. Ed. 2d 66, 2015 U.S. LEXIS 5007.

————

No. 14-9943. Sean Tapp, Petitioner v. James Eckard, Superintendent, State Correctional Institution at Huntingdon.

577 U.S. 1044, 136 S. Ct. 608, 193 L. Ed. 2d 489, 2015 U.S. LEXIS 7712.

December 7, 2015. Petition for rehearing denied.

Former decision, 577 U.S. 841, 136 S. Ct. 75, 193 L. Ed. 2d 70, 2015 U.S. LEXIS 5044.

————

No. 14-10258. Linda Sue Cheek, Petitioner v. United States.

577 U.S. 1044, 136 S. Ct. 609, 193 L. Ed. 2d 489, 2015 U.S. LEXIS 7692.

December 7, 2015. Petition for rehearing denied.

Former decision, 577 U.S. 855, 136 S. Ct. 125, 193 L. Ed. 2d 98, 2015 U.S. LEXIS 6091.

————

No. 14-10281. Ray Turner, Petitioner v. Henry Steward, Warden.

577 U.S. 1044, 136 S. Ct. 609, 193 L. Ed. 2d 489, 2015 U.S. LEXIS 7728.

December 7, 2015. Petition for rehearing denied.

Former decision, 577 U.S. 857, 136 S. Ct. 132, 193 L. Ed. 2d 101, 2015 U.S. LEXIS 5692.

————

No. 14-10328. Ardelia Jones, Petitioner v. Nuttall AFC Company, et al.

577 U.S. 1044, 136 S. Ct. 609, 193 L. Ed. 2d 489, 2015 U.S. LEXIS 7839.

December 7, 2015. Petition for rehearing denied.

Former decision, 577 U.S. 860, 136 S. Ct. 141, 193 L. Ed. 2d 106, 2015 U.S. LEXIS 5899.

No. 14-10420. In re Corey Rowe, Petitioner.

577 U.S. 1044, 136 S. Ct. 609, 193 L. Ed. 2d 490, 2015 U.S. LEXIS 7772.

December 7, 2015. Petition for rehearing denied.

Former decision, 577 U.S. 812, 136 S. Ct. 157, 193 L. Ed. 2d 214, 2015 U.S. LEXIS 4728.

———

No. 14-10444. James Talley, Petitioner v. Jerome B. Simandle, Chief Judge, United States District Court for the District of New Jersey.

577 U.S. 1044, 136 S. Ct. 609, 193 L. Ed. 2d 490, 2015 U.S. LEXIS 7693.

December 7, 2015. Petition for rehearing denied.

Former decision, 577 U.S. 866, 136 S. Ct. 160, 193 L. Ed. 2d 118, 2015 U.S. LEXIS 6343.

———

No. 15-53. Daniel E. Carpenter, Petitioner v. United States.

577 U.S. 1044, 136 S. Ct. 609, 193 L. Ed. 2d 490, 2015 U.S. LEXIS 7738.

December 7, 2015. Petition for rehearing denied.

Former decision, 577 U.S. 871, 136 S. Ct. 196, 193 L. Ed. 2d 126, 2015 U.S. LEXIS 6276.

———

No. 15-112. Susan Skipp-Tittle, Petitioner v. Shawn Tittle.

577 U.S. 1044, 136 S. Ct. 609, 193 L. Ed. 2d 490, 2015 U.S. LEXIS 7746.

December 7, 2015. Petition for rehearing denied.

Former decision, 577 U.S. 874, 136 S. Ct. 228, 193 L. Ed. 2d 132, 2015 U.S. LEXIS 6064.

———

No. 15-160. Alba Nubia Senci, Petitioner v. The Bank of New York Mellon.

577 U.S. 1044, 136 S. Ct. 609, 193 L. Ed. 2d 490, 2015 U.S. LEXIS 7859.

December 7, 2015. Petition for rehearing denied.

Former decision, 577 U.S. 875, 136 S. Ct. 255, 193 L. Ed. 2d 134, 2015 U.S. LEXIS 6275.

———

No. 15-171. James P. DeFazio, et al., Petitioners v. Hollister, Inc., et al.

577 U.S. 1044, 136 S. Ct. 610, 193 L. Ed. 2d 490, 2015 U.S. LEXIS 7689.

December 7, 2015. Petition for rehearing denied.

Former decision, 577 U.S. 923, 136 S. Ct. 325, 193 L. Ed. 2d 230, 2015 U.S. LEXIS 6437.

———

No. 15-279. Kensho Sone, et al., Petitioners v. Harvest Natural Resources, Inc.

577 U.S. 1044, 136 S. Ct. 610, 193 L. Ed. 2d 490, 2015 U.S. LEXIS 7744.

December 7, 2015. Petition for rehearing denied.

Former decision, 577 U.S. 925, 136 S. Ct. 345, 193 L. Ed. 2d 232, 2015 U.S. LEXIS 6558.

No. 15-5157. Anthony Quintin Kelly, Petitioner v. Frank Bishop, Warden, et al.

577 U.S. 1044, 136 S. Ct. 610, 193 L. Ed. 2d 491, 2015 U.S. LEXIS 7824.

December 7, 2015. Petition for rehearing denied.

Former decision, 577 U.S. 885, 136 S. Ct. 194, 193 L. Ed. 2d 153, 2015 U.S. LEXIS 5230.

No. 15-5362. Freddie Crayton, Petitioner v. Florida.

577 U.S. 1044, 136 S. Ct. 610, 193 L. Ed. 2d 491, 2015 U.S. LEXIS 7715.

December 7, 2015. Petition for rehearing denied.

Former decision, 577 U.S. 896, 136 S. Ct. 231, 193 L. Ed. 2d 174, 2015 U.S. LEXIS 4872.

No. 15-5478. Claude V. Jones, Jr., Petitioner v. Leroy Cartledge, Warden.

577 U.S. 1044, 136 S. Ct. 610, 193 L. Ed. 2d 491, 2015 U.S. LEXIS 7701.

December 7, 2015. Petition for rehearing denied.

Former decision, 577 U.S. 903, 136 S. Ct. 252, 193 L. Ed. 2d 187, 2015 U.S. LEXIS 4903.

No. 15-5479. Twana Fisher, Petitioner v. City of Ironton, Ohio.

577 U.S. 1044, 136 S. Ct. 610, 193 L. Ed. 2d 491, 2015 U.S. LEXIS 7857.

December 7, 2015. Petition for rehearing denied.

Former decision, 577 U.S. 925, 136 S. Ct. 321, 193 L. Ed. 2d 233, 2015 U.S. LEXIS 6475.

No. 15-5541. Walter J. Bramage, Petitioner v. Discover Bank.

577 U.S. 1044, 136 S. Ct. 610, 193 L. Ed. 2d 491, 2015 U.S. LEXIS 7854.

December 7, 2015. Petition for rehearing denied.

Former decision, 577 U.S. 927, 136 S. Ct. 325, 193 L. Ed. 2d 235, 2015 U.S. LEXIS 6513.

No. 15-5590. Pauline Moody, Petitioner v. City of Delray Beach, Florida, et al.

577 U.S. 1045, 136 S. Ct. 610, 193 L. Ed. 2d 491, 2015 U.S. LEXIS 7736.

December 7, 2015. Petition for rehearing denied.

Former decision, 577 U.S. 928, 136 S. Ct. 328, 193 L. Ed. 2d 237, 2015 U.S. LEXIS 6425.

No. 15-5747. Charles Todd Clugston, Petitioner v. Mike Batista, Director, Montana Department of Corrections, et al.

577 U.S. 1045, 136 S. Ct. 611, 193 L. Ed. 2d 491, 2015 U.S. LEXIS 7803.

December 7, 2015. Petition for rehearing denied.

Former decision, 577 U.S. 930, 136 S. Ct. 335, 193 L. Ed. 2d 241, 2015 U.S. LEXIS 6473.

No. 15-5911. Jean Mari Lindor, Petitioner v. United States.

577 U.S. 1045, 136 S. Ct. 611, 193 L. Ed. 2d 492, 2015 U.S. LEXIS 7848.

December 7, 2015. Petition for rehearing denied.

Former decision, 577 U.S. 933, 136 S. Ct. 344, 193 L. Ed. 2d 247, 2015 U.S. LEXIS 6589.

No. 15-5975. Manoj Kumar Jha, Petitioner v. United States.

577 U.S. 1045, 136 S. Ct. 611, 193 L. Ed. 2d 492, 2015 U.S. LEXIS 7727.

December 7, 2015. Petition for rehearing denied.

Former decision, 577 U.S. 934, 136 S. Ct. 349, 193 L. Ed. 2d 250, 2015 U.S. LEXIS 6457.

No. 15-6047. Julio Cesar Cardenas, Petitioner v. United States.

577 U.S. 1045, 136 S. Ct. 611, 193 L. Ed. 2d 492, 2015 U.S. LEXIS 7840.

December 7, 2015. Petition for rehearing denied.

Former decision, 577 U.S. 945, 136 S. Ct. 373, 193 L. Ed. 2d 301, 2015 U.S. LEXIS 6651.

No. D-2857. In the Matter of Discipline of Luigi Rosabianca.

577 U.S. 1027, 136 S. Ct. 611, 193 L. Ed. 2d 492, 2015 U.S. LEXIS 7716.

December 7, 2015. Luigi Rosabianca, of New York, New York, is suspended from the practice of law in this Court and a rule will issue, returnable within 40 days, requiring him to show cause why he should not be disbarred from the practice of law in this Court.

No. D-2858. In the Matter of Discipline of Michael S. Sepcich.

577 U.S. 1027, 136 S. Ct. 611, 193 L. Ed. 2d 492, 2015 U.S. LEXIS 7734.

December 7, 2015. Michael S. Sepcich, of Metairie, Louisiana, is suspended from the practice of law in this Court and a rule will issue, returnable within 40 days, requiring him to show cause why he should not be disbarred from the practice of law in this Court.

No. D-2859. In the Matter of Discipline of William Jennings Jefferson.

577 U.S. 1027, 136 S. Ct. 611, 193 L. Ed. 2d 492, 2015 U.S. LEXIS 7737.

December 7, 2015. William Jennings Jefferson, of New Orleans, Louisiana, is suspended from the practice of law in this Court and a rule will issue, returnable within 40 days, requiring him to show cause why he should not be disbarred from the practice of law in this Court.

No. D-2860. In the Matter of Discipline of Alan John Abadie.

577 U.S. 1027, 136 S. Ct. 612, 193 L. Ed. 2d 492, 2015 U.S. LEXIS 7759.

December 7, 2015. Alan John Abadie, of Chalmette, Louisiana, is suspended from the practice of law in this Court and a rule will issue, returnable within 40 days, requiring him to show cause why he should not be disbarred from the practice of law in this Court.

No. D-2861. In the Matter of Discipline of Shauntese Curry Trye.

577 U.S. 1027, 136 S. Ct. 612, 193 L. Ed. 2d 493, 2015 U.S. LEXIS 7801.

December 7, 2015. Shauntese Curry Trye, of Baltimore, Maryland, is suspended from the practice of law in this Court and a rule will issue, returnable within 40 days, requiring her to show cause why she should not be disbarred from the practice of law in this Court.

No. D-2862. In the Matter of Discipline of Gerry G. Zobrist.

577 U.S. 1027, 136 S. Ct. 612, 193 L. Ed. 2d 493, 2015 U.S. LEXIS 7758.

December 7, 2015. Gerry G. Zobrist, of Las Vegas, Nevada, is suspended from the practice of law in this Court and a rule will issue, returnable within 40 days, requiring him to show cause why he should not be disbarred from the practice of law in this Court.

No. D-2863. In the Matter of Discipline of John J. Koresko, V.

577 U.S. 1027, 136 S. Ct. 612, 193 L. Ed. 2d 493, 2015 U.S. LEXIS 7713.

December 7, 2015. John J. Koresko, V, of Bridgeport, Pennsylvania, is suspended from the practice of law in this Court and

a rule will issue, returnable within 40 days, requiring him to show cause why he should not be disbarred from the practice of law in this Court.

Same case below, 944 So. 2d 347.

No. D-2864. In the Matter of Discipline of Donald P. Rosen.

577 U.S. 1027, 136 S. Ct. 612, 193 L. Ed. 2d 493, 2015 U.S. LEXIS 7730.

December 7, 2015. Donald P. Rosen, of Carpentersville, Illinois, is suspended from the practice of law in this Court and a rule will issue, returnable within 40 days, requiring him to show cause why he should not be disbarred from the practice of law in this Court.

No. D-2865. In the Matter of Discipline of Daniel Rozenstrauch.

577 U.S. 1028, 136 S. Ct. 613, 193 L. Ed. 2d 493, 2015 U.S. LEXIS 7768.

December 7, 2015. Daniel Rozenstrauch, of Chicago, Illinois, is suspended from the practice of law in this Court and a rule will issue, returnable within 40 days, requiring him to show cause why he should not be disbarred from the practice of law in this Court.

No. D-2866. In the Matter of Discipline of David E. Neely.

577 U.S. 1028, 136 S. Ct. 613, 193 L. Ed. 2d 493, 2015 U.S. LEXIS 7826.

December 7, 2015. David E. Neely, of Chicago, Illinois, is suspended from the practice of law in this Court and a rule will issue, returnable within 40 days, requiring him to show cause why he should not be disbarred from the practice of law in this Court.

———

No. D-2867. In the Matter of Discipline of Carla Ruth McBeath.

577 U.S. 1028, 136 S. Ct. 613, 193 L. Ed. 2d 494, 2015 U.S. LEXIS 7861.

December 7, 2015. Carla Ruth McBeath, of Fort Lee, New Jersey, is suspended from the practice of law in this Court and a rule will issue, returnable within 40 days, requiring her to show cause why she should not be disbarred from the practice of law in this Court.

———

No. D-2868. In the Matter of Discipline of Cheryl Rose Brawley.

577 U.S. 1028, 136 S. Ct. 613, 193 L. Ed. 2d 494, 2015 U.S. LEXIS 7842.

December 7, 2015. Cheryl Rose Brawley, of Honolulu, Hawaii, is suspended from the practice of law in this Court and a rule will issue, returnable within 40 days, requiring her to show cause why she should not be disbarred from the practice of law in this Court.

———

No. 15-7279 (15A605). Brian Keith Terrell, Petitioner v. Bruce Chatman, Warden.

577 U.S. 1045, 136 S. Ct. 613, 193 L. Ed. 2d 494, 2015 U.S. LEXIS 7869.

December 8, 2015. Application for stay of execution of sentence of death, presented to Justice Thomas, and by him referred to the Court, denied. Petition for writ of certiorari to the Supreme Court of Georgia denied.

———

No. 15-7282 (15A606). Brian Keith Terrell, Petitioner v. Homer Bryson, Commissioner, Georgia Department of Corrections, et al.

577 U.S. 1045, 136 S. Ct. 614, 193 L. Ed. 2d 494, 2015 U.S. LEXIS 7870.

December 8, 2015. Application for stay of execution of sentence of death, presented to Justice Thomas, and by him referred to the Court, denied. Petition for writ of certiorari to the United States Court of Appeals for the Eleventh Circuit denied.

Same case below, 807 F.3d 1276.

———

No. 15-5932 (R46-013). Barry Allan Beach, Petitioner v. Montana.

577 U.S. 1045, 136 S. Ct. 614, 193 L. Ed. 2d 494, 2015 U.S. LEXIS 7871.

December 10, 2015. The petition for writ of certiorari to the Supreme Court of Montana was dismissed today pursuant to Rule 46 of the Rules of this Court.

Same case below, 379 Mont. 74, 348 P.3d 629.

———

No. 14-1468. Danny Birchfield, Petitioner v. North Dakota.

No. 14-1470. William Robert Bernard, Jr., Petitioner v. Minnesota.

No. 14-1507. Steve Michael Beylund, Petitioner v. Grant Levi, Director, North Dakota Department of Transportation.

577 U.S. 1045, 136 S. Ct. 614, 193 L. Ed. 2d 494, 2015 U.S. LEXIS 7877.

December 11, 2015. Petition for writ of certiorari to the Supreme Court of North Dakota granted in No. 14-1468. Petition for writ of certiorari to the Supreme Court of Minnesota granted in No. 14-1470. Petition for writ of certiorari to the Supreme Court of North Dakota granted in No. 14-1507. Cases are consolidated and a total of one hour is allotted for oral argument.

Same cases below, 858 N.W.2d 302 (first judgment); 859 N.W.2d 762 (second judgment); 859 N.W.2d 403 (third judgment).

No. 15-290. United States Army Corps of Engineers, Petitioner v. Hawkes Co., Inc., et al.

577 U.S. 1046, 136 S. Ct. 615, 193 L. Ed. 2d 495, 2015 U.S. LEXIS 7874.

December 11, 2015. Motion of National Association of Home Builders for leave to file a brief as amicus curiae granted. Petition for writ of certiorari to the United States Court of Appeals for the Eighth Circuit granted.

Same case below, 782 F.3d 994.

No. 15-338. Mark J. Sheriff, et al., Petitioners v. Pamela Gillie, et al.

577 U.S. 1045, 136 S. Ct. 614, 193 L. Ed. 2d 495, 2015 U.S. LEXIS 7876.

December 11, 2015. Petition for writ of certiorari to the United States Court of Appeals for the Sixth Circuit granted.

Same case below, 785 F.3d 1091.

No. 15-339. Michael Ross, Petitioner v. Shaidon Blake.

577 U.S. 1045, 136 S. Ct. 614, 193 L. Ed. 2d 495, 2015 U.S. LEXIS 7875.

December 11, 2015. Petition for writ of certiorari to the United States Court of Appeals for the Fourth Circuit granted.

Same case below, 787 F.3d 693.

ANTOINE BRUCE, Petitioner

v

CHARLES E. SAMUELS, JR., et al.

577 U.S. 82, 136 S. Ct. 627, 193 L. Ed. 2d 496, 2016 U.S. LEXIS 620

[No. 14-844]

Argued November 4, 2015. Decided January 12, 2016.

Decision: 28 U.S.C.S. § 1915(b)(2)—which required federal prisoners proceeding in forma pauperis to pay monthly 20 percent of income toward case or appeal's filing fee—called for simultaneous payments when multiple actions were pursued.

Prior history: 411 U.S. App. D.C. 380, 761 F.3d 1, 2014 U.S. App. LEXIS 15000

SUMMARY

Overview: HOLDINGS: [1]-Under 28 U.S.C.S. § 1915(b), monthly installment payments, like the initial partial payment, were to be assessed on a per-case basis as nothing in 28 U.S.C.S. § 1915's current design supported treating a prisoner's second or third action unlike his first lawsuit.

Outcome: Judgment affirmed; Unanimous decision.

HEADNOTES

Classified to United States Supreme Court Digest, Lawyers' Edition

Civil actions — filing fees — installments

L Ed Digest: Prisons and Convicts § 2

1. Under 28 U.S.C.S. § 1915(b), monthly installment payments, like the initial partial payment, are to be assessed on a per-case basis. Nothing in 28 U.S.C.S. § 1915's current design supports treating a prisoner's second or third action unlike his first lawsuit.

Multiple civil actions — filing fees — installments

L Ed Digest: Prisons and Convicts § 2

2. Just as 28 U.S.C.S. § 1915(b)(1) calls for assessment of an initial partial filing fee each time a prisoner brings a civil action or files an appeal, so its allied provision, 28 U.S.C.S. § 1915(b)(2), triggered immediately after, calls for monthly payments of 20 percent of the preceding month's income simultaneously for each action pursued. The other two paragraphs of 28 U.S.C.S. § 1915(b) confirm that the subsection as a whole is written from the perspective of a single case. 28 U.S.C.S. § 1915(b)(3) and (4). There is scant indication that the statute's perspective shifts partway through § 1915(b)(2).

BRUCE v. SAMUELS
(2016) 577 U.S. 82, 136 S. Ct. 627, 193 L. Ed. 2d 496, 2016 U.S. LEXIS 620

RESEARCH REFERENCES

28 U.S.C.S. § 1915(b)

Moore's Federal Practice §§20.10, 53.60, 404.04 (Matthew Bender 3d ed.)

L Ed Digest, Prisons and Convicts § 2

L Ed Index, Forma Pauperis; Prisons and Prisoners

Annotations:

Supreme Court's construction and application of Prison Litigation Reform Act (PLRA) provision (42 U.S.C.S. § 1997e(a), as amended), concerning exhaustion of administrative remedies. 165 L. Ed. 2d 1063.

Supreme Court's construction and application of 28 U.S.C.S. § 1915, providing for federal court proceedings in forma pauperis. 121 L. Ed. 2d 817.

APPEARANCES OF COUNSEL ARGUING CASE

Anthony F. Shelley argued the cause for petitioner.

Nicole A. Saharsky argued the cause for respondents.

SYLLABUS BY REPORTER OF DECISIONS

The Prison Litigation Reform Act of 1995 provides that prisoners qualified to proceed *in forma pauperis* (IFP) must nonetheless pay an initial partial filing fee, set as "20 percent of the greater of" the average monthly deposits in the prisoner's account or the average monthly balance of the account over the preceding six months. 28 U.S.C. § 1915(b)(1). They must then pay the remainder of the fee in monthly installments of "20 percent of the preceding month's income credited to the prisoner's account." § 1915(b)(2). The initial partial fee is assessed on a per-case basis, *i.e.,* each time the prisoner files a lawsuit. The initial payment may not be exacted if the prisoner has no means to pay it,

§ 1915(b)(4), and no monthly installments are required unless the prisoner has more than $10 in his account, § 1915(b)(2). In contest here is the calculation of subsequent monthly installment payments when more than one fee is owed.

Petitioner Antoine Bruce, a federal inmate and a frequent litigant, argued that the monthly filing-fee payments do not become due until filing-fee obligations previously incurred in other cases are satisfied. The D. C. Circuit disagreed, holding that Bruce's monthly payments were due simultaneously with monthly payments in the earlier cases.

Held: Section 1915(b)(2) calls for simultaneous, not sequential, recoupment of multiple monthly installment payments. Pp. 87–91, 193 L. Ed. 2d, at 500-503.

(a) Bruce and the Government present competing interpretations of the IFP statute, which does not explicitly address how multiple filing fees should be paid. In urging a per-prisoner approach under which he would pay 20 percent of his monthly income regardless of the number of cases he has filed, Bruce relies principally on the contrast between the singular "clerk" and the plural "fees" as those nouns appear in § 1915(b)(2), which requires payments to be forwarded "to the clerk of the court . . . until the filing fees are paid." Even when more than one filing fee is owed, Bruce contends, § 1915(b)(2) instructs that only one clerk will receive payment each month. In contrast, the Government urges a per-case approach. Emphasizing that § 1915 as a whole has a single-case focus, providing instructions for *each* case, the Government contends that it would be anomalous to treat paragraph (b)(1)'s initial partial payment, admit-

tedly directed at a single case, differently than paragraph (b)(2)'s subsequent monthly payments. Pp. 87–89, 193 L. Ed. 2d, at 500-502.

(b) Section 1915's text and context support the per-case approach. Just as § 1915(b)(1) calls for assessment of "*an* initial partial filing fee" each time a prisoner "brings *a* civil action or files *an* appeal" (emphasis added), so its allied provision, § 1915(b)(2), calls for monthly 20 percent payments simultaneously for each action pursued. Section 1915(b)(3), which imposes a ceiling on fees permitted "for the commencement of *a* civil action or *an* appeal" (emphasis added), and § 1915(b)(4), which protects the right to bring "*a* civil action or appea[l] *a* . . . judgment" (emphasis added), confirm that subsection (b) as a whole is written from the perspective of a single case. Pp. 89–90, 193 L. Ed. 2d, at 502-503.

761 F.3d 1, affirmed.

Ginsburg, J., delivered the opinion for a unanimous Court.

OPINION OF THE COURT

[577 U.S. 83]

Justice **Ginsburg** delivered the opinion of the Court.

This case concerns the payment of filing fees for civil actions commenced by prisoners in federal courts. Until 1996, indigent prisoners, like other indigent persons, could file a

[577 U.S. 84]

civil action without paying any filing fee. See 28 U.S.C. § 1915(a)(1). In the Prison Litigation Reform Act of 1995 (PLRA), 110 Stat. 1321-66, Congress placed several limitations on prisoner litigation in federal courts. Among those limitations, Congress required pris-

oners qualified to proceed *in forma pauperis* nevertheless to pay an initial partial filing fee. That fee is statutorily set as "20 percent of the greater of" the average monthly deposits in the prisoner's account or the average monthly balance of the account over the preceding six months. § 1915(b)(1). Thereafter, to complete payment of the filing fee, prisoners must pay, in monthly installments, "20 percent of the preceding month's income credited to the prisoner's account." § 1915(b)(2). The initial partial filing fee may not be exacted if the prisoner has no means to pay it, § 1915(b)(4), and no monthly installments are required unless the prisoner has more than $10 in his account, § 1915(b)(2).

It is undisputed that the initial partial filing fee is to be assessed on a per-case basis, *i.e.,* each time the prisoner files a lawsuit. In contest here is the calculation of subsequent monthly installment payments. Petitioner Antoine Bruce urges a per-prisoner approach under which he would pay 20 percent of his monthly income regardless of the number of cases he has filed. The Government urges, and the court below followed, a per-case approach under which a prisoner would pay 20 percent of his monthly income for each case he has filed. Courts of Appeals have divided on which of these two approaches § 1915(b)(2) orders.[1] To resolve the conflict, we granted certiorari. 576 U.S. 1021, 135 S. Ct. 2833, 192 L. Ed. 2d 874 (2015).

[577 U.S. 85]

We hold that [1] monthly installment payments, like the initial partial payment, are to be assessed on a per-case basis. Nothing in § 1915's current design supports treating a prisoner's second or third action unlike his first lawsuit.

I

A

In 1892, Congress enacted the *in forma pauperis* (IFP) statute, now codified at 28 U.S.C. § 1915, "to ensure that indigent litigants have meaningful access to the federal courts." *Neitzke* v. *Williams,* 490 U.S. 319, 324, 109 S. Ct. 1827, 104 L. Ed. 2d 338 (1989). Reacting to "a sharp rise in prisoner litigation," *Woodford* v. *Ngo,* 548 U.S. 81, 84, 126 S. Ct. 2378, 165 L. Ed. 2d 368 (2006), Congress in 1996 enacted the PLRA, which installed a variety of measures "designed to filter out the bad claims [filed by prisoners] and facilitate consideration of the good," *Coleman* v. *Tollefson,* 575 U.S. 532, 535, 135 S. Ct. 1759, 191 L. Ed. 2d 803 (2015) (quoting *Jones* v. *Bock,* 549 U.S. 199, 204, 127 S. Ct. 910, 166 L. Ed. 2d 798 (2007); alteration in original).

Among those measures, Congress required prisoners to pay filing fees for the suits or appeals they launch. The provisions on fee payment, set forth in § 1915(b), read:

"(1) . . . [I]f a prisoner brings a civil action or files an appeal in forma pauperis, the prisoner shall be required to pay the full amount of a filing fee. The court shall assess and, when funds exist, collect, as a partial payment of any court fees required by law, an initial partial filing fee of 20 percent of the greater of—

"(A) the average monthly deposits to the prisoner's account; or

"(B) the average monthly balance in the prisoner's account for the 6-month period immediately preceding the filing of the complaint or notice of appeal.

---

1. Compare *Atchison* v. *Collins,* 288 F.3d 177, 181 (CA5 2002) (*per curiam*); *Newlin* v. *Helman,* 123 F.3d 429, 436 (CA7 1997), overruled in part on other grounds by *Lee* v. *Clinton,* 209 F.3d 1025 (CA7 2000), and *Walker* v. *O'Brien,* 216 F.3d 626 (CA7 2000); *Lefkowitz* v. *Citi-Equity Group, Inc.,* 146 F.3d 609, 612 (CA8 1998); *Christensen* v. *Big Horn Cty. Bd. of Cty. Comm'rs,* 374 Fed. Appx. 821, 829-833 (CA10 2010); and *Pinson* v. *Samuels,* 761 F.3d 1, 7-10 (CADC 2014) (case below) (adopting per-case approach), with *Whitfield* v. *Scully,* 241 F.3d 264, 276-277 (CA2 2001); *Siluk* v. *Merwin,* 783 F.3d 421, 427-436 (CA3 2015); and *Torres* v. *O'Quinn,* 612 F.3d 237, 241-248 (CA4 2010) (adopting per-prisoner approach).

"(2) After payment of the initial partial filing fee, the prisoner shall be required to make monthly payments of 20 percent of the preceding month's income credited to the prisoner's account. The agency having custody of the prisoner shall forward payments from the prisoner's

[577 U.S. 86]

account to the clerk of the court each time the amount in the account exceeds $10 until the filing fees are paid."

The monthly installment scheme described in § 1915(b)(2) also applies to costs awarded against prisoners when they are judgment losers. § 1915(f)(2)(B).

To further contain prisoner litigation, the PLRA introduced a three-strikes provision: Prisoners whose suits or appeals are dismissed three or more times as frivolous, malicious, or failing to state a claim on which relief may be granted are barred from proceeding IFP "unless the prisoner is under imminent danger of serious physical injury." § 1915(g). In other words, for most three strikers, all future filing fees become payable in full upfront.

Congress included in its 1996 overhaul of § 1915 a safety-valve provision to ensure that the fee requirements would not bar access to the courts: "In no event shall a prisoner be prohibited from bringing a civil action or appealing a civil or criminal judgment for the reason that the prisoner has no assets and no means by which to pay the initial partial filing fee." § 1915(b)(4).

B

Petitioner Antoine Bruce, a federal inmate serving a 15-year sentence, is a frequent litigant.[2] In the instant case, Bruce challenges his placement in a special management unit at the Federal Correctional Institution in Talladega, Alabama. *Pinson* v. *Samuels*, 761 F.3d 1, 3-4 (CADC 2014).[3] Bruce had previously incurred filing-fee obligations in other

[577 U.S. 87]

cases and maintained that the monthly filing-fee payments for this case would not become due until those prior obligations were satisfied. *Id.,* at 4, 7. The Court of Appeals for the District of Columbia Circuit, whose decision is before us for review, rejected Bruce's argument. *Id.,* at 8-10. Bruce must make monthly filing-fee payments in this case, the court held, simultaneously with such payments in earlier commenced cases. *Id.,* at 8. We agree with the appeals court that § 1915(b)(2) calls for simultaneous, not sequential, recoupment of multiple filing fees.

II

The IFP statute does not explicitly address whether multiple filing fees (after the initial partial payment) should be paid simultaneously or sequentially. Bruce and the Government present competing interpretations.

---

2. At oral argument, Bruce's counsel informed the Court that Bruce had framed or joined 19 prison-litigation cases, although "the last seven or so have not been filed . . . because [Bruce] had had three strikes by the 12th." Tr. of Oral Arg. 23. See Brief for Respondents 40 (stating that Bruce filed three new lawsuits during the pendency of his case before this Court).

3. The Court of Appeals construed the pleadings in this case as a petition for a writ of mandamus. 761 F.3d, at 3. We assume without deciding that a mandamus petition qualifies as a "civil action" or "appeal" for purposes of 28 U.S.C. § 1915(b).

A

In support of the per-prisoner approach, Bruce relies principally on what he sees as a significant contrast between the singular "clerk" and the plural "fees" as those nouns appear in 28 U.S.C. § 1915(b)(2). That provision requires payments to be forwarded "to the *clerk of the court* . . . until the *filing fees* are paid." *Ibid.* (emphasis added). Even when more than one filing fee is owed, Bruce contends, the statute instructs that only one clerk will receive payment each month; in other words, fee payments are to be made sequentially rather than simultaneously.

The initial partial payment, which is charged on a per-case basis, plus the three-strikes provision, Bruce urges, together suffice to satisfy the PLRA's purpose, which is to "force prisoners to think twice about the case and not just file reflexively," 141 Cong. Rec. 14572 (1995) (remarks of Sen. Kyl). The additional economic disincentive that the per-case approach would occasion, Bruce asserts, could excessively encumber access to federal courts.

[577 U.S. 88]

Furthermore, Bruce points out, the per-case approach breaks down when a prisoner incurs more than five obligations. Nothing will be left in the account to pay the sixth fee, Bruce observes. Necessarily, therefore, its payment will be entirely deferred. Why treat the second obligation unlike the sixth, Bruce asks. Isn't the statute sensibly read to render all monthly payments sequential? Bruce notes in this regard that, under the per-case approach, his ability to use his account to purchase amenities will be progressively curtailed; indeed, the account might be reduced to zero upon his filing or joining a fifth case.

Finally, Bruce argues, administrative difficulties counsel against the per-case approach. Costs could dwarf the monetary yield if prisons, under a per-case regime, were obliged to send as many as five checks to five different courts each month. And the problems faced by state-prison officials—who sometimes must choose which of several claims on a prisoner's income (*e.g.,* child-support, medical copayments) should take precedence— would be exacerbated under a system demanding simultaneous payment of multiple litigation charges.

B

The Government emphasizes that § 1915 as a whole has a single-case focus, providing instructions for *each* case. It would be anomalous, the Government urges, to treat paragraph (b)(1)'s initial partial payment, which Bruce concedes is directed at a single case, differently than paragraph (b)(2)'s subsequent monthly payments. The two paragraphs, the Government observes, are linked by paragraph (b)(2)'s opening clause: "After payment of the initial partial filing fee."

The per-case approach, the Government adds, better comports with the purpose of the PLRA to deter frivolous suits. See *Newlin* v. *Helman,* 123 F.3d 429, 436 (CA7 1997) (Easterbrook, J.) ("Otherwise a prisoner could file multiple suits for the price of one, postponing payment of the fees for later-filed

[577 U.S. 89]

suits until after the end of imprisonment (and likely avoiding them altogether [because fees are often uncollectable on a prisoner's release]).", overruled in part on other grounds by *Lee* v. *Clinton,* 209 F.3d 1025 (CA7 2000), and *Walker* v. *O'Brien,* 216 F.3d 626 (CA7 2000). The

Government further observes that the generally small size of the initial partial fee—here, $0.64, App. to Pet. for Cert. 21a—provides scant disincentive, on its own, for multiple filings.

Responding to Bruce's observation that, for a prisoner with more than five charges, even the per-case approach resorts to sequential payments, the Government agrees, but tells us that this scenario arises infrequently. "[M]ost prisoners," the Government states, "would accrue three strikes (and therefore be required to pay the full filing fees upfront) by the time they incurred the obligation for their sixth case." Brief for Respondents 29.

Finally, answering Bruce's concern that the per-case approach could leave a prisoner without money for amenities, the Government points out that prisons "are constitutionally bound to provide inmates with adequate food, clothing, shelter, and medical care," *id.,* at 48 (citing *Farmer* v. *Brennan*, 511 U.S. 825, 832, 114 S. Ct. 1970, 128 L. Ed. 2d 811 (1994)), and must furnish " 'paper and pen to draft legal documents' and 'stamps to mail them,' " Brief for Respondents 48 (quoting *Bounds* v. *Smith*, 430 U.S. 817, 824, 825, 97 S. Ct. 1491, 52 L. Ed. 2d 72 (1977)). Moreover, the Government notes, the Federal Bureau of Prisons "goes beyond those requirements," providing inmates "articles necessary for main-

taining personal hygiene," and free postage "not only for legal mailings but also to enable the inmate to maintain community ties." Brief for Respondents 48, n. 21 (internal quotation marks omitted).

III

The Circuits following the per-case approach, we conclude, better comprehend the statute. [2] Just as § 1915(b)(1) calls for assessment of "*an* initial partial filing fee" each time a prisoner

[577 U.S. 90]

"brings *a* civil action or files *an* appeal" (emphasis added), so its allied provision, § 1915(b)(2), triggered immediately after, calls for "monthly payments of 20 percent of the preceding month's income" simultaneously for each action pursued. The other two paragraphs of § 1915(b) confirm that the subsection as a whole is written from the perspective of a single case. See § 1915(b)(3) (imposing a ceiling on fees permitted "for the commencement of *a* civil action or *an* appeal" (emphasis added)); § 1915(b)(4) (protecting the right to "brin[g] *a* civil action or appea[l] *a* civil or criminal judgment" (emphasis added)). There is scant indication that the statute's perspective shifts partway through paragraph (2).[4]

Bruce's extratextual points do not warrant a departure from the interpretation suggested by the text and

---

4. Use of the plural "fees" in that paragraph does not persuade us otherwise. Congress has been less than meticulous in its employment of the singular "fee" and the plural "fees," sometimes using those words interchangeably. See, *e.g.,* 28 U.S.C. § 1930(a) ("The parties commencing a case under title 11 shall pay to the clerk . . . the following filing *fees*: [enumerating several options]. In addition to the filing *fee* paid to the clerk, [an additional fee shall be paid]." (emphasis added)); 42 U.S.C. § 1988(b) ("[T]he court . . . may allow the prevailing party . . . a reasonable attorney's *fee* as part of the costs, except that in any action brought against a judicial officer . . . such officer shall not be held liable for any costs, including attorney's *fees* . . . ." (emphasis added)). See also Dictionary Act, 1 U.S.C. § 1 ("In determining the meaning of any Act of Congress, unless the context indicates otherwise—words importing the singular include and apply to several persons, parties, or things; words importing the plural include the singular . . . .").

context. The per-case approach more vigorously serves the statutory objective of containing prisoner litigation, while the safety-valve provision, see *supra,* at 86, 193 L. Ed. 2d, at 500, ensures against denial of access to federal courts. Bruce's administrability concerns carry little weight given reports from several States that the per-case approach is unproblematic.

See Brief for State of Michigan et al. as *Amici Curiae* 18-20.

[577 U.S. 91]

* * *

For the reasons stated, the judgment of the Court of Appeals for the District of Columbia Circuit is affirmed.

TIMOTHY LEE HURST, Petitioner

v

FLORIDA

577 U.S. 92, 136 S. Ct. 616, 193 L. Ed. 2d 504, 2016 U.S. LEXIS 619

[No. 14-7505]

Argued October 13, 2015. Decided January 12, 2016.

Decision: Florida's sentencing scheme, requiring judge to determine at separate hearing whether sufficient aggravating circumstances existed to justify imposing death penalty, violated Federal Constitution's Sixth Amendment, which required jury to find each fact necessary to impose death penalty.

Prior history: 147 So. 3d 435, 2014 Fla. LEXIS 1461

SUMMARY

Overview: HOLDINGS: [1]-Defendant's death sentence violated the Sixth Amendment where the maximum punishment he could have received without any judge-made findings was life in prison without parole, a judge had increased his authorized punishment based on her own factfinding, and the existence of an advisory jury verdict did not impact whether Fla. Stat. § 921.141(3) required a judge to make the critical findings necessary to impose the death penalty; [2]-Spaziano v. Florida, 468 U.S. 447 (1984), and Hildwin v. Florida, 490 U.S. 638 (1989), were overruled to the extent they allowed a sentencing judge to find an aggravating circumstance, independent of a jury's factfinding, that was necessary for imposition of the death penalty; [3]-The State's harmless error assertion was not considered as there was no reason to depart from the usual practice of leaving it for the state court's consideration.

Outcome: Judgment reversed; case remanded. 8-1 decision, 1 concurrence, 1 dissent.

HEADNOTES

Classified to United States Supreme Court Digest, Lawyers' Edition

Death penalty — factfinding — aggravating circumstances

L Ed Digest: Jury § 33.5

1. Florida's sentencing scheme requiring a judge to hold a separate hearing and determine whether sufficient aggravating circumstances existed to justify imposing the death penalty is unconstitutional. The Sixth Amendment requires a jury, not a judge, to find each fact necessary to impose a sentence of death. A jury's mere recommendation is not enough. (Sotomayor, J., joined by Roberts, Ch. J., and Scalia, Kennedy, Thomas, Ginsburg, and Kagan, JJ.)

Crime — standard of proof — jury — capital punishment

L Ed Digest: Constitutional Law §§ 840.9, 848, 848.7

2. The Sixth Amendment provides that in all criminal prosecutions, the accused shall enjoy the right to a speedy and public trial, by an impartial jury. This right, in conjunction with the due process clause, requires that each element of a crime be proved to a jury beyond a reasonable doubt. The Apprendi rule holds that any fact that exposes the defendant to a greater punishment than that authorized by the jury's guilty verdict is an element that must be submitted to a jury. In the years since adoption of the Apprendi rule, it has been applied to instances involving plea bargains, sentencing guidelines, criminal fines, mandatory minimums, and capital punishment. (Sotomayor, J., joined by Roberts, Ch. J., and Scalia, Kennedy, Thomas, Ginsburg, and Kagan, JJ.)

Death penalty — factfinding — aggravating or mitigating circumstances
L Ed Digest: Jury § 33.5

3. Florida does not require the jury to make the critical findings necessary to impose the death penalty. Rather, Florida requires a judge to find these facts. Fla. Stat. § 921.141(3). Although Florida incorporates an advisory jury verdict that Arizona lacked, judicial precedent previously made clear that this distinction is immaterial: It is true that in Florida the jury recommends a sentence, but it does not make specific factual findings with regard to the existence of mitigating or aggravating circumstances and its recommendation is not binding on the trial judge. A Florida trial court no more has the assistance of a jury's findings of fact with respect to sentencing issues than does a trial judge in Arizona. (Sotomayor, J., joined by Roberts, Ch. J.,

and Scalia, Kennedy, Thomas, Ginsburg, and Kagan, JJ.)

Prior decisions — overruling
L Ed Digest: Courts § 776

4. Although the doctrine of stare decisis is of fundamental importance to the rule of law, the United States Supreme Court's precedents are not sacrosanct. The Supreme Court has overruled prior decisions where the necessity and propriety of doing so has been established. And in the Apprendi context, stare decisis does not compel adherence to a decision whose underpinnings have been eroded by subsequent developments of constitutional law. (Sotomayor, J., joined by Roberts, Ch. J., and Scalia, Kennedy, Thomas, Ginsburg, and Kagan, JJ.)

Death penalty — aggravating circumstances — overruling
L Ed Digest: Criminal Law § 93.7; Jury § 33.5

5. Time and subsequent cases have washed away the logic of Spaziano v. Florida, 468 U.S. 447 (1984), and Hildwin v. Florida, 490 U.S. 638 (1989). The decisions are overruled to the extent they allow a sentencing judge to find an aggravating circumstance, independent of a jury's factfinding, that is necessary for imposition of the death penalty. (Sotomayor, J., joined by Roberts, Ch. J., and Scalia, Kennedy, Thomas, Ginsburg, and Kagan, JJ.)

Harmless error — consideration by state court
L Ed Digest: Appeal § 1692.2

6. The United States Supreme Court normally leaves it to state courts to consider whether an error is harmless. (Sotomayor, J., joined by Roberts, Ch. J., and Scalia, Kennedy, Thomas, Ginsburg, and Kagan, JJ.)

Death sentence — factfinding — aggravating circumstances

L Ed Digest: Jury § 33.5

7. The Sixth Amendment protects a defendant's right to an impartial jury. This right requires Florida to base a defendant's death sentence on a jury's verdict, not a judge's factfinding. Florida's sentencing scheme, which required the judge alone to find the existence of an aggravating circumstance, is therefore unconstitutional. (Sotomayor, J., joined by Roberts, Ch. J., and Scalia, Kennedy, Thomas, Ginsburg, and Kagan, JJ.)

RESEARCH REFERENCES

U.S.C.S., Constitution, Amendment 6

26 Moore's Federal Practice § 632.21 (Matthew Bender 3d ed.)

L Ed Digest, Jury § 33.5

L Ed Index, Capital Offenses and Punishment

Annotations:

Rule of Apprendi v. New Jersey (2000) 530 U.S. 466, 147 L. Ed. 2d 435, 120 S. Ct. 2348, and its progeny, as to proof of facts necessary to support criminal sentence—Supreme Court cases. 160 L. Ed. 2d 1163.

Validity of death penalty, under Federal Constitution, as affected by consideration of aggravating or mitigating circumstances—Supreme Court cases. 111 L. Ed. 2d 947.

APPEARANCES OF COUNSEL ARGUING CASE

Seth P. Waxman argued the cause for petitioner.

Allen Winsor argued the cause for respondent.

SYLLABUS BY REPORTER OF DECISIONS

Under Florida law, the maximum sentence a capital felon may receive on the basis of a conviction alone is life imprisonment. He may be sentenced to death, but only if an additional sentencing proceeding "results in findings by the court that such person shall be punished by death." Fla. Stat. § 775.082(1). In that proceeding, the sentencing judge first conducts an evidentiary hearing before a jury. § 921.141(1). Next, the jury, by majority vote, renders an "advisory sentence." § 921.141(2). Notwithstanding that recommendation, the court must independently find and weigh the aggravating and mitigating circumstances before entering a sentence of life or death. § 921.141(3).

(2016) 577 U.S. 92, 136 S. Ct. 616, 193 L. Ed. 2d 504, 2016 U.S. LEXIS 619

A Florida jury convicted petitioner Timothy Hurst of first-degree murder for killing a co-worker and recommended the death penalty. The court sentenced Hurst to death, but he was granted a new sentencing hearing on appeal. At resentencing, the jury again recommended death, and the judge again found the facts necessary to sentence Hurst to death. The Florida Supreme Court affirmed, rejecting Hurst's argument that his sentence violated the Sixth Amendment in light of *Ring* v. *Arizona*, 536 U.S. 584, 122 S. Ct. 2428, 153 L. Ed. 2d 556, in which this Court found unconstitutional an Arizona capital sentencing scheme that permitted a judge rather than the jury to find the facts necessary to sentence a defendant to death.

Held: Florida's capital sentencing scheme violates the Sixth Amendment in light of *Ring*. Pp. 97–103, 193 L. Ed. 2d, at 510-514.

(a) Any fact that "expose[s] the defendant to a greater punishment than that authorized by the jury's guilty verdict" is an "element" that must be submitted to a jury. *Apprendi* v. *New Jersey*, 530 U.S. 466, 494, 120 S. Ct. 2348, 147 L. Ed. 2d 435. Applying *Apprendi* to the capital punishment context, the *Ring* Court had little difficulty concluding that an Arizona judge's independent factfinding exposed Ring to a punishment greater than the jury's guilty verdict authorized. 536 U.S., at 604, 120 S. Ct. 2348, 147 L. Ed. 2d 435. *Ring*'s analysis applies equally here. Florida requires not the jury but a judge to make the critical findings necessary to impose the death penalty. That Florida provides an advisory jury is immaterial. See *Walton* v. *Arizona*, 497 U.S. 639, 648, 110 S. Ct. 3047, 111 L. Ed. 2d 511. As with Ring, Hurst had the maximum authorized punishment he could receive increased by a judge's own factfinding. Pp. 97–99, 193 L. Ed. 2d, at 510-511.

(b) Florida's counterarguments are rejected. Pp. 99–102, 193 L. Ed. 2d, at 511-514.

(1) In arguing that the jury's recommendation necessarily included an aggravating circumstance finding, Florida fails to appreciate the judge's central and singular role under Florida law, which makes the court's findings necessary to impose death and makes the jury's function advisory only. The State cannot now treat the jury's advisory recommendation as the necessary factual finding required by *Ring*. Pp. 99–100, 193 L. Ed. 2d, at 511-512.

(2) Florida's reliance on *Blakely* v. *Washington*, 542 U.S. 296, 124 S. Ct. 2531, 159 L. Ed. 2d 403, is misplaced. There, this Court stated that under *Apprendi*, a judge may impose any sentence authorized "on the basis of the facts . . . admitted by the defendant," 542 U.S., at 303, 124 S. Ct. 2531, 159 L. Ed. 2d 403. Florida alleges that Hurst's counsel admitted the existence of a robbery, but *Blakely* applied *Apprendi* to facts admitted in a guilty plea, in which the defendant necessarily waived his right to a jury trial, while Florida has not explained how Hurst's alleged admissions accomplished a similar waiver. In any event, Hurst never admitted to either aggravating circumstance alleged by the State. Pp. 100–101, 193 L. Ed. 2d, at 512.

(3) That this Court upheld Florida's capital sentencing scheme in *Hildwin* v. *Florida*, 490 U.S. 638, 109

S. Ct. 2055, 104 L. Ed. 2d 728, and *Spaziano* v. *Florida*, 468 U.S. 447, 104 S. Ct. 3154, 82 L. Ed. 2d 340, does not mean that *stare decisis* compels the Court to do so here, see *Alleyne* v. *United States*, 570 U.S. 99, 119, 133 S. Ct. 2151, 186 L. Ed. 2d 314 (Sotomayor, J., concurring). Time and subsequent cases have washed away the logic of *Spaziano* and *Hildwin*. Those decisions are thus overruled to the extent they allow a sentencing judge to find an aggravating circumstance, independent of a jury's factfinding, that is necessary for imposition of the death penalty. Pp. 101–102, 193 L. Ed. 2d, at 512-513.

(4) The State's assertion that any error was harmless is not addressed here, where there is no reason to depart from the Court's normal pattern of leaving such considerations to state courts. P. 102, 193 L. Ed. 2d, at 513.

147 So. 3d 435, reversed and remanded.

Sotomayor, J., delivered the opinion of the Court, in which Roberts, C. J., and Scalia, Kennedy, Thomas, Ginsburg, and Kagan, JJ., joined. Breyer, J., filed an opinion concurring in the judgment. Alito, J., filed a dissenting opinion.

OPINION OF THE COURT

[577 U.S. 94]
Justice **Sotomayor** delivered the opinion of the Court.

A Florida jury convicted Timothy Lee Hurst of murdering his co-worker, Cynthia Harrison. A penalty-phase jury recommended that Hurst's judge impose a death sentence. Notwithstanding this recommendation, Florida law required the judge to hold a separate hearing and determine whether sufficient aggravating circumstances existed to justify imposing the death penalty. The judge so found and sentenced Hurst to death.

[1] We hold this sentencing scheme unconstitutional. The Sixth Amendment requires a jury, not a judge, to find each fact necessary to impose a sentence of death. A jury's mere recommendation is not enough.

I

On May 2, 1998, Cynthia Harrison's body was discovered in the freezer of the restaurant where she worked—bound, gagged, and stabbed over 60 times. The restaurant safe was unlocked and open, missing hundreds of dollars. The State of Florida charged Harrison's co-worker, Timothy Lee Hurst, with her murder. See 819 So. 2d 689, 692-694 (Fla. 2002).

[577 U.S. 95]
During Hurst's 4-day trial, the State offered substantial forensic evidence linking Hurst to the murder. Witnesses also testified that Hurst announced in advance that he planned to rob the restaurant; that Hurst and Harrison were the only people scheduled to work when Harrison was killed; and that Hurst disposed of bloodstained evidence and used stolen money to purchase shoes and rings.

Hurst responded with an alibi defense. He claimed he never made it to work because his car broke down. Hurst told police that he called the restaurant to let Harrison know he would be late. He said she sounded scared and he could hear another person—presumably the real murderer—whispering in the background.

At the close of Hurst's defense, the

judge instructed the jury that it could find Hurst guilty of first-degree murder under two theories: premeditated murder or felony murder for an unlawful killing during a robbery. The jury convicted Hurst of first-degree murder but did not specify which theory it believed.

First-degree murder is a capital felony in Florida. See Fla. Stat. § 782.04(1)(a) (2010). Under state law, the maximum sentence a capital felon may receive on the basis of the conviction alone is life imprisonment. § 775.082(1). "A person who has been convicted of a capital felony shall be punished by death" only if an additional sentencing proceeding "results in findings by the court that such person shall be punished by death." *Ibid.* "[O]therwise such person shall be punished by life imprisonment and shall be ineligible for parole." *Ibid.*

The additional sentencing proceeding Florida employs is a "hybrid" proceeding "in which [a] jury renders an advisory verdict but the judge makes the ultimate sentencing determination." *Ring* v. *Arizona*, 536 U.S. 584, 608, n. 6, 122 S. Ct. 2428, 153 L. Ed. 2d 556 (2002). First, the sentencing judge conducts an evidentiary hearing before a jury. Fla. Stat. § 921.141(1). Next, the jury renders an "advisory sentence" of life or death without specifying

[577 U.S. 96]

the factual basis of its recommendation. § 921.141(2). "Notwithstanding the recommendation of a majority of the jury, the court, after weighing the aggravating and mitigating circumstances, shall enter a sentence of life imprisonment or death." § 921.141(3). If the court imposes death, it must "set forth in writing its findings upon which the

sentence of death is based." *Ibid.* Although the judge must give the jury recommendation "great weight," *Tedder* v. *State*, 322 So. 2d 908, 910 (Fla. 1975) (*per curiam*), the sentencing order must "reflect the trial judge's independent judgment about the existence of aggravating and mitigating factors," *Blackwelder* v. *State*, 851 So. 2d 650, 653 (Fla. 2003) (*per curiam*).

Following this procedure, Hurst's jury recommended a death sentence. The judge independently agreed. See 819 So. 2d, at 694-695. On postconviction review, however, the Florida Supreme Court vacated Hurst's sentence for reasons not relevant to this case. See 18 So. 3d 975 (2009).

At resentencing in 2012, the sentencing judge conducted a new hearing during which Hurst offered mitigating evidence that he was not a "major participant" in the murder because he was at home when it happened. App. 505-507. The sentencing judge instructed the advisory jury that it could recommend a death sentence if it found at least one aggravating circumstance beyond a reasonable doubt: that the murder was especially "heinous, atrocious, or cruel" or that it occurred while Hurst was committing a robbery. *Id.*, at 211-212. The jury recommended death by a vote of 7 to 5.

The sentencing judge then sentenced Hurst to death. In her written order, the judge based the sentence in part on her independent determination that both the heinous-murder and robbery aggravators existed. *Id.*, at 261-263. She assigned "great weight" to her findings as well as to the jury's recommendation of death. *Id.*, at 271.

The Florida Supreme Court affirmed 4 to 3. 147 So. 3d 435 (2014).

As relevant here, the court rejected Hurst's argument

[577 U.S. 97]

that his sentence violated the Sixth Amendment in light of *Ring*, 536 U.S. 584, 122 S. Ct. 2428, 153 L. Ed. 2d 556. *Ring*, the court recognized, "held that capital defendants are entitled to a jury determination of any fact on which the legislature conditions an increase in the maximum punishment." 147 So. 3d, at 445. But the court considered *Ring* inapplicable in light of this Court's repeated support of Florida's capital sentencing scheme in pre-*Ring* cases. 147 So. 3d, at 446-447 (citing *Hildwin* v. *Florida*, 490 U.S. 638, 109 S. Ct. 2055, 104 L. Ed. 2d 728 (1989) (*per curiam*)); see also *Spaziano* v. *Florida*, 468 U.S. 447, 457-465, 104 S. Ct. 3154, 82 L. Ed. 2d 340 (1984). Specifically, in *Hildwin*, this Court held that the Sixth Amendment "does not require that the specific findings authorizing the imposition of the sentence of death be made by the jury." 490 U.S., at 640-641, 109 S. Ct. 2055, 104 L. Ed. 2d 728. The Florida court noted that we have "never expressly overruled *Hildwin*, and did not do so in *Ring*." 147 So. 3d, at 446-447.

Justice Pariente, joined by two colleagues, dissented from this portion of the court's opinion. She reiterated her view that "*Ring* requires any fact that qualifies a capital defendant for a sentence of death to be found by a jury." *Id.*, at 450 (opinion concurring in part and dissenting in part).

We granted certiorari to resolve whether Florida's capital sentencing scheme violates the Sixth Amendment in light of *Ring*, 575 U.S. 902, 135 S. Ct. 1531, 191 L. Ed. 2d 558 (2015). We hold that it does, and reverse.

II

[2] The Sixth Amendment provides: "In all criminal prosecutions, the accused shall enjoy the right to a speedy and public trial, by an impartial jury . . . ." This right, in conjunction with the Due Process Clause, requires that each element of a crime be proved to a jury beyond a reasonable doubt. *Alleyne* v. *United States*, 570 U.S. 99, 104, 133 S. Ct. 2151, 186 L. Ed. 2d 314 (2013). In *Apprendi* v. *New Jersey*, 530 U.S. 466, 494, 120 S. Ct. 2348, 147 L. Ed. 2d 435 (2000), this Court held that any fact that "expose[s] the defendant to a greater punishment than that authorized by the jury's guilty verdict" is an "element" that must be submitted to a jury. In the

[577 U.S. 98]

years since *Apprendi*, we have applied its rule to instances involving plea bargains, *Blakely* v. *Washington*, 542 U.S. 296, 124 S. Ct. 2531, 159 L. Ed. 2d 403 (2004), sentencing guidelines, *United States* v. *Booker*, 543 U.S. 220, 125 S. Ct. 738, 160 L. Ed. 2d 621 (2005), criminal fines, *S. Union Co.* v. *United States*, 567 U.S. 343, 132 S. Ct. 2344, 183 L. Ed. 2d 318 (2012), mandatory minimums, *Alleyne*, 570 U.S., at 117, 133 S. Ct. 2151, 186 L. Ed. 2d 314, and, in *Ring*, 536 U.S. 584, 122 S. Ct. 2428, 153 L. Ed. 2d 556, capital punishment.

In *Ring*, we concluded that Arizona's capital sentencing scheme violated *Apprendi*'s rule because the State allowed a judge to find the facts necessary to sentence a defendant to death. An Arizona jury had convicted Timothy Ring of felony murder. 536 U.S., at 591, 122 S. Ct. 2428, 153 L. Ed. 2d 556. Under state law, "Ring could not be sentenced to death, the statutory maximum penalty for first-degree murder, unless further findings were made." *Id.*, at 592, 122 S.

Ct. 2428, 153 L. Ed. 2d 556. Specifically, a judge could sentence Ring to death only after independently finding at least one aggravating circumstance. *Id.*, at 592-593, 122 S. Ct. 2428, 153 L. Ed. 2d 556. Ring's judge followed this procedure, found an aggravating circumstance, and sentenced Ring to death.

The Court had little difficulty concluding that " 'the required finding of an aggravated circumstance exposed Ring to a greater punishment than that authorized by the jury's guilty verdict.' " *Id.*, at 604, 122 S. Ct. 2428, 153 L. Ed. 2d 556 (quoting *Apprendi*, 530 U.S., at 494, 120 S. Ct. 2348, 147 L. Ed. 2d 435; alterations omitted). Had Ring's judge not engaged in any factfinding, Ring would have received a life sentence. *Ring*, 536 U.S., at 597, 122 S. Ct. 2428, 153 L. Ed. 2d 556. Ring's death sentence therefore violated his right to have a jury find the facts behind his punishment.

The analysis the *Ring* Court applied to Arizona's sentencing scheme applies equally to Florida's. Like Arizona at the time of *Ring*, [3] Florida does not require the jury to make the critical findings necessary to impose the death penalty. Rather, Florida requires a judge to find these facts. Fla. Stat. § 921.141(3). Although Florida incorporates an advisory jury verdict that Arizona lacked, we have previously made clear that this distinction is immaterial: "It is true that

[577 U.S. 99]

in Florida the jury recommends a sentence, but it does not make specific factual findings with regard to the existence of mitigating or aggravating circumstances and its recommendation is not binding on the trial judge. A Florida trial court no more has the assistance of a jury's findings of fact

with respect to sentencing issues than does a trial judge in Arizona." *Walton v. Arizona*, 497 U.S. 639, 648, 110 S. Ct. 3047, 111 L. Ed. 2d 511 (1990); accord, *State v. Steele*, 921 So. 2d 538, 546 (Fla. 2005) ("[T]he trial court alone must make detailed findings about the existence and weight of aggravating circumstances; it has no jury findings on which to rely").

As with Timothy Ring, the maximum punishment Timothy Hurst could have received without any judge-made findings was life in prison without parole. As with Ring, a judge increased Hurst's authorized punishment based on her own factfinding. In light of *Ring*, we hold that Hurst's sentence violates the Sixth Amendment.

III

Without contesting *Ring*'s holding, Florida offers a bevy of arguments for why Hurst's sentence is constitutional. None holds water.

A

Florida concedes that *Ring* required a jury to find every fact necessary to render Hurst eligible for the death penalty. But Florida argues that when Hurst's sentencing jury recommended a death sentence, it "necessarily included a finding of an aggravating circumstance." Brief for Respondent 44. The State contends that this finding qualified Hurst for the death penalty under Florida law, thus satisfying *Ring*. "[T]he additional requirement that a judge *also* find an aggravator," Florida concludes, "only provides the defendant additional protection." Brief for Respondent 22.

The State fails to appreciate the central and singular role the judge plays under Florida law. As described above and by the Florida Supreme Court, the Florida sentencing statute

[577 U.S. 100]

does not make a defendant eligible for death until "findings *by the court* that such person shall be punished by death." Fla. Stat. § 775.082(1) (emphasis added). The trial court *alone* must find "the facts . . . [t]hat sufficient aggravating circumstances exist" and "[t]hat there are insufficient mitigating circumstances to outweigh the aggravating circumstances." § 921.141(3); see *Steele*, 921 So. 2d, at 546. "[T]he jury's function under the Florida death penalty statute is advisory only." *Spaziano* v. *State*, 433 So. 2d 508, 512 (Fla. 1983). The State cannot now treat the advisory recommendation by the jury as the necessary factual finding that *Ring* requires.

B

Florida launches its second salvo at Hurst himself, arguing that he admitted in various contexts that an aggravating circumstance existed. Even if *Ring* normally requires a jury to hear all facts necessary to sentence a defendant to death, Florida argues, "*Ring* does not require jury findings on facts defendants have admitted." Brief for Respondent 41. Florida cites our decision in *Blakely*, 542 U.S. 296, 124 S. Ct. 2531, 159 L. Ed. 2d 403, in which we stated that under *Apprendi*, a judge may impose any sentence authorized "on the basis of the facts reflected in the jury verdict or admitted by the defendant." 542 U.S., at 303, 124 S. Ct. 2531, 159 L. Ed. 2d 403 (emphasis deleted). In light of *Blakely*, Florida points to various instances in which Hurst's counsel allegedly admitted the existence of a robbery. Florida contends that these

"admissions" made Hurst eligible for the death penalty. Brief for Respondent 42-44.

Blakely, however, was a decision applying *Apprendi* to facts admitted in a guilty plea, in which the defendant necessarily waived his right to a jury trial. See 542 U.S., at 310-312, 124 S. Ct. 2531, 159 L. Ed. 2d 403. Florida has not explained how Hurst's alleged admissions accomplished a similar waiver. Florida's argument is also meritless on its own terms. Hurst never admitted to either aggravating circumstance alleged by the State. At most, his counsel simply refrained from challenging the aggravating

[577 U.S. 101]

circumstances in parts of his appellate briefs. See, *e.g.*, Initial Brief for Appellant in No. SC12-1947 (Fla.), p. 24 ("not challeng[ing] the trial court's findings" but arguing that death was nevertheless a disproportionate punishment).

C

The State next argues that *stare decisis* compels us to uphold Florida's capital sentencing scheme. As the Florida Supreme Court observed, this Court "repeatedly has reviewed and upheld Florida's capital sentencing statute over the past quarter of a century." *Bottoson* v. *Moore*, 833 So. 2d 693, 695 (2002) (*per curiam*) (citing *Hildwin*, 490 U.S. 638, 109 S. Ct. 2055, 104 L. Ed. 2d 728; *Spaziano*, 468 U.S. 447, 104 S. Ct. 3154, 82 L. Ed. 2d 340). "In a comparable situation," the Florida court reasoned, "the United States Supreme Court held:

'If a precedent of this Court has direct application in a case, yet appears to rest on reasons rejected in some other line of decisions, the [other courts] should follow the case which directly controls, leaving to this Court the prerogative of over-ruling its own decisions.' " *Bottoson*, 833 So. 2d, at 695 (quoting *Rodriguez de Quijas* v. *Shearson/American Express, Inc.*, 490 U.S. 477, 484, 109 S. Ct. 1917, 104 L. Ed. 2d 526 (1989)); see also 147 So. 3d, at 446-447 (case below).

We now expressly overrule *Spaziano* and *Hildwin* in relevant part.

Spaziano and *Hildwin* summarized earlier precedent to conclude that "the Sixth Amendment does not require that the specific findings authorizing the imposition of the sentence of death be made by the jury." *Hildwin*, 490 U.S., at 640-641, 109 S. Ct. 2055, 104 L. Ed. 2d 728. Their conclusion was wrong, and irreconcilable with *Apprendi*. Indeed, today is not the first time we have recognized as much. In *Ring*, we held that another pre-*Apprendi* decision—*Walton*, 497 U.S. 639, 110 S. Ct. 3047, 111 L. Ed. 2d 511—could not "survive the reasoning of *Apprendi*." 536 U.S., at 603, 122 S. Ct. 2428, 153 L. Ed. 2d 556. *Walton*,

[577 U.S. 102]

for its part, was a mere application of *Hildwin*'s holding to Arizona's capital sentencing scheme. 497 U.S., at 648, 110 S. Ct. 3047, 111 L. Ed. 2d 511.

[4] "Although ' "the doctrine of *stare decisis* is of fundamental importance to the rule of law[,]" . . . [o]ur precedents are not sacrosanct.' . . . '[W]e have overruled prior decisions where the necessity and propriety of doing so has been established.' " *Ring*, 536 U.S., at 608, 122 S. Ct. 2428, 153 L. Ed. 2d 556 (quoting *Patterson* v. *McLean Credit Union*, 491 U.S. 164, 172, 109 S. Ct. 2363, 105 L. Ed. 2d 132 (1989)). And in the *Apprendi* context, we have found that "*stare decisis* does not compel adherence to a decision whose underpinnings' have been 'eroded' by subsequent developments of constitutional law." *Alleyne*, 570 U.S., at 119, 133 S. Ct. 2151, 186 L. Ed. 2d 314 (Sotomayor, J., concurring); see also *United States* v. *Gaudin*, 515 U.S. 506, 519-520, 115 S. Ct. 2310, 132 L. Ed. 2d 444 (1995) (overruling *Sinclair* v. *United States*, 279 U.S. 263, 49 S. Ct. 268, 73 L. Ed. 692 (1929)); *Ring*, 536 U.S., at 609, 122 S. Ct. 2428, 153 L. Ed. 2d 556 (overruling *Walton*, 497 U.S., at 639, 110 S. Ct. 3047, 111 L. Ed. 2d 511); *Alleyne*, 570 U.S., at 116, 133 S. Ct. 2151, 186 L. Ed. 2d 314 (overruling *Harris* v. *United States*, 536 U.S. 545, 122 S. Ct. 2406, 153 L. Ed. 2d 524 (2002)).

[5] Time and subsequent cases have washed away the logic of *Spaziano* and *Hildwin*. The decisions are overruled to the extent they allow a sentencing judge to find an aggravating circumstance, independent of a jury's factfinding, that is necessary for imposition of the death penalty.

D

Finally, we do not reach the State's assertion that any error was harmless. See *Neder* v. *United States*, 527 U.S. 1, 18-19, 119 S. Ct. 1827, 144 L. Ed. 2d 35 (1999) (holding that the failure to submit an uncontested element of an offense to a jury may be harmless). **[6]** This Court normally leaves it to state courts to consider whether an error is harmless, and we see no reason to depart from that pattern here. See *Ring*, 536 U.S., at 609, n. 7, 122 S. Ct. 2428, 153 L. Ed. 2d 556.

* * *

[7] The Sixth Amendment protects a defendant's right to an impartial jury. This right required Florida to base

Timothy Hurst's death sentence on a jury's verdict, not a judge's factfinding.

[577 U.S. 103]

Florida's sentencing scheme, which required the judge alone to find the existence of an aggravating circumstance, is therefore unconstitutional.

The judgment of the Florida Supreme Court is reversed, and the case is remanded for further proceedings not inconsistent with this opinion.

So ordered.

SEPARATE OPINIONS

Justice **Breyer**, concurring in the judgment.

For the reasons explained in my opinion concurring in the judgment in *Ring* v. *Arizona*, 536 U.S. 584, 613-619, 122 S. Ct. 2428, 153 L. Ed. 2d 556 (2002), I cannot join the Court's opinion. As in that case, however, I concur in the judgment here based on my view that "the Eighth Amendment requires that a jury, not a judge, make the decision to sentence a defendant to death." *Id.,* at 614, 122 S. Ct. 2428, 153 L. Ed. 2d 556; see *id.,* at 618, 122 S. Ct. 2428, 153 L. Ed. 2d 556 ("[T]he danger of unwarranted imposition of the [death] penalty cannot be avoided unless 'the decision to impose the death penalty is made by a jury rather than by a single governmental official' " (quoting *Spaziano* v. *Florida,* 468 U.S. 447, 469, 104 S. Ct. 3154, 82 L. Ed. 2d 340 (1984) (Stevens, J., concurring in part and dissenting in part))). No one argues that Florida's juries actually sentence capital defendants to death—that job is left to Florida's judges. See Fla. Stat. § 921.141(3) (2010). Like the majority, therefore, I would reverse the judgment of the Florida Supreme Court.

Justice **Alito**, dissenting.

As the Court acknowledges, "this Court 'repeatedly has reviewed and upheld Florida's capital sentencing statute over the past quarter of a century.' " *Ante,* at 101, 193 L. Ed. 2d,

at 512. And as the Court also concedes, our precedents hold that " 'the Sixth Amendment *does not* require that the specific findings authorizing the imposition of the sentence of death be made by the jury.' " *Ibid.* (quoting *Hildwin* v. *Florida,* 490 U.S. 638, 640-641, 109 S. Ct. 2055, 104 L. Ed. 2d 728 (1989) (*per curiam*); emphasis added); see also *Spaziano* v. *Florida,* 468 U.S. 447, 460, 104 S. Ct. 3154, 82 L. Ed. 2d 340 (1984). The Court

[577 U.S. 104]

now reverses course, striking down Florida's capital sentencing system, overruling our decisions in *Hildwin* and *Spaziano,* and holding that the Sixth Amendment *does* require that the specific findings authorizing a sentence of death be made by a jury. I disagree.

I

First, I would not overrule *Hildwin* and *Spaziano* without reconsidering the cases on which the Court's present decision is based. The Court relies on later cases holding that any fact that exposes a defendant to a greater punishment than that authorized by the jury's guilty verdict is an element of the offense that must be submitted to a jury. *Ante,* at 97–98, 193 L. Ed. 2d, at 510–511. But there are strong reasons to question whether this principle is consistent with the original understanding of the jury trial right. See *Alleyne* v. *United States,* 570 U.S.

99, 133–134, 133 S. Ct. 2151, 186 L. Ed. 2d 314 (2013) (Alito, J., dissenting). Before overruling *Hildwin* and *Spaziano*, I would reconsider the cases, including most prominently *Ring* v. *Arizona*, 536 U.S. 584, 122 S. Ct. 2428, 153 L. Ed. 2d 556 (2002), on which the Court now relies.

Second, even if *Ring* is assumed to be correct, I would not extend it. Although the Court suggests that today's holding follows ineluctably from *Ring*, the Arizona sentencing scheme at issue in that case was much different from the Florida procedure now before us. In *Ring*, the jury found the defendant guilty of felony murder and did no more. It did not make the findings required by the Eighth Amendment before the death penalty may be imposed in a felony-murder case. See *id.*, at 591-592, 594, 122 S. Ct. 2428, 153 L. Ed. 2d 556; *Enmund* v. *Florida*, 458 U.S. 782, 102 S. Ct. 3368, 73 L. Ed. 2d 1140 (1982); *Tison* v. *Arizona*, 481 U.S. 137, 107 S. Ct. 1676, 95 L. Ed. 2d 127 (1987). Nor did the jury find the presence of any aggravating factor, as required for death eligibility under Arizona law. *Ring*, *supra*, at 592-593, 122 S. Ct. 2428, 153 L. Ed. 2d 556. Nor did it consider mitigating factors. And it did not determine whether a capital or noncapital sentence was appropriate. Under that system, the jury played *no* role in the capital sentencing process.

[577 U.S. 105]

The Florida system is quite different. In Florida, the jury sits as the initial and primary adjudicator of the factors bearing on the death penalty. After unanimously determining guilt at trial, a Florida jury hears evidence of aggravating and mitigating circumstances. See Fla. Stat. § 921.141(1) (2010). At the conclusion of this separate sentencing hearing, the jury may recommend a death sentence only if it finds that the State has proved one or more aggravating factors beyond a reasonable doubt and only after weighing the aggravating and mitigating factors. § 921.141(2).

Once the jury has made this decision, the trial court performs what amounts, in practical terms, to a reviewing function. The judge duplicates the steps previously performed by the jury and, while the court can impose a sentence different from that recommended by the jury, the judge must accord the jury's recommendation "great weight." See *Lambrix* v. *Singletary*, 520 U.S. 518, 525-526, 117 S. Ct. 1517, 137 L. Ed. 2d 771 (1997) (recounting Florida law and procedure). Indeed, if the jury recommends a life sentence, the judge may override that decision only if "the facts suggesting a sentence of death [were] so clear and convincing that virtually no reasonable person could differ." *Tedder* v. *State*, 322 So. 2d 908, 910 (Fla. 1975) (*per curiam*). No Florida trial court has overruled a jury's recommendation of a life sentence for more than 15 years.

Under the Florida system, the jury plays a critically important role. Our decision in *Ring* did not decide whether this procedure violates the Sixth Amendment, and I would not extend *Ring* to cover the Florida system.

II

Finally, even if there was a constitutional violation in this case, I would hold that the error was harmless beyond a reasonable doubt. See *Chapman* v. *California*, 386 U.S. 18, 24, 87 S. Ct. 824, 17 L. Ed. 2d 705 (1967). Although petitioner attacks the

Florida system on numerous grounds, the Court's decision is based on a single

[577 U.S. 106]

perceived defect, *i.e.*, that the jury's determination that at least one aggravating factor was proved is not binding on the trial judge. *Ante*, at 98–99, 193 L. Ed. 2d, at 510–511. The Court makes no pretense that this supposed defect could have prejudiced petitioner, and it seems very clear that it did not.

Attempting to show that he might have been prejudiced by the error, petitioner suggests that the jury might not have found the existence of an aggravating factor had it been instructed that its finding was a prerequisite for the imposition of the death penalty, but this suggestion is hard to credit. The jury was told to consider two aggravating factors: that the murder was committed during the course of a robbery and that it was especially "heinous, atrocious, or cruel." App. 212. The evidence in support of both factors was overwhelming.

The evidence with regard to the first aggravating factor—that the murder occurred during the commission of a robbery—was as follows. The victim, Cynthia Harrison, an assistant manager of a Popeye's restaurant, arrived at work between 7 a.m. and 8:30 a.m. on the date of her death. When other employees entered the store at about 10:30 a.m., they found that she had been stabbed to death and that the restaurant's safe was open and the previous day's receipts were missing. At trial, the issue was whether Hurst committed the murder. There was no suggestion that the murder did not occur during the robbery. Any alternative scenario—for example, that Cynthia Harrison was

first murdered by one person for some reason other than robbery and that a second person came upon the scene shortly after the murder and somehow gained access to and emptied the Popeye's safe—is fanciful.

The evidence concerning the second aggravating factor—that the murder was especially "heinous, atrocious, or cruel"—was also overwhelming. Cynthia Harrison was bound, gagged, and stabbed more than 60 times. Her injuries included "facial cuts that went all the way down to the

[577 U.S. 107]

underlying bone," "cuts through the eyelid region" and "the top of her lip," and "a large cut to her neck which almost severed her trachea." *Id.*, at 261. It was estimated that death could have taken as long as 15 minutes to occur. The trial court characterized the manner of her death as follows: "The utter terror and pain that Ms. Harrison likely experienced during the incident is unfathomable. Words are inadequate to describe this death, but the photographs introduced as evidence depict a person bound, rendered helpless, and brutally, savagely, and unmercifully slashed and disfigured. The murder of Ms. Harrison was conscienceless, pitiless, and unnecessarily torturous." *Id.*, at 261-262.

In light of this evidence, it defies belief to suggest that the jury would not have found the existence of either aggravating factor if its finding was binding. More than 17 years have passed since Cynthia Harrison was brutally murdered. In the interest of bringing this protracted litigation to a close, I would rule on the issue of harmless error and would affirm the decision of the Florida Supreme Court.

MEMORANDUM CASES

No. 15-578 (R46-014). In re Juan Deshannon Butler, Petitioner.

577 U.S. 1046, 136 S. Ct. 698, 193 L. Ed. 2d 517, 2015 U.S. LEXIS 8002.

December 14, 2015. The petition for writ of habeas corpus was dismissed today pursuant to Rule 46.1 of the Rules of this Court.

No. 15-6438. Derrick Allen, Petitioner v. Julie L. Jones, Secretary, Florida Department of Corrections.

577 U.S. 1046, 136 S. Ct. 692, 193 L. Ed. 2d 517, 2015 U.S. LEXIS 7996.

December 14, 2015. Motion of petitioner for leave to proceed in forma pauperis denied, and petition for writ of certiorari to the District Court of Appeal of Florida, First District, dismissed. See Rule 39.8.

Same case below, 173 So. 3d 889.

No. 15-6618. Daniel K. Schmidt, Petitioner v. Julie L. Jones, Secretary, Florida Department of Corrections.

577 U.S. 1046, 136 S. Ct. 697, 193 L. Ed. 2d 517, 2015 U.S. LEXIS 7936.

December 14, 2015. Motion of petitioner for leave to proceed in forma pauperis denied, and petition for writ of certiorari to the United States Court of Appeals for the Eleventh Circuit dismissed. See Rule 39.8. As petitioner has repeatedly abused this Court's process, the Clerk is directed not to accept any further petitions in noncriminal matters from petitioner unless the docketing fee required by Rule 38(a) is paid and petition submitted in compliance with Rule 33.1. See Martin v. District of Columbia Court of Appeals, 506 U.S. 1, 113 S. Ct. 397, 121 L. Ed. 2d 305 (1992) (per curiam).

No. 15-648 (15A522). V.L., Petitioner v. E.L., et al.

No. 15-648 (15A532). Tobie J. Smith, Guardian ad Litem, as Representative of Three Minor Children, Applicant v. E.L., et al.

577 U.S. 1046, 136 S. Ct. 701, 193 L. Ed. 2d 517, 2015 U.S. LEXIS 8000.

December 14, 2015. Applications for recall and stay of the Supreme Court of Alabama's Certificate of Judgment, in case No. 1140595, presented to Justice Thomas and by him referred to the Court, granted pending disposition of the petition for writ of certiorari. Should the petition for writ of certiorari be denied, this stay shall terminate automatically. In the event the petition for writ of certiorari is granted, the stay shall terminate upon the issuance of the mandate of this Court.

No. 15M63. Elizabeth A. Mahoney, Petitioner v. The Estate of Richard McDonnell, et al.

577 U.S. 1047, 136 S. Ct. 702, 193 L. Ed. 2d 517, 2015 U.S. LEXIS 7891.

December 14, 2015. Motion to direct the Clerk to file a petition for writ of certiorari out of time denied.

Same case below, 616 Fed. Appx. 500.

No. 15M64. Steven A. Spear, Petitioner v. Amy Kirkland, et al.

577 U.S. 1047, 136 S. Ct. 702, 193 L. Ed. 2d 518, 2015 U.S. LEXIS 7878.

December 14, 2015. Motion for leave to proceed as a veteran denied.

No. 15M65. Loredana Ranza, Petitioner v. Nike, Inc., et al.

577 U.S. 1047, 136 S. Ct. 702, 193 L. Ed. 2d 518, 2015 U.S. LEXIS 7950.

December 14, 2015. Motion for leave to file a petition for writ of certiorari under seal with redacted copies for the public record granted.

Same case below, 793 F.3d 1059.

No. 14-1209. John Sturgeon, Petitioner v. Bert Frost, in His Official Capacity as Alaska Regional Director of the National Park Service, et al.

577 U.S. 1047, 136 S. Ct. 702, 193 L. Ed. 2d 518, 2015 U.S. LEXIS 7924.

December 14, 2015. Motion of petitioner to dispense with printing the joint appendix granted. Motion of Alaska for leave to participate in oral argument as amicus curiae and for divided argument granted.

No. 15-6002. Teddy Moore, Petitioner v. T-Mobile USA, Inc.

577 U.S. 1047, 136 S. Ct. 703, 193 L. Ed. 2d 518, 2015 U.S. LEXIS 7986.

December 14, 2015. Motion of petitioner for reconsideration of order denying leave to proceed in forma pauperis denied.

No. 15-6490. Norman Johnson, Petitioner v. Just Energy.

577 U.S. 1047, 136 S. Ct. 703, 193 L. Ed. 2d 518, 2015 U.S. LEXIS 7979.

December 14, 2015. Motion of petitioner for leave to proceed in forma pauperis denied. Petitioner is allowed until January 4, 2016, within which to pay the docketing fee required by Rule 38(a) and to submit a petition in compliance with Rule 33.1 of the Rules of this Court.

No. 15-6517. Veronique K. Pongo, et al., Petitioners v. Bank of America, et al.

577 U.S. 1047, 136 S. Ct. 703, 193 L. Ed. 2d 518, 2015 U.S. LEXIS 7975.

December 14, 2015. Motion of petitioners for leave to proceed in forma pauperis denied. Petitioners allowed until January 4, 2016, within which to pay the docketing fee required by Rule 38(a) and to submit a petition in compliance with Rule 33.1 of the Rules of this Court.

Same case below, 612 Fed. Appx. 698.

No. 15-420. United States, Petitioner v. Michael Bryant, Jr.

577 U.S. 1048, 136 S. Ct. 690, 193 L. Ed. 2d 518, 2015 U.S. LEXIS 7929.

December 14, 2015. Motion of respondent for leave to proceed in forma pauperis granted. Petition for writ of certiorari to the United States Court of Appeals for the Ninth Circuit granted.

Same case below, 769 F.3d 671.

No. 14-9843. Antoine Lamont Johnson, Petitioner v. United States.

577 U.S. 1048, 136 S. Ct. 688, 193 L. Ed. 2d 519, 2015 U.S. LEXIS 7990.

December 14, 2015. Petition for writ of certiorari to the United States Court of Appeals for the Ninth Circuit denied.

Same case below, 767 F.3d 815.

No. 14-10376. Roger L. Wheeler, Petitioner v. Randy White, Warden.

577 U.S. 1048, 136 S. Ct. 688, 193 L. Ed. 2d 519, 2015 U.S. LEXIS 7905.

December 14, 2015. Petition for writ of certiorari to the United States Court of Appeals for the Sixth Circuit denied.

Same case below, 779 F.3d 366.

No. 15-57. David Paul Hall, Petitioner v. North Carolina.

577 U.S. 1048, 136 S. Ct. 688, 193 L. Ed. 2d 519, 2015 U.S. LEXIS 7932.

December 14, 2015. Petition for writ of certiorari to the Court of Appeals of North Carolina denied.

Same case below, 238 N.C. App. 322, 768 S.E.2d 39.

No. 15-58. City of Los Angeles, California, et al., Petitioners v. Robert Contreras.

577 U.S. 1048, 136 S. Ct. 688, 193 L. Ed. 2d 519, 2015 U.S. LEXIS 7900.

December 14, 2015. Petition for writ of certiorari to the United States Court of Appeals for the Ninth Circuit denied.

Same case below, 603 Fed. Appx. 530.

No. 15-71. Nicky Charune Agnew, Petitioner v. Texas.

577 U.S. 1048, 136 S. Ct. 688, 193 L. Ed. 2d 519, 2015 U.S. LEXIS 7995.

December 14, 2015. Petition for writ of certiorari to the Court of Appeals of Texas, Twelfth District, denied.

No. 15-100. Apple American Group, LLC, Petitioner v. Francisco Salazar.

577 U.S. 1048, 136 S. Ct. 688, 193 L. Ed. 2d 519, 2015 U.S. LEXIS 7904.

December 14, 2015. Petition for writ of certiorari to the Court of Appeal of California, Fourth Appellate District, Division Two, denied.

No. 15-158. Sun-Times Media, LLC, Petitioner v. Scott Dahlstrom, et al.

577 U.S. 1048, 136 S. Ct. 689, 193 L. Ed. 2d 519, 2015 U.S. LEXIS 7882.

December 14, 2015. Petition for writ of certiorari to the United States Court of Appeals for the Seventh Circuit denied.

Same case below, 777 F.3d 937.

Same case below, 602 Fed. Appx. 246.

No. 15-236. CarMax Auto Superstores California, LLC, Petitioner v. Wahid Areso.

577 U.S. 1048, 136 S. Ct. 689, 193 L. Ed. 2d 520, 2015 U.S. LEXIS 7992.

December 14, 2015. Petition for writ of certiorari to the Court of Appeal of California, Second Appellate District, Division One, denied.

No. 15-283. Luis Alberto Galvis Mujica, et al., Petitioners v. Occidental Petroleum Corporation, et al.

577 U.S. 1049, 136 S. Ct. 690, 193 L. Ed. 2d 520, 2015 U.S. LEXIS 7922.

December 14, 2015. Petition for writ of certiorari to the United States Court of Appeals for the Ninth Circuit denied.

Same case below, 771 F.3d 580.

No. 15-266. Juan Carlos Romero-Escobar, Petitioner v. Loretta E. Lynch, Attorney General.

577 U.S. 1048, 136 S. Ct. 689, 193 L. Ed. 2d 520, 2015 U.S. LEXIS 7901.

December 14, 2015. Petition for writ of certiorari to the United States Court of Appeals for the Ninth Circuit denied.

Same case below, 601 Fed. Appx. 484.

No. 15-287. David Hawkins, Petitioner v. Schwan's Home Service, Inc.

577 U.S. 1049, 136 S. Ct. 690, 193 L. Ed. 2d 520, 2015 U.S. LEXIS 7925.

December 14, 2015. Petition for writ of certiorari to the United States Court of Appeals for the Tenth Circuit denied.

Same case below, 778 F.3d 877.

No. 15-267. Fatih Sonmez, Petitioner v. United States.

577 U.S. 1048, 136 S. Ct. 689, 193 L. Ed. 2d 520, 2015 U.S. LEXIS 7960.

December 14, 2015. Petition for writ of certiorari to the United States Court of Appeals for the Fourth Circuit denied.

Same case below, 777 F.3d 684.

No. 15-429. Leo Pelizzo, Petitioner v. Malibu Media, LLC.

577 U.S. 1049, 136 S. Ct. 690, 193 L. Ed. 2d 520, 2015 U.S. LEXIS 7913.

December 14, 2015. Petition for writ of certiorari to the United States Court of Appeals for the Eleventh Circuit denied.

Same case below, 604 Fed. Appx. 879.

No. 15-277. Larry J. Winget, et al., Petitioners v. JPMorgan Chase Bank, N.A.

577 U.S. 1048, 136 S. Ct. 689, 193 L. Ed. 2d 520, 2015 U.S. LEXIS 7970.

December 14, 2015. Petition for writ of certiorari to the United States Court of Appeals for the Sixth Circuit denied.

No. 15-430. Norman Aamodt, et ux., Petitioners v. Landis & Setzler, P.C.

577 U.S. 1049, 136 S. Ct. 690, 193 L. Ed. 2d 520, 2015 U.S. LEXIS 7888.

December 14, 2015. Petition for writ of certiorari to the Superior Court of Pennsylvania, Philadelphia Office, denied.

Same case below, 106 A.3d 172.

No. 15-440. Edmundo C. Diaz, Petitioner v. CitiMortgage, Inc.

577 U.S. 1049, 136 S. Ct. 691, 193 L. Ed. 2d 521, 2015 U.S. LEXIS 7997, reh den 577 U.S. 1231, 136 S. Ct. 1487, 194 L. Ed. 2d 577, 2016 U.S. LEXIS 1907.

December 14, 2015. Petition for writ of certiorari to the Supreme Court of Florida denied.

Same case below, 171 So. 3d 115.

No. 15-442. Robert Hensley, Petitioner v. Gloria Hensley, nka Brinkley.

577 U.S. 1049, 136 S. Ct. 691, 193 L. Ed. 2d 521, 2015 U.S. LEXIS 7909.

December 14, 2015. Petition for writ of certiorari to the Court of Appeals of Washington, Division 1, denied.

Same case below, 184 Wash. App. 1044.

No. 15-443. Anuj Grover, et al., Petitioners v. Choice Hotels International, Inc.

577 U.S. 1049, 136 S. Ct. 691, 193 L. Ed. 2d 521, 2015 U.S. LEXIS 7943.

December 14, 2015. Petition for writ of certiorari to the United States Court of Appeals for the Seventh Circuit denied.

Same case below, 792 F.3d 753.

No. 15-453. Leon V. Bonner, et ux., Petitioners v. City of Brighton, Michigan.

577 U.S. 1049, 136 S. Ct. 691, 193 L. Ed. 2d 521, 2015 U.S. LEXIS 7907.

December 14, 2015. Petition for writ of certiorari to the Court of Appeals of Michigan denied.

No. 15-464. Yi Jing Groeber, Petitioner v. Friedman and Schuman, P.C.

577 U.S. 1049, 136 S. Ct. 695, 193 L. Ed. 2d 521, 2015 U.S. LEXIS 7957, reh den 577 U.S. 1184, 136 S. Ct. 1249, 194 L. Ed. 2d 246, 2016 U.S. LEXIS 1085.

December 14, 2015. Petition for writ of certiorari to the United States Court of Appeals for the Third Circuit denied.

Same case below, 602 Fed. Appx. 69.

No. 15-472. Mary Ellen Kalange, Petitioner v. Douglas J. Suter, et al.

577 U.S. 1049, 136 S. Ct. 695, 193 L. Ed. 2d 521, 2015 U.S. LEXIS 7951.

December 14, 2015. Petition for writ of certiorari to the United States Court of Appeals for the Sixth Circuit denied.

No. 15-475. Ramona Two Shields, et al., Petitioners v. Spencer Wilkinson, Jr., et al.

577 U.S. 1049, 136 S. Ct. 695, 193 L. Ed. 2d 521, 2015 U.S. LEXIS 7946.

December 14, 2015. Petition for writ of certiorari to the United States Court of Appeals for the Eighth Circuit denied.

Same case below, 790 F.3d 791.

No. 15-479. Dante L. Bennett, Petitioner v. Maryland.

577 U.S. 1049, 136 S. Ct. 695, 193 L. Ed. 2d 521, 2015 U.S. LEXIS 7982.

December 14, 2015. Petition for writ of certiorari to the Court of Special Appeals of Maryland denied.

Same case below, 222 Md. App. 706.

No. 15-506. Charles Stanton, Petitioner v. Harold Lassonde, III, et al.

577 U.S. 1049, 136 S. Ct. 697, 193 L. Ed. 2d 522, 2015 U.S. LEXIS 7898.

December 14, 2015. Petition for writ of certiorari to the United States Court of Appeals for the First Circuit denied.

No. 15-524. Daniel J. Herbison, Petitioner v. Chase Bank USA, N.A.

577 U.S. 1049, 136 S. Ct. 697, 193 L. Ed. 2d 522, 2015 U.S. LEXIS 7953.

December 14, 2015. Petition for writ of certiorari to the United States Court of Appeals for the Ninth Circuit denied.

Same case below, 607 Fed. Appx. 737.

No. 15-564. Karen Ahlers, et al., Petitioners v. Rick Scott, Governor of Florida, et al.

577 U.S. 1050, 136 S. Ct. 698, 193 L. Ed. 2d 522, 2015 U.S. LEXIS 7973.

December 14, 2015. Petition for writ of certiorari to the District Court of Appeal of Florida, First District, denied.

Same case below, 169 So. 3d 1164.

No. 15-596. Randal Kent Hansen, Petitioner v. United States.

577 U.S. 1050, 136 S. Ct. 698, 193 L. Ed. 2d 522, 2015 U.S. LEXIS 7879.

December 14, 2015. Petition for writ of certiorari to the United States Court of Appeals for the Eighth Circuit denied.

Same case below, 791 F.3d 863.

No. 15-609. Nicholas Occhiuto, Petitioner v. United States.

577 U.S. 1050, 136 S. Ct. 700, 193 L. Ed. 2d 522, 2015 U.S. LEXIS 7919.

December 14, 2015. Petition for writ of certiorari to the United States Court of Appeals for the First Circuit denied.

Same case below, 784 F.3d 862.

No. 15-621. Bobby W. Ferguson, Petitioner v. United States.

577 U.S. 1050, 136 S. Ct. 700, 193 L. Ed. 2d 522, 2015 U.S. LEXIS 7887.

December 14, 2015. Petition for writ of certiorari to the United States Court of Appeals for the Sixth Circuit denied.

Same case below, 798 F.3d 365.

No. 15-642. OIP Technologies, Inc., Petitioner v. Amazon.com, Inc.

577 U.S. 1050, 136 S. Ct. 701, 193 L. Ed. 2d 522, 2015 U.S. LEXIS 7974.

December 14, 2015. Petition for writ of certiorari to the United States Court of Appeals for the Federal Circuit denied.

Same case below, 788 F.3d 1359.

No. 15-5695. Gary Charles George, Petitioner v. California.

577 U.S. 1050, 136 S. Ct. 689, 193 L. Ed. 2d 522, 2015 U.S. LEXIS 7971.

December 14, 2015. Petition for writ of certiorari to the Court of Appeal of California, Sixth Appellate District, denied.

Same case below, 607 Fed. Appx. 445.

No. 15-6426. Forrest Thomas, III, Petitioner v. Timothy Outlaw, Warden.

577 U.S. 1050, 136 S. Ct. 690, 193 L. Ed. 2d 523, 2015 U.S. LEXIS 7917, reh den 577 U.S. 1184, 136 S. Ct. 1251, 194 L. Ed. 2d 249, 2016 U.S. LEXIS 1222.

December 14, 2015. Petition for writ of certiorari to the United States Court of Appeals for the Fifth Circuit denied.

No. 15-6429. Jason Lee Harris, Petitioner v. Joseph M. Arpaio, Sheriff, Maricopa County, Arizona, et al.

577 U.S. 1050, 136 S. Ct. 691, 193 L. Ed. 2d 523, 2015 U.S. LEXIS 7942.

December 14, 2015. Petition for writ of certiorari to the United States Court of Appeals for the Ninth Circuit denied.

No. 15-6432. James L. Miller, Petitioner v. Amir Kashani, et al.

577 U.S. 1050, 136 S. Ct. 691, 193 L. Ed. 2d 523, 2015 U.S. LEXIS 7978, reh den 577 U.S. 1184, 136 S. Ct. 1251, 194 L. Ed. 2d 249, 2016 U.S. LEXIS 1170.

December 14, 2015. Petition for writ of certiorari to the United States Court of Appeals for the Ninth Circuit denied.

No. 15-6435. Mark Anthony Reed-Bey, Petitioner v. George Pramstaller, et al.

577 U.S. 1050, 136 S. Ct. 692, 193 L. Ed. 2d 523, 2015 U.S. LEXIS 7965.

December 14, 2015. Petition for writ of certiorari to the United States Court of Appeals for the Sixth Circuit denied.

No. 15-6437. Scott Nathon Wehmhoefer, Petitioner v. Unnamed Defendants.

577 U.S. 1050, 136 S. Ct. 692, 193 L. Ed. 2d 523, 2015 U.S. LEXIS 7883.

December 14, 2015. Petition for writ of certiorari to the United States Court of Appeals for the Fifth Circuit denied.

No. 15-6442. Dennis Mickjale Potts, Petitioner v. Jeffrey Beard, Secretary, Florida Department of Corrections and Rehabilitation.

577 U.S. 1050, 136 S. Ct. 692, 193 L. Ed. 2d 523, 2015 U.S. LEXIS 7912.

December 14, 2015. Petition for writ of certiorari to the United States Court of Appeals for the Ninth Circuit denied.

No. 15-6443. Daniel Jon Peterka, Petitioner v. Julie L. Jones, Secretary, Florida Department of Corrections.

577 U.S. 1050, 136 S. Ct. 692, 193 L. Ed. 2d 523, 2015 U.S. LEXIS 7885.

December 14, 2015. Petition for writ of certiorari to the United States Court of Appeals for the Eleventh Circuit denied.

No. 15-6445. Randy Spencer, Petitioner v. Julie L. Jones, Secretary, Florida Department of Corrections, et al.

577 U.S. 1050, 136 S. Ct. 692, 193 L. Ed. 2d 523, 2015 U.S. LEXIS 7949.

December 14, 2015. Petition for writ of certiorari to the United States Court of Appeals for the Eleventh Circuit denied.

No. 15-6449. Peter D. Gache, Petitioner v. Hill Realty Associates, LLC, et al.

577 U.S. 1051, 136 S. Ct. 693, 193 L. Ed. 2d 524, 2015 U.S. LEXIS 7954, reh den 577 U.S. 1185, 136 S. Ct. 1252, 194 L. Ed. 2d 249, 2016 U.S. LEXIS 1048.

December 14, 2015. Petition for writ of certiorari to the United States Court of Appeals for the Second Circuit denied.

No. 15-6459. Vicki L. Marsh, Petitioner v. John L. Wynne, et al.

No. 15-6460. Karen Foster, Petitioner v. John L. Wynne, et al.

577 U.S. 1051, 136 S. Ct. 693, 193 L. Ed. 2d 524, 2015 U.S. LEXIS 7984.

December 14, 2015. Petitions for writs of certiorari to the United States Court of Appeals for the Fourth Circuit denied.

Same cases below, 792 F.3d 469.

No. 15-6462. Marcus Lavern Turner, Petitioner v. Keith Whitener, Correctional Administrator, Alexander Correctional Institution.

577 U.S. 1051, 136 S. Ct. 693, 193 L. Ed. 2d 524, 2015 U.S. LEXIS 7966.

December 14, 2015. Petition for writ of certiorari to the United States Court of Appeals for the Fourth Circuit denied.

Same case below, 603 Fed. Appx. 214.

No. 15-6464. Mary Burns, Petitioner v. Covenant Bank, fka Community Bank of Lawndale.

577 U.S. 1051, 136 S. Ct. 693, 193 L. Ed. 2d 524, 2015 U.S. LEXIS 7881.

December 14, 2015. Petition for writ of certiorari to the Appellate Court of Illinois, First District, denied.

Same case below, 392 Ill. Dec. 364, 32 N.E.3d 672.

No. 15-6469. Patrick Placide, Petitioner v. Julie L. Jones, Secretary, Florida Department of Corrections.

577 U.S. 1051, 136 S. Ct. 693, 193 L. Ed. 2d 524, 2015 U.S. LEXIS 7889.

December 14, 2015. Petition for writ of certiorari to the United States Court of Appeals for the Eleventh Circuit denied.

No. 15-6472. Kevin Saxon, Petitioner v. John B. Lempke.

577 U.S. 1051, 136 S. Ct. 694, 193 L. Ed. 2d 524, 2015 U.S. LEXIS 7976.

December 14, 2015. Petition for writ of certiorari to the United States Court of Appeals for the Second Circuit denied.

Same case below, 618 Fed. Appx. 10.

No. 15-6473. Antonio Soto, Petitioner v. California.

577 U.S. 1051, 136 S. Ct. 694, 193 L. Ed. 2d 524, 2015 U.S. LEXIS 7948.

December 14, 2015. Petition for writ of certiorari to the Court of Appeal of California, Second Appellate District, denied.

No. 15-6482. Christopher John Horton, Petitioner v. North Carolina.

577 U.S. 1051, 136 S. Ct. 694, 193 L. Ed. 2d 524, 2015 U.S. LEXIS 7886.

December 14, 2015. Petition for writ of certiorari to the United States Court of Appeals for the Fourth Circuit denied.

Same case below, 600 Fed. Appx. 156.

No. 15-6484. Joel Ira Furst, Petitioner v. Dannell Malloy, Governor of Connecticut.

577 U.S. 1051, 136 S. Ct. 694, 193 L. Ed. 2d 525, 2015 U.S. LEXIS 7892.

December 14, 2015. Petition for writ of certiorari to the United States Court of Appeals for the Second Circuit denied.

No. 15-6485. Manuel Antonio Gonzalez, III, Petitioner v. Kim Holland, Warden.

577 U.S. 1051, 136 S. Ct. 694, 193 L. Ed. 2d 525, 2015 U.S. LEXIS 7893.

December 14, 2015. Petition for writ of certiorari to the United States Court of Appeals for the Ninth Circuit denied.

No. 15-6488. Michael Hilbert, Petitioner v. Jeffrey Beard, Secretary, California Department of Corrections and Rehabilitation.

577 U.S. 1051, 136 S. Ct. 694, 193 L. Ed. 2d 525, 2015 U.S. LEXIS 7944.

December 14, 2015. Petition for writ of certiorari to the United States Court of Appeals for the Ninth Circuit denied.

No. 15-6496. Daniel K. Miller, Petitioner v. Office of Children, Youth and Families of Allegheny County.

577 U.S. 1051, 136 S. Ct. 703, 193 L. Ed. 2d 525, 2015 U.S. LEXIS 7937, reh

den 578 U.S. 916, 136 S. Ct. 1537, 194 L. Ed. 2d 621, 2016 U.S. LEXIS 2397.

December 14, 2015. Petition for writ of certiorari to the United States Court of Appeals for the Third Circuit denied.

Same case below, 605 Fed. Appx. 99.

No. 15-6510. Buck Richard Crowder, Petitioner v. William Stephens, Director, Texas Department of Criminal Justice, Correctional Institutions Division.

577 U.S. 1051, 136 S. Ct. 696, 193 L. Ed. 2d 525, 2015 U.S. LEXIS 7980.

December 14, 2015. Petition for writ of certiorari to the United States Court of Appeals for the Fifth Circuit denied.

No. 15-6514. Kim Anthony Polonczyk, Petitioner v. Toyota Motor Corporation, et al.

577 U.S. 1051, 136 S. Ct. 696, 193 L. Ed. 2d 525, 2015 U.S. LEXIS 7918.

December 14, 2015. Petition for writ of certiorari to the United States Court of Appeals for the Eleventh Circuit denied.

No. 15-6516. Luis Armando Morales-Lopez, Petitioner v. United States; Sergio Ramirez-Gandarilla, Petitioner v. United States; Jose Ezequiel Munoz-Munoz, Petitioner v. United States; Maria Leticia Gutierrez-Orozco, aka Leticia Gutierrez-Orosco, Petitioner v. United States; Jose Urena-Navarro, Petitioner v. United States; Alfonso Ramirez-Garza, Petitioner v. United States; Juan Angel Torres-Moreno, Petitioner v. United States; Jose Luis Garcia-Guia, aka Miguel Guia-

Llavero, Petitioner v. United States; Pastor Machuca-Secundino, aka Pastor Machuca, Petitioner v. United States; Jose De La Cruz Sepulveda-Gaytan, aka Jose Sepulveda, Petitioner v. United States; Guillermo Gomez-Guerro, Petitioner v. United States; Marcelino Martinez Rubio, Petitioner v. United States; and Baltazar Alejandro Lara-Lorenzo, aka Alejandro Lara-Baltaza, Petitioner v. United States.

577 U.S. 1052, 136 S. Ct. 696, 193 L. Ed. 2d 525, 2015 U.S. LEXIS 7968.

December 14, 2015. Petition for writ of certiorari to the United States Court of Appeals for the Fifth Circuit denied.

Same case below, 613 Fed. Appx. 377 (first judgment); 609 Fed. Appx. 262 (second judgment); 607 Fed. Appx. 442 (third judgment); 610 Fed. Appx. 407 (fourth judgment); 613 Fed. Appx. 372 (fifth judgment); 613 Fed. Appx. 359 (sixth judgment); 613 Fed. Appx. 379 (seventh judgment); 613 Fed. Appx. 371 (eighth judgment); 613 Fed. Appx. 401 (ninth judgment); 613 Fed. Appx. 396 (tenth judgment); 613 Fed. Appx. 408 (eleventh judgment); 613 Fed. Appx. 409 (twelfth judgment); and 609 Fed. Appx. 272 (thirteenth judgment).

No. 15-6544. Heriberto Ramos, Petitioner v. Massachusetts.

577 U.S. 1052, 136 S. Ct. 696, 193 L. Ed. 2d 526, 2015 U.S. LEXIS 7945.

December 14, 2015. Petition for writ of certiorari to the Appeals Court of Massachusetts denied.

Same case below, 87 Mass. App. Ct. 1127, 31 N.E.3d 1192.

No. 15-6586. Robert S. Wilson, Petitioner v. Doug Cook, Warden.

577 U.S. 1052, 136 S. Ct. 696, 193 L. Ed. 2d 526, 2015 U.S. LEXIS 7972.

December 14, 2015. Petition for writ of certiorari to the United States Court of Appeals for the Sixth Circuit denied.

No. 15-6683. Omar Johnson, Petitioner v. Maryland.

577 U.S. 1052, 136 S. Ct. 697, 193 L. Ed. 2d 526, 2015 U.S. LEXIS 7923, reh den 577 U.S. 1185, 136 S. Ct. 1252, 194 L. Ed. 2d 250, 2016 U.S. LEXIS 1042.

December 14, 2015. Petition for writ of certiorari to the Court of Special Appeals of Maryland denied.

Same case below, 224 Md. App. 725.

No. 15-6686. Ricardo A. Asturias, Petitioner v. California.

577 U.S. 1052, 136 S. Ct. 697, 193 L. Ed. 2d 526, 2015 U.S. LEXIS 7931.

December 14, 2015. Petition for writ of certiorari to the Court of Appeal of California, First Appellate District, Division Two, denied.

No. 15-6730. David Silva, Petitioner v. Julie L. Jones, Secretary, Florida Department of Corrections.

577 U.S. 1052, 136 S. Ct. 698, 193 L. Ed. 2d 526, 2015 U.S. LEXIS 7915.

December 14, 2015. Petition for writ of certiorari to the United States Court of Appeals for the Eleventh Circuit denied.

No. 15-6760. Norman Katz, Petitioner v. Jacob J. Lew, Secretary of Treasury.

577 U.S. 1052, 136 S. Ct. 698, 193 L. Ed. 2d 526, 2015 U.S. LEXIS 7916.

December 14, 2015. Petition for writ of certiorari to the United States Court of Appeals for the Ninth Circuit denied.

Same case below, 608 Fed. Appx. 543.

No. 15-6769. Patrick Gelin, Petitioner v. New York.

577 U.S. 1052, 136 S. Ct. 698, 193 L. Ed. 2d 527, 2015 U.S. LEXIS 7967.

December 14, 2015. Petition for writ of certiorari to the Appellate Division, Supreme Court of New York, Second Judicial Department, denied.

Same case below, 128 App. Div. 3d 717, 8 N.Y.S.3d 424.

No. 15-6805. Michael L. Davis, Petitioner v. District of Columbia.

577 U.S. 1052, 136 S. Ct. 699, 193 L. Ed. 2d 527, 2015 U.S. LEXIS 7928, reh den 577 U.S. 1232, 136 S. Ct. 1490, 194 L. Ed. 2d 580, 2016 U.S. LEXIS 1901.

December 14, 2015. Petition for writ of certiorari to the United States Court of Appeals for the District of Columbia Circuit denied.

Same case below, 793 F.3d 120.

No. 15-6837. Jeremiah J. Worm, Petitioner v. Sonja J. Peterson.

577 U.S. 1052, 136 S. Ct. 699, 193 L. Ed. 2d 527, 2015 U.S. LEXIS 7921.

December 14, 2015. Petition for writ of certiorari to the Supreme Court of Montana denied.

Same case below, 379 Mont. 537, 353 P.3d 507.

No. 15-6859. David Hernandez, Petitioner v. Julie L. Jones, Secretary, Florida Department of Corrections.

577 U.S. 1053, 136 S. Ct. 699, 193 L. Ed. 2d 527, 2015 U.S. LEXIS 7906.

December 14, 2015. Petition for writ of certiorari to the United States Court of Appeals for the Eleventh Circuit denied.

No. 15-6865. Shannon L. Gregory, Petitioner v. United States.

577 U.S. 1053, 136 S. Ct. 699, 193 L. Ed. 2d 527, 2015 U.S. LEXIS 7894.

December 14, 2015. Petition for writ of certiorari to the United States Court of Appeals for the Seventh Circuit denied.

Same case below, 795 F.3d 735.

No. 15-6866. Mario Haro, Petitioner v. United States.

577 U.S. 1053, 136 S. Ct. 699, 193 L. Ed. 2d 527, 2015 U.S. LEXIS 7938.

December 14, 2015. Petition for writ of certiorari to the United States Court of Appeals for the Ninth Circuit denied.

Same case below, 617 Fed. Appx. 820.

No. 15-6867. Andre Strum, Petitioner v. Kevin Kauffman, Superintendent, State Correctional Institution at Smithfield, et al.

577 U.S. 1053, 136 S. Ct. 699, 193 L. Ed. 2d 527, 2015 U.S. LEXIS 7987.

December 14, 2015. Petition for writ of certiorari to the United States Court of Appeals for the Third Circuit denied.

Same case below, 785 F.3d 200.

No. 15-6882. Eric Orlando Reese, Petitioner v. United States.

577 U.S. 1053, 136 S. Ct. 700, 193 L. Ed. 2d 528, 2015 U.S. LEXIS 7914.

December 14, 2015. Petition for writ of certiorari to the United States Court of Appeals for the Eleventh Circuit denied.

Same case below, 611 Fed. Appx. 961.

No. 15-6893. Jorge Munoz-Ramon, Petitioner v. United States.

577 U.S. 1053, 136 S. Ct. 700, 193 L. Ed. 2d 528, 2015 U.S. LEXIS 7988.

December 14, 2015. Petition for writ of certiorari to the United States Court of Appeals for the Eighth Circuit denied.

Same case below, 614 Fed. Appx. 857.

No. 15-6902. Juan Carlos Avila-Gonzalez, Petitioner v. United States.

577 U.S. 1053, 136 S. Ct. 700, 193 L. Ed. 2d 528, 2015 U.S. LEXIS 7958.

December 14, 2015. Petition for writ of certiorari to the United States Court of Appeals for the Fifth Circuit denied.

Same case below, 611 Fed. Appx. 801.

No. 15-6920. Sean Jay Widmer, Petitioner v. United States.

577 U.S. 1053, 136 S. Ct. 701, 193 L. Ed. 2d 528, 2015 U.S. LEXIS 7933.

December 14, 2015. Petition for writ of certiorari to the United States Court of Appeals for the Sixth Circuit denied.

No. 15-6997. Lester Johnson, Petitioner v. Julie L. Jones, Secretary, Florida Department of Corrections.

577 U.S. 1053, 136 S. Ct. 701, 193 L. Ed. 2d 528, 2015 U.S. LEXIS 7903.

December 14, 2015. Petition for writ of certiorari to the United States Court of Appeals for the Eleventh Circuit denied.

No. 15-7008. Andre Dothan Dawson, Petitioner v. Florida.

577 U.S. 1053, 136 S. Ct. 701, 193 L. Ed. 2d 528, 2015 U.S. LEXIS 7880.

December 14, 2015. Petition for writ of certiorari to the District Court of Appeal of Florida, Fourth District, denied.

Same case below, 169 So. 3d 1188.

No. 15-469. Michael C. Scher, Petitioner v. City of Las Vegas, Nevada, et al.

577 U.S. 1053, 136 S. Ct. 695, 193 L. Ed. 2d 528, 2015 U.S. LEXIS 7985.

December 14, 2015. Petition for writ of certiorari before judgment to the United States Court of Appeals for the Ninth Circuit denied.

No. 15-538. Allvoice Developments US, LLC, Petitioner v. Microsoft Corp.

577 U.S. 1053, 136 S. Ct. 697, 193 L. Ed. 2d 528, 2015 U.S. LEXIS 7884.

December 14, 2015. Petition for writ of certiorari to the United States Court of

Appeals for the Federal Circuit denied. The Chief Justice took no part in the consideration or decision of this petition.

Same case below, 612 Fed. Appx. 1009.

No. 15-6869. Robert Burke, Petitioner v. United States.

577 U.S. 1053, 136 S. Ct. 700, 193 L. Ed. 2d 529, 2015 U.S. LEXIS 7895.

December 14, 2015. Petition for writ of certiorari to the United States Court of Appeals for the Third Circuit denied. Justice Kagan took no part in the consideration or decision of this petition.

No. 15-651. In re Douglas J. MacNeill, Petitioner.

577 U.S. 1047, 136 S. Ct. 701, 193 L. Ed. 2d 529, 2015 U.S. LEXIS 7941.

December 14, 2015. Petition for writ of habeas corpus denied.

No. 15-7011. In re Justin Wells, Petitioner.

577 U.S. 1047, 136 S. Ct. 702, 193 L. Ed. 2d 529, 2015 U.S. LEXIS 7947, reh den 577 U.S. 1185, 136 S. Ct. 1253, 194 L. Ed. 2d 251, 2016 U.S. LEXIS 1078.

December 14, 2015. Petition for writ of habeas corpus denied.

No. 15-7074. In re Gregory Leon Young, Petitioner.

577 U.S. 1047, 136 S. Ct. 702, 193 L. Ed. 2d 529, 2015 U.S. LEXIS 7920.

December 14, 2015. Petition for writ of habeas corpus denied.

No. 15-465. In re Theodore B. Gould, Petitioner.

577 U.S. 1047, 136 S. Ct. 695, 193 L. Ed. 2d 529, 2015 U.S. LEXIS 7910.

December 14, 2015. Petition for writ of mandamus denied.

No. 14-9012. Gloria Deanna Dickerson, Petitioner v. United Way of New York City, et al.

577 U.S. 1053, 136 S. Ct. 703, 193 L. Ed. 2d 529, 2015 U.S. LEXIS 7977.

December 14, 2015. Petition for rehearing denied.

Former decision, 577 U.S. 829, 136 S. Ct. 33, 193 L. Ed. 2d 47, 2015 U.S. LEXIS 5658.

No. 14-9275. Robert Frazier, Petitioner v. West Virginia.

577 U.S. 1054, 136 S. Ct. 703, 193 L. Ed. 2d 529, 2015 U.S. LEXIS 7969.

December 14, 2015. Petition for rehearing denied.

Former decision, 577 U.S. 829, 136 S. Ct. 35, 193 L. Ed. 2d 48, 2015 U.S. LEXIS 5728.

No. 14-9632. Durwyn Talley, Petitioner v. Christopher L. Gore, et al.

577 U.S. 1054, 136 S. Ct. 704, 193 L. Ed. 2d 529, 2015 U.S. LEXIS 7927.

December 14, 2015. Petition for rehearing denied.

Former decision, 577 U.S. 832, 136 S. Ct. 47, 193 L. Ed. 2d 54, 2015 U.S. LEXIS 5652.

No. 14-9648. Walter Gerald Anderson, Petitioner v. William Stephens, Director, Texas Department of Criminal Justice, Correctional Institutions Division.

577 U.S. 1054, 136 S. Ct. 704, 193 L. Ed. 2d 530, 2015 U.S. LEXIS 7911.

December 14, 2015. Petition for rehearing denied.

Former decision, 577 U.S. 833, 136 S. Ct. 47, 193 L. Ed. 2d 54, 2015 U.S. LEXIS 5880.

No. 14-9823. Carl Dean Sampson, Petitioner v. Robert Patton, Director, Oklahoma Department of Corrections.

577 U.S. 1054, 136 S. Ct. 704, 193 L. Ed. 2d 530, 2015 U.S. LEXIS 7964.

December 14, 2015. Petition for rehearing denied.

Former decision, 577 U.S. 837, 136 S. Ct. 63, 193 L. Ed. 2d 63, 2015 U.S. LEXIS 5601.

No. 14-9869. Michael Paul Ralston, Petitioner v. Texas.

577 U.S. 1054, 136 S. Ct. 704, 193 L. Ed. 2d 530, 2015 U.S. LEXIS 7955.

December 14, 2015. Petition for rehearing denied.

Former decision, 577 U.S. 839, 136 S. Ct. 69, 193 L. Ed. 2d 67, 2015 U.S. LEXIS 5166.

No. 14-9885. Roger R. Adams, Petitioner v. Clark E. Ducart, Warden.

577 U.S. 1054, 136 S. Ct. 704, 193 L. Ed. 2d 530, 2015 U.S. LEXIS 7902.

December 14, 2015. Petition for rehearing denied.

Former decision, 577 U.S. 840, 136 S. Ct. 70, 193 L. Ed. 2d 67, 2015 U.S. LEXIS 5396.

No. 14-9895. Lana K. Williams, Petitioner v. Rex Lee Huha, et al.

577 U.S. 1054, 136 S. Ct. 704, 193 L. Ed. 2d 530, 2015 U.S. LEXIS 7989.

December 14, 2015. Petition for rehearing denied.

Former decision, 577 U.S. 840, 136 S. Ct. 70, 193 L. Ed. 2d 68, 2015 U.S. LEXIS 5154.

No. 14-9934. George Anthony Corrales, Petitioner v. California.

577 U.S. 1054, 136 S. Ct. 704, 193 L. Ed. 2d 530, 2015 U.S. LEXIS 7939.

December 14, 2015. Petition for rehearing denied.

Former decision, 577 U.S. 841, 136 S. Ct. 74, 193 L. Ed. 2d 70, 2015 U.S. LEXIS 5006.

No. 14-9961. Lindsey J. Watson, Petitioner v. Carolyn W. Colvin, Acting Commissioner of Social Security.

577 U.S. 1054, 136 S. Ct. 705, 193 L. Ed. 2d 530, 2015 U.S. LEXIS 7961.

December 14, 2015. Petition for rehearing denied.

Former decision, 577 U.S. 842, 136 S. Ct. 77, 193 L. Ed. 2d 71, 2015 U.S. LEXIS 5469.

————

No. 14-10048. Adelbert H. Warner, II, Petitioner v. United States.

577 U.S. 1054, 136 S. Ct. 705, 193 L. Ed. 2d 531, 2015 U.S. LEXIS 7930.

December 14, 2015. Petition for rehearing denied.

Former decision, 577 U.S. 844, 136 S. Ct. 88, 193 L. Ed. 2d 77, 2015 U.S. LEXIS 5487.

————

No. 14-10364. Jeffrey Scott Hall, Petitioner v. Jody Tallie, et al.

577 U.S. 1054, 136 S. Ct. 705, 193 L. Ed. 2d 531, 2015 U.S. LEXIS 7935.

December 14, 2015. Petition for rehearing denied.

Former decision, 577 U.S. 862, 136 S. Ct. 146, 193 L. Ed. 2d 110, 2015 U.S. LEXIS 5985.

————

No. 14-10456. Robert Ellis Hastings, Petitioner v. United States.

577 U.S. 1054, 136 S. Ct. 705, 193 L. Ed. 2d 531, 2015 U.S. LEXIS 7956.

December 14, 2015. Petition for rehearing denied.

Former decision, 577 U.S. 867, 136 S. Ct. 162, 193 L. Ed. 2d 120, 2015 U.S. LEXIS 6292.

————

No. 15-4. William Hayes Wyttenbach, Petitioner v. R.M.P.

577 U.S. 1054, 136 S. Ct. 705, 193 L. Ed. 2d 531, 2015 U.S. LEXIS 7981.

December 14, 2015. Petition for rehearing denied.

Former decision, 577 U.S. 869, 136 S. Ct. 170, 193 L. Ed. 2d 123, 2015 U.S. LEXIS 5984.

————

No. 15-5016. In re Darrell Burrows, Petitioner.

577 U.S. 1054, 136 S. Ct. 705, 193 L. Ed. 2d 531, 2015 U.S. LEXIS 7991.

December 14, 2015. Petition for rehearing denied.

Former decision, 577 U.S. 812, 136 S. Ct. 172, 193 L. Ed. 2d 214, 2015 U.S. LEXIS 4716.

————

No. 15-5073. Wilbert Patrick Stewart, Petitioner v. William Stephens, Director, Texas Department of Criminal Justice, Correctional Institutions Division.

577 U.S. 1054, 136 S. Ct. 705, 193 L. Ed. 2d 531, 2015 U.S. LEXIS 7962.

December 14, 2015. Petition for rehearing denied.

Former decision, 577 U.S. 881, 136 S. Ct. 300, 193 L. Ed. 2d 145, 2015 U.S. LEXIS 5461.

————

No. 15-5216. Gary M. Brayboy, Petitioner v. Robert Napel, Warden.

577 U.S. 1054, 136 S. Ct. 705, 193 L. Ed. 2d 531, 2015 U.S. LEXIS 7952.

December 14, 2015. Petition for rehearing denied.

Former decision, 577 U.S. 888, 136 S. Ct. 206, 193 L. Ed. 2d 159, 2015 U.S. LEXIS 5470.

No. 15-5269. Danny Ruben, Petitioner v. Timothy Keith, Warden.

577 U.S. 1054, 136 S. Ct. 706, 193 L. Ed. 2d 532, 2015 U.S. LEXIS 7896.

December 14, 2015. Petition for rehearing denied.

Former decision, 577 U.S. 891, 136 S. Ct. 215, 193 L. Ed. 2d 164, 2015 U.S. LEXIS 5492.

No. 15-5354. Jerrin Lavazie Hickman, Petitioner v. Oregon.

577 U.S. 1054, 136 S. Ct. 706, 193 L. Ed. 2d 532, 2015 U.S. LEXIS 7940.

December 14, 2015. Petition for rehearing denied.

Former decision, 577 U.S. 896, 136 S. Ct. 230, 193 L. Ed. 2d 173, 2015 U.S. LEXIS 4847.

No. 15-5395. Timothy M. Strain, Petitioner v. United States District Court for the Middle District of Louisiana.

577 U.S. 1054, 136 S. Ct. 706, 193 L. Ed. 2d 532, 2015 U.S. LEXIS 7897.

December 14, 2015. Petition for rehearing denied.

Former decision, 577 U.S. 898, 136 S. Ct. 300, 193 L. Ed. 2d 177, 2015 U.S. LEXIS 4876.

No. 15-5400. Anthony Dewayne Lester, Petitioner v. William Stephens, Director, Texas Department of Criminal Justice, Correctional Institutions Division.

577 U.S. 1054, 136 S. Ct. 706, 193 L. Ed. 2d 532, 2015 U.S. LEXIS 7934.

December 14, 2015. Petition for rehearing denied.

Former decision, 577 U.S. 898, 136 S. Ct. 238, 193 L. Ed. 2d 178, 2015 U.S. LEXIS 4938.

No. 15-5641. Charles Chukwumeze Eleri, aka Charles C. Eleri, Petitioner v. James D. Hartley, Warden.

577 U.S. 1054, 136 S. Ct. 706, 193 L. Ed. 2d 532, 2015 U.S. LEXIS 7899.

December 14, 2015. Petition for rehearing denied.

Former decision, 577 U.S. 929, 136 S. Ct. 332, 193 L. Ed. 2d 240, 2015 U.S. LEXIS 6436.

No. 15-5662. Carol Johnene Morris, Petitioner v. William Stephens, Director, Texas Department of Criminal Justice, Correctional Institutions Division.

577 U.S. 1054, 136 S. Ct. 706, 193 L. Ed. 2d 532, 2015 U.S. LEXIS 7890.

December 14, 2015. Petition for rehearing denied.

Former decision, 577 U.S. 941, 136 S. Ct. 361, 193 L. Ed. 2d 294, 2015 U.S. LEXIS 6755.

No. 15-5689. Sylvester J. Hoffart, Petitioner v. Scott Wiggins, et al.

577 U.S. 1054, 136 S. Ct. 707, 193 L. Ed. 2d 532, 2015 U.S. LEXIS 7908.

December 14, 2015. Petition for rehearing denied.

Former decision, 577 U.S. 941, 136 S. Ct. 362, 193 L. Ed. 2d 295, 2015 U.S. LEXIS 6705.

No. 15-5703. Willie Bolds, Petitioner v. J. Cavazos, et al.

577 U.S. 1054, 136 S. Ct. 707, 193 L. Ed. 2d 533, 2015 U.S. LEXIS 7993.

December 14, 2015. Petition for rehearing denied.

Former decision, 577 U.S. 942, 136 S. Ct. 363, 193 L. Ed. 2d 295, 2015 U.S. LEXIS 6621.

No. 15-6061. In re John Joseph Tatar, Petitioner.

577 U.S. 1054, 136 S. Ct. 707, 193 L. Ed. 2d 533, 2015 U.S. LEXIS 7983.

December 14, 2015. Petition for rehearing denied.

Former decision, 577 U.S. 937, 136 S. Ct. 374, 193 L. Ed. 2d 307, 2015 U.S. LEXIS 6669.

No. 15-6160. Sylvester Andrews, Petitioner v. United States; and Sylvester Andrews, Petitioner v. United States District Court for the Eastern District of Pennsylvania.

577 U.S. 1054, 136 S. Ct. 707, 193 L. Ed. 2d 533, 2015 U.S. LEXIS 7926.

December 14, 2015. Petition for rehearing denied.

Former decision, 577 U.S. 947, 136 S. Ct. 379, 193 L. Ed. 2d 305, 2015 U.S. LEXIS 6744.

No. 15-292. Rory M. Walsh, Petitioner v. James L. Jones, Jr., et al.

577 U.S. 1054, 136 S. Ct. 707, 193 L. Ed. 2d 533, 2015 U.S. LEXIS 7959.

December 14, 2015. Petition for rehearing denied. Justice Kagan took no part in the consideration or decision of this petition.

Former decision, 577 U.S. 969, 136 S. Ct. 416, 193 L. Ed. 2d 340, 2015 U.S. LEXIS 6772.

No. 15-351. Rory M. Walsh, Petitioner v. Federal Bureau of Investigation, et al.

577 U.S. 1055, 136 S. Ct. 707, 193 L. Ed. 2d 533, 2015 U.S. LEXIS 7963.

December 14, 2015. Petition for rehearing denied. Justice Kagan took no part in the consideration or decision of this petition.

Former decision, 577 U.S. 969, 136 S. Ct. 421, 193 L. Ed. 2d 340, 2015 U.S. LEXIS 6803.

No. 15-7662 (15A699). Oscar Ray Bolin, Jr., Petitioner v. Julie L. Jones, Secretary, Florida Department of Corrections, et al.

577 U.S. 1055, 136 S. Ct. 790, 193 L. Ed. 2d 533, 2016 U.S. LEXIS 1.

January 7, 2016. Application for stay of execution of sentence of death, presented to Justice Thomas, and by him referred to the Court, denied. Petition for writ of certiorari to the United States Court of Appeals for the Eleventh Circuit denied.

Same case below, 628 Fed. Appx. 728.

No. 15-7663 (15A700). Oscar Ray Bolin, Jr., Petitioner v. Florida.

577 U.S. 1055, 136 S. Ct. 790, 193 L. Ed. 2d 534, 2016 U.S. LEXIS 2.

January 7, 2016. Application for stay of execution of sentence of death, presented to Justice Thomas, and by him referred to the Court, denied. Petition for writ of certiorari to the Supreme Court of Florida denied.

Same case below, 184 So. 3d 492.

No. 15-6834 (R46-016). Scott Selmer, Petitioner v. Office of Lawyers Professional Responsibility Board.

577 U.S. 1055, 136 S. Ct. 790, 193 L. Ed. 2d 534, 2016 U.S. LEXIS 8.

January 8, 2016. The petition for writ of certiorari to the Supreme Court of Minnesota was dismissed today pursuant to Rule 46 of the Rules of this Court.

Same case below, 866 N.W.2d 893.

No. 14-770. Bank Markazi, aka The Central Bank of Iran, Petitioner v. Deborah Peterson, et al.

577 U.S. 1055, 136 S. Ct. 790, 193 L. Ed. 2d 534, 2016 U.S. LEXIS 4.

January 8, 2016. Motion of the Solicitor General for leave to participate in oral argument as amicus curiae and for divided argument granted.

No. 14-1280. Jeffrey J. Heffernan, Petitioner v. City of Paterson, New Jersey, et al.

577 U.S. 1055, 136 S. Ct. 790, 193 L. Ed. 2d 534, 2016 U.S. LEXIS 6.

January 8, 2016. Motion of the Solicitor General for leave to participate in oral argument as amicus curiae and for divided argument granted.

No. 14-1406. Nebraska, et al., Petitioners v. Mitch Parker, et al.

577 U.S. 1055, 136 S. Ct. 791, 193 L. Ed. 2d 534, 2016 U.S. LEXIS 3.

January 8, 2016. Joint motion of respondents for divided argument filed out of time granted.

No. 15-108. Commonwealth of Puerto Rico, Petitioner v. Luis M. Sanchez Valle, et al.

577 U.S. 1055, 136 S. Ct. 791, 193 L. Ed. 2d 534, 2016 U.S. LEXIS 7.

January 8, 2016. Motion of the Solicitor General for leave to participate in oral argument as amicus curiae and for divided argument granted.

No. 15-6418. Gregory Welch, Petitioner v. United States.

577 U.S. 1056, 136 S. Ct. 790, 193 L. Ed. 2d 534, 2016 U.S. LEXIS 5.

January 8, 2016. Motion of petitioner for leave to proceed in forma pauperis and petition for writ of certiorari to the United States Court of Appeals for the Eleventh Circuit granted.

KANSAS, Petitioner (No. 14-449)

v

JONATHAN D. CARR

KANSAS, Petitioner (No. 14-450)

v

REGINALD DEXTER CARR, Jr.

KANSAS, Petitioner (No. 14-452)

v

SIDNEY J. GLEASON

577 U.S. 108, 136 S. Ct. 633, 193 L. Ed. 2d 535, 2016 U.S. LEXIS 845

Argued October 7, 2015. Decided January 20, 2016.

Decision: Federal Constitution's Eighth Amendment did not require that capital-sentencing jury be instructed that mitigating circumstances need not be proved beyond reasonable doubt; Constitution did not require severance of joint sentencing proceedings in instant capital case.

Prior history: ON WRITS OF CERTIORARI TO THE SUPREME COURT OF KANSAS, 300 Kan. 340, 329 P.3d 1195, 2014 Kan. LEXIS 431 (No. 14-449); 300 Kan. 1, 331 P.3d 544, 2014 Kan. LEXIS 432 (No. 14-450); 299 Kan. 1127, 329 P.3d 1102, 2014 Kan. LEXIS 426 (No. 14-452)

SUMMARY

Overview: HOLDINGS: [1]-A sentencing court in a capital case was not required to affirmatively instruct the jury that mitigating circumstances need not be proven beyond a reasonable doubt, since the jury was properly informed that aggravating circumstances must be proved beyond a reasonable doubt while mitigating circumstances must only be found to exist, and the instructions repeatedly told the jurors to consider any mitigating factor; [2]-Joint capital-sentencing proceedings did not violate codefendants' right to individualized sentencing determinations since the jury was properly instructed to give separate consideration to each defendant and was provided with defendant-specific instructions for aggravating and mitigating circumstances, and any prejudice from evidence which would have been inadmissible in separate proceedings was extremely speculative.

Outcome: Judgments reversed and cases remanded. 8-1 Decision; 1 Dissent.

HEADNOTES

Classified to United States Supreme Court Digest, Lawyers' Edition

Federal Constitution — state interpretation — criminal defendant

L Ed Digest: Appeal § 553

1. When the U.S. Supreme Court corrects a state court's federal errors, the court returns power to the state, and to its people. The state courts may experiment all they want with their own constitutions, and often do in the wake of the court's decisions. But what a state court cannot do is experiment with the U.S. Constitution and expect to elude the court's review so long as victory goes to the criminal defendant. (Scalia, J., joined by Roberts, Ch. J., and Kennedy, Thomas, Ginsburg, Breyer, Alito, and Kagan, JJ.)

Capital sentencing — ambiguous instructions

L Ed Digest: Criminal Law § 93.7

2. Ambiguity in capital-sentencing instructions gives rise to constitutional error only if there is a reasonable likelihood that the jury has applied the challenged instruction in a way that prevents the consideration of constitutionally relevant evidence. A meager possibility of confusion is not enough. (Scalia, J., joined by Roberts, Ch. J., and Kennedy, Thomas, Ginsburg, Breyer, Alito, and Kagan, JJ.)

Capital case — Eighth Amendment — mitigating evidence

L Ed Digest: Constitutional Law § 848.9; Criminal Law § 93.7

3. The Eighth Amendment is inapposite when each defendant's claim is, at bottom, that the jury considered evidence that would not have been admitted in a severed capital-

sentencing proceeding, and that the joint trial clouded the jury's consideration of mitigating evidence. It is not the role of the Eighth Amendment to establish a special federal code of evidence governing the admissibility of evidence at capital sentencing proceedings. Rather, it is the due process clause that wards off the introduction of unduly prejudicial evidence that would render the trial fundamentally unfair. The test for a constitutional violation attributable to evidence improperly admitted at a capital-sentencing proceeding is whether the evidence so infected the sentencing proceeding with unfairness as to render the jury's imposition of the death penalty a denial of due process. The mere admission of evidence that might not otherwise have been admitted in a severed proceeding does not demand the automatic vacatur of a death sentence. (Scalia, J., joined by Roberts, Ch. J., and Kennedy, Thomas, Ginsburg, Breyer, Alito, and Kagan, JJ.)

Joint capital-sentencing proceedings

L Ed Digest: Criminal Law § 93.1

4. Joint capital-sentencing proceedings are not only permissible but are often preferable when the joined defendants' criminal conduct arises out of a single chain of events. Joint trial may enable a jury to arrive more reliably at its conclusions regarding the guilt or innocence of a particular defendant and to assign fairly the respective responsibilities of each defendant in the sentencing. That the codefendants might have antagonistic theories of mitigation, does not suffice to overcome a state's interest in pro-

moting the reliability and consistency of its judicial process. Limiting instructions often will suffice to cure any risk of prejudice. To forbid joinder in capital-sentencing proceedings would, perversely, increase the odds of wanton and freakish imposition of death sentences. Better that two defendants who have together committed the same crimes be placed side-by-side to have their fates determined by a single jury. (Scalia, J., joined by Roberts, Ch. J., and Kennedy, Thomas, Ginsburg, Breyer, Alito, and Kagan, JJ.)

Vacation of death sentence

L Ed Digest: Appeal § 1692.13

5. It is improper to vacate a death sentence based on pure speculation of fundamental unfairness, rather than reasoned judgment. (Scalia, J., joined by Roberts, Ch. J., and Kennedy, Thomas, Ginsburg, Breyer, Alito, and Kagan, JJ.)

RESEARCH REFERENCES

U.S.C.S., Constitution, Amendments 8, 14

26 Moore's Federal Practice § 632.21 (Matthew Bender 3d ed.)

L Ed Digest, Constitutional Law § 848.7; Criminal Law § 93.7; Evidence § 859

L Ed Index, Capital Offenses and Punishment

Annotations:

Validity of death penalty, under Federal Constitution, as affected by consideration of aggravating or mitigating circumstances—Supreme Court cases. 111 L. Ed. 2d 947.

Supreme Court's views on constitutionality of death penalty and procedures under which it is imposed or carried out. 90 L. Ed. 2d 1001.

SHEPARD'S® Citations Service. For further research of authorities referenced here, use SHEPARD'S to be sure your case or statute is still good law and to find additional authorities that support your position. SHEPARD'S is available exclusively from LexisNexis®.

APPEARANCES OF COUNSEL ARGUING CASE

Derek L. Schmidt argued the cause for petitioner on the burden question.

Stephen R. McAllister argued the cause for petitioner on the severance question.

Rachel P. Kovner argued the cause for the United States, as amicus curiae, by special leave of court, on the severance question.

Jeffrey T. Green argued the cause for respondents in No. 14-449 and No. 14-452 on the burden question.

Neal K. Katyal argued the cause for respondent in No. 14-450 on the burden question.

Frederick Liu argued the cause for respondent in No. 14-450 on the severance question.

Jeffrey T. Green argued the cause for respondent in No. 14-449 on the severance question.

SYLLABUS BY REPORTER OF DECISIONS

A Kansas jury sentenced respondent Sidney Gleason to death for killing a co-conspirator and her boyfriend to cover up the robbery of an elderly man.

A Kansas jury sentenced respondents Reginald and Jonathan Carr, brothers, to death after a joint sentencing proceeding. Respondents were convicted of various charges stemming from a notorious crime spree that culminated in the brutal rape, robbery, kidnaping, and execution-style shooting of five young men and women.

The Kansas Supreme Court vacated the death sentences in each case, holding that the sentencing instructions violated the Eighth Amendment by failing "to affirmatively inform the jury that mitigating circumstances need only be proved to the satisfaction of the individual juror in that juror's sentencing decision and not beyond a reasonable doubt." It also held that the Carrs' Eighth Amendment right "to an individualized capital sentencing determination" was violated by the trial court's failure to sever their sentencing proceedings.

Held:

1. The Eighth Amendment does not require capital-sentencing courts to instruct a jury that mitigating circumstances need not be proved beyond a reasonable doubt. Pp. 117–122, 193 L. Ed. 2d, at 543-546.

(a) Because the Kansas Supreme Court left no doubt that its ruling was based on the Federal Constitution, Gleason's initial argument—that this Court lacks jurisdiction to hear his case because the state court's decision rested on adequate and independent state-law grounds—is rejected. See *Kansas* v. *Marsh*, 548 U.S. 163, 169, 126 S. Ct. 2516, 165 L. Ed. 2d 429. Pp. 117–118, 193 L. Ed. 2d, at 543-544.

(b) This Court's capital-sentencing case law does not support requiring a court to instruct a jury that mitigating circumstances need not be proved beyond a reasonable doubt. See, *e.g.*, *Buchanan* v. *Angelone*, 522 U.S. 269, 275, 118 S. Ct. 757, 139 L. Ed. 2d 702. Nor was such an instruction constitutionally necessary in these particular cases to avoid confusion. Ambiguity in capital-sentencing instructions gives rise to constitutional error only if "there is a reasonable likelihood that the jury has applied the challenged instruction in a way that prevents the consideration of constitutionally relevant evidence," *Boyde* v. *California*, 494 U.S. 370, 380, 110 S. Ct. 1190, 108 L. Ed. 2d 316, a bar not cleared here. Even assuming that it would be unconstitutional to require the defense to prove mitigating circumstances beyond a reasonable doubt, the record belies the defendants' contention that the instructions caused jurors to apply such a standard of proof here. The instructions make clear that both the existence of aggravating circumstances and the conclusion that they outweigh mitigating circumstances must be proved beyond a reasonable doubt but that mitigating circumstances must merely be "found to exist," which does not suggest proof beyond a reasonable doubt. No juror would have reasonably speculated that "beyond a reasonable doubt" was the correct burden for mitigating circumstances. Pp. 118–122, 193 L. Ed. 2d, at 544-546.

2. The Constitution did not require severance of the Carrs' joint sentencing proceedings. The Eighth Amendment is inapposite when a defendant's claim is, at bottom, that evidence was improperly admitted at a capital-sentencing proceeding. The question is whether the allegedly improper evidence "so infected the sentencing proceeding with unfairness as to render the jury's imposition of the death penalty a denial of due process." *Romano* v. *Oklahoma*, 512 U.S. 1, 12, 114 S. Ct. 2004, 129 L. Ed. 2d 1. In light of all the evidence presented at the guilt and penalty phases relevant to the jury's sentencing determination, the contention that the admission of mitigating evidence by one Carr brother could have "so infected" the jury's consideration of the other's sentence as to amount to a denial of due process is beyond the pale. The Court presumes that the jury followed its instructions to "give separate consideration to each defendant." *Bruton* v. *United States*, 391 U.S. 123, 88 S. Ct. 1620, 20 L. Ed. 2d 476, distinguished. Joint proceedings are permissible and often preferable when the joined defendants' criminal conduct arises out of a single chain of events. *Buchanan* v. *Kentucky*, 483 U.S. 402, 418, 107 S. Ct. 2906, 97 L. Ed. 2d 336. Limiting instructions, like those given in the Carrs' proceeding, "often will suffice to cure any risk of prejudice," *Zafiro* v. *United States*, 506 U.S. 534, 539, 113 S. Ct. 933, 122 L. Ed. 2d 317, that might arise from codefendants' "antagonistic" mitigation theories, *id.*, at 538, 113 S. Ct. 933, 122 L. Ed. 2d 317. It is improper to vacate a death sentence based on pure "speculation" of fundamental unfairness, "rather than reasoned judgment." *Romano, supra,* at 13-14, 114 S. Ct. 2004, 129 L. Ed. 2d 1. Only the most extravagant speculation would lead to the conclusion that any supposedly prejudicial evidence rendered the Carr brothers' joint sentencing proceeding fundamentally unfair when their acts of almost inconceivable cruelty and depravity were described in excruciating detail by the sole survivor, who, for two days, relived the Wichita Massacre with the jury. Pp. 122–126, 193 L. Ed. 2d, at 546-549.

No. 14-449, 300 Kan. 340, 329 P.3d 1195; No. 14-450, 300 Kan. 1, 331 P.3d 544; and No. 14-452, 299 Kan. 1127, 329 P.3d 1102, reversed and remanded.

Scalia, J., delivered the opinion of the Court, in which Roberts, C. J., and Kennedy, Thomas, Ginsburg, Breyer, Alito, and Kagan, JJ., joined. Sotomayor, J., filed a dissenting opinion.

OPINION OF THE COURT

[577 U.S. 110]

Justice **Scalia** delivered the opinion of the Court.

The Supreme Court of Kansas vacated the death sentences of Sidney Gleason and brothers Reginald and Jonathan Carr.

[577 U.S. 111]

Gleason killed one of his co-conspirators and her boyfriend to cover up the robbery of an elderly man. The Carrs' notorious Wichita crime spree culminated in the brutal rape, robbery, kidnaping, and execution-style shooting of five young men and women. We first consider whether the Constitution required the sentencing courts to instruct the juries that mitigating circumstances "need not be proved beyond a reasonable doubt." And second, whether the Constitution required severance of the Carrs' joint sentencing proceedings.

I

A

Less than one month after Sidney Gleason was paroled from his sentence for attempted voluntary manslaughter, he joined a conspiracy to rob an elderly man at knifepoint.[1] Gleason and a companion "cut up" the elderly man to get $10 to $35 and a box of cigarettes. 299 Kan. 1127, 1136, 329 P.3d 1102, 1115 (2014). Fearing that their female co-conspirators would snitch, Gleason and his cousin, Damien Thompson, set out to kill co-conspirator Mikiala Martinez. Gleason shot and killed Martinez's boyfriend, and then Gleason and Thompson drove Martinez to a rural location, where Thompson strangled her for five minutes and then shot her in the chest, Gleason standing by and providing the gun for the final shot.

The State ultimately charged Gleason with capital murder for killing Martinez and her boyfriend, first-degree premeditated murder of the boyfriend, aggravating kidnaping of

Martinez, attempted first-degree murder and aggravated robbery of the elderly man, and criminal possession of a firearm. He was convicted on all counts except the attempted first-degree murder charge. *Id.*, at 1134-1135,

[577 U.S. 112]

1146, 329 P.3d, at 1114, 1120. The jury also found that the State proved beyond a reasonable doubt the existence of four aggravating circumstances and unanimously agreed to a sentence of death. *Id.*, at 1146-1147, 329 P.3d, at 1120-1121.

B

In December 2000, brothers Reginald and Jonathan Carr set out on a crime spree culminating in the Wichita Massacre.[2] On the night of December 7, Reginald Carr and an unknown man carjacked Andrew Schreiber, held a gun to his head, and forced him to make cash withdrawals at various ATMs.

On the night of December 11, the brothers followed Linda Ann Walenta, a cellist for the Wichita symphony, home from orchestra practice. One of them approached her vehicle and said he needed help. When she rolled down her window, he pointed a gun at her head. When she shifted into reverse to escape, he shot her three times, ran back to his brother's car, and fled the scene. One of the gunshots severed Walenta's spine, and she died one month later as a result of her injuries.

On the night of December 14, the brothers burst into a triplex at 12727

---

1. The facts for this portion of the opinion come from the Kansas Supreme Court, 299 Kan. 1127, 1134-1147, 329 P.3d 1102, 1113-1121 (2014), and the parties' briefs.

2. The facts for this portion of the opinion come from the Kansas Supreme Court, 300 Kan. 1, 18-38, 331 P.3d 544, 575-586 (2014), and witness testimony. See 21-A Tr. 59-75 (Oct. 7, 2002), 22-B Tr. 39-124 (Oct. 8, 2002), 23-A Tr. 4-118 (Oct. 9, 2002), 23-B Tr. 5-133 (Oct. 9, 2002), and 24-A Tr. 4-93 (Oct. 10, 2002).

Birchwood, where roommates Jason, Brad, and Aaron lived. Jason's girlfriend, Holly, and Heather, a friend of Aaron's, were also in the house. Armed with handguns and a golf club, the brothers forced all five into Jason's bedroom. They demanded that they strip naked and later ordered them into the bedroom closet. They took Holly and Heather from the bedroom, demanded that they perform oral sex and digitally penetrate each other as the Carrs looked on and barked orders. They forced each of the men to have

[577 U.S. 113]

sex with Holly and then with Heather. They yelled that the men would be shot if they could not have sex with the women, so Holly—fearing for Jason's life—performed oral sex on him in the closet before he was ordered out by the brothers.

Jonathan then snatched Holly from the closet. He ordered that she digitally penetrate herself. He set his gun between her knees on the floor. And he raped her. Then he raped Heather.

Reginald took Brad, Jason, Holly, and Aaron one-by-one to various ATMs to withdraw cash. When the victims returned to the house, their torture continued. Holly urinated in the closet because of fright. Jonathan found an engagement ring hidden in the bedroom that Jason was keeping as a surprise for Holly. Pointing his gun at Jason, he had Jason identify the ring while Holly was sitting nearby in the closet. Then Reginald took Holly from the closet, said he was not going to shoot her yet, and raped her on the dining-room floor strewn with boxes of Christmas decorations. He forced her to turn around, ejaculated into her mouth, and forced her to swallow. In a nearby bathroom, Jonathan again raped Heather and then again raped Holly.

At 2 a.m.—three hours after the mayhem began—the brothers decided it was time to leave the house. They attempted to put all five victims in the trunk of Aaron's Honda Civic. Finding that they would not all fit, they jammed the three young men into the trunk. They directed Heather to the front of the car and Holly to Jason's pickup truck, driven by Reginald. Once the vehicles arrived at a snow-covered field, they instructed Jason and Brad, still naked, and Aaron to kneel in the snow. Holly cried, "Oh, my God, they're going to shoot us." Holly and Heather were then ordered to kneel in the snow. Holly went to Jason's side; Heather, to Aaron.

Holly heard the first shot, heard Aaron plead with the brothers not to shoot, heard the second shot, heard the

[577 U.S. 114]

screams, heard the third shot, and the fourth. She felt the blow of the fifth shot to her head, but remained kneeling. They kicked her so she would fall face-first into the snow and ran her over in the pickup truck. But she survived, because a hair clip she had fastened to her hair that night deflected the bullet. She went to Jason, took off her sweater, the only scrap of clothing the brothers had let her wear, and tied it around his head to stop the bleeding from his eye. She rushed to Brad, then Aaron, and then Heather.

Spotting a house with white Christmas lights in the distance, Holly started running toward it for help—naked, skull shattered, and without shoes, through the snow and over barbed-wire fences. Each time a car passed on the nearby road, she feared it was the brothers returning and camouflaged herself by lying down in the snow. She made it to the house, rang the doorbell, knocked. A man

541

opened the door, and she relayed as quickly as she could the events of the night to him, and minutes later to a 911 dispatcher, fearing that she would not live.

Holly lived, and retold this play-by-play of the night's events to the jury. Investigators also testified that the brothers returned to the Birchwood house after leaving the five friends for dead, where they ransacked the place for valuables and (for good measure) beat Holly's dog, Nikki, to death with a golf club.

The State charged each of the brothers with more than 50 counts, including murder, rape, sodomy, kidnaping, burglary, and robbery, and the jury returned separate guilty verdicts. It convicted Reginald of one count of kidnaping, aggravated robbery, aggravated battery, and criminal damage to property for the Schreiber carjacking, and one count of first-degree felony murder for the Walenta shooting. Jonathan was acquitted of all counts related to the Schreiber carjacking but convicted of first-degree felony murder for the Walenta shooting. For the Birchwood murders, the jury convicted

[577 U.S. 115]

each brother of 4 counts of capital murder, 1 count of attempted first-degree murder, 5 counts of aggravated kidnaping, 9 counts of aggravated robbery, 20 counts of rape or attempted rape, 3 counts of aggravated criminal sodomy, 1 count each of aggravated burglary and burglary, 1 count of theft, and 1 count of cruelty to animals. The jury also convicted Reginald of three counts of unlawful possession of a firearm. 300 Kan. 1, 15-16, 331 P.3d 544, 573-574 (2014).

The State sought the death penalty for each of the four Birchwood mur-

ders, and the brothers were sentenced together. The State relied on the guilt-phase evidence, including Holly's two days of testimony, as evidence of four aggravating circumstances: that the defendants knowingly or purposely killed or created a great risk of death to more than one person; that they committed the crimes for the purpose of receiving money or items of monetary value; that they committed the crimes to prevent arrest or prosecution; and that they committed the crimes in an especially heinous, atrocious, or cruel manner. *Id.*, at 258-259, 331 P.3d, at 708. After hearing each brother's case for mitigation, the jury issued separate verdicts of death for Reginald and Jonathan. It found unanimously that the State proved the existence of the four aggravating circumstances beyond a reasonable doubt and that those aggravating circumstances outweighed the mitigating circumstances, justifying four separate verdicts of death for each brother for the murders of Jason, Brad, Aaron, and Heather. App. in No. 14-449 etc., pp. 461-492.

C

The Kansas Supreme Court vacated the death penalties in both cases. It held that the instructions used in both Gleason's and the Carrs' sentencing violated the Eighth Amendment because they "failed to affirmatively inform the jury that mitigating circumstances need only be proved to the satisfaction of the individual juror in that juror's sentencing decision and not beyond a reasonable doubt." 299 Kan., at

[577 U.S. 116]

1196, 329 P.3d, at 1147 (Gleason); 300 Kan., at 303, 331 P.3d, at 733 (Reginald Carr); 300 Kan. 340, 369-370, 329 P.3d 1195, 1213 (2014) (Jonathan Carr). Without that instruction, according to the court, the jury "was left to speculate as to the correct burden of proof for mitigating circumstances, and reasonable jurors might have believed they could not consider mitigating circumstances not proven beyond a reasonable doubt." 299 Kan., at 1197, 329 P.3d, at 1148. This, the court concluded, might have caused jurors to exclude relevant mitigating evidence from their consideration. *Ibid.*

The Kansas Supreme Court also held that the Carrs' death sentences had to be vacated because of the trial court's failure to sever their sentencing proceedings, thereby violating the brothers' Eighth Amendment right "to an individualized capital sentencing determination." 300 Kan., at 275, 331 P.3d, at 717; 300 Kan., at 368, 329 P.3d, at 1212. According to the court, the joint trial "inhibited the jury's individualized consideration of [Jonathan] because of family characteristics tending to demonstrate future dangerousness that he shared with his brother"; and his brother's visible handcuffs prejudiced the jury's consideration of his sentence. 300 Kan., at 275, 331 P.3d, at 717. As for Reginald, he was prejudiced, according to the Kansas Supreme Court, by Jonathan's portrayal of him as the corrupting older brother. *Id.*, at 276, 331 P.3d, at 717. Moreover, Reginald was prejudiced by his brother's cross-examination of their sister, who testified that she thought Reginald had admitted to her that he was the shooter. *Id.*, at 279, 331 P.3d, at 719. (She later backtracked and testified, " 'I don't remember who was, you know, shot by who[m].' " *Ibid.*) The Kansas Supreme Court opined that the presumption that the jury followed its instructions to consider each defendant separately was "defeated

by logic." *Id.*, at 280, 331 P.3d, at 719. "[T]he defendants' joint upbringing in the maelstrom that was their family and their influence on and interactions with one another . . .

[577 U.S. 117]

simply was not amenable to orderly separation and analysis." *Ibid.*, 331 P.3d, at 719-720. The Kansas Supreme Court found itself unable to "say that the death verdict was unattributable, at least in part, to this error." *Id.*, at 282, 331 P.3d, at 720. We granted certiorari. 575 U.S. 934, 135 S. Ct. 1698, 191 L. Ed. 2d 674 (2015).

II

We first turn to the Kansas Supreme Court's contention that the Eighth Amendment required these capital-sentencing courts to instruct the jury that mitigating circumstances need not be proved beyond a reasonable doubt.

A

Before considering the merits of that contention, we consider Gleason's challenge to our jurisdiction. According to Gleason, the Kansas Supreme Court's decision rests on adequate and independent state-law grounds. This argument is a familiar one. We rejected it in *Kansas* v. *Marsh*, 548 U.S. 163, 169, 126 S. Ct. 2516, 165 L. Ed. 2d 429 (2006). Like the defendant in that case, Gleason urges that the decision below rests only on a rule of Kansas law announced in *State* v. *Kleypas*, 272 Kan. 894, 40 P.3d 139 (2001) (*per curiam*)—a rule later reiterated in *State* v. *Scott*, 286 Kan. 54, 183 P.3d 801 (2008) (*per curiam*). As we stated in *Marsh*, "*Kleypas*, itself, rested on federal law." 548 U.S., at 169, 126 S. Ct. 2516, 165 L. Ed. 2d 429. So too does the relevant passage of *Scott*, which rested on *Kleypas*'s discussion of the constitutional rule that jurors need not agree on mitigating circumstances. See *Scott, supra*, at 106-107, 183 P.3d, at 837-838. The Kansas Supreme Court's opinion in this case acknowledged as much, saying that "statements from *Kleypas* implicate the broader Eighth Amendment principle prohibiting barriers that preclude a sentencer's consideration of all relevant mitigating evidence." 299 Kan., at 1195, 329 P.3d, at 1147.

The Kansas Supreme Court's opinion leaves no room for doubt that it was relying on the Federal Constitution. It

[577 U.S. 118]

stated that the instruction it required "protects a capital defendant's *Eighth Amendment* right to individualized sentencing," that the absence of the instruction "implicat[ed] Gleason's right to individualized sentencing under the *Eighth Amendment*," and that vacatur of Gleason's death sentence was the "[c]onsequen[ce]" of *Eighth Amendment* error. *Id.*, at 1196-1197, 329 P.3d, at 1147-1148 (emphasis added).

For this reason, the criticism leveled by the dissent is misdirected. It generally would have been "none of our business" had the Kansas Supreme Court vacated Gleason's and the Carrs' death sentences on state-law grounds. *Marsh*, 548 U.S., at 184, 126 S. Ct. 2516, 165 L. Ed. 2d 429 (Scalia, J., concurring). But it decidedly did not. And when the Kansas Supreme Court time and again invalidates death sentences because it says the Federal Constitution *requires* it, "review by this Court, far from *undermining* state autonomy, is the only possible way to *vindicate* it." *Ibid.* **[1]** "When we correct a state court's federal errors, *we return power to the*

State, and to its people." *Ibid.* The state courts may experiment all they want with their own constitutions, and often do in the wake of this Court's decisions. See Sutton, *San Antonio Independent School District v. Rodriguez And Its Aftermath*, 94 Va. L. Rev. 1963, 1971-1977 (2008). But what a state court cannot do is experiment with our Federal Constitution and expect to elude this Court's review so long as victory goes to the criminal defendant. "Turning a blind eye" in such cases "would change the uniform 'law of the land' into a crazy quilt." *Marsh, supra*, at 185, 126 S. Ct. 2516, 165 L. Ed. 2d 429. And it would enable state courts to blame the unpopular death-sentence reprieve of the most horrible criminals upon the Federal Constitution when it is in fact their own doing.

B

We turn, then, to the merits of the Kansas Supreme Court's conclusion that the Eighth Amendment requires capital-sentencing courts in Kansas "to affirmatively inform the jury that mitigating circumstances need not be proven

[577 U.S. 119]

beyond a reasonable doubt." 299 Kan., at 1197, 329 P.3d, at 1148.

Approaching the question in the abstract, and without reference to our capital-sentencing case law, we doubt whether it is even possible to apply a standard of proof to the mitigating-factor determination (the so-called "selection phase" of a capital-sentencing proceeding). It is possible to do so for the aggravating-factor determination (the so-called "eligibility phase"), because that is a purely factual determination. The facts justifying death set forth in the Kansas statute either did or did not exist— and one can require the finding that they did exist to be made beyond a reasonable doubt. Whether mitigation exists, however, is largely a judgment call (or perhaps a value call); what one juror might consider mitigating another might not. And of course the ultimate question whether mitigating circumstances outweigh aggravating circumstances is mostly a question of mercy—the quality of which, as we know, is not strained. It would mean nothing, we think, to tell the jury that the defendants must deserve mercy beyond a reasonable doubt; or must more-likely-than-not deserve it. It *would* be possible, of course, to instruct the jury that *the facts establishing* mitigating circumstances need only be proved by a preponderance, leaving the judgment whether those facts are indeed mitigating, and whether they outweigh the aggravators, to the jury's discretion without a standard of proof. If we were to hold that the Constitution requires the mitigating-factor determination to be divided into its factual component and its judgmental component, and the former to be accorded a burden-of-proof instruction, we doubt whether that would produce anything but jury confusion. In the last analysis, jurors will accord mercy if they deem it appropriate, and withhold mercy if they do not, which is what our case law is designed to achieve.

In any event, our case law does not require capital-sentencing courts "to affirmatively inform the jury that mitigating

[577 U.S. 120]

circumstances need not be proved beyond a reasonable doubt." *Ibid*. In *Buchanan* v. *Angelone*, 522 U.S. 269, 118 S. Ct. 757, 139 L. Ed. 2d 702 (1998), we upheld a death sentence even though the trial court "failed to provide the jury with ex-

press guidance on the concept of mitigation." *Id*., at 275, 118 S. Ct. 757, 139 L. Ed. 2d 702. Likewise in *Weeks* v. *Angelone*, 528 U.S. 225, 120 S. Ct. 727, 145 L. Ed. 2d 727 (2000), we reaffirmed that the Court has "never held that the State must structure in a particular way the manner in which juries consider mitigating evidence" and rejected the contention that it was constitutionally deficient to instruct jurors to " 'consider a mitigating circumstance if you find there is evidence to support it,' " without additional guidance. *Id*., at 232-233, 120 S. Ct. 727, 145 L. Ed. 2d 727.

Equally unavailing is the contention that even if an instruction that mitigating evidence need not be "proven beyond a reasonable doubt" is not always required, it was constitutionally necessary in *these* cases to avoid confusion. **[2]** Ambiguity in capital-sentencing instructions gives rise to constitutional error only if "there is a *reasonable likelihood* that the jury has applied the challenged instruction in a way that prevents the consideration of constitutionally relevant evidence." *Boyde* v. *California*, 494 U.S. 370, 380, 110 S. Ct. 1190, 108 L. Ed. 2d 316 (1990) (emphasis added). The alleged confusion stemming from the jury instructions used at the defendants' sentencings does not clear that bar. A meager "possibility" of confusion is not enough. *Ibid*.

As an initial matter, the defendants' argument rests on the assumption that it would be unconstitutional to require the defense to prove mitigating circumstances beyond a reasonable doubt. Assuming without deciding that that is the case, the record belies the defendants' contention that the instructions caused jurors to apply that standard of proof. The defendants focus upon the following instruction: "The State has the burden to prove beyond a reasonable doubt that there are one or more aggravating circumstances and that they are not outweighed by any mitigating circumstances

[577 U.S. 121]

found to exist." App. to Pet. for Cert. in No. 14-452, p. 133 (Instr. 8).[3] The juxtaposition of aggravating and mitigating circumstances, so goes the argument, caused the jury to speculate that mitigating circumstances must also be proved beyond a reasonable doubt. 299 Kan., at 1197, 329 P.3d, at 1148. It seems to us quite the opposite. The instruction makes clear that both the existence of aggravating circumstances and the conclusion that they outweigh mitigating circumstances must be proved beyond a reasonable doubt; mitigating circumstances themselves, on the other hand, must merely be "found to exist." That same description, mitigating circumstances *"found to exist,"* is contained in three other instructions, App. to Pet. for Cert. in No. 14-452, at 133 (Instrs. 7, 9, and 10) (emphasis added)—unsurprisingly, since it recites the Kansas statute, see Kan. Stat. Ann. § 21-4624(e) (1995). "Found to exist" certainly does not suggest proof beyond a reasonable doubt. The instructions as a whole distinguish clearly between aggravating and mitigating circumstances: *"The State* has the burden to prove beyond a reasonable doubt that there are one or more aggravating circumstances . . . ," and the jury must decide unanimously that the State met that burden. App. to Pet. for Cert. in No. 14-452, at 133 (Instrs. 8 and 10) (emphasis added). "[M]itigating circumstances," on the other hand, "do not need to be found by all members of the jury" to "be

considered by an individual juror in arriving at his or her sentencing decision." *Id.*, at 131 (Instr. 7). Not once do the instructions say that defense counsel bears the burden of proving the facts constituting a mitigating circumstance beyond a reasonable doubt—nor would that make much sense, since one of the mitigating circumstances is (curiously) "mercy," which simply is not a factual determination.

[577 U.S. 122]

We reject the Kansas Supreme Court's decision that jurors were "left to speculate as to the correct burden of proof for mitigating circumstances." 299 Kan., at 1197, 329 P.3d, at 1148. For the reasons we have described, no juror would reasonably have speculated that mitigating circumstances must be proved by any particular standard, let alone beyond a reasonable doubt. The reality is that jurors do not "pars[e] instructions for subtle shades of meaning in the same way that lawyers might." *Boyde, supra*, at 381, 110 S. Ct. 1190, 108 L. Ed. 2d 316. The instructions repeatedly told the jurors to consider *any* mitigating factor, meaning any aspect of the defendants' background or the circumstances of their offense. Jurors would not have misunderstood these instructions to prevent their consideration of constitutionally relevant evidence.

III

We turn next to the contention that a joint capital-sentencing proceeding in the Carrs' cases violated the defendants' Eighth Amendment right to an "individualized sentencing determination." 300 Kan., at 276, 331 P.3d, at 717.

---

3. The relevant penalty-phase instructions from the Carrs' sentencing proceedings are materially indistinguishable. See App. to Pet. for Cert. in No. 14-450, pp. 501-510.

The Kansas Supreme Court agreed with the defendants that, because of the joint sentencing proceeding, one defendant's mitigating evidence put a thumb on death's scale for the other, in violation of the other's Eighth Amendment rights. *Ibid.* It accepted Reginald's contention that he was prejudiced by his brother's portrayal of him as the corrupting older brother. And it agreed that Reginald was prejudiced by his brother's cross-examination of their sister, who equivocated about whether Reginald admitted to her that he was the shooter. (Reginald has all but abandoned that implausible theory of prejudice before this Court and contends only that the State "likely would not have introduced any such testimony" had he been sentenced alone. Brief for Respondent in No. 14-450, p. 34, n. 3.) Jonathan asserted that he was prejudiced by evidence associating him with his dangerous older brother, which caused the jury to perceive him

[577 U.S. 123]

as an incurable socio-path.[4] Both speculate that the evidence assertedly prejudicial to them would have been inadmissible in severed proceedings under Kansas law. The Kansas Supreme Court also launched a broader attack on the joint proceedings, contending that the joinder rendered it impossible for the jury to consider the Carrs' relative moral culpability and to determine individually whether they were entitled to "mercy." 300 Kan., at 278, 331 P.3d, at 718-719.

Whatever the merits of defendants' procedural objections, we will not shoe-horn them into the Eighth Amendment's prohibition of "cruel and unusual punishments." As the United States as *amicus curiae* intimates, [3] the Eighth Amendment is inapposite when each defendant's claim is, at bottom, that the jury considered evidence that would not have been admitted in a severed proceeding, and that the joint trial clouded the jury's consideration of mitigating evidence like "mercy." Brief for United States 24, n. 8. As we held in *Romano* v. *Oklahoma*, 512 U.S. 1, 114 S. Ct. 2004, 129 L. Ed. 2d 1 (1994), it is not the role of the Eighth Amendment to establish a special "federal code of evidence" governing "the admissibility of evidence at capital sentencing proceedings." *Id.*, at 11-12, 114 S. Ct. 2004, 129 L. Ed. 2d 1. Rather, it is the Due Process Clause that wards off the introduction of "unduly prejudicial" evidence that would "rende[r] the trial fundamentally unfair." *Payne* v. *Tennessee*, 501 U.S. 808, 825, 111 S. Ct. 2597, 115 L. Ed. 2d 720 (1991); see also *Brown* v. *Sanders*, 546 U.S. 212, 220-221, 126 S. Ct. 884, 163 L. Ed. 2d 723 (2006).

The test prescribed by *Romano* for a constitutional violation attributable to evidence improperly admitted at a capital-sentencing proceeding is whether the evidence "so infected the sentencing proceeding with unfairness as to render

[577 U.S. 124]

the jury's imposition of the death penalty a denial of due process." 512 U.S., at 12, 114 S. Ct. 2004, 129 L. Ed. 2d 1. The mere admission of evidence that might not otherwise have been admitted in a

---

4. Jonathan also alleges that he was prejudiced by the jury's witnessing his brother's handcuffs, which his brother requested remain visible before the penalty phase commenced. That allegation is mystifying. That his brother's handcuffs were visible (while his own restraints were not) more likely caused the jury to see Jonathan as the *less* dangerous of the two.

severed proceeding does not demand the automatic vacatur of a death sentence.

In light of all the evidence presented at the guilt and penalty phases relevant to the jury's sentencing determination, the contention that the admission of mitigating evidence by one brother could have "so infected" the jury's consideration of the other's sentence as to amount to a denial of due process is beyond the pale. To begin with, the court instructed the jury that it "must give separate consideration to each defendant," that each was "entitled to have his sentence decided on the evidence and law which is applicable to him," and that any evidence in the penalty phase "limited to only one defendant should not be considered by you as to the other defendant." App. to Pet. for Cert. in No. 14-450, at 501 (Instr. 3). The court gave defendant-specific instructions for aggravating and mitigating circumstances. *Id.*, at 502-508 (Instrs. 5, 6, 7, and 8). And the court instructed the jury to consider the "individual" or "particular defendant" by using four separate verdict forms for each defendant, one for each murdered occupant of the Birchwood house. *Id.*, at 509 (Instr. 10); App. in No. 14-449 etc., at 461-492. We presume the jury followed these instructions and considered each defendant separately when deciding to impose a sentence of death for each of the brutal murders. *Romano, supra*, at 13, 114 S. Ct. 2004, 129 L. Ed. 2d 1.

The contrary conclusion of the Kansas Supreme Court—that the presumption that jurors followed these instructions was "defeated by logic," 300 Kan., at 280, 331 P.3d, at 719—is untenable. The Carrs implausibly liken the prejudice resulting from the joint sentencing proceeding to the prejudice infecting the joint trial in *Bruton* v. *United States*, 391 U.S. 123, 88 S. Ct. 1620, 20 L. Ed. 2d 476 (1968), where the prosecution admitted hearsay evidence of a codefendant's confession implicating the defendant.

[577 U.S. 125]
That particular violation of the defendant's confrontation rights, incriminating evidence of the most persuasive sort, ineradicable, as a practical matter, from the jury's mind, justified what we have described as a narrow departure from the presumption that jurors follow their instructions, *Richardson* v. *Marsh*, 481 U.S. 200, 207, 107 S. Ct. 1702, 95 L. Ed. 2d 176 (1987). We have declined to extend that exception, *id.*, at 211, 107 S. Ct. 1702, 95 L. Ed. 2d 176, and have continued to apply the presumption to instructions regarding mitigating evidence in capital-sentencing proceedings, see, *e.g., Weeks*, 528 U.S., at 234, 120 S. Ct. 727, 145 L. Ed. 2d 727. There is no reason to think the jury could not follow its instruction to consider the defendants separately in this case.

[4] Joint proceedings are not only permissible but are often preferable when the joined defendants' criminal conduct arises out of a single chain of events. Joint trial may enable a jury "to arrive more reliably at its conclusions regarding the guilt or innocence of a particular defendant and to assign fairly the respective responsibilities of each defendant in the sentencing." *Buchanan* v. *Kentucky*, 483 U.S. 402, 418, 107 S. Ct. 2906, 97 L. Ed. 2d 336 (1987). That the codefendants might have "antagonistic" theories of mitigation, *Zafiro* v. *United States*, 506 U.S. 534, 538, 113 S. Ct. 933, 122 L. Ed. 2d 317 (1993), does not suffice to overcome Kansas's "interest in pro-

moting the reliability and consistency of its judicial process," *Buchanan, supra*, at 418, 107 S. Ct. 2906, 97 L. Ed. 2d 336. Limiting instructions, like those used in the Carrs' sentencing proceeding, "often will suffice to cure any risk of prejudice." *Zafiro, supra*, at 539, 113 S. Ct. 933, 122 L. Ed. 2d 317 (citing *Richardson, supra*, at 211, 107 S. Ct. 1702, 95 L. Ed. 2d 176). To forbid joinder in capital-sentencing proceedings would, perversely, *increase* the odds of "wanto[n] and freakis[h]" imposition of death sentences. *Gregg* v. *Georgia*, 428 U.S. 153, 206-207, 96 S. Ct. 2909, 49 L. Ed. 2d 859 (1976) (joint opinion of Stewart, Powell, and Stevens, JJ.). Better that two defendants who have together committed the same crimes be placed side-by-side to have their fates determined by a single jury.

[5] It is improper to vacate a death sentence based on pure "speculation" of fundamental unfairness, "rather than reasoned

[577 U.S. 126]

judgment," *Romano, supra*, at 13-14, 114 S. Ct. 2004, 129 L. Ed. 2d 1. Only the most extravagant speculation would lead to the conclusion that the supposedly prejudicial evidence rendered the Carr brothers' joint sentencing proceeding fundamentally unfair. It is beyond reason to think that the jury's death verdicts were caused by the identification of Reginald as the "corrupter" or of Jonathan as the "corrupted," the jury's viewing of Reginald's handcuffs, or the sister's retracted statement that Reginald fired the final shots. None of that mattered. What these defendants did—acts of almost inconceivable cruelty and depravity—was described in excruciating detail by Holly, who relived with the jury, for two days, the Wichita Massacre. The joint sentencing proceedings did not render the sentencing proceedings fundamentally unfair.

IV

When we granted the State's petition for a writ of certiorari for the Carrs' cases, we declined to review whether the Confrontation Clause, U.S. Const., Amdt. 6, requires that defendants be allowed to cross-examine witnesses whose statements are recorded in police reports referred to by the State in penalty-phase proceedings. The Kansas Supreme Court did not make the admission of those statements a basis for its vacating of the death sentences, but merely "caution[ed]" that in the resentencing proceedings these out-of-court testimonial statements should be omitted, 300 Kan., at 288, 331 P.3d, at 724. We are confident that cross-examination regarding these police reports would not have had the slightest effect upon the sentences. See *Delaware* v. *Van Arsdall*, 475 U.S. 673, 684, 106 S. Ct. 1431, 89 L. Ed. 2d 674 (1986).

* * *

The judgments of the Supreme Court of Kansas are reversed, and these cases are remanded for further proceedings not inconsistent with this opinion.

It is so ordered.

[577 U.S. 127]

SEPARATE OPINION

Justice **Sotomayor**, dissenting.

I respectfully dissent because I do not believe these cases should ever have been reviewed by the Supreme Court. I see no reason to intervene in cases like these—and plenty of reasons not to. Kansas has not violated any federal constitutional right. If anything, the State has overprotected its citizens based on its interpretation of state and federal law. For reasons ably articulated by my predecessors and colleagues and because I worry that cases like these prevent States from serving as necessary laboratories for experimenting with how best to guarantee defendants a fair trial, I would dismiss the writs as improvidently granted.

I

In 2014, the Kansas Supreme Court vacated three death sentences—the sentences of Sidney Gleason and the Carr brothers, Reginald and Jonathan—because of constitutional errors in the penalty phases of their trials.

All three men were tried under jury instructions that did not include language previously mandated by the Kansas Supreme Court. The instructions did not state that, under Kansas' statutory scheme, mitigating circumstances need only be proved to an individual juror's satisfaction and not beyond a reasonable doubt. 299 Kan. 1127, 1192-1197, 329 P.3d 1102, 1145-1148 (2014) (Sidney Gleason); 300 Kan. 1, 302-303, 331 P.3d 544, 732-733 (2014) (Reginald Carr); 300 Kan. 340, 368-369, 329 P.3d 1195, 1213 (2014) (Jonathan Carr). The court found that the instructions therefore both undermined Kansas' state law and created a "reasonable likelihood that the jury . . . applied the challenged instruction in a way that prevents consideration" of mitigating evidence as required by the Federal Constitution. 299 Kan., at 1191-1197, 329 P.3d, at 1144-1148 (quoting *Boyde v. California*, 494 U.S. 370, 380, 110 S. Ct. 1190, 108 L. Ed. 2d 316 (1990)).

The Kansas Supreme Court also vacated the Carr brothers' death sentences because they were jointly tried at the

[577 U.S. 128]

penalty phase. The court concluded that each brother's particular case for mitigation compromised the other brother's case and therefore that trying them jointly violated the Eighth Amendment right to individualized sentencing. The error was not harmless, the Kansas Supreme Court found, because an "especially damning subset" of the evidence presented might not have been admitted in separate penalty proceedings. 300 Kan., at 275-282, 331 P.3d, at 717-720; 300 Kan., at 369-370, 329 P.3d, at 1212.

The Kansas attorney general requested certiorari, alleging that it would best serve the State's interest for a federal court to intervene and correct the Kansas Supreme Court. This Court complied, even though there was no suggestion that the Kansas Supreme Court had violated any federal constitutional right. The majority now reverses the Kansas Supreme Court on both points.

II

A

Even where a state court has wrongly decided an "important question of federal law," this Court's Rule 10, we often decline to grant certiorari, instead reserving such grants for instances where the benefits of hearing a case outweigh the costs of so doing. My colleagues and predecessors have effectively set forth many of the costs of granting certiorari in cases where state courts grant relief to criminal defendants: We risk issuing opinions that, while not strictly advisory, may have little effect if a lower court is able to reinstate its holding as a matter of state law. *Florida* v. *Powell*, 559 U.S. 50, 66, 130 S. Ct. 1195, 175 L. Ed. 2d 1009 (2010) (Stevens, J., dissenting). We expend resources on cases where the only concern is that a State has "'overprotected'" its citizens. *Michigan* v. *Long*, 463 U.S. 1032, 1068, 103 S. Ct. 3469, 77 L. Ed. 2d 1201 (1983) (Stevens, J., dissenting). We intervene in an intrastate dispute between the State's executive and its judiciary rather than entrusting the State's structure of government to sort it out. See *Coleman* v. *Thompson*, 501 U.S.

[577 U.S. 129]

722, 766-767, 111 S. Ct. 2546, 115 L. Ed. 2d 640 (1991) (Blackmun, J., dissenting). And we lose valuable data about the best methods of protecting constitutional rights—a particular concern in cases like these, where the federal constitutional question turns on the "reasonable likelihood" of jury confusion, an empirical question best answered with evidence from many state courts. Cf. *Arizona* v. *Evans*, 514 U.S. 1, 30-31, 115 S. Ct. 1185, 131 L. Ed. 2d 34 (1995) (Ginsburg, J., dissenting).

B

The cases here demonstrate yet another cost of granting certiorari to correct a state court's overprotection of federal rights: In explaining that the Federal Constitution does not protect some particular right, it is natural to buttress the conclusion by explaining why that right is not very important. In so doing, the Court risks discouraging States from adopting valuable procedural protections even as a matter of their own state law.

State experimentation with how best to guarantee a fair trial to criminal defendants is an essential aspect of our federalism scheme. See, *e.g.*, Linde, First Things First: Rediscovering the States' Bill of Rights, 9 U. Balt. L. Rev. 379, 393 (1980). The Federal Constitution guarantees only a minimum slate of protections; States can and do provide individual rights above that constitutional floor. See, *e.g.*, Brennan, The Bill of Rights and the States: the Revival of State Constitutions as Guardians of Constitutional Rights, 61 N. Y. U. L. Rev. 535, 548-550 (1986). That role is particularly important in the criminal arena because state courts preside over many millions more criminal cases than their federal counterparts and so are more likely to identify protections important to a fair trial. Compare Court Statistics Project, Examining the Work of State Courts: An Analysis of 2010 State Court Caseloads 19-21 (2012), with Dept. of Justice, Bureau of Justice Statistics, Federal Justice Statistics 2011-2012, pp. 19-20 (Jan. 2015) (Tables 11 and 12).

[577 U.S. 130]

The majority's opinion in these cases illustrates how an unnecessary grant of certiorari can lead to unexpected costs by disrupting this sort of state experimentation. Take the first question presented in these cases. The majority's actual holding is that the Eighth Amendment does not require an instruction specifying that mitigating factors need not be proved beyond a reasonable doubt. *Ante*, at 119–121, 193 L. Ed. 2d, at 544-546. The Eighth Amendment has nothing to say about whether such an instruction is wise as a question of state law or policy. But the majority nonetheless uses this Court's considerable influence to call into question the logic of specifying *any* burden of proof as to mitigating circumstances. The majority claims that while assessing an aggravating factor is "a purely factual determination," assessing mitigation involves "a judgment call (or perhaps a value call)" and is thus not amenable to burdens of proof. *Ante*, at 119, 193 L. Ed. 2d, at 545. Short of dividing the mitigating factor "into its factual component and its judgmental component," and issuing burden-of-proof instructions only as to the former, the majority wonders "whether it is even possible to apply a standard of proof to the mitigating-factor determination." *Ibid.*

By this observation, and with no experience with the needs of juries, the majority denigrates the many States that *do* specify a burden of proof for the existence of mitigating factors as a matter of state law, presumably under the belief that it is, in fact, "possible" to do so.* Brief for Respondent in No. 14-452, pp. 28-29, and n. 6. Some States even recommend an instruction specifying that mitigating factors need not be proven beyond a reasonable doubt. See, *e.g.*, Idaho

[577 U.S. 131]

Jury Instr., Crim., ICJI 1718, Jury Deliberations (2010); Okla. Jury Instr., Crim, OUJI-CR 4-78 (2015).

The majority's discussion of severance likewise short circuits state experimentation. The majority is not content to hold that the Eighth Amendment does not, strictly speaking, require severance of capital penalty proceedings. Instead, it goes on to explain why joint capital sentencing proceedings are not only permissible under the Federal Constitution but are, in fact, preferable as a policy matter: "Better that two defendants who have together committed the same crimes be placed side-by-side to have their fates determined by a single jury." *Ante*, at 125, 193 L. Ed. 2d, at 549. The majority even intimates that severed proceedings may be worse for defendants: "To forbid joinder in capital-sentencing proceedings would, perversely, *increase* the odds of 'wanto[n] and freakis[h]' imposition of death sentences." *Ibid.* (quoting *Gregg* v. *Georgia*, 428 U.S. 153, 206-207, 96 S. Ct. 2909, 49 L. Ed. 2d 859 (1976) (joint opinion of Stewart, Powell, and Stevens, JJ.).

So much for Ohio's, Georgia's, and Mississippi's sentencing regimes, all of which routinely allow severance at both phases of capital proceedings. See Ga. Code Ann. § 17-8-4 (2013) (upon request, defendants must be tried separately in capital cases); Miss. Code Ann. § 99-15-47 (2015) (same); Ohio Rev. Code Ann. § 2945.20 (Lexis 2014) (capital defendants shall be tried separately unless good cause is shown for a joint trial). There is no evidence that any of those three States adopted a severance regime based on a misunderstanding of the Eighth Amendment. But without any empirical foundation or any basis in experience, the majority asserts that such regimes may increase the odds of arbitrariness.

The majority claims that we " 'return power to the State, and to its people,' " when we explain that the Federal Constitution does not require a particular result. *Ante*, at 118, 193 L. Ed. 2d, at 544 (emphasis deleted). But that is only so when the Court is

---

* I leave aside the merits of the majority's questionable distinction, though I cannot see how the jury's conclusion that the Carr brothers committed their crime "in an especially heinous, atrocious or cruel manner"—one of the aggravating circumstances found by the Carr brothers' jury— involved any less of a judgment or value call than the mitigating circumstances alleged. See 300 Kan. 1, 282-283, 331 P.3d 544, 721 (2014).

able to pass solely on the federal constitutional ground and

[577 U.S. 132]

not the wisdom of a state holding on an equivalent question. Though the Court pretends that it sends back cases like this one with a clean slate, it rarely fully erases its thoughts on the virtues of the procedural protection at issue. By placing a thumb on the scale against a State adopting—even as a matter of state law—procedural protections the Constitution does not require, the Court risks turning the Federal Constitution into a ceiling, rather than a floor, for the protection of individual liberties.

III

I see no reason why these three cases out of the Kansas Supreme Court warranted our intervention given the costs that I have just described and those described by my predecessors and colleagues, see *supra*, at 128–129, 193 L. Ed. 2d, at 550–551. No federal right has been compromised. And nobody disputes that the State of Kansas could, as a matter of state law, reach the same outcome.

Perhaps most importantly, both of the questions on which the Court granted certiorari turn on specific features of Kansas' sentencing scheme. As a result, the Kansas Supreme Court's opinion is unlikely to have much salience for other States. If the Kansas Supreme Court was wrong, its wrong opinion will not subvert federal law on a broader scale.

First, the Kansas court's decision on the jury instruction question aimed to "*both* preserv[e] the [state] statute's favorable distinction *and* protec[t] a capital defendant's Eighth Amendment right to individualized sentencing by ensuring jurors are not precluded from considering all relevant mitigating evidence." 299 Kan., at 1196, 329 P.3d, at 1147 (emphasis added). The Kansas Supreme Court's decision was thus informed by a combination of federal and state considerations. A decision that expressly relies on a State's unique statutory scheme—as did the Kansas Supreme Court's here—has limited potential for influencing other States.

It is not absurd to conclude that a juror unfamiliar with the mechanics of the law might be confused by Kansas' jury

[577 U.S. 133]

instructions, which almost always mention aggravating and mitigating instructions in the same breath. *Id.*, at 1196-1197, 329 P.3d, at 1147-1148. The Kansas Supreme Court's opinion rested largely on the specific language and ordering of that State's instructions. Other States' jury instructions may be less likely to have the same effect.

Moreover, the decision below was made against the unique backdrop of trial courts' failure to implement the Kansas Supreme Court's earlier demands for a change to jury instructions in capital cases. In a 2001 case, the Kansas Supreme Court considered the jury instructions insufficiently confusing to reverse the judgment, but sufficiently confusing to demand higher clarity going forward: "[A]ny instruction dealing with the consideration of mitigating circumstances should state (1) they need to be proved only to the satisfaction of the individual juror in the juror's sentencing decision and not beyond a reasonable doubt and (2) mitigating circumstances do not need to be found by all members of the jury in order to be considered in an individual juror's sentencing decision." *State* v. *Kleypas*, 272 Kan. 894, 1078, 40 P.3d 139, 268.

The Kansas pattern instructions were then revised to include consideration (2), but—"inexplicably," as the court noted in *Gleason*—not consideration (1). 299 Kan., at 1193, 329 P.3d, at 1145. The Kansas Supreme Court reiterated the two requirements for any jury instruction in 2008, see *State* v. *Scott*, 286 Kan. 54, 106-108, 183 P.3d 801, 837, and the pattern instructions were finally changed in 2011, see 299 Kan., at 1193, 329 P.3d, at 1145. But Gleason and the Carr brothers were tried in the 10-year delay between the Kansas Supreme Court's initial admonition and when the jury instructions were finally edited. The Kansas Supreme Court's opinion in *Gleason* may have rested in part on a "broader Eighth Amendment principle," but it also rested on some lower courts' failure to give instructions reflecting the Kansas Supreme Court's "repeated recognition of the required content." *Ibid.*, at 1195, 329 P.3d, at 1146, 1147.

[577 U.S. 134]

Given this context, the Kansas Supreme Court's decision is particularly unlikely to undermine other States or the Federal Constitution.

The same goes for the severance question. The Kansas Supreme Court's decision depended on the "especially damning subset" of the aggravating evidence presented that may not have been admitted in a severed proceeding under Kansas' capital punishment scheme and evidentiary rules, such as evidence that one brother was a bad influence on the other. *Ibid.* But the difference between a joint penalty phase and a severed penalty phase may be of limited significance in States where the same evidence may be admitted in joint and severed proceedings. Cf. *Brown* v. *Sanders*, 546 U.S. 212, 217, 126 S. Ct. 884, 163 L. Ed. 2d 723 (2006); L. Palmer, The Death Penalty in the United States: A Complete Guide to Federal and State Laws 137 (2d ed. 2014). It thus seems to me unlikely that the Kansas Supreme Court's opinion would have proven instructive in other States, even though it was couched in the language of the Federal Constitution.

IV

There may, of course, be rare cases where certiorari is warranted in which a state prosecutor alleges that a State's highest court has overprotected a criminal defendant. These circumstances may include: Where a state court's decision in favor of a criminal defendant implicates another constitutional right, see, *e.g.*, *Nebraska Press Ass'n* v. *Stuart*, 427 U.S. 539, 547, 96 S. Ct. 2791, 49 L. Ed. 2d 683 (1976); where a state court indicates a hostility to applying federal precedents, *Florida* v. *Meyers*, 466 U.S. 380, 383, 104 S. Ct. 1852, 80 L. Ed. 2d 381 (1984) (*per curiam*) (Stevens, J., dissenting); or where a state court's grant of relief is particularly likely to destabilize or significantly interfere with federal policy. None of those circumstances, and no comparable interest, is present in these cases.

The Carr brothers committed acts of "almost inconceivable cruelty and depravity," and the majority is understandably

[577 U.S. 135]

anxious to ensure they receive their just deserts. (So anxious, in fact, that it reaches out to address a question on which we did not grant certiorari at all. *Ante*, at 126, 193 L. Ed. 2d, at 549.) But I do not believe that interest justifies not only "correcting" the Kansas Supreme Court's error but also calling into question the procedures of other States.

The standard adage teaches that hard cases make bad law. See *Northern Securities Co. v. United States*, 193 U.S. 197, 400, 24 S. Ct. 436, 48 L. Ed. 679 (1904) (Holmes, J., dissenting). I fear that these cases suggest a corollary: Shocking cases make too much law. Because I believe the Court should not have granted certiorari here, I respectfully dissent.

[577 U.S. 136]

ROBERT MONTANILE, Petitioner

v

BOARD OF TRUSTEES OF THE NATIONAL ELEVATOR INDUSTRY
HEALTH BENEFIT PLAN

577 U.S. 136, 136 S. Ct. 651, 193 L. Ed. 2d 556, 2016 U.S. LEXIS 843

[No. 14-723]

Argued November 9, 2015. Decided January 20, 2016.

Decision: When participant in Employee Retirement Income Security Act of
1974 (29 U.S.C.S. § 1001 et seq.) plan dissipated whole settlement on
nontraceable items, fiduciary was not allowed to sue to attach participant's
general assets under 29 U.S.C.S. § 1132(a)(3).

Prior history: ON WRIT OF CERTIORARI TO THE UNITED STATES
COURT OF APPEALS FOR THE ELEVENTH CIRCUIT, 593 Fed. Appx.
903, 2014 U.S. App. LEXIS 22438

SUMMARY

Overview: HOLDINGS: [1]-When a participant dissipated the whole settlement on nontraceable items, the fiduciary could not bring a suit to attach the
participant's general assets under § 502(a)(3) of the Employee Retirement
Income Security Act of 1974 (ERISA), 29 U.S.C.S. § 1132(a)(3), because the suit
was not one for appropriate equitable relief; [2]-An ERISA fiduciary's
§ 1132(a)(3) action seeking to enforce an equitable lien by agreement against
the plan participant's assets was equitable in nature where the lien attached
to the settlement funds that the participant recovered in a negligence action,
rather than the participant's general assets, the right to recover money was a
legal remedy, and the fiduciary had sufficient notice of the settlement to have
taken steps to preserve those funds.

Outcome: Judgment reversed and case remanded; 8-1 Decision, 1 Dissent.

HEADNOTES

Classified to United States Supreme Court Digest, Lawyers' Edition

**ERISA — violation — enforce-
ment**

*L Ed Digest: Pensions and Retirement
Funds § 13*

1. See 29 U.S.C.S. § 1132(a)(3),
which authorizes a civil action by an
Employee Retirement Income Security Act of 1974 (ERISA) (29 U.S.C.S.
§ 1001 et seq.) plan participant, ben-

eficiary, or fiduciary to obtain equitable relief to address ERISA or plan
violations or to enforce ERISA or the
plan.

**ERISA participant — attachment
of assets**

*L Ed Digest: Pensions and Retirement
Funds § 13*

2. When a participant dissipates
the whole settlement on nontraceable

items, the fiduciary cannot bring a suit to attach the participant's general assets under § 502(a)(3) of the Employee Retirement Income Security Act of 1974, 29 U.S.C.S. § 1132(a)(3), because the suit is not one for appropriate equitable relief. (Thomas, J., joined by Roberts, Ch. J., and Scalia, Kennedy, Breyer, Alito, Sotomayor, and Kagan JJ.)

ERISA — equitable relief
L Ed Digest: Pensions and Retirement Funds § 13

3. Case law explains that the term equitable relief in § 502(a)(3) of the Employee Retirement Income Security Act of 1974, 29 U.S.C.S. § 1132(a)(3), is limited to those categories of relief that were typically available in equity during the days of the divided bench (meaning, the period before 1938 when courts of law and equity were separate). Under judicial precedents, whether the remedy a plaintiff seeks is legal or equitable depends on (1) the basis for the plaintiff's claim and (2) the nature of the underlying remedies sought. Judicial precedents also prescribe a framework for resolving this inquiry. To determine how to characterize the basis of a plaintiff's claim and the nature of the remedies sought, courts turn to standard treatises on equity, which establish the basic contours of what equitable relief was typically available in premerger equity courts. (Thomas, J., joined by Roberts, Ch. J., and Scalia, Kennedy, Breyer, Alito, Sotomayor, and Kagan JJ.)

Restitution in equity
L Ed Digest: Restitution, Implied Contracts, and Assumpsit Actions § 1

4. Restitution in equity typically involves enforcement of a constructive trust or an equitable lien, where money or property identified as belonging in good conscience to the plaintiff could clearly be traced to particular funds or property in the defendant's possession. (Thomas, J., joined by Roberts, Ch. J., and Scalia, Kennedy, Breyer, Alito, Sotomayor, and Kagan JJ.)

Equity — specific funds
L Ed Digest: Liens § 5

5. Standard equity treatises make clear that a plaintiff could ordinarily enforce an equitable lien only against specifically identified funds that remain in the defendant's possession or against traceable items that the defendant purchased with the funds (e.g., identifiable property like a car). A defendant's expenditure of the entire identifiable fund on nontraceable items (like food or travel) destroys an equitable lien. The plaintiff then may have a personal claim against the defendant's general assets, but recovering out of those assets is a legal remedy, not an equitable one. (Thomas, J., joined by Roberts, Ch. J., and Scalia, Kennedy, Breyer, Alito, Sotomayor, and Kagan JJ.)

Equity — specific fund
L Ed Digest: Liens § 5

6. Equitable remedies are, as a general rule, directed against some specific thing; they give or enforce a right to or over some particular thing rather than a right to recover a sum of money generally out of the defendant's assets. Equitable liens thus are ordinarily enforceable only against a specifically identified fund because an equitable lien is simply a right of a special nature over the thing so that the very thing itself may be proceeded against in an equitable action. This general rule's application to equitable liens includes equitable liens by agreement, which depend on the notion that the contract creates some right or interest in or over specific property, and are enforceable only if the decree of the court can lay hold of that specific property. (Thomas, J., joined by Roberts, Ch. J., and Scalia, Kennedy, Breyer, Alito, Sotomayor, and Kagan JJ.)

Equity — specific fund — dissipation

L Ed Digest: Liens § 5

7. If, instead of preserving the specific fund subject to the equitable lien, the defendant dissipated the entire fund on nontraceable items, that complete dissipation eliminates the lien. Even though the defendant's conduct is wrongful, the plaintiff can not attach the defendant's general assets instead. Absent specific exceptions, where a person wrongfully disposes of the property of another but the property cannot be traced into any product, the other cannot enforce a constructive trust or lien upon any part of the wrongdoer's property. The plaintiff has merely a personal claim against the wrongdoer, a quintessential action at law. (Thomas, J., joined by Roberts, Ch. J., and Scalia, Kennedy, Breyer, Alito, Sotomayor, and Kagan JJ.)

Equity — separate fund — dissipation

L Ed Digest: Liens § 5

8. At equity, a plaintiff ordinarily can not enforce any type of equitable lien if the defendant once possessed a separate, identifiable fund to which the lien attached, but then dissipates it all. The plaintiff can not attach the defendant's general assets instead because those assets are not part of the specific thing to which the lien attaches. This rule applies to equitable

liens by agreement as well as other types of equitable liens. (Thomas, J., joined by Roberts, Ch. J., and Scalia, Kennedy, Breyer, Alito, Sotomayor, and Kagan JJ.)

Equity — specific fund

L Ed Digest: Liens § 5

9. The basic premise of an equitable lien by agreement is that, rather than physically taking the plaintiff's property, the defendant constructively possesses a fund to which the plaintiff is entitled. But the plaintiff must still identify a specific fund in the defendant's possession to enforce the lien. (Thomas, J., joined by Roberts, Ch. J., and Scalia, Kennedy, Breyer, Alito, Sotomayor, and Kagan JJ.)

ERISA — equitable lien

L Ed Digest: Pensions and Retirement Funds § 13

10. Judicial precedent has long rejected the argument that equitable relief under § 502(a)(3) of the Employee Retirement Income Security Act of 1974, 29 U.S.C.S. § 1132(a)(3), means whatever relief a court of equity is empowered to provide in the particular case at issue, including ancillary legal remedies. In many situations an equity court could establish purely legal rights and grant legal remedies which would otherwise be beyond the scope of its authority. But these legal remedies are not relief typically available in equity, and interpreting them as such would eliminate any limit on the meaning of equitable relief and would render the modifier superfluous. As judicial precedent explains, as a general rule, plaintiffs cannot enforce an equitable lien against a defendant's general assets. (Thomas, J., joined by Roberts, Ch. J., and Scalia, Kennedy, Breyer, Alito, Sotomayor, and Kagan JJ.)

ERISA — legal remedies — equitable relief

L Ed Digest: Pensions and Retirement Funds § 13

11. Legal remedies, even legal remedies that a court of equity could sometimes award, are not equitable relief under § 502(a)(3) of the Employee Retirement Income Security Act of 1974, 29 U.S.C.S. § 1132(a)(3). (Thomas, J., joined by Roberts, Ch. J., and Scalia, Kennedy, Breyer, Alito, Sotomayor, and Kagan JJ.)

Equity — swollen-assets theory

L Ed Digest: Liens § 5

12. To the extent that courts endorsed any version of the swollen assets theory, they adopt a more limited rule: that commingling a specifically identified fund, to which a lien attached, with a different fund of the defendant's did not destroy the lien. Instead, that commingling allowed the plaintiff to recover the amount of the lien from the entire pot of money. (Thomas, J., joined by Roberts, Ch. J., and Scalia, Kennedy, Breyer, Alito, Sotomayor, and Kagan JJ.)

Basic purpose

L Ed Digest: Statutes § 100

13. Vague notions of a statute's basic purpose are inadequate to overcome the words of its text regarding the specific issue under consideration. (Thomas, J., joined by Roberts, Ch. J., and Scalia, Kennedy, Breyer, Sotomayor, and Kagan JJ.)

RESEARCH REFERENCES

29 U.S.C.S. § 1132(a)(3)

6 Labor and Employment Law § 154.04 (Matthew Bender)

L Ed Digest, Pensions and Retirement Funds § 13

L Ed Index, Pensions and Retirement

Annotations:

Supreme Court's construction and application of § 502 of Employee Retirement Income Security Act of 1974 (ERISA), as amended (29 U.S.C.S. § 1132), providing for civil enforcement of ERISA. 151 L. Ed. 2d 1083.

SHEPARD'S® Citations Service. For further research of authorities referenced here, use SHEPARD'S to be sure your case or statute is still good law and to find additional authorities that support your position. SHEPARD'S is available exclusively from LexisNexis®.

APPEARANCES OF COUNSEL ARGUING CASE

Peter K. Stris argued the cause for petitioner.

Ginger D. Anders argued the cause for the United States, as amicus curiae, by special leave of court.

Neal K. Katyal argued the cause for respondent.

Employee benefits plans regulated by the Employee Retirement Income Security Act of 1974 (ERISA) often contain subrogation clauses requiring a plan participant to reimburse the plan for medical expenses if the participant later recovers money from a third party for his injuries. Here, petitioner Montanile was seriously injured by a drunk driver, and his ERISA plan paid more than $120,000 for his medical expenses. Montanile later sued the drunk driver, obtaining a $500,000 settlement. Pursuant to the plan's subrogation clause, respondent plan administrator (the Board of Trustees of the National Elevator Industry Health Benefit Plan, or Board), sought reimbursement from the settlement. Montanile's attorney refused that request and subsequently informed the Board that the fund would be transferred from a client trust account to Montanile unless the Board objected. The Board did not respond, and Montanile received the settlement.

Six months later, the Board sued Montanile in Federal District Court under § 502(a)(3) of ERISA, which authorizes plan fiduciaries to file suit "to obtain . . . appropriate equitable relief . . . to enforce . . . the terms of the plan." 29 U.S.C. § 1132(a)(3). The Board sought an equitable lien on any settlement funds or property in Montanile's possession and an order enjoining Montanile from dissipating any such funds. Montanile argued that because he had already spent almost all of the settlement, no identifiable fund existed against which to enforce the lien. The District Court rejected Montanile's argument, and the Eleventh Circuit affirmed, holding that even if Montanile had completely dissipated the fund, the plan was entitled to reimbursement from Montanile's general assets.

Held: When an ERISA-plan participant wholly dissipates a third-party settlement on nontraceable items, the plan fiduciary may not bring suit under § 502(a)(3) to attach the participant's separate assets. Pp. 142–151, 193 L. Ed. 2d, at 564-570.

(a) Plan fiduciaries are limited by § 502(a)(3) to filing suits "to obtain . . . equitable relief." Whether the relief requested "is legal or equitable depends on [1] the basis for [the plaintiff's] claim and [2] the nature of the underlying remedies sought." *Sereboff* v. *Mid Atlantic Medical Services, Inc.,* 547 U.S. 356, 363, 126 S. Ct. 1869, 164 L. Ed. 2d 612. Pp. 142–146, 193 L. Ed. 2d, at 564-566.

(1) This Court's precedents establish that the basis for the Board's claim—the enforcement of a lien created by an agreement to convey a particular fund to another party—is equitable. See *Sereboff,* 547 U.S., at 363-364, 126 S. Ct. 1869, 164 L. Ed. 2d 612. The Court's precedents also establish that the nature of the Board's underlying remedy—enforcement of a lien against " 'specifically identifiable' funds that were within [Montanile's] possession and control," *id.,* 547 U.S. at 362-363, 126 S. Ct. 1869, 164 L. Ed. 2d 612—would also have been equitable had the Board immediately sued to enforce the lien against the fund. But those propositions do not resolve the question here: whether a plan is still seeking an equitable remedy when the defendant has dissipated all of a separate settlement fund, and the plan then seeks to

recover out of the defendant's general assets. Pp. 142–144, 193 L. Ed. 2d, at 564-565.

(2) This Court holds today that a plan is not seeking equitable relief under those circumstances. In pre-merger equity courts, a plaintiff could ordinarily enforce an equitable lien, including, as here, an equitable lien by agreement, only against specifically identified funds that remained in the defendant's possession or against traceable items that the defendant purchased with the funds. See 4 S. Symons, Pomeroy's Equity Jurisprudence § 1234, pp. 693-695. If a defendant dissipated the entire fund on nontraceable items, the lien was eliminated and the plaintiff could not attach the defendant's general assets instead. See Restatement of Restitution § 215(1), p. 866. Pp. 144–146, 193 L. Ed. 2d, at 565-566.

(b) The Board's arguments in favor of the enforcement of an equitable lien against Montanile's general assets are unsuccessful. *Sereboff* does not contain an exception to the general asset-tracing requirement for equitable liens by agreement. See 547 U.S., at 365, 126 S. Ct. 1869, 164 L.

Ed. 2d 612. Nor does historical equity practice support the enforcement of an equitable lien against general assets. And the Board's claim that ERISA's objectives are best served by allowing plans to enforce such liens is a "vague notio[n] of [the] statute's 'basic purpose' . . . inadequate to overcome the words of its text regarding the *specific* issue under consideration." *Mertens* v. *Hewitt Associates,* 508 U.S. 248, 261, 113 S. Ct. 2063, 124 L. Ed. 2d 161. Pp. 146–151, 193 L. Ed. 2d, at 566-569.

(c) The case is remanded for the District Court to determine, in the first instance, whether Montanile kept his settlement fund separate from his general assets and whether he dissipated the entire fund on non-traceable assets. P. 151, 193 L. Ed. 2d, at 569.

593 Fed. Appx. 903, reversed and remanded.

Thomas, J., delivered the opinion of the Court, in which Roberts, C. J., and Scalia, Kennedy, Breyer, Sotomayor, and Kagan, JJ., joined, and in which Alito, J., joined except for Part III-C. Ginsburg, J., filed a dissenting opinion.

OPINION OF THE COURT

[577 U.S. 138]

Justice **Thomas** delivered the opinion of the Court.*

When a third party injures a participant in an employee benefits plan under the Employee Retirement Income Security Act of 1974 (ERISA), 88 Stat. 829, as amended, 29 U.S.C.

§ 1001 *et seq.*, the plan frequently pays covered medical expenses. The terms of these plans often include a subrogation clause requiring a participant to reimburse the plan if the participant later recovers money from the third party for his injuries. And under ERISA § 502(a)(3), 29 U.S.C. § 1132(a)(3), plan fiduciaries can file

---

* Justice Alito joins this opinion, except for Part III-C.

civil suits "to obtain . . . appropriate equitable relief . . . to enforce . . . the terms of the plan."[1]

[577 U.S. 139]

In this case, we consider what happens when a participant obtains a settlement fund from a third party, but spends the whole settlement on nontraceable items (for instance, on services or consumable items like food). We evaluate in particular whether a plan fiduciary can sue under § 502(a)(3) to recover from the participant's remaining assets the medical expenses it paid on the participant's behalf. We hold that, [2] when a participant dissipates the whole settlement on nontraceable items, the fiduciary cannot bring a suit to attach the participant's general assets under § 502(a)(3) because the suit is not one for "appropriate equitable relief." In this case, it is unclear whether the participant dissipated all of his settlement in this manner, so we remand for further proceedings.

I

Petitioner Robert Montanile was a participant in a health benefits plan governed by ERISA and administered by respondent, the Board of Trustees of the National Elevator Industry Health Benefit Plan (Board of Trustees or Board). The plan must pay for certain medical expenses that beneficiaries or participants incur. The plan may demand reimbursement, however, when a participant recovers money from a third party for medical expenses. The plan states: "Amounts that have been recovered by a [participant] from another party are assets of the Plan . . . and are not distributable to any person or entity without the Plan's written release of its subrogation interest." App. 45. The plan also provides that "any amounts" that a participant "recover[s] from another party by award, judgment, settlement or otherwise . . . will promptly be applied first to reimburse the Plan in full for benefits advanced by the Plan . . . and without reduction for attorneys' fees, costs, expenses or damages claimed by the covered person." *Id.*, at 46. Participants must notify the plan and obtain its consent before settling claims.

[577 U.S. 140]

In December 2008, a drunk driver ran through a stop sign and crashed into Montanile's vehicle. The accident severely injured Montanile, and the plan paid at least $121,044.02 for his initial medical care. Montanile signed a reimbursement agreement reaffirming his obligation to reimburse the plan from any recovery he obtained "as a result of any legal action or settlement or otherwise." *Id.*, at 51 (emphasis deleted).

Thereafter, Montanile filed a negligence claim against the drunk driver and made a claim for uninsured motorist benefits under Montanile's car insurance. He obtained a $500,000 settlement. Montanile then paid his attorneys $200,000 and repaid about $60,000 that they had advanced him. Thus, about $240,000 remained of the settlement. Montanile's attorneys held most of that sum in a client trust

---

1. In full, the provision states: [1] "A civil action may be brought— . . . (3) by a participant, beneficiary, or fiduciary (A) to enjoin any act or practice which violates any provision of this subchapter or the terms of the plan, or (B) to obtain other appropriate equitable relief (i) to redress such violations or (ii) to enforce any provisions of this subchapter or the terms of the plan." 29 U.S.C. § 1132(a)(3).

account. This included enough money to satisfy Montanile's obligations to the plan.

The Board of Trustees sought reimbursement from Montanile on behalf of the plan, and Montanile's attorney argued that the plan was not entitled to any recovery. The parties attempted but failed to reach an agreement about reimbursement. After discussions broke down, Montanile's attorney informed the Board that he would distribute the remaining settlement funds to Montanile unless the Board objected within 14 days. The Board did not respond within that time, so Montanile's attorney gave Montanile the remainder of the funds.

Six months after negotiations ended, the Board sued Montanile in District Court under ERISA § 502(a)(3), 29 U.S.C. § 1132(a)(3), seeking repayment of the $121,044.02 the plan had expended on his medical care. The Board asked the court to enforce an equitable lien upon any settlement funds or any property which is " 'in [Montanile's] actual or constructive possession.' " 593 Fed. Appx. 903, 906 (CA11 2014) (quoting complaint). Because Montanile had already taken possession of the settlement funds, the Board also sought an

[577 U.S. 141]

order enjoining Montanile from dissipating any such funds. Montanile then stipulated that he still possessed some of the settlement proceeds.

The District Court granted summary judgment to the Board. No. 12-80746-Civ. (SD Fla., Apr. 18, 2014),

2014 WL 8514011, *1. The court rejected Montanile's argument that, because he had by that time spent almost all of the settlement funds, there was no specific, identifiable fund separate from his general assets against which the Board's equitable lien could be enforced. *Id.*, 2014 WL 8514011 at *8-*11. The court held that, even if Montanile had dissipated some or all of the settlement funds, the Board was entitled to reimbursement from Montanile's general assets. *Id.*, 2014 WL 8514011 at *10-*11. The court entered judgment for the Board in the amount of $121,044.02.

The Court of Appeals for the Eleventh Circuit affirmed. It reasoned that a plan can always enforce an equitable lien once the lien attaches, and that dissipation of the specific fund to which the lien attached cannot destroy the underlying reimbursement obligation. The court therefore held that the plan can recover out of a participant's general assets when the participant dissipates the specifically identified fund. 593 Fed. Appx., at 908.

We granted certiorari to resolve a conflict among the Courts of Appeals over whether an ERISA fiduciary can enforce an equitable lien against a defendant's general assets under these circumstances.[2] 575 U.S. 934, 135 S. Ct. 1700, 191 L. Ed. 2d 675 (2015). We hold that it cannot, and accordingly reverse the judgment of the Eleventh Circuit and remand for further proceedings.

[577 U.S. 142]

---

2. Compare *Thurber* v. *Aetna Life Ins. Co.*, 712 F.3d 654 (CA2 2013), *Funk* v. *CIGNA Group Ins.*, 648 F.3d 182 (CA3 2011), *Cusson* v. *Liberty Life Assurance Co. of Boston*, 592 F.3d 215 (CA1 2010), *Longaberger Co.* v. *Kolt*, 586 F.3d 459 (CA6 2009), and *Gutta* v. *Standard Select Trust Ins. Plans*, 530 F.3d 614 (CA7 2008), with *Treasurer, Trustees of Drury Industries, Inc. Health Care Plan & Trust* v. *Goding*, 692 F.3d 888 (CA8 2012), and *Bilyeu* v. *Morgan Stanley Long Term Disability Plan*, 683 F.3d 1083 (CA9 2012).

II

A

As previously stated, § 502(a)(3) of ERISA authorizes plan fiduciaries like the Board of Trustees to bring civil suits "to obtain other appropriate equitable relief . . . to enforce . . . the terms of the plan." 29 U.S.C. § 1132(a)(3). **[3]** Our cases explain that the term "equitable relief" in § 502(a)(3) is limited to "those categories of relief that were *typically* available in equity" during the days of the divided bench (meaning, the period before 1938 when courts of law and equity were separate). *Mertens* v. *Hewitt Associates*, 508 U.S. 248, 256, 113 S. Ct. 2063, 124 L. Ed. 2d 161 (1993). Under this Court's precedents, whether the remedy a plaintiff seeks "is legal or equitable depends on [(1)] the basis for [the plaintiff's] claim and [(2)] the nature of the underlying remedies sought." *Sereboff* v. *Mid Atlantic Medical Services, Inc.*, 547 U.S. 356, 363, 126 S. Ct. 1869, 164 L. Ed. 2d 612 (2006) (internal quotation marks omitted). Our precedents also prescribe a framework for resolving this inquiry. To determine how to characterize the basis of a plaintiff's claim and the nature of the remedies sought, we turn to standard treatises on equity, which establish the "basic contours" of what equitable relief was typically available in premerger equity courts. *Great-West Life & Annuity Ins. Co.* v. *Knudson*, 534 U.S. 204, 217, 122 S. Ct. 708, 151 L. Ed. 2d 635 (2002).

We have employed this approach in three earlier cases where, as here, the plan fiduciary sought reimbursement for medical expenses after the plan beneficiary or participant recovered money from a third party. Under these precedents, the basis for the Board's claim is equitable. But our cases do not resolve whether the *remedy* the Board now seeks—enforcement of an equitable lien by agreement against the defendant's general assets—is equitable in nature.

First, in *Great-West*, we held that a plan with a claim for an equitable lien was—in the circumstances presented—

[577 U.S. 143]

seeking a legal rather than an equitable remedy. In that case, a plan sought to enforce an equitable lien by obtaining a money judgment from the defendants. The plan could not enforce the lien against the third-party settlement that the defendants had obtained because the defendants never actually possessed that fund; the fund went directly to the defendants' attorneys and to a restricted trust. We held that the plan sought a legal remedy, not an equitable one, even though the plan claimed that the money judgment was a form of restitution. *Id.*, at 208-209, 213-214, 122 S. Ct. 708, 151 L. Ed. 2d 635. We explained that **[4]** restitution in equity typically involved enforcement of "a constructive trust or an equitable lien, where money or property identified as belonging in good conscience to the plaintiff could clearly be traced to particular funds or property in the defendant's possession." *Id.*, at 213, 122 S. Ct. 708, 151 L. Ed. 2d 635. But the restitution sought in *Great-West* was legal—not equitable—because the specific funds to which the fiduciaries "claim[ed] an entitlement . . . [we]re not in [the defendants'] possession." *Id.*, at 214, 122 S. Ct. 708, 151 L. Ed. 2d 635. Since both the basis for the claim and the particular remedy sought were not equitable, the plan could not sue under § 502(a)(3).

Next, in *Sereboff*, we held that both

the basis for the claim and the remedy sought were equitable. The plan there sought reimbursement from beneficiaries who had retained their settlement fund in a separate account. 547 U.S., at 359-360, 126 S. Ct. 1869, 164 L. Ed. 2d 612. We held that the basis for the plan's claim was equitable because the plan sought to enforce an equitable lien by agreement, a type of equitable lien created by an agreement to convey a particular fund to another party. See *id.*, at 363-364, 126 S. Ct. 1869, 164 L. Ed. 2d 612. The lien existed in *Sereboff* because of the beneficiaries' agreement with the plan to convey the proceeds of any third-party settlement. We explained that a claim to enforce such a lien is equitable because the plan "could rely on a familiar rul[e] of equity" to collect—specifically, the rule "that a contract to convey a specific object even before it is acquired will make the contractor a trustee

[577 U.S. 144]

as soon as he gets a title to the thing." *Ibid.* (internal quotation marks omitted; alteration in original). The underlying remedies that the plan sought also were equitable, because the plan "sought specifically identifiable funds that were within the possession and control" of the beneficiaries—not recovery from the beneficiaries' "assets generally." *Id.*, at 362-363, 126 S. Ct. 1869, 164 L. Ed. 2d 612 (internal quotation marks omitted).

Finally, in *US Airways, Inc.* v. *McCutchen*, 569 U.S. 88, 133 S. Ct. 1537, 185 L. Ed. 2d 654 (2013), we reaffirmed our analysis in *Sereboff* and again concluded that a plan sought to enforce an equitable claim by seeking equitable remedies. As in *Sereboff*, "the basis for [the plan's] claim was equitable" because the plan's terms created an equitable lien by agreement on a third-party settlement. See 569 U.S., at 95, 133 S. Ct. 1537, 185 L. Ed. 2d 654 (internal quotation marks omitted). And, as in *Sereboff*, "[t]he nature of the recovery requested" by the plan "was equitable because [it] claimed specifically identifiable funds within the [beneficiaries'] control—that is, a portion of the settlement they had gotten." 569 U.S., at 95, 133 S. Ct. 1537, 185 L. Ed. 2d 654 (internal quotation marks omitted).

Under these principles, the basis for the Board's claim here is equitable: The Board had an equitable lien by agreement that attached to Montanile's settlement fund when he obtained title to that fund. And the nature of the Board's underlying *remedy* would have been equitable had it immediately sued to enforce the lien against the settlement fund then in Montanile's possession. That does not resolve this case, however. Our prior cases do not address whether a plan is still seeking an equitable remedy when the defendant, who once possessed the settlement fund, has dissipated it all, and the plan then seeks to recover out of the defendant's general assets.

B

To resolve this issue, we turn to standard equity treatises. As we explain below, [5] those treatises make clear that a plaintiff could ordinarily enforce an equitable lien only against specifically identified funds that remain in the defendant's

[577 U.S. 145]

possession or against traceable items that the defendant purchased with the funds (*e.g.*, identifiable property like a car). A defendant's expenditure of the entire identifiable fund on nontraceable items (like food or travel) destroys an equitable lien. The plaintiff then may have a personal claim against the defendant's general assets—but recovering out of those assets is a *legal* remedy, not an equitable one.

[6] Equitable remedies "are, as a general rule, directed against some specific thing; they give or enforce a right to or over some particular thing . . . rather than a right to recover a sum of money generally out of the defendant's assets." 4 S. Symons, Pomeroy's Equity Jurisprudence § 1234, p. 694 (5th ed. 1941) (Pomeroy). Equitable liens thus are ordinarily enforceable only against a specifically identified fund because an equitable lien "is simply a right of a special nature *over* the thing . . . so that the very thing itself may be proceeded against in an equitable action." *Id.*, § 1233, at 692; see also Restatement of Restitution § 215, Comment *a*, p. 866 (1936) (Restatement) (enforcement of equitable lien requires showing that the defendant "still holds the property or property which is in whole or in part its product"); 1 D. Dobbs, Law of Remedies § 1.4, p. 19 (2d ed. 1993) (Dobbs) (similar). This general rule's application to equitable liens includes equitable liens by agreement, which depend on "the notion . . . that the contract creates some right or interest in or over specific property," and are enforceable only if "the decree of the court can lay hold of" that specific property. 4 Pomeroy § 1234, at 694-695.

[7] If, instead of preserving the specific fund subject to the lien, the defendant dissipated the entire fund on nontraceable items, that complete dissipation eliminated the lien. Even though the defendant's conduct was wrongful, the plaintiff could not attach the defendant's general assets

instead. Absent specific exceptions not relevant here, "where a person wrongfully dispose[d] of the property of another but the property cannot be traced into any product, the other . . .

[577 U.S. 146]

cannot enforce a constructive trust or lien *upon any part of the wrongdoer's property*." Restatement § 215(1), at 866 (emphasis added); see also *Great-West*, 534 U.S., at 213-214, 122 S. Ct. 708, 151 L. Ed. 2d 635 (citing Restatement § 160). The plaintiff had "merely a personal claim against the wrongdoer"—a quintessential action at law. *Id.*, § 215(1), at 866.

In sum, [8] at equity, a plaintiff ordinarily could not enforce any type of equitable lien if the defendant once possessed a separate, identifiable fund to which the lien attached, but then dissipated it all. The plaintiff could not attach the defendant's general assets instead because those assets were not part of the specific thing to which the lien attached. This rule applied to equitable liens by agreement as well as other types of equitable liens.

III

The Board of Trustees nonetheless maintains that it can enforce its equitable lien against Montanile's general assets. We consider the Board's arguments in turn.

A

First, the Board argues that, while equity courts ordinarily required plaintiffs to trace a specific, identifiable fund in the defendant's possession to which the lien attached, there is an exception for equitable liens by agreement. The Board asserts that equitable liens by agreement require no such tracing, and can be enforced against a defendant's general assets. According to the Board, we recognized this exception in *Sereboff* by distinguishing between equitable restitution (where a lien attaches because the defendant misappropriated property from the plaintiff) and equitable liens by agreement.

The Board misreads *Sereboff*, which left untouched the rule that *all* types of equitable liens must be enforced against a specifically identified fund in the defendant's possession. See 1 Dobbs § 4.3(3), at 601, 603. The question we

[577 U.S. 147]

faced in *Sereboff* was whether plaintiffs seeking an equitable lien by agreement must "identify an asset they originally possessed, which was improperly acquired and converted into property the defendant held." 547 U.S., at 365, 126 S. Ct. 1869, 164 L. Ed. 2d 612. We observed that such a requirement, although characteristic of restitutionary relief, does not "appl[y] to equitable liens by agreement or assignment." *Ibid.* (discussing *Barnes* v. *Alexander*, 232 U.S. 117, 34 S. Ct. 276, 58 L. Ed. 530 (1914)). That is because [9] the basic premise of an equitable lien by agreement is that, rather than physically taking the plaintiff's property, the defendant constructively possesses a fund to which the plaintiff is entitled. But the plaintiff must still identify a specific fund in the defendant's possession to enforce the lien. See *id.*, at 123, 34 S. Ct. 276, 58 L. Ed. 530 ("Having a lien upon the fund, as soon as it was identified they could follow it into the hands of the appellant").

B

Second, the Board contends that historical equity practice supports enforcement of its equitable lien against Montanile's general assets. The Board identifies three methods that equity courts purportedly employed to effectuate this principle: substitute money decrees, deficiency judgments, and the swollen assets doctrine. This argument also fails.

[10] We have long rejected the argument that "equitable relief" under § 502(a)(3) means "whatever relief a court of equity is empowered to provide in the particular case at issue," including ancillary legal remedies. *Mertens,* 508 U.S., at 256, 113 S. Ct. 2063, 124 L. Ed. 2d 161. In "many situations . . . an equity court could establish purely legal rights and grant legal remedies which would otherwise be beyond the scope of its authority." *Ibid.* (internal quotation marks omitted). But these legal remedies were not relief "typically available in equity," and interpreting them as such would eliminate any limit on the meaning of "equitable relief" and would "render the modifier superfluous." *Id.,* at 256, 258, 113 S. Ct. 2063, 124 L. Ed. 2d 161 (emphasis deleted); see also *Great-West, supra,* at 210, 122 S. Ct. 708, 151 L. Ed. 2d 635. As we have explained—and as the

[577 U.S. 148]

Board conceded at oral argument—as a general rule, plaintiffs cannot enforce an equitable lien against a defendant's general assets. See Part II-B, *supra.* The Board contends that there is an exception if the defendant wrongfully dissipates the equitable lien to thwart its enforcement. But none of the Board's examples show that such relief was "typically available" in equity.[3]

The specific methods by which eq-

---

3. The Board also interprets *CIGNA Corp.* v. *Amara*, 563 U.S. 421, 131 S. Ct. 1866, 179 L. Ed. 2d 843 (2011), as all but overruling *Mertens* v. *Hewitt Associates*, 508 U.S. 248, 113 S. Ct. 2063, 124

uity courts might have awarded relief from a defendant's general assets only confirm that the Board seeks legal, not equitable, remedies. While equity courts sometimes awarded money decrees as a substitute for the value of the equitable lien, they were still legal remedies, because they were "wholly pecuniary and personal." 4 Pomeroy § 1234, at 694. The same is true with respect to deficiency judgments. Equity courts could award both of these remedies as part of their ancillary jurisdiction to award complete relief. But the treatises make clear that when equity courts did so, "the rights of the parties are strictly legal, and the final remedy granted is of the kind which might be conferred by a court of law." 1 *id.*, § 231, at 410; see also 1 Dobbs § 2.7, at 180-181, and § 4.3(3), at 602 (similar); New Federal Equity Rules 10 (rev. 5th ed. 1925) (authorizing equity courts to award such relief). But

[577 U.S. 149]

[11] legal remedies— even legal remedies that a court of equity could sometimes award—are not "equitable relief" under § 502(a)(3). See *Mertens, supra,* at 256-258, 113 S. Ct. 2063, 124 L. Ed. 2d 161.

The swollen assets doctrine also does not establish that the relief the Board seeks is equitable. Under the Board's view of this doctrine, even if a defendant spends all of a specifically identified fund, the mere fact that the defendant wrongfully had assets that belonged to another increased the defendant's available assets, and justifies recovery from his general assets. But most equity courts and treatises rejected that theory. See Taft, Note, A Defense of a Limited Use of the Swollen Assets Theory Where Money Has Wrongfully Been Mingled With Other Money, 39 Colum. L. Rev. 172, 175 (1939) (describing the swollen assets doctrine as "often . . . rejected by the courts"); see also Oesterle, Deficiencies of the Restitutionary Right To Trace Misappropriated Property in Equity and in UCC § 9-306, 68 Cornell L. Rev. 172, 189, and n. 33 (1983) (similar). [12] To the extent that courts endorsed any version of the swollen assets theory, they adopted a more limited rule: that commingling a specifically identified fund—to which a lien attached—with a different fund of the defendant's did not destroy the lien. Instead, that commingling allowed the plaintiff to recover the amount of the lien from the entire pot of money. See Restatement § 209, at 844; Scott, The Right To Follow Money Wrongfully Mingled With Other Money, 27 Harv. L. Rev. 125, 125-126 (1913). Thus, even under the version of the swollen assets doctrine adopted by some courts, recovery out of Montanile's general assets—in the absence of commingling—would not have been "typically available" relief.

L. Ed. 2d 161 (1993), and *Great-West Life & Annuity Ins. Co.* v. *Knudson,* 534 U.S. 204, 122 S. Ct. 708, 151 L. Ed. 2d 635 (2002), in favor of the Board's broad interpretation of "equitable relief" under § 502(a)(3). But *CIGNA* reaffirmed that "traditionally speaking, relief that sought a lien or a constructive trust was legal relief, not equitable relief, unless the funds in question were 'particular funds or property in the defendant's possession.' " 563 U.S., at 439, 131 S. Ct. 1866, 179 L. Ed. 2d 843 (quoting *Great-West, supra,* at 213, 122 S. Ct. 708, 151 L. Ed. 2d 635; emphasis deleted). In any event, the Court's discussion of § 502(a)(3) in *CIGNA* was not essential to resolving that case, and—as our later analysis in *US Airways, Inc.* v. *McCutchen,* 569 U.S. 88, 133 S. Ct. 1537, 185 L. Ed. 2d 654 (2013), reinforces—our interpretation of "equitable relief" in *Mertens, Great-West,* and *Sereboff* v. *Mid Atlantic Medical Services, Inc.,* 547 U.S. 356, 126 S. Ct. 1869, 164 L. Ed. 2d 612 (2006), remains unchanged. See *McCutchen, supra,* at 94–95, 133 S. Ct. 1537, 185 L. Ed. 2d 654.

C

Finally, the Board argues that ERISA's objectives—of enforcing plan documents according to their terms and of protecting plan assets—would be best served by allowing plans to enforce equitable liens against a participant's general

[577 U.S. 150]

assets. The Board also contends that, unless plans can enforce reimbursement provisions against a defendant's general assets, plans will lack effective or cost-efficient remedies, and participants will dissipate any settlement as quickly as possible, before fiduciaries can sue.

We have rejected these arguments before, and do so again. **[13]** "[V]ague notions of a statute's 'basic purpose' are . . . inadequate to overcome the words of its text regarding the *specific* issue under consideration." *Mertens*, 508 U.S., at 261, 113 S. Ct. 2063, 124 L. Ed. 2d 161. Had Congress sought to prioritize the Board's policy arguments, it could have drafted § 502(a)(3) to mirror ERISA provisions governing civil actions. One of those provisions, for instance, allows participants and beneficiaries to bring civil actions "to enforce [their] rights under the terms of the plan" and does not limit them to equitable relief. *Great-West*, 534 U.S., at 221, 122 S. Ct. 708, 151 L. Ed. 2d 635 (quoting 29 U.S.C. § 1132(a)(1)(B) (1994 ed.)).

In any event, our interpretation of § 502(a)(3) promotes ERISA's purposes by "allocat[ing] liability for plan-related misdeeds in reasonable proportion to respective actors' power to control and prevent the misdeeds." *Mertens, supra,* at 262, 113 S. Ct. 2063, 124 L. Ed. 2d 161. More than a decade has passed since we decided *Great-West*, and plans have developed safeguards against participants' and beneficiaries' efforts to evade reimbursement obligations. Plans that cover medical expenses know how much medical care that participants and beneficiaries require, and have the incentive to investigate and track expensive claims. Plan provisions—like the ones here—obligate participants and beneficiaries to notify the plan of legal process against third parties and to give the plan a right of subrogation.

The Board protests that tracking and participating in legal proceedings is hard and costly, and that settlements are often shrouded in secrecy. The facts of this case undercut that argument. The Board had sufficient notice of Montanile's settlement to have taken various steps to preserve those funds. Most notably, when negotiations broke down and

[577 U.S. 151]

Montanile's lawyer expressed his intent to disburse the remaining settlement funds to Montanile unless the plan objected within 14 days, the Board could have—but did not—object. Moreover, the Board could have filed suit immediately, rather than waiting half a year.

IV

Because the lower courts erroneously held that the plan could recover out of Montanile's general assets, they did not determine whether Montanile kept his settlement fund separate from his general assets or dissipated the entire fund on nontraceable assets. At oral argument, Montanile's counsel acknowledged "a genuine issue of . . . material fact on how much dissipation there was" and a lack of record evidence as to whether Montanile mixed the settlement fund with his general assets. Tr. of Oral Arg. 4. A remand is necessary so that the District Court can make that determination.

* * *

We reverse the judgment of the

Eleventh Circuit and remand the case for further proceedings consistent with this opinion.

It is so ordered.

SEPARATE OPINION

Justice **Ginsburg**, dissenting.

Montanile received a $500,000 settlement out of which he had pledged to reimburse his health benefit plan for expenditures on his behalf of at least $121,044.02. See *ante*, at 140, 193 L. Ed. 2d, at 562-563. He can escape that reimbursement obligation, the Court decides, by spending the settlement funds rapidly on nontraceable items. See *ante*, at 145–146, 193 L. Ed. 2d, at 565–566. What brings the Court to that bizarre conclusion? As developed in my dissenting opinion in *Great-West Life & Annuity Ins. Co.* v. *Knudson*, 534 U.S. 204, 224-234, 122 S. Ct. 708, 151 L. Ed. 2d 635 (2002), the Court erred

profoundly in that case by reading the work product of a Congress sitting in 1974 as "unravel[ling] forty years of fusion of law and

[577 U.S. 152]

equity, solely by employing the benign sounding word 'equitable' when authorizing 'appropriate equitable relief.'" Langbein, What ERISA Means by "Equitable": The Supreme Court's Trail of Error in *Russell*, *Mertens*, and *Great-West*, 103 Colum. L. Rev. 1317, 1365 (2003). The Court has been persuasively counseled "to confess its error." *Ibid.* I would not perpetuate *Great-West*'s mistake, and would therefore affirm the judgment of the Court of Appeals for the Eleventh Circuit.

CAMPBELL-EWALD COMPANY, Petitioner

v

JOSE GOMEZ

577 U.S. 153, 136 S. Ct. 663, 193 L. Ed. 2d 571, 2016 U.S. LEXIS 846

[No. 14-857]

Argued October 14, 2015. Decided January 20, 2016.

Decision: Federal District Court retained jurisdiction to adjudicate Telephone Consumer Protection Act claim of individual who had filed class action but not yet moved for class certification when he rejected company's settlement offer; company's status as federal contractor did not entitle it to immunity from suit.

Prior history: ON WRIT OF CERTIORARI TO THE UNITED STATES COURT OF APPEALS FOR THE NINTH CIRCUIT, 768 F.3d 871, 2014 U.S. App. LEXIS 18019

SUMMARY

Overview: HOLDINGS: [1]-A class action an individual filed against a company that was hired by the U.S. Navy to develop a multimedia recruiting campaign, which alleged that the company violated the Telephone Consumer Protection Act ("TCPA"), 47 U.S.C.S. § 227(b)(1)(A)(iii), when a subcontractor the company hired sent a text message to the individual without his permission, did not become moot because the individual did not accept an offer of judgment the company filed pursuant to Fed. R. Civ. P. 68 before the individual sought class certification; [2]-Although the United States and its agencies were not subject to the TCPA's prohibitions because no statute lifted their immunity, the company's status as a federal contractor did not render it immune from suit for violating the TCPA by sending text messages to unconsenting recipients.

Outcome: The Supreme Court affirmed the U.S. Court of Appeals for the Ninth Circuit's judgment and remanded the case. 6-3 Decision; 1 concurrence; 2 dissents.

HEADNOTES

Classified to United States Supreme Court Digest, Lawyers' Edition

Settlement offer — effect
L Ed Digest: Release or Right or Claim § 17
 1. An unaccepted settlement offer has no force. Like other unaccepted contract offers, it creates no lasting right or obligation. (Ginsburg, J.,

joined by Kennedy, Breyer, Sotomayor, and Kagan, JJ.)

Telephone calls — automatic dialing — damages
L Ed Digest: Communications § 25
 2. The Telephone Consumer Protec-

tion Act (TCPA), 47 U.S.C.S. § 227(b)(1)(A)(iii), prohibits any person, absent the prior express consent of a telephone-call recipient, from making any call using any automatic telephone dialing system to any telephone number assigned to a paging service or cellular telephone service. A text message to a cellular telephone qualifies as a "call" within the compass of § 227(b)(1)(A)(iii). For damages occasioned by conduct violating the TCPA, § 227(b)(3) authorizes a private right of action. A plaintiff successful in such an action may recover her "actual monetary loss" or $500 for each violation, whichever is greater. Damages may be trebled if a defendant willfully or knowingly violated the TCPA. (Ginsburg, J., joined by Kennedy, Breyer, Sotomayor, and Kagan, JJ.)

Offer of judgment
L Ed Digest: Judgment § 6.5
3. See Fed. R. Civ. P. 68(a), (b), and (d), which apply to a defendant's offer to allow judgment on specified terms, failure to accept such an offer, and payment of costs after an unaccepted offer.

Case or controversy — mootness
L Ed Digest: Courts §§ 236, 762
4. Article III of the Constitution limits federal-court jurisdiction to "cases" and "controversies." U. S. Const. art. III, § 2. The United States Supreme Court has interpreted this requirement to demand that an actual controversy be extant at all stages of review, not merely at the time a complaint is filed. If an intervening circumstance deprives a plaintiff of a personal stake in the outcome of a lawsuit, at any point during litigation, the action can no longer proceed and must be dismissed as moot.

A case becomes moot, however, only when it is impossible for a court to grant any effectual relief whatever to the prevailing party. As long as the parties have a concrete interest, however small, in the outcome of the litigation, the case is not moot. (Ginsburg, J., joined by Kennedy, Breyer, Sotomayor, and Kagan, JJ.)

Settlement offer — rejection — mootness
L Ed Digest: Courts § 762
5. When a plaintiff rejects an offer of settlement—however good the terms—her interest in the lawsuit remains just what it was before. And so too does the court's ability to grant her relief. An unaccepted settlement offer—like any unaccepted contract offer—is a legal nullity, with no operative effect. As every first-year law student learns, the recipient's rejection of an offer leaves the matter as if no offer had ever been made. Nothing in Fed. R. Civ. P. 68 alters that basic principle; to the contrary, that rule specifies that an unaccepted offer is considered withdrawn. Fed. R. Civ. P. 68(b). So assuming the case was live before—because the plaintiff had a stake and the court could grant relief—the litigation carries on, unmooted. (Ginsburg, J., joined by Kennedy, Breyer, Sotomayor, and Kagan, JJ.)

Settlement offer — rejection — mootness
L Ed Digest: Courts § 762
6. Fed. R. Civ. P. 68 hardly supports the argument that an unaccepted settlement offer can moot a complaint. An offer of judgment, the Rule provides, is considered withdrawn if not accepted within 14 days of its service. Fed. R. Civ. P. 68(a), (b). The sole built-in sanction appears in Rule

68(d), which provides that if the ultimate judgment is not more favorable than the unaccepted offer, the offeree must pay the costs incurred after the offer was made. (Ginsburg, J., joined by Kennedy, Breyer, Sotomayor, and Kagan, JJ.)

Certification

L Ed Digest: Class Actions § 16

7. While a class lacks independent status until certified, a would-be class representative with a live claim of her own must be accorded a fair opportunity to show that certification is warranted. (Ginsburg, J., joined by Kennedy, Breyer, Sotomayor, and Kagan, JJ.)

Unaccepted offer — mootness

L Ed Digest: Courts § 762

8. An unaccepted settlement offer or offer of judgment does not moot a plaintiff's case. (Ginsburg, J., joined by Kennedy, Breyer, Sotomayor, and Kagan, JJ.)

Federal statute — immunity of United States

L Ed Digest: Communications § 8.3

9. The United States and its agencies are not subject to the Telephone Consumer Protection Act's, 47 U.S.C.S. § 227(b)(1)(A)(iii), prohibitions because no statute lifts their immunity. (Ginsburg, J., joined by Kennedy, Breyer, Sotomayor, and Kagan, JJ.)

Government contractors — derivative immunity

L Ed Digest: United States § 105.5

10. Government contractors obtain certain immunity in connection with work which they do pursuant to their contractual undertakings with the United States. That immunity, however, unlike the sovereign's, is not absolute. When a contractor violates both federal law and the Government's explicit instructions, no "derivative immunity" shields the contractor from suit by persons adversely affected by the violation. (Ginsburg, J., joined by Kennedy, Breyer, Sotomayor, and Kagan, JJ.)

Immunity from suit

L Ed Digest: Public Officers § 56

11. Qualified immunity may be overcome if a defendant knew or should have known that his conduct violated a right clearly established at the time of the episode in suit. (Ginsburg, J., joined by Kennedy, Breyer, Sotomayor, and Kagan, JJ.)

Favoring non-moving party

L Ed Digest: Summary Judgment and Judgment on Pleadings § 5.7

12. At the pretrial stage of litigation, the United States Supreme Court construes the record in a light favorable to the party seeking to avoid summary disposition. (Ginsburg, J., joined by Kennedy, Breyer, Sotomayor, and Kagan, JJ.)

Federal statute — vicarious liability

L Ed Digest: Communications § 23

13. The Federal Communications Commission has ruled that, under federal common-law principles of agency, there is vicarious liability for Telephone Consumer Protection Act, 47 U.S.C.S. § 227(b)(1)(A)(iii), violations. (Ginsburg, J., joined by Kennedy, Breyer, Sotomayor, and Kagan, JJ.)

RESEARCH REFERENCES

U.S.C.S., Constitution, Article III, § 2

Moore's Federal Practice §§56.26, 68.04, 68.07, 101.93, 101.98A (Matthew Bender)

L Ed Digest, Courts §§236, 236.5, 762; United States § 105.5

L Ed Index, Class Actions or Proceedings; Compromise and Settlement; Moot or Abstract Questions or Matters; Sovereign Immunity; Telephones and Telegraphs

Annotations:

Supreme Court's construction and application of Rule 23 of Federal Rules of Civil Procedure, concerning class actions. 144 L. Ed. 2d 889.

Requirements of Article III of Federal Constitution as affecting standing to challenge particular conduct as violative of federal law—Supreme Court cases. 70 L. Ed. 2d 941.

What circumstances render civil case, or issues arising therein, moot so as to preclude Supreme Court's consideration of their merits. 44 L. Ed. 2d 745.

Supreme Court's view as to what is a "case or controversy" within the meaning of Article III of the Federal Constitution or an "actual controversy" within the meaning of the Declaratory Judgment Act (28 U.S.C.S. § 2201). 40 L. Ed. 2d 783.

Unconstitutional conduct by state or federal officer as affecting governmental immunity from suit in federal court—Supreme Court cases. 12 L. Ed. 2d 1110.

SHEPARD'S® Citations Service. For further research of authorities referenced here, use SHEPARD'S to be sure your case or statute is still good law and to find additional authorities that support your position. SHEPARD'S is available exclusively from LexisNexis®.

APPEARANCES OF COUNSEL ARGUING CASE

Gregory G. Garre argued the cause for petitioner.

Jonathan F. Mitchell argued the cause for respondent.

Anthony A. Yang argued the cause for the United States, as amicus curiae, by special leave of the court.

SYLLABUS BY REPORTER OF DECISIONS

The United States Navy contracted with petitioner Campbell-Ewald Company (Campbell) to develop a multimedia recruiting campaign that included the sending of text messages to young adults, but only if those individuals had "opted in" to receipt of marketing solicitations on topics that included Navy service. Campbell's subcontractor Mindmatics LLC generated a list of cellular phone numbers for consenting 18- to 24-year-old users and then transmitted the Navy's message to over 100,000 recipients, including respondent Jose Gomez, who alleges that he did not consent to receive text messages and, at age 40, was not in the Navy's targeted age group. Gomez filed a nationwide class action, alleging that Campbell violated the Telephone Consumer Protection Act (TCPA), 47 U.S.C. § 227(b)(1)(A)(iii), which prohibits "using any automatic dialing system" to send a text message to a cellular telephone, absent the recipient's prior express consent. He sought treble statutory damages for a willful and knowing TCPA violation and an injunction against Campbell's involvement in unsolicited messaging.

Before the deadline for Gomez to file a motion for class certification, Campbell proposed to settle Gomez's individual claim and filed an offer of judgment pursuant to Federal Rule of Civil Procedure 68. Gomez did not accept the offer and allowed the Rule 68 submission to lapse on expiration of the time (14 days) specified in the Rule. Campbell then moved to dismiss the case pursuant to Rule 12(b)(1) for lack of subject-matter jurisdiction. Campbell argued first that its offer mooted Gomez's individual claim by providing him with complete relief. Next, Campbell urged that Gomez's failure to move for class certification before his individual claim became moot caused the putative class claims to become moot as well. The District Court denied the motion. After limited discovery, the District Court granted Campbell's motion for summary judgment. Relying on Yearsley v. W. A. Ross Constr. Co., 309 U.S. 18, 60 S. Ct. 413, 84 L. Ed. 554, the court held that Campbell, as a contractor acting on the Navy's behalf, acquired the Navy's sovereign immunity from suit under the TCPA. The Ninth Circuit reversed. It agreed that Gomez's case remained live but concluded that Campbell was not entitled to "derivative sovereign immunity" under Yearsley or on any other basis.

Held:

1. An unaccepted settlement offer or offer of judgment does not moot a plaintiff's case, so the District Court retained jurisdiction to adjudicate Gomez's complaint.

Article III's "cases" and "controversies" limitation requires that "an actual controversy . . . be extant at all stages of review, not merely at the time the complaint is filed," *Arizonans for Official English* v. *Arizona*, 520 U.S. 43, 67, 117 S. Ct. 1055, 137 L. Ed. 2d 170 (internal quotation marks omitted), but a case does not become moot as "long as the parties have a concrete interest, however small," in the litigation's outcome, *Chafin* v. *Chafin*, 568 U.S. 165, 172, 133 S. Ct. 1017, 185 L. Ed. 2d 1 (internal quotation marks omitted).

Gomez's complaint was not effaced by Campbell's unaccepted offer to satisfy his individual claim. Under basic principles of contract law, Campbell's settlement bid and Rule 68 offer of judgment, once rejected, had no continuing efficacy. With no settlement offer operative, the parties remained adverse; both retained the same stake in the litigation they had at the outset. Neither Rule 68 nor the 19th-century railroad tax cases, *California* v. *San Pablo & Tulare R. Co.*, 149 U.S. 308, 13 S. Ct. 876, 37 L. Ed. 747, *Little* v. *Bowers*, 134 U.S. 547, 10 S. Ct. 620, 33 L. Ed. 1016, and *San Mateo County*

v. *Southern Pacific R. Co.*, 116 U.S. 138, 6 S. Ct. 317, 29 L. Ed. 589, support the argument that an unaccepted settlement offer can moot a complaint. Pp. 160–166, 193 L. Ed. 2d, at 579-582.

2. Campbell's status as a federal contractor does not entitle it to immunity from suit for its violation of the TCPA. Unlike the United States and its agencies, federal contractors do not enjoy absolute immunity. A federal contractor who simply performs as directed by the Government may be shielded from liability for injuries caused by its conduct. See *Yearsley*, 309 U.S., at 20-21, 60 S. Ct. 413, 84 L. Ed. 554. But no "derivative immunity" exists when the contractor has "exceeded [its] authority" or its authority "was not validly conferred."

Id., at 21, 60 S. Ct. 413, 84 L. Ed. 554. The summary judgment record includes evidence that the Navy authorized Campbell to send text messages only to individuals who had "opted in" to receive solicitations, as required by the TCPA. When a contractor violates both federal law and the Government's explicit instructions, as alleged here, no immunity shields the contractor from suit. Pp. 166–169, 193 L. Ed. 2d, at 583-584.

Ginsburg, J., delivered the opinion of the Court, in which Kennedy, Breyer, Sotomayor, and Kagan, JJ., joined. Thomas, J., filed an opinion concurring in the judgment. Roberts, C. J., filed a dissenting opinion, in which Scalia and Alito, JJ., joined. Alito, J., filed a dissenting opinion.

OPINION OF THE COURT

[577 U.S. 156]

Justice **Ginsburg** delivered the opinion of the Court.

Is an unaccepted offer to satisfy the named plaintiff's individual claim sufficient to render a case moot when the complaint seeks relief on behalf of the plaintiff and a class of persons similarly situated? This question, on which Courts of Appeals have divided, was reserved in *Genesis HealthCare Corp.* v. *Symczyk*, 569 U.S. 66, 72, 73, n. 4, 133 S. Ct. 1523, 185 L. Ed. 2d 636 (2013). We hold today, in accord with Rule 68 of the Federal Rules of Civil Procedure, that [1] an unaccepted settlement offer has no force. Like other unaccepted contract offers, it creates no lasting right or obligation. With the offer off the table, and the defendant's continuing denial of liability, adversity between the parties persists.

This case presents a second ques-

tion. The claim in suit concerns performance of the petitioner's contract with the Federal Government. Does the sovereign's immunity from suit shield the petitioner, a private enterprise, as well? We hold that the petitioner's status as a Government contractor does not entitle it to "derivative sovereign immunity," *i.e.,* the blanket immunity enjoyed by the sovereign.

I

[2] The Telephone Consumer Protection Act (TCPA or Act), 48 Stat. 1064, 47 U.S.C. § 227(b)(1)(A)(iii), prohibits any person, absent the prior express consent of a telephone-call recipient, from "mak[ing] any call . . . using any automatic telephone dialing system . . . to any telephone number assigned to a paging service [or] cellular telephone service." A text message to a cellular telephone, it is

undisputed, qualifies as a "call" within the compass of § 227(b)(1)(A)(iii). 768 F.3d 871, 874 (CA9 2014). For damages occasioned by conduct violating the TCPA, § 227(b)(3) authorizes a private right of action. A plaintiff successful in such an action may recover her "actual monetary loss" or $500 for each violation, "whichever is greater." Damages may be trebled if "the defendant willfully or knowingly violated" the Act.

[577 U.S. 157]

Petitioner Campbell-Ewald Company (Campbell) is a nationwide advertising and marketing communications agency. Beginning in 2000, the United States Navy engaged Campbell to develop and execute a multimedia recruiting campaign. In 2005 and 2006, Campbell proposed to the Navy a campaign involving text messages sent to young adults, the Navy's target audience, encouraging them to learn more about the Navy. The Navy approved Campbell's proposal, conditioned on sending the messages only to individuals who had "opted in" to receipt of marketing solicitations on topics that included service in the Navy. App. 42. In final form, the message read:

> "Destined for something big? Do it in the Navy. Get a career. An education. And a chance to serve a greater cause. For a FREE Navy video call [phone number]." 768 F.3d, at 873.

Campbell then contracted with Mindmatics LLC, which generated a list of cellular phone numbers geared to the Navy's target audience—namely, cellular phone users between the ages of 18 and 24 who had consented to receiving solicitations by text message. In May 2006, Mindmatics transmitted the Navy's message to over 100,000 recipients.

Respondent Jose Gomez was a recipient of the Navy's recruiting message. Alleging that he had never consented to receiving the message, that his age was nearly 40, and that Campbell had violated the TCPA by sending the message (and perhaps others like it), Gomez filed a class-action complaint in the District Court for the Central District of California in 2010. On behalf of a nationwide class of individuals who had received, but had not consented to receipt of, the text message, Gomez sought treble statutory damages, costs, and attorney's fees, also an injunction against Campbell's involvement in unsolicited messaging. App. 16-24.

Prior to the agreed-upon deadline for Gomez to file a motion for class certification, Campbell proposed to settle Gomez's

[577 U.S. 158]

individual claim and filed an offer of judgment pursuant to Federal Rule of Civil Procedure 68. App. to Pet. for Cert. 52a-61a.[1] Campbell offered to pay Gomez his costs, excluding attorney's fees, and $1,503 per message for the May 2006 text message and any other text message

---

1. Federal Rule of Civil Procedure 68 provides, in relevant part:

[3] **"(a) Making an Offer; Judgment on an Accepted Offer.** At least 14 days before the date set for trial, a party defending against a claim may serve on an opposing party an offer to allow judgment on specified terms, with the costs then accrued. If, within 14 days after being served, the opposing party serves written notice accepting the offer, either party may then file the offer and notice of acceptance, plus proof of service. The clerk must then enter judgment.

"(b) Unaccepted Offer. An unaccepted offer is considered withdrawn, but it does not preclude a later offer. Evidence of an unaccepted offer is not admissible except in a proceeding to determine costs.

Gomez could show he had received, thereby satisfying his personal treble-damages claim. *Id.*, at 53a. Campbell also proposed a stipulated injunction in which it agreed to be barred from sending text messages in violation of the TCPA. The proposed injunction, however, denied liability and the allegations made in the complaint, and disclaimed the existence of grounds for the imposition of an injunction. *Id.*, at 56a. The settlement offer did not include attorney's fees, Campbell observed, because the TCPA does not provide for an attorney's-fee award. *Id.*, at 53a. Gomez did not accept the settlement offer and allowed Campbell's Rule 68 submission to lapse after the time, 14 days, specified in the Rule.

Campbell thereafter moved to dismiss the case pursuant to Federal Rule of Civil Procedure 12(b)(1) for lack of subject-matter jurisdiction. No Article III case or controversy remained, Campbell urged, because its offer mooted Gomez's individual claim by providing him with complete relief. Gomez had not moved for class certification before

[577 U.S. 159]

his claim became moot, Campbell added, so the putative class claims also became moot. The District Court denied Campbell's motion. 805 F. Supp. 2d 923 (CD Cal. 2011).[2] Gomez was not dilatory in filing his certification request, the District Court determined; consequently, the court noted, the class claims would "relat[e] back" to the date Gomez filed the complaint. *Id.*, at 930-931.

After limited discovery, Campbell

moved for summary judgment on a discrete ground. The U. S. Navy enjoys the sovereign's immunity from suit under the TCPA, Campbell argued. The District Court granted the motion. Relying on our decision in *Yearsley* v. *W. A. Ross Constr. Co.*, 309 U.S. 18, 60 S. Ct. 413, 84 L. Ed. 554 (1940), the court held that, as a contractor acting on the Navy's behalf, Campbell acquired the Navy's immunity. No. CV 10-02007 DMG (CD Cal., Feb. 22, 2013), App. to Pet. for Cert. 22a-34a, 2013 WL 655237.

The Court of Appeals for the Ninth Circuit reversed the summary judgment entered for Campbell. 768 F.3d 871. The appeals court disagreed with the District Court's ruling on the immunity issue, but agreed that Gomez's case remained live. Concerning Gomez's individual claim, the Court of Appeals relied on its then-recent decision in *Diaz* v. *First American Home Buyers Protection Corp.*, 732 F.3d 948 (2013). *Diaz* held that "an unaccepted Rule 68 offer that would fully satisfy a plaintiff's [individual] claim is insufficient to render th[at] claim moot." *Id.*, at 950. As to the class relief Gomez sought, the Ninth Circuit held that "an unaccepted Rule 68 offer of judgment—for the full amount of the named plaintiff's individual claim and made before the named plaintiff files a motion for class certification—does not moot a class action." 768 F.3d, at 875 (quoting *Pitts* v. *Terrible Herbst, Inc.*, 653 F.3d 1081, 1091-1092 (CA9 2011)).

[577 U.S. 160]

Next, the Court of Appeals held that Campbell was not entitled to "derivative sovereign immunity" un-

"**(d) Paying Costs After an Unaccepted Offer.** If the judgment that the offeree finally obtains is not more favorable than the unaccepted offer, the offeree must pay the costs incurred after the offer was made."

2. Because Campbell had already answered the complaint, the District Court construed Campbell's motion as a request for summary judgment. 805 F. Supp. 2d, at 927, n. 2.

der this Court's decision in *Yearsley* or on any other basis. 768 F.3d, at 879-881. Vacating the District Court's judgment, the Ninth Circuit remanded the case for further proceedings.[3]

We granted certiorari to resolve a disagreement among the Courts of Appeals over whether an unaccepted offer can moot a plaintiff's claim, thereby depriving federal courts of Article III jurisdiction. Compare *Bais Yaakov* v. *Act, Inc.*, 798 F.3d 46, 52 (CA1 2015); *Hooks* v. *Landmark Industries, Inc.*, 797 F.3d 309, 315 (CA5 2015); *Chapman* v. *First Index, Inc.*, 796 F.3d 783, 787 (CA7 2015); *Tanasi* v. *New Alliance Bank*, 786 F.3d 195, 200 (CA2 2015); *Stein* v. *Buccaneers Limited Partnership*, 772 F.3d 698, 703 (CA11 2014); *Diaz*, 732 F.3d, at 954-955 (holding that an unaccepted offer does not render a plaintiff's claim moot), with *Warren* v. *Sessoms & Rogers, P. A.*, 676 F.3d 365, 371 (CA4 2012); *O'Brien* v. *Ed Donnelly Enterprises, Inc.*, 575 F.3d 567, 574-575 (CA6 2009); *Weiss* v. *Regal Collections*, 385 F.3d 337, 340 (CA3 2004) (noting that an unaccepted offer can moot an individual plaintiff's claim). We granted review as well to resolve the federal contractor immunity question Campbell's petition raised. 575 U.S. 1008, 135 S. Ct. 2311, 191 L. Ed. 2d 977 (2015).

II

[4] Article III of the Constitution limits federal-court jurisdiction to "cases" and "controversies." U. S. Const., Art. III, § 2. We have interpreted this requirement to demand that "an actual controversy . . . be extant at all stages of review, not merely at the time the complaint is filed." *Arizonans for Official English* v. *Arizona*, 520 U.S. 43, 67, 117 S. Ct. 1055, 137 L. Ed. 2d 170 (1997) (quoting *Preiser* v. *Newkirk*, 422 U.S. 395, 401, 95 S. Ct. 2330, 45 L. Ed. 2d 272 (1975)). "If an intervening circumstance deprives the plaintiff of a 'personal

[577 U.S. 161]

stake in the outcome of the lawsuit,' at any point during litigation, the action can no longer proceed and must be dismissed as moot." *Genesis HealthCare Corp.*, 569 U.S., at 72, 133 S. Ct. 1523, 185 L. Ed. 2d 636 (quoting *Lewis* v. *Continental Bank Corp.*, 494 U.S. 472, 477-478, 110 S. Ct. 1249, 108 L. Ed. 2d 400 (1990)). A case becomes moot, however, "only when it is impossible for a court to grant any effectual relief whatever to the prevailing party." *Knox* v. *Service Employees*, 567 U.S. 298, 307, 132 S. Ct. 2277, 183 L. Ed. 2d 281 (2012) (internal quotation marks omitted). "As long as the parties have a concrete interest, however small, in the outcome of the litigation, the case is not moot." *Chafin* v. *Chafin*, 568 U.S. 165, 172, 133 S. Ct. 1017, 185 L. Ed. 2d 1 (2013) (internal quotation marks omitted).

In *Genesis HealthCare*, the Court considered a collective action brought by Laura Symczyk, a former employee of Genesis HealthCare Corp. Symczyk sued on behalf of herself and similarly situated employees for alleged violations of the Fair Labor Standards Act of 1938, 29 U.S.C. § 201 *et seq.* In that case, as here, the defendant served the plaintiff with an offer of judgment pursuant to Rule 68 that would have satisfied the plaintiff's individual damages claim. 569 U.S., at 69, 133

---

3. The Court of Appeals stayed its mandate pending proceedings in this Court. App. to Pet. for Cert. 62a-63a.

S. Ct. 1523, 185 L. Ed. 2d 636. Also as here, the plaintiff allowed the offer to lapse by failing to respond within the time specified in the Rule. *Id.,* at ——(70), 133 S. Ct. 1523, 185 L. Ed. 2d 636. But unlike the case Gomez mounted, Symczyk did not dispute in the lower courts that Genesis Health-Care's offer mooted her individual claim. *Id.,* at 72–73, 133 S. Ct. 1523, 185 L. Ed. 2d 636. Because of that failure, the *Genesis HealthCare* majority refused to rule on the issue. Instead, the majority simply assumed, without deciding, that an offer of complete relief pursuant to Rule 68, even if unaccepted, moots a plaintiff's claim. *Id.,* at 73, 133 S. Ct. 1523, 185 L. Ed. 2d 636. Having made that assumption, the Court proceeded to consider whether the action remained justiciable on the basis of the collective-action allegations alone. Absent a plaintiff with a live individual case, the Court concluded, the suit could not be maintained. *Ibid.*

Justice Kagan, writing in dissent, explained that she would have reached the threshold question and would have

[577 U.S. 162]

held that "an unaccepted offer of judgment cannot moot a case." *Id.*, at 81, 33 S. Ct. 1523, 185 L. Ed. 2d 636. She reasoned:

[5] "When a plaintiff rejects such an offer—however good the terms— her interest in the lawsuit remains just what it was before. And so too does the court's ability to grant her relief. An unaccepted settlement offer—like any unaccepted contract offer—is a legal nullity, with no operative effect. As every first-year law student learns, the recipient's rejection of an offer 'leaves the matter as if no offer had ever been made.' *Minneapolis & St. Louis R. Co.* v. *Columbus Rolling Mill,* 119 U.S. 149, 151 [7 S. Ct. 168, 30 L. Ed. 376] (1886). Nothing in Rule 68 alters that basic principle; to the contrary, that rule specifies that '[a]n unaccepted offer is considered withdrawn.' Fed. Rule Civ. Proc. 68(b). So assuming the case was live before—because the plaintiff had a stake and the court could grant relief—the litigation carries on, unmooted." *Ibid.*

We now adopt Justice Kagan's analysis, as has every Court of Appeals ruling on the issue post *Genesis HealthCare.*[4] Accordingly, we hold that Gomez's complaint was not effaced by Campbell's unaccepted offer to satisfy his individual claim.

As earlier recounted, see *supra*, at 157–158, 193 L. Ed. 2d, at 577-578, Gomez commenced an action against Campbell for violation of the TCPA, suing on behalf of himself and others similarly situated. Gomez sought treble statutory damages and an injunction on behalf of a nationwide class, but Campbell's settlement offer proposed relief for Gomez alone, and it did not admit liability.

[577 U.S. 163]

App. to Pet. for Cert. 58a. Gomez rejected Campbell's settlement terms and the offer of judgment.

Under basic principles of contract law, Campbell's settlement bid and Rule 68 offer of judgment, once rejected, had no continuing efficacy. See *Genesis HealthCare*, 569 U.S., at 81,

---

4. See *Bais Yaakov* v. *Act, Inc.*, 798 F.3d 46, 51-52 (CA1 2015); *Hooks* v. *Landmark Industries, Inc.*, 797 F.3d 309, 314-315 (CA5 2015); *Chapman* v. *First Index, Inc.*, 796 F.3d 783, 786-787 (CA7 2015); *Tanasi* v. *New Alliance Bank*, 786 F.3d 195, 199-200 (CA2 2015); *Stein* v. *Buccaneers Limited Partnership*, 772 F.3d 698, 702-703 (CA11 2014); *Diaz* v. *First American Home Buyers Corp.*, 732 F.3d 948, 953-955 (CA9 2013).

133 S. Ct. 1523, 185 L. Ed. 2d 636 (Kagan, J., dissenting). Absent Gomez's acceptance, Campbell's settlement offer remained only a proposal, binding neither Campbell nor Gomez. See App. to Pet. for Cert. 59a ("Please advise whether Mr. Gomez will accept [Campbell's] offer . . . ."). Having rejected Campbell's settlement bid, and given Campbell's continuing denial of liability, Gomez gained no entitlement to the relief Campbell previously offered. See *Eliason* v. *Henshaw*, 4 Wheat. 225, 228, 4 L. Ed. 556 (1819) ("It is an undeniable principle of the law of contracts, that an offer of a bargain by one person to another, imposes no obligation upon the former, until it is accepted by the latter . . . ."). In short, with no settlement offer still operative, the parties remained adverse; both retained the same stake in the litigation they had at the outset.

The Federal Rule in point, [6] Rule 68, hardly supports the argument that an unaccepted settlement offer can moot a complaint. An offer of judgment, the Rule provides, "is considered withdrawn" if not accepted within 14 days of its service. Fed. Rule Civ. Proc. 68(a), (b). The sole built-in sanction: "If the [ultimate] judgment . . . is not more favorable than the unaccepted offer, the offeree must pay the costs incurred after the offer was made." Rule 68(d).

In urging that an offer of judgment can render a controversy moot, Campbell features a trio of 19th-century railroad tax cases: *California* v. *San Pablo & Tulare R. Co.*, 149 U.S. 308, 13 S. Ct. 876, 37 L. Ed. 747 (1893), *Little* v. *Bowers*, 134 U.S. 547, 10 S. Ct. 620, 33 L. Ed. 1016 (1890), and *San Mateo County* v. *Southern Pacific R. Co.*, 116 U.S. 138, 6 S. Ct. 317, 29 L. Ed. 589 (1885). None of those decisions suggests that an *unaccepted* settlement offer can put a plaintiff out of court. In *San Pablo*, California had sued to recover state and county taxes due from a railroad. In response, the railroad had

[577 U.S. 164]

not merely offered to pay the taxes in question. It had actually deposited the full amount demanded in a California bank in the State's name, in accord with a California statute that "extinguished" the railroad's tax obligations upon such payment. 149 U.S., at 313-314, 13 S. Ct. 876, 37 L. Ed. 747. *San Pablo* thus rested on California's substantive law, which required the State to accept a taxpayer's full payment of the amount in controversy. *San Mateo* and *Little* similarly involved actual payment of the taxes for which suit was brought. In all three cases, the railroad's payments had fully satisfied the asserted tax claims, and so extinguished them. *San Mateo*, 116 U.S., at 141-142, 6 S. Ct. 317, 29 L. Ed. 589; *Little*, 134 U.S., at 556, 10 S. Ct. 620, 33 L. Ed. 1016.[5]

[577 U.S. 165]

In contrast to the cases Campbell highlights, when the settlement offer Campbell extended to Gomez expired,

---

5. In addition to *California* v. *San Pablo & Tulare R. Co.*, 149 U.S. 308, 13 S. Ct. 876, 37 L. Ed. 747 (1893), The Chief Justice maintains, two recent decisions of the Court support its position: *Alvarez* v. *Smith*, 558 U.S. 87, 130 S. Ct. 576, 175 L. Ed. 2d 447 (2009), and *Already, LLC* v. *Nike, Inc.*, 568 U.S. 85, 133 S. Ct. 721, 184 L. Ed. 2d 553 (2013). See *post*, at 180–182, 193 L. Ed. 2d, at 591-593 (dissenting opinion). The Court's reasoning in those opinions, however, is consistent with our decision in this case. In *Alvarez*, the Court found moot claims for injunctive and declaratory relief in relation to cars and cash seized by the police. Through separate state-court proceedings, the State had "returned all the cars that it seized," and the plaintiff-property owners

Gomez remained emptyhanded; his TCPA complaint, which Campbell opposed on the merits, stood wholly unsatisfied. Because Gomez's individual claim was not made moot by the expired settlement offer, that claim would retain vitality during the time involved in determining whether the case could proceed on behalf of a class. **[7]** While a class lacks independent status until certified, see *Sosna* v. *Iowa*, 419 U.S. 393, 399, 95 S. Ct. 553, 42 L. Ed. 2d 532 (1975), a would-be class representative with a live claim of her own must be accorded a fair opportunity to show that certification is warranted.

The Chief Justice's dissent asserts that our decision transfers authority from the federal courts and "hands it to the plaintiff." *Post*, at 184, 193 L. Ed. 2d, at 594. Quite the contrary. The dissent's approach would place the defendant in the driver's seat. We encountered a kindred strategy in *U. S. Bancorp Mortgage Co.* v. *Bonner Mall Partnership*, 513 U.S. 18, 115 S. Ct. 386, 130 L. Ed. 2d 233 (1994). The parties in *Bancorp* had reached a voluntary settlement while the case was pending before this Court. *Id.*, at 20,

115 S. Ct. 386, 130 L. Ed. 2d 233. The petitioner then sought vacatur of the Court of Appeals' judgment, contending that it should be relieved from the adverse decision on the ground that the settlement made the dispute moot. The Court rejected this gambit. *Id.*, at 25, 115 S. Ct. 386, 130 L. Ed. 2d 233. Similarly here, Campbell sought to avoid a potential adverse decision, one that could expose it to damages a thousandfold larger than the bid Gomez declined to accept.

In sum, **[8]** an unaccepted settlement offer or offer of judgment does not moot a plaintiff's case, so the District Court

[577 U.S. 166]

retained jurisdiction to adjudicate Gomez's complaint. That ruling suffices to decide this case. We need not, and do not, now decide whether the result would be different if a defendant deposits the full amount of the plaintiff's individual claim in an account payable to the plaintiff, and the court then enters judgment for the plaintiff in that amount. That question is appropriately reserved for a case in which it is not hypothetical.

had "either forfeited any relevant cash or ha[d] accepted as final the State's return of some of it." 558 U.S., at 89, 95-96, 130 S. Ct. 576, 175 L. Ed. 2d 447. *Alvarez* thus resembles the railroad tax cases described above: The *Alvarez* plaintiffs had in fact received all the relief they could claim, all "underlying property disputes" had ended, *id.*, at 89, 130 S. Ct. 576, 175 L. Ed. 2d 447, and as the complaint sought "only declaratory and injunctive relief, not damages," *id.*, at 92, 130 S. Ct. 576, 175 L. Ed. 2d 447, no continuing controversy remained.

Already concerned a trademark owned by Nike. Already sought a declaratory judgment invalidating the trademark. The injury Already asserted was the ongoing threat that Nike would sue for trademark infringement. In response to Already's claim, Nike filed a "Covenant Not to Sue," in which it promised not to bring any trademark claims based on Already's existing or similar footwear designs. 568 U.S., at 88–89, 133 S. Ct. 721, 184 L. Ed. 2d 553. The Court found this covenant sufficient to overcome the rule that "voluntary cessation" is generally inadequate to moot a claim. *Id.*, at 93, 133 S. Ct. 721, 184 L. Ed. 2d 553. True, Nike's covenant was unilateral, but it afforded Already blanket protection from future trademark litigation. *Id.*, at 95, 133 S. Ct. 721, 184 L. Ed. 2d 553. The risk that underpinned Already's standing—the Damocles' sword of a trademark infringement suit—thus ceased to exist given Nike's embracive promise not to sue. In short, in both *Alvarez* and *Already*, the plaintiffs had received full redress for the injuries asserted in their complaints. Here, by contrast, Campbell's revocable offer, far from providing Gomez the relief sought in his complaint, gave him nary a penny.

III

The second question before us is whether Campbell's status as a federal contractor renders it immune from suit for violating the TCPA by sending text messages to unconsenting recipients. **[9]** The United States and its agencies, it is undisputed, are not subject to the TCPA's prohibitions because no statute lifts their immunity. Brief for Petitioner 2; Brief for Respondent 43. Do federal contractors share the Government's unqualified immunity from liability and litigation? We hold they do not.

[10] "[G]overnment contractors obtain certain immunity in connection with work which they do pursuant to their contractual undertakings with the United States." *Brady* v. *Roosevelt S. S. Co.*, 317 U.S. 575, 583, 63 S. Ct. 425, 87 L. Ed. 471 (1943). That immunity, however, unlike the sovereign's, is not absolute. See *id.*, at 580-581, 63 S. Ct. 425, 87 L. Ed. 471. Campbell asserts "derivative sovereign immunity," Brief for Petitioner 35, but can offer no authority for the notion that private persons performing Government work acquire the Government's embracive immunity. When a contractor violates both federal law and the Government's explicit instructions, as here alleged, no "derivative immunity" shields the contractor from suit by persons adversely affected by the violation.

Campbell urges that two of our decisions support its "derivative immunity" defense: *Yearsley*, 309 U.S. 18,

60 S. Ct. 413, 84 L. Ed. 554, and *Filarsky* v. *Delia*, 566 U.S. 377, 132 S. Ct. 1657, 182 L. Ed. 2d 662 (2012). In *Yearsley*, a landowner asserted a claim for damages against a private company whose work building dikes on the Missouri River pursuant

[577 U.S. 167]

to its contract with the Federal Government had washed away part of the plaintiff's land. We held that the contractor was not answerable to the landowner. "[T]he work which the contractor had done in the river bed," we observed, "was all authorized and directed by the Government of the United States" and "performed pursuant to the Act of Congress." 309 U.S., at 20, 60 S. Ct. 413, 84 L. Ed. 554 (internal quotation marks omitted). Where the Government's "authority to carry out the project was validly conferred, that is, if what was done was within the constitutional power of Congress," we explained, "there is no liability on the part of the contractor" who simply performed as the Government directed. *Id.*, at 20-21, 60 S. Ct. 413, 84 L. Ed. 554.[6] The Court contrasted with *Yearsley* cases in which a Government agent had "exceeded his authority" or the authority "was not validly conferred"; in those circumstances, the Court said, the agent could be held liable for conduct causing injury to another. *Id.*, at 21, 60 S. Ct. 413, 84 L. Ed. 554.[7]

In *Filarsky*, we considered whether a private attorney temporarily retained by a municipal government as

---

6. If there had been a taking of the plaintiff's property, the Court noted, "a plain and adequate remedy" would be at hand, *i.e.*, recovery from the United States of "just compensation." *Yearsley*, 309 U.S., at 21, 60 S. Ct. 413, 84 L. Ed. 554.

7. We disagree with the Court of Appeals to the extent that it described *Yearsley* as "establish-[ing] a narrow rule regarding claims arising out of property damage caused by public works projects." 768 F.3d, at 879. Critical in *Yearsley* was not the involvement of public works, but the contractor's performance in compliance with all federal directions.

an investigator could claim qualified immunity in an action brought under 42 U.S.C. § 1983. Finding no distinction in the common law "between public servants and private individuals engaged in public service," we held that the investigator could assert "qualified immunity" in the lawsuit. 566 U.S., at 387, 384, 132 S. Ct. 1657, 182 L. Ed. 2d 662. Qualified immunity reduces the risk that contractors will shy away from government work. But the doctrine is bounded in a way that Campbell's "derivative immunity" plea is not. [11] "Qualified immunity may be overcome . . .

[577 U.S. 168]

if the defendant knew or should have known that his conduct violated a right 'clearly established' at the time of the episode in suit." *Id.*, at 394, 132 S. Ct. 1657, 182 L. Ed. 2d 662 (Ginsburg, J., concurring) (citing *Harlow* v. *Fitzgerald*, 457 U.S. 800, 818, 102 S. Ct. 2727, 73 L. Ed. 2d 396 (1982)). Campbell does not here contend that the TCPA's requirements or the Navy's instructions failed to qualify as "clearly established."

[12] At the pretrial stage of litigation, we construe the record in a light favorable to the party seeking to avoid summary disposition, here, Gomez. *Matsushita Elec. Industrial Co.* v. *Zenith Radio Corp.*, 475 U.S. 574, 587, 106 S. Ct. 1348, 89 L. Ed. 2d 538 (1986). In opposition to summary judgment, Gomez presented evidence that the Navy authorized Campbell to send text messages only to individuals who had "opted in" to receive solicitations. App. 42-44; 768 F.3d, at 874. A Navy representative noted the importance of ensuring that the mes-

sage recipient list be "kosher" (*i.e.,* that all recipients had consented to receiving messages like the recruiting text), and made clear that the Navy relied on Campbell's representation that the list was in compliance. App. 43. See also *ibid.* (noting that Campbell itself encouraged the Navy to use only an opt-in list in order to meet national and local law requirements). In short, the current record reveals no basis for arguing that Gomez's right to remain message-free was in doubt or that Campbell complied with the Navy's instructions.

We do not overlook that subcontractor Mindmatics, not Campbell, dispatched the Navy's recruiting message to unconsenting recipients. But [13] the Federal Communications Commission has ruled that, under federal common-law principles of agency, there is vicarious liability for TCPA violations. *In re Joint Petition Filed by Dish Network, LLC*, 28 FCC Rcd. 6574 (2013). The Ninth Circuit deferred to that ruling, 768 F.3d, at 878, and we have no cause to question it. Campbell's vicarious liability for Mindmatics' conduct, however, in no way advances Campbell's contention that it

[577 U.S. 169]

acquired the sovereign's immunity from suit based on its contract with the Navy.

* * *

For the reasons stated, the judgment of the Court of Appeals for the Ninth Circuit is affirmed, and the case is remanded for further proceedings consistent with this opinion.

It is so ordered.

SEPARATE OPINIONS

Justice **Thomas**, concurring in the judgment.

The Court correctly concludes that an offer of complete relief on a claim does not render that claim moot. But, in my view, the Court does not advance a sound basis for this conclusion. The Court rests its conclusion on modern contract law principles and a recent dissent concerning Federal Rule of Civil Procedure 68. See *ante*, at 160–163, 193 L. Ed. 2d, at 579–581. I would rest instead on the common-law history of tenders. That history—which led to Rule 68—demonstrates that a mere offer of the sum owed is insufficient to eliminate a court's jurisdiction to decide the case to which the offer related. I therefore concur only in the judgment.

I

The text of Article III's case-or-controversy requirement, that requirement's drafting history, and our precedents do not appear to provide sufficiently specific principles to resolve this case. When faced with such uncertainty, it seems particularly important for us to look to how courts traditionally have viewed a defendant's offer to pay the plaintiff's alleged damages. That history—which stretches from the common law directly to Rule 68 and modern settlement offers—reveals one unbroken practice that should resolve this case: A defendant's offer to pay the plaintiff—without more—would not have deprived a court of jurisdiction. Campbell-Ewald's offers thus do not bar federal courts from continuing to hear this case.

[577 U.S. 170]

A

Modern settlement procedure has its origins in the law of tenders, as refined in the 18th and 19th centuries. As with much of the early common law, the law of tenders had many rigid formalities. These formalities make clear that, around the time of the framing, a mere offer of relief was insufficient to deprive a court of jurisdiction.

At common law, a prospective defendant could prevent a case from proceeding, but he needed to provide substantially more than a bare offer. A "mere proposal or proposition" to pay a claim was inadequate to end a case. A. Hunt, A Treatise on the Law of Tender, and Bringing Money Into Court §§ 1-2, 3-4 (1903) (Hunt) (citing cases from the 1800's). Nor would a defendant's "readiness and an ability to pay the money" suffice to end a case. *Holmes* v. *Holmes*, 12 Barb. 137, 144 (N. Y. 1851). Rather, a prospective defendant needed to provide a "tender"—an offer to pay the entire claim before a suit was filed, accompanied by "actually produc[ing]" the sum "at the time of tender" in an "unconditional" manner. M. Bacon, A New Abridgment of the Law 314-315, 321 (1856) (citing cases from the early 1800's).

Furthermore, in state and federal courts, a tender of the amount due was deemed "an admission of a liability" on the cause of action to which the tender related, so any would-be defendant who tried to deny liability could not effectuate a tender. Hunt § 400, at 448; see *Cottier* v. *Stimpson*, 18 F. 689, 691 (Ore. 1883) (explaining that a tender constitutes "an admission of the cause of action"); *The Rossend Castle Dillenback* v. *The Rossend Castle*, 30 F. 462, 464 (SDNY 1887) (same). As one treatise explained, "[a] tender must be of a specific sum which the tenderor *admits* to be due"—"[t]here must be no denial of the debt." Hunt § 242, at 253 (emphasis added). The tender had to offer and actually deliver complete relief.

585

See *id.*, § 2, at 4; *Sheredine* v. *Gaul*, 22 Dallas 190, 191, 1 L. Ed. 344 (Pa. 1792) (defendant must "brin[g] the money into Court"). And an offer to pay less than what was demanded

[577 U.S. 171]

was not a valid tender. See, *e.g.*, *Elderkin* v. *Fellows*, 60 Wis. 339, 340-341, 19 N.W. 101, 102 (1884).

Even when a potential defendant properly effectuated a tender, the case would not necessarily end. At common law, a plaintiff was entitled to "deny that [the tender was] sufficient to satisfy his demand" and accordingly "go on to trial." *Raiford* v. *Governor*, 29 Ala. 382, 384 (1856); see also Hunt § 511, at 595.*

This history demonstrates that, at common law, a defendant or prospective defendant had to furnish far more than a mere offer of settlement to end a case. This history also demonstrates that courts at common law would not have understood a mere offer to strip them of jurisdiction.

B

Although 19th-century state statutes expanded the common-law tender regime, the law retained its essential features. See Bone, "To Encourage Settlement": Rule 68, Offers of Judgment, and the History of the Federal Rules of Civil Procedure, 102 Nw. U. L. Rev. 1561, 1585 (2008) (Bone). These changes, for example, allowed defendants to offer a tender "during the pendency of an action," as well as before it commenced. *Taylor* v. *Brooklyn Elevated R. Co.*, 119 N.Y. 561, 565,

23 N.E. 1106, 1107 (1890); cf. *Colby* v. *Reed*, 99 U.S. 560, 566, 25 L. Ed. 484 (1879) (at common law, generally no "right of tender after action brought"). Statutes also expanded the right of tender to cover types of actions in which damages were not certain. Compare *Dedekam* v. *Vose*, 7 F. Cas. 337, 338 (SDNY 1853) ("[T]ender could not be maintained,

[577 U.S. 172]

according to the strict principles of the common law," in cases where damages were not easily ascertainable), with *Patrick* v. *Illawaco Oyster Co.*, 189 Wash. 152, 155, 63 P.2d 520, 521 (1937) (state statute "extend[ed] the common-law rule" to tort actions).

Nevertheless, state statutes generally retained the core of the common-law tender rules. Most critically for this case, a mere offer remained insufficient to end a lawsuit. See, *e.g.*, *Kilts* v. *Seeber,* 10 How. Pr. 270, 271 (N. Y. 1854) (under New York law, a mere offer was insufficient to preclude litigation). Like the common-law tender rules, state statutes recognized that plaintiffs could continue to pursue litigation by rejecting an offer. See Bone 1586.

C

The offer-of-judgment procedure in Rule 68 was modeled after a provision in the New York Field Code that was enacted in the mid-19th century. See *id.*, at 1583-1584. That code abrogated many of the common-law formalities governing civil procedure. Among its innovations, the code al-

---

* Nevertheless, the common law strongly encouraged a plaintiff to accept a tender by penalizing plaintiffs who improperly rejected them. A plaintiff would not be able to recover any damages that accrued after the tender, nor could he receive the costs of the suit if the jury returned a verdict for either the amount offered or less. See Hunt §§ 363-364, at 403-404. This rule remains today. See Fed. Rule Civ. Proc. 68(d) (taxing costs to plaintiff who fails to recover more than the offer of judgment).

lowed defendants in any cause of action to make an offer in writing to the plaintiff proposing to accept judgment against the defendant for a specified sum. See The Code of Procedure of the State of New York From 1848 to 1871: Comprising the Act as Originally Enacted and the Various Amendments Made Thereto, to the Close of the Session of 1870, § 385, p. 274 (1870). The plaintiff could accept the offer, which would end the litigation, or reject the offer, in which case the offer was considered with drawn without any admission of liability by the defendant. *Ibid.*

In 1938, Rule 68 was adopted as part of the Federal Rules of Civil Procedure, and has subsisted throughout the years without material changes. See Bone 1564. As it did in 1938, Rule 68 now authorizes "a party defending against a claim" to "serve on an opposing party an offer to allow judgment on specified terms." Rule 68(a). Rule 68 also

[577 U.S. 173]

provides a plaintiff the option to accept or reject an offer. If the plaintiff accepts the offer, the "clerk must then enter judgment," but "[a]n unaccepted offer is considered withdrawn." Rules 68(a)-(b). Withdrawn offers (unlike common-law tenders) cannot be used in court as an admission against defendants. Rule 68(b).

D

In light of the history discussed above, a rejected offer does not end the case. And this consistent historical practice demonstrates why Campbell-Ewald's offers do not divest a federal court of jurisdiction to entertain Gomez's suit. Campbell-Ewald made two settlement offers after Gomez sued—one filed with the District Court under Rule 68 and one free-standing settlement offer. But with neither of these offers did the company make payment; it only declared its intent to pay. Because Campbell-Ewald only offered to pay Gomez's claim but took no further steps, the court was not deprived of jurisdiction.

II

Although the Court reaches the right result, I cannot adopt its reasoning. Building on the dissent in *Genesis HealthCare Corp.* v. *Symczyk*, 569 U.S. 66, 133 S. Ct. 1523, 185 L. Ed. 2d 636 (2013), the Court relies on principles of contract law that an unaccepted offer is a legal nullity. But the question here is not whether Campbell-Ewald's offer formed an enforceable contract. The question is whether its continuing offer of complete relief eliminated the case or controversy required by Article III. By looking only to contract law and one recent Rule 68 opinion, the Court fails to confront this broader issue. Instead, I believe that we must resolve the meaning of "case" and "controversy" in Article III by looking to "the traditional, fundamental limitations upon the powers of common-law courts" because "cases" and "controversies" "have virtually no meaning except by reference to that tradition."

[577 U.S. 174]

Honig v. *Doe*, 484 U.S. 305, 340, 108 S. Ct. 592, 98 L. Ed. 2d 686 (1988) (Scalia, J., dissenting).

The Chief Justice's dissent argues that examining whether the requirements of common-law tenders have been met does not answer "whether there is a case or controversy for purposes of Article III." *Post*, at 183, 193 L. Ed. 2d, at 593–594, n. 3. As explained above, however, courts have historically refused to dismiss cases when an offer did not conform to the strict tender rules. The logical implications of The Chief Justice's reasoning are that the common-law tender rules conflict with Article III and that the Constitution bars Article III courts from following those principles. But see *Colby*, 99 U.S., at 566, 25 L. Ed. 484 (stating that, to stop litigation, a party "must adopt the measure prescribed by the common law, except in jurisdictions where a different mode of proceeding is prescribed by statute"). That reasoning, therefore, calls into question the history and tradition that the case-or-controversy requirement embodies.

The Chief Justice also contends that our precedents "plainly establish that an admission of liability is not required for a case to be moot under Article III." *Post*, at 183, 193 L. Ed. 2d, at 594, n. 3. But we need not decide today whether compliance with every common-law formality would be necessary to end a case. The dispositive point is that state and federal courts have not considered a mere offer, without more, sufficient to moot the case. None of the cases cited by The Chief Justice hold that a retrospective claim for money damages can become moot based on a mere offer. *California* v. *San Pablo & Tulare R. Co.*, 149 U.S. 308, 13 S. Ct. 876, 37 L. Ed. 747 (1893), is inapposite because that decision involved a fully tendered offer that extinguished the tax debt under California law. *Id.*, at 313-314. *Alvarez* v. *Smith*, 558 U.S. 87, 130 S. Ct. 576, 175 L. Ed. 2d 447 (2009), and *Already, LLC* v. *Nike, Inc.*, 568 U.S. 88, 133 S. Ct. 721, 184 L. Ed. 2d 553 (2013), are also not on point. Both involved claims for injunctive or declaratory relief that became moot when the defendants ceased causing actual or threatened injury. But whether a claim for prospective relief

is moot is different from the issue in this case, which involves claims for damages to remedy past harms. See, *e.g.*, *Parents Involved in Community Schools* v. *Seattle School Dist. No. 1*, 551 U.S. 701, 720, 127 S. Ct. 2738, 168 L. Ed. 2d 508 (2007) (plaintiff "sought damages in her complaint, which is sufficient to preserve our ability to consider the question"); *Alvarez, supra*, at 92, 130 S. Ct. 576, 175 L. Ed. 2d 447 (suggesting that a "continuing controversy over damages" would mean that the case was not moot).

As explained above, I would follow history and tradition in construing Article III, and so I find that Campbell-Ewald's mere offers did not deprive the District Court of jurisdiction. Accordingly, I concur in the judgment only.

Chief Justice **Roberts**, with whom Justice **Scalia** and Justice **Alito** join, dissenting.

This case is straightforward. Jose Gomez alleges that the marketing firm Campbell-Ewald (Campbell) sent him text messages without his permission, and he requests relief under the Telephone Consumer Protection Act. That Act permits consumers to recover statutory damages for unauthorized text messages. Based on Gomez's allegations, the maximum that he could recover under the Act is $1500 per text message, plus the costs of filing suit. Campbell has offered to pay Gomez that amount, but it turns out he wants more. He wants a federal court to say he is right.

The problem for Gomez is that the federal courts exist to resolve real disputes, not to rule on a plaintiff's entitlement to relief already there for the taking. As this Court has said, "[n]o principle is more fundamental to the judiciary's proper role in our system of government than the constitutional limitation of federal-court jurisdiction to actual cases or controversies." *Raines* v. *Byrd*, 521 U.S. 811, 818, 117 S. Ct. 2312, 138 L. Ed. 2d 849 (1997) (quoting *Simon* v. *Eastern Ky. Welfare Rights Organization*, 426 U.S. 26, 37, 96 S. Ct. 1917, 48 L. Ed. 2d 450 (1976)). If there is no actual case or controversy, the lawsuit is moot, and the power of the federal courts to declare the law has come to an end. Here, the

[577 U.S. 176]

District Court found that Campbell agreed to fully satisfy Gomez's claims. That makes the case moot, and Gomez is not entitled to a ruling on the merits of a moot case.

I respectfully dissent.

I

A

In 1793, President George Washington sent a letter to Chief Justice John jay and the Associate Justices of the Supreme Court, asking for the opinion of the Court on the rights and obligations of the United States with respect to the war between Great Britain and France. The Supreme Court politely—but firmly—refused the request, concluding that "the lines of separation drawn by the Constitution between the three departments of the government" prohibit the federal courts from issuing such advisory opinions. 3 Correspondence and Public Papers of John jay 486-489 (H. Johnston ed. 1890-1893).

That prohibition has remained "the oldest and most consistent thread in the federal law of justiciability." *Flast* v. *Cohen*, 392 U.S. 83, 96, 88 S. Ct.

1942, 20 L. Ed. 2d 947 (1968) (internal quotation marks omitted). And for good reason. It is derived from Article III of the Constitution, which limits the authority of the federal courts to the adjudication of "Cases" or "Controversies." U. S. Const., Art. III, § 2. The case or controversy requirement is at once an important check on the powers of the Federal Judiciary and the source of those powers. In *Marbury* v. *Madison*, 1 Cranch 137, 177, 2 L. Ed. 60 (1803), Chief Justice Marshall established that it is "the province and duty of the judicial department to say what the law is." Not because there is a provision in the Constitution that says so—there isn't. Instead, the federal courts wield that power because they have to decide cases and controversies, and "[t]hose who apply [a] rule to particular cases, must of necessity expound and interpret that rule." *Ibid.* Federal courts may exercise their authority "only in the last resort, and as a necessity

[577 U.S. 177]

in the determination of real, earnest and vital controversy between individuals." *Chicago & Grand Trunk R. Co.* v. *Wellman*, 143 U.S. 339, 345, 12 S. Ct. 400, 36 L. Ed. 176 (1892); see also *Allen* v. *Wright*, 468 U.S. 737, 752, 104 S. Ct. 3315, 82 L. Ed. 2d 556 (1984). "If a dispute is not a proper case or controversy, the courts have no business deciding it, or expounding the law in the course of doing so." *DaimlerChrysler Corp.* v. *Cuno*, 547 U.S. 332, 341, 126 S. Ct. 1854, 164 L. Ed. 2d 589 (2006).

A case or controversy exists when both the plaintiff and the defendant have a "personal stake" in the lawsuit. *Camreta* v. *Greene*, 563 U.S. 692, 701, 131 S. Ct. 2020, 179 L. Ed. 2d 1118 (2011). A plaintiff demonstrates a personal stake by establishing standing to sue, which requires a "personal injury fairly traceable to the defendant's allegedly unlawful conduct and likely to be redressed by the requested relief." *Allen*, 468 U.S., at 751, 104 S. Ct. 3315, 82 L. Ed. 2d 556. A defendant demonstrates a personal stake through "an ongoing interest in the dispute." *Camreta*, 563 U.S., at 701, 131 S. Ct. 2020, 179 L. Ed. 2d 1118.

The personal stake requirement persists through every stage of the lawsuit. It "is not enough that a dispute was very much alive when suit was filed"; the "parties must continue to have a personal stake in the outcome of the lawsuit" to prevent the case from becoming moot. *Lewis* v. *Continental Bank Corp.*, 494 U.S. 472, 477-478, 110 S. Ct. 1249, 108 L. Ed. 2d 400 (1990) (internal quotation marks omitted). If either the plaintiff or the defendant ceases to have a concrete interest in the outcome of the litigation, there is no longer a live case or controversy. A federal court that decides the merits of such a case runs afoul of the prohibition on advisory opinions.

B

Applying those basic principles to this case, it is clear that the lawsuit is moot. All agree that at the time Gomez filed suit, he had a personal stake in the litigation. In his complaint, Gomez alleged that he suffered an injury in fact when he received unauthorized text messages from Campbell. To remedy that injury, he requested $1500 in statutory damages

[577 U.S. 178]

for each unauthorized text message. (It was later determined that he received only one text message.)

What happened next, however, is critical: After Gomez's initial legal volley, Campbell did not return fire. Instead, Campbell responded to the complaint with a freestanding offer to pay Gomez the maximum amount that he could recover under the statute: $1500 per unauthorized text message, plus court costs. Campbell also made an offer of judgment on the same terms under Rule 68 of the Federal Rules of Civil Procedure, which permits a defendant to recover certain attorney's fees if the Rule 68 offer is unaccepted and the plaintiff later recovers no more than the amount of the offer. Crucially, the District Court found that the "parties do not dispute" that Campbell's Rule 68 offer—reflecting the same terms as the freestanding offer—"would have fully satisfied the individual claims asserted, or that could have been asserted," by Gomez. 805 F. Supp. 2d 923, 927 (CD Cal. 2011).

When a plaintiff files suit seeking redress for an alleged injury, and the defendant *agrees* to fully redress that injury, there is no longer a case or controversy for purposes of Article III. After all, if the defendant is willing to remedy the plaintiff's injury without forcing him to litigate, the plaintiff cannot demonstrate an injury in need of redress by the court, and the defendant's interests are not adverse to the plaintiff. At that point, there is no longer any "necessity" to "expound and interpret" the law, *Marbury*, 1 Cranch, at 177, 2 L. Ed. 60, and the federal courts lack authority to hear the case. That is exactly what happened here: Once Campbell offered to fully remedy Gomez's injury, there was no longer any "necessity" for the

District Court to hear the merits of his case, rendering the lawsuit moot.[1]

[577 U.S. 179]

It is true that although Campbell has offered Gomez full relief, Campbell has not yet paid up. That does not affect the mootness inquiry under the facts of this case. Campbell is a multimillion dollar company, and the settlement offer here is for a few thousand dollars. The settlement offer promises "prompt payment," App. to Pet. for Cert. 59a, and it would be mere pettifoggery to argue that Campbell might not make good on that promise. In any event, to the extent there is a question whether Campbell is willing and able to pay, there is an easy answer: have the firm deposit a certified check with the trial court.

II

The Court today holds that Gomez's lawsuit is not moot. According to the Court, "An unaccepted settlement offer—like any unaccepted contract offer—is a legal nullity, with no operative effect." *Ante*, at 162, 193 L. Ed. 2d, at 580 (quoting *Genesis Health-Care Corp.* v. *Symczyk*, 569 U.S. 66, 81, 133 S. Ct. 1523, 185 L. Ed. 2d 636 (2013) (Kagan, J., dissenting)). And so, the Court concludes, if a plaintiff does not feel like accepting the defendant's complete offer of relief, the lawsuit cannot be moot because it is as if no offer had ever been made.

But a plaintiff is not the judge of whether federal litigation is necessary, and a mere *desire* that there be federal litigation—for whatever reason—does not make it *necessary*. When a lawsuit is filed, it is up to the federal court to determine whether a concrete case or controversy exists between

[577 U.S. 180]

the parties. That remains true throughout the litigation. Article III does not require the parties to affirmatively agree on a settlement before a case becomes moot. This Court has long held that when a defendant unilaterally remedies the injuries of the plaintiff, the case is moot—even if the plaintiff disagrees and refuses to settle the dispute, and even if the defendant continues to deny liability.

In *California* v. *San Pablo & Tulare R. Co.*, 149 U.S. 308, 13 S. Ct. 876, 37 L. Ed. 747 (1893), the State of California brought suit against a railroad company for back taxes. Before oral argument in this Court, the railroad offered to pay California the entire sum at issue, "together with interest, penalties and costs." *Id.*, at 313, 13 S. Ct. 876, 37 L. Ed. 747. Although California continued to litigate the case despite the railroad's offer of complete

---

1. The Court does not reach the question whether Gomez's claim for class relief prevents this case from becoming moot. The majority nevertheless suggests that Campbell "sought to avoid a potential adverse decision, one that could expose it to damages a thousandfold larger than the bid Gomez declined to accept." *Ante*, at 165, 193 L. Ed. 2d, at 582. But under this Court's precedents Gomez does not have standing to seek relief based solely on the alleged injuries of others, and Gomez's interest in sharing attorney's fees among class members or in obtaining a class incentive award does not create Article III standing. See *Lewis* v. *Continental Bank Corp.*, 494 U.S. 472, 480, 110 S. Ct. 1249, 108 L. Ed. 2d 400 (1990) (An "interest in attorney's fees is, of course, insufficient to create an Article III case or controversy where none exists on the merits of the underlying claim."); *Steel Co.* v. *Citizens for Better Environment*, 523 U.S. 83, 107, 118 S. Ct. 1003, 140 L. Ed. 2d 210 (1998) ("Obviously, however, a plaintiff cannot achieve standing to litigate a substantive issue by bringing suit for the cost of bringing suit. The litigation must give the plaintiff some other benefit besides reimbursement of costs that are a by-product of the litigation itself.").

relief, the Court concluded that the offer to pay the full sum, in addition to "the deposit of the money in a bank, which by a statute of the State ha[s] the same effect as actual payment and receipt of the money," mooted the case. *Id.*, at 314, 13 S. Ct. 876, 37 L. Ed. 747.

The Court grounded its decision in *San Pablo* on the prohibition against advisory opinions, explaining that "the court is not empowered to decide moot questions or abstract propositions, or to declare, for the government of future cases, principles or rules of law which cannot affect the result as to the thing in issue in the case." *Ibid.* Although the majority here places great weight on Gomez's rejection of Campbell's offer of complete relief, *San Pablo* did not consider the agreement of the parties to be relevant to the question of mootness. As the Court said then, "[n]o stipulation of parties or counsel, whether in the case before the court or in any other case, can enlarge the power, or affect the duty, of the court." *Ibid.*

More recently, in *Alvarez* v. *Smith*, 558 U.S. 87, 130 S. Ct. 576, 175 L. Ed. 2d 447 (2009), the Court found that a plaintiff's refusal to settle a case did not prevent it from becoming moot. In *Alvarez*, Chicago police officers had seized vehicles and cash from six individuals. The individuals filed suit against the city and two officials,

[577 U.S. 181]

claiming that they were entitled to a timely post-seizure hearing to seek the return of their property. The Court of Appeals ruled for the plaintiffs, and this Court granted certiorari.

At oral argument, the parties informed the Court that the cars and some of the cash had been returned, and that the plaintiffs no longer sought the return of the remainder of the cash. *Id.*, at 92, 130 S. Ct. 576, 175 L. Ed. 2d 447. Nevertheless, the plaintiffs—much like Gomez—"continue[d] to dispute the lawfulness of the State's hearing procedures." *Id.*, at 93, 130 S. Ct. 576, 175 L. Ed. 2d 447. Although the plaintiffs refused to settle the case, and the defendants would not concede that the hearing procedures were unlawful, the Court held that the case was moot. As the Court explained, the "dispute is no longer embedded in any actual controversy about the plaintiffs' particular legal rights," and "a dispute solely about the meaning of a law, abstracted from any concrete actual or threatened harm, falls outside the scope of the constitutional words 'Cases' and 'Controversies.' " *Ibid.*

The Court reached a similar conclusion in *Already, LLC* v. *Nike, Inc.*, 568 U.S. 85, 133 S. Ct. 721, 184 L. Ed. 2d 553 (2013). In that case, Nike filed suit alleging that two of Already's athletic shoes violated Nike's Air Force 1 trademark. In response, Already filed a counterclaim alleging that Nike's trademark was invalid. Instead of litigating the counterclaim, Nike issued a *unilateral* covenant not to sue Already. In that covenant, Nike "unconditionally and irrevocably" promised not to raise any trademark or unfair competition claims against Already based on its current shoe designs or any future "colorable imitations" of those designs. *Id.*, at 930, 133 S. Ct. 721, 184 L. Ed. 2d 553. Nike did not, however, admit that its trademark was invalid. After issuing the covenant, Nike asked the District

Court to dismiss the counterclaim as moot. *Id.*, at 89, 133 S. Ct. 721, 184 L. Ed. 2d 553.

Already did not agree to Nike's covenant, and it did not view the covenant as sufficient to protect it from future trademark litigation. Already argued that without judicial resolution of the dispute, "Nike's trademarks [would] hang

[577 U.S. 182]

over Already's operations like a Damoclean sword." *Id.*, at 96, 133 S. Ct. 721, 184 L. Ed. 2d 553. This Court disagreed and dismissed the suit. It found that because Nike had demonstrated "that the covenant encompasses all of [Nike's] allegedly unlawful conduct," and that the "challenged conduct cannot reasonably be expected to recur," the counterclaim was moot. *Id.*, at 94–95, 133 S. Ct. 721, 184 L. Ed. 2d 553.

These precedents reflect an important constitutional principle: The agreement of the plaintiff is not required to moot a case. In *San Pablo*, California did not accept the railroad's money in exchange for settling the State's legal claims; in *Alvarez*, the plaintiffs did not receive their cars and cash in return for an agreement to stop litigating the case; and in *Already*, the eponymous shoe company never agreed to Nike's covenant not to sue. In each of those cases,

despite the plaintiff's desire not to settle, the Court held that the lawsuit was moot.

The majority attempts to distinguish these precedents by emphasizing that the plaintiffs in all three cases received complete relief, but that is not the point. I had thought that the theory of the Court's opinion was that acceptance is required before complete relief will moot a case. But consider the majority's discussion of *Already*: What did Nike's covenant do? It "afforded Already blanket protection from future trademark litigation." *Ante*, at 164, n. 5, 193 L. Ed. 2d, at 581–582. What happened as a result of this complete relief? "The risk that underpinned Already's standing" thus "ceased to exist." *Ibid.* Even though what? Even though "Nike's covenant was unilateral," and not accepted by Already. *Ibid.*

The majority is correct that because Gomez did not accept Campbell's settlement, it is a "legal nullity" as a matter of contract law. The question, however, is not whether there is a contract; it is whether there is a case or controversy under Article III.[2] If the defendant is willing to give the

[577 U.S. 183]

plaintiff everything he asks for, there is no case or controversy to adjudicate, and the lawsuit is moot.[3]

---

2. The majority suggests that this case is analogous to *U. S. Bancorp Mortgage Co.* v. *Bonner Mall Partnership*, 513 U.S. 18, 115 S. Ct. 386, 130 L. Ed. 2d 233 (1994), where the Court declined to vacate a lower court decision that became moot on certiorari when the parties voluntarily settled the case. *Bancorp* is inapposite—it involves the equitable powers of the courts to vacate judgments in moot cases, not the Article III question whether a case is moot in the first place. The premise of *Bancorp* is that it is up to the federal courts—and not the parties—to decide what to do once a case becomes moot. The majority's position, in contrast, would leave it to the plaintiff to decide whether a case is moot.

3. To further support its Article III-by-contract theory of the case, the Court looks to Federal Rule of Civil Procedure 68, which states that an unaccepted offer of judgment "is considered withdrawn." Rule 68(b). But Campbell made Gomez both a Rule 68 offer *and* a freestanding settlement offer. By its terms, Rule 68 does not apply to the latter. The majority's only argument with respect to the freestanding settlement offer is that under the rules of contract law, an

* * *

The case or controversy requirement serves an essential purpose: It ensures that the federal courts expound the law "only in the last resort, and as a necessity." *Allen*, 468 U.S., at 752, 104 S. Ct. 3315, 82 L. Ed. 2d 556 (internal quotation marks omitted). It is the necessity of resolving a live dispute that reconciles the exercise of profound power by unelected judges with the principles of self-governance, ensuring adherence to "the proper— and

[577 U.S. 184]

properly limited—role of the courts in a democratic society." *Id.*, at 750, 104 S. Ct. 3315, 82 L. Ed. 2d 556 (internal quotation marks omitted).

There is no such necessity here. As the District Court found, Campbell offered Gomez full relief. Although Gomez nonetheless wants to continue litigating, the issue is not what the plaintiff *wants*, but what the federal courts may do. It is up to those courts to decide whether each party continues to have the requisite personal stake in the lawsuit, and if not, to dismiss the case as moot. The Court today takes that important responsibility away from the federal courts and hands it to the plaintiff.

The good news is that this case is limited to its facts. The majority holds that an *offer* of complete relief is insufficient to moot a case. The majority does not say that *payment* of complete relief leads to the same result. For aught that appears, the majority's analysis may have come out differently if Campbell had deposited the offered funds with the District Court. See *ante*, at 165–166, 193 L. Ed. 2d, at 582. This Court leaves that question for another day—assuming there are other plaintiffs out there who, like Gomez, won't take "yes" for an answer.

Justice **Alito**, dissenting.

I join The Chief Justice's dissent. I agree that a defendant may extinguish a plaintiff's personal stake in pursuing a claim by offering complete relief on the claim, even if the plaintiff spurns the offer. Our Article III precedents make clear that, for mootness purposes, there is nothing talismanic about the plaintiff's acceptance. *E.g., Already, LLC* v. *Nike, Inc.*, 568 U.S. 85, 133 S. Ct. 721, 184 L. Ed. 2d 553 (2013) (holding that Nike's unilateral covenant not to sue mooted Already's trademark invalidity claim). I write separately to emphasize what I see as the linchpin for finding mootness in this case: There is no real dispute that Campbell would "make good on [its] promise" to pay Gomez the money it offered him if the case were dismissed. *Ante*, at 179, 193 L. Ed. 2d, at 591 (opinion of Roberts, C. J.).

[577 U.S. 185]

Absent this fact, I would be compelled to find that the case is not moot.

---

unaccepted offer is a "legal nullity." *Ante*, at 162, 193 L. Ed. 2d, at 580. As explained, however, under the principles of Article III, an unaccepted offer of complete relief moots a case.

Justice Thomas, concurring in the judgment, would decide the case based on whether there was a formal tender under the common law. This suffers from the same flaw as the majority opinion. The question is not whether the requirements of the common law of tender have been met, but whether there is a case or controversy for purposes of Article III. The Supreme Court cases we have discussed make clear that the two questions are not the same. To cite just one example, Justice Thomas argues that a tender under the common law must include an admission of liability. *Ante*, at 170–171, 193 L. Ed. 2d, at 585-586. Our precedents, however, plainly establish that an admission of liability is not required for a case to be moot under Article III. See *supra*, at at 181–182, 193 L. Ed. 2d, at 592-593. We are not at liberty to proceed as if those Article III precedents do not exist.

Our "voluntary cessation" cases provide useful guidance. Those cases hold that, when a plaintiff seeks to enjoin a defendant's conduct, a defendant's "voluntary cessation of challenged conduct does not ordinarily render a case moot because a dismissal for mootness would permit a resumption of the challenged conduct as soon as the case is dismissed." *Knox* v. *Service Employees*, 567 U.S. 298, 307, 132 S. Ct. 2277, 183 L. Ed. 2d 281 (2012). To obtain dismissal in such circumstances, the defendant must " 'bea[r] the formidable burden of showing that it is absolutely clear the allegedly wrongful behavior could not reasonably be expected to recur.' " *Already, supra,* at 91, 133 S. Ct. 721, 184 L. Ed. 2d 553 (quoting *Friends of the Earth, Inc.* v. *Laidlaw Environmental Services (TOC), Inc.,* 528 U.S. 167, 190, 120 S. Ct. 693, 145 L. Ed. 2d 610 (2000)). We have typically applied that rule in cases involving claims for prospective relief, see *Knox, supra,* at 307, 132 S. Ct. 2277, 183 L. Ed. 2d 281, but the basic principle easily translates to cases, like this one, involving claims for damages: When a defendant offers a plaintiff complete relief on a damages claim, the case will be dismissed as moot if—but only if—it is " 'absolutely clear' " that the plaintiff will be able to receive the offered relief. *Already, supra,* at 95, 133 S. Ct. 721, 184 L. Ed. 2d 553.[1]

Consider an offer of complete relief from a defendant that has no intention of actually paying the promised sums, or from a defendant whose finances are so shaky that it cannot produce the necessary funds. In both instances, there is a question whether the defendant will back up its offer to pay with an actual payment. If those cases were dismissed as moot, the defendant's failure to follow through on its promise to pay would leave the plaintiff forever emptyhanded. In

[577 U.S. 186]

the language of our mootness cases, those cases would *not* be moot because a court could still grant the plaintiff "effectual relief," *Knox, supra,* at 307, 132 S. Ct. 2277, 183 L. Ed. 2d 281 (internal quotation marks omitted)—namely, the relief sought in the first place. The plaintiff retains a "personal stake" in continuing the litigation. *Genesis HealthCare Corp.* v. *Symczyk,* 569 U.S. 66, 71, 133 S. Ct. 1523, 185 L. Ed. 2d 636 (2013) (internal quotation marks omitted). An offer of complete relief thus will not always warrant dismissal.

Campbell urges that a plaintiff could simply move to reopen a dismissed case if a defendant fails to make good on its offer. Reply Brief 10. I assume that is true. But the prospect of having to reopen litigation is precisely why our voluntary cessation cases require defendants to prove, *before* dismissal, that the plaintiff's injury cannot reasonably be expected to recur. I see no reason not to impose a similar burden when a defendant asserts that it has rendered a damages claim moot.

How, then, can a defendant make "absolutely clear" that it will pay the relief it has offered? The most straightforward way is simply to pay over the money. The defendant might hand the plaintiff a certified check or

---

1. I say it must be clear that the plaintiff "will *be able to* receive" the relief, rather than that the plaintiff "*will* receive" the relief, to account for the possibility of an obstinate plaintiff who refuses to take any relief even if the case is dismissed. A plaintiff cannot thwart mootness by refusing complete relief presented on a silver platter.

deposit the requisite funds in a bank account in the plaintiff's name. See *California* v. *San Pablo & Tulare R. Co.*, 149 U.S. 308, 313-314, 13 S. Ct. 876, 37 L. Ed. 747 (1893). Alternatively, a defendant might deposit the money with the district court (or another trusted intermediary) on the condition that the money be released to the plaintiff when the court dismisses the case as moot. See Fed. Rule Civ. Proc. 67; 28 U.S.C. §§ 2041, 2042. In these situations, there will rarely be any serious doubt that the plaintiff can obtain the offered money.[2]

[577 U.S. 187]

While outright payment is the surest way for a defendant to make the requisite mootness showing, I would not foreclose other means of doing so. The question is whether it is certain the defendant will pay, not whether the defendant has already paid. I believe Campbell clears the mark in this case. As The Chief Justice observes, there is no dispute Campbell has the means to pay the few thousand dollars it offered Gomez, and there is no basis "to argue that Campbell might not make good on that promise" if the case were dismissed. *Ante*, at 179, 193 L. Ed. 2d, at 591. Thus, in the circumstances of this case, Campbell's offer of complete relief should have rendered Gomez's damages claim moot.

But the same would not necessarily be true for other defendants, particularly those that face more substantial claims, possess less secure finances, or extend offers of questionable sincerity. Cf. *Already*, 568 U.S., at 105, 133 S. Ct. 721, 184 L. Ed. 2d 553 (Kennedy, J., concurring) (emphasizing the "formidable burden on the party asserting mootness" and noting possible "doubts that Nike's showing [of mootness] would suffice in other circumstances").

The Court does not dispute Campbell's ability or willingness to pay, but nonetheless concludes that its unaccepted offer did not moot Gomez's claim. While I disagree with that result on these facts, I am heartened that the Court appears to endorse the proposition that a plaintiff's claim *is* moot once he has "received full redress" from the defendant for the injuries he has asserted. *Ante*, at 165, n. 5, 193 L. Ed. 2d, at 582 (discussing *Already*, *supra*, and *Alvarez* v. *Smith*, 558 U.S. 87, 130 S. Ct. 576, 175 L. Ed. 2d 447 (2009)).

[577 U.S. 188]

Today's decision thus does not prevent a defendant who actually pays complete relief—either directly to the plaintiff or to a trusted intermediary—from seeking dismissal on mootness grounds.[3]

---

2. Depositing funds with the district court or another intermediary may be particularly attractive to defendants because it would ensure that the plaintiff can obtain the money, yet allow the defendant to reclaim the funds if the court refuses to dismiss the case (for example, because it determines the offer is for less than full relief). Contrary to the views of Gomez's *amicus*, there is no reason to force a defendant to effect an " 'irrevocable transfer of title' " to the funds without regard to whether doing so succeeds in mooting the case. Brief for American Federation of Labor and Congress of Industrial Organizations 10. Likewise, because I believe our precedents "provide sufficiently specific principles to resolve this case," I would not apply the "rigid formalities" of common-law tender in this context. *Ante*, at 169, 170, 193 L. Ed. 2d, at 585, 585 (Thomas, J., concurring in judgment). Article III demands that a plaintiff always have a personal stake in continuing the litigation, and that stake is extinguished if the plaintiff is freely able to obtain full relief in the event the case is dismissed as moot.

3. Although it does not resolve the issue, the majority raises the possibility that a defendant must *both* pay the requisite funds *and* have "the court . . . ente[r] judgment for the plaintiff in that amount." *Ante*, at 166, 193 L. Ed. 2d, at 582. I do not see how that can be reconciled with *Already*, which affirmed an order of dismissal—not judgment for the plaintiff—where the plaintiff had received full relief from the defendant. *Already, LLC v. Nike, Inc.*, 568 U.S. 85, 89–90, 101, 133 S. Ct. 721, 184 L. Ed. 2d 553 (2013).

STEPHEN DUNCAN, WARDEN, Petitioner

v

LAWRENCE OWENS

577 U.S. 189, 136 S. Ct. 651, 193 L. Ed. 2d 598, 2016 U.S. LEXIS 844

[No. 14-1516]

Argued January 12, 2016.Decided January 20, 2016.

Prior history: ON WRIT OF CERTIORARI TO THE UNITED STATES COURT OF APPEALS FOR THE SEVENTH CIRCUIT, 781 F.3d 360, 2015 U.S. App. LEXIS 4739

APPEARANCES OF COUNSEL ARGUING CASE

Carolyn E. Shapiro argued the cause for petitioner.
Barry Levenstam argued the cause for respondent.

PER CURIAM.

The writ of certiorari is dismissed as improvidently granted.

It is so ordered.

HENRY MONTGOMERY, Petitioner

v

LOUISIANA

577 U.S. 190, 136 S. Ct. 718, 193 L. Ed. 2d 599, 2016 U.S. LEXIS 862

[No. 14-280]

Argued October 13, 2015. Decided January 25, 2016.

Decision: Supreme Court had jurisdiction to review state court's refusal to apply retroactively holding, in Miller v. Alabama (2012) 567 U.S. 460, 132 S. Ct. 2455, 183 L. Ed. 2d 407, that Eighth Amendment forbade mandated sentence of life in prison without possibility of parole for juvenile; Miller announced new retroactively-applicable substantive rule.

Prior history: ON WRIT OF CERTIORARI TO THE SUPREME COURT OF LOUISIANA, 141 So. 3d 264, 2014 La. LEXIS 1538

SUMMARY

Overview: HOLDINGS: [1]-When a new substantive rule of constitutional law controlled the outcome of a case, the Constitution required state collateral review courts to give retroactive effect to that rule. The Court therefore had jurisdiction to review the Louisiana courts' decision that the Miller rule did not apply retroactively; [2]-Miller's holding that mandatory life imprisonment without parole for juvenile homicide offenders violated the Eighth Amendment announced a new substantive rule that was retroactive in cases on collateral review; [3]-Giving Miller retroactive effect did not require states to relitigate sentences in every case. Instead, states could remedy Miller violations by permitting juvenile homicide offenders to be considered for parole.

Outcome: Judgment reversed; case remanded. 6-3 decision; two dissents.

HEADNOTES

Classified to United States Supreme Court Digest, Lawyers' Edition

Life sentence — juvenile
L Ed Digest: Criminal Law § 79
1. A juvenile convicted of a homicide offense cannot be sentenced to life in prison without parole absent consideration of the juvenile's special circumstances in light of the principles and purposes of juvenile sentencing. (Kennedy, J., joined by Roberts, Ch. J., and Ginsburg, Breyer, Sotomayor, and Kagan, JJ.)

Life sentence — juvenile
L Ed Digest: Criminal Law § 79
2. Miller v. Alabama holds that mandatory life without parole for juvenile homicide offenders violates the Eighth Amendment's prohibition on cruel and unusual punishments. By making youth (and all that accompanies it) irrelevant to imposition of that harshest prison sentence, mandatory life without parole poses too great a

risk of disproportionate punishment. Miller requires that sentencing courts consider a child's diminished culpability and heightened capacity for change before condemning him or her to die in prison. Although Miller does not foreclose a sentencer's ability to impose life without parole on a juvenile, a lifetime in prison is a disproportionate sentence for all but the rarest of children, those whose crimes reflect "irreparable corruption." (Kennedy, J., joined by Roberts, Ch. J., and Ginsburg, Breyer, Sotomayor, and Kagan, JJ.)

Challenge to sentence — state law
L Ed Digest: Criminal Law § 74

3. In Louisiana there are two principal mechanisms for collateral challenge to the lawfulness of imprisonment. Each begins with a filing in the trial court where the prisoner was convicted and sentenced. La. Code Crim. Proc. Ann. arts. 882, 926 (2008). The first procedure permits a prisoner to file an application for postconviction relief on one or more of seven grounds set forth in the statute. La. Code Crim. Proc. Ann. art. 930.3. The Louisiana Supreme Court has held that none of those grounds provides a basis for collateral review of sentencing errors. Sentencing errors must instead be raised through Louisiana's second collateral review procedure. This second mechanism allows a prisoner to bring a collateral attack on his or her sentence by filing a motion to correct an illegal sentence. art. 882. (Kennedy, J., joined by Roberts, Ch. J., and Ginsburg, Breyer, Sotomayor, and Kagan, JJ.)

Correction of sentence — state law
L Ed Digest: Criminal Law § 74

4. La. Code Crim. Proc. Ann. art 882 (2008) provides that an illegal sentence may be corrected at any time by the court that imposed the sentence. An illegal sentence is primarily restricted to those instances in which the term of the prisoner's sentence is not authorized by the statute or statutes which govern the penalty for the crime of conviction. In the ordinary course Louisiana courts will not consider a challenge to a disproportionate sentence on collateral review; rather, as a general matter, it appears that prisoners must raise Eighth Amendment sentencing challenges on direct review. Louisiana's collateral review courts will, however, consider a motion to correct an illegal sentence based on a decision of the U.S. Supreme Court holding that the Eighth Amendment to the Federal Constitution prohibits a punishment for a type of crime or a class of offenders. (Kennedy, J., joined by Roberts, Ch. J., and Ginsburg, Breyer, Sotomayor, and Kagan, JJ.)

Constitutional rule — state court — federal review
L Ed Digest: Appeal § 523

5. If the Constitution establishes a rule and requires that the rule have retroactive application, then a state court's refusal to give the rule retroactive effect is reviewable by the U.S. Supreme Court. States may not disregard a controlling, constitutional command in their own courts. (Kennedy, J., joined by Roberts, Ch. J., and Ginsburg, Breyer, Sotomayor, and Kagan, JJ.)

New federal constitutional rule — retroactivity
L Ed Digest: Courts § 777.7

6. The plurality opinion in Teague v. Lane sets forth a framework for retroactivity in cases on federal collateral review. Under Teague, a new constitutional rule of criminal procedure does not apply, as a general matter, to convictions that were final when the new rule was announced. Teague recognizes, however, two categories of rules that are not subject to its general retroactivity bar. First, courts must give retroactive effect to new substantive rules of constitutional law. Substantive rules include rules forbidding criminal punishment of certain primary conduct, as well as rules prohibiting a certain category of punishment for a class of defendants because of their status or offense. Although Teague describes new substantive rules as an exception to the bar on retroactive application of procedural rules, substantive rules are more accurately characterized as not subject to the bar. Second, courts must give retroactive effect to new watershed rules of criminal procedure implicating the fundamental fairness and accuracy of the criminal proceeding. Teague requires the retroactive application of new substantive and watershed procedural rules in federal habeas proceedings. (Kennedy, J., joined by Roberts, Ch. J., and Ginsburg, Breyer, Sotomayor, and Kagan, JJ.)

New federal constitutional rule — retroactivity

L Ed Digest: Courts § 777.7

7. When a new substantive rule of constitutional law controls the outcome of a case, the Constitution requires state collateral review courts to give retroactive effect to that rule. Teague's conclusion establishing the retroactivity of new substantive rules is best understood as resting upon constitutional premises. That constitutional command is, like all federal law, binding on state courts. (Ken-

nedy, J., joined by Roberts, Ch. J., and Ginsburg, Breyer, Sotomayor, and Kagan, JJ.)

New federal constitutional rule — retroactivity

L Ed Digest: Courts § 777.7

8. The Constitution requires substantive rules to have retroactive effect regardless of when a conviction became final. (Kennedy, J., joined by Roberts, Ch. J., and Ginsburg, Breyer, Sotomayor, and Kagan, JJ.)

Substantive new federal constitutional rules — retroactivity

L Ed Digest: Courts § 777.7

9. Substantive constitutional rules have been defined as those that place, as a matter of constitutional interpretation, certain kinds of primary, private individual conduct beyond the power of the criminal law-making authority to proscribe. The first exception set forth in Teague should be understood to cover not only rules forbidding criminal punishment of certain primary conduct but also rules prohibiting a certain category of punishment for a class of defendants because of their status or offense. The first exception speaks in terms of substantive categorical guarantees accorded by the Constitution, regardless of the procedures followed. Whether a new rule bars states from proscribing certain conduct or from inflicting a certain punishment, in both cases, the Constitution itself deprives the state of the power to impose a certain penalty. (Kennedy, J., joined by Roberts, Ch. J., and Ginsburg, Breyer, Sotomayor, and Kagan, JJ.)

State enforcement — federal constitutional bar

L Ed Digest: Criminal Law § 70

10. Substantive rules set forth categorical constitutional guarantees that place certain criminal laws and punishments altogether beyond a state's power to impose. It follows that when a state enforces a proscription or penalty barred by the Constitution, the resulting conviction or sentence is, by definition, unlawful. (Kennedy, J., joined by Roberts, Ch. J., and Ginsburg, Breyer, Sotomayor, and Kagan, JJ.)

State procedural rules — federal unconstitutionality — retroactivity

L Ed Digest: Courts § 777.7

11. Procedural rules, in contrast to substantive rules, are designed to enhance the accuracy of a conviction or sentence by regulating the manner of determining the defendant's culpability. Those rules merely raise the possibility that someone convicted with use of the invalidated procedure might have been acquitted otherwise. Even where procedural error has infected a trial, the resulting conviction or sentence may still be accurate; and, by extension, the defendant's continued confinement may still be lawful. For this reason, a trial conducted under a procedure found to be unconstitutional in a later case does not, as a general matter, have the automatic consequence of invalidating a defendant's conviction or sentence. The same possibility of a valid result does not exist where a substantive rule has eliminated a state's power to proscribe the defendant's conduct or impose a given punishment. Even the use of impeccable factfinding procedures could not legitimate a verdict where the conduct being penalized is constitutionally immune from punishment. Nor could the use of flawless sentencing procedures legitimate a punishment where the Constitution immunizes the defendant from the sentence imposed. No circumstances call more for the invocation of a rule of complete retroactivity. (Kennedy, J., joined by Roberts, Ch. J., and Ginsburg, Breyer, Sotomayor, and Kagan, JJ.)

Invalid punishment — new rule — retroactivity

L Ed Digest: Courts § 777.7; Criminal Law § 70

12. A conviction under an unconstitutional law is not merely erroneous, but is illegal and void, and cannot be a legal cause of imprisonment. It is true, if no writ of error lies, the judgment may be final, in the sense that there may be no means of reversing it. But if the laws are unconstitutional and void, the circuit court acquired no jurisdiction of the causes. The same logic governs a challenge to a punishment that the Constitution deprives states of authority to impose. A conviction or sentence imposed in violation of a substantive rule is not just erroneous but contrary to law and, as a result, void. It follows, as a general principle, that a court has no authority to leave in place a conviction or sentence that violates a substantive rule, regardless of whether the conviction or sentence became final before the rule was announced. (Kennedy, J., joined by Roberts, Ch. J., and Ginsburg, Breyer, Sotomayor, and Kagan, JJ.)

Invalid penalty — new rule — retroactivity

L Ed Digest: Courts § 777.7; Criminal Law § 70

13. An unconstitutional law is void, and is as no law. A penalty imposed pursuant to an unconstitutional law is no less void because the prisoner's sentence became final before the law was held unconstitutional. There is no grandfather clause that permits states to enforce punishments the Constitution forbids. To conclude otherwise would undercut the Constitution's substantive guarantees. No circumstances call more for the invocation of a rule of complete retroactivity than when the conduct being penalized is constitutionally immune from punishment. The same principle should govern the application of substantive rules on collateral review. Where a state lacks the power to proscribe a habeas petitioner's conduct, it cannot constitutionally insist that he remain in jail. (Kennedy, J., joined by Roberts, Ch. J., and Ginsburg, Breyer, Sotomayor, and Kagan, JJ.)

State prisoner — Federal Constitution — supremacy clause

L Ed Digest: States, Territories, and Possessions § 47

14. If a state may not constitutionally insist that a prisoner remain in jail on federal habeas review, it may not constitutionally insist on the same result in its own postconviction proceedings. Under the Supremacy Clause of the Constitution, state collateral review courts have no greater power than federal habeas courts to mandate that a prisoner continue to suffer punishment barred by the Constitution. If a state collateral proceeding is open to a claim controlled by federal law, the state court has a duty to grant the relief that federal law requires. Where state collateral review proceedings permit prisoners to challenge the lawfulness of their confinement, states cannot refuse to give retroactive effect to a substantive constitutional right that determines the outcome of that challenge. (Kennedy,

J., joined by Roberts, Ch. J., and Ginsburg, Breyer, Sotomayor, and Kagan, JJ.)

State prisoners — substantive federal constitutional rule — retroactivity

L Ed Digest: Courts § 777.7

15. The retroactive application of substantive rules does not implicate a state's weighty interests in ensuring the finality of convictions and sentences. Teague warns against the intrusiveness of continually forcing the states to marshal resources in order to keep in prison defendants whose trials and appeals conformed to then-existing constitutional standards. This concern has no application in the realm of substantive rules, for no resources marshaled by a state could preserve a conviction or sentence that the Constitution deprives the state of power to impose. (Kennedy, J., joined by Roberts, Ch. J., and Ginsburg, Breyer, Sotomayor, and Kagan, JJ.)

State collateral review — federal constitutional right

L Ed Digest: Criminal Law § 45.5

16. In adjudicating claims under its collateral review procedures a state may not deny a controlling right asserted under the Constitution, assuming the claim is properly presented in the case. (Kennedy, J., joined by Roberts, Ch. J., and Ginsburg, Breyer, Sotomayor, and Kagan, JJ.)

Challenge to sentence — state procedures

L Ed Digest: Criminal Law § 74

17. Louisiana's collateral review procedures are open to claims that a decision of the U.S. Supreme Court has rendered certain sentences illegal, as a substantive matter, under the Eighth Amendment. (Kennedy, J., joined by Roberts, Ch. J., and Ginsburg, Breyer, Sotomayor, and Kagan, JJ.)

New rule — retroactivity
L Ed Digest: Criminal Law § 79

18. Miller v. Alabama announced a substantive rule that is retroactive in cases on collateral review. (Kennedy, J., joined by Roberts, Ch. J., and Ginsburg, Breyer, Sotomayor, and Kagan, JJ.)

Disproportionate punishment
L Ed Digest: Criminal Law § 78

19. Protection against disproportionate punishment is the central substantive guarantee of the Eighth Amendment and goes far beyond the manner of determining a defendant's sentence. (Kennedy, J., joined by Roberts, Ch. J., and Ginsburg, Breyer, Sotomayor, and Kagan, JJ.)

Sentencing of child
L Ed Digest: Criminal Law § 79

20. Children are constitutionally different from adults for purposes of sentencing. These differences result from children's diminished culpability and greater prospects for reform, and are apparent in three primary ways: First, children have a lack of maturity and an underdeveloped sense of responsibility, leading to recklessness, impulsivity, and heedless risk-taking. Second, children are more vulnerable to negative influences and outside pressures, including from their family and peers; they have limited control over their own environment and lack the ability to extricate themselves from horrific, crime-producing settings. And third, a child's character is not as well formed as an adult's; his traits are less fixed and his actions less likely to be evidence of irretrievable depravity. (Kennedy, J.,

Life sentence — juvenile
L Ed Digest: Criminal Law § 79

21. Mandatory life-without-parole sentences for children pose too great a risk of disproportionate punishment. Miller requires that before sentencing a juvenile to life without parole, the sentencing judge take into account how children are different, and how those differences counsel against irrevocably sentencing them to a lifetime in prison. A sentencer might encounter the rare juvenile offender who exhibits such irretrievable depravity that rehabilitation is impossible and life without parole is justified. But in light of children's diminished culpability and heightened capacity for change, appropriate occasions for sentencing juveniles to this harshest possible penalty will be uncommon. (Kennedy, J., joined by Roberts, Ch. J., and Ginsburg, Breyer, Sotomayor, and Kagan, JJ.)

Life sentence — juvenile — substantive rule — retroactivity
L Ed Digest: Criminal Law § 79

22. Miller does more than require a sentencer to consider a juvenile offender's youth before imposing life without parole; it establishes that the penological justifications for life without parole collapse in light of the distinctive attributes of youth. Even if a court considers a child's age before sentencing him or her to a lifetime in prison, that sentence still violates the Eighth Amendment for a child whose crime reflects unfortunate yet transient immaturity. Because Miller determined that sentencing a child to life without parole is excessive for all but the rare juvenile offender whose crime reflects irreparable corruption, it renders life without parole an unconstitutional penalty for a class of defendants because of their status—that is, juvenile offenders whose crimes reflect the transient immaturity of youth. As a result, Miller announced a substantive rule of constitutional law. Like other substantive rules, Miller is retroactive because it necessarily carries a significant risk that a defendant—here, the vast majority of juvenile offenders—faces a punishment that the law cannot impose upon him. (Kennedy, J., joined by Roberts, Ch. J., and Ginsburg, Breyer, Sotomayor, and Kagan, JJ.)

Life sentence — juvenile
L Ed Digest: Criminal Law § 79
23. Miller, it is true, does not bar a punishment for all juvenile offenders, as the U.S. Supreme Court did in Roper or Graham. Miller did bar life without parole, however, for all but the rarest of juvenile offenders, those whose crimes reflect permanent incorrigibility. For that reason, Miller is no less substantive than are Roper and Graham. Before Miller, every juvenile convicted of a homicide offense could be sentenced to life without parole. After Miller, it will be the rare juvenile offender who can receive that same sentence. The only difference between Roper and Graham, on the one hand, and Miller, on the other hand, is that Miller draws a line between children whose crimes reflect transient immaturity and those rare children whose crimes reflect irreparable corruption. The fact that life without parole could be a proportionate sentence for the latter kind of juvenile offender does not mean that all other children imprisoned under a disproportionate sentence have not suffered the deprivation of a substan-

tive right. (Kennedy, J., joined by Roberts, Ch. J., and Ginsburg, Breyer, Sotomayor, and Kagan, JJ.)

Substantive change in law — retroactivity
L Ed Digest: Courts § 777.7
24. There are instances in which a substantive change in the law must be attended by a procedure that enables a prisoner to show that he falls within the category of persons whom the law may no longer punish. Some rules may have both procedural and substantive ramifications. For example, when an element of a criminal offense is deemed unconstitutional, a prisoner convicted under that offense receives a new trial where the government must prove the prisoner's conduct still fits within the modified definition of the crime. In a similar vein, when the Constitution prohibits a particular form of punishment for a class of persons, an affected prisoner receives a procedure through which he can show that he belongs to the protected class. Those procedural requirements do not, of course, transform substantive rules into procedural ones. (Kennedy, J., joined by Roberts, Ch. J., and Ginsburg, Breyer, Sotomayor, and Kagan, JJ.)

Life sentence — juvenile
L Ed Digest: Criminal Law § 79
25. A hearing where youth and its attendant characteristics are considered as sentencing factors is necessary to separate those juveniles who may be sentenced to life without parole from those who may not. The hearing does not replace but rather gives effect to Miller's substantive holding that life without parole is an excessive sentence for children whose crimes reflect transient immaturity. (Kennedy, J., joined by Roberts,

Ch. J., and Ginsburg, Breyer, Soto-mayor, and Kagan, JJ.)

Federal Constitution — new rule — state enforcement

L Ed Digest: Courts § 777.7

26. When a new substantive rule of constitutional law is established, the U.S. Supreme Court is careful to limit the scope of any attendant procedural requirement to avoid intruding more than necessary upon the states' sovereign administration of their criminal justice systems. The Court leaves to the states the task of developing appropriate ways to enforce the constitutional restriction upon their execution of sentences. Fidelity to this important principle of federalism, however, should not be construed to demean the substantive character of the federal right at issue. (Kennedy, J., joined by Roberts, Ch. J., and Ginsburg, Breyer, Sotomayor, and Kagan, JJ.)

Life sentence — child

L Ed Digest: Criminal Law § 79

27. That Miller did not impose a formal factfinding requirement does not leave states free to sentence a child whose crime reflects transient immaturity to life without parole. To the contrary, Miller established that this punishment is disproportionate under the Eighth Amendment. (Kennedy, J., joined by Roberts, Ch. J., and Ginsburg, Breyer, Sotomayor, and Kagan, JJ.)

Life sentence for juvenile — substantive rule — retroactivity

L Ed Digest: Criminal Law § 79

28. Miller announced a substantive rule of constitutional law. The conclusion that Miller states a substantive rule comports with the principles that informed Teague. Teague sought to balance the important goals of finality and comity with the liberty interests of those imprisoned pursuant to rules later deemed unconstitutional. Miller's conclusion that the sentence of life without parole is disproportionate for the vast majority of juvenile offenders raises a grave risk that many are being held in violation of the Constitution. Giving Miller retroactive effect, moreover, does not require states to relitigate sentences, let alone convictions, in every case where a juvenile offender received mandatory life without parole. A state may remedy a Miller violation by permitting juvenile homicide offenders to be considered for parole, rather than by resentencing them. Allowing those offenders to be considered for parole ensures that juveniles whose crimes reflected only transient immaturity— and who have since matured—will not be forced to serve a disproportionate sentence in violation of the Eighth Amendment. (Kennedy, J., joined by Roberts, Ch. J., and Ginsburg, Breyer, Sotomayor, and Kagan, JJ.)

RESEARCH REFERENCES

U.S.C.S., Constitution, Amendment 8

Moore's Federal Practice §§632.20, 671.09, 672.06 (Matthew Bender 3d ed.)

L Ed Digest, Appeal §§523, 698; Courts § 777.7; Criminal Law § 79

L Ed Index, Parole, Probation, and Pardon; Prospective or Retrospective Matters

Annotations:

Supreme Court's views as to retroactive effect of its own decisions announcing new rules as to sentencing in criminal cases. 122 L. Ed. 2d 837.

Duration of prison sentence as constituting cruel and unusual punishment in violation of Federal Constitution's Eighth Amendment—Supreme Court cases. 115 L. Ed. 2d 1169.

United States Supreme Court's views as to retroactive effect of its own decisions announcing new rules. 65 L. Ed. 2d 1219.

Federal constitutional rule against cruel and unusual punishment. 33 L. Ed. 2d 932.

Comment Note: Retroactive or merely prospective operation of new rule adopted by court in overruling precedent—federal cases. 14 L. Ed. 2d 992.

SHEPARD'S® Citations Service. For further research of authorities referenced here, use SHEPARD'S to be sure your case or statute is still good law and to find additional authorities that support your position. SHEPARD'S is available exclusively from LexisNexis®.

APPEARANCES OF COUNSEL ARGUING CASE

Richard D. Bernstein argued the cause, as amicus curiae, appointed by the court.

Mark D. Plaisance argued the cause for petitioner.

Michael R. Dreeben argued the cause for the United States, as amicus curiae, by special leave of court.

S. Kyle Duncan argued the cause for respondent.

SYLLABUS BY REPORTER OF DECISIONS

Petitioner Montgomery was 17 years old in 1963, when he killed a deputy sheriff in Louisiana. The jury returned a verdict of "guilty without capital punishment," which carried an automatic sentence of life without parole. Nearly 50 years after Montgomery was taken into custody, this Court decided that mandatory life without parole for juvenile homicide offenders violates the Eighth Amendment's prohibition on " 'cruel and unusual punishments.' " *Miller* v. *Alabama*, 567 U.S. 460, 465, 132 S. Ct. 2455, 183 L. Ed. 2d 407. Montgomery sought state collateral relief, arguing that *Miller* rendered his mandatory life-without-parole sentence illegal. The trial court denied his motion, and his application for a supervisory writ was denied by the Louisiana Supreme Court, which had previously held that *Miller* does not have retroactive effect in cases on state collateral review.

Held:

1. This Court has jurisdiction to decide whether the Louisiana Supreme Court correctly refused to give

retroactive effect to *Miller*. Pp. 197–205, 193 L. Ed. 2d, at 612-618.

(a) *Teague* v. *Lane*, 489 U.S. 288, 109 S. Ct. 1060, 103 L. Ed. 2d 334, a federal habeas case, set forth a framework for the retroactive application of a new constitutional rule to convictions that were final when the new rule was announced. While the Court held that new constitutional rules of criminal procedure are generally not retroactive, it recognized that courts must give retroactive effect to new watershed procedural rules and to substantive rules of constitutional law. Substantive constitutional rules include "rules forbidding criminal punishment of certain primary conduct" and "rules prohibiting a certain category of punishment for a class of defendants because of their status or offense," *Penry* v. *Lynaugh*, 492 U.S. 302, 330, 109 S. Ct. 2934, 106 L. Ed. 2d 256. Court-appointed *amicus* contends that because *Teague* was an interpretation of the federal habeas statute, not a constitutional command, its retroactivity holding has no application in state collateral review proceedings. However, neither *Teague* nor *Danforth* v. *Minnesota*, 552 U.S. 264, 128 S. Ct. 1029, 169 L. Ed. 2d 859—which concerned only *Teague's* general retroactivity bar for new constitutional rules of criminal procedure—had occasion to address whether States are required as a constitutional matter to give retroactive effect to new substantive rules. Pp. 197–200, 193 L. Ed. 2d, at 612-614.

(b) When a new substantive rule of constitutional law controls the outcome of a case, the Constitution requires state collateral review courts to give retroactive effect to that rule.

This conclusion is established by precedents addressing the nature of substantive rules, their differences from procedural rules, and their history of retroactive application. As *Teague, supra,* at 292, 312, 109 S. Ct. 1060, 103 L. Ed. 2d 334, and *Penry, supra,* at 330, 109 S. Ct. 2934, 106 L. Ed. 2d 256, indicate, substantive rules set forth categorical constitutional guarantees that place certain criminal laws and punishments altogether beyond the State's power to impose. It follows that when a State enforces a proscription or penalty barred by the Constitution, the resulting conviction or sentence is, by definition, unlawful. In contrast, where procedural error has infected a trial, a conviction or sentence may still be accurate and the defendant's continued confinement may still be lawful, see *Schriro* v. *Summerlin*, 542 U.S. 348, 352-353, 124 S. Ct. 2519, 159 L. Ed. 2d 442; for this reason, a trial conducted under a procedure found unconstitutional in a later case does not automatically invalidate a defendant's conviction or sentence. The same possibility of a valid result does not exist where a substantive rule has eliminated a State's power to proscribe the defendant's conduct or impose a given punishment. See *United States* v. *United States Coin & Currency*, 401 U.S. 715, 724, 91 S. Ct. 1041, 28 L. Ed. 2d 434. By holding that new substantive rules are, indeed, retroactive, *Teague* continued a long tradition of recognizing that substantive rules must have retroactive effect regardless of when the defendant's conviction became final; for a conviction under an unconstitutional law "is not merely erroneous, but is illegal and void, and cannot be a legal cause of imprisonment," *Ex parte Siebold*, 100 U.S. 371, 376-377,

25 L. Ed. 717. The same logic governs a challenge to a punishment that the Constitution deprives States of authority to impose, *Penry, supra,* at 330, 109 S. Ct. 2934, 106 L. Ed. 2d 256. It follows that a court has no authority to leave in place a conviction or sentence that violates a substantive rule, regardless of whether the conviction or sentence became final before the rule was announced. This Court's precedents may not directly control the question here, but they bear on the necessary analysis, for a State that may not constitutionally insist that a prisoner remain in jail on federal habeas review may not constitutionally insist on the same result in its own postconviction proceedings. Pp. 200–205, 193 L. Ed. 2d, at 614-618.

2. *Miller*'s prohibition on mandatory life without parole for juvenile offenders announced a new substantive rule that, under the Constitution, is retroactive in cases on state collateral review. The "foundation stone" for *Miller*'s analysis was the line of precedent holding certain punishments disproportionate when applied to juveniles, 567 U.S., at 470, n. 4, 132 S. Ct. 2455, 183 L. Ed. 2d 407. Relying on *Roper* v. *Simmons*, 543 U.S. 551, 125 S. Ct. 1183, 161 L. Ed. 2d 1, and *Graham* v. *Florida*, 560 U.S. 48, 130 S. Ct. 2011, 176 L. Ed. 2d 825, *Miller* recognized that children differ from adults in their "diminished culpability and greater prospects for reform," 567 U.S., at 471, 132 S. Ct. 2455, 183 L. Ed. 2d 407, and that these distinctions "diminish the penological justifications" for imposing life without parole on juvenile offenders, *id.,* at 472, 132 S. Ct. 2455, 183 L. Ed. 2d 407. Because *Miller* determined that sentencing a child to life without parole is excessive for all but " 'the rare juvenile offender whose crime reflects irreparable corruption,' " *id.,* at 479–480, 132 S. Ct. 2455, 183 L. Ed. 2d 407, it rendered life without parole an unconstitutional penalty for "a class of defendants because of their status"—*i.e.,* juvenile offenders whose crimes reflect the transient immaturity of youth, *Penry, supra,* at 330, 109 S. Ct. 2934, 106 L. Ed. 2d 256. *Miller* therefore announced a substantive rule of constitutional law, which, like other substantive rules, is retroactive because it " 'necessarily carr[ies] a significant risk that a defendant' "—here, the vast majority of juvenile offenders—" 'faces a punishment that the law cannot impose upon him.' " *Schriro, supra,* at 352, 124 S. Ct. 2519, 159 L. Ed. 2d 442.

A State may remedy a *Miller* violation by extending parole eligibility to juvenile offenders. This would neither impose an onerous burden on the States nor disturb the finality of state convictions. And it would afford someone like Montgomery, who submits that he has evolved from a troubled, misguided youth to a model member of the prison community, the opportunity to demonstrate the truth of *Miller*'s central intuition—that children who commit even heinous crimes are capable of change. Pp. 206–213, 193 L. Ed. 2d, at 618-623.

2013-1163 (La. 6/20/14), 141 So. 3d 264, reversed and remanded.

Kennedy, J., delivered the opinion of the Court, in which Roberts, C. J., and Ginsburg, Breyer, Sotomayor, and Kagan, JJ., joined. Scalia, J., filed a dissenting opinion, in which Thomas and Alito, JJ., joined. Thomas, J., filed a dissenting opinion.

OPINION OF THE COURT

[577 U.S. 193]

Justice **Kennedy** delivered the opinion of the Court.

This is another case in a series of decisions involving the sentencing of offenders who were juveniles when their crimes were committed. In *Miller* v. *Alabama*, 567 U.S. 460, 132 S. Ct. 2455, 183 L. Ed. 2d 407 (2012), the Court held that [1] a juvenile convicted of a homicide offense could not be sentenced to life in prison without parole absent consideration of the juvenile's special circumstances in light of the principles and purposes of juvenile

[577 U.S. 194]

sentencing. In the wake of *Miller*, the question has arisen whether its holding is retroactive to juvenile offenders whose convictions and sentences were final when *Miller* was decided. Courts have reached different conclusions on this point. Compare, *e.g.*, *Martin* v. *Symmes*, 782 F.3d 939, 943 (CA8 2015); *Johnson* v. *Ponton*, 780 F.3d 219, 224-226 (CA4 2015); *Chambers* v. *State*, 831 N.W.2d 311, 331 (Minn. 2013); and *State* v. *Tate*, 2012-2763, p. 17 (La. 11/5/13), 130 So. 3d 829, 841, with *Diatchenko* v. *District Attorney for Suffolk Dist.*, 466 Mass. 655, 661-667, 1 N.E.3d 270, 278-282 (2013); *Aiken* v. *Byars*, 410 S.C. 534, 548, 765 S.E.2d 572, 578 (2014); *State* v. *Mares*, 2014 WY 126, ¶¶47-63, 335 P.3d 487, 504-508; and *People* v. *Davis*, 2014 IL 115595, ¶41, 6 N.E.3d 709, 722. Certiorari was granted in this case to resolve the question.

I

Petitioner is Henry Montgomery. In 1963, Montgomery killed Charles Hurt, a deputy sheriff in East Baton Rouge, Louisiana. Montgomery was 17 years old at the time of the crime. He was convicted of murder and sentenced to death, but the Louisiana Supreme Court reversed his conviction after finding that public prejudice had prevented a fair trial. *State* v. *Montgomery*, 181 So. 2d 756, 762 (1966).

Montgomery was retried. The jury returned a verdict of "guilty without capital punishment." *State* v. *Montgomery*, 242 So. 2d 818 (La. 1970). Under Louisiana law, this verdict required the trial court to impose a sentence of life without parole. The sentence was automatic upon the jury's verdict, so Montgomery had no opportunity to present mitigation evidence to justify a less severe sentence. That evidence might have included Montgomery's young age at the time of the crime; expert testimony regarding his limited capacity for foresight, self-discipline, and judgment; and his potential for rehabilitation. Montgomery, now 69 years old, has spent almost his entire life in prison.

[577 U.S. 195]

Almost 50 years after Montgomery was first taken into custody, this Court decided [2] *Miller* v. *Alabama*, 567 U.S. 460, 132 S. Ct. 2455, 183 L. Ed. 2d 407. *Miller* held that mandatory life without parole for juvenile homicide offenders violates the Eighth Amendment's prohibition on " 'cruel and unusual punishments.' " *Id.*, at 465, 132 S. Ct. 2455, 183 L. Ed. 2d 407. "By making youth (and all that accompanies it) irrelevant to imposition of that harshest prison sentence," mandatory life without parole "poses too great a risk of disproportionate punishment." *Id.*, at 479, 132 S. Ct. 2455, 183 L. Ed. 2d 407. *Miller* required that sentencing courts consider a child's "diminished culpability and heightened capacity for change" before condemning him or her to die in prison. *Ibid.* Although *Miller* did not foreclose a sentencer's ability to impose life without parole on a juvenile, the Court explained that a lifetime in prison is a disproportionate sentence for all but the rarest of children, those whose crimes reflect " 'irreparable corruption.' " *Id.*, at 479, 132 S. Ct. 2455, 183 L. Ed. 2d 407 (quoting *Roper* v. *Simmons*, 543 U.S. 551, 573, 125 S. Ct. 1183, 161 L. Ed. 2d 1 (2005)).

After this Court issued its decision in *Miller*, Montgomery sought collateral review of his mandatory life-without-parole sentence. **[3]** In Louisiana there are two principal mechanisms for collateral challenge to the lawfulness of imprisonment. Each begins with a filing in the trial court where the prisoner was convicted and sentenced. La. Code Crim. Proc. Ann., Arts. 882, 926 (West 2008). The first procedure permits a prisoner to file an application for postconviction relief on one or more of seven grounds set forth in the statute. Art. 930.3. The Louisiana Supreme Court has held that none of those grounds provides a basis for collateral review of sentencing errors. See *State ex rel. Melinie* v. *State*, 93-1380 (La. 1/12/96), 665 So. 2d 1172 (*per curiam*). Sentencing errors must instead be raised through Louisiana's second collateral review procedure.

This second mechanism allows a prisoner to bring a collateral attack on his or her sentence by filing a motion to correct an illegal sentence. See Art. 882. Montgomery invoked

[577 U.S. 196]

this procedure in the East Baton Rouge Parish District Court.

[4] The state statute provides that

"[a]n illegal sentence may be corrected at any time by the court that imposed the sentence." *Ibid.* An illegal sentence "is primarily restricted to those instances in which the *term* of the prisoner's sentence is not authorized by the statute or statutes which govern the penalty" for the crime of conviction. *State* v. *Mead*, 2014-1051, p. 3 (La. App. 4 Cir. 4/22/15), 165 So. 3d 1044, 1047; see also *State* v. *Alexander*, 2014-0401 (La. 11/7/14), 152 So. 3d 137 (*per curiam*). In the ordinary course Louisiana courts will not consider a challenge to a disproportionate sentence on collateral review; rather, as a general matter, it appears that prisoners must raise Eighth Amendment sentencing challenges on direct review. See *State* v. *Gibbs*, 620 So. 2d 296, 296-297 (La. App. 1993); *Mead*, *supra*, at 1047.

Louisiana's collateral review courts will, however, consider a motion to correct an illegal sentence based on a decision of this Court holding that the Eighth Amendment to the Federal Constitution prohibits a punishment for a type of crime or a class of offenders. When, for example, this Court held in *Graham* v. *Florida*, 560 U.S. 48, 130 S. Ct. 2011, 176 L. Ed. 2d 825 (2010), that the Eighth Amendment bars life-without-parole sentences for juvenile nonhomicide offenders, Louisiana courts heard *Graham* claims brought by prisoners whose sentences had long been final. See, *e.g.*, *State* v. *Shaffer*, 2011-1756, pp. 1-4 (La. 11/23/11), 77 So. 3d 939, 940-942 (*per curiam*) (considering motion to correct an illegal sentence on the ground that *Graham* rendered illegal a life-without-parole sentence for a juvenile nonhomicide offender). Montgomery's motion argued that *Miller* rendered his mandatory life-without-parole sentence illegal.

The trial court denied Montgomery's motion on the ground that *Miller* is not retroactive on collateral review. Montgomery then filed an application for a supervisory writ. The Louisiana Supreme Court denied the application. 2013-1163

[577 U.S. 197]

(6/20/14), 141 So. 3d 264. The court relied on its earlier decision in *State* v. *Tate*, 130 So. 3d 829, which held that *Miller* does not have retroactive effect in cases on state collateral review. Chief Justice Johnson and Justice Hughes dissented in *Tate*, and Chief Justice Johnson again noted her dissent in Montgomery's case.

This Court granted Montgomery's petition for certiorari. The petition presented the question "whether *Miller* adopts a new substantive rule that applies retroactively on collateral review to people condemned as juveniles to die in prison." Pet. for Cert. i. In addition, the Court directed the parties to address the following question: "Do we have jurisdiction to decide whether the Supreme Court of Louisiana correctly refused to give retroactive effect in this case to our decision in *Miller*?" 575 U.S. 911, 135 S. Ct. 1546, 191 L. Ed. 2d 635 (2015).

II

The parties agree that the Court has jurisdiction to decide this case. To ensure this conclusion is correct, the Court appointed Richard D. Bernstein as *amicus curiae* to brief and argue the position that the Court lacks jurisdiction. He has ably discharged his assigned responsibilities.

Amicus argues that a State is under no obligation to give a new rule of constitutional law retroactive effect in its own collateral review proceedings. As those proceedings are created by state law and under the State's plenary control, *amicus* contends, it is for state courts to define applicable principles of retroactivity. Under this view, the Louisiana Supreme Court's decision does not implicate a federal right; it only determines the scope of relief available in a particular type of state proceeding—a question of state law beyond this Court's power to review.

[5] If, however, the Constitution establishes a rule and requires that the rule have retroactive application, then a state court's refusal to give the rule retroactive effect is reviewable by this Court. Cf. *Griffith* v. *Kentucky*, 479 U.S. 314,

[577 U.S. 198]

328, 107 S. Ct. 708, 93 L. Ed. 2d 649 (1987) (holding that on direct review, a new constitutional rule must be applied retroactively "to all cases, state or federal"). States may not disregard a controlling, constitutional command in their own courts. See *Martin* v. *Hunter's Lessee*, 1 Wheat. 304, 340-341, 344, 4 L. Ed. 97 (1816); see also *Yates* v. *Aiken*, 484 U.S. 211, 218, 108 S. Ct. 534, 98 L. Ed. 2d 546 (1988) (when a State has not "placed any limit on the issues that it will entertain in collateral proceedings . . . it has a duty to grant the relief that federal law requires"). *Amicus'* argument therefore hinges on the premise that this Court's retroactivity precedents are not a constitutional mandate.

[6] Justice O'connor's plurality opinion in *Teague* v. *Lane*, 489 U.S. 288, 109 S. Ct. 1060, 103 L. Ed. 2d 334 (1989), set forth a framework for retroactivity in cases on federal collateral review. Under *Teague*, a new constitutional rule of criminal procedure does not apply, as a general matter, to convictions that were final when the new rule was announced. *Teague*

recognized, however, two categories of rules that are not subject to its general retroactivity bar. First, courts must give retroactive effect to new substantive rules of constitutional law. Substantive rules include "rules forbidding criminal punishment of certain primary conduct," as well as "rules prohibiting a certain category of punishment for a class of defendants because of their status or offense." *Penry* v. *Lynaugh*, 492 U.S. 302, 330, 109 S. Ct. 2934, 106 L. Ed. 2d 256 (1989); see also *Teague, supra*, at 307, 109 S. Ct. 1060, 103 L. Ed. 2d 334. Although *Teague* describes new substantive rules as an exception to the bar on retroactive application of procedural rules, this Court has recognized that substantive rules "are more accurately characterized as . . . not subject to the bar." *Schriro* v. *Summerlin*, 542 U.S. 348, 352, n. 4, 124 S. Ct. 2519, 159 L. Ed. 2d 442 (2004). Second, courts must give retroactive effect to new " ' "watershed rules of criminal procedure" implicating the fundamental fairness and accuracy of the criminal proceeding.' " *Id.*, at 352, 124 S. Ct. 2519, 159 L. Ed. 2d 442; see also *Teague*, 489 U.S., at 312-313, 109 S. Ct. 1060, 103 L. Ed. 2d 334.

It is undisputed, then, that *Teague* requires the retroactive application of new substantive and watershed procedural

[577 U.S. 199]

rules in federal habeas proceedings. *Amicus*, however, contends that *Teague* was an interpretation of the federal habeas statute, not a constitutional command; and so, the argument proceeds, *Teague*'s retroactivity holding simply has no application in a State's own collateral review proceedings.

To support this claim, *amicus*

points to language in *Teague* that characterized the Court's task as " 'defin[ing] the scope of the writ.' " *Id.*, at 308, 109 S. Ct. 1060, 103 L. Ed. 2d 334 (quoting *Kuhlmann* v. *Wilson*, 477 U.S. 436, 447, 106 S. Ct. 2616, 91 L. Ed. 2d 364 (1986) (plurality opinion)); see also 489 U.S., at 317, 109 S. Ct. 1060, 103 L. Ed. 2d 334 (White, J., concurring in part and concurring in judgment) ("If we are wrong in construing the reach of the habeas corpus statutes, Congress can of course correct us . . . "); *id.*, at 332, 109 S. Ct. 1060, 103 L. Ed. 2d 334 (Brennan, J., dissenting) ("No new facts or arguments have come to light suggesting that our [past] reading of the federal habeas statute . . . was plainly mistaken").

In addition, *amicus* directs us to *Danforth* v. *Minnesota*, 552 U.S. 264, 128 S. Ct. 1029, 169 L. Ed. 2d 859 (2008), in which a majority of the Court held that *Teague* does not preclude state courts from giving retroactive effect to a broader set of new constitutional rules than *Teague* itself required. 552 U.S., at 266, 128 S. Ct. 1029, 169 L. Ed. 2d 859. The *Danforth* majority concluded that *Teague*'s general rule of nonretroactivity for new constitutional rules of criminal procedure "was an exercise of this Court's power to interpret the federal habeas statute." 552 U.S., at 278, 128 S. Ct. 1029, 169 L. Ed. 2d 859. Since *Teague*'s retroactivity bar "limit[s] only the scope of *federal* habeas relief," the *Danforth* majority reasoned, States are free to make new procedural rules retroactive on state collateral review. 552 U.S., at 281-282, 128 S. Ct. 1029, 169 L. Ed. 2d 859.

Amicus, however, reads too much into these statements. Neither *Teague* nor *Danforth* had reason to address whether States are required as a constitutional matter to give retroactive effect to new substantive or watershed procedural rules. *Teague* originated in a federal, not state, habeas proceeding; so it had no particular reason to discuss whether any part of its holding was required by the Constitution in addition to the federal habeas statute. And *Danforth* held

[577 U.S. 200]

only that *Teague*'s general rule of nonretroactivity was an interpretation of the federal habeas statute and does not prevent States from providing greater relief in their own collateral review courts. The *Danforth* majority limited its analysis to *Teague*'s general retroactivity bar, leaving open the question whether *Teague*'s two exceptions are binding on the States as a matter of constitutional law. 552 U.S., at 278, 128 S. Ct. 1029, 169 L. Ed. 2d 859; see also *id.*, at 277, 128 S. Ct. 1029, 169 L. Ed. 2d 859 ("[T]he case before us now does not involve either of the '*Teague* exceptions' ").

In this case, the Court must address part of the question left open in *Danforth*. The Court now holds that **[7]** when a new substantive rule of constitutional law controls the outcome of a case, the Constitution requires state collateral review courts to give retroactive effect to that rule. *Teague*'s conclusion establishing the retroactivity of new substantive rules is best understood as resting upon constitutional premises. That constitutional command is, like all federal law, binding on state courts. This holding is limited to *Teague*'s first exception for substantive rules; the constitutional status of *Teague*'s exception for watershed rules of procedure need not be addressed here.

This Court's precedents addressing the nature of substantive rules, their differences from procedural rules, and their history of retroactive application establish that **[8]** the Constitution requires substantive rules to have retroactive effect regardless of when a conviction became final.

The category of substantive rules discussed in *Teague* originated in Justice Harlan's approach to retroactivity. *Teague* adopted that reasoning. See 489 U.S., at 292, 312, 109 S. Ct. 1060, 103 L. Ed. 2d 334 (discussing *Mackey* v. *United States*, 401 U.S. 667, 692, 91 S. Ct. 1160, 28 L. Ed. 2d 404 (1971) (opinion concurring in judgments in part and dissenting in part); and *Desist* v. *United States*, 394 U.S. 244, 261, n. 2, 89 S. Ct. 1030, 22 L. Ed. 2d 248 (1969) (dissenting opinion)). **[9]** Justice Harlan defined substantive constitutional rules as "those that place, as a matter of constitutional interpretation, certain kinds of primary, private individual conduct beyond the power of the criminal

[577 U.S. 201]

law-making authority to proscribe." *Mackey, supra,* at 692, 91 S. Ct. 1160, 28 L. Ed. 2d 404. In *Penry* v. *Lynaugh,* decided four months after *Teague,* the Court recognized that "the first exception set forth in *Teague* should be understood to cover not only rules forbidding criminal punishment of certain primary conduct but also rules prohibiting a certain category of punishment for a class of defendants because of their status or offense." 492 U.S., at 330, 109 S. Ct. 2934, 106 L. Ed. 2d 256. *Penry* explained that Justice Harlan's first exception spoke "in terms of substantive categorical guarantees accorded by the Constitution, regardless of the procedures followed." *Id.,* at 329, 109 S. Ct. 2934, 106 L. Ed. 2d 256. Whether a new rule bars States from proscribing certain conduct or from inflicting a certain punishment, "[i]n both cases, the Constitution itself deprives the State of the power to impose a certain penalty." *Id.*, at 330, 109 S. Ct. 2934, 106 L. Ed. 2d 256.

[10] Substantive rules, then, set forth categorical constitutional guarantees that place certain criminal laws and punishments altogether beyond the State's power to impose. It follows that when a State enforces a proscription or penalty barred by the Constitution, the resulting conviction or sentence is, by definition, unlawful. [11] Procedural rules, in contrast, are designed to enhance the accuracy of a conviction or sentence by regulating "the *manner of determining* the defendant's culpability." *Schriro*, 542 U.S., at 353, 124 S. Ct. 2519, 159 L. Ed. 2d 442; *Teague, supra*, at 313, 109 S. Ct. 1060, 103 L. Ed. 2d 334. Those rules "merely raise the possibility that someone convicted with use of the invalidated procedure might have been acquitted otherwise." *Schriro, supra*, at 352, 124 S. Ct. 2519, 159 L. Ed. 2d 442. Even where procedural error has infected a trial, the resulting conviction or sentence may still be accurate; and, by extension, the defendant's continued confinement may still be lawful. For this reason, a trial conducted under a procedure found to be unconstitutional in a later case does not, as a general matter, have the automatic consequence of invalidating a defendant's conviction or sentence.

The same possibility of a valid result does not exist where a substantive rule has eliminated a State's power to proscribe the defendant's conduct or impose a given punishment.

[577 U.S. 202]

"[E]ven the use of impeccable factfinding procedures could not le-

gitimate a verdict" where "the conduct being penalized is constitutionally immune from punishment." *United States* v. *United States Coin & Currency*, 401 U.S. 715, 724, 91 S. Ct. 1041, 28 L. Ed. 2d 434 (1971). Nor could the use of flawless sentencing procedures legitimate a punishment where the Constitution immunizes the defendant from the sentence imposed. "No circumstances call more for the invocation of a rule of complete retroactivity." *Ibid.*

By holding that new substantive rules are, indeed, retroactive, *Teague* continued a long tradition of giving retroactive effect to constitutional rights that go beyond procedural guarantees. See *Mackey, supra*, at 692-693, 91 S. Ct. 1160, 28 L. Ed. 2d 404 (opinion of Harlan, J.) ("[T]he writ has historically been available for attacking convictions on [substantive] grounds"). Before *Brown* v. *Allen*, 344 U.S. 443, 73 S. Ct. 397, 97 L. Ed. 469 (1953), "federal courts would never consider the merits of a constitutional claim if the habeas petitioner had a fair opportunity to raise his arguments in the original proceeding." *Desist*, 394 U.S., at 261, 89 S. Ct. 1030, 22 L. Ed. 2d 248 (Harlan, J., dissenting). Even in the pre-1953 era of restricted federal habeas, however, an exception was made "when the habeas petitioner attacked the constitutionality of the state statute under which he had been convicted. Since, in this situation, the State had no power to proscribe the conduct for which the petitioner was imprisoned, it could not constitutionally insist that he remain in jail." *Id.*, at 261, n. 2, 89 S. Ct. 1030, 22 L. Ed. 2d 248 (dissenting) (citation omitted).

In *Ex parte Siebold*, 100 U.S. 371, 25 L. Ed. 717 (1880), the Court addressed why substantive rules must

615

have retroactive effect regardless of when the defendant's conviction became final. At the time of that decision, "[m]ere error in the judgment or proceedings, under and by virtue of which a party is imprisoned, constitute[d] no ground for the issue of the writ." *Id.*, at 375, 25 L. Ed. 717. Before *Siebold*, the law might have been thought to establish that so long as the conviction and sentence were imposed by a court of competent jurisdiction, no

[577 U.S. 203]

habeas relief could issue. In *Siebold*, however, the petitioners attacked the judgments on the ground that they had been convicted under unconstitutional statutes. The Court explained that if "this position is well taken, it affects the foundation of the whole proceedings." *Id.*, at 376, 25 L. Ed. 717. **[12]** A conviction under an unconstitutional law

"is not merely erroneous, but is illegal and void, and cannot be a legal cause of imprisonment. It is true, if no writ of error lies, the judgment may be final, in the sense that there may be no means of reversing it. But . . . if the laws are unconstitutional and void, the Circuit Court acquired no jurisdiction of the causes." *Id.*, at 376-377, 25 L. Ed. 717.

As discussed, the Court has concluded that the same logic governs a challenge to a punishment that the Constitution deprives States of authority to impose. *Penry*, 492 U.S., at 330, 109 S. Ct. 2934, 106 L. Ed. 2d 256; see also Friendly, Is Innocence Irrelevant? Collateral Attack on Criminal Judgments, 38 U. Chi. L. Rev. 142, 151 (1970) ("Broadly speaking, the original sphere for collateral attack on a conviction was where the tribunal lacked jurisdiction either in the usual sense or because the statute under which the defendant had been pros-

ecuted was unconstitutional or because the sentence was one the court could not lawfully impose" (footnote omitted)). A conviction or sentence imposed in violation of a substantive rule is not just erroneous but contrary to law and, as a result, void. See *Siebold*, 100 U.S., at 376, 25 L. Ed. 717. It follows, as a general principle, that a court has no authority to leave in place a conviction or sentence that violates a substantive rule, regardless of whether the conviction or sentence became final before the rule was announced.

Siebold and the other cases discussed in this opinion, of course, do not directly control the question the Court now answers for the first time. These precedents did not involve a state court's postconviction review of a conviction or sentence

[577 U.S. 204]

and so did not address whether the Constitution requires new substantive rules to have retroactive effect in cases on state collateral review. These decisions, however, have important bearing on the analysis necessary in this case.

In support of its holding that a conviction obtained under an unconstitutional law warrants habeas relief, the *Siebold* Court explained that **[13]** "[a]n unconstitutional law is void, and is as no law." *Ibid.* A penalty imposed pursuant to an unconstitutional law is no less void because the prisoner's sentence became final before the law was held unconstitutional. There is no grandfather clause that permits States to enforce punishments the Constitution forbids. To conclude otherwise would undercut the Constitution's substantive guarantees. Writing for the Court in *United States Coin & Currency*, Justice Harlan made this point when he declared that "[n]o circumstances call more for the invocation of a rule of complete retroactivity" than when "the conduct being penalized is constitutionally immune from punishment." 401 U.S., at 724, 91 S. Ct. 1041, 28 L. Ed. 2d 434. *United States Coin & Currency* involved a case on direct review; yet, for the reasons explained in this opinion, the same principle should govern the application of substantive rules on collateral review. As Justice Harlan explained, where a State lacked the power to proscribe the habeas petitioner's conduct, "it could not constitutionally insist that he remain in jail." *Desist, supra,* at 261, n. 2, 89 S. Ct. 1030, 22 L. Ed. 2d 248 (dissenting opinion).

[14] If a State may not constitutionally insist that a prisoner remain in jail on federal habeas review, it may not constitutionally insist on the same result in its own postconviction proceedings. Under the Supremacy Clause of the Constitution, state collateral review courts have no greater power than federal habeas courts to mandate that a prisoner continue to suffer punishment barred by the Constitution. If a state collateral proceeding is open to a claim controlled by federal law, the state court "has a duty to grant the relief

[577 U.S. 205]

that federal law requires." *Yates,* 484 U.S., at 218, 108 S. Ct. 534, 98 L. Ed. 2d 546. Where state collateral review proceedings permit prisoners to challenge the lawfulness of their confinement, States cannot refuse to give retroactive effect to a substantive constitutional right that determines the outcome of that challenge.

As a final point, it must be noted that [15] the retroactive application of substantive rules does not implicate a State's weighty interests in ensuring the finality of convictions and sentences. *Teague* warned against the intrusiveness of "*continually* forc[ing] the States to marshal resources in order to keep in prison defendants whose trials and appeals conformed to then-existing constitutional standards." 489 U.S., at 310, 109 S. Ct. 1060, 103 L. Ed. 2d 334. This concern has no application in the realm of substantive rules, for no resources marshaled by a State could preserve a conviction or sentence that the Constitution deprives the State of power to impose. See *Mackey,* 401 U.S., at 693, 91 S. Ct. 1160, 28 L. Ed. 2d 404 (opinion of Harlan, J.) ("There is little societal interest in permitting the criminal process to rest at a point where it ought properly never to repose").

[16] In adjudicating claims under its collateral review procedures a State may not deny a controlling right asserted under the Constitution, assuming the claim is properly presented in the case. Louisiana follows these basic Supremacy Clause principles in its postconviction proceedings for challenging the legality of a sentence. [17] The State's collateral review procedures are open to claims that a decision of this Court has rendered certain sentences illegal, as a substantive matter, under the Eighth Amendment. See, *e.g., State* v. *Dyer,* 2011-1758, pp. 1-2 (La. 11/23/11), 77 So. 3d 928, 928-929 (*per curiam*) (considering claim on collateral review that this Court's decision in *Graham* v. *Florida,* 560 U.S. 48, 130 S. Ct. 2011, 176 L. Ed. 2d 825, rendered petitioner's life-without-parole sentence illegal). Montgomery alleges that *Miller* announced a substantive constitutional rule and that the Louisiana Supreme Court erred by failing

to recognize its retroactive effect. This Court has jurisdiction to review that determination.

[577 U.S. 206]

III

This leads to the question whether *Miller*'s prohibition on mandatory life without parole for juvenile offenders indeed did announce a new substantive rule that, under the Constitution, must be retroactive.

As stated above, a procedural rule "regulate[s] only the *manner of determining* the defendant's culpability." *Schriro*, 542 U.S., at 353, 124 S. Ct. 2519, 159 L. Ed. 2d 442. A substantive rule, in contrast, forbids "criminal punishment of certain primary conduct" or prohibits "a certain category of punishment for a class of defendants because of their status or offense." *Penry*, 492 U.S., at 330, 109 S. Ct. 2934, 106 L. Ed. 2d 256; see also *Schriro*, *supra*, at 353, 124 S. Ct. 2519, 159 L. Ed. 2d 442 (A substantive rule "alters the range of conduct or the class of persons that the law punishes"). Under this standard, and for the reasons explained below, [18] *Miller* announced a substantive rule that is retroactive in cases on collateral review.

The "foundation stone" for *Miller*'s analysis was this Court's line of precedent holding certain punishments disproportionate when applied to juveniles. 567 U.S., at 470, n. 4, 132 S. Ct. 2455, 183 L. Ed. 2d 407. Those cases include *Graham* v. *Florida*, *supra*, which held that the Eighth Amendment bars life without parole for juvenile nonhomicide offenders, and *Roper* v. *Simmons*, 543 U.S. 551, 125 S. Ct. 1183, 161 L. Ed. 2d 1, which held that the Eighth Amendment prohibits capital punishment for those under the age of 18 at the time of their crimes. [19] Protection against dispro-portionate punishment is the central substantive guarantee of the Eighth Amendment and goes far beyond the manner of determining a defendant's sentence. See *Graham*, *supra*, at 59, 130 S. Ct. 2011, 176 L. Ed. 2d 825 ("The concept of proportionality is central to the Eighth Amendment"); see also *Weems* v. *United States*, 217 U.S. 349, 367, 30 S. Ct. 544, 54 L. Ed. 793 (1910); *Harmelin* v. *Michigan*, 501 U.S. 957, 997-998, 111 S. Ct. 2680, 115 L. Ed. 2d 836 (1991) (Kennedy, J., concurring in part and concurring in judgment).

Miller took as its starting premise the principle established in *Roper* and *Graham* that [20] "children are constitutionally different from adults for purposes of sentencing." 567

[577 U.S. 207]

U.S., at 471, 132 S. Ct. 2455, 183 L. Ed. 2d 407 (citing *Roper*, *supra*, at 569-570, 125 S. Ct. 1183, 161 L. Ed. 2d 1; and *Graham*, *supra*, at 68, 130 S. Ct. 2011, 176 L. Ed. 2d 825). These differences result from children's "diminished culpability and greater prospects for reform," and are apparent in three primary ways:

"First, children have a 'lack of maturity and an underdeveloped sense of responsibility,' leading to recklessness, impulsivity, and heedless risk-taking. Second, children 'are more vulnerable to negative influences and outside pressures,' including from their family and peers; they have limited 'control over their own environment' and lack the ability to extricate themselves from horrific, crime-producing settings. And third, a child's character is not as 'well formed' as an adult's; his traits are 'less fixed' and his actions less likely to be 'evidence of irretrievable depravity.' " 567 U.S., at

471, 132 S. Ct. 2455, 183 L. Ed. 2d 407 (quoting *Roper*, supra, at 569-570, 125 S. Ct. 1183, 161 L. Ed. 2d 1; alterations, citations, and some internal quotation marks omitted).

As a corollary to a child's lesser culpability, *Miller* recognized that "the distinctive attributes of youth diminish the penological justifications" for imposing life without parole on juvenile offenders. 567 U.S., at 472, 132 S. Ct. 2455, 183 L. Ed. 2d 407. Because retribution "relates to an offender's blameworthiness, the case for retribution is not as strong with a minor as with an adult." *Ibid.* (quoting *Graham*, supra, at 71, 130 S. Ct. 2011, 176 L. Ed. 2d 825; internal quotation marks omitted). The deterrence rationale likewise does not suffice, since "the same characteristics that render juveniles less culpable than adults—their immaturity, recklessness, and impetuosity—make them less likely to consider potential punishment." 567 U.S., at 472, 132 S. Ct. 2455, 183 L. Ed. 2d 407 (internal quotation marks omitted). The need for incapacitation is lessened, too, because ordinary adolescent development diminishes the likelihood that a juvenile offender " 'forever will be a danger to society.' " *Ibid.* (quoting *Graham*, supra, at 72, 130 S. Ct. 2011, 176 L. Ed. 2d 825). Rehabilitation is not a satisfactory rationale, either. Rehabilitation cannot justify the sentence, as life without parole "forswears

[577 U.S. 208]

altogether the rehabilitative ideal." 567 U.S., at 473, 132 S. Ct. 2455, 183 L. Ed. 2d 407 (quoting *Graham*, supra, at 74, 130 S. Ct. 2011, 176 L. Ed. 2d 825).

These considerations underlay the Court's holding in *Miller* that [21] mandatory life-without-parole sen-

tences for children "pos[e] too great a risk of disproportionate punishment." 567 U.S., at 479, 132 S. Ct. 2455, 183 L. Ed. 2d 407. *Miller* requires that before sentencing a juvenile to life without parole, the sentencing judge take into account "how children are different, and how those differences counsel against irrevocably sentencing them to a lifetime in prison." *Id.*, at 480, 132 S. Ct. 2455, 183 L. Ed. 2d 407. The Court recognized that a sentencer might encounter the rare juvenile offender who exhibits such irretrievable depravity that rehabilitation is impossible and life without parole is justified. But in light of "children's diminished culpability and heightened capacity for change," *Miller* made clear that "appropriate occasions for sentencing juveniles to this harshest possible penalty will be uncommon." *Id.*, at 479, 132 S. Ct. 2455, 183 L. Ed. 2d 407.

[22] *Miller*, then, did more than require a sentencer to consider a juvenile offender's youth before imposing life without parole; it established that the penological justifications for life without parole collapse in light of "the distinctive attributes of youth." *Id.*, at 472, 132 S. Ct. 2455, 183 L. Ed. 2d 407. Even if a court considers a child's age before sentencing him or her to a lifetime in prison, that sentence still violates the Eighth Amendment for a child whose crime reflects " 'unfortunate yet transient immaturity.' " *Id.*, at 479, 132 S. Ct. 2455, 183 L. Ed. 2d 407 (quoting *Roper*, supra, at 573, 125 S. Ct. 1183, 161 L. Ed. 2d 1). Because *Miller* determined that sentencing a child to life without parole is excessive for all but " 'the rare juvenile offender whose crime reflects irreparable corruption,' " 567 U.S., at 479–480, 132 S. Ct. 2455, 183 L. Ed. 2d 407 (quoting *Roper*, supra, at 573, 125

S. Ct. 1183, 161 L. Ed. 2d 1), it rendered life without parole an unconstitutional penalty for "a class of defendants because of their status"—that is, juvenile offenders whose crimes reflect the transient immaturity of youth, *Penry*, 492 U.S., at 330, 109 S. Ct. 2934, 106 L. Ed. 2d 256. As a result, *Miller* announced a substantive rule of constitutional law. Like other substantive rules, *Miller* is retroactive because it " 'necessarily carr[ies]

[577 U.S. 209]

a significant risk that a defendant' "—here, the vast majority of juvenile offenders—"faces a punishment that the law cannot impose upon him." *Schriro*, 542 U.S., at 352, 124 S. Ct. 2519, 159 L. Ed. 2d 442 (quoting *Bousley* v. *United States*, 523 U.S. 614, 620, 118 S. Ct. 1604, 140 L. Ed. 2d 828 (1998)).

Louisiana nonetheless argues that *Miller* is procedural because it did not place any punishment beyond the State's power to impose; it instead required sentencing courts to take children's age into account before condemning them to die in prison. In support of this argument, Louisiana points to *Miller*'s statement that the decision "does not categorically bar a penalty for a class of offenders or type of crime—as, for example, we did in *Roper* or *Graham*. Instead, it mandates only that a sentencer follow a certain process—considering an offender's youth and attendant characteristics—before imposing a particular penalty." *Miller, supra*, at 483, 132 S. Ct. 2455, 183 L. Ed. 2d 407. **[23]** *Miller*, it is true, did not bar a punishment for all juvenile offenders, as the Court did in *Roper* or *Graham*. *Miller* did bar life without parole, however, for all but the rarest of juvenile offenders, those whose crimes reflect permanent incorrigibility. For that

reason, *Miller* is no less substantive than are *Roper* and *Graham*. Before *Miller*, every juvenile convicted of a homicide offense could be sentenced to life without parole. After *Miller*, it will be the rare juvenile offender who can receive that same sentence. The only difference between *Roper* and *Graham*, on the one hand, and *Miller*, on the other hand, is that *Miller* drew a line between children whose crimes reflect transient immaturity and those rare children whose crimes reflect irreparable corruption. The fact that life without parole could be a proportionate sentence for the latter kind of juvenile offender does not mean that all other children imprisoned under a disproportionate sentence have not suffered the deprivation of a substantive right.

To be sure, *Miller*'s holding has a procedural component. *Miller* requires a sentencer to consider a juvenile offender's youth and attendant characteristics before determining that

[577 U.S. 210]

life without parole is a proportionate sentence. See 567 U.S., at 483, 132 S. Ct. 2455, 183 L. Ed. 2d 407. Louisiana contends that because *Miller* requires this process, it must have set forth a procedural rule. This argument, however, conflates a procedural requirement necessary to implement a substantive guarantee with a rule that "regulate[s] only the *manner of determining* the defendant's culpability." *Schriro, supra*, at 353, 124 S. Ct. 2519, 159 L. Ed. 2d 442. **[24]** There are instances in which a substantive change in the law must be attended by a procedure that enables a prisoner to show that he falls within the category of persons whom the law may no longer punish. See *Mackey*, 401 U.S., at 692, n. 7, 91 S. Ct. 1160, 28 L. Ed. 2d 404 (opinion of

Harlan, J.) ("Some rules may have both procedural and substantive ramifications, as I have used those terms here"). For example, when an element of a criminal offense is deemed unconstitutional, a prisoner convicted under that offense receives a new trial where the government must prove the prisoner's conduct still fits within the modified definition of the crime. In a similar vein, when the Constitution prohibits a particular form of punishment for a class of persons, an affected prisoner receives a procedure through which he can show that he belongs to the protected class. See, *e.g.*, *Atkins* v. *Virginia*, 536 U.S. 304, 317, 122 S. Ct. 2242, 153 L. Ed. 2d 335 (2002) (requiring a procedure to determine whether a particular individual with an intellectual disability "fall[s] within the range of [intellectually disabled] offenders about whom there is a national consensus" that execution is impermissible). Those procedural requirements do not, of course, transform substantive rules into procedural ones.

The procedure *Miller* prescribes is no different. **[25]** A hearing where "youth and its attendant characteristics" are considered as sentencing factors is necessary to separate those juveniles who may be sentenced to life without parole from those who may not. 567 U.S., at 465, 132 S. Ct. 2455, 183 L. Ed. 2d 407. The hearing does not replace but rather gives effect to *Miller*'s substantive holding that life without parole is an excessive sentence for children whose crimes reflect transient immaturity.

[577 U.S. 211]

Louisiana suggests that *Miller* cannot have made a constitutional distinction between children whose crimes reflect transient immaturity and those whose crimes reflect irreparable corruption because *Miller* did not require trial courts to make a finding of fact regarding a child's incorrigibility. That this finding is not required, however, speaks only to the degree of procedure *Miller* mandated in order to implement its substantive guarantee. **[26]** When a new substantive rule of constitutional law is established, this Court is careful to limit the scope of any attendant procedural requirement to avoid intruding more than necessary upon the States' sovereign administration of their criminal justice systems. See *Ford* v. *Wainwright*, 477 U.S. 399, 416-417, 106 S. Ct. 2595, 91 L. Ed. 2d 335 (1986) ("[W]e leave to the State[s] the task of developing appropriate ways to enforce the constitutional restriction upon [their] execution of sentences"). Fidelity to this important principle of federalism, however, should not be construed to demean the substantive character of the federal right at issue. **[27]** That *Miller* did not impose a formal factfinding requirement does not leave States free to sentence a child whose crime reflects transient immaturity to life without parole. To the contrary, *Miller* established that this punishment is disproportionate under the Eighth Amendment.

For this reason, the death penalty cases Louisiana cites in support of its position are inapposite. See, *e.g.*, *Beard* v. *Banks*, 542 U.S. 406, 408, 124 S. Ct. 2504, 159 L. Ed. 2d 494 (2004) (holding nonretroactive the rule that forbids instructing a jury to disregard mitigating factors not found by a unanimous vote); *O'Dell* v. *Netherland*, 521 U.S. 151, 153, 117 S. Ct. 1969, 138 L. Ed. 2d 351 (1997) (holding nonretroactive the rule providing that, if the prosecutor cites future dangerousness, the defendant may inform the jury of his ineligibility for parole); *Sawyer* v. *Smith,* 497 U.S. 227, 229, 110 S. Ct. 2822, 111 L. Ed. 2d 193 (1990) (holding nonretroactive the rule that forbids suggesting to a capital jury that it is not responsible for a death sentence). Those decisions altered the processes in which States must engage before sentencing a person to death. The processes may have had

[577 U.S. 212]

some effect on the likelihood that capital punishment would be imposed, but none of those decisions rendered a certain penalty unconstitutionally excessive for a category of offenders.

The Court now holds that **[28]** *Miller* announced a substantive rule of constitutional law. The conclusion that *Miller* states a substantive rule comports with the principles that informed *Teague. Teague* sought to balance the important goals of finality and comity with the liberty interests of those imprisoned pursuant to rules later deemed unconstitutional. *Miller*'s conclusion that the sentence of life without parole is disproportionate for the vast majority of juvenile offenders raises a grave risk that many are being held in violation of the Constitution.

Giving *Miller* retroactive effect, moreover, does not require States to relitigate sentences, let alone convictions, in every case where a juvenile offender received mandatory life without parole. A State may remedy a *Miller* violation by permitting juvenile homicide offenders to be considered for parole, rather than by resentencing them. See, *e.g.,* Wyo. Stat. Ann. § 6-10-301(c) (2013) (juvenile homicide offenders eligible for parole after 25 years). Allowing those offenders to be considered for parole ensures that juveniles whose crimes reflected

only transient immaturity—and who have since matured—will not be forced to serve a disproportionate sentence in violation of the Eighth Amendment.

Extending parole eligibility to juvenile offenders does not impose an onerous burden on the States, nor does it disturb the finality of state convictions. Those prisoners who have shown an inability to reform will continue to serve life sentences. The opportunity for release will be afforded to those who demonstrate the truth of *Miller*'s central intuition—that children who commit even heinous crimes are capable of change.

Petitioner has discussed in his submissions to this Court his evolution from a troubled, misguided youth to a model

[577 U.S. 213]

member of the prison community. Petitioner states that he helped establish an inmate boxing team, of which he later became a trainer and coach. He alleges that he has contributed his time and labor to the prison's silkscreen department and that he strives to offer advice and serve as a role model to other inmates. These claims have not been tested or even addressed by the State, so the Court does not confirm their accuracy. The petitioner's submissions are relevant, however, as an example of one kind of evidence that prisoners might use to demonstrate rehabilitation.

* * *

Henry Montgomery has spent each day of the past 46 years knowing he was condemned to die in prison. Perhaps it can be established that, due to exceptional circumstances, this fate was a just and proportionate punishment for the crime he committed as a 17-year-old boy. In light of what this

Court has said in *Roper, Graham*, and *Miller* about how children are constitutionally different from adults in their level of culpability, however, prisoners like Montgomery must be given the opportunity to show their crime did not reflect irreparable corruption; and, if it did not, their hope for some years of life outside prison walls must be restored.

The judgment of the Supreme Court of Louisiana is reversed, and the case is remanded for further proceedings not inconsistent with this opinion.

It is so ordered.

SEPARATE OPINIONS

Justice **Scalia**, with whom Justice **Thomas** and Justice **Alito** join, dissenting.

The Court has no jurisdiction to decide this case, and the decision it arrives at is wrong. I respectfully dissent.

I. Jurisdiction

Louisiana postconviction courts willingly entertain Eighth Amendment claims but, with limited exceptions, apply the

[577 U.S. 214]

law as it existed when the state prisoner was convicted and sentenced. Shortly after this Court announced *Teague* v. *Lane*, 489 U.S. 288, 109 S. Ct. 1060, 103 L. Ed. 2d 334 (1989), the Louisiana Supreme Court adopted *Teague*'s framework to govern the provision of postconviction remedies available to *state* prisoners in its *state* courts as a matter of *state* law. *Taylor* v. *Whitley*, 606 So. 2d 1292 (1992). In doing so, the court stated that it was "not bound" to adopt that federal framework. *Id.*, at 1296. One would think, then, that it is none of our business that a 69-year-old Louisiana prisoner's state-law motion to be resentenced according to *Miller* v. *Alabama*, 567 U.S. 460, 132 S. Ct. 2455, 183 L. Ed. 2d 407 (2012), a case announced almost half a century after his sentence was final, was met with a firm rejection on state-law grounds by the Louisiana Supreme Court. But a majority of this Court, eager to reach the merits of this case, resolves the question of our jurisdiction by deciding that the Constitution *requires* state postconviction courts to adopt *Teague*'s exception for so-called "substantive" new rules and to provide state-law remedies for the violations of those rules to prisoners whose sentences long ago became final. This conscription into federal service of state postconviction courts is nothing short of astonishing.

A

Teague announced that federal courts could not grant habeas corpus to overturn state convictions on the basis of a "new rule" of constitutional law—meaning one announced after the convictions became final—*unless* that new rule was a "substantive rule" or a "watershed rul[e]" of criminal procedure." 489 U.S., at 311, 109 S. Ct. 1060, 103 L. Ed. 2d 334. The *Teague* prescription followed from Justice Harlan's view of the "retroactivity problem" detailed in his separate opinion in *Desist* v. *United States*, 394 U.S. 244, 256, 89 S. Ct. 1030, 22 L. Ed. 2d 248 (1969) (dissenting opinion), and later in *Mackey* v. *United States*, 401 U.S. 667, 675, 91 S. Ct. 1160, 28 L. Ed. 2d 404 (1971) (opinion concurring in judgment in part and dissenting in part). Placing the

[577 U.S. 215]

rule's first exception in context requires more analysis than the majority has applied.

The Court in the mid-20th century was confounded by what Justice Harlan called the "swift pace of constitutional change," *Pickelsimer* v. *Wainwright*, 375 U.S. 2, 4, 84 S. Ct. 80, 11 L. Ed. 2d 41 (1963) (dissenting opinion), as it vacated and remanded many cases in the wake of *Gideon* v. *Wainwright*, 372 U.S. 335, 83 S. Ct. 792, 9 L. Ed. 2d 799 (1963). Justice Harlan called upon the Court to engage in "informed and deliberate consideration" of "whether the States are constitutionally required to apply [*Gideon's*] new rule retrospectively, which may well require the reopening of cases long since finally adjudicated in accordance with then applicable decisions of this Court." *Pickelsimer*, *supra*, at 3, 84 S. Ct. 80, 11 L. Ed. 2d 41. The Court answered that call in *Linkletter* v. *Walker*, 381 U.S. 618, 85 S. Ct. 1731, 14 L. Ed. 2d 601 (1965). *Linkletter* began with the premise "that we are neither required to apply, nor prohibited from applying, a decision retrospectively" and went on to adopt an equitable rule-by-rule approach to retroactivity, considering "the prior history of the rule in question, its purpose and effect, and whether retrospective operation will further or retard its operation." *Id.*, at 629, 85 S. Ct. 1731, 14 L. Ed. 2d 601.

The *Linkletter* framework proved unworkable when the Court began applying the rule-by-rule approach not only to cases on collateral review but also to cases on direct review, rejecting any distinction "between convictions now final" and "convictions at various stages of trial and direct review." *Stovall* v. *Denno*, 388 U.S. 293, 300, 87 S. Ct. 1967, 18 L. Ed. 2d 1199 (1967). It was this rejection that drew Justice Harlan's reproach in *Desist* and later in *Mackey*. He urged that "all 'new' rules of constitutional law must, at a minimum, be applied to all those cases which are still subject to direct review by this Court at the time the 'new' decision is handed down." *Desist*, *supra*, at 258, 89 S. Ct. 1030, 22 L. Ed. 2d 248 (dissenting opinion). "Simply fishing one case from the stream of appellate review, using it as a vehicle for pronouncing new constitutional standards, and then permitting a

[577 U.S. 216]

stream of similar cases subsequently to flow by unaffected by that new rule constitute an indefensible departure from th[e] model of judicial review." *Mackey*, *supra*, at 679, 91 S. Ct. 1160, 28 L. Ed. 2d 404.

The decision in *Griffith* v. *Kentucky*, 479 U.S. 314, 107 S. Ct. 708, 93 L. Ed. 2d 649 (1987), heeded this constitutional concern. The Court jettisoned the *Linkletter* test for cases pending on direct review and adopted for them Justice Harlan's rule of redressability: "[F]ailure to apply a newly declared constitutional rule to criminal cases pending on direct review violates basic norms of *constitutional* adjudication." 479 U.S., at 322, 107 S. Ct. 708, 93 L. Ed. 2d 649 (emphasis added). We established in *Griffith* that this Court must play by our own "old rules"—rules we have settled before the defendant's conviction and sentence become final, even those that are a clear break from existing precedent—for cases pending before us on direct appeal. *Id.*, at 323, 107 S. Ct. 708, 93 L. Ed. 2d 649. Since the *Griffith* rule is constitutionally compelled, we instructed the lower state and federal courts to comply with it as well. *Ibid.*

When *Teague* followed on *Griffith*'s heels two years later, the opinion contained no discussion of "basic norms of constitutional adjudication," *Griffith, supra,* at 322, 107 S. Ct. 708, 93 L. Ed. 2d 649, nor any discussion of the obligations of state courts. Doing away with *Linkletter* for good, the Court adopted Justice Harlan's solution to "the retroactivity problem" for cases pending on collateral review— which he described not as a constitutional problem but as "a problem as to the *scope of the habeas writ.*" *Mackey, supra,* at 684, 91 S. Ct. 1160, 28 L. Ed. 2d 404 (emphasis added). *Teague* held that federal habeas courts could no longer upset state-court convictions for violations of so-called "new rules," not yet announced when the conviction became final. 489 U.S., at 310, 109 S. Ct. 1060, 103 L. Ed. 2d 334. But it allowed for the previously mentioned exceptions to this rule of non-redressability: substantive rules placing " 'certain kinds of primary, private individual conduct beyond the power of the criminal law-making authority to proscribe' " and "watershed rules of criminal procedure." *Id.,* at 311, 109 S. Ct. 1060, 103 L. Ed. 2d 334. Then in *Penry* v. *Lynaugh,* 492 U.S. 302, 109 S. Ct. 2934, 106 L. Ed. 2d 256 (1989),

[577 U.S. 217]

the Court expanded this first exception for substantive rules to embrace new rules "prohibiting a certain category of punishment for a class of defendants because of their status or offense." *Id.,* at 330, 109 S. Ct. 2934, 106 L. Ed. 2d 256.

Neither *Teague* nor its exceptions are constitutionally compelled. Unlike today's majority, the *Teague*-era Court understood that cases on collateral review are fundamentally different from those pending on direct review because of "considerations of finality in the judicial process." *Shea* v. *Louisiana,* 470 U.S. 51, 59-60, 105 S. Ct. 1065, 84 L. Ed. 2d 38 (1985). That line of finality demarcating the constitutionally required rule in *Griffith* from the habeas rule in *Teague* supplies the answer to the not-so-difficult question whether a state postconviction court must remedy the violation of a new substantive rule: No. A state court need only apply the law as it existed at the time a defendant's conviction and sentence became final. See *Griffith, supra,* at 322, 107 S. Ct. 708, 93 L. Ed. 2d 649. And once final, "a new rule cannot reopen a door already closed." *James B. Beam Distilling Co.* v. *Georgia,* 501 U.S. 529, 541, 111 S. Ct. 2439, 115 L. Ed. 2d 481 (1991) (opinion of Souter, J.). Any relief a prisoner might receive in a state court after finality is a matter of grace, not constitutional prescription.

B

The majority can marshal no case support for its contrary position. It creates a constitutional rule where none had been before: "*Teague*'s conclusion establishing the retroactivity of new substantive rules is best understood as resting upon constitutional premises" binding in both federal and state courts. *Ante,* at 200, 193 L. Ed. 2d, at 614. "Best understood." Because of what? Surely not because of its history and derivation.

Because of the Supremacy Clause, says the majority. *Ante,* at 204, 193 L. Ed. 2d, at 616–617. But the Supremacy Clause cannot possibly answer the question before us here. It only elicits another question: What federal law is supreme? Old or new? The majority's champion, Justice Harlan, said the old rules apply for federal habeas review of a state-court conviction: "[T]he

[577 U.S. 218]

habeas court need only apply the constitutional standards that prevailed at the time the original proceedings took place," *Desist,* 394 U.S., at 263, 89 S. Ct. 1030, 22 L. Ed. 2d 248 (dissenting opinion), for a state court cannot "toe the constitutional mark" that does not yet exist, *Mackey,* 401 U.S., at 687, 91 S. Ct. 1160, 28 L. Ed. 2d 404 (opinion of Harlan, J.). Following his analysis, we have clarified time and again—recently in *Greene* v. *Fisher,* 565 U.S. 34, 38–39, 132 S. Ct. 38, 181 L. Ed. 2d 336 (2011)—that *federal* habeas courts are to review state-court decisions against the law and factual record that existed at the time the decisions were made. "Section 2254(d)(1) [of the federal habeas statute] refers, in the past tense, to a state-court adjudication that 'resulted in' a decision that was contrary to, or 'involved' an unreasonable application of, established law. This backward-looking language requires an examination of the state-court decision at the time it was made." *Cullen* v. *Pinholster,* 563 U.S. 170, 181-182, 131 S. Ct. 1388, 179 L. Ed. 2d 557 (2011). How can it possibly be, then, that the Constitution requires a *state* court's review of its own convictions to be governed by "new rules" rather than (what suffices when federal courts review state courts) "old rules"?

The majority relies on the statement in *United States* v. *United States Coin & Currency,* 401 U.S. 715, 91 S. Ct. 1041, 28 L. Ed. 2d 434 (1971), that " '[n]o circumstances call more for the invocation of a rule of complete retroactivity' " than when " 'the conduct

being penalized is constitutionally immune from punishment.' " *Ante,* at 202, 193 L. Ed. 2d, at 615 (quoting 401 U.S., at 724, 91 S. Ct. 1041, 28 L. Ed. 2d 434). The majority neglects to mention that this statement was addressing the "circumstances" of a conviction that "had *not become final,*" *id.,* at 724, n. 13, 91 S. Ct. 1041, 28 L. Ed. 2d 434 (emphasis added), when the "rule of complete retroactivity" was invoked. *Coin & Currency,* an opinion written by (guess whom?) Justice Harlan, merely foreshadowed the rule announced in *Griffith,* that all cases pending on direct review receive the benefit of newly announced rules—better termed "old rules" for such rules were announced *before* finality.

The majority also misappropriates *Yates* v. *Aiken,* 484 U.S. 211, 108 S. Ct. 534, 98 L. Ed. 2d 546 (1988), which reviewed a state habeas petitioner's

[577 U.S. 219]

Fourteenth Amendment claim that the jury instructions at his trial lessened the State's burden to prove every element of his offense beyond a reasonable doubt. That case at least did involve a conviction that was final. But the majority is oblivious to the critical fact that Yates's claim depended upon an *old rule,* settled at the time of his trial. *Id.,* at 217, 108 S. Ct. 534, 98 L. Ed. 2d 546. This Court reversed the state habeas court for its refusal to consider that the jury instructions violated that *old rule. Ibid.* The majority places great weight upon the dictum in *Yates* that the South Carolina habeas court " 'ha[d] a duty to grant the relief that federal law requires.' " *Ante,* at 204–205, 193 L. Ed. 2d, at 616–617 (quoting *Yates, supra,* at 218, 108 S. Ct. 534, 98 L. Ed. 2d 546). It is simply wrong to divorce that dictum from the facts it addressed. In that context, *Yates* merely reinforces the line drawn by *Griffith*: when state courts provide a forum for postconviction relief, they need to play by the "old rules" announced *before* the date on which a defendant's conviction and sentence became final.

The other sleight of hand performed by the majority is its emphasis on *Ex parte Siebold*, 100 U.S. 371, 25 L. Ed. 717 (1880). That case considered a petition for a federal writ of habeas corpus following a federal conviction, and the initial issue it confronted was its jurisdiction. A federal court has no inherent habeas corpus power, *Ex parte Bollman*, 4 Cranch 75, 94, 2 L. Ed. 554 (1807), but only that which is conferred (and limited) by statute, see, *e.g., Felker* v. *Turpin*, 518 U.S. 651, 664, 116 S. Ct. 2333, 135 L. Ed. 2d 827 (1996). As *Siebold* stated, it was forbidden to use the federal habeas writ "as a mere writ of error." 100 U.S., at 375, 25 L. Ed. 717. "The only ground on which this court, or any court, without some special statute authorizing it, [could] give relief on *habeas corpus* to a prisoner under conviction and sentence of another court is the want of jurisdiction in such court over the person or the cause, or some other matter rendering its proceedings void." *Ibid.* Turning to the facts before it, the Court decided it was within its power to hear Siebold's claim, which did not merely protest that the conviction and sentence were "erroneous" but contended that the statute he was convicted of violating was unconstitutional and the conviction therefore

[577 U.S. 220]

void: "[I]f the laws are unconstitutional and void, the Circuit Court acquired no jurisdiction of the causes." *Id.,* at 376-377, 25 L. Ed. 717. *Siebold* is thus a decision that ex-

pands the limits of this Court's power to issue a federal habeas writ for a federal prisoner.

The majority, however, divines from *Siebold* "a general principle" that "a court has no authority to leave in place a conviction or sentence that violates a substantive rule, regardless of whether the conviction or sentence became final before the rule was announced." *Ante*, at 203, 193 L. Ed. 2d, at 616. That is utterly impossible. No "general principle" can rationally be derived from *Siebold* about constitutionally required remedies in state courts; indeed, the opinion does not even speak to constitutionally required remedies in *federal* courts. It is a decision about this Court's statutory power to grant the Original Writ, not about its constitutional obligation to do so. Nowhere in *Siebold* did this Court intimate that relief was constitutionally required—or as the majority puts it, that a court would have had "no authority" to leave in place Siebold's conviction, *ante*, at 203, 193 L. Ed. 2d, at 616.

The majority's sorry acknowledgment that "*Siebold* and the other cases discussed in this opinion, of course, do not directly control the question the Court now answers for the first time," *ibid.*, is not nearly enough of a disclaimer. It is not just that they "do not directly control," but that the dicta cherry picked from those cases are irrelevant; they addressed circumstances fundamentally different from those to which the majority now applies them. Indeed, we know for sure that the author of some of those dicta, Justice Harlan, held views that flatly contradict the majority.

The majority's maxim that "state collateral review courts have no greater power than federal habeas courts to mandate that a prisoner continue to suffer punishment barred by the Constitution," *ante*, at 204, 193 L. Ed. 2d, at 617, begs the question rather than contributes to its solution. Until today, no federal court was *constitutionally obliged* to grant relief for the

[577 U.S. 221]

past violation of a newly announced substantive rule. Until today, it was Congress's prerogative to do away with *Teague*'s exceptions altogether. Indeed, we had left unresolved the question whether Congress had already done that when it amended a section of the habeas corpus statute to add backward-looking language governing the review of state-court decisions. See Antiterrorism and Effective Death Penalty Act of 1996, § 104, 110 Stat. 1219, codified at 28 U.S.C. § 2254(d)(1); *Greene,* 565 U.S., at 39, n., 132 S. Ct. 38, 181 L. Ed. 2d 336. A maxim shown to be more relevant to this case, by the analysis that the majority omitted, is this: The Supremacy Clause does not impose upon state courts a constitutional obligation it fails to impose upon federal courts.

C

All that remains to support the majority's conclusion is that all-purpose Latin canon: *ipse dixit*. The majority opines that because a substantive rule eliminates a State's power to proscribe certain conduct or impose a certain punishment, it has "the automatic consequence of invalidating a defendant's conviction or sentence." *Ante*, at 201, 193 L. Ed. 2d, at 615. What provision of the Constitution could conceivably produce such a result? The Due Process Clause? It surely cannot be a denial of due process for a court to pronounce a final judgment which, though fully in ac-

cord with federal constitutional law at the time, fails to anticipate a change to be made by this Court half a century into the future. The Equal Protection Clause? Both statutory and (increasingly) constitutional laws change. If it were a denial of equal protection to hold an earlier defendant to a law more stringent than what exists today, it would also be a denial of equal protection to hold a later defendant to a law more stringent than what existed 50 years ago. No principle of equal protection requires the criminal law of all ages to be the same.

The majority grandly asserts that "[t]here is no grandfather clause that permits States to *enforce punishments the*

[577 U.S. 222]

Constitution forbids." *Ante*, at 204, 193 L. Ed. 2d, at 616 (emphasis added). Of course the italicized phrase begs the question. There most certainly is a grandfather clause—one we have called *finality*—which says that the Constitution does not require States to revise punishments that were lawful when they were imposed. Once a conviction has become final, whether new rules or old ones will be applied to revisit the conviction is a matter entirely within the State's control; the Constitution has nothing to say about that choice. The majority says that there is no "possibility of a valid result" when a new substantive rule is not applied retroactively. *Ante*, at 201, 193 L. Ed. 2d, at 615. But the whole controversy here arises because many think there *is* a valid result when a defendant has been convicted under the law that existed when his conviction became final. And the States are unquestionably entitled to take that view of things.

The majority's imposition of *Teague*'s

first exception upon the States is all the worse because it does not adhere to that exception as initially conceived by Justice Harlan—an exception for rules that "place, as a matter of constitutional interpretation, certain kinds of primary, private individual *conduct* beyond the power of the criminal law-making authority to proscribe." *Mackey*, 401 U.S., at 692, 91 S. Ct. 1160, 28 L. Ed. 2d 404 (emphasis added). Rather, it endorses the exception as expanded by *Penry*, to include "rules prohibiting a certain category of punishment for a class of defendants because of their status or offense." 492 U.S., at 330, 109 S. Ct. 2934, 106 L. Ed. 2d 256. That expansion empowered and obligated federal (and after today state) habeas courts to invoke this Court's Eighth Amendment "evolving standards of decency" jurisprudence to upset punishments that were constitutional when imposed but are "cruel and unusual," U. S. Const., Amdt. 8, in our newly enlightened society. See *Trop* v. *Dulles*, 356 U.S. 86, 101, 78 S. Ct. 590, 2 L. Ed. 2d 630 (1958). The "evolving standards" test concedes that in 1969 the State had the power to punish Henry Montgomery as it did. Indeed, Montgomery could at that time have been sentenced to death

[577 U.S. 223]

by our yet unevolved society. Even 20 years later, this Court reaffirmed that the Constitution posed no bar to death sentences for juveniles. *Stanford* v. *Kentucky*, 492 U.S. 361, 109 S. Ct. 2969, 106 L. Ed. 2d 306 (1989). Not until our People's "standards of decency" evolved a mere 10 years ago—nearly 40 years after Montgomery's sentence was imposed—did this Court declare the death penalty unconstitutional for juveniles. *Roper* v. *Simmons*, 543 U.S.

551, 125 S. Ct. 1183, 161 L. Ed. 2d 1 (2005). Even then, the Court reassured States that "the punishment of life imprisonment without the possibility of parole is itself a severe sanction," implicitly still available for juveniles. *Id.*, at 572, 125 S. Ct. 1183, 161 L. Ed. 2d 1. And again five years ago this Court left in place this severe sanction for juvenile homicide offenders. *Graham* v. *Florida*, 560 U.S. 48, 69, 130 S. Ct. 2011, 176 L. Ed. 2d 825 (2010). So for the five decades Montgomery has spent in prison, not one of this Court's precedents called into question the legality of his sentence— until the People's "standards of decency," as perceived by five Justices, "evolved" yet again in *Miller*.

Teague's central purpose was to do away with the old regime's tendency to "*continually* forc[e] the States to marshal resources in order to keep in prison defendants whose trials and appeals conformed to then-existing constitutional standards." 489 U.S., at 310, 109 S. Ct. 1060, 103 L. Ed. 2d 334. Today's holding thwarts that purpose with a vengeance. Our everevolving Constitution changes the rules of "cruel and unusual punishments" every few years. In the passage from *Mackey* that the majority's opinion quotes, *ante*, at 205, 193 L. Ed. 2d, at 617, Justice Harlan noted the diminishing force of finality (and hence the equitable propriety—not the constitutional requirement—of disregarding it) when the law punishes nonpunishable *conduct*, see 401 U.S., at 693, 91 S. Ct. 1160, 28 L. Ed. 2d 404. But one cannot imagine a clearer frustration of the sensible policy of *Teague* when the evermoving target of impermissible *punishments* is at issue. Today's holding not only forecloses Congress from eliminating this expansion of *Teague* in federal courts, but also foists this distortion upon the States.

[577 U.S. 224]

II. The Retroactivity of *Miller*

Having created jurisdiction by ripping *Teague*'s first exception from its moorings, converting an equitable rule governing federal habeas relief to a constitutional command governing state courts as well, the majority proceeds to the merits. And here it confronts a second obstacle to its desired outcome. *Miller*, the opinion it wishes to impose upon state postconviction courts, simply does not decree what the first part of the majority's opinion says *Teague*'s first exception requires to be given retroactive effect: a rule "set[ting] forth *categorical* constitutional guarantees that place certain criminal laws and punishments *altogether* beyond the State's power to impose." *Ante*, at 201, 193 L. Ed. 2d, at 615 (emphasis added). No problem. Having distorted *Teague*, the majority simply proceeds to rewrite *Miller*.

The majority asserts that *Miller* "rendered life without parole an unconstitutional penalty for 'a class of defendants because of their status'— that is, juvenile offenders whose crimes reflect the transient immaturity of youth." *Ante*, at 208, 193 L. Ed. 2d, at 620. It insists that *Miller* barred life-without-parole sentences "for all but the rarest of juvenile offenders, those whose crimes reflect permanent incorrigibility. For that reason, *Miller* is no less substantive than are *Roper* and *Graham*." *Ante,* at 209, 193 L. Ed. 2d, at 620. The problem is that *Miller* stated, quite clearly, precisely the opposite: "Our decision does not categorically bar a penalty for a class of offenders or type of crime—as, for example, we did in *Roper* or *Graham*. Instead, it mandates only that a sentencer *follow a certain process*—considering an offender's youth and attendant characteristics—before imposing a particular penalty." 567 U.S., at 483, 132 S. Ct. 2455, 183 L. Ed. 2d 407 (emphasis added).

To contradict that clear statement, the majority opinion quotes passages from *Miller* that assert such things as "mandatory life-without-parole sentences for children 'pos[e] too great a risk of disproportionate punishment' " and " 'appropriate occasions for sentencing juveniles to this harshest possible

[577 U.S. 225]

penalty will be uncommon.' " *Ante*, at 208, 193 L. Ed. 2d, at 585 (quoting *Miller*, *supra*, at 479, 132 S. Ct. 2455, 183 L. Ed. 2d 407). But to say that a punishment might be inappropriate and disproportionate for certain juvenile offenders is not to say that it is unconstitutionally void. All of the statements relied on by the majority do nothing more than express the *reason* why the new, youth-protective *procedure* prescribed by *Miller* is desirable: to deter life sentences for certain juvenile offenders. On the issue of whether *Miller* rendered life-without-parole penalties unconstitutional, it is impossible to get past *Miller*'s unambiguous statement that "[o]ur decision does not categorically bar a penalty for a class of offenders" and "mandates only that a sentencer follow a certain process . . . before imposing a particular penalty." 567 U.S., at 483, 132 S. Ct. 2455, 183 L. Ed. 2d 407. It is plain as day that the majority is not applying *Miller*, but rewriting it.[1]

And the rewriting has consequences beyond merely making *Miller*'s procedural guarantee retroactive. If, indeed, a State is categorically prohibited from imposing life without parole on juvenile offenders whose crimes do not "reflect permanent incorrigibility," then even when the procedures that *Miller* demands are provided the constitutional requirement is not necessarily satisfied. It remains available for the defendant sentenced to life without parole to argue that his crimes did not in fact "reflect permanent incorrigibility." Or as the majority's opinion puts it: "That *Miller* did not impose a formal factfinding requirement does not leave States free to sentence a child[2] whose crime reflects transient immaturity to life without parole. To the contrary,

[577 U.S. 226]

Miller established that this punishment is disproportionate under the Eighth Amendment." *Ante*, at 211, 193 L. Ed. 2d, at 621.

How wonderful. Federal and (like it or not) state judges are henceforth to resolve the knotty "legal" question: whether a 17-year-old who murdered an innocent sheriff's deputy half a century ago was at the time of his trial "incorrigible." Under *Miller*, bear in mind, the inquiry is whether the inmate was seen to be incorrigible when he was sentenced—not whether he has proven corrigible and so can safely be paroled today. What silli-

ness. (And how impossible in practice, see Brief for National District Attorneys Assn. et al. as *Amici Curiae* 9-17.) When in *Lockett* v. *Ohio*, 438 U.S. 586, 608, 98 S. Ct. 2954, 57 L. Ed. 2d 973 (1978), the Court imposed the thitherto unheard-of requirement that the sentencer in capital cases must consider and weigh all "relevant mitigating factors," it at least did not impose the substantive (and hence judicially reviewable) requirement that the aggravators must outweigh the mitigators; it would suffice that the sentencer *thought* so. And, fairly read, *Miller* did the same. Not so with the "incorrigibility" requirement that the Court imposes today to make *Miller* retroactive.

But have no fear. The majority does not seriously expect state and federal collateral-review tribunals to engage in this silliness, probing the evidence of "incorrigibility" that existed decades ago when defendants were sentenced. What the majority expects (and intends) to happen is set forth in the following not-so-subtle invitation: "A State may remedy a *Miller* violation by permitting juvenile homicide offenders to be considered for parole, rather than by resentencing them." *Ante*, at 212, 193 L. Ed. 2d, at 622. Of course. This whole exercise, this whole distortion of *Miller*, is just a devious way of eliminating life without parole for juvenile offenders. The Court might have done that expressly (as we know, the Court can decree *anything*), but that would have been something of an embarrassment. Af-

---

1. It is amusing that the majority's initial description of *Miller* is the same as our own: "[T]he Court held that a juvenile convicted of a homicide offense could not be sentenced to life in prison without parole absent consideration of the juvenile's special circumstances in light of the principles and purposes of juvenile sentencing." *Ante*, at 193–194, 193 L. Ed. 2d, at 610. Only 15 pages later, after softening the reader with 3 pages of obfuscating analysis, does the majority dare to attribute to *Miller* that which *Miller* explicitly denies.

2. The majority presumably regards any person one day short of voting age as a "child."

ter all, one of the justifications the Court gave for decreeing an end to the death penalty for

[577 U.S. 227]

murders (no matter how many) committed by a juvenile was that life without parole was a severe enough punishment. See *Roper*, 543 U.S., at 572, 125 S. Ct. 1183, 161 L. Ed. 2d 1. How could the majority—in an opinion written by the very author of *Roper*—now say *that* punishment is *also* unconstitutional? The Court expressly refused to say so in *Miller*. 567 U.S., at 479, 132 S. Ct. 2455, 183 L. Ed. 2d 407. So the Court refuses again today, but merely makes imposition of that severe sanction a practical impossibility. And then, in Godfather fashion, the majority makes state legislatures an offer they can't refuse: Avoid all the utterly impossible nonsense we have prescribed by simply "permitting juvenile homicide offenders to be considered for parole." *Ante*, at 212, 193 L. Ed. 2d, at 622. Mission accomplished.

Justice **Thomas**, dissenting.

I join Justice Scalia's dissent. I write separately to explain why the Court's resolution of the jurisdictional question, *ante*, at 197–205, 193 L. Ed. 2d, at 612-618, lacks any foundation in the Constitution's text or our historical traditions. We have jurisdiction under 28 U.S.C. § 1257 only if the Louisiana Supreme Court's decision implicates a federal right. That condition is satisfied, the Court holds, because the Constitution purportedly requires state and federal postconviction courts to give "retroactive effect" to new substantive constitutional rules by applying them to overturn long-final convictions and sentences. *Ante*, at 200, 193 L. Ed. 2d, at 614. Because our Constitution and traditions embrace no such right, I respectfully dissent.

I

"[O]ur jurisprudence concerning the 'retroactivity' of 'new rules' of constitutional law is primarily concerned, not with the question whether a constitutional violation occurred, but with the availability or nonavailability of remedies." *Danforth* v. *Minnesota*, 552 U.S. 264, 290-291, 128 S. Ct. 1029, 169 L. Ed. 2d 859 (2008). Accordingly, the issue in this case is not whether prisoners who received mandatory life-without-parole sentences for crimes

[577 U.S. 228]

they committed decades ago as juveniles had an Eighth Amendment right not to receive such a sentence. Rather, the question is how, when, and in what forum that newfound right can be enforced. See *ibid.*

The Court answers that question one way: It says that state postconviction and federal habeas courts are constitutionally required to supply a remedy because a sentence or conviction predicated upon an unconstitutional law is a legal nullity. See *ante*, at 200–205, 193 L. Ed. 2d, at 614-618. But nothing in the Constitution's text or in our constitutional tradition provides such a right to a remedy on collateral review.

A

No provision of the Constitution supports the Court's holding. The Court invokes only the Supremacy Clause, asserting that the Clause deprives state and federal postconviction courts alike of power to leave an unconstitutional sentence in place. *Ante*, at 204–205, 193 L. Ed. 2d, at 616-617. But that leaves the question of what provision of the Constitution supplies that underlying prohibition.

The Supremacy Clause does not do so. That Clause merely supplies a rule of decision: *If* a federal constitutional right exists, that right supersedes any contrary provisions of state law. See Art. VI, cl. 2 ("This Constitution, and the Laws of the United States which shall be made in Pursuance thereof . . . shall be the supreme Law of the Land; and the Judges in every State shall be bound thereby, any Thing in the Constitution or Laws of any State to the Contrary notwithstanding"). Accordingly, as we reaffirmed just last Term, the Supremacy Clause is no independent font of substantive rights. *Armstrong* v. *Exceptional Child Center, Inc.*, 575 U.S. 320, 325, 135 S. Ct. 1378, 191 L. Ed. 2d 471 (2015).

Nor am I aware of any other provision in the Constitution that would support the Court's new constitutional right to retroactivity. Of the natural places to look—Article III, the Due Process Clauses of the Fifth and Fourteenth Amendments,

[577 U.S. 229]

and the Equal Protection Clause of the Fourteenth Amendment—none establishes a right to void an unconstitutional sentence that has long been final.

To begin, Article III does not contain the requirement that the Court announces today. Article III vests "[t]he judicial Power" in this Court and whatever inferior courts Congress creates, Art. III, § 1, and "extend[s]" that power to various "Cases . . . and Controversies," Art. III, § 2. Article III thus defines the scope of *federal* judicial power. It cannot compel *state* postconviction courts to apply new substantive rules retroactively.

Even if the Court's holding were limited to federal courts, Article III would not justify it. The nature of "judicial power" may constrain the retroactivity rules that Article III courts can apply.* But even our broad modern precedents treat Article III as requiring courts to apply new rules only on *direct* review. Thus in *Griffith* v. *Kentucky*, 479 U.S. 314, 107 S. Ct. 708, 93 L. Ed. 2d 649 (1987), the Court suggested—based on Justice Harlan's views—that "after we have decided a new rule in the case selected, the integrity of judicial review requires that we apply that rule to all similar cases pending on direct review." *Id.*, at 322-323, 107 S. Ct. 708, 93 L. Ed. 2d 649. But, as Justice Harlan had explained, that view of Article III has no force on collateral review: "While the entire theoretical underpinnings of judicial review and constitutional supremacy dictate that federal courts having jurisdiction on direct review adjudicate every issue of law . . . fairly implicated by the trial process below and properly presented on appeal, federal courts have never had a similar obligation on habeas corpus." *Mackey* v. *United States*, 401 U.S. 667, 682, 91 S. Ct. 1160, 28 L. Ed. 2d 404 (1971) (opinion concurring in judgment in part and dissenting in part).

[577 U.S. 230]

The Court's holding also cannot be grounded in the Due Process Clause's prohibition on "depriv[ations] . . . of life, liberty, or property, without due process of law." Amdts. V and XIV, § 1. Quite possibly, " '[d]ue process of law' was originally used as a shorthand expression for governmental proceed-

---

* For instance, Article III courts cannot arrive at a holding, refuse to apply it to the case at hand, and limit its application to future cases involving yet-to-occur events. The power to rule prospectively in this way is a quintessentially legislative power. See *Harper* v. *Virginia Dept. of Taxation*, 509 U.S. 86, 106-110, 113 S. Ct. 2510, 125 L. Ed. 2d 74 (1993) (Scalia, J., concurring).

ings according to the 'law of the land' *as it existed at the time of those proceedings.*" *In re Winship*, 397 U.S. 358, 378, 90 S. Ct. 1068, 25 L. Ed. 2d 368 (1970) (Black, J., dissenting) (emphasis added); accord, *Johnson* v. *United States*, 576 U.S. 591, 623, 135 S. Ct. 2551, 192 L. Ed. 2d 569 (2015) (Thomas, J., concurring in judgment). Under that understanding, due process excluded any right to have new substantive rules apply retroactively.

Even if due process required courts to anticipate this Court's new substantive rules, it would not compel courts to revisit settled convictions or sentences on collateral review. We have never understood due process to require further proceedings once a trial ends. The Clause "does not establish any right to an appeal . . . and certainly does not establish any right to collaterally attack a final judgment of conviction." *United States* v. *MacCollom*, 426 U.S. 317, 323, 96 S. Ct. 2086, 48 L. Ed. 2d 666 (1976) (plurality opinion); see *Pennsylvania* v. *Finley*, 481 U.S. 551, 557, 107 S. Ct. 1990, 95 L. Ed. 2d 539 (1987) ("States have no obligation to provide [postconviction] relief"). Because the Constitution does not require postconviction remedies, it certainly does not require postconviction courts to revisit every potential type of error. Cf. *Martinez* v. *Court of Appeal of Cal., Fourth Appellate Dist.*, 528 U.S. 152, 165-166, 120 S. Ct. 684, 145 L. Ed. 2d 597 (2000) (Scalia, J., concurring in judgment) ("Since a State could . . . subject its trial-court determinations to no review whatever, it could *a fortiori* subject them to review which consists of a nonadversarial reexamination of convictions by a panel of government experts").

Nor can the Equal Protection Clause justify requiring courts on collateral review to apply new substantive rules retroactively. That Clause prohibits a State from "deny[ing]

[577 U.S. 231]

to any person within its jurisdiction the equal protection of the laws." Amdt. XIV, § 1. But under our precedents "a classification neither involving fundamental rights nor proceeding along suspect lines . . . cannot run afoul of the Equal Protection Clause if there is a rational relationship between the disparity of treatment and some legitimate governmental purpose." *Armour* v. *Indianapolis,* 566 U.S. 673, 680, 132 S. Ct. 2073, 182 L. Ed. 2d 998 (2012) (internal quotation marks omitted; ellipsis in original).

The disparity the Court eliminates today—between prisoners whose cases were on direct review when this Court announced a new substantive constitutional rule, and those whose convictions had already become final—is one we have long considered rational. "[T]he notion that different standards should apply on direct and collateral review runs throughout our recent habeas jurisprudence." *Wright* v. *West*, 505 U.S. 277, 292, 112 S. Ct. 2482, 120 L. Ed. 2d 225 (1992); see *Brecht* v. *Abrahamson*, 507 U.S. 619, 633-635, 113 S. Ct. 1710, 123 L. Ed. 2d 353 (1993). Thus, our precedents recognize a right to counsel on direct review, but not in collateral proceedings. Compare *Douglas* v. *California*, 372 U.S. 353, 355-358, 83 S. Ct. 814, 9 L. Ed. 2d 811 (1963) (courts must provide counsel on an initial direct appeal), with *Finley, supra*, at 555, 107 S. Ct. 1990, 95 L. Ed. 2d 539 (no such right on habeas). The Fourth Amendment also applies differently on direct and collateral review. Compare *Mapp* v. *Ohio*, 367 U.S. 643,

654-660, 81 S. Ct. 1684, 6 L. Ed. 2d 1081 (1961) (courts on direct review must exclude evidence obtained in violation of the Fourth Amendment), with *Stone* v. *Powell*, 428 U.S. 465, 489-496, 96 S. Ct. 3037, 49 L. Ed. 2d 1067 (1976) (no relitigation of such claims on collateral review).

These distinctions are reasonable. They reflect the "significant costs" of collateral review, including disruption of "the State's significant interest in repose for concluded litigation." *Wright, supra*, at 293, 112 S. Ct. 2482, 120 L. Ed. 2d 225 (internal quotation marks omitted). Our equal protection precedents, therefore, do not compel a uniform rule of retroactivity in direct and collateral proceedings for new substantive constitutional rules.

[577 U.S. 232]

B

The Court's new constitutional right also finds no basis in the history of state and federal postconviction proceedings. Throughout our history, postconviction relief for alleged constitutional defects in a conviction or sentence was available as a matter of legislative grace, not constitutional command.

The Constitution mentions habeas relief only in the Suspension Clause, which specifies that "[t]he Privilege of the Writ of *Habeas Corpus* shall not be suspended, unless when in Cases of Rebellion or Invasion the public Safety may require it." Art. I, § 9, cl. 2 (emphasis added). But that Clause does not specify the scope of the writ. And the First Congress, in prescribing federal habeas jurisdiction in the 1789 Judiciary Act, understood its scope to reflect "the black-letter principle of the common law that the writ was simply not available at all to one convicted of crime by a court of competent jurisdiction." Bator, Finality in

Criminal Law and Federal Habeas Corpus for State Prisoners, 76 Harv. L. Rev. 441, 466 (1963). Early cases echoed that understanding. *E.g., Ex parte Watkins*, 3 Pet. 193, 202, 7 L. Ed. 650 (1830) ("An imprisonment under a judgment cannot be unlawful, unless that judgment be an absolute nullity; and it is not a nullity if the court has general jurisdiction of the subject, although it should be erroneous").

For nearly a century thereafter, this Court understood the Judiciary Act and successor provisions as limiting habeas relief to instances where the court that rendered the judgment lacked jurisdiction over the general category of offense or the person of the prisoner. See *Wright, supra*, at 285, 112 S. Ct. 2482, 120 L. Ed. 2d 225 (recounting history). Federal habeas courts thus afforded no remedy for a claim that a sentence or conviction was predicated on an unconstitutional law. Nor did States. Indeed, until 1836, Vermont made no provision for any state habeas proceedings. See Oaks, Habeas Corpus in the States 1776-1865, 32 U. Chi. L. Rev. 243, 250 (1965). Even when States allowed collateral attacks in state court, review was unavailable

[577 U.S. 233]

if the judgment of conviction was rendered by a court with general jurisdiction over the subject matter and the defendant. *Id.,* at 261-262.

The Court portrays *Ex parte Siebold*, 100 U.S. 371, 25 L. Ed. 717 (1880), as a departure from this history and as the genesis of a constitutional principle that "a conviction obtained under an unconstitutional law warrants habeas relief." *Ante*, at 204, 193 L. Ed. 2d, at 616. But *Siebold*—a case construing the scope of federal habeas review under the 1789 Judiciary Act—does not support the Court's position. *Ante*, at 219–220, 193 L. Ed. 2d, at 626-628 (Scalia, J., dissenting). *Siebold* did not imply that the Constitution requires courts to stop enforcing convictions under an unconstitutional law. Rather, *Siebold* assumed that prisoners would lack a remedy if the federal habeas statute did not allow challenges to such convictions. 100 U.S., at 377, 25 L. Ed. 717 ("It is true, if no writ of error lies, the judgment may be final, in the sense that there may be no means of reversing it").

Moreover, when Congress authorized appeals as a matter of right in federal criminal cases, the Court renounced *Siebold* and stopped entertaining federal habeas challenges to the constitutionality of the statute under which a defendant was sentenced or convicted. See Bator, *supra*, at 473-474, and n. 77. If the Constitution prevented courts from enforcing a void conviction or sentence even after the conviction is final, this Court would have been incapable of withdrawing relief.

The Court's purported constitutional right to retroactivity on collateral review has no grounding even in our mod-ern precedents. In the 1950's, this Court began recognizing many new constitutional rights in criminal proceedings. Even then, however, the Court did not perceive any constitutional right for prisoners to vacate their convictions or sentences on collateral review based on the Court's new interpretations of the Constitution. To the contrary, the Court derived *Miranda* warnings and the exclusionary rule from the Constitution, yet drew the line at creating a constitutional

[577 U.S. 234]

right to retroactivity. *E.g., Linkletter* v. *Walker*, 381 U.S. 618, 629, 85 S. Ct. 1731, 14 L. Ed. 2d 601 (1965) ("[T]he Constitution neither prohibits nor requires retrospective effect. As Justice Cardozo said, 'We think the Federal Constitution has no voice upon the subject' ").

Only in 1987, in *Griffith* v. *Kentucky*, 479 U.S. 314, 107 S. Ct. 708, 93 L. Ed. 2d 649, did this Court change course and hold that the Constitution requires courts to give constitutional rights some retroactive effect. Even then, *Griffith* was a directive only to courts on *direct* review. It held that "a new rule for the conduct of criminal prosecutions is to be applied retroactively to all cases, state or federal, pending on direct review or not yet final." *Id.*, at 328, 107 S. Ct. 708, 93 L. Ed. 2d 649. It said nothing about what happens once a case becomes final. That was resolved in *Teague* v. *Lane*, 489 U.S. 288, 109 S. Ct. 1060, 103 L. Ed. 2d 334 (1989)—which announced the narrow exceptions to the rule against retroactivity on collateral review—but which did so by interpreting the scope of the federal habeas writ, not the Constitution.

II

A

Not only does the Court's novel constitutional right lack any constitutional foundation; the reasoning the Court uses to construct this right lacks any logical stopping point. If, as the Court supposes, the Constitution bars courts from insisting that prisoners remain in prison when their convictions or sentences are later deemed unconstitutional, why can courts let stand a judgment that wrongly decided any constitutional question?

The Court confronted this question when *Siebold* and other cases began expanding the federal habeas statute to encompass claims that a sentence or conviction was constitutionally void. But the Court could not find a satisfactory answer: "A judgment may be erroneous and not void, and it may be erroneous *because* it is void. The distinctions . . . are very nice, and they may fall under the one class or the

[577 U.S. 235]

other as they are regarded for different purposes." *Ex parte Lange*, 18 Wall. 163, 175-176, 21 L. Ed. 872 (1874).

The lack of any limiting principle became apparent as the Court construed the federal habeas statute to supply jurisdiction to address prerequisites to a valid sentence or conviction (like an indictment). See Bator, *supra*, at 467-468, and n. 56, 471. As Justice Bradley, *Siebold*'s author, later observed for the Court: "It is difficult to see why a conviction and punishment under an unconstitutional law is more violative of a person's constitutional rights, than an unconstitutional conviction and punishment under a valid law." *In re Nielsen*, 131 U.S. 176, 183, 9 S. Ct. 672, 33 L. Ed. 118 (1889).

I doubt that today's rule will fare any better. By refashioning *Siebold* as the foundation of a purported constitutional right, the Court transforms an unworkable doctrine into an immutable command. Because Justice Bradley's dicta in *Siebold* was a gloss on the 1789 Judiciary Act, Congress could at least supply a fix to it. But the Court's reinvention of *Siebold* as a constitutional imperative eliminates any room for legislative adjustment.

B

There is one silver lining to today's ruling: States still have a way to miti-gate its impact on their court systems. As the Court explains, States must enforce a constitutional right to remedies on collateral review only if such proceedings are "open to a claim controlled by federal law." *Ante*, at 204, 193 L. Ed. 2d, at 617. State courts, on collateral review, thus must provide remedies for claims under *Miller* v. *Alabama*, 567 U.S. 460, 132 S. Ct. 2455, 183 L. Ed. 2d 407 (2012), only if those courts are open to "claims that a decision of this Court has rendered certain sentences illegal . . . under the Eighth Amendment." *Ante*, at 205, 193 L. Ed. 2d, at 617.

Unlike the rule the Court announces today, this limitation at least reflects a constitutional principle. Only when state courts have chosen to entertain a federal claim can the Supremacy Clause conceivably command a state court to apply

[577 U.S. 236]

federal law. As we explained last Term, private parties have no "constitutional . . . right to enforce federal laws against the States." *Armstrong*, 575 U.S., at 325, 135 S. Ct. 1378, 191 L. Ed. 2d 471. Instead, the Constitution leaves the initial choice to entertain federal claims up to state courts, which are "tribunals over which the government of the Union has no adequate control, and which may be closed to any claim asserted under a law of the United States." *Osborn* v. *Bank of United States*, 9 Wheat. 738, 821, 6 L. Ed. 204 (1824).

States therefore have a modest path to lessen the burdens that today's decision will inflict on their courts. States can stop entertaining claims alleging that this Court's Eighth Amendment decisions invalidated a sentence, and leave federal habeas courts to shoulder the burden of adjudicating such claims in the first instance. Whatever the desirability of that choice, it is one the Constitution allows States to make.

* * *

Today's decision repudiates established principles of finality. It finds no support in the Constitution's text, and cannot be reconciled with our Nation's tradition of considering the availability of postconviction remedies a matter about which the Constitution has nothing to say. I respectfully dissent.

[577 U.S. 237]

MICHAEL MUSACCHIO, Petitioner

v

UNITED STATES

577 U.S. 237, 136 S. Ct. 709, 193 L. Ed. 2d 639, 2016 U.S. LEXIS 972

[No. 14-1095]

Argued November 30, 2015. Decided January 25, 2016.

Decision: Sufficiency-of-evidence challenge had to be assessed against elements of charged crime rather than elements set forth in erroneous jury instruction; accused could not successfully raise statute of limitations bar under 18 U.S.C.S. § 3282(a) for first time on appeal.

Prior history: ON WRIT OF CERTIORARI TO THE UNITED STATES COURT OF APPEALS FOR THE FIFTH CIRCUIT, 590 Fed. Appx. 359, 2014 U.S. App. LEXIS 21358

SUMMARY

Overview: HOLDINGS: [1]-Where the district court's instruction on the elements of conspiracy to make unauthorized access to a computer under 18 U.S.C.S. § 1030(a)(2)(C) incorrectly added the element of exceeding authorized access, and the government failed to object, the sufficiency of the evidence was properly measured against the elements of the charged crime, not against the erroneously heightened instruction; [2]-Defendant could not successfully raise the statute of limitations bar under 18 U.S.C.S. § 3282(a) for the first time on appeal. Section 3282(a) provides a nonjurisdictional defense, and a district court's failure to enforce an unraised limitations defense under § 3282(a) cannot be plain error.

Outcome: Judgment affirmed. Unanimous decision.

HEADNOTES

Classified to United States Supreme Court Digest, Lawyers' Edition

Sufficiency — criminal case
L Ed Digest: Evidence § 980
1. In a criminal case when a jury instruction adds an element to the charged crime and the government fails to object, the sufficiency of the evidence should be assessed against the elements of the charged crime.

Statute of limitations
L Ed Digest: Appeal § 1128
2. The statute-of-limitations defense contained in 18 U.S.C. § 3282(a) (the general federal criminal statute of limitations) may not be successfully raised for the first time on appeal.

Computer — unauthorized access
L Ed Digest: Larceny § 3
3. Under 18 U.S.C.S. § 1030(a)(2)(C), a person commits a crime when he intentionally accesses a computer without authorization or exceeds authorized access, and in doing so obtains information from any protected

computer. The statute thus provides two ways of committing the crime of improperly accessing a protected computer: (1) obtaining access without authorization; and (2) obtaining access with authorization but then using that access improperly. § 1030(a)(2)(C). Section 1030(e)(6) defines "exceeds authorized access."

Crimes
L Ed Digest: Limitation of Actions § 209

4. 18 U.S.C.S. § 3282(a) provides a general five year statute of limitations.

Sufficiency — jury instruction
L Ed Digest: Evidence § 980

5. When a jury instruction sets forth all the elements of the charged crime but incorrectly adds one more element, a sufficiency challenge should be assessed against the elements of the charged crime, not against the erroneously heightened command in the jury instruction.

Sufficiency of evidence — inquiry — due process
L Ed Digest: Appeal § 1463; Constitutional Law §§ 840.1, 840.9

6. Sufficiency review essentially addresses whether the government's case was so lacking that it should not have even been submitted to the jury. On sufficiency review, a reviewing court makes a limited inquiry tailored to ensure that a defendant receives the minimum that due process requires: a meaningful opportunity to defend against the charge against him and a jury finding of guilt beyond a reasonable doubt. The reviewing court considers only the "legal" question whether, after viewing the evidence in the light most favorable to

the prosecution, any rational trier of fact could have found the essential elements of the crime beyond a reasonable doubt. That limited review does not intrude on the jury's role to resolve conflicts in the testimony, to weigh the evidence, and to draw reasonable inferences from basic facts to ultimate facts.

Review — sufficiency of evidence — criminal case
L Ed Digest: Appeal § 1463

7. A reviewing court's limited determination on sufficiency review does not rest on how the jury was instructed. When a jury finds guilt after being instructed on all elements of the charged crime plus one more element, the jury has made all the findings that due process requires. If a jury instruction requires the jury to find guilt on the elements of the charged crime, a defendant will have had a "meaningful opportunity to defend" against the charge. And if the jury instruction requires the jury to find those elements "beyond a reasonable doubt," the defendant has been accorded the procedure that the U.S. Supreme Court has required to protect the presumption of innocence. The government's failure to introduce evidence of an additional element does not implicate the principles that sufficiency review protects. All that a defendant is entitled to on a sufficiency challenge is for the court to make a "legal" determination whether the evidence was strong enough to reach a jury at all. The government's failure to object to the heightened jury instruction thus does not affect the court's review for sufficiency of the evidence.

Law of case — sufficiency of evidence — crime

L Ed Digest: Appeal § 1463; Judgment § 76

8. The law-of-the-case doctrine generally provides that when a court decides upon a rule of law, that decision should continue to govern the same issues in subsequent stages in the same case. The doctrine expresses the practice of courts generally to refuse to reopen what has been decided, but it does not limit courts' power. Thus, the doctrine may describe an appellate court's decision not to depart from a ruling that it made in a prior appeal in the same case. But the doctrine is something of a misnomer when used to describe how an appellate court assesses a lower court's rulings. An appellate court's function is to revisit matters decided in the trial court. When an appellate court reviews a matter on which a party failed to object below, its review may well be constrained by other doctrines such as waiver, forfeiture, and estoppel, as well as by the type of challenge that it is evaluating. But it is not bound by district court rulings under the law-of-the-case doctrine. That doctrine does not bear on how to assess a sufficiency challenge when a jury convicts a defendant after being instructed—without an objection by the government—on all charged elements of a crime plus an additional element.

Statute of limitations

L Ed Digest: Appeal § 1128

9. A defendant cannot successfully raise the statute-of-limitations bar under 18 U.S.C.S. § 3282(a) for the first time on appeal.

Jurisdiction — filing deadlines

L Ed Digest: Courts § 248

10. Statutes of limitations and other filing deadlines ordinarily are not jurisdictional. A court treats a time bar as jurisdictional only if Congress has clearly stated that it is. To determine whether Congress has made the necessary clear statement, the court examines the text, context, and relevant historical treatment of the provision at issue.

Jurisdiction — criminal statute of limitations

L Ed Digest: Courts § 457

11. The statutory text, context, and history establish that 18 U.S.C.S. § 3282(a) imposes a nonjurisdictional defense that becomes part of a case only if a defendant raises it in the district court.

Noncapital crime

L Ed Digest: Limitation of Actions § 209

12. See 18 U.S.C.S. § 3282(a), which provides: "Except as otherwise expressly provided by law, no person shall be prosecuted, tried, or punished for any offense, not capital, unless the indictment is found or the information is instituted within five years next after such offense shall have been committed."

Jurisdiction — criminal statute of limitations

L Ed Digest: Courts § 457

13. Although 18 U.S.C.S. § 3282(a) uses mandatory language, it does not expressly refer to subject-matter jurisdiction or speak in jurisdictional terms. The text of § 3282(a) does not, therefore, provide a clear indication that Congress wanted that provision to be treated as having jurisdictional attributes.

Jurisdiction — criminal cases

L Ed Digest: Courts § 457

14. Federal courts' general criminal subject-matter jurisdiction comes from 18 U.S.C.S. § 3231, which states that the district courts shall have original jurisdiction of all offenses against the laws of the United States. Section 3231 speaks squarely to federal courts' "jurisdiction," in marked contrast to 18 U.S.C.S. § 3282(a), which does not mention "jurisdiction" or a variant of that term. And, nothing in § 3231 conditions its jurisdictional grant on compliance with § 3282(a)'s statute of limitations. This context supports the conclusion that § 3282(a) is not jurisdictional.

Limitations bar — crime
L Ed Digest: Appeal § 1128

15. The history of the limitations bar in 18 U.S.C.S. § 3282(a) demonstrates that it is a defense that becomes part of a case only if the defendant presses it in the District Court. When a defendant introduces the limitations defense into the case, the government then has the right to reply or give evidence on the limitations claim.

Crime — raising defense
L Ed Digest: Limitation of Actions § 209

16. Commission of a federal crime within the statute-of-limitations period is not an element of the offense, and it is up to the defendant to raise the limitations defense. There is a long history of treating the operative language in 18 U.S.C.S. § 3282(a) as providing a nonjurisdictional defense that a defendant must press at trial to insert into the case.

Limitations bar — crime
L Ed Digest: Appeal § 1128

17. Because 18 U.S.C.S. § 3282(a) does not impose a jurisdictional limit, the failure to raise it at or before trial means that it is reviewable on appeal—if at all—only for plain error. Fed. Rule Crim. Proc. 52(b) provides for consideration of a plain error that affects substantial rights even though the error was not brought to the court's attention. However, a district court's failure to enforce an unraised limitations defense under § 3282(a) cannot be a plain error.

Jurisdiction — statute of limitations — burden of proof
L Ed Digest: Appeal § 1128; Evidence § 419.2

18. A statute-of-limitations defense becomes part of a case only if the defendant puts the defense in issue. When a defendant presses a limitations defense, the government then bears the burden of establishing compliance with the statute of limitations by presenting evidence that the crime was committed within the limitations period or by establishing an exception to the limitations period. When a defendant fails to press a limitations defense, the defense does not become part of the case and the government does not otherwise have the burden of proving that it filed a timely indictment. When a defendant does not press the defense, then, there is no error for an appellate court to correct—and certainly no plain error. A defendant thus cannot successfully raise the statute-of-limitations defense in 18 U.S.C.S. § 3282(a) for the first time on appeal.

MUSACCHIO v. UNITED STATES

(2016) 577 U.S. 237, 136 S. Ct. 709, 193 L. Ed. 2d 639, 2016 U.S. LEXIS 972

RESEARCH REFERENCES

18 U.S.C.S. § 3282(a)

Weinstein's Federal Evidence §§107.21, 602.03 (Matthew Bender)

L Ed Digest, Appeal § 1128; Evidence § 980

L Ed Index, Evidence; Limitation of Actions

Annotations:

Lack of evidence supporting conviction of criminal offense as violation of due process clause of Federal Constitution's Fifth or Fourteenth Amendment—Supreme Court cases. 148 L. Ed. 2d 1135.

Supreme Court's views as to what constitute harmless errors or plain errors, under Rule 52 of Federal Rules of Criminal Procedure. 84 L. Ed. 2d 876.

APPEARANCES OF COUNSEL ARGUING CASE

Erik S. Jaffe argued the cause for petitioner.

Roman Martinez argued the cause for respondent.

SYLLABUS BY REPORTER OF DECISIONS

Petitioner Musacchio resigned as president of Exel Transportation Services (ETS) in 2004, but with help from the former head of ETS' information-technology department, he accessed ETS' computer system without ETS' authorization through early 2006. In November 2010, Musacchio was indicted under 18 U.S.C. § 1030(a)(2)(C), which makes it a crime if a person "intentionally accesses a computer without authorization *or* exceeds authorized access" and thereby "obtains . . . information from any protected computer." (Emphasis added.) He was charged in count 1 with conspiring to commit both types of improper access and in count 23 with making unauthorized access "[o]n or about" November 24, 2005. In a 2012 superseding indictment, count 1 dropped the charge of conspiracy to exceed authorized access, and count 2 changed count 23's date to "[o]n or about" November 23-25, 2005. Musacchio never argued in the trial court that his prosecution violated the 5-year statute of limitations applicable to count 2. See § 3282(a). At trial, the Government did not object when the District Court instructed the jury that § 1030(a)(2)(C) "makes it a crime . . . to intentionally access a computer without authorization *and* exceed authorized access" (emphasis added), even though the conjunction "and" added an additional element. The jury found Musacchio guilty on counts 1 and 2. On appeal, he challenged the sufficiency of the evidence supporting his conspiracy conviction and argued, for the first time, that his prosecution on count 2 was barred by § 3282(a)'s statute of limitations. In affirming his conviction, the Fifth Circuit assessed Musacchio's sufficiency challenge against the charged elements of the conspiracy count rather than against the heightened jury instruction, and it concluded that he had waived his statute-of-limitations defense by failing to raise it at trial.

Held:

1. A sufficiency challenge should be assessed against the elements of the charged crime, not against the elements set forth in an erroneous jury instruction. Sufficiency review essentially addresses whether the Government's case was strong enough to reach the jury. A reviewing court conducts a limited inquiry tailored to ensuring that a defendant receives the minimum required by due process: a "meaningful opportunity to defend" against the charge against him and a jury finding of guilt "beyond a reasonable doubt." *Jackson* v. *Virginia*, 443 U.S. 307, 314-315, 99 S. Ct. 2781, 61 L. Ed. 2d 560. It does this by considering only the "legal" question "whether, after viewing the evidence in the light most favorable to the prosecution, *any* rational trier of fact could have found the essential elements of the crime beyond a reasonable doubt." *Id.*, at 319, 99 S. Ct. 2781, 61 L. Ed. 2d 560. A reviewing court's determination thus does not rest on how the jury was instructed. The Government's failure to introduce evidence of an additional element does not implicate these principles, and its failure to object to a heightened jury instruction does not affect sufficiency

review. Because Musacchio does not dispute that he was properly charged with conspiracy to obtain unauthorized access or that the evidence was sufficient to convict him of the charged crime, the Fifth Circuit correctly rejected his sufficiency challenge. Pp. 243–245, 193 L. Ed. 2d, at 647-649.

2. A defendant cannot successfully raise § 3282(a)'s statute-of-limitations bar for the first time on appeal. Pp. 245–249, 193 L. Ed. 2d, at 649-651.

(a) A time bar is jurisdictional only if Congress has "clearly state[d]" that it is. *Sebelius* v. *Auburn Regional Medical Center*, 568 U.S. 145, 153, 133 S. Ct. 817, 184 L. Ed. 2d 627. Here, the "text, context, and relevant historical treatment" of § 3282(a), *Reed Elsevier, Inc.* v. *Muchnick*, 559 U.S. 154, 166, 130 S. Ct. 1237, 176 L. Ed. 2d 18, establish that it imposes a nonjurisdictional defense that becomes part of a case only if a defendant raises it in the district court. The provision does not expressly refer to subject-matter jurisdiction or speak in jurisdictional terms. It thus stands in marked contrast to § 3231, which speaks squarely to federal courts' general criminal subject-matter "jurisdiction" and does not "conditio[n] its jurisdictional grant on" compliance with § 3282(a)'s statute of limitations. *Id.*, at 165, 166, 130 S. Ct. 1237, 176 L. Ed. 2d 18. The history of § 3282(a)'s limitations bar further confirms that the provision does not impose a jurisdictional limit. See *United States* v. *Cook*, 17 Wall. 168, 181, 21 L. Ed. 538; *Smith* v. *United States*, 568 U.S. 106, 112, 133 S. Ct. 714, 184 L. Ed. 2d 570. Pp. 246–248, 193 L. Ed. 2d, at 649-651.

(b) Because § 3282(a) does not impose a jurisdictional limit, the failure to raise the defense at or before trial is reviewable on appeal—if at all—only for plain error. A district court's failure to enforce an unraised limitations defense under § 3282(a) cannot be a plain error, however, because if a defendant fails to press the defense, it does not become part of the case and, thus, there is no error for an appellate court to correct. Pp. 248–249, 193 L. Ed. 2d, at 650-651.

590 Fed. Appx. 359, affirmed.

Thomas, J., delivered the opinion for a unanimous Court.

OPINION OF THE COURT

[577 U.S. 239]

Justice **Thomas** delivered the opinion of the Court.

In this case, the Government failed to object to a jury instruction that erroneously added an element that it had to prove, and petitioner failed to press a statute-of-limitations defense until his appeal. We address two questions arising from the parties' failures to raise timely challenges. We first consider how a court should assess a challenge to the sufficiency of the evidence [1] in a criminal case when a jury instruction adds an element to the charged crime and the Government fails to object. We conclude that the sufficiency of the evidence should be assessed against the elements of the charged crime. We next consider [2] whether the statute-of-limitations defense contained in 18 U.S.C. § 3282(a) (the general federal criminal statute of limitations) may be successfully raised for the first time on appeal. We conclude that it may not be.

I

Petitioner Michael Musacchio served as president of a logistics company, Exel Transportation Services (ETS), until his resignation in 2004. In 2005, he formed a rival company, Total Transportation Services (TTS).

Musacchio was soon joined there by Roy Brown, who previously headed ETS' information-technology department. At TTS, Brown, using a password, continued to access ETS' computer system without ETS' authorization. Brown also gave Musacchio access to ETS' system. This improper access of ETS' system kept on until early 2006.

In November 2010, a grand jury indicted Musacchio under **[3]** 18 U.S.C. § 1030(a)(2)(C). Under that provision, a person commits a crime when he "intentionally accesses a computer

[577 U.S. 240]

without authorization *or* exceeds authorized access," and in doing so "obtains . . . information from any protected computer." (Emphasis added.) The statute thus provides two ways of committing the crime of improperly accessing a protected computer: (1) obtaining access without authorization; and (2) obtaining access with authorization but then using that access improperly. See *ibid.*; § 1030(e)(6) (defining "exceeds authorized access"). Count 1 of the indictment charged Musacchio with conspiring to commit both types of improper access. Count 23 charged him with making unauthorized access to ETS' e-mail server "[o]n or about" November 24, 2005. App. 70-71.[1]

In 2012, the Government filed a superseding indictment amending those charges. Count 1 dropped the charge of conspiracy to exceed authorized access, limiting that charge to conspiracy to make unauthorized access. Count 2 amended the allegations originally contained in count 23 by alleging that Musacchio accessed specific ETS e-mail accounts "[o]n or about" November 23-25, 2005. *Id.,* at 83-84. The Government later filed a second superseding indictment that made no changes relevant here.

Musacchio proceeded to a jury trial. At no time before or during trial did he argue that his prosecution violated the 5-year statute of limitations applicable to count 2. See **[4]** 18 U.S.C. § 3282(a) (providing general 5-year statute of limitations).

For the Government's part, it submitted proposed jury instructions on the conspiracy count before and during the trial. Each set of proposed instructions identified that count as involving "Unauthorized Access to Protected Computer[s]," and none required the jury additionally to find that Musacchio conspired to exceed authorized access to protected

[577 U.S. 241]

computers. Musacchio did not propose instructions on the conspiracy count.

Diverging from the indictment and the proposed instructions, the District Court instructed the jury on count 1 that § 1030(a)(2)(C) "makes it a crime for a person to intentionally access a protected computer without authori-

zation *and* exceed authorized access." App. 168 (emphasis added). The parties agree that this instruction was erroneous: By using the conjunction "and" when referring to both ways of violating § 1030(a)(2)(C), the instruction required the Government to prove an additional element. Yet the Government did not object to this error in the instructions.

The jury found Musacchio guilty on both counts 1 and 2. The District Court sentenced him to 60 months' imprisonment. Musacchio appealed, making the two challenges that he again advances in this Court. First, he challenged the sufficiency of the evidence supporting his conspiracy conviction on count 1. He maintained, moreover, that the sufficiency of the evidence should be assessed against the erroneous jury instruction that included the additional element. Second, he argued, for the first time, that his prosecution on count 2—for unauthorized access—was barred by the 5-year statute of limitations because the superseding indictment was filed seven years after the crime and did not relate back to the timely original indictment.

The Fifth Circuit rejected both challenges and affirmed Musacchio's conviction. 590 Fed. Appx. 359 (2014) (*per curiam*). First, the Court of Appeals concluded that it should assess Musacchio's sufficiency challenge against the charged elements of the conspiracy count, not against the erroneous jury instruction. See *id.,* at 362-363. Under Fifth Circuit precedent, the court explained, erroneously heightened jury instructions generally become the binding "law of

---

1. Counts 2 through 22 charged other defendants with exceeding authorized access to specific e-mail accounts. App. 68-70. Those defendants pleaded guilty, and later indictments dropped those counts.

the case" on appeal. *Id.,* at 362 (internal quotation marks omitted). Circuit precedent supplies an exception, however, when (1) the jury instruction is " 'patently erroneous,' " and (2) " 'the

[577 U.S. 242]

issue is not misstated in the indictment.' " *Ibid.* (quoting *United States* v. *Guevara,* 408 F.3d 252, 258 (CA5 2005)). The Fifth Circuit concluded that those conditions for applying the exception were satisfied. See 590 Fed. Appx., at 362-363. The court explained that the instruction's requirement of an additional element was "an obvious clerical error," and that the indictment correctly charged Musacchio only with "Conspiracy To Make Unauthorized Access to [a] Protected Computer." *Id.,* at 362. Therefore, the Fifth Circuit did not assess Musacchio's sufficiency challenge under the heightened jury instruction. *Id.,* at 362-363. Because Musacchio did not dispute that the evidence was sufficient to support a conviction under the elements set out in the indictment, the Fifth Circuit rejected his challenge. *Id.,* at 363.

Second, the Fifth Circuit rejected Musacchio's statute-of-limitations defense, concluding that he had "waived" the defense by failing to raise it at trial. *Id.,* at 363, 364.

We granted certiorari to resolve two questions that have divided the lower courts. 576 U.S. 1053, 135 S. Ct. 2889, 192 L. Ed. 2d 923 (2015). The first question is whether the sufficiency of the evidence in a criminal case should be measured against the elements described in the jury instructions where those instructions, without objection, require the Government to prove more elements than do the statute and indictment. Compare, *e.g., United States* v. *Romero,* 136 F.3d 1268, 1272-1273 (CA10 1998) (explaining that

sufficiency is measured against heightened jury instructions), with *Guevara, supra,* at 258 (CA5) (adopting an exception to that rule). The second question is whether a statute-of-limitations defense not raised at or before trial is reviewable on appeal. Compare, *e.g., United States* v. *Franco-Santiago,* 681 F.3d 1, 12, and n. 18 (CA1 2012) (limitations defense not raised and preserved before or at trial is reviewable on appeal for plain error), with *United States* v. *Walsh,* 700 F.2d 846, 855-856 (CA2 1983) (limitations defense not properly raised below is not reviewable on appeal).

[577 U.S. 243]

II

We first address how a court should assess a sufficiency challenge when a jury instruction adds an element to the charged crime and the Government fails to object. We hold that, **[5]** when a jury instruction sets forth all the elements of the charged crime but incorrectly adds one more element, a sufficiency challenge should be assessed against the elements of the charged crime, not against the erroneously heightened command in the jury instruction.

That conclusion flows from the nature of a court's task in evaluating a sufficiency-of-the-evidence challenge. **[6]** Sufficiency review essentially addresses whether "the government's case was so lacking that it should not have even been submitted to the jury." *Burks* v. *United States,* 437 U.S. 1, 16, 98 S. Ct. 2141, 57 L. Ed. 2d 1 (1978) (emphasis deleted). On sufficiency review, a reviewing court makes a limited inquiry tailored to ensure that a defendant receives the minimum that due process requires: a "meaningful opportunity to defend" against the charge against him and a jury finding of guilt "beyond a reasonable doubt." *Jackson* v. *Virginia*, 443 U.S. 307, 314-315, 99 S. Ct. 2781, 61 L. Ed. 2d 560 (1979). The reviewing court considers only the "legal" question "whether, after viewing the evidence in the light most favorable to the prosecution, *any* rational trier of fact could have found the essential elements of the crime beyond a reasonable doubt." *Id.*, at 319, 99 S. Ct. 2781, 61 L. Ed. 2d 560 (emphasis in original). That limited review does not intrude on the jury's role "to resolve conflicts in the testimony, to weigh the evidence, and to draw reasonable inferences from basic facts to ultimate facts." *Ibid.*

[7] A reviewing court's limited determination on sufficiency review thus does not rest on how the jury was instructed. When a jury finds guilt after being instructed on all elements of the charged crime plus one more element, the jury has made all the findings that due process requires. If a jury instruction requires the jury to find guilt on the elements of the charged crime, a defendant will have had a "meaningful

[577 U.S. 244]

opportunity to defend" against the charge. *Id.*, at 314, 99 S. Ct. 2781, 61 L. Ed. 2d 560. And if the jury instruction requires the jury to find those elements "beyond a reasonable doubt," the defendant has been accorded the procedure that this Court has required to protect the presumption of innocence. *Id.*, at 314-315, 99 S. Ct. 2781, 61 L. Ed. 2d 560.

The Government's failure to introduce evidence of an additional element does not implicate the principles that sufficiency review protects. All that a defendant is entitled to on a sufficiency challenge is for the court to make a "legal" determination whether the evidence was strong enough to reach a jury at all. *Id.*, at 319, 99 S. Ct. 2781, 61 L. Ed. 2d 560. The Government's failure to object to the heightened jury instruction thus does not affect the court's review for sufficiency of the evidence.[2]

Musacchio does not contest that the indictment here properly charged him with the statutory elements for conspiracy to obtain unauthorized access. The jury instructions required the jury to find all of the elements of that charged offense beyond a reasonable doubt. Nor does he dispute that the evidence was sufficient to convict him of the crime charged in the indictment—of conspiring to make unauthorized access. Accordingly, the Fifth Circuit correctly rejected his sufficiency challenge.

The Fifth Circuit erred, however, in basing that conclusion on the law-of-the-case doctrine. See 590 Fed. Appx., at 362-363. That doctrine does not apply here. [8] The law-of-the-case doctrine generally provides that " 'when a court decides

[577 U.S. 245]

upon a rule of law, that decision should continue to govern the same issues in subsequent stages in the same case.' " *Pepper* v. *United States*, 562 U.S. 476, 506, 131 S. Ct. 1229, 179 L. Ed. 2d 196 (2011)

---

2. In resolving the first question presented, we leave open several matters. First, we express no view on the question whether sufficiency of the evidence at trial must be judged by reference to the elements charged in the indictment, even if the indictment charges one or more elements not required by statute. Second, we do not suggest that the Government adds an element to a crime for purposes of sufficiency review when the indictment charges different means of committing a crime in the conjunctive. Third, we also do not suggest that an erroneous jury instruction cannot result in reversible error just because the evidence was sufficient to support a conviction.

(quoting *Arizona* v. *California*, 460 U.S. 605, 618, 103 S. Ct. 1382, 75 L. Ed. 2d 318 (1983)). The doctrine "expresses the practice of courts generally to refuse to reopen what has been decided," but it does not "limit [courts'] power." *Messenger* v. *Anderson*, 225 U.S. 436, 444, 32 S. Ct. 739, 56 L. Ed. 1152 (1912). Thus, the doctrine may describe an appellate court's decision not to depart from a ruling that it made in a prior appeal in the same case. See C. Wright et al., 18B Federal Practice and Procedure § 4478, p. 646, and n. 16 (2d ed. 2002) (collecting cases). But the doctrine is "something of a misnomer" when used to describe how an appellate court assesses a lower court's rulings. *United States* v. *Wells*, 519 U.S. 482, 487, n. 4, 117 S. Ct. 921, 137 L. Ed. 2d 107 (1997). An appellate court's function *is* to revisit matters decided in the trial court. When an appellate court reviews a matter on which a party failed to object below, its review may well be constrained by other doctrines such as waiver, forfeiture, and estoppel, as well as by the type of challenge that it is evaluating. But it is not bound by district court rulings under the law-of-the-case doctrine. That doctrine does not bear on how to assess a sufficiency challenge when a jury convicts a defendant after being instructed—without an objection by the Government—on all charged elements of a crime plus an additional element.

III

We now consider whether a defendant may successfully raise the statute-of-limitations bar in 18 U.S.C. § 3282(a) for the first time on appeal. Musacchio argues that he may do so, either because § 3282(a) imposes a nonwaivable limit on federal courts'

subject-matter jurisdiction or because a previously unraised limitations claim may constitute plain error that can be noticed on appeal. We disagree with both points, and hold that **[9]** a defendant cannot successfully raise this statute-of-limitations bar for the first time on appeal.

[577 U.S. 246]

A

[10] Statutes of limitations and other filing deadlines "ordinarily are not jurisdictional." *Sebelius* v. *Auburn Regional Medical Center*, 568 U.S. 145, 154, 133 S. Ct. 817, 184 L. Ed. 2d 627 (2013). We treat a time bar as jurisdictional only if Congress has "clearly stated" that it is. *Id.*, at 153, 133 S. Ct. 817, 184 L. Ed. 2d 627; (brackets and internal quotation marks omitted); see, *e.g., Henderson* v. *Shinseki*, 562 U.S. 428, 436, 439, 131 S. Ct. 1197, 179 L. Ed. 2d 159 (2011) (requiring a "clear indication" that a statute is jurisdictional (internal quotation marks omitted)). To determine whether Congress has made the necessary clear statement, we examine the "text, context, and relevant historical treatment" of the provision at issue. *Reed Elsevier, Inc.* v. *Muchnick*, 559 U.S. 154, 166, 130 S. Ct. 1237, 176 L. Ed. 2d 18 (2010).

Congress has not made such a clear statement here. Rather, **[11]** the statutory text, context, and history establish that § 3282(a) imposes a nonjurisdictional defense that becomes part of a case only if a defendant raises it in the district court.

The statutory text suggests that § 3282(a) does not impose a jurisdictional limit. Section 3282(a) provides:

[12] "Except as otherwise expressly provided by law, no person shall be prosecuted, tried, or punished for any offense, not capital, unless the indictment is found or the information is instituted within five years next after such offense shall have been committed."

[13] Although § 3282(a) uses mandatory language, it does not expressly refer to subject-matter jurisdiction or speak in jurisdictional terms. The text of § 3282(a) does not, therefore, provide a "clear indication that Congress wanted that provision to be treated as having jurisdictional attributes." *Henderson, supra*, at 439, 131 S. Ct. 1197, 179 L. Ed. 2d 159.

Context confirms that § 3282(a) does not impose a jurisdictional limit. [14] Federal courts' general criminal subject-matter jurisdiction comes from 18 U.S.C. § 3231, which

[577 U.S. 247]

states: "The district courts . . . shall have original jurisdiction . . . of all offenses against the laws of the United States." Section 3231 speaks squarely to federal courts' "jurisdiction," in marked contrast to § 3282(a), which does not mention "jurisdiction" or a variant of that term. And, nothing in § 3231 "conditions its jurisdictional grant on" compliance with § 3282(a)'s statute of limitations. *Reed Elsevier, supra*, at 165, 130 S. Ct. 1237, 176 L. Ed. 2d 18. This context supports the conclusion that § 3282(a) is not jurisdictional.

[15] The history of the limitations bar in § 3282(a) demonstrates that it is a defense that becomes part of a case only if the defendant presses it in the district court. This Court held in *United States* v. *Cook*, 17 Wall. 168, 21 L. Ed. 538 (1872), that a statute of limitations—identical in all relevant respects to § 3282(a)—was "a matter of defence and must be pleaded or

given in evidence by the accused." *Id.*, at 181, 21 L. Ed. 538; see § 32, 1 Stat. 119 (statute of limitations); see also *Cook, supra,* at 173, and n. *, 21 L. Ed. 538 (citing and describing statute of limitations). When a defendant introduces the limitations defense into the case, the Government then has "the right to reply or give evidence" on the limitations claim. 17 Wall., at 179, 21 L. Ed. 538.

Cook was decided more than 140 years ago, and we have adhered to its holding. Just three Terms ago, we reaffirmed that [16] "[c]ommission of [a federal] crime within the statute-of-limitations period is not an element of the . . . offense," and "it is up to the defendant to raise the limitations defense." *Smith* v. *United States*, 568 U.S. 106, 112, 133 S. Ct. 714, 184 L. Ed. 2d 570 (2013) (citing *Cook*; emphasis deleted); see also *Biddinger* v. *Commissioner of Police of City of New York*, 245 U.S. 128, 135, 38 S. Ct. 41, 62 L. Ed. 193 (1917) ("The statute of limitations is a defense and must be asserted on the trial by the defendant in criminal cases . . ." (citing *Cook*)). There is, in sum, a long history of treating the operative language in § 3282(a) as providing a nonjurisdictional defense that a defendant must press at trial to insert into the case.

[577 U.S. 248]

In keeping with § 3282(a)'s text, context, and history, we conclude that § 3282(a) provides a nonjurisdictional defense, not a jurisdictional limit.

B

[17] Because § 3282(a) does not impose a jurisdictional limit, the failure to raise it at or before trial means that it is reviewable on appeal—if at all—only for plain error. See Fed. Rule Crim. Proc. 52(b) (providing for consideration of "[a] plain error that af-

fects substantial rights" even though the error "was not brought to the court's attention"). We conclude, however, that a district court's failure to enforce an unraised limitations defense under § 3282(a) cannot be a plain error.[3]

As explained above, **[18]** a statute-of-limitations defense becomes part of a case only if the defendant puts the defense in issue. When a defendant presses a limitations defense, the Government *then* bears the burden of establishing compliance with the statute of limitations by presenting evidence that the crime was committed within the limitations period or by establishing an exception to the limitations period. See *Cook, supra,* at 179, 21 L. Ed. 538. When a defendant fails to press a limitations defense, the defense does not become part of the case and the Government does not otherwise have the burden of proving that it filed a timely indictment. When a defendant does not press the defense, then, there is no error for an appellate court to correct—and certainly no plain error.

A defendant thus cannot successfully raise the statute-of-limitations defense in § 3282(a) for the first time on appeal.

[577 U.S. 249]
The Fifth Circuit correctly refused to consider Musacchio's limitations defense here.

* * *

For the foregoing reasons, we affirm the judgment of the Fifth Circuit.

It is so ordered.

---

3. Because we conclude that the failure to enforce § 3282(a)'s limitations defense cannot be plain error, we do not resolve whether the failure to raise that defense in the District Court amounts to waiver (which some courts have held to preclude all appellate review of the defense) or forfeiture (which some courts have held to allow at least plain-error review). See *United States* v. *Franco-Santiago,* 681 F.3d 1, 12, n. 18 (CA1 2012) (collecting cases).

MENOMINEE INDIAN TRIBE OF WISCONSIN, Petitioner

v

UNITED STATES, et al.

577 U.S. 250, 136 S. Ct. 750, 193 L. Ed. 2d 652, 2016 U.S. LEXIS 971

[No. 14-510]

Argued December 1, 2015. Decided January 25, 2016.

Decision: Indian tribe was not entitled to equitable tolling of statute of limitations for filing of Indian Self-Determination and Education Assistance Act (25 U.S.C.S. § 450 et seq.) claims under Contract Disputes Act (41 U.S.C.S. § 7101 et seq.).

Prior history: ON WRIT OF CERTIORARI TO THE UNITED STATES COURT OF APPEALS FOR THE DISTRICT OF COLUMBIA CIRCUIT, 412 U.S. App. D.C. 221, 764 F.3d 51, 2014 U.S. App. LEXIS 16894

SUMMARY

Overview: HOLDINGS: [1]-Equitable tolling did not apply to render timely a portion of an Indian tribe's claim for breach of a contract by the government in failing to make contractual payments to the tribe, since the tribe's mistaken belief that the limitations period was tolled during the pendency of a putative class action by tribes, its mistaken belief that presentment of the claim to a contracting officer was unnecessary, and the risks and expense of litigation did not constitute extraordinary circumstances beyond the tribe's control.

Outcome: Judgment affirmed. Unanimous Decision.

HEADNOTES

Classified to United States Supreme Court Digest, Lawyers' Edition

Indian Self-Determination and Education Assistance Act

L Ed Digest: Indians § 32.2

1. Under the Indian Self-Determination and Education Assistance Act, 25 U.S.C.S. § 450 et seq., Indian tribes may enter into self-determination contracts with federal agencies to take control of a variety of federally funded programs. 25 U.S.C.S. § 450f. A contracting tribe is eligible to receive the amount of money that the government would have otherwise spent on the program, 25 U.S.C.S. § 450j-1(a)(1), as well as reimbursement for reasonable contract support costs, which include administrative and overhead costs associated with carrying out the contracted programs, § 450j-1(a)(2), (3), (5).

Contract disputes

L Ed Digest: United States § 156

2. As part of its mandatory administrative process for resolving government contract disputes, the Contract Disputes Act of 1978 (CDA), 41 U.S.C.S. § 7101 et seq., requires contractors to present each claim they may have to a contracting officer for decision. 41 U.S.C.S. § 7103(a)(1). The CDA includes a 6-year statute of limitations for presentment of each claim. § 7103(a)(4)(A).

Contract with Federal Government — dispute

L Ed Digest: Indians § 32.2

3. Under the Contract Disputes Act of 1978, 41 U.S.C.S. § 7101 et seq., a government contracting officer's decision is generally final, unless challenged through one of the statutorily authorized routes. 41 U.S.C.S. § 7103(g). A contractor dissatisfied with the officer's decision may either take an administrative appeal to a board of contract appeals or file an action for breach of contract in the United States Court of Federal Claims. 41 U.S.C.S. §§7104(a), (b)(1), 7105(b). Both routes then lead to the United States Court of Appeals for the Federal Circuit for any further review. 28 U.S.C.S. § 1295(a)(3); 41 U.S.C.S. § 7107(a)(1); 25 U.S.C.S. § 450m-1(d). Under the Indian Self-Determination and Education Assistance Act, 25 U.S.C.S. § 450 et seq., tribal contractors have a third option. They may file a claim for money damages in federal district court, 25 U.S.C.S. § 450m-1(a), (d), and if they lose, they may pursue an appeal in one of the regional courts of appeals. 28 U.S.C.S. § 1291.

Equitable tolling

L Ed Digest: Limitation of Actions § 220

4. A litigant is entitled to equitable tolling of a statute of limitations only if the litigant establishes two elements: (1) that he has been pursuing his rights diligently; and (2) that some extraordinary circumstance stood in his way and prevented timely filing.

Equitable tolling

L Ed Digest: Limitation of Actions § 220

5. The second prong of the equitable tolling test is met only where the circumstances that caused a litigant's delay are both extraordinary and beyond its control.

Congress' commitment

L Ed Digest: Indians § 1

6. See 25 U.S.C.S. § 450a(b), which declares Congress' commitment to the maintenance of the Federal Government's unique and continuing relationship with, and responsibility to, individual Indian tribes and to the Indian people as a whole.

RESEARCH REFERENCES

25 U.S.C.S. § 450 et seq.; 41 U.S.C.S. § 7101 et seq.

1 Moore's Federal Practice § 3.05 (Matthew Bender 3d ed.)

L Ed Digest, Indians § 32.2; Limitation of Actions §§220, 221

L Ed Index, Indians

Annotations:

Equitable estoppel as precluding reliance on statute of limitations—federal cases. 3 L. Ed. 2d 1886.

APPEARANCES OF COUNSEL ARGUING CASE

Geoffrey D. Strommer argued the cause for petitioner.
Ilana H. Eisenstein argued the cause for respondents.

SYLLABUS BY REPORTER OF DECISIONS

Pursuant to the Indian Self-Determination and Education Assistance Act (ISDA), petitioner Menominee Indian Tribe of Wisconsin contracted with the Indian Health Service (IHS) to operate what would otherwise have been a federal program and to receive an amount of money equal to what the Government would have spent on operating the program itself, including reimbursement for reasonable contract support costs. 25 U.S.C. §§ 450f, 450j-1(a). After other tribal entities successfully litigated complaints against the Federal Government for failing to honor its obligation to pay contract support costs, the Menominee Tribe presented its own contract support claims to IHS in accordance with the Contract Disputes Act of 1978 (CDA), which requires contractors to present each claim to a contracting officer for decision, 41 U.S.C. § 7103(a)(1). The contracting officer denied some of the Tribe's claims because they were not presented within the CDA's 6-year limitations period. See § 7103(a)(4)(A).

The Tribe challenged the denials in Federal District Court, arguing that the limitations period should be tolled for the nearly two years in which a putative class action, brought by Tribes with parallel complaints, was pending. As relevant here, the District Court eventually denied the Tribe's equitable-tolling claim, and the Court of Appeals affirmed, holding that no extraordinary circumstances beyond the Tribe's control caused the delay.

Held: Equitable tolling does not apply to the presentment of petitioner's claims. Pp. 255–259, 193 L. Ed. 2d, at 657-660.

(a) To be entitled to equitable tolling of a statute of limitations, a litigant must establish "(1) that he has been pursuing his rights diligently, and (2) that some extraordinary circumstance stood in his way and prevented timely filing." *Holland* v. *Florida*, 560 U.S. 631, 649, 130 S. Ct. 2549, 177 L. Ed. 2d 130. The Tribe argues that diligence and extraordinary circumstances should be considered together as factors in a unitary test, and it faults the Court of Appeals for declining to consider the Tribe's diligence in connection with its finding that no extraordinary circumstances existed. But this Court has expressly characterized these two components as "elements," not merely factors of indeterminate or commensurable weight, *Pace* v. *DiGuglielmo*, 544 U.S. 408, 418, 125 S. Ct. 1807, 161 L. Ed. 2d 669, and has treated them as such in practice, see *Lawrence* v. *Florida*, 549 U.S. 327, 336-337, 127 S. Ct. 1079, 166 L. Ed. 2d 924. The Tribe also objects to the

Court of Appeals' interpretation of the "extraordinary circumstances" prong as requiring the showing of an "external obstacle" to timely filing. This Court reaffirms that this prong is met only where the circumstances that caused a litigant's delay are both extraordinary *and* beyond its control. Pp. 255–257, 193 L. Ed. 2d, at 657-658.

(b) None of the Tribe's excuses satisfy the "extraordinary circumstances" prong of the test. The Tribe had unilateral authority to present its claims in a timely manner. Its claimed obstacles, namely, a mistaken reliance on a putative class action and a belief that presentment was futile, were not outside the Tribe's control. And the significant risk and expense associated with presenting and litigating its claims are far from extraordinary. Finally, the special relationship between the United States and Indian tribes, as articulated in the ISDA, does not override clear statutory language. Pp. 257–259, 193 L. Ed. 2d, at 659-660.

764 F.3d 51, affirmed.

Alito, J., delivered the opinion for a unanimous Court.

OPINION OF THE COURT

[577 U.S. 251]
Justice **Alito** delivered the opinion of the Court.

Petitioner Menominee Indian Tribe of Wisconsin (Tribe) seeks equitable tolling to preserve contract claims not timely presented to a federal contracting officer. Because the Tribe cannot establish extraordinary circumstances that stood in the way of timely filing, we hold that equitable tolling does not apply.

[577 U.S. 252]

I

Congress enacted the Indian Self-Determination and Education Assistance Act (ISDA), Pub. L. 93-638, 88 Stat. 2203, 25 U.S.C. § 450 *et seq.,* in 1975 to help Indian tribes assume responsibility for aid programs that benefit their members. [1] Under the ISDA, tribes may enter into "self-determination contracts" with federal agencies to take control of a variety of federally funded programs. § 450f. A contracting tribe is eligible to receive the amount of money that the Government would have otherwise spent on the program, see § 450j-1(a)(1), as well as reimbursement for reasonable "contract support costs," which include administrative and overhead costs associated with carrying out the contracted programs, §§ 450j-1(a)(2), (3), (5).

In 1988, Congress amended the ISDA to apply the Contract Disputes Act of 1978 (CDA), 41 U.S.C. § 7101 *et seq.*, to disputes arising under the ISDA. See 25 U.S.C. § 450m-1(d); Indian Self-Determination and Education Assistance Act Amendments of 1988, § 206(2), 102 Stat. 2295. [2] As part of its mandatory administrative process for resolving contract disputes, the CDA requires contractors to present "[e]ach claim" they may have to a contracting officer for decision. 41 U.S.C. § 7103(a)(1). Congress later amended the CDA to include a 6-year statute of limitations for presentment of each claim. Federal Acquisition Streamlining Act of 1994, 41 U.S.C. § 7103(a)(4)(A).

[3] Under the CDA, the contracting officer's decision is generally final, unless challenged through one of

the statutorily authorized routes. § 7103(g). A contractor dissatisfied with the officer's decision may either take an administrative appeal to a board of contract appeals or file an action for breach of contract in the United States Court of Federal Claims. §§ 7104(a), (b)(1), 7105(b). Both routes then lead to the United States Court of Appeals for the Federal Circuit for any further review. 28 U.S.C. § 1295(a)(3); 41 U.S.C. § 7107(a)(1); see 25 U.S.C. § 450m-1(d). Under the ISDA,

[577 U.S. 253]

tribal contractors have a third option. They may file a claim for money damages in federal district court, §§ 450m-1(a), (d), and if they lose, they may pursue an appeal in one of the regional courts of appeals, 28 U.S.C. § 1291.

Tribal contractors have repeatedly complained that the Federal Government has not fully honored its obligations to pay contract support costs. Three lawsuits making such claims are relevant here.

The first was a class action filed by the Ramah Navajo Chapter alleging that the Bureau of Indian Affairs (BIA) systematically underpaid certain contract support costs. *Ramah Navajo Chapter* v. *Lujan*, No. 1:90-cv-0957 (D NM) (filed Oct. 4, 1990). In 1993, Ramah successfully moved for certification of a nationwide class of all tribes that had contracted with the BIA under the ISDA. See Order and Memorandum Opinion in *Ramah Navajo Chapter* v. *Lujan*, No. 1:90-cv-0957, 1993 U.S. Dist. LEXIS 21762 (D NM, Oct. 1, 1993), App. 35-40. The Government argued that each tribe needed to present its claims to a contracting officer before it could partici-

pate in the class. *Id.*, at 37-38. But the trial court held that tribal contractors could participate in the class without presentment, because the suit alleged systemwide flaws in the BIA's contracting scheme, not merely breaches of individual contracts. *Id.*, at 39. The Government did not appeal the certification order, and the *Ramah* class action proceeded to further litigation and settlement.

The second relevant ISDA suit raised similar claims about contract support costs but arose from contracts with the Indian Health Service (IHS). *Cherokee Nation of Okla.* v. *United States*, No. 6:99-cv-0092 (ED Okla.) (filed Mar. 5, 1999). In *Cherokee Nation*, two Tribes filed a putative class action against IHS. On February 9, 2001, the District Court denied class certification without addressing whether tribes would need to present claims to join the class. *Cherokee Nation* v. *United States*, 199 F.R.D. 357, 363-366 (ED Okla.). The two plaintiff Tribes did not appeal the denial

[577 U.S. 254]

of class certification but proceeded to the merits on their own, eventually prevailing before this Court in a parallel suit. See *Cherokee Nation of Okla.* v. *Leavitt*, 543 U.S. 631, 125 S. Ct. 1172, 161 L. Ed. 2d 66 (2005).

The third relevant case is the one now before us. In this case, the Tribe presented its contract support claims (for contract years 1995 through 2004) to IHS on September 7, 2005, shortly after our *Cherokee Nation* ruling. As relevant here, the contracting officer denied the Tribe's claims based on its 1996, 1997, and 1998 contracts because, *inter alia*, those claims were barred by the CDA's 6-year statute of limitations.[1] The Tribe challenged the denials in the United States District Court for the District of Columbia, arguing, based on theories of class-action and equitable tolling, that the limitations period should be tolled for the 707 days that the putative *Cherokee Nation* class had been pending. See *American Pipe & Constr. Co.* v. *Utah*, 414 U.S. 538, 94 S. Ct. 756, 38 L. Ed. 2d 713 (1974) (class-action tolling); *Holland* v. *Florida*, 560 U.S. 631, 130 S. Ct. 2549, 177 L. Ed. 2d 130 (2010) (equitable tolling).

Initially, the District Court held that the limitations period was jurisdictional and thus forbade tolling of any sort. 539 F. Supp. 2d 152, 154, and n. 2 (DC 2008). On appeal, the United States Court of Appeals for the District of Columbia Circuit concluded that the limitations period was not jurisdictional and thus did not necessarily bar tolling. 614 F.3d 519, 526 (2010). But the court held that the Tribe was ineligible for class-action tolling during the pendency of the putative *Cherokee Nation* class, because the Tribe's failure to present its claims to IHS made it "ineligible to participate in the class action at the time class certification [was] denied."

[577 U.S. 255]

614 F.3d, at 527 (applying *American Pipe*). The court then remanded the case to the District Court to determine the Tribe's eligibility for equitable tolling.

On remand, the District Court concluded that the Tribe's asserted reasons for failing to present its claims within the specified time "do not, individually or collectively, amount to an extraordinary circumstance" that could warrant equitable tolling. 841 F. Supp. 2d 99, 107 (DC 2012) (internal quotation marks omitted). This time, the Court of Appeals affirmed. 764 F.3d 51 (CADC 2014). It explained that, "[t]o count as sufficiently 'extraordinary' to support equitable tolling, the circumstances that caused a litigant's delay must have been beyond its control" and "cannot be a product of that litigant's own misunderstanding of the law or tactical mistakes in litigation." *Id.*, at 58. Because none of the Tribe's proffered circumstances was beyond its control, the court held, there were no extraordinary circumstances that could merit equitable tolling.

The Court of Appeals' decision created a split with the Federal Circuit, which granted another tribal entity equitable tolling under similar circumstances. See *Arctic Slope Native Ass'n* v. *Sebelius*, 699 F.3d 1289 (CA Fed. 2012). We granted certiorari to resolve the conflict. 576 U.S. 1083, 135 S. Ct. 2927, 192 L. Ed. 2d 975 (2015).

II

The Court of Appeals denied the Tribe's request for equitable tolling by applying the test that we articulated in *Holland* v. *Florida*, 560 U.S. 631, 130 S. Ct. 2549, 177 L. Ed. 2d 130. **[4]** Under *Holland*, a litigant is entitled to equitable tolling of a statute of limitations only if the litigant establishes two elements: "(1) that he has been pursuing his rights diligently, and (2) that some extraordinary circumstance stood in his way and prevented timely filing." *Id.,* at 649, 130

---

1. Because the contract claims accrued no later than the end of each calendar-year contract, the District Court determined, the statute of limitations for the 1996, 1997, and 1998 contracts had run by January 1st of the years 2003, 2004, and 2005, respectively. 539 F. Supp. 2d 152, 154, n. 1 (DC 2008). The Tribe does not dispute the timing of accrual before this Court.

S. Ct. 2549, 177 L. Ed. 2d 130 (internal quotation marks omitted).

The Tribe calls this formulation of the equitable-tolling test overly rigid, given the doctrine's equitable nature. First, it argues that diligence and extraordinary circumstances

[577 U.S. 256]

should be considered together as two factors in a unitary test, and it faults the Court of Appeals for declining to consider the Tribe's diligence in connection with its finding that no extraordinary circumstances existed. But we have expressly characterized equitable tolling's two components as "elements," not merely factors of indeterminate or commensurable weight. *Pace* v. *DiGuglielmo*, 544 U.S. 408, 418, 125 S. Ct. 1807, 161 L. Ed. 2d 669 (2005) ("Generally, a litigant seeking equitable tolling bears the burden of establishing two elements"). And we have treated the two requirements as distinct elements in practice, too, rejecting requests for equitable tolling where a litigant failed to satisfy one without addressing whether he satisfied the other. See, *e.g.*, *Lawrence* v. *Florida*, 549 U.S. 327, 336-337, 127 S. Ct. 1079, 166 L. Ed. 2d 924 (2007) (rejecting equitable tolling without addressing diligence because habeas petitioner fell "far short of showing 'extraordinary circumstances' "); *Pace, supra*, at 418, 125 S. Ct. 1807, 161 L. Ed. 2d 669 (holding, without resolving litigant's argument that he had "satisfied the extraordinary circumstance test," that, "[e]ven if we were to accept [his argument], he would not be entitled to relief because he has not established the requisite diligence").

Second, the Tribe objects to the Court of Appeals' interpretation of the "extraordinary circumstances" prong as requiring a litigant seeking tolling to show an "external obstacl[e]" to timely filing, *i.e.*, that "the circumstances that caused a litigant's delay must have been beyond its control." 764 F.3d, at 58-59. The Tribe complains that this "external obstacle" formulation amounts to the same kind of " 'overly rigid *per se* approach' " we rejected in *Holland*. Brief for Petitioner 32 (quoting 560 U.S., at 653, 130 S. Ct. 2549, 177 L. Ed. 2d 130). But in truth, the phrase "external obstacle" merely reflects our requirement that a litigant seeking tolling show "that some extraordinary circumstance *stood in his way." Id.*, at 649, 130 S. Ct. 2549, 177 L. Ed. 2d 130 (emphasis added; internal quotation marks omitted). This phrasing in *Holland* (and in *Pace* before that) would make little sense if

[577 U.S. 257]

equitable tolling were available when a litigant was responsible for its *own* delay. Indeed, the diligence prong already covers those affairs within the litigant's control; the extraordinary-circumstances prong, by contrast, is meant to cover matters outside its control. [5] We therefore reaffirm that the second prong of the equitable-tolling test is met only where the circumstances that caused a litigant's delay are both extraordinary *and* beyond its control.[2]

---

2. *Holland* v. *Florida*, 560 U.S. 631, 130 S. Ct. 2549, 177 L. Ed. 2d 130 (2010), is a habeas case, and we have never held that its equitable-tolling test necessarily applies outside the habeas context. Nevertheless, because we agree that the Tribe cannot meet *Holland*'s test, we have no occasion to decide whether an even stricter test might apply to a nonhabeas case. Nor does the Tribe argue that a more generous test than *Holland*'s should apply here.

III

The Tribe offers no circumstances that meet this standard.

Its mistaken reliance on the putative *Cherokee Nation* class action was not an obstacle beyond its control.[3] As the Tribe conceded below, see 614 F.3d, at 526-527, it could not have been a member of the putative *Cherokee Nation* class because it did not present its claims to an IHS contracting officer before class certification was denied. Before then, the Tribe had unilateral authority to present its claims and to join the putative class. Presentment was blocked not by an obstacle outside its control, but by the Tribe's mistaken belief that presentment was unneeded.

The Tribe's mistake, in essence, was its inference that the reasoning of the *Ramah* class certification decision (allowing tribes to participate—without presentment—in the class challenging underpayment of BIA contract support costs) applied to the putative *Cherokee Nation* class. This mistake was fundamentally no different from "a garden variety

[577 U.S. 258]

claim of excusable neglect," *Irwin* v. *Department of Veterans Affairs*, 498 U.S. 89, 96, 111 S. Ct. 453, 112 L. Ed. 2d 435 (1990), "such as a simple 'miscalculation' that leads a lawyer to miss a filing deadline," *Holland, supra*, at 651, 130 S. Ct. 2549, 177 L. Ed. 2d 130 (quoting *Lawrence, supra*, at 336, 127 S. Ct. 1079, 166 L. Ed. 2d 924). And it is quite different from relying on *actually binding* precedent that is subsequently reversed.[4]

The Tribe's other excuses are even less compelling. Its belief that presentment was futile was not an obstacle beyond its control but a species of the same mistake that kept it out of the putative *Cherokee Nation* class. And the fact that there may have been significant risk and expense associated with presenting and litigating its claims is far from extraordinary. As the District Court noted below, "it is common for a litigant to be confronted with significant costs to litigation, limited financial resources, an uncertain outcome based upon an uncertain legal landscape, and impending deadlines. These circumstances are not 'extraordinary.'" 841 F. Supp. 2d, at 107.

Finally, the Tribe also urges us to consider the special relationship between the United States and Indian tribes, as articulated in the ISDA. See 25 U.S.C. § 450a(b) (**[6]** "Congress declares its commitment to the maintenance of the Federal Government's unique and continuing relationship with, and responsibility to, individual Indian tribes and to the Indian people as a whole"). We do not question the "general trust relationship between the United States and the Indian tribes," but any specific obligations the Government may have under that relationship are "governed by statute rather than the common law." *United States* v. *Jicarilla Apache Nation*, 564 U.S. 162, 165, 131 S. Ct. 2313, 180 L. Ed. 2d 187 (2011). The ISDA and CDA establish a clear procedure for the resolution of disputes over ISDA contracts, with an unambiguous 6-year deadline for

[577 U.S. 259]

presentment of claims.

---

3. Because we conclude that the Tribe's mistake of law was not outside its control, we need not decide whether a mistake of law, however reasonable, could ever be extraordinary.

4. The Court of Appeals speculated, without deciding, that such a development might merit tolling, but like that court we have no occasion to decide the question.

The "general trust relationship" does not override the clear language of those statutes.[5]

IV

For these reasons, the judgment of the United States Court of Appeals for the District of Columbia Circuit is affirmed.

It is so ordered.

---

5. Because we hold that there were no extraordinary circumstances, we need not decide whether the Tribe was diligently pursuing its rights. We also need not accept the Tribe's invitation to assess prejudice to the Government, because the absence of prejudice to the opposing party "is not an independent basis for invoking the doctrine [of equitable tolling] and sanctioning deviations from established procedures." *Baldwin County Welcome Center v. Brown*, 466 U.S. 147, 152, 104 S. Ct. 1723, 80 L. Ed. 2d 196 (1984) (*per curiam*). Rather, the absence of prejudice is "a factor to be considered in determining whether the doctrine of equitable tolling should apply *once a factor that might justify such tolling is identified.*" *Ibid.* (emphasis added).

FEDERAL ENERGY REGULATORY COMMISSION, Petitioner (No. 14-840)

v

ELECTRIC POWER SUPPLY ASSOCIATION, et al.

ENERNOC, INC., et al., Petitioners (No. 14-841)

v

ELECTRIC POWER SUPPLY ASSOCIATION, et al.

577 U.S. 260, 136 S. Ct. 760, 193 L. Ed. 2d 661, 2016 U.S. LEXIS 853

Argued October 14, 2015. Decided January 25, 2016.

Decision: Federal Power Act (16 U.S.C.S. § 791a et seq.) authorized Federal Energy Regulatory Commission (FERC) to regulate wholesale market operators' compensation of demand-response bids; FERC's decision to compensate demand-response providers at locational marginal price was not arbitrary and capricious.

Prior history: ON WRITS OF CERTIORARI TO THE UNITED STATES COURT OF APPEALS FOR THE DISTRICT OF COLUMBIA CIRCUIT, 410 U.S. App. D.C. 103, 753 F.3d 216, 2014 U.S. App. LEXIS 9585

SUMMARY

Overview: HOLDINGS: [1]-The Federal Energy Regulatory Commission (FERC) had authority to require wholesale electric market operators to pay the same price to demand response providers for conserving energy as to generators for producing it, so long as consumers actually saved money, since the rule directly affected the wholesale rate which was reduced by displacing higher-priced generation bids; [2]-Although transactions occurring on the wholesale market affected retail rates, the regulatory plan did not invade the states' authority to regulate retail rates since every aspect of the plan happened exclusively on the wholesale market and governed exclusively the wholesale market's rules; [3]-The decision to pay demand response providers at the same price paid to generators was reasonable since FERC engaged in reasoned decisionmaking, weighed competing views, and intelligibly explained the decision.

Outcome: Judgment reversed. 6-2 Decision; 1 Dissent.

HEADNOTES

Classified to United States Supreme Court Digest, Lawyers' Edition

Wholesale electricity — federal regulation — state regulation

L Ed Digest: Energy §§ 19, 21

1. The Federal Power Act, 16 U.S.C.S. § 791a et seq., authorizes the Federal Energy Regulatory Commission (FERC) to regulate the sale of electric energy at wholesale in interstate commerce, including both wholesale electricity rates and any rule or practice affecting such rates. 16 U.S.C.S. §§824(b), 824e(a). But the

law places beyond FERC's power, and leaves to the States alone, the regulation of any other sale—most notably, any retail sale—of electricity. § 824(b). That statutory division generates a steady flow of jurisdictional disputes because—in point of fact if not of law—the wholesale and retail markets in electricity are inextricably linked. (Kagan, J., joined by Roberts, Ch. J., and Kennedy, Ginsburg, Breyer, and Sotomayor, JJ.)

Electricity — federal regulation
L Ed Digest: Energy § 20
2. Under the Federal Power Act (FPA), 16 U.S.C.S. § 791a et seq., the Federal Energy Regulatory Commission (FERC) has authority to regulate the transmission of electric energy in interstate commerce and the sale of electric energy at wholesale in interstate commerce. 16 U.S.C.S. § 824(b)(1). In particular, the FPA obligates FERC to oversee all prices for those interstate transactions and all rules and practices affecting such prices. The statute provides that all rates and charges made, demanded, or received by any public utility for or in connection with interstate transmissions or wholesale sales—as well as all rules and regulations affecting or pertaining to such rates or charges—must be just and reasonable. 16 U.S.C.S. § 824d(a). And if any rate or charge, or any rule, regulation, practice, or contract affecting such rate or charge, falls short of that standard, FERC must rectify the problem: it then shall determine what is just and reasonable and impose the same by order. 16 U.S.C.S. § 824e(a). (Kagan, J., joined by Roberts, Ch. J., and Kennedy, Ginsburg, Breyer, and Sotomayor, JJ.)

Wholesale electricity — federal regulation — state regulation
L Ed Digest: Energy §§ 19, 21
3. Alongside the grants of power to regulate sale of electric energy at wholesale in interstate commerce, the Federal Power Act, 16 U.S.C.S. § 791a et seq., also limits the regulatory reach of the Federal Energy Regulatory Commission (FERC), and thereby maintains a zone of exclusive state jurisdiction. 16 U.S.C.S. § 824(b)(1)—the same provision that gives FERC authority over wholesale sales—states that the subchapter, including its delegation to FERC, shall not apply to any other sale of electric energy. Accordingly, FERC may not regulate either within-state wholesale sales or retail sales of electricity (i.e., sales directly to users). State utility commissions continue to oversee those transactions. (Kagan, J., joined by Roberts, Ch. J., and Kennedy, Ginsburg, Breyer, and Sotomayor, JJ.)

Electricity — federal regulation
L Ed Digest: Energy § 20
4. 18 C.F.R. § 35.28(g)(1)(v) attempts to ensure just and reasonable wholesale electricity rates by requiring market operators to appropriately compensate demand response providers and thus bring about meaningful demand-side participation in the wholesale markets. 16 U.S.C.S. § 824d(a). The rule's most significant provision directs operators, under two specified conditions, to pay locational marginal price for any accepted demand response bid, just as they do for successful supply bids. In other words, the rule requires that demand response providers in those circumstances receive as much for conserving electricity as generators do for producing it. (Kagan, J., joined by

Roberts, Ch. J., and Kennedy, Ginsburg, Breyer, and Sotomayor, JJ.)

Electricity — demand response
L Ed Digest: Energy § 20

5. Two specified conditions ensure that a bid to use less electricity provides the same value to the wholesale market as a bid to make more. First, a demand response bidder must have the capability to provide the service offered; it must, that is, actually be able to reduce electricity use and thereby obviate the operator's need to secure additional power. Second, paying locational marginal price for a demand response bid must be cost-effective, as measured by a standard called the net benefits test. (Kagan, J., joined by Roberts, Ch. J., and Kennedy, Ginsburg, Breyer, and Sotomayor, JJ.)

Electricity — demand response
L Ed Digest: Energy § 20

6. The net benefits test makes certain that accepting a lower-priced demand response bid over a higher-priced supply bid will actually save load-serving entities (LSEs) (i.e., wholesale purchasers) money. In some situations it will not, even though accepting a lower-priced bid (by definition) reduces locational marginal price. That is because (to oversimplify a bit) LSEs share the cost of paying successful bidders, and reduced electricity use makes some LSEs drop out of the market, placing a proportionally greater burden on those that are left. Each remaining LSE may thus wind up paying more even though the total bill is lower; or said otherwise, the costs associated with an LSE's increased share of compensating bids may exceed the savings that the LSE obtains from a lower wholesale price. The net ben-

efits test screens out such counterproductive demand response bids, exempting them from the rule's compensation requirement. What remains are only those offers whose acceptance will result in actual savings to wholesale purchasers (along with more reliable service to end users). (Kagan, J., joined by Roberts, Ch. J., and Kennedy, Ginsburg, Breyer, and Sotomayor, JJ.)

Electricity — public utilities — federal regulation
L Ed Digest: Energy § 22

7. The Federal Power Act (FPA), 16 U.S.C.S. § 791a et seq., delegates responsibility to the Federal Energy Regulatory Commission (FERC) to regulate the interstate wholesale market for electricity—both wholesale rates and the panoply of rules and practices affecting them. The FPA establishes a scheme for federal regulation of the sale of electric energy at wholesale in interstate commerce. 16 U.S.C.S. § 824(b)(1). Under the statute, all rates and charges made, demanded, or received by any public utility for or in connection with interstate wholesale sales shall be just and reasonable; so too shall all rules and regulations affecting or pertaining to such rates or charges. 16 U.S.C.S. § 824d(a). And if FERC sees a violation of that standard, it must take remedial action. More specifically, whenever FERC shall find that any rate or charge—or any rule, regulation, practice, or contract affecting such rate or charge—is unjust or unreasonable, then FERC shall determine the just and reasonable rate, charge, rule, regulation, practice, or contract and impose the same by order. 16 U.S.C.S. § 824e(a). That means FERC has the authority—and, indeed, the duty—to ensure that rules or practices affecting wholesale rates are just and reasonable. (Kagan, J., joined by Roberts, Ch. J., and Kennedy, Ginsburg, Breyer, and Sotomayor, JJ.)

Electricity — wholesale sales

L Ed Digest: Energy § 22

8. 16 U.S.C.S. § 824(b) limits the sale jurisdiction of the Federal Energy Regulatory Commission (FERC) to that at wholesale, reserving regulatory authority over retail sales (as well as intrastate wholesale sales) to the States. § 824(b). FERC cannot take an action transgressing that limit no matter how direct, or dramatic, its impact on wholesale rates. (Kagan, J., joined by Roberts, Ch. J., and Kennedy, Ginsburg, Breyer, and Sotomayor, JJ.)

Scope of review — "arbitrary and capricious" standard

L Ed Digest: Administrative Law § 250

9. The scope of review under the "arbitrary and capricious" standard is narrow. A court is not to ask whether a regulatory decision is the best one possible or even whether it is better than the alternatives. Rather, the court must uphold a rule if the agency has examined the relevant considerations and articulated a satisfactory explanation for its action, including a rational connection between the facts found and the choice made. (Kagan, J., joined by Roberts, Ch. J., and Kennedy, Ginsburg, Breyer, and Sotomayor, JJ.)

RESEARCH REFERENCES

16 U.S.C.S. § 791a et seq.

1 Energy Law and Transactions § 3.03 (Matthew Bender)

L Ed Digest, Energy § 20

L Ed Index, Federal Energy Regulatory Commission

Annotations:

Construction and application of Federal Power Act (16 U.S.C.S. § 791a et seq.) with regard to Indian lands—federal cases. 80 L. Ed. 2d 920.

APPEARANCES OF COUNSEL ARGUING CASE

Donald B. Verrilli, Jr. argued the cause for petitioner in No. 14-840.

Carter G. Phillips argued the cause for petitioners in No. 14-841.

Paul D. Clement argued the cause for respondents.

SYLLABUS BY REPORTER OF DECISIONS

The Federal Power Act (FPA) authorizes the Federal Energy Regulatory Commission (FERC) to regulate "the sale of electric energy at wholesale in interstate commerce," including both wholesale electricity rates and any rule or practice "affecting" such rates. 16 U.S.C. §§ 824(b), 824d(a), 824e(a). But it places beyond FERC's power, leaving to the States alone, the regulation of "any other sale"—that is, any intrastate wholesale sale or, more pertinent here, any retail sale—of electricity. § 824(b).

In an increasingly competitive interstate electricity market, FERC has undertaken to ensure "just and reasonable" wholesale rates, § 824d(a), by encouraging the creation of nonprofit entities to manage regions of the nationwide electricity grid. These wholesale market operators administer their portions of the grid to ensure that the network conducts electricity reliably, and each holds competitive auctions to set wholesale prices. These auctions balance supply and demand continuously by matching bids to provide electricity from generators with orders from utilities and other "load-serving entities" that buy power at wholesale for resale to users. All bids to supply electricity are stacked from lowest to highest, and accepted in that order until all requests for power have been met. Every electricity supplier is paid the price of the highest-accepted bid, known as the locational marginal price (LMP).

In periods of high electricity demand, prices can reach extremely high levels as the least efficient generators have their supply bids accepted in the wholesale market auctions. Not only do rates rise dramatically during these peak periods, but the increased flow of electricity threatens to overload the grid and cause substantial service problems. Faced with these challenges, wholesale market operators devised wholesale demand response programs, which pay consumers for commitments to reduce their use of power during these peak periods. Just like bids to supply electricity, offers from aggregators of multiple users of electricity or large individual consumers to reduce consumption can be bid into the wholesale market auctions. When it costs less to pay consumers to refrain from using power than it does to pay producers to supply more of it, demand response can lower these wholesale prices and increase grid reliability. Wholesale operators began integrating these programs into their markets some 15 years ago and FERC authorized their use. Congress subsequently encouraged further development of demand response.

Spurred on by Congress, FERC issued Order No. 719, which, among other things, requires wholesale market operators to receive demand response bids from aggregators of electricity consumers, except when the state regulatory authority overseeing those users' retail purchases bars demand response participation. 18 CFR § 35.28(g)(1). Concerned that the order had not gone far enough, FERC then issued the rule under review here, Order No. 745. § 35.28(g)(1)(v) (Rule). It requires market operators to pay the same price to demand response providers for conserving energy as to generators for producing it, so long as a "net benefits test," which ensures that accepted bids actually save consumers money, is met. The

Rule rejected an alternative compensation scheme that would have subtracted from LMP the savings consumers receive from not buying electricity in the retail market, a formula known as LMP–G. The Rule also rejected claims that FERC lacked statutory authority to regulate the compensation operators pay for demand response bids.

The Court of Appeals for the District of Columbia Circuit vacated the Rule, holding that FERC lacked authority to issue the order because it directly regulates the retail electricity market, and holding in the alternative that the Rule's compensation scheme is arbitrary and capricious under the Administrative Procedure Act.

Held:

1. The FPA provides FERC with the authority to regulate wholesale market operators' compensation of demand response bids. The Court's analysis proceeds in three parts. First, the practices at issue directly affect wholesale rates. Second, FERC has not regulated retail sales. Taken together, these conclusions establish that the Rule complies with the FPA's plain terms. Third, the contrary view would conflict with the FPA's core purposes. Pp. 276–291, 193 L. Ed. 2d, at 675-684.

(a) The practices at issue directly affect wholesale rates. The FPA has delegated to FERC the authority—and, indeed, the duty—to ensure that rules or practices "affecting" wholesale rates are just and reasonable. §§ 824d(a), 824e(a). To prevent the statute from assuming near-infinite breadth, see, *e.g., New York State Conference of Blue Cross & Blue Shield Plans* v. *Travelers Ins. Co.*, 514 U.S. 645, 655, 115 S. Ct. 1671, 131 L. Ed. 2d 695, this Court adopts the D. C. Circuit's common-sense construction limiting FERC's "affecting" jurisdiction to rules or practices that "*directly* affect the [wholesale] rate," *California Independent System Operator Corp.* v. *FERC*, 372 F.3d 395, 403 (emphasis added). That standard is easily met here. Wholesale demand response is all about reducing wholesale rates; so too the rules and practices that determine how those programs operate. That is particularly true here, as the formula for compensating demand response necessarily lowers wholesale electricity prices by displacing higher-priced generation bids. Pp. 277–279, 193 L. Ed. 2d, at 675-677.

(b) The Rule also does not regulate retail electricity sales in violation of § 824(b). A FERC regulation does not run afoul of § 824(b)'s proscription just because it affects the quantity or terms of retail sales. Transactions occurring on the wholesale market have natural consequences at the retail level, and so too, of necessity, will FERC's regulation of those wholesale matters. That is of no legal consequence. See, *e.g., Mississippi Power & Light Co.* v. *Mississippi ex rel. Moore*, 487 U.S. 354, 365, 370-373, 108 S. Ct. 2428, 101 L. Ed. 2d 322. When FERC regulates what takes place on the wholesale market, as part of carrying out its charge to improve how that market runs, then no matter the effect on retail rates, § 824(b) imposes no bar. Here, every aspect of FERC's regulatory plan happens exclusively on the wholesale market and governs exclusively that market's rules. FERC's justifications for regulating demand response are likewise only about improving the wholesale market. Cf. *Oneok, Inc.* v. *Learjet, Inc.*, 575 U.S. 373, 385, 135 S. Ct. 1591, 191 L. Ed. 2d 511. Pp. 279–288, 193 L. Ed. 2d, at 677-682.

(c) In addition, respondent Electric Power Supply Association's (EPSA) position would subvert the FPA. EPSA's arguments suggest that the entire practice of wholesale demand response falls outside what FERC can regulate, and EPSA concedes that States also lack that authority. But under the FPA, wholesale demand response programs could not go forward if no entity had jurisdiction to regulate them. That outcome would flout the FPA's core purposes of protecting "against excessive prices" and ensuring effective transmission of electric power. *Pennsylvania Water & Power Co.* v. *FPC*, 343 U.S. 414, 418, 72 S. Ct. 843, 96 L. Ed. 1042; see *Gulf States Util. Co.* v. *FPC*, 411 U.S. 747, 758, 93 S. Ct. 1870, 36 L. Ed. 2d 635. The FPA should not be read, against its clear terms, to halt a practice that so evidently enables FERC to fulfill its statutory duties of holding down prices and enhancing reliability in the wholesale energy market. Pp. 288–291, 193 L. Ed. 2d, at 682-684.

2. FERC's decision to compensate demand response providers at LMP— the same price paid to generators— instead of at LMP--G, is not arbitrary and capricious. Under the narrow scope of review in *Motor Vehicle Mfrs. Assn. of United States, Inc.* v. *State Farm Mut. Automobile Ins. Co.*, 463 U.S. 29, 43, 103 S. Ct. 2856, 77 L. Ed. 2d 443, this Court's important but limited role is to ensure that FERC engaged in reasoned decisionmaking—that it weighed competing views, selected a compensation formula with adequate support in the record, and intelligibly explained the reasons for making that decision. Here, FERC provided a detailed explanation of its choice of LMP and responded at length to contrary views. FERC's serious and careful discussion of the issue satisfies the arbitrary and capricious standard. Pp. 291–296, 193 L. Ed. 2d, at 684-687.

753 F.3d 216, reversed and remanded.

Kagan, J., delivered the opinion of the Court, in which Roberts, C. J., and Kennedy, Ginsburg, Breyer, and Sotomayor, JJ., joined. Scalia, J. filed a dissenting opinion, in which Thomas, J., joined. Alito, J., took no part in the consideration or decision of the cases.

OPINION OF THE COURT

[577 U.S. 264]

Justice **Kagan** delivered the opinion of the Court.

[1] The Federal Power Act (FPA or Act), 41 Stat. 1063, as amended, 16 U.S.C. § 791a *et seq.*, authorizes the Federal Energy Regulatory Commission (FERC or Commission) to regulate "the sale of electric energy at wholesale in interstate

[577 U.S. 265]

commerce," including both wholesale electricity rates and any rule or practice "affecting" such rates. §§ 824(b), 824e(a). But the law places beyond FERC's power, and leaves to the States alone, the regulation of "any other sale"—most notably, any retail sale—of electricity. § 824(b). That statutory division generates a steady flow of jurisdictional disputes because—in point of fact if not of law—the wholesale and retail markets in electricity are inextricably linked.

These cases concern a practice called "demand response," in which operators of wholesale markets pay electricity consumers for commitments *not* to use power at certain times. That practice arose because wholesale market operators can sometimes—say, on a muggy August day—offer electricity both more cheaply and more reliably by paying users to dial down their consumption than by paying power plants to ramp up their production. In the regulation challenged here, FERC required those market operators, in specified circumstances, to compensate the two services equivalently—that is, to pay the same price to demand response providers for conserving energy as to generators for making more of it.

Two issues are presented here. First, and fundamentally, does the FPA permit FERC to regulate these demand response transactions at all, or does any such rule impinge on the States' authority? Second, even if FERC has the requisite statutory power, did the Commission fail to justify adequately why demand response providers and electricity producers should receive the same compensation? The court below ruled against FERC on both scores. We disagree.

I

A

Federal regulation of electricity owes its beginnings to one of this Court's decisions. In the early 20th century, state

[577 U.S. 266]

and local agencies oversaw nearly all generation, transmission, and distribution of electricity. But this Court held in *Public Util.*

Comm'n of R. I. v. *Attleboro Steam & Elec. Co.*, 273 U.S. 83, 89-90, 47 S. Ct. 294, 71 L. Ed. 549 (1927), that the Commerce Clause bars the States from regulating certain interstate electricity transactions, including wholesale sales (*i.e.*, sales for resale) across state lines. That ruling created what became known as the "*Attleboro* gap"—a regulatory void which, the Court pointedly noted, only Congress could fill. See *id.,* at 90, 47 S. Ct. 294, 71 L. Ed. 549.

Congress responded to that invitation by passing the FPA in 1935. The Act charged FERC's predecessor agency with undertaking "effective federal regulation of the expanding business of transmitting and selling electric power in interstate commerce." *New York* v. *FERC*, 535 U.S. 1, 6, 122 S. Ct. 1012, 152 L. Ed. 2d 47 (2002) (quoting *Gulf States Util. Co.* v. *FPC,* 411 U.S. 747, 758, 93 S. Ct. 1870, 36 L. Ed. 2d 635 (1973)). **[2]** Under the statute, the Commission has authority to regulate "the transmission of electric energy in interstate commerce" and "the sale of electric energy at wholesale in interstate commerce." 16 U.S.C. § 824(b)(1).

In particular, the FPA obligates FERC to oversee all prices for those interstate transactions and all rules and practices affecting such prices. The statute provides that "[a]ll rates and charges made, demanded, or received by any public utility for or in connection with" interstate transmissions or wholesale sales—as well as "all rules and regulations affecting or pertaining to such rates or charges"—must be "just and reasonable." § 824d(a). And if "any rate [or] charge," or "any rule, regulation, practice, or contract affecting such rate [or] charge[,]" falls short of that standard, the Commission must rectify the problem: It then shall determine what is "just and reasonable" and impose "the same by order." § 824e(a).

[3] Alongside those grants of power, however, the Act also limits FERC's regulatory reach, and thereby maintains a zone of exclusive state jurisdiction. As pertinent here,

[577 U.S. 267]

§ 824(b)(1)—the same provision that gives FERC authority over wholesale sales—states that "this subchapter," including its delegation to FERC, "shall not apply to any other sale of electric energy." Accordingly, the Commission may not regulate either within-state wholesale sales or, more pertinent here, retail sales of electricity (*i.e.*, sales directly to users). See *New York*, 535 U.S., at 17, 23, 122 S. Ct. 1012, 152 L. Ed. 2d 47. State utility commissions continue to oversee those transactions.

Since the FPA's passage, electricity has increasingly become a competitive interstate business, and FERC's role has evolved accordingly. Decades ago, state or local utilities controlled their own power plants, transmission lines, and delivery systems, operating as vertically integrated monopolies in confined geographic areas. That is no longer so. Independent power plants now abound, and almost all electricity flows not through "the local power networks of the past," but instead through an interconnected "grid" of near-nationwide scope. See *id.*, at 7, 122 S. Ct. 1012, 152 L. Ed. 2d 47 ("electricity that enters the grid immediately becomes a part of a vast pool of energy that is constantly moving in interstate commerce," linking producers and users across the country). In this new world, FERC often forgoes the cost-based rate-setting traditionally used to prevent monopolistic pricing. The Commission instead undertakes to ensure "just and reasonable" wholesale rates by enhancing competition—attempting, as we recently explained, "to break down regulatory and economic barriers that hinder a free market in wholesale electricity." *Morgan Stanley Capital Group Inc.* v. *Public Util. Dist. No. 1 of Snohomish Cty.*, 554 U.S. 527, 536, 128 S. Ct. 2733, 171 L. Ed. 2d 607 (2008).

As part of that effort, FERC encouraged the creation of nonprofit entities to manage wholesale markets on a regional basis. Seven such wholesale market operators now serve areas with roughly two-thirds of the country's electricity "load" (an industry term for the amount of electricity used). See FERC, Energy Primer: A Handbook of Energy Market

[577 U.S. 268]

Basics 58-59 (Nov. 2015) (Energy Primer). Each administers a portion of the grid, providing generators with access to transmission lines and ensuring that the network conducts electricity reliably. See *ibid.* And still more important for present purposes, each operator conducts a competitive auction to set wholesale prices for electricity.

These wholesale auctions serve to balance supply and demand on a continuous basis, producing prices for electricity that reflect its value at given locations and times throughout each day. Such a real-time mechanism is needed because, unlike most products, electricity cannot be stored effectively. Suppliers must generate—every day, hour, and minute—the exact amount of power necessary to meet demand from the utilities and other "load-serving entities" (LSEs) that buy power at wholesale for resale to users. To ensure that happens, wholesale market operators obtain (1) orders from LSEs indicating how much electricity they need at various times and (2) bids from generators specifying how much electricity they can produce at those times and how much they will charge for it. Operators accept the generators' bids in order of cost (least expensive first) until they satisfy the LSEs' total demand. The price of the last unit of electricity purchased is then paid to every supplier whose bid was accepted, regardless of its actual offer; and the total cost is split among the LSEs in proportion to how much energy they have ordered. So, for example, suppose that at 9 a.m. on August 15, four plants serving Washington, D. C. can each produce some amount of electricity for, respectively, $10/unit, $20/unit, $30/unit, and $40/unit. And suppose that LSEs' demand at that time and place is met after the operator accepts the three cheapest bids. The first three generators would then all receive $30/unit. That amount is (think back to Econ 101) the marginal cost—*i.e.,* the added cost of meeting another unit of demand—which is the price an efficient market would produce. See 1 A. Kahn, The Economics of Regulation: Principles and Institutions 65-67 (1988). FERC calls

[577 U.S. 269]

that cost (in jargon that will soon become oddly familiar) the locational marginal price, or LMP.[1]

As in any market, when wholesale buyers' demand for electricity increases, the price they must pay rises correspondingly; and in those times of peak load, the grid's reliability may also falter. Suppose that by 2 p.m. on August 15, it is 98 degrees in D. C. In every home, store, or office, people are turning the air conditioning up. To keep providing power to their customers, utilities and other LSEs must ask their market operator for more electricity. To meet that spike in demand, the operator will have to accept more expensive bids from suppliers. The operator, that is, will have to agree to the $40 bid that it spurned before— and maybe, beyond that, to bids of $50 or $60 or $70. In such periods, operators often must call on extremely inefficient generators whose high costs of production cause them to sit idle most of the time. See Energy Primer 41-42. As that happens, LMP—the price paid by *all* LSEs to *all* suppliers—climbs ever higher. And meanwhile, the increased flow of electricity through the grid threatens to overload transmission lines. See *id.,* at 44. As every consumer knows, it is just when the weather is hottest and the need for air conditioning most acute that blackouts, brownouts, and other service problems tend to occur.

Making matters worse, the wholesale electricity market lacks the self-correcting mechanism of other markets. Usually, when the price of a product rises, buyers naturally adjust by reducing how much they purchase. But consumers of electricity—and therefore the utilities and other LSEs buying power for them at wholesale—do not respond to price signals in that way. To use the economic term, demand for electricity is inelastic. That is in part because electricity is a necessity with few ready substitutes: When the temperature

[577 U.S. 270]

reaches 98 degrees, many people see no option but

---

1. To be more precise, LMP generally includes, in addition to the price of the highest-accepted bid, certain costs of moving power through the grid. But those costs are not relevant here, and we therefore disregard them.

to switch on the AC. And still more: Many State regulators insulate consumers from short-term fluctuations in wholesale prices by insisting that LSEs set stable retail rates. See *id.,* at 41, 43-44. That, one might say, short-circuits the normal rules of economic behavior. Even in peak periods, as costs surge in the wholesale market, consumers feel no pinch, and so keep running the AC as before. That means, in turn, that LSEs must keep buying power to send to those users—no matter that wholesale prices spiral out of control and increased usage risks overtaxing the grid.

But what if there were an alternative to that scenario? Consider what would happen if wholesale market operators could induce consumers to refrain from using (and so LSEs from buying) electricity during peak periods. Whenever doing that costs less than adding more power, an operator could bring electricity supply and demand into balance at a lower price. And simultaneously, the operator could ease pressure on the grid, thus protecting against system failures. That is the idea behind the practice at issue here: Wholesale demand response, as it is called, pays consumers for commitments to curtail their use of power, so as to curb wholesale rates and prevent grid breakdowns. See *id.,* at 44-46.[2]

These demand response programs work through the operators' regular auctions. Aggregators of multiple users of electricity, as well as large-scale individual users like factories or big-box stores, submit bids to decrease electricity consumption by a set amount at a set time for a set price. The wholesale market operators treat those offers just like bids from generators to increase supply. The operators, that is, rank order all the bids—both to produce and to refrain from consuming electricity—from least to most expensive, and

[577 U.S. 271]

then accept the lowest bids until supply and demand come into equipoise. And, once again, the LSEs pick up the cost of all those payments. So, to return to our prior example, if a store submitted an offer *not* to use a unit of electricity at 2 p.m. on August 15 for $35, the operator would accept that bid before calling on the generator that offered to produce a unit of power for $40. That would result in a lower LMP—again, wholesale market price—than if the market operator could not avail itself of demand response pledges. See ISO/RTO Council, Harnessing the Power of Demand: How ISOs and RTOs Are Integrating Demand Response Into Wholesale Electricity Markets 40-43 (2007) (estimating that, in one market, a demand response program reducing electricity usage by 3% in peak hours would lead to price declines of 6% to 12%). And it would decrease the risk of blackouts and other service problems.

Wholesale market operators began using demand response some 15 years ago, soon after they assumed the role of overseeing wholesale electricity sales. Recognizing the value of demand response for both system reliability and efficient pricing, they urged FERC to allow them to implement such programs. See, *e.g., PJM Interconnection, L. L. C.,* Order Accepting Tariff Sheets as Modified, 95

---

2. Differently designed demand response programs can operate in retail markets. Some States, for example, either encourage or require utilities to offer "critical-peak rebates" to customers for curtailing electricity use at times of high load. See Energy Primer 45.

FERC ¶61,306 (2001); *California Independent System Operator Corp.*, Order Conditionally Accepting for Filing Tariff Revisions, 91 FERC ¶61,256 (2000). And as demand response went into effect, market participants of many kinds came to view it—in the words of respondent Electric Power Supply Association (EPSA)—as an "important element[ ] of robust, competitive wholesale electricity markets." App. 94, EPSA, Comments on Proposed Rule on Demand Response Compensation in Organized Wholesale Energy Markets (May 12, 2010).

Congress added to the chorus of voices praising wholesale demand response. In the Energy Policy Act of 2005, 119 Stat. 594 (EPAct), it declared as "the policy of the United States" that such demand response "shall be encouraged."

[577 U.S. 272]

§ 1252(f), 119 Stat. 966, 16 U.S.C. § 2642 note. In particular, Congress directed, the deployment of "technology and devices that enable electricity customers to participate in . . . demand response systems shall be facilitated, and unnecessary barriers to demand response participation in energy . . . markets shall be eliminated." *Ibid.*[3]

B

Spurred on by Congress, the Commission determined to take a more active role in promoting wholesale demand response programs. In 2008, FERC issued Order No. 719, which (among other things) requires whole-sale market operators to receive demand response bids from aggregators of electricity consumers, except when the state regulatory authority overseeing those users' retail purchases bars such demand response participation. See 73 Fed. Reg. 64119, ¶154 (codified 18 CFR § 35.28(g)(1) (2015)). That original order allowed operators to compensate demand response providers differently from generators if they so chose. No party sought judicial review.

Concerned that Order No. 719 had not gone far enough, FERC issued the rule under review here in 2011, with one commissioner dissenting. See *Demand Response Competition in Organized Wholesale Energy Markets*, Order No. 745, 76 Fed. Reg. 16658 (Rule) (codified 18 CFR § 35.28(g)(1)(v)). **[4]** The Rule attempts to ensure "just and reasonable"

[577 U.S. 273]

wholesale rates by requiring market operators to appropriately compensate demand response providers and thus bring about "meaningful demand-side participation" in the wholesale markets. 76 Fed. Reg. 16658, ¶1, 16660, ¶10; 16 U.S.C. § 824d(a). The Rule's most significant provision directs operators, under two specified conditions, to pay LMP for any accepted demand response bid, just as they do for successful supply bids. See 76 Fed. Reg. 16666-16669, ¶¶45-67. In other words, the Rule requires that demand response providers in those circum-

---

3. The dissent misreads this subsection of the EPAct in suggesting that it encourages States' use of retail demand response, rather than the wholesale programs at issue here. See *post*, at 303–304, 193 L. Ed. 2d, at 691-692 (opinion of Scalia, J.); n. 2, *supra*. The prior subsection, § 1252(e), as the dissent notes, promotes demand response in the States—but then the EPAct switches gears. Subsection (f) expressly addresses the programs of "regional electricity entit[ies]"—that is, wholesale market operators. Indeed, the provision lists all the markets those operators run: not just the electricity market involved here, but also the "capacity and ancillary service markets." Those are established components of the wholesale system with no counterparts at the state level. See Energy Primer 59.

stances receive as much for conserving electricity as generators do for producing it.

[5] The two specified conditions ensure that a bid to use less electricity provides the same value to the wholesale market as a bid to make more. First, a demand response bidder must have "the capability to provide the service" offered; it must, that is, actually be able to reduce electricity use and thereby obviate the operator's need to secure additional power. *Id.*, at 16666, ¶¶48-49. Second, paying LMP for a demand response bid "must be cost-effective," as measured by a standard called "the net benefits test." *Ibid.*, ¶48. [6] That test makes certain that accepting a lower-priced demand response bid over a higher-priced supply bid will actually save LSEs (*i.e.*, wholesale purchasers) money. In some situations it will not, even though accepting a lower-priced bid (by definition) reduces LMP. That is because (to oversimplify a bit) LSEs share the cost of paying successful bidders, and reduced electricity use makes some LSEs drop out of the market, placing a proportionally greater burden on those that are left. Each remaining LSE may thus wind up paying more even though the total bill is lower; or said otherwise, the costs associated with an LSE's increased share of compensating bids may exceed the savings that the LSE obtains from a lower wholesale price.[4] The net benefits

[577 U.S. 274]

test screens out such counterproductive demand response bids, exempting them from the Rule's compensation requirement.

See *id.*, at 16659, 16666-16667, ¶¶3, 50-53. What remains are only those offers whose acceptance will result in actual savings to wholesale purchasers (along with more reliable service to end users). See *id.*, at 16671, ¶¶78-80.

The Rule rejected an alternative scheme for compensating demand response bids. Several commenters had urged that, in paying a demand response provider, an operator should subtract from the ordinary wholesale price the savings that the provider nets by not buying electricity on the retail market. Otherwise, the commenters claimed, demand response providers would receive a kind of "double-payment" relative to generators. See *id.*, at 16663, ¶24. That proposal, which the dissenting commissioner largely accepted, became known as LMP minus G, or more simply LMP–G, where "G" stands for the retail price of electricity. See *id.*, at 16668, ¶60, 16680 (Moeller, dissenting). But FERC explained that, under the conditions it had specified, the value of an accepted demand response bid to the wholesale market is identical to that of an accepted supply bid because each succeeds in cost-effectively "balanc[ing] supply and demand." *Id.*, at 16667, ¶55. And, the Commission reasoned, that comparable value is what ought to matter given FERC's goal of strengthening competition in the wholesale market: Rates should reflect not the costs that each market participant incurs, but instead the services it provides. See *id.*, at 16668, ¶62. Moreover, the Rule stated, compensating demand re-

---

4. The explanation is a stylized version of the actual phenomenon. In reality, LSEs rarely drop out of the market entirely because of demand response; instead, they will merely order less electricity. But the effect is the same as in the text, because the total cost of accepted bids is spread among LSEs in proportion to the units of electricity they purchase; and as those units decline, each remaining one bears a greater share of the bill.

sponse bids at their actual value—*i.e.*, LMP—will help overcome various technological barriers, including a lack of needed infrastructure, that impede aggregators and large-scale users of electricity

[577 U.S. 275]

from fully participating in demand response programs. See *id.*, at 16667-16668, ¶¶57-58.

The Rule also responded to comments challenging FERC's statutory authority to regulate the compensation operators pay for demand response bids. Pointing to the Commission's analysis in Order No. 719, the Rule explained that the FPA gives FERC jurisdiction over such bids because they "directly affect[ ] wholesale rates." *Id.*, at 16676, ¶112 (citing 74 *id.*, at 37783, ¶47, and 16 U.S.C. § 824d). Nonetheless, the Rule noted, FERC would continue Order No. 719's policy of allowing any state regulatory body to prohibit consumers in its retail market from taking part in wholesale demand response programs. See 76 Fed. Reg. 16676, ¶114; 73 *id.*, at 64119, ¶154. Accordingly, the Rule does not require any "action[ ] that would violate State laws or regulations." 76 *id.*, at 16676, ¶114.

C

A divided panel of the Court of Appeals for the District of Columbia Circuit vacated the Rule as "*ultra vires* agency action." 753 F.3d 216, 225 (2014). The court held that FERC lacked authority to issue the Rule even though "demand response compensation affects the wholesale market." *Id.*, at 221. The Commission's "jurisdiction to regulate practices 'affecting' rates," the court stated, "does not erase the specific limit[ ]" that the FPA imposes on FERC's regulation of retail sales. *Id.*, at 222. And the Rule, the court concluded, exceeds that

limit: In "luring . . . *retail* customers" into the wholesale market, and causing them to decrease "levels of *retail* electricity consumption," the Rule engages in "direct regulation of the retail market." *Id.*, at 223-224.

The Court of Appeals held, alternatively, that the Rule is arbitrary and capricious under the Administrative Procedure Act, 5 U.S.C. § 706(2)(A), because FERC failed to "adequately explain[ ]" why paying LMP to demand response providers "results in just compensation." 753 F.3d, at 225.

[577 U.S. 276]

According to the court, FERC did not "properly consider" the view that such a payment would give those providers a windfall by leaving them with "the full LMP *plus* . . . the savings associated with" reduced consumption. *Ibid.* (quoting *Demand Response Competition in Organized Wholesale Energy Markets: Order on Rehearing and Clarification*, Order No. 745-A (Rehearing Order), 137 FERC ¶61,215, p. 62,316 (2011) (Moeller, dissenting)). The court dismissed out of hand the idea that "comparable contributions [could] be the reason for equal compensation." 753 F.3d, at 225.

Judge Edwards dissented. He explained that the rules governing wholesale demand response have a "direct effect . . . on wholesale electricity rates squarely within FERC's jurisdiction." *Id.*, at 227. And in setting those rules, he argued, FERC did not engage in "direct regulation of the retail market"; rather, "[a]uthority over retail rates . . . remains vested solely in the States." *Id.*, at 234 (internal quotation marks omitted). Finally, Judge Edwards rejected the majority's view that the Rule is arbitrary and capricious. He noted the substantial deference due to the Commission in cases involving ratemaking, and concluded that FERC provided a "thorough" and "reasonable" explanation for choosing LMP as the appropriate compensation formula. *Id.*, at 236-238.

We granted certiorari, 575 U.S. 995, 135 S. Ct. 2049, 191 L. Ed. 2d 954 (2015), to decide whether the Commission has statutory authority to regulate wholesale market operators' compensation of demand response bids and, if so, whether the Rule challenged here is arbitrary and capricious. We now hold that the Commission has such power and that the Rule is adequately reasoned. We accordingly reverse.

II

Our analysis of FERC's regulatory authority proceeds in three parts. First, the practices at issue in the Rule—market operators' payments for demand response commitments—directly affect wholesale rates. Second, in addressing

[577 U.S. 277]

those practices, the Commission has not regulated retail sales. Taken together, those conclusions establish that the Rule complies with the FPA's plain terms. And third, the contrary view would conflict with the Act's core purposes by preventing all use of a tool that no one (not even EPSA) disputes will curb prices and enhance reliability in the wholesale electricity market.[5]

A

[7] The FPA delegates responsibility to FERC to regulate the interstate wholesale market for electricity—both wholesale rates and the panoply of rules and practices affecting them.

As noted earlier, the Act establishes a scheme for federal regulation of "the sale of electric energy at wholesale in interstate commerce." 16 U.S.C. § 824(b)(1); see *supra,* at 266, 193 L. Ed. 2d, at 668. Under the statute, "[a]ll rates and charges made, demanded, or received by any public utility for or in connection with" interstate wholesale sales "shall be just and reasonable"; so too shall "all rules and regulations affecting or pertaining to such rates or charges." § 824d(a). And if FERC sees a violation of that standard, it must take remedial action. More specifically, whenever the Commission "shall find that any rate [or] charge"—or "any rule, regulation, practice, or contract affecting such rate [or] charge"—is "unjust [or] unreasonable," then the Commission "shall determine the just and reasonable rate, charge[,] rule, regulation, practice or contract" and impose "the same by order." § 824e(a). That means FERC has the authority—and, indeed, the duty—to ensure that rules or practices "affecting" wholesale rates are just and reasonable.

Taken for all it is worth, that statutory grant could extend FERC's power to some surprising places. As the court below noted, markets in all electricity's inputs—steel, fuel,

[577 U.S. 278]

and labor most prominent among them—might affect generators' supply of power. See 753 F.3d, at 221; *id.,* at 235 (Edwards, J., dissenting). And for that matter, markets in just about everything—the whole economy, as it were—might influence LSEs' demand. So if indirect

---

5. Because we think FERC's authority clear, we need not address the Government's alternative contention that FERC's interpretation of the statute is entitled to deference under *Chevron U.S.A. Inc.* v. *Natural Resources Defense Council, Inc.*, 467 U.S. 837, 104 S. Ct. 2778, 81 L. Ed. 2d 694 (1984).

or tangential impacts on wholesale electricity rates sufficed, FERC could regulate now in one industry, now in another, changing a vast array of rules and practices to implement its vision of reasonableness and justice. We cannot imagine that was what Congress had in mind.

For that reason, an earlier D. C. Circuit decision adopted, and we now approve, a common-sense construction of the FPA's language, limiting FERC's "affecting" jurisdiction to rules or practices that *"directly* affect the [wholesale] rate." *California Independent System Operator Corp.* v. *FERC*, 372 F.3d 395, 403 (2004) (emphasis added); see 753 F.3d, at 235 (Edwards, J., dissenting). As we have explained in addressing similar terms like "relating to" or "in connection with," a non-hyperliteral reading is needed to prevent the statute from assuming near-infinite breadth. See *New York State Conference of Blue Cross & Blue Shield Plans* v. *Travelers Ins. Co.*, 514 U.S. 645, 655, 115 S. Ct. 1671, 131 L. Ed. 2d 695 (1995) ("If 'relate to' were taken to extend to the furthest stretch of its indeterminacy, then for all practical purposes [the statute] would never run its course"); *Maracich* v. *Spears*, 570 U.S. 48, 59, 133 S. Ct. 2191, 186 L. Ed. 2d 275 (2013) ("The phrase 'in connection with' is essentially indeterminat[e] because connections, like relations, stop nowhere" (internal quotation marks omitted)). The Commission itself incorporated the D. C. Circuit's standard in addressing its authority to issue the Rule. See 76 Fed. Reg. 16676, ¶112 (stating that FERC has jurisdiction because wholesale demand response "directly affects wholesale rates"). We think it right to do the same.

Still, the rules governing wholesale demand response programs meet that standard with room to spare. In general (and as earlier described), wholesale market operators employ

demand response bids in competitive auctions that balance wholesale supply and demand and thereby set wholesale prices. See *supra*, at 270–271, 193 L. Ed. 2d, at 671-672. The operators accept such bids if and only if they bring down the wholesale rate by displacing higher-priced generation. And when that occurs (most often in peak periods), the easing of pressure on the grid, and the avoidance of service problems, further contributes to lower charges. See Brief for Grid Engineers et al. as *Amici Curiae* 26-27. Wholesale demand response, in short, is all about reducing wholesale rates; so too, then, the rules and practices that determine how those programs operate.

And that is particularly true of the formula that operators use to compensate demand response providers. As in other areas of life, greater pay leads to greater participation. If rewarded at LMP, rather than at some lesser amount, more demand response providers will enter more bids capable of displacing generation, thus necessarily lowering wholesale electricity prices. Further, the Commission found, heightened demand response participation will put "downward pressure" on generators' own bids, encouraging power plants to offer their product at reduced prices lest they come away empty-handed from the bidding process. 76 Fed. Reg. 16660, ¶10. That, too, ratchets down the rates wholesale purchasers pay. Compensation for demand response thus directly affects wholesale prices. Indeed, it is hard to think of a practice that does so more.

B

The above conclusion does not end our inquiry into the Commission's statutory authority; to uphold the Rule, we also must determine that it does not regulate *retail* electricity sales. **[8]** That is because, as earlier described, § 824(b) "limit[s] FERC's sale jurisdiction to that at wholesale," reserving regulatory authority over retail sales (as well as intrastate wholesale sales) to the States. *New York*, 535 U.S., at 17, 122 S. Ct. 1012, 152 L. Ed. 2d 47 (emphasis deleted); see 16 U.S.C. § 824(b); *supra,* at

[577 U.S. 280]

266–267, 193 L. Ed. 2d, at 668–669.[6] FERC cannot take an action transgressing that limit no matter how direct, or dramatic, its impact on wholesale rates. Suppose, to take a far-fetched example, that the Commission issued a regulation compelling every consumer to buy a certain amount of electricity on the retail market. Such a rule would necessarily determine the load purchased on the wholesale market too, and thus would alter wholesale prices. But even given that ineluctable consequence, the regulation would exceed FERC's authority, as defined in § 824(b), because it specifies terms of sale at retail— which is a job for the States alone.[7]

[577 U.S. 281]

Yet a FERC regulation does not run afoul of § 824(b)'s proscription just because it affects—even substantially—the quantity or terms of retail sales. It is a fact of economic life that the wholesale and retail markets in electricity, as in every other known product, are not hermetically sealed from each other. To the contrary,

---

6. EPSA additionally cites § 824(a) as constraining the Commission's authority, see Brief for Respondent EPSA et al. 25, 31, 43 (Brief for Respondents), but that provision adds nothing to the analysis. Section 824(a), the FPA's "declaration of policy," states that federal regulation of electricity is to "extend only to those matters which are not subject to regulation by the States." We have often explained that this declaration serves only to frame the Act's basic structure and purpose. See, *e.g., New York*, 535 U.S., at 22, 122 S. Ct. 1012, 152 L. Ed. 2d 47 (Section 824(a) "broadly expresse[s] [the Act's] purpose" (quoting *FPC* v. *Southern Cal. Edison Co.*, 376 U.S. 205, 215, 84 S. Ct. 644, 11 L. Ed. 2d 638 (1964))); *id.,* at 215, 84 S. Ct. 644, 11 L. Ed. 2d 638 (Section 824(a) is "merely a 'policy declaration . . . of great generality' " (quoting *Connecticut Light & Power Co.* v. *FPC*, 324 U.S. 515, 527, 65 S. Ct. 749, 89 L. Ed. 1150 (1945))). That means, as applied to the issue here, that § 824(a) merely points toward the division of regulatory authority that § 824(b) carries out. The operative provision is what counts.

7. The dissent disputes this framing of the issue, but its criticism (made by neither EPSA nor its *amici*) is irrelevant to deciding this case. According to the dissent, the FPA prohibits FERC from regulating not only retail sales of electricity (as we agree) but also any other sales of electricity aside from wholesale sales. See *post,* at 297–299, 193 L. Ed. 2d, at 687–689. But the dissent turns out not to argue that the Rule regulates some kind of non-retail, non-wholesale sale of electric energy (whatever that might be). Rather, the dissent claims that the Rule regulates retail sales, see *post,* at 299–301, 193 L. Ed. 2d, at 689-690—exactly the point that we address, and reject, in the following pages. And in any event, the dissent's framing of the issue is wrong if and to the extent it posits some undefined category of other electricity sales falling within neither FERC's nor the States' regulatory authority. Sales of electric energy come in two varieties: wholesale and retail. The very case the dissent relies on recognizes that fact by referring to "other sales, that is, to direct sales for consumptive use." *Panhandle Eastern Pipe Line Co.* v. *Public Serv. Comm'n of Ind.*, 332 U.S. 507, 516, 68 S. Ct. 190, 92 L. Ed. 128 (1947). FERC regulates interstate wholesale sales of electricity; the States regulate retail sales of electricity. And FERC may also regulate, as it did here, practices and rules affecting wholesale prices—that is, matters beyond wholesale sales themselves—so long as, in doing so, it does not trespass on the States' authority to regulate retail sales of electric power. See *supra,* at 266–267, 193 L. Ed. 2d, at 668–669.

transactions that occur on the wholesale market have natural consequences at the retail level. And so too, of necessity, will FERC's regulation of those wholesale matters. Cf. *Oneok, Inc.* v. *Learjet, Inc.*, 575 U.S. 373, 387, 135 S. Ct. 1591, 194 L. Ed. 2d 511 (2015) (noting that in the similarly structured world of natural gas regulation, a "Platonic ideal" of strict separation between federal and state realms cannot exist). When FERC sets a wholesale rate, when it changes wholesale market rules, when it allocates electricity as between wholesale purchasers—in short, when it takes virtually any action respecting wholesale transactions—it has some effect, in either the short or the long term, on retail rates. That is of no legal consequence. See, *e.g., Mississippi Power & Light Co.* v. *Mississippi ex rel. Moore*, 487 U.S. 354, 365, 370-373, 108 S. Ct. 2428, 101 L. Ed. 2d 322 (1988) (holding that an order regulating wholesale purchases fell within FERC's jurisdiction, and preempted contrary state action, even though it clearly affected retail prices); *Nantahala Power & Light Co.* v. *Thornburg*, 476 U.S. 953, 959-961, 970, 106 S. Ct. 2349, 90 L. Ed. 2d 943 (1986) (same); *FPC* v. *Louisiana Power & Light Co.*, 406 U.S. 621, 636-641, 92 S. Ct. 1827, 32 L. Ed. 2d 369 (1972) (holding similarly in the natural gas context). When FERC regulates what takes place on the wholesale market, as part of carrying out its charge to improve how that market runs,

[577 U.S. 282]

then no matter the effect on retail rates, § 824(b) imposes no bar.

And in setting rules for demand response, that is all FERC has done. The Commission's Rule addresses— and addresses only—transactions occurring on the wholesale market. Recall once again how demand response works—and forgive the coming italics. See *supra,* at 270–271, 193 L. Ed. 2d, at 671-672. *Wholesale* market operators administer the entire program, receiving every demand response bid made. Those operators accept such a bid at the mandated price when (and only when) the bid provides value to the *wholesale* market by balancing supply and demand more "cost-effective[ly]"—*i.e.,* at a lower cost to *wholesale* purchasers— than a bid to generate power. 76 Fed. Reg. 16659, 16666, ¶¶2, 48. The compensation paid for a successful bid (LMP) is whatever the operator's auction has determined is the marginal price of *wholesale* electricity at a particular location and time. See *id.,* at 16659, ¶2. And those footing the bill are the same *wholesale* purchasers that have benefited from the lower *wholesale* price demand response participation has produced. See *id.,* at 16674, ¶¶99-100. In sum, whatever the effects at the retail level, every aspect of the regulatory plan happens exclusively on the wholesale market and governs exclusively that market's rules.

What is more, the Commission's justifications for regulating demand response are all about, and only about, improving the wholesale market. Cf. *Oneok,* 575 U.S., at 385, 135 S. Ct. 1591, 194 L. Ed. 2d 511 (considering "the *target* at which [a] law *aims*" in determining whether a State is properly regulating retail or, instead, improperly regulating wholesale sales). In Order No. 719, FERC explained that demand response participation could help create a "well-functioning competitive wholesale electric energy market" with "reduce[d] wholesale power prices" and "enhance[d] reliability." 73 Fed. Reg. 64103, ¶16. And in the Rule under review, FERC expanded on that theme. It listed the several ways in which "demand response in organized

[577 U.S. 283]

wholesale energy markets can help improve the functioning and competitiveness of those markets": by replacing high-priced, inefficient generation; exerting "downward pressure" on "generator bidding strategies"; and "support[ing] system reliability." 76 *id.*, at 16660, ¶10; see Notice of Proposed Rulemaking for Order No. 745, 75 *id.*, at 15363-15364, ¶4 (2010) (noting similar aims); *supra,* at 270–271, 193 L. Ed. 2d, at 671–672. FERC, that is, focused wholly on the benefits that demand response participation (in the wholesale market) could bring to the wholesale market. The retail market figures no more in the Rule's goals than in the mechanism through which the Rule operates.

EPSA's primary argument that FERC has usurped state power (echoed in the dissent) maintains that the Rule "effectively," even though not "nominal[ly]," regulates retail prices. See, *e.g.,* Brief for Respondents 1, 10, 23-27, 35-39; Tr. of Oral Arg. 26, 30; *post,* at 299–301, 193 L. Ed. 2d, at 689-690. The argument begins on universally accepted ground: Under § 824(b), only the States, not FERC, can set retail rates. See, *e.g., FPC* v. *Conway Corp.*, 426 U.S. 271, 276, 96 S. Ct. 1999, 48 L. Ed. 2d 626 (1976). But as EPSA concedes, that tenet alone cannot make its case, because FERC's Rule does not set actual rates: States continue to make or approve all retail rates, and in doing so may insulate them from price fluctuations in the wholesale market. See Brief for

Respondents 39. Still, EPSA contends, rudimentary economic analysis shows that the Rule does the "functional equivalen[t]" of setting—more particularly, of raising—retail rates. *Id.,* at 36. That is because the opportunity to make demand response bids in the wholesale market changes consumers' calculations. In deciding whether to buy electricity at retail, economically-minded consumers now consider *both* the cost of making such a purchase *and* the cost of forgoing a possible demand response payment. So, EPSA explains, if a factory can buy electricity for $10/unit, but can earn $5/unit for *not* buying power at peak times, then the effective retail rate at those times is $15/unit: the $10 the factory paid

[577 U.S. 284]

at retail plus the $5 it passed up. See *id.,* at 10. And by thus increasing effective retail rates, EPSA concludes, FERC trespasses on the States' ground.

The modifier "effective" is doing quite a lot of work in that argument—more work than any conventional understanding of rate-setting allows. The standard dictionary definition of the term "rate" (as used with reference to prices) is "[a]n amount paid or charged for a good or service." Black's Law Dictionary 1452 (10th ed. 2014); see, *e.g.,* 13 Oxford English Dictionary 208-209 (2d ed. 1989) ("rate" means "price," "cost," or "sum paid or asked for a . . . thing"). To set a retail electricity rate is thus to establish the amount of money a consumer will hand over in exchange for power. Nothing in § 824(b) or any other part of the FPA suggests a more expansive notion, in which FERC sets a rate for electricity merely by altering consumers' incentives to purchase that product.[8] And neither does anything in this Court's caselaw. Our decisions uniformly speak about rates, for electricity and all else, in only their most prosaic, garden-variety sense. As the Solicitor General summarized that view, "the rate is what it is." Tr. of Oral Arg. 7. It is the price paid, not the price paid *plus* the cost of a forgone economic opportunity.

Consider a familiar scenario to see what is odd about EPSA's theory. Imagine that a flight is overbooked. The airline offers passengers $300 to move to a later plane that has extra seats. On EPSA's view, that offer adds $300—the

[577 U.S. 285]

cost of not accepting the airline's proffered payment—to the price of every continuing passenger's ticket. So a person who originally spent $400 for his ticket, and decides to reject the airline's proposal, paid an "effective" price of $700. But would any passenger getting off the plane say he had paid $700 to fly? That is highly unlikely. And airline lawyers and regulators (including many, we are sure, with economics Ph. D.'s) appear to share that common-sensical view. It is in fact illegal to "increase the price" of "air transportation . . . after [such] air transportation has been purchased by the consumer." 14 CFR § 399.88(a) (2015). But it is a safe bet that no airline has ever gotten into trouble by offering a payment not to fly.[9]

And EPSA's "effective price increase" claim fares even worse when it comes to payments not to use electricity. In EPSA's universe, a wholesale demand response program raises retail rates by compelling consumers to "pay" the price of forgoing demand response compensation. But such a consumer would be even more surprised than our air traveler to learn of that price hike, because the natural consequence of wholesale demand response programs is to bring *down* retail rates. Once again, wholesale market operators accept demand response bids only if those offers lower the wholesale price. See *supra,* at 270–271, 193 L. Ed. 2d, at 671–672. And when wholesale

[577 U.S. 286]

prices go down, retail prices tend to follow, because state regulators can, and mostly do, insist that wholesale buyers eventually pass on their savings to consumers. EPSA's theoretical construct thus

---

8. The dissent offers, alternatively, a definition of "price," but that only further proves our point. "Price," says the dissent, is "[t]he amount of money or other consideration asked for or given in exchange for something else." *Post,* at 300, 193 L. Ed. 2d, at 690 (quoting Black's Law Dictionary 1380). But the "effective" rates posited by EPSA and the dissent do not meet that test. If $10 is the actual rate for a unit of retail electricity, that is the only amount either "asked for" or "given" in exchange for power. A retail customer is asked to pay $10 by its LSE, and if it buys that electricity, it gives the LSE that same $10. By contrast, the $15 "effective" rate is neither asked for nor given by anyone.

9. The dissent replaces our simple, real-world example with a convoluted, fictitious one—but once again merely confirms our point. Suppose, the dissent says, that an airline cancels a passenger's $400 ticket; gives him a refund plus an extra $300; and then tells him that if he wants to repurchase the ticket, he must pay $700. Aha!, says the dissent—isn't the price now $700? See *post,* at 300–301, 193 L. Ed. 2d, at 689–690. Well, yes it is, because that is now the *actual* amount the passenger will have to hand over to the airline to receive a ticket in exchange (or in the dissent's definition of price, the amount "asked for" and "given," see n. 8, *supra*). In other words, in search of an intuitive way to explain its "effective rate" theory, the dissent must rely on an "actual rate" hypothetical. But all that does is highlight the distance, captured in the law, between real prices (reflecting amounts paid) and effective ones (reflecting opportunity costs).

runs headlong into the real world of electricity sales—where the Rule does anything but increase retail prices.

EPSA's second argument that FERC intruded into the States' sphere is more historical and purposive in nature. According to EPSA, FERC deliberately "lured [retail customers] into the[ ] wholesale markets"—and, more, FERC did so "only because [it was] dissatisfied with the States' exercise of their undoubted authority" under § 824(b) to regulate retail sales. Brief for Respondents 23; see *id.*, at 2-3, 31, 34. In particular, EPSA asserts, FERC disapproved of "many States' continued preference" for stable pricing—that is, for insulating retail rates from short-term fluctuations in wholesale costs. *Id.*, at 28. In promoting demand response programs—or, in EPSA's somewhat less neutral language, in "forc[ing] retail customers to respond to wholesale price signals"—FERC acted "for the express purpose of overriding" that state policy. *Id.*, at 29, 49.

That claim initially founders on the true facts of how wholesale demand response came about. Contra EPSA, the Commission did not invent the practice. Rather, and as described earlier, the impetus came from wholesale market operators. See *supra,* at 271, 193 L. Ed. 2d, at 671. In designing their newly organized markets, those operators recognized almost at once that demand response would lower wholesale electricity prices and improve the grid's reliability. So they quickly sought, and obtained, FERC's approval to institute such programs. Demand response, then, emerged not as a Commission power grab, but instead as a market-generated innovation for more optimally balancing wholesale electricity supply and demand.

And when, years later (after Congress, too, endorsed the practice), FERC began to play a more proactive role, it did

[577 U.S. 287]

so for the identical reason: to enhance the wholesale, not retail, electricity market. Like the market operators, FERC saw that sky-high demand in peak periods threatened network breakdowns, compelled purchases from inefficient generators, and consequently drove up wholesale prices. See, *e.g.,* 73 Fed. Reg. 64103, ¶16; 76 *id.*, at 16660, ¶10; see *supra,* at 269–270, 193 L. Ed. 2d, at 670-671. Addressing those problems—which demand response does—falls within the sweet spot of FERC's statutory charge. So FERC took action promoting the practice. No doubt FERC recognized connections, running in both directions, between the States' policies and its own. The Commission understood that by insulating consumers from price fluctuations, States contributed to the wholesale market's difficulties in optimally balancing supply and demand. See 76 Fed. Reg. 16667-16668, ¶¶57, 59; *supra,* at 269–270, 193 L. Ed. 2d, at 670-671. And FERC realized that increased use of demand response in that market would (by definition) inhibit retail sales otherwise subject to State control. See 73 Fed. Reg. 64167. But nothing supports EPSA's more feverish idea that the Commission's interest in wholesale demand response emerged from a yen to usurp State authority over, or impose its own regulatory agenda on, retail sales. In promoting demand response, FERC did no more than follow the dictates of its regulatory mission to improve the competitiveness, efficiency, and reliability of the wholesale market.

Indeed, the finishing blow to both of EPSA's arguments comes from FERC's notable solicitude toward the States. As explained earlier, the Rule allows any State regulator to prohibit its consumers from making demand response bids in the wholesale market. See 76 *id.*, at 16676, ¶114; 73 *id.*, at 64119, ¶154; *supra,* at 275, 193 L. Ed. 2d, at 674. Although claiming the ability to negate such state decisions, the Commission chose not to do so in recognition of the linkage between wholesale and retail markets and the States' role in overseeing retail sales. See 76 Fed. Reg. 16676, ¶¶112-114. The veto power thus granted to the States belies EPSA's view that FERC aimed

[577 U.S. 288]

to "obliterate[ ]" their regulatory authority or "override" their pricing policies. Brief for Respondents 29, 33. And that veto gives States the means to block whatever "effective" increases in retail rates demand response programs might be thought to produce. Wholesale demand response as implemented in the Rule is a program of cooperative federalism, in which the States retain the last word. That feature of the Rule removes any conceivable doubt as to its compliance with § 824(b)'s allocation of federal and state authority.

C

One last point, about how EPSA's position would subvert the FPA.

EPSA's jurisdictional claim, as may be clear by now, stretches very far. Its point is not that this single Rule, relating to compensation levels, exceeds FERC's power. Instead, EPSA's arguments—that rewarding energy conservation raises effective retail rates and that "luring" consumers onto wholesale markets aims to disrupt state policies—suggest that the entire practice of wholesale demand response falls outside what FERC can regulate. EPSA proudly embraces that point: FERC, it declares, "has no business regulating 'demand response' at all." *Id.*, at 24. Under EPSA's theory, FERC's earlier Order No. 719, although never challenged, would also be ultra vires because it requires operators to open their markets to demand response bids. And more: FERC could not even approve an operator's voluntary plan to administer a demand response program. See Tr. of Oral Arg. 44. That too would improperly allow a retail customer to participate in a wholesale market.

Yet state commissions could not regulate demand response bids either. EPSA essentially concedes this point. See Brief for Respondents 46 ("That may well be true"). And so it must. The FPA "leaves no room either for direct state regulation of the prices of interstate wholesales" or for regulation that "would indirectly achieve the same result." *Northern Natural Gas Co.* v. *State Corporation Comm'n of*

[577 U.S. 289]

Kan., 372 U.S. 84, 91, 83 S. Ct. 646, 9 L. Ed. 2d 601 (1963). A State could not oversee offers, made in a wholesale market operator's auction, that help to set wholesale prices. Any effort of that kind would be preempted.

And all of that creates a problem. If neither FERC nor the States can regulate wholesale demand response, then by definition no one can. But under the Act, no electricity transaction can proceed unless it is regulable by someone. As earlier described, Congress passed the FPA precisely to eliminate vacuums of authority over the electricity markets. See *supra,* at 265–266, 193 L. Ed. 2d, at 668-669. The Act makes federal and state powers "complementary" and "comprehensive," so that "there [will] be no 'gaps' for private interests to subvert the public welfare." *Louisiana Power & Light Co.,* 406 U.S., at 631, 92 S. Ct. 1827, 32 L. Ed. 2d 369. Or said otherwise, the statute prevents the creation of any regulatory "no man's land." *FPC* v. *Transcontinental Gas Pipe Line Corp.,* 365 U.S. 1, 19, 81 S. Ct. 435, 5 L. Ed. 2d 377 (1961); see *id.,* at 28. Some entity must have jurisdiction to regulate each and every practice that takes place in the electricity markets, demand response no less than any other.[10]

For that reason, the upshot of EPSA's view would be to extinguish the wholesale demand response program in its entirety. Under the FPA, each market operator must submit

[577 U.S. 290]

to FERC all its proposed rules and procedures. See 16 U.S.C. §§ 824d(c)-(d); 18 CFR §§ 35.28(c)(4), 35.3(a)(1). Assume that, as EPSA argues, FERC could not authorize any demand response program as part of that package. Nor could FERC simply allow such plans to go into effect without its consideration and approval. There are no "off the books" programs in the wholesale electricity markets—be-

cause, once again, there is no regulatory "no man's land." *Transcontinental,* 365 U.S., at 19, 81 S. Ct. 435, 5 L. Ed. 2d 377. The FPA mandates that FERC review, and ensure the reasonableness of, every wholesale rule and practice. See 16 U.S.C. §§ 824d(a), 824e(a); *supra,* at 266, 277, 193 L. Ed. 2d, at 668–669, 675. If FERC could not carry out that duty for demand response, then those programs could not go forward.

And that outcome would flout the FPA's core objects. The statute aims to protect "against excessive prices" and ensure effective transmission of electric power. *Pennsylvania Water & Power Co.* v. *FPC,* 343 U.S. 414, 418, 72 S. Ct. 843, 96 L. Ed. 1042 (1952); see *Gulf States Util. Co.* v. *FPC,* 411 U.S. 747, 758, 93 S. Ct. 1870, 36 L. Ed. 2d 635 (1973). As shown above, FERC has amply explained how wholesale demand response helps to achieve those ends, by bringing down costs and preventing service interruptions in peak periods. See *supra,* at 282, 193 L. Ed. 2d, at 678. No one taking part in the rulemaking process—not even EPSA—seriously challenged that account. Even as he objected to FERC's compensation formula, Commissioner Moeller noted the unanimity of opinion as to demand response's value: "[N]owhere did I review any comment or hear any testimony that questioned the benefit

---

10. The dissent contests this point (complaining that our decades' worth of precedents affirming it partly rely on legislative history), but the example the dissent offers in response misses the mark. See *post,* at 301–303, 193 L. Ed. 2d, at 690-692. The dissent hypothesizes a rule enabling generators to sell directly to consumers and fixing all generation, transmission, and retail rates. But of course neither FERC nor the States could issue such a rule: If FERC did so, it would interfere with the States' authority over retail sales and rates as well as (most) generation; if a State did so, it would interfere with FERC's power over transmission. Thus, to implement such a scheme, the States would need to do some things and FERC to do others. And if the one or the other declined to cooperate, then the full scheme could not proceed. But that just goes to show that the FPA divides regulatory power over electricity matters between FERC and the States. The example does nothing to demonstrate that some electricity transactions can proceed outside any regulator's authority.

of having demand response resources participate in the organized wholesale energy markets. On this point, there is no debate." 76 Fed. Reg. 16679; see also App. 82, EPSA, Comments on Proposed Rule (avowing "full[ ] support" for demand response participation in wholesale markets because of its "economic and operational" benefits).[11] Congress itself

[577 U.S. 291]

agreed, "encourag[ing]" greater use of demand response participation at the wholesale level. EPAct § 1252(f), 119 Stat. 966. That undisputed judgment extinguishes any last flicker of life in EPSA's argument. We will not read the FPA, against its clear terms, to halt a practice that so evidently enables the Commission to fulfill its statutory duties of holding down prices and enhancing reliability in the wholesale energy market.

III

These cases present a second, narrower question: Is FERC's decision to compensate demand response providers at LMP—the same price paid to generators—arbitrary and capricious? Recall here the basic issue. See *supra*, at 272–275, 193 L. Ed. 2d, at 672-674. Wholesale market operators pay a single price—LMP—for all successful bids to supply electricity at a given time and place. The Rule orders operators to pay the identical price for

a successful bid to conserve electricity so long as that bid can satisfy a "net benefits test"—meaning that it is sure to bring down costs for wholesale purchasers. In mandating that payment, FERC rejected an alternative proposal under which demand response providers would receive LMP minus G (LMP–G), where G is the retail rate for electricity. According to EPSA and others favoring that approach,

[577 U.S. 292]

demand response providers get a windfall—a kind of "double-payment"—unless market operators subtract the savings associated with conserving electricity from the ordinary compensation level. 76 Fed. Reg. 16663, ¶24. EPSA now claims that FERC failed to adequately justify its choice of LMP rather than LMP–G.

In reviewing that decision, we may not substitute our own judgment for that of the Commission. [9] The "scope of review under the 'arbitrary and capricious' standard is narrow." *Motor Vehicle Mfrs. Assn. of United States, Inc.* v. *State Farm Mut. Automobile Ins. Co.*, 463 U.S. 29, 43, 103 S. Ct. 2856, 77 L. Ed. 2d 443 (1983). A court is not to ask whether a regulatory decision is the best one possible or even whether it is better than the alternatives. Rather, the court must uphold a rule if the agency has "examine[d] the relevant [considerations]

---

11. EPSA now contends that wholesale demand response is unnecessary because state regulators can adopt programs to reduce demand at the retail level. See Brief for Respondents 46-47. For example, States can insist that utilities give rebates to customers for not using energy at certain times. See n. 2, *supra*. But according to both the Commission and market participants, state-level programs cannot offer nearly the same benefits as wholesale demand response because individual utilities lack the regional scope and real-time information needed to identify when demand response will lower prices and ensure reliability system-wide. See 73 Fed. Reg. 64103, ¶18; Energy Primer 45-46; Brief for NRG Energy, Inc., as *Amicus Curiae* 20-22. Similarly, FERC addressed and rejected the dissent's suggestion that wholesale market operators could pay LSEs to reduce their electricity purchases: Because LSEs lose revenues whenever demand goes down, any demand response programs targeting those actors would be highly inefficient. See FERC, Assessment of Demand Response and Advanced Metering 72 (2006); Tr. of Oral Arg. 56 (Solicitor General noting that LSEs engaged in demand response would be "cannibaliz[ing] their own profits").

and articulate[d] a satisfactory explanation for its action[,] including a rational connection between the facts found and the choice made." *Ibid.* (internal quotation marks omitted). And nowhere is that more true than in a technical area like electricity rate design: "[W]e afford great deference to the Commission in its rate decisions." *Morgan Stanley*, 554 U.S., at 532, 128 S. Ct. 2733, 171 L. Ed. 2d 607.

Here, the Commission gave a detailed explanation of its choice of LMP. See 76 Fed. Reg. 16661-16669, ¶¶18-67. Relying on an eminent regulatory economist's views, FERC chiefly reasoned that demand response bids should get the same compensation as generators' bids because both provide the same value to a wholesale market. See *id.*, at 16662-16664, 16667-16668, ¶¶20, 31, 57, 61; see also App. 829-851, Reply Affidavit of Dr. Alfred E. Kahn (Aug. 30, 2010) (Kahn Affidavit). FERC noted that a market operator needs to constantly balance supply and demand, and that either kind of bid can perform that service cost-effectively—*i.e.*, in a way that lowers costs for wholesale purchasers. See 76 Fed. Reg. 16667-16668, ¶¶56, 61. A compensation system, FERC concluded, therefore should place the two kinds of bids "on

[577 U.S. 293]

a competitive par." *Id.*, at 16668, ¶61 (quoting Kahn Affidavit); see also App. 830, Kahn Affidavit (stating that "economic efficiency requires" compensating the two equally given their equivalent function in a "competitive power market[ ]"). With both supply and demand response available on equal terms, the operator will select whichever bids, of whichever kind, provide the needed electricity at the lowest possible cost. See Rehearing Order, 137 FERC, at 62,301-62,302, ¶68 ("By ensuring that both . . . re-

ceive the same compensation for the same service, we expect the Final Rule to enhance the competitiveness" of wholesale markets and "result in just and reasonable rates").

That rationale received added support from FERC's adoption of the net benefits test. The Commission realized during its rulemaking that in some circumstances a demand response bid—despite reducing the wholesale rate—does *not* provide the same value as generation. See 76 Fed. Reg. 16664-16665, ¶38. As described earlier, that happens when the distinctive costs associated with compensating a demand response bid exceed the savings from a lower wholesale rate: The purchaser then winds up paying more than if the operator had accepted the best (even though higher priced) supply bid available. See *supra*, at 273–274, 193 L. Ed. 2d, at 673. And so FERC developed the net benefits test to filter out such cases. See 76 Fed. Reg. 16666-16667, ¶¶50-53. With that standard in place, LMP is paid only to demand response bids that benefit wholesale purchasers—in other words, to those that function as "cost-effective alternative[s] to the next highest-bid generation." *Id.*, at 16667, ¶54. Thus, under the Commission's approach, a demand response provider will receive the same compensation as a generator only when it is in fact providing the same service to the wholesale market. See *ibid.*, ¶53.

The Commission responded at length to EPSA's contrary view that paying LMP, even in that situation, will overcompensate demand response providers because they are also "effectively receiv[ing] 'G,' the retail rate that they do not

[577 U.S. 294]

need to pay." *Id.*, at 16668, ¶60. FERC explained

that compensation ordinarily reflects only the value of the service an entity provides—not the costs it incurs, or benefits it obtains, in the process. So when a generator presents a bid, "the Commission does not inquire into the costs or benefits of production." *Ibid.*, ¶62. Different power plants have different cost structures. And, indeed, some plants receive tax credits and similar incentive payments for their activities, while others do not. See Rehearing Order, 137 FERC, at 62,301, ¶65, and n. 122. But the Commission had long since decided that such matters are irrelevant: Paying LMP to all generators—although some then walk away with more profit and some with less—"encourages more efficient supply and demand decisions." 76 Fed. Reg. 16668, ¶62 (internal quotation marks omitted). And the Commission could see no economic reason to treat demand response providers any differently. Like generators, they too experience a range of benefits and costs—both the benefits of not paying for electricity and the costs of not using it at a certain time. But, FERC again concluded, that is immaterial: To increase competition and optimally balance supply and demand, market operators should compensate demand response providers, like generators, based on their contribution to the wholesale system. See *ibid.*; 137 FERC, at 62,300, ¶60.

Moreover, FERC found, paying LMP will help demand response providers overcome certain barriers to participation in the wholesale market. See 76 Fed. Reg. 16667-16668, ¶¶57-59. Commenters had detailed significant start-up expenses associated with demand response, including the cost of installing necessary metering technology and energy management systems. See *id.*, at 16661, ¶18, 16667-16668, ¶57; see also, *e.g.*, App. 356, Viridity Energy, Inc., Comments on Proposed Rule on Demand Response Compensation in Organized Wholesale Energy Markets (May 13, 2010) (noting the "capital investments and operational changes needed" for demand response participation). The Commission agreed that

[577 U.S. 295]

such factors inhibit potential demand responders from competing with generators in the wholesale markets. See 76 Fed. Reg. 16668, ¶59. It concluded that rewarding demand response at LMP (which is, in any event, the price reflecting its value to the market) will encourage that competition and, in turn, bring down wholesale prices. See *ibid.*

Finally, the Commission noted that determining the "G" in the formula LMP–G is easier proposed than accomplished. See *ibid.*, ¶63. Retail rates vary across and even within States, and change over time as well. Accordingly, FERC concluded, requiring market operators to incorporate G into their prices, "even though perhaps feasible," would "create practical difficulties." *Ibid.* Better, then, not to impose that administrative burden.

All of that together is enough. The Commission, not this or any other court, regulates electricity rates. The disputed question here involves both technical understanding and policy judgment. The Commission addressed that issue seriously and carefully, providing reasons in support of its position and responding to the principal alternative advanced. In upholding that action, we do not discount the cogency of EPSA's arguments in favor of LMP–G. Nor do we say that in opting for LMP instead,

FERC made the better call. It is not our job to render that judgment, on which reasonable minds can differ. Our important but limited role is to ensure that the Commission engaged in reasoned decisionmaking—that it weighed competing views, selected a compensation formula with adequate support in the record, and intelligibly explained the reasons for making that choice. FERC satisfied that standard.

IV

FERC's statutory authority extends to the Rule at issue here addressing wholesale demand response. The Rule governs a practice directly affecting wholesale electricity rates. And although (inevitably) influencing the retail market too,

[577 U.S. 296]

the Rule does not intrude on the States' power to regulate retail sales. FERC set the terms of transactions occurring in the organized wholesale markets, so as to ensure the reasonableness of wholesale prices and the reliability of the interstate grid—just as the FPA contemplates. And in choosing a compensation formula, the Commission met its duty of reasoned judgment. FERC took full account of the alternative policies proposed, and adequately supported and explained its decision. Accordingly, we reverse the judgment of the Court of Appeals for the District of Columbia Circuit and remand the cases for further proceedings consistent with this opinion.

It is so ordered.

Justice **Alito** took no part in the consideration or decision of these cases.

SEPARATE OPINION

Justice **Scalia**, with whom Justice **Thomas** joins, dissenting.

I believe the Federal Power Act (FPA or Act), 16 U.S.C. § 791a *et seq.*, prohibits the Federal Energy Regulatory Commission (FERC) from regulating the demand response of retail purchasers of power. I respectfully dissent from the Court's holding to the contrary.

I

A

I agree with the majority that FERC has the authority to regulate practices "affecting" wholesale rates. §§ 824d(a), 824e(a); *Mississippi Power & Light Co.* v. *Mississippi ex rel. Moore*, 487 U.S. 354, 371, 108 S. Ct. 2428, 101 L. Ed. 2d 322 (1988). I also agree that this so-called "affecting" jurisdiction cannot be limitless. And I suppose I could even live with the Court's "direct effect" test as a reasonable limit. *Ante*, at 278, 193 L. Ed. 2d, at 676. But as the majority recognizes, *ante*, at 279–280, 193 L. Ed. 2d, at 677, that extratextual limit on the "affecting" jurisdiction merely supplements, not supplants,

[577 U.S. 297]

limits that are already contained in the statutory text and structure. I believe the Court misconstrues the primary statutory limit. (Like the majority, I think that deference under *Chevron U.S.A. Inc.* v. *Natural Resources Defense Council, Inc.*, 467 U.S. 837, 104 S. Ct. 2778, 81 L. Ed. 2d 694 (1984), is unwarranted because the statute is clear.)

The Act grants FERC authority to regulate the "generation . . . [and] transmission of electric energy in interstate commerce and the sale of such energy at wholesale." § 824(a). Yet the majority frames the issue

687

thusly: "[T]o uphold the [r]ule, we also must determine that it does not regulate *retail* electricity sales." *Ante*, at 279, 193 L. Ed. 2d, at 677. That formulation inverts the proper inquiry. The pertinent question under the Act is whether the rule regulates sales "*at wholesale*." If so, it falls within FERC's regulatory authority. If not, the rule is unauthorized whether or not it happens to regulate "*retail* electricity sales"; for, with exceptions not material here, the FPA prohibits FERC from regulating "*any other* sale of electric energy" that is *not* at wholesale. § 824(b)(1) (emphasis added). (The majority wisely ignores FERC's specious argument that the demand-response rule does not regulate any sale, wholesale or retail. See Brief for Petitioner in No. 14-840, p. 39. Paying someone *not* to conclude a transaction that otherwise would without a doubt have been concluded is most assuredly a regulation of that transaction. Cf. *Gonzales* v. *Raich*, 545 U.S. 1, 39-40, 125 S. Ct. 2195, 162 L. Ed. 2d 1 (2005) (Scalia, J., concurring in judgment).)

Properly framing the inquiry matters not because I think there exists "some undefined category of . . . electricity sales" that is "non-retail [and] non-wholesale," *ante,* at 280, n. 7, 193 L. Ed. 2d, at 677,*

[577 U.S. 298]

but because a proper framing of the inquiry is important to establish the default presumption regarding the scope of FERC's authority. While the majority would find every sale of electric energy to be *within* FERC's authority to regulate *unless* the transaction is demonstrably a retail sale, the statute actually *excludes* from FERC's jurisdiction all sales of electric energy *except* those that are demonstrably sales at wholesale.

So what, exactly, is a "sale of electric energy at wholesale"? We need not guess, for the Act provides a definition: "a sale of electric energy to any person *for resale*." § 824(d) (emphasis added). No matter how many times the majority incants and italicizes the word "wholesale," *ante*, at 282–283, 193 L. Ed. 2d, at 678-679, nothing can change the fact that the vast majority of (and likely all) demand-response participants—"[a]ggregators of multiple users of electricity, as well as large-scale individual users like factories or big-box stores," *ante*, at 270, 193 L. Ed. 2d, at 671—*do not resell electric energy*; they consume it themselves. FERC's own definition of demand response is aimed at energy *consumers*, not resellers. 18 CFR § 35.28(b)(4) (2015).

It is therefore quite beside the point that the challenged "[r]ule addresses—and addresses only—transactions occurring on the wholesale market," *ante*, at 282, 193 L. Ed. 2d, at 678. For FERC's regulatory authority over electric-energy sales depends not on which "market" the "transactions occu[r] on" (whatever that means), but rather on the *identity of the putative purchaser*. If the purchaser is one who resells electric energy to other customers, the transaction is one "at wholesale" and thus within FERC's authority. If not, then not. Or so, at least, says the statute.

---

*Although the majority dismisses this possibility, in fact it appears to think that demand response is in that category: It rejects the conclusion that the demand-response rule regulates retail sales, *ante*, at 279–286, 193 L. Ed. 2d, at 677-681, yet also implicitly rejects the conclusion that it regulates wholesale sales—otherwise why rely on FERC's "affecting" jurisdiction to rescue the rule's legitimacy?

As we long ago said of the parallel provision in the Natural Gas Act, 15 U.S.C. § 717, "[t]he line of the statute [i]s thus clear and complete. It cut[s] sharply and cleanly between sales for resale and direct sales for consumptive uses. No exceptions [a]re made in either category for particular uses, quantities, or otherwise." *Panhandle Eastern Pipe Line Co.* v. *Public Serv. Comm'n of Ind.*, 332

[577 U.S. 299]

U.S. 507, 517, 68 S. Ct. 190, 92 L. Ed. 128 (1947). The majority makes no textual response to this plain reading of the statute.

The demand-response bidders here indisputably do not resell energy to other customers. It follows that the rule does not regulate electric-energy sales "at wholesale," and 16 U.S.C. § 824(b)(1) therefore forbids FERC to regulate these demand-response transactions. See *New York* v. *FERC*, 535 U.S. 1, 17, 122 S. Ct. 1012, 152 L. Ed. 2d 47 (2002). That is so whether or not those transactions "directly affect" wholesale rates; as we recently said in another context, we will not adopt a construction that "needlessly produces a contradiction in the statutory text." *Shapiro* v. *McManus, ante,* at 43, 136 S. Ct. 450, 193 L. Ed. 2d 279 (2015). A faithful application of that principle would compel the conclusion that FERC may not "do under [§§ 824d(a) and 824e(a)] what [it] is forbidden to do under [§ 824(b)(1)]." *Ante,* at 44, 136 S. Ct. 450, 193 L. Ed. 2d 279.

B

The analysis could stop there. But the majority is wrong even on its own terms, for the rule at issue here does in fact regulate *"retail* electricity sales," which are indisputably "matters . . . subject to regulation by the States" and therefore off-limits to FERC. § 824(a); see *FPC* v. *Conway Corp.,* 426 U.S. 271, 276, 96 S. Ct. 1999, 48 L. Ed. 2d 626 (1976); *Panhandle Eastern Pipe Line Co., supra,* at 517-518, 68 S. Ct. 190, 92 L. Ed. 2d 128. The demand-response participants are retail customers—they purchase electric energy solely for their own consumption. And FERC's demand-response scheme is intentionally "designed to induce lower consumption of electric energy"—in other words, to induce a reduction in *"retail* electricity sales"—by offering "incentive payments" to those customers. 18 CFR § 35.28(b)(4). The incentive payments effectively increase the retail price of electric energy for participating customers because they must now account for the opportunity cost of using, as opposed to abstaining from using, more energy. In other words, it literally *costs them more* to buy energy on the retail market. In the court below, FERC conceded that offering

[577 U.S. 300]

credits to retail customers to reduce their electricity consumption "would be an impermissible intrusion into the retail market" because it would in effect regulate retail rates. 753 F.3d 216, 223 (CADC 2014). Demand-response incentive payments are identical in substance.

The majority resists this elementary economic conclusion (notwithstanding its own exhortation to "think back to Econ 101," *ante,* at 268, 193 L. Ed. 2d, at 670). Why? Because its self-proclaimed "common-sensical" view dictates otherwise. *Ante,* at 285, 193 L. Ed. 2d, at 680. Maybe the easiest way to see the majority's error is to take its own example: an airline passenger who rejects a $300 voucher for taking a later flight. Consider the following formulation of that example, indistinguishable in substance from the majority's formulation. (Indistinguishable because the hypothetical passenger has exactly the same options and outcomes available to him.) Suppose the airline said to the passenger: "We have proactively canceled your ticket and refunded $400 to your account; and because we have inconvenienced you, we have also deposited an extra $300. The money is yours to use as you like. But if you insist on repurchasing a ticket on the same flight, you must not only pay us $400, but return the $300 too." *Now* what is the effective price of the ticket? Sometimes an allegedly commonsensical intuition is just that—an intuition, often mistaken.

Moving closer to home, recall that demand-response participants must choose either to purchase a unit of energy at the prevailing retail price (say $10) or to withhold from purchasing that unit and receive instead an incentive payment (of say $5). The two options thus present a choice between having a unit of energy, on the one hand, and having $15 more in the bank, on the other. To repeat: take the energy, be $15 poorer; forgo the energy, be $15 richer. Is that not the very definition of price? See Black's Law Dictionary 1380 (10th ed. 2014) ("[t]he amount of money or other consideration asked for or given in exchange for something else"). In fact, is that not *the majority's* definition of price? *Ante,*

[577 U.S. 301]

at 284, 193 L. Ed. 2d, at 679 ("the amount of money a consumer will hand over in exchange for power").

In any event, the majority appears to recognize that the effective price is indeed $15—just as the effective price of the airline ticket in the hypotheti-cal is $700. *Ante,* at 285, n. 9, 193 L. Ed. 2d, at 680. That recognition gives away the game. For FERC is prohibited not just from directly setting or modifying retail *prices*; it is prohibited from regulating retail *sales*, no matter the means. *Panhandle Eastern Pipe Line Co., supra,* at 517, 68 S. Ct. 190, 92 L. Ed. 2d 128. Whether FERC sets the "real" retail price (to use the majority's idiosyncratic terminology, *ante,* at 285, n. 9, 193 L. Ed. 2d, at 680) or the "effective" retail price is immaterial; either way, the rule—*by design*—induces demand-response participants to forgo retail electric-energy purchases they otherwise would have made. As noted, even FERC conceded that offering credits to retail customers would impermissibly regulate retail sales. The majority blithely overlooks this concession in favor of its own myopic view of retail pricing—all the while evading the inconvenient fact that fiddling with the effective retail price of electric energy, be it through incentive payments or hypothetical credits, *regulates retail sales* of electric energy no less than does direct ratesetting.

C

The majority cites dicta in several of our opinions expressing the assumption that state jurisdiction and federal jurisdiction under FERC cover the field, so that there is no regulatory "gap"; one entity or the other "must have jurisdiction to regulate each and every practice that takes place in the electricity markets." *Ante,* at 289, 193 L. Ed. 2d, at 683. The cases that express such a principle, with respect to the Federal Power Act and its companion the Natural Gas Act, base it (no surprise) on legislative history. See, *e.g., FPC* v. *Louisiana Power & Light Co.,* 406 U.S. 621, 631, 92 S. Ct. 1827, 32 L. Ed. 2d 369 (1972); *FPC* v.

Transcontinental Gas Pipe Line Corp., 365 U.S. 1, 19, 81 S. Ct. 435, 5 L. Ed. 2d 377 (1961); *Panhandle Eastern Pipe Line Co.*, 332 U.S., at 517-518, and

[577 U.S. 302]

n. 13, 68 S. Ct. 190, 92 L. Ed. 2d 128. One would *expect* the congressional proponents of legislation to assert that it is "comprehensive" and leaves no stone unturned. But even if one is a fan of legislative history, surely one cannot rely upon such generalities in determining what a statute actually *does*. Whether it is "comprehensive" and leaves not even the most minor regulatory "gap" surely depends on what it says and not on what its proponents hoped to achieve. I cannot imagine a more irrational interpretive principle than the following, upon which the majority evidently relies:

"[W]hen a dispute arises over whether a given transaction is within the scope of federal or state regulatory authority, we are not inclined to approach the problem negatively, thus raising the possibility that a 'no man's land' will be created. That is to say, in a borderline case where congressional authority is not explicit we must ask whether state authority can practicably regulate a given area and, if we find that it cannot, then we are impelled to decide that federal authority governs." *Transcontinental Gas Pipe Line Corp.*, *supra*, at 19-20, 81 S. Ct. 435, 5 L. Ed. 2d 377 (citation omitted).

That extravagant and otherwise-unheard-of method of establishing regulatory jurisdiction was not necessary to the judgments that invoked it, and should disappear in the Court's memory hole.

Suppose FERC decides that eliminating the middleman would benefit the public, and therefore promulgates a rule allowing electric-energy generators to sell directly to retail consumers across state lines and fixing generation, transmission, and retail rates for such sales. I think it obvious this hypothetical scheme would be forbidden to FERC. Yet just as surely the States could not enact it either, for only FERC has authority to regulate "the transmission of electric energy in interstate commerce." 16 U.S.C. § 824(b)(1); see also *New York*, 535 U.S., at 19-20, 122 S. Ct. 1012, 152 L. Ed. 2d 47. Is this a regulatory

[577 U.S. 303]

"gap"? Has the generator-to-consumer sales scheme fallen into a regulatory "no man's land"? *Must* FERC therefore be allowed to implement this scheme on its own? Applying the majority's *logic* would yield nothing but "yesses." Yet the majority acknowledges that neither FERC nor the States have regulatory jurisdiction over this scheme. *Ante*, at 289, n. 10, 193 L. Ed. 2d, at 683. Such sales transactions, involving a mix of retail and wholesale players—*as the demand-response scheme does*—can be regulated (if at all) only by joint action. I would not call that a "problem," *ante*, at 289, 193 L. Ed. 2d, at 682; I would call it an inevitable consequence of the federal-state division created by the FPA.

The majority is evidently distraught that affirming the decision below "would . . . extinguish the wholesale demand response program in its entirety." *Ibid.* Alarmist hyperbole. Excluding FERC jurisdiction would at most eliminate *this particular flavor* of FERC-regulated demand response. Nothing prevents FERC from tweaking its demand-response scheme by requiring incentive payments to be offered to *wholesale* customers, rather than retail ones. Brief for Respondent Electric Power Supply Assn. (EPSA) et al. 47-48; Brief for Respondents Midwest Load-Serving Entities 10-11. And retail-level demand-response programs, run by the States, do and would continue to exist. See Brief for Respondent EPSA et al. 46-47; Brief for Respondents Midwest Load-Serving Entities 6-11. In fact Congress seemed to presuppose that *States*, not FERC, would run such programs: The relevant provisions of the Energy Policy Act of 2005, 119 Stat. 594 *et seq*, are intended "to encourage *States* to coordinate, on a regional basis, *State* energy policies to provide reliable and affordable demand response services." § 1252(e)(1), *id.*, at 965, codified at 16 U.S.C. § 2642 note (emphasis added). That statute also imposes several duties on the Secretary of Energy to assist States in implementing demand-response programs. §§ 1252(e)(2), (e)(3), 119 Stat. 965-966. In context, § 1252(f)

[577 U.S. 304]

of the 2005 Act is therefore best read as directing the Secretary to eliminate "unnecessary barriers" to *States'* adopting and implementing demand-response systems—and not, as the majority contends, as "praising *wholesale* demand response" systems to be deployed and regulated by FERC, *ante*, at 271, 193 L. Ed. 2d, at 671–672 (emphasis added).

Moreover, the rule itself allows States to forbid their retail customers to participate in the existing demand-response scheme. 18 CFR § 35.28(g)(1)(i)(A); see Brief for Petitioner in No. 14-840, at 43. The majority accepts FERC's argument that this is merely a matter of grace, and claims that it puts the "finishing blow" to respondents' argument that 16 U.S.C. § 824(b)(1) prohibits the

scheme. *Ante*, at 287, 193 L. Ed. 2d, at 682. Quite the contrary. Remember that the majority believes FERC's authority derives from 16 U.S.C. §§ 824d(a) and 824e(a), the grants of "affecting" jurisdiction. Yet those provisions impose a *duty* on FERC to ensure that "all rules and regulations affecting or pertaining to [wholesale] rates or charges *shall be just and reasonable*." § 824d(a) (emphasis added); see § 824e(a) (similar); *Conway Corp.*, 426 U.S., at 277-279, 96 S. Ct. 1999, 48 L. Ed. 2d 626. If inducing retail customers to participate in wholesale demand-response transactions is necessary to render wholesale rates "just and reasonable," how can FERC, consistent with its statutory mandate, permit States to thwart such participation? See Brief for United States as *Amicus Curiae* 20-21, in *Hughes* v. *Talen Energy Marketing, LLC*, No. 14-614 etc., now pending before the Court (making an argument similar to ours); cf. *New England Power Co.* v. *New Hampshire*, 455 U.S. 331, 339-341, 102 S. Ct. 1096, 71 L. Ed. 2d 188 (1982). Although not legally relevant, the fact that FERC—ordinarily so jealous of its regulatory authority, see Brief for United States as *Amicus Curiae* in No. 14-614 etc.—is willing to let States opt out of its demand-response scheme serves to highlight just how far the rule intrudes into the retail electricity market.

[577 U.S. 305]

II

Having found the rule to be within FERC's authority, the Court goes on to hold that FERC's choice of compensating demand-response bidders with the "locational marginal price" is not arbitrary and capricious. There are strong arguments that it is. Brief for Robert L. Borlick et al. as *Amici*

Curiae 5-34. Since, however, I believe FERC's rule is ultra vires I have neither need nor desire to analyze whether, if it were not ultra vires, it would be reasonable.

* * *

For the foregoing reasons, I respectfully dissent.

[577 U.S. 306]

MELENE JAMES, Petitioner

v

CITY OF BOISE, IDAHO, et al.

577 U.S. 306, 136 S. Ct. 685, 193 L. Ed. 2d 694, 2016 U.S. LEXIS 947

[No. 15-493]

Decided January 25, 2016.

Prior history: ON PETITION FOR WRIT OF CERTIORARI TO THE SUPREME COURT OF IDAHO, 158 Idaho 713, 351 P.3d 1171, 2015 Ida. LEXIS 130

SYLLABUS BY REPORTER OF DECISIONS

For text of added syllabus for this case see p 814F, infra.

[577 U.S. 306]

PER CURIAM.

Under federal law, a court has discretion to "allow the prevailing party, other than the United States, a reasonable attorney's fee" in a civil rights lawsuit filed under 42 U.S.C. § 1983. 42 U.S.C. § 1988(b). In *Hughes* v. *Rowe*, 449 U.S. 5, 101 S. Ct. 173, 66 L. Ed. 2d 163 (1980) (*per curiam*), this Court interpreted § 1988 to permit a prevailing defendant in such a suit to recover fees only if "the plaintiff's action was frivolous, unreasonable, or without foundation." *Id.*, at 14, 101 S. Ct. 173, 66 L. Ed. 2d 163 (quoting *Christiansburg Garment Co.* v. *EEOC*, 434 U.S. 412, 421, 98 S. Ct. 694, 54 L. Ed. 2d 648 (1978) (internal quotation marks omitted)).

In the decision below, the Idaho Supreme Court concluded that it was not bound by this Court's interpretation of § 1988 in *Hughes*. According to that court, "[a]lthough the Supreme Court may have the authority to limit the discretion of lower federal courts, it does not have the authority to limit the discretion of state courts where such limitation is not

[577 U.S. 307]

contained in the statute." 158 Idaho 713, 734, 351 P.3d 1171, 1192 (2015). The court then proceeded to award attorney's fees

under § 1988 to a prevailing defendant without first determining that "the plaintiff's action was frivolous, unreasonable, or without foundation." The court's fee award rested solely on its interpretation of federal law; the court explicitly refused to award fees under state law. *Id.*, at 734-735, 351 P.3d, at 1192-1193. We grant certiorari, and now reverse.

Section 1988 is a federal statute. "It is this Court's responsibility to say what a [federal] statute means, and once the Court has spoken, it is the duty of other courts to respect that understanding of the governing rule of law." *Nitro-Lift Technologies, L.L.C.* v. *Howard*, 568 U.S. 17, 21, 133 S. Ct. 500, 184 L. Ed. 2d 328 (2012) (*per curiam*) (quoting *Rivers* v. *Roadway Express, Inc.*, 511 U.S. 298, 312, 114 S. Ct. 1510, 128 L. Ed. 2d 274 (1994) internal quotation marks omitted). And for good reason. As Justice Story explained 200 years ago, if state courts were permitted to disregard this Court's rulings on federal law, "the laws, the treaties, and the constitution of the United States would be different in different states, and might, perhaps, never have precisely the same construction, obligation, or efficacy, in any two states. The public

694

mischiefs that would attend such a state of things would be truly deplorable." *Martin* v. *Hunter's Lessee*, 1 Wheat. 304, 348, 4 L. Ed. 97 (1816).

The Idaho Supreme Court, like any other state or federal court, is bound by this Court's interpretation of federal law. The state court erred in concluding otherwise. The judgment of the Idaho Supreme Court is reversed, and the case is remanded for further proceedings not inconsistent with this opinion.

It is so ordered.

AMGEN INC., et al., Petitioners

v

STEVE HARRIS, et al.

577 U.S. 308, 136 S. Ct. 758, 193 L. Ed. 2d 696, 2016 U.S. LEXIS 891

[No. 15-278]

Decided January 25, 2016.

Decision: Former corporate employees, who had participated in plans that qualified under ERISA provision (29 U.S.C.S. § 1107(d)(3)(A)) as eligible individual account plans, failed to state claim under ERISA (29 U.S.C.S. § 1001 et seq.) for breach of fiduciary duties.

Prior history: ON PETITION FOR WRIT OF CERTIORARI TO THE UNITED STATES COURT OF APPEALS FOR THE NINTH CIRCUIT, 788 F.3d 916, 2015 U.S. App. LEXIS 9695

SUMMARY

Overview: HOLDINGS: [1]-Where stockholders, former employees who participated in plans that offered ownership in employer stock, alleged that fiduciaries breached their fiduciary duties, including the duty of prudence, under the Employee Retirement Income Security Act of 1974, 29 U.S.C.S. § 1001 et seq., and the appellate court, initially and on remand, reversed the dismissal of the complaint, remand was warranted because the Supreme Court did not find sufficient facts and allegations to state a claim for breach of the duty of prudence; [2]-The appellate court failed to assess whether the complaint in its current form plausibly alleged that a prudent fiduciary in the same position could not have concluded that the alternative action, involving removing the employer stock fund from the list of investment options, would do more harm than good.

Outcome: Judgment reversed and case remanded for further proceedings. 9-0 per curiam decision.

SUBJECT OF ANNOTATION

Beginning on page 861, infra

Fiduciary duties under Employee Retirement Income Security Act of 1974, as amended (ERISA) (29 U.S.C.S. § 1001 et seq.)— Supreme Court cases

---

HEADNOTES

Classified to United States Supreme Court Digest, Lawyers' Edition

Fiduciary duties — presumption

L Ed Digest: Evidence § 185; Pensions and Retirement Funds § 12

1. Regarding Employee Retirement Income Security Act of 1974 (ERISA), 29 U.S.C.S. § 1001 et seq., fiduciaries who administer employee stock ownership plans, such ERISA fiduciaries are not entitled to a presumption of prudence but are subject to the same duty of prudence that applies to ERISA fiduciaries in general, except that they need not diversify the fund's assets.

[See annotation p 861, infra]

Fiduciary duties — prudence

L Ed Digest: Pensions and Retirement Funds § 12

2. Notwithstanding the lack of a presumption of prudence, Fifth Third

Bancorp v. Dudenhoeffer noted that Congress sought to encourage the creation of employee stock-ownership plans, a purpose that the decision recognized may come into tension with the Employee Retirement Income Security Act of 1974's, 29 U.S.C.S. § 1001 et seq., general duty of prudence. Moreover, employee stock ownership plan fiduciaries confront unique challenges given the potential for conflict that arises when fiduciaries are alleged to have imprudently failed to act on inside information they had about the value of the employer's stock.

[See annotation p 861, infra]

Fiduciary duties — prudence

L Ed Digest: Pensions and Retirement Funds § 12

3. To state a claim for breach of the duty of prudence on the basis of inside information, a plaintiff must plausibly allege an alternative action that the defendant could have taken that would have been consistent with the securities laws and that a prudent fiduciary in the same circumstances would not have viewed as more likely to harm the fund than to help it. Courts should determine whether the complaint itself states a claim satisfying that liability standard: Lower courts faced with such claims should also consider whether the complaint has plausibly alleged that a prudent fiduciary in the defendant's position could not have concluded that stopping purchases—which the market might take as a sign that insider fiduciaries viewed the employer's stock as a bad investment—or publicly disclosing negative information would do more harm than good to the fund by causing a drop in the stock price and a concomitant drop in the value of the stock already held by the fund.

[See annotation p 861, infra]

RESEARCH REFERENCES

29 U.S.C.S. § 1001 et seq.

6 Labor and Employment Law § 153.06 (Matthew Bender)

L Ed Digest, Pensions and Retirement Funds § 12

L Ed Index, Pensions and Retirement

Annotations:

When do individuals or entities act as covered fiduciaries, for purposes of Employee Retirement Income Security Act of 1974, as amended (ERISA) (29 U.S.C.S. § 1001 et seq.)—Supreme Court cases. 142 L. Ed. 2d 1043.

SYLLABUS BY REPORTER OF DECISIONS

For text of added syllabus for this case see p 814G, infra.

OPINION OF THE COURT

[577 U.S. 308]

Per Curiam.

The Court considers for the second time the Ninth Circuit's determination that respondent stockholders' complaint states a claim against petitioner fiduciaries for breach of the duty of prudence. The first time, the Court vacated and remanded in light of *Fifth Third Bancorp* v. *Dudenhoeffer*, 573 U.S. 409, 134 S. Ct. 2459, 189 L. Ed. 2d 457 (2014), a case which set forth the standards for stating

[577 U.S. 309]

a claim for breach of the duty of prudence against fiduciaries who manage employee stock ownership plans (ESOPs). On remand, the Ninth Circuit reiterated its conclusion that the complaint states such a claim. The Court now reverses and remands.

The stockholders are former employees of Amgen Inc. and its subsidiary Amgen Manufacturing, Limited, who participated in plans that qualified under 29 U.S.C. § 1107(d)(3)(A) as eligible individual account plans. Like ESOPs, these plans offer ownership in employer stock as an option to employees. The parties agree that the decision in *Fifth Third* is fully applicable to the plans at issue here. See 788 F.3d 916, 935 (2014).

All of the plans had holdings in the Amgen Common Stock Fund (composed, unsurprisingly, of Amgen common stock) during the relevant period. The value of Amgen stock fell, and in 2007, the stockholders filed a class action against petitioner fiduciaries alleging that they had breached their fiduciary duties, including the duty of prudence, under the Employee Retirement Income Security Act of 1974 (ERISA), 88 Stat. 829, as amended, 29 U.S.C. § 1001 *et seq.* The

District Court granted the fiduciaries' motion to dismiss, and the Ninth Circuit reversed, *Harris* v. *Amgen, Inc.*, 738 F.3d 1026 (2013). The fiduciaries sought certiorari.

While that petition was pending, this Court issued a decision that concerned the duty of prudence owed by ERISA fiduciaries who administer ESOPs. That decision, *Fifth Third*, held that **[1]** such ERISA fiduciaries are not entitled to a presumption of prudence but are "subject to the same duty of prudence that applies to ERISA fiduciaries in general, except that they need not diversify the fund's assets." 573 U.S., at 412, 134 S. Ct. 2459, 189 L. Ed. 2d 457.

[2] Notwithstanding the lack of a presumption of prudence, *Fifth Third* noted that "Congress sought to encourage the creation of" ESOPs, *id.,* at 424, 134 S. Ct. 2459, 189 L. Ed. 2d 457, a purpose that the decision recognized may come into tension with ERISA's general

[577 U.S. 310]

duty of prudence. Moreover, ESOP fiduciaries confront unique challenges given "the potential for conflict" that arises when fiduciaries are alleged to have imprudently "fail[ed] to act on inside information they had about the value of the employer's stock." *Id.,* at 423, 134 S. Ct. 2459, 189 L. Ed. 2d 457. *Fifth Third* therefore laid out standards to help "divide the plausible sheep from the meritless goats," *id.,* at 425, 134 S. Ct. 2459, 189 L. Ed. 2d 457:

[3] "To state a claim for breach of the duty of prudence on the basis of inside information, a plaintiff must plausibly allege an alternative action that the defendant could have taken that would have been consistent with the securities laws and that a prudent fiduciary in the same circumstances would not have viewed as more likely to harm the fund than to help it." *Id.*, at 428, 134 S. Ct. 2459, 189 L. Ed. 2d 457.

It further clarified that courts should determine whether the complaint itself states a claim satisfying that liability standard:

"[L]ower courts faced with such claims should also consider whether the complaint has plausibly alleged that a prudent fiduciary in the defendant's position could not have concluded that stopping purchases—which the market might take as a sign that insider fiduciaries viewed the employer's stock as a bad investment—or publicly disclosing negative information would do more harm than good to the fund by causing a drop in the stock price and a concomitant drop in the value of the stock already held by the fund." *Id.*, at 429–430, 134 S. Ct. 2459, 189 L. Ed. 2d 457 (emphasis added).

In the matter that is once again before the Court here, following the issuance of *Fifth Third*, the Court granted the fiduciaries' first petition for a writ of certiorari, vacated the judgment, and remanded for further proceedings consistent with that decision. *Amgen Inc.* v. *Harris*, 573 U.S. 942, 134 S. Ct. 2870, 189 L. Ed. 2d 828 (2014). On remand, the Ninth Circuit reversed again the dismissal of the complaint and denied the fiduciaries' petition

[577 U.S. 311]

for rehearing en banc. See 788 F.3d 916. The fiduciaries once more sought certiorari.

The Court now holds that the Ninth Circuit failed to properly evaluate the complaint. That court explained that its previous opinion (that is, the one it issued before *Fifth Third* was decided) "had already assumed" the standards for ERISA fiduciary liability laid out by this Court in *Fifth Third*. 788 F.3d, at 940. And it reasoned that the complaint at issue here satisfies those standards because when "the federal securities laws require disclosure of material information," it is "quite plausible" that removing the Amgen Common Stock Fund "from the list of investment options" would not "caus[e] undue harm to plan participants." *Id.*, at 937-938. The Ninth Circuit, however, failed to assess whether the complaint in its current form "has plausibly alleged" that a prudent fiduciary in the same position "could not have concluded" that the alternative action "would do more harm than good." *Fifth Third, supra,* at 429–430, 134 S. Ct. 2459, 189 L. Ed. 2d 457.

The Ninth Circuit's proposition that removing the Amgen Common Stock Fund from the list of investment options was an alternative action that could plausibly have satisfied *Fifth Third*'s standards may be true. If so, the facts and allegations supporting that proposition should appear in the stockholders' complaint. Having examined the complaint, the Court has not found sufficient facts and allegations to state a claim for breach of the duty of prudence.

Although the Ninth Circuit did not correctly apply *Fifth Third*, the stockholders are the masters of their complaint. The Court leaves to the District Court in the first instance whether the stockholders may amend it in order to adequately plead a claim for breach of the duty of prudence guided by the standards provided in *Fifth Third*.

The petition for certiorari is granted.

The judgment of the Ninth Circuit is reversed, and the case is remanded for further proceedings consistent with this opinion.

It is so ordered.

MEMORANDUM CASES

No. 15-378. The Ritz-Carlton Development Company, Inc., et al., Petitioners v. Krishna Narayan, et al.

577 U.S. 1056, 136 S. Ct. 799, 193 L. Ed. 2d 701, 2016 U.S. LEXIS 288.

January 11, 2016. On petition for writ of certiorari to the Supreme Court of Hawaii. Petition for writ of certiorari granted. Judgment vacated, and case remanded to the Supreme Court of Hawaii for further consideration in light of DIRECTV, Inc. v. Imburgia, 577 U.S. 47, 136 S. Ct. 463, 193 L. Ed. 2d 365 (2015).

Same case below, 136 Hawaii 23, 356 P.3d 1043.

No. 15-379. The Ritz-Carlton Development Company, Inc., et al., Petitioners v. Virendra Nath, et al.

577 U.S. 1056, 136 S. Ct. 799, 193 L. Ed. 2d 701, 2016 U.S. LEXIS 45.

January 11, 2016. On petition for writ of certiorari to the Supreme Court of Hawaii. Petition for writ of certiorari granted. Judgment vacated, and case remanded to the Supreme Court of Hawaii for further consideration in light of DIRECTV, Inc. v. Imburgia, 577 U.S. 47, 136 S. Ct. 463, 193 L. Ed. 2d 365 (2015).

Same case below, 136 Hawaii 23, 356 P.3d 1043.

No. 15-406. The Ritz-Carlton Development Company, Inc., et al., Petitioners v. Krishna Narayan, et al.

577 U.S. 1056, 136 S. Ct. 800, 193 L. Ed. 2d 701, 2016 U.S. LEXIS 365.

January 11, 2016. On petition for writ of certiorari to the Supreme Court of Hawaii. Petition for writ of certiorari granted. Judgment vacated, and case remanded to the Supreme Court of Hawaii for further consideration in light of DIRECTV, Inc. v. Imburgia, 577 U.S. 47, 136 S. Ct. 463, 193 L. Ed. 2d 365 (2015).

Same case below, 135 Hawaii 327, 350 P.3d 995.

No. 15-6565. Elbert Phillip Long, Petitioner v. John D. Minton, Jr., Chief Justice, Supreme Court of Kentucky, et al.

577 U.S. 1056, 136 S. Ct. 805, 193 L. Ed. 2d 701, 2016 U.S. LEXIS 615.

January 11, 2016. Motion of petitioner for leave to proceed in forma pauperis denied, and petition for writ of certiorari to the United States Court of Appeals for the Sixth Circuit dismissed. See Rule 39.8.

No. 15-6581. Melinda Gabriella Valenzuela, Petitioner v. S. Johnson, et al.

577 U.S. 1056, 136 S. Ct. 806, 193 L. Ed. 2d 701, 2016 U.S. LEXIS 293.

January 11, 2016. Motion of petitioner for leave to proceed in forma pauperis denied, and petition for writ of certiorari to the United States Court of Appeals for the Ninth Circuit dismissed. See Rule 39.8.

No. 15-6582. Melinda Gabriella Valenzuela, Petitioner v. Maricopa County Correctional Health Services, et al.

577 U.S. 1056, 136 S. Ct. 878, 193 L. Ed. 2d 702, 2016 U.S. LEXIS 534.

January 11, 2016. Motion of petitioner for leave to proceed in forma pauperis denied, and petition for writ of certiorari to the United States Court of Appeals for the Ninth Circuit dismissed. See Rule 39.8.

No. 15-6674. David Webb, Petitioner v. Janine M. Kern, et al.

577 U.S. 1056, 136 S. Ct. 813, 193 L. Ed. 2d 702, 2016 U.S. LEXIS 466.

January 11, 2016. Motion of petitioner for leave to proceed in forma pauperis denied, and petition for writ of certiorari to the United States Court of Appeals for the Eighth Circuit dismissed. See Rule 39.8.

No. 15-6762. Jeffrey R. LeBlanc, Petitioner v. Keith Barber.

577 U.S. 1056, 136 S. Ct. 825, 193 L. Ed. 2d 702, 2016 U.S. LEXIS 608.

January 11, 2016. Motion of petitioner for leave to proceed in forma pauperis denied, and petition for writ of certiorari to the United States Court of Appeals for the Sixth Circuit dismissed. See Rule 39.8.

No. 15-6763. Jeffrey R. LeBlanc, Petitioner v. United States.

577 U.S. 1057, 136 S. Ct. 878, 193 L. Ed. 2d 702, 2016 U.S. LEXIS 238.

January 11, 2016. Motion of petitioner for leave to proceed in forma pauperis denied, and petition for writ of certiorari to the United States Court of Appeals for the Sixth Circuit dismissed. See Rule 39.8.

No. 15-6764. Jeffrey R. LeBlanc, Petitioner v. Jerome W. Zimmer, Jr.

577 U.S. 1057, 136 S. Ct. 825, 193 L. Ed. 2d 702, 2016 U.S. LEXIS 578.

January 11, 2016. Motion of petitioner for leave to proceed in forma pauperis denied, and petition for writ of certiorari to the United States Court of Appeals for the Sixth Circuit dismissed. See Rule 39.8.

No. 15-6765. Jeffrey R. LeBlanc, Petitioner v. Larry S. Royster.

577 U.S. 1057, 136 S. Ct. 825, 193 L. Ed. 2d 702, 2016 U.S. LEXIS 252.

January 11, 2016. Motion of petitioner for leave to proceed in forma pauperis denied, and petition for writ of certiorari to the United States Court of Appeals for the Sixth Circuit dismissed. See Rule 39.8.

No. 15-6766. Jeffrey R. LeBlanc, Petitioner v. Connie L. Branch.

577 U.S. 1057, 136 S. Ct. 825, 193 L. Ed. 2d 702, 2016 U.S. LEXIS 576.

January 11, 2016. Motion of petitioner for leave to proceed in forma pauperis denied, and petition for writ of certiorari to the United States Court of Appeals for the Sixth Circuit dismissed. See Rule 39.8.

No. 15-6860. Tyrone Leslie Farris, Petitioner v. J. Frazier, et al.

577 U.S. 1057, 136 S. Ct. 833, 193 L. Ed. 2d 703, 2016 U.S. LEXIS 538.

January 11, 2016. Motion of petitioner for leave to proceed in forma pauperis denied, and petition for writ of certiorari to the United States Court of Appeals for the Tenth Circuit dismissed. See Rule 39.8. As petitioner has repeatedly abused this Court's process, the Clerk is directed not to accept any further petitions in non-criminal matters from petitioner unless the docketing fees required by Rule 38(a) is paid and petition submitted in compliance with Rule 33.1. See Martin v. District of Columbia Court of Appeals, 506 U.S. 1, 113 S. Ct. 397, 121 L. Ed. 2d 305 (1992) (per curiam).

Same case below, 599 Fed. Appx. 851.

No. 15-6879. Tracy Nixon, Petitioner v. 301st Judicial Court, Dallas County, Texas.

577 U.S. 1057, 136 S. Ct. 835, 193 L. Ed. 2d 703, 2016 U.S. LEXIS 429.

January 11, 2016. Motion of petitioner for leave to proceed in forma pauperis denied, and petition for writ of certiorari to the Supreme Court of Texas dismissed. See Rule 39.8. As petitioner have repeatedly abused this Court's process, the Clerk is directed not to accept any further petitions in noncriminal matters from petitioner unless the docketing fees required by Rule 38(a) is paid and petition submitted in compliance with Rule 33.1. See Martin v. District of Columbia Court of Appeals, 506 U.S. 1, 113 S. Ct. 397, 121 L. Ed. 2d 305 (1992) (per curiam).

No. 15-6932. Christopher Stoller, Petitioner v. Consumer Financial Protection Bureau, et al.

577 U.S. 1057, 136 S. Ct. 879, 193 L. Ed. 2d 703, 2016 U.S. LEXIS 536.

January 11, 2016. Motion of petitioner for leave to proceed in forma pauperis denied, and petition for writ of certiorari to the United States Court of Appeals for the District of Columbia Circuit dismissed. See Rule 39.8. As petitioner has repeatedly abused this Court's process, the Clerk is directed not to accept any further petitions in noncriminal matters from petitioner unless the docketing fee required by Rule 38(a) is paid and petition submitted in compliance with Rule 33.1. See Martin v. District of Columbia Court of Appeals, 506 U.S. 1, 113 S. Ct. 397, 121 L. Ed. 2d 305 (1992) (per curiam).

No. 15A567. Sidney Bender, Applicant v. Barack H. Obama, President of the United States, et al.

577 U.S. 1058, 136 S. Ct. 871, 193 L. Ed. 2d 703, 2016 U.S. LEXIS 41.

January 11, 2016. Application for a temporary injunction pending the disposition of the petition for a writ of certiorari, addressed to Justice Scalia and referred to the Court, denied.

No. 15M66. Travis Ray Thompson, Petitioner v. G. Alvarez, et al.

577 U.S. 1058, 136 S. Ct. 871, 193 L. Ed. 2d 703, 2016 U.S. LEXIS 77.

January 11, 2016. Motion to direct the Clerk to file a petition for writ of certiorari out of time denied.

Same case below, 586 Fed. Appx. 390.

———

No. 15M67. Russell Allen, Petitioner v. United States.

577 U.S. 1058, 136 S. Ct. 871, 193 L. Ed. 2d 704, 2016 U.S. LEXIS 169.

January 11, 2016. Motion to direct the Clerk to file a petition for writ of certiorari out of time denied.

———

No. 15M68. Carmon E. Warren, Petitioner v. J. Shawnego.

577 U.S. 1058, 136 S. Ct. 871, 193 L. Ed. 2d 704, 2016 U.S. LEXIS 43.

January 11, 2016. Motion to direct the Clerk to file a petition for writ of certiorari out of time denied.

Same case below, 599 Fed. Appx. 725.

———

No. 15M69. Phillip A. Hamilton, Petitioner v. United States.

577 U.S. 1058, 136 S. Ct. 871, 193 L. Ed. 2d 704, 2016 U.S. LEXIS 25.

January 11, 2016. Motion to direct the Clerk to file a petition for writ of certiorari out of time denied.

Same case below, 589 Fed. Appx. 96.

———

No. 15M70. Scott A. Frye, Petitioner v. Luther Strange, Attorney General of Alabama.

577 U.S. 1058, 136 S. Ct. 871, 193 L. Ed. 2d 704, 2016 U.S. LEXIS 35.

January 11, 2016. Motion to direct the Clerk to file a petition for writ of certiorari out of time denied.

———

No. 15M71. Corey A. McDowell Bey, Petitioner v. Richard Vega.

577 U.S. 1058, 136 S. Ct. 872, 193 L. Ed. 2d 704, 2016 U.S. LEXIS 92.

January 11, 2016. Motion to direct the Clerk to file a petition for writ of certiorari out of time denied.

Same case below, 588 Fed. Appx. 923.

———

No. 15M72. Mario Sentelle Cavin, Petitioner v. Michigan.

577 U.S. 1058, 136 S. Ct. 872, 193 L. Ed. 2d 704, 2016 U.S. LEXIS 186.

January 11, 2016. Motion to direct the Clerk to file a petition for writ of certiorari out of time denied.

Same case below, 497 Mich. 1028, 863 N.W.2d 312.

———

No. 15M73. Bob Bejarano, Petitioner v. Jeff Macomber, Warden.

577 U.S. 1058, 136 S. Ct. 872, 193 L. Ed. 2d 704, 2016 U.S. LEXIS 306.

January 11, 2016. Motion to direct the Clerk to file a petition for writ of certiorari out of time denied.

———

No. 15M74. Deborah Ann Nardella, Petitioner v. Philadelphia Gas Works, et al.

577 U.S. 1058, 136 S. Ct. 872, 193 L. Ed. 2d 704, 2016 U.S. LEXIS 160.

January 11, 2016. Motion to direct the Clerk to file a petition for writ of certiorari out of time denied.

Same case below, 621 Fed. Appx. 105.

No. 14-10154. Stephen L. Voisine and William E. Armstrong, III, Petitioners v. United States.

577 U.S. 1058, 136 S. Ct. 872, 193 L. Ed. 2d 705, 2016 U.S. LEXIS 164.

January 11, 2016. Motion of petitioners for appointment of counsel granted and Virginia G. Villa, Esq., of St. Croix Falls, Wisconsin, is appointed to serve as counsel for the petitioners in this case.

No. 15-513. State Farm Fire and Casualty Company, Petitioner v. United States ex rel. Cori Rigsby, et al.

577 U.S. 1058, 136 S. Ct. 872, 193 L. Ed. 2d 705, 2016 U.S. LEXIS 84.

January 11, 2016. The Solicitor General is invited to file a brief in this case expressing the views of the United States.

Same case below, 794 F.3d 457.

No. 15-5776. Barbara Ellen Sherrill, Petitioner v. Estate of Thomas Michael Pico, Jr.

577 U.S. 1058, 136 S. Ct. 873, 193 L. Ed. 2d 705, 2016 U.S. LEXIS 224.

January 11, 2016. Motion of petitioner for reconsideration of order denying leave to proceed in forma pauperis denied.

No. 15-6082. Jose J. Hernandez, Petitioner v. Dignity Health.

577 U.S. 1058, 136 S. Ct. 873, 193 L. Ed. 2d 705, 2016 U.S. LEXIS 256.

January 11, 2016. Motion of petitioner for reconsideration of order denying leave to proceed in forma pauperis denied.

No. 15-6127. Van Lee Brewer, Petitioner v. William Stephens, Director, Texas Department of Criminal Justice, Correctional Institutions Division.

577 U.S. 1058, 136 S. Ct. 873, 193 L. Ed. 2d 705, 2016 U.S. LEXIS 162.

January 11, 2016. Motion of petitioner for reconsideration of order denying leave to proceed in forma pauperis denied.

No. 15-6177. David E. Hill, Petitioner v. Rudolph Contreras, Judge, United States District Court for the District of Columbia.

577 U.S. 1059, 136 S. Ct. 873, 193 L. Ed. 2d 705, 2016 U.S. LEXIS 137.

January 11, 2016. Motion of petitioner for reconsideration of order denying leave to proceed in forma pauperis denied.

No. 15-6205. Stephen W. Carlson, Petitioner v. Mark Dayton, Governor of Minnesota, et al.

577 U.S. 1059, 136 S. Ct. 873, 193 L. Ed. 2d 705, 2016 U.S. LEXIS 51.

January 11, 2016. Motion of petitioner for reconsideration of order denying leave to proceed in forma pauperis denied.

No. 15-6538. Renea J. Chafe, Petitioner v. Florida Department of Children and Families.

577 U.S. 1059, 136 S. Ct. 873, 193 L. Ed. 2d 706, 2016 U.S. LEXIS 325.

January 11, 2016. Motion of petitioner for reconsideration of order denying leave to proceed in forma pauperis denied.

No. 15-6566. Kimberly T. Spence, Petitioner v. Carl J. Willis, II.

577 U.S. 1059, 136 S. Ct. 874, 193 L. Ed. 2d 706, 2016 U.S. LEXIS 147.

January 11, 2016. Motion of petitioner for leave to proceed in forma pauperis denied. Petitioner is allowed until February 1, 2016, within which to pay the docketing fees required by Rule 38(a) and to submit a petition in compliance with Rule 33.1 of the Rules of this Court.

Same case below, 602 Fed. Appx. 927.

No. 15-6567. Kimberly T. Spence, Petitioner v. Carl J. Willis, II.

577 U.S. 1059, 136 S. Ct. 874, 193 L. Ed. 2d 706, 2016 U.S. LEXIS 52.

January 11, 2016. Motion of petitioner for leave to proceed in forma pauperis denied. Petitioner is allowed until February 1, 2016, within which to pay the docketing fees required by Rule 38(a) and to submit a petition in compliance with Rule 33.1 of the Rules of this Court.

No. 15-6578. Cynthia E. Collie, Petitioner v. South Carolina Commission on Lawyer Conduct, et al.

577 U.S. 1059, 136 S. Ct. 874, 193 L. Ed. 2d 706, 2016 U.S. LEXIS 67.

January 11, 2016. Motion of petitioner for leave to proceed in forma pauperis

denied. Petitioner is allowed until February 1, 2016, within which to pay the docketing fees required by Rule 38(a) and to submit a petition in compliance with Rule 33.1 of the Rules of this Court.

Same case below, 410 S.C. 556, 765 S.E.2d 835.

No. 15-6632. Edward Avila, Petitioner v. County of Hidalgo, Texas.

577 U.S. 1059, 136 S. Ct. 874, 193 L. Ed. 2d 706, 2016 U.S. LEXIS 34.

January 11, 2016. Motion of petitioner for leave to proceed in forma pauperis denied. Petitioner is allowed until February 1, 2016, within which to pay the docketing fees required by Rule 38(a) and to submit a petition in compliance with Rule 33.1 of the Rules of this Court.

Same case below, 606 Fed. Appx. 269.

No. 15-6660. Eddie Rivera, Petitioner v. Charles Creech.

577 U.S. 1059, 136 S. Ct. 874, 193 L. Ed. 2d 706, 2016 U.S. LEXIS 276, reh den 578 U.S. 942, 136 S. Ct. 1706, 194 L. Ed. 2d 803, 2016 U.S. LEXIS 2483.

January 11, 2016. Motion of petitioner for leave to proceed in forma pauperis denied. Petitioner is allowed until February 1, 2016, within which to pay the docketing fees required by Rule 38(a) and to submit a petition in compliance with Rule 33.1 of the Rules of this Court.

Same case below, 220 N.J. 575, 108 A.3d 635.

No. 15-6673. Katherine Kessel-Revis, Petitioner v. Texas.

577 U.S. 1059, 136 S. Ct. 874, 193 L. Ed. 2d 706, 2016 U.S. LEXIS 281.

January 11, 2016. Motion of petitioner for leave to proceed in forma pauperis

denied. Petitioner is allowed until February 1, 2016, within which to pay the docketing fees required by Rule 38(a) and to submit a petition in compliance with Rule 33.1 of the Rules of this Court.

No. 15-6761. Leonard P. Machulas, Petitioner v. United States.

577 U.S. 1059, 136 S. Ct. 875, 193 L. Ed. 2d 707, 2016 U.S. LEXIS 225.

January 11, 2016. Motion of petitioner for leave to proceed in forma pauperis denied. Petitioner is allowed until February 1, 2016, within which to pay the docketing fees required by Rule 38(a) and to submit a petition in compliance with Rule 33.1 of the Rules of this Court.

Same case below, 621 Fed. Appx. 629.

No. 15-6816. Bolarinwa Okezie, Petitioner v. Nicholas Leonard, et al.

577 U.S. 1059, 136 S. Ct. 875, 193 L. Ed. 2d 707, 2016 U.S. LEXIS 351.

January 11, 2016. Motion of petitioner for leave to proceed in forma pauperis denied. Petitioner is allowed until February 1, 2016, within which to pay the docketing fees required by Rule 38(a) and to submit a petition in compliance with Rule 33.1 of the Rules of this Court.

Same case below, 611 Fed. Appx. 788.

No. 15-6827. Michelle Lynne Emery, Petitioner v. Bryan Alan Bogle, et al.

577 U.S. 1059, 136 S. Ct. 875, 193 L. Ed. 2d 707, 2016 U.S. LEXIS 95.

January 11, 2016. Motion of petitioner for leave to proceed in forma pauperis

---

denied. Petitioner is allowed until February 1, 2016, within which to pay the docketing fees required by Rule 38(a) and to submit a petition in compliance with Rule 33.1 of the Rules of this Court.

No. 15-6840. James R. Thomas, Jr., et ux., Petitioners v. Chattahoochee Judicial Circuit, et al.

577 U.S. 1059, 136 S. Ct. 875, 193 L. Ed. 2d 707, 2016 U.S. LEXIS 274.

January 11, 2016. Motion of petitioners for leave to proceed in forma pauperis denied. Petitioners are allowed until February 1, 2016, within which to pay the docketing fees required by Rule 38(a) and to submit a petition in compliance with Rule 33.1 of the Rules of this Court.

No. 15-6853. Ryan J. Duerst, Petitioner v. Placer County, California, et al.

577 U.S. 1059, 136 S. Ct. 875, 193 L. Ed. 2d 707, 2016 U.S. LEXIS 279.

January 11, 2016. Motion of petitioner for leave to proceed in forma pauperis denied. Petitioner is allowed until February 1, 2016, within which to pay the docketing fees required by Rule 38(a) and to submit a petition in compliance with Rule 33.1 of the Rules of this Court.

No. 15-6863. Barbara Fletcher, et vir, Petitioners v. Park County, Montana.

577 U.S. 1059, 136 S. Ct. 876, 193 L. Ed. 2d 707, 2016 U.S. LEXIS 339.

January 11, 2016. Motion of petitioners for leave to proceed in forma pauperis denied. Petitioners are allowed until February 1, 2016, within which to pay the docketing fees required by Rule 38(a) and to submit a petition in compliance with Rule 33.1 of the Rules of this Court.

Same case below, 379 Mont. 538, 353 P.3d 508.

No. 15-6880. Beverly V. Andrews, Petitioner v. Superior Court of California, Los Angeles County, et al.

577 U.S. 1059, 136 S. Ct. 876, 193 L. Ed. 2d 708, 2016 U.S. LEXIS 273.

January 11, 2016. Motion of petitioner for leave to proceed in forma pauperis denied. Petitioner is allowed until February 1, 2016, within which to pay the docketing fees required by Rule 38(a) and to submit a petition in compliance with Rule 33.1 of the Rules of this Court.

No. 15-6896. Charles G. Kinney, Petitioner v. Michele R. Clark.

577 U.S. 1059, 136 S. Ct. 876, 193 L. Ed. 2d 708, 2016 U.S. LEXIS 226.

January 11, 2016. Motion of petitioner for leave to proceed in forma pauperis denied. Petitioner is allowed until February 1, 2016, within which to pay the docketing fees required by Rule 38(a) and to submit a petition in compliance with Rule 33.1 of the Rules of this Court.

No. 15-6897. Charles G. Kinney, Petitioner v. Eric Chomsky, et al.

577 U.S. 1059, 136 S. Ct. 876, 193 L. Ed. 2d 708, 2016 U.S. LEXIS 37.

January 11, 2016. Motion of petitioner for leave to proceed in forma pauperis

denied. Petitioner is allowed until February 1, 2016, within which to pay the docketing fees required by Rule 38(a) and to submit a petition in compliance with Rule 33.1 of the Rules of this Court.

No. 14-1168. Roger L. Smith, Petitioner v. Aegon Companies Pension Plan.

577 U.S. 1061, 136 S. Ct. 791, 193 L. Ed. 2d 708, 2016 U.S. LEXIS 47.

January 11, 2016. Petition for writ of certiorari to the United States Court of Appeals for the Sixth Circuit denied.

Same case below, 769 F.3d 922.

No. 14-1531. Kimberley Cowser-Griffin, Executrix of the Estate of David Griffin, Petitioner v. Sandra D. T. Griffin.

577 U.S. 1061, 136 S. Ct. 791, 193 L. Ed. 2d 708, 2016 U.S. LEXIS 333.

January 11, 2016. Petition for writ of certiorari to the Supreme Court of Virginia denied.

Same case below, 289 Va. 189, 771 S.E.2d 660.

No. 14-9962. Alan L. Burnett, II, Petitioner v. Caren C. Burnett.

577 U.S. 1061, 136 S. Ct. 791, 193 L. Ed. 2d 708, 2016 U.S. LEXIS 40, reh den 577 U.S. 1184, 136 S. Ct. 1249, 194 L. Ed. 2d 246, 2016 U.S. LEXIS 1187.

January 11, 2016. Petition for writ of certiorari to the Court of Appeals of Ohio, Sandusky County, denied.

No. 14-10427. Manuel Arzola, Petitioner v. Massachusetts.

577 U.S. 1061, 136 S. Ct. 792, 193 L. Ed. 2d 709, 2016 U.S. LEXIS 130.

January 11, 2016. Petition for writ of certiorari to the Supreme Judicial Court of Massachusetts denied.

Same case below, 470 Mass. 809, 26 N.E.3d 185.

No. 15-25. Sierra Pacific Power Company, et al., Petitioners v. Nevada Department of Taxation, et al.

577 U.S. 1061, 136 S. Ct. 792, 193 L. Ed. 2d 709, 2016 U.S. LEXIS 53.

January 11, 2016. Petition for writ of certiorari to the Supreme Court of Nevada denied.

Same case below, 130 Nev. 940, 338 P.3d 1244.

No. 15-68. Johnmichael O'Hare, et al., Petitioners v. Glen Harris, Individually, and P.P.A. as Guardian for K. H., a Minor.

577 U.S. 1061, 136 S. Ct. 792, 193 L. Ed. 2d 709, 2016 U.S. LEXIS 168.

January 11, 2016. Petition for writ of certiorari to the United States Court of Appeals for the Second Circuit denied.

Same case below, 770 F.3d 224.

No. 15-111. Zwicker & Associates, P.C., et al., Petitioners v. Dawson W. Wise.

577 U.S. 1061, 136 S. Ct. 793, 193 L. Ed. 2d 709, 2016 U.S. LEXIS 259.

January 11, 2016. Petition for writ of certiorari to the United States Court of Appeals for the Sixth Circuit denied.

Same case below, 780 F.3d 710.

No. 15-126. Michael R. Griep, Petitioner v. Wisconsin.

577 U.S. 1061, 136 S. Ct. 793, 193 L. Ed. 2d 709, 2016 U.S. LEXIS 337.

January 11, 2016. Petition for writ of certiorari to the Supreme Court of Wisconsin denied.

Same case below, 361 Wis. 2d 657, 863 N.W.2d 567.

No. 15-141. American Freedom Defense Initiative, et al., Petitioners v. Massachusetts Bay Transportation Authority, et al.

577 U.S. 1061, 136 S. Ct. 793, 193 L. Ed. 2d 709, 2016 U.S. LEXIS 336.

January 11, 2016. Petition for writ of certiorari to the United States Court of Appeals for the First Circuit denied.

Same case below, 781 F.3d 571.

No. 15-181. Steven Edward Ross, Petitioner v. United States.

577 U.S. 1061, 136 S. Ct. 794, 193 L. Ed. 2d 709, 2016 U.S. LEXIS 44.

January 11, 2016. Petition for writ of certiorari to the United States Court of Appeals for the Fourth Circuit denied.

Same case below, 602 Fed. Appx. 113.

No. 15-182. Desmond Farmer, Petitioner v. United States.

577 U.S. 1062, 136 S. Ct. 794, 193 L. Ed. 2d 710, 2016 U.S. LEXIS 245.

January 11, 2016. Petition for writ of certiorari to the United States Court of Appeals for the Fourth Circuit denied.

Same case below, 599 Fed. Appx. 525.

No. 15-196. Electronic Privacy Information Center, Petitioner v. Department of Homeland Security.

577 U.S. 1062, 136 S. Ct. 876, 193 L. Ed. 2d 710, 2016 U.S. LEXIS 98.

January 11, 2016. Petition for writ of certiorari to the United States Court of Appeals for the District of Columbia Circuit denied.

Same case below, 777 F.3d 518.

No. 15-216. Udren Law Offices, P.C., Petitioner v. Dale Kaymark.

577 U.S. 1062, 136 S. Ct. 794, 193 L. Ed. 2d 710, 2016 U.S. LEXIS 258.

January 11, 2016. Petition for writ of certiorari to the United States Court of Appeals for the Third Circuit denied.

Same case below, 783 F.3d 168.

No. 15-253. Katherine Lea Stanfield, Petitioner v. Idaho.

577 U.S. 1062, 136 S. Ct. 794, 193 L. Ed. 2d 710, 2016 U.S. LEXIS 275.

January 11, 2016. Petition for writ of certiorari to the Supreme Court of Idaho denied.

Same case below, 158 Idaho 327, 347 P.3d 175.

No. 15-259. Chuck Zamiara, et al., Petitioners v. Kevin King.

577 U.S. 1062, 136 S. Ct. 794, 193 L. Ed. 2d 710, 2016 U.S. LEXIS 189.

January 11, 2016. Petition for writ of certiorari to the United States Court of Appeals for the Sixth Circuit denied.

Same case below, 788 F.3d 207.

No. 15-280. Sam Francis Foundation, et al., Petitioners v. Christies, Inc., et al.

577 U.S. 1062, 136 S. Ct. 795, 193 L. Ed. 2d 710, 2016 U.S. LEXIS 150.

January 11, 2016. Petition for writ of certiorari to the United States Court of Appeals for the Ninth Circuit denied.

Same case below, 784 F.3d 1320.

No. 15-289. Anthony Thompson, Petitioner v. Loretta E. Lynch, Attorney General.

577 U.S. 1062, 136 S. Ct. 795, 193 L. Ed. 2d 710, 2016 U.S. LEXIS 340.

January 11, 2016. Petition for writ of certiorari to the United States Court of Appeals for the Sixth Circuit denied.

Same case below, 788 F.3d 638.

No. 15-308. City of New York, New York, Petitioner v. Alan Newton.

577 U.S. 1062, 136 S. Ct. 795, 193 L. Ed. 2d 710, 2016 U.S. LEXIS 185.

January 11, 2016. Petition for writ of certiorari to the United States Court of Appeals for the Second Circuit denied.

Same case below, 779 F.3d 140.

No. 15-314. Retirement Board of the Policemen's Annuity and Benefit Fund of the City of Chicago, et al., Petitioners v. The Bank of New York Mellon.

577 U.S. 1062, 136 S. Ct. 796, 193 L. Ed. 2d 711, 2016 U.S. LEXIS 179.

January 11, 2016. Petition for writ of certiorari to the United States Court of Appeals for the Second Circuit denied.

Same case below, 775 F.3d 154.

No. 15-321. Patricia Caplinger, Petitioner v. Medtronic, Inc., et al.

577 U.S. 1062, 136 S. Ct. 796, 193 L. Ed. 2d 711, 2016 U.S. LEXIS 36.

January 11, 2016. Petition for writ of certiorari to the United States Court of Appeals for the Tenth Circuit denied.

Same case below, 784 F.3d 1335.

No. 15-348. Ekaterini Alexopoulos, et vir, Petitioners v. Gordon Hargrove and James, P.A., et al.

577 U.S. 1062, 136 S. Ct. 797, 193 L. Ed. 2d 711, 2016 U.S. LEXIS 65, reh den 577 U.S. 1231, 136 S. Ct. 1486, 194 L. Ed. 2d 577, 2016 U.S. LEXIS 1918.

January 11, 2016. Petition for writ of certiorari to the District Court of Appeal of Florida, Fourth District, denied.

Same case below, 195 So. 3d 385.

No. 15-349. Nestle U.S.A., Inc., et al., Petitioners v. John Doe I, et al.

577 U.S. 1062, 136 S. Ct. 798, 193 L. Ed. 2d 711, 2016 U.S. LEXIS 120.

January 11, 2016. Petition for writ of certiorari to the United States Court of Appeals for the Ninth Circuit denied.

Same case below, 766 F.3d 1013.

No. 15-370. Clifford D. Bercovich and Howard Webber, Petitioners v. United States.

577 U.S. 1062, 136 S. Ct. 799, 193 L. Ed. 2d 711, 2016 U.S. LEXIS 358.

January 11, 2016. Petition for writ of certiorari to the United States Court of Appeals for the Ninth Circuit denied.

Same case below, 615 Fed. Appx. 416.

No. 15-376. Maricopa County, Arizona, Petitioner v. Manuel De Jesus Ortega Melendres, et al.

577 U.S. 1062, 136 S. Ct. 799, 193 L. Ed. 2d 711, 2016 U.S. LEXIS 134.

January 11, 2016. Petition for writ of certiorari to the United States Court of Appeals for the Ninth Circuit denied.

Same case below, 784 F.3d 1254.

No. 15-410. Nelson J. Mezerhane, Petitioner v. Republica Bolivariana de Venezuela, et al.

577 U.S. 1063, 136 S. Ct. 800, 193 L. Ed. 2d 711, 2016 U.S. LEXIS 24.

January 11, 2016. Petition for writ of certiorari to the United States Court of Appeals for the Eleventh Circuit denied.

Same case below, 785 F.3d 545.

No. 15-432. Gary Heinz, Michael Welty, and Peter Ghavami, Petitioners v. United States.

577 U.S. 1063, 136 S. Ct. 801, 193 L. Ed. 2d 712, 2016 U.S. LEXIS 167.

January 11, 2016. Petition for writ of certiorari to the United States Court of Appeals for the Second Circuit denied.

Same case below, 790 F.3d 365 and 607 Fed. Appx. 53.

No. 15-461. SpeedTrack, Inc., Petitioner v. Office Depot, Inc. et al.

577 U.S. 1063, 136 S. Ct. 801, 193 L. Ed. 2d 712, 2016 U.S. LEXIS 308.

January 11, 2016. Petition for writ of certiorari to the United States Court of Appeals for the Federal Circuit denied.

Same case below, 791 F.3d 1317.

No. 15-466. Cox Communications, Inc., Petitioner v. Richard Healy.

577 U.S. 1063, 136 S. Ct. 801, 193 L. Ed. 2d 712, 2016 U.S. LEXIS 239.

January 11, 2016. Petition for writ of certiorari to the United States Court of Appeals for the Tenth Circuit denied.

Same case below, 790 F.3d 1112.

No. 15-473. Jeffrey Sorensen, Petitioner v. WD-40 Company.

577 U.S. 1063, 136 S. Ct. 801, 193 L. Ed. 2d 712, 2016 U.S. LEXIS 133.

January 11, 2016. Petition for writ of certiorari to the United States Court of Appeals for the Seventh Circuit denied.

Same case below, 792 F.3d 712.

No. 15-484. Ernest S. Hendry, Jr., et ux., Petitioners v. The Georgelas Group, Inc., et al.

577 U.S. 1063, 136 S. Ct. 802, 193 L. Ed. 2d 712, 2016 U.S. LEXIS 111.

January 11, 2016. Petition for writ of certiorari to the United States Court of Appeals for the Fourth Circuit denied.

Same case below, 603 Fed. Appx. 222.

No. 15-485. Mark Warren Tetzlaff, Petitioner v. Educational Credit Management Corporation.

577 U.S. 1063, 136 S. Ct. 803, 193 L. Ed. 2d 712, 2016 U.S. LEXIS 61.

January 11, 2016. Petition for writ of certiorari to the United States Court of Appeals for the Seventh Circuit denied.

Same case below, 794 F.3d 756.

No. 15-489. Tomeko A. Gordon, et al., Petitioners v. City of New York, New York, et al.

577 U.S. 1063, 136 S. Ct. 804, 193 L. Ed. 2d 712, 2016 U.S. LEXIS 138.

January 11, 2016. Petition for writ of certiorari to the United States Court of Appeals for the Second Circuit denied.

Same case below, 612 Fed. Appx. 629.

Same case below, 779 F.3d 1254.

No. 15-490. David A. Brown, Petitioner v. Lower Brule Community Development Enterprise, LLC, et al.

577 U.S. 1063, 136 S. Ct. 804, 193 L. Ed. 2d 713, 2016 U.S. LEXIS 54.

January 11, 2016. Petition for writ of certiorari to the United States Court of Appeals for the Second Circuit denied.

Same case below, 606 Fed. Appx. 626.

No. 15-492. Linda Ash, et al., Petitioners v. Anderson Merchandisers LLC, et al.

577 U.S. 1063, 136 S. Ct. 804, 193 L. Ed. 2d 713, 2016 U.S. LEXIS 366.

January 11, 2016. Petition for writ of certiorari to the United States Court of Appeals for the Eighth Circuit denied.

Same case below, 799 F.3d 957.

No. 15-495. The Original Talk Radio Network, Inc., Petitioner v. Michael Wiener, aka Michael Savage, et al.

577 U.S. 1063, 136 S. Ct. 804, 193 L. Ed. 2d 713, 2016 U.S. LEXIS 50.

January 11, 2016. Petition for writ of certiorari to the United States Court of Appeals for the Ninth Circuit denied.

Same case below, 620 Fed. Appx. 568.

No. 15-499. U.S. Bank N.A., Petitioner v. Maury Rosenberg.

577 U.S. 1063, 136 S. Ct. 805, 193 L. Ed. 2d 713, 2016 U.S. LEXIS 357.

January 11, 2016. Petition for writ of certiorari to the United States Court of Appeals for the Eleventh Circuit denied.

No. 15-500. Peggy Willis, Petitioner v. Anne Marie Mobley.

577 U.S. 1063, 136 S. Ct. 805, 193 L. Ed. 2d 713, 2016 U.S. LEXIS 48.

January 11, 2016. Petition for writ of certiorari to the District Court of Appeal of Florida, Fifth District, denied.

Same case below, 171 So. 3d 739.

No. 15-501. Jordan M. Tonkin, Petitioner v. Shadow Management, Inc., dba Platinum Plus.

577 U.S. 1064, 136 S. Ct. 805, 193 L. Ed. 2d 713, 2016 U.S. LEXIS 158.

January 11, 2016. Petition for writ of certiorari to the United States Court of Appeals for the Fourth Circuit denied.

Same case below, 605 Fed. Appx. 194.

No. 15-502. Debra Feaster, Petitioner v. Federal Express Corporation.

577 U.S. 1064, 136 S. Ct. 807, 193 L. Ed. 2d 713, 2016 U.S. LEXIS 128.

January 11, 2016. Petition for writ of certiorari to United States Court of Appeals for the Fourth Circuit denied.

Same case below, 599 Fed. Appx. 63.

No. 15-504. Veronica B. D'Antignac, Petitioner v. Deere & Company, dba John Deere Commercial Products, Inc.

577 U.S. 1064, 136 S. Ct. 808, 193 L. Ed. 2d 713, 2016 U.S. LEXIS 96, reh den 577 U.S. 1184, 136 S. Ct. 1249, 194 L. Ed. 2d 247, 2016 U.S. LEXIS 1109.

January 11, 2016. Petition for writ of certiorari to the United States Court of Appeals for the Eleventh Circuit denied.

Same case below, 604 Fed. Appx. 875.

Same case below, 107 A.3d 228.

No. 15-509. Tata Consultancy Services Ltd., et al., Petitioners v. County of Orange, California.

577 U.S. 1064, 136 S. Ct. 808, 193 L. Ed. 2d 714, 2016 U.S. LEXIS 298.

January 11, 2016. Petition for writ of certiorari to the United States Court of Appeals for the Ninth Circuit denied.

Same case below, 784 F.3d 520.

No. 15-512. Delmer M. Ackels, Petitioner v. Kerwin Krause, et al.

577 U.S. 1064, 136 S. Ct. 808, 193 L. Ed. 2d 714, 2016 U.S. LEXIS 391.

January 11, 2016. Petition for writ of certiorari to the Supreme Court of Alaska denied.

No. 15-514. Omayra Mulero-Carrillo, et al., Petitioners v. Alejandro Roman-Hernandez, et al.

577 U.S. 1064, 136 S. Ct. 808, 193 L. Ed. 2d 714, 2016 U.S. LEXIS 62.

January 11, 2016. Petition for writ of certiorari to the United States Court of Appeals for the First Circuit denied.

Same case below, 790 F.3d 99.

No. 15-515. Drew Rizzo, Petitioner v. Pennsylvania.

577 U.S. 1064, 136 S. Ct. 877, 193 L. Ed. 2d 714, 2016 U.S. LEXIS 141.

January 11, 2016. Petition for writ of certiorari to the Superior Court of Pennsylvania, Philadelphia Office, denied.

No. 15-516. Loan Phuong, Petitioner v. Jason E. Thompson, et al.

577 U.S. 1064, 136 S. Ct. 809, 193 L. Ed. 2d 714, 2016 U.S. LEXIS 58, reh den 577 U.S. 1184, 136 S. Ct. 1249, 194 L. Ed. 2d 247, 2016 U.S. LEXIS 1193.

January 11, 2016. Petition for writ of certiorari to the Supreme Court of Virginia denied.

No. 15-520. Janice S. Haagensen, Personal Representative of the Estate of Myrtle Shelburne Haagensen, Petitioner v. Michael J. Wherry, Visiting Judge, Lawrence County Court of Common Pleas, Pennsylvania, et al.

577 U.S. 1064, 136 S. Ct. 809, 193 L. Ed. 2d 714, 2016 U.S. LEXIS 177, reh den 577 U.S. 1231, 136 S. Ct. 1487, 194 L. Ed. 2d 578, 2016 U.S. LEXIS 1915.

January 11, 2016. Petition for writ of certiorari to the United States Court of Appeals for the Third Circuit denied.

Same case below, 610 Fed. Appx. 210.

No. 15-521. Victoria Giampa, Petitioner v. Bryce C. Duckworth, et al.

577 U.S. 1064, 136 S. Ct. 809, 193 L. Ed. 2d 714, 2016 U.S. LEXIS 38.

January 11, 2016. Petition for writ of certiorari to the United States Court of Appeals for the Ninth Circuit denied.

Same case below, 586 Fed. Appx. 284.

No. 15-526. James Phillips, Petitioner v. Joseph E. Ternes, Jr., et al.

577 U.S. 1064, 136 S. Ct. 811, 193 L. Ed. 2d 715, 2016 U.S. LEXIS 30.

January 11, 2016. Petition for writ of certiorari to the United States Court of Appeals for the Sixth Circuit denied.

Same case below, 788 F.3d 650.

No. 15-528. Michigan, Petitioner v. Adam Benjamin Stevens.

577 U.S. 1064, 136 S. Ct. 811, 193 L. Ed. 2d 715, 2016 U.S. LEXIS 285.

January 11, 2016. Petition for writ of certiorari to the Court of Appeals of Michigan denied.

Same case below, 498 Mich. 162, 869 N.W.2d 233.

No. 15-529. Gary Tsirelman, Petitioner v. Howard Zucker, Commissioner, New York Department of Health, et al.

577 U.S. 1064, 136 S. Ct. 811, 193 L. Ed. 2d 715, 2016 U.S. LEXIS 368.

January 11, 2016. Petition for writ of certiorari to the United States Court of Appeals for the Second Circuit denied.

Same case below, 794 F.3d 310.

No. 15-531. Jeanette Doal, Petitioner v. Central Intelligence Agency, et al.

577 U.S. 1065, 136 S. Ct. 811, 193 L. Ed. 2d 715, 2016 U.S. LEXIS 74, reh den 577 U.S. 1184, 136 S. Ct. 1249, 194 L. Ed. 2d 247, 2016 U.S. LEXIS 1092.

January 11, 2016. Petition for writ of certiorari to the United States Court of Appeals for the Second Circuit denied.

Same case below, 613 Fed. Appx. 63.

No. 15-532. John Doe 2, et al., Petitioners v. John W. Rosa.

577 U.S. 1065, 136 S. Ct. 811, 193 L. Ed. 2d 715, 2016 U.S. LEXIS 197.

January 11, 2016. Petition for writ of certiorari to the United States Court of Appeals for the Fourth Circuit denied.

Same case below, 795 F.3d 429.

No. 15-534. Hongyan Li, Petitioner v. United States.

577 U.S. 1065, 136 S. Ct. 813, 193 L. Ed. 2d 715, 2016 U.S. LEXIS 97.

January 11, 2016. Petition for writ of certiorari to the United States Court of Appeals for the Fifth Circuit denied.

Same case below, 619 Fed. Appx. 298.

No. 15-535. Patrick Koffley, Petitioner v. Jo Benson Fogel.

577 U.S. 1065, 136 S. Ct. 814, 193 L. Ed. 2d 715, 2016 U.S. LEXIS 249, reh den 577 U.S. 1184, 136 S. Ct. 1249, 194 L. Ed. 2d 247, 2016 U.S. LEXIS 1107.

January 11, 2016. Petition for writ of certiorari to the Court of Special Appeals of Maryland denied.

Same case below, 219 Md. App. 712 and 219 Md. App. 714.

No. 15-536. Stephen D. Chamberlain, Petitioner v. Judith C. Chamberlain.

577 U.S. 1065, 136 S. Ct. 814, 193 L. Ed. 2d 715, 2016 U.S. LEXIS 192.

January 11, 2016. Petition for writ of certiorari to the Court of Special Appeals of Maryland denied.

Same case below, 222 Md. App. 708.

No. 15-539. Randolph H. Guthrie, III, Petitioner v. City of New York, New York, et al.

577 U.S. 1065, 136 S. Ct. 877, 193 L. Ed. 2d 716, 2016 U.S. LEXIS 144.

January 11, 2016. Petition for writ of certiorari to the United States Court of Appeals for the Eleventh Circuit denied.

Same case below, 618 Fed. Appx. 612.

No. 15-544. Bruce Keene, Petitioner v. Gerald Rossi, et al.

577 U.S. 1065, 136 S. Ct. 814, 193 L. Ed. 2d 716, 2016 U.S. LEXIS 104.

January 11, 2016. Petition for writ of certiorari to the Court of Appeals of Michigan denied.

Same case below, 306 Mich. App. 252, 856 N.W.2d 556.

No. 15-546. Vivian Braxton, et vir, Petitioners v. Apperson, Crump & Maxwell, PLC, et al.

577 U.S. 1065, 136 S. Ct. 817, 193 L. Ed. 2d 716, 2016 U.S. LEXIS 63.

January 11, 2016. Petition for writ of certiorari to the United States Court of Appeals for the Sixth Circuit denied.

No. 15-548. Wesley Eugene Perkins, Petitioner v. Texas.

577 U.S. 1065, 136 S. Ct. 817, 193 L. Ed. 2d 716, 2016 U.S. LEXIS 90.

January 11, 2016. Petition for writ of certiorari to the Court of Appeals of Texas, Third District, denied.

No. 15-552. Pierre Mentor, Petitioner v. Limor Rosenberg, et al.

577 U.S. 1065, 136 S. Ct. 817, 193 L. Ed. 2d 716, 2016 U.S. LEXIS 70.

January 11, 2016. Petition for writ of certiorari to the District Court of Appeal of Florida, Third District, denied.

Same case below, 163 So. 3d 1209.

No. 15-554. Debra M. Stevenson, et al., Petitioners v. First American Title Insurance Company, et al.

577 U.S. 1065, 136 S. Ct. 820, 193 L. Ed. 2d 716, 2016 U.S. LEXIS 101.

January 11, 2016. Petition for writ of certiorari to the United States Court of Appeals for the District of Columbia Circuit denied.

Same case below, 789 F.3d 197.

No. 15-562. NECA-IBEW Pension Trust Fund, et al., Petitioners v. Kenneth D. Lewis, et al.

577 U.S. 1065, 136 S. Ct. 821, 193 L. Ed. 2d 716, 2016 U.S. LEXIS 262.

January 11, 2016. Petition for writ of certiorari to the United States Court of Appeals for the Second Circuit denied.

Same case below, 607 Fed. Appx. 79.

No. 15-570. Jola Kimca and Ejldin Kimca, et al., Petitioners v. Loretta E. Lynch, Attorney General.

577 U.S. 1065, 136 S. Ct. 822, 193 L. Ed. 2d 716, 2016 U.S. LEXIS 219.

January 11, 2016. Petition for writ of certiorari to the United States Court of Appeals for the Second Circuit denied.

Same case below, 610 Fed. Appx. 54.

No. 15-575. Solomon Upshaw, Petitioner v. United States.

577 U.S. 1066, 136 S. Ct. 822, 193 L. Ed. 2d 717, 2016 U.S. LEXIS 611.

January 11, 2016. Petition for writ of certiorari to the United States Court of Appeals for the Federal Circuit denied.

Same case below, 615 Fed. Appx. 949.

No. 15-576. Jennifer Tian, Petitioner v. Aspen Technology, Inc.

577 U.S. 1066, 136 S. Ct. 822, 193 L. Ed. 2d 717, 2016 U.S. LEXIS 88.

January 11, 2016. Petition for writ of certiorari to the United States Court of Appeals for the First Circuit denied.

No. 15-579. Lothian Cassidy, LLC, et al., Petitioners v. Bruce Ransom, et al.

577 U.S. 1066, 136 S. Ct. 822, 193 L. Ed. 2d 717, 2016 U.S. LEXIS 33.

January 11, 2016. Petition for writ of certiorari to the United States Court of Appeals for the Fifth Circuit denied.

No. 15-581. Jonathan Adams Thomas, Petitioner v. Jeh Johnson, Secretary of Homeland Security.

577 U.S. 1066, 136 S. Ct. 822, 193 L. Ed. 2d 717, 2016 U.S. LEXIS 69.

January 11, 2016. Petition for writ of certiorari to the United States Court of Appeals for the Fifth Circuit denied.

Same case below, 788 F.3d 177.

No. 15-582. Dinh Ton That, Petitioner v. Alders Maintenance Association.

577 U.S. 1066, 136 S. Ct. 823, 193 L. Ed. 2d 717, 2016 U.S. LEXIS 60, reh den 577 U.S. 1184, 136 S. Ct. 1250, 194 L. Ed. 2d 247, 2016 U.S. LEXIS 1257.

January 11, 2016. Petition for writ of certiorari to the Court of Appeal of California, Fourth Appellate District, Division Three, denied.

No. 15-586. Paul D. Ceglia, Petitioner v. Mark Elliot Zuckerberg, et al.

577 U.S. 1066, 136 S. Ct. 823, 193 L. Ed. 2d 717, 2016 U.S. LEXIS 59.

January 11, 2016. Petition for writ of certiorari to the United States Court of Appeals for the Second Circuit denied.

Same case below, 600 Fed. Appx. 34.

No. 15-589. United States ex rel. Harry Barko, Petitioner v. Kellogg Brown & Root, Inc., et al.

577 U.S. 1066, 136 S. Ct. 823, 193 L. Ed. 2d 717, 2016 U.S. LEXIS 56.

January 11, 2016. Petition for writ of certiorari to the United States Court of Appeals for the District of Columbia Circuit denied.

Same case below, 796 F.3d 137.

No. 15-593. Michael Tesler, Petitioner v. Susan Cacace, et al.

577 U.S. 1066, 136 S. Ct. 823, 193 L. Ed. 2d 717, 2016 U.S. LEXIS 364, reh den 577 U.S. 1208, 136 S. Ct. 1402, 194 L. Ed. 2d 382, 2016 U.S. LEXIS 1615.

January 11, 2016. Petition for writ of certiorari to the United States Court of Appeals for the Second Circuit denied.

Same case below, 607 Fed. Appx. 87.

No. 15-594. Martha Chavis, Individually and on Behalf of the Estate of Kevin Jones, Deceased, Petitioner v. Leland Borden.

577 U.S. 1066, 136 S. Ct. 823, 193 L. Ed. 2d 718, 2016 U.S. LEXIS 193.

January 11, 2016. Petition for writ of certiorari to the United States Court of Appeals for the Fifth Circuit denied.

Same case below, 621 Fed. Appx. 283.

No. 15-598. Arizona Libertarian Party, et al., Petitioners v. Michele Reagan, Arizona Secretary of State.

577 U.S. 1066, 136 S. Ct. 823, 193 L. Ed. 2d 718, 2016 U.S. LEXIS 614.

January 11, 2016. Petition for writ of certiorari to the United States Court of Appeals for the Ninth Circuit denied.

Same case below, 798 F.3d 723.

No. 15-601. Luis Enrique Platas-Hernandez, Petitioner v. Loretta E. Lynch, Attorney General.

577 U.S. 1066, 136 S. Ct. 824, 193 L. Ed. 2d 718, 2016 U.S. LEXIS 20.

January 11, 2016. Petition for writ of certiorari to the United States Court of Appeals for the Ninth Circuit denied.

Same case below, 611 Fed. Appx. 404.

No. 15-602. Rodney K. Morgan, et al., Petitioners v. Global Traffic Technologies LLC.

577 U.S. 1066, 136 S. Ct. 824, 193 L. Ed. 2d 718, 2016 U.S. LEXIS 327.

January 11, 2016. Petition for writ of certiorari to the United States Court of Appeals for the Federal Circuit denied.

Same case below, 620 Fed. Appx. 895.

No. 15-603. Milge H. Menchu, Petitioner v. Loretta E. Lynch, Attorney General.

577 U.S. 1066, 136 S. Ct. 824, 193 L. Ed. 2d 718, 2016 U.S. LEXIS 139, reh den 577 U.S. 1184, 136 S. Ct. 1250, 194 L. Ed. 2d 247, 2016 U.S. LEXIS 1298.

January 11, 2016. Petition for writ of certiorari to the United States Court of Appeals for the Ninth Circuit denied.

Same case below, 592 Fed. Appx. 645.

No. 15-604. Daniel Brink, et al., Petitioners v. Continental Insurance Company, et al.

577 U.S. 1066, 136 S. Ct. 824, 193 L. Ed. 2d 718, 2016 U.S. LEXIS 68.

January 11, 2016. Petition for writ of certiorari to the United States Court of Appeals for the District of Columbia Circuit denied.

Same case below, 787 F.3d 1120.

No. 15-605. Dorian Cheeks, Petitioner v. Freeport Pancake House, Inc., et al.

577 U.S. 1067, 136 S. Ct. 824, 193 L. Ed. 2d 718, 2016 U.S. LEXIS 356.

January 11, 2016. Petition for writ of certiorari to the United States Court of Appeals for the Second Circuit denied.

Same case below, 796 F.3d 199.

No. 15-612. John Ryskamp, Petitioner v. Commissioner of Internal Revenue.

577 U.S. 1067, 136 S. Ct. 834, 193 L. Ed. 2d 719, 2016 U.S. LEXIS 246.

January 11, 2016. Petition for writ of certiorari to the United States Court of Appeals for the District of Columbia Circuit denied.

Same case below, 797 F.3d 1142.

No. 15-614. Paul Dorsey, Petitioner v. James P. Tennille, et al.

No. 15-615. Sikora Nelson, Petitioner v. James P. Tennille, et al.

577 U.S. 1067, 136 S. Ct. 835, 193 L. Ed. 2d 719, 2016 U.S. LEXIS 55.

January 11, 2016. Petitions for writs of certiorari to the United States Court of Appeals for the Tenth Circuit denied.

Same cases below, 785 F.3d 422.

No. 15-617. Kwan Ho Wu, aka Shui-Hui Wei, Petitioner v. Loretta E. Lynch, Attorney General.

577 U.S. 1067, 136 S. Ct. 837, 193 L. Ed. 2d 719, 2016 U.S. LEXIS 344.

January 11, 2016. Petition for writ of certiorari to the United States Court of Appeals for the Third Circuit denied.

Same case below, 612 Fed. Appx. 140.

No. 15-632. Jeffrey Cutler, Petitioner v. Department of Health and Human Services, et al.

577 U.S. 1067, 136 S. Ct. 877, 193 L. Ed. 2d 719, 2016 U.S. LEXIS 372.

January 11, 2016. Petition for writ of certiorari to the United States Court of Appeals for the District of Columbia Circuit denied.

Same case below, 797 F.3d 1173.

No. 15-634. Lauri Huffman, Petitioner v. Speedway LLC.

577 U.S. 1067, 136 S. Ct. 838, 193 L. Ed. 2d 719, 2016 U.S. LEXIS 73.

January 11, 2016. Petition for writ of certiorari to the United States Court of Appeals for the Sixth Circuit denied.

Same case below, 621 Fed. Appx. 792.

No. 15-647. Phillip Ransom, Petitioner v. Anthony Grisafe, et al.

577 U.S. 1067, 136 S. Ct. 838, 193 L. Ed. 2d 719, 2016 U.S. LEXIS 28.

January 11, 2016. Petition for writ of certiorari to the United States Court of Appeals for the Eighth Circuit denied.

Same case below, 790 F.3d 804.

No. 15-656. Kyung Choi, Petitioner v. Ray Mabus, Secretary of the Navy.

577 U.S. 1067, 136 S. Ct. 842, 193 L. Ed. 2d 719, 2016 U.S. LEXIS 600.

January 11, 2016. Petition for writ of certiorari to the United States Court of Appeals for the Ninth Circuit denied.

Same case below, 617 Fed. Appx. 669.

Same case below, 609 Fed. Appx. 235.

No. 15-669. Yi Hong Chen, Petitioner v. Loretta E. Lynch, Attorney General.

577 U.S. 1067, 136 S. Ct. 849, 193 L. Ed. 2d 720, 2016 U.S. LEXIS 156.

January 11, 2016. Petition for writ of certiorari to the United States Court of Appeals for the Second Circuit denied.

No. 15-670. Darin A. Jones, Petitioner v. Merit Systems Protection Board.

577 U.S. 1067, 136 S. Ct. 877, 193 L. Ed. 2d 720, 2016 U.S. LEXIS 227.

January 11, 2016. Petition for writ of certiorari to the United States Court of Appeals for the Federal Circuit denied.

Same case below, 597 Fed. Appx. 1083.

No. 15-671. Rochester City Lines, Co., Petitioner v. City of Rochester, Minnesota, et al.

577 U.S. 1067, 136 S. Ct. 849, 193 L. Ed. 2d 720, 2016 U.S. LEXIS 116.

January 11, 2016. Petition for writ of certiorari to the Supreme Court of Minnesota denied.

Same case below, 868 N.W.2d 655.

No. 15-678. Dwight Bowling, Petitioner v. United States.

577 U.S. 1067, 136 S. Ct. 850, 193 L. Ed. 2d 720, 2016 U.S. LEXIS 80.

January 11, 2016. Petition for writ of certiorari to the United States Court of Appeals for the Fifth Circuit denied.

No. 15-679. Soorajnie Singh, as Next Friend for Rovin Singh, et al., Petitioners v. Caribbean Airlines Limited.

577 U.S. 1068, 136 S. Ct. 850, 193 L. Ed. 2d 720, 2016 U.S. LEXIS 26.

January 11, 2016. Petition for writ of certiorari to the United States Court of Appeals for the Eleventh Circuit denied.

Same case below, 798 F.3d 1355.

No. 15-687. Isaac Lee Hykes, Petitioner v. Jacob J. Lew, Secretary of the Treasury.

577 U.S. 1068, 136 S. Ct. 855, 193 L. Ed. 2d 720, 2016 U.S. LEXIS 76.

January 11, 2016. Petition for writ of certiorari to the United States Court of Appeals for the Sixth Circuit denied.

No. 15-690. Layne Energy, Inc., et al., Petitioners v. Richard Catron.

577 U.S. 1068, 136 S. Ct. 855, 193 L. Ed. 2d 720, 2016 U.S. LEXIS 607.

January 11, 2016. Petition for writ of certiorari to the United States Court of Appeals for the Tenth Circuit denied.

No. 15-691. Lakshmi Arunachalam, Petitioner v. JPMorgan Chase & Co.

577 U.S. 1068, 136 S. Ct. 856, 193 L. Ed. 2d 720, 2016 U.S. LEXIS 301, reh den 577 U.S. 1209, 136 S. Ct. 1403, 194 L. Ed. 2d 383, 2016 U.S. LEXIS 1648.

January 11, 2016. Petition for writ of certiorari to the United States Court of Appeals for the Federal Circuit denied.

Same case below, 600 Fed. Appx. 774.

No. 15-695. Sofjan Bahaudin, Petitioner v. Eric K. Fanning, Acting Secretary of the Army.

577 U.S. 1068, 136 S. Ct. 856, 193 L. Ed. 2d 721, 2016 U.S. LEXIS 57.

January 11, 2016. Petition for writ of certiorari to the United States Court of Appeals for the Ninth Circuit denied.

No. 15-697. Ilanit Rubin, Petitioner v. Fannie Mae, et al.

577 U.S. 1068, 136 S. Ct. 857, 193 L. Ed. 2d 721, 2016 U.S. LEXIS 81.

January 11, 2016. Petition for writ of certiorari to the United States Court of Appeals for the Sixth Circuit denied.

Same case below, 587 Fed. Appx. 273.

No. 15-699. Kenneth Lester Mullikin, Jr., Petitioner v. United States.

577 U.S. 1068, 136 S. Ct. 857, 193 L. Ed. 2d 721, 2016 U.S. LEXIS 350.

January 11, 2016. Petition for writ of certiorari to the United States Court of Appeals for the Sixth Circuit denied.

No. 15-702. Wayne Walker, Petitioner v. United States.

577 U.S. 1068, 136 S. Ct. 857, 193 L. Ed. 2d 721, 2016 U.S. LEXIS 270.

January 11, 2016. Petition for writ of certiorari to the United States Court of Appeals for the Eleventh Circuit denied.

Same case below, 799 F.3d 1361.

No. 15-705. Brent Bollinger, Petitioner v. Kansas.

577 U.S. 1068, 136 S. Ct. 858, 193 L. Ed. 2d 721, 2016 U.S. LEXIS 602.

January 11, 2016. Petition for writ of certiorari to the Supreme Court of Kansas denied.

Same case below, 302 Kan. 309, 352 P.3d 1003.

No. 15-713. Henry J. Lazniarz, et ux., Petitioners v. Commissioner of Internal Revenue.

577 U.S. 1068, 136 S. Ct. 862, 193 L. Ed. 2d 721, 2016 U.S. LEXIS 64.

January 11, 2016. Petition for writ of certiorari to the United States Court of Appeals for the Eighth Circuit denied.

Same case below, 597 Fed. Appx. 900.

No. 15-718. Cassandra Cean, Petitioner v. United States.

577 U.S. 1068, 136 S. Ct. 863, 193 L. Ed. 2d 721, 2016 U.S. LEXIS 265.

January 11, 2016. Petition for writ of certiorari to the United States Court of Appeals for the Second Circuit denied.

Same case below, 621 Fed. Appx. 44.

No. 15-733. Lester Roger Decker, Petitioner v. United States.

577 U.S. 1068, 136 S. Ct. 867, 193 L. Ed. 2d 721, 2016 U.S. LEXIS 296.

January 11, 2016. Petition for writ of certiorari to the United States Court of Appeals for the Ninth Circuit denied.

Same case below, 624 Fed. Appx. 959.

No. 15-5096. Jose Armando Bran, Petitioner v. United States.

577 U.S. 1068, 136 S. Ct. 792, 193 L. Ed. 2d 722, 2016 U.S. LEXIS 117.

January 11, 2016. Petition for writ of certiorari to the United States Court of Appeals for the Fourth Circuit denied.

Same case below, 776 F.3d 276.

No. 15-5156. Rance M. Strunk, et ux., Petitioners v. Wells Fargo Bank, N.A., et al.

577 U.S. 1068, 136 S. Ct. 792, 193 L. Ed. 2d 722, 2016 U.S. LEXIS 32.

January 11, 2016. Petition for writ of certiorari to the United States Court of Appeals for the Third Circuit denied.

Same case below, 614 Fed. Appx. 586.

No. 15-5267. Jarrell Neal, Petitioner v. Louisiana.

577 U.S. 1069, 136 S. Ct. 793, 193 L. Ed. 2d 722, 2016 U.S. LEXIS 108.

January 11, 2016. Petition for writ of certiorari to the Supreme Court of Louisiana denied.

Same case below, 168 So. 3d 391.

No. 15-5399. Steven Lloyd Mosley, Petitioner v. California.

577 U.S. 1069, 136 S. Ct. 793, 193 L. Ed. 2d 722, 2016 U.S. LEXIS 383.

January 11, 2016. Petition for writ of certiorari to the Supreme Court of California denied.

Same case below, 60 Cal. 4th 1044, 185 Cal. Rptr. 3d 251, 344 P.3d 788.

No. 15-5421. Constandino Argyris, Petitioner v. New York.

577 U.S. 1069, 136 S. Ct. 793, 193 L. Ed. 2d 722, 2016 U.S. LEXIS 46.

January 11, 2016. Petition for writ of certiorari to the Court of Appeals of New York denied.

Same case below, 24 N.Y.3d 1138, 3 N.Y.S.3d 711, 27 N.E.3d 425.

No. 15-5645. Diane King, Petitioner v. Department of the Army.

577 U.S. 1069, 136 S. Ct. 794, 193 L. Ed. 2d 722, 2016 U.S. LEXIS 264.

January 11, 2016. Petition for writ of certiorari to the United States Court of Appeals for the Federal Circuit denied.

Same case below, 602 Fed. Appx. 812.

No. 15-5985. Paul Glen Everett, Petitioner v. Julie L. Jones, Secretary, Florida Department of Corrections.

577 U.S. 1069, 136 S. Ct. 795, 193 L. Ed. 2d 722, 2016 U.S. LEXIS 194.

January 11, 2016. Petition for writ of certiorari to the United States Court of Appeals for the Eleventh Circuit denied.

Same case below, 779 F.3d 1212.

No. 15-6037. Christopher L. Roalson, Petitioner v. Wisconsin.

577 U.S. 1069, 136 S. Ct. 795, 193 L. Ed. 2d 722, 2016 U.S. LEXIS 261.

January 11, 2016. Petition for writ of certiorari to the Court of Appeals of Wisconsin, District III, denied.

Same case below, 356 Wis. 2d 327, 855 N.W.2d 492.

Same case below, 462 S.W.3d 389.

No. 15-6068. Amna Salahuddin, Petitioner v. Zoning Hearing Board of West Chester, et al.

577 U.S. 1069, 136 S. Ct. 797, 193 L. Ed. 2d 723, 2016 U.S. LEXIS 100, reh den 577 U.S. 1184, 136 S. Ct. 1250, 194 L. Ed. 2d 248, 2016 U.S. LEXIS 1059.

January 11, 2016. Petition for writ of certiorari to the Commonwealth Court of Pennsylvania denied.

Same case below, 103 A.3d 888.

No. 15-6070. Gary S. Roup, Petitioner v. Commercial Research, LLC.

577 U.S. 1069, 136 S. Ct. 797, 193 L. Ed. 2d 723, 2016 U.S. LEXIS 123.

January 11, 2016. Petition for writ of certiorari to the Supreme Court of Colorado denied.

Same case below, 349 P.3d 273, 2015 CO 38.

No. 15-6090. Candido Antomattei, Petitioner v. United States.

577 U.S. 1069, 136 S. Ct. 797, 193 L. Ed. 2d 723, 2016 U.S. LEXIS 153.

January 11, 2016. Petition for writ of certiorari to the United States Court of Appeals for the Second Circuit denied.

Same case below, 607 Fed. Appx. 33.

No. 15-6098. Robert Carl Foley and Ralph Baze, Petitioners v. Steve Beshear, Governor of Kentucky, et al.

577 U.S. 1069, 136 S. Ct. 797, 193 L. Ed. 2d 723, 2016 U.S. LEXIS 29.

January 11, 2016. Petition for writ of certiorari to the Supreme Court of Kentucky denied.

No. 15-6110. Ronald Hammons, Petitioner v. United States; andAnthony Nix, Petitioner v. United States.

577 U.S. 1069, 136 S. Ct. 797, 193 L. Ed. 2d 723, 2016 U.S. LEXIS 222.

January 11, 2016. Petition for writ of certiorari to the United States Court of Appeals for the Eleventh Circuit denied.

No. 15-6191. Richard E. Lynch, Petitioner v. Julie L. Jones, Secretary, Florida Department of Corrections, et al.

577 U.S. 1069, 136 S. Ct. 798, 193 L. Ed. 2d 723, 2016 U.S. LEXIS 106.

January 11, 2016. Petition for writ of certiorari to the United States Court of Appeals for the Eleventh Circuit denied.

Same case below, 776 F.3d 1209.

No. 15-6198. Samuel Steven Fields, Petitioner v. Kentucky.

577 U.S. 1069, 136 S. Ct. 798, 193 L. Ed. 2d 723, 2016 U.S. LEXIS 89.

January 11, 2016. Petition for writ of certiorari to the Supreme Court of Kentucky denied.

No. 15-6211. Joseph White, Petitioner v. Detroit East Community Mental Health, et al.

577 U.S. 1069, 136 S. Ct. 798, 193 L. Ed. 2d 723, 2016 U.S. LEXIS 294, reh den 577 U.S. 1209, 136 S. Ct. 1403, 194 L. Ed. 2d 383, 2016 U.S. LEXIS 1635.

January 11, 2016. Petition for writ of certiorari to the Court of Appeals of Michigan denied.

No. 15-6301. Yesid Rios Suarez, Petitioner v. United States.

577 U.S. 1070, 136 S. Ct. 800, 193 L. Ed. 2d 724, 2016 U.S. LEXIS 27.

January 11, 2016. Petition for writ of certiorari to the United States Court of Appeals for the Second Circuit denied.

Same case below, 791 F.3d 363 and 615 Fed. Appx. 5.

No. 15-6360. Terrence James Jackson, Petitioner v. United States.

577 U.S. 1070, 136 S. Ct. 800, 193 L. Ed. 2d 724, 2016 U.S. LEXIS 187.

January 11, 2016. Petition for writ of certiorari to the United States Court of Appeals for the Eleventh Circuit denied.

Same case below, 614 Fed. Appx. 438.

No. 15-6361. Ramon Dellosantos, Petitioner v. United States.

No. 15-6407. Richard W. Szpyt, Petitioner v. United States.

577 U.S. 1070, 136 S. Ct. 800, 193 L. Ed. 2d 724, 2016 U.S. LEXIS 154.

January 11, 2016. Petitions for writs of certiorari to the United States Court of Appeals for the First Circuit denied.

Same cases below, 785 F.3d 31.

No. 15-6493. Tom Lan, Petitioner v. Comcast Corporation, LLC.

577 U.S. 1070, 136 S. Ct. 801, 193 L. Ed. 2d 724, 2016 U.S. LEXIS 42, reh den

577 U.S. 1185, 136 S. Ct. 1252, 194 L. Ed. 2d 250, 2016 U.S. LEXIS 1185.

January 11, 2016. Petition for writ of certiorari to the Court of Appeal of California, First Appellate District, Division Five, denied.

No. 15-6504. Ron Brady, Jr., Petitioner v. Brian E. Williams, Sr., Warden.

577 U.S. 1070, 136 S. Ct. 801, 193 L. Ed. 2d 724, 2016 U.S. LEXIS 22.

January 11, 2016. Petition for writ of certiorari to the United States Court of Appeals for the Ninth Circuit denied.

No. 15-6506. William Beasley, Petitioner v. Jeffrey Woods, Warden.

577 U.S. 1070, 136 S. Ct. 802, 193 L. Ed. 2d 724, 2016 U.S. LEXIS 181.

January 11, 2016. Petition for writ of certiorari to the United States Court of Appeals for the Sixth Circuit denied.

No. 15-6508. Austin Bernard, III, Petitioner v. Burl Cain, Warden.

577 U.S. 1070, 136 S. Ct. 802, 193 L. Ed. 2d 724, 2016 U.S. LEXIS 616.

January 11, 2016. Petition for writ of certiorari to the United States Court of Appeals for the Fifth Circuit denied.

No. 15-6518. Simon F. Ranteesi, Petitioner v. Eric Arnold, Warden.

577 U.S. 1070, 136 S. Ct. 802, 193 L. Ed. 2d 724, 2016 U.S. LEXIS 49, reh den 577 U.S. 1185, 136 S. Ct. 1252, 194 L. Ed. 2d 250, 2016 U.S. LEXIS 1194.

January 11, 2016. Petition for writ of certiorari to the United States Court of Appeals for the Ninth Circuit denied.

No. 15-6521. Terry Lee Lattimore, Petitioner v. Jacqueline Banks, Superintendent, South Mississippi Correctional Institution.

577 U.S. 1070, 136 S. Ct. 802, 193 L. Ed. 2d 725, 2016 U.S. LEXIS 612.

January 11, 2016. Petition for writ of certiorari to the United States Court of Appeals for the Fifth Circuit denied.

No. 15-6535. Orlando Samuel McKeithen, Petitioner v. Cathy Jackson, et al.

577 U.S. 1070, 136 S. Ct. 802, 193 L. Ed. 2d 725, 2016 U.S. LEXIS 375.

January 11, 2016. Petition for writ of certiorari to the United States Court of Appeals for the Eleventh Circuit denied.

Same case below, 606 Fed. Appx. 937.

No. 15-6536. Gerord Robinson, Petitioner v. Randall Haas, Warden.

577 U.S. 1070, 136 S. Ct. 803, 193 L. Ed. 2d 725, 2016 U.S. LEXIS 113.

January 11, 2016. Petition for writ of certiorari to the United States Court of Appeals for the Sixth Circuit denied.

No. 15-6539. Larry Denson, Jr., Petitioner v. Stan Shepard, Warden.

577 U.S. 1070, 136 S. Ct. 803, 193 L. Ed. 2d 725, 2016 U.S. LEXIS 603.

January 11, 2016. Petition for writ of certiorari to the Superior Court of Georgia, Montgomery County, denied.

No. 15-6540. Kenneth Kelley, Petitioner v. Thomas Winn, Warden.

577 U.S. 1070, 136 S. Ct. 803, 193 L. Ed. 2d 725, 2016 U.S. LEXIS 152.

January 11, 2016. Petition for writ of certiorari to the United States Court of Appeals for the Sixth Circuit denied.

No. 15-6541. Earl Lee Wright, Petitioner v. Marshall L. Fisher, Commissioner, Mississippi Department of Corrections.

577 U.S. 1070, 136 S. Ct. 803, 193 L. Ed. 2d 725, 2016 U.S. LEXIS 199.

January 11, 2016. Petition for writ of certiorari to the United States Court of Appeals for the Fifth Circuit denied.

No. 15-6548. John David Battaglia, Petitioner v. William Stephens, Director, Texas Department of Criminal Justice, Correctional Institutions Division.

577 U.S. 1071, 136 S. Ct. 803, 193 L. Ed. 2d 725, 2016 U.S. LEXIS 236.

January 11, 2016. Petition for writ of certiorari to the United States Court of Appeals for the Fifth Circuit denied.

Same case below, 621 Fed. Appx. 781.

No. 15-6552. Alan Canillo Loon, Petitioner v. Michigan.

577 U.S. 1071, 136 S. Ct. 804, 193 L. Ed. 2d 725, 2016 U.S. LEXIS 39.

January 11, 2016. Petition for writ of certiorari to the Court of Appeals of Michigan denied.

No. 15-6563. Willie Bolds, Petitioner v. California.

577 U.S. 1071, 136 S. Ct. 804, 193 L. Ed. 2d 726, 2016 U.S. LEXIS 146.

January 11, 2016. Petition for writ of certiorari to the Supreme Court of California denied.

No. 15-6574. Kildgret Burce, Petitioner v. Vance Laughlin, Warden, et al.

577 U.S. 1071, 136 S. Ct. 805, 193 L. Ed. 2d 726, 2016 U.S. LEXIS 284.

January 11, 2016. Petition for writ of certiorari to the United States Court of Appeals for the Eleventh Circuit denied.

No. 15-6575. Carolyn Butler, Petitioner v. David Whitten, et al.

577 U.S. 1071, 136 S. Ct. 806, 193 L. Ed. 2d 726, 2016 U.S. LEXIS 31.

January 11, 2016. Petition for writ of certiorari to the Court of Appeals of Texas, Second District, denied.

No. 15-6579. Tomas Zavalidroga, et al., Petitioners v. Oneida County Sheriff's Department, et al.

577 U.S. 1071, 136 S. Ct. 806, 193 L. Ed. 2d 726, 2016 U.S. LEXIS 165, reh den

577 U.S. 1185, 136 S. Ct. 1252, 194 L. Ed. 2d 250, 2016 U.S. LEXIS 1230.

January 11, 2016. Petition for writ of certiorari to the United States Court of Appeals for the Second Circuit denied.

No. 15-6583. Jeremy Alan Williams, Petitioner v. Maurice Warrior, Interim Warden.

577 U.S. 1071, 136 S. Ct. 806, 193 L. Ed. 2d 726, 2016 U.S. LEXIS 114.

January 11, 2016. Petition for writ of certiorari to the United States Court of Appeals for the Tenth Circuit denied.

Same case below, 782 F.3d 1184.

No. 15-6587. Mark Wallace, Petitioner v. New York.

577 U.S. 1071, 136 S. Ct. 806, 193 L. Ed. 2d 726, 2016 U.S. LEXIS 314.

January 11, 2016. Petition for writ of certiorari to the Appellate Division, Supreme Court of New York, Second Judicial Department, denied.

Same case below, 128 App. Div. 3d 866, 7 N.Y.S.3d 610.

No. 15-6588. Daron Thomas, Petitioner v. Billy Cape, Sheriff, Pulaski County, Georgia.

577 U.S. 1071, 136 S. Ct. 806, 193 L. Ed. 2d 726, 2016 U.S. LEXIS 161.

January 11, 2016. Petition for writ of certiorari to the United States Court of Appeals for the Eleventh Circuit denied.

No. 15-6591. Chokchai Krongkiet, Petitioner v. Jeffrey Beard, Secretary, California Department of Corrections and Rehabilitation.

577 U.S. 1071, 136 S. Ct. 807, 193 L. Ed. 2d 727, 2016 U.S. LEXIS 235.

January 11, 2016. Petition for writ of certiorari to the United States Court of Appeals for the Ninth Circuit denied.

Same case below, 597 Fed. Appx. 416.

No. 15-6594. Gregorio Ortiz, Petitioner v. Court of Appeal of California, Second Appellate District, et al.

577 U.S. 1071, 136 S. Ct. 807, 193 L. Ed. 2d 727, 2016 U.S. LEXIS 234.

January 11, 2016. Petition for writ of certiorari to the Supreme Court of California denied.

No. 15-6597. Nancy Johnson, Petitioner v. Santa Clara County, California.

577 U.S. 1071, 136 S. Ct. 807, 193 L. Ed. 2d 727, 2016 U.S. LEXIS 228, reh den 577 U.S. 1231, 136 S. Ct. 1488, 194 L. Ed. 2d 578, 2016 U.S. LEXIS 1909.

January 11, 2016. Petition for writ of certiorari to the United States Court of Appeals for the Ninth Circuit denied.

No. 15-6605. Christopher Diaz, Petitioner v. David M. Unger, Superintendent, Wyoming Correctional Facility.

577 U.S. 1071, 136 S. Ct. 807, 193 L. Ed. 2d 727, 2016 U.S. LEXIS 135.

January 11, 2016. Petition for writ of certiorari to the United States Court of Appeals for the Second Circuit denied.

No. 15-6607. Andre Staton, Petitioner v. Pennsylvania.

577 U.S. 1072, 136 S. Ct. 807, 193 L. Ed. 2d 727, 2016 U.S. LEXIS 19.

January 11, 2016. Petition for writ of certiorari to the Supreme Court of Pennsylvania, Eastern District, denied.

Same case below, 632 Pa. 400, 120 A.3d 277.

No. 15-6619. Ladon Churn, Petitioner v. Unknown Parkkila, et al.

577 U.S. 1072, 136 S. Ct. 808, 193 L. Ed. 2d 727, 2016 U.S. LEXIS 369.

January 11, 2016. Petition for writ of certiorari to the United States Court of Appeals for the Sixth Circuit denied.

No. 15-6620. King Edward Williams, Petitioner v. Julie L. Jones, Secretary, Florida Department of Corrections.

577 U.S. 1072, 136 S. Ct. 808, 193 L. Ed. 2d 727, 2016 U.S. LEXIS 237.

January 11, 2016. Petition for writ of certiorari to the United States Court of Appeals for the Eleventh Circuit denied.

No. 15-6626. Eric Maxton, Petitioner v. John Kerestes, Superintendent, State Correctional Institution at Mahanoy, et al.

577 U.S. 1072, 136 S. Ct. 809, 193 L. Ed. 2d 727, 2016 U.S. LEXIS 248.

January 11, 2016. Petition for writ of certiorari to the United States Court of Appeals for the Third Circuit denied.

No. 15-6628. Randy R. Carson, Petitioner v. Wayne Millus.

577 U.S. 1072, 136 S. Ct. 809, 193 L. Ed. 2d 728, 2016 U.S. LEXIS 320.

January 11, 2016. Petition for writ of certiorari to the United States Court of Appeals for the Fifth Circuit denied.

Same case below, 621 Fed. Appx. 787.

No. 15-6630. Francyne J. Cooper, Petitioner v. Director, Office of Workers' Compensation Programs, Department of Labor, et al.

577 U.S. 1072, 136 S. Ct. 809, 193 L. Ed. 2d 728, 2016 U.S. LEXIS 204, reh den 577 U.S. 1231, 136 S. Ct. 1488, 194 L. Ed. 2d 579, 2016 U.S. LEXIS 1887.

January 11, 2016. Petition for writ of certiorari to the United States Court of Appeals for the Fourth Circuit denied.

Same case below, 602 Fed. Appx. 127.

No. 15-6633. Theresa Barnett, Petitioner v. David S. Crockett, et al.

577 U.S. 1072, 136 S. Ct. 810, 193 L. Ed. 2d 728, 2016 U.S. LEXIS 170, reh den 577 U.S. 1209, 136 S. Ct. 1403, 194 L. Ed. 2d 383, 2016 U.S. LEXIS 1625.

January 11, 2016. Petition for writ of certiorari to the Court of Appeals of Texas, Fifth District, denied.

No. 15-6638. Tia Smith, Petitioner v. American Mortgage Network, et al.

577 U.S. 1072, 136 S. Ct. 810, 193 L. Ed. 2d 728, 2016 U.S. LEXIS 107.

January 11, 2016. Petition for writ of certiorari to the Supreme Court of California denied.

No. 15-6640. J. P., Petitioner v. Florida Department of Children and Families, et al.

577 U.S. 1072, 136 S. Ct. 877, 193 L. Ed. 2d 728, 2016 U.S. LEXIS 210.

January 11, 2016. Petition for writ of certiorari to the District Court of Appeal of Florida, Third District denied.

Same case below, 206 So. 3d 53.

No. 15-6641. George Peterson, Petitioner v. Ken Cameron, Superintendent, State Correctional Institution at Houtzdale, et al.

577 U.S. 1072, 136 S. Ct. 810, 193 L. Ed. 2d 728, 2016 U.S. LEXIS 110.

January 11, 2016. Petition for writ of certiorari to the United States Court of Appeals for the Third Circuit denied.

No. 15-6642. Renard Truman Polk, Petitioner v. Nevada, et al.

577 U.S. 1072, 136 S. Ct. 810, 193 L. Ed. 2d 728, 2016 U.S. LEXIS 21.

January 11, 2016. Petition for writ of certiorari to the Supreme Court of Nevada denied.

No. 15-6643. Hector Genaro Pacheco, Petitioner v. F. Foulk, Warden.

577 U.S. 1072, 136 S. Ct. 810, 193 L. Ed. 2d 728, 2016 U.S. LEXIS 87.

January 11, 2016. Petition for writ of certiorari to the United States Court of Appeals for the Ninth Circuit denied.

No. 15-6646. Floyd Hamilton and Ruth Johnson, Petitioners v. United States.

577 U.S. 1072, 136 S. Ct. 810, 193 L. Ed. 2d 729, 2016 U.S. LEXIS 125, reh den 577 U.S. 1231, 136 S. Ct. 1488, 194 L. Ed. 2d 579, 2016 U.S. LEXIS 1926.

January 11, 2016. Petition for writ of certiorari to the United States Court of Appeals for the Fifth Circuit denied.

Same case below, 606 Fed. Appx. 237.

No. 15-6648. James Garrett Freeman, Petitioner v. William Stephens, Director, Texas Department of Criminal Justice, Correctional Institutions Division.

577 U.S. 1072, 136 S. Ct. 811, 193 L. Ed. 2d 729, 2016 U.S. LEXIS 251.

January 11, 2016. Petition for writ of certiorari to the United States Court of Appeals for the Fifth Circuit denied.

Same case below, 614 Fed. Appx. 180.

No. 15-6653. Paul Joseph Zeedyk, Petitioner v. William Stephens, Director, Texas Department of Criminal Justice, Correctional Institutions Division.

577 U.S. 1073, 136 S. Ct. 812, 193 L. Ed. 2d 729, 2016 U.S. LEXIS 23.

January 11, 2016. Petition for writ of certiorari to the United States Court of Appeals for the Fifth Circuit denied.

No. 15-6654. Michael Addison, Petitioner v. New Hampshire.

577 U.S. 1073, 136 S. Ct. 812, 193 L. Ed. 2d 729, 2016 U.S. LEXIS 381.

January 11, 2016. Petition for writ of certiorari to the Supreme Court of New Hampshire denied.

Same case below, 167 N.H. 562, 116 A.3d 551.

No. 15-6659. Tod Jack, Petitioner v. Jesse Panuccio.

577 U.S. 1073, 136 S. Ct. 812, 193 L. Ed. 2d 729, 2016 U.S. LEXIS 143.

January 11, 2016. Petition for writ of certiorari to the United States Court of Appeals for the Fourth Circuit denied.

Same case below, 610 Fed. Appx. 287.

No. 15-6661. Jonathan Mano, Petitioner v. Neil McDowell, Warden.

577 U.S. 1073, 136 S. Ct. 812, 193 L. Ed. 2d 729, 2016 U.S. LEXIS 85.

January 11, 2016. Petition for writ of certiorari to the United States Court of Appeals for the Ninth Circuit denied.

No. 15-6663. William Terry Smith, Petitioner v. John Haugen, et al.

577 U.S. 1073, 136 S. Ct. 812, 193 L. Ed. 2d 729, 2016 U.S. LEXIS 263.

January 11, 2016. Petition for writ of certiorari to the United States Court of Appeals for the Ninth Circuit denied.

Same case below, 599 Fed. Appx. 322.

No. 15-6664. Paul K. Kusak, Petitioner v. Eileen Creeden, et al.

577 U.S. 1073, 136 S. Ct. 812, 193 L. Ed. 2d 729, 2016 U.S. LEXIS 401.

January 11, 2016. Petition for writ of certiorari to the United States Court of Appeals for the Second Circuit denied.

No. 15-6666. Christopher Ryan White-head, Petitioner v. South Carolina.

577 U.S. 1073, 136 S. Ct. 813, 193 L. Ed. 2d 730, 2016 U.S. LEXIS 119.

January 11, 2016. Petition for writ of certiorari to the Supreme Court of South Carolina denied.

No. 15-6667. Devinche Javon Albritton, Petitioner v. Virginia.

577 U.S. 1073, 136 S. Ct. 813, 193 L. Ed. 2d 730, 2016 U.S. LEXIS 380.

January 11, 2016. Petition for writ of certiorari to the Supreme Court of Virginia denied.

No. 15-6668. Winston Bontrager, Petitioner v. United States.

577 U.S. 1073, 136 S. Ct. 813, 193 L. Ed. 2d 730, 2016 U.S. LEXIS 347.

January 11, 2016. Petition for writ of certiorari to the United States Court of Appeals for the Ninth Circuit denied.

Same case below, 610 Fed. Appx. 665.

No. 15-6672. Rogelio Villareal Villanueva, Petitioner v. Scott Frauenheim, Warden.

577 U.S. 1073, 136 S. Ct. 813, 193 L. Ed. 2d 730, 2016 U.S. LEXIS 487.

January 11, 2016. Petition for writ of certiorari to the United States Court of Appeals for the Ninth Circuit denied.

No. 15-6675. George E. Kersey, Petitioner v. New Hampshire, et al.

577 U.S. 1073, 136 S. Ct. 814, 193 L. Ed. 2d 730, 2016 U.S. LEXIS 315.

January 11, 2016. Petition for writ of certiorari to the United States Court of Appeals for the First Circuit denied.

No. 15-6677. Gerald Franklin, Petitioner v. Georgia.

577 U.S. 1073, 136 S. Ct. 814, 193 L. Ed. 2d 730, 2016 U.S. LEXIS 105.

January 11, 2016. Petition for writ of certiorari to the Supreme Court of Georgia denied.

No. 15-6681. Marco Devon Jiles, Petitioner v. Gregory McLaughlin, Warden.

577 U.S. 1073, 136 S. Ct. 814, 193 L. Ed. 2d 730, 2016 U.S. LEXIS 386.

January 11, 2016. Petition for writ of certiorari to the United States Court of Appeals for the Eleventh Circuit denied.

No. 15-6682. Kevin Lewis, Petitioner v. John Soto, Warden.

577 U.S. 1073, 136 S. Ct. 814, 193 L. Ed. 2d 730, 2016 U.S. LEXIS 311, reh den 577 U.S. 1241, 136 S. Ct. 1510, 194 L. Ed. 2d 598, 2016 U.S. LEXIS 2205.

January 11, 2016. Petition for writ of certiorari to the United States Court of Appeals for the Ninth Circuit denied.

No. 15-6684. Ngoc Duong, aka Danny Duong, Petitioner v. United States.

577 U.S. 1073, 136 S. Ct. 815, 193 L. Ed. 2d 731, 2016 U.S. LEXIS 338.

January 11, 2016. Petition for writ of certiorari to the United States Court of Appeals for the Ninth Circuit denied.

Same case below, 619 Fed. Appx. 580.

No. 15-6685. Michael Thomas Cupp, Petitioner v. United States.

577 U.S. 1074, 136 S. Ct. 815, 193 L. Ed. 2d 731, 2016 U.S. LEXIS 213.

January 11, 2016. Petition for writ of certiorari to the United States Court of Appeals for the Fifth Circuit denied.

Same case below, 611 Fed. Appx. 237.

No. 15-6687. Eugene French, Petitioner v. Alan Carter, Warden, et al.

577 U.S. 1074, 136 S. Ct. 815, 193 L. Ed. 2d 731, 2016 U.S. LEXIS 367.

January 11, 2016. Petition for writ of certiorari to the United States Court of Appeals for the Eleventh Circuit denied.

Same case below, 790 F.3d 1259.

No. 15-6688. Barry Lefkovitch, Petitioner v. California.

577 U.S. 1074, 136 S. Ct. 815, 193 L. Ed. 2d 731, 2016 U.S. LEXIS 441.

January 11, 2016. Petition for writ of certiorari to the Court of Appeal of California, Second Appellate District, Division Six, denied.

No. 15-6689. Lawrence Higgins, Petitioner v. Texas.

577 U.S. 1074, 136 S. Ct. 815, 193 L. Ed. 2d 731, 2016 U.S. LEXIS 406.

January 11, 2016. Petition for writ of certiorari to the Court of Criminal Appeals of Texas denied.

No. 15-6693. Roberto Armendariz Sandoval, Petitioner v. United States.

577 U.S. 1074, 136 S. Ct. 815, 193 L. Ed. 2d 731, 2016 U.S. LEXIS 456.

January 11, 2016. Petition for writ of certiorari to the United States Court of Appeals for the Fifth Circuit denied.

Same case below, 610 Fed. Appx. 438.

No. 15-6694. Allen Preston, Petitioner v. Mary Attebury.

577 U.S. 1074, 136 S. Ct. 816, 193 L. Ed. 2d 731, 2016 U.S. LEXIS 345, reh den 577 U.S. 1241, 136 S. Ct. 1511, 194 L. Ed. 2d 598, 2016 U.S. LEXIS 2250.

January 11, 2016. Petition for writ of certiorari to the United States Court of Appeals for the Eighth Circuit denied.

No. 15-6695. Geremy Ford, Petitioner v. Pennsylvania.

577 U.S. 1074, 136 S. Ct. 816, 193 L. Ed. 2d 731, 2016 U.S. LEXIS 180.

January 11, 2016. Petition for writ of certiorari to the Superior Court of Pennsylvania, Philadelphia Office, denied.

Same case below, 105 A.3d 45.

No. 15-6696. Walter Hoskins, IV, Petitioner v. John Fayram, Warden.

577 U.S. 1074, 136 S. Ct. 816, 193 L. Ed. 2d 732, 2016 U.S. LEXIS 183, reh den 577 U.S. 1209, 136 S. Ct. 1403, 194 L. Ed. 2d 383, 2016 U.S. LEXIS 1623.

January 11, 2016. Petition for writ of certiorari to the United States Court of Appeals for the Eighth Circuit denied.

No. 15-6697. Anthony D. Hayes, Sr., Petitioner v. Dwight Cowans, et al.

577 U.S. 1074, 136 S. Ct. 816, 193 L. Ed. 2d 732, 2016 U.S. LEXIS 94.

January 11, 2016. Petition for writ of certiorari to the United States Court of Appeals for the Sixth Circuit denied.

No. 15-6699. Tommy May, Petitioner v. Daniel Schnurr, Warden.

577 U.S. 1074, 136 S. Ct. 816, 193 L. Ed. 2d 732, 2016 U.S. LEXIS 126.

January 11, 2016. Petition for writ of certiorari to the Court of Appeals of Kansas denied.

Same case below, 345 P.3d 296.

No. 15-6700. Margarette Foules, Petitioner v. Santa Clara County Federal Credit Union.

577 U.S. 1074, 136 S. Ct. 816, 193 L. Ed. 2d 732, 2016 U.S. LEXIS 272.

January 11, 2016. Petition for writ of certiorari to the Court of Appeal of California, Sixth Appellate District, denied.

No. 15-6701. Christopher L. Griffith, Petitioner v. Brenda Cash, Warden, et al.

577 U.S. 1074, 136 S. Ct. 817, 193 L. Ed. 2d 732, 2016 U.S. LEXIS 109.

January 11, 2016. Petition for writ of certiorari to the United States Court of Appeals for the Ninth Circuit denied.

No. 15-6706. Jamie Shawn McCall, Petitioner v. Andy Shock, Sheriff, Faulkner County, Arkansas.

577 U.S. 1074, 136 S. Ct. 817, 193 L. Ed. 2d 732, 2016 U.S. LEXIS 163.

January 11, 2016. Petition for writ of certiorari to the United States Court of Appeals for the Eighth Circuit denied.

No. 15-6708. Leopoldo Cardenas-Bucio, Petitioner v. United States.

577 U.S. 1074, 136 S. Ct. 817, 193 L. Ed. 2d 732, 2016 U.S. LEXIS 449.

January 11, 2016. Petition for writ of certiorari to the United States Court of Appeals for the Fifth Circuit denied.

Same case below, 615 Fed. Appx. 207.

No. 15-6709. Gregory Alan Kokal, Petitioner v. Julie L. Jones, Secretary, Florida Department of Corrections, et al.

577 U.S. 1074, 136 S. Ct. 818, 193 L. Ed. 2d 732, 2016 U.S. LEXIS 142.

January 11, 2016. Petition for writ of certiorari to the United States Court of Appeals for the Eleventh Circuit denied.

No. 15-6710. Stephen Le, Petitioner v. Steven E. Racette, Superintendent, Great Meadow Correctional Facility.

577 U.S. 1075, 136 S. Ct. 878, 193 L. Ed. 2d 733, 2016 U.S. LEXIS 172.

January 11, 2016. Petition for writ of certiorari to the United States Court of Appeals for the Second Circuit denied.

No. 15-6711. Everette Lewis Johnson, Petitioner v. Harold W. Clarke, Director, Virginia Department of Corrections.

577 U.S. 1075, 136 S. Ct. 818, 193 L. Ed. 2d 733, 2016 U.S. LEXIS 418.

January 11, 2016. Petition for writ of certiorari to the United States Court of Appeals for the Fourth Circuit denied.

Same case below, 604 Fed. Appx. 288.

No. 15-6712. Irwin Dewayne Gaines, Petitioner v. William Stephens, Director, Texas Department of Criminal Justice, Correctional Institutions Division.

577 U.S. 1075, 136 S. Ct. 818, 193 L. Ed. 2d 733, 2016 U.S. LEXIS 395.

January 11, 2016. Petition for writ of certiorari to the United States Court of Appeals for the Fifth Circuit denied.

No. 15-6713. David Hardy, Petitioner v. William Alfred Adams, et al.

577 U.S. 1075, 136 S. Ct. 818, 193 L. Ed. 2d 733, 2016 U.S. LEXIS 196.

January 11, 2016. Petition for writ of certiorari to the United States Court of Appeals for the Sixth Circuit denied.

No. 15-6714. Roland Damond Foster, Petitioner v. Burl Cain, Warden.

577 U.S. 1075, 136 S. Ct. 818, 193 L. Ed. 2d 733, 2016 U.S. LEXIS 157.

January 11, 2016. Petition for writ of certiorari to the United States Court of Appeals for the Fifth Circuit denied.

No. 15-6716. Nathaniel Harris, Petitioner v. Georgia.

577 U.S. 1075, 136 S. Ct. 818, 193 L. Ed. 2d 733, 2016 U.S. LEXIS 497.

January 11, 2016. Petition for writ of certiorari to the Supreme Court of Georgia denied.

No. 15-6717. Michelle Kronenberg, Petitioner v. Ohio.

577 U.S. 1075, 136 S. Ct. 818, 193 L. Ed. 2d 733, 2016 U.S. LEXIS 218, reh den 577 U.S. 1231, 136 S. Ct. 1488, 194 L. Ed. 2d 579, 2016 U.S. LEXIS 1921.

January 11, 2016. Petition for writ of certiorari to the Court of Appeals of Ohio, Cuyahoga County, denied.

No. 15-6718. Dean C. Rodriguez, Petitioner v. Jeffrey Beard, Secretary, California Department of Corrections and Rehabilitation.

577 U.S. 1075, 136 S. Ct. 819, 193 L. Ed. 2d 733, 2016 U.S. LEXIS 211, reh den 577 U.S. 1209, 136 S. Ct. 1403, 194 L. Ed. 2d 383, 2016 U.S. LEXIS 1633.

January 11, 2016. Petition for writ of certiorari to the United States Court of Appeals for the Ninth Circuit denied.

No. 15-6722. Joan Leslie Gates, Petitioner v. North Dakota.

577 U.S. 1075, 136 S. Ct. 819, 193 L. Ed. 2d 734, 2016 U.S. LEXIS 271, reh den 577 U.S. 1231, 136 S. Ct. 1488, 194 L. Ed. 2d 579, 2016 U.S. LEXIS 1872.

January 11, 2016. Petition for writ of certiorari to the Supreme Court of North Dakota denied.

Same case below, 865 N.W.2d 816.

No. 15-6723. Stephen Floyd, Petitioner v. Lisa Gorcyca.

577 U.S. 1075, 136 S. Ct. 819, 193 L. Ed. 2d 734, 2016 U.S. LEXIS 360.

January 11, 2016. Petition for writ of certiorari to the United States Court of Appeals for the Sixth Circuit denied.

No. 15-6724. Corey Sanders, Petitioner v. Wendy Kelley, Director, Arkansas Department of Correction.

577 U.S. 1075, 136 S. Ct. 819, 193 L. Ed. 2d 734, 2016 U.S. LEXIS 290.

January 11, 2016. Petition for writ of certiorari to the United States Court of Appeals for the Eighth Circuit denied.

No. 15-6725. Cuong Phu Le, Petitioner v. Texas.

577 U.S. 1075, 136 S. Ct. 819, 193 L. Ed. 2d 734, 2016 U.S. LEXIS 216.

January 11, 2016. Petition for writ of certiorari to the Court of Criminal Appeals of Texas denied.

Same case below, 463 S.W.3d 872.

No. 15-6733. Christopher A. Henry, Petitioner v. Martin Vasquez, et al.

577 U.S. 1075, 136 S. Ct. 819, 193 L. Ed. 2d 734, 2016 U.S. LEXIS 184.

January 11, 2016. Petition for writ of certiorari to the United States Court of Appeals for the Second Circuit denied.

No. 15-6734. Joseph Lee Bell, Jr., Petitioner v. Laura Gramling Perez, et al.

577 U.S. 1075, 136 S. Ct. 820, 193 L. Ed. 2d 734, 2016 U.S. LEXIS 457, reh den 578 U.S. 942, 136 S. Ct. 1707, 194 L. Ed. 2d 803, 2016 U.S. LEXIS 2548.

January 11, 2016. Petition for writ of certiorari to the United States Court of Appeals for the Seventh Circuit denied.

Same case below, 612 Fed. Appx. 849.

No. 15-6740. Charles Matthew Saenz, Petitioner v. Texas.

577 U.S. 1076, 136 S. Ct. 820, 193 L. Ed. 2d 734, 2016 U.S. LEXIS 530.

January 11, 2016. Petition for writ of certiorari to the Court of Criminal Appeals of Texas denied.

No. 15-6745. Warren Scott, III, Petitioner v. Cornel Hubert.

577 U.S. 1076, 136 S. Ct. 820, 193 L. Ed. 2d 734, 2016 U.S. LEXIS 103.

January 11, 2016. Petition for writ of certiorari to the United States Court of Appeals for the Fifth Circuit denied.

Same case below, 610 Fed. Appx. 433.

No. 15-6746. Lavert Cox, Petitioner v. California.

577 U.S. 1076, 136 S. Ct. 820, 193 L. Ed. 2d 735, 2016 U.S. LEXIS 291.

January 11, 2016. Petition for writ of certiorari to the Court of Appeal of California, Fifth Appellate District, denied.

No. 15-6747. Maurice Clay, Petitioner v. David Bergh, Warden.

577 U.S. 1076, 136 S. Ct. 821, 193 L. Ed. 2d 735, 2016 U.S. LEXIS 617.

January 11, 2016. Petition for writ of certiorari to the United States Court of Appeals for the Sixth Circuit denied.

No. 15-6748. Anthony Anniversary Edwards, Petitioner v. California.

577 U.S. 1076, 136 S. Ct. 821, 193 L. Ed. 2d 735, 2016 U.S. LEXIS 400.

January 11, 2016. Petition for writ of certiorari to the Supreme Court of California denied.

No. 15-6750. Arthur Lee Manning, Petitioner v. Michael Bowersox, Warden.

577 U.S. 1076, 136 S. Ct. 821, 193 L. Ed. 2d 735, 2016 U.S. LEXIS 398.

January 11, 2016. Petition for writ of certiorari to the United States Court of Appeals for the Eighth Circuit denied.

No. 15-6751. Gregory Allen Mines, Petitioner v. Anthony Barber, et al.

577 U.S. 1076, 136 S. Ct. 821, 193 L. Ed. 2d 735, 2016 U.S. LEXIS 393.

January 11, 2016. Petition for writ of certiorari to the United States Court of Appeals for the Eleventh Circuit denied.

Same case below, 610 Fed. Appx. 838.

No. 15-6754. Donaldo Zavaleta, Petitioner v. David Bergh, Warden.

577 U.S. 1076, 136 S. Ct. 822, 193 L. Ed. 2d 735, 2016 U.S. LEXIS 328.

January 11, 2016. Petition for writ of certiorari to the United States Court of Appeals for the Sixth Circuit denied.

No. 15-6756. Garry Jones, Petitioner v. Willie Smith, Warden.

577 U.S. 1076, 136 S. Ct. 878, 193 L. Ed. 2d 735, 2016 U.S. LEXIS 124.

January 11, 2016. Petition for writ of certiorari to the United States Court of Appeals for the Sixth Circuit denied.

Same case below, 801 F.3d 556.

No. 15-6757. Howard Walter Thomas, Petitioner v. Randy Lee, Warden.

577 U.S. 1076, 136 S. Ct. 825, 193 L. Ed. 2d 735, 2016 U.S. LEXIS 464.

January 11, 2016. Petition for writ of certiorari to the United States Court of Appeals for the Sixth Circuit denied.

Same case below, 615 Fed. Appx. 271.

Same case below, 618 Fed. Appx. 938.

No. 15-6767. Michael Allen Griffin, Petitioner v. Julie L. Jones, Secretary, Florida Department of Corrections, et al.

577 U.S. 1076, 136 S. Ct. 825, 193 L. Ed. 2d 736, 2016 U.S. LEXIS 394.

January 11, 2016. Petition for writ of certiorari to the United States Court of Appeals for the Eleventh Circuit denied.

Same case below, 787 F.3d 1086.

No. 15-6774. Cornell Stricklen, Petitioner v. Sherry Burt, Warden.

577 U.S. 1076, 136 S. Ct. 826, 193 L. Ed. 2d 736, 2016 U.S. LEXIS 83.

January 11, 2016. Petition for writ of certiorari to the United States Court of Appeals for the Sixth Circuit denied.

No. 15-6778. Elbert Kirby, Jr., Petitioner v. Linda G. Morrissey, Judge, District Court of Oklahoma, Tulsa County, et al.

577 U.S. 1076, 136 S. Ct. 826, 193 L. Ed. 2d 736, 2016 U.S. LEXIS 461.

January 11, 2016. Petition for writ of certiorari to the Supreme Court of Oklahoma denied.

No. 15-6779. Gabriel Esparza, Petitioner v. James Falk, Warden, et al.

577 U.S. 1076, 136 S. Ct. 826, 193 L. Ed. 2d 736, 2016 U.S. LEXIS 127.

January 11, 2016. Petition for writ of certiorari to the United States Court of Appeals for the Tenth Circuit denied.

No. 15-6784. James Crosby, Petitioner v. Julie L. Jones, Secretary, Florida Department of Corrections, et al.

577 U.S. 1076, 136 S. Ct. 826, 193 L. Ed. 2d 736, 2016 U.S. LEXIS 504.

January 11, 2016. Petition for writ of certiorari to the United States Court of Appeals for the Eleventh Circuit denied.

No. 15-6788. Michael Smith, Petitioner v. New York.

577 U.S. 1077, 136 S. Ct. 826, 193 L. Ed. 2d 736, 2016 U.S. LEXIS 198.

January 11, 2016. Petition for writ of certiorari to the Appellate Division, Supreme Court of New York, First Judicial Department, denied.

Same case below, 126 App. Div. 3d 534, 5 N.Y.S.3d 89.

No. 15-6789. Isador Alexander Piper, Petitioner v. California.

577 U.S. 1077, 136 S. Ct. 827, 193 L. Ed. 2d 736, 2016 U.S. LEXIS 122.

January 11, 2016. Petition for writ of certiorari to the Court of Appeal of California, Sixth Appellate District, denied.

No. 15-6790. Sergei Portnoy, Petitioner v. City of Woodland, California, et al.

577 U.S. 1077, 136 S. Ct. 827, 193 L. Ed. 2d 736, 2016 U.S. LEXIS 121.

January 11, 2016. Petition for writ of certiorari to the United States Court of Appeals for the Ninth Circuit denied.

Same case below, 611 Fed. Appx. 921.

No. 15-6792. Desean Lewis, Petitioner v. Illinois.

577 U.S. 1077, 136 S. Ct. 827, 193 L. Ed. 2d 737, 2016 U.S. LEXIS 166.

January 11, 2016. Petition for writ of certiorari to the Appellate Court of Illinois, First District, denied.

No. 15-6794. Theotis Thornton, Petitioner v. Wendy Kelley, Director, Arkansas Department of Correction.

577 U.S. 1077, 136 S. Ct. 827, 193 L. Ed. 2d 737, 2016 U.S. LEXIS 266.

January 11, 2016. Petition for writ of certiorari to the United States Court of Appeals for the Eighth Circuit denied.

No. 15-6796. Lee Ander Tillman, Jr., Petitioner v. Josie Gastelo, Acting Warden.

577 U.S. 1077, 136 S. Ct. 827, 193 L. Ed. 2d 737, 2016 U.S. LEXIS 316, reh den 578 U.S. 916, 136 S. Ct. 1537, 194 L. Ed. 2d 621, 2016 U.S. LEXIS 2306.

January 11, 2016. Petition for writ of certiorari to the United States Court of Appeals for the Ninth Circuit denied.

No. 15-6797. James Thivel, Petitioner v. Kim Butler, Warden.

577 U.S. 1077, 136 S. Ct. 827, 193 L. Ed. 2d 737, 2016 U.S. LEXIS 491.

January 11, 2016. Petition for writ of certiorari to the United States Court of Appeals for the Seventh Circuit denied.

No. 15-6801. Ignacio Serrano, Petitioner v. Florida.

577 U.S. 1077, 136 S. Ct. 828, 193 L. Ed. 2d 737, 2016 U.S. LEXIS 409.

January 11, 2016. Petition for writ of certiorari to the Supreme Court of Florida denied.

Same case below, 163 So. 3d 513.

No. 15-6802. Eddie Ryan Lewis, Petitioner v. Mary Berghuis, Warden.

577 U.S. 1077, 136 S. Ct. 828, 193 L. Ed. 2d 737, 2016 U.S. LEXIS 233.

January 11, 2016. Petition for writ of certiorari to the United States Court of Appeals for the Sixth Circuit denied.

No. 15-6808. Anthony L. Jackson, Petitioner v. Larry Denney, Warden.

577 U.S. 1077, 136 S. Ct. 828, 193 L. Ed. 2d 737, 2016 U.S. LEXIS 260.

January 11, 2016. Petition for writ of certiorari to the United States Court of Appeals for the Eighth Circuit denied.

No. 15-6809. Homer Ray Roseberry, Petitioner v. Arizona.

577 U.S. 1077, 136 S. Ct. 828, 193 L. Ed. 2d 737, 2016 U.S. LEXIS 517.

January 11, 2016. Petition for writ of certiorari to the Supreme Court of Arizona denied.

Same case below, 237 Ariz. 507, 353 P.3d 847.

No. 15-6810. Franklin Sandoval Nelson, Petitioner v. Jon S. Flemmer, Judge, Fifth Circuit Court of South Dakota, et al.

577 U.S. 1077, 136 S. Ct. 828, 193 L. Ed. 2d 738, 2016 U.S. LEXIS 459.

January 11, 2016. Petition for writ of certiorari to the United States Court of Appeals for the Eighth Circuit denied.

No. 15-6811. Michael McCall, Petitioner v. Julie L. Jones, Secretary, Florida Department of Corrections, et al.

577 U.S. 1077, 136 S. Ct. 828, 193 L. Ed. 2d 738, 2016 U.S. LEXIS 190.

January 11, 2016. Petition for writ of certiorari to the United States Court of Appeals for the Eleventh Circuit denied.

No. 15-6812. Jerome McFadden, Petitioner v. Dennis Bush, Warden.

577 U.S. 1077, 136 S. Ct. 828, 193 L. Ed. 2d 738, 2016 U.S. LEXIS 359, reh den 577 U.S. 1231, 136 S. Ct. 1488, 194 L. Ed. 2d 579, 2016 U.S. LEXIS 1908.

January 11, 2016. Petition for writ of certiorari to the United States Court of Appeals for the Fourth Circuit denied.

Same case below, 610 Fed. Appx. 309.

No. 15-6813. David Lee Jones, Petitioner v. Wendy Kelley, Director, Arkansas Department of Correction.

577 U.S. 1078, 136 S. Ct. 829, 193 L. Ed. 2d 738, 2016 U.S. LEXIS 173.

January 11, 2016. Petition for writ of certiorari to the United States Court of Appeals for the Eighth Circuit denied.

No. 15-6815. Edward Oberwise, Petitioner v. Julie L. Jones, Secretary, Florida Department of Corrections, et al.

577 U.S. 1078, 136 S. Ct. 829, 193 L. Ed. 2d 738, 2016 U.S. LEXIS 201.

January 11, 2016. Petition for writ of certiorari to the United States Court of Appeals for the Eleventh Circuit denied.

No. 15-6817. Irvin Shay Viers, Petitioner v. Stan Shepard, Warden.

577 U.S. 1078, 136 S. Ct. 829, 193 L. Ed. 2d 738, 2016 U.S. LEXIS 78, reh den 577 U.S. 1231, 136 S. Ct. 1488, 194 L. Ed. 2d 579, 2016 U.S. LEXIS 1888.

January 11, 2016. Petition for writ of certiorari to the United States Court of Appeals for the Eleventh Circuit denied.

Same case below, 605 Fed. Appx. 933.

No. 15-6822. Robert T. Allen, aka Thomas L. Duncan, aka Tommy L. Fitzgerald, Petitioner v. Dennis A. Rolf, Judge, Circuit Court of Missouri, Lafayette and Saline Counties.

577 U.S. 1078, 136 S. Ct. 829, 193 L. Ed. 2d 738, 2016 U.S. LEXIS 253.

January 11, 2016. Petition for writ of certiorari to the Supreme Court of Missouri denied.

No. 15-6823. Autry Earl Barney, Petitioner v. Congoleum Corporation, et al.

577 U.S. 1078, 136 S. Ct. 829, 193 L. Ed. 2d 738, 2016 U.S. LEXIS 361, reh den 577 U.S. 1231, 136 S. Ct. 1488, 194 L. Ed. 2d 579, 2016 U.S. LEXIS 1886.

January 11, 2016. Petition for writ of certiorari to the United States Court of Appeals for the Third Circuit denied.

No. 15-6824. Lisa Kay Brumfiel, Petitioner v. U.S. Bank N.A., et al.

577 U.S. 1078, 136 S. Ct. 830, 193 L. Ed. 2d 739, 2016 U.S. LEXIS 606.

January 11, 2016. Petition for writ of certiorari to the United States Court of Appeals for the Tenth Circuit denied.

Same case below, 618 Fed. Appx. 933.

No. 15-6828. Norman E. Caison, Petitioner v. Julie L. Jones, Secretary, Florida Department of Corrections.

577 U.S. 1078, 136 S. Ct. 830, 193 L. Ed. 2d 739, 2016 U.S. LEXIS 75.

January 11, 2016. Petition for writ of certiorari to the Supreme Court of Florida denied.

Same case below, 177 So. 3d 1263.

No. 15-6829. Tina M. Emerson, Petitioner v. Asa Hutchinson, Governor of Arkansas.

577 U.S. 1078, 136 S. Ct. 830, 193 L. Ed. 2d 739, 2016 U.S. LEXIS 115.

January 11, 2016. Petition for writ of certiorari to the United States Court of Appeals for the Eighth Circuit denied.

No. 15-6830. Michael Lynn Bradden, Petitioner v. Texas (two judgments).

577 U.S. 1078, 136 S. Ct. 830, 193 L. Ed. 2d 739, 2016 U.S. LEXIS 310.

January 11, 2016. Petition for writ of certiorari to the Court of Criminal Appeals of Texas denied.

No. 15-6831. Cassandra C. Olague, Petitioner v. County of Sacramento, California, et al.

577 U.S. 1078, 136 S. Ct. 830, 193 L. Ed. 2d 739, 2016 U.S. LEXIS 512.

January 11, 2016. Petition for writ of certiorari to the United States Court of Appeals for the Ninth Circuit denied.

Same case below, 601 Fed. Appx. 557.

No. 15-6832. Ronald A. Nurse, Petitioner v. Richmond County Sheriff's Department, et al.

577 U.S. 1078, 136 S. Ct. 831, 193 L. Ed. 2d 739, 2016 U.S. LEXIS 450.

January 11, 2016. Petition for writ of certiorari to the United States Court of Appeals for the Eleventh Circuit denied.

No. 15-6833. James Murray, Petitioner v. Jean Toal.

577 U.S. 1078, 136 S. Ct. 831, 193 L. Ed. 2d 739, 2016 U.S. LEXIS 269.

January 11, 2016. Petition for writ of certiorari to the United States Court of Appeals for the Third Circuit denied.

No. 15-6835. Benjamin Taylor, Petitioner v. Florida.

577 U.S. 1078, 136 S. Ct. 831, 193 L. Ed. 2d 739, 2016 U.S. LEXIS 502.

January 11, 2016. Petition for writ of certiorari to the District Court of Appeal of Florida, Fifth District, denied.

Same case below, 336 P.3d 922.

No. 15-6839. Daniel Loren Jenkins, Petitioner v. John Myrick, Superintendent, Two Rivers Correctional Institution.

577 U.S. 1078, 136 S. Ct. 831, 193 L. Ed. 2d 740, 2016 U.S. LEXIS 448.

January 11, 2016. Petition for writ of certiorari to the United States Court of Appeals for the Ninth Circuit denied.

No. 15-6841. Charles Rembert, Petitioner v. Illinois.

577 U.S. 1079, 136 S. Ct. 831, 193 L. Ed. 2d 740, 2016 U.S. LEXIS 212.

January 11, 2016. Petition for writ of certiorari to the Appellate Court of Illinois, First District, denied.

No. 15-6843. Richard Litschewski, Petitioner v. Robert Dooley, Warden, et al.

577 U.S. 1079, 136 S. Ct. 832, 193 L. Ed. 2d 740, 2016 U.S. LEXIS 424.

January 11, 2016. Petition for writ of certiorari to the United States Court of Appeals for the Eighth Circuit denied.

Same case below, 792 F.3d 1012.

No. 15-6845. Aaron Alvarez, Petitioner v. Kansas.

577 U.S. 1079, 136 S. Ct. 832, 193 L. Ed. 2d 740, 2016 U.S. LEXIS 286.

January 11, 2016. Petition for writ of certiorari to the Court of Appeals of Kansas denied.

No. 15-6846. Nick Alfred Aguilar, Petitioner v. Texas.

577 U.S. 1079, 136 S. Ct. 832, 193 L. Ed. 2d 740, 2016 U.S. LEXIS 91.

January 11, 2016. Petition for writ of certiorari to the United States Court of Appeals for the Fifth Circuit denied.

Same case below, 612 Fed. Appx. 245.

No. 15-6847. Leo M. Abby, Petitioner v. Mitch Perry, Warden.

577 U.S. 1079, 136 S. Ct. 832, 193 L. Ed. 2d 740, 2016 U.S. LEXIS 501.

January 11, 2016. Petition for writ of certiorari to the United States Court of Appeals for the Sixth Circuit denied.

No. 15-6849. David Hardy, Petitioner v. Unknown Thompson, et al.

577 U.S. 1079, 136 S. Ct. 832, 193 L. Ed. 2d 740, 2016 U.S. LEXIS 322.

January 11, 2016. Petition for writ of certiorari to the United States Court of Appeals for the Sixth Circuit denied.

No. 15-6852. Edward Charles, III, Petitioner v. California.

577 U.S. 1079, 136 S. Ct. 832, 193 L. Ed. 2d 740, 2016 U.S. LEXIS 433.

January 11, 2016. Petition for writ of certiorari to the Supreme Court of California denied.

Same case below, 61 Cal. 4th 308, 188 Cal. Rptr. 3d 282, 349 P.3d 990.

———————

No. 15-6856. David Hardy, Petitioner v. Unknown Peterman, et al.

577 U.S. 1079, 136 S. Ct. 833, 193 L. Ed. 2d 741, 2016 U.S. LEXIS 299.

January 11, 2016. Petition for writ of certiorari to the United States Court of Appeals for the Sixth Circuit denied.

———————

No. 15-6858. Timothy Earl Green, Petitioner v. Dennis Bush, Warden.

577 U.S. 1079, 136 S. Ct. 833, 193 L. Ed. 2d 741, 2016 U.S. LEXIS 422.

January 11, 2016. Petition for writ of certiorari to the United States Court of Appeals for the Fourth Circuit denied.

Same case below, 601 Fed. Appx. 235.

———————

No. 15-6861. Michael D. Hickingbottom, Petitioner v. Indiana.

577 U.S. 1079, 136 S. Ct. 833, 193 L. Ed. 2d 741, 2016 U.S. LEXIS 131.

January 11, 2016. Petition for writ of certiorari to the Court of Appeals of Indiana, Fifth District, denied.

Same case below, 26 N.E.3d 684.

———————

No. 15-6862. Sean Fields, Petitioner v. Nancy Giroux, Superintendent, State Correctional Institution at Albion, et al.

577 U.S. 1079, 136 S. Ct. 833, 193 L. Ed. 2d 741, 2016 U.S. LEXIS 220.

January 11, 2016. Petition for writ of certiorari to the United States Court of Appeals for the Third Circuit denied.

———————

No. 15-6864. Thomas G., Petitioner v. Sonya G.

577 U.S. 1079, 136 S. Ct. 834, 193 L. Ed. 2d 741, 2016 U.S. LEXIS 289.

January 11, 2016. Petition for writ of certiorari to the Supreme Court of Alaska denied.

———————

No. 15-6868. Joe Seals, Petitioner v. Michael Capra, Superintendent, Sing Sing Correctional Facility.

577 U.S. 1079, 136 S. Ct. 834, 193 L. Ed. 2d 741, 2016 U.S. LEXIS 255.

January 11, 2016. Petition for writ of certiorari to the United States Court of Appeals for the Second Circuit denied.

———————

No. 15-6871. Franklin S. Nelson, Petitioner v. Jon S. Flemmer, Judge, et al.

577 U.S. 1079, 136 S. Ct. 834, 193 L. Ed. 2d 741, 2016 U.S. LEXIS 191.

January 11, 2016. Petition for writ of certiorari to the United States Court of Appeals for the Eighth Circuit denied.

———————

No. 15-6872. Saul A. Rojas, Petitioner v. California.

577 U.S. 1079, 136 S. Ct. 834, 193 L. Ed. 2d 741, 2016 U.S. LEXIS 178.

January 11, 2016. Petition for writ of certiorari to the Supreme Court of California denied.

No. 15-6873. Charles Elvis Raby, Petitioner v. Texas.

577 U.S. 1079, 136 S. Ct. 834, 193 L. Ed. 2d 742, 2016 U.S. LEXIS 151.

January 11, 2016. Petition for writ of certiorari to the Court of Criminal Appeals of Texas denied.

No. 15-6876. L.B., Petitioner v. S.T., et al.

577 U.S. 1080, 136 S. Ct. 834, 193 L. Ed. 2d 742, 2016 U.S. LEXIS 159, reh den 577 U.S. 1209, 136 S. Ct. 1404, 194 L. Ed. 2d 383, 2016 U.S. LEXIS 1639.

January 11, 2016. Petition for writ of certiorari to the District of Columbia Court of Appeals denied.

Same case below, 120 A.3d 89.

No. 15-6877. Richard Fairchild, Petitioner v. Maurice Warrior, Interim Warden.

577 U.S. 1080, 136 S. Ct. 835, 193 L. Ed. 2d 742, 2016 U.S. LEXIS 423.

January 11, 2016. Petition for writ of certiorari to the United States Court of Appeals for the Tenth Circuit denied.

Same case below, 784 F.3d 702.

No. 15-6881. Charlie Lewis, Petitioner v. Michelle Smith, Warden.

577 U.S. 1080, 136 S. Ct. 836, 193 L. Ed. 2d 742, 2016 U.S. LEXIS 93.

January 11, 2016. Petition for writ of certiorari to the United States Court of Appeals for the Eighth Circuit denied.

No. 15-6884. Debra Lee Jeffery, Petitioner v. California, et al.

577 U.S. 1080, 136 S. Ct. 836, 193 L. Ed. 2d 742, 2016 U.S. LEXIS 132.

January 11, 2016. Petition for writ of certiorari to the United States Court of Appeals for the Ninth Circuit denied.

No. 15-6885. Thomas A. Kidwell, Petitioner v. Charles L. Ryan, Director, Arizona Department of Corrections, et al.

577 U.S. 1080, 136 S. Ct. 836, 193 L. Ed. 2d 742, 2016 U.S. LEXIS 490, reh den 578 U.S. 916, 136 S. Ct. 1537, 194 L. Ed. 2d 622, 2016 U.S. LEXIS 2378.

January 11, 2016. Petition for writ of certiorari to the United States Court of Appeals for the Ninth Circuit denied.

Same case below, 601 Fed. Appx. 546.

No. 15-6886. Walter E. Johnson Jr., Petitioner v. Burl Cain, Warden.

577 U.S. 1080, 136 S. Ct. 836, 193 L. Ed. 2d 742, 2016 U.S. LEXIS 440.

January 11, 2016. Petition for writ of certiorari to the United States Court of Appeals for the Fifth Circuit denied.

No. 15-6887. Eric Dean Krieger, Petitioner v. Minnesota.

577 U.S. 1080, 136 S. Ct. 836, 193 L. Ed. 2d 742, 2016 U.S. LEXIS 99.

January 11, 2016. Petition for writ of certiorari to the United States Court of Appeals for the Eighth Circuit denied.

No. 15-6888. Marquitta Littlebear, Petitioner v. Oklahoma.

577 U.S. 1080, 136 S. Ct. 836, 193 L. Ed. 2d 743, 2016 U.S. LEXIS 397.

January 11, 2016. Petition for writ of certiorari to the Court of Criminal Appeals of Oklahoma denied.

No. 15-6891. Jamar B. Perry, Petitioner v. Michael Wenerowicz, Superintendent, State Correctional Institution at Graterford, et al.

577 U.S. 1080, 136 S. Ct. 837, 193 L. Ed. 2d 743, 2016 U.S. LEXIS 208.

January 11, 2016. Petition for writ of certiorari to the United States Court of Appeals for the Third Circuit denied.

No. 15-6892. Etumai Felix Mtoched, Petitioner v. Loretta E. Lynch, Attorney General.

577 U.S. 1080, 136 S. Ct. 837, 193 L. Ed. 2d 743, 2016 U.S. LEXIS 202.

January 11, 2016. Petition for writ of certiorari to the United States Court of Appeals for the Ninth Circuit denied.

Same case below, 786 F.3d 1210.

No. 15-6894. Frederick Miller, Petitioner v. David Sexton, Warden.

577 U.S. 1080, 136 S. Ct. 837, 193 L. Ed. 2d 743, 2016 U.S. LEXIS 254.

January 11, 2016. Petition for writ of certiorari to the United States Court of Appeals for the Sixth Circuit denied.

No. 15-6895. Bynum Rayfield, Petitioner v. Willie Eagleton, Warden.

577 U.S. 1080, 136 S. Ct. 837, 193 L. Ed. 2d 743, 2016 U.S. LEXIS 182.

January 11, 2016. Petition for writ of certiorari to the United States Court of Appeals for the Fourth Circuit denied.

Same case below, 608 Fed. Appx. 135.

No. 15-6898. Maricela Ramirez, Petitioner v. Melanie Parker, et al.

577 U.S. 1080, 136 S. Ct. 837, 193 L. Ed. 2d 743, 2016 U.S. LEXIS 447, reh den 577 U.S. 1185, 136 S. Ct. 1252, 194 L. Ed. 2d 250, 2016 U.S. LEXIS 1227.

January 11, 2016. Petition for writ of certiorari to the United States Court of Appeals for the Ninth Circuit denied.

No. 15-6901. Larry E. Clark, Petitioner v. Anthony Foxx, Secretary of Transportation, et al.

577 U.S. 1080, 136 S. Ct. 838, 193 L. Ed. 2d 743, 2016 U.S. LEXIS 442.

January 11, 2016. Petition for writ of certiorari to the United States Court of Appeals for the Fifth Circuit denied.

No. 15-6908. Paul Kenneth Kusak, Petitioner v. Samuel Lambadola, et al.

577 U.S. 1081, 136 S. Ct. 839, 193 L. Ed. 2d 743, 2016 U.S. LEXIS 331.

January 11, 2016. Petition for writ of certiorari to the United States Court of Appeals for the Second Circuit denied.

No. 15-6909. Paul K. Kusak, Petitioner v. Robert Klein, et al.

577 U.S. 1081, 136 S. Ct. 839, 193 L. Ed. 2d 744, 2016 U.S. LEXIS 175.

January 11, 2016. Petition for writ of certiorari to the United States Court of Appeals for the Second Circuit denied.

No. 15-6912. Louis Peoples, Jr., Petitioner v. James Falk, Warden, et al.

577 U.S. 1081, 136 S. Ct. 839, 193 L. Ed. 2d 744, 2016 U.S. LEXIS 214.

January 11, 2016. Petition for writ of certiorari to the United States Court of Appeals for the Tenth Circuit denied.

Same case below, 613 Fed. Appx. 752.

No. 15-6915. Josean Clemente, Petitioner v. United States.

577 U.S. 1081, 136 S. Ct. 839, 193 L. Ed. 2d 744, 2016 U.S. LEXIS 378.

January 11, 2016. Petition for writ of certiorari to the United States Court of Appeals for the First Circuit denied.

No. 15-6921. Sheryl Taylor, Petitioner v. Memphis Area Legal Services, et al.

577 U.S. 1081, 136 S. Ct. 839, 193 L. Ed. 2d 744, 2016 U.S. LEXIS 223.

January 11, 2016. Petition for writ of certiorari to the United States Court of Appeals for the Sixth Circuit denied.

No. 15-6923. Pedio Vaigasi, Petitioner v. Solow Management Corporation, et al.

No. 15-6924. Pedio Vaigasi, Petitioner v. Solow Management Corporation, et al.

577 U.S. 1081, 136 S. Ct. 840, 193 L. Ed. 2d 744, 2016 U.S. LEXIS 232.

January 11, 2016. Petitions for writs of certiorari to the United States Court of Appeals for the Second Circuit denied.

No. 15-6926. Paul A. Lewis, Petitioner v. Robert A. McDonald, Secretary of Veterans Affairs.

577 U.S. 1081, 136 S. Ct. 840, 193 L. Ed. 2d 744, 2016 U.S. LEXIS 390.

January 11, 2016. Petition for writ of certiorari to the United States Court of Appeals for the Fourth Circuit denied.

Same case below, 621 Fed. Appx. 163.

No. 15-6928. Marshall Reedom, Jr., Petitioner v. Department of the Treasury, et al.

577 U.S. 1081, 136 S. Ct. 840, 193 L. Ed. 2d 744, 2016 U.S. LEXIS 155.

January 11, 2016. Petition for writ of certiorari to the United States Court of Appeals for the First Circuit denied.

No. 15-6929. Gina Brasher Langley, Petitioner v. Internal Revenue Service.

577 U.S. 1081, 136 S. Ct. 840, 193 L. Ed. 2d 744, 2016 U.S. LEXIS 129.

January 11, 2016. Petition for writ of certiorari to the United States Court of Appeals for the Eleventh Circuit denied.

Same case below, 612 Fed. Appx. 585.

No. 15-6930. Bozorgmehr Pouyeh, Petitioner v. Board of Trustees of the University of Alabama, et al.

577 U.S. 1081, 136 S. Ct. 840, 193 L. Ed. 2d 745, 2016 U.S. LEXIS 500, reh den 577 U.S. 1185, 136 S. Ct. 1253, 194 L. Ed. 2d 251, 2016 U.S. LEXIS 1303.

January 11, 2016. Petition for writ of certiorari to the United States Court of Appeals for the Eleventh Circuit denied.

Same case below, 625 Fed. Appx. 495.

No. 15-6933. Cypriah Diaz, Petitioner v. John Kerestes, Superintendent, State Correctional Institution at Mahanoy, et al.

577 U.S. 1081, 136 S. Ct. 841, 193 L. Ed. 2d 745, 2016 U.S. LEXIS 493.

January 11, 2016. Petition for writ of certiorari to the United States Court of Appeals for the Third Circuit denied.

No. 15-6934. Gregory Devonte Robertson, Petitioner v. United States.

577 U.S. 1081, 136 S. Ct. 841, 193 L. Ed. 2d 745, 2016 U.S. LEXIS 482.

January 11, 2016. Petition for writ of certiorari to the United States Court of Appeals for the Fourth Circuit denied.

Same case below, 612 Fed. Appx. 196.

No. 15-6935. Anna Margarita Sandoval, Petitioners v. United States.

577 U.S. 1081, 136 S. Ct. 841, 193 L. Ed. 2d 745, 2016 U.S. LEXIS 278.

January 11, 2016. Petition for writ of certiorari to the United States Court of Appeals for the Ninth Circuit denied.

Same case below, 617 Fed. Appx. 645.

No. 15-6936. Phillip Dominic Casciola, Petitioner v. Julie L. Jones, Secretary, Florida Department of Corrections, et al.

577 U.S. 1081, 136 S. Ct. 841, 193 L. Ed. 2d 745, 2016 U.S. LEXIS 496.

January 11, 2016. Petition for writ of certiorari to the United States Court of Appeals for the Eleventh Circuit denied.

No. 15-6940. Jonathan Cornish, Petitioner v. United States.

577 U.S. 1082, 136 S. Ct. 841, 193 L. Ed. 2d 745, 2016 U.S. LEXIS 465.

January 11, 2016. Petition for writ of certiorari to the United States Court of Appeals for the Fourth Circuit denied.

Same case below, 600 Fed. Appx. 104.

No. 15-6941. Raymond Clark, Petitioner v. California.

577 U.S. 1082, 136 S. Ct. 842, 193 L. Ed. 2d 745, 2016 U.S. LEXIS 416, reh den 577 U.S. 1232, 136 S. Ct. 1489, 194 L. Ed. 2d 580, 2016 U.S. LEXIS 1903.

January 11, 2016. Petition for writ of certiorari to the Supreme Court of California denied.

No. 15-6945. Richard DeCaro, Petitioner v. United States.

577 U.S. 1082, 136 S. Ct. 842, 193 L. Ed. 2d 745, 2016 U.S. LEXIS 136.

January 11, 2016. Petition for writ of certiorari to the United States Court of Appeals for the Eighth Circuit denied.

Same case below, 593 Fed. Appx. 605.

No. 15-6946. Gennaro Rauso, Petitioner v. United States.

577 U.S. 1082, 136 S. Ct. 842, 193 L. Ed. 2d 746, 2016 U.S. LEXIS 387.

January 11, 2016. Petition for writ of certiorari to the United States Court of Appeals for the Third Circuit denied.

No. 15-6947. Criss E. Duncan, Petitioner v. United States.

577 U.S. 1082, 136 S. Ct. 842, 193 L. Ed. 2d 746, 2016 U.S. LEXIS 480.

January 11, 2016. Petition for writ of certiorari to the United States Court of Appeals for the Seventh Circuit denied.

No. 15-6948. Miguel De La Cruz-Quintana, Petitioner v. United States.

577 U.S. 1082, 136 S. Ct. 842, 193 L. Ed. 2d 746, 2016 U.S. LEXIS 435.

January 11, 2016. Petition for writ of certiorari to the United States Court of Appeals for the Fifth Circuit denied.

Same case below, 613 Fed. Appx. 366.

No. 15-6951. Charles Nolon Bush, Petitioner v. United States.

577 U.S. 1082, 136 S. Ct. 843, 193 L. Ed. 2d 746, 2016 U.S. LEXIS 319.

January 11, 2016. Petition for writ of certiorari to the United States Court of Appeals for the Ninth Circuit denied.

Same case below, 594 Fed. Appx. 389.

No. 15-6952. Edgardo Barron-Espinosa, Petitioner v. United States.

577 U.S. 1082, 136 S. Ct. 843, 193 L. Ed. 2d 746, 2016 U.S. LEXIS 102.

January 11, 2016. Petition for writ of certiorari to the United States Court of Appeals for the Fourth Circuit denied.

Same case below, 608 Fed. Appx. 140.

No. 15-6954. Joseph Coppola, Petitioner v. Terry O'Brien, Warden.

577 U.S. 1082, 136 S. Ct. 843, 193 L. Ed. 2d 746, 2016 U.S. LEXIS 546, reh den 577 U.S. 1232, 136 S. Ct. 1489, 194 L. Ed. 2d 580, 2016 U.S. LEXIS 1891.

January 11, 2016. Petition for writ of certiorari to the United States Court of Appeals for the Fourth Circuit denied.

Same case below, 616 Fed. Appx. 80.

No. 15-6960. Troy Brandon Woodard, Petitioner v. United States.

577 U.S. 1082, 136 S. Ct. 843, 193 L. Ed. 2d 746, 2016 U.S. LEXIS 446.

January 11, 2016. Petition for writ of certiorari to the United States Court of Appeals for the Fourth Circuit denied.

Same case below, 614 Fed. Appx. 101.

No. 15-6961. David E. Bowers, Jr., Petitioner v. William Pollard, Warden.

577 U.S. 1082, 136 S. Ct. 843, 193 L. Ed. 2d 746, 2016 U.S. LEXIS 171.

January 11, 2016. Petition for writ of certiorari to the United States Court of Appeals for the Seventh Circuit denied.

No. 15-6962. Billy Gene Jefferson, Jr., Petitioner v. United States.

577 U.S. 1082, 136 S. Ct. 844, 193 L. Ed. 2d 747, 2016 U.S. LEXIS 283.

January 11, 2016. Petition for writ of certiorari to the United States Court of Appeals for the Fourth Circuit denied.

Same case below, 621 Fed. Appx. 757.

No. 15-6964. Marco Maurice Heath, Petitioner v. United States.

577 U.S. 1082, 136 S. Ct. 844, 193 L. Ed. 2d 747, 2016 U.S. LEXIS 329.

January 11, 2016. Petition for writ of certiorari to the United States Court of Appeals for the Eleventh Circuit denied.

Same case below, 622 Fed. Appx. 843.

No. 15-6967. Armando Gonzalez-Martinez, Petitioner v. United States.

577 U.S. 1082, 136 S. Ct. 844, 193 L. Ed. 2d 747, 2016 U.S. LEXIS 413.

January 11, 2016. Petition for writ of certiorari to the United States Court of Appeals for the Eleventh Circuit denied.

Same case below, 612 Fed. Appx. 587.

No. 15-6969. Glen Lee Green, Petitioner v. United States.

577 U.S. 1082, 136 S. Ct. 844, 193 L. Ed. 2d 747, 2016 U.S. LEXIS 610.

January 11, 2016. Petition for writ of certiorari to the United States Court of Appeals for the Ninth Circuit denied.

Same case below, 623 Fed. Appx. 848.

No. 15-6970. Braulio Gonzalez-Tejeda, Petitioner v. United States.

577 U.S. 1083, 136 S. Ct. 844, 193 L. Ed. 2d 747, 2016 U.S. LEXIS 140.

January 11, 2016. Petition for writ of certiorari to the United States Court of Appeals for the Ninth Circuit denied.

Same case below, 599 Fed. Appx. 734.

No. 15-6973. Dorian Shareef Fowler, Petitioner v. United States.

577 U.S. 1083, 136 S. Ct. 844, 193 L. Ed. 2d 747, 2016 U.S. LEXIS 295.

January 11, 2016. Petition for writ of certiorari to the United States Court of Appeals for the Ninth Circuit denied.

Same case below, 542 Fed. Appx. 647.

No. 15-6974. Portie A. Robertson, Petitioner v. Pennsylvania.

577 U.S. 1083, 136 S. Ct. 845, 193 L. Ed. 2d 747, 2016 U.S. LEXIS 200.

January 11, 2016. Petition for writ of certiorari to the Superior Court of Pennsylvania, Philadelphia Office, denied.

Same case below, 125 A.3d 444.

No. 15-6976. Keith Brooks, Petitioner v. Rick Raemisch, Executive Director, Colorado Department of Corrections, et al.

577 U.S. 1083, 136 S. Ct. 845, 193 L. Ed. 2d 747, 2016 U.S. LEXIS 506.

January 11, 2016. Petition for writ of certiorari to the United States Court of Appeals for the Tenth Circuit denied.

Same case below, 613 Fed. Appx. 773.

Same case below, 599 Fed. Appx. 777.

No. 15-6977. Jimmy Bernard Barkley, Petitioner v. United States.

577 U.S. 1083, 136 S. Ct. 845, 193 L. Ed. 2d 748, 2016 U.S. LEXIS 431.

January 11, 2016. Petition for writ of certiorari to the United States Court of Appeals for the Eleventh Circuit denied.

Same case below, 615 Fed. Appx. 557.

No. 15-6978. Brandon Allen, Petitioner v. United States.

577 U.S. 1083, 136 S. Ct. 845, 193 L. Ed. 2d 748, 2016 U.S. LEXIS 542.

January 11, 2016. Petition for writ of certiorari to the United States Court of Appeals for the Eleventh Circuit denied.

No. 15-6979. James J. Briscoe, Petitioner v. Ian Wallace, Warden.

577 U.S. 1083, 136 S. Ct. 845, 193 L. Ed. 2d 748, 2016 U.S. LEXIS 547.

January 11, 2016. Petition for writ of certiorari to the United States Court of Appeals for the Eighth Circuit denied.

No. 15-6982. Bladimir Perez, Petitioner v. United States.

577 U.S. 1083, 136 S. Ct. 845, 193 L. Ed. 2d 748, 2016 U.S. LEXIS 437.

January 11, 2016. Petition for writ of certiorari to the United States Court of Appeals for the Ninth Circuit denied.

No. 15-6983. Eric Alberto Lewis, Petitioner v. United States.

577 U.S. 1083, 136 S. Ct. 846, 193 L. Ed. 2d 748, 2016 U.S. LEXIS 370.

January 11, 2016. Petition for writ of certiorari to the United States Court of Appeals for the Fifth Circuit denied.

Same case below, 603 Fed. Appx. 306.

No. 15-6984. Varnador Sutton, Petitioner v. United States.

577 U.S. 1083, 136 S. Ct. 846, 193 L. Ed. 2d 748, 2016 U.S. LEXIS 217.

January 11, 2016. Petition for writ of certiorari to the United States Court of Appeals for the Seventh Circuit denied.

No. 15-6985. Jesse James Baldwin, Jr., Petitioner v. United States.

577 U.S. 1083, 136 S. Ct. 846, 193 L. Ed. 2d 748, 2016 U.S. LEXIS 495.

January 11, 2016. Petition for writ of certiorari to the United States Court of Appeals for the Fourth Circuit denied.

Same case below, 620 Fed. Appx. 150.

No. 15-6986. Kim Davis Beckstrom, Petitioner v. United States.

577 U.S. 1083, 136 S. Ct. 846, 193 L. Ed. 2d 748, 2016 U.S. LEXIS 323.

January 11, 2016. Petition for writ of certiorari to the United States Court of Appeals for the Tenth Circuit denied.

Same case below, 618 Fed. Appx. 361.

Same case below, 599 Fed. Appx. 750.

No. 15-6987. Willie Bailey, Petitioner v. United States.

577 U.S. 1083, 136 S. Ct. 846, 193 L. Ed. 2d 749, 2016 U.S. LEXIS 498.

January 11, 2016. Petition for writ of certiorari to the United States Court of Appeals for the Sixth Circuit denied.

Same case below, 634 Fed. Appx. 473.

No. 15-6989. Evalina Walls, Petitioner v. Dillon County Detention Center.

577 U.S. 1083, 136 S. Ct. 846, 193 L. Ed. 2d 749, 2016 U.S. LEXIS 392.

January 11, 2016. Petition for writ of certiorari to the United States Court of Appeals for the Fourth Circuit denied.

Same case below, 612 Fed. Appx. 696.

No. 15-6993. Flavio Gutierrez Rubio, Petitioner v. United States.

577 U.S. 1083, 136 S. Ct. 847, 193 L. Ed. 2d 749, 2016 U.S. LEXIS 467.

January 11, 2016. Petition for writ of certiorari to the United States Court of Appeals for the Ninth Circuit denied.

Same case below, 601 Fed. Appx. 514.

No. 15-6994. Ivan Lopez-Ilustre, Petitioner v. United States.

577 U.S. 1084, 136 S. Ct. 847, 193 L. Ed. 2d 749, 2016 U.S. LEXIS 324.

January 11, 2016. Petition for writ of certiorari to the United States Court of Appeals for the Ninth Circuit denied.

No. 15-6998. Amilcar Matias-Torres, Petitioner v. United States.

577 U.S. 1084, 136 S. Ct. 847, 193 L. Ed. 2d 749, 2016 U.S. LEXIS 477, reh den 577 U.S. 1241, 136 S. Ct. 1511, 194 L. Ed. 2d 598, 2016 U.S. LEXIS 2142.

January 11, 2016. Petition for writ of certiorari to the United States Court of Appeals for the First Circuit denied.

No. 15-6999. Gilbert Lopez, Petitioner v. United States.

577 U.S. 1084, 136 S. Ct. 847, 193 L. Ed. 2d 749, 2016 U.S. LEXIS 247.

January 11, 2016. Petition for writ of certiorari to the United States Court of Appeals for the Third Circuit denied.

No. 15-7000. Sandra Rumanek, Petitioner v. Independent School Management, Inc.

577 U.S. 1084, 136 S. Ct. 847, 193 L. Ed. 2d 749, 2016 U.S. LEXIS 176.

January 11, 2016. Petition for writ of certiorari to the United States Court of Appeals for the Third Circuit denied.

Same case below, 619 Fed. Appx. 71.

No. 15-7002. Jose Luis Cruz, Petitioner v. Harold W. Clarke, Director, Virginia Department of Corrections.

577 U.S. 1084, 136 S. Ct. 847, 193 L. Ed. 2d 749, 2016 U.S. LEXIS 215.

January 11, 2016. Petition for writ of certiorari to the United States Court of Appeals for the Fourth Circuit denied.

Same case below, 610 Fed. Appx. 259.

No. 15-7006. Narcisa Veliz Novack, Petitioner v. United States.

577 U.S. 1084, 136 S. Ct. 848, 193 L. Ed. 2d 750, 2016 U.S. LEXIS 533.

January 11, 2016. Petition for writ of certiorari to the United States Court of Appeals for the Second Circuit denied.

Same case below, 623 Fed. Appx. 538.

No. 15-7007. Luis Montoya-Correa, Petitioner v. United States.

577 U.S. 1084, 136 S. Ct. 848, 193 L. Ed. 2d 750, 2016 U.S. LEXIS 342.

January 11, 2016. Petition for writ of certiorari to the United States Court of Appeals for the Fifth Circuit denied.

Same case below, 612 Fed. Appx. 786.

No. 15-7010. Martha Lupita James, Petitioner v. United States.

577 U.S. 1084, 136 S. Ct. 848, 193 L. Ed. 2d 750, 2016 U.S. LEXIS 385.

January 11, 2016. Petition for writ of certiorari to the United States Court of Appeals for the Ninth Circuit denied.

Same case below, 607 Fed. Appx. 752.

No. 15-7012. Derek Thomas, Petitioner v. United States.

577 U.S. 1084, 136 S. Ct. 848, 193 L. Ed. 2d 750, 2016 U.S. LEXIS 244.

January 11, 2016. Petition for writ of certiorari to the United States Court of Appeals for the Second Circuit denied.

Same case below, 788 F.3d 345.

No. 15-7014. Joseph Lee Ollie, Petitioner v. United States.

577 U.S. 1084, 136 S. Ct. 848, 193 L. Ed. 2d 750, 2016 U.S. LEXIS 205.

January 11, 2016. Petition for writ of certiorari to the United States Court of Appeals for the Third Circuit denied.

Same case below, 624 Fed. Appx. 807.

No. 15-7016. Francisco Cedillo-Martinez, Petitioner v. United States.

577 U.S. 1084, 136 S. Ct. 849, 193 L. Ed. 2d 750, 2016 U.S. LEXIS 425.

January 11, 2016. Petition for writ of certiorari to the United States Court of Appeals for the Fifth Circuit denied.

Same case below, 613 Fed. Appx. 385.

No. 15-7018. David Allen Nichols, Petitioner v. Jeffrey Beard, Secretary, California Department of Corrections and Rehabilitation.

577 U.S. 1084, 136 S. Ct. 849, 193 L. Ed. 2d 750, 2016 U.S. LEXIS 313.

January 11, 2016. Petition for writ of certiorari to the United States Court of Appeals for the Ninth Circuit denied.

Same case below, 617 Fed. Appx. 721.

No. 15-7019. Sherinette Wannamaker, aka Sheri Wannamaker, Petitioner v. Marian Boulware, Warden.

577 U.S. 1084, 136 S. Ct. 849, 193 L. Ed. 2d 750, 2016 U.S. LEXIS 349, reh den 578 U.S. 916, 136 S. Ct. 1537, 194 L. Ed. 2d 622, 2016 U.S. LEXIS 2317.

January 11, 2016. Petition for writ of certiorari to the United States Court of Appeals for the Fourth Circuit denied.

Same case below, 612 Fed. Appx. 686.

Same case below, 613 Fed. Appx. 370.

———

———

No. 15-7020. Jermaine A. Williams, Petitioner v. Steven Johnson, Administrator, New Jersey State Prison, et al.

577 U.S. 1084, 136 S. Ct. 849, 193 L. Ed. 2d 751, 2016 U.S. LEXIS 206, reh den 578 U.S. 916, 136 S. Ct. 1538, 194 L. Ed. 2d 622, 2016 U.S. LEXIS 2279.

January 11, 2016. Petition for writ of certiorari to the United States Court of Appeals for the Third Circuit denied.

———

No. 15-7025. Juan Manuel Carbajal-Moreno, Petitioner v. United States.

577 U.S. 1084, 136 S. Ct. 850, 193 L. Ed. 2d 751, 2016 U.S. LEXIS 548.

January 11, 2016. Petition for writ of certiorari to the United States Court of Appeals for the Tenth Circuit denied.

Same case below, 619 Fed. Appx. 767.

———

No. 15-7028. Jorge Fabian Buck-Soltero, Petitioner v. United States.

577 U.S. 1085, 136 S. Ct. 850, 193 L. Ed. 2d 751, 2016 U.S. LEXIS 451.

January 11, 2016. Petition for writ of certiorari to the United States Court of Appeals for the Fifth Circuit denied.

Same case below, 628 Fed. Appx. 246.

———

No. 15-7029. Orlin Jimenez-Archaga, Petitioner v. United States.

577 U.S. 1085, 136 S. Ct. 850, 193 L. Ed. 2d 751, 2016 U.S. LEXIS 453.

January 11, 2016. Petition for writ of certiorari to the United States Court of Appeals for the Fifth Circuit denied.

No. 15-7031. Marco Antonio Ortiz-Varela, Petitioner v. United States.

577 U.S. 1085, 136 S. Ct. 850, 193 L. Ed. 2d 751, 2016 U.S. LEXIS 241.

January 11, 2016. Petition for writ of certiorari to the United States Court of Appeals for the Fifth Circuit denied.

Same case below, 613 Fed. Appx. 350.

———

No. 15-7033. Paul Norris, Jr., Petitioner v. Wendy Kelley, Director, Arkansas Department of Correction.

577 U.S. 1085, 136 S. Ct. 851, 193 L. Ed. 2d 751, 2016 U.S. LEXIS 230.

January 11, 2016. Petition for writ of certiorari to the United States Court of Appeals for the Eighth Circuit denied.

———

No. 15-7034. Albert Guzman, Petitioner v. United States.

577 U.S. 1085, 136 S. Ct. 851, 193 L. Ed. 2d 751, 2016 U.S. LEXIS 379.

January 11, 2016. Petition for writ of certiorari to the United States Court of Appeals for the Fifth Circuit denied.

Same case below, 614 Fed. Appx. 745.

———

No. 15-7036. Tyrone Hunter, Petitioner v. United States.

577 U.S. 1085, 136 S. Ct. 851, 193 L. Ed. 2d 751, 2016 U.S. LEXIS 559.

January 11, 2016. Petition for writ of certiorari to the United States Court of Appeals for the Second Circuit denied.

Same case below, 770 F.3d 582.

No. 15-7037. Roger D. Hughes, Petitioner v. Julie L. Jones, Secretary, Florida Department of Corrections, et al.

577 U.S. 1085, 136 S. Ct. 851, 193 L. Ed. 2d 752, 2016 U.S. LEXIS 543.

January 11, 2016. Petition for writ of certiorari to the United States Court of Appeals for the Eleventh Circuit denied.

Same case below, 610 Fed. Appx. 829.

No. 15-7045. Samuel Gray, Petitioner v. United States.

577 U.S. 1085, 136 S. Ct. 852, 193 L. Ed. 2d 752, 2016 U.S. LEXIS 71.

January 11, 2016. Petition for writ of certiorari to the United States Court of Appeals for the Eleventh Circuit denied.

Same case below, 622 Fed. Appx. 788.

No. 15-7039. James Earl Gunnell, Petitioner v. United States.

577 U.S. 1085, 136 S. Ct. 851, 193 L. Ed. 2d 752, 2016 U.S. LEXIS 145.

January 11, 2016. Petition for writ of certiorari to the United States Court of Appeals for the Eighth Circuit denied.

Same case below, 775 F.3d 1079.

No. 15-7046. Marcus Chatman, Petitioner v. United States.

577 U.S. 1085, 136 S. Ct. 852, 193 L. Ed. 2d 752, 2016 U.S. LEXIS 82.

January 11, 2016. Petition for writ of certiorari to the United States Court of Appeals for the Eleventh Circuit denied.

Same case below, 610 Fed. Appx. 942.

No. 15-7041. Kingy Ossarius Holden, Petitioner v. United States.

577 U.S. 1085, 136 S. Ct. 851, 193 L. Ed. 2d 752, 2016 U.S. LEXIS 112.

January 11, 2016. Petition for writ of certiorari to the United States Court of Appeals for the Eleventh Circuit denied.

Same case below, 603 Fed. Appx. 744.

No. 15-7047. Roger Lee Lockamy, Petitioner v. United States.

577 U.S. 1085, 136 S. Ct. 852, 193 L. Ed. 2d 752, 2016 U.S. LEXIS 66.

January 11, 2016. Petition for writ of certiorari to the United States Court of Appeals for the Fourth Circuit denied.

Same case below, 613 Fed. Appx. 227.

No. 15-7042. Christopher Michael Horton, Petitioner v. United States.

577 U.S. 1085, 136 S. Ct. 852, 193 L. Ed. 2d 752, 2016 U.S. LEXIS 499.

January 11, 2016. Petition for writ of certiorari to the United States Court of Appeals for the Seventh Circuit denied.

No. 15-7048. Jacques Maddox, Petitioner v. United States.

577 U.S. 1085, 136 S. Ct. 852, 193 L. Ed. 2d 752, 2016 U.S. LEXIS 257.

January 11, 2016. Petition for writ of certiorari to the United States Court of Appeals for the Eleventh Circuit denied.

Same case below, 803 F.3d 1215.

No. 15-7051. John Maurice Henoud, Petitioner v. Craig Apker, Warden.

577 U.S. 1085, 136 S. Ct. 852, 193 L. Ed. 2d 753, 2016 U.S. LEXIS 486.

January 11, 2016. Petition for writ of certiorari to the United States Court of Appeals for the Fourth Circuit denied.

Same case below, 621 Fed. Appx. 734.

No. 15-7052. Hector Herrera-Sifuentes, Petitioner v. United States.

577 U.S. 1085, 136 S. Ct. 853, 193 L. Ed. 2d 753, 2016 U.S. LEXIS 79.

January 11, 2016. Petition for writ of certiorari to the United States Court of Appeals for the Fifth Circuit denied.

No. 15-7054. Kelvin Jerod Holman, Petitioner v. United States.

577 U.S. 1086, 136 S. Ct. 853, 193 L. Ed. 2d 753, 2016 U.S. LEXIS 473.

January 11, 2016. Petition for writ of certiorari to the United States Court of Appeals for the Fourth Circuit denied.

Same case below, 607 Fed. Appx. 302.

No. 15-7055. Francisco Gonzalez Uribe, Petitioner v. United States.

577 U.S. 1086, 136 S. Ct. 853, 193 L. Ed. 2d 753, 2016 U.S. LEXIS 174.

January 11, 2016. Petition for writ of certiorari to the United States Court of Appeals for the Second Circuit denied.

No. 15-7056. Joshua Hampton, Petitioner v. United States.

577 U.S. 1086, 136 S. Ct. 853, 193 L. Ed. 2d 753, 2016 U.S. LEXIS 601.

January 11, 2016. Petition for writ of certiorari to the United States Court of Appeals for the Eleventh Circuit denied.

No. 15-7057. Jose Santiago Hernandez-Lopez, Petitioner v. United States.

577 U.S. 1086, 136 S. Ct. 853, 193 L. Ed. 2d 753, 2016 U.S. LEXIS 300.

January 11, 2016. Petition for writ of certiorari to the United States Court of Appeals for the Fourth Circuit denied.

Same case below, 602 Fed. Appx. 921.

No. 15-7059. Curtis J. Neeley, Jr., Petitioner v. Louis Jerry Edwards, et al.

577 U.S. 1086, 136 S. Ct. 853, 193 L. Ed. 2d 753, 2016 U.S. LEXIS 86.

January 11, 2016. Petition for writ of certiorari to the United States Court of Appeals for the Eighth Circuit denied.

No. 15-7060. Tia D. McPike-McDyess, Petitioner v. JPMorgan Chase Bank, N.A., et al.

577 U.S. 1086, 136 S. Ct. 854, 193 L. Ed. 2d 753, 2016 U.S. LEXIS 377.

January 11, 2016. Petition for writ of certiorari to the United States Court of Appeals for the Sixth Circuit denied.

No. 15-7061. Missouri ex rel. Kenneth G. Middleton, Petitioner v. Ronda Pash, Superintendent, Crossroads Correctional Center.

577 U.S. 1086, 136 S. Ct. 854, 193 L. Ed. 2d 754, 2016 U.S. LEXIS 353.

January 11, 2016. Petition for writ of certiorari to the Supreme Court of Missouri denied.

No. 15-7062. Arthur Smith, Petitioner v. United States.

577 U.S. 1086, 136 S. Ct. 854, 193 L. Ed. 2d 754, 2016 U.S. LEXIS 478.

January 11, 2016. Petition for writ of certiorari to the United States Court of Appeals for the Sixth Circuit denied.

Same case below, 624 Fed. Appx. 385.

No. 15-7063. Donald Green, Petitioner v. United States.

577 U.S. 1086, 136 S. Ct. 854, 193 L. Ed. 2d 754, 2016 U.S. LEXIS 221.

January 11, 2016. Petition for writ of certiorari to the United States Court of Appeals for the Second Circuit denied.

No. 15-7064. Roderick Gunn, Petitioner v. United States.

577 U.S. 1086, 136 S. Ct. 854, 193 L. Ed. 2d 754, 2016 U.S. LEXIS 519.

January 11, 2016. Petition for writ of certiorari to the United States Court of Appeals for the Second Circuit denied.

No. 15-7065. Darryl Solomon Hope, Petitioner v. United States.

577 U.S. 1086, 136 S. Ct. 854, 193 L. Ed. 2d 754, 2016 U.S. LEXIS 72.

January 11, 2016. Petition for writ of certiorari to the United States Court of Appeals for the Eleventh Circuit denied.

No. 15-7066. Larry E. Clark, Petitioner v. Anthony Foxx, Secretary of Transportation, et al.

577 U.S. 1086, 136 S. Ct. 854, 193 L. Ed. 2d 754, 2016 U.S. LEXIS 250.

January 11, 2016. Petition for writ of certiorari to the United States Court of Appeals for the Fifth Circuit denied.

No. 15-7067. Erdinc Coskun, Petitioner v. United States.

577 U.S. 1086, 136 S. Ct. 855, 193 L. Ed. 2d 754, 2016 U.S. LEXIS 335.

January 11, 2016. Petition for writ of certiorari to the United States Court of Appeals for the Fifth Circuit denied.

Same case below, 623 Fed. Appx. 663.

No. 15-7068. Shawn Reaves, Petitioner v. South Carolina.

577 U.S. 1086, 136 S. Ct. 855, 193 L. Ed. 2d 754, 2016 U.S. LEXIS 518.

January 11, 2016. Petition for writ of certiorari to the Supreme Court of South Carolina denied.

Same case below, 414 S.C. 118, 777 S.E.2d 213.

No. 15-7071. Kevin W. Williams, Petitioner v. United States.

577 U.S. 1086, 136 S. Ct. 855, 193 L. Ed. 2d 755, 2016 U.S. LEXIS 524.

January 11, 2016. Petition for writ of certiorari to the United States Court of Appeals for the Ninth Circuit denied.

No. 15-7076. Craig Price, Petitioner v. Ashbel T. Wall, II, Director, Rhode Island Department of Corrections, et al.

577 U.S. 1087, 136 S. Ct. 855, 193 L. Ed. 2d 755, 2016 U.S. LEXIS 526.

January 11, 2016. Petition for writ of certiorari to the United States Court of Appeals for the First Circuit denied.

No. 15-7080. Jason Walker, Petitioner v. United States.

577 U.S. 1087, 136 S. Ct. 856, 193 L. Ed. 2d 755, 2016 U.S. LEXIS 434.

January 11, 2016. Petition for writ of certiorari to the United States Court of Appeals for the Fifth Circuit denied.

No. 15-7081. Trey Michael Boykin, Petitioner v. United States.

577 U.S. 1087, 136 S. Ct. 856, 193 L. Ed. 2d 755, 2016 U.S. LEXIS 452.

January 11, 2016. Petition for writ of certiorari to the United States Court of Appeals for the Eighth Circuit denied.

Same case below, 794 F.3d 939.

No. 15-7088. Thomas Gioeli, Petitioner v. United States.

577 U.S. 1087, 136 S. Ct. 856, 193 L. Ed. 2d 755, 2016 U.S. LEXIS 505.

January 11, 2016. Petition for writ of certiorari to the United States Court of Appeals for the Second Circuit denied.

Same case below, 796 F.3d 176.

No. 15-7089. Francisco Martin Flores, Petitioner v. United States.

577 U.S. 1087, 136 S. Ct. 856, 193 L. Ed. 2d 755, 2016 U.S. LEXIS 550.

January 11, 2016. Petition for writ of certiorari to the United States Court of Appeals for the Eleventh Circuit denied.

Same case below, 615 Fed. Appx. 639.

No. 15-7091. Bart Wayne Johnson, Petitioner v. Alabama.

577 U.S. 1087, 136 S. Ct. 857, 193 L. Ed. 2d 755, 2016 U.S. LEXIS 586.

January 11, 2016. Petition for writ of certiorari to the Court of Criminal Appeals of Alabama denied.

Same case below, 256 So. 3d 684.

No. 15-7099. Carlos Velazco, Petitioner v. Julie L. Jones, Secretary, Florida Department of Corrections.

577 U.S. 1087, 136 S. Ct. 857, 193 L. Ed. 2d 755, 2016 U.S. LEXIS 242.

January 11, 2016. Petition for writ of certiorari to the United States Court of Appeals for the Eleventh Circuit denied.

No. 15-7100. Thomas Patrick Keelan, Petitioner v. United States.

577 U.S. 1087, 136 S. Ct. 857, 193 L. Ed. 2d 756, 2016 U.S. LEXIS 302.

January 11, 2016. Petition for writ of certiorari to the United States Court of Appeals for the Eleventh Circuit denied.

Same case below, 786 F.3d 865.

No. 15-7105. Luis A. Colon, Petitioner v. United States.

577 U.S. 1087, 136 S. Ct. 858, 193 L. Ed. 2d 756, 2016 U.S. LEXIS 549.

January 11, 2016. Petition for writ of certiorari to the United States Court of Appeals for the Third Circuit denied.

No. 15-7108. Pedro De La Rosa-Soto, Petitioner v. United States.

577 U.S. 1087, 136 S. Ct. 858, 193 L. Ed. 2d 756, 2016 U.S. LEXIS 407.

January 11, 2016. Petition for writ of certiorari to the United States Court of Appeals for the Ninth Circuit denied.

Same case below, 600 Fed. Appx. 558.

No. 15-7109. Metaphyzic El-Ectromagnetic Supreme-El, fka Antonio Edward McLean, Petitioner v. Harold W. Clarke, Director, Virginia Department of Corrections.

577 U.S. 1087, 136 S. Ct. 878, 193 L. Ed. 2d 756, 2016 U.S. LEXIS 520.

January 11, 2016. Petition for writ of certiorari to the United States Court of Appeals for the Fourth Circuit denied.

Same case below, 610 Fed. Appx. 279.

No. 15-7110. Frederick Alphonso Demetre Irby, Petitioner v. Robert M. Stevenson, Warden.

577 U.S. 1087, 136 S. Ct. 858, 193 L. Ed. 2d 756, 2016 U.S. LEXIS 444.

January 11, 2016. Petition for writ of certiorari to the United States Court of Appeals for the Fourth Circuit denied.

Same case below, 610 Fed. Appx. 278.

No. 15-7111. Steven Fishman, Petitioner v. United States.

577 U.S. 1087, 136 S. Ct. 858, 193 L. Ed. 2d 756, 2016 U.S. LEXIS 594, reh den 577 U.S. 1241, 136 S. Ct. 1511, 194 L. Ed. 2d 598, 2016 U.S. LEXIS 2253.

January 11, 2016. Petition for writ of certiorari to the United States Court of Appeals for the Tenth Circuit denied.

Same case below, 608 Fed. Appx. 711.

No. 15-7112. Ronald Fuentes-Majano, Petitioner v. United States.

577 U.S. 1087, 136 S. Ct. 858, 193 L. Ed. 2d 756, 2016 U.S. LEXIS 362.

January 11, 2016. Petition for writ of certiorari to the United States Court of Appeals for the Sixth Circuit denied.

No. 15-7113. Salvatore P. Cordovano, Petitioner v. Florida, et al.

577 U.S. 1087, 136 S. Ct. 859, 193 L. Ed. 2d 757, 2016 U.S. LEXIS 371.

January 11, 2016. Petition for writ of certiorari to the United States Court of Appeals for the Eleventh Circuit denied.

No. 15-7114. Maurice Xavier Cruell, Petitioner v. United States.

577 U.S. 1088, 136 S. Ct. 859, 193 L. Ed. 2d 757, 2016 U.S. LEXIS 565.

January 11, 2016. Petition for writ of certiorari to the United States Court of Appeals for the Fourth Circuit denied.

No. 15-7117. Jean Rene Duperval, Petitioner v. United States.

577 U.S. 1088, 136 S. Ct. 859, 193 L. Ed. 2d 757, 2016 U.S. LEXIS 510.

January 11, 2016. Petition for writ of certiorari to the United States Court of Appeals for the Eleventh Circuit denied.

Same case below, 777 F.3d 1324.

No. 15-7120. Scott Heddings, Petitioner v. United States.

577 U.S. 1088, 136 S. Ct. 859, 193 L. Ed. 2d 757, 2016 U.S. LEXIS 494.

January 11, 2016. Petition for writ of certiorari to the United States Court of Appeals for the Ninth Circuit denied.

Same case below, 598 Fed. Appx. 500.

No. 15-7121. John G. Krantz, Petitioner v. United States.

577 U.S. 1088, 136 S. Ct. 859, 193 L. Ed. 2d 757, 2016 U.S. LEXIS 305.

January 11, 2016. Petition for writ of certiorari to the United States Court of Appeals for the Eleventh Circuit denied.

No. 15-7123. Michael Attilio Mangarella, Petitioner v. United States.

577 U.S. 1088, 136 S. Ct. 859, 193 L. Ed. 2d 757, 2016 U.S. LEXIS 540, reh den 577 U.S. 1241, 136 S. Ct. 1511, 194 L. Ed. 2d 598, 2016 U.S. LEXIS 2203.

January 11, 2016. Petition for writ of certiorari to the United States Court of Appeals for the Fourth Circuit denied.

Same case below, 589 Fed. Appx. 89.

No. 15-7125. Muhammad Leach, Petitioner v. Tabb Bickell, Superintendent, State Correctional Institution at Huntingdon, et al.

577 U.S. 1088, 136 S. Ct. 860, 193 L. Ed. 2d 757, 2016 U.S. LEXIS 529.

January 11, 2016. Petition for writ of certiorari to the United States Court of Appeals for the Third Circuit denied.

No. 15-7137. Kenneth Tyrone Murray, Petitioner v. United States.

577 U.S. 1088, 136 S. Ct. 860, 193 L. Ed. 2d 757, 2016 U.S. LEXIS 483.

January 11, 2016. Petition for writ of certiorari to the United States Court of Appeals for the Ninth Circuit denied.

No. 15-7141. Pedro Garcia and Gonzalo Ramirez, Petitioners v. United State.

577 U.S. 1088, 136 S. Ct. 860, 193 L. Ed. 2d 758, 2016 U.S. LEXIS 514.

January 11, 2016. Petition for writ of certiorari to the United States Court of Appeals for the Tenth Circuit denied.

Same case below, 793 F.3d 1194.

No. 15-7142. David Belvin Gilmore, Petitioner v. United States.

577 U.S. 1088, 136 S. Ct. 860, 193 L. Ed. 2d 758, 2016 U.S. LEXIS 567.

January 11, 2016. Petition for writ of certiorari to the United States Court of Appeals for the Fifth Circuit denied.

Same case below, 613 Fed. Appx. 436.

No. 15-7145. Jose Lagos-Maradiaga, Petitioner v. United States; Alejandro Morales-Vega, aka Alejandro Morales, Petitioner v. United States; Ramon Machuca-Anzaldo, Petitioner v. United States; Manuel De Jesus Martinez, Petitioner v. United States; Orlando Raudel Nunez-Pena, Petitioner v. United States; Martin Netro-De Leon, Petitioner v. United States; Esteban Corona-Rosales, Petitioner v. United States; Rene Vargas-Alvarez, Petitioner v. United States; Joel Salgado-Padilla, Petitioner v. United States; Luis Javier Cantu-Moreno, Petitioner v. United States; Carlos Luna-Erives, Petitioner v. United States; Ruben Paredes-Carmona, Petitioner v. United States; Pedro Cruz-Granados, Petitioner v. United States; Gabriel Garcia-Gaona, Petitioner v. United States; Rodrigo Sanchez-Rodriguez, Petitioner v. United States; Frankie Celso Villagran-Pecina, aka Antonio Quintanilla, Petitioner v. United States; Julio Cesar Perez-De La Rosa, Petitioner v. United States;

Juan Carlos Aramburo-Moreno, Petitioner v. United States; Juan Jose Gomez-Lopez, Petitioner v. United States; and Rogelio Mora-Patino, Petitioner v. United States.

577 U.S. 1088, 136 S. Ct. 860, 193 L. Ed. 2d 758, 2016 U.S. LEXIS 566.

January 11, 2016. Petition for writ of certiorari to the United States Court of Appeals for the Fifth Circuit denied.

Same case below, 615 Fed. Appx. 185 (first judgment); 620 Fed. Appx. 322 (second judgment); 617 Fed. Appx. 370 (third judgment); 617 Fed. Appx. 361 (fourth judgment); 620 Fed. Appx. 320 (fifth judgment); 620 Fed. Appx. 337 (sixth judgment); 620 Fed. Appx. 324 (seventh judgment); 619 Fed. Appx. 426 (eighth judgment); 619 Fed. Appx. 439 (ninth judgment); 619 Fed. Appx. 428 (tenth judgment); 620 Fed. Appx. 328 (eleventh judgment); 620 Fed. Appx. 341 (twelfth judgment); 617 Fed. Appx. 356 (thirteenth judgment); 617 Fed. Appx. 360 (fourteenth judgment); 617 Fed. Appx. 357 (fifteenth judgment); 620 Fed. Appx. 333 (sixteenth judgment); 619 Fed. Appx. 436 (seventeenth judgment); 620 Fed. Appx. 327 (eighteenth judgment); 620 Fed. Appx. 328 (nineteenth judgment); and 617 Fed. Appx. 359 (twentieth judgment).

No. 15-7146. Gary Daniel Bartley, Petitioner v. United States.

577 U.S. 1089, 136 S. Ct. 861, 193 L. Ed. 2d 758, 2016 U.S. LEXIS 348.

January 11, 2016. Petition for writ of certiorari to the United States Court of Appeals for the Tenth Circuit denied.

Same case below, 618 Fed. Appx. 439.

No. 15-7147. Jesse Keith Wiggins, Petitioner v. Julie L. Jones, Secretary, Florida Department of Corrections.

577 U.S. 1089, 136 S. Ct. 861, 193 L. Ed. 2d 758, 2016 U.S. LEXIS 396.

January 11, 2016. Petition for writ of certiorari to the United States Court of Appeals for the Eleventh Circuit denied.

No. 15-7150. Edmundo Guerrero-Gonzalez, Petitioner v. United States.

577 U.S. 1089, 136 S. Ct. 861, 193 L. Ed. 2d 759, 2016 U.S. LEXIS 343.

January 11, 2016. Petition for writ of certiorari to the United States Court of Appeals for the Fifth Circuit denied.

Same case below, 614 Fed. Appx. 779.

No. 15-7154. David Elijah Rhodes, Sr., Petitioner v. Donald Beckwith, Warden.

577 U.S. 1089, 136 S. Ct. 861, 193 L. Ed. 2d 759, 2016 U.S. LEXIS 557, reh den 578 U.S. 956, 136 S. Ct. 1730, 194 L. Ed. 2d 826, 2016 U.S. LEXIS 2898.

January 11, 2016. Petition for writ of certiorari to the United States Court of Appeals for the Fourth Circuit denied.

Same case below, 604 Fed. Appx. 302.

No. 15-7160. Mark K. Arness, Petitioner v. United States.

577 U.S. 1089, 136 S. Ct. 861, 193 L. Ed. 2d 759, 2016 U.S. LEXIS 572.

January 11, 2016. Petition for writ of certiorari to the United States Court of Appeals for the Armed Forces denied.

Same case below, 74 M.J. 441.

No. 15-7162. Thomas Reid DeCarlo, Petitioner v. United States.

577 U.S. 1089, 136 S. Ct. 862, 193 L. Ed. 2d 759, 2016 U.S. LEXIS 516.

January 11, 2016. Petition for writ of certiorari to the United States Court of Appeals for the Sixth Circuit denied.

No. 15-7168. Gustavo Garcia-Gonzalez, Petitioner v. United States.

577 U.S. 1089, 136 S. Ct. 862, 193 L. Ed. 2d 759, 2016 U.S. LEXIS 513.

January 11, 2016. Petition for writ of certiorari to the United States Court of Appeals for the Ninth Circuit denied.

Same case below, 791 F.3d 1175.

No. 15-7169. Matthew Joseph Guevara, Petitioner v. Colorado.

577 U.S. 1089, 136 S. Ct. 862, 193 L. Ed. 2d 759, 2016 U.S. LEXIS 605.

January 11, 2016. Petition for writ of certiorari to the Court of Appeals of Colorado denied.

No. 15-7170. Winston Womble, Petitioner v. United States.

577 U.S. 1089, 136 S. Ct. 862, 193 L. Ed. 2d 759, 2016 U.S. LEXIS 355.

January 11, 2016. Petition for writ of certiorari to the United States Court of Appeals for the Third Circuit denied.

No. 15-7171. James Thomas Webb, Petitioner v. United States.

577 U.S. 1089, 136 S. Ct. 862, 193 L. Ed. 2d 759, 2016 U.S. LEXIS 522, reh den 577 U.S. 1185, 136 S. Ct. 1253, 194 L. Ed. 2d 251, 2016 U.S. LEXIS 1003.

January 11, 2016. Petition for writ of certiorari to the United States Court of Appeals for the Fourth Circuit denied.

Same case below, 601 Fed. Appx. 189.

No. 15-7178. Randy B. McGowan, Petitioner v. Maine.

577 U.S. 1089, 136 S. Ct. 863, 193 L. Ed. 2d 760, 2016 U.S. LEXIS 484.

January 11, 2016. Petition for writ of certiorari to the Supreme Judicial Court of Maine denied.

No. 15-7180. Tam Tran Nguyen, Petitioner v. United States.

577 U.S. 1089, 136 S. Ct. 863, 193 L. Ed. 2d 760, 2016 U.S. LEXIS 188.

January 11, 2016. Petition for writ of certiorari to the United States Court of Appeals for the Eleventh Circuit denied.

No. 15-7185. Eric Lance Whitson, Petitioner v. United States.

577 U.S. 1089, 136 S. Ct. 863, 193 L. Ed. 2d 760, 2016 U.S. LEXIS 376.

January 11, 2016. Petition for writ of certiorari to the United States Court of Appeals for the Sixth Circuit denied.

No. 15-7187. Nakia Heath Keller, Petitioner v. United States.

577 U.S. 1089, 136 S. Ct. 863, 193 L. Ed. 2d 760, 2016 U.S. LEXIS 438, reh den 578 U.S. 942, 136 S. Ct. 1707, 194 L. Ed. 2d 804, 2016 U.S. LEXIS 2575.

January 11, 2016. Petition for writ of certiorari to the United States Court of Appeals for the Fourth Circuit denied.

Same case below, 622 Fed. Appx. 228.

No. 15-7191. David Adeyemi Adeyi, Petitioner v. Robert A. McDonald, Secretary of Veterans Affairs.

577 U.S. 1090, 136 S. Ct. 863, 193 L. Ed. 2d 760, 2016 U.S. LEXIS 382.

January 11, 2016. Petition for writ of certiorari to the United States Court of Appeals for the Federal Circuit denied.

Same case below, 606 Fed. Appx. 1002.

No. 15-7193. Rances Ulices Amaya, Petitioner v. United States.

577 U.S. 1090, 136 S. Ct. 864, 193 L. Ed. 2d 760, 2016 U.S. LEXIS 537.

January 11, 2016. Petition for writ of certiorari to the United States Court of Appeals for the Fourth Circuit denied.

Same case below, 616 Fed. Appx. 93.

No. 15-7195. Harold Steven Abbott, Petitioner v. United States.

577 U.S. 1090, 136 S. Ct. 864, 193 L. Ed. 2d 760, 2016 U.S. LEXIS 568.

January 11, 2016. Petition for writ of certiorari to the United States Court of Appeals for the Eleventh Circuit denied.

Same case below, 613 Fed. Appx. 817.

No. 15-7201. Eugenio Perez-Perez, Petitioner v. United States.

577 U.S. 1090, 136 S. Ct. 864, 193 L. Ed. 2d 760, 2016 U.S. LEXIS 481.

January 11, 2016. Petition for writ of certiorari to the United States Court of Appeals for the First Circuit denied.

Same case below, 626 Fed. Appx. 8.

No. 15-7206. Oscar Omar Lobo-Lopez, Petitioner v. United States.

577 U.S. 1090, 136 S. Ct. 864, 193 L. Ed. 2d 761, 2016 U.S. LEXIS 303.

January 11, 2016. Petition for writ of certiorari to the United States Court of Appeals for the Fourth Circuit denied.

Same case below, 607 Fed. Appx. 332.

No. 15-7208. Ernesto Monell, Petitioner v. United States.

577 U.S. 1090, 136 S. Ct. 864, 193 L. Ed. 2d 761, 2016 U.S. LEXIS 458.

January 11, 2016. Petition for writ of certiorari to the United States Court of Appeals for the First Circuit denied.

Same case below, 801 F.3d 34.

No. 15-7212. Ronald Larose, Petitioner v. United States.

577 U.S. 1090, 136 S. Ct. 865, 193 L. Ed. 2d 761, 2016 U.S. LEXIS 420.

January 11, 2016. Petition for writ of certiorari to the United States Court of Appeals for the Eleventh Circuit denied.

Same case below, 609 Fed. Appx. 629.

No. 15-7213. Danny Keel, Petitioner v. Kansas.

577 U.S. 1090, 136 S. Ct. 865, 193 L. Ed. 2d 761, 2016 U.S. LEXIS 268.

January 11, 2016. Petition for writ of certiorari to the Supreme Court of Kansas denied.

Same case below, 302 Kan. 560, 357 P.3d 251.

No. 15-7214. Lee Ervin Dale, Petitioner v. United States.

577 U.S. 1090, 136 S. Ct. 865, 193 L. Ed. 2d 761, 2016 U.S. LEXIS 521.

January 11, 2016. Petition for writ of certiorari to the United States Court of Appeals for the Eleventh Circuit denied.

Same case below, 618 Fed. Appx. 494.

No. 15-7218. J. Jefferson Crook, Petitioner v. Pedro Galaviz, et al.

577 U.S. 1090, 136 S. Ct. 865, 193 L. Ed. 2d 761, 2016 U.S. LEXIS 528.

January 11, 2016. Petition for writ of certiorari to the United States Court of Appeals for the Fifth Circuit denied.

Same case below, 616 Fed. Appx. 747.

No. 15-7219. Marcus Clark, Petitioners v. John Kerestes, Superintendent, State Correctional Institution at Mahanoy, et al.

577 U.S. 1090, 136 S. Ct. 865, 193 L. Ed. 2d 761, 2016 U.S. LEXIS 554.

January 11, 2016. Petition for writ of certiorari to the United States Court of Appeals for the Third Circuit denied.

No. 15-7226. Raymond Mendez, Petitioner v. United States.

577 U.S. 1090, 136 S. Ct. 865, 193 L. Ed. 2d 761, 2016 U.S. LEXIS 419.

January 11, 2016. Petition for writ of certiorari to the United States Court of Appeals for the Ninth Circuit denied.

Same case below, 628 Fed. Appx. 923.

No. 15-7228. Richard Shannon, Petitioner v. United States.

577 U.S. 1090, 136 S. Ct. 866, 193 L. Ed. 2d 762, 2016 U.S. LEXIS 243.

January 11, 2016. Petition for writ of certiorari to the United States Court of Appeals for the Sixth Circuit denied.

Same case below, 803 F.3d 778.

No. 15-7229. Juan Manuel Cantero-Perez, Petitioner v. United States.

577 U.S. 1090, 136 S. Ct. 866, 193 L. Ed. 2d 762, 2016 U.S. LEXIS 455.

January 11, 2016. Petition for writ of certiorari to the United States Court of Appeals for the Fifth Circuit denied.

Same case below, 614 Fed. Appx. 796.

No. 15-7230. Leonardo Jabalera-Chavira, Petitioner v. United States.

577 U.S. 1090, 136 S. Ct. 866, 193 L. Ed. 2d 762, 2016 U.S. LEXIS 354.

January 11, 2016. Petition for writ of certiorari to the United States Court of Appeals for the Fifth Circuit denied.

Same case below, 613 Fed. Appx. 448.

No. 15-7233. Sheri Rosenbaum, Petitioner v. United States.

577 U.S. 1091, 136 S. Ct. 866, 193 L. Ed. 2d 762, 2016 U.S. LEXIS 373.

January 11, 2016. Petition for writ of certiorari to the United States Court of Appeals for the Sixth Circuit denied.

No. 15-7235. Marvin Lewis Adams, Petitioner v. United States.

577 U.S. 1091, 136 S. Ct. 866, 193 L. Ed. 2d 762, 2016 U.S. LEXIS 432, reh den 577 U.S. 1209, 136 S. Ct. 1404, 194 L. Ed. 2d 384, 2016 U.S. LEXIS 1640.

January 11, 2016. Petition for writ of certiorari to the United States Court of Appeals for the Eleventh Circuit denied.

No. 15-7236. Morris Dabbs, aka Ray Dabbs, Petitioner v. United States.

577 U.S. 1091, 136 S. Ct. 866, 193 L. Ed. 2d 762, 2016 U.S. LEXIS 427.

January 11, 2016. Petition for writ of certiorari to the United States Court of Appeals for the Fourth Circuit denied.

Same case below, 615 Fed. Appx. 143.

No. 15-7241. Torrie Brumfield, Petitioner v. United States.

577 U.S. 1091, 136 S. Ct. 867, 193 L. Ed. 2d 762, 2016 U.S. LEXIS 436.

January 11, 2016. Petition for writ of certiorari to the United States Court of Appeals for the Fifth Circuit denied.

Same case below, 615 Fed. Appx. 184.

No. 15-7243. Francisco Mercedes, Petitioner v. United States.

577 U.S. 1091, 136 S. Ct. 867, 193 L. Ed. 2d 762, 2016 U.S. LEXIS 389.

January 11, 2016. Petition for writ of certiorari to the United States Court of Appeals for the First Circuit denied.

Same case below, 612 Fed. Appx. 565.

No. 15-7247. Brian Woodings, Petitioner v. United States.

577 U.S. 1091, 136 S. Ct. 867, 193 L. Ed. 2d 763, 2016 U.S. LEXIS 460.

January 11, 2016. Petition for writ of certiorari to the District of Columbia Court of Appeals denied.

Same case below, 122 A.3d 945.

No. 15-7257. John A. Champion, Petitioner v. Ronnie R. Holt, Warden.

577 U.S. 1091, 136 S. Ct. 868, 193 L. Ed. 2d 763, 2016 U.S. LEXIS 267.

January 11, 2016. Petition for writ of certiorari to the United States Court of Appeals for the District of Columbia Circuit denied.

No. 15-7248. William H. True, Petitioner v. United States.

577 U.S. 1091, 136 S. Ct. 867, 193 L. Ed. 2d 763, 2016 U.S. LEXIS 532.

January 11, 2016. Petition for writ of certiorari to the District of Columbia Court of Appeals denied.

Same case below, 116 A.3d 938.

No. 15-7258. Ruben Judas Ruiz-Vazquez, Petitioner v. United States; Gonzalo Ismael Sobrevilla-Revolloso, Petitioner v. United States; Heriberto Ezequiel Martinez-Garza, Petitioner v. United States; April Zalest Ravell, Petitioner v. United States; Isaac Medina, Petitioner v. United States; Cesar Cuevas-Medina, Petitioner v. United States; Jesus Hernan De La Paz, Petitioner v. United States; Fernando De La Garza-Garza, Petitioner v. United States; and Ivan Hernandez, Petitioner v. United States.

No. 15-7251. Keith Tywane Barnett, Petitioner v. United States.

577 U.S. 1091, 136 S. Ct. 867, 193 L. Ed. 2d 763, 2016 U.S. LEXIS 443.

January 11, 2016. Petition for writ of certiorari to the District of Columbia Court of Appeals denied.

Same case below, 122 A.3d 946.

577 U.S. 1091, 136 S. Ct. 868, 193 L. Ed. 2d 763, 2016 U.S. LEXIS 558.

January 11, 2016. Petition for writ of certiorari to the United States Court of Appeals for the Fifth Circuit denied.

Same case below, 620 Fed. Appx. 339 (first judgment); 620 Fed. Appx. 340 (second judgment); 617 Fed. Appx. 368 (third judgment); 619 Fed. Appx. 440 (fourth judgment); 619 Fed. Appx. 431 (fifth judgment); 619 Fed. Appx. 433 (sixth judgment); 620 Fed. Appx. 332 (seventh judgment); 620 Fed. Appx. 333 (eighth judgment); and 620 Fed. Appx. 326 (ninth judgment).

No. 15-7253. Kara Singleton Adams, Petitioner v. United States.

577 U.S. 1091, 136 S. Ct. 868, 193 L. Ed. 2d 763, 2016 U.S. LEXIS 388.

January 11, 2016. Petition for writ of certiorari to the United States Court of Appeals for the Eleventh Circuit denied.

No. 15-7259. Marcos Cornejo-Macias, aka Macias Cornejo, aka Marco Cornejo, aka Marcos Cornejo, aka Littleman Cornejo, aka Marcos Littleman, Petitioner v. United States.

577 U.S. 1091, 136 S. Ct. 868, 193 L. Ed. 2d 764, 2016 U.S. LEXIS 374.

January 11, 2016. Petition for writ of certiorari to the United States Court of Appeals for the Ninth Circuit denied.

Same case below, 616 Fed. Appx. 287.

No. 15-7265. Michael Brown, Petitioner v. United States.

577 U.S. 1091, 136 S. Ct. 869, 193 L. Ed. 2d 764, 2016 U.S. LEXIS 287.

January 11, 2016. Petition for writ of certiorari to the United States Court of Appeals for the Eleventh Circuit denied.

Same case below, 625 Fed. Appx. 945.

No. 15-7272. James Andrew Washington, Petitioner v. United States.

577 U.S. 1092, 136 S. Ct. 869, 193 L. Ed. 2d 764, 2016 U.S. LEXIS 405.

January 11, 2016. Petition for writ of certiorari to the United States Court of Appeals for the Eleventh Circuit denied.

Same case below, 612 Fed. Appx. 546.

No. 15-7280. Darren Cephas, Petitioner v. United States.

577 U.S. 1092, 136 S. Ct. 869, 193 L. Ed. 2d 764, 2016 U.S. LEXIS 445.

January 11, 2016. Petition for writ of certiorari to the United States Court of Appeals for the Third Circuit denied.

No. 14-1467. Richard Glover, Petitioner v. Richard Mathis, et al.

577 U.S. 1092, 136 S. Ct. 791, 193 L. Ed. 2d 764, 2016 U.S. LEXIS 470.

January 11, 2016. Motion of Nevada Public Agency Insurance Pool, et al. for leave to file a brief as amici curiae granted. Petition for writ of certiorari to the United States Court of Appeals for the Ninth Circuit denied.

Same case below, 591 Fed. Appx. 635.

No. 15-54. Nancy Schott, Petitioner v. Peter Wenk, et ux.

577 U.S. 1092, 136 S. Ct. 792, 193 L. Ed. 2d 764, 2016 U.S. LEXIS 593.

January 11, 2016. Motion of Ohio School Boards Association, et al. for leave to file a brief as amici curiae granted. Petition for writ of certiorari to the United States Court of Appeals for the Sixth Circuit denied.

Same case below, 783 F.3d 585.

No. 15-305. Lito Martinez Asignacion, Petitioner v. Rickmers Genoa Schiffahrtsgesellschaft mbH & Cie KG.

577 U.S. 1092, 136 S. Ct. 795, 193 L. Ed. 2d 764, 2016 U.S. LEXIS 553.

January 11, 2016. Motion of International Transport Workers' Federation, and Seafarers' Rights International for leave to file a brief as amici curiae granted. Motion of Global Maritime Ministries, Inc. of New Orleans, Louisiana, et al. for leave to file a brief as amici curiae granted.

Petition for writ of certiorari to the United States Court of Appeals for the Fifth Circuit denied.

Same case below, 783 F.3d 1010.

No. 15-328. David Lawson, Petitioner v. Sun Microsystems, Inc.

577 U.S. 1092, 136 S. Ct. 796, 193 L. Ed. 2d 765, 2016 U.S. LEXIS 591.

January 11, 2016. Petition for writ of certiorari to the United States Court of Appeals for the Seventh Circuit denied. Justice Alito took no part in the consideration or decision of this petition.

Same case below, 791 F.3d 754.

No. 15-331. TIFD III-E, LLC, Petitioner v. United States.

577 U.S. 1092, 136 S. Ct. 796, 193 L. Ed. 2d 765, 2016 U.S. LEXIS 560.

January 11, 2016. Petition for writ of certiorari to the United States Court of Appeals for the Second Circuit denied. Justice Sotomayor and Justice Kagan took no part in the consideration or decision of this petition.

Same case below, 604 Fed. Appx. 69.

No. 15-353. Don Eugene Siegelman, Petitioner v. United States.

577 U.S. 1092, 136 S. Ct. 798, 193 L. Ed. 2d 765, 2016 U.S. LEXIS 428.

January 11, 2016. Petition for writ of certiorari to the United States Court of Appeals for the Eleventh Circuit denied. Justice Kagan took no part in the consideration or decision of this petition.

Same case below, 786 F.3d 1322.

No. 15-365. Juanita Perez, et al., Petitioners v. The Fredericksburg Care Company, LP.

577 U.S. 1092, 136 S. Ct. 798, 193 L. Ed. 2d 765, 2016 U.S. LEXIS 577.

January 11, 2016. Motion of The Texas Chapters of the American Board of Trial Advocates, et al. for leave to file a brief as amici curiae granted. Petition for writ of certiorari to the Supreme Court of Texas denied.

Same case below, 461 S.W.3d 513.

No. 15-367. Bear Valley Mutual Water Company, et al., Petitioners v. Sally Jewell, Secretary of the Interior, et al.

577 U.S. 1092, 136 S. Ct. 799, 193 L. Ed. 2d 765, 2016 U.S. LEXIS 426.

January 11, 2016. Motion of Pacific Legal Foundation for leave to file a brief as amicus curiae granted. Motion of Association of California Water Agencies, et al. for leave to file a brief as amici curiae granted. Petition for writ of certiorari to the United States Court of Appeals for the Ninth Circuit denied.

Same case below, 790 F.3d 977.

No. 15-387. John Doe, Petitioner v. Board of County Commissioners of Payne County, Oklahoma, et al.

577 U.S. 1093, 136 S. Ct. 878, 193 L. Ed. 2d 765, 2016 U.S. LEXIS 203.

January 11, 2016. Motion of The Iraq and Afghanistan Veterans of America for leave to file a brief as amicus curiae granted. Petition for writ of certiorari to the United States Court of Appeal for the Tenth Circuit denied.

Same case below, 613 Fed. Appx. 743.

No. 15-555. Sidney Bender, Petitioner v. Barack H. Obama, President of the United States, et al.

577 U.S. 1093, 136 S. Ct. 820, 193 L. Ed. 2d 766, 2016 U.S. LEXIS 292.

January 11, 2016. Petition for writ of certiorari before judgment denied.

No. 15-600. Ortho-McNeil-Janssen Pharmaceuticals, Inc., fka Janssen Pharmaceutical, Inc., and/or Janssen, L.P., et al., Petitioners v. South Carolina ex rel. Alan Wilson, Attorney General.

577 U.S. 1093, 136 S. Ct. 824, 193 L. Ed. 2d 766, 2016 U.S. LEXIS 515.

January 11, 2016. Petition for writ of certiorari to the Supreme Court South Carolina denied. Justice Alito took no part in the consideration or decision of this petition.

Same case below, 414 S.C. 33, 777 S.E.2d 176.

No. 15-721. Laura M. Watson, Petitioner v. Florida Judicial Qualifications Commission.

577 U.S. 1093, 136 S. Ct. 863, 193 L. Ed. 2d 766, 2016 U.S. LEXIS 575.

January 11, 2016. Motion of Dr. Philip Busey, et al. for leave to file a brief as

amici curiae granted. Petition for writ of certiorari to the Supreme Court of Florida denied.

Same case below, 174 So. 3d 364.

No. 15-6050. James Eric Jones, Petitioner v. Tamyra Jarvis, Warden.

577 U.S. 1093, 136 S. Ct. 796, 193 L. Ed. 2d 766, 2016 U.S. LEXIS 584.

January 11, 2016. Petition for writ of certiorari to the United States Court of Appeals for the Eleventh Circuit denied. Justice Kagan took no part in the consideration or decision of this petition.

Same case below, 598 Fed. Appx. 678.

No. 15-6753. Prentiss B. Davis, Petitioner v. The Boeing Company, et al.

577 U.S. 1093, 136 S. Ct. 821, 193 L. Ed. 2d 766, 2016 U.S. LEXIS 527.

January 11, 2016. Petition for writ of certiorari to the United States Court of Appeals for the Ninth Circuit denied. Justice Alito took no part in the consideration or decision of this petition.

Same case below, 604 Fed. Appx. 565.

No. 15-6836. Charles Edward Turner, Petitioner v. Lawrence Mahally, Superintendent, State Correctional Institution at Dallas, et al.

577 U.S. 1093, 136 S. Ct. 831, 193 L. Ed. 2d 766, 2016 U.S. LEXIS 297.

January 11, 2016. Petition for writ of certiorari to the United States Court of

Appeals for the Third Circuit denied. Justice Alito took no part in the consideration or decision of this petition.

———

No. 15-6907. John David Richards, Petitioner v. Ron Barnes, Warden.

577 U.S. 1093, 136 S. Ct. 839, 193 L. Ed. 2d 767, 2016 U.S. LEXIS 511.

January 11, 2016. Petition for writ of certiorari to the United States Court of Appeals for the Ninth Circuit denied. Justice Breyer took no part in the consideration or decision of this petition.

———

No. 15-6937. Bruno Choiniere, Petitioner v. United States.

577 U.S. 1093, 136 S. Ct. 841, 193 L. Ed. 2d 767, 2016 U.S. LEXIS 472.

January 11, 2016. Petition for writ of certiorari to the United States Court of Appeals for the Seventh denied. Justice Kagan took no part in the consideration or decision of this petition.

———

No. 15-6953. Mario N. Baker, Petitioner v. United States.

577 U.S. 1094, 136 S. Ct. 843, 193 L. Ed. 2d 767, 2016 U.S. LEXIS 408.

January 11, 2016. Petition for writ of certiorari to the United States Court of Appeals for the Fourth Circuit denied. Justice Kagan took no part in the consideration or decision of this petition. Same case below, 610 Fed. Appx. 263.

———

No. 15-7004. Jerome Williams, Jr., Petitioner v. United States.

577 U.S. 1094, 136 S. Ct. 848, 193 L. Ed. 2d 767, 2016 U.S. LEXIS 489.

January 11, 2016. Petition for writ of certiorari to the United States Court of Appeals for the Seventh Circuit denied. Justice Kagan took no part in the consideration or decision of this petition.

———

No. 15-7262. Demarcis L. March, Petitioner v. United States.

577 U.S. 1094, 136 S. Ct. 868, 193 L. Ed. 2d 767, 2016 U.S. LEXIS 569.

January 11, 2016. Petition for writ of certiorari to the United States Court of Appeals for the Eighth Circuit denied. Justice Kagan took no part in the consideration or decision of this petition.

———

No. 15-7276. Rickey Lee Scott, Petitioner v. United States.

577 U.S. 1094, 136 S. Ct. 869, 193 L. Ed. 2d 767, 2016 U.S. LEXIS 229.

January 11, 2016. Petition for writ of certiorari to the United States Court of Appeals for the Fifth Circuit denied. Justice Kagan took no part in the consideration or decision of this petition.

Same case below, 624 Fed. Appx. 850.

———

No. 15-759. In re Anthony Allen Williams, Petitioner.

577 U.S. 1060, 136 S. Ct. 870, 193 L. Ed. 2d 767, 2016 U.S. LEXIS 590.

January 11, 2016. Petition for writ of habeas corpus denied.

No. 15-7194. In re William F. Batter, Petitioner.

577 U.S. 1060, 136 S. Ct. 864, 193 L. Ed. 2d 768, 2016 U.S. LEXIS 277.

January 11, 2016. Petition for writ of habeas corpus denied.

No. 15-7239. In re Nathan Rena Johnson, Petitioner.

577 U.S. 1060, 136 S. Ct. 867, 193 L. Ed. 2d 768, 2016 U.S. LEXIS 341, reh den 578 U.S. 916, 136 S. Ct. 1538, 194 L. Ed. 2d 622, 2016 U.S. LEXIS 2347.

January 11, 2016. Petition for writ of habeas corpus denied.

No. 15-7311. In re Warren Parks, Petitioner.

577 U.S. 1060, 136 S. Ct. 870, 193 L. Ed. 2d 768, 2016 U.S. LEXIS 599.

January 11, 2016. Petition for writ of habeas corpus denied.

No. 15-7327. In re Ronald Spangler, Petitioner.

577 U.S. 1060, 136 S. Ct. 870, 193 L. Ed. 2d 768, 2016 U.S. LEXIS 595, reh den 577 U.S. 1185, 136 S. Ct. 1253, 194 L. Ed. 2d 251, 2016 U.S. LEXIS 996.

January 11, 2016. Petition for writ of habeas corpus denied.

No. 15-7369. In re Tracy A. Peters, Petitioner.

577 U.S. 1060, 136 S. Ct. 870, 193 L. Ed. 2d 768, 2016 U.S. LEXIS 421.

January 11, 2016. Petition for writ of habeas corpus denied.

No. 15-7399. In re Larry Walthall, Petitioner.

577 U.S. 1060, 136 S. Ct. 870, 193 L. Ed. 2d 768, 2016 U.S. LEXIS 561.

January 11, 2016. Petition for writ of habeas corpus denied.

No. 15-626. In re Ronnie Glenn Triplett, Petitioner.

577 U.S. 1060, 136 S. Ct. 838, 193 L. Ed. 2d 768, 2016 U.S. LEXIS 304.

January 11, 2016. Petition for writ of habeas corpus denied. Justice Kagan took no part in the consideration or decision of this petition.

No. 15-646. In re Willie B. Sharp, Petitioner.

577 U.S. 1060, 136 S. Ct. 838, 193 L. Ed. 2d 768, 2016 U.S. LEXIS 597.

January 11, 2016. Motion of Law Professors for leave to file a brief as amici curiae granted. Petition for writ of habeas corpus denied.

No. 15-7309. In re Andrew Cox, Petitioner.

577 U.S. 1060, 136 S. Ct. 869, 193 L. Ed. 2d 768, 2016 U.S. LEXIS 583.

January 11, 2016. Motion of petitioner for leave to proceed in forma pauperis denied, and petition for writ of habeas corpus dismissed. See Rule 39.8.

No. 15-7398. In re Alejandro Rodriguez, Petitioner.

577 U.S. 1060, 136 S. Ct. 870, 193 L. Ed. 2d 769, 2016 U.S. LEXIS 474.

January 11, 2016. Motion of petitioner for leave to proceed in forma pauperis denied, and petition for writ of habeas corpus dismissed. See Rule 39.8.

No. 15-498. In re Cheryl A. Wolf, et al., Petitioners.

577 U.S. 1060, 136 S. Ct. 805, 193 L. Ed. 2d 769, 2016 U.S. LEXIS 492, reh den 577 U.S. 1184, 136 S. Ct. 1249, 194 L. Ed. 2d 246, 2016 U.S. LEXIS 1332.

January 11, 2016. Petition for writ of mandamus denied.

No. 15-758. In re Anthony Allen Williams, Petitioner.

577 U.S. 1060, 136 S. Ct. 870, 193 L. Ed. 2d 769, 2016 U.S. LEXIS 471.

January 11, 2016. Petition for writ of mandamus denied.

No. 15-6731. In re Santiago Strickland, Petitioner.

577 U.S. 1060, 136 S. Ct. 819, 193 L. Ed. 2d 769, 2016 U.S. LEXIS 404.

January 11, 2016. Petition for writ of mandamus denied.

No. 15-6857. In re James Kevin Ruppert, Petitioner.

577 U.S. 1060, 136 S. Ct. 833, 193 L. Ed. 2d 769, 2016 U.S. LEXIS 411, reh den 577 U.S. 1231, 136 S. Ct. 1489, 194 L. Ed. 2d 579, 2016 U.S. LEXIS 1889.

January 11, 2016. Petition for writ of mandamus denied.

No. 15-7058. In re Jeffrey Nathan Schirripa, Petitioner.

577 U.S. 1060, 136 S. Ct. 853, 193 L. Ed. 2d 769, 2016 U.S. LEXIS 596.

January 11, 2016. Petition for writ of mandamus denied.

No. 15-625. In re Ronnie Glenn Triplett, Petitioner.

577 U.S. 1060, 136 S. Ct. 838, 193 L. Ed. 2d 769, 2016 U.S. LEXIS 402.

January 11, 2016. Petition for writ of mandamus denied. Justice Kagan took no part in the consideration or decision of this petition.

No. 15-6743. In re Wei Zhou, Petitioner.

577 U.S. 1060, 136 S. Ct. 820, 193 L. Ed. 2d 769, 2016 U.S. LEXIS 280, reh den 578 U.S. 916, 136 S. Ct. 1537, 194 L. Ed. 2d 621, 2016 U.S. LEXIS 2399.

January 11, 2016. Petition for writ of mandamus and/or prohibition denied.

No. 15-6786. In re Rayshon Thomas, Petitioner.

577 U.S. 1061, 136 S. Ct. 826, 193 L. Ed. 2d 769, 2016 U.S. LEXIS 613.

January 11, 2016. Motion of petitioner for leave to proceed in forma pauperis denied, and petition for writ of mandamus and/or prohibition dismissed. See Rule 39.8.

**No. 15-6814. In re Stephen G. Krae-
mer, Petitioner.**

577 U.S. 1060, 136 S. Ct. 829, 193 L.
Ed. 2d 770, 2016 U.S. LEXIS 574.

January 11, 2016. Petition for writ of
mandamus and/or prohibition denied.

**No. 15-6825. In re Michael Boone, Pe-
titioner.**

577 U.S. 1060, 136 S. Ct. 830, 193 L.
Ed. 2d 770, 2016 U.S. LEXIS 503.

January 11, 2016. Petition for writ of
mandamus denied. Justice Kagan took no
part in the consideration or decision of
this petition.

**No. 15-6878. In re Carmen E. Camp-
bell, Petitioner.**

577 U.S. 1060, 136 S. Ct. 835, 193 L.
Ed. 2d 770, 2016 U.S. LEXIS 580.

January 11, 2016. Motion of petitioner
for leave to proceed in forma pauperis
denied, and petition for writ of mandamus
dismissed. See Rule 39.8.

**No. 15-7078. In re Vincent A. Williams,
Petitioner.**

577 U.S. 1061, 136 S. Ct. 856, 193 L.
Ed. 2d 770, 2016 U.S. LEXIS 535, reh den
577 U.S. 1185, 136 S. Ct. 1253, 194 L. Ed.
2d 251, 2016 U.S. LEXIS 1158.

January 11, 2016. Petition for writ of
prohibition denied.

**No. 15-7267. In re Jesus Delrio, Peti-
tioner.**

577 U.S. 1061, 136 S. Ct. 869, 193 L.
Ed. 2d 770, 2016 U.S. LEXIS 209, reh den
577 U.S. 1185, 136 S. Ct. 1253, 194 L. Ed.
2d 251, 2016 U.S. LEXIS 992.

January 11, 2016. Petition for writ of
prohibition denied.

**No. 14-1446. Albert J. Ragge, Jr., Peti-
tioner v. Webster Bank, N.A.**

577 U.S. 1094, 136 S. Ct. 879, 193 L.
Ed. 2d 770, 2016 U.S. LEXIS 523.

January 11, 2016. Petition for rehearing denied.

Former decision, 577 U.S. 823, 136 S.
Ct. 104, 193 L. Ed. 2d 37, 2015 U.S.
LEXIS 5399.

**No. 14-1529. Edward Lilly, Petitioner
v. Lewiston-Porter Central School
District, et al.**

577 U.S. 1094, 136 S. Ct. 879, 193 L.
Ed. 2d 770, 2016 U.S. LEXIS 240.

January 11, 2016. Petition for rehearing denied.

Former decision, 577 U.S. 827, 136 S.
Ct. 156, 193 L. Ed. 2d 44, 2015 U.S.
LEXIS 5556.

**No. 14-8890. Mario Flavio Garcia, Pe-
titioner v. Kathleen Allison, Warden
(two judgments).**

577 U.S. 1094, 136 S. Ct. 879, 193 L.
Ed. 2d 770, 2016 U.S. LEXIS 414.

January 11, 2016. Petition for rehearing denied.

Former decision, 575 U.S. 1001, 135 S. Ct. 2060, 191 L. Ed. 2d 964, 2015 U.S. LEXIS 3115.

No. 14-9586. John Randall Futch, Petitioner v. United States.

577 U.S. 1094, 136 S. Ct. 879, 193 L. Ed. 2d 771, 2016 U.S. LEXIS 430.

January 11, 2016. Petition for rehearing denied.

Former decision, 576 U.S. 1010, 135 S. Ct. 2819, 192 L. Ed. 2d 858, 2015 U.S. LEXIS 3856.

No. 14-9731. Hugo Romare Jones, Petitioner v. Harold W. Clarke, Director, Virginia Department of Corrections.

577 U.S. 1094, 136 S. Ct. 879, 193 L. Ed. 2d 771, 2016 U.S. LEXIS 581.

January 11, 2016. Petition for rehearing denied.

Former decision, 577 U.S. 835, 136 S. Ct. 56, 193 L. Ed. 2d 58, 2015 U.S. LEXIS 5822.

No. 14-9754. Michael Tony Velez, Petitioner v. New York.

577 U.S. 1094, 136 S. Ct. 880, 193 L. Ed. 2d 771, 2016 U.S. LEXIS 415.

January 11, 2016. Petition for rehearing denied.

Former decision, 577 U.S. 835, 136 S. Ct. 57, 193 L. Ed. 2d 59, 2015 U.S. LEXIS 5871.

No. 14-9791. In re Michael Schneider, Petitioner.

577 U.S. 1094, 136 S. Ct. 880, 193 L. Ed. 2d 771, 2016 U.S. LEXIS 462.

January 11, 2016. Petition for rehearing denied.

Former decision, 577 U.S. 814, 136 S. Ct. 61, 193 L. Ed. 2d 218, 2015 U.S. LEXIS 4712.

No. 14-9863. Frank Shawnte Allen, Petitioner v. Dave Davey, Warden.

577 U.S. 1094, 136 S. Ct. 880, 193 L. Ed. 2d 771, 2016 U.S. LEXIS 531.

January 11, 2016. Petition for rehearing denied.

Former decision, 577 U.S. 839, 136 S. Ct. 68, 193 L. Ed. 2d 66, 2015 U.S. LEXIS 5139.

No. 14-9879. Rodney T. Kralovetz, Petitioner v. Marion Spearman, Warden.

577 U.S. 1094, 136 S. Ct. 880, 193 L. Ed. 2d 771, 2016 U.S. LEXIS 587.

January 11, 2016. Petition for rehearing denied.

Former decision, 577 U.S. 840, 136 S. Ct. 70, 193 L. Ed. 2d 67, 2015 U.S. LEXIS 5056.

No. 14-9894. John Albert Estrada, Petitioner v. Texas.

577 U.S. 1094, 136 S. Ct. 880, 193 L. Ed. 2d 771, 2016 U.S. LEXIS 410.

January 11, 2016. Petition for rehearing denied.

Former decision, 577 U.S. 840, 136 S. Ct. 70, 193 L. Ed. 2d 68, 2015 U.S. LEXIS 5512.

———

No. 14-10081. Cecilia Aranda, Petitioner v. Dal-Tile Corporation.

577 U.S. 1094, 136 S. Ct. 880, 193 L. Ed. 2d 772, 2016 U.S. LEXIS 463.

January 11, 2016. Petition for rehearing denied.

Former decision, 577 U.S. 846, 136 S. Ct. 93, 193 L. Ed. 2d 79, 2015 U.S. LEXIS 5061.

———

No. 14-10130. Duwane Shackelford, Petitioner v. William Stephens, Director, Texas Department of Criminal Justice, Correctional Institutions Division.

577 U.S. 1094, 136 S. Ct. 880, 193 L. Ed. 2d 772, 2016 U.S. LEXIS 399.

January 11, 2016. Petition for rehearing denied.

Former decision, 577 U.S. 849, 136 S. Ct. 102, 193 L. Ed. 2d 85, 2015 U.S. LEXIS 5001.

———

No. 14-10141. Merlene Jordan, Petitioner v. Carolyn W. Colvin, Acting Commissioner of Social Security.

577 U.S. 1094, 136 S. Ct. 880, 193 L. Ed. 2d 772, 2016 U.S. LEXIS 485.

January 11, 2016. Petition for rehearing denied.

Former decision, 577 U.S. 849, 136 S. Ct. 105, 193 L. Ed. 2d 86, 2015 U.S. LEXIS 5052.

———

No. 14-10215. Lisa Meriweather, Petitioner v. Wells Fargo Bank, N.A., et al.

577 U.S. 1094, 136 S. Ct. 881, 193 L. Ed. 2d 772, 2016 U.S. LEXIS 564.

January 11, 2016. Petition for rehearing denied.

Former decision, 577 U.S. 853, 136 S. Ct. 118, 193 L. Ed. 2d 93, 2015 U.S. LEXIS 6065.

———

No. 14-10256. Jeffrey R. Weinhaus, Petitioner v. Missouri.

577 U.S. 1094, 136 S. Ct. 881, 193 L. Ed. 2d 772, 2016 U.S. LEXIS 525.

January 11, 2016. Petition for rehearing denied.

Former decision, 577 U.S. 855, 136 S. Ct. 125, 193 L. Ed. 2d 97, 2015 U.S. LEXIS 5637.

———

No. 14-10282. Sebryne Walthall, aka Se'Bryne Walthall, Petitioner v. Gregory McQuiggen, Warden, et al.

577 U.S. 1094, 136 S. Ct. 881, 193 L. Ed. 2d 772, 2016 U.S. LEXIS 507.

January 11, 2016. Petition for rehearing denied.

Former decision, 577 U.S. 857, 136 S. Ct. 132, 193 L. Ed. 2d 101, 2015 U.S. LEXIS 5668.

———

No. 14-10287. Sylvester Rollins, Petitioner v. Louisiana Department of Corrections Officials, et al.

577 U.S. 1095, 136 S. Ct. 881, 193 L. Ed. 2d 772, 2016 U.S. LEXIS 556.

January 11, 2016. Petition for rehearing denied.

Former decision, 577 U.S. 857, 136 S. Ct. 298, 193 L. Ed. 2d 102, 2015 U.S. LEXIS 5718.

No. 14-10354. Kenneth Lee Lawshea, Petitioner v. Wendy Kelley, Director, Arkansas Department of Correction.

577 U.S. 1095, 136 S. Ct. 881, 193 L. Ed. 2d 773, 2016 U.S. LEXIS 551.

January 11, 2016. Petition for rehearing denied.

Former decision, 577 U.S. 861, 136 S. Ct. 145, 193 L. Ed. 2d 109, 2015 U.S. LEXIS 5698.

No. 14-10389. In re Ricky Dewayne Booth, Petitioner.

577 U.S. 1095, 136 S. Ct. 881, 193 L. Ed. 2d 773, 2016 U.S. LEXIS 330.

January 11, 2016. Petition for rehearing denied.

Former decision, 577 U.S. 812, 136 S. Ct. 150, 193 L. Ed. 2d 214, 2015 U.S. LEXIS 4743.

No. 14-10413. Eric Laquince Brown, Petitioner v. Tim Perez, Warden.

577 U.S. 1095, 136 S. Ct. 881, 193 L. Ed. 2d 773, 2016 U.S. LEXIS 412.

January 11, 2016. Petition for rehearing denied.

Former decision, 577 U.S. 865, 136 S. Ct. 155, 193 L. Ed. 2d 115, 2015 U.S. LEXIS 6235.

No. 14-10473. John P. Tomkins, Petitioner v. United States.

577 U.S. 1095, 136 S. Ct. 881, 193 L. Ed. 2d 773, 2016 U.S. LEXIS 403.

January 11, 2016. Petition for rehearing denied.

Former decision, 577 U.S. 955, 136 S. Ct. 402, 193 L. Ed. 2d 314, 2015 U.S. LEXIS 6928.

No. 15-104. Eduardo Nunez, et ux., Petitioners v. CitiMortgage, Incorporated, Successor by Merger to ABN AMRO Mortgage Group, Inc.

577 U.S. 1095, 136 S. Ct. 882, 193 L. Ed. 2d 773, 2016 U.S. LEXIS 363.

January 11, 2016. Petition for rehearing denied.

Former decision, 577 U.S. 873, 136 S. Ct. 223, 193 L. Ed. 2d 131, 2015 U.S. LEXIS 6239.

No. 15-192. Glenn Henderson, Petitioner v. Town of Hope Mills, North Carolina, et al.

577 U.S. 1095, 136 S. Ct. 882, 193 L. Ed. 2d 773, 2016 U.S. LEXIS 582.

January 11, 2016. Petition for rehearing denied.

Former decision, 577 U.S. 924, 136 S. Ct. 331, 193 L. Ed. 2d 230, 2015 U.S. LEXIS 6416.

No. 15-200. Kenneth J. Taggart, Petitioner v. GMAC Mortgage, LLC, et al.

577 U.S. 1095, 136 S. Ct. 882, 193 L. Ed. 2d 773, 2016 U.S. LEXIS 334.

January 11, 2016. Petition for rehearing denied.

Former decision, 577 U.S. 939, 136 S. Ct. 358, 193 L. Ed. 2d 290, 2015 U.S. LEXIS 6694.

No. 15-262. Martha Echeverry, Petitioner v. Deutsche Bank National Trust Company.

577 U.S. 1095, 136 S. Ct. 882, 193 L. Ed. 2d 774, 2016 U.S. LEXIS 544.

January 11, 2016. Petition for rehearing denied.

Former decision, 577 U.S. 957, 136 S. Ct. 410, 193 L. Ed. 2d 316, 2015 U.S. LEXIS 6976.

No. 15-295. Raymond H. Pierson, III, Petitioner v. Bruce S. Rogow, et al.

577 U.S. 1095, 136 S. Ct. 882, 193 L. Ed. 2d 774, 2016 U.S. LEXIS 592.

January 11, 2016. Petition for rehearing denied.

Former decision, 577 U.S. 957, 136 S. Ct. 416, 193 L. Ed. 2d 317, 2015 U.S. LEXIS 6942.

No. 15-299. Anthony J. Russo, Petitioner v. New York City Department of Education.

577 U.S. 1095, 136 S. Ct. 882, 193 L. Ed. 2d 774, 2016 U.S. LEXIS 609.

January 11, 2016. Petition for rehearing denied.

Former decision, 577 U.S. 957, 136 S. Ct. 416, 193 L. Ed. 2d 317, 2015 U.S. LEXIS 6916.

No. 15-311. Michael Houston and Steve Houston, Petitioners v. Vernetta Queen, et al.

577 U.S. 1095, 136 S. Ct. 882, 193 L. Ed. 2d 774, 2016 U.S. LEXIS 508.

January 11, 2016. Petition for rehearing denied.

Former decision, 577 U.S. 986, 136 S. Ct. 503, 193 L. Ed. 2d 397, 2015 U.S. LEXIS 7199.

No. 15-322. Lewis Wu, et ux., Petitioners v. Capital One, N.A., et al.

577 U.S. 1095, 136 S. Ct. 883, 193 L. Ed. 2d 774, 2016 U.S. LEXIS 231.

January 11, 2016. Petition for rehearing denied.

Former decision, 577 U.S. 986, 136 S. Ct. 506, 193 L. Ed. 2d 397, 2015 U.S. LEXIS 7204.

No. 15-332. Joseph W. Lewicki, Jr., et al., Petitioners v. Washington County, Pennsylvania, et al.

577 U.S. 1095, 136 S. Ct. 883, 193 L. Ed. 2d 774, 2016 U.S. LEXIS 541.

January 11, 2016. Petition for rehearing denied.

Former decision, 577 U.S. 986, 136 S. Ct. 507, 193 L. Ed. 2d 397, 2015 U.S. LEXIS 7193.

No. 15-392. James W. Hall, Petitioner v. Edward L. Gilbert, et al.

577 U.S. 1095, 136 S. Ct. 883, 193 L. Ed. 2d 774, 2016 U.S. LEXIS 439.

January 11, 2016. Petition for rehearing denied.

Former decision, 577 U.S. 958, 136 S. Ct. 428, 193 L. Ed. 2d 320, 2015 U.S. LEXIS 6863.

———

No. 15-393. Bridget M. Long, Petitioner v. Libertywood Nursing Center, et al.

577 U.S. 1095, 136 S. Ct. 883, 193 L. Ed. 2d 775, 2016 U.S. LEXIS 317.

January 11, 2016. Petition for rehearing denied.

Former decision, 577 U.S. 986, 136 S. Ct. 513, 193 L. Ed. 2d 398, 2015 U.S. LEXIS 7178.

———

No. 15-413. Andrew Searcy, Jr., Petitioner v. Merit Systems Protection Board.

577 U.S. 1095, 136 S. Ct. 883, 193 L. Ed. 2d 775, 2016 U.S. LEXIS 539.

January 11, 2016. Petition for rehearing denied.

Former decision, 577 U.S. 976, 136 S. Ct. 497, 193 L. Ed. 2d 351, 2015 U.S. LEXIS 7088.

———

No. 15-5044. Robert Lee Ortega, Petitioner v. William Stephens, Director, Texas Department of Criminal Justice, Correctional Institutions Division.

577 U.S. 1095, 136 S. Ct. 883, 193 L. Ed. 2d 775, 2016 U.S. LEXIS 579.

January 11, 2016. Petition for rehearing denied.

Former decision, 577 U.S. 879, 136 S. Ct. 176, 193 L. Ed. 2d 142, 2015 U.S. LEXIS 5334.

———

No. 15-5074. Rene Rivas, Jr., Petitioner v. William Stephens, Direc-

tor, Texas Department of Criminal Justice, Correctional Institutions Division.

577 U.S. 1095, 136 S. Ct. 883, 193 L. Ed. 2d 775, 2016 U.S. LEXIS 207.

January 11, 2016. Petition for rehearing denied.

Former decision, 577 U.S. 881, 136 S. Ct. 180, 193 L. Ed. 2d 145, 2015 U.S. LEXIS 5323.

———

No. 15-5125. In re Ramon Williamson, Petitioner.

577 U.S. 1095, 136 S. Ct. 884, 193 L. Ed. 2d 775, 2016 U.S. LEXIS 604.

January 11, 2016. Petition for rehearing denied.

Former decision, 577 U.S. 812, 136 S. Ct. 190, 193 L. Ed. 2d 214, 2015 U.S. LEXIS 4731.

———

No. 15-5209. Thomas Williams, Petitioner v. Illinois.

577 U.S. 1095, 136 S. Ct. 884, 193 L. Ed. 2d 775, 2016 U.S. LEXIS 469.

January 11, 2016. Petition for rehearing denied.

Former decision, 577 U.S. 888, 136 S. Ct. 205, 193 L. Ed. 2d 158, 2015 U.S. LEXIS 5419.

———

No. 15-5246. Eugenia Woodard, Petitioner v. Fortress Insurance Company, et al.

577 U.S. 1095, 136 S. Ct. 884, 193 L. Ed. 2d 775, 2016 U.S. LEXIS 312.

January 11, 2016. Petition for rehearing denied.

Former decision, 577 U.S. 890, 136 S. Ct. 211, 193 L. Ed. 2d 162, 2015 U.S. LEXIS 5485.

————

No. 15-5403. Jeffrey R. LeBlanc, Petitioner v. Macomb Regional Facility.

577 U.S. 1095, 136 S. Ct. 884, 193 L. Ed. 2d 776, 2016 U.S. LEXIS 332.

January 11, 2016. Petition for rehearing denied.

Former decision, 577 U.S. 898, 136 S. Ct. 238, 193 L. Ed. 2d 178, 2015 U.S. LEXIS 4957.

————

No. 15-5434. Jeffrey R. LeBlanc, Petitioner v. Kalamazoo County Sheriff's Department.

577 U.S. 1096, 136 S. Ct. 884, 193 L. Ed. 2d 776, 2016 U.S. LEXIS 488.

January 11, 2016. Petition for rehearing denied.

Former decision, 577 U.S. 900, 136 S. Ct. 245, 193 L. Ed. 2d 182, 2015 U.S. LEXIS 4817.

————

No. 15-5440. Jeffrey R. LeBlanc, Petitioner v. Michigan Department of Corrections.

577 U.S. 1096, 136 S. Ct. 884, 193 L. Ed. 2d 776, 2016 U.S. LEXIS 479.

January 11, 2016. Petition for rehearing denied.

Former decision, 577 U.S. 901, 136 S. Ct. 300, 193 L. Ed. 2d 183, 2015 U.S. LEXIS 4886.

————

No. 15-5496. Gardell Cowart, Petitioner v. Stu Sherman, Warden.

577 U.S. 1096, 136 S. Ct. 884, 193 L. Ed. 2d 776, 2016 U.S. LEXIS 307.

January 11, 2016. Petition for rehearing denied.

Former decision, 577 U.S. 926, 136 S. Ct. 322, 193 L. Ed. 2d 233, 2015 U.S. LEXIS 6450.

————

No. 15-5518. Richard A. Thurston, Petitioner v. Maryland.

577 U.S. 1096, 136 S. Ct. 884, 193 L. Ed. 2d 776, 2016 U.S. LEXIS 195.

January 11, 2016. Petition for rehearing denied.

Former decision, 577 U.S. 904, 136 S. Ct. 256, 193 L. Ed. 2d 190, 2015 U.S. LEXIS 4836.

————

No. 15-5534. Richard Layne LaBelle, Petitioner v. United States.

577 U.S. 1096, 136 S. Ct. 885, 193 L. Ed. 2d 776, 2016 U.S. LEXIS 384.

January 11, 2016. Petition for rehearing denied.

Former decision, 577 U.S. 905, 136 S. Ct. 258, 193 L. Ed. 2d 190, 2015 U.S. LEXIS 4826.

————

No. 15-5542. Jerry Neil Alfred, Petitioner v. Julie L. Jones, Secretary, Florida Department of Corrections, et al.

577 U.S. 1096, 136 S. Ct. 885, 193 L. Ed. 2d 776, 2016 U.S. LEXIS 509.

January 11, 2016. Petition for rehearing denied.

Former decision, 577 U.S. 927, 136 S. Ct. 325, 193 L. Ed. 2d 235, 2015 U.S. LEXIS 6440.

No. 15-5554. Jeffrey R. LeBlanc, Petitioner v. Kalamazoo County, Michigan.

577 U.S. 1096, 136 S. Ct. 885, 193 L. Ed. 2d 777, 2016 U.S. LEXIS 352.

January 11, 2016. Petition for rehearing denied.

Former decision, 577 U.S. 905, 136 S. Ct. 260, 193 L. Ed. 2d 192, 2015 U.S. LEXIS 5977.

No. 15-5597. Brandon Michael Pickens, Petitioner v. Brad Perritt, Superintendent, Lumberton Correctional Institution.

577 U.S. 1096, 136 S. Ct. 885, 193 L. Ed. 2d 777, 2016 U.S. LEXIS 468.

January 11, 2016. Petition for rehearing denied.

Former decision, 577 U.S. 928, 136 S. Ct. 329, 193 L. Ed. 2d 238, 2015 U.S. LEXIS 6395.

No. 15-5612. Thomas Chambliss, Petitioner v. United States.

577 U.S. 1096, 136 S. Ct. 885, 193 L. Ed. 2d 777, 2016 U.S. LEXIS 309.

January 11, 2016. Petition for rehearing denied.

Former decision, 577 U.S. 907, 136 S. Ct. 265, 193 L. Ed. 2d 195, 2015 U.S. LEXIS 6144.

No. 15-5622. Terence O'Neal Boyd, Petitioner v. Mississippi.

577 U.S. 1096, 136 S. Ct. 885, 193 L. Ed. 2d 777, 2016 U.S. LEXIS 585.

January 11, 2016. Petition for rehearing denied.

Former decision, 577 U.S. 929, 136 S. Ct. 331, 193 L. Ed. 2d 239, 2015 U.S. LEXIS 6417.

No. 15-5698. Frank D. Maki, Petitioner v. New York, et al.

577 U.S. 1096, 136 S. Ct. 885, 193 L. Ed. 2d 777, 2016 U.S. LEXIS 589.

January 11, 2016. Petition for rehearing denied.

Former decision, 577 U.S. 941, 136 S. Ct. 362, 193 L. Ed. 2d 295, 2015 U.S. LEXIS 6656.

No. 15-5706. Roswitha Ann Savoie, Petitioner v. Ric Bradshaw, Sheriff, Palm Beach County, Florida, et al.

577 U.S. 1096, 136 S. Ct. 885, 193 L. Ed. 2d 777, 2016 U.S. LEXIS 417.

January 11, 2016. Petition for rehearing denied.

Former decision, 577 U.S. 942, 136 S. Ct. 363, 193 L. Ed. 2d 295, 2015 U.S. LEXIS 6674.

No. 15-5719. Brad Bolton, Petitioner v. United States.

577 U.S. 1096, 136 S. Ct. 886, 193 L. Ed. 2d 777, 2016 U.S. LEXIS 573.

January 11, 2016. Petition for rehearing denied.

Former decision, 577 U.S. 942, 136 S. Ct. 364, 193 L. Ed. 2d 296, 2015 U.S. LEXIS 6629.

————

No. 15-5720. Kai Brost, Petitioner v. Iowa.

577 U.S. 1096, 136 S. Ct. 886, 193 L. Ed. 2d 778, 2016 U.S. LEXIS 282.

January 11, 2016. Petition for rehearing denied.

Former decision, 577 U.S. 942, 136 S. Ct. 364, 193 L. Ed. 2d 296, 2015 U.S. LEXIS 6602.

————

No. 15-5839. In re GwanJun Kim, Petitioner.

577 U.S. 1096, 136 S. Ct. 886, 193 L. Ed. 2d 778, 2016 U.S. LEXIS 563.

January 11, 2016. Petition for rehearing denied.

Former decision, 577 U.S. 954, 136 S. Ct. 409, 193 L. Ed. 2d 341, 2015 U.S. LEXIS 6774.

————

No. 15-5842. Joel Carter, Petitioner v. Michigan Department of Corrections, et al.

577 U.S. 1096, 136 S. Ct. 886, 193 L. Ed. 2d 778, 2016 U.S. LEXIS 552.

January 11, 2016. Petition for rehearing denied.

Former decision, 577 U.S. 961, 136 S. Ct. 439, 193 L. Ed. 2d 324, 2015 U.S. LEXIS 6856.

————

No. 15-5845. Bennie K. Ellison, Petitioner v. Joseph G. Kazmierski, Su-

pervising Judge, Circuit Court of Illinois, Cook County, et al.

577 U.S. 1096, 136 S. Ct. 886, 193 L. Ed. 2d 778, 2016 U.S. LEXIS 618.

January 11, 2016. Petition for rehearing denied.

Former decision, 577 U.S. 961, 136 S. Ct. 410, 193 L. Ed. 2d 324, 2015 U.S. LEXIS 7022.

————

No. 15-5847. Chester Staples, Petitioner v. Texas.

577 U.S. 1096, 136 S. Ct. 886, 193 L. Ed. 2d 778, 2016 U.S. LEXIS 545.

January 11, 2016. Petition for rehearing denied.

Former decision, 577 U.S. 961, 136 S. Ct. 410, 193 L. Ed. 2d 324, 2015 U.S. LEXIS 6853.

————

No. 15-5860. Corielle Johnson, Petitioner v. Leslie Beak, et al.

577 U.S. 1096, 136 S. Ct. 886, 193 L. Ed. 2d 778, 2016 U.S. LEXIS 588.

January 11, 2016. Petition for rehearing denied.

Former decision, 577 U.S. 961, 136 S. Ct. 411, 193 L. Ed. 2d 325, 2015 U.S. LEXIS 6876.

————

No. 15-5884. Carline M. Curry, Petitioner v. Martin Berger, et al.

577 U.S. 1096, 136 S. Ct. 886, 193 L. Ed. 2d 778, 2016 U.S. LEXIS 476.

January 11, 2016. Petition for rehearing denied.

Former decision, 577 U.S. 962, 136 S. Ct. 413, 193 L. Ed. 2d 326, 2015 U.S. LEXIS 6885.

———

No. 15-5889. Zane Balsam, Petitioner v. United States.

577 U.S. 1096, 136 S. Ct. 887, 193 L. Ed. 2d 779, 2016 U.S. LEXIS 562.

January 11, 2016. Petition for rehearing denied.

Former decision, 577 U.S. 932, 136 S. Ct. 342, 193 L. Ed. 2d 246, 2015 U.S. LEXIS 6484.

———

No. 15-5891. Shuntrell Jones, Petitioner v. United States.

577 U.S. 1096, 136 S. Ct. 887, 193 L. Ed. 2d 779, 2016 U.S. LEXIS 571.

January 11, 2016. Petition for rehearing denied.

Former decision, 577 U.S. 932, 136 S. Ct. 342, 193 L. Ed. 2d 246, 2015 U.S. LEXIS 6461.

———

No. 15-5943. James Spencer, aka Troy Buxton, Petitioner v. United States.

577 U.S. 1096, 136 S. Ct. 887, 193 L. Ed. 2d 779, 2016 U.S. LEXIS 570.

January 11, 2016. Petition for rehearing denied.

Former decision, 577 U.S. 933, 136 S. Ct. 346, 193 L. Ed. 2d 248, 2015 U.S. LEXIS 6393.

———

No. 15-5974. Marcia L. Jackson, Petitioner v. Park Place Condominiums Association, Inc.

577 U.S. 1096, 136 S. Ct. 887, 193 L. Ed. 2d 779, 2016 U.S. LEXIS 475.

January 11, 2016. Petition for rehearing denied.

Former decision, 577 U.S. 977, 136 S. Ct. 484, 193 L. Ed. 2d 355, 2015 U.S. LEXIS 7123.

———

No. 15-5986. Sher Qureshi, Petitioner v. New York (two judgments).

577 U.S. 1096, 136 S. Ct. 887, 193 L. Ed. 2d 779, 2016 U.S. LEXIS 318.

January 11, 2016. Petition for rehearing denied.

Former decision, 577 U.S. 978, 136 S. Ct. 485, 193 L. Ed. 2d 355, 2015 U.S. LEXIS 7084.

———

No. 15-6025. Lonnie Goodrich, Petitioner v. United States.

577 U.S. 1096, 136 S. Ct. 887, 193 L. Ed. 2d 779, 2016 U.S. LEXIS 321.

January 11, 2016. Petition for rehearing denied.

Former decision, 577 U.S. 944, 136 S. Ct. 371, 193 L. Ed. 2d 300, 2015 U.S. LEXIS 6717.

———

No. 15-6056. Leon Michael T. Kornegay, Petitioner v. New York, et al.

577 U.S. 1096, 136 S. Ct. 887, 193 L. Ed. 2d 779, 2016 U.S. LEXIS 326.

January 11, 2016. Petition for rehearing denied.

Former decision, 577 U.S. 978, 136 S. Ct. 486, 193 L. Ed. 2d 356, 2015 U.S. LEXIS 7108.

———

No. 15-6218. Christopher Barksdale, Petitioner v. United States District Court for the Northern District of Ohio.

577 U.S. 1096, 136 S. Ct. 887, 193 L. Ed. 2d 779, 2016 U.S. LEXIS 555.

January 11, 2016. Petition for rehearing denied.

Former decision, 577 U.S. 1012, 136 S. Ct. 569, 193 L. Ed. 2d 437, 2015 U.S. LEXIS 7577.

———

No. 15-6227. Terrell Taylor, Petitioner v. Karen Crowley, Superintendent, Orleans Correctional Facility.

577 U.S. 1096, 136 S. Ct. 888, 193 L. Ed. 2d 780, 2016 U.S. LEXIS 346.

January 11, 2016. Petition for rehearing denied.

Former decision, 577 U.S. 990, 136 S. Ct. 512, 193 L. Ed. 2d 404, 2015 U.S. LEXIS 7296.

———

No. 15-6234. Steven Lee, Petitioner v. Paul Hymowitz, et al.

577 U.S. 1097, 136 S. Ct. 888, 193 L. Ed. 2d 780, 2016 U.S. LEXIS 598.

January 11, 2016. Petition for rehearing denied.

Former decision, 577 U.S. 1012, 136 S. Ct. 546, 193 L. Ed. 2d 437, 2015 U.S. LEXIS 7533.

———

No. 15-6249. Mark Brown, Petitioner v. United States.

577 U.S. 1097, 136 S. Ct. 888, 193 L. Ed. 2d 780, 2016 U.S. LEXIS 454.

January 11, 2016. Petition for rehearing denied.

Former decision, 577 U.S. 966, 136 S. Ct. 426, 193 L. Ed. 2d 333, 2015 U.S. LEXIS 6967.

———

No. 15-6255. Kinoll McCormick, Petitioner v. Lawrence Mahally, Super-

intendent, State Correctional Institution at Dallas, et al.

577 U.S. 1097, 136 S. Ct. 888, 193 L. Ed. 2d 780, 2016 U.S. LEXIS 16.

January 11, 2016. Petition for rehearing denied.

Former decision, 577 U.S. 990, 136 S. Ct. 512, 193 L. Ed. 2d 404, 2015 U.S. LEXIS 7265.

———

No. 15-6259. Robert Lee Johnson, Petitioner v. Department of Labor, et al.

577 U.S. 1097, 136 S. Ct. 888, 193 L. Ed. 2d 780, 2016 U.S. LEXIS 9.

January 11, 2016. Petition for rehearing denied.

Former decision, 577 U.S. 990, 136 S. Ct. 512, 193 L. Ed. 2d 404, 2015 U.S. LEXIS 7280.

———

No. 15-6348. Kendrick Jermaine Fulton, Petitioner v. United States.

577 U.S. 1097, 136 S. Ct. 888, 193 L. Ed. 2d 780, 2016 U.S. LEXIS 18.

January 11, 2016. Petition for rehearing denied.

Former decision, 577 U.S. 967, 136 S. Ct. 431, 193 L. Ed. 2d 335, 2015 U.S. LEXIS 6835.

———

No. 15-6367. Donald Sullivan, Petitioner v. United States.

577 U.S. 1097, 136 S. Ct. 888, 193 L. Ed. 2d 780, 2016 U.S. LEXIS 12.

January 11, 2016. Petition for rehearing denied.

Former decision, 577 U.S. 979, 136 S. Ct. 491, 193 L. Ed. 2d 358, 2015 U.S. LEXIS 7140.

No. 15-6420. Antonio M. Taylor, Petitioner v. United States.

577 U.S. 1097, 136 S. Ct. 888, 193 L. Ed. 2d 781, 2016 U.S. LEXIS 15.

January 11, 2016. Petition for rehearing denied.

Former decision, 577 U.S. 968, 136 S. Ct. 436, 193 L. Ed. 2d 339, 2015 U.S. LEXIS 6802.

No. 15-6564. Kenneth J. Rowe, Petitioner v. United States.

577 U.S. 1097, 136 S. Ct. 889, 193 L. Ed. 2d 781, 2016 U.S. LEXIS 11.

January 11, 2016. Petition for rehearing denied.

Former decision, 577 U.S. 993, 136 S. Ct. 521, 193 L. Ed. 2d 410, 2015 U.S. LEXIS 7177.

No. 14-1385. Bianka Cruz, Petitioner v. Citibank, N.A.

577 U.S. 1097, 136 S. Ct. 889, 193 L. Ed. 2d 781, 2016 U.S. LEXIS 14.

January 11, 2016. Motion of petitioner for leave to file a petition for rehearing denied.

Former decision, 577 U.S. 820, 136 S. Ct. 73, 193 L. Ed. 2d 32, 2015 U.S. LEXIS 5070.

No. 15-78. Alejandro Mirabal, Petitioner v. HSBC Bank USA, N.A.

577 U.S. 1097, 136 S. Ct. 889, 193 L. Ed. 2d 781, 2016 U.S. LEXIS 13.

January 11, 2016. Motion of petitioner for leave to file a petition for rehearing denied.

Former decision, 577 U.S. 872, 136 S. Ct. 199, 193 L. Ed. 2d 129, 2015 U.S. LEXIS 6207.

No. 15-97. Yurania Dolz, Petitioner v. CitiMortgage, Inc.

577 U.S. 1097, 136 S. Ct. 889, 193 L. Ed. 2d 781, 2016 U.S. LEXIS 10.

January 11, 2016. Motion of petitioner for leave to file a petition for rehearing denied.

Former decision, 577 U.S. 873, 136 S. Ct. 218, 193 L. Ed. 2d 131, 2015 U.S. LEXIS 6330.

No. D-2851. In the Matter of Disbarment of Gerald Isadore Katz.

577 U.S. 1058, 136 S. Ct. 889, 193 L. Ed. 2d 781, 2016 U.S. LEXIS 17.

January 11, 2016. Disbarment entered.

Former order, 577 U.S. 952, 136 S. Ct. 442, 193 L. Ed. 2d 343, 2015 U.S. LEXIS 6813.

No. 15-655 (R46-015). Heath S. Downs and Judy Probart Long, Petitioners v. Alan Van Orden, as Personal Representative of the Estate of Crystal Rhea Bannister, et al.

577 U.S. 1097, 136 S. Ct. 889, 193 L. Ed. 2d 782, 2016 U.S. LEXIS 621.

January 12, 2016. The petition for writ of certiorari to the United States Court of Appeals for the Ninth Circuit was dismissed today pursuant to Rule 46 of the Rules of this Court.

Same case below, 609 Fed. Appx. 474.

———

No. 14-1418. David A. Zubik, et al., Petitioners v. Sylvia Burwell, Secretary of Health and Human Services, et al.

No. 14-1453. Priests for Life, et al., Petitioners v. Department of Health and Human Services, et al.

No. 14-1505. Roman Catholic Archbishop of Washington, et al., Petitioners v. Sylvia Burwell, Secretary of Health and Human Services, et al.

No. 15-35. East Texas Baptist University, et al., Petitioners v. Sylvia Burwell, Secretary of Health and Human Services, et al.

No. 15-105. Little Sisters of the Poor Home for the Aged, Denver, Colorado, et al., Petitioners v. Sylvia Burwell, Secretary of Health and Human Services, et al.

No. 15-119. Southern Nazarene University, et al., Petitioners v. Sylvia Burwell, Secretary of Health and Human Services, et al.

No. 15-191. Geneva College, Petitioner v. Sylvia Burwell, Secretary of Health and Human Services, et al.

577 U.S. 1097, 136 S. Ct. 891, 193 L. Ed. 2d 782, 2016 U.S. LEXIS 623.

January 15, 2016. Motion of petitioners for divided argument and enlargement of time for oral argument granted.

———

No. 15-6418. Gregory Welch, Petitioner v. United States.

577 U.S. 1098, 136 S. Ct. 892, 193 L. Ed. 2d 782, 2016 U.S. LEXIS 634.

January 15, 2016. Helgi C. Walker, Esq., of Washington, D.C., is invited to brief and argue this case, as amicus curiae, in support of the judgment below. Briefs of other amici curiae in support of affirmance are to be filed within 7 days after the filing of the brief of the Court-appointed amicus curiae.

No. 14-9496. Elijah Manuel, Petitioner v. City of Joliet, Illinois, et al.

577 U.S. 1098, 136 S. Ct. 890, 193 L. Ed. 2d 783, 2016 U.S. LEXIS 627.

January 15, 2016. Motion of petitioner for leave to proceed in forma pauperis granted. Petition for writ of certiorari to the United States Court of Appeals for the Seventh Circuit granted.

Same case below, 590 Fed. Appx. 641.

No. 15-214. Joseph P. Murr, et al., Petitioners v. Wisconsin, et al.

577 U.S. 1098, 136 S. Ct. 890, 193 L. Ed. 2d 783, 2016 U.S. LEXIS 622.

January 15, 2016. Petition for writ of certiorari to the Court of Appeals of Wisconsin, District III, granted.

Same case below, 359 Wis. 2d 675, 859 N.W.2d 628.

No. 15-375. Supap Kirtsaeng, dba Bluechristine99, Petitioner v. John Wiley & Sons, Inc.

577 U.S. 1098, 136 S. Ct. 890, 193 L. Ed. 2d 783, 2016 U.S. LEXIS 629.

January 15, 2016. Petition for writ of certiorari to the United States Court of Appeals for the Second Circuit granted.

Same case below, 605 Fed. Appx. 48.

No. 15-415. Encino Motorcars, LLC, Petitioner v. Hector Navarro, et al.

577 U.S. 1098, 136 S. Ct. 890, 193 L. Ed. 2d 783, 2016 U.S. LEXIS 635.

January 15, 2016. Petition for writ of certiorari to the United States Court of Appeals for the Ninth Circuit granted.

Same case below, 780 F.3d 1267.

No. 15-446. Cuozzo Speed Technologies, LLC, Petitioner v. Michelle K. Lee, Under Secretary of Commerce for Intellectual Property and Director, Patent and Trademark Office.

577 U.S. 1098, 136 S. Ct. 890, 193 L. Ed. 2d 783, 2016 U.S. LEXIS 632.

January 15, 2016. Petition for writ of certiorari to the United States Court of Appeals for the Federal Circuit granted.

Same case below, 793 F.3d 1268.

No. 15-457. Microsoft Corporation, Petitioner v. Seth Baker, et al.

577 U.S. 1099, 136 S. Ct. 890, 193 L. Ed. 2d 783, 2016 U.S. LEXIS 637.

January 15, 2016. Petition for writ of certiorari to the United States Court Appeals of Appeals for the Ninth Circuit granted limited to the following question: Whether a federal court of appeals has jurisdiction under both Article III and 28 U.S.C. §1291 to review an order denying class certification after the named plaintiffs voluntarily dismiss their individual claims with prejudice.

Same case below, 797 F.3d 607.

No. 15-474. Robert F. McDonnell, Petitioner v. United States.

577 U.S. 1099, 136 S. Ct. 891, 193 L. Ed. 2d 784, 2016 U.S. LEXIS 625.

January 15, 2016. Petition for writ of certiorari to the United States Court of Appeals for the Fourth Circuit granted limited to Question 1 presented by the petition.

Same case below, 792 F.3d 478.

No. 15-577. Trinity Lutheran Church of Columbia, Inc., Petitioner v. Sara Parker Pauley, Director, Missouri Department of Natural Resources.

577 U.S. 1098, 136 S. Ct. 891, 193 L. Ed. 2d 784, 2016 U.S. LEXIS 633.

January 15, 2016. Petition for writ of certiorari to the United States Court of Appeals for the Eighth Circuit granted.

Same case below, 788 F.3d 779.

MEMORANDUM CASES

No. 15-85. Medtronic Sofamor Danek USA, Inc., et al., Petitioners v. NuVasive, Inc.

577 U.S. 1099, 136 S. Ct. 893, 193 L. Ed. 2d 785, 2016 U.S. LEXIS 686.

January 19, 2016. On petition for writ of certiorari to the United States Court of Appeals for the Federal Circuit. Petition for writ of certiorari granted. Judgment vacated, and case remanded to the United States Court of Appeals for the Federal Circuit for further consideration in light of Commil USA, LLC v. Cisco Systems, Inc., 575 U.S. 632, 135 S. Ct. 1920, 191 L. Ed. 2d 883 (2015).

Same case below, 778 F.3d 1365.

No. 15-6957. Cedric Greene, Jr., Petitioner v. California, et al.

577 U.S. 1099, 136 S. Ct. 904, 193 L. Ed. 2d 785, 2016 U.S. LEXIS 793.

January 19, 2016. Motion of petitioner for leave to proceed in forma pauperis denied, and petition for writ of certiorari to the United States Court of Appeals for the Ninth Circuit dismissed. See Rule 39.8.

No. 15-7124. Sukit Kumvachirapitag, Petitioner v. Barack H. Obama, President of the United States.

577 U.S. 1099, 136 S. Ct. 907, 193 L. Ed. 2d 785, 2016 U.S. LEXIS 800.

January 19, 2016. Motion of petitioner for leave to proceed in forma pauperis

denied, and petition for writ of certiorari to the United States Court of Appeals for the Ninth Circuit dismissed. See Rule 39.8.

Same case below, 617 Fed. Appx. 804.

No. 15-7326. Richard Vieux, Petitioner v. United States.

577 U.S. 1099, 136 S. Ct. 914, 193 L. Ed. 2d 785, 2016 U.S. LEXIS 797.

January 19, 2016. Motion of petitioner for leave to proceed in forma pauperis denied, and petition for writ of certiorari to the United States Court of Appeals for the Eleventh Circuit dismissed. See Rule 39.8. As the petitioner has repeatedly abused this Court's process, the Clerk is directed not to accept any further petitions in noncriminal matters from petitioner unless the docketing fee required by Rule 38(a) is paid and the petition is submitted in compliance with Rule 33.1. See Martin v. District of Columbia Court of Appeals, 506 U.S. 1, 113 S. Ct. 397, 121 L. Ed. 2d 305 (1992) (per curiam). Justice Kagan took no part in the consideration or decision of this motion and this petition.

Same case below, 616 Fed. Appx. 891.

No. 15-7352. Ebrahim Adkins, Petitioner v. United States District Court for the District of Kansas.

577 U.S. 1100, 136 S. Ct. 925, 193 L. Ed. 2d 785, 2016 U.S. LEXIS 777.

January 19, 2016. Motion of petitioner for leave to proceed in forma pauperis

denied, and petition for writ of certiorari to the United States Court of Appeals for the Tenth Circuit dismissed. See Rule 39.8.

No. 15A551. Keli'i Akina, et al., Applicants v. Hawaii, et al.

577 U.S. 1100, 136 S. Ct. 922, 193 L. Ed. 2d 786, 2016 U.S. LEXIS 796.

January 19, 2016. Motion of applicants Keli'i Akina, et al. for civil contempt denied.

No. 15M75. Robert Biros, Petitioner v. Kathleen Kane, Attorney General of Pennsylvania, et al.

577 U.S. 1100, 136 S. Ct. 922, 193 L. Ed. 2d 786, 2016 U.S. LEXIS 687.

January 19, 2016. Motion for leave to file a petition for writ of certiorari under seal granted.

No. 15-497. Stacy Fry, et vir, as Next Friends of Minor E. F., Petitioners v. Napoleon Community Schools, et al.

577 U.S. 1100, 136 S. Ct. 923, 193 L. Ed. 2d 786, 2016 U.S. LEXIS 820.

January 19, 2016. The Solicitor General is invited to file a brief in this case expressing the views of the United States.

Same case below, 788 F.3d 622.

No. 15-5495. Juan Enriquez, Petitioner v. William Stephens, Director, Texas Department of Criminal Justice, Correctional Institutions Division.

577 U.S. 1100, 136 S. Ct. 923, 193 L. Ed. 2d 786, 2016 U.S. LEXIS 683.

January 19, 2016. Motion of petitioner for reconsideration of order denying leave to proceed in forma pauperis denied.

No. 15-5648. Landry Dixon, Petitioner v. 24th District Court of Louisiana, et al.

577 U.S. 1100, 136 S. Ct. 923, 193 L. Ed. 2d 786, 2016 U.S. LEXIS 657.

January 19, 2016. Motion of petitioner for reconsideration of order denying leave to proceed in forma pauperis denied.

No. 15-6142. Thomas H. Clay, Petitioner v. William Stephens, Director, Texas Department of Criminal Justice, Correctional Institutions Division.

577 U.S. 1100, 136 S. Ct. 923, 193 L. Ed. 2d 786, 2016 U.S. LEXIS 752.

January 19, 2016. Motion of petitioner for reconsideration of order denying leave to proceed in forma pauperis denied.

No. 15-6244. Darrell J. Moore, Sr., Petitioner v. Rudolf Montiel, et al.

577 U.S. 1100, 136 S. Ct. 923, 193 L. Ed. 2d 786, 2016 U.S. LEXIS 678.

January 19, 2016. Motion of petitioner for reconsideration of order denying leave to proceed in forma pauperis denied.

MEMORANDUM CASES

No. 15-6492. Pio Peter Zammit, Petitioner v. City of New Baltimore, Michigan.

577 U.S. 1101, 136 S. Ct. 923, 193 L. Ed. 2d 787, 2016 U.S. LEXIS 705.

January 19, 2016. Motion of petitioner for reconsideration of order denying leave to proceed in forma pauperis denied.

No. 15-6890. Edward Stewart, Petitioner v. Treasure Bay Casino.

577 U.S. 1101, 136 S. Ct. 924, 193 L. Ed. 2d 787, 2016 U.S. LEXIS 715.

January 19, 2016. Motion of petitioner for leave to proceed in forma pauperis denied. Petitioner is allowed until February 9, 2016, within which to pay the docketing fee required by Rule 38(a) and to submit a petition in compliance with Rule 33.1 of the Rules of this Court.

Same case below, 622 Fed. Appx. 337.

No. 15-6916. Charles G. Kinney, Petitioner v. Susan Steele, et al.

577 U.S. 1101, 136 S. Ct. 924, 193 L. Ed. 2d 787, 2016 U.S. LEXIS 778.

January 19, 2016. Motion of petitioner for leave to proceed in forma pauperis denied. Petitioner is allowed until February 9, 2016, within which to pay the docketing fee required by Rule 38(a) and to submit a petition in compliance with Rule 33.1 of the Rules of this Court.

No. 15-7093. Samuel Thomas Phifer, Petitioner v. Sevenson Environmental Services, Inc., et al.

577 U.S. 1101, 136 S. Ct. 924, 193 L. Ed. 2d 787, 2016 U.S. LEXIS 684.

January 19, 2016. Motion of petitioner for leave to proceed in forma pauperis denied. Petitioner is allowed until February 9, 2016, within which to pay the docketing fee required by Rule 38(a) and to submit a petition in compliance with Rule 33.1 of the Rules of this Court.

Same case below, 619 Fed. Appx. 153.

No. 15-7153. Rungrudee Suteerachanon, Petitioner v. McDonald's Restaurants of Maryland, Inc.

577 U.S. 1101, 136 S. Ct. 924, 193 L. Ed. 2d 787, 2016 U.S. LEXIS 667.

January 19, 2016. Motion of petitioner for leave to proceed in forma pauperis denied. Petitioner is allowed until February 9, 2016, within which to pay the docketing fee required by Rule 38(a) and to submit a petition in compliance with Rule 33.1 of the Rules of this Court.

Same case below, 607 Fed. Appx. 339.

No. 15-7304. Gennaro Rauso, Petitioner v. United States.

577 U.S. 1101, 136 S. Ct. 924, 193 L. Ed. 2d 787, 2016 U.S. LEXIS 741.

January 19, 2016. Motion of petitioner for leave to proceed in forma pauperis denied. Petitioner is allowed until February 9, 2016, within which to pay the docketing fee required by Rule 38(a) and to submit a petition in compliance with Rule 33.1 of the Rules of this Court.

No. 15-7406. Terrance Williams, Petitioner v. United States.

577 U.S. 1101, 136 S. Ct. 925, 193 L. Ed. 2d 787, 2016 U.S. LEXIS 713.

January 19, 2016. Motion of petitioner for leave to proceed in forma pauperis

denied. Petitioner is allowed until February 9, 2016, within which to pay the docketing fee required by Rule 38(a) and to submit a petition in compliance with Rule 33.1 of the Rules of this Court.

Same case below, 124 A.3d 149.

_____

No. 15-458. Rocky Dietz, Petitioner v. Hillary Bouldin.

577 U.S. 1101, 136 S. Ct. 896, 193 L. Ed. 2d 788, 2016 U.S. LEXIS 673.

January 19, 2016. Petition for writ of certiorari to the United States Court of Appeals for the Ninth Circuit granted.

Same case below, 794 F.3d 1093.

_____

No. 15-628. Bassam Yacoub Salman, Petitioner v. United States.

577 U.S. 1101, 136 S. Ct. 899, 193 L. Ed. 2d 788, 2016 U.S. LEXIS 662.

January 19, 2016. Petition for writ of certiorari to the United States Court of Appeals for the Ninth Circuit granted limited to Question 1 presented by the petition.

Same case below, 792 F.3d 1087.

_____

No. 15-674. United States, et al., Petitioners v. Texas, et al.

577 U.S. 1101, 136 S. Ct. 906, 193 L. Ed. 2d 788, 2016 U.S. LEXIS 841.

January 19, 2016. Petition for writ of certiorari to the United States Court of Appeals for the Fifth Circuit granted. In addition to the questions presented by the petition, the parties are directed to brief and argue the following question: "Whether the Guidance violates the Take Care Clause of the Constitution, Art. II, § 3."

Same case below, 809 F.3d 134.

_____

No. 15-6092. Richard Mathis, Petitioner v. United States.

577 U.S. 1101, 136 S. Ct. 894, 193 L. Ed. 2d 788, 2016 U.S. LEXIS 710.

January 19, 2016. Motion of petitioner for leave to proceed in forma pauperis granted. Petition for writ of certiorari to the United States Court of Appeals for the Eighth Circuit granted.

Same case below, 786 F.3d 1068.

_____

No. 14-8071. Brandon Bernard, Petitioner v. United States.

577 U.S. 1101, 136 S. Ct. 892, 193 L. Ed. 2d 788, 2016 U.S. LEXIS 648.

January 19, 2016. Petition for writ of certiorari to the United States Court of Appeals for the Fifth Circuit denied.

Same case below, 762 F.3d 467.

_____

No. 15-170. Ryan Morris, Petitioner v. United States.

577 U.S. 1102, 136 S. Ct. 893, 193 L. Ed. 2d 788, 2016 U.S. LEXIS 743.

January 19, 2016. Petition for writ of certiorari to the United States Court of Appeals for the First Circuit denied.

Same case below, 784 F.3d 870.

No. 15-186. Antwaine Lamar McCoy, Petitioner v. United States.

577 U.S. 1102, 136 S. Ct. 894, 193 L. Ed. 2d 789, 2016 U.S. LEXIS 758.

January 19, 2016. Petition for writ of certiorari to the United States Court of Appeals for the Fourth Circuit denied.

Same case below, 589 Fed. Appx. 169.

No. 15-362. Elenilson J. Ortiz-Franco, Petitioner v. Loretta E. Lynch, Attorney General.

577 U.S. 1102, 136 S. Ct. 894, 193 L. Ed. 2d 789, 2016 U.S. LEXIS 798.

January 19, 2016. Petition for writ of certiorari to the United States Court of Appeals for the Second Circuit denied.

Same case below, 782 F.3d 81.

No. 15-428. Jan Miller, Petitioner v. Federal Election Commission.

577 U.S. 1102, 136 S. Ct. 895, 193 L. Ed. 2d 789, 2016 U.S. LEXIS 761.

January 19, 2016. Petition for writ of certiorari to the United States Court of Appeals for the District of Columbia Circuit denied.

Same case below, 793 F.3d 1.

No. 15-447. Julius H. Schoeps, et al., Petitioners v. Free State of Bavaria, Federal Republic of Germany.

577 U.S. 1102, 136 S. Ct. 895, 193 L. Ed. 2d 789, 2016 U.S. LEXIS 669, reh den 577

U.S. 1231, 136 S. Ct. 1487, 194 L. Ed. 2d 578, 2016 U.S. LEXIS 1884.

January 19, 2016. Petition for writ of certiorari to the United States Court of Appeals for the Second Circuit denied.

Same case below, 611 Fed. Appx. 32.

No. 15-448. Joseph M. Beck, in His Official Capacity as Chairperson of the Arkansas State Medical Board, et al., Petitioners v. Louis Jerry Edwards, et al.

577 U.S. 1102, 136 S. Ct. 895, 193 L. Ed. 2d 789, 2016 U.S. LEXIS 646.

January 19, 2016. Petition for writ of certiorari to the United States Court of Appeals for the Eighth Circuit denied.

Same case below, 786 F.3d 1113.

No. 15-450. Nikolay Ivanov Angov, Petitioner v. Loretta E. Lynch, Attorney General.

577 U.S. 1102, 136 S. Ct. 896, 193 L. Ed. 2d 789, 2016 U.S. LEXIS 835.

January 19, 2016. Petition for writ of certiorari to the United States Court of Appeals for the Ninth Circuit denied.

Same case below, 788 F.3d 896.

No. 15-451. Firefighters' Retirement System, et al., Petitioners v. Citco Group Limited, et al.

577 U.S. 1102, 136 S. Ct. 896, 193 L. Ed. 2d 789, 2016 U.S. LEXIS 815.

January 19, 2016. Petition for writ of certiorari to the United States Court of Appeals for the Fifth Circuit denied.

Same case below, 796 F.3d 520.

Same case below, 793 F.3d 771.

No. 15-456. Joannie Jefferson, et al., Petitioners v. Certain Underwriters of Lloyd's, London.

577 U.S. 1102, 136 S. Ct. 896, 193 L. Ed. 2d 790, 2016 U.S. LEXIS 704.

January 19, 2016. Petition for writ of certiorari to the United States Court of Appeals for the Fifth Circuit denied.

No. 15-468. David J. Whelan, et ux., Petitioners v. Judith A. Pascale, et al.

577 U.S. 1102, 136 S. Ct. 896, 193 L. Ed. 2d 790, 2016 U.S. LEXIS 746.

January 19, 2016. Petition for writ of certiorari to the United States Court of Appeals for the Second Circuit denied.

Same case below, 610 Fed. Appx. 19.

No. 15-480. Town of Mocksville, North Carolina, et al., Petitioners v. Kenneth L. Hunter, et al.

577 U.S. 1102, 136 S. Ct. 897, 193 L. Ed. 2d 790, 2016 U.S. LEXIS 666.

January 19, 2016. Petition for writ of certiorari to the United States Court of Appeals for the Fourth Circuit denied.

Same case below, 789 F.3d 389.

No. 15-505. Kirkland Townsend, Petitioner v. HSBC Bank USA, N.A.

577 U.S. 1102, 136 S. Ct. 897, 193 L. Ed. 2d 790, 2016 U.S. LEXIS 688.

January 19, 2016. Petition for writ of certiorari to the United States Court of Appeals for the Seventh Circuit denied.

No. 15-560. Boehringer Ingelheim Pharmaceuticals, Inc., Petitioner v. Federal Trade Commission.

577 U.S. 1102, 136 S. Ct. 925, 193 L. Ed. 2d 790, 2016 U.S. LEXIS 692.

January 19, 2016. Petition for writ of certiorari to the United States Court of Appeals for the District of Columbia Circuit denied.

Same case below, 414 U.S. App. D.C. 188, 778 F.3d 142.

No. 15-567. Alps South, LLC, Petitioner v. The Ohio Willow Wood Company.

577 U.S. 1102, 136 S. Ct. 897, 193 L. Ed. 2d 790, 2016 U.S. LEXIS 742.

January 19, 2016. Petition for writ of certiorari to the United States Court of Appeals for the Federal Circuit denied.

Same case below, 787 F.3d 1379.

No. 15-613. Martha Rodriguez, Petitioner v. American Home Mortgage Servicing.

577 U.S. 1103, 136 S. Ct. 898, 193 L. Ed. 2d 790, 2016 U.S. LEXIS 716, reh den 577 U.S. 1231, 136 S. Ct. 1487, 194 L. Ed. 2d 578, 2016 U.S. LEXIS 1870.

January 19, 2016. Petition for writ of certiorari to the District Court of Appeal of Florida, Fourth District, denied.

Same case below, 195 So. 3d 390.

No. 15-616. MedImmune, LLC, Petitioner v. Board of Trustees of the University of Massachusetts, dba University of Massachusetts Biologic Laboratories.

577 U.S. 1103, 136 S. Ct. 898, 193 L. Ed. 2d 791, 2016 U.S. LEXIS 780.

January 19, 2016. Petition for writ of certiorari to the Court of Special Appeals of Maryland denied.

Same case below, 223 Md. App. 777 and 223 Md. App. 781.

No. 15-618. George Varriale, Petitioner v. Maryland.

577 U.S. 1103, 136 S. Ct. 898, 193 L. Ed. 2d 791, 2016 U.S. LEXIS 840.

January 19, 2016. Petition for writ of certiorari to the Court of Appeals of Maryland denied.

Same case below, 444 Md. 400, 119 A.3d 824.

No. 15-619. Soudabeh White, Petitioner v. Malcolm White.

577 U.S. 1103, 136 S. Ct. 899, 193 L. Ed. 2d 791, 2016 U.S. LEXIS 739.

January 19, 2016. Petition for writ of certiorari to the Supreme Court of Virginia denied.

No. 15-624. Gregory Pellerin, Petitioner v. Nevada County, California, et al.

577 U.S. 1103, 136 S. Ct. 899, 193 L. Ed. 2d 791, 2016 U.S. LEXIS 689.

January 19, 2016. Petition for writ of certiorari to the United States Court of Appeals for the Ninth Circuit denied.

Same case below, 635 Fed. Appx. 345.

No. 15-629. Herman Hoffman, et ux., Petitioners v. Texas.

577 U.S. 1103, 136 S. Ct. 899, 193 L. Ed. 2d 791, 2016 U.S. LEXIS 717.

January 19, 2016. Petition for writ of certiorari to the County Court at Law 2, Montgomery County, Texas, denied.

No. 15-633. Tyrone Duff, et ux., Petitioners v. Richard W. Lewis, et al.

577 U.S. 1103, 136 S. Ct. 899, 193 L. Ed. 2d 791, 2016 U.S. LEXIS 706, reh den 577 U.S. 1208, 136 S. Ct. 1403, 194 L. Ed. 2d 382, 2016 U.S. LEXIS 1627.

January 19, 2016. Petition for writ of certiorari to the United States Court of Appeals for the Ninth Circuit denied.

No. 15-636. Javier Carrillo, et al., Petitioners v. Deutsche Bank National Trust Company, as Trustee.

577 U.S. 1103, 136 S. Ct. 900, 193 L. Ed. 2d 791, 2016 U.S. LEXIS 775, reh den 577 U.S. 1241, 136 S. Ct. 1510, 194 L. Ed. 2d 598, 2016 U.S. LEXIS 2262.

January 19, 2016. Petition for writ of certiorari to the Supreme Court of Florida denied.

Same case below, 171 So. 3d 114.

No. 15-637. Energy-Intensive Manufacturers Working Group on Greenhouse Gas Regulation, Petitioner v. Environmental Protection Agency, et al.

577 U.S. 1103, 136 S. Ct. 900, 193 L. Ed. 2d 791, 2016 U.S. LEXIS 751.

January 19, 2016. Petition for writ of certiorari to the United States Court of Appeals for the District of Columbia Circuit denied.

Same case below, 606 Fed. Appx. 6.

No. 15-643. Joseph M. Arpaio, Sheriff, Maricopa County, Arizona, Petitioner v. Barack H. Obama, President of the United States, et al.

577 U.S. 1103, 136 S. Ct. 900, 193 L. Ed. 2d 792, 2016 U.S. LEXIS 736, reh den 577 U.S. 1184, 136 S. Ct. 1250, 194 L. Ed. 2d 247, 2016 U.S. LEXIS 1168.

January 19, 2016. Petition for writ of certiorari to the United States Court of Appeals for the District of Columbia Circuit denied.

Same case below, 797 F.3d 11.

No. 15-644. Nancy Dolan, Petitioner v. Penn Millers Insurance Company, et al.

577 U.S. 1103, 136 S. Ct. 900, 193 L. Ed. 2d 792, 2016 U.S. LEXIS 816.

January 19, 2016. Petition for writ of certiorari to the United States Court of Appeals for the Third Circuit denied.

Same case below, 625 Fed. Appx. 91.

No. 15-658. Christopher Hadsell, Petitioner v. Catherine Hadsell.

577 U.S. 1103, 136 S. Ct. 902, 193 L. Ed. 2d 792, 2016 U.S. LEXIS 745.

January 19, 2016. Petition for writ of certiorari to the Court of Appeal of California, First Appellate District, denied.

No. 15-661. Joel D. Joseph, Petitioner v. Richard S. Bernstein, et al.

577 U.S. 1103, 136 S. Ct. 902, 193 L. Ed. 2d 792, 2016 U.S. LEXIS 721.

January 19, 2016. Petition for writ of certiorari to the United States Court of Appeals for the Eleventh Circuit denied.

Same case below, 612 Fed. Appx. 551.

No. 15-663. Jeffrey F. Kratz, Petitioner v. CitiMortgage Inc.

577 U.S. 1104, 136 S. Ct. 903, 193 L. Ed. 2d 792, 2016 U.S. LEXIS 738, reh den 577 U.S. 1209, 136 S. Ct. 1403, 194 L. Ed. 2d 382, 2016 U.S. LEXIS 1617.

January 19, 2016. Petition for writ of certiorari to the Superior Court of Pennsylvania, Philadelphia Office, denied.

Same case below, 108 A.3d 122.

No. 15-688. Mark David Frankel, Petitioner v. Wells Fargo Bank, N.A.

577 U.S. 1104, 136 S. Ct. 906, 193 L. Ed. 2d 792, 2016 U.S. LEXIS 718.

January 19, 2016. Petition for writ of certiorari to the Superior Court of Pennsylvania, Harrisburg Office, denied.

Same case below, 120 A.3d 392.

No. 15-701. Terrance Ross Willaman, Petitioner v. Erie Satellite Office of the Bureau of Alcohol, Tobacco, Firearms and Explosives.

577 U.S. 1104, 136 S. Ct. 907, 193 L. Ed. 2d 792, 2016 U.S. LEXIS 723.

January 19, 2016. Petition for writ of certiorari to the United States Court of Appeals for the Third Circuit denied.

Same case below, 620 Fed. Appx. 88.

No. 15-714. Victor Martinez, et al., Petitioners v. Florida Department of Agriculture and Consumer Services.

577 U.S. 1104, 136 S. Ct. 908, 193 L. Ed. 2d 792, 2016 U.S. LEXIS 787.

January 19, 2016. Petition for writ of certiorari to the Supreme Court of Florida denied.

Same case below, 177 So. 3d 1268.

No. 15-717. Eric D. Dixon, Petitioner v. Disciplinary Board of the Supreme Court of New Mexico, et al.

577 U.S. 1104, 136 S. Ct. 909, 193 L. Ed. 2d 793, 2016 U.S. LEXIS 825.

January 19, 2016. Petition for writ of certiorari to the Supreme Court of New Mexico denied.

No. 15-724. Edgar Nivia, et al., Petitioners v. Aurora Loan Services, LLC, et al.

577 U.S. 1104, 136 S. Ct. 909, 193 L. Ed. 2d 793, 2016 U.S. LEXIS 707.

January 19, 2016. Petition for writ of certiorari to the United States Court of Appeals for the Eleventh Circuit denied.

Same case below, 620 Fed. Appx. 822.

No. 15-738. Roderick Lee Mitchell, Petitioner v. Texas Medical Board.

577 U.S. 1104, 136 S. Ct. 910, 193 L. Ed. 2d 793, 2016 U.S. LEXIS 823.

January 19, 2016. Petition for writ of certiorari to the Court of Appeals of Texas, Third District, denied.

No. 15-752. Copley Fund, Inc., Petitioner v. Securities and Exchange Commission.

577 U.S. 1104, 136 S. Ct. 913, 193 L. Ed. 2d 793, 2016 U.S. LEXIS 838.

January 19, 2016. Petition for writ of certiorari to the United States Court of Appeals for the District of Columbia Circuit denied.

Same case below, 796 F.3d 131.

No. 15-756. Loredana Ranza, Petitioner v. Nike, Inc., et al.

577 U.S. 1104, 136 S. Ct. 915, 193 L. Ed. 2d 793, 2016 U.S. LEXIS 794.

January 19, 2016. Petition for writ of certiorari to the United States Court of Appeals for the Ninth Circuit denied.

Same case below, 793 F.3d 1059.

No. 15-760. Christopher S. Schloff, Petitioner v. United States.

577 U.S. 1104, 136 S. Ct. 915, 193 L. Ed. 2d 793, 2016 U.S. LEXIS 670.

January 19, 2016. Petition for writ of certiorari to the United States Court of Appeals for the Armed Forces denied.

Same case below, 74 M.J. 312.

No. 15-761. Donna Lesher, et al., Petitioners v. Troy Ellison, as Personal Representative of the Estate of Eugene Ellison, Deceased.

577 U.S. 1104, 136 S. Ct. 915, 193 L. Ed. 2d 793, 2016 U.S. LEXIS 672.

January 19, 2016. Petition for writ of certiorari to the United States Court of Appeals for the Eighth Circuit denied.

Same case below, 796 F.3d 910.

No. 15-800. William Douglas Brown, et ux., Petitioners v. Smith McCausland.

577 U.S. 1104, 136 S. Ct. 919, 193 L. Ed. 2d 793, 2016 U.S. LEXIS 748.

January 19, 2016. Petition for writ of certiorari to the Supreme Court of Appeals of West Virginia denied.

No. 15-823. Mira Overseas Consulting Ltd., et al., Petitioners v. Muse Family Enterprises, et al.

577 U.S. 1104, 136 S. Ct. 922, 193 L. Ed. 2d 794, 2016 U.S. LEXIS 731.

January 19, 2016. Petition for writ of certiorari to the Court of Appeal of California, Second Appellate District, Division Two, denied.

Same case below, 237 Cal. App. 4th 378, 187 Cal. Rptr. 3d 858.

No. 15-5115. Jared R. Clark, Petitioner v. Federal Labor Relations Authority.

577 U.S. 1105, 136 S. Ct. 893, 193 L. Ed. 2d 794, 2016 U.S. LEXIS 724.

January 19, 2016. Petition for writ of certiorari to the United States Court of Appeals for the District of Columbia Circuit denied.

Same case below, 782 F.3d 701.

No. 15-6022. Billy R. Irick, Petitioner v. Wayne Carpenter, Warden.

577 U.S. 1105, 136 S. Ct. 894, 193 L. Ed. 2d 794, 2016 U.S. LEXIS 677.

January 19, 2016. Petition for writ of certiorari to the United States Court of Appeals for the Sixth Circuit denied.

No. 15-6081. Charles Ray Hooper, Petitioner v. United States.

577 U.S. 1105, 136 S. Ct. 894, 193 L. Ed. 2d 794, 2016 U.S. LEXIS 744.

January 19, 2016. Petition for writ of certiorari to the United States Court of Appeals for the Fifth Circuit denied.

Same case below, 621 Fed. Appx. 770.

No. 15-6119. Tyrone Cade, Petitioner v. Texas.

577 U.S. 1105, 136 S. Ct. 894, 193 L. Ed. 2d 794, 2016 U.S. LEXIS 770.

January 19, 2016. Petition for writ of certiorari to the Court of Criminal Appeals of Texas denied.

No. 15-6221. Robert Mitchell Jennings, Petitioner v. William Stephens, Director, Texas Department of Criminal Justice, Correctional Institutions Division.

577 U.S. 1105, 136 S. Ct. 895, 193 L. Ed. 2d 794, 2016 U.S. LEXIS 722.

January 19, 2016. Petition for writ of certiorari to the United States Court of Appeals for the Fifth Circuit denied.

Same case below, 617 Fed. Appx. 315.

No. 15-6236. Christina M. Kitterman, Petitioner v. United States.

577 U.S. 1105, 136 S. Ct. 895, 193 L. Ed. 2d 794, 2016 U.S. LEXIS 784.

January 19, 2016. Petition for writ of certiorari to the United States Court of Appeals for the Eleventh Circuit denied.

Same case below, 618 Fed. Appx. 963.

No. 15-6557. Gustavo Julian Garcia, Petitioner v. William Stephens, Director, Texas Department of Criminal Justice, Correctional Institutions Division.

577 U.S. 1105, 136 S. Ct. 897, 193 L. Ed. 2d 795, 2016 U.S. LEXIS 714.

January 19, 2016. Petition for writ of certiorari to the United States Court of Appeals for the Fifth Circuit denied.

Same case below, 793 F.3d 513.

No. 15-6883. Andre Michael Leteve, Petitioner v. Arizona.

577 U.S. 1105, 136 S. Ct. 898, 193 L. Ed. 2d 795, 2016 U.S. LEXIS 799.

January 19, 2016. Petition for writ of certiorari to the Supreme Court of Arizona denied.

Same case below, 237 Ariz. 516, 354 P.3d 393.

No. 15-6899. Nathaniel L. Johnson, Petitioner v. Delaware, et al.

577 U.S. 1105, 136 S. Ct. 898, 193 L. Ed. 2d 795, 2016 U.S. LEXIS 701.

January 19, 2016. Petition for writ of certiorari to the United States Court of Appeals for the Third Circuit denied.

No. 15-6900. Jason Jermarr Johnson, Petitioner v. P. D. Brazelton, Warden.

577 U.S. 1105, 136 S. Ct. 898, 193 L. Ed. 2d 795, 2016 U.S. LEXIS 755.

January 19, 2016. Petition for writ of certiorari to the United States Court of Appeals for the Ninth Circuit denied.

No. 15-6903. Demetrius M. Boyd, Petitioner v. Gary A. Boughton, Warden.

577 U.S. 1105, 136 S. Ct. 899, 193 L. Ed. 2d 795, 2016 U.S. LEXIS 806.

January 19, 2016. Petition for writ of certiorari to the United States Court of Appeals for the Seventh Circuit denied.

Same case below, 798 F.3d 490.

No. 15-6906. Idelfonso Cardelle, Petitioner v. Wilmington Trust, N.A.

577 U.S. 1105, 136 S. Ct. 900, 193 L. Ed. 2d 795, 2016 U.S. LEXIS 675, reh den 577 U.S. 1231, 136 S. Ct. 1489, 194 L. Ed. 2d 580, 2016 U.S. LEXIS 1890.

January 19, 2016. Petition for writ of certiorari to the District Court of Appeal of Florida, Third District, denied.

Same case below, 195 So. 3d 380.

No. 15-6910. Joshua Nickerson, Petitioner v. F. Foulk, Warden.

577 U.S. 1105, 136 S. Ct. 900, 193 L. Ed. 2d 795, 2016 U.S. LEXIS 754.

January 19, 2016. Petition for writ of certiorari to the United States Court of Appeals for the Ninth Circuit denied.

No. 15-6911. Patricia Parker, Petitioner v. Exeter Finance Corporation.

577 U.S. 1106, 136 S. Ct. 901, 193 L. Ed. 2d 795, 2016 U.S. LEXIS 747.

January 19, 2016. Petition for writ of certiorari to the United States Court of Appeals for the Fifth Circuit denied.

No. 15-6913. Ahmed Shaker, Petitioner v. Correctional Care Solutions Medical Advisor, et al.

577 U.S. 1106, 136 S. Ct. 901, 193 L. Ed. 2d 796, 2016 U.S. LEXIS 661.

January 19, 2016. Petition for writ of certiorari to the United States Court of Appeals for the Third Circuit denied.

No. 15-6914. Donald Richard, Petitioner v. Gary C. Mohr, et al.

577 U.S. 1106, 136 S. Ct. 901, 193 L. Ed. 2d 796, 2016 U.S. LEXIS 654, reh den 577 U.S. 1231, 136 S. Ct. 1489, 194 L. Ed. 2d 580, 2016 U.S. LEXIS 1911.

January 19, 2016. Petition for writ of certiorari to the United States Court of Appeals for the Sixth Circuit denied.

No. 15-6917. Jeffrey A. Weisheit, Petitioner v. Indiana.

577 U.S. 1106, 136 S. Ct. 901, 193 L. Ed. 2d 796, 2016 U.S. LEXIS 795.

January 19, 2016. Petition for writ of certiorari to the Supreme Court of Indiana denied.

Same case below, 26 N.E.3d 3.

No. 15-6919. Billy Wayne Williams, Petitioner v. William Stephens, Director, Texas Department of Criminal Justice, Correctional Institutions Division.

577 U.S. 1106, 136 S. Ct. 901, 193 L. Ed. 2d 796, 2016 U.S. LEXIS 783.

January 19, 2016. Petition for writ of certiorari to the United States Court of Appeals for the Fifth Circuit denied.

No. 15-6922. Lutrica Thompkins, Petitioner v. Joseph Brown, et al.

577 U.S. 1106, 136 S. Ct. 901, 193 L. Ed. 2d 796, 2016 U.S. LEXIS 732, reh den 578 U.S. 916, 136 S. Ct. 1537, 194 L. Ed. 2d 622, 2016 U.S. LEXIS 2423.

January 19, 2016. Petition for writ of certiorari to the Court of Appeals of Michigan denied.

No. 15-6925. Angela Rigdon, Petitioner v. Mississippi.

577 U.S. 1106, 136 S. Ct. 902, 193 L. Ed. 2d 796, 2016 U.S. LEXIS 826.

January 19, 2016. Petition for writ of certiorari to the Supreme Court of Mississippi denied.

Same case below, 126 So. 3d 931.

No. 15-6927. John Eric Sims, Petitioner v. Louisiana.

577 U.S. 1106, 136 S. Ct. 902, 193 L. Ed. 2d 796, 2016 U.S. LEXIS 810.

January 19, 2016. Petition for writ of certiorari to the Supreme Court of Louisiana denied.

Same case below, 175 So. 3d 398.

No. 15-6938. Ignacio Cervantes Chavez, Petitioner v. Los Angeles County, California, et al.

577 U.S. 1106, 136 S. Ct. 902, 193 L. Ed. 2d 796, 2016 U.S. LEXIS 711.

January 19, 2016. Petition for writ of certiorari to the United States Court of Appeals for the Ninth Circuit denied.

Same case below, 599 Fed. Appx. 792.

No. 15-6939. Billy S. Campbell, Petitioner v. Ohio.

577 U.S. 1106, 136 S. Ct. 902, 193 L. Ed. 2d 797, 2016 U.S. LEXIS 740.

January 19, 2016. Petition for writ of certiorari to the Court of Appeals of Ohio, Butler County, denied.

No. 15-6942. Raymond Earl Carr, Petitioner v. William Stephens, Director, Texas Department of Criminal Justice, Correctional Institutions Division, et al.

577 U.S. 1106, 136 S. Ct. 903, 193 L. Ed. 2d 797, 2016 U.S. LEXIS 760.

January 19, 2016. Petition for writ of certiorari to the United States Court of Appeals for the Fifth Circuit denied.

No. 15-6943. Mark Cowder, Petitioner v. Brian H. Thompson, Superintendent, State Correctional Institution at Mercer.

577 U.S. 1106, 136 S. Ct. 903, 193 L. Ed. 2d 797, 2016 U.S. LEXIS 789, reh den 577 U.S. 1241, 136 S. Ct. 1511, 194 L. Ed. 2d 598, 2016 U.S. LEXIS 2193.

January 19, 2016. Petition for writ of certiorari to the United States Court of Appeals for the Third Circuit denied.

No. 15-6944. Richard Carlton Davidson, Petitioner v. California.

577 U.S. 1106, 136 S. Ct. 903, 193 L. Ed. 2d 797, 2016 U.S. LEXIS 819.

January 19, 2016. Petition for writ of certiorari to the Court of Appeal of California, Sixth Appellate District, denied.

No. 15-6949. Rejeanne M. Bernier, Petitioner v. Court of Appeal of California, Fourth Appellate District, Division One, et al.

577 U.S. 1106, 136 S. Ct. 903, 193 L. Ed. 2d 797, 2016 U.S. LEXIS 803.

January 19, 2016. Petition for writ of certiorari to the Supreme Court of California denied.

No. 15-6950. Corey Levon Beckham, Petitioner v. Charles H. Allen, Warden.

577 U.S. 1107, 136 S. Ct. 903, 193 L. Ed. 2d 797, 2016 U.S. LEXIS 831.

January 19, 2016. Petition for writ of certiorari to the Supreme Court of Virginia denied.

No. 15-6958. Bray Jibril Murray, Petitioner v. Tom Wolf, Governor of Pennsylvania, et al.

577 U.S. 1107, 136 S. Ct. 904, 193 L. Ed. 2d 797, 2016 U.S. LEXIS 785.

January 19, 2016. Petition for writ of certiorari to the United States Court of Appeals for the Third Circuit denied.

No. 15-6959. Gabriel Lucian Roman, Petitioner v. Los Angeles Department of Public Social Services, et al.

577 U.S. 1107, 136 S. Ct. 904, 193 L. Ed. 2d 797, 2016 U.S. LEXIS 680.

January 19, 2016. Petition for writ of certiorari to the United States Court of Appeals for the Ninth Circuit denied.

Same case below, 617 Fed. Appx. 726.

Same case below, 121 A.3d 1281.

No. 15-6963. Ricky Smith, Sr., Petitioner v. Georgia.

577 U.S. 1107, 136 S. Ct. 904, 193 L. Ed. 2d 798, 2016 U.S. LEXIS 786.

January 19, 2016. Petition for writ of certiorari to the Supreme Court of Georgia denied.

Same case below, 297 Ga. 214, 773 S.E.2d 209.

No. 15-6965. Dale Ray Hurd, Petitioner v. California.

577 U.S. 1107, 136 S. Ct. 904, 193 L. Ed. 2d 798, 2016 U.S. LEXIS 664.

January 19, 2016. Petition for writ of certiorari to the Court of Appeal of California, Second Appellate District, denied.

No. 15-6966. Annamaria Magno Gana, Petitioner v. California.

577 U.S. 1107, 136 S. Ct. 904, 193 L. Ed. 2d 798, 2016 U.S. LEXIS 842.

January 19, 2016. Petition for writ of certiorari to the Court of Appeal of California, Fourth Appellate District, Division Three, denied.

Same case below, 236 Cal. App. 4th 598, 186 Cal. Rptr. 3d 724.

No. 15-6968. Wade R. Hoover, Petitioner v. Maine.

577 U.S. 1107, 136 S. Ct. 905, 193 L. Ed. 2d 798, 2016 U.S. LEXIS 804.

January 19, 2016. Petition for writ of certiorari to the Supreme Judicial Court of Maine denied.

No. 15-6971. Christopher A. Henry, Petitioner v. Patricia Allen, et al.

577 U.S. 1107, 136 S. Ct. 905, 193 L. Ed. 2d 798, 2016 U.S. LEXIS 828.

January 19, 2016. Petition for writ of certiorari to the United States Court of Appeals for the Second Circuit denied.

No. 15-6975. Charles Edward Jones, Petitioner v. Florida.

577 U.S. 1107, 136 S. Ct. 905, 193 L. Ed. 2d 798, 2016 U.S. LEXIS 700.

January 19, 2016. Petition for writ of certiorari to the District Court of Appeal of Florida, Third District, denied.

Same case below, 173 So. 3d 900.

No. 15-6980. Gerald Beelby, Petitioner v. Lori Gidley, Warden.

577 U.S. 1107, 136 S. Ct. 905, 193 L. Ed. 2d 798, 2016 U.S. LEXIS 836.

January 19, 2016. Petition for writ of certiorari to the United States Court of Appeals for the Sixth Circuit denied.

No. 15-6981. John O. Study, Petitioner v. Richard Brown, Superintendent, Wabash Valley Correctional Facility.

577 U.S. 1107, 136 S. Ct. 905, 193 L. Ed. 2d 798, 2016 U.S. LEXIS 767, reh den 578 U.S. 942, 136 S. Ct. 1707, 194 L. Ed. 2d 803, 2016 U.S. LEXIS 2578.

January 19, 2016. Petition for writ of certiorari to the United States Court of Appeals for the Seventh Circuit denied.

No. 15-6991. April Juarez, Petitioner v. Millicent Warren, Warden.

577 U.S. 1107, 136 S. Ct. 905, 193 L. Ed. 2d 799, 2016 U.S. LEXIS 769.

January 19, 2016. Petition for writ of certiorari to the United States Court of Appeals for the Sixth Circuit denied.

No. 15-6995. Chad Dias, Petitioner v. Suzanne M. Peery, Acting Warden.

577 U.S. 1107, 136 S. Ct. 906, 193 L. Ed. 2d 799, 2016 U.S. LEXIS 771.

January 19, 2016. Petition for writ of certiorari to the United States Court of Appeals for the Ninth Circuit denied.

No. 15-6996. Dwight Erwin Taylor, Petitioner v. Carmen Palmer, Warden.

577 U.S. 1107, 136 S. Ct. 906, 193 L. Ed. 2d 799, 2016 U.S. LEXIS 699.

January 19, 2016. Petition for writ of certiorari to the United States Court of Appeals for the Sixth Circuit denied.

Same case below, 623 Fed. Appx. 783.

No. 15-7001. Andre C. T. Wells, Petitioner v. Indiana.

577 U.S. 1107, 136 S. Ct. 906, 193 L. Ed. 2d 799, 2016 U.S. LEXIS 776.

January 19, 2016. Petition for writ of certiorari to the Court of Appeals of Indiana, Fourth District, denied.

Same case below, 30 N.E.3d 1256.

No. 15-7035. Robert Edward Holdridge, Petitioner v. California.

577 U.S. 1108, 136 S. Ct. 906, 193 L. Ed. 2d 799, 2016 U.S. LEXIS 656.

January 19, 2016. Petition for writ of certiorari to the Court of Appeal of California, Sixth Appellate District, denied.

No. 15-7095. Angel Pabon, Petitioner v. John Kerestes, Superintendent, State Correctional Institution at Mahanoy, et al.

577 U.S. 1108, 136 S. Ct. 907, 193 L. Ed. 2d 799, 2016 U.S. LEXIS 658.

January 19, 2016. Petition for writ of certiorari to the United States Court of Appeals for the Third Circuit denied.

No. 15-7098. Robert Yell, Petitioner v. Randy White, Warden.

577 U.S. 1108, 136 S. Ct. 907, 193 L. Ed. 2d 799, 2016 U.S. LEXIS 805.

January 19, 2016. Petition for writ of certiorari to the United States Court of Appeals for the Sixth Circuit denied.

No. 15-7104. Daniel J. Levitan, Petitioner v. David Morgan, Sheriff, Escambia County, Florida.

577 U.S. 1108, 136 S. Ct. 907, 193 L. Ed. 2d 799, 2016 U.S. LEXIS 734, reh den 577 U.S. 1209, 136 S. Ct. 1404, 194 L. Ed. 2d 384, 2016 U.S. LEXIS 1643.

January 19, 2016. Petition for writ of certiorari to the District Court of Appeal of Florida, First District, denied.

Same case below, 172 So. 3d 872.

No. 15-7128. Peter King, Petitioner v. New York.

577 U.S. 1108, 136 S. Ct. 908, 193 L. Ed. 2d 800, 2016 U.S. LEXIS 766.

January 19, 2016. Petition for writ of certiorari to the Appellate Division, Supreme Court of New York, Fourth Judicial Department, denied.

No. 15-7130. Jonathan Cardenas, Petitioner v. Gary Swarthout, Warden.

577 U.S. 1108, 136 S. Ct. 908, 193 L. Ed. 2d 800, 2016 U.S. LEXIS 829.

January 19, 2016. Petition for writ of certiorari to the United States Court of Appeals for the Ninth Circuit denied.

No. 15-7135. Pedro Ramirez-Rivera, Petitioner v. United States.

No. 15-7374. Jose Laureano-Salgado, Petitioner v. United States.

577 U.S. 1108, 136 S. Ct. 908, 193 L. Ed. 2d 800, 2016 U.S. LEXIS 812.

January 19, 2016. Petitions for writs of certiorari to the United States Court of Appeals for the First Circuit denied.

Same cases below, 800 F.3d 1.

No. 15-7148. Jakiem Lance Wilson, Petitioner v. North Carolina.

577 U.S. 1108, 136 S. Ct. 908, 193 L. Ed. 2d 800, 2016 U.S. LEXIS 830, reh den 577 U.S. 1185, 136 S. Ct. 1253, 194 L. Ed. 2d 251, 2016 U.S. LEXIS 1156.

January 19, 2016. Petition for writ of certiorari to the Court of Appeals of North Carolina denied.

No. 15-7159. William Robert Gray, Jr., Petitioner v. R. C. Lee, Warden.

577 U.S. 1108, 136 S. Ct. 908, 193 L. Ed. 2d 800, 2016 U.S. LEXIS 750.

January 19, 2016. Petition for writ of certiorari to the United States Court of Appeals for the Fourth Circuit denied.

Same case below, 608 Fed. Appx. 172.

No. 15-7173. Toby Carl McAdam, Petitioner v. United States.

577 U.S. 1108, 136 S. Ct. 909, 193 L. Ed. 2d 800, 2016 U.S. LEXIS 649.

January 19, 2016. Petition for writ of certiorari to the United States Court of Appeals for the Ninth Circuit denied.

Same case below, 599 Fed. Appx. 305.

No. 15-7192. Daniel J. Bowers, Petitioner v. Massachusetts.

577 U.S. 1108, 136 S. Ct. 909, 193 L. Ed. 2d 800, 2016 U.S. LEXIS 730.

January 19, 2016. Petition for writ of certiorari to the Appeals Court of Massachusetts denied.

Same case below, 87 Mass. App. Ct. 1131, 32 N.E.3d 370.

No. 15-7198. Debra Lynette Johnson, Petitioner v. General Motors Corporation.

577 U.S. 1108, 136 S. Ct. 910, 193 L. Ed. 2d 800, 2016 U.S. LEXIS 782.

January 19, 2016. Petition for writ of certiorari to the United States Court of Appeals for the Sixth Circuit denied.

No. 15-7203. Hernan Orozco, Petitioner v. Aleksandr Reznichenko.

577 U.S. 1108, 136 S. Ct. 909, 193 L. Ed. 2d 801, 2016 U.S. LEXIS 728.

January 19, 2016. Petition for writ of certiorari to the Court of Appeal of California, Fifth Appellate District, denied.

No. 15-7223. Christopher Todisco, Petitioner v. Massachusetts.

577 U.S. 1108, 136 S. Ct. 910, 193 L. Ed. 2d 801, 2016 U.S. LEXIS 708.

January 19, 2016. Petition for writ of certiorari to the Appeals Court of Massachusetts denied.

Same case below, 87 Mass. App. Ct. 1117, 30 N.E.3d 133.

No. 15-7225. Cesilio Ramirez, Petitioner v. Illinois.

577 U.S. 1109, 136 S. Ct. 910, 193 L. Ed. 2d 801, 2016 U.S. LEXIS 697.

January 19, 2016. Petition for writ of certiorari to the Appellate Court of Illinois, First District, denied.

No. 15-7227. Shawn Spivey, Petitioner v. New Jersey.

577 U.S. 1109, 136 S. Ct. 910, 193 L. Ed. 2d 801, 2016 U.S. LEXIS 753.

January 19, 2016. Petition for writ of certiorari to the Superior Court of New Jersey, Appellate Division, denied.

No. 15-7237. Jamey D. Cope, Petitioner v. Joseph P. Meko, Warden.

577 U.S. 1109, 136 S. Ct. 910, 193 L. Ed. 2d 801, 2016 U.S. LEXIS 685.

January 19, 2016. Petition for writ of certiorari to the United States Court of Appeals for the Sixth Circuit denied.

No. 15-7254. Lester Johnson, Petitioner v. Julie L. Jones, Secretary, Florida Department of Corrections.

577 U.S. 1109, 136 S. Ct. 909, 193 L. Ed. 2d 801, 2016 U.S. LEXIS 709.

January 19, 2016. Petition for writ of certiorari to the United States Court of Appeals for the Eleventh Circuit denied.

No. 15-7271. Paul Toler, Petitioner v. Julie L. Jones, Secretary, Florida Department of Corrections, et al.

577 U.S. 1109, 136 S. Ct. 911, 193 L. Ed. 2d 801, 2016 U.S. LEXIS 698.

January 19, 2016. Petition for writ of certiorari to the United States Court of Appeals for the Eleventh Circuit denied.

No. 15-7281. Coy Lee Coleman, Jr., Petitioner v. Julie L. Jones, Secretary, Florida Department of Corrections.

577 U.S. 1109, 136 S. Ct. 911, 193 L. Ed. 2d 801, 2016 U.S. LEXIS 821.

January 19, 2016. Petition for writ of certiorari to the United States Court of Appeals for the Eleventh Circuit denied.

No. 15-7284. Mike C. Matson, Petitioner v. Joel Hrabe.

577 U.S. 1109, 136 S. Ct. 911, 193 L. Ed. 2d 802, 2016 U.S. LEXIS 691.

January 19, 2016. Petition for writ of certiorari to the United States Court of Appeals for the Tenth Circuit denied.

Same case below, 612 Fed. Appx. 926.

No. 15-7287. Ferdinand-Sanchez Montes, Petitioner v. Florida.

577 U.S. 1109, 136 S. Ct. 911, 193 L. Ed. 2d 802, 2016 U.S. LEXIS 663.

January 19, 2016. Petition for writ of certiorari to the District Court of Appeal of Florida, Fifth District, denied.

Same case below, 177 So. 3d 624.

No. 15-7296. Jeffrey Dale St. John, Petitioner v. United States.

No. 15-7314. Lawrence Dale St. John, Petitioner v. United States.

577 U.S. 1109, 136 S. Ct. 911, 193 L. Ed. 2d 802, 2016 U.S. LEXIS 733.

January 19, 2016. Petitions for writs of certiorari to the United States Court of Appeals for the Fifth Circuit denied.

Same cases below, 625 Fed. Appx. 661.

No. 15-7299. Victor Hugo Lee-Gutierrez, Petitioner v. United States.

577 U.S. 1109, 136 S. Ct. 911, 193 L. Ed. 2d 802, 2016 U.S. LEXIS 652.

January 19, 2016. Petition for writ of certiorari to the United States Court of Appeals for the Fifth Circuit denied.

Same case below, 615 Fed. Appx. 175.

No. 15-7301. Juan Manuel Marquez-Esquivel, aka Juan Marquez, Petitioner v. United States.

577 U.S. 1109, 136 S. Ct. 912, 193 L. Ed. 2d 802, 2016 U.S. LEXIS 668.

January 19, 2016. Petition for writ of certiorari to the United States Court of Appeals for the Fifth Circuit denied.

Same case below, 615 Fed. Appx. 197.

No. 15-7303. Bob Sam Castleman, Petitioner v. United States.

577 U.S. 1109, 136 S. Ct. 912, 193 L. Ed. 2d 802, 2016 U.S. LEXIS 756.

January 19, 2016. Petition for writ of certiorari to the United States Court of Appeals for the Eighth Circuit denied.

Same case below, 795 F.3d 904.

No. 15-7305. Jacob Drummondo-Farias, Petitioner v. United States.

577 U.S. 1109, 136 S. Ct. 912, 193 L. Ed. 2d 802, 2016 U.S. LEXIS 725.

January 19, 2016. Petition for writ of certiorari to the United States Court of Appeals for the Ninth Circuit denied.

Same case below, 622 Fed. Appx. 616.

No. 15-7312. Megan Nichole Hanson Mosteller, Petitioner v. United States.

577 U.S. 1109, 136 S. Ct. 912, 193 L. Ed. 2d 802, 2016 U.S. LEXIS 682, reh den 577 U.S. 1232, 136 S. Ct. 1489, 194 L. Ed. 2d 580, 2016 U.S. LEXIS 1896.

January 19, 2016. Petition for writ of certiorari to the United States Court of Appeals for the Fourth Circuit denied.

Same case below, 741 F.3d 503.

No. 15-7315. Francisco J. Velez-Soto, Petitioner v. United States.

577 U.S. 1110, 136 S. Ct. 912, 193 L. Ed. 2d 803, 2016 U.S. LEXIS 813.

January 19, 2016. Petition for writ of certiorari to the United States Court of Appeals for the First Circuit denied.

No. 15-7316. Ferrell Damon Scott, Petitioner v. United States.

577 U.S. 1110, 136 S. Ct. 913, 193 L. Ed. 2d 803, 2016 U.S. LEXIS 763.

January 19, 2016. Petition for writ of certiorari to the United States Court of Appeals for the Fifth Circuit denied.

Same case below, 576 Fed. Appx. 409.

No. 15-7317. Stanton Mylo Hales, Petitioner v. United States.

577 U.S. 1110, 136 S. Ct. 913, 193 L. Ed. 2d 803, 2016 U.S. LEXIS 773.

January 19, 2016. Petition for writ of certiorari to the United States Court of Appeals for the Sixth Circuit denied.

Same case below, 615 Fed. Appx. 375.

No. 15-7319. Francisco Hernandez-Diaz, Petitioner v. United States.

577 U.S. 1110, 136 S. Ct. 913, 193 L. Ed. 2d 803, 2016 U.S. LEXIS 757.

January 19, 2016. Petition for writ of certiorari to the United States Court of Appeals for the Fifth Circuit denied.

Same case below, 615 Fed. Appx. 171.

No. 15-7320. Blessing Sydney Iwuala, Petitioner v. United States.

577 U.S. 1110, 136 S. Ct. 913, 193 L. Ed. 2d 803, 2016 U.S. LEXIS 762.

January 19, 2016. Petition for writ of certiorari to the United States Court of Appeals for the First Circuit denied.

Same case below, 789 F.3d 1.

No. 15-7321. Amir Ali Faraz, Petitioner v. United States.

577 U.S. 1110, 136 S. Ct. 913, 193 L. Ed. 2d 803, 2016 U.S. LEXIS 814.

January 19, 2016. Petition for writ of certiorari to the United States Court of Appeals for the Fourth Circuit denied.

Same case below, 626 Fed. Appx. 395.

No. 15-7324. Matthew Steven Howard, Petitioner v. United States.

577 U.S. 1110, 136 S. Ct. 914, 193 L. Ed. 2d 803, 2016 U.S. LEXIS 781.

January 19, 2016. Petition for writ of certiorari to the United States Court of Appeals for the Eleventh Circuit denied.

Same case below, 625 Fed. Appx. 934.

No. 15-7325. Owusu Ananeh Firempong, Petitioner v. United States.

577 U.S. 1110, 136 S. Ct. 914, 193 L. Ed. 2d 803, 2016 U.S. LEXIS 729.

January 19, 2016. Petition for writ of certiorari to the United States Court of Appeals for the Ninth Circuit denied.

Same case below, 624 Fed. Appx. 497.

Same case below, 616 Fed. Appx. 742.

No. 15-7328. Donald Jones, Jr., Petitioner v. United States.

577 U.S. 1110, 136 S. Ct. 916, 193 L. Ed. 2d 804, 2016 U.S. LEXIS 792.

January 19, 2016. Petition for writ of certiorari to the United States Court of Appeals for the Fifth Circuit denied.

Same case below, 615 Fed. Appx. 229.

No. 15-7330. Elton Ray Jones, Petitioner v. United States.

577 U.S. 1110, 136 S. Ct. 914, 193 L. Ed. 2d 804, 2016 U.S. LEXIS 660.

January 19, 2016. Petition for writ of certiorari to the United States Court of Appeals for the Fifth Circuit denied.

Same case below, 615 Fed. Appx. 213.

No. 15-7335. Lester Keith Gunter, Petitioner v. United States.

577 U.S. 1110, 136 S. Ct. 914, 193 L. Ed. 2d 804, 2016 U.S. LEXIS 839.

January 19, 2016. Petition for writ of certiorari to the United States Court of Appeals for the Fourth Circuit denied.

Same case below, 615 Fed. Appx. 162.

No. 15-7337. James Ward Davis, Petitioner v. United States.

577 U.S. 1110, 136 S. Ct. 915, 193 L. Ed. 2d 804, 2016 U.S. LEXIS 772.

January 19, 2016. Petition for writ of certiorari to the United States Court of Appeals for the Fifth Circuit denied.

No. 15-7338. Jeffrey John Cummings-Avila, Petitioner v. United States.

577 U.S. 1110, 136 S. Ct. 915, 193 L. Ed. 2d 804, 2016 U.S. LEXIS 671.

January 19, 2016. Petition for writ of certiorari to the United States Court of Appeals for the First Circuit denied.

Same case below, 797 F.3d 45.

No. 15-7340. Jesus Manuel Meza-Garcia, Petitioner v. United States.

577 U.S. 1110, 136 S. Ct. 915, 193 L. Ed. 2d 804, 2016 U.S. LEXIS 694.

January 19, 2016. Petition for writ of certiorari to the United States Court of Appeals for the Fifth Circuit denied.

Same case below, 619 Fed. Appx. 429.

No. 15-7357. Audrey Louis Johnson, Jr., Petitioner v. United States.

577 U.S. 1110, 136 S. Ct. 916, 193 L. Ed. 2d 804, 2016 U.S. LEXIS 681.

January 19, 2016. Petition for writ of certiorari to the United States Court of Appeals for the Sixth Circuit denied.

No. 15-7358. Prince Martin Mayele, Petitioner v. United States.

577 U.S. 1111, 136 S. Ct. 916, 193 L. Ed. 2d 804, 2016 U.S. LEXIS 788.

January 19, 2016. Petition for writ of certiorari to the United States Court of Appeals for the Ninth Circuit denied.

Same case below, 616 Fed. Appx. 314.

Same case below, 626 Fed. Appx. 589.

No. 15-7361. Sandy James Oates, Petitioner v. United States.

577 U.S. 1111, 136 S. Ct. 916, 193 L. Ed. 2d 805, 2016 U.S. LEXIS 659.

January 19, 2016. Petition for writ of certiorari to the United States Court of Appeals for the Fourth Circuit denied.

Same case below, 618 Fed. Appx. 172.

No. 15-7372. Arnulfo Galvan Mireles, Petitioner v. United States.

577 U.S. 1111, 136 S. Ct. 917, 193 L. Ed. 2d 805, 2016 U.S. LEXIS 759.

January 19, 2016. Petition for writ of certiorari to the United States Court of Appeals for the Fifth Circuit denied.

Same case below, 616 Fed. Appx. 133.

No. 15-7362. William Miller, Petitioner v. United States.

577 U.S. 1111, 136 S. Ct. 916, 193 L. Ed. 2d 805, 2016 U.S. LEXIS 702.

January 19, 2016. Petition for writ of certiorari to the United States Court of Appeals for the Eighth Circuit denied.

Same case below, 796 F.3d 843.

No. 15-7373. Isaiah Edmondson, Petitioner v. United States.

577 U.S. 1111, 136 S. Ct. 917, 193 L. Ed. 2d 805, 2016 U.S. LEXIS 827.

January 19, 2016. Petition for writ of certiorari to the United States Court of Appeals for the Sixth Circuit denied.

No. 15-7377. David Jordan, Petitioner v. United States.

577 U.S. 1111, 136 S. Ct. 917, 193 L. Ed. 2d 805, 2016 U.S. LEXIS 774.

January 19, 2016. Petition for writ of certiorari to the United States Court of Appeals for the First Circuit denied.

Same case below, 619 Fed. Appx. 1.

No. 15-7363. Adelfo Vizcarra-Serrano, Petitioner v. United States.

577 U.S. 1111, 136 S. Ct. 916, 193 L. Ed. 2d 805, 2016 U.S. LEXIS 749.

January 19, 2016. Petition for writ of certiorari to the United States Court of Appeals for the Fifth Circuit denied.

Same case below, 624 Fed. Appx. 874.

No. 15-7379. Fabio Moreno Vargas, et al., Petitioners v. United States.

577 U.S. 1111, 136 S. Ct. 917, 193 L. Ed. 2d 805, 2016 U.S. LEXIS 808.

January 19, 2016. Petition for writ of certiorari to the United States Court of Appeals for the Third Circuit denied.

Same case below, 629 Fed. Appx. 415.

No. 15-7371. Ernest William Singleton, Petitioner v. United States.

577 U.S. 1111, 136 S. Ct. 917, 193 L. Ed. 2d 805, 2016 U.S. LEXIS 653.

January 19, 2016. Petition for writ of certiorari to the United States Court of Appeals for the Sixth Circuit denied.

No. 15-7381. Dennis Gray Williams, Petitioner v. United States.

577 U.S. 1111, 136 S. Ct. 918, 193 L. Ed. 2d 806, 2016 U.S. LEXIS 832.

January 19, 2016. Petition for writ of certiorari to the United States Court of Appeals for the Eleventh Circuit denied.

Same case below, 790 F.3d 1240.

No. 15-7383. Joshua Cavazos, Petitioner v. Illinois.

577 U.S. 1111, 136 S. Ct. 918, 193 L. Ed. 2d 806, 2016 U.S. LEXIS 809.

January 19, 2016. Petition for writ of certiorari to the Appellate Court of Illinois, Second District, denied.

Same case below, 40 N.E.3d 92.

No. 15-7385. Joseph Jenkins, Petitioner v. United States.

577 U.S. 1111, 136 S. Ct. 918, 193 L. Ed. 2d 806, 2016 U.S. LEXIS 655.

January 19, 2016. Petition for writ of certiorari to the District of Columbia Court of Appeals denied.

Same case below, 113 A.3d 535.

No. 15-7387. Toussaint Kirkland, Petitioner v. United States.

577 U.S. 1111, 136 S. Ct. 918, 193 L. Ed. 2d 806, 2016 U.S. LEXIS 665.

January 19, 2016. Petition for writ of certiorari to the District of Columbia Court of Appeals denied.

Same case below, 117 A.3d 1042.

No. 15-7388. Jason Jones, Petitioner v. United States.

577 U.S. 1111, 136 S. Ct. 918, 193 L. Ed. 2d 806, 2016 U.S. LEXIS 679.

January 19, 2016. Petition for writ of certiorari to the United States Court of Appeals for the Tenth Circuit denied.

Same case below, 608 Fed. Appx. 712.

No. 15-7390. Mario Serna, Petitioner v. James W. Gray, Commandant, United States Disciplinary Barracks, Fort Leavenworth.

577 U.S. 1111, 136 S. Ct. 918, 193 L. Ed. 2d 806, 2016 U.S. LEXIS 650.

January 19, 2016. Petition for writ of certiorari to the United States Court of Appeals for the Tenth Circuit denied.

No. 15-7393. Roberto Berrones-Vargas, Petitioner v. United States.

577 U.S. 1112, 136 S. Ct. 919, 193 L. Ed. 2d 806, 2016 U.S. LEXIS 791.

January 19, 2016. Petition for writ of certiorari to the United States Court of Appeals for the Fifth Circuit denied.

Same case below, 616 Fed. Appx. 135.

No. 15-7397. Ella B. Vinson, Petitioner v. Ohio.

577 U.S. 1112, 136 S. Ct. 919, 193 L. Ed. 2d 806, 2016 U.S. LEXIS 645.

January 19, 2016. Petition for writ of certiorari to the Court of Appeals of Ohio, Franklin County, denied.

No. 15-7410. Bodie B. Witzlib, Petitioner v. United States.

577 U.S. 1112, 136 S. Ct. 919, 193 L. Ed. 2d 807, 2016 U.S. LEXIS 768.

January 19, 2016. Petition for writ of certiorari to the United States Court of Appeals for the Seventh Circuit denied.

Same case below, 796 F.3d 799.

No. 15-7414. Byron Keith Brown, Petitioner v. United States.

577 U.S. 1112, 136 S. Ct. 919, 193 L. Ed. 2d 807, 2016 U.S. LEXIS 834.

January 19, 2016. Petition for writ of certiorari to the United States Court of Appeals for the Fourth Circuit denied.

Same case below, 614 Fed. Appx. 120.

No. 15-7418. Walter Louis Bridges, Jr., Petitioner v. United States.

577 U.S. 1112, 136 S. Ct. 919, 193 L. Ed. 2d 807, 2016 U.S. LEXIS 720.

January 19, 2016. Petition for writ of certiorari to the United States Court of Appeals for the Sixth Circuit denied.

Same case below, 626 Fed. Appx. 620.

No. 15-7421. Byron Cole, Petitioner v. United States.

577 U.S. 1112, 136 S. Ct. 920, 193 L. Ed. 2d 807, 2016 U.S. LEXIS 807.

January 19, 2016. Petition for writ of certiorari to the District of Columbia Court of Appeals denied.

Same case below, 117 A.3d 583.

No. 15-7428. Charles Malouff, Jr., Petitioner v. United States.

577 U.S. 1112, 136 S. Ct. 920, 193 L. Ed. 2d 807, 2016 U.S. LEXIS 695, reh den 577 U.S. 1232, 136 S. Ct. 1489, 194 L. Ed. 2d 580, 2016 U.S. LEXIS 1880.

January 19, 2016. Petition for writ of certiorari to the United States Court of Appeals for the Fifth Circuit denied.

Same case below, 613 Fed. Appx. 432.

No. 15-7429. Eric D. Foreman, Petitioner v. United States.

577 U.S. 1112, 136 S. Ct. 920, 193 L. Ed. 2d 807, 2016 U.S. LEXIS 693.

January 19, 2016. Petition for writ of certiorari to the District of Columbia Court of Appeals denied.

Same case below, 114 A.3d 631.

No. 15-7433. Rafael Galan-Olavarria, Petitioner v. United States.

577 U.S. 1112, 136 S. Ct. 920, 193 L. Ed. 2d 807, 2016 U.S. LEXIS 674.

January 19, 2016. Petition for writ of certiorari to the United States Court of Appeals for the First Circuit denied.

Same case below, 799 F.3d 134.

No. 15-7439. Matthew Norman Simpson, Petitioner v. United States.

577 U.S. 1112, 136 S. Ct. 920, 193 L. Ed. 2d 807, 2016 U.S. LEXIS 817.

January 19, 2016. Petition for writ of certiorari to the United States Court of Appeals for the Fifth Circuit denied.

Same case below, 796 F.3d 548.

No. 15-7443. Naeem Deonte Jones, et al., Petitioners v. United States.

577 U.S. 1112, 136 S. Ct. 920, 193 L. Ed. 2d 808, 2016 U.S. LEXIS 712.

January 19, 2016. Petition for writ of certiorari to the United States Court of Appeals for the Fourth Circuit denied.

Same case below, 625 Fed. Appx. 194.

No. 15-7444. Joseph Jesus Lopez, Petitioner v. United States.

577 U.S. 1112, 136 S. Ct. 921, 193 L. Ed. 2d 808, 2016 U.S. LEXIS 737.

January 19, 2016. Petition for writ of certiorari to the United States Court of Appeals for the Sixth Circuit denied.

No. 15-7450. James Ramsey, Petitioner v. Linda Stephenson, Warden.

577 U.S. 1112, 136 S. Ct. 921, 193 L. Ed. 2d 808, 2016 U.S. LEXIS 726.

January 19, 2016. Petition for writ of certiorari to the United States Court of Appeals for the Sixth Circuit denied.

No. 15-7452. James Bates, Petitioner v. United States.

577 U.S. 1112, 136 S. Ct. 921, 193 L. Ed. 2d 808, 2016 U.S. LEXIS 833.

January 19, 2016. Petition for writ of certiorari to the District of Columbia Court of Appeals denied.

Same case below, 113 A.3d 535.

No. 15-7454. Betsy Elizabeth Duranty-Moore, aka Elizabeth Sarah Collins, aka Betsy Duranty, aka Betsy Elizabeth Duranty, aka Betsy Moore, aka Betsy Elizabeth Proebstle, Petitioner v. United States.

577 U.S. 1112, 136 S. Ct. 921, 193 L. Ed. 2d 808, 2016 U.S. LEXIS 802.

January 19, 2016. Petition for writ of certiorari to the United States Court of Appeals for the Ninth Circuit denied.

Same case below, 616 Fed. Appx. 330.

No. 15-7455. Ira C. Jackson, Petitioner v. United States.

577 U.S. 1112, 136 S. Ct. 921, 193 L. Ed. 2d 808, 2016 U.S. LEXIS 837, reh den 577 U.S. 1232, 136 S. Ct. 1489, 194 L. Ed. 2d 580, 2016 U.S. LEXIS 1865.

January 19, 2016. Petition for writ of certiorari to the United States Court of Appeals for the Eleventh Circuit denied.

No. 15-7459. Miguel Angel Cuevas, Petitioner v. United States.

577 U.S. 1113, 136 S. Ct. 921, 193 L. Ed. 2d 808, 2016 U.S. LEXIS 676.

January 19, 2016. Petition for writ of certiorari to the United States Court of Appeals for the Eighth Circuit denied.

No. 15-7462. Michael Rocky Lane, Petitioner v. United States.

577 U.S. 1113, 136 S. Ct. 921, 193 L. Ed. 2d 808, 2016 U.S. LEXIS 811.

January 19, 2016. Petition for writ of certiorari to the United States Court of Appeals for the Ninth Circuit denied.

Same case below, 616 Fed. Appx. 328.

No. 15-7486. Terrence Eugene Priestley, Petitioner v. United States.

577 U.S. 1113, 136 S. Ct. 922, 193 L. Ed. 2d 809, 2016 U.S. LEXIS 647.

January 19, 2016. Petition for writ of certiorari to the United States Court of Appeals for the Fifth Circuit denied.

Same case below, 618 Fed. Appx. 222.

No. 15-7491. John Villalonga, Petitioner v. United States.

577 U.S. 1113, 136 S. Ct. 922, 193 L. Ed. 2d 809, 2016 U.S. LEXIS 818.

January 19, 2016. Petition for writ of certiorari to the United States Court of Appeals for the Eleventh Circuit denied.

Same case below, 615 Fed. Appx. 945.

No. 15-122. Ruth Calderon-Cardona, et al., Petitioners v. The Bank of New York Mellon, et al.

577 U.S. 1113, 136 S. Ct. 893, 193 L. Ed. 2d 809, 2016 U.S. LEXIS 779.

January 19, 2016. Motion of The Levin Judgment Creditors for leave to file a brief as amicus curiae granted. Petition for writ of certiorari to the United States Court of Appeals for the Second Circuit denied.

Same case below, 770 F.3d 993.

No. 15-125. Jeannette Fuller Hausler, as Successor Personal Representative of the Estate of Robert Otis Fuller, Deceased, Petitioner v. JPMorgan Chase Bank, N.A., et al.

577 U.S. 1113, 136 S. Ct. 893, 193 L. Ed. 2d 809, 2016 U.S. LEXIS 790.

January 19, 2016. Motion of The Levin Judgment Creditors for leave to file a brief as amicus curiae granted. Petition for writ of certiorari to the United States Court of Appeals for the Second Circuit denied. Justice Alito took no part in the consideration or decision of this motion and this petition.

Same case below, 770 F.3d 207.

No. 15-374. Kansas, Petitioner v. Luis A. Aguirre.

577 U.S. 1113, 136 S. Ct. 895, 193 L. Ed. 2d 809, 2016 U.S. LEXIS 690.

January 19, 2016. Motion of respondent for leave to proceed in forma pauperis granted. Petition for writ of certiorari to the Supreme Court of Kansas denied.

Same case below, 301 Kan. 950, 349 P.3d 1245.

No. 15-449. Johnson & Johnson, et al., Petitioners v. Lisa Reckis, et vir.

577 U.S. 1113, 136 S. Ct. 896, 193 L. Ed. 2d 809, 2016 U.S. LEXIS 801.

January 19, 2016. Petition for writ of certiorari to the Supreme Judicial Court of Massachusetts denied. Justice Alito took no part in the consideration or decision of this petition.

Same case below, 471 Mass. 272, 28 N.E.3d 445.

No. 15-470. William A. Livingston, Petitioner v. Pat Frank, Clerk, Circuit Court of Hillsborough County, Florida, et al.

577 U.S. 1113, 136 S. Ct. 897, 193 L. Ed. 2d 810, 2016 U.S. LEXIS 822.

January 19, 2016. Motion of Cato Institute for leave to file a brief as amicus curiae granted. Motion of Owners' Counsel of America for leave to file a brief as amicus curiae granted. Petition for writ of certiorari to the District Court of Appeal of Florida, Second District, denied.

Same case below, 150 So. 3d 239.

No. 15-543. Matt Sissel, Petitioner v. Department of Health and Human Services, et al.

577 U.S. 1113, 136 S. Ct. 925, 193 L. Ed. 2d 810, 2016 U.S. LEXIS 703.

January 19, 2016. Motion of Daniel G. Anderson, et al. for leave to file a brief as amici curiae out of time is denied. Petition for writ of certiorari to the United States Court of Appeals for the District of Columbia Circuit denied.

Same case below, 411 U.S. App. D.C. 301, 760 F.3d 1.

No. 15-7118. Robert Earl Tippens, Jr., Petitioner v. Virginia.

577 U.S. 1114, 136 S. Ct. 907, 193 L. Ed. 2d 810, 2016 U.S. LEXIS 727.

January 19, 2016. Petition for writ of certiorari before judgment denied.

No. 15-7351. Bernard Barnett, Petitioner v. United States.

577 U.S. 1114, 136 S. Ct. 916, 193 L. Ed. 2d 810, 2016 U.S. LEXIS 644.

January 19, 2016. Petition for writ of certiorari to the United States Court of Appeals for the Second Circuit denied. Justice Sotomayor took no part in the consideration or decision of this petition.

No. 15-7463. Derrek Pannell, Petitioner v. United States.

577 U.S. 1114, 136 S. Ct. 922, 193 L. Ed. 2d 810, 2016 U.S. LEXIS 696.

January 19, 2016. Petition for writ of certiorari to the United States Court of Appeals for the Second Circuit denied. Justice Kagan took no part in the consideration or decision of this petition.

No. 14-9909. Claretha Ross, Petitioner v. Pamela H. Cobb.

577 U.S. 1114, 136 S. Ct. 925, 193 L. Ed. 2d 810, 2016 U.S. LEXIS 765.

January 19, 2016. Petition for rehearing denied.

Former decision, 577 U.S. 840, 136 S. Ct. 72, 193 L. Ed. 2d 68, 2015 U.S. LEXIS 5047.

No. 15-5855. Edgar Keaton Martin, Petitioner v. United States.

577 U.S. 1114, 136 S. Ct. 925, 193 L. Ed. 2d 810, 2016 U.S. LEXIS 643.

January 19, 2016. Petition for rehearing denied.

Former decision, 577 U.S. 931, 136 S. Ct. 340, 193 L. Ed. 2d 244, 2015 U.S. LEXIS 6467.

No. 15-6026. John Ivy, Petitioner v. Richard Brown, Superintendent, Wabash Valley Correctional Facility.

577 U.S. 1114, 136 S. Ct. 926, 193 L. Ed. 2d 811, 2016 U.S. LEXIS 764.

January 19, 2016. Petition for rehearing denied.

Former decision, 577 U.S. 988, 136 S. Ct. 505, 193 L. Ed. 2d 400, 2015 U.S. LEXIS 7170.

No. 15-6125. Jonathan Eugene Brunson, Petitioner v. Felix Taylor, Warden.

577 U.S. 1114, 136 S. Ct. 926, 193 L. Ed. 2d 811, 2016 U.S. LEXIS 719.

January 19, 2016. Petition for rehearing denied.

Former decision, 577 U.S. 964, 136 S. Ct. 421, 193 L. Ed. 2d 330, 2015 U.S. LEXIS 7004.

No. 15-6158. David V. Alston, Petitioner v. Kean University, et al.

577 U.S. 1114, 136 S. Ct. 926, 193 L. Ed. 2d 811, 2016 U.S. LEXIS 651.

January 19, 2016. Petition for rehearing denied.

Former decision, 577 U.S. 989, 136 S. Ct. 511, 193 L. Ed. 2d 403, 2015 U.S. LEXIS 7229.

No. 15-6237. Corielle Johnson, Petitioner v. Jeffrey Dauphanus, et al.

577 U.S. 1114, 136 S. Ct. 926, 193 L. Ed. 2d 811, 2016 U.S. LEXIS 638.

January 19, 2016. Petition for rehearing denied.

Former decision, 577 U.S. 1012, 136 S. Ct. 546, 193 L. Ed. 2d 437, 2015 U.S. LEXIS 7641.

No. 15-6393. James Mario Pridgen, Petitioner v. John Kerestes, Superintendent, State Correctional Institution at Mahanoy, et al.

577 U.S. 1114, 136 S. Ct. 926, 193 L. Ed. 2d 811, 2016 U.S. LEXIS 641.

January 19, 2016. Petition for rehearing denied.

Former decision, 577 U.S. 1015, 136 S. Ct. 553, 193 L. Ed. 2d 442, 2015 U.S. LEXIS 7621.

No. 15-6590. Seidy Maria Tiburcio, Petitioner v. United States Capitol.

577 U.S. 1114, 136 S. Ct. 926, 193 L. Ed. 2d 811, 2016 U.S. LEXIS 639.

January 19, 2016. Petition for rehearing denied.

Former decision, 577 U.S. 1017, 136 S. Ct. 558, 193 L. Ed. 2d 445, 2015 U.S. LEXIS 7616.

No. 15-6791. Leonard Moore, Petitioner v. United States.

577 U.S. 1114, 136 S. Ct. 926, 193 L. Ed. 2d 811, 2016 U.S. LEXIS 642.

January 19, 2016. Petition for rehearing denied.

Former decision, 577 U.S. 1037, 136 S. Ct. 602, 193 L. Ed. 2d 481, 2015 U.S. LEXIS 7696.

No. D-2852. In the Matter of James Francis Donohue.

577 U.S. 1100, 136 S. Ct. 926, 193 L. Ed. 2d 812, 2016 U.S. LEXIS 640.

January 19, 2016. James Francis Donohue, of Butler, Pennsylvania, having requested to resign as a member of the Bar of this Court, it is ordered that his name be stricken from the roll of attorneys admitted to the practice of law before this Court. The Rule to Show Cause, issued on November 2, 2015, is discharged.

No. 15-7777 (15A750). In re Richard Allen Masterson, Petitioner.

577 U.S. 1114, 136 S. Ct. 927, 193 L. Ed. 2d 812, 2016 U.S. LEXIS 850.

January 20, 2016. Application for stay of execution of sentence of death, presented to Justice Scalia, and by him referred to the Court, denied. Petition for writ of habeas corpus denied.

No. 15-7767 (15A743). Richard Allen Masterson, Petitioner v. Texas.

577 U.S. 1114, 136 S. Ct. 927, 193 L. Ed. 2d 812, 2016 U.S. LEXIS 848.

January 20, 2016. Application for stay of execution of sentence of death, presented to Justice Scalia, and by him re-

ferred to the Court, denied. Petition for writ of certiorari to the Court of Criminal Appeals of Texas denied.

No. 15-7768 (15A744). Richard Allen Masterson, Petitioner v. Texas.

577 U.S. 1114, 136 S. Ct. 927, 193 L. Ed. 2d 812, 2016 U.S. LEXIS 849.

January 20, 2016. Application for stay of execution of sentence of death, presented to Justice Scalia, and by him referred to the Court, denied. Petition for writ of certiorari to the 178th District Court of Texas, Harris County, denied.

No. 15-7769 (15A745). Richard Allen Masterson, Petitioner v. Texas.

577 U.S. 1115, 136 S. Ct. 927, 193 L. Ed. 2d 812, 2016 U.S. LEXIS 847.

January 20, 2016. Application for stay of execution of sentence of death, presented to Justice Scalia, and by him referred to the Court, denied. Petition for writ of certiorari to the Court of Criminal Appeals of Texas denied.

No. 15-7786 (15A755). Christopher Eugene Brooks, Petitioner v. Alabama.

577 U.S. 1115, 136 S. Ct. 708, 193 L. Ed. 2d 812, 2016 U.S. LEXIS 852.

January 21, 2016. Application for stay of execution of sentence of death, presented to Justice Thomas, and by him referred to the Court, denied. Petition for writ of certiorari to the Supreme Court of Alabama denied.

MEMORANDUM CASES

Justice **Sotomayor**, with whom Justice **Ginsburg** joins, concurring in the denial of certiorari.

This Court's opinion upholding Alabama's capital sentencing scheme was based on *Hildwin* v. *Florida*, 490 U.S. 638, 109 S. Ct. 2055, 104 L. Ed. 2d 728 (1989) (*per curiam*), and *Spaziano* v. *Florida*, 468 U.S. 447, 104 S. Ct. 3154, 82 L. Ed. 2d 340 (1984), two decisions we recently overruled in *Hurst* v. *Florida*, 577 U.S. 92, 136 S. Ct. 616, 193 L. Ed. 2d 504 (2016). See *Harris* v. *Alabama*, 513 U.S. 504, 115 S. Ct. 1031, 130 L. Ed. 2d 1004 (1995). I nonetheless vote to deny certiorari in this particular case because I believe procedural obstacles would have prevented us from granting relief.

Justice **Breyer**, dissenting from denial of application for stay of execution and petition for certiorari.

Christopher Eugene Brooks was sentenced to death in accordance with Alabama's procedures, which allow a jury to render an "advisory verdict" that "is not binding on the court." Ala. Code § 13A-5-47(e) (2006). For the reasons explained in my opinions concurring in the judgment in *Hurst* v. *Florida, ante,* at 103, 136 S. Ct. 616, 193 L. Ed. 2d 504, and *Ring* v. *Arizona,* 536 U.S. 584, 613-619, 122 S. Ct. 2428, 153 L. Ed. 2d 556 (2002), and my dissenting opinion in *Schriro* v. *Summerlin*, 542 U.S. 348, 358-366, 124 S. Ct. 2519, 159 L. Ed. 2d 442 (2004), I dissent from the order of the Court to deny the application for stay of execution and the petition for a writ of certiorari.

Moreover, we have recognized that Alabama's sentencing scheme is "much like" and "based on Florida's sentencing scheme." *Harris* v. *Alabama*, 513 U.S. 504, 508, 115 S. Ct. 1031, 130 L. Ed. 2d 1004 (1995). Florida's scheme is unconstitutional. See *Hurst, ante,* at 103, 136 S. Ct. 616, 193 L. Ed. 2d 504 (Breyer, J., concurring in judgment). The unfairness inherent in treating this case differently from others which used similarly unconstitutional procedures only underscores the need to reconsider the validity of capital punishment under the Eighth Amendment. See *Glossip* v. *Gross*, 576 U.S. 863, 908–909, 135 S. Ct. 2726, 192 L. Ed. 2d 761 (2015) (Breyer, J., dissenting). I respectfully dissent.

No. 15-7787 (15A756). Christopher E. Brooks, Petitioner v. Jefferson S. Dunn, Commissioner, Alabama Department of Corrections.

577 U.S. 1116, 136 S. Ct. 979, 193 L. Ed. 2d 813, 2016 U.S. LEXIS 851.

January 21, 2016. Application for stay of execution of sentence of death, presented to Justice Thomas, and by him referred to the Court, denied. Petition for writ of certiorari to the United States Court of Appeals for the Eleventh Circuit denied.

Same case below, 810 F.3d 812.

MARYLAND, Petitioner

v

JAMES KULBICKI

577 U.S. 1, 136 S. Ct. 2, 193 L. Ed. 2d 1, 2015 U.S. LEXIS 4693

[No. 14-848]

Decided October 5, 2015.

EDITOR'S NOTE: The following syllabus was added after the slip opinion was issued.

SYLLABUS BY REPORTER OF DECISIONS

At respondent Kulbicki's 1995 murder trial, the State of Maryland's ballistics expert testified, based on Comparative Bullet Lead Analysis (CBLA), that bullet fragments from the crime scene were similar in composition to a fragment found in Kulbicki's truck and a bullet found in his gun. The jury convicted Kulbicki of first-degree murder. Years later, after CBLA was discredited and abandoned as a mode of ballistics analysis, Kulbicki argued on state postconviction review that his trial attorneys were ineffective because they had not questioned CBLA's legitimacy. The Court of Appeals of Maryland held that trial counsel's failure to discover a 1991 report coauthored by the State's expert witness, to identify a methodological flaw contained therein, and to use that flaw to cast doubt on CBLA during cross-examination amounted to deficient performance. Concluding further that counsel's deficiency was prejudicial, the court set aside Kulbicki's conviction and ordered a new trial.

Held: Kulbicki's trial attorneys were not constitutionally ineffective.

Under the "rule of contemporary assessment of counsel's conduct," *Lockhart* v. *Fretwell*, 506 U.S. 364, 372, 113 S. Ct. 838, 122 L. Ed. 2d 180, the Maryland Court of Appeals should have "judge[d] the reasonableness of counsel's challenged conduct . . . viewed as of the time of counsel's conduct," *Strickland* v. *Washington*, 466 U.S. 668, 690, 104 S. Ct. 2052, 80 L. Ed. 2d 674. Had it done so, it would have acknowledged that counsel's failure to poke methodological holes in a then-uncontroversial mode of ballistics analysis did not amount to deficient performance. There is no reason to believe that a diligent search would have discovered the supposedly crucial 1991 report. The State Court of Appeals' demand for something close to "perfect advocacy" is far more than the "reasonable competence" the Sixth Amendment right to counsel guarantees. *Yarborough* v. *Gentry*, 540 U.S. 1, 8, 124 S. Ct. 1, 157 L. Ed. 2d 1.

Certiorari granted; 440 Md. 33, 99 A.3d 730, reversed.

MULLENIX v. LUNA

[577 U.S. 7]

CHADRIN LEE MULLENIX, Petitioner

v

BEATRICE LUNA, Individually and as Representative of the ESTATE OF
ISRAEL LEIJA, JR., et al.

577 U.S. 7, 136 S. Ct. 305, 193 L. Ed. 2d 255, 2015 U.S. LEXIS 7160

[No. 14-1143]

Decided November 9, 2015.

EDITOR'S NOTE: The following syllabus was added after the slip opinion
was issued.

SYLLABUS BY REPORTER OF DECISIONS

Israel Leija, Jr., led officers on a high-speed car chase in an attempt to evade service of an arrest warrant. During the chase, he twice told a police dispatcher that he had a gun and would shoot officers if they did not abandon their pursuit. The dispatcher relayed the threats, together with a report that Leija might be intoxicated, to all concerned officers, including petitioner Chadrin Mullenix, who had driven ahead to an overpass above the interstate. Once there, Mullenix discussed with other officers the idea of shooting Leija's car to disable it, even though he had not been trained in this tactic and had not attempted it before. Mullenix nonetheless took up a shooting position and learned that another officer was beneath the overpass. As Leija approached, Mullenix fired multiple shots, killing Leija. Respondents sued Mullenix under 42 U.S.C. § 1983, alleging that he had violated the Fourth Amendment by using excessive force against Leija. Mullenix moved for summary judgment on the ground of qualified immunity, but the District Court denied the motion. The Fifth Circuit affirmed, concluding that Mullenix was not entitled to qualified immunity because the law clearly established "that a reasonable officer would have known that the use of deadly force, absent a sufficiently substantial and immediate threat, violated the Fourth Amendment." 773 F.3d 712, 725.

Held: Because the constitutional rule applied by the Fifth Circuit was not " 'beyond debate,' " *Stanton* v. *Sims,* 571 U.S. 3, 6, 134 S. Ct. 3, 187 L. Ed. 2d 341, the Fifth Circuit wrongly decided that Mullenix was not entitled to qualified immunity. In assessing whether Mullenix violated clearly established statutory or constitutional rights of which a reasonable person would have known, the court improperly defined the clearly established law at a high level of generality rather than asking whether the violative nature of the particular conduct is clearly established. *Ashcroft* v. *al-Kidd,* 563 U.S. 731, 742, 131 S. Ct. 2074, 179 L. Ed. 2d 1149. Here, Mullenix confronted a reportedly intoxicated fugitive, set on avoiding capture through high-speed vehicular flight, who twice during his flight had threatened to shoot police officers, and who was moments away from encountering an officer underneath the overpass. Far from clarifying the issue, this Court's excessive force cases involving car chases reveal the hazy legal backdrop against which Mullenix acted. See *Brosseau* v. *Haugen*, 543 U.S. 194, 125 S. Ct. 596, 160 L. Ed. 2d 583; *Scott* v. *Harris*, 550 U.S. 372, 127 S. Ct. 1769, 167 L. Ed. 2d 686; and *Plumhoff* v. *Rickard*, 572 U.S. 765, 134 S. Ct. 2012, 188 L. Ed. 2d 1056. Nor have cases decided by lower courts since *Brosseau* clearly established that deadly force is inappropriate in response to conduct like Leija's. Finally, the fact that the danger Leija represented was less substantial than the threats that courts have previously found sufficient to justify deadly force says little, if anything, about whether such force was reasonable in the circumstances here because qualified immunity protects actions in "the 'hazy border between excessive and acceptable force.'" *Brosseau*, 573 U.S., at 201, 134 S. Ct. 2259, 189 L. Ed. 2d 262 (quoting *Saucier* v. *Katz*, 533 U.S. 194, 206, 121 S. Ct. 2151, 150 L. Ed. 2d 272).

Certiorari granted; 773 F.3d 712, reversed.

RANDY WHITE, WARDEN, Petitioner

v

ROGER L. WHEELER

577 U.S. 73, 136 S. Ct. 456, 193 L. Ed. 2d 384, 2015 U.S. LEXIS 7998

[No. 14-1372]

Decided December 14, 2015.

EDITOR'S NOTE: The following syllabus was added after the slip opinion was issued.

SYLLABUS BY REPORTER OF DECISIONS

During the jury selection process in respondent Roger Wheeler's state murder trial, the prosecution moved to strike Juror 638 for cause based on his inconsistent replies to the question whether he could consider voting to impose the death penalty. The trial judge initially found the juror unproblematic but, after deliberating and reviewing the relevant testimony, excused the juror, concluding that he could not give sufficient assurance of neutrality or impartiality in considering whether the death penalty should be imposed. Respondent was convicted and sentenced to death, and the Kentucky Supreme Court affirmed. After exhausting available state postconviction procedures, respondent sought a writ of habeas corpus in Federal District Court, asserting, *inter alia*, that the trial court erred in striking Juror 638. The District Court dismissed the petition, but the Sixth Circuit granted relief as to respondent's sentence, holding that the exclusion of Juror 638 was an unreasonable application of *Witherspoon* v. *Illinois*, 391 U.S. 510, 88 S. Ct. 1770, 20 L. Ed. 2d 776, *Wainwright* v. *Witt*, 469 U.S. 412, 105 S. Ct. 844, 83 L. Ed. 2d 841, and their progeny.

Held: The Sixth Circuit's determination contravenes this Court's controlling precedents. Under the Antiterrorism and Effective Death Penalty Act of 1996, federal habeas review of respondent's claim—much like that of an ineffective-assistance-of-counsel claim—must be " ' "doubly deferential." ' " *Burt* v. *Titlow*, 571 U.S. 12, 15, 134 S. Ct. 10, 187 L. Ed. 2d 348. The Court of Appeals did not afford the proper deference to the state-court ruling. Juror 638's statement that he was "not absolutely certain whether [he] could realistically consider" the death penalty, App. to Pet. for Cert. 132a, was a reasonable basis for the trial judge's conclusion that the juror was unable to give that penalty fair consideration. Her decision to excuse Juror 638 thus did not violate clearly established federal law. See, *e.g.*, *Witt, supra*, at 425–426, 105 S. Ct. 844, 83 L. Ed. 2d 841. Nor was the Kentucky Supreme Court's ruling that there was no error " 'beyond any possibility for fairminded disagreement.' " *White* v. *Woodall*, 572 U.S. 415, 420, 134 S. Ct. 1697, 188 L. Ed. 2d 698. The Sixth Circuit's suggestion that a trial judge is entitled to less deference for having deliberated after her initial ruling is wrong. While a trial court's contemporaneous assessment of a juror's demeanor and its bearing on how to interpret or understand the juror's responses are entitled to substantial deference, see *Uttecht* v. *Brown*, 551 U.S. 1, 17, 127 S. Ct. 2218, 167 L. Ed. 2d 1014, a trial court ruling is likewise entitled to deference when made after a careful review of a formal transcript or recording.

Certiorari granted; 779 F.3d 366, reversed and remanded.

MELENE JAMES, Petitioner

v

CITY OF BOISE, IDAHO, et al.

577 U.S. 306, 136 S. Ct. 685, 193 L. Ed. 2d 694, 2016 U.S. LEXIS 947

[No. 15-493]

Decided January 25, 2016.

EDITOR'S NOTE: The following syllabus was added after the slip opinion was issued.

SYLLABUS BY REPORTER OF DECISIONS

In *Hughes* v. *Rowe*, 449 U.S. 5, 101 S. Ct. 173, 66 L. Ed. 2d 163, this Court determined that 42 U.S.C. § 1988 permits a prevailing defendant in a civil rights lawsuit filed under § 1983 to recover fees only if "the plaintiff's action was frivolous, unreasonable, or without foundation," 449 U.S., at 14, 101 S. Ct. 173, 66 L. Ed. 2d 163. The Idaho Supreme Court concluded that it was not bound by *Hughes* and awarded attorney's fees under § 1988 to a prevailing defendant without first making the determination required by *Hughes*.

Held: The Idaho Supreme Court is bound by this Court's interpretation of federal law and erred in concluding otherwise. " 'It is this Court's responsibility to say what a [federal] statute means, and once the Court has spoken, it is the duty of other courts to respect that understanding of the governing rule of law.' " *Nitro-Lift Technologies, L. L. C.* v. *Howard*, 568 U.S. 17, 21, 133 S. Ct. 500, 184 L. Ed. 2d 328.

Certiorari granted; 158 Idaho 713, 351 P.3d 1171, reversed and remanded.

AMGEN INC., et al., Petitioners

v

STEVE HARRIS, et al.

577 U.S. 308, 136 S. Ct. 758, 193 L. Ed. 2d 696, 2016 U.S. LEXIS 891

[No. 15-278]

Decided January 25, 2016.

EDITOR'S NOTE: The following syllabus was added after the slip opinion was issued.

SYLLABUS BY REPORTER OF DECISIONS

Respondent stockholders are former Amgen employees who participated in plans that qualified under the Employee Retirement Income Security Act of 1974 (ERISA) as eligible individual account plans and that, like employee stock ownership plans (ESOPs), offered employer stock as an option. They filed a class action alleging that petitioner fiduciaries had breached their fiduciary duties, including the duty of prudence. The District Court granted petitioners' motion to dismiss, but the Ninth Circuit reversed. This Court vacated that judgment and remanded the case in light of *Fifth Third Bancorp* v. *Dudenhoeffer*, 573 U.S. 409, 134 S. Ct. 2459, 189 L. Ed. 2d 457, where the Court held that ERISA fiduciaries who administer ESOPs are not entitled to a presumption of prudence but are "subject to the same duty of prudence that applies to ERISA fiduciaries in general, except that they need not diversify the fund's assets," *id.*, at 412, 134 S. Ct. 2459, 189 L. Ed. 2d 457, and instructed lower courts faced with such claims to determine whether the complaint itself "has plausibly alleged" facts sufficient to satisfy the liability standard, *id.*, at 429, 134 S. Ct. 2459, 189 L. Ed. 2d 457. On remand, the Ninth Circuit again reversed

Held: The Ninth Circuit failed to properly evaluate the stockholders' complaint by failing to assess whether the complaint in its current form "plausibly allege[s]" a claim for breach of the duty of prudence. This Court's examination of that complaint has not found sufficient facts and allegations to state such a claim. On remand, the District Court should determine in the first instance whether the stockholders may amend their complaint in order to adequately plead a claim for breach of the duty of prudence guided by the standards provided in *Fifth Third*.

Certiorari granted; 788 F.3d 916, reversed and remanded.

SURVEY OF THE TERM
AND
ANNOTATIONS

FOR CASES REPORTED IN THIS VOLUME

The annotations herein, prepared by the Editors, are indexed in the "Index to Decisions and Annotations" appearing at the end of this volume. For additional annotation references, consult appropriate topics and sections in the United States Supreme Court Digest, Lawyers' Edition, and consult the L. Ed General Index to Decisions, Annotations, and Digest.

SURVEY OF THE 2015-2016 TERM

by

Gary Knapp, M.B.A., J.D.

§ 1. Generally; statistics

The Supreme Court's 2015-2016 Term began on October 5, 2015, and adjourned on October 3, 2016.

It is noted that Justice Scalia died on February 13, 2016. Born in 1936, he had taken his seat as an Associate Justice on September 26, 1986.

Statistics issued by the Office of the Clerk of the Supreme Court show that, as of the court's beginning its summer recess on June 28, 2016, (1) 7,535 cases appeared on the Supreme Court's docket for the 2015-2016 Term; and (2) of these, 1,060 were carried over from the prior term, and 6,475 were docketed during the 2015-2016 Term.

Of the 7,535 cases on the docket during the 2015-2016 Term, 6,277 nonoriginal cases were disposed of by (1) the court's denial of review, (2) the court's dismissal, or (3) withdrawal. Another 145 nonoriginal cases were summarily decided. A total of 998 cases, including 7 original cases, were not acted upon, or remained undisposed of.

There were 114 cases available for argument during the 2015-2016 Term, of which 82 cases were argued and 1 case was dismissed or remanded without argument, leaving 31 cases still available for argument. Of the 82 cases that were argued, 70 were disposed of by signed opinions and 12 were disposed of by per curiam opinions.

§ 2. Leading decisions

In vacating criminal convictions of a former governor of Virginia, and in remanding the case to a lower federal court for further proceedings, the Supreme Court held that setting up a meeting, calling another public official, or hosting an event did not, standing alone, qualify as an "official act" exchanged for something of value in violation of 18 U.S.C.S. § 201 (McDonnell v. United States (2016, US) 136 S. Ct. 2355, 195 L. Ed. 2d 639, 2016 U.S. LEXIS 4062, infra § 9). In another case involving interpretation of a federal statute, the Supreme Court decided that reckless domestic assault qualified as a "misdemeanor crime of domestic violence" under 18 U.S.C.S. § 922(g)(9), which prohibited anyone with a conviction for a crime of domestic violence from possessing a firearm (Voisine v. United States (2016, US) 136 S. Ct. 2272, 195 L. Ed. 2d 736, 2016 U.S. LEXIS 4061, infra § 22).

In light of the positions asserted by the parties in their supplemental briefs that had been requested by the Supreme Court—after oral argument concerning the questions whether (1) Department of Health and Human Services (HHS) regulations, interpreting the Patient Protection and Affordable Care Act of 2010 to require specified employers' health insurance plans to cover certain contraceptive methods, violated the Religious Freedom Restoration Act of 1993 (RFRA) (42 U.S.C.S. § 2000bb et seq.) by allegedly forcing religious not-for-profit employers to act in violation of their sincerely held religious beliefs, (2) the alleged availability of a regulatory method for not-for-profit religious employers to comply with HHS' contraceptive mandate eliminated either the asserted substantial burden on religious exercise or the RFRA violation allegedly recognized in Burwell v. Hobby Lobby Stores, Inc. (2014) 573 U.S. 682, 134 S. Ct. 2751, 189 L. Ed. 2d 675, 2014 U.S. LEXIS 4505, and (3) HHS satisfied RFRA's test for overriding sincerely held religious objections in circumstances where HHS allegedly insisted that overriding the religious objection would not fulfill HHS' regulatory objective of providing no-cost contraceptives to the objector's employees—vacated the judgments below and remanded to the respective Federal Courts of Appeals, which were instructed to afford the parties on remand an opportunity to arrive at an approach that accommodated petitioners' religious exercise while insuring that women covered by petitioners' health plans received full and equal health coverage, including contraceptive coverage (Zubik v. Burwell (2016) 578 U.S. 403, 136 S. Ct. 1557, 194 L. Ed. 2d 696, 2016 U.S. LEXIS 3047, infra § 23).

The Supreme Court held that the Federal Constitution's full faith and credit clause (Art. IV, § 1) required the Alabama courts to respect a Georgia court's final judgment of adoption that made a woman a legal parent of the children that she and another woman—who had given birth to the children—had raised together from birth before the women separated while residing in Alabama, where, after the separation, the non-birth parent asked the Alabama courts to enforce the Georgia judgment and grant her custody or visitation rights (V.L. v. E.L. (2016) 577 U.S. 404, 136 S. Ct. 1017, 194 L. Ed. 2d 92, 2016 U.S. LEXIS 1653, infra § 4).

As to federal constitutional amendments, the court determined that (1) the Fourth Amendment permitted warrantless breath tests, but not warrantless blood tests, incident to lawful arrests for suspected drunk driving (Birchfield v. North Dakota (2016) 579 U.S. 438, 136 S. Ct. 2160, 195 L. Ed. 2d 560, 2016 U.S. LEXIS 4058, infra § 34); (2) the Fifth Amendment's double jeopardy clause barred Puerto Rico and the United States from successively prosecuting an individual for the same conduct under equivalent criminal laws, because Puerto Rico and the United States were not separate sovereigns, since the ultimate source of Puerto Rico's prosecutorial power was the Federal Government (Puerto Rico v. Sanchez Valle (2016) 579 U.S. 59, 136 S. Ct. 1863, 195 L. Ed. 2d 179, 2016 U.S. LEXIS 3773, infra § 15); and (3) the use of Indian-tribal-court convictions, with respect to which an indigent accused had not been provided with appointed counsel and had received prison sentences not exceeding 1 year, as predicate offenses for the accused's conviction in federal court as a habitual domestic-violence offender under 18 U.S.C.S. § 117(a) did not violate the accused's right to the assistance of counsel under the Sixth Amendment, because the tribal-court convictions had occurred in proceedings that complied with the Indian Civil Rights Act of 1968, which in 25 U.S.C.S. § 1302(c)(2), gave indigent defendants a right to appointed counsel only with respect to sentences exceeding 1 year (United States v. Bryant (2016) 579 U.S.

140, 136 S. Ct. 1954, 195 L. Ed. 2d 317, 2016 U.S. LEXIS 3775, infra § 7).

The Supreme Court held that a Texas statute that required a physician who performed abortions to have admitting privileges at a hospital within 30 miles of the facility where the abortions were performed, and a Texas statute that required the facility to meet surgical-center standards, constituted an undue burden on abortion access that violated the due process clause of the Federal Constitution's Fourteenth Amendment (Whole Woman's Health v. Hellerstedt (2016, US) 136 S. Ct. 2292, 195 L. Ed. 2d 665, 2016 U.S. LEXIS 4063, infra § 3). Moreover, the court held that the University of Texas at Austin's undergraduate admissions program— which (1) offered admission to any student who graduated in the top 10 percent of any Texas high school class, and (2) filled the remainder of the incoming freshman class on the combined basis of SAT scores, high school academic performance, and a "Personal Achievement Index" that contained numerous factors, including race— was lawful under the Fourteenth Amendment's equal protection clause (Fisher v. Univ. of Tex. (2016, US) 136 S. Ct. 2198, 195 L. Ed. 2d 511, 2016 U.S. LEXIS 4059, infra § 10). Also, in a case that apparently involved alleged violation of the Fourteenth Amendment's equal protection clause, the Supreme Court held that a state court, in denying habeas corpus relief sought by a state prisoner who had been convicted of murder and sentenced to death, erred in holding that the prisoner had failed to show purposeful racially discriminatory jury selection where the state had used peremptory challenges to strike all 4 qualified black prospective jurors, as copies of the file used by the prosecution during the prisoner's trial contained (1) the jury venire list on which the names of each black prospective juror were highlighted in bright green, with a legend indicating that the highlighting "represents Blacks"; (2) a draft affidavit comparing black prospective jurors and concluding, "If it comes down to having to pick one of the black jurors, [this one] might be okay"; (3) notes identifying black prospec-

tive jurors as "B" with numbers; (4) notes with "N" (for "no") appearing next to the names of all black prospective jurors; (5) a list titled "[D]efinite NO's" containing 6 names, including the names of all of the qualified black prospective jurors; and (6) questionnaires filled out by 5 prospective black jurors, on which each juror's response indicating his or her race had been circled (Foster v. Chatman (2016) 578 U.S. 488, 136 S. Ct. 1737, 195 L. Ed. 2d 1, 2016 U.S. LEXIS 3486, infra § 36).

§ 3. Abortion

The court held that a Texas statute that required a physician who performed abortions to have admitting privileges at a hospital within 30 miles of the facility where the abortions were performed, and a Texas statute that required the facility to meet surgical-center standards, constituted an undue burden on abortion access that violated the due process clause of the Federal Constitution's Fourteenth Amendment. [Whole Woman's Health v. Hellerstedt (2016, US) 136 S. Ct. 2292, 195 L. Ed. 2d 665, 2016 U.S. LEXIS 4063.]

§ 4. Adoption

The Supreme Court held that the Federal Constitution's full faith and credit clause (Art. IV, § 1) required the Alabama courts to respect a Georgia court's final judgment of adoption that made a woman a legal parent of the children that she and another woman—who had given birth to the children—had raised together from birth before the women separated while residing in Alabama, where, after the separation, the non-birth parent asked the Alabama courts to enforce the Georgia judgment and grant her custody or visitation rights. [V.L. v. E.L. (2016) 577 U.S. 404, 136 S. Ct. 1017, 194 L. Ed. 2d 92, 2016 U.S. LEXIS 1653.]

§ 5. Aliens

For purposes of removal from the United States under 8 U.S.C.S. § 1227(a)(2)(A)(iii) of an alien who had committed an aggravated felony, a state crime having every element of a listed federal crime except a connection to interstate or foreign commerce was determined by the

Supreme Court to be an aggravated felony as defined in 8 U.S.C.S. § 1101(a)(43). [Torres v. Lynch (2016) 578 U.S. 452, 136 S. Ct. 1619, 194 L. Ed. 2d 737, 2016 U.S. LEXIS 3351.]

§ 6. Arbitration

It was held that the interpretation, by a state appellate court—which refused to enforce a contract's arbitration provision—of the contract phrase "law of your state" (1) did not place arbitration contracts on an equal footing with all other contracts, and (2) was pre-empted by the Federal Arbitration Act (9 U.S.C.S. § 1 et seq.). [DIRECTV, Inc. v. Imburgia (2015) 577 U.S. 47, 136 S. Ct. 463, 193 L. Ed. 2d 365, 2015 U.S. LEXIS 7999.]

§ 7. Assistance of counsel

According to the Supreme Court, counsel for an accused who was convicted in state trial court of murder were not ineffective in violation of the Federal Constitution's Sixth Amendment in failing to question the legitimacy of Comparative Bullet Lead Analysis (CBLA), where a Federal Bureau of Investigation agent testified as the state's CBLA expert at the accused's trial—and where, years later in a different case, a state appellate court held that CBLA evidence was not generally accepted by the scientific community and was therefore inadmissible at trial—as (1) at the time of the accused's trial, the validity of CBLA was widely accepted; and (2) there had been offered no support for the conclusion that the accused's counsel were constitutionally required to predict the demise of CBLA. [Maryland v. Kulbicki (2015) 577 U.S. 1, 136 S. Ct. 2, 193 L. Ed. 2d 1, 2015 U.S. LEXIS 4693.]

The Supreme Court decided that a court order that, under 18 U.S.C.S. § 1345—which authorized the freezing before trial of certain assets that belonged to an accused who was charged with violating federal health care or banking laws—froze assets that were untainted by the charged crime violated the accused's right to counsel under the Federal Constitution's Sixth Amendment insofar as the order pre-vented the accused from paying her lawyer. [Luis v. United States (2016) 578 U.S. 5, 136 S. Ct. 1083, 194 L. Ed. 2d 256, 2016 U.S. LEXIS 2272.]

It was decided that an accused who had been convicted in a state court of possession with intent to deliver cocaine was not entitled to federal habeas corpus relief under 28 U.S.C.S. § 2254(d)(1) on the basis of allegedly ineffective assistance of counsel in violation of the Federal Constitution's Sixth Amendment on direct appeal, since a state court's decision that appellate counsel's failure to assert that there had been violations at trial of the Sixth Amendment's confrontation clause and right to effective assistance of counsel was not contrary to, and did not involve, an unreasonable application of, clearly established federal law as determined by the Supreme Court. [Woods v. Etherton (2016) 578 U.S. 113, 136 S. Ct. 1149, 194 L. Ed. 2d 333, 2016 U.S. LEXIS 2277.]

According to the Supreme Court, the use of Indian-tribal-court convictions, with respect to which an indigent accused had not been provided with appointed counsel and had received prison sentences not exceeding 1 year, as predicate offenses for the accused's conviction in federal court as a habitual domestic-violence offender under 18 U.S.C.S. § 117(a) did not violate the accused's right to the assistance of counsel under the Federal Constitution's Sixth Amendment, because the tribal-court convictions had occurred in proceedings that complied with the Indian Civil Rights Act of 1968, which in 25 U.S.C.S. § 1302(c)(2), gave indigent defendants a right to appointed counsel only with respect to sentences exceeding 1 year. [United States v. Bryant (2016) 579 U.S. 140, 136 S. Ct. 1954, 195 L. Ed. 2d 317, 2016 U.S. LEXIS 3775.]

§ 8. Bankruptcy

The court held that the "actual fraud" bar to debt discharge under § 523(a)(2)(A) of the Bankruptcy Code (11 U.S.C.S. § 523(a)(2)(A)) encompassed fraudulent-conveyance schemes even when those schemes did not involve false representation. [Husky Int'l Elecs., Inc. v. Ritz (2016)

578 U.S. 355, 136 S. Ct. 1581, 194 L. Ed. 2d 655, 2016 U.S. LEXIS 3048.]

It was held that Puerto Rico (1) was a "state" for purposes of § 903(1) of Bankruptcy Code (11 U.S.C.S. § 903(1)); and (2) therefore, was barred from enacting a municipal bankruptcy scheme to restructure the debt of its insolvent public utilities. [Puerto Rico v. Franklin Cal. Tax-Free Trust (2016) 579 U.S. 115, 136 S. Ct. 1938, 195 L. Ed. 2d 298, 2016 U.S. LEXIS 3777.]

§ 9. Bribery

In a case that involved a former governor of Virginia, the court held that setting up a meeting, calling another public official, or hosting an event did not, standing alone, qualify as an "official act" exchanged for something of value in violation of 18 U.S.C.S. § 201. [McDonnell v. United States (2016, US) 136 S. Ct. 2355, 195 L. Ed. 2d 639, 2016 U.S. LEXIS 4062.]

§ 10. College admissions

The court held that the University of Texas at Austin's undergraduate admissions program—which (1) offered admission to any student who graduated in the top 10 percent of any Texas high school class; and (2) filled the remainder of the incoming freshman class on the combined basis of SAT scores, high school academic performance, and a "Personal Achievement Index" that contained numerous factors, including race—was lawful under the equal protection clause of the Federal Constitution's Fourteenth Amendment. [Fisher v. Univ. of Tex. (2016, US) 136 S. Ct. 2198, 195 L. Ed. 2d 511, 2016 U.S. LEXIS 4059.]

§ 11. Copyright

It was held that when deciding whether to award attorneys' fees under § 505 of the Copyright Act (17 U.S.C.S. § 505) to the prevailing party in a copyright case, a Federal District Court had to give substantial weight to the objective reasonableness of the losing party's position while taking into account all other circumstances relevant to granting fees. [Kirtsaeng v. John Wiley & Sons, Inc. (2016)

579 U.S. 197, 136 S. Ct. 1979, 195 L. Ed. 2d 368, 2016 U.S. LEXIS 3922.]

§ 12. Damages

The Supreme Court determined that a Federal District Court properly had certified and maintained a class of employees under Rule 23(b)(3) of the Federal Rules of Civil Procedure and a Fair Labor Standards Act provision (29 U.S.C.S. § 216), where, to support alleged liability and damages, the employees primarily relied on work-time estimates resulting from a study performed by an industrial relations expert. [Tyson Foods, Inc. v. Bouaphakeo (2016) 577 U.S. 442, 136 S. Ct. 1036, 194 L. Ed. 2d 124, 2016 U.S. LEXIS 2134.]

The Supreme Court concluded that the Federal Constitution's full faith and credit clause (Art. IV, § 1) did not permit a Nevada state court to apply a rule of Nevada law that awarded damages against California that were greater than the Nevada court could have awarded against Nevada in similar circumstances. [Franchise Tax Bd. v. Hyatt (2016) 578 U.S. 171, 136 S. Ct. 1277, 194 L. Ed. 2d 431, 2016 U.S. LEXIS 2796.]

It was held that a Federal District Court Judge (1) had a limited inherent power to rescind a jury discharge order and recall a jury—all members of which remained in the courtroom building—in a civil case for further deliberations after identifying an error, concerning damages, in the jury's verdict; and (2) did not abuse that power when he (a) recalled jurors, (b) gave them supplemental instructions pursuant to Rule 51(b)(3) of the Federal Rules of Civil Procedure, and (c) directed them to deliberate based on those instructions. [Dietz v. Bouldin (2016) 579 U.S. 40, 136 S. Ct. 1885, 195 L. Ed. 2d 161, 2016 U.S. LEXIS 3772.]

The Supreme Court decided that the 2-part test used by the United States Court of Appeals for the Federal Circuit to determine whether to award enhanced damages under 35 U.S.C.S. § 284 for patent infringement was not consistent with § 284, because the test required a finding of objective recklessness and required that recklessness be proved by clear and convincing evidence, while patent-infringement litigation had always been governed by a preponderance-of-the-evidence standard. [Halo Elecs., Inc. v. Pulse Elecs., Inc. (2016) 579 U.S. 93, 136 S. Ct. 1923, 195 L. Ed. 2d 278, 2016 U.S. LEXIS 3776.]

§ 13. Debt collection

Assuming for the sake of argument that special counsel were not state officers within the meaning of a Fair Debt Collection Practices Act provision (15 U.S.C.S. § 1692e)—which barred "debt collectors" from using any false, deceptive, or misleading representation or means, but in 15 U.S.C.S. § 1692a(6)(C), said that the Act did not apply to any state officer or employee to the extent that collecting or attempting to collect any debt was in the performance of the person's official duties—the Supreme Court held that the use by special counsel, who had been appointed by the Ohio Attorney General to act on the Attorney General's behalf by collecting debts owed to the state, of the Attorney General's letterhead on debt-collection letters sent by special counsel did not offend § 1692e. [Sheriff v. Gillie (2016) 578 U.S. 317, 136 S. Ct. 1594, 194 L. Ed. 2d 625, 2016 U.S. LEXIS 3050.]

§ 14. Disclosure of evidence

According to the Supreme Court, an accused had been denied his due-process rights under the Federal Constitution's Fourteenth Amendment at his state criminal trial by the prosecution's failure to disclose evidence that allegedly supported the accused's assertion of innocence. [Wearry v. Cain (2016) 577 U.S. 385, 136 S. Ct. 1002, 194 L. Ed. 2d 78, 2016 U.S. LEXIS 1654.]

§ 15. Double jeopardy

The court held that the double jeopardy clause of the Federal Constitution's Fifth Amendment barred Puerto Rico and the United States from successively prosecuting an individual for the same conduct under equivalent criminal laws, because Puerto Rico and the United States were not separate sovereigns, since the ulti-

mate source of Puerto Rico's prosecutorial power was the Federal Government. [Puerto Rico v. Sanchez Valle (2016) 579 U.S. 59, 136 S. Ct. 1863, 195 L. Ed. 2d 179, 2016 U.S. LEXIS 3773.]

§ 16. Elections and voting

It was held that parties alleging that Maryland's 2011 congressional redistricting plan burdened their right of political association under the Federal Constitution's First Amendment were entitled under 28 U.S.C.S. § 2284 to make their case before a three-judge Federal District Court. [Shapiro v. McManus (2015) 577 U.S. 39, 136 S. Ct. 450, 193 L. Ed. 2d 279, 2015 U.S. LEXIS 7868.]

The court held that under the "one-person, one-vote" principle of the equal protection clause of the Federal Constitution's Fourteenth Amendment, a state or locality was allowed to draw its legislative districts on the basis of total population, rather than being required to draw such districts on the basis of the population of eligible voters. [Evenwel v. Abbott (2016) 578 U.S. 54, 136 S. Ct. 1120, 194 L. Ed. 2d 291, 2016 U.S. LEXIS 2278.]

The Supreme Court decided that a Federal District Court had not erred in holding that an Arizona legislative redistricting plan did not violate the equal protection clause of the Federal Constitution's Fourteenth Amendment, where (1) after the 2010 census, Arizona's independent redistricting commission, comprising two Republicans, two Democrats, and one independent, redrew Arizona's legislative districts, with guidance from legal counsel, mapping specialists, a statistician, and a Voting Rights Act of 1965 specialist; (2) the initial plan had a maximum population deviation of 4.07 percent; and (3) the commission adopted a revised plan with an 8.8 percent deviation on a 3-to-2 vote, with the Republican members dissenting. [Harris v. Ariz. Indep. Redistricting Comm'n (2016) 578 U.S. 253, 136 S. Ct. 1301, 194 L. Ed. 2d 497, 2016 U.S. LEXIS 2798.]

With respect to a redistricting plan for a congressional district that was alleged to be unconstitutional racial gerrymandering, some intervenors were held to lack standing under the Federal Constitution's Article III to pursue an appeal to defend the plan, where none of the intervenors resided in or represented the district, as they failed to establish injury in fact that was fairly traceable to the challenged conduct and was likely to be redressed by a favorable decision. [Wittman v. Personhuballah (2016) 578 U.S. 539, 136 S. Ct. 1732, 195 L. Ed. 2d 37, 2016 U.S. LEXIS 3353]

§ 17. Energy

The court held that (1) the Federal Power Act (16 U.S.C.S. § 791a et seq.) gave the Federal Energy Regulatory Commission (FERC) authority to regulate wholesale market operators' compensation of demand-response bids; and (2) FERC's decision to compensate demand-response providers at the locational marginal price—the price of the highest accepted bid—was not arbitrary and capricious. [FERC v. Elec. Power Supply Ass'n (2016) 577 U.S. 260, 136 S. Ct. 760, 193 L. Ed. 2d 661, 2016 U.S. LEXIS 853.]

The court determined that a state program under which the contract price to build and operate a power plant was the developer's bid price was pre-empted by federal law because the program disregarded the interstate wholesale rate that the Federal Energy Regulatory Commission required. [Hughes v. Talen Energy Mktg., LLC (2016) 578 U.S. 150, 136 S. Ct. 1288, 194 L. Ed. 2d 414, 2016 U.S. LEXIS 2797.]

§ 18. Environmental law

According to the Supreme Court, the United States Army Corps of Engineers' approved "jurisdictional determination" that the property at issue contained "waters of the United States" protected by the Clean Water Act (33 U.S.C.S. § 1251 et seq.) was a final agency action that was judicially reviewable under the Administrative Procedure Act (5 U.S.C.S. § 500 et seq.). [United States Army Corps of Eng'rs v. Hawkes Co. (2016) 578 U.S. 590, 136 S. Ct. 1807, 195 L. Ed. 2d 77, 2016 U.S. LEXIS 3489.]

§ 19. False Claims Act

The court concluded that an implied-false-certification theory was allowed to be the basis for liability under a False Claims Act provision (31 U.S.C.S. § 3729(a)(1)(A)) for a claim's specific misleading representations. [Universal Health Servs. v. United States (2016) 579 U.S. 176, 136 S. Ct. 1989, 195 L. Ed. 2d 348, 2016 U.S. LEXIS 3920.]

§ 20. Federal jurisdiction

It was held that a Federal District Court retained jurisdiction under the Federal Constitution's Article III, § 2, to adjudicate the claim of an individual who had filed a class action alleging that a company had violated a Telephone Consumer Protection Act provision (47 U.S.C.S. § 227(b)(1)(A)(iii)), but had not yet moved for class certification when he rejected a settlement offer from the company, because an unaccepted settlement offer or offer of judgment did not moot a plaintiff's case. [Campbell-Ewald Co. v. Gomez (2016) 577 U.S. 153, 136 S. Ct. 663, 193 L. Ed. 2d 571, 2016 U.S. LEXIS 846.]

The United States Supreme Court held that it had jurisdiction to decide whether the Supreme Court of Louisiana correctly had refused to give retroactive effect to the decision, in Miller v. Alabama (2012, US) 132 S. Ct. 2455, 183 L. Ed. 2d 407, 2012 U.S. LEXIS 4873, that the Federal Constitution's Eighth Amendment forbade a sentencing scheme that mandated life in prison without the possibility of parole for a juvenile offender. [Montgomery v. Louisiana (2016) 577 U.S. 190, 136 S. Ct. 718, 193 L. Ed. 2d 599, 2016 U.S. LEXIS 862.]

The Supreme Court determined that for purposes of federal-court jurisdiction that was based on diversity of citizenship, the citizenship of a real estate investment trust, which sought to remove from state to federal court an action against the trust, was based on the citizenship of its members, which included its shareholders. [Americold Realty Trust v. ConAgra Foods, Inc. (2016) 577 U.S. 378, 136 S. Ct. 1012, 194 L. Ed. 2d 71, 2016 U.S. LEXIS 1652.]

It was decided that a Federal District Court did not have jurisdiction under § 27 of the Securities Exchange Act 1934 (15 U.S.C.S. § 78aa)—which granted federal courts exclusive jurisdiction "of all suits in equity and actions at law brought to enforce any liability or duty created by [the Act] or the rules and regulations thereunder"—over an action filed against some financial institutions in state court by an entity's former shareholders who alleged that the institutions, which sought to remove the action to federal court, had violated state law by devaluing the entity through "naked short sales" of its stock, as (1) 28 U.S.C.S. § 1331, which granted District Courts jurisdiction of "all civil actions arising under" federal law, did not confer jurisdiction in the case at hand; and (2) the jurisdictional test established by § 27 was the same as § 1331's test for deciding whether a case arose under federal law. [Merrill Lynch, Pierce, Fenner & Smith, Inc. v. Manning (2016) 578 U.S. 374, 136 S. Ct. 1562, 194 L. Ed. 2d 671, 2016 U.S. LEXIS 3049.]

§ 21. Federal Tort Claims Act

The court held that 28 U.S.C.S. § 2676—which provided that a judgment in a 28 U.S.C.S § 1346(b) suit barred a claimant's Federal Tort Claims Act (FTCA) suit, based on same subject matter, against a federal employee whose act or omission gave rise to the claim—did not apply to claims that had been dismissed as 28 U.S.C.S. § 2680 exceptions to FTCA coverage. [Simmons v. Himmelreich (2016) 578 U.S. 621, 136 S. Ct. 1843, 195 L. Ed. 2d 106, 2016 U.S. LEXIS 3613.]

§ 22. Firearms

The Supreme Court determined that reckless domestic assault qualified as a "misdemeanor crime of domestic violence" under 18 U.S.C.S. § 922(g)(9), which prohibited anyone with a conviction for a crime of domestic violence from possessing a firearm. [Voisine v. United States (2016, US) 136 S. Ct. 2272, 195 L. Ed. 2d 736, 2016 U.S. LEXIS 4061.]

§ 23. Health insurance

The Supreme Court, in light of the positions asserted by the parties in their supplemental briefs that had been requested by the Supreme Court—after oral argument concerning the questions whether (1) Department of Health and Human Services (HHS) regulations, interpreting the Patient Protection and Affordable Care Act of 2010 to require specified employers' health insurance plans to cover certain contraceptive methods, violated the Religious Freedom Restoration Act of 1993 (RFRA) (42 U.S.C.S. § 2000bb et seq.) by allegedly forcing religious not-for-profit employers to act in violation of their sincerely held religious beliefs, (2) the alleged availability of a regulatory method for not-for-profit religious employers to comply with HHS' contraceptive mandate eliminated either (a) the asserted substantial burden on religious exercise, or (b) the RFRA violation allegedly recognized in Burwell v. Hobby Lobby Stores, Inc. (2014, US) 134 S. Ct. 2751, 189 L. Ed. 2d 675, 2014 U.S. LEXIS 4505, and (3) HHS satisfied RFRA's test for overriding sincerely held religious objections in circumstances where HHS allegedly insisted that overriding the religious objection would not fulfill HHS' regulatory objective of providing no-cost contraceptives to the objector's employees—vacated the judgments below and remanded to the respective Federal Courts of Appeals, which were instructed to afford the parties on remand an opportunity to arrive at an approach that accommodated petitioners' religious exercise while insuring that women covered by petitioners' health plans received full and equal health coverage, including contraceptive coverage. [Zubik v. Burwell (2016) 578 U.S. 403, 136 S. Ct. 1557, 194 L. Ed. 2d 696, 2016 U.S. LEXIS 3047.]

§ 24. Hobbs Act

The court held that an accused could be convicted of conspiring to violate the Hobbs Act (18 U.S.C.S. § 1951)—which in § 1951(b)(2), defined extortion as involving the consensual obtaining of property "from another"—on the basis of proof that the accused had reached an agreement with the owner of the property in question to obtain that property under color of official right, since proof that the alleged conspirators agreed to obtain property from someone outside the conspiracy was not required. [Ocasio v. United States (2016) 578 U.S. 282, 136 S. Ct. 1423, 194 L. Ed. 2d 520, 2016 U.S. LEXIS 2932.]

The court concluded that the prosecution in a Hobbs Act (18 U.S.C.S. § 1951) robbery case satisfied the Act's interstate-commerce element by introducing evidence that the accused's gang intentionally had targeted drug dealers to obtain drugs and drug proceeds. [Taylor v. United States (2016) 579 U.S. 301, 136 S. Ct. 2074, 195 L. Ed. 2d 456, 2016 U.S. LEXIS 3928.]

§ 25. Immunity from suit

The court held that a police officer was entitled to qualified immunity from a 42 U.S.C.S. § 1983 civil-rights action alleging that he had violated the Federal Constitution's Fourth Amendment by using excessive force in shooting and killing a reportedly intoxicated fugitive—who was fleeing in a motor vehicle at high speed, twice threatened to kill officers, and was racing toward another officer's location before the vehicle reached a spike strip placed on the road—since it was not beyond debate that the officer had acted unreasonably in the unclear border between excessive and acceptable force. [Mullenix v. Luna (2015) 577 U.S. 7, 136 S. Ct. 305, 193 L. Ed. 2d 255, 2015 U.S. LEXIS 7160.]

The Supreme Court decided that a contention by an American passenger, who sued for injury against an Austrian state-owned railway, that her claims were "based upon" the railway's entire railway enterprise, for purposes of 28 U.S.C.S. § 1605(a)(2)'s commercial-activity exception to sovereign immunity, was forfeited because that argument had not been presented to any lower court. [OBB Personenverkehr AG v. Sachs (2015) 577 U.S. 27, 136 S. Ct. 390, 193 L. Ed. 2d 269, 2015 U.S. LEXIS 7670.]

The court concluded that a company's status as a federal contractor did not entitle the company to immunity from suit for its alleged violation of a Telephone Consumer Protection Act provision (47 U.S.C.S. § 227(b)(1)(A)(iii)), because when a federal contractor violated both federal law and the government's explicit instructions, as alleged in the instant case, no immunity shielded the contractor from suit. [Campbell-Ewald Co. v. Gomez (2016) 577 U.S. 153, 136 S. Ct. 663, 193 L. Ed. 2d 571, 2016 U.S. LEXIS 846.]

§ 26. Labor and employment

The Supreme Court held that a Federal District Court properly had certified and maintained a class of employees under Rule 23(b)(3) of the Federal Rules of Civil Procedure and a Fair Labor Standards Act provision (29 U.S.C.S. § 216), where, to support alleged liability and damages, the employees primarily relied on work-time estimates resulting from a study performed by an industrial relations expert. [Tyson Foods, Inc. v. Bouaphakeo (2016) 577 U.S. 442, 136 S. Ct. 1036, 194 L. Ed. 2d 124, 2016 U.S. LEXIS 2134.]

The court held that when a public employer demoted an employee out of a desire to prevent the employee from engaging in protected political activity, the employee was entitled to challenge that unlawful action under the Federal Constitution's First Amendment in a civil rights action under 42 U.S.C.S. § 1983 even if the employer's actions were based on a factual mistake about the employee's behavior. [Heffernan v. City of Paterson (2016) 578 U.S. 266, 136 S. Ct. 1412, 194 L. Ed. 2d 508, 2016 U.S. LEXIS 2924.]

A favorable ruling on the merits in employment-discrimination actions under Title VII of the Civil Rights Act of 1964, 42 U.S.C.S. § 2000e et seq., was not, according to the Supreme Court, a necessary predicate to a finding that a defendant was a prevailing party entitled to an award of attorneys' fees. [CRST Van Expedited, Inc. v. EEOC (2016) 578 U.S. 419, 136 S. Ct. 1642, 194 L. Ed. 2d 707, 2016 U.S. LEXIS 3350.]

The court held that 29 C.F.R. § 1614.105(a)(1)'s 45-day limitations period for initiating a constructive-discharge claim with an Equal Employment Opportunity counselor under Title VII of the

Civil Rights Act of 1964 (42 U.S.C.S. § 2000e et seq.) began when the employee gave notice of the employee's resignation. [Green v. Brennan (2016) 578 U.S. 547, 136 S. Ct. 1769, 195 L. Ed. 2d 44, 2016 U.S. LEXIS 3484.]

It was held that a federal administrative agency's regulation, which was inconsistent with the agency's earlier positions without a reasoned explanation for the departure, was not entitled to deference in deciding whether a car dealership's service advisors were exempt from overtime requirements under 29 U.S.C.S. § 213(b)(10)(A). [Encino Motorcars, LLC v. Navarro (2016) 579 U.S. 211, 136 S. Ct. 2117, 195 L. Ed. 2d 382, 2016 U.S. LEXIS 3924.]

§ 27. —pensions and retirement funds

The court held that when a participant in an Employee Retirement Income Security Act of 1974 (29 U.S.C.S. § 1001 et seq.) plan dissipated a whole settlement on nontraceable items, a plan fiduciary was not allowed to sue to attach the participant's general assets under 29 U.S.C.S. § 1132(a)(3). [Montanile v. Bd. of Trs. of the Nat'l Elevator Indus. Health Ben. Plan (2016) 577 U.S. 136, 136 S. Ct. 651, 193 L. Ed. 2d 556, 2016 U.S. LEXIS 843.]

The Supreme Court decided that some former employees of a corporation and its subsidiary—which employees had participated in plans that qualified under an Employee Retirement Income Security Act of 1974 (ERISA) provision (29 U.S.C.S. § 1107(d)(3)(A)) as eligible individual account plans—failed to state a claim under ERISA (29 U.S.C.S. § 1001 et seq.) for breach of fiduciary duties. [Amgen Inc. v. Harris (2016) 577 U.S. 308, 136 S. Ct. 758, 193 L. Ed. 2d 696, 2016 U.S. LEXIS 891.]

According to the court, the Employee Retirement Income Security Act of 1974 (ERISA) (29 U.S.C.S. § 1001 et seq.), through 29 U.S.C.S. § 1144(a), pre-empted a Vermont health-care-database statute as applied to ERISA plans, since the state statute imposed duties that were inconsistent with ERISA's central design to pro-vide a single uniform national scheme for ERISA administration. [Gobeille v. Liberty Mut. Ins. Co. (2016) 577 U.S. 312, 136 S. Ct. 936, 194 L. Ed. 2d 20, 2016 U.S. LEXIS 1612.]

§ 28. Military veterans

The Supreme Court held that the contracting procedures in 38 U.S.C.S. § 8127(d)—which provided that contracting officers at the Department of Veterans Affairs "shall award" contracts on the basis of competition restricted to small businesses owned by veterans whenever there was a reasonable expectation that two or more such businesses would bid for the contract at a fair and reasonable price that offered best value to the United States—were mandatory and applied to all of the Department's contract determinations. [Kingdomware Techs., Inc. v. United States (2016) 579 U.S. 162, 136 S. Ct. 1969, 195 L. Ed. 2d 334, 2016 U.S. LEXIS 3921.]

§ 29. Native Americans

The court concluded that Indian tribe was not entitled to equitable tolling of the statute of limitations for the filing of Indian Self-Determination and Education Assistance Act (25 U.S.C.S. § 450 et seq.) claims under the Contract Disputes Act (41 U.S.C.S. § 7101 et seq.). [Menominee Indian Tribe v. United States (2016) 577 U.S. 250, 136 S. Ct. 750, 193 L. Ed. 2d 652, 2016 U.S. LEXIS 971.]

The court held that an Alaska National Interest Lands Conservation Act of 1980 provision (16 U.S.C.S. § 3103(c))—which provided: "No lands which, before, on, or after December 2, 1980, are conveyed to the State, to any Native Corporation, or to any private party shall be subject to the regulations applicable solely to public lands within such units"—did not necessarily prohibit the National Park Service from exercising regulatory control over state, native corporation, and private Alaska land located within National Park System boundaries. [Sturgeon v. Frost (2016) 577 U.S. 424, 136 S. Ct. 1061, 194 L. Ed. 2d 108, 2016 U.S. LEXIS 2135.]

The Supreme Court determined that an 1882 federal statute (22 Stat. 341) that authorized the Secretary of the Interior to survey, appraise, and sell roughly 50,000 acres located in the 300,000-acre Omaha Indian Reservation—where an individual purchased a tract under the terms of the statute and established a village on the tract—did not diminish the reservation. [Nebraska v. Parker (2016) 577 U.S. 481, 136 S. Ct. 1072, 194 L. Ed. 2d 152, 2016 U.S. LEXIS 2132.]

§ 30. Patents

It was decided that the 2-part test used by the United States Court of Appeals for the Federal Circuit to determine whether to award enhanced damages under 35 U.S.C.S. § 284 for patent infringement was not consistent with § 284, because the test required a finding of objective recklessness and required that recklessness be proved by clear and convincing evidence, while patent-infringement litigation had always been governed by a preponderance-of-the-evidence standard. [Halo Elecs., Inc. v. Pulse Elecs., Inc. (2016) 579 U.S. 93, 136 S. Ct. 1923, 195 L. Ed. 2d 278, 2016 U.S. LEXIS 3776.]

The court held that (1) 35 U.S.C.S. § 314 barred judicial review of routine claims that involved the Patent and Trademark Office's decision to institute inter partes review; and (2) 37 C.F.R. § 42.100(b), which required the broadest-reasonable-construction standard in patent-claim interpretation, was a reasonable exercise of the Patent and Trademark Office's rulemaking authority. [Cuozzo Speed Techs., LLC v. Lee (2016) 579 U.S. 261, 136 S. Ct. 2131, 195 L. Ed. 2d 423, 2016 U.S. LEXIS 3927.]

§ 31. Prisoners

The court held that 28 U.S.C.S. § 1915(b)(2)—which required federal prisoners who were proceeding in forma pauperis to pay monthly 20 percent of their existing income toward a federal case or appeal's filing fee until satisfying the entire fee—called for simultaneous, not sequential, recoupment of multiple monthly installment payments. [Bruce v. Samuels (2016) 577 U.S. 82, 136 S. Ct. 627, 193 L. Ed. 2d 496, 2016 U.S. LEXIS 620.]

It was held that a Federal Court of Appeals had erred in determining that a state court's denial of a state prisoner's petition for federal habeas corpus relief under 28 U.S.C.S. § 2254 was not on the merits and was therefore subject to de novo, rather than deferential, review, as a presumption—that where the last reasoned opinion on the claim in question explicitly imposed a procedural default, a later decision rejecting the claim was not on the merits—had been amply refuted in the instant case. [Kernan v. Hinojosa (2016) 578 U.S. 412, 136 S. Ct. 1603, 194 L. Ed. 2d 701, 2016 U.S. LEXIS 3051.]

The Supreme Court decided that there was no common-law "special circumstances" exception that relieved a prison inmate of the obligation, under a Prison Litigation Reform Act provision (42 U.S.C.S. § 1997e(a)), to exhaust administrative remedies when (allegedly) the inmate erroneously believed that he had satisfied exhaustion by participating in an internal investigation. [Ross v. Blake (2016) 578 U.S. 632, 136 S. Ct. 1850, 195 L. Ed. 2d 117, 2016 U.S. LEXIS 3614.]

§ 32. Procedural default

According to the Supreme Court, procedural default, because a state criminal defendant's claim could have been raised earlier on direct appeal, of a claim raised for the first time on state collateral review barred federal habeas corpus review of the claim. [Johnson v. Lee (2016) 578 U.S. 605, 136 S. Ct. 1802, 195 L. Ed. 2d 92, 2016 U.S. LEXIS 3488.]

§ 33. Racketeering

The court held that a civil action under a Racketeer Influenced and Corrupt Organizations Act (RICO) provision (18 U.S.C.S. § 1964(c)) by plaintiffs who waived any claims for domestic injuries was not maintainable, because RICO did not apply extraterritorially under § 1964(c). [RJR Nabisco, Inc. v. European Cmty. (2016) 579 U.S. 325, 136 S. Ct. 2090, 195 L. Ed. 2d 476, 2016 U.S. LEXIS 3925.]

§ 34. Search and seizure

The Supreme Court held that in accordance with the attenuation doctrine, an outstanding arrest warrant that was discovered during a federally unconstitutional investigatory stop was a critical intervening circumstance that rendered evidence that a police officer seized incident to the arrest admissible under the Federal Constitution's Fourth Amendment. [Utah v. Strieff (2016) 579 U.S. 232, 136 S. Ct. 2056, 195 L. Ed. 2d 400, 2016 U.S. LEXIS 3926.]

The court held that the Federal Constitution's Fourth Amendment permitted warrantless breath tests, but not warrantless blood tests, incident to lawful arrests for suspected drunk driving. [Birchfield v. North Dakota (2016) 579 U.S. 438, 136 S. Ct. 2160, 195 L. Ed. 2d 560, 2016 U.S. LEXIS 4058.]

§ 35. Sentencing

The United States Supreme Court held that it had jurisdiction to decide whether the Supreme Court of Louisiana correctly had refused to give retroactive effect to the decision, in Miller v. Alabama (2012, US) 132 S. Ct. 2455, 183 L. Ed. 2d 407, 2012 U.S. LEXIS 4873, that the Federal Constitution's Eighth Amendment forbade a sentencing scheme that mandated life in prison without the possibility of parole for a juvenile offender. [Montgomery v. Louisiana (2016) 577 U.S. 190, 136 S. Ct. 718, 193 L. Ed. 2d 599, 2016 U.S. LEXIS 862.]

The court determined that an accused who was convicted of possessing child pornography in violation of 18 U.S.C.S. § 2252(a)(4) was subject to 18 U.S.C.S. § 2252(b)(2)'s mandatory 10-year minimum sentence—which was triggered by, among other matters, prior state convictions for crimes "relating to aggravated sexual abuse, sexual abuse, or abusive sexual conduct involving a minor or ward"—because the accused's prior state-court conviction for first-degree sexual abuse involving his adult girlfriend was encompassed by § 2252(b)(2). [Lockhart v. United States (2016) 577 U.S. 347, 136 S. Ct. 958, 194 L. Ed. 2d 48, 2016 U.S. LEXIS 1611.]

According to the Supreme Court, Johnson v. United States (2015, US) 135 S. Ct.

2551, 192 L. Ed. 2d 569, 2015 U.S. LEXIS 4251—which held that imposing an increased sentence under the residual clause of 18 U.S.C.S. § 924(e)(2)(B) violated the Federal Constitution's Fifth Amendment guarantee of due process—announced a new substantive rule of federal constitutional law that applied retroactively to cases that were on collateral review at the time of that decision. [Welch v. United States (2016) 578 U.S. 120, 136 S. Ct. 1257, 194 L. Ed. 2d 387, 2016 U.S. LEXIS 2451.]

It was held that courts reviewing alleged errors in application of the Federal Sentencing Guidelines (18 U.S.C.S. Appx.) were not allowed to apply a categorical "additional evidence" rule in cases where a Federal District Court had applied an incorrect sentence range but had sentenced the defendant within the correct range. [Molina-Martinez v. United States (2016) 578 U.S. 189, 136 S. Ct. 1338, 194 L. Ed. 2d 444, 2016 U.S. LEXIS 2800.]

The court decided that the speedy-trial clause of the Federal Constitution's Sixth Amendment's did not apply to a 14-month gap between the conviction and sentencing of a defendant who had pleaded guilty to domestic-assault charges, because the guarantee of a speedy trial did not apply once a defendant had been found guilty at trial or had pleaded guilty. [Betterman v. Montana (2016) 578 U.S. 437, 136 S. Ct. 1609, 194 L. Ed. 2d 723, 2016 U.S. LEXIS 3349.]

It was held that a defendant had been improperly sentenced under an Armed Career Criminal Act provision (18 U.S.C.S. § 924(e))—on the basis of a prior state burglary convictions for which elements included unlawful entry into a building, structure, or land, water, or air vehicle—because (1) the alternate means of committing burglary depending on what was entered were broader than the elements of generic burglary, which included only entry into a structure or building; and (2) thus, the defendant's burglary convictions were not predicate crimes under the Act. [Mathis v. United States (2016, US) 136 S. Ct. 2243, 195 L. Ed. 2d 604, 2016 U.S. LEXIS 4060.]

§ 36. —death

The United States Supreme Court held that for purposes of a petition for habeas corpus relief under 28 U.S.C.S. § 2254(d)(1), the Supreme Court of Kentucky had not unreasonably applied clearly established federal law when it concluded that the exclusion of a juror, who gave equivocal answers when asked if he could impose the death penalty if the accused in the instant capital case was convicted, did not violate the Federal Constitution's Sixth Amendment. [White v. Wheeler (2015) 577 U.S. 73, 136 S. Ct. 456, 193 L. Ed. 2d 384, 2015 U.S. LEXIS 7998.]

The court held that a Florida sentencing scheme, which required a judge to determine at a separate hearing whether sufficient aggravating circumstances existed to justify imposing the death penalty, violated the Federal Constitution's Sixth Amendment, because (1) the Sixth Amendment required a jury, not a judge, to find each fact necessary to impose the death penalty; and (2) a jury's mere recommendation was not enough. [Hurst v. Florida (2016) 577 U.S. 92, 136 S. Ct. 616, 193 L. Ed. 2d 504, 2016 U.S. LEXIS 619.]

The court decided that (1) the Federal Constitution's Eighth Amendment— which prohibited cruel and unusual punishments—did not require that a capital-sentencing jury be instructed that mitigating circumstances need not be proved beyond a reasonable doubt; and (2) the Constitution did not require severance of two defendants' joint sentencing proceedings in a state capital case, since (a) the Eighth Amendment was inapposite when a defendant's claim was, at bottom, that evidence improperly had been admitted at a capital-sentencing proceeding, and (b) any allegedly improperly-admitted evidence did not create unfairness that caused imposition of the death penalty to violate due process. [Kansas v. Carr (2016) 577 U.S. 108, 136 S. Ct. 633, 193 L. Ed. 2d 535, 2016 U.S. LEXIS 845.]

The Supreme Court held that a state court, in denying habeas corpus relief sought by a state prisoner who had been convicted of murder and sentenced to death, erred in holding that the prisoner had failed to show purposeful racially discriminatory jury selection where the state had used peremptory challenges to strike all 4 qualified black prospective jurors, as copies of the file used by the prosecution during the prisoner's trial contained (1) the jury venire list on which the names of each black prospective juror were highlighted in bright green, with a legend indicating that the highlighting "represents Blacks"; (2) a draft affidavit comparing black prospective jurors and concluding, "If it comes down to having to pick one of the black jurors, [this one] might be okay"; (3) notes identifying black prospective jurors as "B" with numbers; (4) notes with "N" (for "no") appearing next to the names of all black prospective jurors; (5) a list titled "[D]efinite NO's" containing 6 names, including the names of all of the qualified black prospective jurors; and (6) questionnaires filled out by 5 prospective black jurors, on which each juror's response indicating his or her race had been circled. [Foster v. Chatman (2016) 578 U.S. 488, 136 S. Ct. 1737, 195 L. Ed. 2d 1, 2016 U.S. LEXIS 3486]

According to the Supreme Court, a state criminal defendant was entitled to a jury instruction that the defendant's only alternative sentence to death was life imprisonment without possibility of parole, where the state had suggested, during the penalty phase of the defendant's trial, that the defendant could be dangerous. [Lynch v. Arizona (2016) 578 U.S. 613, 136 S. Ct. 1818, 195 L. Ed. 2d 99, 2016 U.S. LEXIS 3487.]

The refusal by an appellate judge—who, as district attorney, had approved a request to seek the death penalty for an accused—to recuse himself from review of the accused's death sentence was held (1) to violated the due process clause of the Federal Constitution's Fourteenth Amendment; and (2) not to be amenable to harmless-error review, regardless of whether the judge's vote to reinstate the sentence was dispositive. [Williams v. Pennsylvania (2016) 579 U.S. 1, 136 S. Ct. 1899, 195 L. Ed. 2d 132, 2016 U.S. LEXIS 3774.]

§ 37. Separation of powers

The Supreme Court held that § 502 of the Iran Threat Reduction and Syria Human Rights Act of 2012 (22 U.S.C.S. § 8772), which (allegedly) effectively directed a particular result in a single pending federal case, did not violate the separation of powers between the federal legislative and judicial branches under the Federal Constitution's Article III. [Bank Markazi v. Peterson (2016) 578 U.S. 212, 136 S. Ct. 1310, 194 L. Ed. 2d 463, 2016 U.S. LEXIS 2799.]

§ 38. Sex-offender registration

The court decided that a Sex Offender Registration and Notification Act provision (42 U.S.C.S. § 16913(a)) did not require a sex offender who resided in a foreign country to update the offender's registration in the American jurisdiction where the offender formerly resided. [Nichols v. United States (2016) 578 U.S. 104, 136 S. Ct. 1113, 194 L. Ed. 2d 324, 2016 U.S. LEXIS 2276.]

§ 39. Standing to sue

With respect to the question whether Congress had authority to confer standing under the Federal Constitution's Article III upon a plaintiff (who allegedly had suffered no concrete harm and, therefore, could not otherwise invoke the jurisdiction of a federal court) by authorizing a private right of action assertedly based on a bare violation of a federal statute—the Supreme Court vacated a Federal Court of Appeals' judgment and remanded the case for further proceedings, because the Court of Appeals' Article III standing analysis was incomplete, since the Court of Appeals had failed to consider the concreteness aspect of the injury-in-fact requirement. [Spokeo, Inc. v. Robins (2016) 578 U.S. 330, 136 S. Ct. 1540, 194 L. Ed. 2d 635, 2016 U.S. LEXIS 3046.]

§ 40. Sufficiency of evidence

The court concluded that (1) a sufficiency-of-the-evidence challenge had to be assessed against the elements of the charged crime rather than the elements set forth in an erroneous jury instruction; and (2) an accused could not successfully raise the statute of limitations bar under 18 U.S.C.S. § 3282(a) for the first time on appeal. [Musacchio v. United States (2016) 577 U.S. 237, 136 S. Ct. 709, 193 L. Ed. 2d 639, 2016 U.S. LEXIS 972.]

ANNOTATION

Supreme Court's views as to application or applicability of doctrine of qualified immunity in action under 42 U.S.C.S. § 1983, or in Bivens action, seeking damages for alleged civil rights violations involving law enforcement activities or treatment of prisoners

by

Gary Knapp, M.B.A., J.D.

TABLE OF CONTENTS

OUTLINE OF ANNOTATION

B. State and Local Actors

§ 7. Entitled to immunity
§ 8. Issue not decided

III. Treatment of Prisoners

§ 9. Entitled to immunity
§ 10. Not entitled to immunity
§ 11. Issue not decided

RESEARCH REFERENCES

Annotations

See the related annotations listed in § 1[b].

Federal Statutes, Constitution, and Court Rules

U.S.C.S., Constitution, Amendments 1, 4, 5, 8, 14; 42 U.S.C.S. § 1983

Encyclopedias, Treatises, and Specialized Services

5 Antieau on Local Government Law § 77.04 (Matthew Bender 2d ed.)

1 Civil Rights Actions ¶¶ 2A.01, 2A.04, 2A.06, 2A.07 (Matthew Bender)

Digests and Indexes

L Ed Digest, Civil Rights § 32.5; Public Officers § 56; Search and Seizure § 32; United States § 107.3

L Ed Index, Qualified Immunity

SHEPARD'S® Citations Service. For further research of authorities referenced here, use SHEPARD'S to be sure your case or statute is still good law and to find additional authorities that support your position. SHEPARD'S is available exclusively from LexisNexis®.

Electronic Search Query

(qualified immunity) and (1983 or Bivens)

Law Review Articles

Magun, A Changing Landscape for Pretrial Detainees? The Potential Impact of Kingsley v. Hendrickson on Jail-Suicide Litigation. 116 Colum. L. Rev. 2059 (December, 2016).

Shannon, Reasonableness as Corrections Reform in Kingsley v. Hendrickson. 62 Loy. L. Rev. 577 (Summer, 2016).

Kinports, The Supreme Court's Quiet Expansion of Qualified Immunity. 100 Minn. L. Rev. Headnotes 62 (2016).

Dawson, Qualified Immunity for Officers' Reasonable Reliance on Lawyers' Advice. 110 Nw. U.L. Rev. 525 (2016).

Nielson and Walker, The New Qualified Immunity. 89 S. Cal. L. Rev. 1 (November, 2015).

Gross, Judge, Jury, and Executioner: The Excessive Use of Deadly Force by Police Officers. 21 Tex. J. on C.L. & C.R. 155 (Spring, 2016).

Grosst, Unguided Missiles: Why the Supreme Court Should Prohibit Police Officers from Shooting at Moving Vehicles. 163 U. Pa. L. Rev. Online 135 (2016).

TABLE OF CASES

Hunter v. Bryant (1991) 502 U.S. 224, 112 S. Ct. 534, 116 L. Ed. 2d 589, 1991
    U.S. LEXIS 7262—§§ 3, 5

Kingsley v. Hendrickson (2015) 576 U.S. 389, 135 S. Ct. 2466, 192 L. Ed. 2d
    416, 2015 U.S. LEXIS 4073—§§ 3, 11

Kisela v. Hughes (2018) 584 U.S. ___, 138 S. Ct. 1148, 200 L. Ed. 2d 449, 2018
    U.S. LEXIS 2066—§§ 3, 7

Malley v. Briggs (1986) 475 U.S. 335, 106 S. Ct. 1092, 89 L. Ed. 2d 271, 1986
    U.S. LEXIS 29—§§ 3, 8

Messerschmidt v. Millender (2012) 565 U.S. 535, 132 S. Ct. 1235, 182 L. Ed.
    2d 47, 2012 U.S. LEXIS 1687—§§ 3, 7

Mitchell v. Forsyth (1985) 472 U.S. 511, 105 S. Ct. 2806, 86 L. Ed. 2d 411,
    1985 U.S. LEXIS 113—§§ 3, 4

Mullenix v. Luna (2015) 577 U.S. ___, 136 S. Ct. 305, 193 L. Ed. 2d 255, 2015
    U.S. LEXIS 7160—§§ 3, 7

Pearson v. Callahan (2009) 555 U.S. 223, 129 S. Ct. 808, 172 L. Ed. 2d 565,
    2009 U.S. LEXIS 591—§§ 2[b], 3, 7

Plumhoff v. Rickard (2014) 572 U.S. 765, 134 S. Ct. 2012, 188 L. Ed. 2d 1056,
    2014 U.S. LEXIS 3816—§§ 3, 7

Procunier v. Navarette (1978) 434 U.S. 555, 98 S. Ct. 855, 55 L. Ed. 2d 24,
    1978 U.S. LEXIS 60—§ 9

Reichle v. Howards (2012) 566 U.S. 658, 132 S. Ct. 2088, 182 L. Ed. 2d 985,
    2012 U.S. LEXIS 4132—§§ 3, 5

Ryburn v. Huff (2012) 565 U.S. 469, 132 S. Ct. 987, 181 L. Ed. 2d 966, 2012
    U.S. LEXIS 910—§ 7

Saucier v. Katz (2001) 533 U.S. 194, 121 S. Ct. 2151, 150 L. Ed. 2d 272, 2001
    U.S. LEXIS 4664—§§ 3, 6[a]

Scott v. Harris (2007) 550 U.S. 372, 127 S. Ct. 1769, 167 L. Ed. 2d 686, 2007
    U.S. LEXIS 4748—§ 2[b]

Stanton v. Sims (2013) 571 U.S. 3, 134 S. Ct. 3, 187 L. Ed. 2d 341, 2013 U.S.
    LEXIS 7773—§§ 3, 7

Taylor v. Barkes (2015) 575 U.S. 822, 135 S. Ct. 2042, 192 L. Ed. 2d 78, 2015
    U.S. LEXIS 3715—§§ 3, 9

Taylor v. Riojas (2020) 592 U.S. ___, 141 S. Ct. ___, 208 L. Ed. 2d 164, 2020
    U.S. LEXIS 5193—§ 10

Tolan v. Cotton (2014) 572 U.S. 650, 134 S. Ct. 1861, 188 L. Ed. 2d 895, 2014
    U.S. LEXIS 3112—§§ 3, 8

Van de Kamp v. Goldstein (2009) 555 U.S. 335, 129 S. Ct. 855, 172 L. Ed. 2d
    706, 2009 U.S. LEXIS 10—§ 1[a]

White v. Pauly (2017) 580 U.S. ___, 137 S. Ct. 548, 196 L. Ed. 2d 463, 2017
    U.S. LEXIS 5—§§ 3, 7

Wilson v. Layne (1999) 526 U.S. 603, 119 S. Ct. 1692, 143 L. Ed. 2d 818, 1999
    U.S. LEXIS 3633—§§ 3, 4, 6[a], 7

Wood v. Moss (2014) 572 U.S. 744, 134 S. Ct. 2056, 188 L. Ed. 2d 1039, 2014
U.S. LEXIS 3614—§§ 3, 5

Ziglar v. Abbasi (2017) 582 U.S. ___, 137 S. Ct. 1843, 198 L. Ed. 2d 290, 2017
U.S. LEXIS 3874—§ 9

I. Preliminary and General Matters

§ 1. Introduction

[a] Scope

This annotation.[1] collects and analyzes the cases in which the United States
Supreme Court made determinations concerning the application or applicability of the doctrine of qualified immunity in actions under 42 U.S.C.S. § 1983,[2]
or in a Bivens action,[3] seeking damages for alleged civil rights violations
involving law enforcement activities or the treatment of prisoners. This annotation does not cover qualified immunity in cases not involving law enforcement activities or the treatment of prisoners[4] or the questions whether (1) the
asserted federal rights existed, and, if so, had been violated by the defendants
claiming qualified immunity; (2) the defendants were entitled to absolute immunity;[5] or (3) a superior officer or government entity might be vicariously liable for the alleged misconduct of a subordinate.[6]

[b] Related annotations

When does local government or local governmental agency become liable,
under 42 U.S.C.S. § 1983, for alleged violation of civil rights—Supreme Court
cases. 178 L. Ed. 2d 905.

---

1. This annotation supersedes § 7 of the annotation at 116 L. Ed. 2d 965.
2. For the text of 42 U.S.C.S. § 1983, see § 1[c], infra.
3. For purposes of this annotation, a "Bivens" action refers to an implied damages
action for a federal agent's alleged violation of an individual's rights under federal law.
The term is derived from the Supreme Court's holding in Bivens v. Six Unknown
Named Agents of Federal Bureau of Narcotics (1971) 403 U.S. 388, 91 S. Ct. 1999, 29
L. Ed. 2d 619, 1971 U.S. LEXIS 23, that a violation of the Federal Constitution's
Fourth Amendment by a federal agent acting under color of the agent's authority
would give rise to a cause of action for damages consequent upon the agent's
unconstitutional conduct.
4. As to qualified immunity in cases not involving law enforcement activities or
treatment of prisoners, see the annotation at 116 L. Ed. 2d 965.
5. As to absolute prosecutorial immunity from liability for damages for alleged violations of civil rights, see the annotation at 172 L. Ed. 2d 905.
6. As to a state or federal officer's unconstitutional conduct affecting governmental
immunity from suit in a federal court, see the annotation at 12 L. Ed. 2d 1110. For a
case involving asserted supervisory responsibility for subordinates' alleged civil-rights
violations, see, for example, Van de Kamp v. Goldstein (2009) 555 U.S. 335, 129 S. Ct.
855, 172 L. Ed. 2d 706, 2009 U.S. LEXIS 10, in which the Supreme Court held that a
former district attorney and a deputy district attorney were entitled to absolute immunity from a 42 U.S.C.S. § 1983 action asserting that supervision, training, or
information-system management that they provided was constitutionally inadequate.

Supreme Court's views as to extent of prosecutorial immunity from liability for damages for alleged violations of civil rights. 172 L. Ed. 2d 905.

Supreme Court's views as to extent, under Federal Constitution, of privileges and immunities of United States President or former President, by reason of that office, as to judicial proceedings or process. 137 L. Ed. 2d 1135.

Validity, construction, and application of 18 U.S.C.S. §§ 241 and 242 (and similar predecessor provisions), providing criminal liability for conspiring to deprive, or depriving, person of civil rights—Supreme Court cases. 137 L. Ed. 2d 1091.

When will private right of action for damages ([93]Bivens&cdquot; action) be implied from provision of Federal Constitution—Supreme Court cases. 127 L. Ed. 2d 715.

Supreme Court's views as to application or applicability of doctrine of qualified immunity in action under 42 U.S.C.S. § 1983, or in Bivens action, seeking damages for alleged civil rights violations. 116 L. Ed. 2d 965.

Supreme Court's views as to who is "person" under civil rights statute (42 U.S.C.S. § 1983) providing private right of action for violation of federal rights. 105 L. Ed. 2d 721.

Supreme Court's views as to when person is acting "under color of" state law, within meaning of civil rights statute (42 U.S.C.S. § 1983) providing private right of action for violation of federal rights. 101 L. Ed. 2d 987.

Supreme Court's views as to measure or elements of damages recoverable in federal civil rights action under 42 U.S.C.S. § 1983. 91 L. Ed. 2d 647.

Supreme Court's construction of Civil Rights Act of 1871 (42 U.S.C.S. § 1983) providing private right of action for violation of federal rights. 43 L. Ed. 2d 833.

Unconstitutional conduct by state or federal officer as affecting governmental immunity from suit in federal court—Supreme Court cases. 12 L. Ed. 2d 1110.

[c] Text of § 1983

The text of 42 U.S.C.S. § 1983 provides as follows:

§ 1983. Civil action for deprivation of rights

Every person who, under color of any statute, ordinance, regulation, custom, or usage, of any State or Territory or the District of Columbia, subjects, or causes to be subjected, any citizen of the United States or other person within the jurisdiction thereof to the deprivation of any rights, privileges, or immunities secured by the Constitution and laws, shall be liable to the party injured in an action at law, suit in equity, or other proper proceeding for redress, except that in any action brought against a judicial officer for an act or omission taken in such officer's judicial capacity, injunctive relief shall not be granted unless a declaratory decree was violated or declaratory relief was unavailable. For the purposes of this section, any Act of Congress applicable exclusively to the District of Columbia shall be considered to be a statute of the District of Columbia.

§ 2. Background, summary, and comment

[a] Generally

Although liability under 42 U.S.C.S. § 1983 may be restricted by § 1983's limitation to action under color of state law, the Supreme Court, pursuant to its leading decision in Bivens v. Six Unknown Named Agents of Federal Bureau of Narcotics (1971) 403 U.S. 388, 91 S. Ct. 1999, 29 L. Ed. 2d 619, 1971 U.S. LEXIS 23, has established that, even in the absence of federal legislation expressly creating a cause of action, a damages action may be brought against federal agents for at least some alleged violations of federal rights. Also, the court has established an objective test under which government officials performing discretionary functions generally are entitled to qualified immunity from liability in § 1983 and Bivens actions insofar as such officials' challenged conduct does not violate clearly established federal statutory or constitutional rights of which a reasonable person would have known at the time of the challenged conduct (§ 3, infra).

As to Bivens actions against federal law enforcement officers, the Supreme Court held (1) in cases involving a federal attorney, that the attorney was entitled to qualified immunity (§ 4, infra); and (2) in cases involving Secret Service agents, that the agents were entitled to qualified immunity (§ 5, infra). As to other federal law enforcement officers, the court (1) held the officers in question were entitled to qualified immunity in some circumstances (§ 6[a], infra), but not in other circumstances (§ 6[b], infra); and (2) in remanding a case for determination whether a particular officer was entitled to qualified immunity, said that a Federal Court of Appeals had misapplied the principles of qualified immunity in the case (§ 6[c], infra).

With respect to § 1983 actions against state or local law enforcement officers, the Supreme Court (1) in particular circumstances, decided that the officers in question were entitled to qualified immunity (§ 7, infra); and (2) in other circumstances, made holdings concerning qualified immunity without determining whether the officers in question were entitled to such immunity (§ 8, infra).

In cases involving § 1983 actions alleging violations of federal rights in regard to the treatment of prisoners, the Supreme Court held that (1) prison officers were entitled to qualified immunity in some circumstances (§ 9, infra); but (2) prison officers were not entitled to qualified immunity, at the summary-judgment stage, in other circumstances (§ 10, infra). In other § 1983 or Bivens actions involving the treatment of prisoners, the court made holdings with respect to qualified immunity without deciding whether the officers in question were entitled to such immunity (§ 11, infra).

[b] Practice pointers

Counsel representing a client being sued under 42 U.S.C.S. § 1983 or in a Bivens action may be able to defend successfully the client without addressing the issue of qualified immunity by showing that the client's conduct in question did not violate a federal constitutional right. See, for example, Scott v. Harris (2007) 550 U.S. 372, 127 S. Ct. 1769, 167 L. Ed. 2d 686, 2007 U.S. LEXIS 4748, in which the Supreme Court said that in resolving questions of qualified immunity, courts were required to resolve a threshold question as to whether, taken in the light most favorable to the party asserting the injury, did the facts alleged show that an officer's conduct violated a federal constitutional right. According to the Supreme Court in Scott v. Harris, (1) this had to be the initial inquiry; and (2) only if a court found a violation of such a right, the next, sequential step was to ask whether the right was clearly established in light of the specific context of the case. However, see also, for example, Pearson v. Callahan (2009) 555 U.S. 223, 129 S. Ct. 808, 172 L. Ed. 2d 565, 2009 U.S. LEXIS 591, in which the Supreme Court, on reconsidering, determined that (1) while the two-step sequence was often appropriate, it should no longer be regarded as mandatory; and (2) the judges of the Federal District Courts and the Federal Courts of Appeals should be permitted to exercise their sound discretion in deciding which of the two prongs of the qualified immunity analysis should be addressed first in light of the circumstances in the particular case at hand.

§ 3. Clearly established rights of which reasonable person would have known

The following Supreme Court cases, involving claims with respect to law enforcement activities or the treatment of prisoners, support application of an objective test under which government officials performing discretionary functions generally are entitled to qualified immunity from liability in 42 U.S.C.S. § 1983 and Bivens actions insofar as such officials' challenged conduct does not violate clearly established federal statutory or constitutional rights of which a reasonable person would have known at the time of the challenged conduct: Mitchell v. Forsyth (1985) 472 U.S. 511, 105 S. Ct. 2806, 86 L. Ed. 2d 411, 1985 U.S. LEXIS 113; Cleavinger v. Saxner (1985) 474 U.S. 193, 106 S. Ct. 496, 88 L. Ed. 2d 507, 1985 U.S. LEXIS 148; Malley v. Briggs (1986) 475 U.S. 335, 106 S. Ct. 1092, 89 L. Ed. 2d 271, 1986 U.S. LEXIS 29; Anderson v. Creighton (1987) 483 U.S. 635, 107 S. Ct. 3034, 97 L. Ed. 2d 523, 1987 U.S. LEXIS 2894; Hunter v. Bryant (1991) 502 U.S. 224, 112 S. Ct. 534, 116 L. Ed. 2d 589, 1991 U.S. LEXIS 7262; Elder v. Holloway (1994) 510 U.S. 510, 114 S. Ct. 1019, 127 L. Ed. 2d 344, 1994 U.S. LEXIS 1865; Conn v. Gabbert (1999) 526 U.S. 286, 119 S. Ct. 1292, 143 L. Ed. 2d 399, 1999 U.S. LEXIS 2345; Wilson v. Layne (1999) 526 U.S. 603, 119 S. Ct. 1692, 143 L. Ed. 2d 818, 1999 U.S. LEXIS 3633; Hanlon v. Berger (1999) 526 U.S. 808, 119 S. Ct. 1706, 143 L. Ed. 2d 978, 1999 U.S. LEXIS 3634; Saucier v. Katz (2001) 533 U.S. 194, 121 S. Ct. 2151, 150 L. Ed. 2d 272, 2001 U.S. LEXIS 4664; Hope v. Pelzer (2002) 536 U.S. 730, 122 S. Ct. 2508, 153 L. Ed. 2d 666, 2002 U.S. LEXIS

4884; Groh v. Ramirez (2004) 540 U.S. 551, 124 S. Ct. 1284, 157 L. Ed. 2d 1068, 2004 U.S. LEXIS 1624; Brosseau v. Haugen (2004) 543 U.S. 194, 125 S. Ct. 596, 160 L. Ed. 2d 583, 2004 U.S. LEXIS 8275; Pearson v. Callahan (2009) 555 U.S. 223, 129 S. Ct. 808, 172 L. Ed. 2d 565, 2009 U.S. LEXIS 591; Camreta v. Greene (2011) 563 U.S. 692, 131 S. Ct. 2020, 179 L. Ed. 2d 1118, 2011 U.S. LEXIS 4016; Ashcroft v. al-Kidd (2011) 563 U.S. 731, 131 S. Ct. 2074, 179 L. Ed. 2d 1149, 2011 U.S. LEXIS 4021; Messerschmidt v. Millender (2012) 565 U.S. 535, 132 S. Ct. 1235, 182 L. Ed. 2d 47, 2012 U.S. LEXIS 1687; Reichle v. Howards (2012) 566 U.S. 658, 132 S. Ct. 2088, 182 L. Ed. 2d 985, 2012 U.S. LEXIS 4132; Stanton v. Sims (2013) 571 U.S. 3, 134 S. Ct. 3, 187 L. Ed. 2d 341, 2013 U.S. LEXIS 7773; Tolan v. Cotton (2014) 572 U.S. 650, 134 S. Ct. 1861, 188 L. Ed. 2d 895, 2014 U.S. LEXIS 3112; Wood v. Moss (2014) 572 U.S. 744, 134 S. Ct. 2056, 188 L. Ed. 2d 1039, 2014 U.S. LEXIS 3614; Plumhoff v. Rickard (2014) 572 U.S. 765, 134 S. Ct. 2012, 188 L. Ed. 2d 1056, 2014 U.S. LEXIS 3816; Carroll v. Carman (2014) 574 U.S. 13, 135 S. Ct. 348, 190 L. Ed. 2d 311, 2014 U.S. LEXIS 7430; City & Cnty. of San Francisco v. Sheehan (2015) 575 U.S. 600, 135 S. Ct. 1765, 191 L. Ed. 2d 856, 2015 U.S. LEXIS 3200; Taylor v. Barkes (2015) 575 U.S. 822, 135 S. Ct. 2042, 192 L. Ed. 2d 78, 2015 U.S. LEXIS 3715; Kingsley v. Hendrickson (2015) 576 U.S. 389, 135 S. Ct. 2466, 192 L. Ed. 2d 416, 2015 U.S. LEXIS 4073; Mullenix v. Luna (2015) 577 U.S. ___, 136 S. Ct. 305, 193 L. Ed. 2d 255, 2015 U.S. LEXIS 7160; White v. Pauly (2017) 580 U.S. ___, 137 S. Ct. 548, 196 L. Ed. 2d 463, 2017 U.S. LEXIS 5; Hernandez v. Mesa (2017) 582 U.S. ___, 137 S. Ct. 2003, 198 L. Ed. 2d 625, 2017 U.S. LEXIS 4059; District of Columbia v. Wesby (2018) 583 U.S. ___, 138 S. Ct. 577, 199 L. Ed. 2d 453, 2018 U.S. LEXIS 760; Kisela v. Hughes (2018) 584 U.S. ___, 138 S. Ct. 1148, 200 L. Ed. 2d 449, 2018 U.S. LEXIS 2066; and City of Escondido v. Emmons (2019) 586 U.S. ___, 139 S. Ct. 500, 202 L. Ed. 2d 455, 2019 U.S. LEXIS 11.

Thus, in Wilson v. Layne (1999) 526 U.S. 603, 119 S. Ct. 1692, 143 L. Ed. 2d 818, 1999 U.S. LEXIS 3633, infra §§ 6[a] and 7, which involved a "media ride-along" during an attempt to execute arrest warrants, the Supreme Court said that under both Bivens and 42 U.S.C.S. § 1983, a plaintiff was allowed to seek money damages from government officials who had violated the plaintiff's rights under the Federal Constitution's Fourth Amendment. However, the court further indicated that government officials performing discretionary functions generally were granted qualified immunity that shielded them from liability for civil damages under Bivens and § 1983 insofar as the officials' conduct did not violate clearly established federal statutory or constitutional rights of which a reasonable person would have known. According to the court, the qualified immunity analysis was identical under either cause of action.

Where the Supreme Court held that a warrant to search a family's house was invalid, and a search of the house pursuant to the warrant, by a team of federal and local law enforcement officers led by an agent of the (then) United States Bureau of Alcohol, Tobacco and Firearms, was clearly unreasonable, in violation of the Federal Constitution's Fourth Amendment, in Groh v.

Ramirez (2004) 540 U.S. 551, 124 S. Ct. 1284, 157 L. Ed. 2d 1068, 2004 U.S. LEXIS 1624, infra § 6[b], the court concluded that, even though the warrant indicated that a Federal Magistrate Judge had found probable cause to conduct the search, the agent was not entitled to qualified immunity from the Bivens suit brought by the family against the agent, because (1) the agent's entitlement to qualified immunity depended on whether the right that had been transgressed had been clearly established at the time in question, that is, whether it would have been clear to a reasonable officer that the officer's conduct was unlawful in the situation confronted by the officer; and (2) the warrant in question was so facially deficient, in failing to particularize the place to be searched or the things to be seized, that the executing officers could not reasonably have presumed the warrant to be valid.

In Mullenix v. Luna (2015) 577 U.S. ___, 136 S. Ct. 305, 193 L. Ed. 2d 255, 2015 U.S. LEXIS 7160, infra § 7, which involved a 42 U.S.C.S. § 1983 claim of excessive force, the Supreme Court, with respect to the doctrine of qualified immunity shielding government officials from civil liability so long as their conduct did not violate a clearly established federal statutory or constitutional right of which a reasonable person would have known, said that a clearly established right was one that was sufficiently clear so that every reasonable official would have understood that what the official was doing violated that right. According to the Supreme Court, qualified immunity protected all but the plainly incompetent or those who knowingly violated the law. Indicating that courts were not to define clearly established law at a high level of generality, the Supreme Court noted that the dispositive question was whether the violative nature of particular conduct was clearly established. The court said that the inquiry had to be undertaken in light of the specific context of each case, and that such specificity was especially important in the context of the Federal Constitution's Fourth Amendment.

Stating, in City of Escondido v. Emmons (2019) 586 U.S. ___, 139 S. Ct. 500, 202 L. Ed. 2d 455, 2019 U.S. LEXIS 11, infra §§ 7, 8, that qualified immunity in a 42 U.S.C.S. § 1983 action attached when the conduct of the public official in question did not violate clearly established statutory or constitutional rights of which a reasonable person would have known, the Supreme Court added, with respect to the Federal Constitution's Fourth Amendment, that such a clearly established right had to be defined with specificity, particularly in excessive-force cases. According to the court, it was sometimes difficult for an officer to determine how the relevant legal doctrine would apply to a particular situation, and the answer to this question depended very much on the facts of each case. Observing that police officers were entitled to qualified immunity unless existing precedent squarely governed the specific facts at issue, the Supreme Court said that it did not suffice for a court simply to state that an officer was not allowed to not use unreasonable and excessive force, to deny qualified immunity, and then to remit the case for a trial on the question of reasonableness. The Supreme Court said that it had stressed the need to identify a case where an officer acting under similar circumstances had been held to have violated the Fourth Amendment. It was observed that while there did not have to be a case directly on point, existing precedent had to place the lawfulness of the particular action beyond debate. The court noted that (1) there could be the rare obvious case where the unlawfulness of an officer's conduct was sufficiently clear even though existing precedent did not address similar circumstances; but (2) a body of relevant case law was usually necessary to clearly establish the answer.

II. Law Enforcement Activities

A. Federal Actors

§ 4. Attorneys

In the following cases, the Supreme Court decided that a federal attorney was entitled to qualified immunity in a Bivens action seeking damages for the attorney's alleged violation of federal civil rights in regard to a law enforcement activity.

According to the Supreme Court in Mitchell v. Forsyth (1985) 472 U.S. 511, 105 S. Ct. 2806, 86 L. Ed. 2d 411, 1985 U.S. LEXIS 113, a Federal District Court had erroneously denied a former United States Attorney General summary judgment on the ground of qualified immunity from damages liability for a Bivens claim that the Attorney General's November 1970 authorization of a warrantless wiretap of a telephone on domestic security grounds had violated the Federal Constitution's Fourth Amendment guarantee against unreasonable searches and seizures. The Supreme Court reasoned that, even though the doctrine of executive authority to conduct such wiretaps had not long survived the expiration of the wiretap in question, it did not follow that the authorization in question had violated law that was clearly established at the time. The Supreme Court reversed a Federal Court of Appeals' judgment to the extent that the effect of that judgment was to leave standing the District Court's qualified immunity decision. The record showed that the wiretap had been installed shortly after the authorization and had stayed in place until January 1971, during which time the government had intercepted several conversations between the wiretap's subject and the plaintiff. The Supreme Court decided that the District Court's handling of the case precluded any suggestion that the wiretap had been authorized for (1) criminal investigatory purposes, or (2) some purpose unrelated to national security. While referring to a holding in a 1972 Supreme Court case that wiretaps aimed at gathering intelligence regarding a domestic threat to national security were unconstitutional, the Supreme Court reasoned that the decisive fact in the case at hand was not that the Attorney General's position had turned out to be incorrect, but that the question had been open when he had acted, where (1) as of November 1970, the Justice Departments of six successive administrations had considered warrantless, domestic security wiretaps to be constitutional, and two Federal District Courts had accepted that position; (2) in 1967, the Supreme Court had expressly left open the possibility that the Justice Department's view was correct; (3) although a 1968 federal statute had attempted to fashion wiretapping rules meeting constitutional requirements, Congress had expressly disclaimed any attempt to limit the President's national-security wiretapping powers; and (4) in the 1972 case, the Supreme Court had (a) found the issue sufficiently doubtful to warrant the exercise of the court's discretionary jurisdiction, and (b) explicitly recognized that the question was one that had yet to receive the definitive answer that the question demanded. While the court added that it did not intend to suggest that an official was always immune from liability for a warrantless search merely because the warrant requirement had never explicitly been held to apply to a search conducted in identical circumstances, the court said that, in cases where there was a legitimate question whether an exception to the warrant requirement existed, it could not be said that a warrantless search violated clearly established law.

In Hanlon v. Berger (1999) 526 U.S. 808, 119 S. Ct. 1706, 143 L. Ed. 2d 978, 1999 U.S. LEXIS 3634, the Supreme Court determined that an assistant United States attorney was entitled to qualified immunity from damages liability in a Bivens action brought against the attorney for asserted violation of the Federal Constitution's Fourth Amendment with respect to news media representatives' allegedly accompanying federal agents during the agents' execution of a search warrant at a ranch, as (1) the Supreme Court's holding in Wilson v. Layne (1999) 526 U.S. 603, 119 S. Ct. 1692, 143 L. Ed. 2d 818, 1999 U.S. LEXIS 3633 (decided on same day as the case at hand), infra § 6[a], made it clear that the Fourth Amendment's prohibition of the taking by the police of media representatives or other third parties into a home during the execution of a warrant when the presence of the third parties in the home was not in aid of execution of the warrant was not clearly established at the time of the search in question in Wilson; and (2) the parties in the case at hand had not called the Supreme Court's attention to any decisions that would have made the relevant law any clearer about a year later at the time of the search in question in the case at hand, which involved a multiple-vehicle caravan consisting of government agents and a crew of photographers and reporters from a cable news network, where the agents had executed the search warrant while accompanied by the media crew, which had observed the officers and had recorded the officers' conduct in executing the warrant. A judgment against defendants including the attorney was vacated, and the case was remanded.

The Supreme Court determined in Ashcroft v. al-Kidd (2011) 563 U.S. 731, 131 S. Ct. 2074, 179 L. Ed. 2d 1149, 2011 U.S. LEXIS 4021, that a former Attorney General of the United States was entitled to qualified immunity from a Bivens action brought by a former detainee who alleged that, after the September 11, 2001, terrorist attacks, the then-Attorney General had unconstitutionally authorized federal officials to detain terrorism suspects using a federal material-witness statute (18 U.S.C.S. § 3144), where the detainee asserted that this detention policy was a pretext that had led to his material-witness arrest as he was boarding a plane to Saudi Arabia. The court reversed a judgment that had upheld the Attorney General's motion to dismiss on grounds of absolute and qualified immunity, as the court said that the objectively reasonable arrest and detention of the detainee pursuant to a validly obtained warrant could not be challenged under the Federal Constitution's Fourth Amendment as being unconstitutional on the basis of allegations that arresting authority had an improper motive. The detainee remained in federal custody for 16 days and on supervised release until a terrorism suspect's trial concluded 14 months later. However, prosecutors never called the detainee as a witness. Rejecting the view that "programmatic purpose" was relevant to Fourth Amendment analysis of programs of seizures without probable cause, the court said that (1) the existence of a judicial warrant based on individualized suspicion took the case outside the domain of suspicionless intrusions pursuant to a general scheme; and (2) because the detainee conceded that individualized suspicion supported the issuance of the material-witness arrest warrant, and he did not assert that his arrest would have been unconstitutional absent the alleged pretextual use of the warrant, there was no Fourth Amendment violation. According to the court, (1) at the time of the detainee's arrest, not a single judicial opinion had held that pretext could render an objectively reasonable arrest pursuant to a material-witness warrant unconstitutional; and (2) the Attorney General deserved qualified immunity even if it was assumed, contrafactually, that his alleged detention policy violated the Fourth Amendment.

§ 5. Secret Service agents

Secret Service agents involved in the following cases were held by the Supreme Court to be entitled to qualified immunity in Bivens actions seeking damages for alleged violations of federal civil rights.

With respect to an individual's Bivens claim for damages against two United States Secret Service agents, to the effect that the agents' arrest of the individual for threatening the President of the United States had violated the Federal Constitution's Fourth Amendment due to an alleged lack of probable cause, the Supreme Court held in Hunter v. Bryant (1991) 502 U.S. 224, 112 S. Ct. 534, 116 L. Ed. 2d 589, 1991 U.S. LEXIS 7262, that—even if it was assumed for the purposes of argument that the agents, as well as a magistrate, had erred in concluding that probable cause existed to arrest the individual— the agents were entitled to qualified immunity, because the agents' decision was reasonable, even if mistaken. The court observed that when the agents had arrested the individual, he had (1) written a letter containing references to an assassination scheme directed against the President; (2) been cognizant of the President's whereabouts; (3) made an oral statement, around a time when the President was traveling in Germany, that "[h]e should have been assassinated in Bonn"; and (4) refused to answer questions about whether the individual intended to harm the President. On the basis of this information, the court observed, the magistrate in question had ordered the individual to be held without bond. The Supreme Court granted the agents' petition for certiorari, reversed a judgment upholding a denial of qualified immunity, and remanded the case. According to the Supreme Court, its cases had established that qualified immunity shielded the agents from suit if a reasonable officer could have believed the arrest to be lawful, in light of clearly established law and the information that the arresting officers possessed. Even law enforcement officials who reasonably but mistakenly believed that probable cause was present were entitled to immunity from suit, the court said. The court added that (1) the qualified-immunity standard's accommodation for reasonable error existed because officials should not err always on the side of caution for fear of being sued; and (2) the national experience taught that such a principle was no more important than when the specter of Presidential assassination was raised.

Two Secret Service agents were entitled to qualified immunity from a Bivens action brought against the agents by an arrestee who alleged that his arrest, by one of the agents following the arrestee's confrontation with the Vice President of the United States in a public area to express displeasure over war in Iraq, violated the free-speech clause of the Federal Constitution's First Amendment, according to the Supreme Court in Reichle v. Howards (2012) 566 U.S. 658, 132 S. Ct. 2088, 182 L. Ed. 2d 985, 2012 U.S. LEXIS 4132. Noting that the arrestee asserted that the arrest was in retaliation for his criticism of the Vice President, the court reversed a judgment that had rejected the agent's qualified-immunity defense, as the court said that at the time of arrest, it was not clearly established that an arrest supported by probable cause could give rise to a First Amendment violation. The court observed that it had held in an earlier case that a plaintiff could not state a First Amendment retaliatory-prosecution claim if probable cause supported the charges. According to the court, for qualified-immunity purposes at the time in question in the instant case, it was at least arguable that the rule in the earlier case extended to retaliatory arrests, as the earlier case injected uncertainty into the law governing retaliatory arrests, particularly in light of its rationale and the close relationship between retaliatory arrest and prosecution claims. That uncertainty was only confirmed by subsequent appellate decisions that disagreed over whether that reasoning applied similarly to retaliatory arrests, the Supreme Court said.

It was decided by the Supreme Court in Wood v. Moss (2014) 572 U.S. 744, 134 S. Ct. 2056, 188 L. Ed. 2d 1039, 2014 U.S. LEXIS 3614, that two Secret Service agents, who allegedly had required that a group of protesters against the President of the United States be moved farther from the President than a group of pro-President demonstrators, were entitled to qualified immunity from a Bivens suit alleging that the agents had violated the protesters' rights of free speech protected by the Federal Constitution's First Amendment. Reversing a judgment that had upheld a judgment denying the agents' motion to dismiss, the Supreme Court observed that none of its prior decision would have alerted the agents, when they engaged in crowd control around the President, that they bore First Amendment obligation to insure that groups with different viewpoints were at comparable locations at all times. When the President made an unscheduled stop for dinner at an inn, the agents, in establishing a security perimeter, ordered the protesters moved from their original location in front of the inn. The court said that a map of the area undermined the protesters' allegations that viewpoint discrimination was the sole reason for the agents' directions, since the map corroborated that, because of their location, the protesters posed a potential security risk to the President, while the supporters, because of their location, did not. Because the protesters, but not the supporters, were within weapons range of the President, the protesters could not plausibly have argued that the agents had no valid security reason to order that the protesters be moved, the court said.

§ 6. Other actors

[a] Entitled to immunity

In the following cases, the Supreme Court determined that the federal law enforcement officers in question were entitled to qualified immunity in Bivens actions seeking damages for alleged violations of federal civil rights.

The Supreme Court held in Wilson v. Layne (1999) 526 U.S. 603, 119 S. Ct. 1692, 143 L. Ed. 2d 818, 1999 U.S. LEXIS 3633, that even though a "media ride-along"—in which representatives of the news media accompanied a team of federal and county law enforcement officers during the officers' attempt to execute arrest warrants in a private home—violated the Federal Constitution's Fourth Amendment, the federal officers were entitled to qualified immunity from damages liability in a Bivens action brought by residents of the home against those federal officers, because the Fourth Amendment right in question was not clearly established when the ride-along occurred. In affirming a judgment upholding the officers' qualified-immunity defense, the court said that (1) the Fourth Amendment prohibited the police from taking media representatives or other third parties into a home during the execution of a warrant when the presence of the third parties in the home was not in aid of execution of the warrant; and (2) it was conceded that the news media representatives involved in the case at hand had neither engaged in execution of the warrants in question nor assisted the officers in their task. However, the court pointed out that, at the time of the ride-along at issue, there were no judicial opinions holding that the practice of media ride-alongs became unlawful when a home was entered.

The Supreme Court decided in Hanlon v. Berger (1999) 526 U.S. 808, 119 S. Ct. 1706, 143 L. Ed. 2d 978, 1999 U.S. LEXIS 3634, that some special agents of the United States Fish and Wildlife Service were entitled to qualified immunity from damages liability in a Bivens action brought against the agents for asserted violation of the Federal Constitution's Fourth Amendment by news media representatives' alleged accompaniment of the agents during the agents' execution of a search warrant at a ranch. The Supreme Court observed that (1) its holding in Wilson v. Layne (decided on same day as the instant case), supra, made it clear that the Fourth Amendment's prohibition of the taking by the police of media representatives or other third parties into a home during the execution of a warrant when the presence of the third parties in the home was not in aid of execution of the warrant was not clearly established at the time of the search in question in Wilson; and (2) the parties in the instant case had not called the Supreme Court's attention to any decisions that would have made the relevant law any clearer at the time of the search in question in the instant case about a year later. Noting that the instant case involved a multiple-vehicle caravan consisting of government agents and a crew of photographers and reporters from a cable news network, the Hanlon court pointed out that the agents had executed the search warrant while accompanied by the media crew, which had observed the officers and had recorded the officers' conduct in executing the warrant.

According to the Supreme Court in Saucier v. Katz (2001) 533 U.S. 194, 121 S. Ct. 2151, 150 L. Ed. 2d 272, 2001 U.S. LEXIS 4664, a military police officer who was alleged to have used excessive force in arresting an animal-rights protester was entitled to qualified immunity from a Bivens action concerning alleged violation of the protester's rights under the Federal Constitution's Fourth Amendment, where the protester, who had attempted to approach the Vice President of United States and to unfurl a banner when the Vice President spoke at a military base, was (1) seized by military police, including the officer in question, as the protester approached a fence that separated the public from the speaking platform; and (2) allegedly shoved or thrown into a military van. In reversing a judgment denying qualified immunity, the court said that the question whether the asserted right was clearly established at the time in question had to be addressed in light of the specific context of the case rather than as a broad proposition. According to the court, if the officer's mistake as to what the law required with respect to force used to make an arrest was reasonable, then the officer was entitled to the defense of qualified immunity. The court concluded that the mistake was reasonable, as the officer had a duty to protect the safety and security of the Vice President, and there was no clearly established rule prohibiting the officer from acting as he did.

[b] Not entitled to immunity

It was held by the Supreme Court in the following cases that the federal law enforcement officers in question were not entitled to qualified immunity in Bivens actions seeking damages for alleged violations of federal civil rights.

In Groh v. Ramirez (2004) 540 U.S. 551, 124 S. Ct. 1284, 157 L. Ed. 2d 1068, 2004 U.S. LEXIS 1624, the Supreme Court affirmed a judgment holding that an agent of the (then) United States Bureau of Alcohol, Tobacco and Firearms was not entitled to qualified immunity in a Bivens action alleging that a search, led by the agent, of a family's house pursuant to a warrant violated the Federal Constitution's Fourth Amendment. According to the court, the search was clearly unreasonable, in violation of the Fourth Amendment, even though the warrant indicated that a Federal Magistrate Judge had found probable cause to conduct the search, where the agent had (1) prepared and signed a warrant application stating that the search was for specified weapons, explosives, and records; (2) supported the application with detailed affidavit setting forth the agent's basis for believing that such items were in house; and (3) presented these documents, along with a warrant form completed by the agent, to the Magistrate Judge. The court noted that the warrant (1) in portions calling for a description of "person or property" described only the house; and (2) did not incorporate, by reference, the itemized list in the application. Observing that the fact that the application adequately described the things to be seized did not save the warrant from its facial invalidity, and that the Magistrate Judge's authorization of the search did not render it constitutional, the court said that the search was presumptively unreasonable. According to the court, the agent was not entitled to qualified immunity, because no reasonable officer could have (1) believed that a warrant that plainly did not comply with the Fourth Amendment's particularity requirements was valid; or (2) been unaware of the basic rule that, absent consent or exigency, a warrantless search was presumptively unconstitutional.

On certiorari with respect to the cross-border shooting, by a United States agent standing on United States soil, of a Mexican alien standing on Mexican soil, in Hernandez v. Mesa (2017) 582 U.S. ___, 137 S. Ct. 2003, 198 L. Ed. 2d 625, 2017 U.S. LEXIS 4059, the Supreme Court determined that (1) it was appropriate to remand for further proceedings on the question of a possible Bivens remedy, where the Federal Court of Appeals below had not had the opportunity to consider how a recent Supreme Court decision in another case might bear on the case at hand; (2) it would be imprudent for the Supreme Court to resolve the issue whether, under the circumstances, the alien had any rights under the Federal Constitution's Fourth Amendment; and (3) the United States agent was not entitled to qualified immunity on the basis of the alien's nationality and extent of his United States ties, where these factors were unknown to the agent at time of the shooting of the alien. According to the Supreme Court, facts that an officer learned after the incident in question ended were not relevant to the immunity question. The court vacated a judgment granting the agent qualified immunity.

☆ COMMENT: In Hernandez v. Mesa (2020) 589 U.S. ___, 140 S. Ct. 735, 206 L. Ed. 2d 29, 2020 U.S. LEXIS 1361, a later decision in this case, the Supreme Court held—without appearing to determine possible qualified immunity—that with respect to some claims under the Federal Constitution's Fourth and Fifth Amendments, Bivens did not extend to creating a damages remedy for a cross-border shooting by a federal agent from the United States into Mexico.

[c] Issue not decided

In remanding the following case for determination whether a Federal Bureau of Investigation agent was entitled to qualified immunity in a Bivens action seeking damages for alleged violation of federal civil rights, the Supreme Court concluded that a Federal Court of Appeals had misapplied the principles of qualified immunity in the case.

In a case involving a Bivens claim for damages against a Federal Bureau of Investigation agent for alleged violations of the Federal Constitution's

Fourth Amendment guarantee against unreasonable searches and seizures through the agent's participation in a warrantless search of the plaintiffs' home, the Supreme Court in Anderson v. Creighton (1987) 483 U.S. 635, 107 S. Ct. 3034, 97 L. Ed. 2d 523, 1987 U.S. LEXIS 2894—in vacating a Federal Court of Appeals' judgment to the effect that the agent was not entitled to summary judgment on qualified immunity grounds, and in remanding the case—left for determination on remand the question whether the agent was entitled to qualified immunity, but (1) agreed with the agent's contention that the Court of Appeals had misapplied the principles of qualified immunity; and (2) held that the relevant question in the instant case was the objective, although fact-specific, question whether a reasonable officer could have believed the agent's warrantless search to be lawful in light of clearly established law and the information that the searching officers possessed. The Supreme Court added that the agent's subjective beliefs about the search were irrelevant. The record showed that the search had been conducted because the agent believed that a bank robbery suspect might be found in the home, but that the suspect had not been found there. According to the Supreme Court, even though it was firmly established that the Fourth Amendment was violated by a warrantless search that was not supported by probable cause and exigent circumstances, the conclusion did not immediately follow that the search in question was objectively unreasonable, where (1) it was inevitable that law enforcement officers would in some cases reasonably or mistakenly conclude that probable cause was present; (2) in such cases, these officers— like other officials who acted in ways that the officials reasonably believed to be lawful—ought not to be held personally liable; and (3) the same was true of officers' conclusions regarding exigent circumstances. Thus, the court observed, the determination whether it was objectively reasonable to conclude that a given search was supported by probable cause and exigent circumstances would often require examination of the information possessed by the searching officials. Also, the court rejected several suggested alternatives, which, in progressively narrower circumstances, would have denied qualified immunity (1) to all officials who violated the Fourth Amendment, and thus searched and seized unreasonably; (2) to officials who conducted unlawful warrantless searches; or (3) in a position allegedly—but perhaps dubiously— based on English common law, to police officers who conducted unlawful warrantless searches of innocent third parties' homes in search of fugitives. The court said that it was unwilling to "Balkanize" the rule of qualified immunity by carving exceptions at the level of detail that the plaintiffs proposed.

B. State and Local Actors

§ 7. Entitled to immunity

In the following cases, the Supreme Court decided that the state or local law enforcement officers in question were entitled to qualified immunity in 42 U.S.C.S. § 1983 actions seeking damages for alleged violations of federal civil rights.

Although concluding that a "media ride-along"—in which representatives of the news media accompanied a team of federal and county law enforcement officers during the officers' attempt to execute arrest warrants in a private home—violated the Federal Constitution's Fourth Amendment, in Wilson v. Layne (1999) 526 U.S. 603, 119 S. Ct. 1692, 143 L. Ed. 2d 818, 1999 U.S. LEXIS 3633, the Supreme Court held that the county officers were entitled to qualified immunity from damages liability in a 42 U.S.C.S. § 1983 action brought by residents of the home against those county officers, as the Fourth Amendment right in question was not clearly established at the time of the ride-along. Stating that the Fourth Amendment prohibited the police from taking media representatives or other third parties into a home during the execution of a warrant when the presence of the third parties in the home was not in aid of execution of the warrant, the court added that it was conceded that the news media representatives involved in the instant case had neither engaged in execution of the warrants in question nor assisted the officers in their task. However, the court noted that at the time of the ride-along at issue there were no judicial opinions holding that the practice of media ride-alongs became unlawful when a home was entered.

In Brosseau v. Haugen (2004) 543 U.S. 194, 125 S. Ct. 596, 160 L. Ed. 2d 583, 2004 U.S. LEXIS 8275, the Supreme Court held that for purposes of determining whether a summary judgment properly had been granted to a local police officer in a 42 U.S.C.S. § 1983 action alleging excessive force in violation of the Federal Constitution's Fourth Amendment, the officer was entitled to qualified immunity from the § 1983 action. The action was brought by a driver whom the officer allegedly had shot in the back while the driver was attempting to flee in a motor vehicle when the officer attempted to arrest the driver, who locked himself in the vehicle and had ignored the officer's commands, issued at gun point, to get out of the vehicle. After the officer shattered the driver's-side window, unsuccessfully attempted to grab the car keys, and struck the driver on the head with the officer's gun, the driver began to drive away. The officer, who then fired one shot through a window of the vehicle, hitting the driver in the back, later explained that she shot the driver because she was fearful for other police officers whom she believed were in the immediate area on foot, as well as for occupied vehicles in the driver's path and any other citizens who might have been in the area. The court concluded that, even if material facts were construed in light most favorable to the driver, and regardless of whether the officer's alleged conduct had violated the driver's rights under the Fourth Amendment, caselaw clearly showed that the qualified-immunity issue was one in which the result depended very much on the facts of each case, and that the cases suggested that the officer's actions fell in the hazy border between excessive and acceptable force and did not clearly establish that the officer's conduct had violated the Fourth Amendment. A judgment that had reversed a summary judgment for the officer was reversed.

It was held in Pearson v. Callahan (2009) 555 U.S. 223, 129 S. Ct. 808, 172 L. Ed. 2d 565, 2009 U.S. LEXIS 591, that police officers who had relied on the consent-once-removed doctrine—which (assertedly) permitted a warrantless police entry into a home when consent to enter had been granted to an undercover officer who had observed contraband in plain view—to conduct a warrantless search of an accused's house, to which an informant had been voluntarily admitted, were entitled to qualified immunity from the accused's 42 U.S.C.S. § 1983 suit, because it was not clearly established at time of the search that the officers' conduct in relying on the consent-once-removed doctrine violated the Federal Constitution's Fourth Amendment. The § 1983 action was brought after a state appellate court had vacated the accused's conviction for possession and distribution of drugs that he had sold to an undercover informant whom he voluntarily had admitted into his house. Reversing a judgment to the effect that the officers were not entitled to qualified immunity, the Supreme Court said that qualified immunity balanced the need to hold public officials accountable when they exercised power irresponsibly against the need to shield public officials from harassment, distraction, and liability when they performed their duties reasonably, and that the protection of qualified immunity applied regardless of whether a government official's error was a mistake of law, a mistake of fact, or a mistake based on mixed questions of law and fact. As to the officers reasonably believing that the consent-once-removed doctrine had authorized the officers' conduct, it was noted that it was not clearly established at the time they conducted the search that their conduct was unconstitutional, where at that time, (1) the consent-once-removed doctrine had been accepted by the highest court of two states and three Federal Courts of Appeals; and (2) not one Federal Court of Appeals had issued a contrary decision. According to the Supreme Court, the officers were entitled to rely on these cases, even though the Court of Appeals in the federal Circuit where the officers were located had not at the time ruled on consent-once-removed entries.

In Ryburn v. Huff (2012) 565 U.S. 469, 132 S. Ct. 987, 181 L. Ed. 2d 966, 2012 U.S. LEXIS 910, the Supreme Court held that some police officers were entitled to qualified immunity from a 42 U.S.C.S. § 1983 suit alleging that the officers' warrantless entry into a home violated the Federal Constitution's Fourth Amendment, as the officers' belief that entry of the home was necessary to avoid injury to themselves or others was reasonable when judged from the proper perspective, under a Federal District Court's findings in the instant case, of a reasonable officer who was forced to make a split-second decision in response to a rapidly unfolding chain of events that culminated with the mother of a high school student—who, according to the school's principal, was rumored to have threatened to "shoot up" the school—turning and running into the home after refusing to answer question about guns. The court reversed a judgment finding that qualified immunity was not available to the officers, and remanded for entry of a judgment in favor of the officers. The court decided that a reasonable police officer in the circumstances in question could have read precedent to mean that the Fourth Amendment permitted the officer to enter a residence if he had a reasonable basis for concluding that there was an imminent threat of violence. The principal (1) told the officers that many parents, after hearing the rumor about the student, had decided to keep their children at home; (2) expressed concern for the safety of the other students; and (3) requested that the officers investigate the threat. When the officers went to the student's house in an attempt to interview him, the mother, after answering the door and being asked if there were guns in the house, ran back into the house while being questioned. Observing that the officers had learned at the school that the student had been a victim of bullying, and had been absent from school for 2 days, the court determined that circumstances had led the officers to believe that there could have been weapons inside the house, and that family members or the officers were in danger.

It was held in Messerschmidt v. Millender (2012) 565 U.S. 535, 132 S. Ct. 1235, 182 L. Ed. 2d 47, 2012 U.S. LEXIS 1687, that some police officers were entitled to qualified immunity from a suit under 42 U.S.C.S. § 1983 alleging that a search warrant by which a magistrate had authorized the officers' search of home was invalid under the Federal Constitution's Fourth Amendment, as the alleged invalidity was not so obvious that any reasonable officer would have recognized it despite the magistrate's approval. After a suspect's ex-girlfriend told the police that the suspect was a gang member, had shot at her with a pistol-gripped sawed-off shotgun, and might be staying at the home of his former foster mother, the officers obtained a warrant to search that home for all firearms and gang-related materials. Referring to the allegation that the search warrant was not supported by probable cause, the court said that even if the warrant had been invalid, it was not so obviously lacking in probable cause that the officers could be considered plainly incompetent for concluding otherwise, because (1) a reasonable officer could have concluded that there would have been additional illegal guns among others that the suspect owned, given his possession of one illegal gun, his gang membership, his willingness to use the gun to kill someone, and his concern about the police; (2) it would not have been unreasonable for an officer to believe that evidence regarding the suspect's gang affiliation would prove helpful in prosecuting him; and (3) the officers had sought and obtained approval of the warrant application from a superior and a deputy district attorney before submitting the application to the magistrate. The court reversed a judgment denying the officer's defense of qualified immunity.

The Supreme Court reversed a judgment holding that a police officer was entitled to qualified immunity from a homeowner's suit under 42 U.S.C.S. § 1983 alleging that the officer had violated the Federal Constitution's Fourth Amendment by entering, without a warrant, the owner's yard to pursue an individual who was suspected of having committed a misdemeanor, in Stanton v. Sims (2013) 571 U.S. 3, 134 S. Ct. 3, 187 L. Ed. 2d 341, 2013 U.S. LEXIS 7773, where the court said that case law at the time in question was sharply divided over whether such entry violated the Fourth Amendment. When the officer and his partner, responding to a call about a disturbance, approached the place where the disturbance had been reported, the suspect, ignoring the officer's order to stop, fled through the gate of a wooden fence that was more

than 6 feet tall, enclosed the owner's front yard, and blocked the officer's view
of the yard. When the officer, made a "split-second decision" and kicked open
the gate, it struck and injured the owner, who, unbeknownst to the officer,
was standing behind the gate. The Supreme Court said that the law at the
time the officer made his split-second decision to enter the yard consisted of
(1) two Supreme Court opinions that were equivocal on the lawfulness of the
officer's entry; (2) two state appellate-court opinions affirmatively authorizing
the entry; (3) a state lower-court opinion that was readily distinguishable;
and (4) two Federal District Court opinions granting qualified immunity in
the wake of that lower-court opinion. Given this sharp division over the issue,
the Supreme Court concluded that, although the officer might have been
mistaken in believing that his actions were justified, he was not plainly
incompetent and, thus, was entitled to qualified immunity.

In Plumhoff v. Rickard (2014) 572 U.S. 765, 134 S. Ct. 2012, 188 L. Ed. 2d
1056, 2014 U.S. LEXIS 3816, the Supreme Court determined that some police
officers, who had shot the driver of a fleeing vehicle to put an end to a car
chase, were entitled to qualified immunity from a 42 U.S.C.S. § 1983 suit alleging the officers had used excessive force, in violation of the Federal
Constitution's Fourth Amendment. When the driver sped away from a traffic
stop, and the officers pursued him, the vehicles swerved through traffic at
high speeds, an officer fired three shots into the driver's car, and as the driver
continued fleeing, officers fired 12 more shots toward his car. The driver and
his passenger died from some combination of gunshot wounds and injuries
suffered in the crash that ended the chase. The Supreme Court determined
that the officers were entitled to qualified immunity as to the Fourth Amendment excessive force claim asserted by the driver's daughter because (1) the
officers did not violate the Fourth Amendment, since the driver's flight posed
a grave public safety risk, and the officers acted reasonably in using deadly
force to end that risk; and (2) moreover, no clearly established law precluded
the officers' conduct at the time in question. The court reversed a judgment
that had upheld a judgment denying the officers' motion for summary judgment on the basis of qualified immunity.

According to the Supreme Court in Carroll v. Carman (2014) 574 U.S. 13,
135 S. Ct. 348, 190 L. Ed. 2d 311, 2014 U.S. LEXIS 7430, a state police officer was entitled to qualified immunity in a 42 U.S.C.S. § 1983 suit alleging
violation of the Federal Constitution's Fourth Amendment, because the officer
did not violate clearly established federal law when he knocked on, and
permissibly entered a home through, a rear sliding-glass door. When the officer and a partner, without a warrant, went to the home to investigate a
reported theft of a car and two loaded handguns, they (1) knocked on the
sliding-glass door, which opened onto a ground-level deck, and (2) told the
woman who answered the door the name of the person for whom they were
looking. After she said that the person was not there, the officers requested
permission to search the house, and the woman consented. Reversing a judgment of the United States Court of Appeals for the Third Circuit to the effect
that the officer was not entitled to qualified immunity, the Supreme Court

said that, even if it was assumed for the sake of argument that a controlling circuit precedent could constitute clearly established federal law, the Third Circuit misapplied its own decision from an earlier case when it found that the earlier case had established a clear rule that a "knock and talk" exception to the warrant requirement had to begin at a front door.

In City & Cnty. of San Francisco v. Sheehan (2015) 575 U.S. 600, 135 S. Ct. 1765, 191 L. Ed. 2d 856, 2015 U.S. LEXIS 3200, the Supreme Court concluded that two police officers, who were dispatched to a group home after receiving a report that a mentally ill resident was acting erratically and had threatened to kill a social worker, were entitled to qualified immunity from the resident's 42 U.S.C.S. § 1983 action seeking recovery for injuries suffered as result of the officers' alleged use of excessive force against the resident, in violation of the Federal Constitution's Fourth Amendment. When the officers, who had been dispatched to help escort the resident to a facility for temporary evaluation and treatment, first entered the resident's room, she grabbed a knife and threatened to kill them, and they retreated and closed the door. When they re-entered the room, the resident, knife in hand, again confronted them, and after pepper spray proved ineffective, the officers shot the resident multiple times and arrested her. With respect to the officers' allegedly violating the Fourth Amendment by failing to accommodate the resident's disability, the court reasoned that, regardless of whether a right to such accommodation existed, it was not clearly established at the time of the arrest. The court reversed a judgment in part, to the extent that the judgment held that the officers were not entitled to qualified immunity.

Reversing a judgment upholding the denial of a police officer's motion for summary judgment in a 42 U.S.C.S. § 1983 suit, in Mullenix v. Luna (2015) 577 U.S. ___, 136 S. Ct. 305, 193 L. Ed. 2d 255, 2015 U.S. LEXIS 7160, the Supreme Court held that the officer was entitled to qualified immunity, where it was alleged that he had violated the Federal Constitution's Fourth Amendment by using excessive force in shooting and killing a reportedly intoxicated fugitive who (1) was fleeing in a motor vehicle at a high speed; (2) twice threatened to kill police officers; and (3) was racing toward another officer's location before the vehicle reached a spike strip that had been placed on the road by the police. The defendant officer raised with his colleagues the idea of shooting at the car in order to disable it, although the officer neither had received training in this tactic nor previously attempted it. He fired six shots, and it was later determined that four shots had struck the fugitive's upper body, while there was no evidence that any had hit the car's radiator, hood, or engine block. Pointing out that, for purposes of the qualified-immunity issue, a clearly established right was one that was sufficiently clear that every reasonable official would have understood that what he was doing violated that right, the court said that, although a case directly on point was not required, existing precedent had to have placed the statutory or constitutional question beyond debate. In the instant case, the court concluded that it was not beyond debate whether the officer had acted unreasonably in the unclear border between excessive and acceptable force.

In White v. Pauly (2017) 580 U.S. ___, 137 S. Ct. 548, 196 L. Ed. 2d 463, 2017 U.S. LEXIS 5, the Supreme Court vacated a judgment to the effect that a police officer was not entitled to qualified immunity in a 42 U.S.C.S. § 1983 action alleging that the officer violated the right, under the Federal Constitution's Fourth Amendment, of an armed occupant of a house to be free from excessive force, where, having arrived late at an ongoing police action, and having witnessed shots being fired by one of several individuals in the house, which was surrounded by other officers, the officer, without warning, had fatally shot the occupant. According to the Supreme Court, the record described by a Federal Court of Appeals did not show that the officer had violated clearly established federal law, as no settled Fourth Amendment principle required the officer to second-guess the earlier steps already taken by his fellow officers or to shout a warning to the armed occupant before shooting. At the time of the shooting, constitutional issue in question was not beyond debate, the court said.

In District of Columbia v. Wesby (2018) 583 U.S. ___, 138 S. Ct. 577, 199 L. Ed. 2d 453, 2018 U.S. LEXIS 760, the Supreme Court held that police officers who arrested some late-night partygoers for trespassing in a vacant home owned by someone other than any of the partygoers—where after giving conflicting stories for their presence, some partygoers said that they had been invited by a person who was not the owner and was not present, and where the owner told the officers that he had not authorized entry by anyone—(1) had probable cause under the Federal Constitution's Fourth Amendment for the arrests; and (2) were entitled to qualified immunity from a civil rights suit under 42 U.S.C.S. § 1983, because the relevant law was not clearly established at the time of the arrests. According to the court, a reasonable officer could have concluded that there was probable cause to believe the partygoers knew that they did not have permission to be in the house. The court said that the officers had probable cause to arrest the partygoers because (1) the officers found a group of people who claimed to be having a bachelor party with no bachelor, in a near-empty house, with strippers in the living room and sexual activity in the bedroom; and (2) the people fled at the first sign of police. Reversing a judgment to the effect that the officers were not entitled to qualified immunity, the court observed that even if the court assumed that the officers lacked probable cause to arrest the partygoers, the officers were entitled to qualified immunity because they reasonably but mistakenly had concluded that probable cause was present.

The Supreme Court determined in Kisela v. Hughes (2018) 584 U.S. ___, 138 S. Ct. 1148, 200 L. Ed. 2d 449, 2018 U.S. LEXIS 2066, that a city police officer who shot a person who was holding a large kitchen knife, had taken steps toward another person standing nearby, and had refused to drop the knife after at least two commands to do so, was entitled to qualified immunity from a civil rights suit under 42 U.S.C.S. § 1983, because the shooting did not violate law that was clearly established at the time of the shooting. The court said that even if it assumed that a violation of the Federal Constitution's Fourth Amendment had occurred, the police officer was at least entitled to qualified immunity because this case was far from an obvious one in which any competent officer would have known that shooting respondent to protect her roommate would have violated the Fourth Amendment, where the person holding the knife was within striking distance of her roommate and the situation unfolded in less than a minute. Noting that it was sometimes difficult for a law enforcement officer to determine how the relevant legal doctrine would apply to the factual situation that the officer confronted, the court added that (1) use of excessive force was an area of law in which the result depended very much on the facts of each case; (2) police officers were entitled to qualified immunity unless existing precedent squarely governed the specific facts at issue; and (3) precedent involving similar facts could help move a case beyond the otherwise hazy border between excessive and acceptable force and thereby provide an officer notice that a specific use of force was unlawful. The court reversed a judgment to the effect that the officer in question was not entitled to qualified immunity.

Reversing a Federal Court of Appeals' judgment to the extent that it denied one police officer qualified immunity in a 42 U.S.C.S. § 1983 action, alleging that two police officers had used excessive force, in violation of the Federal Constitution's Fourth Amendment, in City of Escondido v. Emmons (2019) 586 U.S. ___, 139 S. Ct. 500, 202 L. Ed. 2d 455, 2019 U.S. LEXIS 11, infra § 8, the Supreme Court said that (1) the Court of Appeals had offered no explanation for its decision regarding the officer as to whom Supreme Court was reversing; and (2) the Court of Appeals' denial of qualified immunity for this officer was erroneous, and quite puzzling, in light of a Federal District Court's conclusions that only the other officer was involved in the excessive-force claim and that the plaintiff had failed to identify contrary evidence.

§ 8. Issue not decided

In the following cases involving 42 U.S.C.S. § 1983 actions alleging violations of federal civil rights by state or local law enforcement officers, the Supreme Court made holdings concerning qualified immunity without determining whether the officers in question were entitled to such immunity.

When it was alleged that a defendant police officer had caused the plaintiffs to be unconstitutionally arrested by presenting a judge with a complaint and a supporting affidavit that failed to establish probable cause, the officer would not be entitled to qualified immunity if it was obvious that no reasonably competent officer would have concluded that a warrant should have issued, but if officers of reasonable competence could have disagreed on this issue, then immunity should be recognized, the Supreme Court stated in Malley v. Briggs (1986) 475 U.S. 335, 106 S. Ct. 1092, 89 L. Ed. 2d 271, 1986 U.S. LEXIS 29, which involved a 42 U.S.C.S. § 1983 damages action. According to the court, the same objective-reasonableness standard that the court had applied in a 1982 case in the context of a criminal suppression-of-evidence hearing defined the qualified immunity of an officer whose request for a warrant allegedly caused an unconstitutional arrest, which meant that only where the warrant application was so lacking in indicia of probable cause as to render official belief in its existence unreasonable, would the shield of immunity be lost. The Supreme Court rejected a proposal that an officer's act of applying for a warrant would be objectively reasonable if the officer believed that the facts alleged in the affidavit were true. Instead, the court continued, the question was whether a reasonably well-trained officer in the position of the defendant in question would have known that (1) the affidavit failed to establish probable cause; and (2) the officer ought not to have applied for the warrant. If such was the case, the court observed, then the application was not objectively reasonable, because the application created an unnecessary danger of unlawful arrest, as the nation did not have an ideal system. Where a magistrate acted mistakenly in issuing a warrant but within the range of professional competence of a magistrate, the officer who requested the warrant could not be held liable, the court said, but if no officer of reasonable competence would have requested the warrant, then (1) the magistrate's action indicated gross incompetence or neglect of duty; and (2) an officer could not excuse the officer's own default by pointing to the magistrate's greater incompetence. However, in affirming a judgment that had reversed a directed verdict in favor of a particular police officer, and in remanding the case, the Supreme Court (1) declined to decide whether the conduct of that officer had been objectively reasonable; and (2) left the issue to be resolved on remand.

In Tolan v. Cotton (2014) 572 U.S. 650, 134 S. Ct. 1861, 188 L. Ed. 2d 895, 2014 U.S. LEXIS 3112, the Supreme Court held that a Federal Court of Appeals had erred in affirming in a 42 U.S.C.S. § 1983 action, on the basis of qualified immunity, a summary judgment for a police officer who allegedly had used excessive force, in violation of the Federal Constitution's Fourth Amendment, in firing three bullets at a car-theft suspect when he was unarmed on his parent's front porch about 15 to 20 feet away from the officer, as the Court of Appeals had failed to view the evidence in the light most favorable to the suspect with respect to the central facts of case. Vacating the Court of Appeals' judgment, and remanding for further proceedings, the Supreme Court concluded that the Court of Appeals, by failing to credit evidence that contradicted some of its key factual conclusions, had improperly weighed the evidence and resolved disputed issues in favor of the moving party, where, the Court of Appeals ought to have acknowledged and credited the suspect's evidence concerning the lighting, his mother's demeanor, whether he shouted words that were an overt threat, and his positioning during the shooting. The suspect's father instructed him to lie down, which he did, and his mother told the officer that the car in question belonged to the family. The parties disagreed as to what happened next, as (1) the mother, the suspect, and another party testified that the officer pushed the mother against the garage door, while (2) the officer testified that when he was escorting the mother to the garage, she flipped her arm up and told him to get his hands off her. The parties agreed that the suspect exclaimed, "[G]et your fucking hands off my mom," and that the officer then fired three shots at the suspect.

Vacating a Federal Court of Appeals' judgment to the extent that it denied one police officer qualified immunity in a 42 U.S.C.S. § 1983 action, alleging that two police officers, responding to a 911 call—which led them to the apartment resided in by a husband and wife, their children, and an apparently unrelated person—had used excessive force, in violation of the Federal Constitution's Fourth Amendment, in City of Escondido v. Emmons (2019) 586 U.S. ___, 139 S. Ct. 500, 202 L. Ed. 2d 455, 2019 U.S. LEXIS 11, supra § 7, the Supreme Court concluded that a Federal Court of Appeals had erred by defining the clearly established right at issue in the case too generally. When a man, who was later learned by the officers to be the wife's father, exited the apartment and attempted to pass the officer with respect to whom the judgment was vacated, this officer stopped the man, took him quickly to the ground, and handcuffed him. This officer did not hit the man or display any weapon, and a recording showed that the man was not in any visible or audible pain as a result of the takedown or while on the ground. Within a few minutes, officers helped the man up and arrested him for a misdemeanor offense of resisting and delaying a police officer. According to the Supreme Court, the Court of Appeals' entire relevant analysis of the qualified-immunity question consisted of a quote from the Court of Appeals' opinion in an earlier case stating that the right to be free of excessive force was clearly established at the time of the events in question.

III. Treatment of Prisoners

§ 9. Entitled to immunity

Under particular circumstances involving the treatment of prisoners, the Supreme Court held that state prison officers were entitled to qualified immunity in 42 U.S.C.S. § 1983 actions alleging that the officers had violated federal civil rights.

See Procunier v. Navarette (1978) 434 U.S. 555, 98 S. Ct. 855, 55 L. Ed. 2d 24, 1978 U.S. LEXIS 60, which was decided when the Supreme Court was still using a two-part, "subjective" and "objective" test for qualified immunity from damages liability—prior to the court's limitation to a single-part, objective test (§ 3, supra)—where the court (1) held that defendant state prison officers had satisfied both test parts, so as to be entitled to qualified immunity from a prisoner's 42 U.S.C.S. § 1983 claim that the defendant's alleged interference in 1971-1972 with the prisoner's outgoing mail had violated the prisoner's asserted rights under the Federal Constitution's First and Fourteenth Amendments; and (2) reasoned, as to the objective part of the test, that (a) whether the state of the law was measured by reference to the opinions of the Supreme Court, of the Federal Courts of Appeals, or of the local Federal District Court, there had been in 1971-1972 no clearly established First and Fourteenth Amendment right with respect to the correspondence of convicted prisoners, and (b) the officials and officers could not reasonably be expected to have been aware of a constitutional right that had not yet been declared. The Supreme Court reversed a judgment in favor of the prisoner with respect to that claim.

The Supreme Court determined in Taylor v. Barkes (2015) 575 U.S. 822, 135 S. Ct. 2042, 192 L. Ed. 2d 78, 2015 U.S. LEXIS 3715, that the warden of a state prison and the commissioner of the state department of corrections were entitled to qualified immunity from a 42 U.S.C.S. § 1983 suit alleging that those prison officials had violated the Federal Constitution's Eighth Amendment prohibition of cruel and unusual punishment by failing to prevent a pretrial detainee's suicide. Reversing a judgment to the effect that the officials were not entitled to a summary judgment based on qualified immunity, the court noted that at the time of the suicide, no Supreme Court decision had established a right to proper implementation of adequate suicide prevention protocols or had even discussed suicide screening or prevention protocols. A nurse at the prison employed a suicide screening form that was based on a model form that had been developed by the National Commission on Correctional Health Care and listed 17 suicide risk factors, where, if the inmate's responses and the nurse's observations had indicated that at least eight factors were present, or if certain serious risk factors had been present, then the nurse would have been expected to notify a physician and initiate suicide prevention measures. The detainee indicated that he (1) had a history of psychiatric treatment; (2) was on medication; (3) had attempted suicide in 2003; but (4) was not currently thinking about killing himself. Because only two of the 17 risk factors were apparent, the nurse gave the detainee a "routine" referral to mental health services and did not initiate any special suicide prevention measures. The detainee was placed in a cell by himself.

See Ziglar v. Abbasi (2017) 582 U.S. ___, 137 S. Ct. 1843, 198 L. Ed. 2d 290, 2017 U.S. LEXIS 3874, in which the Supreme Court, while holding that some alien federal detainees' putative-class-action claims under the Federal Constitution's Fourth and Fifth Amendments challenging confinement conditions allegedly imposed after the September 11 terrorist attacks could not proceed as Bivens claims, also held that executive officials and wardens were entitled to qualified immunity to the civil conspiracy claims asserted in the detainees' 42 U.S.C.S. § 1985(3) action, as reasonable officials could not have predicted that § 1985(3)—which imposed liability on two or more persons who conspired for the purpose of depriving any person or class of persons of the equal protection of the laws—prohibited their joint consultation and resulting policies. The court affirmed the part of a judgment that had dismissed the claims against the wardens and vacated the part of the judgment that had allowed the claims against the wardens to go forward.

§ 10. Not entitled to immunity

The Supreme Court has held that state prison guards were not entitled to qualified immunity, at the summary-judgment stage, in a particular 42 U.S.C.S. § 1983 action alleging that the guards had violated an inmate's federal civil right.

Three state-prison guards were not entitled to qualified immunity, at the summary-judgment stage, from an inmate's 42 U.S.C.S. § 1983 damages claim that was based on the guards' alleged participation on two occasions in

1995 of the handcuffing of the inmate to a prison "hitching post," according to the Supreme Court in Hope v. Pelzer (2002) 536 U.S. 730, 122 S. Ct. 2508, 153 L. Ed. 2d 666, 2002 U.S. LEXIS 4884. One handcuffing to the post, which was a horizontal bar supposedly placed between 45 and 57 inches from the ground in a location exposed to the sun, occurred following an argument with another inmate and lasted approximately 2 hours, while the second handcuffing followed a wrestling match with a guard and lasted approximately 7 hours. On the second occasion, the inmate remained shirtless while the sun burned his skin, and he was given water only once or twice and was given no bathroom breaks. The court concluded that the guards had violated a clearly established right, under the Federal Constitution's Eighth Amendment prohibition against cruel and unusual punishments, of which a reasonable person would have known in 1995, as (1) any safety concerns had long since abated by the time the inmate was handcuffed to the hitching post; and (2) despite the clear lack of an emergency situation, the guards knowingly had subjected the inmate to a substantial risk of physical harm, to unnecessary pain caused by the handcuffs and the restricted position of confinement, to unnecessary exposure to the heat of the sun, to prolonged thirst and taunting, and to a deprivation of bathroom breaks that created a risk of particular discomfort and humiliation. The court reversed a summary judgment that had been granted in favor of the guards on the basis of the view that they were entitled to qualified immunity.

See Taylor v. Riojas (2020) 592 U.S. ___, 141 S. Ct. ___, 208 L. Ed. 2d 164, 2020 US LEXIS 5193, in which the Supreme Court (1) held that a Federal Court of Appeals erred in granting some state correctional officers qualified immunity from a prisoner's claim (apparently under 42 U.S.C.S. § 1983) that the officers had (allegedly) confined the prisoner in shockingly unsanitary cells, in asserted violation of the Federal Constitution's Eighth Amendment prohibition against cruel and unusual punishment; and (2) noted that at the case's summary-judgment stage, the facts subject to genuine dispute were viewed in the light most favorable to the prisoner's claim. The Supreme Court vacated a judgment against the prisoner and remanded for further proceedings.

§ 11. Issue not decided

In the following 42 U.S.C.S. § 1983 or Bivens actions alleging that officers had violated federal civil rights in regard to the treatment of prisoners, the Supreme Court made holdings concerning qualified immunity without deciding whether the officers in question were entitled to such immunity.

See Cleavinger v. Saxner (1985) 474 U.S. 193, 106 S. Ct. 496, 88 L. Ed. 2d 507, 1985 U.S. LEXIS 148, a Bivens-claim case where the Supreme Court—in holding that qualified rather than absolute immunity, from personal damages liability for actions that violated the Federal Constitution, was available to members of a federal prison's "Institution Discipline Committee," who heard cases in which inmates were charged with rules infractions—said that (1) all that the committee members needed to do was to follow the clear and simple

MULLENIX v. LUNA
Reported p 255, supra

constitutional requirements set out in a particular 1974 Supreme Court case; and (2) then, the members ought to have no reason to fear substantial harassment and liability. However, in affirming a judgment against particular committee members, the court for procedural reasons did not determine whether those members were entitled to qualified immunity.

Where a pretrial detainee brought a 42 U.S.C.S. § 1983 action alleging that two officers at a county jail violated the due process clause of the Federal Constitution's Fourteenth Amendment by using excessive force when they removed him from his cell after he refused to comply with their instructions, in Kingsley v. Hendrickson (2015) 576 U.S. 389, 135 S. Ct. 2466, 192 L. Ed. 2d 416, 2015 U.S. LEXIS 4073, the Supreme Court held that a Federal Court of Appeals had erred by entering a judgment holding that the law required a subjective inquiry into the officers' state of mind when they removed the detainee from his cell. The Supreme Court vacated the Court of Appeals' judgment and remanded the case, as the Supreme Court (1) noted that the officers would be entitled to qualified immunity unless they had violated a clearly established right, such that it would have been clear to a reasonable officer that the conduct in question was unlawful; and (2) said that this standard was objective, not subjective.

ANNOTATION

Fiduciary duties under Employee Retirement Income Security Act of 1974, as amended (ERISA) (29 U.S.C.S. § 1001 et seq.)—Supreme Court cases

by

Gary Knapp, M.B.A., J.D.

TABLE OF CONTENTS

Outline of Annotation
Research References
Table of Cases Cited in Annotation
Text of Annotation

OUTLINE OF ANNOTATION

§ 9. Breach shown or propriety not shown

§ 10. Breach not shown

IV. Remedies

§ 11. Available

§ 12. Not available

RESEARCH REFERENCES

Annotations

See the related annotations listed in § 1[b].

Federal Statutes, Constitution, and Court Rules

29 U.S.C.S. §§ 1104, 1106, 1109, 1132(a)

Encyclopedias, Treatises, and Specialized Services

6 Labor and Employment Law §§ 153.02-153.06 (Matthew Bender)

Digests and Indexes

L Ed Digest, Pensions and Retirement Funds § 12

L Ed Index, Pensions and Retirement

> **SHEPARD'S®** Citations Service. For further research of authorities referenced here, use SHEPARD'S to be sure your case or statute is still good law and to find additional authorities that support your position. SHEPARD'S is available exclusively from LexisNexis®.

Electronic Search Query

erisa and (fiduciary w/15 (dut! or responsibilit!))

Law Review Articles

Grosbard, The Duty To Inform in the Post-Dudenhoeffer World of ERISA. 117 Colum. L. Rev. 79 (January, 2017).

Langdon, For Whom the Plan Tolls: Tatum v. RJR Pension Investment Committee and the Emergence of Exacting Scrutiny Awaiting Fiduciaries in Breach in the ERISA Litigation Landscape Post Dudenhoeffer. 49 Creighton L. Rev. 437 (March, 2016).

Medill, Regulating ERISA Fiduciary Outsourcing. 102 Iowa L. Rev. 505 (January, 2017).

Muir and Stein, Two Hats, One Head, No Heart: The Anatomy of the ERISA Settlor/Fiduciary Distinction. 93 N.C.L. Rev. 459 (2015).

Shea, Better Go It Alone: An Extension of Fiduciary Duties for Investment Fund Managers in Securities Class Action Opt-Outs. 6 Wm. & Mary Bus. L. Rev. 255 (February, 2015).

ERISA—FIDUCIARY DUTIES
193 L. Ed. 2d 861

TABLE OF CASES

I. Preliminary Matters

§ 1. Introduction

[a] Scope

This annotation[1] collects and analyzes the cases in which the United States
Supreme Court made determinations with respect to fiduciary duties—what
the duties consist of, what constitutes a breach of the duties, and what
remedies are available in the event of a breach—under the Employee Retirement Income Security Act of 1974, as amended (ERISA) (29 U.S.C.S. § 1001
et seq.).[2] All other ERISA-related issues are outside the scope of this annotations.[3]

[b] Related annotations

Supreme Court's construction and application of § 502 of Employee Retirement Income Security Act of 1974 (ERISA), as amended (29 U.S.C.S. § 1132),
providing for civil enforcement of ERISA. 151 L. Ed. 2d 1083.

When do individuals or entities act as covered fiduciaries, for purposes of
Employee Retirement Income Security Act of 1974, as amended (ERISA) (29
U.S.C.S. § 1001 et seq.)—Supreme Court cases. 142 L. Ed. 2d 1043.

Supreme Court's construction and application of § 302 of Labor Management Relations Act of 1947, as amended (29 U.S.C.S. § 186), concerning
restrictions on financial transactions. 124 L. Ed. 2d 789.

When is state or local law pre-empted by Employee Retirement Income
Security Act of 1974, as amended (ERISA) (29 U.S.C.S. § 1001 et seq.)—
Supreme Court cases. 121 L. Ed. 2d 783.

Supreme Court's views as to proper remedies for unfair labor practices
under National Labor Relations Act (29 U.S.C.S. § 151 et seq.). 74 L. Ed. 2d
1112.

---

1. This annotation supersedes § 10 of the annotation at 151 L. Ed. 2d 1083.
2. Generally, in the text of this annotation, the Employee Retirement Income
Security Act of 1974 is referred to simply as ERISA.
3. As to general coverage of other ERISA-related issues, see, for example, the annotations at 121 L. Ed. 2d 783 (pre-emption under ERISA of state or local law), 142
L. Ed. 2d 1043 (entities constituting fiduciaries under ERISA), and 151 L. Ed. 2d 1083
(civil enforcement of ERISA under 29 U.S.C.S. § 1132).

Supreme Court's view as to weight and effect to be given, on subsequent judicial construction, to prior administrative construction of statute. 39 L. Ed. 2d 942.

The doctrine of primary administrative jurisdiction as defined and applied by the Supreme Court. 38 L. Ed. 2d 796.

The Supreme Court and the post-Erie federal common law. 31 L. Ed. 2d 1006.

[c] Statutory text

The text of § 404(a) of the Employee Retirement Income Security Act of 1974 (29 U.S.C.S. § 1104(a)) provides as follows:

§ 1104. Fiduciary duties

(a) Prudent man standard of care.

(1) Subject to sections 403(c) and (d), 4042, and 4044 [29 U.S.C.S. §§ 1103(c), (d), 1342, 1344], a fiduciary shall discharge his duties with respect to a plan solely in the interest of the participants and beneficiaries and—

(A) for the exclusive purpose of:

(i) providing benefits to participants and their beneficiaries; and

(ii) defraying reasonable expenses of administering the plan;

(B) with the care, skill, prudence, and diligence under the circumstances then prevailing that a prudent man acting in a like capacity and familiar with such matters would use in the conduct of an enterprise of a like character and with like aims;

(C) by diversifying the investments of the plan so as to minimize the risk of large losses, unless under the circumstances it is clearly prudent not to do so; and

(D) in accordance with the documents and instruments governing the plan insofar as such documents and instruments are consistent with the provisions of this title and title IV.

(2) In the case of an eligible individual account plan (as defined in section 407(d)(3) [29 U.S.C.S. § 11107(d)(3)]), the diversification requirement of paragraph (1)(C) and the prudence requirement (only to the extent that it requires diversification) of paragraph (1)(B) is not violated by acquisition or holding of qualifying employer real property or qualifying employer securities (as defined in section 407(d)(4) and (5) [29 U.S.C.S. § 1107(d)(4) and (5)]).

The text of § 406 of the Employee Retirement Income Security Act of 1974 (29 U.S.C.S. § 1106) provides as follows:

§ 1106. Prohibited transactions

(a) Transactions between plan and party in interest. Except as provided in section 408 29 U.S.C.S. § 1108]:

(1) A fiduciary with respect to a plan shall not cause the plan to engage in a transaction, if he knows or should know that such transaction constitutes a direct or indirect—

(A) sale or exchange, or leasing, of any property between the plan and a party in interest;

(B) lending of money or other extension of credit between the plan and a party in interest;

(C) furnishing of goods, services, or facilities between the plan and a party in interest;

(D) transfer to, or use by or for the benefit of, a party in interest, of any assets of the plan; or

(E) acquisition, on behalf of the plan, of any employer security or employer real property in violation of section 407(a) [29 U.S.C.S. § 1107(a)].

(2) No fiduciary who has authority or discretion to control or manage the assets of a plan shall permit the plan to hold any employer security or employer real property if he knows or should know that holding such security or real property violates section 407(a) [29 U.S.C.S. § 11107(a)].

(b) Transactions between plan and fiduciary. A fiduciary with respect to a plan shall not—

(1) deal with the assets of the plan in his own interest or for his own account,

(2) in his individual or in any other capacity act in any transaction involving the plan on behalf of a party (or represent a party) whose interests are adverse to the interests of the plan or the interests of its participants or beneficiaries, or

(3) receive any consideration for his own personal account from any party dealing with such plan in connection with a transaction involving the assets of the plan.

(c) Transfer of real or personal property to plan by party in interest. A transfer of real or personal property by a party in interest to a plan shall be treated as a sale or exchange if the property is subject to a mortgage or similar lien which the plan assumes or if it is subject to a mortgage or similar lien which a party-in-interest placed on the property within the 10-year period ending on the date of the transfer.

The text of § 409 of the Employee Retirement Income Security Act of 1974 (29 U.S.C.S. § 1109) provides as follows:

§ 1109. Liability for breach of fiduciary duty

(a) Any person who is a fiduciary with respect to a plan who breaches any of the responsibilities, obligations, or duties imposed upon fiduciaries by this title shall be personally liable to make good to such plan any losses to the plan resulting from each such breach, and to restore to such plan any profits of such fiduciary which have been made through use of assets of the plan by the fiduciary, and shall be subject to such other equitable or remedial relief as the court may deem appropriate, including removal of such fiduciary. A fiduciary may also be removed for a violation of section 411 of this Act [29 U.S.C.S. § 1111].

(b) No fiduciary shall be liable with respect to a breach of fiduciary duty under this title if such breach was committed before he became a fiduciary or after he ceased to be a fiduciary.

The text of §§ 502(a)(1), 502(a)(2), and 502(a)(3) of the Employee Retirement Income Security Act of 1974 (29 U.S.C.S. §§ 1132(a)(1), 1132(a)(2), and 1132(a)(3)) provides as follows:

§ 1132. Civil enforcement

(a) Persons empowered to bring a civil action. A civil action may be brought—

(1) by a participant or beneficiary—

(A) for the relief provided for in subsection (c) of this section, or

(B) to recover benefits due to him under the terms of his plan, to enforce his rights under the terms of the plan, or to clarify his rights to future benefits under the terms of the plan;

(2) by the Secretary, or by a participant, beneficiary or fiduciary for appropriate relief under section 409 [29 U.S.C.S. § 1109];

(3) by a participant, beneficiary, or fiduciary (A) to enjoin any act or practice which violates any provision of this title or the terms of the plan, or (B) to obtain other appropriate equitable relief (i) to redress such violations or (ii) to enforce any provisions of this title or the terms of the plan;

§ 2. Background, summary, and comment

[a] Generally

The Supreme Court has referred §§ 401-414 of ERISA (29 U.S.C.S. §§ 1101-1114) as ERISA's fiduciary-responsibility provisions.[4] As to the general duties imposed on ERISA fiduciaries under these provisions, the court (1) indicated in many cases that, under the law of trusts, incorporated into ERISA, a fiduciary of an ERISA plan has a general duty of loyalty to the plan's participants and beneficiaries (§ 3, infra); (2) said that fiduciary duties under ERISA to the participants and beneficiaries of an ERISA plan include a duty to avoid transactions that are likely to injure the ERISA plan (§ 4, infra); and (3) indicated that, to a substantial extent, Congress incorporated into ERISA fiduciary duties that were imposed under federal labor-relations law (§ 5, infra). As to more specific ERISA fiduciary duties, the court described a

---

4. For example, see Firestone Tire & Rubber Co. v. Bruch (1989) 489 U.S. 101, 109 S. Ct. 948, 103 L. Ed. 2d 80, 1989 U.S. LEXIS 599, and Curtiss-Wright Corp. v. Schoonejongen (1995) 514 U.S. 73, 115 S. Ct. 1223, 131 L. Ed. 2d 94, 1995 U.S. LEXIS 1807.

number of such duties, including, for example, a duty to avoid conflicts of interest and a duty to avoid underfunded liabilities (§ 6[a], infra). Also, the court held that except for not being required to diversify the fund's assets, fiduciaries of employee stock ownership plans (ESOPs) were subject to the duty of prudence that was applicable under § 404(a)(1)(B) of ERISA (29 U.S.C.S. § 1104(a)(1)(B)) to fiduciaries generally (§ 6[b], infra).

The Supreme Court made some determinations with respect to the effect, if any, of various types of ERISA-plan documents on fiduciary duties concerning the plan (§ 7, infra). Moreover, the court decided in one case that in order to be held liable under ERISA, a fiduciary who was a transferee in an unlawful property transaction had to be demonstrated to have had actual or constructive knowledge of the circumstances that rendered the transaction unlawful (§ 8, infra).

Depending on the circumstances in each case, the Supreme Court decided in some cases that particular fiduciary acts constituted, or could constitute, breach of fiduciary duties under ERISA (§ 9, infra), while the court determined in other cases that an alleged breach of fiduciary duties under ERISA had not been shown (§ 10, infra). Also depending on the circumstances, the court determined that a particular remedy was available under ERISA for the breach of fiduciary duties alleged in some cases (§ 11, infra), while the court concluded that a particular remedy was not available under ERISA for the breach of fiduciary duties alleged in other cases (§ 12, infra).

[b] Practice pointers

Counsel in a case involving a fiduciary's alleged breach of fiduciary duties under ERISA is advised to be aware of the possible issue whether the action or inaction in question occurred when the fiduciary was acting in a fiduciary capacity. In Beck v. PACE Int'l Union (2007) 551 U.S. 96, 127 S. Ct. 2310, 168 L. Ed. 2d 1, 2007 U.S. LEXIS 7716, the Supreme Court indicated that an employer's fiduciary duties under ERISA were implicated only when the employer acted in its fiduciary capacity. Which hat the employer proverbially was wearing, the court said, (1) depended upon the nature of the function performed; and (2) was an inquiry that was aided by the common law of trusts, which served as ERISA's backdrop.

It is suggested that counsel keep in mind that in Firestone Tire & Rubber Co. v. Bruch (1989) 489 U.S. 101, 109 S. Ct. 948, 103 L. Ed. 2d 80, 1989 U.S. LEXIS 599, and Metro. Life Ins. Co. v. Glenn (2008) 554 U.S. 105, 128 S. Ct. 2343, 171 L. Ed. 2d 299, 2008 U.S. LEXIS 5030, the Supreme Court indicated that (1) principles of trust law required courts to conduct judicial review of a challenge, under 29 U.S.C.S. § 1132(a)(1)(B), to a denial of ERISA-plan benefits on the basis of a plan interpretation by a plan fiduciary, under a de novo standard unless the plan provided to the contrary; (2) where the plan provided to the contrary by granting the fiduciary discretionary authority to determine eligibility for benefits, trust principles made a deferential standard of review appropriate; and (3) if a benefit plan gave discretion to a fiduciary who was operating under a conflict of interest, then that conflict had to be weighed as a factor in determining whether there had been an abuse of discretion.

Counsel for either side in an ERISA case in federal court should be aware that some parties may need to show standing. For example, in Thole v. U.S. Bank, N.A. (2020) 590 U.S. ___, 140 S. Ct. 1615, 207 L. Ed. 2d 85, 2020 U.S. LEXIS 3030, the Supreme Court held that because some participants in a defined-benefit retirement plan had no concrete stake in an ERISA suit for alleged mismanagement of the plan, the participants lacked standing under the Federal Constitution's Article III, where, according to the court, the plan guaranteed the participants a fixed payment each month regardless of the plan's value or the investment decisions of the plan's fiduciaries.

II. General Matters

A. Duties Imposed

§ 3. Loyalty

The Supreme Court indicated in the following cases that, under the law of trusts, a fiduciary of an ERISA plan has a general duty of loyalty to the plan's participants and beneficiaries.

In NLRB v. Amax Coal Co., Div. of Amax, Inc. (1981) 453 U.S. 322, 101 S. Ct. 2789, 69 L. Ed. 2d 672, 1981 U.S. LEXIS 130, and reh. den. 453 U.S. 950, 102 S. Ct. 26, 69 L. Ed. 2d 1036, infra § 4, the Supreme Court said that, although § 408(c)(3) of ERISA (29 U.S.C.S. § 1108(c)(3)) permitted a trustee of an employee benefit fund to serve as an agent or representative of a union or employer, the provision did not limit such a person's duty to follow the law's fiduciary standards while performing the person's responsibilities as trustee. While indicating that ERISA essentially codified the strict fiduciary standards imposed on pension plan trustees by § 302(c)(5) of the Labor Management Relations Act (29 U.S.C.S. § 186(c)(5))—which permitted employers and unions to create employer-financed trust funds for the benefit of employees so long as employees and employers were equally represented by the trustees of the funds—the court said that an employee benefit fund trustee was a fiduciary whose duty to the trust beneficiaries was required to overcome any loyalty to the interest to the party that appointed the trustee. The court noted that (1) under principles of equity, a trustee bore an unwavering duty of complete loyalty to the beneficiary of the trust, to the exclusion of the interests of all other parties; and (2) to deter a trustee from all temptation and to prevent any possible injury to the beneficiary, the rule against a trustee dividing the trustee's loyalties had to be enforced with uncompromising rigidity. According to the court, a fiduciary could not contend that, although he had conflicting interests, he served his masters equally well or that his primary loyalty was not weakened by the pull of his secondary one.

While holding that an employer who participated in a multiemployer benefit plan that was governed by ERISA was required to allow trustees of the plan to conduct an audit involving the records of employees whom the employer denied were participants in the plan, where such an audit was within the trustees' authority outlined in the trust documents, in Central States, Southeast & Southwest Areas Pension Fund v. Central Transp. (1985) 472 U.S. 559, 105 S. Ct. 2833, 86 L. Ed. 2d 447, 1985 U.S. LEXIS 114, reh. den. 473 U.S. 926, 106 S. Ct. 17, 87 L. Ed. 2d 696, 1985 U.S. LEXIS 2872, infra § 10, the Supreme Court said that it had no occasion in the case at hand to analyze what sort of factual showing would have been necessary to a claim that a particular auditing program was being conducted in a manner that violated ERISA's fiduciary duties of loyalty or care.

According to the Supreme Court in Mass. Mut. Life Ins. Co. v. Russell (1985) 473 U.S. 134, 105 S. Ct. 3085, 87 L. Ed. 2d 96, 1985 U.S. LEXIS 85, infra § 12, which involved alleged breach of a fiduciary duty to pay ERISA plan benefits, ERISA established duties of loyalty and care for fiduciaries. Stating that with regard to loyalty, the principal provision was § 406 of ERISA (29 U.S.C.S. § 1106), which generally prohibited self-dealing and sales or exchanges between a plan and parties in interest or disqualified persons, the court pointed out that in the same vein, § 408(c)(2) of ERISA (29 U.S.C.S. § 1108(c)(2)) prohibited compensating fiduciaries who were fulltime employees of unions or employers.

In Firestone Tire & Rubber Co. v. Bruch (1989) 489 U.S. 101, 109 S. Ct. 948, 103 L. Ed. 2d 80, 1989 U.S. LEXIS 599, infra § 6[a], which involved a dispute over an employer's failure to disclose information about an ERISA plan, the Supreme Court, noting that it was the general intent of Congress to incorporate much of the fiduciary law of the Labor Management Relations Act (LMRA) (29 U.S.C.S. § 141 et seq.) into ERISA, said that ERISA, like the LMRA, imposed a duty of loyalty on the fiduciaries and administrators of employee benefit plans. The court stated that ERISA's legislative history confirmed that §§ 401-414 of ERISA (29 U.S.C.S. §§ 1101-1114), which were the statute's fiduciary-responsibility provisions, codified and made applicable to ERISA fiduciaries certain principles developed in the evolution of the law of trusts.

In Varity Corp. v. Howe (1996) 516 U.S. 489, 116 S. Ct. 1065, 134 L. Ed. 2d 130, 1996 U.S. LEXIS 1954, infra § 11, the Supreme Court, noting that § 404(a)(1) of ERISA (29 U.S.C.S. § 1104(a)(1)) required a fiduciary to discharge duties with respect to a plan solely in the interest of the participants and beneficiaries, said that (1) to participate knowingly and significantly in deceiving an ERISA plan's beneficiaries in order to save the employer money at the beneficiaries' expense was not to act solely in the interest of the participants and beneficiaries; and (2) lying was inconsistent with the duty of loyalty owed by all fiduciaries and codified in § 1104(a)(1). The court said that, in interpreting the fiduciary duties imposed upon employee benefit plan administrators by ERISA, the court sometimes would consider the requirements of fiduciaries as developed in the common law of trusts as a starting point, after which it had to be determined whether, or to what extent, ERISA's language, structure, or purposes required departure from common-law trust requirements, which included a fiduciary duty of loyalty. While recognizing that the fiduciary duties under ERISA drew much of their content from the common law of trusts, the court said that ERISA's standards and procedural protections partly reflected a congressional determination that the common law of trusts did not offer completely satisfactory protection. Even with respect to the trust-like fiduciary standards that ERISA imposed, the Supreme Court said, Congress expected that the courts would interpret the fiduciary standards while bearing in mind the special nature and purpose of employee-benefit plans as the courts developed a federal common law of rights and obligations under ERISA.

While reversing, in Pegram v. Herdrich (2000) 530 U.S. 211, 120 S. Ct. 2143, 147 L. Ed. 2d 164, 2000 U.S. LEXIS 3964, a judgment to the effect that mixed treatment-and-eligibility decisions made by a health maintenance organization, acting through its physician employees, were fiduciary acts under ERISA, the Supreme Court said that the common law of trusts— understood as including what once had been the distinct rules of equity— imposed upon fiduciaries a duty of loyalty to guarantee beneficiaries' interests. According to the court, (1) the most fundamental duty owed by the trustee to the beneficiaries of a trust was the duty of loyalty, which required a trustee to administer the trust solely in the interest of the beneficiaries; and (2) therefore, a fiduciary of a health care plan that was covered by ERISA was obligated to act exclusively in the interest of a beneficiary of the plan. However, the court indicated that ERISA allowed a plan fiduciary, when not acting as a fiduciary, to act adversely to the interests of plan beneficiaries, as a fiduciary might have financial interests adverse to the beneficiaries of an employee benefit plan. The court said that employers could be ERISA fiduciaries and still take actions to the disadvantage of employee beneficiaries, when the employers acted as employers by, for example, firing a beneficiary for reasons unrelated to an ERISA plan, or acted as plan sponsors by, for example, modifying the terms of a plan as allowed by ERISA to provide less generous benefits. While stating that there was no apparent reason to conclude on the basis of the ERISA provisions that this tension was permissible for only an employer or plan sponsor, to the exclusion of persons who provided services to an ERISA plan, the court noted that ERISA required, however, that a fiduciary with two hats wear only one at a time and wear the fiduciary hat when making fiduciary decisions.

In Harris Trust & Sav. Bank v. Salomon Smith Barney Inc. (2000) 530 U.S. 238, 120 S. Ct. 2180, 147 L. Ed. 2d 187, 2000 U.S. LEXIS 3962, infra § 8, which involved a suit brought by an ERISA plan's trustee and its administrator against a nonfiduciary of the plan, the Supreme Court indicated that a fiduciary of an ERISA plan had a general duty of loyalty to the plan's beneficiaries under § 404(a) of ERISA (29 U.S.C.S. § 1104(a)).

It was pointed out in Metro. Life Ins. Co. v. Glenn (2008) 554 U.S. 105, 128 S. Ct. 2343, 171 L. Ed. 2d 299, 2008 U.S. LEXIS 5030, infra § 6[a], that in determining the appropriate standard of review under § 502(a)(1)(B) of ERISA (29 U.S.C.S. § 1132(a)(1)(B)), a court (1) ought to be guided by principles of trust law; (2) in doing so, ought to analogize a plan administrator to the trustee of a common-law trust; and (3) ought to consider a benefit determination to be a fiduciary act, which was an act in which the administrator owed a special duty of loyalty to the plan beneficiaries.

In Fifth Third Bancorp v. Dudenhoeffer (2014) 573 U.S. 409, 134 S. Ct. 2459, 189 L. Ed. 2d 457, 2014 U.S. LEXIS 4495, infra § 6[b], the Supreme Court acknowledged the court's indication in Central States, Southeast & Southwest Areas Pension Fund v. Central Transp., supra, that § 404(a)(1) of ERISA (29 U.S.C.S. § 1104(a)(1)) imposed strict standards of trustee conduct that were derived from the common law of trusts, and that the most prominent of such standards were a standard of loyalty and a standard of care.

§ 4. Injury to plan

In the following cases, the Supreme Court indicated that fiduciary duties under ERISA to the participants and beneficiaries of an ERISA plan include a duty to avoid transactions that are likely to injure the ERISA plan.

In Lockheed Corp. v. Spink (1996) 517 U.S. 882, 116 S. Ct. 1783, 135 L. Ed. 2d 153, 1996 U.S. LEXIS 3717, infra § 10, the Supreme Court indicated that Congress had enacted § 406 of ERISA (29 U.S.C.S. § 1106)—which, in § 1106(a)(1)(D), prohibited a fiduciary of an ERISA plan from causing the plan to engage in a transaction if the fiduciary knew or should have known that such transaction constituted a direct or indirect transfer to, or use by or for the benefit of a party in interest, of any plan assets—to bar categorically a transaction that was likely to injure an ERISA plan.

Reversing, on other grounds, a judgment holding that ERISA's 6-year limitations period, for a civil action concerning a multiemployer pension plan, under 29 U.S.C.S. § 1451(f)(1) commenced on the due date for an employer's first installment payment of withdrawal liability to such a plan, in Bay Area Laundry & Dry Cleaning Pension Trust Fund v. Ferbar Corp. (1997) 522 U.S. 192, 118 S. Ct. 542, 139 L. Ed. 2d 553, 1997 U.S. LEXIS 7501, the Supreme Court pointed out that pension funds had a financial imperative to act quickly, since (1) the contributions lost when an employer withdrew would not be replaced with withdrawal liability payments until the employer's plan calculated those payments and served a demand on the employer, and (2) as time passed, the likelihood that the plan would never receive payment increased. According to the court, if a plan trustees' delay in calculating withdrawal liability threatened the plan's financial position, then that delay could constitute a breach of fiduciary duty actionable at the instance of the plan's beneficiaries.

The Supreme Court said in Harris Trust & Sav. Bank v. Salomon Smith Barney Inc. (2000) 530 U.S. 238, 120 S. Ct. 2180, 147 L. Ed. 2d 187, 2000 U.S. LEXIS 3962, infra § 8—which involved a suit brought by an ERISA plan's trustee and its administrator against a nonfiduciary of the plan—that pursuant to § 406(a) of ERISA (29 U.S.C.S. § 1106(a)), a fiduciary's general duty of loyalty to a plan's beneficiaries, under § 404(a) of ERISA (29 U.S.C.S. § 1104(a)), was supplemented by categorically barring certain transactions that were deemed likely to injure the plan.

See Amgen Inc. v. Harris (2016) 577 U.S. ___, 136 S. Ct. 758, 193 L. Ed. 2d 696, 2016 U.S. LEXIS 891, infra § 10, in which the Supreme Court, with respect to ERISA fiduciaries who administered employee stock ownership plans, said that to state a claim for breach of the duty of prudence on the basis of inside information, a plaintiff had to plausibly allege (1) an alternative action that the defendant could have taken that would have been consistent with the securities laws; and (2) that a prudent fiduciary in the same circumstances would not have viewed as more likely to harm the fund than to help it. The Supreme Court indicated that lower courts faced with such claims ought to (1) determine whether the complaint stated a claim satisfying that liability standard; and (2) consider whether the complaint had plausibly alleged that a prudent fiduciary in the defendant's position could not have concluded that stopping purchases—which the market might take as a sign that insider fiduciaries viewed the employer's stock as a bad investment—or publicly disclosing negative information would do more harm than good to the fund by causing a drop in the stock price and a concomitant drop in the value of the stock already held by the fund.

§ 5. Labor-relations-law standards

The Supreme Court has indicated that, to a substantial degree, Congress incorporated into ERISA fiduciary duties imposed under federal labor-relations law.

In holding that employer-selected trustees of a fund created under § 302(c)(5) of the Labor Management Relations Act (29 U.S.C.S. § 186(c)(5)) were not "representatives" of employer for purposes of § 8(b)(1)(B) of the National Labor Relations Act (29 U.S.C.S. § 158(b)(1)(B))—which (1) made it an unfair labor practice for a labor union to coerce an employer in the selection of a collective bargaining representative, and (2) permitted employers and unions to create employer-financed trust funds for the benefit of employees so long as employees and employers were equally represented by the trustees of the funds—the Supreme Court, in NLRB v. Amax Coal Co., Div. of Amax, Inc. (1981) 453 U.S. 322, 101 S. Ct. 2789, 69 L. Ed. 2d 672, 1981 U.S. LEXIS 130, and reh. den. 453 U.S. 950, 102 S. Ct. 26, 69 L. Ed. 2d 1036, stated that ERISA essentially codified the strict fiduciary standards that a pension plan trustee was required to meet under § 186(c)(5), where (1) § 404(a)(1) of ERISA (29 U.S.C.S. § 1104(a)(1)) required a trustee to discharge his duties solely in the interest of the participants and beneficiaries; (2) § 406(b)(2) of ERISA (29 U.S.C.S. § 1106(b)(2)) prohibited a trustee from acting in any transaction involving the plan on behalf of a party (or representing a party) whose interests were adverse to the interests of the plan or the interests of its participants or beneficiaries; and (3) § 405(a) of ERISA (29 U.S.C.S. § 1105(a)) imposed on each trustee an affirmative duty to prevent every other trustee of the same fund from breaching fiduciary duties, including the duty to act solely on behalf of the beneficiaries. A coal company, along with the other members of a multiemployer group, agreed to contribute to a labor union's national pension and welfare trust funds that were administered by three trustees, one selected by the union, one by the members of the multiemployer group, and one by the other trustees. The company did not join the national multiemployer group with respect to one of the company's mines, and the union initiated a strike intended to compel the company to establish a multiemployer bargaining unit for that mine and to agree to a new contract under which members of the new employer unit would contribute to the national trust funds. The court reversed a judgment holding that management-appointed trustees had acted both as fiduciaries of employees and funds beneficiaries and as agents of the appointing employer.

According to the Supreme Court in Firestone Tire & Rubber Co. v. Bruch (1989) 489 U.S. 101, 109 S. Ct. 948, 103 L. Ed. 2d 80, 1989 U.S. LEXIS 599, infra § 6[a], which involved a dispute over an employer's failure to disclose information about an ERISA plan, Congress generally had intended to incorporate much of the fiduciary law of the Labor Management Relations Act (LMRA) (29 U.S.C.S. § 141 et seq.) into ERISA. ERISA, like the LMRA, imposed a duty of loyalty on the fiduciaries and administrators of employee benefit plans, the court said.

§ 6. Particular duties

[a] Generally

The following Supreme Court cases specify some particular fiduciary duties that are imposed under ERISA.

In Central States, Southeast & Southwest Areas Pension Fund v. Central Transp. (1985) 472 U.S. 559, 105 S. Ct. 2833, 86 L. Ed. 2d 447, 1985 U.S. LEXIS 114, reh. den. 473 U.S. 926, 106 S. Ct. 17, 87 L. Ed. 2d 696, 1985 U.S. LEXIS 2872, infra § 10, in which the Supreme Court held that an employer who participated in a multiemployer benefit plan that was governed by ERISA was required to allow trustees of the plan to conduct an audit involving the records of employees whom the employer denied were participants in the plan, where such an audit was within the trustees' authority outlined in the trust documents, the court said that under ERISA, a benefit plan trustee had the duty of determining who was a plan participant and a responsibility for assuring full and prompt collection of contributions owed to the plan. According to the court, ERISA trustees had a fiduciary duty to (1) inform participants and beneficiaries of their rights; (2) gain immediate use of trust assets for the benefit of the trust; (3) avoid the time and expense of litigation; and (4) avoid unfunded liabilities that might eventually prove uncollectable as a result of insolvencies. The court observed that ERISA's structure made it clear that Congress had not intended for government enforcement powers to lessen the responsibilities of plan fiduciaries. Moreover, the court said that, although ERISA granted the Secretary of Labor broad investigatory powers, neither the structure nor the legislative history of ERISA showed any congressional intent that plans ought to rely primarily on centralized federal monitoring of employer contribution requirements.

In Mass. Mut. Life Ins. Co. v. Russell (1985) 473 U.S. 134, 105 S. Ct. 3085, 87 L. Ed. 2d 96, 1985 U.S. LEXIS 85, infra § 12, which involved alleged breach of a fiduciary duty to pay ERISA plan benefits, the Supreme Court indicated that the principal fiduciary duties imposed on ERISA-plan trustees related to the proper management, administration, and investment of fund assets, the maintenance of proper records, the disclosure of specified information, and the avoidance of conflicts of interest.

While affirming a judgment to the extent that the judgment held that de novo review applied where some of an employer's former employees brought against the employer an action seeking to recover severance benefits under § 502(a)(1)(B) of ERISA (29 U.S.C.S. § 1132(a)(1)(B)), and to recover damages under § 502(c)(1)(B) of ERISA (29 U.S.C.S. § 1132(c)(1)(B)) for the employer's failure to disclose some requested information concerning their benefits under the employer's ERISA plans, in Firestone Tire & Rubber Co. v. Bruch (1989) 489 U.S. 101, 109 S. Ct. 948, 103 L. Ed. 2d 80, 1989 U.S. LEXIS 599, the Supreme Court indicated that ERISA-plan fiduciaries had a duty to avoid conflicts of interest. Also, according to the court, the fact that an administrator or fiduciary of an employee benefit plan covered by ERISA was operating under a conflict of interest had to be weighed as a factor in determining whether there had been an abuse of discretion, where the plan gave the administrator or fiduciary discretion to make decisions concerning the plan.

See Curtiss-Wright Corp. v. Schoonejongen (1995) 514 U.S. 73, 115 S. Ct. 1223, 131 L. Ed. 2d 94, 1995 U.S. LEXIS 1807, in which the Supreme Court, while reversing, on other grounds, a judgment holding invalid an ERISA plan's reservation clause that concerned the procedure for amending the plan, said that (1) having an amendment procedure gave plan administrators, the people who managed the plan on a day-to-day basis, a mechanism for sorting out, from among the occasional corporate communications that passed through their offices and that conflicted with the existing plan terms, the bona fide amendments from those that were not; and (2) plan administrators might have a statutory responsibility to do this sorting out. The court referred to § 404(a)(1)(D) of ERISA (29 U.S.C.S. § 1104(a)(1)(D)), which imposed on plan administrators a duty to run the plan in accordance with the documents and instruments governing the plan insofar as such documents and instruments were consistent with the provisions of ERISA. In addition, the court said that the fact that Congress may have had plan administrators in mind was suggested by the fact that § 402(b)(3) of ERISA (29 U.S.C.S. § 1102(b)(3)), and § 402(b) of ERISA (29 U.S.C.S. § 1102(b)) more generally, was located in the §§ 401-414 fiduciary-responsibility part of ERISA (29 U.S.C.S. §§ 1101-1114).

In Pegram v. Herdrich (2000) 530 U.S. 211, 120 S. Ct. 2143, 147 L. Ed. 2d 164, 2000 U.S. LEXIS 3964, supra § 3, the Supreme Court indicated that a fiduciary of an ERISA plan had a duty to avoid conflicts of interest. While indicating that ERISA allowed a plan fiduciary, when not acting as a fiduciary, to act adversely to the interests of plan beneficiaries—where, for example, an employer that was an ERISA fiduciary could fire a beneficiary for reasons unrelated to an ERISA plan, and, if acting as the plan sponsor, could modify the terms of a plan as allowed by ERISA to provide less generous benefits—the court stated that ERISA required, however, that a fiduciary with two hats wear only one at a time and wear the fiduciary hat when making fiduciary decisions.

While reversing a judgment to the effect that causes of action brought in state court by ERISA-plan beneficiaries alleging that their plans' failure to cover certain medical services violated a state statute were not pre-empted by § 502(a)(1)(B) of ERISA (29 U.S.C.S. § 1132(a)(1)(B)), in Aetna Health Inc. v. Davila (2004) 542 U.S. 200, 124 S. Ct. 2488, 159 L. Ed. 2d 312, 2004 U.S. LEXIS 4571, the Supreme Court said because a benefit determination under an ERISA plan was generally a fiduciary act, a benefit determination was part of the ordinary fiduciary responsibilities connected to the administration of a plan. In the court's view, (1) the fact that a benefits determination might be infused with medical judgments did not alter this result, since a trustee managing a medical trust undoubtedly had to make administrative decisions that required the exercise of medical judgment; and (2) ERISA—which, in § 3(21)(A)(3) (29 U.S.C.S. § 1002(21)(A)(3)), defined a fiduciary as any person to the extent that the person had any discretionary authority or discretionary responsibility in administration of an employee benefit plan—and ERISA's implementing regulations confirmed this interpretation. The court concluded that the fact that § 503 of ERISA (29 U.S.C.S. § 1133) required plans to afford a reasonable opportunity to any participant whose claim for benefits had been denied for review by the appropriate named fiduciary of the decision denying the claim strongly suggests that the ultimate decisionmaker regarding an award of plan benefits had to be a fiduciary acting as a fiduciary.

According to the Supreme Court in LaRue v. DeWolff, Boberg & Assocs. (2008) 552 U.S. 248, 128 S. Ct. 1020, 169 L. Ed. 2d 847, 2008 U.S. LEXIS 2014, infra § 11, the principal statutory duties imposed on fiduciaries by § 409(a) of ERISA (29 U.S.C.S. § 1109(a)) related to the proper management, administration, and investment of fund assets, with an eye toward insuring that the benefits authorized by the plan ultimately were paid to participants and beneficiaries.

In Metro. Life Ins. Co. v. Glenn (2008) 554 U.S. 105, 128 S. Ct. 2343, 171 L. Ed. 2d 299, 2008 U.S. LEXIS 5030, it was held that where the entity that administered an ERISA plan both determined whether an employee was eligible for benefits and paid the benefits out of the entity's pocket, this dual role created a conflict of interest that court ought to consider as a factor when reviewing a denial of benefits under the plan. The court said that the significance of this factor would depend upon the circumstances of the particular case. In the case at hand, the record indicated that an insurance company was an administrator and the insurer of an employer's ERISA-covered long-term disability insurance plan that gave the insurer (as administrator) discretion to determine the validity of employees' benefits claims and provided that the insurer (as insurer) would pay the claims. An employee was granted an initial 24 months of benefits under the plan following a diagnosis of a heart disorder. The insurer encouraged her to apply for, and she began receiving, Social Security disability benefits that were based on a Social Security Administration determination that she could do no work. However, when the insurer had to determine whether the employee could work, in order to establish eligibility for extended ERISA plan benefits, the insurer found her capable of doing sedentary work and denied her the extended benefits. A judgment that had set aside this benefits denial was affirmed.

In holding that a claim that an ERISA plan's fiduciaries had breached their duty of prudence by offering funds that had higher costs than the costs of materially identical funds was not barred by the running of the general limitations period of § 413(a) of ERISA (29 U.S.C.S. § 1113(a))—which generally prohibited commencement of an action under ERISA for breach of fiduciary duty after the earlier of 6 years after (1) the date of the last action that constituted a part of the alleged breach, or (2) in the case of an omission, the latest date on which the fiduciary could have cured the breach—after the higher-priced funds were first offered, the Supreme Court in Tibble v. Edison Int'l (2015) 575 U.S. 523, 135 S. Ct. 1823, 191 L. Ed. 2d 795, 2015 U.S. LEXIS 3171, infra § 11, supported this holding by stating that, under trust law, fiduciaries had a continuing duty to monitor trust investments and remove imprudent ones. According to the court, (1) this continuing duty existed apart from a trustee's duty to exercise prudence in selecting investments at the outset; and (2) rather than assuming that if investments were legal and proper for retention at the beginning of the trust, or when purchased, they would remain so indefinitely, the trustee was required to systematically consider all the investments of the trust at regular intervals to insure that they were appropriate. Commenting that a trustee's duties applied not only in making investments but also in monitoring and reviewing them, which was to be done in a manner that was reasonable and appropriate to the particular investments, courses of action, and strategies involved, the court added that the Uniform Prudent Investor Act confirmed that managing embraced monitoring and that a trustee had continuing responsibility for oversight of the suitability of investments already made. When a trust estate included assets that were inappropriate as trust investments, the trustee ordinarily had a duty to dispose of those assets within a reasonable time, the court said.

[b] Employee stock ownership plans (ESOPs)

In the following cases, the Supreme Court expressed the view that except for not being required to diversify the fund's assets, fiduciaries of employee stock ownership plans (ESOPs) were subject to the duty of prudence that was applicable under § 404(a)(1)(B) of ERISA (29 U.S.C.S. § 1104(a)(1)(B)) to fiduciaries generally.

According to the Supreme Court in Fifth Third Bancorp v. Dudenhoeffer (2014) 573 U.S. 409, 134 S. Ct. 2459, 189 L. Ed. 2d 457, 2014 U.S. LEXIS

4495, fiduciaries of employee stock ownership plans (ESOPs) were—except for not being required to diversify the fund's assets—subject to the duty of prudence that was applicable under § 404(a)(1)(B) of ERISA (29 U.S.C.S. § 1104(a)(1)(B)) to fiduciaries generally. Vacating a judgment holding that ESOP fiduciaries were entitled to a presumption of prudence, the court said that Congress had recognized that ESOPs were designed to invest primarily in the stock of the participants' employer, meaning that the plans were not prudently diversified. It was noted that (1) § 404(a)(2) of ERISA (29 U.S.C.S. § 1104(a)(2)) established the extent to which the duties imposed by § 404(a)(1) of ERISA (29 U.S.C.S. § 1104(a)(1)) were loosened in the ESOP context to insure that employers were permitted and encouraged to offer ESOPs, and that § 1104(a)(2) made no reference to a special presumption in favor of ESOP fiduciaries but, instead, simply modified the duties imposed by § 1104(a)(1) in a precisely delineated way. According to the court, an ERISA fiduciary usually was not imprudent to assume that a major stock market provided the best estimate of the value of the stocks traded on it that was available to the fiduciary. Indicating that the duty of prudence, under the ERISA, as under the common law of trusts, did not require a fiduciary to break the law, the court added that federal securities laws were violated when a corporate insider traded in the securities of the insider's corporation on the basis of material, nonpublic information. Moreover, the Supreme Court said that where a complaint faulted fiduciaries for failing to decide, on the basis of the inside information, to refrain from making additional stock purchases or for failing to disclose that information to the public so that the stock would no longer be overvalued, additional considerations arose, as courts ought to consider the extent to which an obligation based on ERISA either to refrain on the basis of inside information from making a planned trade or to disclose inside information to the public could conflict with the complex insider trading and corporate disclosure requirements imposed by the federal securities laws or with the objectives of those laws. To state a claim for breach of the duty of prudence under § 1104(a)(1)(B) on the basis of inside information, the court said, a plaintiff had to plausibly allege an alternative action that the defendant could have taken that would have been consistent with the securities laws and that a prudent fiduciary in the same circumstances would not have viewed as more likely to harm the fund than to help it.

In Amgen Inc. v. Harris (2016) 577 U.S. ___, 136 S. Ct. 758, 193 L. Ed. 2d 696, 2016 U.S. LEXIS 891, infra § 10, the Supreme Court said that rather than being entitled to a presumption of prudence under ERISA, fiduciaries who administered employee stock ownership plans (ESOPs) were subject to the same duty of prudence that applied to ERISA fiduciaries in general, except that ESOP fiduciaries were not required to diversify the fund's assets. Referring to the court's indication in Fifth Third Bancorp v. Dudenhoeffer, supra, that Congress had sought to encourage the creation of ESOPs, which encouragement might come into tension with ERISA's general duty of prudence, the court said that ESOP fiduciaries confronted unique challenges, given the potential for conflict that arose when fiduciaries were alleged to have imprudently failed to act on inside information that they had about the value of the employer's stock.

See Ret. Plans Comm. of IBM v. Jander (2020) 589 U.S. ___, 140 S. Ct. 592, 205 L. Ed. 2d 432, 2020 U.S. LEXIS 527, which involved fiduciaries of an employee stock ownership plan (ESOP), where the Supreme Court (1) quoted from Fifth Third Bancorp v. Dudenhoeffer, supra; (2) vacated a Federal Court of Appeals' judgment; (3) remanded the case; and (4) left it to the Court of Appeals whether to determine the merits of some arguments involving (asserted) fiduciary duty under ERISA.

B. Other Matters

§ 7. Plan documents

In the following cases, the Supreme Court made some determinations concerning the effect of various types of ERISA-plan documents on fiduciary duties with respect to the plan.

The Supreme Court, in Central States, Southeast & Southwest Areas Pension Fund v. Central Transp. (1985) 472 U.S. 559, 105 S. Ct. 2833, 86 L. Ed. 2d 447, 1985 U.S. LEXIS 114, reh. den. 473 U.S. 926, 106 S. Ct. 17, 87 L. Ed. 2d 696, 1985 U.S. LEXIS 2872, infra § 10, decided that an employer who participated in a multiemployer benefit plan that was governed by ERISA had to allow trustees of the plan to conduct an audit involving the records of employees whom the employer denied were participants in the plan, as such an audit was within the trustees' authority outlined in the trust documents. However, the court made the general observation that trust documents could not excuse trustees from their duties under ERISA. Such documents, the court said, generally had to be construed in light of ERISA's policies.

In CIGNA Corp. v. Amara (2011) 563 U.S. 421, 131 S. Ct. 1866, 179 L. Ed. 2d 843, 2011 U.S. LEXIS 3540, infra § 12, where a class of participants in an ERISA plan brought against their employer an action alleging that the employer had changed the plan, to the detriment of the participants, without adequate disclosures, the Supreme Court said that, although § 102(a) of ERISA (29 U.S.C.S. § 1022(a)) obliged plan administrators to furnish summary plan descriptions, § 1022(a) did not suggest that information about the plan provided by summary plan descriptions was part of the plan. Thus indicating that a summary plan description was not part of an ERISA plan's terms, the court said that the opposition to this position could not be squared with ERISA's division of authority between (1) a plan's sponsor, who created the plan's basic terms and conditions, executed a written instrument containing those terms and conditions, and provided in that instrument an amendment procedure; and (2) the plan's administrator, a fiduciary who managed the plan, followed its terms, and provided participants with summary plan descriptions. According to the court, ERISA carefully distinguished these roles, and there was no reason to believe that the statute intended to mix the responsibilities by giving the administrator the power to set plan terms indirectly in the summary plan descriptions, even when, as in the instant case, the administrator also was the plan sponsor. Moreover, the court observed that it was difficult to reconcile an interpretation that would make the language of a summary plan description legally binding with ERISA's basic summary-plan-description objective of clear, simple communication.

The Supreme Court observed in Fifth Third Bancorp v. Dudenhoeffer (2014) 573 U.S. 409, 134 S. Ct. 2459, 189 L. Ed. 2d 457, 2014 U.S. LEXIS 4495, supra § 6[b], that § 504(a)(1)(D) of ERISA (29 U.S.C.S. § 1104(a)(1)(D))—which required a fiduciary to discharge fiduciary duties with respect to an ERISA plan in accordance with the documents and instruments governing the plan insofar as those documents and instruments were consistent with certain federal statutory provisions including ERISA—made clear that the ERISA fiduciary duty of prudence trumped the instructions of a plan document, such as an instruction to invest exclusively in employer stock even if financial goals demanded the contrary. It was noted that by contrast to the rule at common law, trust documents could not excuse trustees from their duties under ERISA.

§ 8. Knowledge of unlawfulness

The Supreme Court concluded in the following case that in order to be held liable under ERISA, a fiduciary who was a transferee in an unlawful property transaction had to be demonstrated to have had actual or constructive knowledge of the circumstances that rendered the transaction unlawful.

While reversing a judgment holding that authorization, under § 502(a)(3) of ERISA (29 U.S.C.S. § 1132(a)(3)), of a civil action for appropriate equitable relief did not extend to a suit against a nonfiduciary party in interest to a transaction that was barred by § 406(a) of ERISA (29 U.S.C.S. § 1106(a)), in Harris Trust & Sav. Bank v. Salomon Smith Barney Inc. (2000) 530 U.S. 238, 120 S. Ct. 2180, 147 L. Ed. 2d 187, 2000 U.S. LEXIS 3962, the Supreme Court held that to be held liable under ERISA, a transferee in an unlawful property transaction had to be demonstrated to have had actual or constructive knowledge of the circumstances that rendered the transaction unlawful. Those circumstances, the court said, involved a showing that the plan fiduciary, with actual or constructive knowledge of the facts satisfying the elements of a § 1106(a) transaction, had caused the plan to engage in the transaction. The case involved an action under § 1132(a)(3) by a plan's trustee and its administrator against a nonfiduciary who allegedly was a party in interest who had entered into a transaction that was prohibited by § 1106(a).

III. Breach of Duties

§ 9. Breach shown or propriety not shown

In the following cases, the Supreme Court decided that particular fiduciary acts constituted, or could constitute, breach of fiduciary duties under ERISA.

In Varity Corp. v. Howe (1996) 516 U.S. 489, 116 S. Ct. 1065, 134 L. Ed. 2d 130, 1996 U.S. LEXIS 1954, the Supreme Court decided that where an employer, which was the administrator of its ERISA plan, presented its employees with material concerning their employee benefits and the benefits offered by a newly created corporate entity, and encouraged the employees to voluntarily transfer their benefits to the new entity's plan, violated the fiduciary obligations imposed by ERISA upon the plan's administrator to discharge its duties with respect to the plan solely in the interest of plan participants and beneficiaries, by knowingly and significantly deceiving the employees about the financial viability of the new entity and the future of the new entity's benefits plan, in order to save the employer money at the expense of the beneficiaries.

See Bay Area Laundry & Dry Cleaning Pension Trust Fund v. Ferbar Corp. (1997) 522 U.S. 192, 118 S. Ct. 542, 139 L. Ed. 2d 553, 1997 U.S. LEXIS 7501—which involved ERISA's 6-year limitations period, for a civil action concerning a multiemployer pension plan, under 29 U.S.C.S. § 1451(f)(1) —where the Supreme Court, in a case decided on other grounds, indicated that if a delay, by the trustees of an ERISA plan, in calculating an employer's liability for withdrawal from a multiemployer plan threatened the plan's financial position, then that delay could constitute a breach of fiduciary duty that was actionable at the instance of the plan's beneficiaries.

§ 10. Breach not shown

In the following cases involving alleged breach of fiduciary duties imposed under ERISA, the Supreme Court determined that a breach had not been shown.

In Central States, Southeast & Southwest Areas Pension Fund v. Central Transp. (1985) 472 U.S. 559, 105 S. Ct. 2833, 86 L. Ed. 2d 447, 1985 U.S. LEXIS 114, reh. den. 473 U.S. 926, 106 S. Ct. 17, 87 L. Ed. 2d 696, 1985 U.S. LEXIS 2872, the Supreme Court concluded that the trustees of several large multiemployer benefit plans governed by ERISA did not violate their fiduciary duties by seeking to conduct an audit that was to encompass, among other subjects, determination of who were eligible plan participants. The court noted that under ERISA, a benefit plan trustee had the duty of determining who was a plan participant and a responsibility for assuring full and prompt collection of contributions owed to the plan. Reversing a judgment to the effect that the audit request required reasonable cause, the court said that given Congress' vision of the proper administration of ERISA plans, the court had little difficulty holding that the requested audit was well within the authority of the trustees as outlined in the trust documents. The court pointed out that it did not hold that under ERISA a benefit plan's interests in fully identifying participants and beneficiaries required that it conduct the sort of audit in question. Rather, the court held merely that the trust documents gave the fiduciaries the right to request the audit in the instant case.

It was held in Lockheed Corp. v. Spink (1996) 517 U.S. 882, 116 S. Ct. 1783, 135 L. Ed. 2d 153, 1996 U.S. LEXIS 3717, that § 406(a)(1)(D) of ERISA (29 U.S.C.S. § 1106(a)(1)(D)), which prohibited a fiduciary from causing an employee benefit plan to engage in a transaction that transferred plan assets

to a party in interest or involved the use of plan assets for the benefit of a
party in interest, did not prevent an employer from amending its ERISA plan
to condition the receipt of benefits, under an early-retirement program, upon
a program participant's waiver of employment-related claims, as, among other
matters, the payment of benefits pursuant to an amended plan, regardless of
what the plan required of the employee in return for those benefits, did not
constitute a prohibited transaction under § 1106(a)(1)(D). The Supreme Court
said that § 1106(a)(1)(D) did not in direct terms include the payment of
benefits by a plan administrator, and that the payment of benefits conditioned
on plan performance could not reasonably be said to share the characteristic
of transactions identified in § 1106(a)(1)(D), which generally involved uses of
plan assets that were potentially harmful to the plan. Moreover, the court
said that there was no basis in § 1106(a)(1)(D) for distinguishing a valid from
an invalid quid pro quo between a plan sponsor and a plan participant, since
§ 1106(a)(1)(D) did not address what an employer could ask an employee to do
in return for benefits. An employer made some previously excluded employees
members of the employer's ERISA plan, while making it clear that these
employees would not receive credit under the plan for earlier service years.
Subsequently, the employer added to the plan two programs that offered
increased pension benefits to employees who would retire early in exchange
for their waiver of any employment claims against the employer. The court
reversed a judgment to the effect that the employer had violated
§ 1106(a)(1)(D) by amending the plan with respect to early-retirement benefits.

See Hughes Aircraft Co. v. Jacobson (1999) 525 U.S. 432, 119 S. Ct. 755,
142 L. Ed. 2d 881, 1999 U.S. LEXIS 753, where (1) an employer's defined
benefit retirement plan allegedly required mandatory contributions from all
participating employees and required employer contributions to the extent
necessary to fund plan benefits, but allowed the employer to suspend its
contributions so long as doing so did not create an accumulated funding
deficiency in the plan under ERISA; and (2) the Supreme Court said that even
if the court assumed that a sham transaction might implicate a fiduciary duty,
then the incidental benefits conferred upon the employer—which had suspended its plan contributions in light of an accumulated plan surplus—when
it amended the plan were not impermissible under ERISA. The court reversed
a judgment to the effect that the retirees involved in the instant case had alleged several causes of action under ERISA.

The Supreme Court decided in Beck v. PACE Int'l Union (2007) 551 U.S.
96, 127 S. Ct. 2310, 168 L. Ed. 2d 1, 2007 U.S. LEXIS 7716, that an employer's
decision not to terminate its pension plans by merger with a labor union's
plan did not constitute a breach of fiduciary duties under ERISA, because 29
U.S.C.S. § 1341(b)(3)(A) did not permit merger as a method of terminating a
single-employer defined-benefit plan. The employer rejected the merger proposed by the union and opted instead for a standard termination through the
purchase of annuities. Reversing a judgment to the effect that the employer's
directors had breached their fiduciary duties by neglecting to give diligent

consideration to the merger proposal, the court stated that an employer's decision whether to terminate an ERISA plan was a settlor function that was immune from ERISA's fiduciary obligations, and that, because decisions regarding the form or structure of a plan were generally settlor functions, the decision to merge plans was normally a plan sponsor's decision as well. It was noted that Congress nowhere had expressly provided for merger as a permissible means of plan termination under ERISA, and that merger was fundamentally different from termination of an employee benefit plan, as merger represented continuation rather than cessation of the ERISA regime. Moreover, the court said that the fact that a transfer of assets could occur in anticipation of a termination of an employee benefit plan did not render that transfer a termination.

In Kennedy v. Plan Adm'r for DuPont Sav. & Inv. Plan (2009) 555 U.S. 285, 129 S. Ct. 865, 172 L. Ed. 2d 662, 2009 U.S. LEXIS 869, the Supreme Court concluded that the administrator of an ERISA plan had done its fiduciary duty by paying plan benefits to a covered decedent's former spouse, who had waived the benefits in a divorce decree, since the decedent had not removed her as a plan beneficiary, and the spouse had not expressly disclaimed benefits in accordance with the terms of the plan. The court affirmed a judgment holding that the former spouse was entitled to the benefits, where the executrix of the decedent's estate alleged that the plan administrator improperly had distributed plan benefits to the former spouse. The court noted that (1) § 402 of ERISA (29 U.S.C.S. § 1102) required every employee benefit plan to be established and maintained pursuant to a written instrument specifying the basis on which payments were made to and from the plan; and (2) ERISA provided no exemption from an administrator's duty under § 404(a)(1)(D) of ERISA (29 U.S.C.S. § 1104(a)(1)(D)) to pay plan benefits in accordance with the documents and instruments governing the plan. Moreover, the court said that § 502(a)(1)(B) of ERISA (29 U.S.C.S. 1132(a)(1)(B)) reinforced the directive to pay the benefits with its with its provision that a participant or beneficiary was allowed to bring a cause of action to recover benefits due to the beneficiary under the terms of the beneficiary's plan.

In Amgen Inc. v. Harris (2016) 577 U.S. ___, 136 S. Ct. 758, 193 L. Ed. 2d 696, 2016 U.S. LEXIS 891, the Supreme Court held that some former employees of a corporation, which employees had participated in plans that qualified under § 407(d)(3)(A) of ERISA (29 U.S.C.S. § 1107(d)(3)(A)) as eligible individual account plans, failed to state a claim under ERISA for breach of fiduciary duties, including the duty of prudence, with respect to plan fiduciaries' management of the plans. Because the court did not find sufficient facts and allegations to state a claim for breach of the duty of prudence, the court (1) reversed a judgment holding the former employees' complaint stated a claim; and (2) remanded the case for further proceedings. According to the court, the proposition that removing the employer's common stock fund from the list of investment options under the plan was an alternative action that plausibly could have been less harmful to the plan funds than were the fiduciaries' acts that allegedly violated their duties might be true. The

Supreme Court indicated that (1) facts and allegations supporting that proposition did not appear in the former employees' complaint, but (2) the Supreme Court was leaving it to the Federal District Court involved in the case to decide in the first instance whether to allow the former employees to amend their complaint accordingly.

IV. Remedies

§ 11. Available

The Supreme Court determined in the following cases that a particular remedy was available under ERISA for the breach of fiduciary duties alleged.

The Supreme Court in Varity Corp. v. Howe (1996) 516 U.S. 489, 116 S. Ct. 1065, 134 L. Ed. 2d 130, 1996 U.S. LEXIS 1954, supra § 9, affirmed a judgment to the effect that individual beneficiaries of an ERISA plan for which the employer that offered the plan was the administrator were permitted to sue for equitable relief under § 502(a)(3) of ERISA (29 U.S.C.S. § 1132(a)(3)), where the court concluded that the employer had violated its fiduciary duties by deliberately misleading the beneficiaries. The court, stating that its decision in Mass. Mut. Life Ins. Co. v. Russell (1985) 473 U.S. 134, 105 S. Ct. 3085, 87 L. Ed. 2d 96, 1985 U.S. LEXIS 85, infra § 12—that individual actions were not allowed to be brought under § 1132(a)(2)—could be distinguished in the circumstances of the case at hand, observed that the language of § 1132(a)(3) was broad enough to cover individual relief for breach of a fiduciary obligation. According to the Varity court, (1) the structure of § 1132 suggested that § 1132(a)(3) was a catchall provision that acted as a safety net, offering appropriate equitable relief for injuries caused by violations that § 1132 did not elsewhere adequately remedy; (2) ERISA's basic purposes favored a reading of § 1132(a)(3) that provided the plaintiffs with a remedy; and (3) potential concerns that permitting individuals to enforce fiduciary obligations owed directly to them threatened to increase costs of benefit plans and to discourage employers from offering such plans seemed unlikely to materialize.

In LaRue v. DeWolff, Boberg & Assocs. (2008) 552 U.S. 248, 128 S. Ct. 1020, 169 L. Ed. 2d 847, 2008 U.S. LEXIS 2014, the Supreme Court concluded that § 502(a)(2) of ERISA (29 U.S.C.S. § 1132(a)(2)) authorized a participant in a defined-contribution pension plan to sue a fiduciary whose alleged misconduct had impaired the value of plan assets in the participant's individual account. Thus, the court vacated a judgment holding that § 1132(a)(2) provided remedies only for entire plans, in a case where a pension-plan participant alleged that his former employer had breached its fiduciary duty as plan administrator by failing to follow the participant's investment directions. The court said that ERISA-plan trustees who breached their fiduciary duties were chargeable with any profit that would have accrued to the trust estate—including profits forgone because a trustee had failed to purchase specific property that it was the trustee's duty to purchase—if there had been no breach. For purposes of establishing breach with respect to defined-contribution plans,

fiduciary misconduct did not have to threaten the solvency of the entire plan
to reduce benefits below the amount that participants would otherwise
receive, the court said. The court observed that regardless of whether a
fiduciary breach diminished plan assets that payable to all participants and
beneficiaries, or only to persons who were tied to particular individual accounts, the breach created the kind of harms that concerned the drafters of
§ 409(a) of ERISA (29 U.S.C.S. § 1109(a)), which imposed liability for breach
of fiduciary duty.

Although holding in CIGNA Corp. v. Amara (2011) 563 U.S. 421, 131 S. Ct.
1866, 179 L. Ed. 2d 843, 2011 U.S. LEXIS 3540, infra § 12, that § 502(a)(1)(B)
of ERISA (29 U.S.C.S. § 1132(a)(1)(B)) did not authorize a Federal District
Court's reformation of an employer's ERISA plan that allegedly had been
changed by the employer, to the detriment of plan participants, without
adequate disclosures, the Supreme Court also held that § 502(a)(3) of ERISA
(29 U.S.C.S. § 1132(a)(3)) authorized such reformation under an equity
standard, as such reformation was consistent with the authorization in
§ 1132(a)(3) to provide appropriate equitable relief. The Supreme Court said
that (1) it had interpreted the term "appropriate equitable relief" in
§ 1132(a)(3) as referring to those categories of relief that, prior to the merger
of law and equity, typically had been available in equity; (2) the instant case
was the kind of lawsuit that, before prior to the merger of law and equity,
could have been brought only in a court of equity, in which the remedies
available were traditionally considered equitable remedies; (3) the District
Court's affirmative and negative injunctions in the instant case obviously fell
within this category; and (4) other relief that had been ordered by the District
Court resembled forms of traditional equitable relief.

It was held in Tibble v. Edison Int'l (2015) 575 U.S. 523, 135 S. Ct. 1823,
191 L. Ed. 2d 795, 2015 U.S. LEXIS 3171, that a claim that an ERISA plan's
fiduciaries had breached their duty of prudence by offering funds that had
higher costs than the costs of materially identical funds was not barred by the
running of the general limitations period of § 413(a) of ERISA (29 U.S.C.S.
§ 1113(a))—which generally prohibited commencement of an action under
ERISA for breach of fiduciary duty after the earlier of 6 years after (1) the
date of the last action that constituted a part of the alleged breach, or (2) in
the case of an omission, the latest date on which the fiduciary could have
cured the breach—after the higher-priced funds were first offered, because
under trust law, fiduciaries had a continuing duty to monitor trust investments and remove imprudent ones. In 2007, beneficiaries of an ERISA plan
brought against plan fiduciaries a suit seeking to recover damages for alleged
losses suffered by the plan as a result of, among other matters, the fiduciaries'
adding three mutual funds to the plan in 1999, when, according to the
beneficiaries, materially identical lower-priced funds were available. Vacating
a judgment to the effect that the beneficiaries' suit was untimely, the court
indicated that (1) § 404(a)(1) of ERISA (29 U.S.C.S. § 1104(a)(1)) required a
fiduciary to discharge the fiduciary's responsibility with the care, skill,
prudence, and diligence that a prudent person acting in a like capacity and

familiar with such matters would use; (2) the Supreme Court often had noted
that an ERISA fiduciary's duty was derived from the common law of trusts;
and (3) in determining the contours of an ERISA fiduciary's duty, courts often
had to look to the law of trusts.

§ 12. Not available

The Supreme Court determined in the following cases that a particular
remedy was not available under ERISA for the breach of fiduciary duties alleged.

In Mass. Mut. Life Ins. Co. v. Russell (1985) 473 U.S. 134, 105 S. Ct. 3085,
87 L. Ed. 2d 96, 1985 U.S. LEXIS 85, the Supreme Court concluded that under
§ 409(a) of ERISA (29 U.S.C.S. § 1109(a)), which established liability for
breach of fiduciary duty, a plan participant or beneficiary did not have a cause
of action against a fiduciary for extracontractual compensatory or punitive
damages allegedly caused by improper or untimely processing of benefit
claims, because (1) nothing in § 1109 provided express authority for an award
of extracontractual damages to a beneficiary; and (2) since Congress had not
intended the judiciary to imply such a private right of action, recovery for a
violation of § 1109 inured to the benefit of the plan as a whole rather than to
an individual beneficiary. An employee, who was a beneficiary under two
ERISA plans administered by her employer, alleged that the employer had
breached its fiduciary duty by failing to make timely benefit payments to the
employee. While reversing a judgment holding that the employee had alleged
a cause of action under § 1109, the court observed that given that the
employee relied entirely on § 1109(a) and expressly disclaimed reliance on
§ 502(a)(3) of ERISA (29 U.S.C.S. § 1132(a)(3)), the court had no occasion to
consider whether any other ERISA provision authorized recovery of extracontractual damages. Also, the court did not need to address the issue
whether a breach of the employer's fiduciary duties had occurred.

In Guidry v. Sheet Metal Workers Nat'l Pension Fund (1990) 493 U.S. 365,
110 S. Ct. 680, 107 L. Ed. 2d 782, 1990 U.S. LEXIS 484, the Supreme Court
concluded that § 206(d)(1) of ERISA (29 U.S.C.S. § 1056(d)(1))—which generally prohibited assignment or alienation of pension benefits—prohibited imposition of a constructive trust, in favor of a local labor union that had a judgment against its former chief executive officer to recover a portion of the union
funds that had been embezzled by the officer, on the benefits from the three
union pension plans from which the officer was eligible to receive benefits,
despite the fact that § 409(a) of ERISA (29 U.S.C.S. § 1109(a)) authorized
courts to provide appropriate equitable or remedial relief against a pension
plan fiduciary who had breached a fiduciary duty to the plan. The court said
that § 1056(d)(1) prohibited a constructive-trust remedy unless some exception to the general ban under § 1056(d)(1) was applicable, and that the officer
had not been found to have breached any fiduciary duty to the plans. Assuming, without deciding, that § 501(b) of the Labor-Management Reporting and
Disclosure Act (LMRDA) (29 U.S.C.S. § 501(b))—which provided a private
right of action to recover damages or secure other appropriate relief for the

benefit of a labor organization—might authorize imposition of a constructive trust, the court said that such authorization did not override § 1056(d)(1). Moreover, the court said that it was inappropriate to approve any generalized equitable exceptions to § 1056(d)(1) even if that decision prevented some plan participants and beneficiaries from securing relief for the wrongs done them. A judgment upholding imposition of a constructive trust was reversed.

See Mertens v. Hewitt Assocs. (1993) 508 U.S. 248, 113 S. Ct. 2063, 124 L. Ed. 2d 161, 1993 U.S. LEXIS 3742, in which the Supreme Court, rejecting an argument under § 502(a)(3) of ERISA (29 U.S.C.S. § 1132(a)(3)), held that ERISA did not authorize a suit by some retired pension-plan participants for money damages against a nonfiduciary actuary who allegedly participated knowingly in a breach of fiduciary duty by the plan's fiduciaries. The court affirmed a judgment in favor of the actuary.

While holding in CIGNA Corp. v. Amara (2011) 563 U.S. 421, 131 S. Ct. 1866, 179 L. Ed. 2d 843, 2011 U.S. LEXIS 3540, supra § 11, that § 502(a)(3) of ERISA (29 U.S.C.S. § 1132(a)(3)) authorized a Federal District Court's reformation, under an equity standard, of an employer's ERISA plan that allegedly had been changed by the employer, to the detriment of plan participants, without adequate disclosures, the Supreme Court also held that § 502(a)(1)(B) of ERISA (29 U.S.C.S. § 1132(a)(1)(B)) did not authorize such reformation. The court noted that (1) § 1132(a)(1)(B) provided only for enforcement of the plan's terms and not for changing the terms; and (2) the allegedly misleading disclosures by the employer were not enforceable plan terms.

INDEX TO
DECISIONS AND ANNOTATIONS

INDEX TO DECISIONS AND ANNOTATIONS --
193 L Ed 2d

Ind-1

EVIDENCE. —Cont'd
crime, rather than elements set forth in erroneous jury instruction, 193 L Ed 2d 639, 577 US 237, 136 S Ct 750.

F

FEDERAL ENERGY REGULATORY COMMISSION.
Electricity.
Demand response bids, wholesale market operators' compensation of.
Authority to regulate and validity of regulation, 193 L Ed 2d 661, 577 US 260, 136 S Ct 760.

FOREIGN SOVEREIGN IMMUNITIES ACT.
Commercial exception.
Train station in Austria, claimed injuries at.
Eurail pass purchase in United States, inapplicability of exception on basis of, 193 L Ed 2d 269, 577 US 27, 136 S Ct 390.

FORMA PAUPERIS.
Payments, 26 L Ed 2d 586, 399 US 235, 90 S Ct 2018, 28 L Ed 2d 130, 401 US 395, 91 S Ct 668, 34 L Ed 2d 626, 409 US 434, 93 S Ct 631, 193 L Ed 2d 496, 577 US 82, 136 S Ct 627.

I

INDIANS.
Limitation of actions.
Claims against United States, 64 L Ed 318, 251 US 382, 40 S Ct 181, 193 L Ed 2d 652, 577 US 250, 136 S Ct 718.

L

LEGISLATIVE APPORTIONMENT.
Three-judge court.
Requirement in reapportionment suit, 18 L Ed 2d 643, 387 US 97, 87 S Ct 1544, 193 L Ed 2d 279, 577 US 39, 136 S Ct 450.

LIMITATION OF ACTIONS.
Appeal and error.
General federal criminal statute as not to be raised successfully for first time on appeal, 193 L Ed 2d 639, 577 US 237, 136 S Ct 750.

P

PAROLE, PROBATION, AND PARDON.
Children and minors.

PAROLE, PROBATION, AND PARDON. —Cont'd
Retroactivity of decision prohibiting mandatory sentence of life imprisonment without possibility of parole, 193 L Ed 2d 599, 577 US 190, 136 S Ct 758.

PENSIONS AND RETIREMENT.
Employee Retirement Income Security Act.
Fiduciaries.
Dissipation by participant of settlement on nontraceable items.
Attachment of general assets, suit not allowed for, 193 L Ed 2d 556, 577 US 136, 136 S Ct 651.
Failure to state claim for breach of duty of prudence, 193 L Ed 2d 696, 577 US 308, 136 S Ct 709.
Fiduciary duties under Employee Retirement Income Security Act of 1974, as amended (ERISA) (29 U.S.C.S. § 1001 et seq.)—Supreme Court cases, 193 L Ed 2d 861 (anno).

Q

QUALIFIED IMMUNITY.
Application or applicability of qualified immunity doctrine in action under 42 USCS § 1983, or in Bivens action, seeking damages for alleged civil rights violations, involving law enforcement activities or treatment of prisoners, 193 L Ed 2d 831 (anno).
High speed police chase.
Shooting from overpass at vehicle and killing driver.
Officer as entitled to qualified immunity, 193 L Ed 2d 255, 577 US 7, 136 S Ct 305.

T

TELEPHONES AND TELEGRAPHS.
Jurisdiction.
Telephone Consumer Protection Act.
Unaccepted settlement offer as not mooting case.
Federal contractor which allegedly violated government's instructions as not immune from suit, 193 L Ed 2d 571, 577 US 153, 136 S Ct 663.

THREE-JUDGE COURTS.
Convening of court.
Refusal to convene, 42 L Ed 2d 249, 419 US 90, 95 S Ct 289, 193 L Ed 2d 279, 577 US 39, 136 S Ct 450.